Biopsychology

Fourth Edition

John P. J. Pinel

UNIVERSITY OF BRITISH COLUMBIA

Allyn and Bacon
BOSTON
LONDON
TORONTO
SYDNEY
TOKYO
SINGAPORE

To Maggie and Greg for your love,
care, and support.

Executive Editor:
Carolyn Merrill

Series Editorial Assistant:
Lara Zeises

Director of Marketing:
Joyce Nilsen

Production Manager:
Elaine Ober

Composition and Prepress Buyer:
Linda Cox

Manufacturing Buyer:
Megan Cochran

Cover Administrator:
Linda Knowles

Editorial-Production Services:
Margaret Pinette

Photo Researcher:
Sarah Evertson, ImageQuest

Text Designer:
Randall Goodall, Seventeenth Street Studios

Illustrators:
William C. Ober, Claire W. Garrison, Mark Lefkowitz,
Schneck-DePippo Graphics, Frank Forney, Illustrious
Interactive, Academy Artworks, LM Graphics, Leo
Harrington, Phil Oliver, Adrienne Lehmann

Cover Designer:
Studio Nine

Copyright © 2000, 1997, 1993, 1990 by Allyn & Bacon
A Pearson Education Company
160 Gould Street
Needham Heights, MA 02494

Library of Congress Cataloging-in-Publication Data
Pinel, John P. J.
    Biopsychology / John P. J. Pinel. — 4th ed.
        p.   cm.
    Include bibliographical references and index.
    ISBN 0-205-28992-4 (hardcover)
    1. Psychobiology.   I. Title.
QP360.P463   1999
612.8—dc21   99-25001
                                                                               CIP

Printed in the United States of America
10 9 8 7 6 5 4 3 2 1   RRD-ROA   02 01 00 99

Illustration and photo credits appear on page 543, which constitutes a continuation of the copyright page.

Brief Contents

Contents

16 LATERALIZATION, LANGUAGE, AND THE SPLIT BRAIN 434

17 BIOPSYCHOLOGY OF STRESS AND ILLNESS 465

Preface

The fourth edition of *Biopsychology* is a clear, engaging introduction to current biopsychological theory and research. It is intended for use as a primary text in one- or two-semester courses in biopsychology—variously entitled Biopsychology, Physiological Psychology, Brain and Behavior, Psychobiology, Behavioral Neuroscience, or Behavioral Neurobiology.

The defining feature of *Biopsychology* is its unique combination of biopsychological science and personal, reader-oriented discourse. It is a textbook that is "untextbooklike." Rather than introducing biopsychology in the usual textbook fashion, it weaves the fundamentals of biopsychology together with clinical case studies, social issues, personal implications, and humorous anecdotes. It tries to be a friendly mentor who speaks directly to the reader and enthusiastically relates recent advances in biopsychological science.

My intention was that the personality of *Biopsychology* would be more than mere window dressing. I hope that *Biopsychology*'s engaging pedagogical approach facilitates the acquisition and retention of information, so that it delivers more biopsychology and more enjoyment for less effort.

Writing this preface is the final step in my preparation of this edition. It marks the end of a year in which I have dedicated myself to further strengthening *Biopsychology*'s strong points, dealing with areas needing improvement, and keeping it abreast of important advances in the field. The following sections of this preface describe the major features of this edition.

Features That Have Carried Over from Previous Editions

The following are features of the first three editions of *Biopsychology* that have been maintained and strengthened in this edition.

■ **AN EMPHASIS ON BEHAVIOR** In some biopsychological textbooks, the coverage of neurophysiology, neurochemistry, and neuroanatomy subverts the coverage of behavioral research. *Biopsychology* gives top billing to behavior: It stresses that neuroscience is a team effort and that the unique contribution made by biopsychologists to this team effort is their behavioral expertise.

■ **A BROAD DEFINITION OF BIOPSYCHOLOGY** Biopsychology is the study of the biology of behavior. *Biopsychology* focuses on the neural mechanisms of behavior, but also emphasizes the evolution, genetics, and adaptiveness of behavioral processes.

■ **EXTENSIVE COVERAGE OF CLINICAL AND HUMAN RESEARCH** *Biopsychology* provides more than the customary coverage of clinical case studies and research on human subjects. One of *Biopsychology*'s dominant themes is that diversity is an important feature of biopsychological research: that major advances in biopsychological science often result from the convergence of pure and applied research and from the convergence of research involving human and nonhuman subjects.

■ **A FOCUS ON THE SCIENTIFIC METHOD** *Biopsychology* emphasizes important, but frequently misunderstood, points about the scientific method. The following are three of them: (1) The scientific method is a means of answering questions that is as applicable to daily life as it is to the laboratory. (2) The scientific method is fun—it is basically the same method that is used by detectives to solve crimes. (3) Widely accepted scientific theories are current best estimates, not statements of absolute fact.

■ **AN INTEGRATIVE APPROACH** *Biopsychology* has not taken the modular approach, dispensing biopsychology as a series of brief independent subject modules. *Biopsychology*'s approach is integrative. It creates a strong fabric of research findings and ideas by weaving together related subject areas and research findings into chapters of intermediate length.

■ **AN EMPHASIS ON PERSONAL AND SOCIAL RELEVANCE** Several chapters of *Biopsychology*—particularly those on eating, sleeping, sex, and drug addiction—carry strong personal and social messages. In these chapters, students are encouraged to consider the relevance of biopsychological research to their lives outside the classroom.

■ **WIT AND ENTHUSIASM** In my experience, biopsychology laboratories are places of enthusiasm, dedication, and good humor. *Biopsychology* communicates these important aspects of "biopsychological life."

■ILLUSTRATIONS The illustrations in *Biopsychology* are special. This is because each illustration was conceptualized and designed by a scientist–artist team who were uniquely qualified to create illustrations to clarify and reinforce the text. This uniquely qualified team was my wife, Maggie, with occasional suggestions from me.

Changes to This Edition

Biopsychology is one of the most rapidly progressing fields of science. This edition of *Biopsychology* has kept abreast of recent developments; it contains approximately 430 references to articles that have been published since the last edition. Indeed, these additions have dictated changes to many parts of this text. The following is a list of some of the topics that receive more or better coverage in this edition than in the last:

- cognitive neuroscience
- thinking about evolution
- mitochondrial DNA
- the human genome project
- functions of the autonomic nervous system
- metabotropic and ionotropic receptors
- ligands and ligand-gated channels
- human brain scanning
- approaches to neuropsychological testing
- genetic engineering
- transgenetic animal models
- necrosis and apoptosis
- ischemic brain damage
- search for a Parkinson's gene
- two streams of visual cortical analysis
- secondary auditory cortex
- anterior cingulate cortex and pain
- conscious awareness
- selective attention
- change blindness
- secondary motor cortex
- somatotopic organization of the motor cortex
- cerebellum and learning
- ob/ob mice
- leptin
- calorie restriction and health
- neuroanatomy of osmoreceptors
- update on the notorious case of ablatio penis

- sexual attraction
- genetics of circadian rhythms
- polyphasic sleep and sleep reduction
- melatonin and sleep
- theories of hippocampal function
- functional brain imaging and memory
- memory and the striatum
- theories of drug conditioning
- methamphetamine and ecstasy
- stem cells
- human studies of neuroplasticity
- genetic treatments of brain disorders
- dyslexia
- functional brain imaging and language
- lateralization of memory
- diathesis-stress model
- ulcers, infection, and stress
- culture and depression
- beneficial effects of sleep deprivation on depression

Learning Aids

Biopsychology has four features that are expressly designed to help students learn and remember the material:

- boldfaced **key terms** and their **marginal definitions**—additional key terms of less importance appear in italics;
- **study exercises** that occur in the chapters at key transition points, where students can benefit most from pausing to consolidate preceding material before continuing;
- **food-for-thought discussion questions** at the end of each chapter;
- **appendices,** which serve as convenient sources of important information that is too detailed for some students of biopsychology.

Ancillary Materials Available with Biopsychology

■TEST BANK The test bank for this edition of *Biopsychology* comprises more than 2000 multiple-choice questions. The difficulty of each item is rated—easy, moderate, or difficult—to assist instructors with their test construction. The test bank is prepared by John Pinel.

■ **INSTRUCTOR'S MANUAL**   The instructor's manual, skillfully prepared by Mike Mana for *Biopsychology*, includes a set of lecture notes. The instructor's manual is available on disk.

■ **STUDY GUIDE**   Each chapter of the study guide prepared by Michael Mana of Western Washington University includes three sections. Section I is composed of "jeopardy" study items—named after the popular television quiz show. The jeopardy study items are arranged in two columns: questions on the left and answers on the right. Sometimes there is nothing in the space to the right of a question, and the student's task is to write the correct answer. Sometimes there is nothing in the space to the left of an answer, and the student's task is to write in the correct question. Once the jeopardy study items are completed, the student has a list of questions and answers that summarize the main points of the chapter, conveniently arranged for bidirectional studying.

Section II of each chapter is composed of essay study questions. Spaces are provided for the student to write outlines of the correct answers to each question. The essay study questions encourage students to consider general issues.

Section III of each chapter is a practice examination. Students are advised to use their results on the practice examination to guide the final stages of their preparation for in-class examinations.

In addition, Allyn and Bacon's Digital Image Archive for Physiological Psychology is available to adopters of the book. This Instructor's Resource, available on CD-ROM from your local A&B sales representative, provides over 250 full color images from the text and from other sources. Finally, we are happy to provide a new resource for both students and instructors at http://www.abacon.com/pinel. Students will find multiple-choice questions that will allow them to "practice" taking exams on line, as well as web links and activities. Instructors will find helpful information about integrating technology in the classroom as well as up-to-date web links and updates about the newest research in biopsychology and the other neurosciences.

■ **BIOPSYCHOLOGY VIDEO**   Instructors who adopt *Biopsychology* can obtain a new 60-minute biopsychology videotape. Based on the *Films for the Humanities* series, this video provides students with glimpses of important biopsychological phenomena such as sleep recording, growing axons, memory testing in monkeys, the formation of synapses, gender differences in brain structure, human amnesic patients, rewarding brain stimulation, and brain scans.

Additional ancillary materials are also available to instructors. Please consult your local Allyn and Bacon representative for details.

Acknowledgments

I wrote *Biopsychology*, but Maggie Edwards made important contributions to all other aspects of the manuscript preparation. Her role in the preparation of the art warrants special acknowledgment. Users of this book will come to recognize that its illustrations are special: The illustrations are so finely attuned to the writing that it appears as if the author must be a talented designer who designed them himself—but I'm not, and I didn't. The illustrations were all designed by Maggie after discussion, debate, and, in some cases, argument with me. You see, Maggie is a professional artist with an extensive background in psychology who also happens to be my partner in life. Maggie took a year from her own successful career to help me achieve a level of illustration that is normally out of reach of writers who are not lucky enough to share their lives with such a talented and dedicated person. I thank her on behalf of the many students who will benefit from her contribution.

Allyn and Bacon did a remarkable job of producing this book. They shared my dream of a textbook that meets the highest standards of pedagogy but is still personal, attractive, and enjoyable. Thank you to Bill Barke, Carolyn Merrill, and the other executives at Allyn and Bacon for having faith in *Biopsychology* and providing the financial and personal support necessary for it to stay at the forefront of its field. A special thank you goes to Elaine Ober and Margaret Pinette for coordinating the entire production effort—an excruciatingly difficult and often thankless job.

I thank the following biopsychology instructors for providing Allyn and Bacon with reviews of *Biopsychology*. Their comments led to significant improvements in this edition.

Michael Babcock, Montana State
    University-Bozeman
Carol Batt, Sacred Heart University
Michelle Butler, Colorado State University
John Conklin, Camosun College
Gregory Ervin, Brigham Young University
Allison Fox, University of Wollongong
Thomas Goettsche, SAS Institute, Inc.
Mary Gotch, Solano College
Tony Jelsma, Atlantic Baptist University
Ora Kofman, Ben Gurion University of the Niger
Louis Koppel, Utah State University
Victoria Littlefield, Augsburg College
Charles Malsbury, Memorial University
Russ Morgan, Western Illinois University
Henry Morlock, SUNY Plattsburg
Michael Peters, University of Guelph
Melody Smith Harrington, St. Gregory's University

David Soderquist, University of North Carolina at Greensboro

Michael Stoloff, James Madison University

Linda Walsh, University of Northern Iowa

In addition, I would like to thank the following people who both responded to surveys sent by the publisher and completed reviews of early draft changes of this edition and who all helped shape the scope of the revision:

Reviewers for the Fourth Edition:

Donald Peter Cain, University of Western Ontario

Arnold M. Golub, California State University–Sacramento

Kenneth Guttman, Citrus College

Charles Kutscher, Syracuse University

Dallas Treit, University of Alberta

Michael P. Matthews, Drury College

Survey Respondents for the Third Edition:

L. Joseph Acher, Baylor University

Thomas Bennett, Colorado State University

Linda Brannon, McNeese State University

Peter Brunjes, University of Virginia

Deborah A. Carroll, Southern Connecticut State University

Robert B. Fischer, Ball State University

Arnold M. Golub, California State University–Sacramento

Mary Gotch, Solano College

Theresa D. Hernandez, University of Colorado

Cindy Ellen Herzog, Frostburg State University

Roger Johnson, Ramapo College

John Jonides, University of Michigan

Jon Kahane, Springfield College

Craig Kinsley, University of Richmond

Charles Kutscher, Syracuse University

Linda Lockwood, Metropolitan State College of Denver

Lin Myers, California State University–Stanislaus

Lauretta Park, Clemson University

Ted Parsons, University of Wisconsin–Platteville

David Robbins, Ohio Wesleyan University

Jeanne Ryan, SUNY–Plattsburgh

Stuart Tousman, Rockford College

Dallas Treit, University of Alberta

Dennis Vincenzi, University of Central Florida

Jon Williams, Kenyon College

David Yager, University of Maryland

To the Student

In the 1960s, I was, in the parlance of the times, "turned on" by an undergraduate course in biopsychology. I could not imagine anything more interesting than a field of science dedicated to studying the relation between psychological processes and the brain. My initial fascination led to a long career as a student, researcher, and teacher of biopsychological science. *Biopsychology* is my attempt to share this fascination with you.

I have tried to make *Biopsychology* a different kind of textbook, a textbook that includes clear, concise, and well-organized explanations of the key points but is still interesting to read—a book from which you might suggest a suitable chapter to an interested friend or relative. To accomplish this goal, I thought about what kind of textbook I would have liked when I was a student, and I decided immediately to avoid the stern formality and ponderous style of conventional textbook writing.

I wanted *Biopsychology* to have a relaxed and personal style. In order to accomplish this, I imagined that you and I were chatting as I wrote, and that I was telling you—usually over a glass of something—about the interesting things that go on in the field of biopsychology. Imagining these chats kept my writing from drifting back into conventional "textbookese," and it never let me forget that I was writing this book for you, the student.

I hope that *Biopsychology* teaches you much, and that reading it generates in you the same personal feeling that writing it did in me. If you are so inclined, I welcome your comments and suggestions. You can contact me at the Department of Psychology, University of British Columbia, Vancouver, B.C., Canada, V6T 1Z4 or at the following e-mail address:

jpinel@cortex.psych.ubc.ca

Biopsychology as a Neuroscience

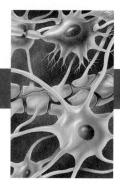

he appearance of the human brain is far from impressive (see Figure 1.1). The human brain is a squishy, wrinkled, walnut-shaped hunk of tissue weighing about 1.3 kilograms. It looks more like something that you might find washed up on a beach than like one of the wonders of the world—which it surely is. Despite its disagreeable external appearance, the human brain is an amazingly intricate network of **neurons** (cells that receive and transmit electro-chemical signals). Contemplate for a moment the complexity of your own brain's neural circuits. Consider the 100 billion neurons in complex array, the estimated 100 trillion connections among them, and the almost infinite number of paths that neural signals can follow through this morass.

The complexity of the human brain is hardly surprising, considering what it can do. An organ capable of creating a *Mona Lisa*, an artificial limb, and a supersonic aircraft; of traveling to the moon and to the depths of the sea; and of experiencing the wonders of an alpine sunset, a newborn infant, and a reverse slam dunk must itself be complex. Paradoxically, **neuroscience** (the scientific study of the nervous system) may prove to be the brain's ultimate challenge: Does the brain have the capacity to understand something as complex as itself?

Neuroscience comprises several related disciplines. The primary purpose of this chapter is to introduce you to one of them: biopsychology. Each of this chapter's seven sections characterizes biopsychology from a different perspective.

Before you proceed to the body of this chapter, I would like to tell you about Jimmie G. Biopsychologists have learned much about the brain from the study of human victims of brain damage—and you will too. But it is important that you do not grow insensitive to their personal tragedy. The case of Jimmie G. introduces you to it.

[In 1975] Jimmie was a fine-looking man, with a curly bush of grey hair, a healthy and handsome forty-nine-year-old. He was cheerful, friendly, and warm.

"Hiya, Doc!" he said. "Nice morning! Do I take this chair here?" . . . He spoke of the houses where his family had lived. . . . He spoke of school and school days, the friends he'd had, and his special fondness for mathematics and science . . . he was seventeen, had just graduated from high school when he

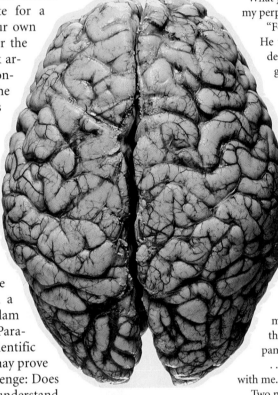

Figure 1.1 The human brain.

was drafted in 1943. . . . He remembered the names of the various submarines on which he had served, their missions, where they were stationed, the names of his shipmates. . . . But there for some reason his reminiscences stopped. . . .

. . . I was very struck by the change of tense in his recollections as he passed from his school days to his days in the navy. He had been using the past tense, but now used the present. . . .

A sudden, improbable suspicion seized me.

"What year is this, Mr. G.?" I asked, concealing my perplexity under a casual manner.

"Forty-five, man. What do you mean?" He went on, "We've won the war, FDR's dead, Truman's at the helm. There are great times ahead."

"And you, Jimmie, how old would you be?" . . .

"Why, I guess I'm nineteen, Doc. I'll be twenty next birthday."

Looking at the grey-haired man before me, I had an impulse for which I have never forgiven myself. . . .

"Here," I said, and thrust a mirror toward him. "Look in the mirror and tell me what you see. . . ."

He suddenly turned ashen and gripped the sides of the chair. "Jesus Christ," he whispered. "Christ, what's going on? What's happened to me? Is this a nightmare? Am I crazy? Is this a joke?"—and he became frantic, panicked.

. . . I stole away, taking the hateful mirror with me.

Two minutes later I re-entered the room. . . . "Hiya, Doc!" he said. "Nice morning! You want to talk to me—do I take this chair here?" There was no sign of recognition on his frank, open face.

"Haven't we met before, Mr. G.?" I asked casually.

"No, I can't say we have. Quite a beard you got there. I wouldn't forget you, Doc!"

. . . "Where do you think you are?"

"I see these beds, and these patients everywhere. Looks like a sort of hospital to me. But hell, what would I be doing in a hospital—and with all these old people, years older than me. . . . Maybe I *work* here. . . . If I don't work here, I've been *put* here. Am I a patient, am I sick and don't know it, Doc? It's crazy, it's scary. . . ."

On intelligence testing he showed excellent ability. He was quick-witted, observant, and logical, and had no difficulty solving complex problems and puzzles—no difficulty, that is, if they could be done quickly. If much time was required, he forgot what he was doing. . . .

Homing in on his memory, I found an extreme and extraordinary loss of recent memory—so that whatever was said or shown to him was apt to be forgotten in a few seconds' time. Thus I laid out my watch, my tie, and my glasses

BIOPSYCHOLOGY AS A NEUROSCIENCE

on the desk, covered them, and asked him to remember these. Then, after a minute's chat, I asked him what I had put under the cover. He remembered none of them—or indeed that I had even asked him to remember. I repeated the test, this time getting him to write down the names of the three objects; again he forgot, and when I showed him the paper with his writing on it he was astounded. . . .

"What is this?" I asked, showing him a photo in the magazine I was holding.

"It's the moon," he replied.

"No, it's not," I answered. "It's a picture of the earth taken from the moon."

"Doc, you're kidding! Someone would've had to get a camera up there! . . . how the hell would you do that?" . . .

He was becoming fatigued, and somewhat irritable and anxious, under the continuing pressure of anomaly and contradiction, and their fearful implications. . . . And I myself was wrung with emotion—it was heartbreaking . . . to think of his life lost in limbo, dissolving.

He is, as it were . . . isolated in a single moment of being, with a moat . . . of forgetting all round him. . . . He is a man without a past (or future), stuck in a constantly changing, meaningless moment. (pp. 22–28)[1]

Remember Jimmie G.; you will encounter him again, later in this chapter.

1.1 What Is Biopsychology?

Biopsychology is the scientific study of the biology of behavior—see Dewsbury (1991). Some refer to this field as *psychobiology, behavioral biology, behavioral neuroscience;* but I prefer the term *biopsychology* because it denotes a biological approach to the study of psychology rather than a psychological approach to the study of biology: Psychology commands center stage in this text.

Psychology is the scientific study of behavior—the scientific study of all overt activities of the organism as well as all the internal processes that are presumed to underlie them (e.g., learning, memory, motivation, perception, and emotion).

The study of the biology of behavior has a long history, but biopsychology did not coalesce into a major neuroscientific discipline until this century. Although it is not possible to specify the exact date of biopsychology's birth, the publication of *The Organization of Behavior* in 1949 by D. O. Hebb played a key role in its emergence (see Milner, 1993; Milner & White, 1987). In his book, Hebb (see Figure 1.2) developed the first comprehensive theory of how complex psychological phenomena, such as perceptions, emotions, thoughts, and memories, might be produced by brain activity. In so doing, Hebb's theory did much to discredit the view that psychological functioning is too complex to have its roots in the physiology and chemistry of the brain. Hebb based his theory on experiments involving both humans and laboratory animals, on clinical case studies, and on logical arguments developed from his own insightful observations of daily life. This eclectic approach has become a hallmark of biopsychological inquiry.

Figure 1.2 D. O. Hebb.
(Photograph courtesy of McGill University.)

[1]From *The Man Who Mistook His Wife for a Hat and Other Clinical Tales* (pp. 22–28) by Oliver Sacks. Copyright © 1970, 1981, 1983, 1984, 1985 by Oliver Sacks. Reprinted by permission of Summit Books, a division of Simon & Schuster, Inc.

Neurons. Cells of the nervous system that are specialized for receiving and transmitting electrochemical signals.

Neuroscience. The scientific study of the nervous system.

Biopsychology. The scientific study of the biology of behavior.

In comparison to physics, chemistry, and biology, biopsychology is an infant—a raucous, healthy, rapidly growing infant, but nonetheless an infant. In this book, you will reap the benefits of biopsychology's youth. Because biopsychology does not have a long and complex history, you will be able to move directly to the excitement of current research.

1.2 What Is the Relation between Biopsychology and the Other Disciplines of Neuroscience?

Neuroscience is a team effort, and biopsychologists are important members of the team. This section of the chapter further defines biopsychology by discussing its relation to other neuroscientific disciplines.

Biopsychologists are neuroscientists who bring to their research a knowledge of behavior and of the methods of behavioral research. It is their behavioral orientation and expertise that make their unique contribution to neuroscience. You will be able to better appreciate the importance of this contribution if you consider that the ultimate purpose of the nervous system is to produce and control behavior.

Biopsychology is an integrative discipline. Biopsychologists draw together knowledge from the other neuroscientific disciplines and apply it to the study of behavior. The following are a few of the disciplines of neuroscience that are particularly relevant to biopsychology:

Neuroanatomy. The study of the structure of the nervous system (see Chapter 3).

Neurochemistry. The study of the chemical bases of neural activity (see Chapter 4).

Neuroendocrinology. The study of interactions between the nervous system and the endocrine system (see Chapters 11 and 17).

Neuropathology. The study of nervous system disorders (see Chapter 6).

Neuropharmacology. The study of the effects of drugs on neural activity (see Chapters 4, 13, and 17).

Neurophysiology. The study of the functions and activities of the nervous system (see Chapter 4).

Recently, I assessed biopsychology's contribution to neuroscience by recording the departmental affiliation of a random sample of neuroscientists selected from the membership directory of the **Society for Neuroscience,** a major international association of neuroscientists with over 24,000 members. The results are presented in Table 1.1. Clearly, the contribution of biopsychology to neuroscience is substantial; about 16 percent of the members of the society listed psychology as their primary departmental affiliation. Moreover, a published analysis of the graduate-student members of the Society of Neuroscience suggests that biopsychology's major contribution to neuroscience is likely to continue (Davis et al., 1988)—see Figure 1.3.

Table 1.1	Departmental Affiliations of Members of the Society for Neuroscience	
Departmental Affiliation		**Percentage of Sample**
Psychology		16.1
Physiology		14.3
Pharmacology		12.5
Biology		11.2
Anatomy		11.2
Neurology		6.7
Psychiatry		5.8
Neuroscience/Neurobiology		5.3
Neurosurgery		3.1
Pathology		3.1
Veterinary Medicine		1.8
Others		8.9
		100.0

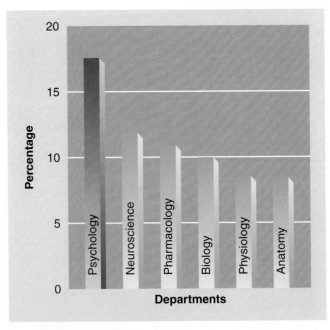

Figure 1.3 The departmental affiliation of graduate-student members of the Society for Neuroscience. Only academic departments contributing over 5% of the graduate-student members are listed. (Adapted from Davis et al., 1988.)

1.3 What Types of Research Characterize the Biopsychological Approach?

Although biopsychology is only one of many disciplines that contribute to neuroscience, it is itself broad and diverse. Biopsychologists study many different phenomena, and they approach their research in many different ways. In order to characterize biopsychological research, this section discusses three major dimensions along which approaches to biopsychological research vary. Biopsychological research can involve either human or nonhuman subjects; it can take the form of either formal experiments or nonexperimental studies; and it can be either pure or applied.

Human and Nonhuman Subjects

Both human and nonhuman animals are the subject of biopsychological research. Of the nonhumans, rats are the most common subjects; however, mice, cats, dogs, and nonhuman primates are also widely studied.

Humans have several advantages over other animals as experimental subjects of biopsychological research: They can follow instructions, they can report their subjective experiences, and their cages are easier to clean. Of course, I am joking about the cages, but the joke does serve to draw attention to one advantage that humans have over other species of experimental subjects: Humans are often cheaper. Because only the highest standards of animal care are acceptable, the cost of maintaining an animal laboratory can be prohibitive for all but the most well-funded researchers.

Of course, the greatest advantage that humans have as subjects in a field aimed at understanding the intricacies of human brain function is that they have human brains. In fact, you might wonder why biopsychologists would bother studying nonhuman subjects at all. The answer lies in the evolutionary continuity of the brain. The brains of humans differ from the brains of other mammals primarily in their overall size and the extent of their cortical development. In other words, the differences between the brains of humans and those of related species are more quantitative than qualitative, and thus many of the principles of human brain function can be derived from the study of nonhumans (see Kolb & Whishaw, 1996).

Conversely, nonhuman animals have three advantages over humans as subjects in biopsychological research. The first is that the brains and behavior of nonhuman subjects are more simple than those of human subjects. Hence, the study of nonhuman species is

more likely to reveal fundamental brain–behavior interactions. The second is that insights frequently arise from the **comparative approach,** the study of biological processes by comparing different species. For example, comparing the behavior of species that do not have a cerebral cortex with the behavior of species that do can provide valuable clues about cortical function. The third is that it is possible to conduct research on laboratory animals that, for ethical reasons, is not possible on human subjects. This is not to say that the study of nonhuman animals is not governed by a strict code of ethics (see Institute of Laboratory Animal Resources, 1996)—it is. However, there are fewer ethical constraints on the study of laboratory species than on the study of humans.

In my experience, most biopsychologists display considerable concern for their subjects whether they are of their own species or not; however, ethical issues are not left to the discretion of the individual researcher. All biopsychological research, whether it involves human or nonhuman subjects, is regulated by independent committees according to strict ethical guidelines: "Researchers cannot escape the logic that if the animals we observe are reasonable models of our own most intricate actions, then they must be respected as we would respect our own sensibilities" (Ulrich, 1991, p. 197).

Experiments and Nonexperiments

Biopsychological research involves both experiments and nonexperimental studies. Two common types of nonexperimental studies are quasiexperimental studies and case studies.

■ **EXPERIMENTS** The experiment is the method used by scientists to find out what causes what, and, as such, it is

---

Neuroanatomy. The study of the structure of the nervous system.
Neurochemistry. The study of the chemical bases of neural activity.
Neuroendocrinology. The study of the interactions between the nervous system and the endocrine system.
Neuropathology. The study of nervous system disorders.

Neuropharmacology. The study of the effects of drugs on neural activity.
Neurophysiology. The study of the functions and activities of the nervous system.
Society for Neuroscience. A major international association of neuroscientists.
Comparative approach. The study of biological processes by comparison of different species.

almost single-handedly responsible for our modern way of life. It is paradoxical that a method capable of such complex feats is itself so simple. To conduct an experiment involving living subjects, the experimenter first designs two or more conditions under which the subjects will be tested. Usually, a different group of subjects is tested under each condition (**between-subjects design**), but sometimes it is possible to test the same group of subjects under each condition (**within-subjects design**). The experimenter assigns the subjects to conditions, administers the treatments, and measures the outcome in such a way that there is only one relevant difference between the conditions that are being compared. This difference between the conditions is called the **independent variable.** The variable that is measured by the experimenter to assess the effect of the independent variable is called the **dependent variable.**

Why is it critical that there be no differences between conditions other than the independent variable? The reason is that when there is more than one difference that could affect the dependent variable, it is difficult to determine whether it was the independent variable or the unintended difference—called a **confounded variable**—that led to the observed effects on the dependent variable. Although the experimental method is conceptually simple, eliminating all confounded variables can be quite difficult. Readers of research papers must be constantly on the alert for confounded variables that have gone unnoticed by the experimenters themselves.

An experiment by Lester and Gorzalka (1988) illustrates the experimental method in action. The experiment was a demonstration of the **Coolidge effect.** The Coolidge effect is the fact that a copulating male who becomes incapable of continuing to copulate with one sex partner can often recommence copulating with a new sex partner (see Figure 1.4). Before your imagination starts running wild, I should mention that the subjects in Lester and Gorzalka's experiment were hamsters, not students from the undergraduate subject pool.

Lester and Gorzalka argued that the Coolidge effect had not been demonstrated in females because it is more difficult to conduct well-controlled Coolidge-effect experiments in females—not because females do not display a Coolidge effect. The confusion, according to Lester and Gorzalka, stemmed from the fact that the males of most mammalian species become sexually fatigued more readily than do the females. As a result, attempts to demonstrate the Coolidge effect in females are often confounded by the fatigue of the males. When, in the midst of copulation, a female is provided with a new sex partner, the increase in her sexual receptivity could be either a legitimate Coolidge effect or a reaction to the greater vigor of the new male. Because female mammals usually display little sexual fatigue,

Figure 1.4 President Calvin Coolidge and Mrs. Grace Coolidge. Many students think that the Coolidge effect is named after a biopsychologist named Coolidge. It is named after President Calvin Coolidge, of whom the following story is told. (If the story isn't true, it should be.) During a tour of a poultry farm, Mrs. Coolidge inquired of the farmer how his farm managed to produce so many eggs with such a small number of roosters. The farmer proudly explained that his roosters performed their duty dozens of times each day.

"Perhaps you could point that out to Mr. Coolidge," replied the first lady in a pointedly loud voice.

The President, overhearing the remark, asked the farmer, "Does each rooster service the same hen each time?"

"No," replied the farmer, "there are many hens for each rooster."

"Perhaps you could point that out to Mrs. Coolidge," replied the President.

this confounded variable is not a serious problem in demonstrations of the Coolidge effect in males.

Lester and Gorzalka devised a clever procedure to control for this confounded variable. At the same time that a female subject was copulating with one male (the familiar male), the other male to be used in the test (the unfamiliar male) was copulating with another female. Then, both males were given a rest while the female was copulating with a third male. Finally, the female subject was tested with either the familiar male or the unfamil-

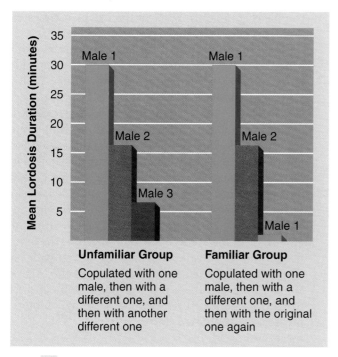

Figure 1.5 The experimental design and results of Lester and Gorzalka (1988). On the third test, the female hamsters were more sexually receptive to unfamiliar males than they were to the males with which they had copulated on the first test.

iar male. The dependent variable was the amount of time that the female displayed **lordosis** (the arched-back, rump-up, tail-diverted posture of female rodent sexual receptivity) during each sex test. As Figure 1.5 illustrates, the females responded more vigorously to the unfamiliar males than they did to the familiar males during the third test, despite the fact that both the unfamiliar and familiar males were equally fatigued and both mounted the females with equal vigor. This experiment illustrates the importance of good experimental design as well as a theme of Chapter 11: that males and females are more similar than most people appreciate.

■ **QUASIEXPERIMENTAL STUDIES** It is not possible for biopsychologists to bring the experimental method to bear on all problems of interest to them. There are frequently physical or ethical impediments that make it impossible to assign subjects to particular conditions or to administer the conditions once the subjects have been assigned to them. For example, experiments on the causes of brain damage in human alcoholics are not feasible because it would not be ethical to assign a subject to a condition that involves years of alcohol consumption. (Some of you may be more concerned about the ethics of assigning subjects to a control condition that involves years of sobriety.) In such prohibitive situations, biopsychologists sometimes conduct **quasi-**

experimental studies—studies of groups of subjects who have been exposed to the conditions of interest in the real world. These studies have the appearance of experiments, but they are not true experiments because potential confounded variables have not been controlled—for example, by the random assignment of subjects to conditions.

In one quasiexperimental study, a team of researchers compared 100 detoxified male alcoholics from an alcoholism treatment unit with 50 male non-drinkers obtained from various sources (Acker et al., 1984). The alcoholics as a group performed more poorly on various tests of perceptual, motor, and cognitive ability, and their brain scans revealed extensive brain damage. Although this quasiexperimental study seems like an experiment, it is not. Because the subjects themselves decided which group they would be in—by drinking alcohol or not—the researchers had no means of ensuring that exposure to alcohol was the only variable that distinguished the two groups. Can you think of differences other than exposure to alcohol that could reasonably be expected to exist between a group of alcoholics and a group of abstainers—differences that could have contributed to the neuroanatomical or intellectual differences that were observed between them? There are several. For example, alcoholics as a group tend to be more poorly educated, more prone to accidental head injury, more likely to use other drugs, and more likely to have poor diets. Accordingly, quasiexperimental studies have revealed that alcoholics tend to have more brain damage than nonalcoholics, but they have not proved why.

Have you forgotten Jimmie G.? He was a product of long-term alcohol consumption.

■ **CASE STUDIES** Studies that focus on a single case or subject are called **case studies.** Because they focus on a single case, they often provide a more in-depth picture than

---

Between-subjects design. An experimental design in which a different group of subjects is tested under each condition.

Within-subjects design. An experimental design in which the same subjects are tested under each condition.

Independent variable. The difference between experimental conditions that is arranged by the experimenter.

Dependent variable. The variable measured by the experimenter—the variable that is affected by the independent variable.

Confounded variable. An unintended difference between the conditions of an experiment

that could have affected the dependent variable.

Coolidge effect. The fact that a copulating male who becomes incapable of continuing to copulate with one sex partner can often recommence copulating with a new sex partner.

Lordosis. The arched-back, rump-up, tail-diverted posture of female rodent sexual receptivity.

Quasiexperimental studies. Studies that have the appearance of experiments but are not true experiments because potential confounded variables have not been controlled.

Case studies. Studies that focus on a single case or subject.

that provided by an experiment or a quasiexperimental study, and they are an excellent source of testable hypotheses. On the other hand, a major problem with case studies is their **generalizability**—the degree to which their results can be applied to other cases. Because humans differ from one another in both brain function and behavior, it is important to be skeptical of any biopsychological theory based entirely on a few case studies.

Pure and Applied Research

Biopsychological research can be either pure or applied. Pure and applied research differ in a number of respects, but they are distinguished less by their own attributes than by the motives of the individuals involved in their pursuit. **Pure research** is research motivated primarily by the curiosity of the researcher—it is done solely for the purpose of acquiring knowledge. In contrast, **applied research** is research intended to bring about some direct benefit to humankind.

Many scientists believe that pure research will ultimately prove to be of more practical benefit than applied research. Their view is that applications flow readily from an understanding of basic principles and that attempts to move directly to application without first gaining a basic understanding are shortsighted. Of course, it is not necessary for a research project to be completely pure or completely applied; many research programs have elements of both approaches.

One important difference between pure and applied research is that pure research is more vulnerable to the vagaries of political regulation because politicians and the voting public have difficulty understanding why research of no immediate practical benefit should be supported. If the decision were yours, would you be willing to grant hundreds of thousands of dollars to support the study of squid *motor neurons* (neurons that control muscles), learning in recently hatched geese, the activity of single nerve cells in the visual systems of monkeys, the hormones released by the *hypothalamus* (a small neural structure at the base of the brain) of pigs and sheep, or the function of the *corpus callosum* (the large neural pathway that connects the left and right halves of the brain)? Which, if any, of these projects would you consider worthy of support? Each of these seemingly esoteric projects was supported, and each earned a Nobel Prize for its author.

Table 1.2 lists some of the Nobel Prizes awarded for research related to the brain and behavior. The purpose of this list is to give you a general sense of the official recognition that behavioral and brain research has received, not to have you memorize the list. You will learn later in the chapter that, when it comes to evaluating science, the Nobel committee has been far from infallible.

Table 1.2   Some of the Nobel Prizes Awarded for Studies Related to the Nervous System or Behavior

Nobel Winner	Date	Accomplishment
Ivan Pavlov	1904	Research on the physiology of digestion
Camillo Golgi and Santiago Ramón y Cajal	1906	Research on the structure of the nervous system
Charles Sherrington and Edgar Adrian	1932	Discoveries about the functions of neurons
Henry Dale and Otto Loewi	1936	Discoveries about the transmissions of nerve impulses
Joseph Erlanger and Herbert Gasser	1944	Research on the functions of single nerve fibers
Walter Hess	1949	Research on the role of the brain in controlling behavior
Egas Moniz	1949	Development of prefrontal lobotomy
Georg von Békésy	1961	Research on the auditory system
John Eccles, Alan Hodgkin, and Andrew Huxley	1963	Research on the ionic basis of neural transmission
Ragnor Granit, Haldan Hartline, and George Wald	1967	Research on the chemistry and physiology of the visual system
Bernard Katz, Ulf von Euler, and Julius Axelrod	1970	Discoveries related to synaptic transmission
Karl Von Frisch, Konrad Lorenz, and Nikolass Tinbergen	1973	Studies of animal behavior
Roger Guillemin and Andrew Schally	1977	Discoveries related to hormone production by the brain
Herbert Simon	1979	Research on human cognition
Roger Sperry	1981	Research on differences between the cerebral hemispheres
David Hubel and Torsten Wiesel	1981	Research on information processing in the visual system
Rita Levi-Montalcini and Stanley Cohen	1986	Discovery and study of nerve and epidermal growth factors
Erwin Neher and Bert Sakmann	1991	Research on ion channels
Alfred Gilman and Martin Rodbell	1994	Discovery of G-protein coupled receptors

1.4 What Are the Divisions of Biopsychology?

As you have just learned, biopsychologists conduct their research in a variety of fundamentally different ways. Biopsychologists who take the same approaches to their research tend to publish their research in the same journals, attend the same scientific meetings, and belong to the same professional societies. The particular approaches to biopsychology that have flourished and grown have gained wide recognition as separate divisions of biopsychological research. The purpose of this section of the chapter is to give you a clearer sense of biopsychology and its diversity by describing six of its major divisions: (1) physiological psychology, (2) psychopharmacology, (3) neuropsychology, (4) psychophysiology, (5) cognitive neuroscience, and (6) comparative psychology. For simplicity, they are presented as distinct approaches; but there is much overlap among them, and many biopsychologists regularly follow more than one approach.

Physiological Psychology

Physiological psychology is the division of biopsychology that studies the neural mechanisms of behavior through the direct manipulation of the brain in controlled experiments—surgical and electrical methods of brain manipulation are most common. The subjects of physiological psychology research are almost always laboratory animals, because the focus on direct brain manipulation and controlled experiments precludes the use of human subjects in most instances. There is also a tradition of pure research in physiological psychology; the emphasis is usually on research that contributes to the development of theories of the neural control of behavior rather than on research that is of immediate practical benefit.

Psychopharmacology

Psychopharmacology is similar to physiological psychology, except that it focuses on the manipulation of neural activity and behavior with drugs. In fact, many of the early psychopharmacologists were simply physiological psychologists who moved into drug research, and many of today's biopsychologists identify closely with both approaches. However, the study of the effects of drugs on the brain and behavior has become so specialized that psychopharmacology is widely regarded as a separate discipline.

A substantial portion of psychopharmacological research is applied (see Brady, 1993). Although drugs are sometimes used by psychopharmacologists to study the basic principles of brain–behavior interaction, the purpose of many psychopharmacological experiments is to develop therapeutic drugs (see Chapter 17) or to reduce drug abuse (see Chapter 13). Psychopharmacologists study the effects of drugs on laboratory species—and on humans, if the ethics of the situation permits it.

Neuropsychology

Neuropsychology is the study of the psychological effects of brain damage in human patients. Obviously, human subjects cannot ethically be exposed to experimental treatments that endanger normal brain function. Consequently, neuropsychology deals almost exclusively with case studies and quasiexperimental studies of patients with brain damage resulting from disease, accident, or neurosurgery. The outer layer of the cerebral hemispheres—the **cerebral cortex**—is most likely to be damaged by accident or surgery; this is one reason why neuropsychology has focused on this important part of the human brain.

Neuropsychology is the most applied of the biopsychological subdisciplines; the neuropsychological assessment of human patients, even when part of a program of pure research, is always done with an eye toward benefiting them in some way. Neuropsychological tests facilitate diagnosis and thus help the attending physician prescribe effective treatment (see Benton,

---

Generalizability. The degree to which the results of a study can be applied to other individuals or situations.

Pure research. Research motivated primarily by the curiosity of the researcher.

Applied research. Research that is intended to bring about some direct benefit to humankind.

Physiological psychology. The division of biopsychology that studies the neural mechanisms of behavior by directly manipulating the nervous systems of nonhuman animal subjects in controlled experiments.

Psychopharmacology. The division of biopsychology that studies the effects of drugs on the brain and behavior.

Neuropsychology. The division of biopsychology that studies the psychological effects of brain damage in human patients.

Cerebral cortex. The layer of neural tissue covering the cerebral hemispheres of humans and other mammals.

1994). They can also be an important basis for patient care and counseling; Kolb and Whishaw (1990) described such an application:

> Mr. R., a 21-year-old left-handed man, struck his head on the dashboard in a car accident. . . . Prior to his accident Mr. R. was an honor student at a university, with plans to attend professional or graduate school. However, a year after the accident he had become a mediocre student who had particular trouble completing his term papers on time. . . . He was referred for a neurological exam by his family physician, but it proved negative and an EEG and a CT scan failed to demonstrate any abnormality. He was referred to us for neuropsychological assessment, which revealed several interesting facts.
>
> First, Mr. R. was one of about one-third of left-handers whose language functions are represented in the right rather than left hemisphere. . . . In addition, although Mr. R. had a superior IQ, his verbal memory and reading speed were only low-average, which is highly unusual for a person of his intelligence and education. These deficits indicated that his right temporal lobe may have been slightly damaged in the car accident, resulting in an impairment of his language skills. On the basis of our neuropsychological investigation we were able to recommend vocations to Mr. R. that did not require superior verbal memory skills, and he is currently studying architecture. (p. 128)[2]

Psychophysiology

Psychophysiology is the division of biopsychology that studies the relation between physiological activity and

[2]From *Fundamentals of Human Neuropsychology*, 3rd Edition, by Bryan Kolb and Ian Q. Whishaw. Copyright © 1980, 1985, 1990 W. H. Freeman and Company. Reprinted with permission.

psychological processes in human subjects (see Andreassi, 1989). Because the subjects of psychophysiological research are human, psychophysiological recording procedures are typically noninvasive; that is, the physiological activity is recorded from the surface of the body. The usual measure of brain activity is the scalp **electroencephalogram (EEG).** Other common psychophysiological measures are muscle tension, eye movement, and several types of autonomic nervous system activity (e.g., heart rate, blood pressure, pupil dilation, and electrical conductance of the skin). The **autonomic nervous system** is the division of the nervous system that regulates the body's inner environment.

Most psychophysiological research focuses on understanding the physiology of psychological processes, such as attention, emotion, and information processing, but there have also been a number of interesting clinical applications of the psychophysiological method (see Iacono, 1985). For example, psychological experiments have indicated that schizophrenics have difficulty smoothly tracking a moving object such as a pendulum (Iacono & Koenig, 1983)—see Figure 1.6.

Cognitive Neuroscience

Cognitive neuroscience is the youngest division of biopsychology, but it is currently among the most active and exciting. Cognitive neuroscientists study the neural bases of **cognition,** a term that generally refers to higher intellectual processes such as thought, memory, attention, and complex perceptual processes. Because of its focus on cognition, most cognitive neuroscience research involves human subjects; and because

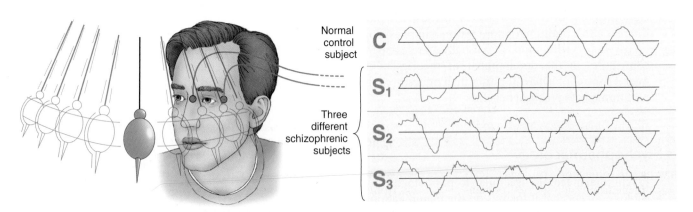

Figure 1.6 Visual tracking of a pendulum by a normal control subject (top) and three schizophrenics. (Adapted from "Features That Distinguish the Smooth-Pursuit Eye-Tracking Performance of Schizophrenic, Affective-Disorder, and Normal Individuals" by W. G. Iacono and W. G. R. Koenig, 1983, *Journal of Abnormal Psychology, 92,* p. 39. Copyright 1983 by the American Psychological Association. Reprinted by permission.)

of its focus on human subjects, its major method is noninvasive recording rather than the direct manipulation of the brain.

The major method of cognitive neuroscience is functional brain imaging (recording images of the activity of the living human brain; see Chapter 5) while the subjects are engaged in particular cognitive activities. For example, in Figure 1.7 you will notice how an area of the left cerebral cortex became active when the subject tapped a finger of her right hand.

Because the theory and methods of cognitive neuroscience are so complex and interesting to people in so many fields, most cognitive neuroscientific research is an interdisciplinary collaboration among individuals with different types of training. For example, in addition to conventionally trained biopsychologists, cognitive psychologists, computing and mathematics experts, and various types of neuroscientists commonly contribute to the field. Cognitive neuroscience research sometimes involves noninvasive electrophysiological recording, and sometimes it focuses on subjects with brain pathology; in these cases, the boundaries of cognitive neuroscience with psychophysiology and neuropsychology, respectively, are blurry.

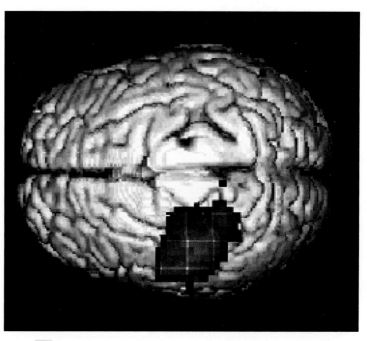

Figure 1.7 Functional brain imaging, the major method of cognitive neuroscience. This functional brain image shows the top of the brain and illustrates the area of the left hemisphere that became active when the subject repeatedly tapped her index finger. (Courtesy of Peter Liddle, Department of Psychiatry, University of British Columbia.)

Comparative Psychology

Although most biopsychologists study the neural mechanisms of behavior, there is more to biopsychology than this. As Dewsbury (1991) asserted:

> The "biology" in "psychobiology" should include the whole-animal approaches of ethology, ecology, evolution . . . as well as the latest in physiological methods and thought. . . . The "compleat psychobiologist" should use whatever explanatory power can be found with modern physiological techniques, but never lose sight of the problems that got us going in the first place: the integrated behavior of whole, functioning, adapted organisms. (p. 198)

The division of biopsychology that deals generally with the biology of behavior, rather than specifically with the neural mechanisms of behavior, is **comparative psychology**. Comparative psychologists compare the behavior of different species and focus on the genetics, evolution, and adaptiveness of behavior (see Timberlake, 1993).

Historically, comparative psychologists have focused on the experimental investigation of animal behavior in controlled laboratory environments. However, modern comparative psychology also encompasses

ethological research—the study of animal behavior in its natural environment. Also, in the last decade, as major advances have been made in the field of genetics, advances in *behavior genetics* (study of the genetics of behavior and other psychological processes) have kept apace.

In case you have forgotten, the purpose of this section has been to characterize biopsychology and its diversity by describing its divisions. You will learn much more about the exciting progress being made by the various divisions of biopsychology in subsequent chapters.

Psychophysiology. The division of biopsychology that studies the relation between physiological activity and psychological processes in human subjects by noninvasive recording.

Electroencephalogram (EEG). A measure of the general electrical activity of the brain, often recorded through the scalp.

Autonomic nervous system. The division of the nervous system that regulates the body's inner environment.

Cognitive neuroscience. A division of biopsychology that focuses on the use of functional brain imaging to study human cognition.

Cognition. Complex intellectual processes such as thought, memory, attention, and perceptual processing.

Comparative psychology. The division of biopsychology that studies the evolution, genetics, and adaptiveness of behavior, often by using the comparative method.

Ethological research. The study of animal behavior in its natural environment.

To make sure that you understand the distinctions among the five biopsychological approaches, fill in each of the following blanks. If you have difficulty, review the preceding section before continuing.

1. A biopsychologist who studies the memory deficits of human patients with brain damage would likely identify with the division of biopsychology termed _____ .

2. Psychologists who study the physiological correlates of psychological processes by recording physiological signals from the surface of the human body are often referred to as _____ .

3. The biopsychological research of _____ _____ frequently involves the direct

manipulation or recording of the neural activity of laboratory animals by various invasive surgical, electrical, and chemical means.

4. The division of biopsychology that focuses on the study of the effects of drugs on behavior is often referred to as _____ .

5. Although _____ can be considered to be a division of biopsychology because it focuses on the neural bases of cognition, it is a collaborative interdisciplinary field.

6. _____ are biopsychologists who study the genetics, evolution, and adaptiveness of behavior, often by using the comparative method.

Converging Operations: How Do Biopsychologists Work Together?

Because none of the six biopsychological approaches to research is without its shortcomings, major biopsychological issues are rarely resolved by a single experiment or even by a single series of experiments taking the same general approach. Progress is most rapid when different approaches are focused on a single problem in such a way that the strengths of one approach compensate for the weaknesses of the others; this is called **converging operations.**

Consider, for example, the relative strengths and weaknesses of neuropsychology and physiological psychology in the study of the psychological effects of damage to the human cerebral cortex. In this instance, the strength of the neuropsychological approach is that it deals directly with human patients; its weakness is that its focus on human patients precludes experiments. In contrast, the strength of the physiological psychology approach is that it can bring the power of

the experimental method and neuroscientific technology to bear on the question through research on nonhuman animals; its weakness is that the relevance of research on laboratory animals to human neuropsychological deficits is always open to question. Clearly these two approaches complement each other well; together they can answer questions that neither can answer individually.

To examine converging operations in action, let's return to the case of Jimmie G. The neuropsychological disorder from which Jimmie G. suffered was first described in the late 1800s by S. S. Korsakoff, a Russian physician, and subsequently became known as **Korsakoff's syndrome.** The primary symptom of Korsakoff's syndrome is severe memory loss, which is made all the more heartbreaking—as you have seen in Jimmie G.'s case—by the fact that its sufferers are often otherwise quite capable. Because Korsakoff's syndrome commonly occurs in alcoholics, it was initially believed to be a direct consequence of the toxic effects of alcohol on the brain. This conclusion proved to be a good illustration of the inadvisability of basing causal conclusions on quasiexperimental research. Subsequent research showed that Korsakoff's syndrome is largely

The answers are (1) neuropsychology, (2) psychophysiologists, (3) physiological psychologists, (4) psychopharmacology, (5) cognitive neuroscience, and (6) comparative psychologists.

caused by the brain damage associated with *thiamine* (vitamin B$_1$) deficiency—see Butterworth, Kril, and Harper (1993) and Lishman (1990).

The first support for the thiamine-deficiency interpretation of Korsakoff's syndrome came from the discovery of the syndrome in malnourished persons who consumed little or no alcohol. Additional support came from experiments in which thiamine-deficient rats were compared with otherwise identical groups of control rats. The thiamine-deficient rats displayed memory deficits and patterns of brain damage similar to those observed in human alcoholics (Knoth & Mair, 1991; Mair, Knoth, et al., 1991; Mair, Otto, et al., 1991). Alcoholics often develop Korsakoff's syndrome because most of their caloric intake comes in the form of alcohol, which lacks vitamins, and because alcohol interferes with the metabolism of what little thiamine they do consume (Rindi, 1989). However, alcohol has been shown to accelerate the development of brain damage in thiamine-deficient rats, so it may have a direct toxic effect on the brain as well (Zimitat et al., 1990). The point of all this (in case you have forgotten) is that progress in biopsychology typically comes from converging operations—in this case, from the convergence of neuropsychological case studies, quasiexperiments on human subjects, and controlled experiments on laboratory animals. The strength of biopsychology lies in its diversity.

So what has all this research done for Jimmie G. and others like him? Today, alcoholics are often counseled to stop drinking and are treated with massive doses of thiamine. The thiamine limits the development of further brain damage and often leads to a slight improvement in the patient's condition; but unfortunately, brain damage, once produced, is permanent. In some parts of the world, the fortification of alcoholic beverages with thiamine has been seriously considered (Wodak, Richmond, & Wilson, 1990). What do you think of this plan?

1.6 Scientific Inference: How Do Biopsychologists Study the Unobservable Workings of the Brain?

Scientific inference is the fundamental method of biopsychology and of most other sciences—it is what makes being a scientist fun. This section provides further insight into the nature of biopsychology by defining, illustrating, and discussing scientific inference.

The scientific method is a system of finding out things by careful observation, but many of the processes studied by scientists cannot be observed. For example, scientists use empirical (observational) methods to study ice ages, gravity, evaporation, electricity, and nuclear fission—none of which can be directly observed; their effects can be observed, but the processes themselves cannot. Biopsychology is no different from other sciences in this respect. One of its main goals is to characterize, through empirical methods, the unobservable processes by which the nervous system controls behavior.

The empirical method that biopsychologists and other scientists use to study the unobservable is called **scientific inference.** The scientists carefully measure key events that they can observe and then use these measures as a basis for logically inferring the nature of events that they cannot observe. Like a detective carefully gathering clues from which to recreate an unwitnessed crime, a biopsychologist carefully gathers relevant measures of behavior and neural activity from which to infer the nature of the neural processes that regulate behavior. The fact that the neural mechanisms of behavior cannot be directly observed and must be studied through scientific inference is what makes biopsychological research such a challenge—and, as I said before, so much fun.

To illustrate scientific inference, I have selected a research project in which you can participate. By making a few simple observations about your own visual abilities under different conditions, you will be able to discover the principle by which your brain translates the movement of images on your retinas into perceptions of movement (see Figure 1.8 on page 14). One feature of the mechanism is immediately obvious. Hold your hand in front of your face, and then move its image across your retinas by moving your eyes, by moving your hand, or by moving both at once. You will notice that only those movements of the retinal image that are produced by the movement of your hand are translated into the sight of motion; movements of the retinal image that are produced by your own eye movements are not. Obviously, there must be a part of your brain that monitors the movements of your retinal image and subtracts from the total those image movements that

Converging operations. The use of several research approaches to solve a single problem.
Korsakoff's syndrome. A neuropsychological disorder that is common in alcoholics, the primary symptom of which is a disturbance of memory.

Scientific inference. The logical process by which observable events are used to infer the properties of unobservable events.

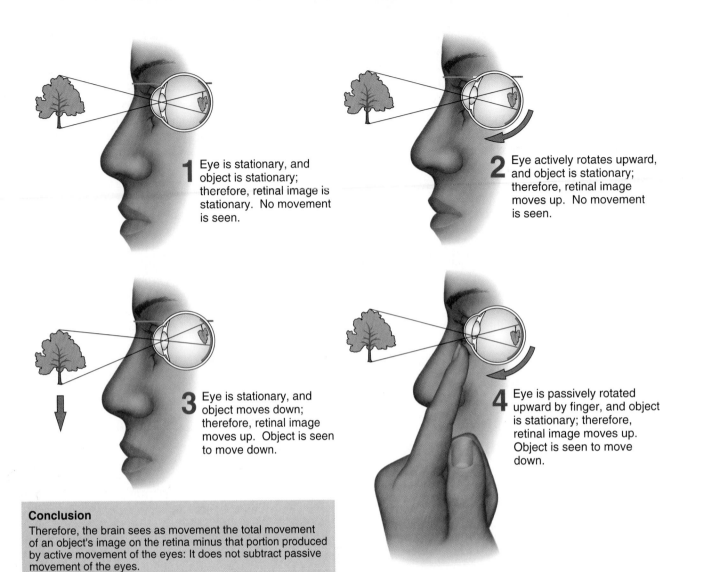

1 Eye is stationary, and object is stationary; therefore, retinal image is stationary. No movement is seen.

2 Eye actively rotates upward, and object is stationary; therefore, retinal image moves up. No movement is seen.

3 Eye is stationary, and object moves down; therefore, retinal image moves up. Object is seen to move down.

4 Eye is passively rotated upward by finger, and object is stationary; therefore, retinal image moves up. Object is seen to move down.

Conclusion
Therefore, the brain sees as movement the total movement of an object's image on the retina minus that portion produced by active movement of the eyes: It does not subtract passive movement of the eyes.

Figure 1.8 The perception of motion under four different conditions.

are produced by your own eye movements, leaving the remainder to be perceived as motion.

Now, let's try to characterize the nature of the information about your eye movements that is used by your brain in its perception of motion (see Bridgeman, Van der Heijden, & Velichkovsky, 1994). Try the following. Shut one eye, then rotate your other eye slightly upward by gently pressing on your lower eyelid with your fingertip. What do you see? You see all of the objects in your visual field moving downward. Why? It seems that the brain mechanism that is responsible for the perception of motion does not consider eye movement per se. It considers only those eye movements that are actively produced by neural signals from the brain to the eye muscles, not those that are passively produced by external means (e.g., by your finger). Thus when your eye was moved passively, your brain assumed that it had remained still and attributed the

movement of your retinal image to the movement of objects in your visual field.

It is possible to trick the visual system in the opposite way; instead of the eyes being moved when no active signals have been sent to the eye muscles, the eyes can be held stationary despite the brain's attempts to move them. Because this experiment involves paralyzing the eye muscles, you cannot participate. Hammond, Merton, and Sutton (1956) injected the active ingredient of *curare*, the paralytic substance with which some South American natives coat their blow darts, into the eye muscles of their subject—who was Merton himself. What do you think Merton saw when he tried to move his eyes? He saw the stationary visual world moving in the same direction as his attempted eye movements. If a visual object is focused on part of your retina, and it stays focused there despite the fact that you have moved your eyes to the right, it too must have moved to the right. Consequently, when Merton sent signals to his eye muscles to move his eyes to the right, his brain assumed that the movement had been carried out, and it perceived stationary objects as moving to the right. The point of this example is that biopsychologists can learn much about the activities of the brain without being able to directly observe them—and so can you.

What Is Bad Science, and How Do You Spot It?

Scientists, like other people, make mistakes; and biopsychologists are no exception. In fact, two features of biopsychological inquiry make it particularly susceptible to error. The first is that biopsychological research has such a wide appeal that it invites the participation of those who have had little or no experience with its complexities. The second is that it is often difficult to be objective when studying biopsychological phenomena. Whether we realize it or not, we all have many preconceptions about the brain and behavior ingrained in our thinking. Accordingly, this, the final section of the chapter, completes the task of defining biopsychology by discussing two of its well-documented errors.

You might wonder why a book about biopsychology would dwell, even momentarily, on errors in biopsychological research. There are two reasons. One reason is that understanding biopsychology's past errors provides important insights into what biopsychology is today—the standards and methods of a discipline frequently grow out of its mistakes. The other reason is that an understanding of biopsychology's errors will help you to become a better consumer of biopsychological science—it will imbue you with an appropriate degree of skepticism and the skills necessary to evaluate for yourself the validity of various claims. In other words, one purpose of this final section of Chapter 1 is to improve your BS detection skills—*BS*, of course, stands for bad science. Following are two historic examples of flawed biopsychological analysis.

Case 1

José Delgado demonstrated to a group of newspaper reporters a remarkable new procedure for controlling aggression. Delgado strode into a Spanish bull ring carrying only a red cape and a small radio transmitter. With the transmitter, he could activate a battery-powered stimulator that had previously been mounted on the horns of the other inhabitant of the ring. As the raging bull charged, Delgado calmly activated the stim-

ulator and sent a weak train of electrical current from the stimulator through an electrode that had been implanted in the caudate nucleus deep in the bull's brain. The bull immediately veered from its charge. After a few such interrupted charges, the bull stood tamely as Delgado swaggered about the ring. According to Delgado, this demonstration marked a significant scientific breakthrough—the discovery of a caudate taming center and the fact that stimulation of this structure could eliminate aggressive behavior, even in bulls specially bred for their ferocity.

To those present at this carefully orchestrated event and to most of the millions who subsequently read about it, Delgado's conclusion was compelling. Surely, if caudate stimulation could stop the charge of a raging bull, the caudate must be a taming center. It was even suggested that caudate stimulation through implanted electrodes might be an effective treatment for human psychopaths. What do you think?

■ **ANALYSIS OF CASE 1** The fact of the matter is that Delgado's demonstration provided little or no support for his conclusion. It should have been obvious to anyone who did not get caught up in the provocative nature of Delgado's media event that there are numerous ways in which brain stimulation can abort a bull's charge, most of which are more simple, and thus more probable, than the one suggested by Delgado. For example, the stimulation may have simply rendered the bull confused, dizzy, nauseous, sleepy, or temporarily blind rather than nonaggressive; or the stimulation could have been painful. Clearly, any observation that can be interpreted in so many different ways provides little support for any one interpretation. When there are several possible interpretations for a behavioral observation, the rule is to give precedence to the simplest one; this rule is called **Morgan's Canon.** The following

> **Morgan's Canon.** The rule that the simplest possible interpretation for a behavioral result should be given precedence.

comments of Valenstein (1973) provide a reasoned view of Delgado's demonstration:

> Actually there is no good reason for believing that the stimulation had any direct effect on the bull's aggressive tendencies. An examination of the film record makes it apparent that the charging bull was stopped because as long as the stimulation was on it was forced to turn around in the same direction continuously. After examining the film, any scientist with knowledge in this field could conclude only that the stimulation had been activating a neural pathway controlling movement. (p. 98)
>
> . . . he [Delgado] seems to capitalize on every individual effect his electrodes happen to produce and presents little, if any, experimental evidence that his impression of the underlying cause is correct. (p. 103)
>
> . . . his propensity for dramatic, albeit ambiguous, demonstrations has been a constant source of material for those whose purposes are served by exaggerating the omnipotence of brain stimulation. (p. 99)

Case 2

In 1949, Dr. Egas Moniz was awarded the Nobel Prize in Physiology and Medicine for the development of **prefrontal lobotomy**—a surgical procedure in which the connections between the prefrontal lobes and the rest of the brain are cut—as a treatment for mental illness. The **prefrontal lobes** are the large areas, left and right, at the very front of the brain (see Figure 1.9). Moniz's discovery was based on the report that Becky, a chimpanzee that frequently became upset when she made errors during the performance of a food-rewarded task, did not do so following the creation of a large *bilateral lesion* (an area of damage to both sides of the brain) of her prefrontal lobes. After hearing about this isolated observation at a scientific meeting in 1935, Moniz persuaded neurosurgeon Almeida Lima to operate on a series of psychiatric patients; Almeida cut out six large cores of prefrontal tissue with a surgical device called a **leucotome** (see Figure 1.10).

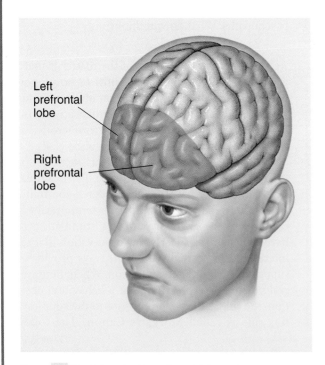

Left prefrontal lobe

Right prefrontal lobe

Figure 1.9 The left and right prefrontal lobes, whose connections to the rest of the brain are disrupted by prefrontal lobotomy.

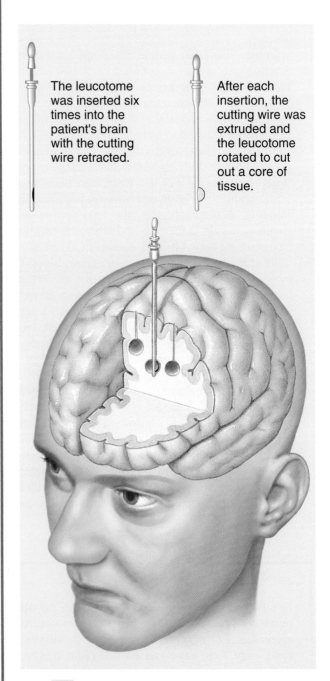

The leucotome was inserted six times into the patient's brain with the cutting wire retracted.

After each insertion, the cutting wire was extruded and the leucotome rotated to cut out a core of tissue.

Figure 1.10 The prefrontal lobotomy procedure developed by Moniz and Lima.

Following Moniz's claims that prefrontal surgery was therapeutically successful and had no significant side effects, there was a rapid proliferation of various forms of prefrontal psychosurgery (see O'Callaghan & Carroll, 1982; Valenstein, 1980, 1986). One such variation was **transorbital lobotomy,** which was developed in Italy and then popularized in the United States by Walter Freeman in the late 1940s. It involved inserting an ice-pick–like device under the eyelid, driving it through the orbit (the eye socket) with a few taps of a mallet, and pushing it into the frontal lobes, where it was waved back and forth to sever the connections between the prefrontal lobes and the rest of the brain (see Figure 1.11). This operation was frequently performed in the surgeon's office.

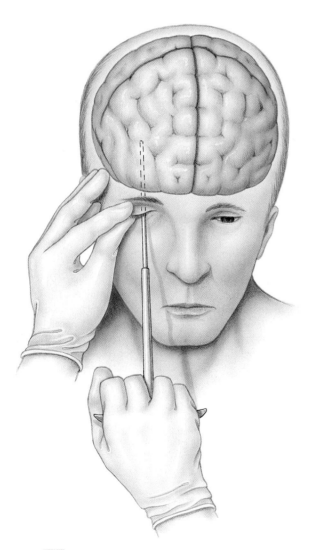

Figure 1.11 The transorbital procedure for performing prefrontal lobotomy.

■ **ANALYSIS OF CASE 2** Incredible as it may seem, Moniz's program of psychosurgery was largely based on the observation of a single chimpanzee in a single situation, thus displaying a complete lack of appreciation for the diversity of brain and behavior, both within and between species. No program of psychosurgery should ever be initiated without a thorough assessment of the effects of the surgery on a large sample of subjects from various nonhuman mammalian species.

A second major weakness in the scientific case for prefrontal psychosurgery was the failure of Moniz and others to carefully evaluate the consequences of the surgery in the first patients to undergo the operation. The early reports that the operation was therapeutically successful were based on the impressions of the individuals who were the least objective—the physicians who had prescribed the surgery. Patients were frequently judged as improved if they were more manageable, and little effort was made to evaluate more important aspects of their psychological adjustment or to document the existence of adverse side effects.

Eventually, it became clear that prefrontal lobotomies are of little therapeutic benefit and that they produce a wide range of undesirable side effects, such as amorality, lack of foresight, emotional unresponsiveness, epilepsy, and urinary incontinence. This led to the abandonment of frontal lobotomy in many parts of the world—but not before over 40,000 patients had been lobotomized in the United States alone. Still, prefrontal lobotomies continue to be performed in some countries.

Some regard sound scientific methods as unnecessary obstacles in the paths of patients seeking treatment and therapists striving to provide it. However, the practice of prefrontal lobotomy should caution us against abandoning science for expediency. Only by observing the rules of science can scientists protect the public from bogus scientific claims (Carroll, 1984).

There is a somber postscript to this story. Moniz was shot by one of his patients. The bullet became lodged in his spine, rendering him *paraplegic* (paralyzed below the waist).

Prefrontal lobotomy. A surgical procedure in which the connections between the prefrontal lobes and the rest of the brain are cut as a treatment for mental illness.

Prefrontal lobes. The large areas, left and right, at the very front of the brain.

Leucotome. Any one of the various surgical devices used for performing lobotomies—*leucotomy* is another word for lobotomy.

Transorbital lobotomy. A prefrontal lobotomy performed with a cutting instrument inserted through the orbit or eye socket.

CONCLUSION

The general purpose of this chapter was to define *biopsychology* and to whet your appetite for more of it. Biopsychology was characterized from seven different perspectives, each corresponding to a section of the chapter. First, you learned that biopsychology is the study of the biology of behavior (1.1), that biopsychology is a major discipline of neuroscience (1.2), that biopsychological research is conducted in a variety of different ways (1.3), and that biopsychology comprises six fundamentally different divisions: physiological psychology, psychopharmacology, neuropsychology, psychophysiology, cognitive neuroscience, and compara-

tive psychology (1.4). Then, you were introduced to two important principles of biopsychological research: converging operations (1.5) and scientific inference (1.6). Finally, you were provided with two examples of bad biopsychology, which illustrated the importance of adhering to the fundamental principles of scientific inquiry and of greeting claims of major scientific breakthroughs with a healthy degree of skepticism (1.7).

You are about to enter a world of amazing discoveries and intriguing ideas: the world of biopsychology. I hope that your brain enjoys learning about itself.

FOOD FOR THOUGHT

1. Chapter 1 tells you in general conceptual terms what biopsychology is. Another, and perhaps better, way of defining biopsychology is to describe what biopsychologists do. Ask your instructor what she or he did to become a biopsychologist and what she or he does each workday. I think that you will be surprised. Is your instructor predominantly a physiological psychologist, a psychopharmacologist, a neuropsychologist, a psychophysiologist, a cognitive neuroscientist, or a comparative psychologist?

2. What ethical considerations should guide biopsychological research on nonhuman animals? How should

these ethical considerations differ from those that should guide biopsychological research on humans? See the chapter's Additional Reading section.

3. In retrospect, the entire prefrontal lobotomy episode is shocking. How could physicians, who are generally intelligent, highly educated, and dedicated to helping their patients, participate in such a travesty? How could somebody win a Nobel Prize for developing a form of surgery that left over 40,000 mental cripples in the United States alone? Why did this happen? Could it happen today?

KEY TERMS

Applied research (*p. 8*)
Autonomic nervous system (*p. 10*)
Between-subjects design (*p. 6*)
Biopsychology (*p. 3*)
Case studies (*p. 7*)
Cerebral cortex (*p. 9*)
Cognition (*p. 10*)
Cognitive neuroscience (*p. 10*)
Comparative approach (*p. 5*)
Comparative psychology (*p. 11*)

Confounded variable (*p. 6*)
Converging operations (*p. 12*)
Coolidge effect (*p. 6*)
Dependent variable (*p. 6*)
Electroencephalogram (EEG) (*p. 10*)
Ethological research (*p. 11*)
Generalizability (*p. 8*)
Independent variable (*p. 6*)
Korsakoff's syndrome (*p. 12*)
Leucotome (*p. 16*)
Lordosis (*p. 7*)

Morgan's Canon (*p. 15*)
Neuroanatomy (*p. 4*)
Neurochemistry (*p. 4*)
Neuroendocrinology (*p. 4*)
Neurons (*p. 2*)
Neuropathology (*p. 4*)
Neuropharmacology (*p. 4*)
Neurophysiology (*p. 4*)
Neuropsychology (*p. 9*)
Neuroscience (*p. 2*)
Physiological psychology (*p. 9*)

Prefrontal lobes (*p. 16*)
Prefrontal lobotomy (*p. 16*)
Psychopharmacology (*p. 9*)
Psychophysiology (*p. 10*)
Pure research (*p. 8*)
Quasiexperimental studies (*p. 7*)
Scientific inference (*p. 13*)
Society for Neuroscience (*p. 4*)
Transorbital lobotomy (*p. 17*)
Within-subjects design (*p. 6*)

ADDITIONAL READING

Each of the following books provides an excellent introduction to one of the six biopsychological subdisciplines:

Andreassi, J. L. (1989). *Psychophysiology: Human behavior and physiological response*. Hillsdale, NJ: Erlbaum.

Carlson, N. R. (1994). *Physiology of behavior* (5th ed.). Boston: Allyn & Bacon.

Dewsbury, D. A. (1990). *Contemporary issues in comparative psychology*. Sunderland, MA: Sinauer.

Kolb, B., & Whishaw, I. Q. (1996). *Fundamentals of human neuropsychology* (4th ed.). New York: Freeman.

Julien, R. M. (1996). *A primer of drug action* (7th ed.). New York: Freeman.

Posner, M. I., & Raichle, M. E. (1994). *Images of mind.* New York: Scientific American Library.

This book provides an excellent historic overview of the topic of psychosurgery:

Valenstein, E. S. (1986). *Great and desperate cures: The rise and decline of psychosurgery and other radical treatments for mental illness.* New York: Basic Books.

The following article is a good discussion of what biopsychology is and how it is related to the other neurosciences:

Davis, H. P., Rosenzweig, M. R., Becker, L. A., & Sather, K. J. (1988). Biological psychology's relationships to psychology and neuroscience. *American Psychologist, 43,* 359–371.

This article argues convincingly that biopsychology is more than the study of the neural basis of behavior:

Dewsbury, D. A. (1991). Psychobiology. *American Psychologist, 46,* 198–205.

The following articles deal with the ethics of research on nonhuman animals:

Institute of Laboratory Animal Resources: Commission on Life Sciences (1996). *Guide for the care and use of laboratory animals.* Washington: National Academy Press.

Miller, N. E. (1991). Commentary on Ulrich: Need to check truthfulness of statements by opponents of animal research. *Psychological Science, 6,* 422–424.

Ulrich, R. E. (1991). Commentary: Animal rights, animal wrongs, and the question of balance. *Psychological Science, 2,* 197–201.

Finally, as the door to neuroscientific information on the World Wide Web, check out the *Neuroguide* site at the following address (see also Burke & Benson, 1997):

http://www.neuroguide.com

Evolution, Genetics, and Experience:
Asking the Right Questions about the
Biology of Behavior

We all tend to think about things in ways that have been ingrained in us by our **Zeitgeist** (pronounced "ZYTE-gyste"), the general intellectual climate of our culture. That is why this is a particularly important chapter for you. You see, you are the intellectual product of a Zeitgeist that promotes ways of thinking about the biological bases of behavior that are inconsistent with the facts. The primary purpose of this chapter is to help you bring your thinking about the biology of behavior in line with modern biopsychological science.

Most textbook chapters focus on answers. This chapter focuses on questions—the questions that people tend to ask about the biology of behavior. It tries to teach you to ask the right questions about the biology of behavior by describing why biopsychologists have abandoned traditional questions in favor of more insightful alternatives. Asking the right questions is the first step toward getting the right answers.

2.1 Thinking about the Biology of Behavior: From Dichotomies to Relations and Interactions

We tend to ignore the subtleties, inconsistencies, and complexities of our existence and to think in terms of simple, mutually exclusive dichotomies: right–wrong, good–bad, attractive–unattractive, and so on. The allure of this way of thinking is its simplicity.

The tendency to think about behavior in terms of dichotomies is illustrated by two kinds of questions that people commonly ask about behavior: (1) Is it physiological, or is it psychological? (2) Is it inherited, or is it learned? Both questions have proved to be misguided; yet they are among the most common kinds of questions asked in biopsychology classrooms. That is why I am dwelling on them here.

Is It Physiological, or Is It Psychological?

The idea that human processes fall into one of two categories, physiological or psychological, grew out of a 17th-century conflict between science and the Roman Church. For much of the history of Western civilization, truth was whatever was decreed to be true by the Church. Then, in about 1400, things started to change. The famines, plagues, and marauding armies that had repeatedly swept Europe during the middle ages subsided, and interest turned to art, commerce, and scholarship—this was the period of the *Renaissance*, or rebirth (1400 to 1700). Some Renaissance scholars were not content to follow the dictates of the Church; instead, they started to study things directly by observing them—and so it was that modern science was born.

Much of the scientific knowledge that accumulated during the Renaissance was at odds with Church dogma. However, the conflict was resolved by the prominent French philosopher René Descartes (pronounced "day CART"). Descartes (1596–1650) proposed a philosophy that, in a sense, gave one part of the universe to science and the other part to the Church. He argued that the universe is composed of two elements: (1) physical matter, which behaves according to the laws of nature and is thus a suitable object of scientific investigation; and (2) the human mind (soul or spirit), which lacks physical substance, controls human behavior, obeys no natural laws, and is thus the appropriate purview of the Church. The human body, including the brain, was assumed to be entirely physical, and so were nonhuman animals.

Cartesian dualism, as Descartes's philosophy became known, was sanctioned by the Roman Church, and so the idea that the human brain and the mind are separate entities became widely accepted. It has survived to this day, despite the intervening centuries of scientific progress. Most people now understand that human behavior has a physiological basis, but many still cling to the dualistic assumption that there is a category of human activity that somehow transcends the human brain.

Is It Inherited, or Is It Learned?

The tendency to think in terms of dichotomies extends to the way people think about the development of behavioral capacities. For centuries, scholars have debated whether humans and other animals inherit their behavioral capacities or whether they acquire them through learning. This issue is commonly referred to as the **nature–nurture issue.**

Zeitgeist. The general intellectual climate of a culture.
Cartesian dualism. The philosophical position of Descartes, who argued that the universe is composed of two elements: physical matter and the human mind.

Nature–nurture issue. The debate about the relative contributions of nature (genes) and nurture (experience) to the behavioral capacities of individuals.

Most of the early North American experimental psychologists were totally committed to the nurture (learning) side of the nature–nurture issue. The degree of this commitment is illustrated by the oft-cited words of John B. Watson, the father of *behaviorism:*

> We have no real evidence of the inheritance of [behavioral] traits. I would feel perfectly confident in the ultimately favorable outcome of careful upbringing of a healthy, well-formed baby born of a long line of crooks, murderers and thieves, and prostitutes. Who has any evidence to the contrary?
>
> . . . Give me a dozen healthy infants, well-formed, and my own specified world to bring them up in and I'll guarantee to take any one at random and train him to become any type of specialist I might select—doctor, lawyer, artist, merchant-chief and, yes even beggar-man and thief. (Watson, 1930, pp. 103–104)

At the same time that experimental psychology was taking root in North America, **ethology** (the study of animal behavior in the wild) was becoming the dominant approach to the study of behavior in Europe. European ethology, in contrast to North American experimental psychology, focused on the study of **instinctive behaviors** (behaviors that occur in all like members of a species, even when there seems to have been no opportunity for them to have been learned), and it emphasized the role of nature, or inherited factors, in behavioral development. For example, Tinbergen and Perdeck (1950) studied the tendency of newly hatched herring-gull chicks to peck at the red dot on the bills of their parents, which caused the parents to regurgitate a yummy meal of half-digested fish. Because instinctive behaviors do not seem to be learned, the early ethologists assumed that they are entirely inherited. They were wrong, but then so were the early experimental psychologists.

Problems with Thinking about the Biology of Behavior in Terms of Traditional Dichotomies

The physiological-or-psychological and nature-or-nurture questions are based on incorrect ways of thinking about the biology of behavior, and a new generation of questions is directing the current boom in biopsychological research. What is wrong with these old ways of thinking about the biology of behavior, and what are the new ways?

■ **PHYSIOLOGICAL-OR-PSYCHOLOGICAL THINKING RUNS INTO DIFFICULTY** Not long after Descartes's mind–brain dualism was officially sanctioned by the Roman Church, it started to come under public attack.

> In 1747, Julien Offroy de la Mettrie anonymously published a pamphlet that scandalized Europe. . . . La Mettrie fled to Berlin, where he was forced to live in exile for the rest of his life. His crime? He had argued that thought was produced by the brain—a dangerous assault, in the eyes of his contemporaries. . . . Not for the last time, the science of human mind had outgrown human imagination. (Corsi, 1991, cover)

Although many people still believe that there is a purely psychological category of human activity that transcends the human brain, two kinds of evidence indicate otherwise. First, numerous studies have shown that even the most complex psychological processes (e.g., memory, emotion, and self-awareness) can be modified by damage to or stimulation of the higher regions of the brain (see Kosslyn & Andersen, 1992). Second, some nonhuman species have been found to possess abilities that were once assumed to be purely psychological and thus purely human (see Cheney & Seyfarth, 1992). The following two quotations illustrate these two kinds of evidence; both quotations deal with the study of self-awareness.

The first quotation describes Oliver Sacks's (1985) case of "the man who fell out of bed."[1] He—the patient, not Sacks—was suffering from **asomatognosia,** a deficiency in the awareness of parts of one's own body. Asomatognosia typically involves the left side of the body and usually results from damage to the *right parietal lobe* (see Figure 2.1). The second quotation describes G. G. Gallup's (1983) demonstrations of self-awareness in chimpanzees (see Parker, Mitchell, & Boccia, 1994; and Figure 2.2)[2].

> He had felt fine all day, and fallen asleep towards evening. When he woke up he felt fine too, until he moved in the bed. Then he found, as he put it, "someone's leg" in the bed—*a severed human leg,* a horrible thing! He was stunned, at first, with amazement and disgust. . . . [Then] he had a brainwave. . . . Obviously one of the nurses . . . had stolen into the Dissecting Room and nabbed a leg, and then slipped it under his bedclothes as a joke. . . . *When he threw it out of bed, he somehow came after it—and now it was attached to him.*
>
> "Look at it!" he cried. . . . "Have you ever seen such a creepy, horrible thing?" . . .
>
> "Easy!" I said. "Be calm! Take it easy!" . . .
>
> " . . . why . . . " he asked irritably, belligerently.
>
> "Because it's *your* leg," I answered. "Don't you know your own leg?" . . .
>
> . . . "Ah Doc!" he said. "You're fooling me! You're in cahoots with that nurse." . . .
>
> "Listen," I said. "I don't think you're well. Please allow us to return you to bed. But I want to ask you one final question. If this—this thing—is *not* your left leg . . . then where is your own left leg?"

[1]From *The Man Who Mistook His Wife for a Hat and Other Clinical Tales* (pp. 53–55) by Oliver Sacks, 1985. New York: Summit Books. Copyright © 1970, 1981, 1983, 1984, 1985 by Oliver Sacks. Reprinted by permission of Summit Books, a division of Simon & Schuster, Inc.

[2]From *Toward a Comparative Psychology of Mind* (pp. 474–477) by G. G. Gallup, Jr. In R. L. Mellgren, ed., *Animal Cognition and Behavior.* Amsterdam: North-Holland Publishing Co. Copyright © 1983. Reprinted by permission of North-Holland Publishing Co. and G. G. Gallup, Jr.

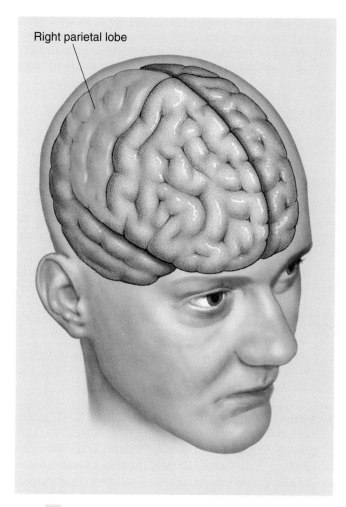

Right parietal lobe

Figure 2.1 Asomatognosia typically involves damage to the right parietal lobe.

Figure 2.2 The reactions of chimpanzees to their own images indicate that they are self-aware. In this photo, the chimpanzee is reacting to the bright red, odorless dye that was painted on its eyebrow ridge while it was anesthetized.

(Photograph by Donna Bierschwale, courtesy of the New Iberia Research Center.)

Once more he became pale—so pale that I thought he was going to faint. "I don't know," he said. "I have no idea. It's disappeared. It's gone. It's nowhere to be found." (Sacks, 1985, pp. 53–55)

An organism is self-aware to the extent that it can be shown capable of becoming the object of its own attention. . . . One way to assess an organism's capacity to become the object of its own attention is to confront it with a mirror.

. . . I gave a number of group-reared, preadolescent chimpanzees individual exposure to themselves in mirrors. . . . Invariably, their first reaction to the mirror was to respond as if they were seeing another chimpanzee. . . . After about two days, however, . . . they . . . started to use the mirror to groom and inspect parts of their bodies they had not seen before, and progressively began to experiment with the reflection by making faces, looking at themselves upside down, and assuming unusual postures while monitoring the results in the mirror. . . .

So in an attempt to provide a more convincing demonstration of self-recognition, I devised an unobtrusive and more rigorous test. . . . [E]ach chimpanzee was anesthetized. . . . I carefully painted the uppermost portion of an eyebrow ridge and the top half of the opposite ear with a bright red, odorless, alcohol soluble dye. . . .

Following recovery from anesthesia . . . the mirror was then reintroduced as an explicit test of self-recognition. Upon seeing their painted faces in the mirror, all the chimpanzees showed repeated mark-directed responses, consisting of attempts to touch and inspect marked areas on their eyebrow and ear while watching the image. In addition, there was over a three-fold increase in viewing time. . . . Several chimpanzees also showed noteworthy attempts to visually examine and smell the fingers which had been used to touch these facial marks. I suspect that you would respond pretty much the same way, if upon awakening one morning you saw yourself in the mirror with red spots on your face. (Gallup, 1983, pp. 474–477)

■ NATURE-OR-NURTURE THINKING RUNS INTO DIFFICULTY The history of nature-or-nurture thinking can be summed up by paraphrasing Mark Twain: "Reports of its death have been greatly exaggerated." Each time it has been discredited, it has resurfaced in a slightly modified form. First, factors other than genetics and learning were shown to influence behavioral development; factors such as the fetal environment, nutrition, stress, and sensory stimulation also proved to be influential. This led to a broadening of the concept of nurture to include a variety of experiential factors in

Ethology. The study of the behavior of animals in their natural environments.
Instinctive behaviors. Behaviors that occur in all like members of a species, even when there seems to have been no oppor-
tunity for them to have been learned.
Asomatognosia. A deficiency in awareness of one's own body that is produced by brain damage.

addition to learning. In effect, it changed the nature-or-nurture dichotomy from "genetic factors or learning" to "genetic factors or experience."

Next, it was argued convincingly that behavior always develops under the combined control of both nature and nurture (see Johnston, 1987; Rutter, 1997), not under the control of one or the other. Faced with this discovery, many people merely substituted one kind of nature–nurture thinking for another. They stopped asking, "Is it genetic or is it the result of experience?" and started asking, "How much of it is genetic, and how much of it is the result of experience?"

Like earlier versions of the nature–nurture question, the how-much-of-it-is-genetic-and-how-much-of-it-is-the-result-of-experience version is fundamentally flawed. The problem is that it is based on the premise that genetic factors and experiential factors combine in an additive fashion—that a behavioral capacity, such as intelligence, is created through the combination or mixture of so many parts of genetics and so many parts of experience, rather than through the interaction of genetics and experience. Once you learn more about how genetic factors and experience interact, you will better appreciate the folly of this assumption. For the time being, however, let me illustrate its weakness with a metaphor embedded in an anecdote:

> One of my students told me that she had read that intelligence was one-third genetic and two-thirds experience, and she wondered whether this was true. She must have been puzzled when I began my response by describing an alpine experience. "I was lazily wandering up a summit ridge when I heard an unexpected sound. Ahead, with his back to me, was a young man sitting on the edge of a precipice, blowing into a peculiar musical instrument. I sat down behind him on a large sun-soaked rock, ate my lunch, and shared his experience with him. Then, I got up and wandered back down the ridge, leaving him undisturbed."
>
> I put the following question to my student: "If I wanted to get a better understanding of this music, would it be reasonable for me to begin by asking how much of it came from the musician and how much of it came from the instrument?"
>
> "That would be dumb," she said. "The music comes from both; it makes no sense to ask how much comes from the musician and how much comes from the instrument. Somehow the music results from the interaction of the two together. You would have to ask about the interaction."

"That's exactly right," I said. "Now, do you see why . . . "

"Don't say any more," she interrupted. "I see what you're getting at. Intelligence is the product of the interaction of genes and experience, and it is dumb to try to find how much comes from genes and how much comes from experience."

"And the same is true of any other behavioral trait," I added.

Several days later, the student strode into my office, reached into her pack, and pulled out a familiar object. "I believe that this is your mystery musical instrument," she said. "It's a Peruvian panpipe." She was right . . . again.

The point of this metaphor, in case you have forgotten, is to illustrate why it is nonsensical to try to understand interactions between two factors by asking how much each factor contributes. We would not ask how much the musician and how much the panpipe contributes to panpipe music; we would not ask how much the water and how much the temperature contributes to evaporation; and we would not ask how much the male and how much the female contributes to copulation. Similarly, we shouldn't ask how much genetic and experiential factors contribute to behavioral development. In each case, the answers lie in understanding the nature of the interactions.

■ A MODEL OF THE BIOLOGY OF BEHAVIOR So far in this section, you have learned why people tend to think about the biology of behavior in terms of dichotomies, and you have learned some of the reasons why this way of thinking is inappropriate. Now, let's look at the way of thinking about the biology of behavior that has been adopted by many biopsychologists (see Kimble, 1989). It is illustrated in Figure 2.3. Like other powerful ideas, it is simple and logical. This five-stage model boils down to the single premise that all behavior is the product of interactions among three factors: (1) the organism's genetic endowment, which is a product of its evolution; (2) its experience; and (3) its perception of the current situation. Please examine the model carefully, and consider its implications.

The next three sections of this chapter deal with three elements of this model of behavior: evolution, genetics, and the interaction of genetics and experience in behavioral development. The final section deals with the genetics of human psychological differences.

2.2 Human Evolution

Modern biology began in 1859 with the publication of Charles Darwin's *On the Origin of Species.* In this monumental work, Darwin described his theory of evolution—the single most influential theory in the biological sciences. Darwin was not the first to suggest that species **evolve** (undergo gradual orderly change) from

EVOLUTION, GENETICS, AND EXPERIENCE: ASKING THE RIGHT QUESTIONS ABOUT THE BIOLOGY OF BEHAVIOR

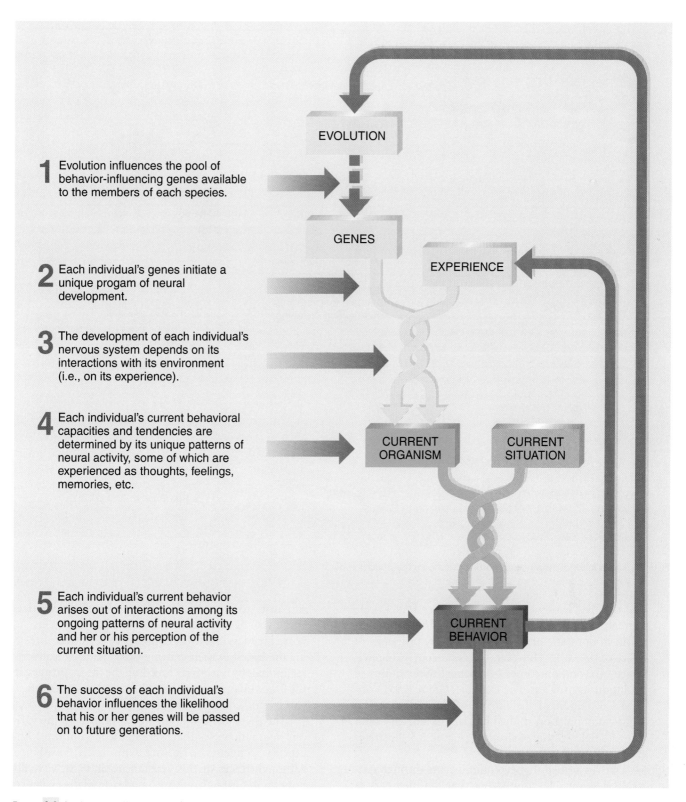

1 Evolution influences the pool of behavior-influencing genes available to the members of each species.

2 Each individual's genes initiate a unique progam of neural development.

3 The development of each individual's nervous system depends on its interactions with its environment (i.e., on its experience).

4 Each individual's current behavioral capacities and tendencies are determined by its unique patterns of neural activity, some of which are experienced as thoughts, feelings, memories, etc.

5 Each individual's current behavior arises out of interactions among its ongoing patterns of neural activity and her or his perception of the current situation.

6 The success of each individual's behavior influences the likelihood that his or her genes will be passed on to future generations.

EVOLUTION

GENES

EXPERIENCE

CURRENT ORGANISM

CURRENT SITUATION

CURRENT BEHAVIOR

Figure 2.3 A schematic illustration of the way that many biopsychologists think about the biology of behavior.

preexisting species; but he was the first to amass a large body of supporting evidence, and he was the first to suggest how evolution occurs.

Darwin presented three kinds of evidence to support his assertion that species evolve: (1) He documented the evolution of fossil records through progressively more recent geological layers. (2) He described striking structural similarities among living species (e.g., a human's hand, a bird's wing, and a cat's paw), which suggested

Evolve. To undergo gradual orderly change.

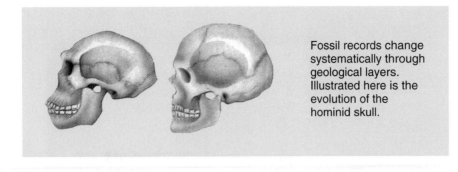
Fossil records change systematically through geological layers. Illustrated here is the evolution of the hominid skull.

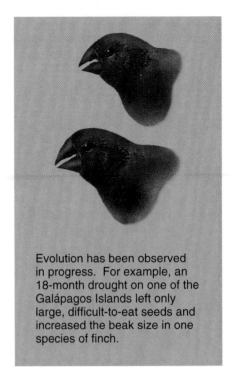
Evolution has been observed in progress. For example, an 18-month drought on one of the Galápagos Islands left only large, difficult-to-eat seeds and increased the beak size in one species of finch.

Major changes have been created in domestic plants and animals by programs of selective breeding.

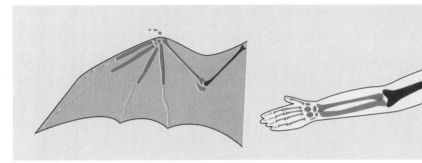
There are striking structural similarities among diverse living species (e.g., between a human arm and a bat's wing).

Figure 2.4 Four kinds of evidence supporting the theory that species evolve.

that they had evolved from common ancestors. (3) He pointed to the major changes that had been brought about in domestic plants and animals by programs of selective breeding. However, the most convincing evidence of evolution comes from direct observations of evolution in progress. For example, Grant (1991) observed evolution of the finches of the Galápagos Islands—a population studied by Darwin himself—after only a single season of drought. Figure 2.4 illustrates these four kinds of evidence.

Darwin argued that evolution occurs through **natural selection.** He pointed out that the members of each species vary greatly in their structure, physiology, and behavior, and that the heritable traits that are associated with high rates of survival and reproduction are the most likely ones to be passed on to future generations. He argued that natural selection, when repeated generation after generation, leads to the evolution of species that are better adapted to surviving and reproducing in their particular environmental niche. Darwin called this process *natural selection* to emphasize its

similarity to the artificial selective breeding practices employed by breeders of domestic animals. Just as horse breeders create faster horses by selectively breeding the fastest of their existing stock, nature creates fitter animals by selectively breeding the fittest. **Fitness,** in the Darwinian sense, is the ability of an organism to survive and contribute its genes to the next generation.

The theory of evolution was at odds with the various dogmatic views that were embedded in the 19th-century Zeitgeist, so it met with initial resistance. Although traces of this resistance still exist, virtually none comes from people who understand the evidence:

Evolution by natural selection meets no significant opposition within biological science. The principle of natural selection has a logical necessity to it; indeed, some have argued that it is a tautology rather than an empirical law . . . [S]ubsequent development of biology in major new areas like genetics and biochemistry has only reinforced Darwin's conclusion that the facts make a belief in the theory of evolution by natural selection "inescapable." (Daly & Wilson, 1983, p. 7)

Figure 2.5 Two massive bull elephant seals challenging one another. Dominant bull elephant seals copulate more frequently than those that are lower in the dominance hierarchy. (Adapted from McCann, 1981.)

Evolution and Behavior

Some behaviors play an obvious role in evolution. For example, the ability to find food, avoid predation, and defend one's young obviously increases an animal's ability to pass on its genes to future generations. Other behaviors play a role that is less obvious but no less important; two examples are social dominance and courtship display.

■ **SOCIAL DOMINANCE** The males of many social species establish a stable *hierarchy of social dominance* through combative encounters with other males. In some species, these encounters often involve physical damage; in others, they involve mainly posturing and threatening until one of the two combatants backs down. The dominant male usually wins encounters with all other males of the group; the number 2 male usually wins encounters with all males except the dominant male; and so on down the line. Once a hierarchy is established, hostilities diminish because the low-ranking males learn to avoid or quickly submit to the dominant males. Because most of the fighting goes on between males competing for positions high in the social hierarchy, low-ranking males fight little; hence the lower levels of the hierarchy tend to be only vaguely recognizable.

Why is social dominance an important factor in evolution? One reason is that in some species dominant males copulate more than nondominant males and thus are more effective in passing on their characteristics to future generations. McCann (1981) studied the effect of social dominance on the rate of copulation in 10 bull elephant seals that cohabited the same breeding beach. Figure 2.5 illustrates how these massive animals challenge

each other by raising themselves to full height and pushing chest to chest. Usually, the smaller of the two backs down; if it does not, a vicious neck-biting battle ensues. McCann found that the dominant male accounted for about 37% of the copulations during the study, whereas poor number 10 accounted for only about 1% (see Figure 2.5).

Another reason why social dominance is an important factor in evolution is that in some species dominant females are more likely to produce more, and more healthy, offspring. For example, Pusey, Williams, and Goodall (1997) found that high-ranking female chimpanzees produced more offspring and that these offspring were more likely to survive to sexual maturity. They attributed these advantages to the fact that higher-ranking female chimpanzees are more likely to maintain access to productive food foraging areas.

■ **COURTSHIP DISPLAY** An intricate series of courtship displays precedes copulation in many species (see Figure 2.6 on page 28). The male approaches the female and signals his interest. His signal (which may be olfactory, visual, auditory, or tactual) may elicit a signal in the female, which may elicit another response in the male, and so on until copulation ensues. But copulation is unlikely to occur if one of the pair fails to react appropriately to the signals of the other.

Courtship displays are thought to promote the evolution of new species. Let me explain. A **species** is a group of organisms that is reproductively isolated from other organisms; that is, the members of one species can produce fertile offspring only by mating with members of the same species. A new species begins to branch off from an existing species when some barrier discourages breeding between a subpopulation of the existing species and the remainder of the species. Once such a reproductive barrier forms, the subpopulation evolves independently of the remainder of the species until cross-fertilization becomes impossible.

The reproductive barrier may be geographic; for example, a few birds may fly together to an isolated island, where many generations of their offspring breed among themselves and evolve into a separate species. Alterna-

Natural selection. The idea that heritable traits that are associated with high rates of survival and reproduction are preferentially passed on to future generations.

Fitness. The ability of an organism to survive and contribute its genes to the next generation.

Species. A group of organisms that is reproductively isolated from other organisms; the members of one species cannot produce fertile offspring by mating with members of other species.

Figure 2.6 A courtship display of the male great frigatebird.

Figure 2.7 Florida walking catfish, which travel on land by propelling themselves with their fins.

tively—to get back to the main point—the reproductive barrier may be behavioral. A few members of a species may develop different courtship displays, and these may form a reproductive barrier between themselves and the rest of their **conspecifics** (members of the same species).

Course of Human Evolution

By studying fossil records and comparing current species, we humans have looked back in time and pieced together the evolutionary history of our species—although some of the details are still controversial. Human evolution, as it is currently understood, is summarized in this section.

■**EVOLUTION OF VERTEBRATES** Complex multicellular water-dwelling organisms first appeared on earth about 600 million years ago (Vermeij, 1996). About 150 million years later, the first chordates evolved. **Chordates** (pronounced "KOR dates") are animals with dorsal nerve cords (large nerves that run along the center of the back, or *dorsum*); they are 1 of the 20 or so large categories, or *phyla* (pronounced "FY la"), into which zoologists group animal species. The first chordates with spinal bones to protect their dorsal nerve cords evolved about 25 million years later. The spinal bones are called *vertebrae* (pronounced "VERT eh bray"), and the chordates that possess them are called **vertebrates.** The first vertebrates were primitive bony fishes. Today, there are seven classes of vertebrates: three classes of fishes, plus amphibians, reptiles, birds, and mammals.

■**EVOLUTION OF AMPHIBIANS** About 410 million years ago, the first bony fishes ventured out of the water. Fishes that could survive on land for brief periods of time had two great advantages: They could escape from stagnant pools to nearby fresh water, and they could take advantage of terrestrial food sources (see Figure 2.7). The advantages of life on land were so great that natural selection transformed the fins and gills of bony fishes to legs and lungs, respectively—and so

it was that the first **amphibians** evolved about 400 million years ago. Amphibians (e.g., frogs, toads, and salamanders) in their larval form must live in the water; only adult amphibians can survive on land.

■**EVOLUTION OF REPTILES** About 300 million years ago, reptiles (e.g., lizards, snakes, and turtles) evolved from amphibians. Reptiles were the first vertebrates to lay shell-covered eggs and to be covered by dry scales. Both of these adaptations reduced the reliance of reptiles on watery habitats. A reptile does not have to spend the first stage of its life in the watery environment of a pond or lake; instead it spends the first stage of its life in the watery environment of a shell-covered egg. And once hatched, a reptile can live far from water, because its dry scales greatly reduce water loss through its water-permeable skin.

■**EVOLUTION OF MAMMALS** About 180 million years ago, during the height of the age of dinosaurs, a new class of vertebrates evolved from one line of small reptiles. The females of this new class fed their young with secretions from special glands called *mammary glands,* and thus the members of this line are called **mammals** after these glands. Eventually, mammals stopped laying eggs; instead, the females nurtured their young in the watery environment of their bodies until the young were mature enough to be born. The *duck-billed platypus* is one surviving mammalian species that lays eggs.

Spending the first stage of life inside one's mother proved to have considerable survival value; it provided the long-term security and environmental stability nec-

---

Conspecifics. Members of the same species.
Chordates. Animals with dorsal nerve chords.
Vertebrates. Chordates that possess spinal bones.
Amphibians. Species that spend their larval phase in water and their adult phase on land.

Mammals. Species whose young are fed from mammary glands.
Primates. One of 14 different orders of mammals; there are five families of primates: prosimians, New-World monkeys, Old-World monkeys, apes, and hominids.

EVOLUTION, GENETICS, AND EXPERIENCE: ASKING THE RIGHT QUESTIONS ABOUT THE BIOLOGY OF BEHAVIOR

essary for complex programs of development to unfold. Today, there are 14 different orders of mammals. The one to which we belong is the order **primates**. We humans—in our usual humble way—named our order after the Latin *primus*, which means "first" or "foremost." There are five families of primates: prosimians, New-World monkeys, Old-World monkeys, apes, and hominids. Examples of the five primate families appear in Figure 2.8.

APE
Silver-Backed Lowland Gorilla

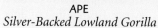

OLD-WORLD MONKEY
Hussar Monkey

PROSIMIAN
Tarsus Monkey

NEW-WORLD MONKEY
Squirrel Monkey

HOMINID
Human

Figure 2.8 Examples of the five different families of primates.

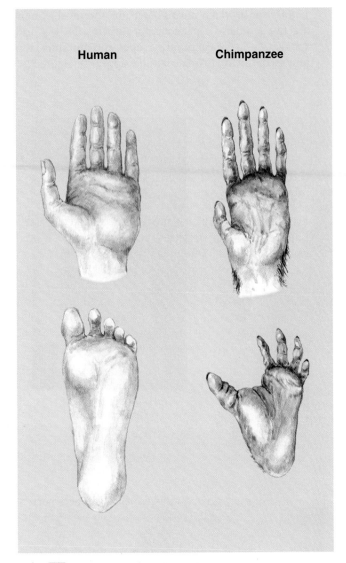

Figure 2.9 A comparison of the feet and hands of a human and a chimpanzee.

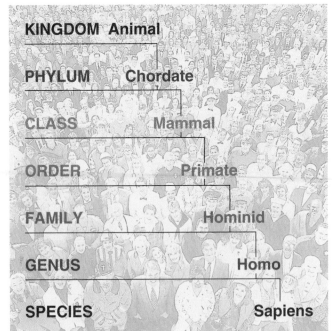

Figure 2.10 The taxonomy of the human species.

Apes (gibbons, orangutans, gorillas, and chimpanzees) are thought to have evolved from a line of Old-World monkeys. Like Old-World monkeys, apes have long arms and grasping hind feet that are specialized for arboreal travel, and they have opposable thumbs that are not long enough to be of much use for precise manipulation (see Figure 2.9). Unlike Old-World monkeys, apes have no tails and can walk upright for short distances. Chimpanzees are the closest living relatives of humans; approximately 99% of the genetic material is identical in the two species (see O'Neill, Murphy, & Gallagher, 1994).

■ EMERGENCE OF HUMANKIND The **hominids** are the family of primates that includes humans; it is composed of two genera (the plural of genus): *Australopithecus* and *Homo* (*Homo erectus* and *Homo sapiens*). However, humans (*Homo sapiens*) are the only surviving hominid species. The *taxonomy* (classification) of the human species is illustrated in Figure 2.10.

The fossil and genetic evidence suggests that the Australopithecines evolved about 6 million years ago in Africa from a line of apes (*australo* means "southern," and *pithecus* means "ape")—from the same line of apes that evolved into chimpanzees in West Africa (see Leakey & Walker, 1997). Several species of *Australopithecus* are thought to have roamed the plains of Africa in small groups for about 5 million years before becoming extinct. Australopithecines were only about 1.3 meters (4 feet) tall, and they had small brains; but analysis of their pelvis and leg bones indicates that their posture was as upright as yours or mine. Any doubts about their upright posture were erased by the discovery of the fossilized footprints pictured in Figure 2.11.

The first *Homo* species, **Homo erectus,** is thought to have evolved from a species of *Australopithecus* about 1.5 million years ago. It was so named because of the incorrect initial assumption that its predecessors were stooped. The most distinctive feature of the *Homo erectus* skull is its large brain cavity (about 850 cubic centimeters), larger than that of *Australopithecus* (about 500 cc), but smaller than that of modern humans (about 1,350 cc). *Homo erectus* used fire and tools (see Susman, 1994) and coexisted in Africa with *Australopithecus* for about 2 million years, until *Australopithecus* died out. *Homo erectus* spread through Europe and Asia (Tattersall, 1997).

About 200,000 years ago (Pääbo, 1995), *Homo erectus* was gradually replaced in the fossil record by modern humans (*Homo sapiens*). Paradoxically, although

EVOLUTION, GENETICS, AND EXPERIENCE: ASKING THE RIGHT QUESTIONS ABOUT THE BIOLOGY OF BEHAVIOR

Figure 2.11 Fossilized footprints of Australopithecine hominids who strode across African volcanic ash about 3.6 million years ago. They left a 70-meter trail, which was discovered in 1978. There were two adults and a child; the child walked in the footsteps of the adults.

the big three human attributes—big brain, upright posture, and free hands with a workable opposing thumb—have been with us for hundreds of thousands of years, most human accomplishments are of recent origin. Artistic artifacts (e.g., wall paintings and carvings) did not appear until about 25,000 years ago, ranching and farming were not established until about 10,000 years ago, and writing did not appear until about 3,000 years ago.

Thinking about Human Evolution

Figure 2.12 on page 32 illustrates the main branches of vertebrate evolution. As you examine it, put hu-

man evolution into perspective by considering the following seven often-misunderstood points about evolution.

1. Evolution does not proceed in a single line. Although it is common to think of an evolutionary ladder or scale, a far better metaphor for evolution is a dense bush.

2. We humans have little reason to claim evolutionary supremacy. We are the last surviving species of a family (i.e., hominids) that has existed for only a blip of evolutionary time.

3. Evolution does not always proceed slowly and gradually. Rapid evolutionary changes (i.e., in a few generations) can be triggered by sudden changes in the environment (see Potts, 1996) or by adaptive genetic mutations (see Elena, Cooper, & Lenski, 1996). Whether human evolution occurred gradually or suddenly is still a matter of intense debate among *paleontologists* (those who scientifically study fossils)—see Kerr (1996). About the time that hominids evolved, there was a sudden cooling of the earth leading to a decrease in African forests and an increase in African grasslands. This may have accelerated human evolution.

4. Few products of evolution have survived to the present day—only the tips of the evolutionary bush have survived. Fewer than 1% of all known species are still in existence.

5. Evolution does not progress to preordained perfection—evolution is a tinkerer, not an architect. Increases in adaptation occur through changes to existing programs of development; and the results, although improvements in their particular environmental context, are never perfect designs. For example, the fact that mammalian sperm do not develop effectively at body temperature led to the evolution of the scrotum—hardly a perfect solution to any design problem.

6. Not all existing behaviors or structures are adaptive. Often evolution occurs through changes in developmental programs that lead to several related characteristics, only one of which might be adaptive. Also, behaviors or structures that were once adaptive might become nonadaptive or maladaptive if the environment changes.

Hominids. The family of primates that includes *Homo sapiens* (humans), *Homo erectus,* and *Australopithecus.*
Homo erectus. The first *Homo* species, thought to have evolved from *Australopithecus* about 1.5 million years ago and to have evolved into *Homo sapiens* about 200,000 years ago.

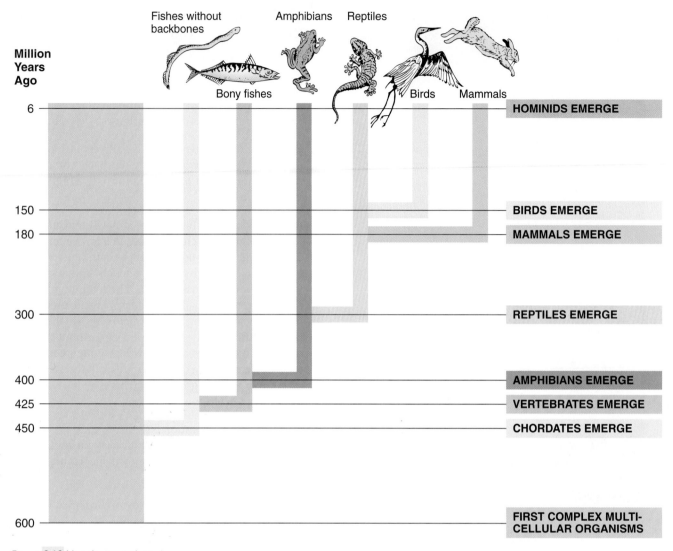

Figure 2.12 Vertebrate evolution.

7. Similarities among species do not necessarily mean that they have common evolutionary origins. Structures that are similar because they have a common evolutionary origin are termed **homologous**—for example, a bird's wing and a human's arm, although used for different things, have a basic underlying similarity of skeletal structure that suggest a common evolutionary ancestor (see Burke & Feduccia, 1997). In contrast, structures that perform similar functions but are not homologous are termed **analogous**—for example, a bird's wing and a bee's wing serve a common function but have few other similarities. Analogous structures result from **convergent evolution,** the evolution of similar solutions to the same environmental demands by unrelated species.

Evolution of the Human Brain

Early research on the evolution of the human brain focused on size. This research was stimulated by the as-

sumption that brain size and intellectual capacity are closely related—an assumption that ran into two problems. First, it was shown that modern humans, whom modern humans believe to be the most intelligent of all creatures, do not have the biggest brains. At 1,350 grams, humans rank far behind whales and elephants, whose brains weigh between 5,000 and 8,000 grams (Harvey & Krebs, 1990). Second, the brains of deceased intellectuals (e.g., Einstein) were found to be no match for their gigantic intellects. Healthy adult human brains vary greatly in size—between about 1,000 and 2,000 grams—but there is no clear relationship between brain size and intelligence.

One obvious problem in relating brain size to intelligence is the fact that larger animals tend to have larger brains, presumably because larger bodies require more brain tissue to control and regulate them. Thus the fact that large men tend to have larger brains than small men, that men tend to have larger brains than women, and that elephants have larger brains than humans does not

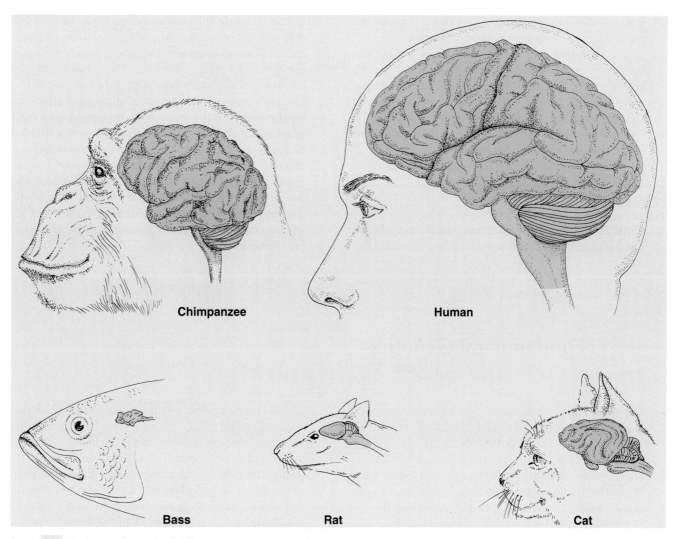

Figure 2.13 The brains of animals of different evolutionary age. Cerebrums are shown in beige; brain stems are shown in blue.

suggest anything about the relative intelligence of these populations. This has led to the proposal that brain weight expressed as a percentage of total body weight might be a better measure of intellectual capacity. This measure allows humans (2.33%) to take their rightful place ahead of elephants (0.20%), but it also allows both humans and elephants to be surpassed by that intellectual giant of the animal kingdom, the shrew (3.33%).

A more reasonable approach to the study of brain evolution has been to compare the evolution of different brain regions (Finlay & Darlington, 1995; Killackey, 1995). For example, it has been informative to consider the evolution of the **brain stem** separately from the evolution of the **cerebrum** (cerebral hemispheres). In general, the brain stem regulates reflex activities that are critical for survival (e.g., heart rate, respiration, and blood glucose level), whereas the cerebrum is involved in more complex adaptive processes such as learning, perception, and motivation.

Figure 2.13 is a schematic representation of the relative size of the brain stems and cerebrums of several species that are living ancestors of species from which humans evolved. This figure makes three important points about the evolution of the human brain. The first is that it has increased in size during evolution; the second is that most of the increase in size has occurred in the cerebrum; and the third is that there has been an increase in the number of **convolutions**—folds on the cerebral

---

Homologous. Having a similar structure because of a common evolutionary ancestor (e.g., a human's arm and a bird's wing are homologous).

Analogous. Having a similar structure because of convergent evolution (e.g., a bird's wing and a bee's wing are analogous).

Convergent evolution. The evolution of similar solutions to the same environmental demands by unrelated species.

Brain stem. The part of the brain on which the cerebral hemispheres rest; in general, it regulates reflex activities that are critical for survival (e.g., heart rate and respiration).

Cerebrum. The portion of the brain that sits on the brain stem; in general, it plays a role in complex adaptive processes (e.g., learning, perception, and motivation).

Convolutions. Folds on the surface of the cerebral hemispheres.

surface—that has greatly increased the volume of the cerebral cortex (the outermost layer of cerebral tissue).

More significant than the differences among the brains of various related species are the similarities. All brains are constructed of neurons, and the neural structures that compose the brains of one species can almost always be found in the brains of related species. For example, the brains of humans, monkeys, rats, and mice contain the same gross structures.

Conclusion

In this section, you have been confronted by two indisputable facts of life: (1) that we humans, like other living animals, are the cumulative products of over 600 million years of adaptation; and (2) that we humans are related to all other animal species—in some cases more closely than we like to admit. These two truths are foundations on which two approaches to biopsychological research rest. Biopsychologists often study behavior and neural mechanisms by considering their adaptability and the environmental pressures that led to their evolution—this is called the **functional approach** (see Tooby & Cosmides, 1995). And biopsychologists often try to learn about the behaviors and neural mechanisms of one species, usually humans, by studying the behaviors and neural mechanisms of related species—this is called the **comparative approach** (see Preuss, 1995).

2.3 Fundamental Genetics

Darwin did not understand two of the key facts on which his theory of evolution was based. He did not understand why conspecifics differ from one another, and he did not understand how anatomical, physiological, and behavioral characteristics are passed from parent to offspring. While Darwin puzzled over these questions, there was an unread manuscript in his files that contained the answers. It had been sent to him by an unknown Augustinian monk, Gregor Mendel. Unfortunately for Darwin (1809–1882) and for Mendel (1822–1884), the significance of Mendel's research was not recognized until the early part of this century, well after both of their deaths.

Mendelian Genetics

Mendel studied inheritance in pea plants. In designing his experiments, he made two wise decisions. He decided to study dichotomous traits, and he decided to begin his experiments by crossing the offspring of true-breeding lines. **Dichotomous traits** are traits that occur in one form or the other, never in combination. For example, seed color is a dichotomous pea plant trait: Every pea plant has either brown seeds or white seeds. **True-breeding lines** are breeding lines in which interbred members always produce offspring with the same trait (e.g., brown seeds), generation after generation.

In one of his early experiments, Mendel studied the inheritance of seed color: brown or white. He began by cross breeding the offspring of a line of pea plants that had bred true for brown seeds with the offspring of a line of pea plants that had bred true for white seeds. The offspring of this cross all had brown seeds. Then Mendel bred these first-generation offspring with one another, and he found that about three-quarters of the resulting second-generation offspring had brown seeds and about one-quarter had white seeds. Mendel repeated this experiment many times with various pairs of dichotomous pea plant traits, and each time the result was the same. One trait, which Mendel called the **dominant trait,** appeared in all of the first-generation offspring; the other trait, which he called the **recessive trait,** appeared in about one-quarter of the second-generation offspring. Mendel would have obtained a similar result if he had conducted an experiment with true-breeding lines of brown-eyed (dominant) and blue-eyed (recessive) humans.

The results of Mendel's experiment challenged the central premise upon which all previous ideas about inheritance had rested: that offspring inherit the traits of their parents. Somehow, the recessive trait (white seeds) was passed on to one-quarter of the second-generation pea plants by first-generation pea plants that did not themselves possess it. An organism's observable traits are referred to as its **phenotype;** the traits that it can pass on to its offspring through its genetic material are referred to as its **genotype.**

Mendel devised a theory to explain his results. It comprised four ideas. First, Mendel proposed that there are two kinds of inherited factors for each dichotomous trait—for example, that a brown-seed factor and a white-seed factor control seed color. Today, we call each inherited factor a **gene.** Second, Mendel proposed that each organism possesses two genes for each of its dichotomous traits; for example, each pea plant possesses either two brown-seed genes, two white-seed genes, or one of each.

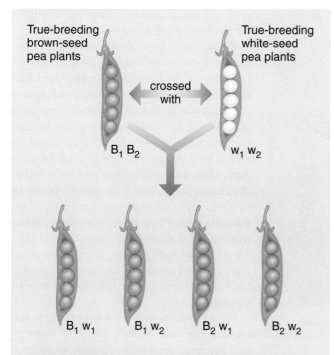

True-breeding brown-seed pea plants

crossed with

True-breeding white-seed pea plants

B_1 B_2

w_1 w_2

B_1 w_1 B_1 w_2 B_2 w_1 B_2 w_2

FIRST CROSS
One parent had two dominant brown-seed genes (B_1 B_2); the other had two recessive white-seed genes (w_1 w_2). Therefore, all offspring had one brown-seed gene and one white-seed gene (B_1 w_1, B_1 w_2, B_2 w_1, or B_2 w_2). Because the brown-seed gene is dominant, all had brown seeds.

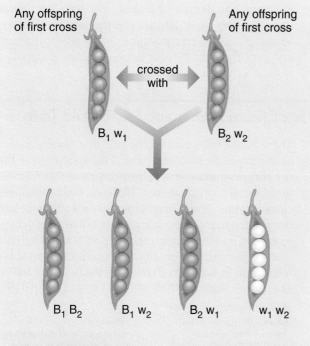

Any offspring of first cross

crossed with

Any offspring of first cross

B_1 w_1

B_2 w_2

B_1 B_2 B_1 w_2 B_2 w_1 w_1 w_2

SECOND CROSS
Each parent had one brown-seed gene and one white-seed gene. Therefore, 25% of the offspring had two brown-seed genes (B_1 B_2), 50% had a brown-seed gene and a white-seed gene (B_1 w_2 or B_2 w_1), and 25% had two white-seed genes (w_1 w_2). Because the brown-seed gene is dominant, 75% had brown seeds.

Figure 2.14 How Mendel's theory accounts for the results of his experiment on the inheritance of seed color in pea plants.

The two genes that control the same trait are called **alleles** (pronounced "a-LEELZ"). Organisms that possess two identical genes for a trait are said to be **homozygous** for that trait; those that possess two different genes for a trait are said to be **heterozygous** for that trait. Third, Mendel proposed that one of the two kinds of genes for each dichotomous trait dominates the other in heterozygous organisms. For example, pea plants with a brown-seed gene and a white-seed gene always have brown seeds because the brown-seed gene always dominates the white-seed gene. And fourth, Mendel proposed that for each trait each organism randomly inherits one of its "father's" two factors and one of its "mother's" two factors. Figure 2.14 illustrates how Mendel's theory accounts for the result of his experiment on the inheritance of seed color in pea plants.

Chromosomes, Reproduction, and Linkage

It was not until the early 1900s that genes were found to be located on **chromosomes**—the threadlike structures in the *nucleus* of each cell. Chromosomes occur in matched pairs, and each species has a characteristic number of pairs in each of its body cells; humans have 23 pairs. The two genes (alleles) that control each trait are situated at the same locus, one on each chromosome of a particular pair.

The process of cell division that produces **gametes** (egg cells and sperm cells) is called **meiosis** (pronounced "my-OH-sis"). In meiosis, the chromosomes divide, and one chromosome of each pair goes to each of the two

Functional approach. The study of behavior and neural mechanisms by consideration of their adaptiveness and of the environmental pressures that led to their evolution.

Comparative approach. Learning about behaviors and neural mechanisms (or about other biological processes) by comparing species.

Dichotomous traits. Traits that occur in one form or the other, never in combination.

True-breeding lines. Breeding lines in which interbred members always produce offspring with the same trait, generation after generation.

Dominant trait. The trait of a dichotomous pair that is expressed in the phenotypes of heterozygous individuals.

Recessive trait. The trait of a dichotomous pair that is not expressed in the phenotype of heterozygous individuals.

Phenotype. An organism's observable traits.

Genotype. The traits that an organism can pass on to its offspring in its genetic material.

Gene. A unit of inheritance; for example, the section of a chromosome that controls the synthesis of one protein.

Alleles. The two genes that control the same trait.

Homozygous. Possessing two identical genes for a particular trait.

Heterozygous. Possessing two different genes for a particular trait.

Chromosomes. Threadlike genetic structures in the cell nucleus; each chromosome is a DNA molecule.

Gametes. Egg cells and sperm cells.

Meiosis. The process of cell division that produces cells (e.g., egg cells and sperm cells) with half the chromosomes of the parent cell.

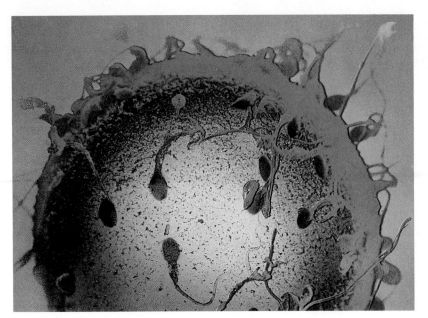
Figure 2.15 Fertilization. A sperm cell attaches itself to the surface of an egg cell.

gametes that results from the division. As a result, each gamete has only half the usual number of chromosomes (23 in humans); and when a sperm cell and an egg cell combine during fertilization (see Figure 2.15), a **zygote** (a fertilized egg cell) with the full complement of chromosomes is produced. All other cell division in the body occurs by **mitosis** (pronounced "my-TOE-sis"). Just prior to mitotic division, the number of chromosomes doubles so that when the division occurs, both daughter cells end up with the full complement of chromosomes. Figure 2.16 illustrates meiosis, fertilization, and mitosis.

Meiosis accounts for much of the genetic diversity within each species. In humans, for example, each meiotic division produces two gametes; each gamete contains 1 chromosome from each of the 23 pairs contained in each body cell. Because each of the 23 pairs is randomly sorted into the two gametes, each human can produce gametes with 2^{23} (8,388,608) different combinations of chromosomes.

The first comprehensive study of **linkage** was published in 1915 by Morgan and his colleagues. They found that there are four different clusters of fruit fly genes. If the gene for one trait in a cluster was inherited from one parent, that fruit fly had a higher probability (greater than 0.5) of inheriting genes for other traits in the cluster from the same parent. Because fruit flies have four pairs of chromosomes, Morgan and his colleagues concluded that linkage occurs between traits that are encoded on the same chromosome. They were correct; in every species in which linkage has been assessed, the number of clusters of linked traits has been found to equal the number of pairs of chromosomes.

If genes are passed from generation to generation on chromosomes, why are the genes on the same chromo-

some not always inherited together? The linkage between pairs of genes on a single chromosome varies from almost complete (close to 1.0) to just above chance (just over 0.5).

Morgan and his colleagues proposed that **crossing over** provided the solution to the puzzle of partial linkage. Figure 2.17 on page 38 illustrates how crossing over works. During the first stage of meiosis, after the chromosomes have replicated, they line up in their pairs. Then they usually cross over one another at random points, break apart at the points of contact, and exchange sections of chromosome. As a result, parents rarely pass on intact chromosomal clusters of genes to their children. Each of your gametes contains chromosomes that are unique spliced-together combinations of chromosomes inherited from your mother and father.

The phenomenon of crossing over is important for two reasons. First, by ensuring that chromosomes are not passed intact from generation to generation, crossovers increase the diversity of the species; in a sense, crossing over shuffles the genetic deck before the chromosomes are randomly dealt out to the next generation. Second, the study of crossovers was the first means by which geneticists could construct **gene maps.** Because each crossover occurs at a random point along the length of a chromosome, the degree of linkage between two genes indicates how close they are together on the chromosome. Crossovers rarely occur between adjacent genes, and they frequently occur between genes at opposite ends of a chromosome.

Sex Chromosomes and Sex-Linked Traits

There is one exception to the rule that chromosomes always come in matched pairs. That exception is the **sex chromosomes**—the pair of chromosomes that determines an individual's sex. There are two types of sex chromosomes, X and Y, and the two look different and carry different genes. Female mammals have two X chromosomes, and male mammals have an X and a Y. Traits that are influenced by genes on the sex chromosomes are referred to as **sex-linked traits.** Virtually all sex-linked

Zygote. A fertilized egg cell.
Mitosis. The process of cell division that produces cells with the same number of chromosomes as the parent cell.
Linkage. The tendency for traits that are encoded on the same chromosome to be inherited together.
Crossing over. The exchange of sections between pairs of chro-

mosomes during the first stage of meiosis.
Gene maps. Maps that indicate the relative positions of genes along a chromosome.
Sex chromosomes. The pair of chromosomes that determine an individual's sex: XX for a female and XY for a male.
Sex-linked traits. Traits that are influenced by genes on the sex chromosomes.

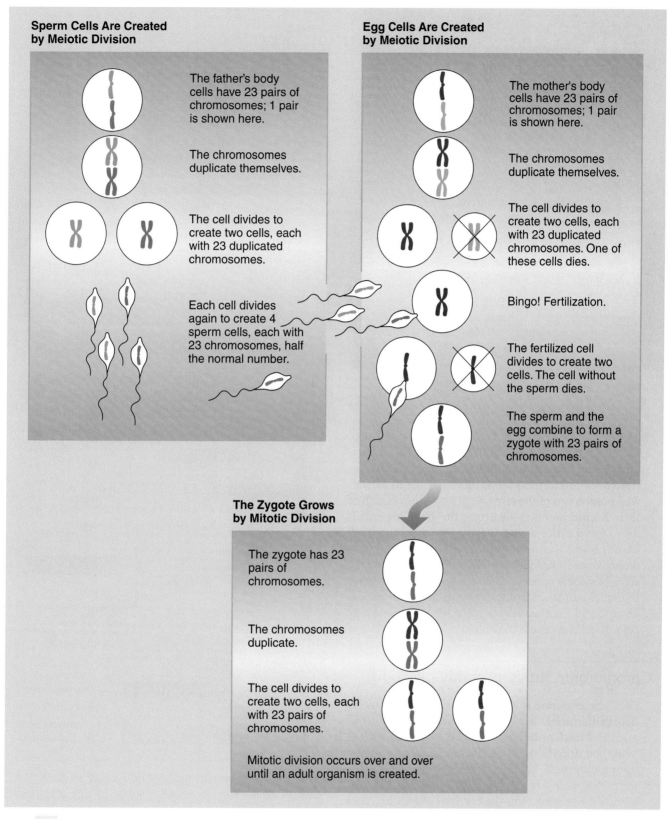

Sperm Cells Are Created by Meiotic Division

The father's body cells have 23 pairs of chromosomes; 1 pair is shown here.

The chromosomes duplicate themselves.

The cell divides to create two cells, each with 23 duplicated chromosomes.

Each cell divides again to create 4 sperm cells, each with 23 chromosomes, half the normal number.

Egg Cells Are Created by Meiotic Division

The mother's body cells have 23 pairs of chromosomes; 1 pair is shown here.

The chromosomes duplicate themselves.

The cell divides to create two cells, each with 23 duplicated chromosomes. One of these cells dies.

Bingo! Fertilization.

The fertilized cell divides to create two cells. The cell without the sperm dies.

The sperm and the egg combine to form a zygote with 23 pairs of chromosomes.

The Zygote Grows by Mitotic Division

The zygote has 23 pairs of chromosomes.

The chromosomes duplicate.

The cell divides to create two cells, each with 23 pairs of chromosomes.

Mitotic division occurs over and over until an adult organism is created.

Figure 2.16 Meiotic cell division, fertilization, and mitotic cell division.

traits are controlled by genes on the X chromosome because the Y chromosome is small and carries few genes other than those that cause an individual to develop into a male (see Rice, 1994).

Traits that are controlled by genes on the X chromosome occur more frequently in one sex than the other. If the trait is dominant, it occurs more frequently in females. Females have twice the chance of inheriting the

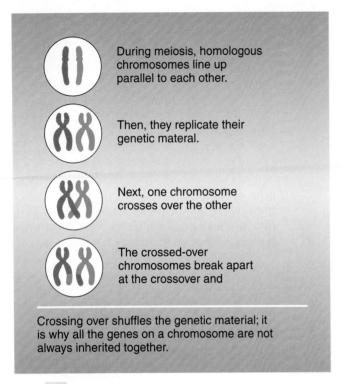

During meiosis, homologous chromosomes line up parallel to each other.

Then, they replicate their genetic materal.

Next, one chromosome crosses over the other

The crossed-over chromosomes break apart at the crossover and

Crossing over shuffles the genetic material; it is why all the genes on a chromosome are not always inherited together.

Figure 2.17 Crossing over.

dominant gene because they have twice the number of X chromosomes. In contrast, recessive sex-linked traits occur more frequently in males. The reason is that recessive sex-linked traits are manifested only in females who possess two of the recessive genes—one on each of their X chromosomes—whereas the traits are manifested in all males who possess the gene because they have only one X chromosome. The classic example of a recessive sex-linked trait is color blindness. Because the color blindness gene is quite rare, females almost never inherit two of them and thus almost never possess the disorder; in contrast, every male who possesses one color blindness gene is colorblind.

Chromosome Structure and Replication

Each chromosome is a double-stranded molecule of **deoxyribonucleic acid (DNA)**. Each strand is a sequence of **nucleotide bases** attached to a chain of *phosphate* and *deoxyribose*; there are four nucleotide bases: *adenine, thymine, guanine,* and *cytosine.* It is the sequence of these bases on each chromosome that constitutes the genetic code—just as the sequence of letters constitutes the code of our language.

The two strands that compose each chromosome are coiled around each other and bonded together by the attraction of adenine for thymine and guanine for cytosine. This specific bonding pattern has an important consequence: The two strands that compose each chromosome are exact complements of each other. For ex-

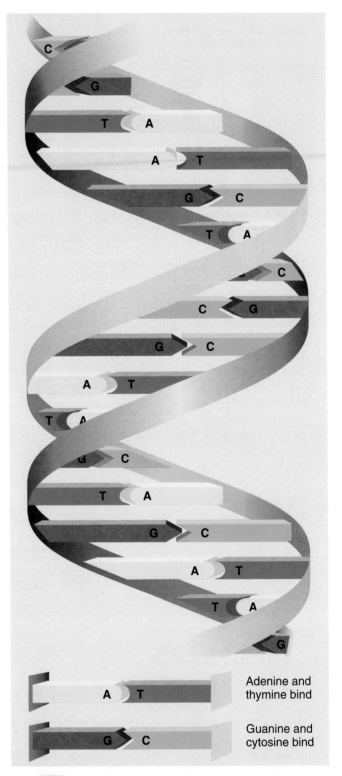

Adenine and thymine bind

Guanine and cytosine bind

Figure 2.18 A schematic illustration of the structure of a DNA molecule. Notice the complementary binding of nucleotide bases: thymine to adenine, and guanine to cytosine.

ample, the sequence of adenine, guanine, thymine, cytosine, and guanine on one strand is always attached to the complementary sequence of thymine, cytosine, adenine, guanine, and cytosine on the other. Figure 2.18 illus-

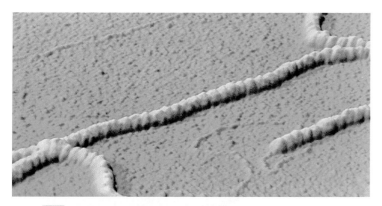

Figure 2.19 A scanning electron microscope image of DNA molecules.

The control of **gene expression** by operator genes is an important process because it determines how a cell will develop and how it will function once it reaches maturity. Operator genes are like switches; and, like switches, they can be regulated in two ways. Some operator genes are normally off, and they are regulated by **DNA-binding proteins** that turn them on; others are normally on, and they are regulated by DNA-binding proteins that turn them up, down, or off. Many of the DNA-binding proteins that control operator genes are influenced by signals received by the cell from its environment (see Darnell, 1997). This, then, is a major mechanism by which experience interacts with genes to influence development.

The expression of a structural gene begins when it is activated by its operator gene. The process is illustrated in Figure 2.21 on page 41. First, the small section of the chromosome that contains the structural gene unravels, and the unraveled section of one of the DNA strands serves as a template for the transcription of a short strand of **ribonucleic acid (RNA)**. RNA is like DNA except that it has uracil bases instead of thymine bases and a phosphate and ribose backbone instead of a phosphate and deoxyribose backbone. The strand of transcribed RNA is called **messenger RNA** because it carries the genetic code from the nucleus of the cell. Once it has left the nucleus, the messenger RNA attaches itself to one of the many **ribosomes** in the cell's *cytoplasm* (the clear inner fluid of the cell). The ribosome then moves along the strand of messenger RNA, translating the genetic code as it proceeds.

Each group of three consecutive nucleotide bases along the messenger RNA strand is called a **codon.**

trates the structure of DNA. Figure 2.19 is a computer enhancement of the surface of several DNA molecules.

Replication is a critical process of the DNA molecule. Without it, mitotic cell division would not be possible. Figure 2.20 on page 40 illustrates how DNA replication works. The two strands of DNA start to unwind. Then the exposed nucleotide bases on each of the two strands attract loose complementary bases from the fluid of the nucleus. Thus, when the unwinding is complete, two double-stranded DNA molecules, both of which are identical to the original, have been created.

Chromosome replication does not always go according to plan; there may be errors. Sometimes, these errors are gross errors. For example, in *Down syndrome*, which you will learn about in Chapter 6, there is an extra chromosome in each cell. But more commonly, errors in duplication take the form of **mutations**—accidental alterations in individual genes. In most cases, mutations disappear from the genetic pool within a few generations because the organisms that inherit them are less fit. However, in rare instances, mutations increase fitness and in so doing contribute to rapid evolution.

The Genetic Code and Gene Expression

There are several different kinds of genes. The most prevalent are the **structural genes**—genes that contain the information necessary for the synthesis of a single protein. **Proteins** are long chains of **amino acids;** they control the physiological activities of cells and are important components of their structure. All the cells in the body (e.g., brain cells, hair cells, and bone cells) contain exactly the same structural genes. How then do different kinds of cells develop? The answer lies in another category of genes, the **operator gene.** Each operator gene controls a structural gene or a group of related structural genes; its function is to determine whether or not each of its structural genes initiates the synthesis of a protein (i.e., whether or not the structural gene will be *expressed* and at what rate).

Deoxyribonucleic acid (DNA). Double-stranded, coiled molecules of genetic material; chromosomes.

Nucleotide bases. A class of molecules that includes adenine, thymine, guanine, and cytosine—the constituents of the genetic code.

Replication. The process by which the DNA molecule duplicates itself.

Mutations. Abnormal genes that are created by accidents of chromosome duplication.

Structural genes. Genes that contain the information required for the synthesis of a particular protein.

Proteins. Long chains of amino acids.

Amino acids. The chemical elements from which proteins are synthesized.

Operator gene. A short segment of DNA that determines whether or not messenger RNA will be transcribed

from adjacent structural genes.

Gene expression. The production of the protein specified by a particular gene.

DNA-binding proteins. Proteins that bind to DNA molecules and in so doing either induce or block gene expression.

Ribonucleic acid (RNA). A molecule that is similar to DNA except that it has uracil nucleotide bases and a phosphate and ribose backbone.

Messenger RNA. The strands of RNA that are transcribed from DNA and direct the synthesis of proteins.

Ribosome. A structure in the cytoplasm that reads the genetic code from strands of messenger RNA.

Codon. A group of three consecutive nucleotide bases on a DNA molecule; each codon specifies the particular amino acid that is to be added to an amino acid chain during protein synthesis.

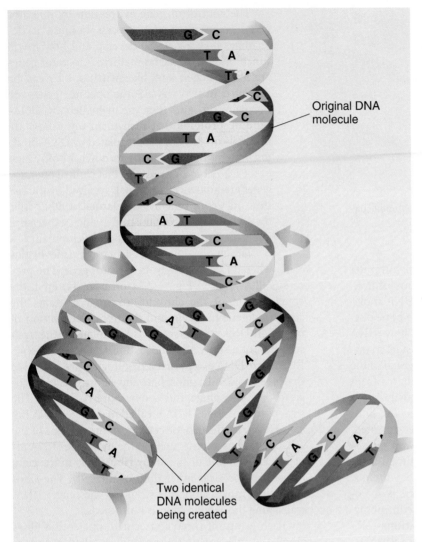

Figure 2.20 DNA replication. As the two strands of the original DNA molecule unwind, the nucleotide bases on each strand attract loose complementary bases. Once the unwinding is complete, two DNA molecules, each identical to the first, have been created.

Original DNA molecule

Two identical DNA molecules being created

Each codon instructs the ribosome to add 1 of the 20 different kinds of amino acids to the protein that it is constructing; for example, the sequence guanine-guanine-adenine instructs the ribosome to add the amino acid glycine. Each kind of amino acid is carried to the ribosome by molecules of **transfer RNA;** and as the ribosome reads a codon, it attracts a transfer RNA molecule that is attached to the appropriate amino acid. The ribosome reads codon after codon and adds amino acid after amino acid until it reaches a codon that tells it the protein is complete, whereupon the completed protein is released into the cytoplasm. Thus, the process of gene expression involves two phases: the *transcription* of the DNA base-sequence code to an RNA base-sequence code and the *translation* of the RNA base-sequence code into a sequence of amino acids.

Human Genome Project

Arguably the most ambitious scientific project of all time began in 1990. Known as the **human genome project,** it is a loosely knit collaboration of major research institutions and individual research teams in many different countries. Its first goal was the construction of a detailed physical map of each of the human chromosomes, to facilitate the identification of the approximately 200,000 genes in the human genome. This has now been accomplished (Lander, 1996).

The physical mapping was done as follows. First, samples of the chromosome of interest were exposed to enzymes that broke them into many small segments. Next, the segments were cloned so that the researchers would have an unlimited supply of each. Then, the segments were exposed to chemical markers that uniquely labeled specific loci along their length. Finally, the patterns of markers on the segments were examined in an effort to locate identical patterns on two segments—an indication that they were overlapping segments of the same chromosome. Once a chromosome was physically mapped, banks of short cloned DNA segments of known location along the chromosome became available to scientists interested in studying them.

Now that physical maps of all the human chromosomes have been determined, the human genome project has turned its efforts to identifying the base sequence of each of the estimated 100,000 human genes. About half of them have been characterized so far (Rowen, Mahairas, & Hood, 1997). This massive task will be completed by about 2005; using one typographical character for each base, the resulting information will fill approximately 400,000 pages (see Beardsley, 1996). An ancillary goal of the project is to map the mouse genome; the mouse is the favorite mammalian subject of genetic research.

Transfer RNA. Molecules of RNA that carry amino acids to ribosomes during protein synthesis; each kind of amino acid is carried by a different kind of transfer RNA molecule.

Human genome project. The international effort to construct a detailed map of the human chromosomes.

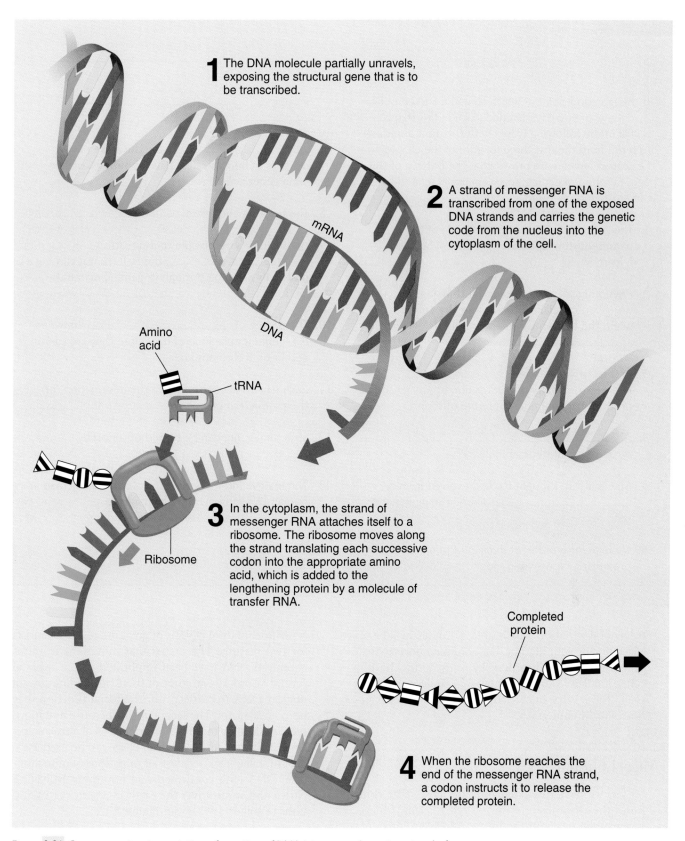

1 The DNA molecule partially unravels, exposing the structural gene that is to be transcribed.

mRNA

DNA

Amino acid

tRNA

2 A strand of messenger RNA is transcribed from one of the exposed DNA strands and carries the genetic code from the nucleus into the cytoplasm of the cell.

Ribosome

3 In the cytoplasm, the strand of messenger RNA attaches itself to a ribosome. The ribosome moves along the strand translating each successive codon into the appropriate amino acid, which is added to the lengthening protein by a molecule of transfer RNA.

Completed protein

4 When the ribosome reaches the end of the messenger RNA strand, a codon instructs it to release the completed protein.

Figure 2.21 Gene expression: transcription of a section of DNA into a complementary strand of messenger RNA, then the translation of the messenger RNA strand into a protein.

The mapping and sequencing of the human and mouse genomes will provide genetic materials, knowledge, and techniques necessary for rapid progress in the diagnosis, treatment, and prevention of genetically based disorders. It will also be a boon to behavioral scientists interested in the contributions of genes to normal

SELF TEST

This is a good point at which to pause and consolidate what you have learned so far in this chapter. Fill in the following blanks with the most appropriate terms from the first three sections of the chapter. The correct answers are provided at the bottom of this page. Before proceeding, review material related to your errors and omissions.

1. The _____ side of the nature–nurture controversy is that all behavior is learned.

2. Physiological-or-psychological thinking was given official recognition in the 1600s when the Roman Church sanctioned _____ .

3. In the Darwinian sense, _____ refers to the ability of an organism to survive and produce large numbers of fertile offspring.

4. A _____ is a group of reproductively isolated organisms.

5. Mammals are thought to have evolved from _____ about 180 million years ago.

6. There are five different families of primates: prosimians, New-World monkeys, Old-World monkeys, _____ , and _____ .

7. _____ are the closest living relatives of humans; they have about 99% of the same genetic material.

8. The first hominids were _____ .

9. An organism's observable traits are its _____ ; the traits that it can pass to its offspring through its genetic material are its _____ .

10. The degree of _____ between two genes is a measure of how close they are together on a chromosome.

11. Each structural gene contains the information for the production of a single _____ .

12. Structural genes can be turned off or on by _____ genes.

13. The massive international effort to physically map human chromosomes is known as the _____ project.

behavioral variation. Much of this progress will be realized during your lifetime. For example, efforts to treat genetically based disorders by substituting healthy genes for flawed ones are now well under way (Marshall, 1995). What once seemed the stuff of science fiction is within our grasp.

Mitochondrial DNA

So far, we have discussed only the DNA that composes the chromosomes in the cell nucleus. Indeed, you may be left with the impression from introductory texts that all the DNA is in the nucleus: It isn't. The cells' mitochondria also contain DNA (i.e., *mitochondrial DNA*). **Mitochondria** are the energy-generating structures located in the cytoplasm of every cell. All mitochondrial genes are inherited from one's mother.

Mitochondrial DNA is of great interest to scientists for two reasons. The first is that mutations in mitochondrial DNA have been implicated in the cause of several disorders—in some of these cases, mutations of nuclear DNA that affect mitochondrial function may be a causal factor. The second is that because mutations seem to develop in mitochondrial DNA at a reasonably consistent rate, mitochondrial DNA can be used as an evolutionary clock. Analysis of mutations of mitochondrial DNA have confirmed that hominids evolved in Africa and spread over the earth in a series of migrations (Wallace, 1997)—see Figure 2.22.

The answers are (1) nurture, (2) Cartesian dualism, (3) fitness, (4) species, (5) reptiles, (6) apes, hominids, (7) chimpanzees, (8) Australopithecines, (9) phenotype, genotype, (10) linkage, (11) protein, (12) operator, (13) human genome.

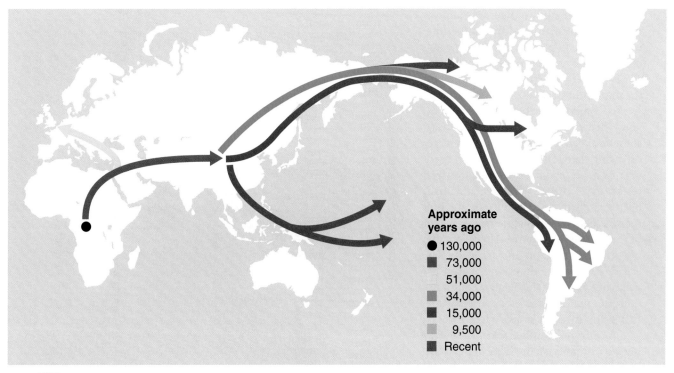

Figure 2.22 The analysis of mitochondrial DNA indicates that hominids evolved in Africa and spread over the earth in a series of migrations.
(Adapted from Wallace, 1997.)

Behavioral Development: The Interaction of Genetic Factors and Experience

This section of the chapter provides three classic examples of how genetic factors and experience interact to direct behavioral ontogeny. **Ontogeny** is the development of individuals through their life span. **Phylogeny**, in contrast, is the evolutionary development of species through the ages.

Selective Breeding of "Maze-Bright" and "Maze-Dull" Rats

You have already learned in this chapter that nature-or-nurture thinking dominated the study of behavior during the first half of this century and that most psychologists of that era assumed that behavior develops largely through learning. Tryon (1934) undermined this assumption by showing that behavioral traits can be selectively bred.

Tryon focused his selective-breeding experiments on the very behavior that had been the focus of early psychologists in their investigations of learning: the maze running of laboratory rats. Tryon began by training a large heterogeneous group of laboratory rats to run a complex maze; the rats received a food reward when they reached the goal box. Tryon then mated the females and males that least frequently entered incorrect alleys during training—he referred to these rats as *maze-bright*. And he bred the females and males that most frequently entered incorrect alleys during training—he referred to these rats as *maze-dull*.

When the offspring of the maze-bright and of the maze-dull rats matured, their maze-learning performance was assessed. Then, the brightest of the maze-bright offspring were mated with one another and so were the dullest of the maze-dull offspring. This selective breeding procedure was continued for 21 generations, and the descendants of Tryon's original strains are available today to those interested in studying them. By

---

Mitochondria. The energy-generating, DNA-containing structures of each cell's cytoplasm.

Ontogeny. The development of individuals through their life span.
Phylogeny. The evolutionary development of species.

the eighth generation, there was almost no overlap in the maze-learning performance of the two strains. With a few exceptions, the worst of the maze-bright strain made fewer errors than the best of the maze-dull strain (see Figure 2.23).

To control for the possibility that good maze-running performance was somehow being passed from parent to offspring through learning, Tryon used a *cross-fostering control procedure:* He tested maze-bright offspring that had been reared by maze-dull parents and maze-dull offspring that had been reared by maze-bright parents. However, the offspring of maze-bright rats made few errors even when they were reared by maze-dull rats, and the offspring of maze-dull rats made many errors even when they were reared by maze-bright rats.

Since Tryon's seminal selective-breeding experiments, many behavioral traits have been selectively bred. Among them are open-field activity in mice, susceptibility to alcohol-induced sleep in mice, susceptibility to alcohol-withdrawal seizures in mice, nest building in mice, avoidance learning in rats, and mating in fruit flies. Indeed, it appears that any measurable behavioral trait that varies among members of a species can be selectively bred.

An important general point made by studies of selective breeding is that selective breeding based on one behavioral trait usually brings a host of other behavioral traits along with it. This indicates that the behavioral trait used as the criterion for selective breeding is not the only behavioral trait that is influenced by the genes segregated by the breeding. Thus, in order to characterize the behavioral function of the segregated genes, it is necessary to compare the performance of the selectively bred strains on a variety of tests. For example, Searle (1949) compared maze-dull and maze-bright rats on 30 different behavioral tests and found that they differed on many of them; the pattern of differences suggested that the maze-bright rats were superior maze learners not because they were more intelligent but because they were less emotional.

Selective-breeding studies have proved that genes influence the development of behavior. This conclusion in no way implies that experience does not. This point was clearly illustrated by Cooper and Zubek (1958) in a classic study of maze-bright and maze-dull rats. The researchers reared maze-bright and maze-dull rats in one of two environments: (1) an impoverished environment (a barren wire-mesh group cage) or (2) an enriched environment (a wire-mesh group cage that contained tunnels, ramps, visual displays, and other objects designed to stim-

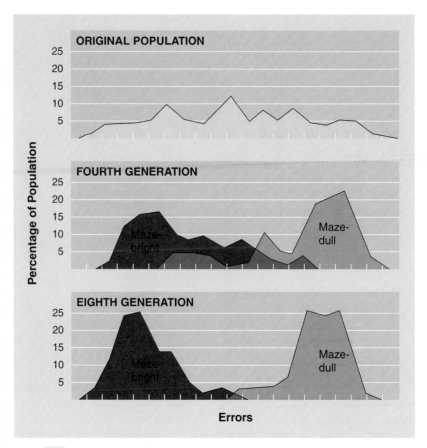

Figure 2.23 Selective breeding of maze-bright and maze-dull strains of rats by Tryon (1934).

ulate interest). When the maze-dull rats reached maturity, they made significantly more errors than the maze-bright rats only if they had been reared in the impoverished environment (see Figure 2.24). Apparently, enriched early environments can overcome the negative effects of disadvantaged genes. Indeed, rats reared in enriched environments develop thicker cerebral cortexes than those reared in impoverished environments (Bennett et al., 1964).

Phenylketonuria: A Single-Gene Metabolic Disorder

In contrast to what you might expect, it is often easier to understand the genetics of a behavioral disorder than it is to understand the genetics of normal behavior. The reason is that many genes influence the development of a normal behavioral trait, but it often takes only one abnormal gene to screw it up (see Plomin, 1995). A good example of this point is the neurological disorder **phenylketonuria (PKU).**

PKU was discovered in 1934 when a Norwegian dentist, Asbjörn Fölling, noticed a peculiar odor in the urine of his two mentally retarded children. He correctly assumed that the odor was related to their disorder, and he had their urine analyzed. High levels of **phenylpyruvic acid** were found in both samples. Spurred on by his dis-

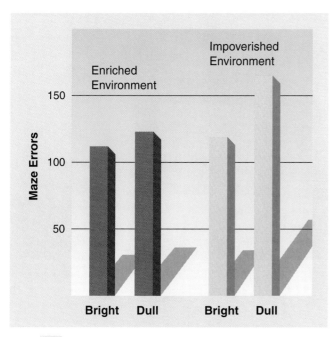

Figure 2.24 Maze-dull rats did not make significantly more errors than maze-bright rats when they were both reared in an enriched environment.

(Adapted from Cooper & Zubek, 1958).

covery, Fölling identified other retarded children who had abnormally high levels of urinary phenylpyruvic acid, and he concluded that this subpopulation of retarded children was suffering from the same disorder. In addition to mental retardation, the symptoms of PKU include vomiting, seizures, hyperactivity, and hyperirritability.

The pattern of transmission of PKU through the family trees of afflicted individuals indicates that it is transmitted by a single gene mutation. About 1 in 100 people of European descent carry the PKU gene; but because the gene is recessive, PKU develops only in homozygous individuals (those who inherit a PKU gene from both their mother and their father). In the United States, about 1 in 10,000 white infants is born with PKU; the incidence is much lower among black infants.

The biochemistry of PKU turned out to be reasonably straightforward. PKU homozygotes lack *phenylalanine hydroxylase,* an enzyme that is required for the conversion of the amino acid *phenylalanine* to *tyrosine.* As a result, phenylalanine accumulates in the body; and levels of *dopamine,* a neurotransmitter normally synthesized from tyrosine, are low. The consequence is abnormal brain development.

Like other behavioral traits, the behavioral symptoms of PKU result from an interaction between genetic and environmental factors: between the PKU gene and diet. Accordingly, in most modern hospitals, the blood of each newborn infant is routinely screened for a high phenylalanine level. If the level is high, the infant is immediately placed on a special phenylalanine-reduced diet; this diet reduces both the amount of phenylalanine

in the blood and the development of mental retardation. The timing of the treatment is extremely important. The phenylalanine-reduced diet does not significantly reduce the development of mental retardation in PKU homozygotes unless it is initiated within the first few weeks of life; conversely, the restriction of phenylalanine in the diet is usually relaxed in late childhood, with few obvious adverse consequences. The period of development, usually early in life, during which a particular experience must occur to have a major effect on development is its **sensitive period.**

Diamond and her colleagues (e.g., Diamond et al., 1997) showed that early application of the standard phenylalanine-reduced diet reduces, but does not prevent, the development of cognitive deficits. PKU children on the special diet performed more poorly than healthy children on several tests of cognitive ability. This finding is consistent with the fact that the blood levels of phenylalanine in PKU children on the standard phenylalanine-reduced diets tend to remain above normal. The cognitive deficits observed by Diamond and her colleagues (e.g., deficits in the ability to inhibit inappropriate responses) suggest prefrontal lobe damage. Diamond recommends putting all PKU children with elevated phenylalanine levels on stricter phenylalanine-reduced diets.

Development of Birdsong

In the spring, the songs of male songbirds threaten conspecific male trespassers and attract potential mates. The males of each species sing similar songs that are readily distinguishable from the songs of other species (see Marler & Nelson, 1992), and there are recognizable local dialects within each species (see King & West, 1990).

Studies of the ontogenetic development of birdsong suggest that birdsong develops in two phases (see Marler, 1991; Nottebohm, 1991). The first phase, called the **sensory phase,** begins several days after hatching. Although the young birds do not sing during this phase, they form memories of the adult songs they hear—usually sung by their own male relatives—that later guide the development of their own singing. The young males of many songbird species are genetically prepared to acquire the songs of their own species during the sensory phase. They cannot readily acquire the

Phenylketonuria (PKU). A neurological disorder whose symptoms are vomiting, seizures, hyperactivity, hyperirritability, mental retardation, and high levels of phenylpyruvic acid in the urine.

Phenylpyruvic acid. A substance that is found in abnormally high concentrations in the urine of those suffering from phenylketonuria.

Sensitive period. The period of development during which a particular experience must occur to have a major effect on development.

Sensory phase. The first of the two phases of birdsong development, during which young birds do not sing but form memories of the adult songs they hear.

Figure 2.25 Male zebra finches (age-limited song learners) and male canaries (open-ended song learners) are common subjects of research on birdsong development. (Illustration kindly provided by *Trends in Neuroscience;* original photograph by Arturo Alvarez-Buylla.)

songs of other species; nor can they acquire the songs of their own species if they do not hear them during the sensory phase (see Petrinovich, 1990). Males who do not hear the songs of their own species early in their lives may later develop a song, but it is likely to be highly abnormal with only a few recognizable features of their species' mature songs.

The second phase of birdsong development, the **sensorimotor phase,** begins when the juvenile males begin to twitter subsongs (the immature songs of young birds), usually when they are several months old. During this phase, the rambling vocalizations of subsongs are gradually refined until they resemble the songs of the birds' earlier adult tutors. Auditory feedback is necessary for the development of singing during the sensorimotor phase; unless the young birds are able to hear themselves sing, their subsongs do not develop into adult songs. However, once stable adult song has crystallized, songbirds are much less dependent on hearing for normal song production; the disruptive effects of deafening on adult song are usually less severe, and they require several months to be fully realized (Nordeen & Nordeen, 1992).

When it comes to the retention of their initial crystallized adult songs, there are two common patterns among songbird species. Most songbird species, such as the widely studied zebra finches and white-crowned sparrows, are *age-limited learners;* in these species, adult songs, once crystallized, remain unchanged for the rest of the birds' lives. In contrast, some species are *open-ended learners;* they are able to add new songs to their repertoire throughout their lives. For example, at the end of each mating season, male canaries return from a period of stable song to a period of plastic song—a period during which they can add new songs for the next mating season. Male zebra finches (age-limited learners) and male canaries (open-ended learners) are shown in Figure 2.25.

Figure 2.26 is a simplified version of the neural circuit that controls birdsong in the canary. It has two

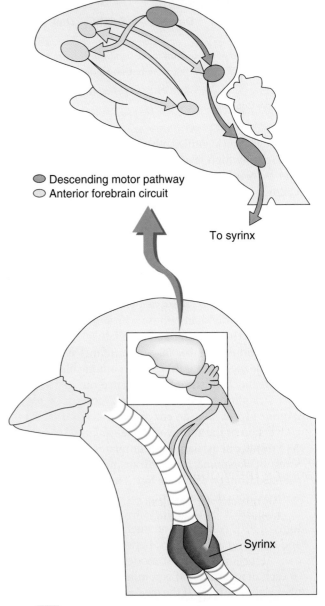

Figure 2.26 The neural circuit responsible for the production and learning of song in the male canary.

● Descending motor pathway
○ Anterior forebrain circuit

To syrinx

Syrinx

EVOLUTION, GENETICS, AND EXPERIENCE: ASKING THE RIGHT QUESTIONS ABOUT THE BIOLOGY OF BEHAVIOR

major components: the *descending motor pathway* and the anterior forebrain pathway. The descending motor pathway descends from the high vocal center on each side of the brain to the *syrinx* (voice box) on the same side; it mediates song production. The *anterior forebrain pathway* mediates song learning (Doupe, 1993; Vicario, 1991).

The canary song circuit is remarkable in four respects (Nottebohm, 1991). First, the left descending motor circuit plays a more important role in singing than the right descending motor circuit (which duplicates the left-hemisphere dominance for language in humans). Second, the high vocal center is four times larger in male canaries than in females. Third, each spring, as the male canary prepares its new repertoire of songs for the summer seduction, the song-control structures of its brain double in size, only to shrink back in the fall; this springtime burst of brain growth and singing is triggered by elevated levels of the hormone testosterone that result from the increasing daylight. Fourth, the seasonal increase in size of the song-control brain structures results from the growth of new neurons, not from an increase in the size of existing ones—a result that is remarkable because the growth of new neurons in adult vertebrates was until recently assumed to be impossible.

The Genetics of Human Psychological Differences

So far, this chapter has focused on three topics—human evolution, genetics, and the interaction of genetics and experience in the ontological development of psychological traits. All three topics converge on one fundamental question: Why are we the way we are? You have learned that each of us is a product of gene–experience interactions and that the effects of genes and experience on individual development are inseparable—remember the metaphor of the musical mountaineer and the panpipe. In view of the fact that I have emphasized these points at every opportunity throughout the chapter, I am certain that you appreciate them by now. However, I am raising them again one last time because this final section of the chapter focuses on a developmental issue that is fundamentally different from the ones that we have been discussing.

Development of the Individual versus Development of Differences among Individuals

So far, this chapter has dealt with the development of the individual. The remainder of the chapter deals with the development of differences among individuals. In the development of the individual, the effects of genes and experience are inseparable. In the development of differences among individuals, they are separable. This distinction is extremely important, but it confuses many people. Let me return to the mountaineer-and-panpipe metaphor to explain it.

The music of an individual panpipe musician is the product of the interaction of the musician and the panpipe, and it is nonsensical to ask what proportion of the music is produced by the musician and what proportion by the panpipe. However, if we measured the panpipe playing of a large sample of subjects, we could statistically estimate the degree to which the differences among them in the quality of their music resulted from differences in the subjects themselves as opposed to differences in their instruments. For example, if we selected 100 Peruvians at random and gave each a test on a professional-quality panpipe, we would likely find that most of the variation in the quality of the music resulted from differences in the subjects, some being experienced players and some never having played before. In the same way, behavioral geneticists measure a behavioral attribute of a group of subjects (e.g., the IQ of human subjects) and ask what proportion of the variation among the subjects resulted from genetic differences as opposed to experiential differences.

To assess the relative contributions of genes and experience to the development of differences in psychological attributes, behavioral geneticists study individuals of varying genetic similarity. For example, they often compare **identical twins** (monozygotic twins), who developed from the same zygote and thus

Sensorimotor phase. The second of the two phases of birdsong development, during which juvenile birds progress from subsong to adult song.

Identical twins. Twins that develop from the same zygote and are thus genetically identical; monozygotic twins.

are genetically identical, with **fraternal twins** (dizygotic twins), who developed from two zygotes and thus are no more similar than any pair of siblings. Studies of identical and fraternal twins who have been separated at infancy by adoption are particularly informative about the relative contributions of genetics and experience to differences in human psychological development. The most extensive of such studies is the Minnesota Study of Twins Reared Apart (see Bouchard et al., 1990; Bouchard, 1994).

Minnesota Study of Twins Reared Apart

The Minnesota Study of Twins Reared Apart involved 59 pairs of identical twins and 47 pairs of fraternal twins who had been reared apart, as well as many pairs of identical and fraternal twins who had been reared together. Their ages ranged from 19 to 68 years. Each twin was brought to the University of Minnesota for approximately 50 hours of testing, which focused on the assessment of intelligence and personality. Would the identical twins reared apart prove to be similar because they were genetically identical, or would they prove to be different because they had been brought up in different family environments?

The identical twins proved to be similar in both intelligence and personality, whether they had been reared together or apart. For example, the average correlation between the intelligence quotients (IQs) of identical twins on the Wechsler Adult Intelligence Scale was about 0.85 for those who had been reared together and about 0.70 for those who had been reared apart (see Figure 2.27); the correlations for fraternal twins have not yet been published. The high correlation coefficients for identical twins indicate that genetic differences were major contributing factors to the observed differences between the subjects' IQs.

The results of the Minnesota study have been widely disseminated by the popular press. Unfortunately, the meaning of the results has often been distorted. Sometimes, the misrepresentation of science by the popular press does not matter—at least not much. This is not one of those times. People's misbeliefs about the origins of human intelligence and personality are often translated into inappropriate and discriminatory social attitudes and practices. The news story "Twins Prove Intelligence and Personality Inherited" illustrates how the results of the Minnesota study have been misrepresented to the public.

This story is misleading in four ways. You should have no difficulty spotting the first; it oozes nature-

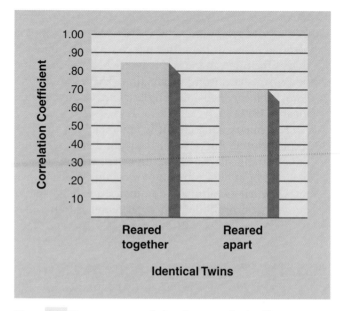

Figure 2.27 The average correlations between the intelligence quotients of identical twins in the Minnesota study.

or-nurture thinking and all of the misconceptions associated with it. Second, by focusing on the similarities of Bob and Bob, the story creates the impression that Bob and Bob (and the other monozygotic pairs of twins reared apart) are virtually identical. They are not. It is easy to come up with a long list of similarities between any two people if one asks them enough questions and ignores the dissimilarities. Third, the story creates the impression that the results of the Minnesota study are revolutionary. On the contrary, the importance of the Minnesota study lies mainly in the fact that it constitutes a particularly thorough confirmation of the results of previous adoption studies (see Plomin, 1990). Fourth, the story creates the false impression that the results of the Minnesota study make some general point about the relative contributions of genes and experience to the development of intelligence and personality in individuals. They do not, and neither do the results of any other adoption study. Bouchard and his colleagues estimated the heritability of IQ to be 0.70, but they did not conclude that IQ is 70% genetic. A **heritability estimate** is an estimate of the proportion of variability occurring in a particular trait in a particular study that resulted from the genetic variation in that study. Thus heritability estimates tell us about the contribution of genetic differences to phenotypic differences among subjects; they have nothing to say about the relative contributions of genes and experience to the development of individuals.

The magnitude of a study's heritability estimate depends on the amount of genetic and environmental

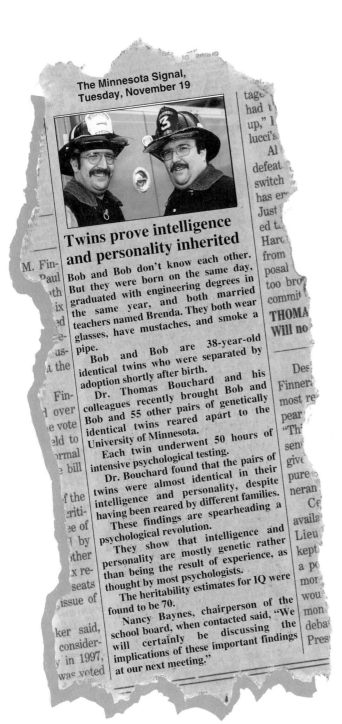

The Minnesota Signal,
Tuesday, November 19

Twins prove intelligence and personality inherited

Bob and Bob don't know each other. But they were born on the same day, graduated with engineering degrees in the same year, and both married teachers named Brenda. They both wear glasses, have mustaches, and smoke a pipe.

Bob and Bob are 38-year-old identical twins who were separated by adoption shortly after birth.

Dr. Thomas Bouchard and his colleagues recently brought Bob and Bob and 55 other pairs of genetically identical twins reared apart to the University of Minnesota.

Each twin underwent 50 hours of intensive psychological testing.

Dr. Bouchard found that the pairs of twins were almost identical in their intelligence and personality, despite having been reared by different families.

These findings are spearheading a psychological revolution.

They show that intelligence and personality are mostly genetic rather than being the result of experience, as thought by most psychologists.

The heritability estimates for IQ were found to be 70.

Nancy Baynes, chairperson of the school board, when contacted said, "We will certainly be discussing the implications of these important findings at our next meeting."

---

variation from which it was calculated, and it cannot be applied to other kinds of situations. For example, in the Minnesota study, there was relatively little environmental variation. All subjects were raised in industrialized countries (e.g., Great Britain, Canada, and the United States) by parents who could meet the strict standards required for adoption. Accordingly, most of the variation in the subjects' intelligence and personality resulted from genetic variation. If the twins had been separately adopted by European royalty, African Bushmen, Hungarian Gypsies, Los Angeles rap stars, London advertising executives, and Argentinian army officers, the resulting heritability estimates for IQ and personality would likely have been much lower. Bouchard et al. emphasize this point in their papers. Still, selective-breeding studies in laboratory animals and twin studies in humans have revealed no psychological differences that do not have a significant genetic component—even in twins over 80 years old (McClearn et al., 1997).

A commonly overlooked point about the role of genetic factors in the development of human psychological differences is that genetic differences promote psychological differences by influencing experience (see Plomin & Neiderhiser, 1992). At first, this statement seems paradoxical because we have been conditioned to think of genes and experience as separate developmental influences. However, there is now ample evidence that individuals of similar genetic endowment tend to seek out similar environments and experiences. For example, individuals whose genetic endowments promote aggression are likely to become involved in aggressive activities (e.g., football or competitive fighting), and these experiences are likely to further contribute to the development of aggressive tendencies.

Fraternal twins. Twins that develop from different zygotes and thus are no more likely to be similar than any pair of siblings; dizygotic twins.

Heritability estimate. An estimate of the proportion of variability occurring in a particular trait in a particular study that resulted from the genetic variation among the subjects in that study.

CONCLUSION

In this chapter, you first learned how to think productively about the biology of behavior. You learned that biopsychologists have rejected conventional physiological-or-psychological and nature-or-nurture dichotomies in favor of more enlightened alternatives. They view all behavior and the psychological processes that underlie it as products of neural activity shaped by the interaction among genes, which are the products of evolution, experience, and the current situation (2.1). Then, you learned about the course of human evolution (2.2), about fundamental genetics (2.3), and about the interaction of genetic factors and experience in behavioral development (2.4). Finally, you learned about the genetics of human intellectual and personality differences (2.5).

FOOD FOR THOUGHT

1. Nature-or-nurture thinking about intelligence is sometimes used as an excuse for racial discrimination. How can the interactionist approach, which has been championed in this chapter, be used as a basis for arguing against discriminatory practices?

2. Imagine that you are a biopsychology instructor. One of your students asks you whether depression is physiological or psychological. What would you say?

3. Modern genetics can prevent the tragedy of a life doomed by heredity; embryos can now be screened for some genetic diseases. But what constitutes a disease? Should genetic testing be used to select a child's characteristics? If so, what characteristics?

4. In the year 2030, a major company demands that all prospective executives take a gene test. As a result, some lose their jobs, and others fail to qualify for health insurance. Discuss.

KEY TERMS

Alleles *(p. 35)*
Amino acids *(p. 39)*
Amphibians *(p. 28)*
Analogous *(p. 32)*
Asomatognosia *(p. 22)*
Brain stem *(p. 33)*
Cartesian dualism *(p. 21)*
Cerebrum *(p. 33)*
Chordates *(p. 28)*
Chromosomes *(p. 35)*
Codon *(p. 39)*
Comparative approach *(p. 34)*
Conspecifics *(p. 28)*
Convergent evolution *(p. 32)*
Convolutions *(p. 33)*
Crossing over *(p. 36)*
Deoxyribonucleic acid (DNA) *(p. 38)*
Dichotomous traits *(p. 34)*

DNA-binding proteins *(p. 39)*
Dominant trait *(p. 34)*
Ethology *(p. 22)*
Evolve *(p. 24)*
Fitness *(p. 26)*
Fraternal twins *(p. 48)*
Functional approach *(p. 34)*
Gametes *(p. 35)*
Gene *(p. 34)*
Gene expression *(p. 39)*
Gene maps *(p. 36)*
Genotype *(p. 34)*
Heritability estimate *(p. 48)*
Heterozygous *(p. 35)*
Hominids *(p. 30)*
Homo erectus (p. 30)
Homologous *(p. 32)*
Homozygous *(p. 35)*
Human genome project *(p. 40)*

Identical twins *(p. 47)*
Instinctive behaviors *(p. 22)*
Linkage *(p. 36)*
Mammals *(p. 28)*
Meiosis *(p. 35)*
Messenger RNA *(p. 39)*
Mitochodria *(p. 42)*
Mitosis *(p. 36)*
Mutations *(p. 39)*
Natural selection *(p. 26)*
Nature–nurture issue *(p. 21)*
Nucleotide bases *(p. 38)*
Ontogeny *(p. 43)*
Operator gene *(p. 39)*
Phenotype *(p. 34)*
Phenylketonuria (PKU) *(p. 44)*
Phenylpyruvic acid *(p. 44)*
Phylogeny *(p. 43)*
Primates *(p. 29)*

Proteins *(p. 39)*
Recessive trait *(p. 34)*
Replication *(p. 39)*
Ribonucleic acid (RNA) *(p. 39)*
Ribosomes *(p. 39)*
Sensitive period *(p. 45)*
Sensorimotor phase *(p. 46)*
Sensory phase *(p. 45)*
Sex chromosomes *(p. 36)*
Sex-linked traits *(p. 36)*
Species *(p. 27)*
Structural genes *(p. 39)*
Transfer RNA *(p. 40)*
True-breeding lines *(p. 34)*
Vertebrates *(p. 28)*
Zeitgeist *(p. 21)*
Zygote *(p. 36)*

ADDITIONAL READING

The following articles focus on current issues in the study of human evolution:

Coppens, Y. (1994, May). East side story: The origin of humankind. *Scientific American, 270,* 88–95.

Leakey, M., & Walker, A. (1997, June). Early hominid fossils from Africa. *Scientific American, 276,* 74–79.

Tattersall, I. (1997, April). Out of Africa again . . . and again? *Scientific American, 276,* 60–67.

The following articles provide an excellent introduction to the human genome project:

Beardsley, T. (1996, March). Trends in human genetics: Vital data. *Scientific American, 274,* 100–105.

Lander, E. S. (1996). The new genomics: Global views of biology. *Science, 274,* 536–539.

Wallace, D. C. (1997, August). Mitochondrial DNA in aging and disease. *Scientific American, 277,* 40–47.

The following articles straighten out some common misconceptions about the biology of behavior:

Johnston, T. D. (1987). The persistence of dichotomies in the study of behavioral development. *Developmental Review, 7,* 149–182.

Plomin, T. R. (1995). Molecular genetics and psychology. *Current Directions in Psychological Science, 4,* 114–117.

Preuss, T. M. (1995). The argument from animals to humans in cognitive neuroscience. In M. S. Gazzaniga (Ed.), *The Cognitive Neurosciences.* Cambridge, MA: MIT Press.

Rutter, M. L. (1997). Nature–nurture integration: The example of antisocial behavior. *American Psychologist, 52,* 390–398.

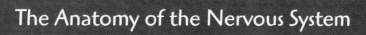

The Anatomy of the Nervous System

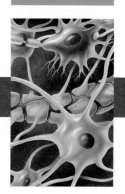

In order to understand what the brain does, it is essential to understand what it is—to know the names and locations of its major parts and how they are connected to one another. This chapter introduces you to these fundamentals of brain anatomy.

Before you begin this chapter, I want to apologize for the lack of foresight displayed by early neuroanatomists in their choice of names for neuroanatomical structures—but, then, how could they have anticipated that Latin and Greek, universal languages of the educated in their day, would not be compulsory university fare in our time? To help you, I have provided the literal English meanings of many of the neuroanatomical terms, and I have kept this chapter as brief and to the point as possible by covering only the most important structures. Still, there is no denying that this chapter will require extra effort. I can assure you, however, that it is effort well expended. Knowledge of your brain's basic structure is the necessary first step in understanding its psychological functions.

3.1 General Layout of the Nervous System

Divisions of the Nervous System

The vertebrate nervous system is composed of two divisions: the central nervous system and the peripheral nervous system (see Figure 3.1). The **central nervous system (CNS)** is the division of the nervous system that is located within the skull and spine. **The peripheral nervous system (PNS)** is the division that is located outside the skull and spine.

The central nervous system is composed of two divisions: the brain and the spinal cord. The *brain* is the part of the CNS that is located in the skull; the *spinal cord* is the part that is located in the spine.

The peripheral nervous system is also composed of two divisions: the somatic nervous system and the autonomic nervous system. The **somatic nervous system (SNS)** is the part of the PNS that interacts with the external environment. It is composed of **afferent nerves** that carry sensory signals from the skin, skeletal muscles, joints, eyes, ears, and so on, to the central nervous system and **efferent nerves** that carry motor signals from the central nervous system to the skeletal muscles. The **autonomic nervous system (ANS)** is the part of the peripheral nervous system that participates in the regulation of the internal environment. It is composed of afferent nerves that carry sensory signals from internal organs to the CNS and efferent nerves that carry motor signals from the CNS to internal organs. You will not confuse the terms *afferent* and *efferent* if you remember that many words that involve the idea of going toward something—in this case, going toward the CNS—begin with an *a* (e.g., advance, approach, arrive) and that many words that involve the idea of going away from something begin with an *e* (e.g., exit, embark, escape).

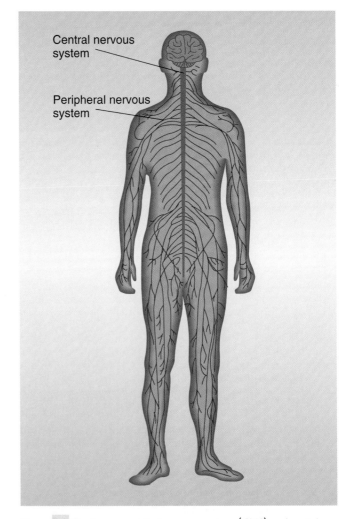

Central nervous system

Peripheral nervous system

Figure 3.1 The human central nervous system (CNS) and peripheral nervous system (PNS). The CNS is represented in red; the PNS in blue.

The autonomic nervous system has two kinds of efferent nerves: sympathetic nerves and parasympathetic nerves. The **sympathetic nerves** are those autonomic motor nerves that project from the CNS in the *lumbar* (small of the back) and *thoracic* (chest area) regions of the spine. The **parasympathetic nerves** are those autonomic motor nerves that project from the brain and *sacral* (lower back) region of the spine. See Appendix I. (Ask your instructor to specify the degree to which you are responsible for material in the appendices.) All sympathetic and parasympathetic nerves are two-stage neural paths: The sympathetic and parasympathetic neurons project from the CNS and go only part of the way to the target organs before they *synapse* onto other neurons (second-stage neurons) that carry the signals the rest of the way. However, the sympathetic and parasympathetic systems differ in that the sympathetic neurons that project from the CNS synapse on second-stage neurons at a substantial distance from their target organs, whereas the parasympathetic neurons that project from the CNS synapse near their target organs on very short second-stage neurons (see Appendix I).

The conventional view of the respective functions of the sympathetic and parasympathetic systems stresses three important principles: (1) that sympathetic nerves stimulate, organize, and mobilize energy resources in threatening situations, whereas parasympathetic nerves act to conserve energy; (2) that each autonomic target organ receives opposing sympathetic and parasympathetic input, and its activity is thus controlled by relative levels of sympathetic and parasympathetic activity; and (3) that sympathetic changes are indicative of psychological arousal, whereas parasympathetic changes are indicative of psychological relaxation. Although these principles are generally correct, there are significant exceptions to each of them (see Blessing, 1997; Hugdahl, 1996)—see Appendix II.

Most of the nerves of the peripheral nervous system project from the spinal cord, but there are 12 pairs of exceptions: the 12 pairs of **cranial nerves,** which project from the brain. They are numbered in sequence from front to back. The cranial nerves include purely sensory nerves such as the olfactory nerves (I) and the optic nerves (II), but most contain both sensory and motor fibers. The longest cranial nerves are the vagus nerves (X), which contain motor and sensory fibers traveling to and from the gut. The 12 pairs of cranial nerves and their targets are illustrated in Appendix III; their functions are listed in Appendix IV. The autonomic motor fibers of the cranial nerves are parasympathetic.

Figure 3.2 on page 54 summarizes the major divisions of the nervous system. Notice that the nervous system is a system of twos.

Meninges, Ventricles, and Cerebrospinal Fluid

The brain and spinal cord (the CNS) are the most protected organs in the body. They are encased in bone and covered by three protective membranes, the three **meninges** (pronounced "men IN gees"). The outer *meninx* (which, believe it or not, is the singular of *meninges*) is a tough membrane called the **dura mater** (tough mother). Immediately inside the dura mater is the fine **arachnoid membrane** (spiderweb-like membrane). Beneath the arachnoid membrane is a space called the **subarachnoid space,** which contains many large blood vessels and cerebrospinal fluid; then comes the innermost meninx, the delicate **pia mater** (pious mother), which adheres to the surface of the CNS.

Also protecting the CNS is the **cerebrospinal fluid (CSF),** which fills the subarachnoid space, the central canal of the spinal cord, and the cerebral ventricles of the brain. The **central canal** is a small central channel that runs the length of the spinal cord; the **cerebral ventricles** are the four large internal chambers of the brain: the two lateral ventricles, the third ventricle, and the fourth ventricle (see Figure 3.3 on page 54).

Central nervous system (CNS). The portion of the nervous system within the skull and spine.

Peripheral nervous system (PNS). The portion of the nervous system outside the skull and spine.

Somatic nervous system (SNS). The part of the peripheral nervous system that interacts with the external environment.

Afferent nerves. Nerves that carry sensory signals to the central nervous system; sensory nerves.

Efferent nerves. Nerves that carry motor signals from the central nervous system to the skeletal muscles or internal organs.

Autonomic nervous system (ANS). The part of the peripheral nervous system that participates in the regulation of the body's internal environment.

Sympathetic nerves. Those motor nerves of the autonomic nervous system that project from the CNS in the lumbar and thoracic areas of the spinal cord.

Parasympathetic nerves. Those motor nerves of the autonomic nervous system that project from the brain (as components of cranial nerves) or from the sacral region of the spinal cord.

Cranial nerves. The 12 pairs of nerves extending from the brain (e.g., the optic nerves, the olfactory nerves, and the vagus nerves).

Meninges. The three protective membranes that cover the brain and spinal cord.

Dura mater. The tough outer meninx.

Arachnoid membrane. The meninx that is located between the dura mater and the pia mater and has the appearance of a gauzelike spiderweb.

Subarachnoid space. The space beneath the arachnoid membrane; it contains many large blood vessels and cerebrospinal fluid.

Pia mater. The delicate, innermost meninx.

Cerebrospinal fluid (CSF). The colorless fluid that fills the subarachnoid space, the central canal, and the cerebral ventricles.

Central canal. The small CSF-filled passage that runs the length of the spine.

Cerebral ventricles. The four CSF-filled internal chambers of the brain: the two lateral ventricles, the third ventricle, and the fourth ventricle.

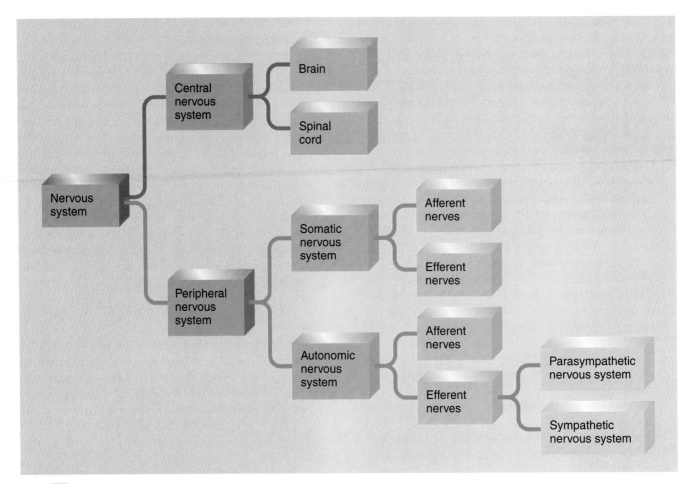

Figure 3.2 The major divisions of the nervous system.

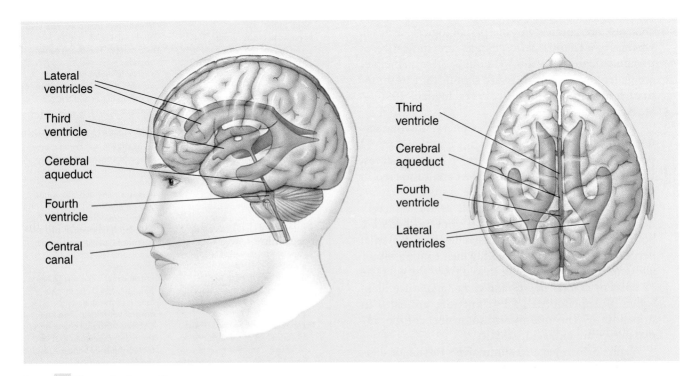

Figure 3.3 The cerebral ventricles.

The cerebrospinal fluid supports and cushions the brain. These functions are all too apparent to patients who have had some of their cerebrospinal fluid drained away; they suffer raging headaches and experience stabbing pain each time they jerk their heads.

Cerebrospinal fluid is continuously produced by the **choroid plexuses**—networks of small blood vessels that protrude into the ventricles from their pia mater lining (see Spector & Johanson, 1989). The excess CSF fluid is continuously absorbed from the subarachnoid space into large blood-filled spaces, or *dural sinuses,* which run through the dura mater and drain into the large jugular veins of the neck. Figure 3.4 illustrates the absorption of cerebrospinal fluid from the subarachnoid space into the large sinus that runs along the top of the brain between the two cerebral hemispheres.

Occasionally, the flow of cerebrospinal fluid is blocked by a tumor near one of the narrow channels that link the ventricles—for example, near the **cerebral aqueduct,** which connects the third and fourth ventricles. The resulting buildup of fluid in the ventricles causes the walls of the ventricles, and thus the entire brain, to expand, producing a condition called *hydrocephalus* (water head). Hydrocephalus is treated by draining the excess fluid from the ventricles and trying to remove the obstruction.

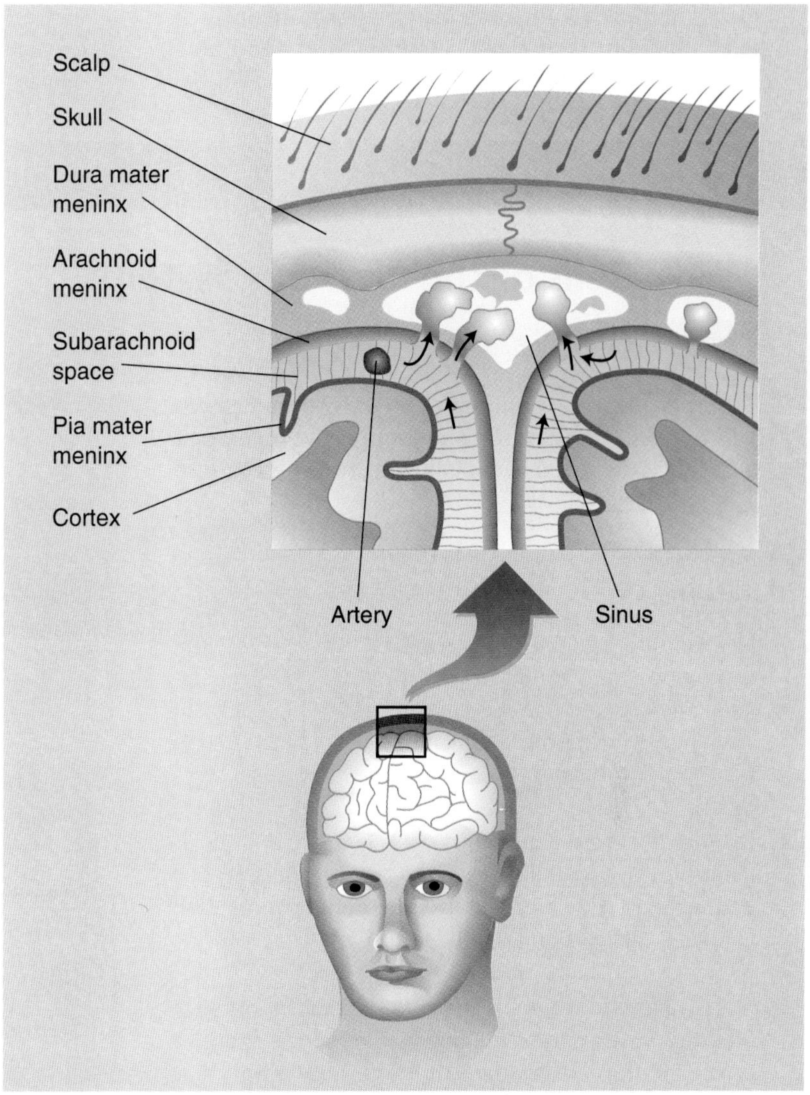

Figure 3.4 The absorption of cerebrospinal fluid from the subarachnoid space (blue) into a major sinus. Note the three meninges.

Blood–Brain Barrier

The brain is a finely tuned electrochemical organ whose function can be severely disturbed by the introduction of certain kinds of chemicals. Fortunately, there is a mechanism that impedes the passage of many toxic substances from the blood into the brain: the **blood–brain barrier.** This barrier is a consequence of the special structure of cerebral blood vessels. In the rest of the body, the cells that compose the walls of blood vessels are loosely packed; as a result, most molecules pass readily through them into surrounding tissue. In the brain, however, the cells of the blood vessel walls are tightly packed, thus forming a barrier to the passage of many molecules—particularly proteins and other large molecules (see Goldstein & Betz, 1986).

The blood–brain barrier does not impede the passage of all large molecules. Some large molecules that are critical for normal brain function (e.g., glucose) are actively transported through cerebral blood vessel walls. Also, the blood vessel walls in some areas of the brain allow certain large molecules to pass through

Choroid plexuses. The networks of capillaries that protrude into the ventricles and continuously produce cerebrospinal fluid.
Cerebral aqueduct. The narrow channel that connects the third and fourth ventricles.

Blood–brain barrier. The mechanism that keeps certain toxic substances in the blood from penetrating cerebral neural tissue.

them unimpeded; for example, sex hormones, which have difficulty permeating some parts of the brain, readily enter parts of the brain involved in sexual be-havior. The degree to which psychoactive drugs influence psychological processes depends on the ease with which they penetrate the blood–brain barrier.

3.2 Cells of the Nervous System

The cells of the nervous system are of two fundamentally different types: neurons and supportive cells. Their anatomy is discussed in the following two subsections.

Anatomy of Neurons

Neurons are cells that are specialized for the reception, conduction, and transmission of electrochemical signals. They come in an incredible variety of shapes and sizes; however, many are similar to the one illustrated in Figures 3.5 and 3.6.

▪ **EXTERNAL ANATOMY OF NEURONS** Figure 3.5 is an illustration of the major external features of a typical neuron. For your convenience, the definition of each feature is included in the illustration.

▪ **INTERNAL ANATOMY OF NEURONS** Figure 3.6 on page 58 is an illustration of the major internal features of a typical neuron. Again, the definition of each feature is included in the illustration.

▪ **NEURON CELL MEMBRANE** The neuron cell membrane is composed of a *lipid bilayer*—two layers of fat molecules (see Figure 3.7 on page 59). Embedded in the lipid bilayer are numerous protein molecules that are the basis of many of the cell membrane's functional properties. Some membrane proteins are *channel proteins,* through which certain molecules can pass; others are *signal proteins,* which transfer a signal to the inside of the neuron when particular molecules bind to their exterior.

▪ **CLASSES OF NEURONS** Figure 3.8 on page 59 illustrates a way of classifying neurons that is based on the number of processes emanating from their cell bodies. A neuron with more than two processes extending from its cell body is classified as a **multipolar neuron;** most neurons are multipolar. A neuron with one process extending from its cell body is classified as a **unipolar neuron,** and a neuron with two processes extending from its cell body is classified as a **bipolar neuron.** Neurons with short axons or no axons at all are called **interneurons;** their function is to integrate the neural activity within a single brain structure, not to conduct signals from one structure to another.

In general, there are two kinds of gross neural structures in the nervous system: those composed primarily of cell bodies and those composed primarily of axons. In the central nervous system, clusters of cell bodies are called **nuclei** (singular *nucleus*); in the peripheral nervous system, they are called **ganglia** (singular *ganglion*). (Note that the word *nucleus* has two different neuroanatomical meanings; it is a structure in the neuron cell body and a cluster of cell bodies in the CNS.) In the central nervous system, bundles of axons are called **tracts;** in the peripheral nervous system, they are called **nerves.**

Supportive Cells of the Nervous System: Glial Cells and Satellite Cells

Neurons are not the only cells in the nervous system. In the central nervous system, they are provided with physical and functional support by **glial cells;** in the peripheral nervous system, they are provided with physical and functional support by **satellite cells.** Among their many supportive functions, glial cells and satellite cells form a physical matrix that holds neural circuits together (*glia* means "glue"), and they absorb dead cells and other debris.

Multipolar neuron. A neuron with more than two processes emanating from its cell body.

Unipolar neuron. A neuron with one process emanating from its cell body.

Bipolar neuron. A neuron with two processes extending from its cell body.

Interneurons. Neurons whose processes are contained within a single brain structure; neurons with short axons or no axons at all.

Nuclei. The DNA-containing structures of cells; also, clusters of neuronal cell bodies in the central nervous system.

Ganglia. Clusters of neuronal cell bodies in the peripheral nervous system.

Tracts. Bundles of axons in the central nervous system.

Nerves. Bundles of axons in the peripheral nervous system.

Glial cells. The supportive cells of the central nervous system.

Satellite cells. The supportive cells of the peripheral nervous system.

Astroglia (astrocytes). Large, star-shaped glial cells that provide a supportive matrix for neurons in the central nervous system and are thought to play a role in the transfer of molecules from blood to CNS neurons.

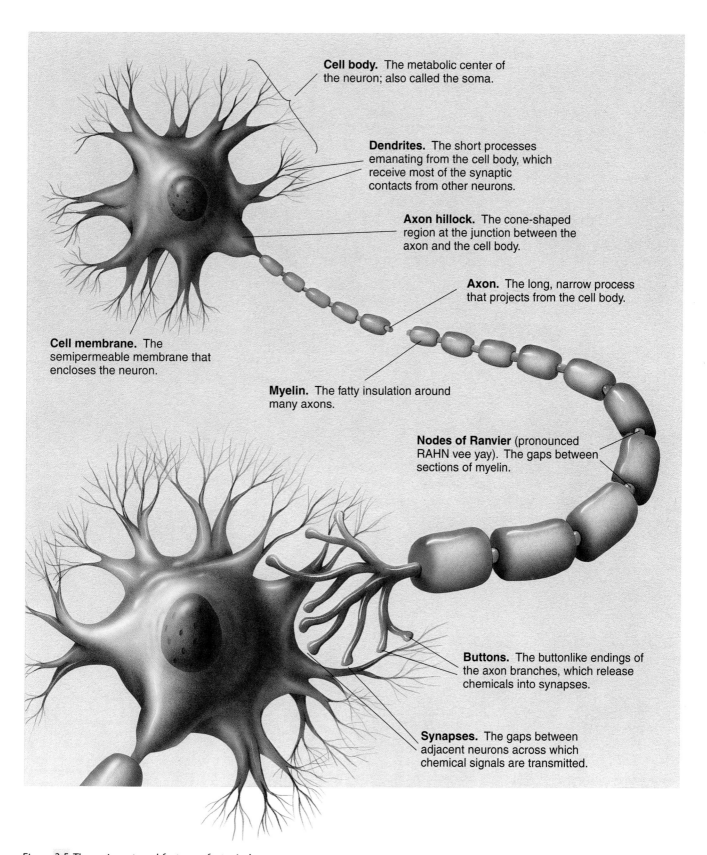

Figure 3.5 The major external features of a typical neuron.

Cell body. The metabolic center of the neuron; also called the soma.

Dendrites. The short processes emanating from the cell body, which receive most of the synaptic contacts from other neurons.

Axon hillock. The cone-shaped region at the junction between the axon and the cell body.

Axon. The long, narrow process that projects from the cell body.

Cell membrane. The semipermeable membrane that encloses the neuron.

Myelin. The fatty insulation around many axons.

Nodes of Ranvier (pronounced RAHN vee yay). The gaps between sections of myelin.

Buttons. The buttonlike endings of the axon branches, which release chemicals into synapses.

Synapses. The gaps between adjacent neurons across which chemical signals are transmitted.

The largest glial cells are called **astroglia,** or **astrocytes** (see Chan-Ling & Stone, 1991; Kimelberg & Norenberg, 1989), because they are star-shaped (*astron* means "star"). The armlike processes of astroglia cover the outer surface of blood vessels that course through the brain; they also contact neuron cell bodies.

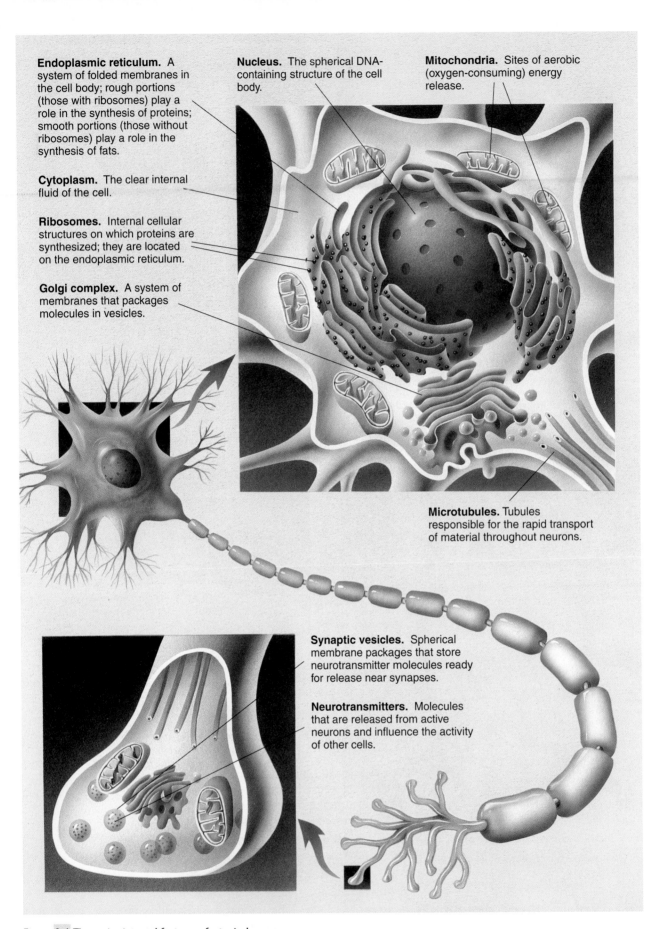

Endoplasmic reticulum. A system of folded membranes in the cell body; rough portions (those with ribosomes) play a role in the synthesis of proteins; smooth portions (those without ribosomes) play a role in the synthesis of fats.

Cytoplasm. The clear internal fluid of the cell.

Ribosomes. Internal cellular structures on which proteins are synthesized; they are located on the endoplasmic reticulum.

Golgi complex. A system of membranes that packages molecules in vesicles.

Nucleus. The spherical DNA-containing structure of the cell body.

Mitochondria. Sites of aerobic (oxygen-consuming) energy release.

Microtubules. Tubules responsible for the rapid transport of material throughout neurons.

Synaptic vesicles. Spherical membrane packages that store neurotransmitter molecules ready for release near synapses.

Neurotransmitters. Molecules that are released from active neurons and influence the activity of other cells.

Figure 3.6 The major internal features of a typical neuron.

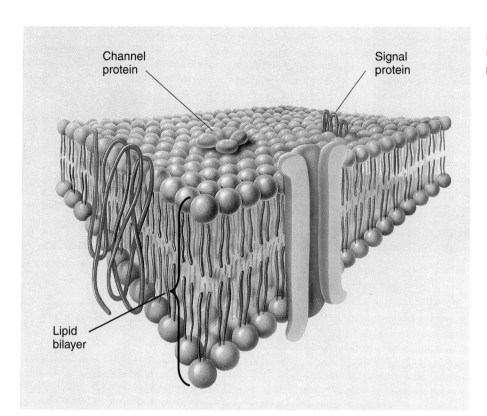

Figure 3.7 The cell membrane: A lipid bilayer with signal proteins and channel proteins embedded in it.

Channel protein

Signal protein

Lipid bilayer

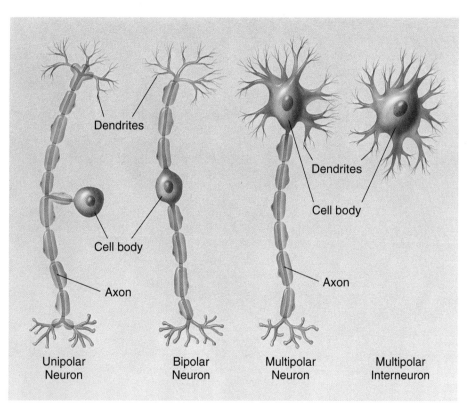

Figure 3.8 A unipolar neuron, a bipolar neuron, a multipolar neuron, and an interneuron.

Dendrites

Dendrites

Cell body

Cell body

Axon

Axon

Unipolar Neuron

Bipolar Neuron

Multipolar Neuron

Multipolar Interneuron

Accordingly, astroglia are thought to play a role in the passage of chemicals from the blood into neurons (see Figure 3.9 on page 60).

Oligodendroglia, or **oligodendrocytes,** are another class of glial cells; they send out processes that wrap around the axons of some neurons of the central nervous system. These processes are rich in *myelin,* a fatty insulating substance, and the myelin sheaths that

Oligodendroglia (oligodendrocytes). Glial cells that myelinate axons of the central nervous system.

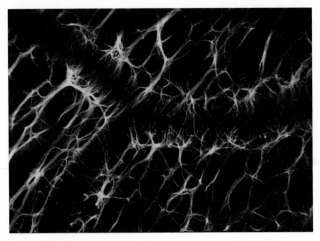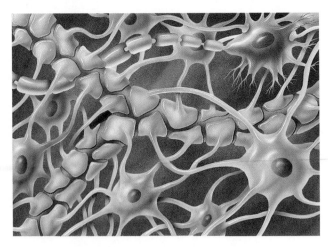

Figure 3.9 Astrocytes. Astrocytes have an affinity for blood vessels, and they form a supportive matrix for neurons. The photograph on the left is of a slice of brain tissue stained with a glial stain; the unstained channels are blood vessels. The illustration on the right shows how the feet of astrocytes cover blood vessels and contact neurons by illustrating how the photograph in the left panel would look in three dimensions. Compare the two panels.

(Photograph courtesy of T. Chan-Ling.)

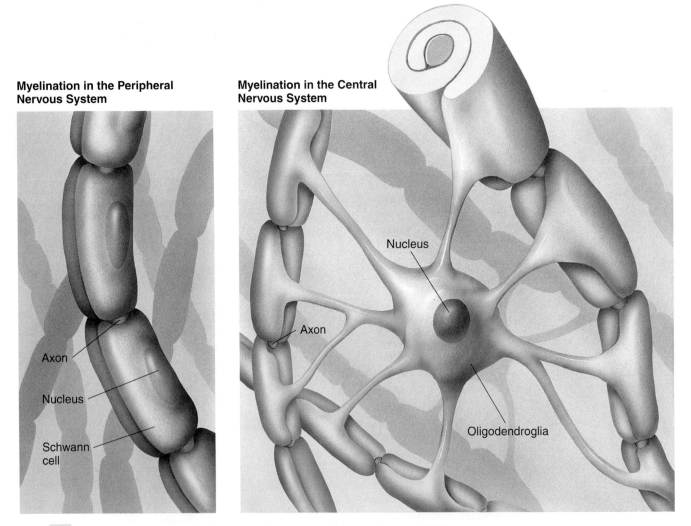

Myelination in the Peripheral Nervous System

Myelination in the Central Nervous System

Nucleus

Axon

Axon

Nucleus

Schwann cell

Oligodendroglia

Figure 3.10 The myelination of CNS axons by an oligodendrocyte and the myelination of PNS axons by Schwann cells.

3 THE ANATOMY OF THE NERVOUS SYSTEM

they form increase the speed and efficiency of axonal conduction. A similar function is performed by **Schwann cells** (a class of satellite cells) in the peripheral nervous system. Oligodendroglia and Schwann cells are illustrated in Figure 3.10. Notice that each Schwann cell constitutes one myelin segment, whereas each oligodendroglia cell constitutes several segments, often on more than one axon. Another important difference between Schwann cells and oligodendroglia is that only Schwann cells can guide axonal *regeneration* (regrowth) after damage. That is why there is normally little axonal regeneration in the mammalian CNS.

3.3 Neuroanatomical Techniques and Directions

The major problem in visualizing neurons is not their minuteness. The major problem is that neurons are so tightly packed and their axons and dendrites so intricately intertwined that looking through a microscope at unprepared neural tissue reveals almost nothing about them. The key to the study of neuroanatomy lies in preparing neural tissue in a variety of ways, each of which permits a clear view of a different aspect of neural structure, and then combining the knowledge obtained from each of the preparations. This section of the chapter first describes a few of the most common neuroanatomical techniques, then explains the system of directions that neuroanatomists use to describe the location of structures in vertebrate nervous systems.

Neuroanatomical Techniques

■ GOLGI STAIN The greatest blessing to befall neuroscience in its early years was the accidental discovery of the **Golgi stain** by Camillo Golgi (pronounced "GOLE-jee"), an Italian physician, in the early 1870s. Golgi was trying to stain the meninges by exposing a block of neural tissue to potassium dichromate and silver nitrate, when he noticed an amazing thing. For some unknown reason, the silver chromate created by the chemical reaction invaded a few neurons in each slice of tissue and stained each invaded neuron entirely black. This discovery made it possible to see individual neurons for the first time, although only in silhouette (see Figure 3.11). Stains that totally dye all neurons on a slide reveal nothing of their structure because the neurons are so tightly packed.

■ NISSL STAIN Although the Golgi stain permits an excellent view of the silhouettes of the few neurons that take up the stain, it provides no indication of the number of neurons in an area or the nature of their inner structure. The first neural staining procedure to overcome these shortcomings was the **Nissl stain,** which was developed by Franz Nissl, a German psychiatrist, in the 1880s. The most common dye used in the Nissl

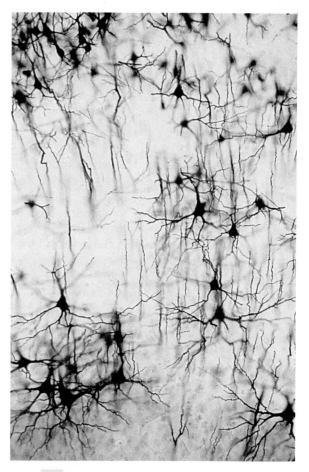

Figure 3.11 Neural tissue that has been stained by the Golgi method. Because only a few neurons take up the stain, their silhouettes are revealed in great detail but their internal details are invisible. Usually, only part of a neuron is captured in a single slice.

(Ed Reschke © Peter Arnold, Inc.)

Schwann cells. Satellite cells whose myelin-rich processes wrap around axons in the peripheral nervous system.

Golgi stain. A neural stain that completely darkens a few of the neurons in each slice of tissue, thereby revealing their silhouettes.

Nissl stain. A neural stain that has an affinity for structures of neural cell bodies.

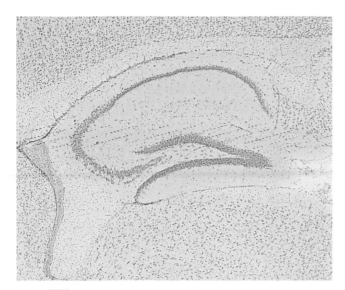

Figure 3.12 Neural tissue that has been stained by the Nissl method. A Nissl-stained section (slice) of the mouse hippocampus, a structure that plays an important role in learning and memory. Notice the densely stained cell body layers.

(Courtesy of Jerold J. M. Chun, M. D., Ph.D.)

method is cresyl violet. Cresyl violet and other Nissl dyes penetrate all cells on a slide, but they bind effectively only to structures in neuron cell bodies. Thus one can estimate the number of cell bodies in an area by counting the number of Nissl-stained dots. Figure 3.12 is a photograph of a slice of brain tissue stained with cresyl violet. Notice that only the layers composed mainly of neuron cell bodies are densely stained.

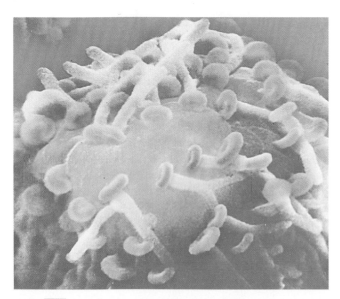

Figure 3.13 A color-enhanced scanning electron micrograph of a neuron cell body (green) studded with terminal buttons (orange). Each neuron receives numerous synaptic contacts.

(Courtesy of Jerold J. M. Chun, M. D., Ph.D.)

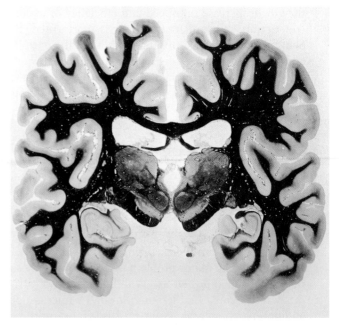

Figure 3.14 A myelin-stained section of the human brain. Notice that the white matter is stained black but that the cortex and other nuclear groups are relatively unstained.

(From *Fundamental Neuroanatomy* by Walle J. H. Nauta and Michael Feirtag. Copyright © 1986 W. H. Freeman and Company. Reprinted with permission.)

■ **ELECTRON MICROSCOPY** A neuroanatomical technique that provides information about the details of neuronal structure is **electron microscopy** (pronounced "my-CROSS-cuh-pee"). Because of the nature of light, the limit of magnification in light microscopy is about 1,500 times, a level of magnification that is insufficient to reveal the fine anatomical details of neurons. Greater detail can be obtained by first coating thin slices of neural tissue with an electron-absorbing substance that is taken up by different parts of neurons to different degrees, then passing a beam of electrons through the tissue onto a photographic film. The result is an *electron micrograph,* which captures neuronal structure in exquisite detail (see Figure 4.12). A *scanning electron microscope* provides spectacular electron micrographs in three dimensions (see Figure 3.13), but is not capable of as much magnification as a conventional electron microscope.

■ **MYELIN STAINS** The first stains specifically developed for studying axons were **myelin stains**—stains that selectively dye the sheaths of myelinated axons. Figure 3.14 is a myelin-stained coronal section of the human brain. Notice that the subcortical white matter, which is composed largely of myelinated axons, is stained,

---

Electron microscopy. A technique used to study the fine details of cellular structure.

Myelin stains. Stains that selectively dye the sheaths of myelinated axons.

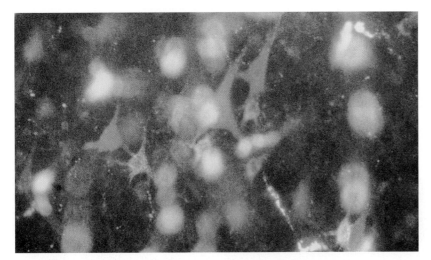

Figure 3.15 Retrograde tracing. Injection of a red fluorescent dye (rhodamine dextrans) into one visual cortex of a cat was taken up by neural buttons in the area and transported back to their cell bodies. In this section, stained red are the neural cell bodies in the contralateral visual cortex whose axons projected via the corpus callosum to the site of the injection.

(Courtesy of Joanne Matsubara, Department of Ophthalmology, University of British Columbia.)

while the cerebral cortex and various subcortical nuclear groups are not. Although myelin stains are useful for visualizing myelinated areas of the CNS, they are not very useful for tracking the pathways of individual axons—for three reasons. First, the stains are of no use in tracking unmyelinated axons. Second, because the initial segment and terminal branches of myelinated axons are not myelinated, the stains cannot reveal exactly where a myelinated axon originates or where it terminates. Third, because all myelinated axons are stained indiscriminately, once a myelinated axon becomes intermingled with others, it is impossible to trace it through a series of slices. Modern neuroanatomical tracing techniques circumvent these problems.

■ **NEUROANATOMICAL TRACING TECHNIQUES** Neuroanatomical tracing techniques are of two types: anterograde (forward) tracing methods and retrograde (backward) tracing methods. *Anterograde tracing methods* are used when an investigator wants to trace the paths of axons projecting away from cell bodies located in a particular area. The investigator injects into the area one of several chemicals commonly used for anterograde tracing—chemicals that are taken up by

cell bodies and then transported forward along their axons to their terminal buttons. After a few days, the brain is removed and sliced; the slices are then treated to reveal the locations of the injected chemical. *Retrograde tracing methods* work in reverse; they are used when an investigator wants to trace the paths of axons projecting into a particular area. The investigator injects into the area one of several chemicals commonly used for retrograde tracing—chemicals that are taken up by terminal buttons and then transported backward along their axons to their cell bodies. After a few days, the brain is removed and sliced; the slices are then treated to reveal the locations of the injected chemical (see Figure 3.15).

Directions in the Vertebrate Nervous System

Directions in the vertebrate nervous system are described in relation to the orientation of the spinal cord. This system is straightforward for most vertebrates, as Figure 3.16 indicates. The vertebrate nervous system

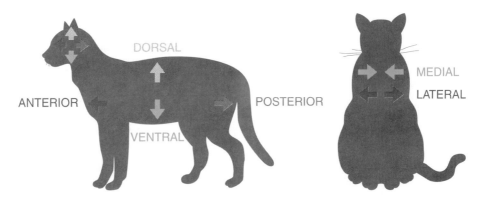

Figure 3.16 Anatomical directions in a representative vertebrate.

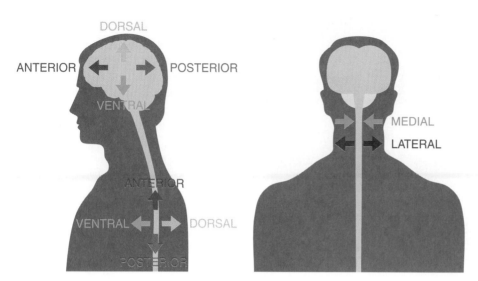

Figure 3.17 Anatomical directions in a human. Notice that the directions in the cerebral hemisphere are rotated by 90° because of the unconventional upright posture of humans.

has three axes: anterior-posterior, dorsal-ventral, and medial-lateral. First, **anterior** means toward the nose end (the anterior end), and **posterior** means toward the tail end (the posterior end); these same directions are sometimes referred to as *rostral* and *caudal*, respectively. Second, **dorsal** means toward the surface of the back or the top of the head (the dorsal surface), and **ventral** means toward the surface of the chest or the bottom of the head (the ventral surface). Third, **medial** means toward the midline of the body, and **lateral** means away from the midline toward the body's lateral surfaces.

We humans complicate this simple three-axis (anterior-posterior, ventral-dorsal, medial-lateral) system of neuroanatomical directions by insisting on walking around on our hind legs, thus changing the orientation of our brains in relation to our spines. You can save yourself a lot of confusion if you remember that the system of vertebrate neuroanatomical directions was adapted for use in humans in such a way that the terms used to describe the positions of various body surfaces are the same in humans as they are in more typical, non-upright vertebrates. Specifically, notice that the top of the human head and the back of the human body are both referred to as *dorsal* even though they are in different directions, and the bottom of the human head and the front of the human body are both referred to as *ventral* even though they are in different directions (see Figure 3.17). To circumvent this complication, the terms **superior** and **inferior** are often used to refer to the top and bottom of the primate head, respectively.

In the next few pages, you will be seeing drawings of sections (slices) of the brain cut in one of three different planes: **horizontal sections, frontal** (also termed *coronal*) **sections,** and **sagittal sections.** These three planes are illustrated in Figure 3.18. A section cut down the center of the brain, between the two hemispheres, is

called a *midsagittal section.* A section cut at a right angle to any long, narrow structure, such as the spinal cord or a nerve, is called a **cross section.**

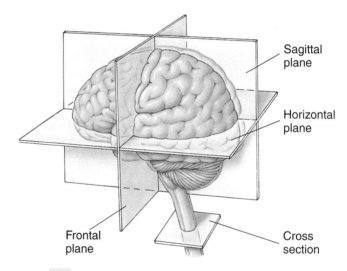

Figure 3.18 Horizontal, frontal (coronal), and sagittal planes in the human brain and a cross section of the human spinal cord.

Anterior. Toward the nose end of a vertebrate.	**Superior.** Toward the top of the primate brain.
Posterior. Toward the tail end of a vertebrate or toward the back of the head.	**Inferior.** Toward the bottom of the primate brain.
Dorsal. Toward the surface of the back of a vertebrate or toward the top of the head.	**Horizontal sections.** Any slices of brain tissue cut in a plane that is parallel to the top of the brain.
Ventral. Toward the stomach surface of a vertebrate, or toward the bottom of the head.	**Frontal sections.** Any slices of brain tissue cut in a plane that is parallel to the face; also termed *coronal section.*
Medial. Toward the midline of the body.	**Sagittal sections.** Any slices of brain tissue cut in a plane that is parallel to the side of the brain.
Lateral. Away from the midline of the body and toward the body's lateral surfaces.	**Cross sections.** Sections cut at a right angle to any long narrow structure.

To test your comprehension and retention of the first three sections of this chapter, draw a line between each term in column 1 and the appropriate phrase in column 2.

The correct answers are provided at the bottom of this page. Before proceeding, review material related to your incorrect answers.

1.	Autonomic nervous system	a.	Packets of neurotransmitter molecules
2.	Cerebral aqueduct	b.	PNS minus the somatic nervous system
3.	Axon hillock	c.	Connects the 3rd and 4th ventricles
4.	Dorsal	d.	Stains cell bodies
5.	Cell membrane	e.	Top of a vertebrate's head
6.	Cranial nerves	f.	Outer meninx
7.	Superior or dorsal	g.	Between the cell body and axon
8.	Cell body	h.	Contains the nucleus of a neuron
9.	Synaptic vesicles	i.	Olfactory, visual, and vagus
10.	Oligodendroglia	j.	Myelinate CNS axons
11.	Nissl	k.	A slice down the center of the brain
12.	Dura mater	l.	Top of the primate head
13.	Midsagittal section	m.	Silhouette
14.	Golgi	n.	Lipid bilayer

3.4 Spinal Cord

In the first three sections of this chapter, you learned about the divisions of the nervous system, the cells that compose it, and some of the neuroanatomical techniques that are used to study it. This section begins your ascent of the human CNS by focusing on the spinal cord. The final two sections of the chapter focus on the brain.

In cross section, it is apparent that the spinal cord comprises two different areas (see Figure 3.19): an inner H-shaped core of gray matter and a surrounding area of white matter. *Gray matter* is composed largely of cell bodies and unmyelinated interneurons, whereas *white matter* is composed largely of myelinated axons. (It is the myelin that gives the white matter its glossy white sheen.) The two dorsal arms of the spinal gray

The answers are (1) b, (2) c, (3) g, (4) e, (5) n, (6) i, (7) l, (8) h, (9) a, (10) j, (11) d, (12) f, (13) k, (14) m.

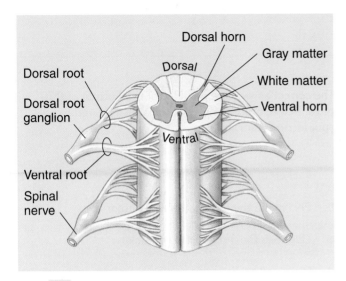

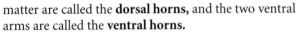

Figure 3.19 The dorsal and ventral roots of the spinal cord.

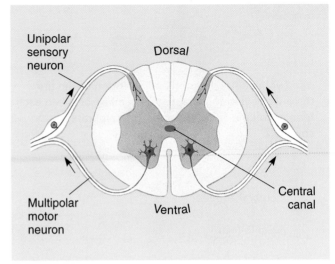

Figure 3.20 A schematic cross section of the spinal cord.

matter are called the **dorsal horns,** and the two ventral arms are called the **ventral horns.**

Pairs of *spinal nerves* are attached to the spinal cord—one on the left and one on the right—at 31 different levels of the spine. As Figure 3.19 shows, each of these 62 spinal nerves divides as it nears the cord, and its axons are joined to the cord via one of two roots: the *dorsal root* or the *ventral root.*

All dorsal root axons, whether somatic or automatic, are sensory (afferent) unipolar neurons with their cell bodies grouped together just outside the cord to form the *dorsal root ganglia.* Many of their synaptic terminals are in the dorsal horns of the spinal gray matter (see Figure 3.20). In contrast, the neurons of the ventral root are motor (efferent) multipolar neurons with their cell bodies in the ventral horns. Those that are part of the somatic nervous system project to skeletal muscles; those that are part of the autonomic nervous system project to ganglia, where they synapse on neurons that in turn project to internal organs (heart, stomach, liver, etc.). See Appendix I.

3.5 The Five Major Divisions of the Brain

A necessary step in learning to live in an unfamiliar city is learning the names and locations of its major neighborhoods or districts. Those who possess this information can easily communicate the general location of any destination in the city. This section of the chapter introduces you to the five "neighborhoods," or divisions, of the brain—for much the same reason.

To understand why the brain is considered to be composed of five divisions, it is necessary to understand its early development. In the vertebrate embryo, the tissue that eventually develops into the CNS is recognizable as a fluid-filled tube (see Figure 3.21). The first indications of the developing brain are three swellings that occur at the anterior end of this tube. These three swellings eventually develop into the adult *forebrain, midbrain,* and *hindbrain.*

Before birth, the initial three swellings in the neural tube become five (see Figure 3.21). This occurs because the forebrain swelling grows into two different swellings, and so does the hindbrain swelling. From anterior to posterior, the five swellings that compose the developing brain at birth are the *telencephalon,* the *diencephalon,* the *mesencephalon* (or midbrain), the *metencephalon,* and the *myelencephalon* (encephalon means "within the head"). These swellings ultimately develop into the five divisions of the adult brain. As a student, I memorized their order by remembering that the *te*lencephalon is on the *top* and that the other four divisions are arrayed below it in alphabetical order.

Figure 3.22 illustrates the locations of the telencephalon, diencephalon, mesencephalon, metencephalon, and myelencephalon in the adult human brain. Notice that in humans, as in other higher vertebrates, the telencephalon (the left and right *cerebral hemispheres*) undergoes the greatest growth during development. The other four divisions of the brain are often referred to collectively as the **brain stem**—the stem on which the cerebral hemispheres sit. The myelencephalon is often referred to as the *medulla.*

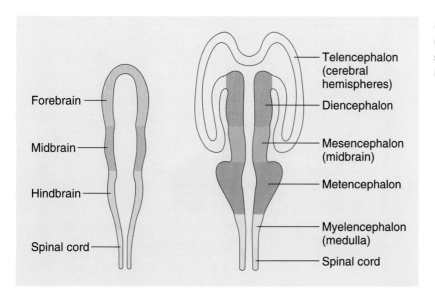

Figure 3.21 The early development of the mammalian brain as illustrated in schematic horizontal sections. Compare with the adult human brain in Figure 3.22.

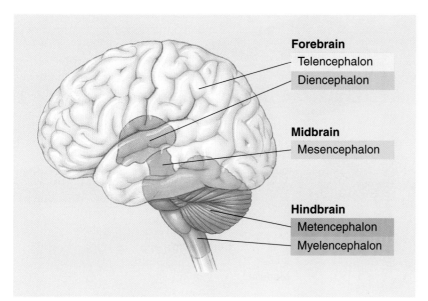

Figure 3.22 The divisions of the adult human brain.

Forebrain
Telencephalon
Diencephalon

Midbrain
Mesencephalon

Hindbrain
Metencephalon
Myelencephalon

 Major Structures of the Brain

Now that you have learned the five major divisions of the brain, it is time to introduce you to their major structures. This section of the chapter begins its survey of brain structures in the myelencephalon, then ascends through the other divisions to the telencephalon. Rather than being defined in the key term boxes, the boldfaced brain structures introduced in this section are defined by Figure 3.32 at the end of the section.

Dorsal horns. The two dorsal arms of the spinal gray matter.
Ventral horns. The two ventral arms of the spinal gray matter.

Brain stem. The myelencephalon, the metencephalon, the mesencephalon, and the diencephalon.

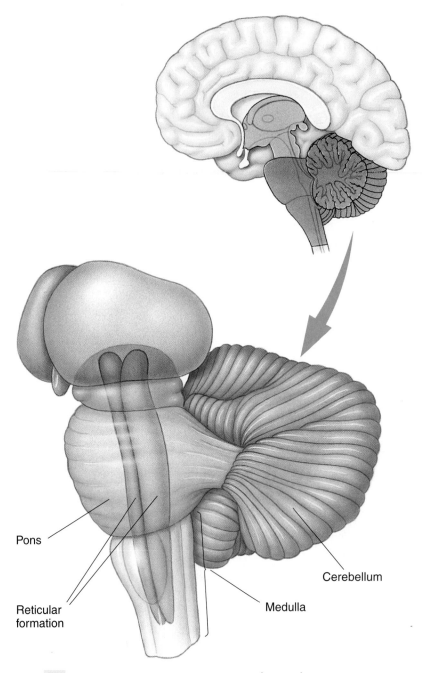

Figure 3.23 Structures of the human myelencephalon (medulla) and metencephalon.

Myelencephalon

Not surprisingly, the **myelencephalon** (or **medulla**), the most posterior division of the brain, is composed largely of tracts carrying signals between the rest of the brain and the body. An interesting part of the myelencephalon from a psychological perspective is the **reticular formation** (see Figure 3.23). It is a complex network of about 100 tiny nuclei that occupies the central core of the brain stem from the posterior boundary of the myelencephalon to the anterior boundary of the midbrain. It is so named because of its netlike appearance (*reticulum* means "little net"). Sometimes, the

reticular formation is referred to as the *reticular activating system* because parts of it seem to play a role in arousal. The various nuclei of the reticular formation are involved in a variety of functions, however—including sleep, attention, movement, the maintenance of muscle tone, and various cardiac, circulatory, and respiratory reflexes. Accordingly, referring to this collection of nuclei as a system can be misleading.

Metencephalon

The **metencephalon,** like the myelencephalon, houses many ascending and descending tracts and part of the

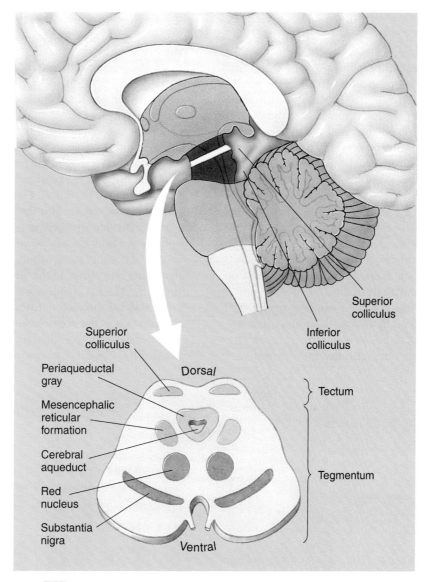

Figure 3.24 The human mesencephalon (midbrain).

reticular formation. These structures create a bulge, called the **pons,** on the brain stem's ventral surface. The pons is one major division of the metencephalon; the other is the cerebellum ("little brain")—see Figure 3.23. The **cerebellum** is the large, convoluted structure on the brain stem's dorsal surface. It is an important sensorimotor structure; cerebellar damage eliminates the ability to precisely control one's movements and to adapt them to changing conditions.

Mesencephalon

The **mesencephalon,** like the metencephalon, has two divisions. The two divisions of the mesencephalon are the tectum and the tegmentum (see Figure 3.24). The **tectum** ("roof") is the dorsal surface of the midbrain. In mammals, the tectum is composed of two pairs of bumps, the *colliculi* ("little hills"). The posterior pair, called the **inferior colliculi,** have an auditory function; the anterior pair, called the **superior colliculi,** have a visual function. In lower vertebrates, the function of the tectum is entirely visual; thus the tectum is referred to as the *optic tectum.*

The **tegmentum** is the division of the mesencephalon ventral to the tectum. In addition to the reticular formation and tracts of passage, the tegmentum contains three colorful structures that are of particular interest to biopsychologists: the periaqueductal gray, the substantia nigra, and the red nucleus (see Figure 3.24). The **periaqueductal gray** is the gray matter situated around the *cerebral aqueduct,* the duct connecting the third and fourth ventricles; it is of special interest because of its role in mediating the analgesic (pain-reducing) effects of opiate drugs. The **substantia nigra** ("black substance") and the **red nucleus** are both important components of the sensorimotor system.

Diencephalon

The **diencephalon** is composed of two structures: the thalamus and the hypothalamus (see Figure 3.25). The **thalamus** is the large, two-lobed structure that constitutes the top of the brain stem. One lobe sits on each side of the third ventricle, and the two lobes are joined by the **massa intermedia,** which runs through the ventricle. Visible on the surface of the thalamus are white *lamina* (layers) that are composed of myelinated axons.

The thalamus comprises many different pairs of nuclei, most of which project to the cortex. Some are *sensory relay nuclei*—nuclei that receive signals from sensory receptors, process them, and then transmit them to the appropriate areas of sensory cortex. For example, the **lateral geniculate nuclei,** the **medial geniculate nuclei,** and the **ventral posterior nuclei** are important relay stations in the visual, auditory, and somatosensory systems, respectively (see Figure 3.25). The various thalamic nuclei are illustrated in Appendix V.

The **hypothalamus** is located just below the anterior thalamus (*hypo* means "below")—see Figure 3.26. It plays an important role in the regulation of several motivated behaviors. It exerts its effects in part by regulating the release of hormones from the **pituitary gland,** which dangles from it on the ventral surface of the brain. The literal meaning of *pituitary gland* is "snot gland"; it was discovered in a gelatinous state behind the nose of an unembalmed cadaver and was incorrectly assumed to be the main source of nasal mucus.

In addition to the pituitary gland, two other structures appear on the inferior surface of the hypothalamus: the optic chiasm and the mammillary bodies (see Figure 3.26). The **optic chiasm** is the point at which the *optic nerves* from each eye come together. The X-shape is created because some of the axons of the optic nerve **decussate** (cross over to the other side of the brain) via the optic chiasm. The decussating fibers are said to be **contralateral** (projecting from one side of the body to the other), and the nondecussating fibers are said to be **ipsilateral** (staying on the same side of the body). The **mammillary bodies** are a pair of spherical hypothala-

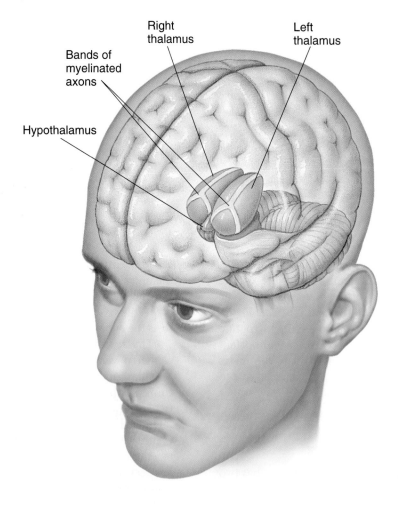

Figure 3.25 The human diencephalon.

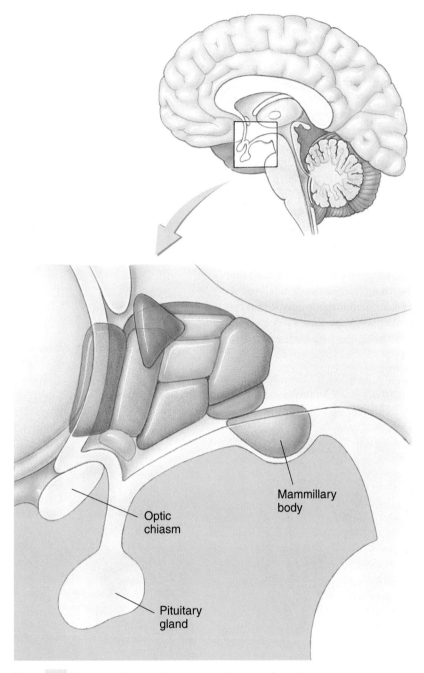

Figure 3.26 The human hypothalamus, optic chiasm, and pituitary.

mic nuclei located on the inferior surface of the hypothalamus, just behind the pituitary. The mammillary bodies and the other nuclei of the hypothalamus are illustrated in Appendix VI.

Telencephalon

The **telencephalon** is the largest division of the human brain, and it mediates its most complex functions. It initiates voluntary movement, interprets sensory input, and mediates complex cognitive processes such as learning, speaking, and problem solving.

Decussate. To cross over to the other side of the brain.
Contralateral. Projecting from one side of the body to the other.
Ipsilateral. On the same side of the body.

■ **CEREBRAL CORTEX** The cerebral hemispheres are covered by a layer of tissue called the **cerebral cortex** (cerebral bark). In humans, the cerebral cortex is deeply convoluted (furrowed)—see Figure 3.27. The *convolutions* have the effect of increasing the amount of cerebral cortex without increasing the overall volume of the brain. Not all mammals have convoluted cortexes; most mammals are *lissencephalic* (smooth-brained). It was once believed that the number and size of cortical convolutions determined a species's intellectual capacities; however, the number and size of cortical convolutions appear to be related more to body size. Every large mammal has an extremely convoluted cortex.

The large furrows in a convoluted cortex are called **fissures,** and the small ones are called *sulci* (singular *sulcus*). The ridges between fissures and sulci are called **gyri** (singular *gyrus*). It is apparent in Figure 3.27 that the cerebral hemispheres are almost completely separated by the largest of the fissures: the **longitudinal fissure.** The cerebral hemispheres are directly connected by only a few tracts spanning the longitudinal fissure;

these hemisphere-connecting tracts are called **cerebral commissures.** The largest cerebral commissure, the **corpus callosum,** is clearly visible in Figure 3.27.

As Figure 3.28 indicates, the two major landmarks on the lateral surface of each hemisphere are the **central fissure** and the **lateral fissure.** These fissures partially divide each hemisphere into four lobes: the **frontal lobe,** the **parietal lobe** (pronounced "pa RYE e

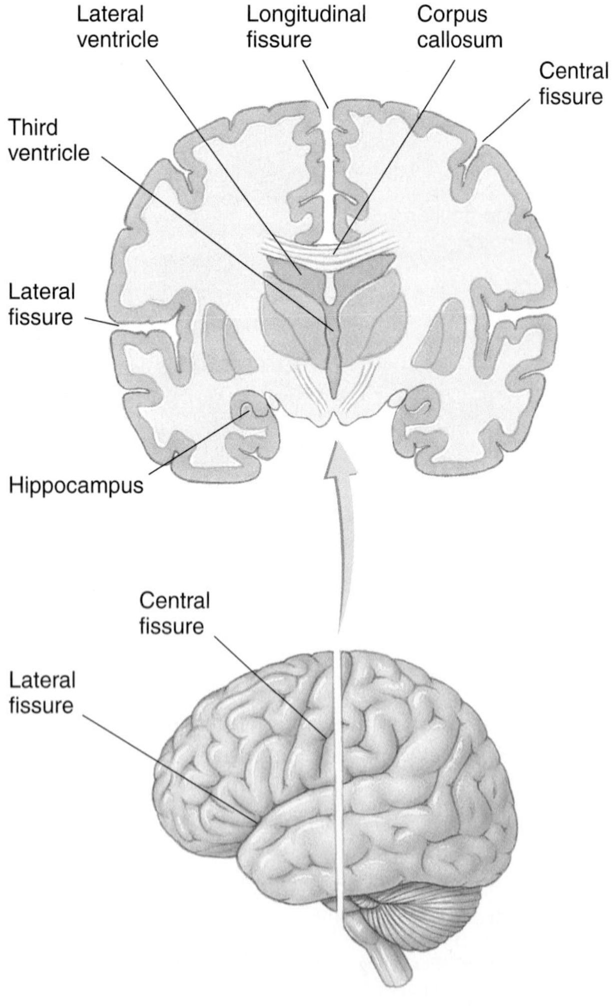

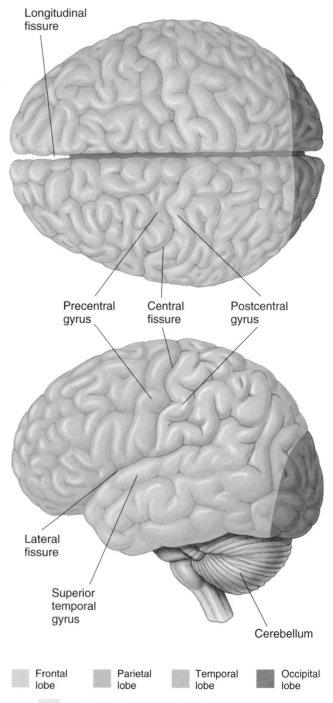

Figure 3.28 The lobes of the cerebral hemispheres.

Figure 3.27 The major fissures of the human cerebral hemispheres.

THE ANATOMY OF THE NERVOUS SYSTEM

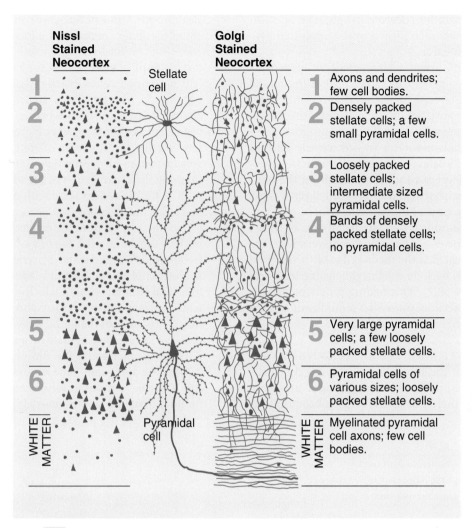

Nissl Stained Neocortex

1
2
3
4
5
6

WHITE MATTER

Stellate cell

Pyramidal cell

Golgi Stained Neocortex

WHITE MATTER

1 Axons and dendrites; few cell bodies.
2 Densely packed stellate cells; a few small pyramidal cells.
3 Loosely packed stellate cells; intermediate sized pyramidal cells.
4 Bands of densely packed stellate cells; no pyramidal cells.
5 Very large pyramidal cells; a few loosely packed stellate cells.
6 Pyramidal cells of various sizes; loosely packed stellate cells.

Myelinated pyramidal cell axons; few cell bodies.

Figure 3.29 The six layers of neocortex.
(Adapted from Rakic, 1979.)

tal"), the **temporal lobe,** and the **occipital lobe** (pronounced "ok SIP i tal"). Among the largest gyri are the **precentral gyri,** which contain motor cortex; the **postcentral gyri,** which contain somatosensory (body-sensation) cortex; and the **superior temporal gyri,** which contain auditory cortex. The function of occipital cortex is entirely visual.

About 90 percent of human cerebral cortex is **neocortex** (new cortex); that is, it is six-layered cortex of relatively recent evolution. By convention, the layers of neocortex are numbered I through VI, starting at the surface. Figure 3.29 illustrates two adjacent sections of neocortex. One has been stained with a Nissl stain to reveal the number and shape of its cell bodies; the other has been stained with a Golgi stain to reveal the silhouettes of a small proportion of its neurons.

Three important characteristics of neocortex anatomy are apparent from the sections in Figure 3.29. First, it is apparent that there are two fundamentally different kinds of cortical neurons: pyramidal (pyramid-shaped) cells and stellate (star-shaped) cells. **Pyramidal cells** are large multipolar neurons with pyramid-shaped cell bodies, a large dendrite called an *apical dendrite* that extends from the apex of the pyramid straight towards the cortex surface, and a very long axon. In contrast, **stellate cells** are small star-shaped interneurons (neurons with short axons). Second, it is apparent that the six layers of neocortex differ from one another in terms of the size and density of their cell bodies and the relative proportion of pyramidal and stellate cell bodies that they contain. Third, it is apparent that many long axons and dendrites course vertically (i.e., at right angles to the cortical layers) through the neocortex. This vertical flow of information is the basis of the neocortex's

---

Pyramidal cells. Large cortical multipolar neurons with a pyramid-shaped cell body, an apical dendrite, and a long axon.

Stellate cells. Small star-shaped cortical interneurons with short axons.

columnar organization; neurons in a given vertical column of neocortex often form a mini circuit that performs a single function.

A fourth important characteristic of neocortex anatomy is not apparent in Figure 3.29: Although all neocortex is six-layered, there are variations in the layers from area to area. For example, because the stellate cells of layer IV are specialized for receiving sensory signals from the thalamus, layer IV is extremely thick in areas of sensory cortex. Conversely, because the pyramidal cells of layer V conduct signals from the neocortex to the brain stem and spinal cord, layer V is extremely thick in areas of motor cortex.

The **hippocampus** is one important area of cortex that is not neocortex—it has only three layers. The hippocampus is located at the medial edge of the cerebral cortex as it folds back on itself in the medial temporal lobe (see Figure 3.27). This folding produces a shape that is, in cross section, somewhat reminiscent of a sea horse (*hippocampus* means "sea horse").

■ **THE LIMBIC SYSTEM AND THE BASAL GANGLIA** Although much of the subcortical portion of the telencephalon is taken up by axons projecting to and from the neocortex, there are several large subcortical nuclear groups. Some of them are considered to be part of either the *limbic system* or the *basal ganglia motor system*. Don't be misled by the word *system* in these contexts; it implies a level of certainty that is unwarranted. It is not entirely clear exactly what these hypothetical systems do, exactly which structures should be included in them, or even whether it is appropriate to view them as unitary systems. Nevertheless, if not taken too literally, the concepts of *limbic system* and *basal ganglia motor system* provide a useful means of conceptualizing the organization of the subcortex.

The **limbic system** is a circuit of midline structures that circle the thalamus (*limbic* means "ring"). The limbic system is involved in the regulation of motivated behaviors—including the four Fs of motivation: fleeing, feeding, fighting, and sexual behavior. (This joke is as old as biopsychology itself, but it is a good one.) In addition to several structures about which you have already read (e.g., the mammillary bodies and the hippocampus), major structures of the limbic system include the amygdala, the fornix, the cingulate cortex, and the septum.

Let's begin tracing the limbic circuit (see Figure 3.30) at the **amygdala**—the almond-shaped nucleus in the anterior temporal lobe (*amygdala* means "almond"). Posterior to the amygdala is the hippocampus,

Figure 3.30 The major structures of the limbic system: amygdala, hippocampus, cingulate cortex, fornix, septum, and mammillary body.

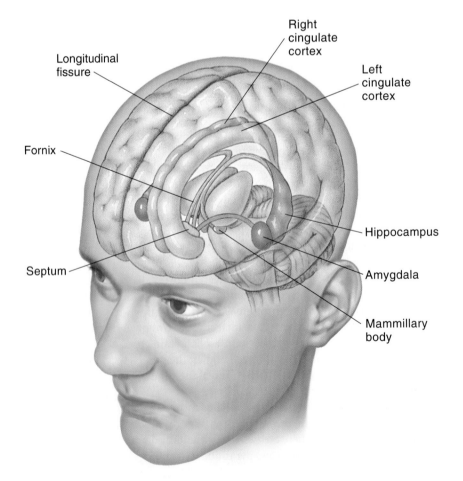

Longitudinal fissure

Right cingulate cortex

Left cingulate cortex

Fornix

Hippocampus

Septum

Amygdala

Mammillary body

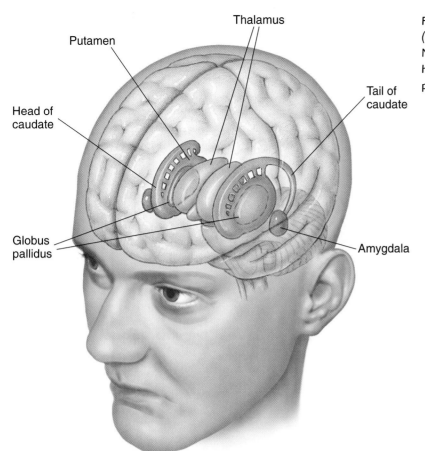

Putamen

Thalamus

Head of
caudate

Tail of
caudate

Globus
pallidus

Amygdala

Figure 3.31 The basal ganglia: amygdala, striatum (caudate plus putamen), and globus pallidus. Note: In this view, the right globus pallidus is largely hidden behind the right thalamus; the left globus pallidus is totally hidden behind the left putamen.

which runs beneath the thalamus in the medial temporal lobe. Next in the ring are the **cingulate cortex** and the **fornix.** The cingulate cortex is the large area of neocortex in the **cingulate gyrus** on the medial surface of the cerebral hemispheres, just superior to the corpus callosum; it encircles the dorsal thalamus (*cingulate* means "encircling"). The fornix, the major tract of the limbic system, also encircles the dorsal thalamus; it leaves the dorsal end of the hippocampus and sweeps forward in an arc coursing along the superior surface of the third ventricle and terminating in the septum and mammillary bodies (*fornix* means "arc"). The **septum** is a midline nucleus that is located at the anterior tip of the cingulate cortex. Several tracts connect the septum and mammillary bodies with the amygdala and hippocampus, thereby completing the limbic ring.

The **basal ganglia** are illustrated in Figure 3.31. As we did with the limbic system, let's begin our examination of the basal ganglia with the amygdala (pronounced "a MIG dah lah"), which is considered to be part of both systems. Sweeping out of each amygdala, first in a posterior direction and then in an anterior direction, is the long tail-like **caudate** nucleus (*caudate* means "tail-like"). Each caudate nucleus forms an al-

most complete circle; in its center, connected to it by a series of fiber bridges, is the **putamen** (pronounced "pew TAY men"). Together, the caudate nucleus and putamen, which both have a striped appearance, are known as the **striatum** ("striped structure"). The remaining structure of the basal ganglia is the pale circular structure known as the globus pallidus ("pale globe"). The **globus pallidus** is located medial to the putamen, between the putamen and the thalamus.

The basal ganglia play a major role in the performance of voluntary motor responses. Of particular interest is a pathway that projects to the striatum from the substantia nigra of the midbrain. *Parkinson's disease,* a disorder that is characterized by rigidity, tremors, and poverty of voluntary movement, is associated with the deterioration of this pathway.

Figure 3.32 on page 76 summarizes the major key-term brain divisions and structures—those that have appeared in boldface in this section.

Columnar organization. The functional organization of the neocortex in vertical columns; the cells in each column form a mini circuit that performs a single function.

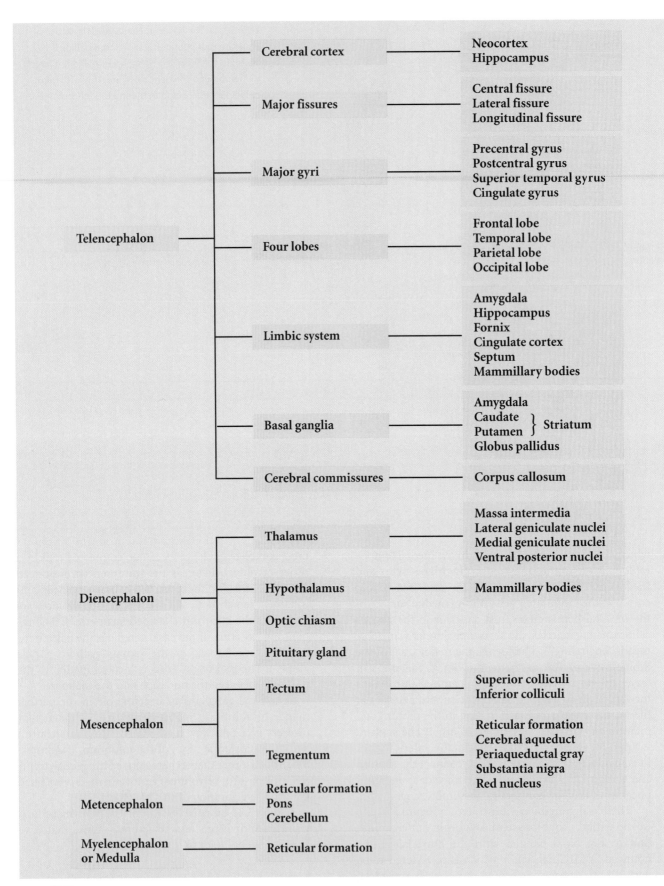

Telencephalon
- Cerebral cortex
  - Neocortex
  - Hippocampus
- Major fissures
  - Central fissure
  - Lateral fissure
  - Longitudinal fissure
- Major gyri
  - Precentral gyrus
  - Postcentral gyrus
  - Superior temporal gyrus
  - Cingulate gyrus
- Four lobes
  - Frontal lobe
  - Temporal lobe
  - Parietal lobe
  - Occipital lobe
- Limbic system
  - Amygdala
  - Hippocampus
  - Fornix
  - Cingulate cortex
  - Septum
  - Mammillary bodies
- Basal ganglia
  - Amygdala
  - Caudate } Striatum
  - Putamen
  - Globus pallidus
- Cerebral commissures
  - Corpus callosum

Diencephalon
- Thalamus
  - Massa intermedia
  - Lateral geniculate nuclei
  - Medial geniculate nuclei
  - Ventral posterior nuclei
- Hypothalamus
  - Mammillary bodies
- Optic chiasm
- Pituitary gland

Mesencephalon
- Tectum
  - Superior colliculi
  - Inferior colliculi
- Tegmentum
  - Reticular formation
  - Cerebral aqueduct
  - Periaqueductal gray
  - Substantia nigra
  - Red nucleus

Metencephalon
- Reticular formation
- Pons
- Cerebellum

Myelencephalon or Medulla
- Reticular formation

Figure 3.32 Summary of major brain structures. This is a diagram of brain anatomy key terms. It contains all the brain anatomy key terms that appear in boldface in this chapter.

If you have not previously studied the gross anatomy of the brain, your own brain is probably straining under the burden of new terms. It is time to pause and assess your progress. Test your knowledge of the brain by labeling the following midsagittal view of a real human brain. It is a bit more difficult to label the real thing than the color-coded illustrations that you have been seeing.

The correct answers are provided at the bottom of the page. Before proceeding, review material related to your errors and omissions. Notice Figure 3.32; it includes all the brain structures that have appeared in this chapter in bold type, and thus it is an excellent vehicle for review.

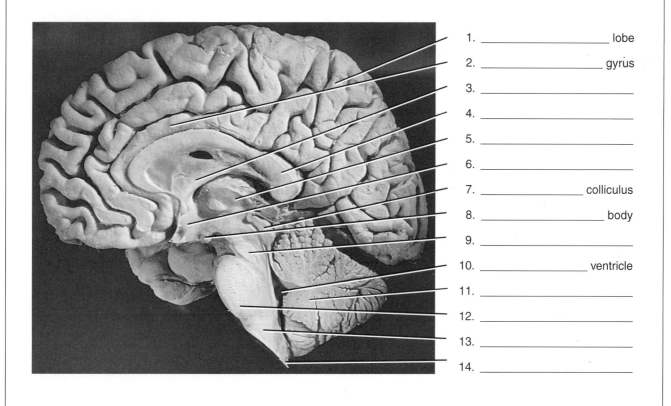

1. _____ lobe
2. _____ gyrus
3. _____
4. _____
5. _____
6. _____
7. _____ colliculus
8. _____ body
9. _____
10. _____ ventricle
11. _____
12. _____
13. _____
14. _____

CONCLUSION

The first three sections of this chapter introduced you to the general layout of the nervous system (3.1), to the cells that compose it (3.2), and to the neuroanatomical techniques that are used to study it (3.3). The final three sections introduced you to the names and locations of the central nervous system's major structures: First, you learned about the structures of the spinal cord (3.4); then you learned about the brain's five major divisions (3.5); and finally, you learned about the brain's major nuclei and tracts (3.6).

Figure 3.33 on page 78 concludes this chapter for reasons that too often get lost in the shuffle of neuroanatomical terms and technology. I have included it here to illustrate the beauty of the brain and the art of those who study its structure. I hope you are inspired by it. I wonder what thoughts these neural circuits once contained.

The answers are (1) parietal, (2) cingulate, (3) fornix, (4) corpus callosum, (5) thalamus, (6) hypothalamus, (7) superior, (8) mammillary, (9) tegmentum, (10) fourth, (11) cerebellum, (12) pons, (13) medulla or myelencephalon, (14) spinal cord.

Figure 3.33 The art of neuroanatomical staining. These pyramidal cells were stained with a Golgi stain and then with a Nissl stain. Clearly visible are the pyramid-shaped cell bodies and apical dendrites of the pyramidal cells. Each pyramidal cell has a long, narrow axon; here they project off the bottom of the slide.

(Courtesy of Miles Herkenham, Unit of Functional Neuro-anatomy, National Institute of Mental Health, Bethesda, MD.)

FOOD FOR THOUGHT

1. Which of the following extreme positions do you think is closer to the truth? (a) The primary goal of all psychological research should be to relate psychological phenomena to the anatomy of neural circuits. (b) Psychologists should leave the study of neuroanatomy to neuroanatomists.

2. Perhaps the most famous mistake in the history of biopsychology was made by Olds and Milner (see Chapter 13). They botched an electrode implantation, and the tip of the stimulation electrode ended up in an unknown structure in the brain of a rat. When they subsequently tested the effects of electrical stimulation of this unknown structure, they made a fantastic discovery: The rat seemed to find the brain stimulation extremely pleasurable. In fact, the rat would press a lever for hours at an extremely high rate if every press produced a brief stimulation to its brain through the electrode. If you had accidentally stumbled on this intracranial self-stimulation phenomenon, what neuroanatomical procedures would you have used to identify the stimulation site and the neural circuits involved in the pleasurable effects of the stimulation?

Afferent nerves *(p. 52)*
Amygdala *(p. 74)*
Anterior *(p. 64)*
Arachnoid membrane *(p. 53)*
Astroglia (astrocytes) *(p. 57)*
**Autonomic nervous system
(ANS)** *(p. 52)*
Axon *(p. 57)*
Axon hillock *(p. 57)*
Basal ganglia *(p. 75)*
Bipolar neuron *(p. 56)*
Blood–brain barrier *(p. 55)*
Brain stem *(p. 66)*
Buttons *(p. 57)*
Caudate *(p. 75)*
Cell body *(p. 57)*
Cell membrane *(p. 57)*
Central canal *(p. 53)*
Central fissure *(p. 72)*
Central nervous system (CNS)
(p. 52)
Cerebellum *(p. 69)*
Cerebral aqueduct *(p. 55, 69)*
Cerebral commissure *(p. 72)*
Cerebral cortex *(p. 72)*
Cerebral ventricles *(p. 53)*
Cerebrospinal fluid (CSF)
(p. 53)
Choroid plexuses *(p. 55)*
Cingulate cortex *(p. 75)*
Cingulate gyrus *(p. 75)*
Columnar organization
(p. 74)
Contralateral *(p. 70)*
Corpus collosum *(p. 72)*

Cranial nerves *(p. 53)*
Cross sections *(p. 64)*
Cytoplasm *(p. 58)*
Decussate *(p. 70)*
Dendrites *(p. 57)*
Diencephalon *(p. 70)*
Dorsal *(p. 64)*
Dorsal horns *(p. 66)*
Dura mater *(p. 53)*
Efferent nerves *(p. 52)*
Electron microscopy *(p. 62)*
Endoplasmic reticulum *(p. 58)*
Fissures *(p. 72)*
Fornix *(p. 75)*
Frontal lobe *(p. 72)*
Frontal sections *(p. 64)*
Ganglia *(p. 56)*
Glial cells *(p. 56)*
Globus pallidus *(p. 75)*
Golgi complex *(p. 58)*
Golgi stain *(p. 61)*
Gyri *(p. 72)*
Hippocampus *(p. 74)*
Horizontal sections *(p. 64)*
Hypothalamus *(p. 70)*
Inferior *(p. 64)*
Inferior colliculi *(p. 69)*
Interneurons *(p. 56)*
Ipsilateral *(p. 70)*
Lateral *(p. 64)*
Lateral fissure *(p. 72)*
Lateral geniculate nuclei
(p. 70)
Limbic system *(p. 74)*
Longitudinal fissure *(p. 72)*

Mammillary bodies *(p. 70)*
Massa intermedia *(p. 70)*
Medial *(p. 64)*
Medial geniculate nuclei
(p. 70)
Meninges *(p. 53)*
Mesencephalon *(p. 69)*
Metencephalon *(p. 68)*
Microtubules *(p. 58)*
Mitochondria *(p. 58)*
Multipolar neuron *(p. 56)*
Myelencephalon (medulla)
(p. 68)
Myelin *(p. 57)*
Myelin stains *(p. 62)*
Neocortex *(p. 73)*
Nerves *(p. 56)*
Neurotransmitters *(p. 58)*
Nissl stain *(p. 61)*
Nodes of Ranvier *(p. 57)*
Nuclei *(p. 56)*
Nucleus *(p. 58)*
Occipital lobe *(p. 73)*
**Oligodendroglia
(oligodendrocytes)** *(p. 59)*
Optic chiasm *(p. 70)*
Parasympathetic nerves
(p. 53)
Parietal lobe *(p. 72)*
Periaqueductal gray *(p. 69)*
**Peripheral nervous system
(PNS)** *(p. 52)*
Pia mater *(p. 53)*
Pituitary gland *(p. 70)*
Pons *(p. 69)*

Postcentral gyri *(p. 73)*
Posterior *(p. 64)*
Precentral gyri *(p. 73)*
Putamen *(p. 75)*
Pyramidal cells *(p. 73)*
Red nucleus *(p. 69)*
Reticular formation *(p. 68)*
Ribosomes *(p. 58)*
Sagittal sections *(p. 64)*
Satellite cells *(p. 56)*
Schwann cells *(p. 61)*
Septum *(p. 75)*
Somatic nervous system (SNS)
(p. 52)
Stellate cells *(p. 73)*
Striatum *(p. 75)*
Subarachnoid space *(p. 53)*
Substantia nigra *(p. 69)*
Superior *(p. 64)*
Superior colliculi *(p. 69)*
Superior temporal gyri *(p. 73)*
Sympathetic nerves *(p. 53)*
Synapses *(p. 57)*
Synaptic vesicles *(p. 58)*
Tectum *(p. 69)*
Tegmentum *(p. 69)*
Telencephalon *(p. 71)*
Temporal lobe *(p. 73)*
Thalamus *(p. 70)*
Tracts *(p. 56)*
Unipolar neuron *(p. 56)*
Ventral *(p. 64)*
Ventral horns *(p. 66)*
Ventral posterior nuclei *(p. 70)*

ADDITIONAL READING

I recommend the following three books for those who are looking for a more detailed introduction to human neuroanatomy. The first is a wonderfully illustrated historical introduction to the brain; the second is a particularly clear neuroanatomy text; and the third is a classic collection of neuroanatomical illustrations:

Corsi, P. (1991). *The enchanted loom: Chapters in the history of neuroscience.* New York: Oxford University Press.

Nauta, W. J. H., & Feirtag, M. (1986). *Fundamental neuroanatomy.* New York: Freeman.

Netter, F. H. (1962). *The CIBA collection of medical illustrations: Vol. 1. The nervous system.* New York: CIBA.

I recommend the following book as a reference for those interested in the intricacies of human neuroanatomy:

Paxinos, G. (ed.) (1990). *The human nervous system.* New York: Harcourt Brace Jovanovich.

Finally, for those students who have found the topic of neuroanatomy particularly difficult and would benefit from a simple and effective introduction that complements this chapter, I recommend the following book—one of my personal favorites, for obvious reasons:

Pinel, J. P. J., & Edwards, M. E. (1998). *A colorful introduction to the anatomy of the human brain.* Boston: Allyn & Bacon.

4

Neural Conduction
and Synaptic Transmission

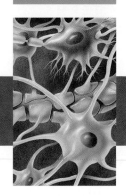

hapter 3 introduced you to the anatomy of neurons. This chapter introduces you to their function—it is a chapter about how neurons conduct and transmit electrochemical signals. It begins with a description of how signals are generated in resting neurons; then it follows the signals as they are conducted through neurons and transmitted across synapses to other neurons.

The Lizard will help you appreciate why a knowledge of neural conduction and synaptic transmission is an integral part of biopsychology. *The Lizard* is the title of a case study of a patient with Parkinson's disease, Roberto Garcia d'Orta:

> "I have become a lizard," he began. "A great lizard frozen in a dark, cold, strange world."
>
> His name was Roberto Garcia d'Orta. He was a tall thin man in his sixties, but like most patients with Parkinson's disease, he appeared to be much older than his actual age. Not many years before, he had been an active, vigorous business man. Then it happened—not all at once, not suddenly, but slowly, subtly, insidiously. Now he turned like a piece of granite, walked in slow shuffling steps, and spoke in a monotonous whisper.
>
> What had been his first symptom?
>
> A tremor.
>
> Had his tremor been disabling?
>
> "No," he said. "My hands shake worse when they are doing nothing at all"—a symptom called tremor-at-rest.
>
> The other symptoms of Parkinson's disease are not quite so benign. They can change a vigorous man into a lizard. These include rigid muscles, a marked poverty of spontaneous movements, difficulty in starting to move, and slowness in executing voluntary movements once they have been initiated.
>
> The term "reptilian stare" is often used to describe the characteristic lack of blinking and the widely opened eyes gazing out of a motionless face, a set of features that seems more reptilian than human. Truly a lizard in the eyes of the world.

What was happening in Mr. d'Orta's brain? A small group of nerve cells called the *substantia nigra* (black substance) were unaccountably dying. These neurons make a particular chemical neurotransmitter called dopamine, which they deliver to another part of the brain, known as the striatum. As the cells of the substantia nigra die, the amount of dopamine they can deliver goes down. The striatum helps control movement, and to do that normally, it needs dopamine. (Paraphrased from Klawans, 1990, pp. 53–57)[1]

Dopamine is not an effective treatment for Parkinson's disease because it does not readily penetrate the blood–brain barrier. However, knowledge of dopaminergic transmission has led to the development of an effective treatment: L-DOPA, the chemical precursor of dopamine, which readily penetrates the blood–brain barrier and is converted to dopamine once inside the brain.

Mr. d'Orta's neurologist prescribed L-DOPA, and it worked. He still had a bit of tremor; but his voice became stronger, his feet no longer shuffled, his reptilian stare faded away, and he was once again able to perform with ease many of the activities of daily life (e.g., eating, bathing, writing, speaking, and even making love with his wife). Mr. d'Orta had been destined to spend the rest of his life trapped inside a body that was becoming increasingly difficult to control, but his life sentence was repealed.

Keep Mr. d'Orta in mind as you read this chapter. His situation will remind you that normal neural activity is necessary for normal psychological activity, and it will serve as an example of the potential clinical benefits of understanding neural function. A knowledge of neural conduction and synaptic transmission is a major asset for any psychologist; it is a must for any biopsychologist.

4.1 The Neuron's Resting Membrane Potential

One key to understanding neural function is the **membrane potential,** the difference in electrical charge between the inside and the outside of a cell.

Recording the Membrane Potential

To record a neuron's membrane potential, it is necessary to position the tip of one electrode inside the neuron and the tip of another electrode outside the neuron in the extracellular fluid. Although the size of the extracellular electrode is not critical, it is paramount that the tip of the intracellular electrode be fine enough to pierce the neural membrane without severely damaging it. The intracellular electrodes are called **microelectrodes;** their

[1]Paraphrased from *Newton's Madness: Further Tales of Clinical Neurology* by Harold L. Klawans. New York: Harper & Row, © Harold Klawans, 1990.

Membrane potential. The difference in electrical charge between the inside and the outside of a cell.

Microelectrodes. Extremely fine recording electrodes, which are used for intracellular recording.

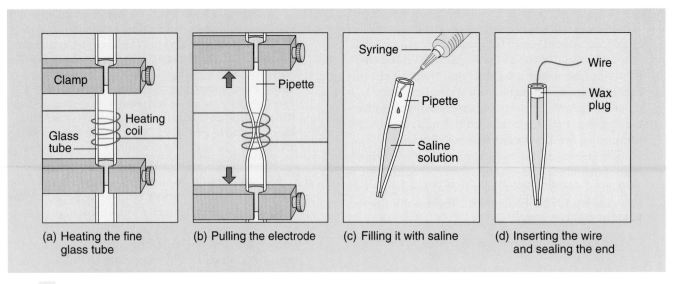

Figure 4.1 The construction of a microelectrode. The point of the microelectrode is invisible to the naked eye, so fine that it can penetrate a neuron without seriously damaging it.

(a) Heating the fine glass tube

(b) Pulling the electrode

(c) Filling it with saline

(d) Inserting the wire and sealing the end

Clamp

Heating coil

Glass tube

Pipette

Syringe

Pipette

Saline solution

Wire

Wax plug

tips are less than one thousandth of a millimeter in diameter—much too small to be seen by the naked eye.

To construct a microelectrode (see Figure 4.1), a fine glass tube is melted in the center and then suddenly pulled apart by an automated *microelectrode puller*. The infinitesimally small, but still hollow, point at which the tube separates serves as the electrode tip. The tube is then filled with a concentrated salt solution through which neural signals can be recorded. The construction of the microelectrode is completed by inserting a wire into the solution through the larger end and sealing it. The solution does not leak from the electrode tip because the opening is too small for even a single molecule to escape.

One method of recording a membrane potential is to connect the intracellular and extracellular electrodes by wires to an **oscilloscope**—a device that displays differences in the electrical potential at the two electrodes over time. The differences are displayed as vertical displacements of a glowing spot that sweeps across a fluorescent screen. Because the spot on an oscilloscope screen is produced by a beam of electrons, which has little inertia to overcome, an oscilloscope can accurately display even the most rapid changes in membrane potential. Figure 4.2 illustrates how a membrane potential is recorded on an oscilloscope.

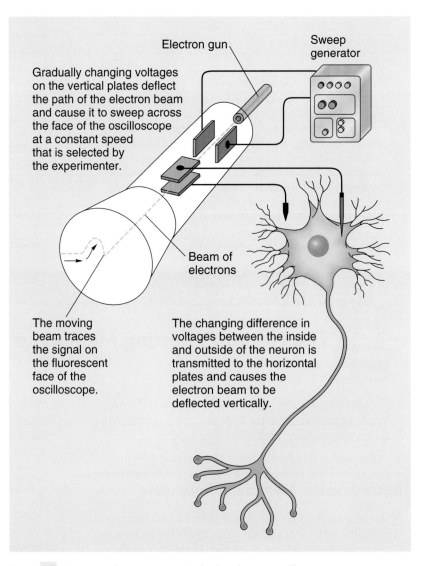

Electron gun

Sweep generator

Gradually changing voltages on the vertical plates deflect the path of the electron beam and cause it to sweep across the face of the oscilloscope at a constant speed that is selected by the experimenter.

Beam of electrons

The moving beam traces the signal on the fluorescent face of the oscilloscope.

The changing difference in voltages between the inside and outside of the neuron is transmitted to the horizontal plates and causes the electron beam to be deflected vertically.

Figure 4.2 How a membrane potential is displayed on an oscilloscope.

Resting Membrane Potential

When both electrode tips are in the extracellular fluid, the voltage difference between them is zero. However, when the tip of the intracellular electrode is inserted into a neuron, a steady potential of about –70 millivolts (mV) is registered on the oscilloscope screen. This indicates that the potential inside the resting neuron is about 70 mV less than that outside the neuron. This steady membrane potential of about –70 mV is called the neuron's **resting potential.** In its resting state, with the –70 mV charge built up across its membrane, a neuron is said to be *polarized.*

The Ionic Basis of the Resting Potential

Why are resting neurons polarized? Like all salts in solution, the salts in neural tissue separate into positively and negatively charged particles called **ions.** The resting potential results from the fact that the ratio of negative to positive charges is greater inside the neuron than outside. Why this unequal distribution of charges occurs can be understood in terms of the interaction of four factors: two forces that act to distribute ions equally throughout the intracellular and extracellular fluids of the nervous system and two features of the neural membrane that counteract these homogenizing forces.

The first of the two homogenizing forces is *random motion.* The ions in neural tissue are in constant random motion, and particles in random motion tend to become evenly distributed because they are more likely to move down their *concentration gradients* than up them; that is, they are more likely to move from areas of high concentration to areas of low concentration than vice versa. The second force that promotes the even distribution of ions is *electrostatic pressure.* Any accumulation of charges, positive or negative, in one area tends to be dispersed by the repulsion of like charges in the vicinity and the attraction of opposite charges concentrated elsewhere.

Despite the continuous homogenizing effects of random movement and electrostatic pressure, no single class of ions is distributed equally on the two sides of the neural membrane. Four kinds of ions contribute significantly to the resting potential: sodium ions (Na^+), potassium ions (K^+), chloride ions (Cl^-), and various negatively charged protein ions. The concentration of both Na^+ and Cl^- ions is greater outside a resting neuron than inside, whereas K^+ ions are more concentrated on the inside. The negatively charged protein ions are synthesized inside the neuron and, for the most part, they stay there. See Figure 4.3. By the way, the symbols for sodium and potassium were derived from their Latin equivalents: *natrium* (Na^+) and *kalium* (K^+), respectively.

Two properties of the neural membrane are responsible for the unequal distribution of Na^+, K^+, Cl^-, and

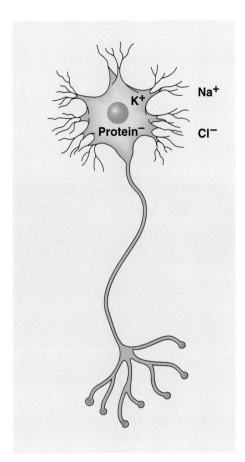

Figure 4.3 In its resting state, more Na^+ and Cl^- ions are outside the resting neuron than inside, and more K^+ ions and protein$^-$ ions are inside the neuron than outside.

protein ions in resting neurons. One of these properties is passive, that is, it does not involve the consumption of energy. The other is active and does involve the consumption of energy. The passive property of the neural membrane that contributes to the unequal disposition of ions is its differential permeability to Na^+, K^+, Cl^-, and protein ions. In resting neurons, K^+ and Cl^- ions pass readily through the neural membrane, Na^+ ions pass through it with difficulty, and the negatively charged protein ions do not pass through it at all. Ions pass through the neural membrane at specialized pores called **ion channels,** each of which is specialized for the passage of particular ions.

In the 1950s, the classic experiments of neurophysiologists Alan Hodgkin and Andrew Huxley provided the first evidence that an energy-consuming process is involved in the maintenance of the resting potential.

Oscilloscope. A device used for recording membrane potentials.
Resting potential. The steady membrane potential of a neuron at rest, usually about –70 mV.

Ions. Positively or negatively charged particles.
Ion channels. Pores in membranes through which specific ions pass.

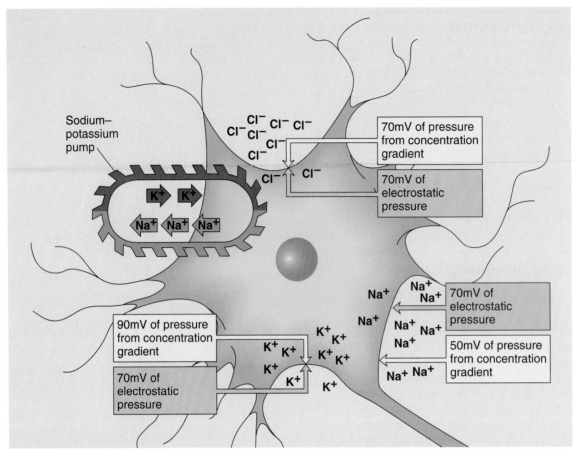

Figure 4.4 The passive and active forces that influence the distribution of Na⁺, K⁺, and Cl⁻ ions across the neural membrane. Passive forces continuously drive K⁺ ions out of the resting neuron and Na⁺ ions in; therefore, K⁺ ions must be actively pumped in and Na⁺ ions must be actively pumped out to maintain the resting equilibrium.

Hodgkin and Huxley began by wondering why the high extracellular concentrations of Na^+ and Cl^- ions and the high intracellular concentration of K^+ ions were not eliminated by pressure for them to move down their concentration gradients to the side of lesser concentration. Could the electrostatic pressure of -70 mV across the membrane be the counteracting force that maintained the unequal distribution of ions? To answer this question, Hodgkin and Huxley calculated for each of the three ions the electrostatic charge that would be required to offset the pressure for them to move down their concentration gradients.

For Cl^- ions, this calculated electrostatic charge was -70 mV, the same as the actual resting potential. Hodgkin and Huxley thus concluded that when neurons are at rest, the unequal distribution of Cl^- ions across the neural membrane is maintained in equilibrium by the balance between the 70 mV force driving Cl^- ions down their concentration gradient into the neuron and the 70 mV of electrostatic pressure driving them out.

The situation turned out to be different for the K^+ ions. Hodgkin and Huxley calculated that 90 mV of electrostatic pressure would be required to keep intracellular K^+ ions from moving down their concentra-

tion gradient and leaving the neuron—some 20 mV more than the actual resting potential.

In the case of Na^+ ions, the situation was much more extreme because the forces of both the concentration gradient and the electrostatic gradient act in the same direction. In the resting neuron, the concentration of Na^+ ions outside the neuron creates 50 mV of pressure for Na^+ ions to move down their concentration gradient into the neuron, which is added to the 70 mV of electrostatic pressure for them to move in the same direction. Thus a whopping total of 120 mV of pressure is trying to force Na^+ ions into resting neurons.

Sodium–potassium pumps. Active transport mechanisms that pump Na^+ ions out of neurons and K^+ ions in.

Depolarize. To decrease the membrane potential.

Hyperpolarize. To increase the membrane potential.

Excitatory postsynaptic potentials (EPSPs). Graded postsynaptic depolarizations, which increase the likelihood that

an action potential will be generated.

Inhibitory postsynaptic potentials (IPSPs). Graded postsynaptic hyperpolarizations, which decrease the likelihood that an action potential will be generated.

Graded responses. Responses whose magnitude is indicative of the magnitude of the stimuli that induce them.

Subsequent experiments confirmed Hodgkin and Huxley's calculations. They showed that K⁺ ions are continuously being driven out of resting neurons by the 20 mV of pressure and that, despite the high resistance of the cell membrane to the passage of Na⁺ ions, the Na⁺ ions are continuously being driven in by the 120 mV of pressure. Why, then, do the intracellular and extracellular concentrations of Na⁺ and K⁺ remain constant in resting neurons? Hodgkin and Huxley discovered that there are active mechanisms in the cell membrane to counteract the *influx* (inflow) of Na⁺ ions by pumping Na⁺ ions out as rapidly as they leak in and to counteract the *efflux* (outflow) of K⁺ ions by pumping K⁺ ions in as rapidly as they leak out. Figure 4.4 summarizes Hodgkin and Huxley's findings and conclusions.

It was subsequently discovered that the transport of Na⁺ ions out of neurons and the transport of K⁺ ions into them are not independent processes. Sodium and potassium transport is performed by energy-consuming transport mechanisms in the cell membrane that continually exchange three Na⁺ ions inside the neuron for two K⁺ ions outside. These mechanisms are commonly referred to as **sodium–potassium pumps.**

Table 4.1 summarizes the major factors that are responsible for maintaining the differences between the intracellular and extracellular concentrations of Na⁺, K⁺, and Cl⁻ ions in resting neurons. These differences plus the negatively charged protein ions, which are trapped inside the neuron, are largely responsible for the resting membrane potential.

Now that you understand these basic properties of the resting neuron, you are prepared to consider how neurons respond to input.

Table 4.1	The Factors Responsible for Maintaining the Differences in the Intracellular and Extracellular Concentrations of Na⁺, K⁺, and Cl⁻ Ions in Resting Neurons
Na⁺	Na⁺ ions are driven into the neurons by both the high concentration of Na⁺ ions outside the neuron and the negative internal resting charge of –70 mV. However, the membrane is resistant to the passive diffusion of Na⁺, and the sodium–potassium pump is thus able to maintain the high external concentration of Na⁺ ions by pumping them out at the same slow rate as they leak in.
K⁺	K⁺ ions are driven out of the neuron by their high internal concentration, although this pressure is partially offset by the internal negative charge. Despite the minimum pressure for the K⁺ ions to leave the neuron, they do so at a substantial rate because the membrane offers little resistance to their passage. To maintain the high internal concentration of K⁺ ions, mechanisms in the cell membrane pump K⁺ ions into neurons at the same rate as they diffuse out.
Cl⁻	There is little resistance in the neural membrane to the passage of Cl⁻ ions. Thus Cl⁻ ions are readily forced out of the neuron by the negative internal charge. As chloride ions begin to accumulate on the outside, there is increased pressure for them to move down their concentration gradient back into the neuron. When the point is reached where the electrostatic pressure for Cl⁻ to move out of the neuron is equal to the pressure for them to move back in, the distribution of Cl⁻ ions is held in equilibrium. This point of equilibrium occurs at –70 mV.

Generation and Conduction of Postsynaptic Potentials

When neurons fire, they release from their terminal buttons chemicals called *neurotransmitters,* which diffuse across the synaptic clefts and interact with specialized receptor molecules on the receptive membranes of the next neurons in the circuit. When neurotransmitter molecules bind to postsynaptic receptors, they typically have one of two effects, depending on the structure of both the neurotransmitter and the receptor in question. They may **depolarize** the receptive membrane (decrease the resting membrane potential—from –70 to –67 mV, for example) or they may **hyperpolarize** it (increase the resting membrane potential—from –70 to –72 mV, for example).

Postsynaptic depolarizations are called **excitatory postsynaptic potentials** (**EPSPs**) because, as you will

soon learn, they increase the likelihood that the neuron will fire. Postsynaptic hyperpolarizations are called **inhibitory postsynaptic potentials** (**IPSPs**) because they decrease the likelihood that the neuron will fire. Both EPSPs and IPSPs are **graded responses.** This means that the amplitudes of EPSPs and IPSPs are proportional to the intensity of the signals that elicit them; weak signals elicit small postsynaptic potentials and strong signals elicit large ones.

EPSPs and IPSPs travel passively from their sites of generation at synapses, usually on the dendrites or cell body, in much the same way that electrical signals travel through a cable. Accordingly, the transmission of postsynaptic potentials has two important characteristics.

First, it is rapid—so rapid that it can be assumed to be instantaneous for most purposes. It is important not to confuse the duration of EPSPs and IPSPs with their rate of transmission; although the duration of EPSPs and IPSPs varies considerably, all postsynaptic potentials, whether brief or enduring, are transmitted at great speed. Second, the transmission of EPSPs and IPSPs is *decremental*; EPSPs and IPSPs decrease in amplitude as they travel through the neuron, just as a sound wave grows fainter as it travels through air.

4.3 Integration of Postsynaptic Potentials and Generation of Action Potentials

The postsynaptic potentials created at a single synapse typically have little effect on the firing of the postsynaptic neuron. The receptive areas of most neurons are covered with thousands of synapses, and whether or not a neuron fires is determined by the net effect of their activity. More specifically, whether or not a neuron fires depends on the balance between the excitatory and inhibitory signals reaching its **axon hillock**—the conical structure at the junction between the cell body and the axon.

The graded EPSPs and IPSPs created by the action of neurotransmitters at particular receptive sites on the neural membrane are conducted instantly and decrementally to the axon hillock. If the sum of the depolarizations and hyperpolarizations reaching the axon hillock at any time is sufficient to depolarize the membrane to a level referred to as its **threshold of excitation**—usually about –65 mV—an action potential is generated at the axon hillock. The **action potential (AP)** is a massive momentary—about 1 millisecond—reversal of the membrane potential from about –70 to about +50 mV. Unlike postsynaptic potentials, action potentials are not graded responses; their magnitude is not related in any way to the intensity of the stimuli that elicit them. To the contrary, they are **all-or-none responses;** that is, they either occur full-blown or do not occur at all. See Figure 4.5 for an illustration of an EPSP, an IPSP, and an AP.

In effect, each multipolar neuron adds together all the graded excitatory and inhibitory postsynaptic potentials reaching its axon hillock and decides to fire or not to fire on the basis of their sum. Adding or combining a number of individual signals into one overall signal is called **integration.** Neurons integrate incoming signals in two ways: over space and over time.

Figure 4.6 illustrates the three possible combinations of **spatial summation.** It shows how local EPSPs that are produced simultaneously on different parts of the receptive membrane sum to form a greater EPSP, how simultaneous IPSPs sum to form a greater IPSP, and how simultaneous EPSPs and IPSPs sum to cancel each other out.

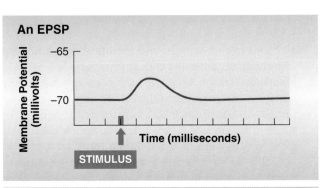

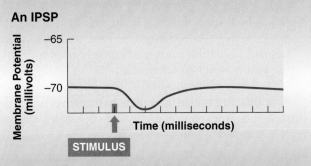

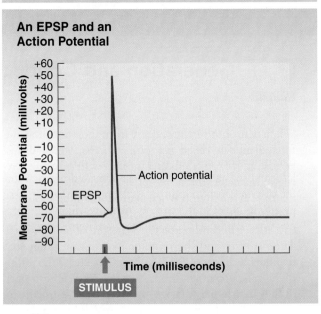

Figure 4.5 An EPSP, an IPSP, and an EPSP followed by an AP.

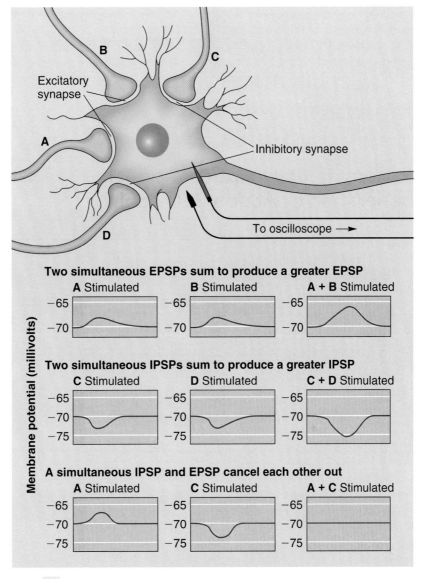

Figure 4.6 The three possible combinations of spatial summation.

Figure 4.7 on page 88 illustrates **temporal summation.** It shows how postsynaptic potentials produced in rapid succession at the same synapse sum to form a greater signal. The reason that stimulations of a neuron can summate over time is that the postsynaptic potentials they produce often outlast them. Thus, if a particular synapse is activated and then activated again before the original postsynaptic potential has completely dissipated, the effect of the second stimulus will be superimposed on the lingering postsynaptic potential produced by the first. Accordingly, it is possible for a brief subthreshold excitatory stimulus to fire a neuron if it is administered twice in rapid succession. In the same way, an inhibitory synapse activated twice in rapid succession can produce a greater IPSP than that produced by a single stimulation.

Each neuron continuously integrates signals over both time and space as it is continually bombarded with

Axon hillock. The conical structure at the junction between the axon and cell body, where action potentials are normally generated.

Threshold of excitation. The level of depolarization at the axon hillock necessary to generate an action potential, usually about −65 mV.

Action potential (AP). The firing of a neuron; a massive momentary change in the membrane potential from about −70 mV to about +50 mV.

All-or-none responses. Responses that are not graded; responses that occur full-blown or not at all.

Integration. Adding or combining a number of individual signals into one overall signal.

Spatial summation. The integration of signals that occur at different sites on the neuron.

Temporal summation. The integration of neural signals that occur at different times on the same neuron.

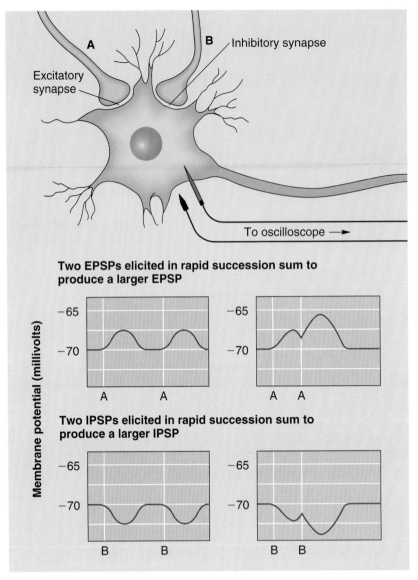

A **B** Inhibitory synapse

Excitatory synapse

To oscilloscope →

Two EPSPs elicited in rapid succession sum to produce a larger EPSP

−65

−70

A   A

−65

−70

A A

Two IPSPs elicited in rapid succession sum to produce a larger IPSP

−65

−70

B   B

−65

−70

B B

Membrane potential (millivolts)

Figure 4.7 The two possible combinations of temporal summation.

stimuli through the thousands of synapses covering its dendrites and cell body. Remember that although schematic diagrams of neural circuitry rarely include neurons with more than a few representative synaptic contacts, most neurons receive thousands of synaptic contacts. The location of a synapse on a receptive membrane is an important factor in determining its potential to influence neural firing. Because EPSPs and IPSPs are transmitted decrementally, synapses near the axon hillock trigger zone have the most influence on the firing of the neuron.

In some ways, the firing of a neuron is like the firing of a gun. Both are all-or-none reactions triggered by graded responses. As a trigger is squeezed, it gradually moves back until it causes the gun to fire; as a neuron is stimulated, it becomes less polarized until

the threshold of excitation is reached and the neuron fires. Furthermore, the firing of a gun and neural firing are both all-or-none events. Just as squeezing a trigger harder does not make the bullet travel faster or farther, stimulating a neuron more intensely does not increase the speed or amplitude of the resulting action potential.

Voltage-activated ion channels. Ion channels that open and close in response to changes in the membrane potential.

Absolute refractory period. A brief period (typically 1 to 2 milliseconds) after the initiation of an action potential during which it is impossible to elicit

another action potential in the same neuron.

Relative refractory period. A period after the absolute refractory period during which a higher-than-normal amount of stimulation is necessary to make a neuron fire.

Conduction of Action Potentials

Ionic Basis of Action Potentials

How are action potentials produced, and how are they conducted along the axon? The answer to both questions is basically the same: through the action of **voltage-activated ion channels**—ion channels that open or close in response to changes in the voltage of the membrane potential.

Recall that the membrane potential of a neuron at rest is relatively constant despite the great pressure for Na^+ ions to flow into the cell. This is because the resting membrane is relatively impermeable to Na^+ ions and because those few that leak in are pumped out. But things suddenly change when the membrane potential at the axon hillock is reduced to the threshold of excitation. The voltage-activated sodium channels in the hillock membrane open wide, and Na^+ ions rush in, suddenly driving the membrane potential from about –70 to about +50 mV. The rapid change in the membrane potential that is associated with the *influx* of Na^+ ions then triggers the opening of voltage-activated potassium channels. At this point, K^+ ions near the membrane are driven out of the cell through these channels—first by their relatively high internal concentration and then, when the action potential is near its peak, by the positive internal charge. After about 1 mil-

lisecond, the sodium channels close. This marks the end of the *rising phase* of the action potential and the beginning of *repolarization* by the continued efflux of K^+ ions. Once repolarization has been achieved, the potassium channels gradually close. Because they close gradually, too many K^+ ions flow out of the neuron, and it is left hyperpolarized for a brief period of time. Figure 4.8 illustrates the timing of the opening and closing of the sodium and potassium channels during an action potential.

The number of ions that flow through the membrane during an action potential is extremely small in relation to the total number inside and around the neuron. The action potential involves only those ions right next to the membrane. Therefore, a single action potential has little effect on the relative concentrations of various ions inside and outside the neuron, and the resting ion concentrations next to the membrane are rapidly reestablished by the random movement of ions. The sodium–potassium pump plays only a minor role in the reestablishment of the resting potential.

Refractory Periods

There is a brief period of about 1 to 2 milliseconds after the initiation of an action potential during which it is impossible to elicit a second one. This period is called the **absolute refractory period.** The absolute refractory period is followed by the **relative refractory period**—the period during which it is possible to fire the neuron again, but only by applying higher-than-normal levels of stimulation. The end of the relative refractory period is the point at which the amount of stimulation necessary to fire a neuron returns to baseline.

The refractory period is responsible for two important characteristics of neural activity. First, it is responsible for the fact that action potentials normally travel along axons in only one direction. Because the portions of an axon over which an action potential has just traveled

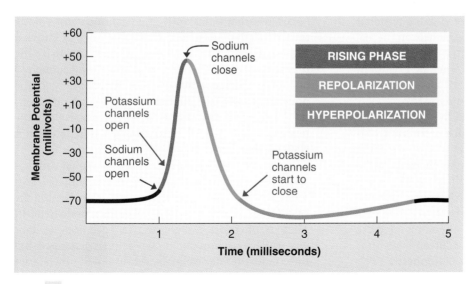

Figure 4.8 The opening and closing of voltage-activated sodium and potassium channels during the three phases of the action potential: *rising phase, repolarization,* and *hyperpolarization.*

are left momentarily refractory, an action potential cannot reverse direction. Second, it is responsible for the fact that the rate of neural firing is related to the intensity of the stimulation. If a neuron is subjected to a high level of continual stimulation, it fires and then fires again as soon as its absolute refractory period is over—a maximum of about 1,000 times per second. However, if the level of stimulation is of an intensity just sufficient to fire the neuron when it is at rest, the neuron does not fire again until both the absolute and the relative refractory periods have run their course. Intermediate levels of stimulation produce intermediate rates of neural firing.

Conduction of Action Potentials

The conduction of action potentials along an axon differs from the conduction of EPSPs and IPSPs in two important ways. First, the conduction of action potentials along an axon is *nondecremental;* action potentials do not grow weaker as they travel along the axonal membrane. Second, action potentials are conducted more slowly than postsynaptic potentials.

The reason for these two differences is that the conduction of EPSPs and IPSPs is passive, whereas the axonal conduction of action potentials is largely active. Once an action potential has been generated at the axon hillock, it travels passively along the axonal membrane to the adjacent voltage-activated sodium channels, which have yet to open. The arrival of the electrical signal opens these channels, thereby allowing Na^+ ions to rush into the neuron and generate a full-blown action potential on this portion of the membrane. This signal is then conducted passively to the next sodium channels, where another action potential is actively triggered. These events are repeated again and again until a full-blown action potential is triggered in the terminal buttons. However, because the ion channels on the axonal membrane are so close together, it is usual to think of axonal conduction as a single wave of excitation spreading actively at a constant speed along the axon, rather than as a series of discrete events.

The wave of excitation triggered by the generation of an action potential on the hillock membrane also spreads back through the cell body and dendrites of the neuron. However, because the sodium channels of the cell body and dendrites are not voltage-activated, the conduction of action potentials back through the cell body and dendrites appears to be passive. Although little is currently known about the functions of these backward action potentials, they are currently the subject of much conjecture (e.g., Eilers & Konnerth, 1997; Sejnowski, 1997).

The following analogy may help you appreciate the major characteristics of axonal conduction. Consider a row of mousetraps on a wobbly shelf, all of them set and ready to be triggered. Each trap stores energy by holding back its striker against the pressure of the spring, in the same way that each sodium channel stores energy by holding back Na^+ ions, which are under pressure to move down their concentration and electrostatic gradients into the neuron. When the first trap in the row is triggered, the vibration is transmitted passively through the shelf, and the next trap is sprung—and so on down the line.

The nondecremental nature of action potential conduction is readily apparent from this analogy; the last trap on the shelf strikes with no less intensity than did the first. This analogy also illustrates the refractory period: A trap cannot respond again until it has been reset, just as a section of axon cannot fire again until it has been repolarized. Furthermore, the row of traps can transmit in either direction, just like an axon. If electrical stimulation of sufficient intensity is applied to the terminal end of an axon, an action potential will be generated and will travel along the axon back to the cell body; this is called **antidromic conduction.** Axonal conduction in the natural direction—from cell body to terminal buttons—is called **orthodromic conduction.**

Conduction in Myelinated Axons

In Chapter 3, you learned that the axons of many neurons are insulated from the extracellular fluid by segments of fatty tissue called *myelin.* In myelinated axons, ions can pass through the axonal membrane only at the **nodes of Ranvier**—the gaps between adjacent myelin segments. How, then, are action potentials transmitted in myelinated axons?

When an action potential is generated at the axon hillock of a myelinated axon, the signal is conducted passively—that is, instantly and decrementally—along the first segment of myelin to the first node of Ranvier. Although the signal is somewhat diminished by the time it reaches the first node, it is still strong enough to open the voltage-activated sodium channels at the node and to generate another full-blown action potential. This action potential is conducted passively to the next node, where another full-blown action potential is elicited, and so on.

Myelination increases the speed of axonal conduction. Because conduction along the myelinated segments of the axon is passive, it occurs instantly, and the signal thus "jumps" down the axon from node to node. There is, of course, a slight delay at each node of Ranvier while the action potential is actively generated, but the conduction in myelinated axons is still much faster than in unmyelinated axons, in which passive conduction plays a less prominent role. The transmission of action potentials in myelinated axons is called **saltatory conduction** (*saltare* means "to skip or jump").

The Velocity of Axonal Conduction

At what speed are action potentials conducted along an axon? The answer to this question depends on two properties of the axon. Conduction is faster in large-diameter axons, and—as you have just learned—it is faster in those that are myelinated. Mammalian *motor neurons* (neurons that synapse on skeletal muscles) are large and myelinated; thus some can conduct at speeds of 100 meters per second (about 224 miles per hour). In contrast, small, unmyelinated axons conduct action potentials at about 1 meter per second.

There is a misconception about the velocity of motor neuron action potentials in humans. The maximum velocity of motor neuron action potentials was found to be about 100 meters per second in cats, and since then it has been assumed to be the same in humans: It is not. The maximum velocity of conduction in human motor neurons is about 60 meters per second (Peters & Brooke, 1998).

Conduction in Neurons without Axons

Action potentials are the means by which axons conduct all-or-none signals nondecrementally over relatively long distances. Thus, to keep what you have just learned about action potentials in perspective, it is important for you to remember that many neurons in the mammalian brain do not have axons and thus do not display action potentials.

Neural conduction in these *interneurons* is entirely by graded, decrementally conducted potentials (Juusola et al., 1998).

4.5 Synaptic Transmission: Chemical Transmission of Signals from One Neuron to Another

You have learned in this chapter how postsynaptic potentials are generated on the receptive membrane of resting neurons, how these graded potentials are conducted passively to the axon hillock, how the sum of these graded potentials can trigger action potentials, and how these all-or-none potentials are actively conducted down the axon to the terminal buttons. In the remaining sections of this chapter, you will learn how action potentials arriving at terminal buttons trigger the release of neurotransmitters into synapses and how neurotransmitters carry signals to other cells. This section provides an overview of five aspects of synaptic transmission: (1) the structure of synapses; (2) the synthesis, packaging, and transport of neurotransmitter molecules; (3) the release of neurotransmitter molecules; (4) the activation of receptors by neurotransmitter molecules; and (5) the reuptake, enzymatic degradation, and recycling of neurotransmitter molecules.

Structure of Synapses

Most communication among neurons occurs across synapses such as the one illustrated in Figure 4.9 on page 92. Neurotransmitter molecules are released from buttons into synaptic clefts, where they induce EPSPs or IPSPs in other neurons by binding to receptors in their postsynaptic membranes. The synapses featured in Figure 4.9 are *axodendritic synapses*—synapses of axon terminal buttons on dendrites. Many axoden-

dritic synapses terminate on **dendritic spines** (see Figure 3.33)—small synaptic buds that cover the surfaces of many dendrites (see Harris & Kater, 1994). Also common are *axosomatic synapses*—synapses of axon terminal buttons on *somas* (cell bodies).

Although axodendritic and axosomatic synapses are the most common synaptic arrangements, there are several other kinds. For example, there are *dendrodendritic synapses,* which are interesting because they are often capable of transmission in either direction; and there are *axoaxonal synapses,* which are interesting because some of them mediate presynaptic inhibition (see Wu & Saggau, 1997). **Presynaptic inhibition** is compared with **postsynaptic inhibition** in Figure 4.10 on page 93.

Antidromic conduction. Axonal conduction opposite to the normal direction; conduction from axon terminals back toward the cell body.

Orthodromic conduction. Axonal conduction in the normal direction; conduction from the cell body toward the terminal buttons.

Nodes of Ranvier. The gaps in axonal myelin.

Saltatory conduction. Conduction of an action potential from node to node down a myelinated axon.

Dendritic spines. Specialized dendritic buds on which axodendritic synapses often occur.

Presynaptic inhibition. A form of inhibition that selectively reduces a neuron's responsiveness to specific synaptic input; it is mediated by excitatory axoaxonal synapses.

Postsynaptic inhibition. A form of inhibition that reduces a neuron's responsiveness to all excitatory synaptic inputs.

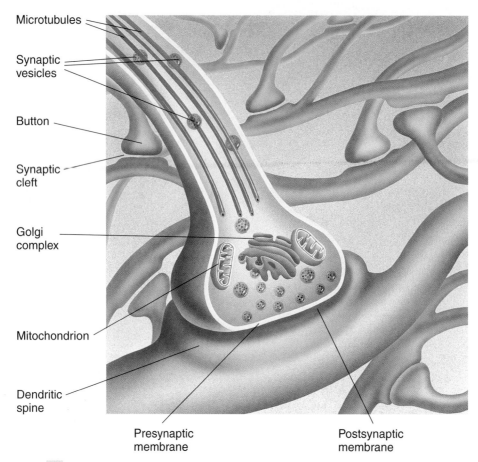

Microtubules

Synaptic
vesicles

Button

Synaptic
cleft

Golgi
complex

Mitochondrion

Dendritic
spine

Presynaptic
membrane

Postsynaptic
membrane

Figure **4.9** The anatomy of a typical synapse.

The synapses depicted in Figure 4.9 are **directed synapses**—synapses at which the site of neurotransmitter release and the site of neurotransmitter reception are in close proximity. This is a common arrangement, but there are also many nondirected synapses in the nervous system. **Nondirected synapses** are synapses at which the site of release is at some distance from the site of reception. One type of nondirected synapse is depicted in Figure 4.11 on page 94. In this type of arrangement, neurotransmitter molecules are released from a series of varicosities along the axon and its branches and thus are widely dispersed to surrounding targets. These synapses are often referred to as *string-of-beads synapses* because of their appearance.

Synthesis, Packaging, and Transport of Neurotransmitter Molecules

Neurotransmitter molecules are of two basic types: small and large (see Matteoli & DeCamilli, 1991). The small neurotransmitters are of several types; large neurotransmitters are all peptides. **Peptides** are amino acid chains that are composed of 10 or fewer amino acids; in

effect, they are short proteins. They may be small for proteins, but they are large for neurotransmitters.

Small-molecule neurotransmitters are typically synthesized in the cytoplasm of the button and packaged in **synaptic vesicles** by the button's **Golgi complex** (see Rothman & Orci, 1996). Once filled with neurotransmitter, the vesicles are stored in clusters right next to the presynaptic membrane. In contrast, peptide neurotransmitters, like other proteins, are assembled in the cytoplasm of the cell body on *ribosomes*; then they are packaged in vesicles by the cell body's Golgi complex and transported by *microtubules* to the terminal buttons at a rate of about 40 centimeters per

Directed synapses. Synapses at which the site of neurotransmitter release and the receptor sites on the postsynaptic membrane are in close proximity.
Nondirected synapses. Synapses at which the site of neurotransmitter release and the target site are not close together.
Peptides. Short chains of amino acids, some of which function as neurotransmitters.

Synaptic vesicles. Small spherical membranes that store neurotransmitter molecules and release them into the synaptic cleft.
Golgi complex. Structures in the cell bodies and buttons of neurons that package neurotransmitters and other molecules in vesicles.

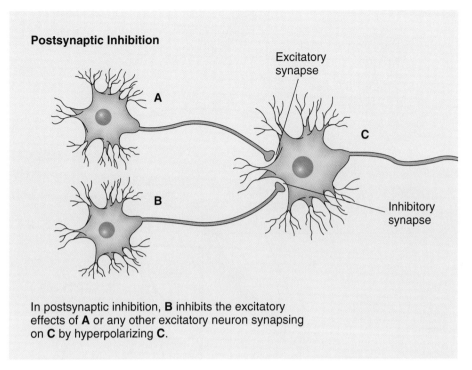

Postsynaptic Inhibition

A

B

Excitatory synapse

C

Inhibitory synapse

In postsynaptic inhibition, **B** inhibits the excitatory effects of **A** or any other excitatory neuron synapsing on **C** by hyperpolarizing **C**.

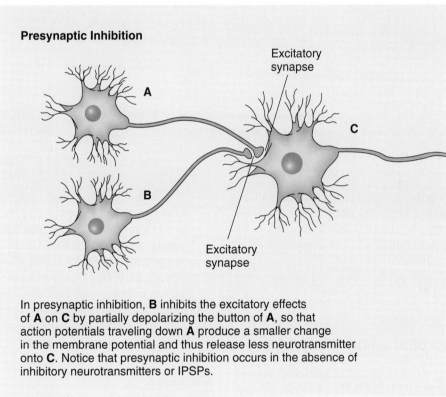

Presynaptic Inhibition

A

B

Excitatory synapse

C

Excitatory synapse

In presynaptic inhibition, **B** inhibits the excitatory effects of **A** on **C** by partially depolarizing the button of **A**, so that action potentials traveling down **A** produce a smaller change in the membrane potential and thus release less neurotransmitter onto **C**. Notice that presynaptic inhibition occurs in the absence of inhibitory neurotransmitters or IPSPs.

Figure 4.10 Presynaptic and postsynaptic inhibition.

day (see Vallee & Bloom, 1991). The vesicles that contain large-molecule neurotransmitters are larger than those that contain small-molecule neurotransmitters, and they do not congregate as closely as the other vesicles to the presynaptic membrane (see Thureson-Klein & Klein, 1990).

It may have escaped your notice that the button illustrated in Figure 4.9 contains synaptic vesicles of two sizes. This means that it contains two neurotransmitters: a peptide neurotransmitter in the larger vesicles and a small-molecule neurotransmitter in the smaller vesicles. It was once believed that each neuron

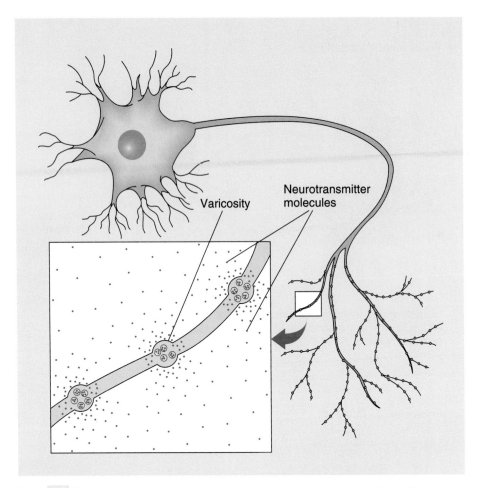

Figure **4.11** Nondirected neurotransmitter release. Some neurons release neurotransmitter molecules diffusely from varicosities along the axon and its branches.

synthesizes and releases only one neurotransmitter, but it is now clear that many neurons contain two neurotransmitters—a situation that is referred to as **coexistence.** So far, almost all documented cases of coexistence have involved one small-molecule neurotransmitter and one peptide neurotransmitter (see Jung & Scheller, 1991).

Release of Neurotransmitter Molecules

Exocytosis—the process of neurotransmitter release—is illustrated in Figure 4.12 (see Matthews, 1996). When a neuron is at rest, synaptic vesicles that contain small-molecule neurotransmitters congregate next to sections of the presynaptic membrane that are particularly rich in *calcium channels*. When stimulated by action potentials, the voltage-activated calcium channels open, and Ca^{++} ions enter the button. The entry of the Ca^{++} ions causes the synaptic vesicles to fuse with the presynaptic membrane and empty their contents into the synaptic cleft (see Bennett, 1997; Matthews & von Gersdorff, 1996).

The exocytosis of small-molecule neurotransmitters differs from the exocytosis of peptide neurotransmitters in one important respect. Small-molecule neurotransmitters are typically released in a pulse each time an action potential triggers a momentary influx of Ca^{++} ions through the presynaptic membrane; in contrast, peptide neurotransmitters are typically released gradually in response to general increases in the level of intracellular Ca^{++} ions, such as might occur during a general increase in the rate of neuron firing.

The Activation of Receptors by Neurotransmitter Molecules

Once released, neurotransmitter molecules produce signals in postsynaptic neurons by binding to **receptors** in the postsynaptic membrane (see Changeux, 1993). Each receptor is a protein that contains binding sites for only particular neurotransmitters; thus a neurotransmitter can influence only those cells that have

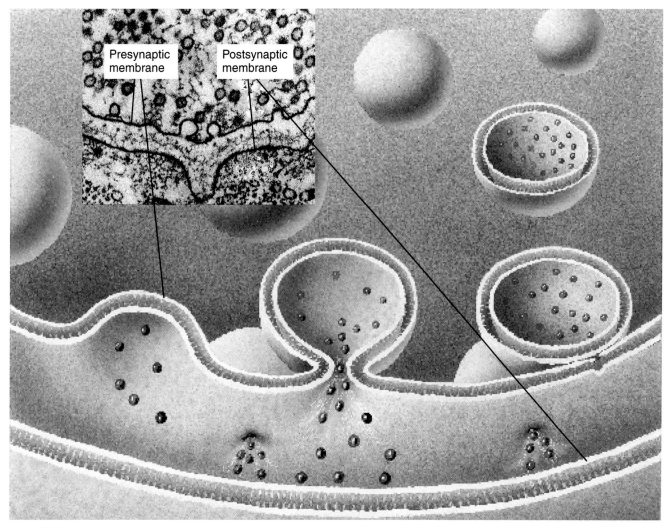

Figure 4.12 Schematic and photographic illustrations of exocytosis.
(The photomicrograph was reproduced from J.E. Heuser et al., *Journal of Cell Biology*, 1979, *81*, 275–300 by copyright permission of The Rockefeller University Press.)

Labels on image: Presynaptic membrane / Postsynaptic membrane

receptors for it. Any molecule that binds to another is referred to as its **ligand,** and a neurotransmitter is thus said to be a ligand of its receptor.

It was initially assumed that there would be only one type of receptor for each neurotransmitter, but this has not proved to be the case. As more receptors have been identified, it has become clear that most neurotransmitters bind to several different types of receptors. The different types of receptors to which a particular neurotransmitter can bind are called the **receptor subtypes** for that neurotransmitter. The various receptor subtypes for a neurotransmitter are typically located in different brain areas, and they typically respond to the neurotransmitter in different ways. Thus, one advantage of receptor subtypes is that they enable a neurotransmitter to transmit different kinds of messages to different parts of the brain.

The binding of a neurotransmitter to one of its receptor subtypes can influence a postsynaptic neuron in one of two fundamentally different ways, depending on whether the receptor is ionotropic or metabotropic. **Ionotropic receptors** are those receptors that are associated with ligand-activated ion channels; **metabotropic receptors** are those receptors that are associated with signal proteins and *G proteins (guanosine-triphosphate–sensitive proteins)*—see Figure 4.13 on page 96.

Coexistence. The presence of more than one neurotransmitter in the same neuron.

Exocytosis. The process of releasing a neurotransmitter.

Receptors. Proteins that include binding sites for particular neurotransmitters; neurotransmitters influence target cells by binding to receptors in the cells' membrane.

Ligand. A molecule that binds to another molecule; neuro-transmitters are ligands of their receptors.

Receptor subtypes. Different classes of receptors to which the same neurotransmitter binds.

Ionotropic receptors. Receptors that are associated with ligand-activated ion channels.

Metabotropic receptors. Receptors that are associated with signal proteins and G proteins.

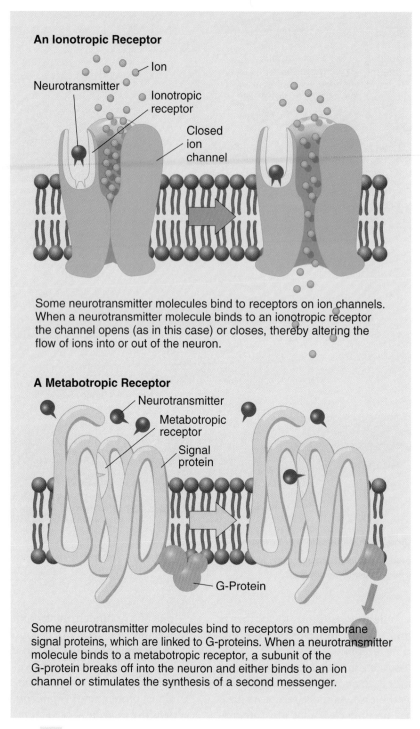

An Ionotropic Receptor

Neurotransmitter

Ion

Ionotropic receptor

Closed ion channel

Some neurotransmitter molecules bind to receptors on ion channels. When a neurotransmitter molecule binds to an ionotropic receptor the channel opens (as in this case) or closes, thereby altering the flow of ions into or out of the neuron.

A Metabotropic Receptor

Neurotransmitter

Metabotropic receptor

Signal protein

G-Protein

Some neurotransmitter molecules bind to receptors on membrane signal proteins, which are linked to G-proteins. When a neurotransmitter molecule binds to a metabotropic receptor, a subunit of the G-protein breaks off into the neuron and either binds to an ion channel or stimulates the synthesis of a second messenger.

Figure 4.13 Ion–channel linked receptors and G-protein linked receptors.

When a neurotransmitter molecule binds to an ionotropic receptor, the associated ion channel usually opens or closes immediately, thereby inducing an immediate postsynaptic potential. For example, in some neurons, EPSPs (depolarizations) occur because the neurotransmitter opens sodium channels, thereby increasing the flow of Na^+ ions into the neuron. In contrast, IPSPs (hyperpolarizations) often occur because

Second messenger. A chemical synthesized in a neuron in response to the binding of a neurotransmitter to a metabotropic receptor in its cell membrane.

Autoreceptors. Receptors, often on the presynaptic membrane, that are sensitive to a neuron's own neurotransmitter.

Reuptake. The more common of the two mechanisms for deactivating a released neurotransmitter.

Enzymatic degradation. The breakdown of chemicals by enzymes—one of the two mechanisms for deactivating released neurotransmitters.

the neurotransmitter opens potassium channels or chloride channels, thereby increasing the flow of K$^+$ ions out of the neuron or the flow of Cl$^-$ ions into it, respectively.

Metabotropic receptors are more prevalent than ionotropic receptors, and their effects are slower to develop, longer-lasting, more diffuse, and more varied (see Linder & Gilman, 1992). There are many different kinds of metabotropic receptors, but each is attached to a signal protein that winds its way back and forth through the cell membrane seven times. The metabotropic receptor is attached to a portion of the signal protein outside the neuron; the G protein is attached to a portion of the signal protein inside the neuron.

When a neurotransmitter binds to a metabotopic receptor, a subunit of the associated G protein breaks away. Then, one of two things happens, depending on the particular G protein: The subunit may move along the inside surface of the membrane and bind to a nearby ion channel, thereby inducing an EPSP or IPSP (see Clapham, 1994); or it may trigger the synthesis of a chemical called a **second messenger** (neurotransmitters are considered to be the *first messengers*). Once created by a G protein, a second messenger diffuses through the cytoplasm and does one of three things: It binds to ion channels, thereby inducing an EPSP or an IPSP; it directly influences the metabolic activities of the cell; or it enters the nucleus and binds to the DNA, thereby influencing gene expression. Thus, although a common consequence of a neurotransmitter binding to a receptor is a brief EPSP or IPSP, neurotransmitters can also have radical long-lasting effects via second messengers.

Differences between small-molecule and peptide neurotransmitters in patterns of release and receptor binding suggest that they serve different functions.

Small-molecule neurotransmitters tend to be released into directed synapses and to activate either ionotropic receptors or metabotropic receptors that act directly on ion channels. In contrast, peptides tend to be released diffusely and bind to metabotropic receptors that act through second messengers. Consequently, the function of small-molecule neurotransmitters appears to be the transmission of rapid, brief excitatory or inhibitory signals to adjacent cells; and the function of peptide neurotransmitters appears to be the transmission of slow, diffuse, long-lasting signals.

One type of metabotropic receptors—autoreceptors—warrants special mention. **Autoreceptors** are metabotropic receptors that have two unconventional characteristics: They bind to their neuron's own neurotransmitter molecules; and they are located on the presynaptic, rather than the postsynaptic, membrane. Their usual function is to monitor the number of neurotransmitter molecules in the synapse, to reduce subsequent release when the levels are high, and to increase subsequent release when they are low.

Reuptake, Enzymatic Degradation, and Recycling

If nothing intervened, a neurotransmitter molecule would remain active in the synapse, in effect clogging that channel of communication. However, two mechanisms terminate synaptic messages and keep that from happening. These two message-terminating mechanisms are **reuptake** and **enzymatic degradation** (see Figure 4.14).

Two Mechanisms of Neurotransmitter Deactivation

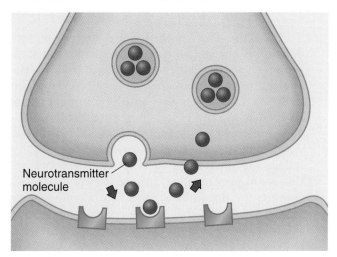

Reuptake

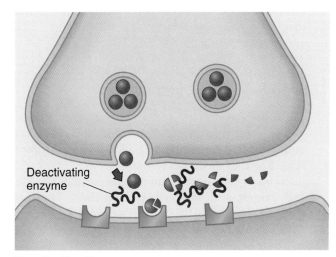

Deactivating Enzymes

Figure 4.14 The two mechanisms of terminating neurotransmitter action in the synapse: reuptake and enzymatic degradation.

Reuptake is the more common of the two deactivating mechanisms. The majority of neurotransmitters, once released, are almost immediately drawn back into the presynaptic buttons (see Clements et al., 1992), repackaged in vesicles by the Golgi complex, and rereleased—over and over again.

In contrast, other neurotransmitters are degraded (broken apart) in the synapse by **enzymes**—chemicals that stimulate or inhibit chemical reactions without directly participating in them. For example, *acetylcholine,* one of the few neurotransmitters for which enzymatic degradation is the main mechanism of synaptic deactivation, is broken down by the enzyme **acetylcholinesterase.** Many of the breakdown products of enzymatic degradation are reabsorbed by the presynaptic button and used in the synthesis of more neurotransmitter molecules.

Neurons also recycle their synaptic vesicles (see Cremona & De Camilli, 1997; Jahn & Südhof, 1994). This is why terminal buttons do not grow steadily bigger as multitudes of vesicles keep adding themselves to the presynaptic membrane during exocytosis. Bits of button membrane continually break off into the button cytoplasm from the region near its boundary with its axon branch. Once in the button cytoplasm, the bits of button membrane are recycled by the resident Golgi complex into small synaptic vesicles.

4.6 The Neurotransmitters

Now that you understand the basics of neurotransmitter function, let's take a look at some of the neurotransmitter substances. There are four classes of small-molecule neurotransmitters: the *amino acids,* the *monoamines,* the recently discovered *soluble gases,* and *acetylcholine.* In addition, there is the one class of large-molecule neurotransmitters: the *neuropeptides.* Most neurotransmitters produce either excitation or inhibition, not both; but a few produce excitation when they bind to some of their receptor subtypes and inhibition when they bind to others. All of the neurotransmitter classes and individual neurotransmitters that appear in this section in bold print are defined by Figure 4.17 at the end of this section rather than appearing with definitions in the margins.

Amino Acid Neurotransmitters

The neurotransmitters in the vast majority of fast-acting, directed synapses in the central nervous system are **amino acids**—the molecular building blocks of proteins. The four most widely acknowledged amino acid neurotransmitters are **glutamate, aspartate, glycine, and gamma-aminobutyric acid (GABA).** The first three are common in the proteins we consume, whereas GABA is synthesized by a simple modification of the structure of glutamate. Glutamate is the most prevalent excitatory neurotransmitter in the mammalian central nervous system; GABA is the most prevalent inhibitory neurotransmitter.

Monoamine Neurotransmitters

Monoamines are another class of small-molecule neurotransmitters. Each is synthesized from a single amino acid—hence the name *monoamine* (one amine). Monoamine neurotransmitters are slightly larger than amino acid neurotransmitters, and their effects tend to be more diffuse. The monoamines are present in small groups of neurons whose cell bodies are, for the most part, located in the brain stem. These neurons often have highly branched axons with many *varicosities* (string-of-beads axons), from which monoamine neurotransmitters are diffusely released into the extracellular fluid (see Figures 4.11 and 4.15).

There are four monoamine neurotransmitters: **dopamine, norepinephrine, epinephrine,** and **serotonin.** They are subdivided into two groups, **catecholamines** and **indolamines,** on the basis of their structure. Dopamine, norepinephrine, and epinephrine are catecholamines. Each is synthesized from the amino acid *tyrosine.* Tyrosine is converted to *L-DOPA,* which in turn is converted to dopamine. Neurons that release norepinephrine have an extra enzyme (one that is not present in dopaminergic neurons), which converts the dopamine in them to norepinephrine. Similarly, neurons that release epinephrine have all the enzymes present in neurons that release norepinephrine, along with an extra enzyme that converts norepinephrine to epinephrine (see Figure 4.16). In contrast to the other monoamines, *serotonin* (also called *5-hydroxytryptamine,* or *5-HT*) is synthesized

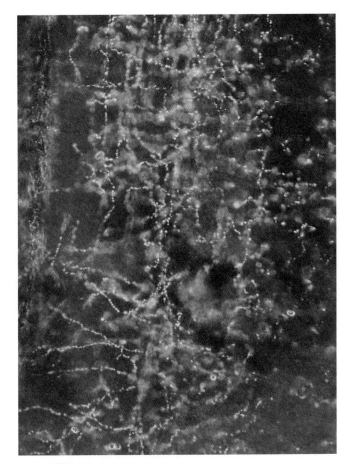

Figure 4.15 *String-of-beads noradrenergic nerve fibers in rat cere-bellar cortex. The bright beaded structures represent sites in these multiply branched axons where the monoamine neurotransmitter norepinephrine is stored in high concentration and released into the surrounding extracellular fluid.*

(Courtesy of Floyd E. Bloom, M.D., The Scripps Research Institute, La Jolla, California.)

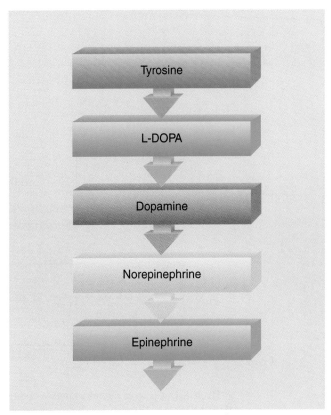

Figure 4.16 *The steps in the synthesis of catecholamines from tyrosine.*

from the amino acid *tryptophan* and is classified as an indolamine.

Neurons that release norepinephrine are called *noradrenergic;* those that release epinephrine are called *adrenergic.* There are two reasons for this naming. One is that epinephrine and norepinephrine used to be called *adrenaline* and *noradrenaline,* respectively, by many scientists, until a drug company registered *Adrenalin* as a brand name. The other reason will become apparent to you if you try to say *norepinephrinergic.*

Soluble-Gas Neurotransmitters

Another class of small-molecule neurotransmitters, the **soluble gases,** has only recently been discovered; so far, the class includes **nitric oxide** and **carbon monoxide.** The soluble gases do not act like the other neurotrans-

mitters (Brenman & Bredt, 1997; Hölscher, 1997). They are produced in the neural cytoplasm; and once produced, they immediately diffuse through the cell membrane into the extracellular fluid and then into nearby cells. They easily pass through cell membranes because they are soluble in lipids. Once in other cells, they stimulate the production of a second messenger and are immediately broken down. They are difficult to study because they exist for only a few seconds.

At some synapses, nitric oxide has been shown to mediate *retrograde transmission.* That is, at some synapses, nitrous oxide transmits feedback signals from the postsynaptic neuron back to the presynaptic neuron.

Acetylcholine

Acetylcholine (Ach) is a small-molecule neurotransmitter that is in one major respect like a professor who is late for lecture: It is in a class by itself. It is created by

Enzymes. Chemicals that stimulate or inhibit chemical reactions without directly participating in them.

Acetylcholinesterase. The enzyme that breaks down acetylcholine.

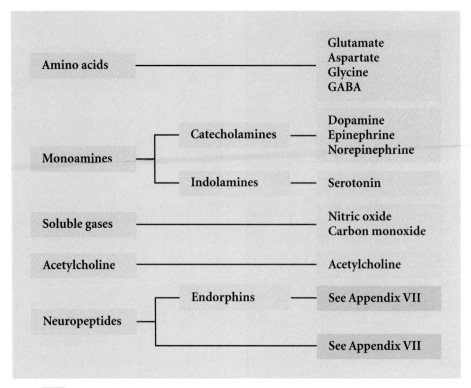

Figure 4.17 Classes of neurotransmitters and the particular neurotransmitters that are introduced in this chapter. This diagram contains all the neurotransmitter classes and all the neurotransmitters that appear in boldface in this chapter, and thus it substitutes for their key term definitions.

adding an *acetyl group* to a *choline molecule.* Acetylcholine is the neurotransmitter at neuromuscular junctions, at many of the synapses in the autonomic nervous system, and at synapses in several parts of the central nervous system. As you learned in the last section, acetylcholine is broken down in the synapse by the enzyme *acetylcholinesterase.* Neurons that release acetylcholine are said to be *cholinergic.*

Neuropeptides

Over 50 peptides currently qualify as neurotransmitters or putative neurotransmitters (see some of them in Appendix VII). A *putative neurotransmitter* is a suspected neurotransmitter—one for which the evidence is strong but not yet unequivocal.

Peptides that play a role in neurotransmission are referred to as **neuropeptides.** Among the most interesting neuropeptides are the **endorphins;** endorphins are endogenous opiates (literally, opiumlike chemicals that are produced within the body). The existence of endorphins was first suggested by the discovery that opiate drugs (e.g., opium, morphine, and heroin) bind to receptors in the brain (Pert, Snowman, & Snyder, 1974); presumably, there would not be receptors in the brain for substances that are not themselves produced by the body. This suggestion was subsequently confirmed by the discovery of

several different endorphins and several subtypes of the endorphin receptor. Endorphins activate neural systems that produce *analgesia* (pain supression) and neural systems that mediate (underlie) the experience of pleasure. These effects are presumably why opiate drugs are so addictive.

Neuropeptides are often referred to as neuromodulators. A *neuromodulator* is a chemical transmitter that does not itself induce signals in other cells; instead, it adjusts the sensitivity of populations of cells to the excitatory and inhibitory signals at fast-acting directed synapses. The concept of neuromodulation is an important one, and there is evidence that some neuropeptides act as neuromodulators under some conditions. However, at present, the evidence does not warrant indiscriminately referring to all neuropeptides as neuromodulators.

Figure 4.17 summarizes the neurotransmitters that were introduced in this section.

Agonists. Drugs that facilitate the effects of a particular neurotransmitter.
Antagonists. Drugs that inhibit the effects of a particular neurotransmitter.
Receptor blockers. Antagonistic drugs that bind to postsynaptic receptors without activating them and block the access of the usual neurotransmitter.

To review the neurotransmitters to which you have just been introduced, fill in the blanks in the following paragraph. The correct answers are provided at the bottom of this page. Before proceeding, review material related to your errors and omissions.

Amino acids are the neurotransmitters in the vast majority of (1)_____-acting, directed synapses. Four amino acids are widely recognized neurotransmitters: (2)_____ , (3)_____ , (4)_____ , and (5)_____ . In contrast to the amino acid neurotransmitters, the (6)_____ are small-molecule neurotransmitters with slower, more diffuse effects; they be-

long to one of two categories: (7)_____ or indolamines. Belonging to the former category are epinephrine, (8)_____ , and (9)_____ ; (10)_____ is the only neurotransmitter belonging to the latter category. The neuropeptides, which are short chains of (11)_____ , are the only class of large-molecule neurotransmitters. (12)_____ , the neurotransmitter at neuromuscular junctions, is a neurotransmitter in a class by itself. Finally, there are the recently discovered (13) _____ neurotransmitters, nitric oxide and carbon monoxide.

4.7 Pharmacology of Synaptic Transmission

The more that neuroscientists have discovered about synaptic transmission, the more that it has been possible for them to develop drugs to modify it in specific ways. The effects of synaptic-transmission–altering drugs on psychological processes is currently one of the most productive topics of biopsychological research. This research taught us a great deal about the neural bases of psychological processes. Also, it has led to the development of effective pharmacologic treatments for psychological disorders—recall the improvement of Roberto Garcia d'Orta. This section completes the chapter by explaining some of the ways drugs influence psychological processes through their effects on synaptic transmission.

Drugs have two fundamentally different kinds of effects on synaptic transmission: They facilitate it or they inhibit it. Drugs that facilitate the effects of a particular neurotransmitter are said to be **agonists** of that neurotransmitter. Drugs that inhibit the effects of a particular neurotransmitter are said to be its **antagonists.**

How Drugs Influence Synaptic Transmission

Although the synthesis, release, and action of neurotransmitters vary somewhat from neurotransmitter to neurotransmitter, the following seven general processes are common to most: (1) synthesis of the neurotransmitter, (2) storage in vesicles, (3) breakdown in the cytoplasm of any neurotransmitter that leaks from the vesicles, (4) exocytosis, (5) inhibitory feedback via autoreceptors, (6) activation of postsynaptic receptors, and (7) deactivation. Figure 4.18 on page 102 illustrates these seven processes, and Figure 4.19 on page 103 illustrates some ways that agonistic and antagonistic drugs influence them. For example, some agonists bind to postsynaptic receptors and activate them, whereas some antagonistic drugs, called **receptor blockers,** bind to postsynaptic receptors without activating them and, in so doing, block the access of the usual neurotransmitter.

Psychoactive Drugs: Four Examples

You will encounter many psychoactive drugs, their psychological effects, and their mechanisms of action in future chapters. Here are four examples: two agonists, cocaine and the benzodiazepines; and two antagonists, atropine and curare.

The answers are (1) fast; (2, 3, 4, 5) glutamate, aspartate, glycine, and GABA, in any order; (6) monoamines; (7) catecholamines; (8, 9) norepinephrine and dopamine, in either order; (10) serotonin; (11) amino acids; (12) Acetylcholine; and (13) soluble gas.

Seven Steps in Neurotransmitter Action

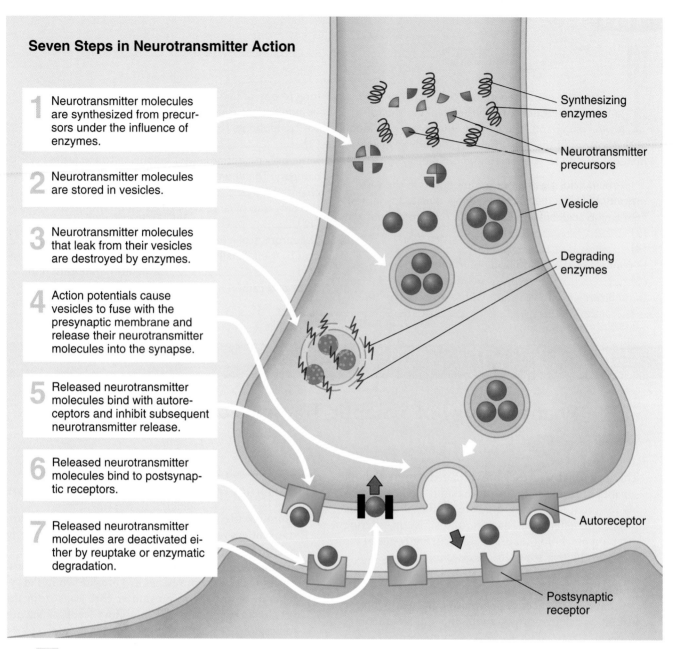

1. Neurotransmitter molecules are synthesized from precursors under the influence of enzymes.

2. Neurotransmitter molecules are stored in vesicles.

3. Neurotransmitter molecules that leak from their vesicles are destroyed by enzymes.

4. Action potentials cause vesicles to fuse with the presynaptic membrane and release their neurotransmitter molecules into the synapse.

5. Released neurotransmitter molecules bind with autoreceptors and inhibit subsequent neurotransmitter release.

6. Released neurotransmitter molecules bind to postsynaptic receptors.

7. Released neurotransmitter molecules are deactivated either by reuptake or enzymatic degradation.

Synthesizing enzymes

Neurotransmitter precursors

Vesicle

Degrading enzymes

Autoreceptor

Postsynaptic receptor

Figure 4.18 Seven common processes in neurotransmitter aciton. The processes are (1) synthesis, (2) storage in vesicles, (3) breakdown of any neurotransmitter leaking from the vesicles, (4) exocytosis, (5) inhibitory feedback via autoreceptors, (6) activation of postsynaptic receptors, and (7) deactivation.

■ **COCAINE** Cocaine is a potent catecholamine agonist that is highly addictive. It increases the activity of both dopamine and norepinephrine by blocking their reuptake from the synapse into the presynaptic button. Accordingly, when there are high levels of cocaine in the brain, molecules of dopamine and norepinephrine, once released into the synapse, continue to activate postsynaptic receptors because their primary method of deactivation has been blocked. This produces a variety of psychological effects, including euphoria, loss of appetite, and insomnia. It is also responsible for the addictive potential of cocaine (see Chapter 13).

■ **BENZODIAZEPINES** *Chlordiazepoxide* (marketed under the name *Librium*) and *diazepam* (marketed under the name *Valium*) belong to a class of drugs called benzodiazepines. **Benzodiazepines** have *anxiolytic* (anxiety-reducing), *sedative* (sleep-inducing), and *anticonvulsant* effects. They appear to exert their anxiolytic effects by serving as GABA agonists. Benzodiazepines bind to one subtype of the GABA receptor, the ionotropic $GABA_A$ receptor (see Macdonald & Olsen, 1994), but they do not exert their agonistic effect by mimicking GABA's actions. Benzodiazepine molecules do not bind to the $GABA_A$ receptor at the same site at which GABA

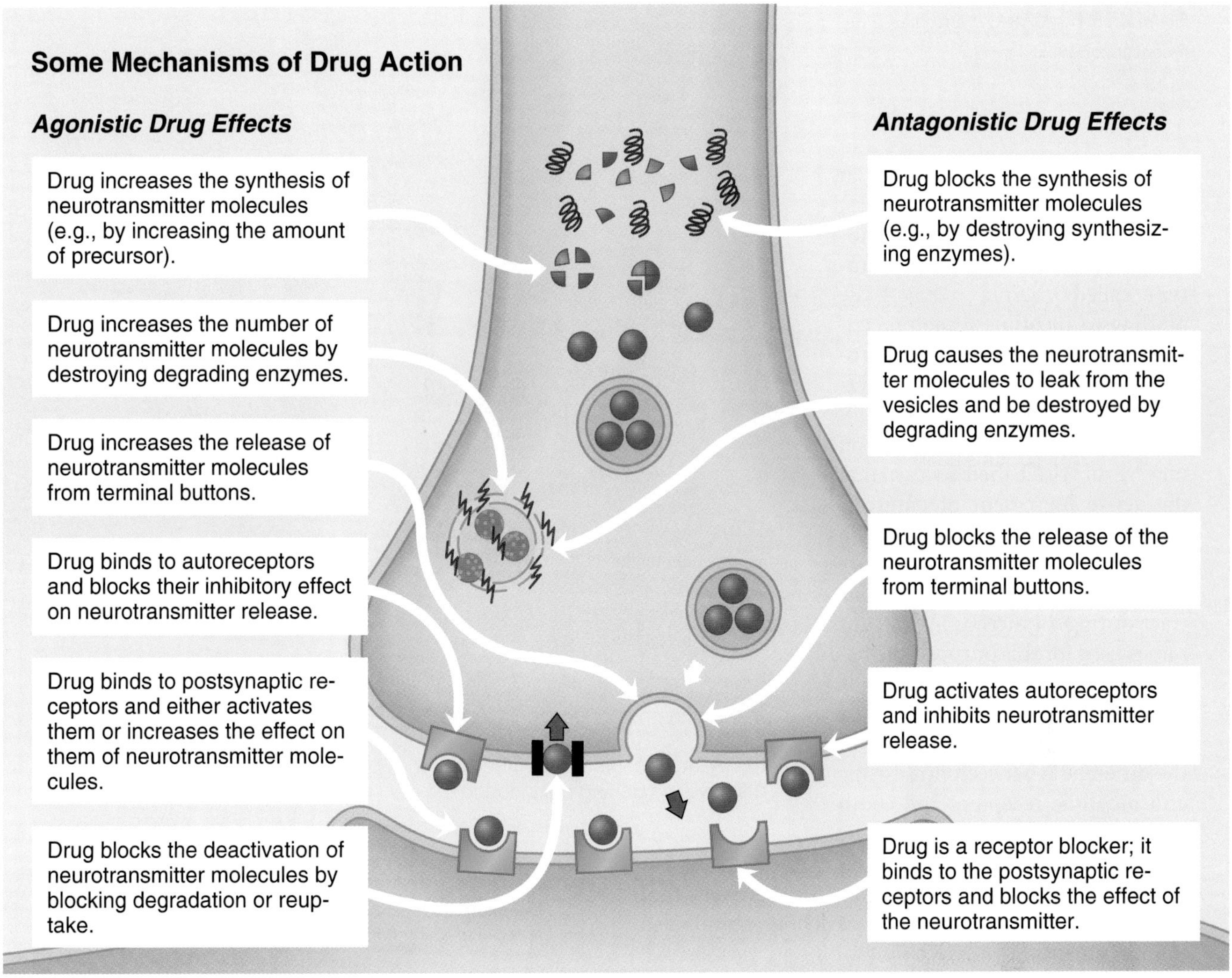

Some Mechanisms of Drug Action

Agonistic Drug Effects

Drug increases the synthesis of neurotransmitter molecules (e.g., by increasing the amount of precursor).

Drug increases the number of neurotransmitter molecules by destroying degrading enzymes.

Drug increases the release of neurotransmitter molecules from terminal buttons.

Drug binds to autoreceptors and blocks their inhibitory effect on neurotransmitter release.

Drug binds to postsynaptic receptors and either activates them or increases the effect on them of neurotransmitter molecules.

Drug blocks the deactivation of neurotransmitter molecules by blocking degradation or reuptake.

Antagonistic Drug Effects

Drug blocks the synthesis of neurotransmitter molecules (e.g., by destroying synthesizing enzymes).

Drug causes the neurotransmitter molecules to leak from the vesicles and be destroyed by degrading enzymes.

Drug blocks the release of the neurotransmitter molecules from terminal buttons.

Drug activates autoreceptors and inhibits neurotransmitter release.

Drug is a receptor blocker; it binds to the postsynaptic receptors and blocks the effect of the neurotransmitter.

Figure 4.19 Some mechanisms of agonistic and antagonistic drug effects.

molecules bind. Instead they bind to another part of the molecule; and by so doing, they increase the binding of GABA molecules to the receptor and thus increase GABA's inhibitory effects by increasing the influx of chloride ions and hyperpolarizing the neuron (see Figure 4.20 on page 104).

The fact that there are benzodiazepine binding sites on the GABA$_A$ receptor suggests that the brain may produce its own benzodiazepinelike chemical. But despite a concerted effort, an endogenous benzodiazepine has yet to be identified.

■ ATROPINE Many of the drugs that are used in research and in medicine are extracts of plants that have long been used for medicinal and recreational purposes. For example, in the time of Hippocrates, the Greeks consumed extracts of the belladonna plant to treat stomach ailments and to make themselves more attractive. Greek women believed that its pupil-dilating effects enhanced their beauty (*belladonna* means "beautiful

lady"). **Atropine** is the active ingredient of belladonna. It is a receptor blocker that exerts its antagonist effect by binding to a metabotropic subtype of acetylcholine receptors called *muscarinic receptors,* thereby blocking the effects of acetylcholine on them. Many muscarinic receptors are located in the brain; the disruptive effect of high doses of atropine on memory was one of the earliest clues that cholinergic mechanisms play a role in memory (see Chapter 14).

■ CURARE South American Indians have long used **curare**—an extract of a certain class of woody vines—to kill their game and occasionally their enemies. Like atropine,

Cocaine. A potent catecholamine agonist that is highly addictive.

Benzodiazepines. A class of GABA agonists with anxiolytic, sedative, and anticonvulsant properties.

Atropine. A receptor blocker at muscarinic cholinergic synapses.

Curare. A blocker of nicotinic cholinergic synapses that produces paralysis by blocking transmission at neuromuscular junctions.

Figure 4.20 The GABA$_A$–benzodiazepine receptor complex.

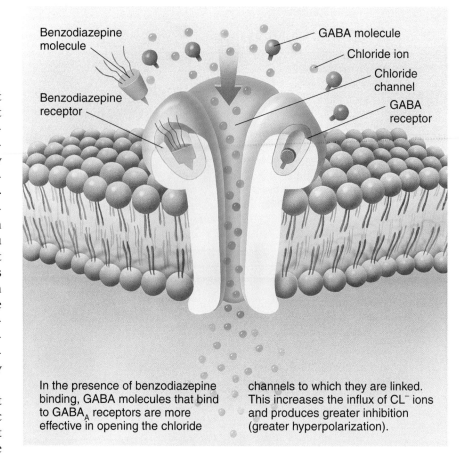

Benzodiazepine molecule

Benzodiazepine receptor

GABA molecule

Chloride ion

Chloride channel

GABA receptor

In the presence of benzodiazepine binding, GABA molecules that bind to GABA$_A$ receptors are more effective in opening the chloride channels to which they are linked. This increases the influx of CL$^-$ ions and produces greater inhibition (greater hyperpolarization).

curare is a receptor blocker at cholinergic synapses, but it acts at a different subtype of acetylcholine receptors: an ionotropic subtype called *nicotinic receptors.* By binding to nicotinic receptors, curare blocks transmission at **neuromuscular junctions,** thus paralyzing its recipients and killing them by blocking their respiration. You may be surprised, then, to learn that the active ingredient of curare is sometimes administered to human patients during surgery to ensure that patients' muscles do not contract during an incision. When curare is used for this purpose, the patient's breathing must be artificially maintained by a respirator.

You may be wondering about the differences between muscarinic and nicotinic receptors and about the significance of their names. The existence of these cholinergic receptor subtypes was inferred from the discovery that some of the receptors to which acetylcholine binds also bind to *muscarine,* whereas others bind to *nicotine.*

Neuromuscular junctions. The synapses of a motor neuron on a muscle.

CONCLUSION

The function of the nervous system, like the function of any circuit, depends on how signals travel through it. Accordingly, an understanding of the basic principles of neural conduction and synaptic transmission is a prerequisite to the study of the neural bases of behavior. This chapter has introduced you to these basic principles. First, you learned why neurons in their resting state have a charge, called the resting potential, built up across their cell membranes (4.1). Then, you learned about the excitatory and inhibitory signals that are conducted from postsynaptic membranes to the axon hillock (4.2), where they elicit action potentials if their integrated value exceeds the threshold of excitation (4.3). Next, the conduction of action potentials along myelinated and unmyelinated axons was described (4.4). The final three sections of the chapter dealt with synaptic transmission: how signals are transmitted from one neuron to another by chemical neurotransmitters (4.5), the various classes of chemical neurotransmitters (4.6), and the ways in which drugs influence synaptic transmission (4.7). *The Lizard,* the story of Roberto Garcia d'Orta, was the glue that held this chapter together; it demonstrated the relevance of neural conduction and synaptic transmission to the study of psychological function.

FOOD FOR THOUGHT

1. Just as computers operate on binary (yes–no) signals, the all-or-none action potential is the basis of neural communication. The human brain is thus nothing more than a particularly complex computer. Discuss.

2. How have the findings described in this chapter changed your understanding of brain function?

3. Why is it important for biopsychologists to understand neural conduction and synaptic transmission? Is it important for all psychologists to have such knowledge? Discuss.

KEY TERMS

Absolute refractory period *(p. 89)*
Acetylcholine *(p. 99)*
Acetylcholinesterase *(p. 98)*
Action potential (AP) *(p. 86)*
Agonists *(p. 101)*
All-or-none responses *(p. 86)*
Amino acids *(p. 98)*
Antagonists *(p. 101)*
Antidromic conduction *(p. 90)*
Asparate *(p. 98)*
Atropine *(p. 103)*
Autoreceptors *(p. 97)*
Axon hillock *(p. 86)*
Benzodiazepines *(p. 102)*
Carbon monoxide *(p. 99)*
Catecholamines *(p. 98)*
Cocaine *(p. 102)*
Coexistence *(p. 94)*
Curare *(p. 103)*
Dendritic spines *(p. 91)*

Depolarize *(p. 85)*
Directed synapses *(p. 92)*
Dopamine *(p. 98)*
Endorphins *(p. 100)*
Enzymatic degradation *(p. 97)*
Enzymes *(p. 98)*
Epinephrine *(p. 98)*
Excitatory postsynaptic potentials (EPSPs) *(p. 85)*
Exocytosis *(p. 94)*
Gamma-aminobutyric acid (GABA) *(p. 98)*
Glutamate *(p. 98)*
Glycine *(p. 98)*
Golgi complex *(p. 92)*
Graded responses *(p. 85)*
Hyperpolarize *(p. 85)*
Indolamines *(p. 98)*
Inhibitory postsynaptic potentials (IPSPs) *(p. 85)*
Integration *(p. 86)*

Ion channels *(p. 83)*
Ionotropic receptors *(p. 95)*
Ions *(p. 83)*
Ligand *(p. 95)*
Membrane potential *(p. 81)*
Metabotropic receptors *(p. 95)*
Microelectrodes *(p. 81)*
Monoamines *(p. 98)*
Neuromuscular junctions *(p. 104)*
Neuropeptides *(p. 100)*
Nitric oxide *(p. 99)*
Nodes of Ranvier *(p. 90)*
Nondirected synapses *(p. 92)*
Norepinephrine *(p. 98)*
Orthodromic conduction *(p. 90)*
Oscilloscope *(p. 82)*
Peptides *(p. 92)*
Postsynaptic inhibition *(p. 91)*
Presynaptic inhibition *(p. 91)*

Receptor blocker *(p. 101)*
Receptor subtypes *(p. 95)*
Receptors *(p. 94)*
Relative refractory period *(p. 89)*
Resting potential *(p. 83)*
Reuptake *(p. 97)*
Saltatory conduction *(p. 90)*
Second messenger *(p. 97)*
Serotonin *(p. 98)*
Sodium–potassium pumps *(p. 85)*
Soluble gases *(p. 99)*
Spatial summation *(p. 86)*
Synaptic vesicles *(p. 92)*
Temporal summation *(p. 87)*
Threshold of excitation *(p. 86)*
Voltage-activated ion channels *(p. 89)*

ADDITIONAL READING

For a systematic introduction to neural conduction and synaptic transmission that is much more detailed than that provided by this chapter, the following text is hard to beat:

Kandel, E. R., Schwartz, J. H., & Jessell, T. M. (1991). *Principles of neural science* (3rd ed.). Norwalk, CT: Appleton & Lange.

Scientific American is one of the few scientific journals that can be purchased at your local newsstand. It specializes in making the research of the world's greatest scientists accessible to the educated public in beautifully illustrated, well-written articles. The following are several that are relevant to this chapter:

Changeux, J. P. (1993, November). Chemical signaling in the brain. *Scientific American, 269,* 58–62.

Gottlieb, D. I. (1988, February). GABAergic neurons. *Scientific American, 258,* 82–89.

Linder, M. E., & Gilman, A. G. (1992, July). G proteins. *Scientific American, 267,* 56–65.

Neher, E., & Sakmann, B. (1992, March). The patch clamp technique. *Scientific American, 266,* 44–51.

Rothman, J. E., & Orci, L. (1996, March). Budding vesicles in living cells. *Scientific American, 274,* 70–75.

Snyder, S. H., & Bredt, D. S. (1992, May). Biological roles of nitric oxide. *Scientific American, 266,* 68–77.

The following book provides a thorough overview of neurotransmitters, drugs, and neuropsychological disorders:

Strange, P. G. (1992). *Brain biochemistry and brain disorders.* New York: Oxford University Press.

5

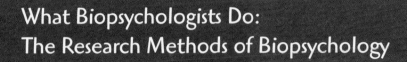

What Biopsychologists Do:
The Research Methods of Biopsychology

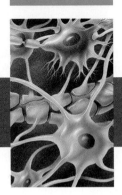

C hapters 1 and 2 introduced you to the general interests, ideas, and approaches that characterize biopsychology. In Chapters 3 and 4, your introduction to biopsychology was temporarily curtailed while background material in neuroanatomy, neurophysiology, and neurochemistry was presented. This chapter gets down to the nitty-gritty of biopsychology; it describes the specific day-to-day activities of the biopsychology laboratory. It is intended to prepare you for future chapters and to sharpen your understanding of biopsychology by describing how biopsychologists do their research.

The organization of this chapter reflects biopsychology's intrinsic duality. The chapter has two major parts: one dealing with methods of studying the nervous system and the other dealing with methods of studying behavior.

5.1 Methods of Visualizing the Living Human Brain

Prior to the early 1970s, biopsychological research was impeded by the inability to obtain images of the organ of primary interest: the living human brain. Conventional X-ray photography is next to useless for this purpose. For an X-ray photograph to be taken, an X-ray beam is passed through an object and then onto a photographic plate. Each of the molecules through which the beam passes absorbs some of the radiation; thus only the unabsorbed portions of the beam reach the photographic plate. X-ray photography is therefore effective in characterizing internal structures that differ substantially from their surroundings in the degree to which they absorb X-rays—for example, a revolver in a suitcase full of clothes or a bone in flesh. However, by the time an X-ray beam has passed through the numerous overlapping structures of the brain, which differ only slightly from one another in their ability to absorb X-rays, it carries little information about the shape of the individual structures through which it has passed.

Contrast X-Rays

Although next to useless for visualizing the brain itself, X-ray photography has long been used to visualize two compartments within the brain: the cerebral ventricular system and the cerebral circulatory system. The visualization is done with **contrast X-ray techniques**—X-ray techniques that involve the injection of a substance that effectively absorbs X-rays (a *radiopaque substance*) into one of the compartments. This injection heightens the contrast between the compartment and the surrounding brain tissue.

One contrast X-ray technique, **pneumoencephalography,** involves temporarily replacing some of the cerebrospinal fluid with air. Because air is radiopaque, the ventricles and fissures of the brain are clearly visible in the subsequent contrast X-ray photograph, which is called a *pneumoencephalogram.* A local deformation of a ventricle or a fissure may indicate the location of a tumor, and a general increase in the size of the ventricles and fissures is indicative of diffuse brain *atrophy* (degeneration).

Another contrast X-ray technique is **cerebral angiography**—a procedure for visualizing the cerebral circulatory system by infusing a radiopaque dye through a cerebral artery during X-ray photography (see Figure 5.1 on page 108). Cerebral angiograms are most useful for localizing vascular damage, but the displacement of blood vessels from their normal position can indicate the location of a tumor.

X-Ray Computed Tomography

In the early 1970s, the study of the living human brain was revolutionized by the introduction of computed tomography. **Computed tomography (CT)** is a computer-assisted X-ray procedure that can be used to visualize the brain and other internal structures of the

---

Contrast X-ray techniques. X-ray techniques that involve the injection of a radiopaque substance into structures to make them visible on an X-ray photograph.

Pneumoencephalography. A contrast X-ray technique that involves temporarily replacing some of the cerebrospinal fluid with air.

Cerebral angiography. A contrast X-ray technique for visualizing the cerebral circulatory system by infusing a radiopaque dye through a cerebral artery.

Computed tomography (CT). A computer-assisted X-ray procedure that can be used to visualize the brain and other inner parts of the living body.

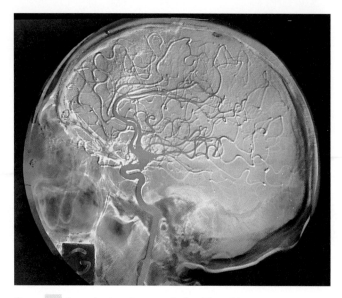

Figure 5.1 A cerebral angiogram of a healthy subject.

vidual X-ray photographs as they rotate. The meager information in each X-ray photograph is combined by a computer to generate a CT scan of one horizontal section of the brain (see Figure 5.3). Then, the X-ray tube and detector are moved along the axis of the patient's body to another level of the brain, and the process is repeated. Scans of eight or nine horizontal brain sections are typically obtained from a patient; combined, they provide a three-dimensional representation of the brain.

Magnetic Resonance Imaging

The success of computed tomography stimulated the development of other techniques for obtaining images of the inside of the living body. Among these techniques is **magnetic resonance imaging (MRI)**—a procedure in which high-resolution images are constructed from the measurement of waves that hydrogen atoms emit when they are activated by radio-frequency waves in a magnetic field. MRI provides clearer images of the brain than does CT (see Moonen et al., 1990). A color-coded two-dimensional MRI scan of the midsagittal brain is illustrated in Figure 5.4.

In addition to high resolution, MRI can provide images in three dimensions. Figure 5.5 on page 110 is a three-dimensional MRI scan.

living body. During cerebral computed tomography, the neurological patient lies with his or her head positioned in the center of a large cylinder, as depicted in Figure 5.2. On one side of the cylinder is an X-ray tube that projects an X-ray beam through the head to an X-ray detector mounted on the other side. The X-ray tube and detector automatically rotate around the head of the patient at one level of the brain, taking many indi-

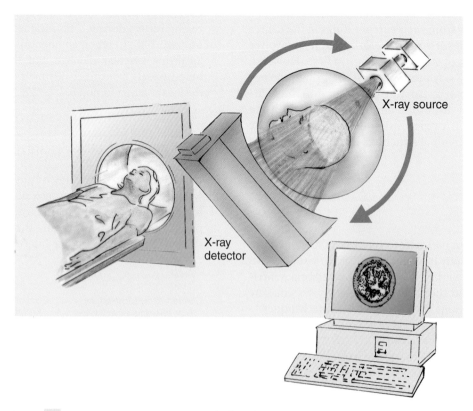

X-ray source

X-ray detector

Figure 5.2 Cerebral computed tomography (CT).

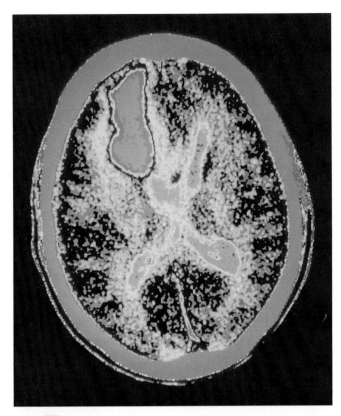

Figure 5.3 A CT scan. Notice the tumor in the left frontal lobe (by convention, posterior is toward the bottom of the scan).

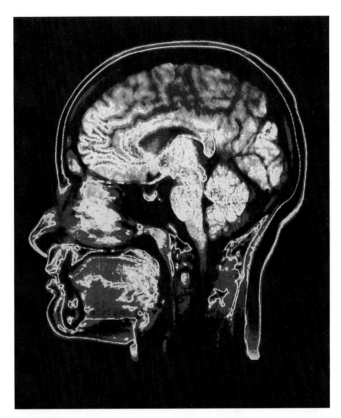

Figure 5.4 A color-enhanced midsagittal MRI scan.

Positron Emission Tomography

Positron emission tomography (PET) is a brain-imaging technique that has been widely used in biopsychological research because it provides images of brain activity rather than brain structure. In one common version of PET, radioactive **2-deoxyglucose (2-DG)** is injected into the patient's *carotid artery* (an artery of the neck that feeds the ipsilateral cerebral hemisphere). Because of its similarity to glucose, the primary metabolic fuel of the brain, 2-deoxyglucose is rapidly taken up by active (energy-consuming) neurons. However, unlike glucose, 2-deoxyglucose cannot be metabolized; it thus accumulates in active neurons until it is gradually broken down. Each PET scan is an image of the levels of radioactivity (indicated by color coding) in various parts of one horizontal level of the brain. Thus, if a PET scan is taken of a patient who engages in an activity such as reading for about 45 seconds after the 2-DG injection, the resulting scan will indicate the areas at that brain level that were most active during the 45 seconds of activity (see Figure 5.6 on page 111). Usually, several different levels of the brain are scanned so that the extent of brain activity can be better assessed.

Another PET procedure (see Turner, 1995) takes advantage of the fact that there is an increase in blood flow to active areas of the brain because active neurons often release *nitric oxide*, a vasodilator (Iadecola, 1993). Accordingly, if radioactive water is injected into the brain's circulatory system as the subject engages in some activity, the PET scan will indicate the areas in which blood flow is increased during the activity (see Raichle, 1994).

Notice from Figure 5.6 that PET scans are not images of the brain. Each PET scan is merely a colored map of the amount of radioactivity in each of the tiny square pixels that compose the scan. One can only estimate exactly how each pixel maps onto a particular brain structure.

Magnetic resonance imaging (MRI). A procedure in which high-resolution images of the structures of the living brain are constructed from the measurement of waves that hydrogen atoms emit when they are activated by radio-frequency waves in a magnetic field.

Positron emission tomography (PET). A technique for visualizing the activity in the brain by measuring the accumulation of radioactive 2-deoxyglucose (2-DG) or radioactive water in the various regions of the brain.

2-deoxyglucose (2-DG). A substance similar to glucose that is taken up by active neurons and accumulates in them because, unlike glucose, it cannot be used by neurons as a source of energy.

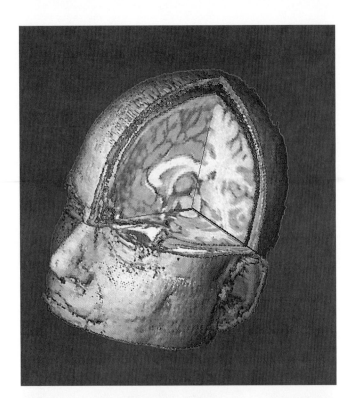

Figure 5.5 Structural magnetic resonance imaging (MRI).

MRI can be used to provide 3-dimensional images of the entire brain. (Courtesy of Bruce Forster and Robert Hare, University of British Columbia.)

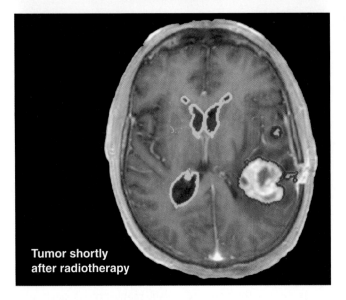

Tumor shortly after radiotherapy

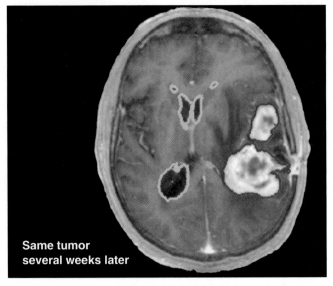

Same tumor several weeks later

MRI can be used to provide 2-dimensional images of brain slices. Here we see the same brain slice shortly after and several weeks after radiotherapy (ventricles oulined in yellow); the therapy has not stopped the growth of the tumor (outlined in red). (Adapted from Calmon et al., in press; courtesy of Neil Roberts, University of Liverpool.)

Functional MRI

Recently, MRI technology has been applied with great success to the measurement of brain activity (see Cohen & Bookheimer, 1994). **Functional MRI** produces images of the increase in oxygen flow in the blood to active areas of the brain. It has four advantages over PET: (1) Nothing has to be injected into the subject; (2) it provides both structural and functional information in the same image; (3) its spatial resolution is better; and (4) it can be used to produce three-dimensional images of activity in the entire brain. Functional MRIs are illustrated in Figure 5.7.

Functional MRI. A magnetic resonance imaging technique for measuring brain activity.

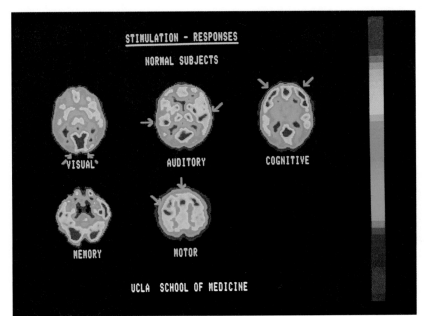

Figure 5.6 A series of PET scans. Each scan is a horizontal section recorded during a different psychological activity. Areas of high activity are indicated by reds and yellows. For example, notice the high level of activity in the visual cortex of the occipital lobe when the subject scanned a visual display.

(From "Positron Tomography: Human Brain Function and Biochemistry" by Michael E. Phelps and John C. Mazziotta, *Science, 228* [9701], May 17, 1985, p. 804. Copyright 1985 by the AAAS. Reprinted by permission. Courtesy of Drs. Michael E. Phelps and John Mazziotta, UCLA School of Medicine.)

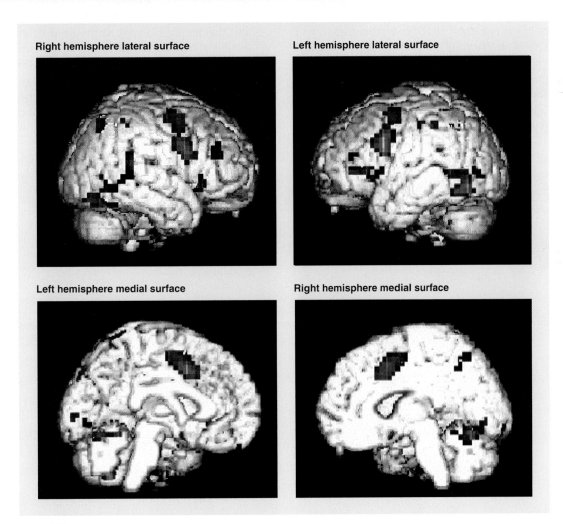

Figure 5.7 Functional magnetic resonance images (fMRIs). These images illustrate the areas of cortex that became more active when the subjects observed strings of letters and were asked to specify which strings were words; control subjects viewed strings of asterisks (Liddle et al., in press). These fMRIs illustrate surface activity; but images of sections through the brain can also be displayed.

(Courtesy of Peter Liddle, Department of Psychiatry, University of British Columbia.)

Recording Human Psychophysiological Activity

In psychophysiological studies of human subjects, physiological activity is usually recorded from the surface of the body. This section of the chapter describes five of the most widely studied psychophysiological measures: one measure of brain activity (the scalp EEG), two measures of somatic nervous system activity (muscle tension and eye movement), and two measures of autonomic nervous system activity (skin conductance and cardiovascular activity).

Scalp Electroencephalography

The *electroencephalogram (EEG)* is a gross measure of the electrical activity of the brain. It is recorded through large electrodes by a device called an *electroencephalograph (EEG machine),* and the technique is called **electroencephalography.** In EEG studies of human subjects, each channel of EEG activity is usually recorded between two disk-shaped electrodes, about half the size of a dime, that are taped to the scalp. In *bipolar recording,* both electrodes are placed over active sites. In *monopolar recording,* one of the two electrodes is placed over the target site and the other is attached to the subject at a point of relative electrical silence—for example, an earlobe.

The scalp EEG signal reflects the sum of electrical events throughout the head. These events include action potentials and postsynaptic potentials, as well as electrical signals from the skin, muscles, blood, and eyes. Thus the utility of the scalp EEG does not lie in its ability to provide an unclouded view of neural activity. Its value as a research and diagnostic tool rests on the fact that some EEG wave forms are associated with particular states of consciousness or particular types of cerebral pathology. For example, **alpha waves** are regular 8- to 12-per-second high-amplitude waves that are associated with relaxed wakefulness. A few examples of EEG wave forms and their psychological correlates are presented in Figure 5.8.

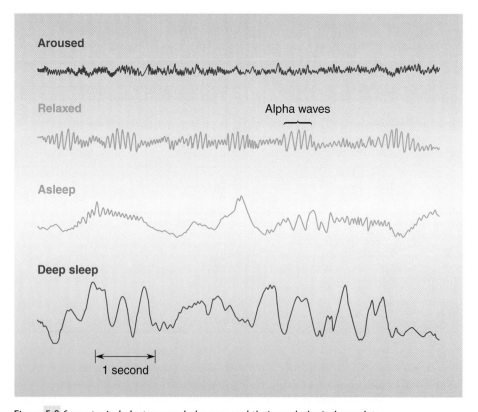

Figure 5.8 Some typical electroencephalograms and their psychological correlates.

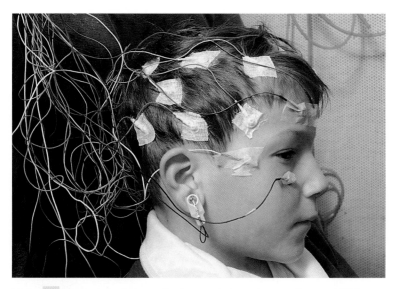

Figure 5.9 Electroencephalography. It is usual to simultaneously record EEG signals from many pairs of scalp electrodes.

Because EEG signals decrease in amplitude as they spread from their source, a comparison of signals recorded from various sites on the scalp can sometimes indicate the origin of particular waves. This is why it is usual to record EEG activity from many sites simultaneously (see Figure 5.9).

In some cases, psychophysiologists are more interested in the EEG waves that accompany certain psychological events than they are in the background EEG signal. These accompanying EEG waves are generally referred to as **event-related potentials (ERPs).** One commonly studied type of event-related potential is the **sensory evoked potential**—the change in the cortical EEG signal that is elicited by the momentary presentation of a sensory stimulus. As Figure 5.10 on page 114 illustrates, the cortical EEG that follows a sensory stimulus has two components: the response to the stimulus (the signal) and the ongoing background EEG activity (the noise). The *signal* is the part of any recording that is of interest; the *noise* is the part that isn't. The problem in recording sensory evoked potentials is that the noise of the background EEG is often so great that the sensory evoked potential is masked. Measuring a sensory evoked potential can be like measuring a whisper at a rock concert.

A method used to reduce the noise of the background EEG is **signal averaging.** First, a subject's response to a stimulus, such as a click, is recorded many—let's say 1,000—times. Then, a computer identifies the millivolt value of each of the 1,000 traces at their starting points (i.e., at the click) and calculates the mean of these 1,000 scores. Next, it considers the value of each of the 1,000 traces 1 millisecond (msec) from their start, for example, and calculates the mean of these values. It repeats this process at the 2-msec mark,

the 3-msec mark, and so on. When these averages are plotted, the average response evoked by the click is more apparent because the random background EEG is canceled out by the averaging. See Figure 5.10, which illustrates the averaging of an auditory evoked potential.

The analysis of *average evoked potentials (AEPs)* focuses on the various peaks or waves in the averaged signal. Each wave is characterized by its direction, positive or negative, and by its latency. For example, the **P300 wave** illustrated in Figure 5.11 on page 114 is the positive wave that occurs about 300 msec after a momentary stimulus that has considerable meaning for the subject (Sutton & Ruchkin, 1984). In contrast, the small waves recorded in the first few milliseconds after a stimulus are not influenced by the meaning of the stimulus. These small waves are called **far-field potentials** because, although they are recorded from the scalp, they originate far away in the sensory nuclei of the brain stem.

Scalp electroencephalography can do something that even the amazing functional MRI techniques cannot: Scalp electroencephalography can follow neural activity in real time. Although increases in neural activity begin to occur a few milliseconds after a triggering experience—and are recorded instantly by scalp electroencephalography—it takes several seconds for the resulting changes in blood flow to develop and individual MRI images are typically based on many seconds of recording. The ability to record neural responses in real time is important: If we are ever to understand the sequences of cerebral events that underlie human cognition, we must be able to follow these events as they unfold.

Although electroencephalography scores high points when it comes to *temporal resolution* (ability to detect differences in time), until recently it has failed miserably when it comes to *spatial resolution* (the ability to detect differences in spatial location). With conventional elec-

Electroencephalography. A procedure for recording the gross electrical activity of the brain through large electrodes, which in humans are usually taped to the surface of the scalp.

Alpha waves. Regular 8- to 12-per-second high-amplitude cortical EEG waves that typically occur during relaxed wakefulness.

Event-related potentials (ERPs). The EEG waves that regularly accompany certain psychological events.

Sensory evoked potential. A change in the electrical activity of the brain that is elicited by the momentary presentation of a sensory stimulus.

Signal averaging. A method of increasing the signal-to-noise ratio by reducing background noise.

P300 wave. The positive EEG wave that usually occurs about 300 msec after a momentary stimulus that has considerable meaning for the subject.

Far-field potentials. EEG signals recorded in an attenuated form at a distance far from their source—for example, brain stem potentials recorded from the scalp.

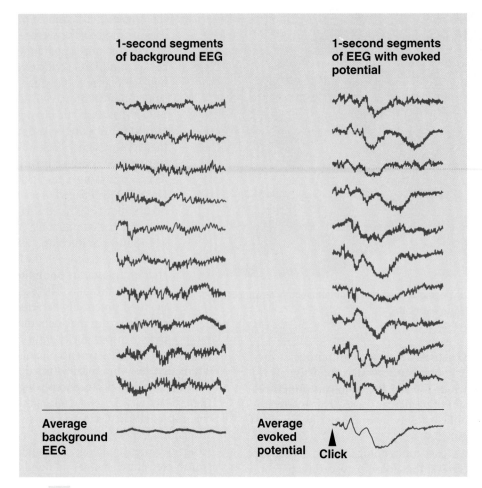

Figure 5.10 The averaging of an auditory evoked potential. Averaging increases the signal–to–noise ratio.

troencephalographic procedures, one can only roughly estimate the source of a particular signal. However, newer techniques employing sophisticated computer

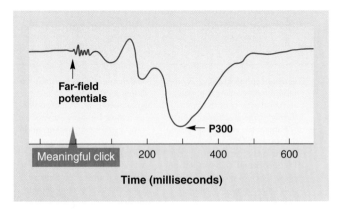

Figure 5.11 An average auditory evoked potential. Notice the P300 wave. This wave occurs only if the stimulus has meaning for the subject; in this case, the click signals the imminent delivery of a reward. By convention, positive EEG waves are always shown as downward deflections.

software and involving many more electrodes can accurately locate the source of signals. The spatial resolution of these new techniques is sufficient to enable the amplitude of evoked EEG signals recorded on the cortex to be color coded and plotted on the surface of a three-dimensional MRI scan (Gevins et al., 1995). This useful marriage of techniques is illustrated in Figure 5.12.

Muscle Tension

Each skeletal muscle is composed of millions of thread-like muscle fibers. Each muscle fiber contracts in an all-or-none fashion when activated by the motor neuron that innervates it. At any given time, a few fibers in each resting muscle are likely to be contracting, thus maintaining the overall tone (tension) of the muscle. Movement results when a large number of fibers contract at the same time. The tension of stationary muscles is a commonly employed measure of a person's psychological arousal.

Electromyography is the usual procedure for measuring muscle tension. The resulting record is called

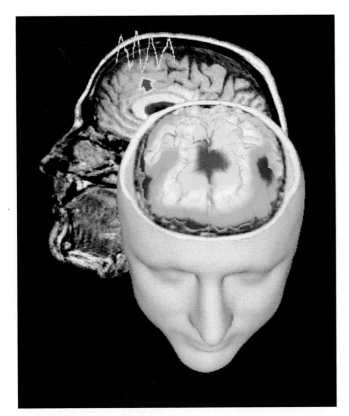

Figure 5.12 The marriage of electroencephalography and magnetic resonance imaging: The distribution of EEG signals can be represented on a structural cerebral MRI. Plotted in this illustration is the distribution of theta waves recorded while the subjects worked on a memory task. The highest incidence of theta waves (indicated by red in the three-dimensional MRI of the dorsal brain surface and by blue on the midsagittal section) occurred in the anterior cingulate cortex.

(Alan Gevins, EEG Systems Laboratory & SAM Technology, San Francisco.)

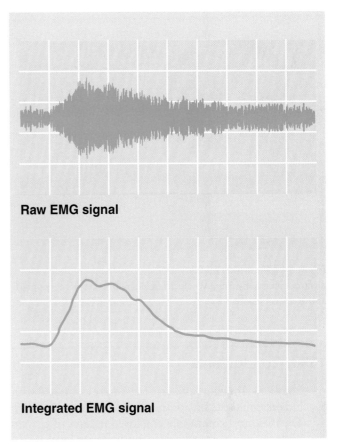

Raw EMG signal

Integrated EMG signal

Figure 5.13 The relation between a raw EMG signal and its integrated version. The subject tensed the muscle beneath the electrodes and then gradually relaxed it.

an *electromyogram (EMG)*. EMG activity is usually recorded between two electrodes taped to the surface of the skin over the muscle of interest. An EMG record is presented in Figure 5.13. You will notice from this figure that the main correlate of an increase in muscle contraction is an increase in the amplitude of the raw EMG signal, which reflects the number of fibers contracting at any one time.

Most psychophysiologists do not work with raw EMG signals; they convert them instead to a more workable form (i.e., they *integrate* the raw signals). The raw signal is fed into a computer that calculates the total amount of EMG spiking per unit of time—in consecutive 0.1-second intervals, for example. The integrated signal (i.e., the total EMG activity per unit of time) is then plotted. The result is a smooth curve, the amplitude of which is a simple, continuous measure of the level of muscle tension over time (see Figure 5.13).

Eye Movement

The electrophysiological technique for recording eye movements is called **electrooculography,** and the resulting record is called an *electrooculogram (EOG)*. Electrooculography is based on the fact that there is a steady potential difference between the front (positive) and back (negative) of the eyeball. Because of this steady potential, when the eye moves, a change in the electrical potential can be recorded between electrodes placed around the eye. It is usual to record EOG activity between two electrodes placed on each side of the eye to measure its horizontal movements and between two electrodes placed above and below the eye to measure its vertical movements (see Figure 5.14 on page 116).

Electromyography. A procedure for recording the gross electrical discharges of muscles.

Electrooculography. A procedure for recording eye movements through electrodes placed around the eye.

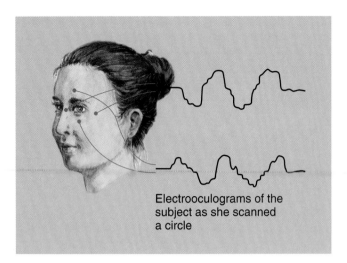

Electrooculograms of the subject as she scanned a circle

Figure 5.14 The typical placement of electrodes around the eye for electrooculography. The two electrooculogram traces were recorded as the subject scanned a circle.

Skin Conductance

Emotional thoughts and experiences are associated with increases in the ability of the skin to conduct electricity. The two most commonly employed indexes of *electrodermal activity* are the **skin conductance level (SCL)** and the **skin conductance response (SCR).** The SCL is a measure of the background level of skin conductance that is associated with a particular situation, whereas the SCR is a measure of the transient changes in skin conductance that are associated with discrete experiences.

The physiological bases of skin conductance changes are not fully understood, but there is considerable evidence implicating the sweat glands (see Boucsein, 1992). Although the main function of sweat glands is to cool the body, these glands tend to become active in emotional situations. Sweat glands are distributed over most of the body surface; but, as you are almost certainly aware, those of the hands, feet, armpits, and forehead are particularly responsive to emotional stimuli.

Cardiovascular Activity

The presence in our language of phrases such as *chicken-hearted, white with fear,* and *blushing bride* indicates that modern psychophysiologists were not the first to recognize the relationship between *cardiovascular activity* and emotion. The cardiovascular system has two parts: the blood vessels and the heart. It is a system for distributing oxygen and nutrients to the tissues of the body, removing metabolic wastes, and transmitting chemical messages. Three different measures of cardiovascular activity are frequently employed in psychophysiological research: heart rate, arterial blood pressure, and local blood volume.

■**HEART RATE** The electrical signal that is associated with each heartbeat can be recorded through electrodes placed on the chest. The recording is called an **electrocardiogram** (abbreviated either **ECG,** for obvious reasons, or **EKG,** from the original German). The average resting heart rate of a healthy adult is about 70 beats per minute, but it increases abruptly at the sound, or thought, of a dental drill.

■**BLOOD PRESSURE** Measuring arterial blood pressure involves two independent measurements: a measurement of the peak pressure during the periods of heart contraction, the *systoles,* and a measurement of the minimum pressure during the periods of relaxation, the *diastoles.* Blood pressure is usually expressed as a ratio of systolic over diastolic blood pressure in millimeters of mercury (mmHg). The normal resting blood pressure for an adult is about 130/70 mmHg. A chronic blood pressure of more than 140/90 mmHg is viewed as a serious health hazard and is called **hypertension.**

You have likely had your blood pressure measured with a *sphygmomanometer*—a crude device composed of a hollow cuff, a rubber bulb for inflating it, and a pressure gauge for measuring the pressure in the cuff (*sphygmos* means "pulse"). More reliable, fully automated methods are used in research.

■**BLOOD VOLUME** Changes in the volume of blood in particular parts of the body are associated with psychological events. The best-known example of such a change is the engorgement of the genitals that is associated with sexual arousal in both males and females. **Plethysmography** refers to the various techniques for measuring changes in the volume of blood in a particular part of the body (*plethysmos* means "an enlargement").

One method of measuring these changes is to record the volume of the target tissue by wrapping a strain gauge around it. Although this method has utility in measuring blood flow in fingers or similarly shaped organs, the possibilities for employing it are somewhat limited. Another plethysmographic method is to shine a light through the tissue under investigation and to measure the amount of the light that is absorbed by it. The more blood there is in a structure, the more light it will absorb.

Changes in the amounts of blood in particular parts of the body (including the brain) can occur because the cardiovascular system is connected in parallel (see Figure 5.15), rather than being a single closed loop of vessels. The selective distribution of blood to various tissues is accomplished by the activity of *sphincter muscles* (muscles whose contraction closes a body channel) in the walls of the *arterioles* (small arteries). Constriction of particular arterioles reduces the blood flowing to areas of the body supplied by them; conversely, dilation increases it.

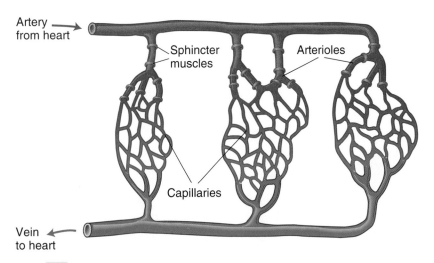

Figure 5.15 An illustration of the parallel structure of the circulatory system. This parallel structure permits the amount of blood flow to particular parts of the body to be increased or decreased by the contraction or relaxation of various arteriole sphincters.

Invasive Physiological Research Methods

Efforts to study brain–behavior relations in human subjects are impeded by the necessity of adhering to lines of research that involve no direct interaction with the organ of interest: the brain. We turn now from a consideration of the *noninvasive techniques* employed in research on living human brains to a consideration of more direct techniques. This section introduces some of the physiological methods commonly employed in biopsychological studies of laboratory animals.

Most physiological techniques used in biopsychological research on laboratory animals fall into one of three categories: lesion methods, electrical stimulation methods, and invasive recording methods. Each of these three methods is discussed in this section of the chapter, but it begins with a description of *stereotaxic surgery*.

Stereotaxic Surgery

Stereotaxic surgery is the first step in many biopsychological experiments. *Stereotaxic surgery* is the means by which experimental devices are precisely positioned in the depths of the brain. Two things are required in stereotaxic surgery: an atlas to provide directions to the target site and an instrument for getting there.

The **stereotaxic atlas** is used to locate brain structures in much the same way that a geographic atlas is used to locate geographic landmarks. There is, however, one important difference. In contrast to the surface of the earth, which has only two dimensions, the brain

has three. Accordingly, the brain is represented in a stereotaxic atlas by a series of individual maps, one per page, each representing the structure of a single, two-dimensional frontal brain slice. In stereotaxic atlases, all distances are given in millimeters from a designated reference point. In some rat atlases, the reference point is **bregma**—the point on top of the skull where two of the major *sutures* (seams in the skull) intersect.

The **stereotaxic instrument** has two parts: a *head holder,* which firmly holds each subject's brain in the prescribed position and orientation; and an *electrode holder,* which holds the device to be inserted. The electrode holder can be moved in three dimensions—anterior–posterior, dorsal–ventral, or lateral–medial—by a system of precision gears. The implantation by

Skin conductance level (SCL). The steady level of skin conductance associated with a particular situation.

Skin conductance response (SCR). The transient change in skin conductance associated with a brief experience.

Electrocardiogram (ECG or EKG). A recording of the electrical activity of the heart.

Hypertension. Chronically high blood pressure.

Plethysmography. Measuring changes in the volume of blood in a part of the body.

Stereotaxic atlas. A three-dimensional map of the brain that is used to determine coordinates for stereotaxic surgery.

Bregma. A landmark on the surface of the skull that is commonly used as a reference point in stereotaxic surgery on rats.

Stereotaxic instrument. A device for performing stereotaxic surgery, composed of two parts: a head holder and an electrode holder.

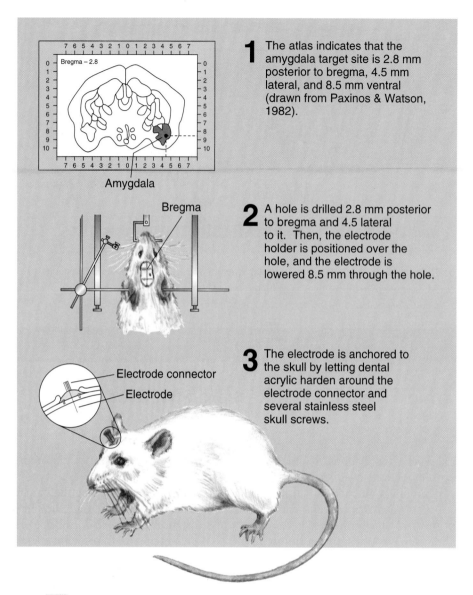

1 The atlas indicates that the amygdala target site is 2.8 mm posterior to bregma, 4.5 mm lateral, and 8.5 mm ventral (drawn from Paxinos & Watson, 1982).

Bregma – 2.8

Amygdala

Bregma

2 A hole is drilled 2.8 mm posterior to bregma and 4.5 lateral to it. Then, the electrode holder is positioned over the hole, and the electrode is lowered 8.5 mm through the hole.

Electrode connector
Electrode

3 The electrode is anchored to the skull by letting dental acrylic harden around the electrode connector and several stainless steel skull screws.

Figure 5.16 Stereotaxic surgery: Implanting an electrode in the rat amygdala.

stereotaxic surgery of an electrode in the amygdala of a rat is illustrated in Figure 5.16.

Lesion Methods

Those of you with an unrelenting drive to dismantle objects to see how they work will appreciate the lesion method. In this method, a part of the brain is removed, damaged, or destroyed; then, the behavior of the subject is carefully assessed in an effort to determine the functions of the lesioned structure. Four types of lesions are discussed here: aspiration lesions, radio-frequency lesions, knife cuts, and cryogenic blockade.

■ **ASPIRATION LESIONS** When a lesion is to be made in an area of cortical tissue that is accessible to the eyes and instruments of the surgeon, **aspiration** is frequently the method of choice. The cortical tissue is drawn off by suction through a fine-tipped handheld glass pipette. Because the underlying white matter is slightly more resistant to suction than the cortical tissue itself, a skilled surgeon can delicately peel off the layers of cortical tissue from the surface of the brain, leaving the underlying white matter and major blood vessels undamaged.

■ **RADIO-FREQUENCY LESIONS** Small subcortical lesions are commonly made by passing *radio-frequency current* (high-frequency current) through the target tissue from the tip of a stereotaxically positioned electrode. The heat from the current destroys the tissue. The size and shape of the lesion are determined by the duration and intensity of the current and the configuration of the electrode tip.

■ **KNIFE CUTS** *Sectioning* (cutting) is used to eliminate conduction in a nerve or tract. A tiny, well-placed cut can

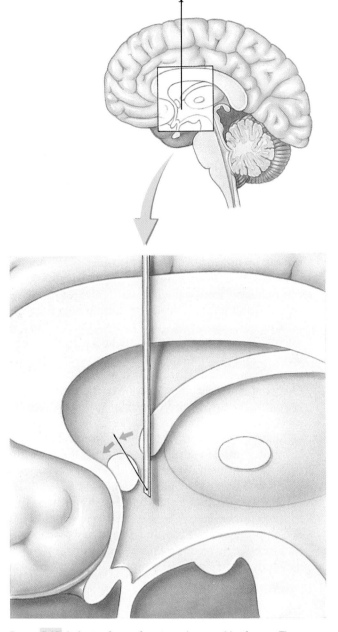

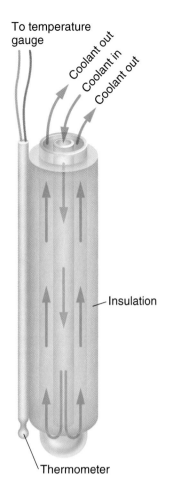

Figure 5.18 A cryoprobe. The cryoprobe is implanted in the brain; then, the brain area at the uninsulated tip of the cryoprobe is cooled while the effects on behavior are assessed. Cryoprobes are slender so that they can be implanted in the brain without causing substantial damage; they are typically constructed of two gauges of hypodermic tubing.

Figure 5.17 A device for performing subcortical knife cuts. The device is stereotaxically positioned in the brain; then, the blade swings out to make the cut. Here we see the anterior commissure being sectioned.

unambiguously accomplish this task without producing extensive damage to surrounding tissue. How does one insert a knife into the brain to make a cut without severely damaging the overlying tissue? The method is depicted in Figure 5.17.

■ CRYOGENIC BLOCKADE An alternative to destructive lesions is **cryogenic blockade.** When coolant is pumped through an implanted *cryoprobe,* such as the one depicted in Figure 5.18, neurons near the tip are cooled until they stop firing. The temperature is maintained above the freezing level so there is no structural dam-

age. Then, when the tissue is allowed to warm up, normal neural activity returns. A cryogenic blockade is functionally similar to a lesion in that it eliminates the contribution of a particular area of the brain to the ongoing behavior of the subject. This is why cryogenic blockades are sometimes referred to as *reversible lesions.* Reversible lesions can also be produced with microinjections of local anesthetics, such as *lidocaine,* into the brain (See Floresco, Seamans, & Phillips, 1997).

■ INTERPRETING LESION EFFECTS Before you leave this section on lesions, a word of caution is in order. Lesion effects are deceptively difficult to interpret. Because the structures of the brain are small, convoluted, and tightly packed together, even a highly skilled surgeon cannot completely destroy a structure without producing significant damage to adjacent structures. There is, however, an unfortunate tendency to lose sight of this fact. For example, a lesion that leaves major portions of

---

Aspiration. A lesion technique in which tissue is drawn off by suction through the tip of a glass pipette.

Cryogenic blockade. The temporary elimination of neural activity in an area of the brain by cooling the area with a cryoprobe.

the amygdala intact and damages an assortment of neighboring structures comes to be thought of simplistically as an *amygdala lesion*. Such an apparently harmless abstraction can be misleading in two ways. If you believe that all lesions referred to as "amygdala lesions" include damage to no other brain structure, you may incorrectly attribute all of their behavioral effects to amygdala damage; conversely, if you believe that all lesions referred to as "amygdala lesions" include the entire amygdala, you may incorrectly conclude that the amygdala does not participate in behaviors uninfluenced by the lesion.

■ **BILATERAL AND UNILATERAL LESIONS** As a general principle—but one with several notable exceptions—the behavioral effects of *unilateral lesions* (lesions restricted to one half of the brain) are much milder than those of symmetrical *bilateral lesions* (lesions involving both sides of the brain), particularly in nonhuman species. Indeed, behavioral effects of unilateral lesions to some brain structures can be difficult to detect. As a result, most experimental studies of lesion effects are studies of bilateral, rather than unilateral, lesions.

Electrical Stimulation

Clues about the function of a neural structure can be obtained by stimulating it electrically. Electrical brain stimulation is usually delivered across the two tips of a *bipolar electrode*—two insulated wires wound tightly together and cut at the end. Weak pulses of current produce an immediate increase in the firing of neurons near the tip of the electrode.

Electrical stimulation of the brain is an important biopsychological research tool because it often has behavioral effects, usually opposite to those produced by a lesion to the same site. It can elicit a number of species-common behavioral sequences, including eating, drinking, attacking, copulating, and sleeping. The particular behavioral response that is elicited depends on the location of the electrode tip, the parameters of the current, and the test environment in which the stimulation is administered.

Invasive Electrophysiological Recording Methods

This section describes four invasive electrophysiological recording methods: intracellular unit recording, extracellular unit recording, multiple-unit recording, and invasive EEG recording. See Figure 5.19 for an example of each method.

■ **INTRACELLULAR UNIT RECORDING** A method discussed at length in Chapter 4, *intracellular unit recording* provides a moment-by-moment record of the graded fluctuations in one neuron's membrane potential. Most experiments using this recording procedure are performed on chemically immobilized animals because it is next to impossible to keep the tip of a microelectrode positioned inside a neuron of a freely moving animal.

■ **EXTRACELLULAR UNIT RECORDING** It is possible to record the action potentials of a neuron through a microelectrode whose tip is positioned in the extracellular fluid next to it. Each time the neuron fires, a blip is recorded on the oscilloscope. Accordingly, *extracellular unit recording* provides a record of the firing of a neuron but no information about the neuron's membrane potential. It is difficult, but not impossible, to record extracellularly from a single neuron in a freely moving animal without the electrode tip shifting away from the neuron, but it can be accomplished with special flexible microelectrodes that can shift slightly with the brain. Initially, extracellular unit recording involved recording from one neuron at a time, each at the tip of a separately implanted electrode. However, it is now possible to simultaneously record extracellular signals from up to 100 or so neurons by analyzing the correlations among the signals picked up through several different electrodes implanted in the same general area. Most theories of the neural mediation of complex behavioral processes assume that they are encoded by relations among the firing of many functionally related neurons—together referred to as *ensembles* (see Deadwyler & Hampson, 1995). Accordingly, studying psychological processes by recording from single neurons can be like studying an animated computer image one pixel at a time.

■ **MULTIPLE-UNIT RECORDING** In *multiple-unit recording*, the electrode tip is larger than that of a microelectrode; thus it picks up signals from many neurons. (The larger the electrode, the more neurons contribute to the signal.) The action potentials picked up by the electrode are fed into an integrating circuit, which adds them together. A multiple-unit recording is a graph of the total number of recorded action potentials per unit of time (e.g., per 0.1 second).

■ **INVASIVE EEG RECORDING** In laboratory animals, EEG signals are recorded through large implanted electrodes rather than through scalp electrodes. Cortical EEG signals are frequently recorded through stainless steel skull screws, whereas subcortical EEG signals are typically recorded through stereotaxically implanted wire electrodes.

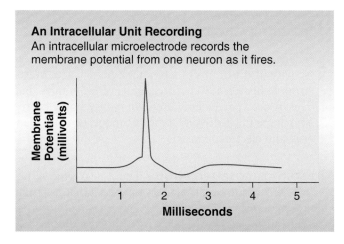

An Intracellular Unit Recording
An intracellular microelectrode records the membrane potential from one neuron as it fires.

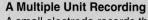

A Multiple Unit Recording
A small electrode records the action potentials of many nearby neurons. These are added up and plotted. In this example, firing in the area of the electrode tip gradually declined and then suddenly increased.

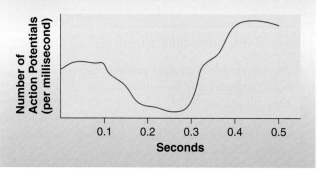

An Extracellular Unit Recording
An extracellular microelectrode records the electrical disturbance that is created each time that an adjacent neuron fires.

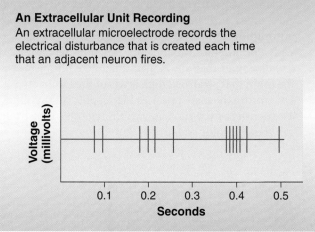
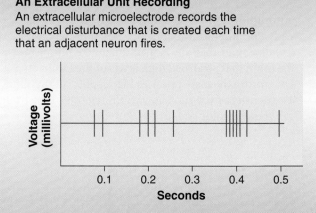

An Invasive EEG Recording
A large implanted electrode picks up general changes in electrical brain activity. The EEG signal is not related to neural firing in any obvious way.

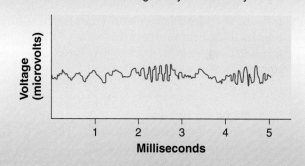

Figure 5.19 Four methods of recording electrical activity of the nervous system.

5.4 Pharmacological Research Methods

The major research strategy of psychopharmacology is to administer drugs that either increase or decrease the effects of particular neurotransmitters and to observe the behavioral consequences. You learned in the preceding chapter how *agonists* and *antagonists* affect neurotransmitter systems. Described here are the various routes of drug administration, several methods of using chemicals to make selective brain lesions, and three methods of measuring the chemical activity of the brain that are particularly useful in biopsychological research.

Routes of Drug Administration

In most psychopharmacological experiments, drugs are administered in one of the following ways: (1) They are fed to the subject; (2) they are injected through a tube into the stomach (*intragastrically*); or (3) they are injected hypodermically into the peritoneal cavity of the abdomen (*intraperitonally, IP*), into a large muscle (*intramuscularly, IM*), into the fatty tissue beneath the skin (*subcutaneously, SC*), or into a large surface vein (*intra-*

venously, IV). A problem with these peripheral routes of administration is that many drugs do not readily pass through the blood–brain barrier. To overcome this problem, drugs can be injected in small amounts through a fine, hollow needle, called a **cannula,** that has been stereotaxically implanted in the brain.

Selective Chemical Lesions

The effects of surgical, electrolytic, and cryogenic lesions are frequently difficult to interpret because they affect all neurons in the target area. In some cases, it is possible to make more selective lesions by injecting **neurotoxins** (neural poisons) that have an affinity for certain components of the nervous system. There are many selective neurotoxins. For example, when *kainic acid* and *ibotenic acid* are administered by microinjection, they are preferentially taken up by cell bodies at the tip of the cannula and destroy those neurons, while leaving neurons with axons passing through the area largely unscathed. Another widely used selective neurotoxin is *6-hydroxydopamine (6-OHDA).* It is taken up only by those neurons that release the neurotransmitters *norepinephrine* or *dopamine;* it leaves other neurons at the injection site undamaged.

Measuring Chemical Activity of the Brain

There are many procedures for measuring the chemical activity of the brains of laboratory animals (see Westerink & Justice, 1991). Three kinds of techniques that have proved particularly useful in biopsychological research are the 2-deoxyglucose technique, cerebral dialysis, and electrochemistry.

■ **2-DEOXYGLUCOSE TECHNIQUE** The *2-deoxyglucose (2-DG)* technique entails placing an animal that has been injected with radioactive 2-DG in a test situation in which it engages in the behavior of interest. Because 2-DG is similar in structure to glucose—the brain's main source of energy—neurons active during the test absorb it at a high rate but do not metabolize it. After the subject engages in the behavior, it is killed, and its brain is removed and sliced. The slices are then subjected to **autoradiography** (see Figure 5.20); they are coated with a photographic emulsion, stored in the dark for a few days, and then developed much like film. Areas of the brain that absorbed high levels of the radioactive 2-DG during the test appear as black spots on the slides. The density of the spots in various regions of the brain can then be color coded.

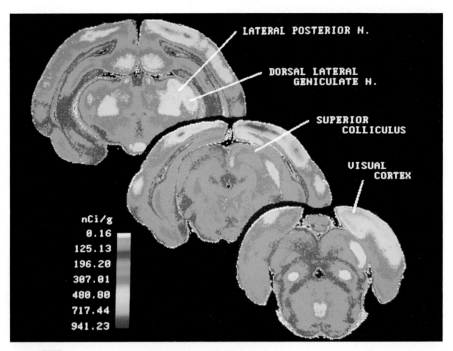

Figure 5.20 The 2-deoxyglucose technique. The accumulation of radioactivity is shown in three frontal sections taken from the brain of a Richardson's ground squirrel. The subject was injected with radioactive 2-deoxyglucose; then, for 45 minutes it viewed brightly illuminated black and white stripes through its left eye while its right eye was covered. Because the ground squirrel visual system is largely crossed, most of the radioactivity accumulated in the visual structures of the right hemisphere (the hemisphere on your right).

(Courtesy of Rod Cooper, Department of Psychology, University of Calgary.)

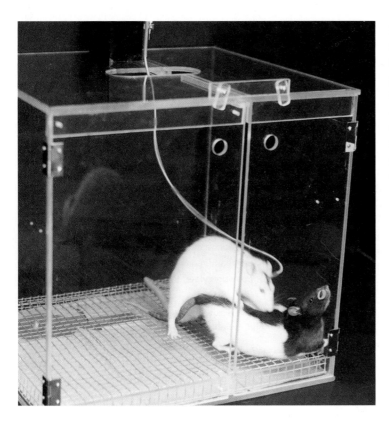

Figure 5.21 Electrochemistry. The male rat is mounting the female as extracellular dopamine levels in its nucleus accumbens are being monitored by electrochemistry. Dopamine levels begin to increase in the males once they are given access to receptive females, and they increase further during copulation (Fiorino et al., 1997). Notice that the male (*albino*) and female (*hooded*) are of different strains, and notice the sexually receptive posture (*lordosis*) of the female.

(Photograph courtesy of Dennis Fiorino, Department of Psychology, University of British Columbia.)

■ **CEREBRAL DIALYSIS** The **cerebral dialysis** procedure is a method of measuring the extracellular concentration of specific neurochemicals in behaving animals (see Robinson & Justice, 1991)—most other techniques for measuring neurochemicals require that the animals be killed so that samples can be extracted. Cerebral dialysis involves the implantation in the brain of a fine tube with a short semipermeable section. The semipermeable section is positioned in the brain structure of interest so the extracellular chemicals from the structure will diffuse into the tube. Once in the tube, they can be collected for freezing, storage, and later analysis; or they can be carried in solution directly to a *chromatograph*—a device for measuring the chemical constituents of liquids and gases.

Figure 5.21 shows a rat copulating while samples of the extracellular fluid of its brain are being collected by cerebral dialysis, one sample every few seconds. The investigators in this study (Fiorino, Coury, & Phillips, 1997) found that levels of dopamine in the nucleus accumbens were elevated while the rats were anticipating or engaging in sex.

■ **ELECTROCHEMISTRY** **Electrochemistry** is another method of recording the extracellular concentration of neurochemicals in behaving animals (see Blaha et al., 1990; Blaha & Jung, 1991). *Electrochemistry* is a general term that refers to several techniques of inferring the concentration of particular neurochemicals at the tip of specially constructed electrodes from changes in the flow of weak currents through them under various conditions. Electrochemistry has been used most extensively to measure the release of *dopamine.*

Locating Neurotransmitters and Receptors in the Brain

A key step in trying to understand the psychological function of a particular neurotransmitter or receptor is finding out where it is located in the brain. Two of the techniques available for this purpose are immunocytochemistry and in situ hybridization. Each involves exposing brain slices to a labeled *ligand* of the molecule under investigation (the ligand of a molecule is another molecule that binds to it).

Cannula. A fine tube, such as a hypodermic needle, that is implanted in the body for the purpose of introducing or extracting substances.

Neurotoxins. Neural poisons.

Autoradiography. The technique of photographically developing brain slices that have been exposed to a radioactively labeled substance such as 2-DG so that regions of high uptake are visible on the brain slices.

Cerebral dialysis. A method for recording changes in brain chemistry in behaving animals; a tube with a short semipermeable section is implanted in the brain, and extracellular neurochemicals are continuously drawn off for analysis through the semipermeable section.

Electrochemistry. A variety of techniques for inferring the concentration of particular neurochemicals (e.g., dopamine) at the tip of specially constructed electrodes from changes in the flow of weak currents through them under various conditions.

■IMMUNOCYTOCHEMISTRY When a foreign protein (an *antigen*) is injected into an animal, the animal creates *antibodies* that bind to it and then help the body remove or destroy it; this is known as the body's *immune reaction*. Neurochemists have created stocks of antibodies to most of the brain's peptide neurotransmitters and receptors. **Immunocytochemistry** is a procedure for locating particular neuroproteins in the brain by labeling antibodies with a dye or radioactive element and then exposing slices of brain tissue to the labeled antibodies (see Figure 5.22). Regions of dye or radioactivity accumulation in the brain slices mark the locations of the target neuroprotein.

Because all enzymes are proteins and because only those neurons that release a particular neurotransmitter are likely to contain all the enzymes required for its synthesis, immunocytochemistry can be used to locate neurotransmitters by binding to their enzymes. This is done by exposing brain slices to labeled antibodies that bind to enzymes located in only those neurons that contain the neurotransmitter of interest (see Figure 5.23).

■IN SITU HYBRIDIZATION Another technique for locating peptides and other proteins in the brain is **in situ hybridization.** This technique takes advantage of the fact that all peptides and proteins are transcribed from sequences of nucleotide bases on strands of messenger RNA (see Chapter 2). The nucleotide base sequences that direct the synthesis of many neuroproteins have been identified, and hybrid strands of mRNA with the complementary base sequences have been artificially created. In situ hybridization (see Fig-

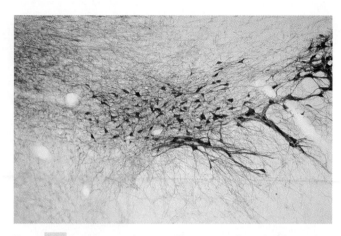

Figure 5.23 Immunocytochemistry. This section through the rat substantia nigra reveals dopaminergic neurons that have taken up the antibody for tyrosine hydroxylase, the enzyme that converts tyrosine to L-DOPA.

(Courtesy of Mark Klitenick and Chris Fibiger, Department of Psychiatry, University of British Columbia.)

ure 5.24) involves the following steps. First, hybrid RNA strands with the base sequence complementary to the mRNA that directs the synthesis of the target neuroprotein are obtained. Next, the hybrid RNA strands are labeled with a dye or radioactive element. Finally, the brain slices are exposed to the labeled hybrid RNA strands; they bind to the complementary mRNA strands marking the location of neurons that release the target neuroprotein.

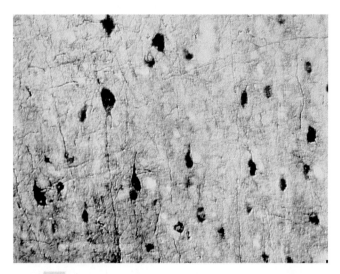

Figure 5.22 Immunocytochemistry. This section through the cat visual cortex reveals GABAergic inhibitory interneurons that have taken up the antibody for GABA.

(Courtesy of Joanne Matsubara, Department of Ophthalmology, University of British Columbia.)

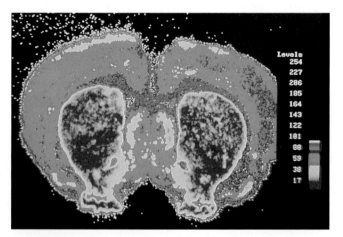

Figure 5.24 In situ hybridization. This color-coded frontal section through the rat brain reveals high concentrations of mRNA expression for the endorphin preproenkephalon in the striatum. In this illustration, the lowest levels (in red and yellow) indicate the highest concentrations.

(Courtesy of Ningning Guo and Chris Fibiger, Department of Psychiatry, University of British Columbia.)

Genetic Engineering

Genetics is a science that has made amazing progress in the last decade, and biopsychologists are reaping the benefits. For example, gene knockout techniques and gene replacement techniques have been used by biopsychologists for modifying the genetic makeup of subjects to study the effects of genes on behavior (see Plomin et al., 1997). Although these two techniques are still largely limited to use in simple invertebrates, both have recently been adapted for use in the mouse, the favored mammalian subject of geneticists.

Gene Knockout Techniques

Gene knockout techniques are procedures for creating organisms that lack the particular gene under investigation. Once these subjects have been created, efforts are made to identify and then investigate any observable neural or behavioral anomalies they might possess. Mice that are the products of gene knockout techniques are referred to as *knockout mice.* This term often makes me smile, as images of little mice with boxing gloves momentarily flit through my mind.

Knockout mice are created first by deleting the gene of interest in a few embryonic cells in culture; this is done by deleting the base sequences from the segment of the chromosome known to contain the gene. Second, the abnormal cells are transferred to a developing mouse embryo. And third, once the embryos develop into mature mice, the mice are bred to create mice that are *homozygous* for the knocked-out gene.

There has been much enthusiasm for gene knockout technology, and hundreds of gene knockout studies are currently in progress (Plomin et al., 1997). However, several authorities (e.g., Crusio, 1996; Gerlai, 1996; Lathe, 1996) have warned that the results of behavioral studies of knockout mice may be more difficult to interpret than first anticipated. The following are four of the warnings that they have issued. First, most behavioral traits are *polymorphic* traits (traits that are influenced by the activities of many interacting genes); consequently, the elimination of a behavioral trait by a gene knockout can at best identify only one small genetic contribution to the behavior. Second, elimination of a gene often influences the expression of other genes; as a result, any observed change in the *phenotype* (observable traits) in knockout mice may be only indirectly related to the knocked-out gene. Third, the expression of many genes is influenced by experience; thus, the effects of some gene knockouts may depend on the mouse's experience. And fourth, the DNA of control littermates differs from the DNA of knockout mice in terms of genes in addition to the target genes. This is because the knockout cells are typically derived from one strain and injected into a different one; as a result, the section of DNA around the knocked-out gene tends to be inherited from the implanted cells, whereas the same section of DNA in the control littermates tends to be inherited from the recipients.

Gene Replacement Techniques

It is now possible to replace one gene with another in mice. **Gene replacement techniques** are creating some interesting possibilities for developmental research. For example, it is now possible to remove pathological genes from human cells and insert them in mice (mice that contain the genetic material of another species are called **transgenic mice**). Also, it is now possible to replace a gene with one that is identical except for the addition of a few bases that can act as a switch, turning the gene off or on in response to particular chemicals. These chemicals can be used to activate or suppress a gene at a particular point in development or in a particular brain structure (see Mayford et al., 1996). Gene knockout and gene replacement technologies are certainly amazing; how much they will teach us about psychological development awaits to be determined.

Immunocytochemistry. A procedure for locating particular proteins in the brain by labeling antibodies to the neuroproteins with a dye or radioactive element and then exposing slices of brain tissue to the labeled antibodies.

In situ hybridization. A technique for locating particular proteins in the brain: Molecules that bind to the mRNA that directs the synthesis of the target protein are synthesized; then these ligands are labeled, and brain slices are exposed to them.

Gene knockout techniques. Procedures for creating organisms that lack a particular gene.

Gene replacement techniques. Procedures for creating organisms in which a particular gene has been deleted and replaced with another.

Transgenic mice. Mice into which the genetic material of another species has been introduced.

The research methods of biopsychology illustrate a psychological disorder suffered by many scientists. I call it "unabbreviaphobia"—the fear of leaving any term left unabbreviated. As a means of reviewing Part 1 of this chapter, write out the following abbreviations in full.

1. CT: _____

2. MRI: _____

3. PET: _____

4. 2-DG: _____

5. EEG: _____

6. ERP: _____

7. AEP: _____

8. EMG: _____

9. EOG: _____

10. SCL: _____

11. SCR: _____

12. ECG: _____

13. EKG: _____

14. IP: _____

15. IM: _____

16. IV: _____

17. SC: _____

18. 6-OHDA: _____

PART 2 / THE BEHAVIORAL RESEARCH METHODS OF BIOPSYCHOLOGY

We turn now from the methods used by biopsychologists to study the nervous system to those that deal with the behavioral side of biopsychology. As we progress through this section of the chapter, it will become apparent that a fundamental difference between behavior and the nervous system is reflected in the nature of the methods used in their investigation. This difference is one of visibility. The nervous system and its activities are not ordinarily observable, whereas behavior is continuously on display in all its diversity and complexity. In essence, behavior is the overt expression of covert neural activity.

Because of the inherent invisibility of neural activity, the primary objective of the methods used in its investigation is to render the unobservable observable. In contrast, the major objectives of behavioral research methods are to control, to simplify, and to

objectify. A single set of such procedures developed for the investigation of a particular behavioral phenomenon is commonly referred to as a **behavioral paradigm.** Each behavioral paradigm normally comprises a method for producing the behavioral phenomenon under investigation and a method for objectively measuring it.

There is an unfortunate tendency to underestimate both the critical role that effective behavioral paradigms play in the progress of neuroscience and the ingenuity and effort required to develop them. Perhaps this is a consequence of behavior's visibility—we all seem to undervalue the familiar. Do not make this mistake! Remember that behavior is the ultimate manifestation of nervous system activity. In the final analysis, the purpose of all neural activity is the production of behavior. Studying it is no simple matter.

The answers are (1) computed tomography, (2) magnetic resonance imaging, (3) positron emission tomography, (4) 2-deoxyglucose, (5) electroencephalogram, (6) event-related potential, (7) average evoked potential, (8) electromyogram, (9) electrooculogram, (10) skin conductance level, (11) skin conductance response, (12) electrocardiogram, (13) electrocardiogram, (14) intraperitoneal, (15) intramuscular, (16) intravenous, (17) subcutaneous, and (18) 6-hydroxydopamine.

Neuropsychological Testing

A patient suspected of suffering from some sort of nervous system dysfunction is usually referred to a *neurologist*, who assesses simple sensory and motor functions. More subtle changes in perceptual, emotional, motivational, or cognitive functions are the domain of the *neuropsychologist*.

Because neuropsychological testing is so time consuming, it is typically prescribed for only a small portion of brain-damaged patients. This is unfortunate; the results of neuropsychological testing can help brain-damaged patients in three important ways: (1) by assisting in the diagnosis of neural disorders, particularly in cases in which brain imaging, EEG, and neurological testing have proved equivocal; (2) by serving as a basis for counseling and caring for the patients; or (3) by providing a basis for objectively evaluating the effectiveness of the treatment and the seriousness of its side effects.

Modern Approach to Neuropsychological Testing

In the last half century, the nature of neuropsychological testing has changed radically. Indeed, the dominant approach to psychological testing has evolved through three distinct phases: the *single-test approach*, the *standardized-test-battery approach*, and the modern *customized-test-battery approach*.

■ **SINGLE-TEST APPROACH** Before the 1950s, the few existing neuropsychological tests were designed to detect the presence of brain damage; in particular, the goal of these early tests was to discriminate between patients with psychological problems resulting from structural brain damage and those with psychological problems resulting from functional, rather than structural, changes to the brain. This approach proved unsuccessful, in large part because no single test could be developed that would be sensitive to all the varied and complex psychological symptoms that could potentially occur in a brain-damaged patient.

■ **STANDARDIZED-TEST-BATTERY APPROACH** The standardized-test-battery approach to neuropsychological testing grew out of the failures of the single-test approach, and by the 1960s, it was predominant. The objective stayed the same—to identify brain-damaged patients—but the testing now involved standardized batteries of tests rather than a single test. The most widely used standardized test battery has been the *Halstead-Reitan Neuropsychological Test Battery*. The Halstead-Reitan is a collection of tests that tend to be performed poorly by brain-damaged patients in relation to other patients or healthy control subjects; the scores on each test are added together to form a single aggregate score. An aggregate score below the designated cutoff leads to a diagnosis of brain damage. The standardized-test-battery approach has proved only marginally successful; standardized test batteries discriminate effectively between neurological patients and healthy patients, but they are not so good at discriminating between neurological patients and psychiatric patients.

■ **THE CUSTOMIZED-TEST-BATTERY APPROACH** The modern customized-test-battery approach began to be used routinely in a few elite neuropsychological research institutions in the 1960s. This approach proved highly successful in research, and it soon spread to clinical practice. It predominates today in both the research laboratory and the neurological ward.

The objective of modern neuropsychological testing is not merely to identify patients with brain damage; the objective is to characterize the nature of the psychological deficits of each brain-damaged patient. So how does the modern approach to neuropsychological testing work? It usually begins in the same way for all patients: with a common battery of tests selected by the neuropsychologist to provide an indication of the general nature of the neuropsychological symptoms. Then, depending on the results of the common test battery, the neuropsychologist selects a series of tests customized to each patient in an effort to characterize in more detail the general symptoms revealed by the common battery. For example, if a patient were found to have a memory problem by the test battery, subsequent tests would include those designed to reveal the specific nature of the memory problem.

The tests used in the modern customized-test-battery approach differ in three respects from earlier tests. First, the modern tests are specifically designed to measure aspects of psychological function that have been

---

Behavioral paradigm. A single set of procedures developed for the investigation of a particular behavioral phenomenon.

spotlighted by modern theories and data. For example, modern theories, and the evidence on which they are based, suggest that the mechanisms of short-term and long-term memory are totally different; thus the testing of patients with memory problems virtually always involves specific tests of both short-term and long-term memory. Second, the interpretation of the tests often does not rest entirely on how well the patient does; unlike early neuropsychological tests, modern tests often require the neuropsychologist to assess the cognitive strategy that the patient employs in performing the test. Brain damage often changes the strategy that a neuropsychological patient uses to perform a test without lowering the overall score. Third, the customized-test-battery approach requires more skillful examination. Skill and knowledge are often required to select just the right battery of tests to expose a patient's deficits and to identify qualitative differences in cognitive strategy.

Tests of the Common Neuropsychological Test Battery

Because the modern approach to neuropsychological testing typically involves two phases—a battery of general tests given to all patients followed by a series of specific tests customized to each patient—the following examples of neurological tests are presented in two subsections. First are some tests that are often administered as part of the initial common test battery, and second are some tests that might be used by a neuropsychologist to investigate in more depth particular problems revealed by the common battery.

■ **INTELLIGENCE** Although the overall *intelligence quotient* (IQ) is a notoriously poor measure of brain damage, a test of general intelligence is nearly always included in the battery of neuropsychological tests routinely given to all patients. Many neuropsychological assessments begin with the **Wechsler Adult Intelligence Scale (WAIS).** This is because knowing a patient's IQ can help the neuropsychologist interpret the results of other tests. Also, a skilled neuropsychologist can sometimes draw inferences about a patient's neuropsychological dysfunction from the pattern of deficits on the various subtests of the WAIS. For example, low scores on subtests of verbal ability tend to be associated with left hemisphere damage, whereas right hemisphere damage tends to reduce scores on performance subtests. The 11 subtests of the WAIS are illustrated in Table 5.1.

■ **MEMORY** One weakness of the WAIS is that it often fails to detect memory deficits, despite including two tests specifically designed to test memory function. The information test of the WAIS assesses memory for general knowledge (e.g., who is Queen Elizabeth?), and the

Table 5.1 The 11 Subtests of the Wechsler Adult Intelligence Scale (WAIS)

VERBAL SUBTESTS

Information Read to the subject are 29 questions of general information—for example, questions like: "Who is the president of the United States?"

Digit-span Three digits are read to the subject at one-second intervals, and the subject is asked to repeat them in the same order. Two trials are given at three digits, four digits, five digits, and so on until the subject fails both trials at one level.

Vocabulary The subject is asked to define a list of 35 words that range in difficulty.

Arithmetic The subject is presented with 14 arithmetic questions and must answer them without the benefit of pencil and paper.

Comprehension The subject is asked 16 questions that test the ability to understand general principles—for example, questions like: "Why should people vote?"

Similarities The subject is presented with pairs of items and is asked to explain how the items in each pair are similar.

PERFORMANCE SUBTESTS

Picture-completion The subject must identify the important part missing from 20 drawings—for example, drawings like a squirrel with no tail.

Picture-arrangement The subject is presented with 10 sets of cartoon drawings and is asked to arrange each set so it will tell a sensible story.

Block-design The subject is presented with blocks that are red on two sides, white on two sides, and half red and half white on the other two. The subject is shown pictures of nine patterns and is asked to duplicate them by arranging the blocks appropriately.

Object-assembly The subject is asked to put together the pieces of four jigsaw puzzles to form familiar objects.

Digit-symbol The subject is presented with a key that matches each of a series of symbols with a different digit. On the lower part of the page is a series of digits, and the subject is given 90 seconds to write the correct symbol next to as many digits as possible.

digit-span test determines the longest sequence of random digits that can be correctly repeated 50% of the time by the patient—most people have a digit span of 7. However, these two forms of memory are among the least likely to be disrupted by brain damage—patients with seriously disturbed memories often have no deficits on either the information or digit-span subtests of the WAIS. Be that as it may, memory problems rarely escape unnoticed. If present, they may be detected by other tests that are included in the common test battery; they may be noticed by the neuropsychologist during discussions with the patient; or they may be reported by the patient or the family of the patient.

■ **LANGUAGE** If a neuropsychological patient has taken the WAIS, deficits in the use of language can be inferred from a low aggregate score on the six verbal subtests. If the WAIS has not been taken, patients can be quickly screened for language-related deficits with the **token test.** Twenty tokens of two different shapes (squares and circles), two different sizes (large and small), and five different colors (white, black, yellow, green, and red) are placed on a table in front of the subject. The test begins with the examiner reading simple instructions—for example, "Touch a red square"—and the subject trying to follow them. Then, the test progresses to more difficult instructions, such as, "Touch the small, red circle and then the large, green square." Finally, the subject is asked to read the instructions aloud and follow them.

■ **LANGUAGE LATERALIZATION** It is usual for one hemisphere to participate more than the other in language-related activities. In most people, the left hemisphere is dominant for language, but in some, the right hemisphere is dominant. A test of language lateralization is often included in the common test because knowing which hemisphere is dominant for language is often useful in interpreting the results of other tests. Furthermore, a test of language lateralization is virtually always given to patients before any surgery that might encroach on the cortical language areas. The results are used to plan the surgery, trying to avoid the language areas if possible.

There are two widely used tests of language lateralization. The sodium amytal test (Wada, 1949) is one, and the dichotic listening test (Kimura, 1973) is the other.

The **sodium amytal test** involves injecting the anesthetic sodium amytal into either the left or right carotid artery of the neck. This temporarily anesthetizes the ipsilateral hemisphere while leaving the contralateral hemisphere largely unaffected. Several tests of language function are quickly administered while the ipsilateral hemisphere is anesthetized. Later, the process is repeated for the other side of the brain. When the injection is on the side dominant for language, the patient is completely mute for about 2 minutes. When the injection is on the nondominant side, there are only a few minor speech problems. Because the sodium amytal test is invasive, it can be administered only for medical reasons—usually to determine the dominant language hemisphere prior to brain surgery.

In the standard version of the **dichotic listening test,** sequences of spoken digits are presented to subjects through stereo headphones. Three digits are presented to one ear at the same time that three different digits are presented to the other ear. Then the subjects are asked to report as many of the six digits as they can. Kimura found that subjects correctly report more of the digits heard by the ear contralateral to their dominant hemisphere for language, as determined by the sodium amytal test.

Tests of Specific Neuropsychological Function

Following analysis of the results of a neuropsychological patient's performance on the common test battery, the neuropsychologist selects a series of specific tests to clarify the nature of the general problems exposed by the common battery. There are hundreds of tests that might be selected: The following are a few of them and some of the considerations that might influence their selection.

■ **MEMORY** Following the discovery of a memory impairment by the common test battery, at least four fundamental questions about the memory impairment must be answered: (1) Do the memory impairments involve *short-term memory, long-term memory,* or both? (2) Are any impairments to long-term memory *anterograde* (affecting the retention of things learned after the damage), *retrograde* (affecting the retention of things learned before the damage), or both? (3) Do any deficits in long-term memory involve *semantic memory* (memory for knowledge of the world) or *episodic memory* (memory for personal experiences)? (4) Are any deficits in long-term memory deficits of *explicit memory* (memories of which the patient is aware and can thus express verbally), *implicit memory* (memories that are demonstrated by the improved performance of the patient without the patient being conscious of them), or both?

Many amnesic patients display severe deficits in explicit memory with no deficits at all in implicit memory. **Repetition priming tests** have proven instrumental in the assessment and study of this pattern. Patients are first shown a list of words and asked to study them; they are not asked to remember them. Then, at a later time, they are asked to complete a list of word fragments, many of which are fragments of words from the

---

Wechsler Adult Intelligence Scale (WAIS). A widely used test of general intelligence.

Digit-span test. A classic test of verbal short-term memory that assesses the ability of subjects to immediately repeat sequences of random digits of various lengths.

Token test. A preliminary test of language deficits that involves following verbal instructions to touch or move tokens of different colors and shapes.

Sodium amytal test. A test involving the anesthetization of first one hemisphere and then the other to determine which hemisphere plays the dominant role in language.

Dichotic listening test. A test of language lateralization in which patients simultaneously hear two different sequences of digits, one sequence in each ear.

Repetition priming tests. Tests that are used to assess implicit memory in neuropsychological patients.

initial list. For example, if "purple" had been in the initial test, "pu__p__ __" could be one of the test word fragments. Amnesic patients often complete the fragments as well as healthy control subjects. But—and this is the really important part—they often have no conscious memory of any of the words in the initial list or even of ever having seen the list. In other words, they display good implicit memory of experiences without explicit memories of them.

■ **LANGUAGE** If a neuropsychological patient turns out to have language-related deficits on the common test battery, a complex series of tests is administered to clarify the nature of the problem. For example, if there is a speech problem, there may be one of three fundamentally different problems: problems of *phonology* (the rules governing the sounds of the language), problems of *syntax* (the grammar of the language), or problems of *semantics* (the meanings of the language). Because brain-damaged patients may have one of these problems but not the others, it is imperative that the testing of all neuropsychological patients with speech problems include tests of each of these three capacities.

Reading aloud can be disrupted in different ways by brain damage, and follow-up tests must be employed that can differentiate between the different patterns of disruption. Some *dyslexic* patients (those with reading problems) remember the rules of pronunciation but have difficulties pronouncing words that do not follow rules and must be pronounced from memory of the specific words (e.g., *come* and *tongue*). Other dyslexic patients pronounce simple familiar words based on memory but have lost the ability to apply the rules of pronunciation—they cannot pronounce nonwords such as *trapple* or *fleeming*.

■ **FRONTAL-LOBE FUNCTION** Injuries to the frontal lobes are common, and the **Wisconsin Card Sorting Test** (see Figure 5.25) is a component of many customized test batteries because it is sensitive to frontal-lobe damage. On each Wisconsin card is either one symbol or two, three, or four identical symbols. The symbols are all either triangles, stars, circles, or crosses; and they are all either red, green, yellow, or blue. At the beginning of the test, the patient is confronted with four stimulus cards that differ from one another in form, color, and number. The task is to correctly sort cards from a deck into piles in front of the stimulus cards. However, the patient does not know whether to sort by form, by color, or by number. The patient begins by guessing and is told after each card has been sorted whether it was sorted correctly or incorrectly. At first, the task is to learn to sort by color. But as soon as the patient makes several consecutive correct responses, the sorting principle is changed to shape or number without any indication other than the fact that responses based on color

Figure 5.25 The Wisconsin Card Sorting Test. This woman is just starting the test; in front of which of the four test cards should she place her first card? She must guess until she can learn which principle—color, shape, or number—should guide her sorting.

become incorrect. Thereafter, each time a new sorting principle is learned, the principle is changed.

Patients with damage to their frontal lobes often continue to sort on the basis of one sorting principle for 100 or more trials after it has become incorrect. They seem to have great difficulty learning and remembering that previously appropriate guidelines for effective behavior are no longer appropriate, a problem called *perseveration*.

Wisconsin Card Sorting Test. A neuropsychological test that evaluates a patient's ability to remember that previously learned rules of behavior are no longer effective and to learn to respond to new rules.

Cognitive neuroscience. An approach to studying the neural bases of cognitive processes that involves a collaboration between cognitive psychologists, computer scientists, and neuroscientists.

Constituent cognitive processes. Simple cognitive processes that combine to produce complex cognitive processes.

Paired-image subtraction technique. Using PET and functional MRI to locate constituent cognitive processes in the brain by producing an image of the difference in brain activity associated with two cognitive tasks that differ in terms of a single constituent cognitive process.

5.7 Behavioral Methods of Cognitive Neuroscience

Cognitive neuroscience is predicated on two related assumptions (see Sarter, Berntson, & Cacioppo, 1996). The first premise is that each complex cognitive process results from the combined activity of simple cognitive processes called **constituent cognitive processes.** The second premise is that each constituent cognitive process is mediated by neural activity in a particular area of the brain. One of the main goals of cognitive neuroscience is to identify the parts of the brain that mediate various constituent cognitive processes.

Computer scientists have made two important contributions to the cognitive neuroscience team effort. First, by developing computer models of complex cognitive processes (e.g., of artificial intelligence), they have provided indications of how constituent processes might interact to produce them. Second, they have provided the computer expertise that has fueled the recent development of techniques for applying PET and functional MRI technology to cognitive neuroscience research.

With the central role played by PET and functional MRI in cutting-edge cognitive neuroscience research, the **paired-image subtraction technique** has become one of the key behavioral research methods in cognitive neuroscience research (see Posner & Raichle, 1994). Let me illustrate this technique with an example from a PET study of single-word processing by Petersen and colleagues (1988). Petersen and his colleagues were interested in locating the parts of the brain that enable a subject to make a word association (to respond to a printed word by saying a related word). You might think this would be an easy task to accomplish by having a subject perform a word-association task while a PET image of the subject's brain is recorded. The problem with this approach is that many parts of the brain that would be active during the test period would have nothing to do with the constituent cognitive process of forming a word association; much of the activity recorded would be associated with other processes such as seeing the words, reading the words, and speaking. The paired-image subtraction technique was developed to deal with this problem.

The paired-image subtraction technique involves obtaining PET or functional MRI images during several different cognitive tasks. Ideally, the tasks are designed so that pairs of them differ from each other in terms of only a single constituent cognitive process. Then, the brain activity associated with that process can be estimated by subtracting the activity in the image associated with one of the two tasks from the activity in the image associated with the other. For example, in one of the tasks in the Petersen et al. study, subjects spent a minute reading aloud printed nouns as they appeared on a screen; in another, they observed the same nouns on the screen but responded to each of them by saying aloud an associated verb (e.g., *truck—drive*). Then, Petersen and his colleagues subtracted the activity in the images that they recorded during the two tasks to obtain a *difference image.*

The difference image illustrated the areas of the brain that were specifically involved in the constituent cognitive process of forming the word association; the activity associated with fixating on the screen, seeing the nouns, saying the words, and so on was eliminated by the subtraction (see Figure 5.26).

Figure 5.26 The paired–image subtraction technique, which is commonly employed in cognitive neuroscience. Here we see that the brain of the subject is generally active when the subject looks at a flickering checkerboard pattern (stimulation condition). However, if the activity that occurred when the subject stared at a blank screen is subtracted, it becomes apparent that the perception of the flashing checkerboard pattern was associated with an increase in activity in the occipital lobe. The individual difference images of five subjects were averaged to produce the ultimate mean difference image.

(PET scans courtesy of Marcus Raichle, Mallinckrodt Institute of Radiology, Washington University Medical Center.)

Another problem involved in using PET and functional MRI to locate constituent cognitive processes is the *noise* associated with random cerebral events that occur during the test—for example, thinking about a sudden pang of hunger, noticing a fly on the screen, or wondering whether the test will last much longer. The noise created by such events can be significantly reduced with a technique discussed earlier in this chapter: *signal averaging.* By averaging the difference images obtained from repetitions of the same tests, the researchers can greatly increase the *signal-to-noise ratio.* It is standard practice to average the images obtained from several subjects; the resulting averaged difference image emphasizes areas of activity that are common to most of the subjects and deemphasizes areas of activity that are peculiar to a few of them (see Figure 5.26). This is a potential problem, but in at least one PET study (Hunton et al., 1996), the average PET scans were found to be quite similar to the PET scans of individual subjects.

5.8 Biopsychological Paradigms of Animal Behavior

Noteworthy examples of the behavioral paradigms used to study the biopsychology of laboratory species are provided here under three headings: (1) paradigms for the assessment of species-common behaviors, (2) traditional conditioning paradigms, and (3) seminatural animal learning paradigms. In each case, the focus is on methods used to study the behavior of the laboratory rat, the most common subject of biopsychological research.

Paradigms for Assessment of Species-Common Behaviors

Many of the behavioral paradigms that are used in biopsychological research are used to study species-common behaviors. **Species-common behaviors** are those that are displayed by virtually all members of a species, or at least by all those of the same age and sex. Commonly studied species-common behaviors include grooming, swimming, eating, drinking, copulating, fighting, and nest building. Described here are the open-field test, tests of aggressive and defensive behavior, and tests of sexual behavior.

■ **OPEN-FIELD TEST** In the **open-field test** the subject is placed in a large, barren chamber, and its activity is recorded. It is usual to measure general activity either with an automated activity recorder or by drawing lines on the floor of the chamber and counting the number of line-crossings during the test. It is also common in the open-field test to count the number of *boluses* (pieces of excrement) that were dropped by an animal during the test. Low activity scores and high bolus counts are frequently used as indicators of fearfulness. Fearful rats are highly **thigmotaxic;** that is, they rarely venture away from the walls of the test chamber and rarely engage in such activities as rearing and grooming. Rats are often fearful when they are first placed in a strange open field, but this fearfulness usually declines with repeated exposure to the same open field.

■ **TESTS OF AGGRESSIVE AND DEFENSIVE BEHAVIOR** Typical patterns of aggressive and defensive behavior can be observed and measured during combative encounters between the dominant male rat of an established colony and a smaller male intruder (see Blanchard & Blanchard, 1988). This is called the **colony–intruder paradigm.** The behaviors of the dominant male are considered to be aggressive and those of the hapless intruder defensive. The dominant male of the colony (the *alpha male*) moves sideways toward the intruder, with its hair erect. When it nears the intruder, it tries to push the intruder off balance and to deliver bites to its back and flanks. The defender tries to protect its back and flanks by rearing up on its hind legs and pushing the attacker away with its forepaws or by rolling onto its back. Thus piloerection, lateral approach, and flank-and back-biting indicate conspecific aggression in the rat; freezing, boxing (rearing and pushing away), and rolling over indicate defensiveness. Some tests of rat defensive behavior assess reactivity to the experimenter rather than to another rat. For example, it is common to rate the resistance of a rat to being picked up—no resistance being the lowest category and biting the highest—and to use the score as one measure of defensiveness (Kalynchuk et al., 1997).

The **elevated plus maze** is a test of defensiveness that is commonly used to study the *anxiolytic* (antianxiety) effects of drugs in rats. It is a four-armed plus-sign-shaped maze that is typically mounted 50 centimeters above the floor. Two of the arms of the maze have sides, and two do not. The measure of defensiveness, or anxiety, is the proportion of time the rats spend in the protected closed arms rather than on the exposed arms. Anxiolytic drugs such as the *benzodiazepines* significantly increase the proportion of time that rats spend on the open arms (see Pellow et al., 1985).

■ TESTS OF SEXUAL BEHAVIOR Most attempts to study the physiological bases of rat sexual behavior have focused on the copulatory act itself. The male mounts the female from behind and clasps her hindquarters. If the female is receptive, she responds by assuming the **lordosis** posture; that is, she sticks her hindquarters in the air, she bends her back in a U, and she deflects her tail to the side. During some mounts, the male inserts his penis into the female's vagina; this act is called **intromission.** After intromission, the male dismounts by jumping backwards. He then returns a few seconds later to mount and intromit once again. Following about 10 such cycles of mounting, intromitting, and dismounting, the male mounts, intromits, and **ejaculates** (ejects his sperm).

Three common measures of male rat sexual behavior are the number of mounts required to achieve intromission, the number of intromissions required to achieve ejaculation, and the interval between ejaculation and the reinitiation of mounting. The most common measures of female rat sexual behavior are the **lordosis quotient** (the proportion of mounts that elicit lordosis) and the degree of back bending during lordosis.

Traditional Conditioning Paradigms

Learning paradigms play a major role in biopsychological research for three reasons. The first is that learning is a phenomenon of primary interest to psychologists. The second is that learning paradigms provide an effective technology for producing and controlling animal behavior. Because animals cannot follow instructions from the experimenter, it is often necessary to train them to behave in a fashion consistent with the goals of the experiment. The third reason is that it is possible to infer much about the sensory, motor, motivational, and cognitive state of an animal from its ability to learn various tasks and to perform various learned responses.

If you have taken a previous course in psychology, you will likely be familiar with the Pavlovian and operant conditioning paradigms. In the **Pavlovian conditioning paradigm,** the experimenter pairs an initially neutral stimulus called a *conditional stimulus* (e.g., a tone or a light) with an *unconditional stimulus* (e.g., meat powder)—a stimulus that elicits an *unconditional* (reflexive) *response* (e.g., salivation). As a result of these pairings, the conditional stimulus eventually acquires the capacity, when administered alone, to elicit a *conditional response* (e.g., salivation)—a response that is often, but not always, similar to the unconditional response.

In the **operant conditioning paradigm,** the rate at which a particular voluntary response (such as a lever press) is emitted is increased by *reinforcement* or decreased by *punishment.* One of the most widely used operant conditioning paradigms in biopsychology is the self-stimulation paradigm. In the **self-stimulation paradigm,** animals press a lever to administer reinforcing electrical stimulation to certain "pleasure centers" in their brains. Another operant conditioning paradigm that is widely used in biopsychology is the **drug self-administration paradigm,** in which animals inject drugs into themselves through implanted cannulas by pressing a lever.

Seminatural Animal Learning Paradigms

In addition to Pavlovian and operant conditioning paradigms, biopsychologists use animal learning paradigms that have been specifically designed to mimic situations that an animal might encounter in its natural environment. Each of the following "seminatural" animal learning paradigms is discussed in the following paragraphs: the conditioned taste aversion, radial arm maze, Morris water maze, and conditioned defensive burying paradigms.

■ CONDITIONED TASTE AVERSION A **conditioned taste aversion** is the aversion that develops to tastes of food whose consumption has been followed by illness (see Garcia & Koelling, 1966). In the standard conditioned taste aversion experiment, rats receive an *emetic* (a nausea-inducing drug) after they consume a food with an unfamiliar taste. On the basis of this single conditioning trial, the rats learn to avoid the taste.

Species-common behaviors. Behaviors that are displayed in the same manner by virtually all like members of a species.

Open-field test. Scoring the behavior of an animal in a large, barren chamber.

Thigmotaxic. Tending to stay near the walls of an open field.

Colony–intruder paradigm. A paradigm for the study of aggressive and defensive behavior in male rats; a small male intruder rat is placed in an established colony in order to study the aggressive responses of the colony's alpha male and the defensive responses of the intruder.

Elevated plus maze. A test of defensiveness or anxiety in rats that assesses the tendency of rats to avoid the two open arms of an elevated plus-sign-shaped maze.

Lordosis. The female rat's rump-up, tail-to-the-side posture of sexual receptivity.

Intromission. Insertion of the penis into the vagina.

Ejaculates. Ejects sperm.

Lordosis quotient. The proportion of mounts that produce lordosis.

Pavlovian conditioning paradigm. A paradigm in which the experimenter pairs an initially neutral stimulus (conditional stimulus) with a stimulus (unconditional stimulus) that elicits a reflexive response (unconditional response); after several pairings, the neutral stimulus elicits a response (conditional response).

Operant conditioning paradigm. A paradigm in which the rate of a particular voluntary response is increased by reinforcement or decreased by punishment.

Self-stimulation paradigm. A paradigm in which animals press a lever to administer reinforcing electrical stimulation to their own brains.

Drug self-administration paradigm. An operant conditioning paradigm in which animals press a lever to administer reinforcing drugs to themselves.

Conditioned taste aversion. The aversion developed by animals to tastes that have been followed by illness.

The ability of rats to readily learn the relationship between a particular taste and subsequent illness unquestionably increases their chances of survival in their natural environment, where potentially edible substances are not routinely screened by government agencies. Rats and many other animals are *neophobic* (afraid of new things); thus, when they first encounter a new food, they consume it in only small quantities. If they subsequently become ill, they will not consume it again. Conditioned aversions also develop to familiar tastes, but these typically require more than a single trial to be learned.

Humans also develop conditioned taste aversions. Cancer patients have been reported to develop aversions to foods consumed before nausea-inducing chemotherapy (Bernstein & Webster, 1980). Many of you will be able to testify on the basis of personal experience about the effectiveness of conditioned taste aversions. I still have vivid memories of a long-ago batch of laboratory punch that I overzealously consumed after eating two pieces of blueberry pie. But that is another story—albeit a particularly colorful one.

> The 1950s was a time of sock hops, sodas at Al's, crewcuts, and drive-in movies. In the animal-behavior laboratory, it was a time of lever presses, key pecks, and shuttles made in response to flashing lights, tones, and geometric patterns. Then, along came rock 'n' roll and research on conditioned taste aversion: Things have not been the same since.

These words communicate just how much the study of conditioned taste aversion changed the thinking of psychologists about conditioning. It challenged three widely accepted principles of learning (see Revusky & Garcia, 1970) that had grown out of research on traditional operant and Pavlovian conditioning paradigms. First, it challenged the view that animal conditioning is always a gradual step-by-step process; robust taste aversions can be established in only a single trial. Second, it showed that *temporal contiguity* is not essential for conditioning; rats acquire taste aversions even when they do not become ill until several hours after eating. Third, it challenged the *principle of equipotentiality*—the view that conditioning proceeds in basically the same manner regardless of the particular stimuli and responses under investigation. Rats appear to be particularly well prepared to learn associations between tastes and illness; it is only with great difficulty that they learn relations between the color of food and nausea or between taste and footshock.

■ **RADIAL ARM MAZE** The radial arm maze taps the well-developed spatial abilities of rodents. The survival of rats in the wild depends on their ability to navigate quickly and accurately through their environment and to learn which locations in it are likely to contain food and water. This task is much more complex for a rodent than it is for us. Most of us obtain food from locations

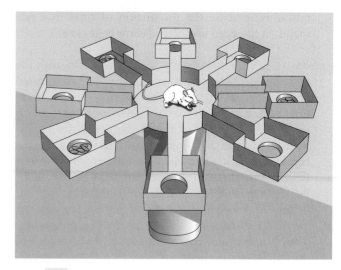

Figure 5.27 A radial arm maze.

where the supply is continually replenished; we go to the market confident that we will find enough food to satisfy our needs. In contrast, the foraging rat must learn, and retain, a complex pattern of spatially coded details. It must not only learn where morsels of food are likely to be found but must also remember which of these sites it has recently stripped of their booty so as not to revisit them too soon. Designed by Olton and Samuelson (1976) to study these spatial abilities, the **radial arm maze** (see Figure 5.27) is an array of arms—usually eight or more—radiating from a central starting area. At the end of each arm is a food cup, which may or may not be baited, depending on the purpose of the experiment.

In one version of the radial arm maze paradigm, rats are placed each day in a radial arm maze that has the same arms baited each day. After a few days of experience, rats rarely visit unbaited arms at all, and they rarely visit baited arms more than once in the same day—even when control procedures make it impossible for them to recognize odors left during previous visits to an arm or to make their visits in a systematic sequence. Because the arms are identical, rats must orient themselves in the maze with reference to external room cues; thus their performance can be disrupted by rotation of the maze or by changes in the appearance of the room.

■ **MORRIS WATER MAZE** Another seminatural learning paradigm that has been designed to study the spatial abilities of rats is the **Morris water maze** (Morris, 1981). The rats are placed in a circular, featureless pool of cool milky water, in which they must swim until they discover the escape platform—which is invisible just beneath the surface of the water. The rats are allowed to rest on the platform before being returned to the water for another trial. Despite the fact that the starting point is varied from trial to trial, the rats learn after only a few trials to swim directly to the platform, presumably by using spatial cues from the room as a reference. The Morris water maze has proved extremely useful for assessing the navigational skills of lesioned or drugged animals (e.g., Kolb, 1989).

■ CONDITIONED DEFENSIVE BURYING
Yet another seminatural learning paradigm that is useful in biopsychological research is the conditioned defensive burying paradigm (e.g., Pinel & Mana, 1989; Pinel & Treit, 1978). In the **conditioned defensive burying** experiments, rats receive a single aversive stimulus (e.g., a shock, airblast, or noxious odor) from an object mounted on the wall of the chamber just above the floor, which is littered with bedding material. After a single trial, almost every rat learns that the test object is a threat and responds by spraying bedding material at the test object with its head and forepaws (see Figure 5.28). Treit has shown that antianxiety drugs reduce the amount of conditioned defensive burying and has used the paradigm to study the neurochemistry of anxiety (e.g., Treit, 1987). The burying response does not develop normally in rats that have been reared in cages with wire-mesh floors rather than bedding-covered floors (Pinel et al., 1989).

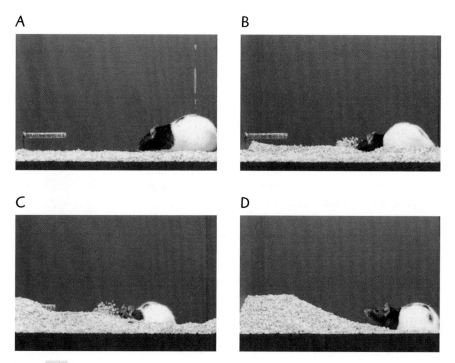

Figure 5.28 A rat burying a test object from which it has just received a single mild shock. (Photograph by Jack Wong.)

Radial arm maze. A maze in which several arms radiate out from a central starting chamber; it is commonly used to study spatial learning in rats.
Morris water maze. A pool of milky water with a goal plat- form invisible just beneath its surface; it is used to study the ability of rats to learn spatial locations.
Conditioned defensive burying. The burial of a source of aversive stimulation by rodents.

CONCLUSION

This chapter has introduced you to the research methods of biopsychology. In Part 1—the "brain half" of the chapter—you learned about methods of visualizing the living human brain (5.1); about noninvasive methods of recording human physiological activity (5.2); about invasive lesion, stimulation, and recording methods that are used in biopsychological research on laboratory animals (5.3); about pharmacological research methods that are used in biopsychological research (5.4), and about methods of genetic engineering (5.5). In Part 2—the "behavior half" of the chapter—you learned about neuropsychological testing (5.6), behavioral research methods of cognitive neuroscience (5.7), and biopsychological paradigms of animal behavior (5.8).

Before you leave the chapter, you need to appreciate that to be effective these methods must be used to-

gether. Seldom, if ever, is an important biopsychological issue resolved by a single set of methods. The reason for this is that neither the methods used to manipulate the brain nor the methods used to assess the behavioral consequences of these manipulations are totally selective; there are no methods of manipulating the brain that change only a single aspect of brain function, and there are no measures of behavior that reflect only a single psychological process. Accordingly, lines of research that use a single set of methods can often be interpreted in more than one way and thus cannot provide unequivocal evidence for any one interpretation. Typically, important research questions are resolved only when several methods are brought to bear on a single problem. This approach, as you learned in Chapter 1, is called *converging operations*.

FOOD FOR THOUGHT

1. The current rate of progress in the development of new and better brain scanning devices will soon render behavioral tests of brain damage obsolete. Discuss.

2. You are taking a physiological psychology laboratory course, and your instructor gives you two rats: one rat with a lesion in an unknown structure and one normal rat. How would you test the rats to determine which has the lesion? How would your approach differ from what you might use to test a human patient suspected of having brain damage?

KEY TERMS

2-deoxyglucose (2-DG) *(p. 109)*
Alpha waves *(p. 112)*
Aspiration *(p. 118)*
Autoradiography *(p. 122)*
Behavioral paradigm *(p. 126)*
Bregma *(p. 117)*
Cannula *(p. 122)*
Cerebral angiography *(p. 107)*
Cerebral dialysis *(p. 123)*
Cognitive neuroscience *(p. 131)*
Colony–intruder paradigm *(p. 132)*
Computed tomography (CT) *(p. 107)*
Conditioned defensive burying paradigm *(p. 135)*
Conditioned taste aversion *(p. 133)*
Constituent cognitive processes *(p. 131)*
Contrast X-ray techniques *(p. 107)*
Cryogenic blockade *(p. 119)*

Dichotic listening test *(p. 129)*
Digit-span test *(p. 128)*
Drug self-administration paradigm *(p. 133)*
Ejaculates *(p. 133)*
Electrocardiogram (ECG or EKG) *(p. 116)*
Electrochemistry *(p. 123)*
Electroencephalography *(p. 112)*
Electromyography *(p. 114)*
Electrooculography *(p. 115)*
Elevated plus maze *(p. 132)*
Event-related potentials (ERPs) *(p. 113)*
Far-field potentials *(p. 113)*
Functional MRI *(p. 110)*
Gene knockout techniques *(p. 125)*
Gene replacement techniques *(p. 125)*
Hypertension *(p. 116)*
Immunocytochemistry *(p. 124)*
In situ hybridization *(p. 124)*

Intromission *(p. 133)*
Lordosis *(p. 133)*
Lordosis quotient *(p. 133)*
Magnetic resonance imaging (MRI) *(p. 108)*
Morris water maze *(p. 134)*
Neurotoxins *(p. 122)*
Open-field test *(p. 132)*
Operant conditioning paradigm *(p. 133)*
P300 wave *(p. 113)*
Paired-image subtraction technique *(p. 131)*
Pavlovian conditioning paradigm *(p. 133)*
Plethysmography *(p. 116)*
Pneumoencephalography *(p. 107)*
Positron emission tomography (PET) *(p. 109)*
Radial arm maze *(p. 134)*
Repetition priming tests *(p. 129)*

Self-stimulation paradigm *(p. 133)*
Sensory evoked potential *(p. 113)*
Signal averaging *(p. 113)*
Skin conductance level (SCL) *(p. 116)*
Skin conductance response (SCR) *(p. 116)*
Sodium amytal test *(p. 129)*
Species-common behaviors *(p. 132)*
Stereotaxic atlas *(p. 117)*
Stereotaxic instrument *(p. 117)*
Thigmotaxic *(p. 132)*
Token test *(p. 129)*
Transgenic mice *(p. 125)*
Wechsler Adult Intelligence Scale (WAIS) *(p. 128)*
Wisconsin Card Sorting Test *(p. 130)*

ADDITIONAL READING

The following are provocative discussions of two behavioral testing strategies:

Jacobs, W. J., Blackburn, J. R., Buttrick, M., Harpur, T. J., Kennedy, D., Mana, M. J., MacDonald, M. A., McPherson, L. M., Paul, D., & Pfaus, J. G. (1988). Observations. *Psychobiology, 16,* 3–19.

Whishaw, I. Q., Kolb, B., & Sutherland, R. J. (1983). The analysis of behavior in the laboratory rat. In T. E. Robinson (Ed.), *Behavioral approaches to brain research.* New York: Oxford University Press.

This is an interesting, colorful, and simple introduction to modern brain-imaging techniques and to the emerging field of cognitive neuroscience:

Posner, M. I., & Raichle, M. E. (1994). *Images of the mind.* New York: Scientific American Library.

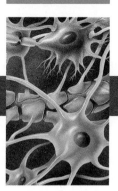

Human Brain Damage and Animal Models

6

The study of human brain damage has two major goals: the furtherance of our understanding of the functions of the healthy human brain and the development of effective strategies for treatment. This chapter is an introduction to human brain damage that focuses on both of these goals.

The first section of this chapter describes common causes of human brain damage; the second section describes several major neuropsychological disorders; and the third, and final, section discusses the investigation of human neuropsychological disorders through the study of animal models. But first the case of Professor P. introduces you to the personal tragedy that underlies the academic discourse that follows.

One night Professor P. sat at his desk staring at a drawing of the cranial nerves, much like the one in Appendix III, of this book. As he mulled over the location and function of each cranial nerve (see Appendix IV), the painful truth became impossible for him to deny. The irony of the situation was that Professor P. was a neuroscientist, all too familiar with what he was experiencing.

His symptoms started subtly, with slight deficits in balance. He probably wouldn't have even noticed them except that his experience as a mountaineer had taught him to pay attention to such things. Professor P. chalked these occasional lurches up to aging—after all, he thought to himself, he was past his prime, and things like this happen. Similarly, his doctor didn't seem to think that it was a problem worth looking into, but Professor P. monitored his symptoms carefully nevertheless. Three years later, his balance problems still unabated, Professor P. really started to worry. He was trying to talk with a colleague on the phone but was not having much success because of what he thought was a bad connection. Then, he changed the phone to his other ear, and all of a sudden, the faint voice on the other end became louder. He tried this switch several times over the ensuing days, and the conclusion became inescapable: Professor P. was going deaf in his right ear.

Professor P. immediately made an appointment with his GP, who referred him to a specialist. After a cursory and poorly controlled hearing test, the specialist gave him good news. "You're fine, Professor P.; lots of people experience hearing loss when they reach middle age, and your problems are not serious enough to worry about." To this day, Professor P. regrets that he did not insist on a second opinion; his problem would have been so much easier to deal with at that stage.

It was about one year later that Professor P. sat staring at the illustration of the cranial nerves. By then he had begun to experience numbness on the right side of his mouth; he was having minor problems swallowing; and his right tear ducts were not releasing enough tears.

There he sat staring at the point where the auditory and vestibular nerves come together to form the 8th cranial nerve (the auditory-vestibular nerve). He knew it was there, and he knew that it was large enough to be affecting the 5th, 6th, 7th, 9th, and 10th cranial nerves as well, but he didn't know what it was: a tumor, a stroke, an angioma, an infection? Was he going to die? Was his death going to be terrible and lingering as his brain and intellect gradually deteriorated?

He didn't make an appointment with his doctor right away. A friend of his was conducting a brain MRI study, and Professor P. volunteered to be a control subject, knowing that his problem would show up on the scan. It did: a large tumor sitting, as predicted, on the right 8th cranial nerve.

Then, MRI in hand, Professor P. went to his GP, who referred him to a neurologist, who in turn referred him to a neurosurgeon. Several stressful weeks later, Professor P. found himself on life support in the intensive care unit of his local hospital, hands tied to the bed and tubes emanating seemingly from every part of his body. You see, the tumor was so convoluted that it took 6 hours to remove; and during the 6 hours that Professor P.'s brain was exposed, air entered his circulatory system, and he developed pneumonia. Near death and hallucinating from the morphine, Professor P. thought he heard his wife, Maggie, calling for help and tried to go to her assistance: That is why he was tied down. One gentle morphine-steeped professor was no match for five burly nurses intent on saving his life.

Professor P.'s 8th cranial nerve was transected during his surgery, which has left him permanently deaf and without vestibular function on the right side. He was also left with partial hemifacial paralysis, including serious blinking and tearing problems, but these facial symptoms have largely cleared up.

Professor P. has now returned to his students, his research, and his writing, hoping that the tumor was completely removed and that he will not have to endure another surgery. Indeed, at the very moment that I am writing these words, Professor P. is working on the forthcoming edition of his textbook. . . . If it has not yet occurred to you, I am Professor P.

Tumor (neoplasm). A mass of cells that grows independently of the rest of the body.

Meningiomas. Tumors that grow between the meninges.

Encapsulated tumors. Tumors that grow within their own membrane.

Benign tumors. Tumors that are surgically removable with little risk of further growth in the body.

Infiltrating tumors. Tumors that grow diffusely through surrounding tissue.

Malignant tumors. Tumors that may continue to grow in the body even after attempted surgical removal.

Metastatic tumors. Tumors that originate in one organ and spread to another.

Causes of Brain Damage

This section of the chapter provides an introduction to six causes of brain damage: brain tumors, cerebrovascular disorders, closed-head injuries, infections of the brain, neurotoxins, and genetic factors. It concludes with a discussion of programmed cell death, which mediates many forms of brain damage.

Brain Tumors

A **tumor** or **neoplasm** (literally, "new growth") is a mass of cells that grows independently of the rest of the body. In other words, it is a cancer.

About 20% of tumors found in the human brain are **meningiomas** (see Figure 6.1)—tumors that grow between the *meninges,* the three membranes that cover the central nervous system. All meningiomas are **encapsulated tumors**—tumors that grow within their own membrane. As a result, they are particularly easy to identify on a CAT scan, they can influence the function of the brain only by the pressure they exert on surrounding tissue, and they are almost always **benign tumors**—tumors that are surgically removable with little risk of further growth in the body.

Unfortunately, encapsulation is the exception rather than the rule when it comes to brain tumors. With the exception of meningiomas, most brain tumors are infiltrating. **Infiltrating tumors** are those that grow diffusely through surrounding tissue. As a result, they are usually **malignant tumors;** it is difficult to remove them completely, and any cancerous tissue that remains after surgery continues to grow.

About 10% of brain tumors do not originate in the brain. They grow from infiltrating tumor fragments carried to the brain by the bloodstream from some other part of the body. (The brain is a particularly fertile ground for tumor growth.) These tumors are called **metastatic tumors;** *metastasis* refers to the transmission of disease from one organ to another. Most metastatic brain tumors originate as cancers of the lungs. Obviously, the chance of recovering from a cancer that has already attacked two or more separate sites is slim at best. Figure 6.2 on page 140 illustrates the ravages of metastasis.

Infiltrating brain tumors are usually untreatable, but there is reason for optimism. Tumor growth results from the dysfunction of mechanisms that regulate normal cell division and growth. It has been discovered that normal cells contain *tumor suppressor genes,* which become dysfunctional during the growth of certain types of tumors. Efforts to understand and treat tumor growth are focusing on these genes (see Sager, 1989; Weinberg, 1991).

Fortunately, my tumor was encapsulated. Encapsulated tumors that grow on the 8th cranial nerve are referred to as *acoustic neuromas* (neuromas are tumors

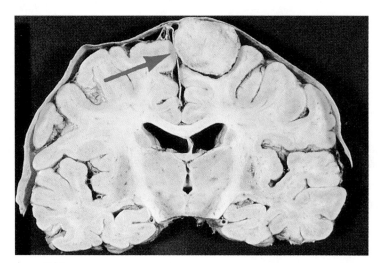

Figure **6.1** A meningioma.

(Courtesy of Kenneth Berry, Head of Neuropathology, Vancouver General Hospital.)

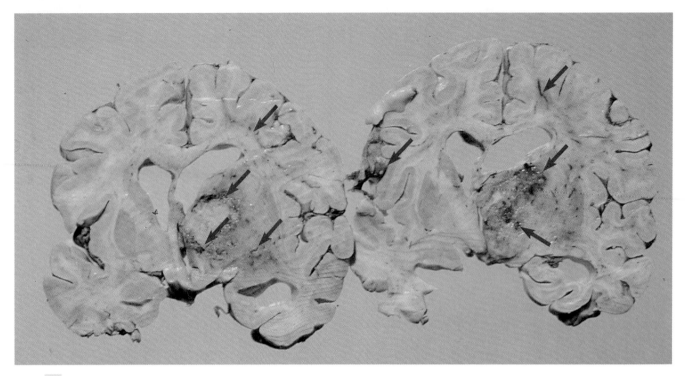

Figure 6.2 Multiple metastatic brain tumors. The arrows indicate some of the more advanced areas of metastatic tumor development.

that grow on nerves or tracts). Figure 6.3 is an MRI scan of my acoustic neuroma, the very same scan that I took to my neurosurgeon.

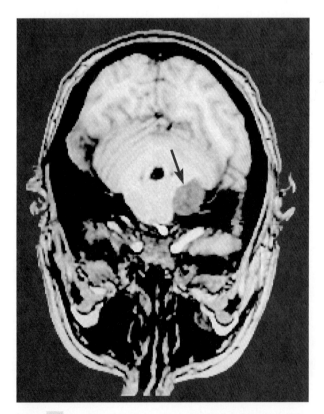

Figure 6.3 An MRI of Professor P.'s acoustic neuroma. The arrow indicates the tumor.

Cerebrovascular Disorders

Strokes are sudden-onset cerebrovascular disorders that cause brain damage. Two types of cerebrovascular disorders lead to strokes: cerebral hemorrhage and cerebral ischemia (pronounced "iss-KEEM-ee-a"). In the United States, stroke is the third leading cause of death and the most common cause of adult disability. Common consequences of stroke are amnesia, aphasia (language difficulties), paralysis, and coma (see Zivin & Choi, 1991). The area of dead or dying tissue produced by a stroke is called an *infarct*.

■ **CEREBRAL HEMORRHAGE** Cerebral hemorrhage (bleeding in the brain) occurs when a cerebral blood vessel ruptures and blood seeps into the surrounding neural tissue and damages it. Bursting aneurysms are a common cause of intracerebral hemorrhage. An **aneurysm** is a pathological balloonlike dilation that forms in the wall of a blood vessel at a point where the elasticity of the vessel wall is defective. Aneurisms can be **congenital** (present at birth) or can result from exposure to vascular poisons or infection. Individuals who have aneurysms should make every effort to avoid high blood pressure.

■ **CEREBRAL ISCHEMIA** Cerebral ischemia is a disruption of the blood supply to an area of the brain. The three main causes of cerebral ischemia are thrombosis, embolism, and arteriosclerosis. In **thrombosis,** a plug

6 HUMAN BRAIN DAMAGE AND ANIMAL MODELS

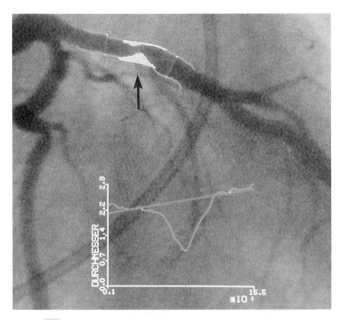

Figure 6.4 An angiogram that illustrates narrowing of the carotid artery (see arrow), the main pathway of blood to the brain. Compare this angiogram with the normal angiogram in Figure 5.1.

and Ca^{++} ions to enter the postsynaptic neurons. The glutamate receptors that are most involved in this reaction are the **NMDA (N-methyl-D-aspartate) receptors.** The excessive internal concentrations of Na$^+$ and Ca^{++} ions affect the postsynaptic neurons in two ways: They trigger the release of excessive amounts of glutamate from them, thus spreading the toxic cascade to yet other neurons; and they trigger a sequence of reactions that ultimately kills the postsynaptic neurons. (See Figure 6.5 on page 142.)

Ischemia-induced brain damage has three important properties (Krieglstein, 1997). First, it takes a while to develop. Soon after a temporary cerebral ischemic episode, say an episode 10 minutes in duration, there usually is little or no evidence of brain damage; however, substantial neuron loss can often be detected several days later. Second, ischemia-induced brain damage does not occur equally in all parts of the brain; particularly susceptible are neurons in certain areas of the hippocampus. Third, the mechanisms of ischemia-induced brain damage vary somewhat from structure to structure.

An exciting implication of the discovery that excessive glutamate release causes much of the brain damage associated with stroke is the possibility of preventing stroke-related brain damage by blocking the glutaminergic cascade. Indeed, it has already been shown that *NMDA receptor blockers* or *calcium-channel blockers* administered immediately after a stroke can substantially reduce the subsequent development of brain damage in experimental animals (e.g., Kogure & Kogure, 1997; Nicoletti et al., 1996). The search is now on for a therapeutic drug that is effective and safe for use in human stroke victims (see Plum, 1997).

Closed-Head Injuries

It is not necessary for the skull to be penetrated for the brain to be seriously damaged. In fact, any blow to the head should be treated with extreme caution, particu-

called a *thrombus* is formed and blocks blood flow at the site of its formation. A thrombus may be composed of a blood clot, fat, oil, an air bubble, tumor cells, or any combination thereof. **Embolism** is similar except that the plug, called an *embolus* in this case, is carried by the blood from a larger vessel, where it was formed, to a smaller one, where it becomes lodged; in essence, an embolus is just a thrombus that has taken a trip. In **arteriosclerosis,** the walls of blood vessels thicken and the channels narrow, usually as the result of fat deposits; this narrowing can eventually lead to complete blockage of the blood vessels. The *angiogram* in Figure 6.4 illustrates partial blockage of one carotid artery.

Paradoxically, some of the brain's own neurotransmitters, specifically the *excitatory amino acids,* play a key role in the development of ischemia-produced brain damage (see Schousboe et al., 1997; Szatkowski & Attwell, 1994). It was once assumed—quite reasonably—that the disruption of the oxygen and glucose supply was the key causal factor in stroke-related brain damage; however, it now appears that much of the brain damage associated with stroke is a consequence of excessive release of excitatory amino acid neurotransmitters, in particular **glutamate,** the brain's most prevalent excitatory neurotransmitter.

Here is how this mechanism is thought to work (see Rothman, 1994; Zivin & Choi, 1991). After a blood vessel becomes blocked, many of the blood-deprived neurons become overactive and release excessive quantities of glutamate. The excessive glutamate in turn overactivates glutamate receptors in the membranes of postsynaptic neurons. Then, the overactivity of the postsynaptic glutamate receptors allows large numbers of Na$^+$

Strokes. Sudden-onset cerebrovascular disorders that cause brain damage.

Cerebral hemorrhage. Bleeding in the brain.

Aneurysm. A pathological balloonlike dilation that forms in the wall of a blood vessel at a point where the elasticity of the vessel wall is defective.

Congenital. Present at birth.

Cerebral ischemia. A disruption of blood supply to an area of the brain.

Thrombosis. The blockage of blood flow by a plug (a thrombus) at the site of its formation.

Embolism. The blockage of blood flow in a smaller blood vessel by a plug that was formed in a larger blood vessel and carried by the bloodstream to the smaller one.

Arteriosclerosis. A condition in which blood vessels are blocked by the accumulation of fat deposits in the vessel walls.

Glutamate. The brain's most prevalent exitatory neurotransmitter, whose excessive release causes much of the brain damage resulting from cerebral ischemia.

NMDA (N-methyl-D-aspartate) receptors. Glutamate receptors that play a key role in the development of stroke-induced brain damage.

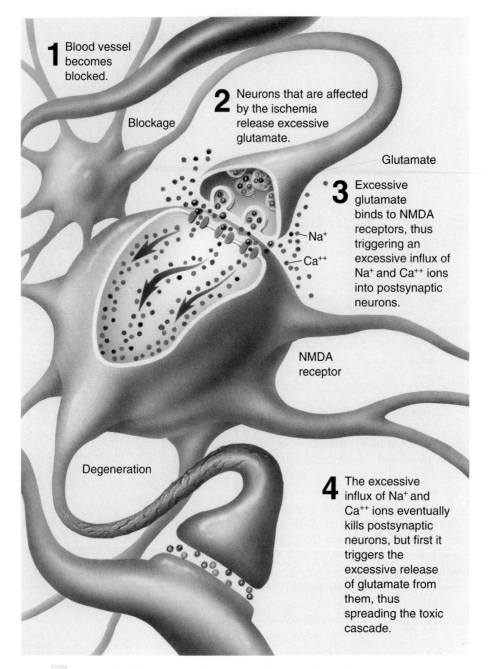

Figure 6.5 The cascade of events by which the stroke-induced release of glutamate kills neurons.

larly when confusion, sensorimotor disturbances, or loss of consciousness ensues. Brain injuries produced by blows that do not penetrate the skull are called *closed-head injuries.*

Contusions are closed-head injuries that involve damage to the cerebral circulatory system. Such damage produces internal hemorrhaging, which results in a hematoma. A **hematoma** is a localized collection of clotted blood in an organ or tissue—in other words, a bruise.

It is paradoxical that the very hardness of the skull, which protects the brain from penetrating injuries, is the major factor in the development of contusions.

Contusions from closed-head injuries occur when the brain slams against the inside of the skull. As Figure 6.6 illustrates, blood from such injuries can accumulate in the *subdural space*—the space between the dura mater and arachnoid membrane—and severely distort the surrounding neural tissue.

It may surprise you to learn that contusions frequently occur on the side of the brain opposite the side struck by a blow. The reason for such so-called **contrecoup injuries** is that the blow causes the brain to strike the inside of the skull on the other side of the head.

When there is a disturbance of consciousness following a blow to the head and there is no evidence of a

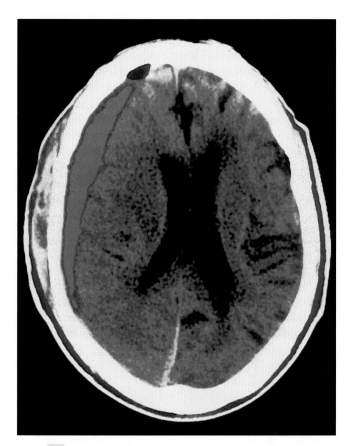

Figure 6.6 A CAT scan of a subdural hematoma. Notice that the subdural hematoma has displaced the left lateral ventricle.

contusion or other structural damage, the diagnosis is **concussion.** It is commonly assumed that concussions entail a temporary disruption of normal cerebral function with no long-term damage. However, the punch-drunk syndrome suggests otherwise. The **punch-drunk syndrome** is the **dementia** (general intellectual deterioration) and cerebral scarring that is observed in boxers and other individuals who experience repeated concussions. If there were no damage associated with a single concussion, the effects of many concussions could not summate to produce severe damage. One of the most dangerous aspects of concussion is the complacency with which it is regarded. Flippant references to it, such as "having one's bell rung," do little to communicate its hazards.

> Jerry Quarry thumps his hard belly with both fists. Smiles at the sound. Like a stone against a tree.
>
> "Feel it," he says proudly, punching himself again and again.
>
> He pounds big, gnarled fists into meaty palms. Cocks his head. Stares. Vacant blue eyes. Punch-drunk at 50. Medical name: *Dementia pugilistic* [punch-drunk syndrome]. Cause: Thousands of punches to the head.
>
> A top heavyweight contender in the 1960s and '70s, Quarry now needs help shaving, showering, putting on shoes and socks. Soon, probably, diapers. His older brother, James,

cuts meat into little pieces so he won't choke. Jerry smiles like a kid. Shuffles like an old man.

> Slow, slurred speech. Random thoughts snagged on branches in a dying brain. Memories twisted. Voices no one else hears. (Steve Wilstein, Associated Press, 1995)

Infections of the Brain

An invasion of the brain by microorganisms is a *brain infection,* and the resulting inflammation is **encephalitis.** There are two common types of brain infections: bacterial infections and viral infections.

■ **BACTERIAL INFECTIONS** When bacteria infect the brain, they often lead to the formation of *cerebral abscesses*—pockets of pus in the brain. They also often attack and inflame the meninges, creating a disorder known as **meningitis.** Penicillin and other antibiotics are no panacea for bacterial brain infections. They can eliminate the infection, but they cannot reverse brain damage that has already been produced.

Syphilis is one bacterial brain infection you have likely heard about. Syphilis bacteria are passed from infected to noninfected individuals through contact with genital sores. The infecting bacteria then go into a dormant stage for several years before they become virulent and attack many parts of the body, including the brain. The syndrome of insanity and dementia that results from a syphilitic infection is called **general paresis.**

Syphilis has a particularly interesting history (see Klawans, 1990). The first Europeans to visit America stripped the natives of their gold and left smallpox in return. But the deal was not totally one-sided; the booty carried back to Europe by Columbus's sailors and the adventurers that followed included a cargo of syphilis bacteria. Until then, syphilis had been restricted to the Americas, but it was quickly distributed to the rest of the world.

■ **VIRAL INFECTIONS** There are two types of viral infections of the nervous system—neurotropic and pantropic. **Neurotropic infections** have a particular affin-

---

Contusions. Closed-head injuries that involve bleeding.
Hematoma. A bruise.
Contrecoup injuries. Contusions that occur on the side of the brain opposite to the side of a blow.
Concussion. The situation in which there is a disturbance of consciousness following a blow to the head with no cerebral bleeding or obvious structural damage.
Punch-drunk syndrome. The psychological disturbances that result from repeated concussions.
Dementia. General intellectual deterioration.
Encephalitis. The inflammation associated with brain infection.
Meningitis. Inflammation of the meninges, usually caused by bacterial infection.
General paresis. The insanity and intellectual deterioration resulting from syphilitic infection.
Neurotropic infections. Viral infections that have a particular affinity for neural tissue.

ity for neural tissue. **Pantropic infections** attack neural tissue but not preferentially.

Rabies, which is usually transmitted through the bite of a rabid animal, is a well-known example of a neurotropic viral infection. The fits of rage caused by the virus's effects on the brain increase the probability that rabid animals that normally attack by biting (e.g., dogs, cats, raccoons, bats, and mice) will spread the disorder. Although the effects of the rabies virus on the brain are ultimately lethal, the virus does have one redeeming feature: It does not usually attack the brain for at least a month after it has been contracted, thus allowing time for a preventive vaccination.

The *mumps* and *herpes* viruses are common examples of pantropic viruses. They typically attack other tissues of the body, but they can spread into the brain—with dire consequences.

Neurotoxins

The nervous system can be damaged by exposure to any one of a variety of toxic chemicals, which can enter general circulation from the gastrointestinal tract, from the lungs, or through the skin. For example, heavy metals such as mercury and lead can accumulate in the brain and permanently damage it, producing a **toxic psychosis** (chronic insanity produced by a neurotoxin). Have you ever wondered why Alice in Wonderland's Mad Hatter was a mad hatter and not a mad something else? In 18th- and 19th-century England, hatmakers were commonly driven mad by the *mercury* employed in the preparation of the felt used to make hats. In a similar vein, the word *crackpot* originally referred to the toxic psychosis observed in people—primarily the British poor—who steeped their tea in cracked ceramic pots with *lead* cores.

Sometimes, the very drugs used to treat neurological disorders prove to have toxic effects. Some of the antipsychotic drugs introduced in the early 1950s provide an example of distressing scope. By the late 1950s, millions of psychotic patients were being maintained on these drugs. However, the initial enthusiasm for these drugs was tempered by the discovery that many of the patients eventually developed a motor disorder termed **tardive dyskinesia (TD).** Its primary symptoms are involuntary smacking and sucking movements of the lips, thrusting and rolling of the tongue, lateral jaw movements, and puffing of the cheeks. Unfortunately, tardive dyskinesia is not responsive to treatment. Once it has developed, even lowering the dose of the offending drug does not help; in fact, it sometimes makes the symptoms worse. Safer antipsychotic drugs have now been developed.

Brain damage from the neurotoxic effects of recreational drugs is also a serious problem. You learned in Chapter 1 that alcohol produces brain damage through a combination of its direct toxic effects and its effects on thiamine metabolism. Do you remember the case of Jimmie G.? You will learn more about the neurotoxic effects of recreational drugs in Chapter 13.

Some neurotoxins are *endogenous* (produced by the patient's own body). For example, the body can produce antibodies that can cause various types of disorders by attacking components of the nervous system (see Newsom-Davis & Vincent, 1991). Multiple sclerosis, an example of such an *autoimmune disorder,* is a consequence of antibodies that attack their body's own myelin. It is described in detail later in the chapter.

Genetic Factors

Normal human cells have 23 pairs of chromosomes; however, sometimes accidents of cell division occur, and the fertilized egg ends up with an abnormal chromosome or with an abnormal number of normal chromosomes. Then, as the fertilized egg divides and redivides, these chromosomal anomalies are duplicated in every cell of the body.

A common example of a disorder caused by such a genetic accident is **Down syndrome,** which occurs in 0.15% of all live births. This syndrome is associated with an extra chromosome in pair 21. The consequences of the superfluous chromosome are unfortunate. In addition to a characteristic disfigurement—flattened skull and nose, folds of skin over the inner corners of the eyes, and short fingers (see Figure 6.7)—intellectual development is retarded, and there are often serious medical complications. The probability of giving birth to a child with Down syndrome increases with advancing maternal age.

Few neuropsychological diseases of genetic origin are the result of faulty chromosomal duplication. Most are caused by abnormal recessive genes that are passed from parent to offspring. (In Chapter 2, you learned about one such disorder, *phenylketonuria.*) Inherited neuropsychological disorders are rarely associated with faulty dominant genes because dominant genes that disturb neuropsychological function tend to be eliminated from the gene pool—every individual who carries one is at a major survival and reproductive disadvantage. In contrast, individuals who inherit one abnormal recessive gene do not develop the disorder, and the gene is likely to be passed on to future generations; only individuals who inherit two of these genes are affected.

There are, however, two situations in which neurological disorders are associated with dominant genes. One is the case in which an abnormal dominant gene manifests itself only in rare environmental circumstances. The other is the case in which an abnormal dominant gene is not expressed until the individual is well past puberty. The gene for *Huntington's disease* is a dominant gene of this type.

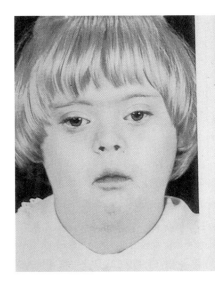 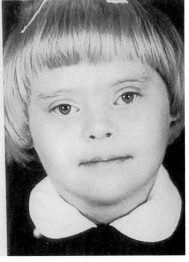

Figure 6.7 A child with Down syndrome before and after plastic surgery. The purpose of these photographs is not to promote cosmetic surgery but to challenge our culture's reaction to patients with Down syndrome. The little girl on the left and the little girl on the right are the same girl; they deserve the same respect and consideration.

(Courtesy of Kenneth E. Salyer, Director, International Craniofacial Institute.)

Rapid progress is being made in locating and characterizing the faulty genes that are associated with some neuropsychological disorders. Once this goal is achieved, it will open up a variety of new treatment and prevention strategies, such as splicing in healthy genes to replace faulty ones and developing specific DNA-binding proteins that can enter neurons and block the expression of faulty genes.

Programmed Cell Death

One of the reasons why humans and other animals stay healthy and function effectively is that neurons and other cells that become redundant or dysfunctional kill themselves by committing suicide (Ameisen, 1996; Duke, Ojcius, & Young, 1996). Cell death by activation of a cell's genetic program for suicide is called *programmed cell death* or **apoptosis** (pronounced "AP oh TOE sis"). Neural apoptosis is particularly prevalent in early development but continues through the life span.

Apoptosis is currently a major focus of research. It is of major interest to those investigators interested in brain plasticity and development—as you will learn in Chapter 15. However, its discussion in this chapter stems from the fact that it has been implicated as a major factor in brain damage. Indeed, the six causes of brain damage that have already been discussed in this chapter (tumors, cerebrovascular disorders, closed-head injuries, infections, toxins, and genetic factors), each produces its effect, in part, by activating genetic programs of cell self-destruction.

Neurons and other cells die in two fundamentally different ways: They can actively kill themselves by apoptosis, or they can passively die by injury, a process called *necrosis*. Necrotic and apoptotic cell death differ in major respects. In necrotic cell death, an injury causes cells to swell and rupture. The region of the damage then becomes inflamed; the inflammatory response involves an influx of cells of the immune system that ultimately ingest the ruptured cells. In apoptotic cell death, cells begin to shrink and shrivel under genetic control and are ultimately consumed by local cells, involving no inflammatory response. In addition, necrotic and apoptotic cell death involve the cell nucleus in different ways. In necrotic cell death, the nucleus is not grossly affected until the very end; in apoptotic cell death, changes in nuclear structure are among the first observable changes.

Necrotic and apoptotic cell death occur at vastly different rates. For example, cerebral ischemia may induce areas of necrotic death, which are largely complete in a few hours, whereas the neurons around the areas of necrotic death may undergo apoptotic death, which is not complete for several days (see Kogure & Kogure, 1997). Accordingly, a massive research effort is currently underway to develop antiapoptosis drugs that could be administered after cerebral ischemia or other cerebral trauma to limit the brain damage. Efforts to block apoptotic neuron death have focused both on membrane receptors that turn on the genetic programs of cell death and on the genetic programs themselves. Several positive results have been reported in laboratory species, but as yet no major unambiguous successes have been reported in human patients (see Nicoletti et al., 1996; Plum, 1997).

Pantropic infections. Viral infections that can infect brain tissue but have no preference for it.

Toxic psychosis. Psychiatric disturbance that is caused by exposure to toxic chemicals.

Tardive dyskinesia (TD). A motor disorder that results from chronic use of certain antipsychotic drugs.

Down syndrome. A disorder associated with the presence of an extra chromosome in pair 21, resulting in disfigurement and mental retardation.

Apoptosis. Programmed cell death.

Neuropsychological Diseases

The preceding section focused on the causes of neuropsychological diseases. This section focuses on the neuropsychological diseases themselves.

It is not always easy to decide whether an individual has a neuropsychological disease. Is an individual who performs poorly on intelligence tests, sleeps longer than most, or displays aggressive behavior in inappropriate contexts suffering from a disorder of the brain, or does the person simply represent the extreme of normal biological function?

The problem of *differential diagnosis*—of deciding which particular neural disorder a patient has—is even more thorny. Each neuropsychological patient displays a unique array of complex behavioral symptoms—no two neuropsychological patients display exactly the same pattern of symptoms. Physicians and scientists search for clusters of neuropsychological symptoms that tend to occur together. When they identify a recurring cluster, they coin a term for it. This term and the cluster of symptoms it represents come to be thought of as a neuropsychological disease. The assumptions on which this approach is based are that all patients with a particular cluster of symptoms will prove to have the same underlying neural pathology and that the pathology will prove in each case to have the same causes. These assumptions do not always turn out to be correct. As more is found out about patients with a particular cluster of neuropsychological symptoms, it is usually necessary to redefine the disorder—by excluding some cases, including others, or dividing the disorder into subtypes. The more that is known about the causes and neural bases of a neuropsychological disorder, the more accurately it can be diagnosed; and the more accurately it can be diagnosed, the more readily its causes and neural bases can be identified.

Epilepsy, Parkinson's disease, Huntington's disease, multiple sclerosis, and Alzheimer's disease are the neuropsychological diseases that are discussed in this section.

Epilepsy

The primary symptom of **epilepsy** is the epileptic seizure, but not all persons who suffer seizures are considered to have epilepsy. It is not uncommon for an otherwise healthy person to have a seizure during temporary illness or following exposure to a convulsive agent. The label *epilepsy* is applied to only those pa-

tients whose seizures appear to be generated by their own chronic brain dysfunction. About 1% of the population are diagnosed as epileptic at some point in their lives.

In view of the fact that epilepsy is characterized by epileptic seizures—or, more accurately, by spontaneously recurring epileptic seizures—you might think that the task of diagnosing epilepsy would be an easy one. But you would be wrong. The task is made difficult by the diversity and complexity of epileptic seizures. You are probably familiar with seizures that take the form of **convulsions** (motor seizures); these often involve tremors (*clonus*), rigidity (*tonus*), and loss of both balance and consciousness. But many seizures do not take this form; instead, they involve subtle changes of thought, mood, or behavior that are not easily distinguishable from normal ongoing activity. In such cases, the diagnosis of epilepsy rests heavily on electroencephalographic evidence.

The value of scalp electroencephalography in suspected cases of epilepsy stems from the fact that epileptic seizures are associated with bursts of high-amplitude EEG spikes, which are often apparent in the scalp EEG during an attack (see Figure 6.8), and from the fact that individual spikes often punctuate the scalp EEGs of epileptics between attacks. Although the observation of spontaneous epileptic discharges is incon-

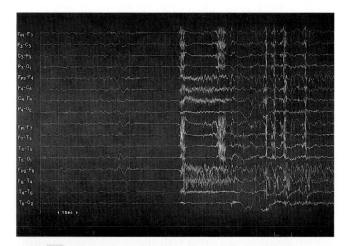

Figure 6.8 Cortical electroencephalogram (EEG) record from various locations on the scalp during the beginning of a complex partial seizure. The letters and numbers to the left of each trace indicate the conventional locations of the electrodes over the frontal (F), temporal (T), parietal (P), and occipital (O) lobes.

Figure 6.9 The bursting of an epileptic neuron, recorded by extracellular unit recording.

trovertible evidence of epilepsy, the failure to observe them does not always mean that the patient is not epileptic. It could mean that the patient is epileptic but did not happen to experience epileptic discharges during the test or that epileptic discharges did occur during the test but were not recorded through the scalp electrodes.

Some epileptics experience peculiar psychological changes just before a convulsion. These changes, called **epileptic auras,** may take many different forms—for example, a bad smell, a specific thought, a vague feeling of familiarity, a hallucination, or a tightness of the chest. Epileptic auras are important for two reasons. First, the nature of the auras provides clues concerning the location of the epileptic focus. Second, because the epileptic auras experienced by a particular patient are often similar from attack to attack, they warn the patient of an impending convulsion. For most people, the warning is an advantage; but for some it can become an experience of dread, as the normal parts of their brains struggle to keep in touch with reality.

Once an individual has been diagnosed as epileptic, it is usual to assign the epilepsy to one of two general categories—*partial epilepsy* or *generalized epilepsy*—and then to one of their respective subcategories. The various seizure types are so different from one another that there are many who believe that epilepsy is best viewed not as a single disease but as a number of different, but related, diseases. Supporting this view is the fact that epilepsy has no single cause; almost any kind of brain disturbance can cause seizures. The diagnosis of the two general categories of epilepsy depends on which of the two types of seizures—partial or generalized—is more prevalent.

■ PARTIAL SEIZURES A **partial seizure** is a seizure that does not involve the entire brain. For reasons unknown, the epileptic neurons at a focus begin to discharge together in bursts, and it is this synchronous bursting of neurons (see Figure 6.9) that produces epileptic spiking in the EEG. The synchronous activity may stay restricted to the focus until the seizure is over, or it may spread to healthy areas of the brain—but, in the case of partial seizures, not to the entire brain. The specific behavioral symptoms of a partial epileptic seizure depend on where the disruptive discharges begin and into what structures they spread. Because par-

tial seizures do not involve the entire brain, they are not usually accompanied by a total loss of consciousness or equilibrium.

There are two major categories of partial seizures: simple and complex. **Simple partial seizures** are partial seizures whose symptoms are primarily sensory or motor or both; they are sometimes called *Jacksonian seizures* after the famous 19th-century neurologist Hughlings Jackson. As the epileptic discharges spread through the sensory or motor areas of the brain, the symptoms spread systematically through the body.

In contrast, **complex partial seizures** are often restricted to the temporal lobes, and those who experience them are said to have *temporal lobe epilepsy.* Complex partial seizures typically begin with an aura, which may develop into a psychomotor attack. In a **psychomotor attack,** the patient engages in compulsive, repetitive, simple behaviors commonly referred to as *automatisms* (e.g., doing and undoing a button) or in more complex behaviors that appear almost normal. The diversity of psychomotor attacks is illustrated by the following four cases reported by Lennox (1960):

A war veteran subject to many automatisms read in the newspaper about a man who had embraced a woman in a park, followed her into a women's toilet, and then boarded a bus. From the description given, he realized he was the man.

One morning a doctor left home to answer an emergency call from the hospital and returned several hours later, a trifle confused, feeling as though he had experienced a bad dream. At the hospital he had performed a difficult . . . [operation] with his usual competence, but later had done and said things deemed inappropriate.

Epilepsy. A neurological disorder characterized by spontaneously recurring seizures.

Convulsions. Motor seizures.

Epileptic auras. Psychological symptoms that precede the onset of a convulsion.

Partial seizures. Seizures that do not involve the entire brain.

Simple partial seizures. Partial seizures in which the symptoms are primarily sensory or motor or both.

Complex partial seizures. Seizures that are characterized by various complex psychological phenomena and are thought to result from temporal lobe discharges.

Psychomotor attack. An epileptic attack in which the patient engages in compulsive behaviors that, although inappropriate, have the appearance of normal behaviors.

A young man, a music teacher, when listening to a concert, walked down the aisle and onto the platform, circled the piano, jumped to the floor, did a hop, skip, and jump up the aisle, and regained his senses when part way home. He often found himself on a trolley [bus] far from his destination.

A man in an attack went to his employer and said, "I have to have more money or [I] quit." Later, to his surprise, he found that his salary had been raised. (pp. 237–238)

Although patients appear to be conscious throughout their psychomotor attacks, they usually have little or no subsequent recollection of them. About half of all cases of epilepsy are of the complex partial variety—the temporal lobes are particularly susceptible to epileptic discharges.

■ **GENERALIZED SEIZURES** **Generalized seizures** involve the entire brain. Some begin as focal discharges that gradually spread through the entire brain. In other cases, the discharges seem to begin almost simultaneously in all parts of the brain. Such sudden-onset generalized seizures may result from diffuse pathology or may begin focally in a structure, such as the thalamus, that projects to many parts of the brain.

Like partial seizures, generalized seizures occur in many forms. One is the **grand mal** (literally "big trouble") **seizure.** The primary symptoms of a grand mal seizure are loss of consciousness, loss of equilibrium, and a violent *tonic-clonic convulsion*—a convulsion involving both tonus and clonus. Tongue biting, urinary incontinence, and *cyanosis* (turning blue from excessive extraction of oxygen from the blood during the convulsion) are common manifestations of grand mal convulsions. The **hypoxia** (shortage of oxygen supply to tissue, for example to the brain) that accompanies a grand mal convulsion can itself cause brain damage, some of which develops slowly after the attack and is mediated by the excessive release of excitatory amino acids.

A second major category of generalized seizure is the **petit mal** (literally "small trouble") **seizure.** Petit mal seizures are not associated with convulsions; their primary behavioral symptom is the *petit mal absence*—a disruption of consciousness that is associated with a cessation of ongoing behavior, a vacant look, and sometimes fluttering eyelids. The EEG of a petit mal seizure is different from that of other seizures; it is a bilaterally symmetrical **3-per-second spike-and-wave discharge** (see Figure 6.10). Petit mal seizures are most common in children, and they frequently cease at puberty. They often go undiagnosed; thus children with petit mal epilepsy are sometimes considered to be "daydreamers" by their parents and teachers and "space cadets" by their playmates.

Although there is no cure for epilepsy, the frequency and severity of seizures can often be reduced by anticonvulsant medication. Brain surgery is prescribed only in life-threatening situations.

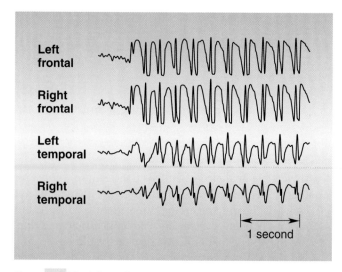

Figure 6.10 The bilaterally symmetrical, 3-per-second spike-and-wave EEG discharge that is associated with petit mal epileptic attacks.

Parkinson's Disease

Parkinson's disease is a movement disorder of middle and old age that affects about 0.5% of the population (see Youdim & Riederer, 1997). Its initial symptoms are mild—perhaps no more than a slight stiffness or tremor of the fingers—but they inevitably increase in severity with advancing years. The most common symptoms of the full-blown disorder are a tremor that is pronounced during inactivity but not during voluntary movement or sleep, muscular rigidity, difficulty initiating movement, slowness of movement, and a masklike face. There is typically little or no intellectual impairment. Parkinson's disease victims are normal-thinking people trapped inside bodies they cannot control. Do you remember from Chapter 4 the case of the "lizard"—Roberto Garcia d'Orta?

Like epilepsy, Parkinson's disease seems to have no single cause; faulty genes, brain infections, strokes, tumors, traumatic brain injury, and neurotoxins have all been implicated in specific cases. However, in the majority of cases, no cause is obvious and there is no family history of the disorder (see Calne et al., 1987).

Parkinson's disease is associated with degeneration of the **substantia nigra**—the midbrain nucleus whose neurons project via the **nigrostriatal pathway** to the **striatum** of the basal ganglia. The neurotransmitter of substantia nigra neurons is *dopamine,* and there is almost a total lack of dopamine in the substantia nigras and striatums of long-term Parkinson's patients.

As you saw in the case of d'Orta, the symptoms of Parkinson's disease can be alleviated by injections of **L-DOPA**—the chemical from which dopamine is synthesized. However, L-DOPA is rarely a permanent solution; it typically becomes less and less effective with use, until its side effects outweigh its benefits. This is exactly what happened to d'Orta. L-DOPA therapy did give him a 3-year respite from his disease, but ultimately it became totally ineffective. His prescription was then changed to another dopamine agonist, and again his condition improved—but again the improvement was only temporary. You will return to d'Orta's roller-coaster case in Chapter 15, which will describe how, as a last resort, dopamine-releasing cells were transplanted into d'Orta's brain.

A cure for Parkinson's disease may lie in the not-too-distant future; several important findings of the therapeutic significance have been reported in the last few years. One particularly important finding was the discovery of a gene mutation associated with a rare form of Parkinson's disease in four different families (Polymeropoulos et al., 1997); this rare form has an early age of onset and runs in families. Although this same gene mutation is unlikely to be a causal factor in the vast majority of Parkinson's cases, it does provide an important clue about the nature of the changes that underlie the disorder. Another important recent finding relevant to the treatment of Parkinson's disease was the discovery of a receptor in the nuclei of dopaminergic neurons that initiates the synthesis of dopamine (Zetterström et al., 1997). Agonists for this receptor could conceivably be of value in treating Parkinson's disease by increasing dopamine synthesis.

Huntington's Disease

Like Parkinson's disease, **Huntington's disease** is a progressive motor disorder of middle and old age; unlike Parkinson's disease, it is rare, it has a strong genetic basis, and it is always associated with severe dementia. At first, the motor symptoms of Huntington's disease take the form of increased fidgetiness; but they slowly grow worse, until the behavior of the patient is characterized by the incessant involuntary performance of a variety of rapid, complex, jerky movements that involve entire limbs rather than individual muscles. Huntington's disease is sometimes called *Huntington's chorea* because the twisting, writhing, grimacing movements displayed by some Huntington's patients have a dancelike quality. (*Chorea* means "dance," as in *chorus line* and *choreography*.)

Huntington's disease is passed from generation to generation by a single dominant gene; thus all of the individuals carrying the gene develop the disorder, as do about half their offspring. The Huntington's gene is readily passed from parent to child because the first symptoms of the disease do not appear until the parent is well past the peak reproductive years (at about age 40). There is no cure; and death occurs approximately 15 years after the appearance of the first symptoms. Autopsy reveals selective degeneration of the striatum and cerebral cortex (see DiFiglia et al., 1997).

The abnormal dominant gene that causes Huntington's disease was identified and characterized in 1993 by the Huntington's Disease Collaborative Research Group. In addition, the abnormal protein produced by the Huntington's gene has been isolated and characterized (see Albin & Tagle, 1995; MacDonald & Gusella, 1996; Paulson & Fischbeck, 1996). The effect of this protein, which has been termed "huntingtin," has not yet been determined. Curiously, huntingtin is produced in all parts of the brain, yet brain damage is largely restricted to the striatum and cerebral hemisphere.

If one of your parents were to develop Huntington's disease, the chance would be 50/50 that you too would develop it. If you were in such a situation, would you want to know whether or not you would suffer the same fate? Medical geneticists have discovered the location of the lethal Huntington's gene (see Wexler, Rose, & Housman, 1991). They have also developed a test that can tell relatives of Huntington's patients whether they too are carrying the gene (Gilliam, Gusella, & Lehrach, 1987; Martin, 1987). Some choose to take the test, and some do not. One advantage of the test is that it permits the relatives of Huntington's patients who have not inherited the gene to have children without the fear of passing on the disorder.

Much of the early research on Huntington's disease was aimed at tracing the family trees of those with the disorder. The first recorded cases of the disease occurred in 1630 in the town of Bures, England (Vessie, 1932). At that time, afflicted individuals were judged to be witches and were executed. Many North American cases of Huntington's disease can be traced to two families who fled Bures. Once in North America, these unfortunates were dealt with more humanely: Only one of them was hanged. In the last few decades, the prevalence of Huntington's disease has declined as a result of genetic counseling.

Generalized seizures. Seizures that involve the entire brain.

Grand mal seizure. A seizure whose symptoms are loss of consciousness, loss of equilibrium, and a violent tonic-clonic convulsion.

Hypoxia. Shortage of oxygen supply to tissue, for example to the brain.

Petit mal seizure. A generalized seizure that is characterized by a disturbance of consciousness and a 3-per-second spike-and-wave EEG discharge.

3-per-second spike-and-wave discharge. The characteristic EEG of the petit mal seizure.

Parkinson's disease. A movement disorder that is associated with degeneration of dopaminergic neurons in the nigrostriatal pathway.

Substantia nigra. The dopaminergic midbrain nucleus that degenerates in cases of Parkinson's disease.

Nigrostriatal pathway. The pathway along which axons from the substantia nigra project to the striatum.

Striatum. The structure of the basal ganglia that is the terminal of the dopaminergic nigrostriatal pathway.

L-DOPA. The chemical precursor of dopamine, which is used in the treatment of Parkinson's disease.

Huntington's disease. A progressive terminal disorder of motor and intellectual function that is produced in adulthood by a dominant gene.

Mr. Walter S. Miller
1500 N. Severn-Langdon Rd.
Manchester, Connecticut 22022
Z9/900-854
August 5, 1991

Dr. John P.J. Pinel
Department of Psychology
University of British Columbia
Vancouver, B.C. Canada V6T.,1Y7.

Dear Dr. Pinel:

I am worried about my children and their future. In fact, I am worried sick. After reading your book I feel that you are my friend and I have nowhere else to turn.

My wife came down with Huntington's disease 7 years ago, and today she can't walk or take care of herself. I have three young children. Where can I take them to see if they have inherited my wife's infected cells? I am presently incarcerated, which adds to my psychological pain. I look to be released soon, and could take my wife and kids just about any wheres to find help and get answers.

Any kind of advice that you could give us would be greatly appreciated by me and my family. I wish to thank you for any assistance that you can give.

God bless you and give you and yours His love and peace! I remain with warmest personal regards.

Very truly yours,

Walter S. Miller

Walter S. Miller

WSM:

THE UNIVERSITY OF BRITISH COLUMBIA

Department of Psychology
2136 West Mall
Vancouver, B. C. Canada V6T 1Z4
Tel: (604) 822–2755
Fax: (604) 822–6923

November 25, 1991

Mr. Walter S. Miller
1500 N. Severn-Langdon Road
Manchester, Connecticut 22022
U.S.A.

Dear Mr. Miller:

I was saddened to learn of your unhappy state of affairs. In requesting my advice, I hope that you understand that I am a scientist, not a physician. In any case, the following is my assessment.

If your wife does in fact have Huntington's disease and not some other neurological disorder, each of your children has a 50/50 chance of developing Huntington's disease in adulthood. I am sure that you are aware that there is currently no cure.

I advise you to seek the advice of a local neurologist, who can explain your options to you and provide you with the advice and support that you sorely need. You must decide whether or not to subject your children to the tests that are required to determine whether or not they are carrying the Huntington's gene. One option would be to wait for your children to reach legal age and then allow them to make the decision for themselves. Some people whose parents develop Huntington's disease decide to take the test; others decide not to. In either case, it is extremely important for them not to risk passing on the Huntington's gene to future generations.

I am sorry that I cannot provide you with a more optimistic assessment, but your children's situation is too serious for me to be less than totally frank. Again, please consult a neurologist as soon as possible.

Do not lose hope. There is a chance (1/8) that none of your children is carrying the Huntington's gene. I wish you, your wife, and your children good fortune.

Cordially,

John Pinel

John P. J. Pinel
Professor

Shortly after the first edition of this textbook appeared in print, I received the letter reproduced on the facing page. I have altered it slightly to protect the identity of its author and his family. It speaks for itself.

Multiple Sclerosis

Multiple sclerosis (MS), a progressive disease of CNS myelin, typically begins in early adult life. First, there are microscopic areas of degeneration on myelin sheaths; but eventually there is a breakdown of both the myelin and the associated axons, along with the development of many areas of hard scar tissue (*sclerosis* means "hardening"). Figure 6.11 illustrates degeneration in the white matter of a patient with multiple sclerosis.

Diagnosing multiple sclerosis is difficult because the nature and severity of the disorder depends on the number, size, and position of the sclerotic lesions. Furthermore, in some cases there are lengthy periods of remission (up to 2 years), during which the patient seems almost normal; but these are usually just oases in the progression of the disorder. Common symptoms of advanced multiple sclerosis are urinary incontinence, visual disturbances, muscular weakness, numbness, tremor, and **ataxia** (loss of motor coordination).

Epidemiological studies of multiple sclerosis have provided evidence of the environmental and genetic factors that influence its development. **Epidemiology** is the study of the various factors, such as diet, geographic location, age, sex, and race, that influence the distribution of a disease in the general population.

Evidence that environmental factors influence the development of multiple sclerosis comes from the finding that the incidence of multiple sclerosis is far greater in people who spent their childhood in a cool climate, even if they subsequently moved to a warm climate. In contrast, evidence of genetic involvement comes from the finding that multiple sclerosis is rare among certain groups, such as gypsies and Asians, even when they live in environments in which the incidence of the disease is high in other groups. Further evidence of a genetic factor in multiple sclerosis comes from comparisons of the concordance of the disease in *monozygotic* (identical) twins (about 36%) and *dizygotic* (fraternal) twins (about 12%). Studies of the DNA of patients with multiple sclerosis suggest that there are several genes that play roles in predisposing people to the disorder.

A model of multiple sclerosis can be induced in laboratory animals by injecting them with myelin and a preparation that stimulates the body's immune reaction (see Wekerle, 1993). Because the resulting disorder, which is termed **experimental autoimmune encephalomyelitis,** is similar in some respects to multiple sclerosis, it has led to the view that multiple sclerosis results from a faulty immune reaction that attacks the body's own myelin as if it were a foreign substance (see Allegretta et al., 1990). Many researchers believe that this faulty *autoimmune reaction* is the result of a slow-acting infection contracted early in life. There is currently no effective treatment for multiple sclerosis.

Alzheimer's Disease

Alzheimer's disease is the most common cause of *dementia*. It sometimes appears in individuals as young as 40, but the likelihood of its manifestation becomes greater with advancing years. About 3% of the general population over the age of 65 suffer from the disease, and the proportion is about 10% in those over 85.

Alzheimer's disease is progressive. Its early stages are characterized by depression and a general decline in cognitive ability; its intermediate stages are marked by irritability, anxiety, and deterioration of speech; and in its advanced stages, the patient deteriorates to the point that even simple responses such as swallowing and controlling the bladder are difficult. Alzheimer's disease is terminal.

Because Alzheimer's disease is not the only cause of severe dementia, it cannot be diagnosed with certainty on the basis of its behavioral symptoms—definitive diagnosis of Alzheimer's disease must await autopsy. The

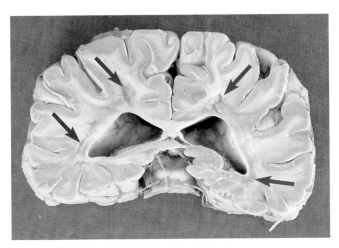

Figure 6.11 Areas of sclerosis (see arrows) in the white matter of a patient with MS.

Multiple sclerosis (MS). A progressive disease of the CNS myelin.

Ataxia. Loss of motor coordination.

Epidemiology. The study of factors that influence the distribution of a disease in the general population.

Experimental autoimmune encephalomyelitis. A model of multiple sclerosis that can be induced in laboratory animals by injecting them with myelin and a preparation that stimulates the body's immune system.

Alzheimer's disease. The major cause of dementia in old age, characterized by neurofibrillary tangles, amyloid plaques, and neuron loss.

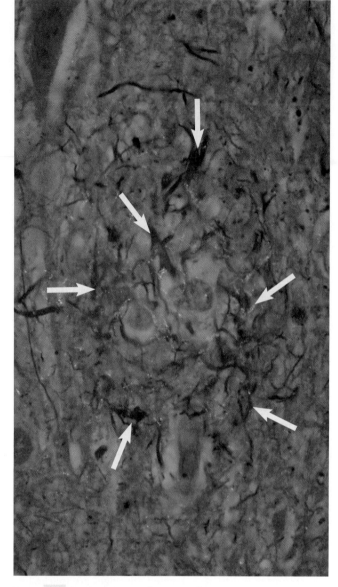

Figure 6.12 Amyloid plaques (see arrows) in the brain of a patient with Alzheimer's disease.

medial temporal lobe structures such as the *entorhinal cortex, amygdala,* and *hippocampus*—all structures that are involved in various aspects of memory. And on the lateral surface of the cerebral hemispheres, they are most prevalent in the inferior temporal cortex, posterior parietal cortex, and prefrontal cortex—all areas that mediate complex cognitive functions. (See Figure 6.13.)

There is a major difficulty in studying the genetics of Alzheimer's disease: Its carriers often die of natural causes before their Alzheimer's symptoms can be manifested. Nevertheless, it is now clear that Alzheimer's disease does have a major genetic component. People with an Alzheimer's victim in their immediate family have a 50% chance of being stricken by the disease if they survive into their 80s and 90s (Breitner, 1990).

Because of the difficulties involved in studying the genetics of late-onset diseases, most of the research on the genetics of Alzheimer's disease has focused on early-onset forms of the disease (Dewji & Singer, 1996). A major discovery was the location of a gene mutation on chromosome 21 that is associated with the early-onset form of the disease (Goate et al., 1991). It makes sense that the disease would be caused by a defect on chromosome 21: The gene responsible for the production of amyloid is on this chromosome, and many Down patients, who have an extra chromosome 21, develop Alzheimer's disease in adulthood. However, in some families, the early onset form of the disorder has been linked to a mutation on chromosome 14; and in other families, it has been linked to a mutation on chromosome 1 (see Roses, 1996; Selkoe, 1997). The fact that three different Alzheimer's genes have already been discovered even though only a few families with the disorder have been systematically studied suggests that many different genes can dispose one to Alzheimer's disease. Nevertheless, the discovery of the three genes is an important accomplishment: The structure and function of the proteins produced by these three genes will, once identified, provide important clues about the nature of the brain pathology associated with Alzheimer's disease.

Although there are currently no effective treatments for Alzheimer's disease, evidence suggests that over-the-counter anti-inflammatory medications, such as aspirin or Advil, might prove useful in retarding its development (McGeer, Schulzer, & McGeer, 1996). Several studies have found the incidence of Alzheimer's disease to be lower than usual among elderly patients taking anti-inflammatory drugs for the treatment of arthritis.

two defining characteristics of the disease are neurofibrillary tangles and amyloid plaques. *Neurofibrillary tangles* are threadlike tangles of protein in the neural cytoplasm, and *amyloid plaques* are clumps of scar tissue composed of degenerating neurons and a protein called **amyloid.** In addition, there is substantial neuron loss. The presence of amyloid plaques in the brain of a patient who died of Alzheimer's disease is illustrated in Figure 6.12.

Although neurofibrillary tangles (see Goedert, 1993), amyloid plaques (see Selkoe, 1991), and neuron loss (see O'Banion, Coleman, & Callahan, 1994) tend to occur throughout the brains of Alzheimer's patients, they are more prevalent in some areas than others. For example, they are particularly prevalent in

Amyloid. A protein that is found in clumps of degenerating neurons in Alzheimer's patients.

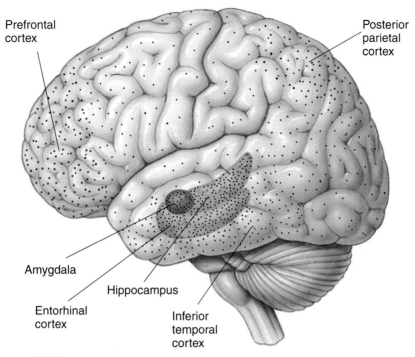

Prefrontal cortex

Posterior parietal cortex

Amygdala

Hippocampus

Entorhinal cortex

Inferior temporal cortex

Figure 6.13 The typical distribution of neurofibrillary tangles and amyloid plaques in the brains of patients with advanced Alzheimer's disease.

(Based on Selkoe, 1991, and Goedert, 1993.)

SELF TEST

Test your knowledge of neuropsychological disorders by filling in the following blanks. The correct answers are provided at the bottom of this page. Before proceeding, review material related to your errors and omissions.

1. The two major categories of epileptic seizures are _____ and _____ .

2. The disorder characterized by tremor at rest is _____ disease.

3. _____ disease is passed from generation to generation by a single dominant gene.

4. Parkinson's disease is associated with degeneration in the _____ dopamine pathway.

5. Experimental autoimmune encephalomyelitis is an animal model of _____ _____ .

6. The most common cause of dementia is _____ disease.

7. _____ attacks are complex partial seizures that are similar in many respects to normal behavior.

8. Alzheimer's disease is associated with _____ syndrome.

9. Two major neuropathological symptoms of Alzheimer's disease are _____ tangles and _____ plaques.

The answers are (1) partial and generalized in either order, (2) Parkinson's, (3) Huntington's, (4) nigrostriatal, (5) multiple sclerosis, (6) Alzheimer's, (7) Psychomotor, (8) Down, and (9) neurofibrillary and amyloid.

Animal Models of Human Neuropsychological Diseases

The first two sections of this chapter focused on neuropsychological diseases and their causes, but they also provided some glimpses into the ways in which researchers have attempted to solve the many puzzles of neurological dysfunction. This section focuses on one of these ways: the experimental investigation of animal models. Because the experimentation necessary to identify the neuropathological basis of human neuropsychological disorders is seldom possible on the patients themselves, animal models of the disorders play a particularly important role in their investigation.

Three types of animal models are used in medical research: homologous, isomorphic, and predictive (Kornetsky, 1977). **Homologous animal models** are disorders in animals that duplicate human disorders in every respect; the *etiology* (causes), symptoms, and prognosis of a homologous model resemble those of the human disorder. **Isomorphic animal models** resemble human disorders, but are artificially produced in the laboratory in a way that does not reflect normal etiology. Finally, **predictive animal models** do not resemble the human disorders but are of value in predicting some aspects of the disorders, such as their response to various drugs.

In a sense, the three types of animal models represent a hierarchy. A predictive model enables one to make certain predictions about the disorder it models. An isomorphic model permits predictions and the study of underlying mechanisms. A homologous model serves as a basis for studying all aspects of a disorder, including its causes. Accordingly, to understand a model's potential uses and limitations, it is important to recognize which type of model it is.

It is difficult to judge how closely animal models mirror neuropsychological disorders, because we do not fully understand the causes and mechanisms of the disorders. It is clear, however, that even the best animal models of neuropsychological disorders display only some of the features of the disorders that they are modeling. Consequently, animal models must be employed with caution. Studying an animal model is like exploring a section of an unknown maze. One enters an unfamiliar section with little more than a hope that its exploration will prove fruitful, and it is only after each of its arms has been carefully explored that it is possible to know whether the decision to enter the section was wise. In the same way, it is not possible to evaluate various animal models of neuropsychological dysfunction that are currently under investigation until each has been thoroughly explored. Surely, only a few animal models will

lead toward the goals of understanding and prevention, but only time and effort can tell which ones these are.

Completing this chapter is a discussion of three animal models that are currently the focus of intensive investigation: the kindling model of epilepsy, the transgenic mouse model of Alzheimer's disease, and the MPTP model of Parkinson's disease. I would classify each as partially isomorphic: They resemble the human disorder in some ways but not in others.

Kindling Model of Epilepsy

In 1969, Goddard, McIntyre, and Leech delivered one mild electrical stimulation per day to rats through implanted amygdalar electrodes. There was no behavioral response to the first few stimulations, but soon each stimulation began to elicit a convulsive response. The first convulsions were mild, involving only a slight tremor of the face. However, with each subsequent stimulation, the elicited convulsions became more generalized, until each convulsion involved the entire body. Each of these fully generalized kindled convulsions in rats was characterized by the following progression of symptoms: facial tremor, rhythmic jaw movements, rhythmic head nodding, forelimb clonus, rearing up on the hind legs, and falling (e.g., Racine, 1972; 1978). The progressive development and intensification of convulsions elicited by a series of periodic brain stimulations became known as the **kindling phenomenon.**

Although kindling is most frequently studied in rats subjected to repeated amygdalar stimulation, it is a remarkably general phenomenon. For example, kindling has been reported in mice (Leech & McIntyre, 1976), rabbits (Tanaka, 1972), cats (Adamec, 1990), dogs (Wauquier, Ashton, & Melis, 1979), and various primates (Wada, 1990a). Moreover, kindling can be produced by the repeated stimulation of many brain sites other than the amygdala, and it can be produced by the repeated application of initially subconvulsive doses of convulsive chemicals (Cain, 1986; Mori & Wada, 1990; Post et al., 1990).

There are many interesting features of kindling (see Racine & Burnham, 1984; Wada, 1990b), but two warrant emphasis. The first is that the neural changes underlying kindling are permanent. A subject that has been kindled and then left unstimulated for several months still responds to each low-intensity stimulation with a generalized convulsion (Goddard, McIntyre, & Leech,

1969; Wada & Sato, 1974). The second is that kindling is produced by distributed, as opposed to massed, stimulations. If the intervals between successive stimulations are shorter than an hour or two, it usually requires many more stimulations to kindle a subject; and under normal circumstances, no kindling at all occurs at intervals of less than about 20 minutes (Racine et al., 1973).

Much of the interest in kindling stems from the fact that it models epilepsy in two ways. First, the convulsions elicited in kindled animals are similar in many respects to those observed in some types of human epilepsy. Second, the kindling phenomenon itself is comparable to the **epileptogenesis** (the development, or genesis, of epilepsy) that can follow a head injury: Some individuals who at first appear to have escaped serious injury after a blow to the head begin to experience convulsions a few weeks later, and these convulsions sometimes begin to recur more and more frequently and with greater and greater intensity.

Many studies have been conducted in order to determine which drugs block the kindling of motor convulsions and which block the elicitation of convulsions in animals that have already been kindled (e.g., Pinel, Kim, & Mana, 1990). The study of Racine, Livingston, and Joaquin (1975) is a particularly good example of this type of study. In this study, an anticonvulsant commonly used in the treatment of human epileptics, *diphenylhydantoin* (Dilantin), blocked convulsions elicited in kindled rats by neocortical stimulation but not those elicited by amygdalar stimulation. Conversely, another commonly used anticonvulsant, *diazepam* (Valium), blocked kindled convulsions elicited by amygdalar stimulation, but had no effect on neocortical kindled convulsions. These findings suggest that the response of human epileptics to various anticonvulsant drugs may depend on the location of the epileptic focus.

It must be stressed that the kindling model as it is applied in most laboratories is not isomorphic in one important respect. You will recall from earlier in this chapter that epilepsy is a disease in which epileptic attacks recur spontaneously; in contrast, kindled convulsions are elicited. However, a model that overcomes this shortcoming has been developed in several species. If subjects are kindled for a very long time—about 300 stimulations in rats—a syndrome can be induced that is truly epileptic, in the sense that the subjects begin to display spontaneous seizures and continue to display them even after the regimen of stimulation is curtailed (e.g., Pinel, 1981; Shouse et al., 1990; Wada, Sato, & Corcoran, 1974).

Transgenic Mouse Model of Alzheimer's Disease

Perhaps the most exciting recent development in the study of Alzheimer's disease has been the development

of the transgenic model of the disorder. **Transgenic** refers to animals into which the genes of another species have been introduced.

One difficulty in studying Alzheimer's disease is that only humans and a few related primates develop amyloid plaques, considered by many to be the primary symptom of the disorder. As a result, experimental studies of Alzheimer's disease have been difficult to conduct, and fundamental questions of causation have been difficult to address. For example, the causal role of amyloid deposits in Alzheimer's disease has not yet been sorted out: Some investigators believe that amyloid deposition triggers neuron degeneration, thereby causing the behavioral symptoms; others believe that the amyloid plaques are the result, not the cause, of the neural degeneration. This lack of progress in answering fundamental causal questions about Alzheimer's disease is why the development of the transgenic mouse model of the disorder is such an important contribution.

There are several forms of the transgenic Alzheimer's model. In the most promising of these models, the one developed by Hsiao and her colleagues (1996), genes for human amyloid are injected into newly fertilized mouse eggs, which are then injected into a foster mother to develop. The injected genes are not the genes that carry the code for human amyloid; they are genes that accelerate its synthesis.

When the transgenic mice mature, their brains contain many amyloid plaques like those of human Alzheimer's patients. Moreover, the distribution of the amyloid plaques is comparable to that observed in human Alzheimer's patients, with the highest concentrations occurring in the hippocampus and surrounding areas.

What makes the transgenic mice of Hsiao and her colleagues particularly promising models of human Alzheimer's disease is that they display deficits on tests of memory. In particular, Hsiao et al. found that they displayed deficits on two memory tasks known to be sensitive to hippocampal damage. The transgenic mice displayed significant deficits on both the *spontaneous alternation task*, a task in which the subjects must learn to alternate their selections between the right and left

---

Homologous animal models. Disorders in animals that duplicate human disorders in every respect.

Isomorphic animal models. Disorders in animals that resemble human disorders but are artificially produced in the laboratory.

Predictive animal models. Animal models that do not resemble the human disorders in key respects but are of value in predicting some aspect of the disorders.

Kindling phenomenon. The progressive development and intensification of convulsions elicited by a series of periodic low-intensity stimulations—most commonly by daily electrical stimulations to the amygdala.

Epileptogenesis. Development of epilepsy.

Transgenic. Containing the genes of another species, which have been implanted there for research purposes.

arms of a simple Y-shaped maze, and the *Morris water maze task,* a task in which the subjects must learn to swim to a platform hidden beneath the surface of milky water (see Chapter 5).

Soon it will be possible to block the amyloid synthesis in these transgenic mice to see whether this prevents the memory deficit. If it does, this will be the best evidence yet that the amyloid plaques cause the memory problems of Alzheimer's patients.

MPTP Model of Parkinson's Disease

The preeminent animal model of Parkinson's disease grew out of an unfortunate incident that occurred in the early 1980s:

Parkinson's disease . . . rarely occurs before the age of 50. It was somewhat of a surprise then to see a group of young drug addicts at our hospital in 1982 who had developed symptoms of severe and what proved to be irreversible parkinsonism. The only link between these patients was the recent use of a new "synthetic heroin." They exhibited virtually all of the typical motor features of Parkinson's disease, including the classic triad of bradykinesia (slowness of movement), tremor and rigidity of their muscles. Even the subtle features, such as seborrhea (oiliness of the skin) and micrographia (small handwriting), that are typical of Parkinson's disease were present. After tracking down samples of this substance, the offending agent was tentatively identified as 1-methyl-4-phenyl-1,2,3,6-tetrahydropyridine or **MPTP**.... After nearly two and a half years, there has been no sign of remission, and most are becoming increasingly severe management problems. (Langston, 1985, p. 79)

Researchers immediately tried to turn the misfortune of these few to the advantage of many by developing a much-needed animal model of Parkinson's disease (Langston, 1986). It was quickly established that nonhuman primates respond like humans to MPTP (Burns et al., 1983; Langston et al., 1984), but attempts to develop a rodent model have been less successful. Rodents treated with MPTP develop some mild symptoms of Parkinson's disease, but the symptoms do not persist for more than a few weeks (Duvoisin et al., 1986).

The brains of primates exposed to MPTP have cell loss to the substantia nigra similar to that observed in the brains of Parkinson's patients. Considering that the substantia nigra is the major source of the brain's dopamine, it is not surprising that the level of dopamine is greatly reduced in both the MPTP model and in the naturally occurring disorder. However, it is curious that in a few monkeys MPTP produces a major

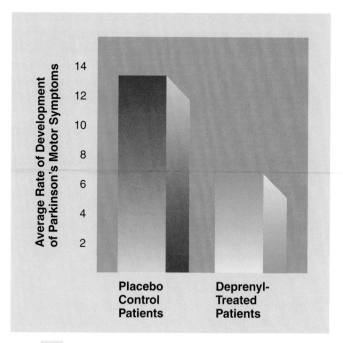

Figure 6.14 Average rate of motor symptom development in early Parkinson's patients treated with deprenyl (a monoamine oxidase inhibitor) or with a placebo. Deprenyl slowed the progression of the disease by 50%.

(Based on Tetrud and Langston, 1989.)

depletion of dopamine without producing any gross motor symptoms (Taylor et al., 1990).

The development of the MPTP animal model has already started to benefit patients with Parkinson's disease. For example, it was discovered that **deprenyl,** a monoamine agonist, blocks the effects of MPTP in an animal model. Deprenyl is a **monoamine oxidase (MAO) inhibitor;** that is, it increases the level of dopamine and other monoamines by inhibiting the activity of *monoamine oxidase*—an enzyme in monoaminergic neurons that breaks down any monoamine molecules that are not stored in vesicles. It was subsequently shown that deprenyl administered to early Parkinson's patients greatly retards the progression of the disease (Tetrud & Langston, 1989)—see Figure 6.14.

MPTP. A neurotoxin that produces a disorder in primates that is similar to Parkinson's disease.

Deprenyl. A monoamine oxidase inhibitor that has been shown to retard the development of Parkinson's disease.

Monoamine oxidase (MAO) inhibitor. A drug that increases the activity of monoamine neurotransmitters by inhibiting monoamine oxidase—an enzyme in neurons that breaks down monoamines.

CONCLUSION

This chapter began with the case of Professor P., the ironic case of the biopsychologist who diagnosed his

own brain tumor and lived to write the fourth edition of his textbook. Then, it discussed the causes of brain damage (6.1), common neuropsychological diseases (6.2), and animal models of these diseases (6.3). The following case history of a 30-year-old woman who was poisoned by MPTP (Ballard, Tetrud, & Langston, 1985) completes the circle:

> During the first 4 days of July 1982, . . . [she] used 4½ grams of a "new synthetic heroin." The substance was injected IV [intravenously] three or four times daily and caused a burning sensation at the site of injection. . . .
>
> She had brief auditory hallucinations and visual distortions with larger doses. After 3 days of use, she felt "weak" and "slow," but used the drug for another day. Four days later, she was described by family as sitting quietly without moving all day, staring into space "like a zombie." She later said that she felt fully alert during this period and was aware of the environment, but had difficulty initiating speech and could move only with great effort. She also noted intermittent "shaking" of the left arm. Her family provided total care for her, including all dressing, feeding, and bathing.
>
> On July 21, 1982, she was admitted to our neurobehavioral unit. She had the appearance of a "wax doll," sitting immobile with head and arms held in flexion. General examination [revealed] . . . facial seborrhea [oiliness] . . . , a breakdown of horizontal smooth [visual] pursuit, . . . infrequent blinking, continuous drooling, . . . and difficulty initiating speech. Tongue protrusion was slow, limited to about 1 cm. Voluntary movements were profoundly slowed. Left to herself, she remained motionless. . . . A resting tremor of 5 to 6 Hz in the right hand and foot disappeared on volitional movement. . . . She could not rise from a chair without assistance. Gait was shuffling, with small steps, loss of associated movement . . . and loss of postural reflexes. Sensation was normal. The remainder of the neurologic examination was normal, including mental status. . . .
>
> After 2 years of treatment, there has been no improvement in her parkinsonism, and she has suffered a variety of therapeutic complications. (pp. 949–951)[1]

Before leaving this chapter, pause for a moment to contemplate the plight of this woman, of Roberto Garcia d'Orta, and of others who suffer from advanced Parkinson's disease or MPTP poisoning. These are intelligent, alert, sensitive people—people just like you—who are trapped inside bodies that do not work. Compare this to the plight of Alzheimer's patients with severe dementia. Which is worse?

---

[1]From "Permanent Human Parkinsonism Due to 1-methyl-4-phenyl-1,2,3,6-tetrahydropyridine (MPTP): Seven Cases" by P. A. Ballard, J. W. Tetrud, and J. W. Langston, 1985, *Neurology, 35,* 949–956. Reprinted by permission.

FOOD FOR THOUGHT

1. An epileptic is brought to trial for assault. The lawyer argues that her client is not a criminal and that the assaults in question were psychomotor attacks. She points out that her client takes her medication faithfully, but that it does not help. The prosecution lawyer argues that the defendant has a long history of violent assault and must be locked up. What do you think that the judge should do?

2. Describe a bizarre incident you have observed that you think in retrospect might have been a psychomotor or petit mal attack.

3. The more that is known about a disorder, the easier it is to diagnose; and the more accurately that it can be diagnosed, the easier it is to find things out about it. Explain and discuss.

KEY TERMS

Alzheimer's disease (p. 151)
Amyloid (p. 152)
Aneurysm (p. 140)
Apoptosis (p. 145)
Arteriosclerosis (p. 141)
Ataxia (p. 151)
Benign tumors (p. 139)
Cerebral hemorrhage (p. 140)
Cerebral ischemia (p. 140)
Complex partial seizures (p. 147)
Concussion (p. 143)
Congenital (p. 140)
Contrecoup injuries (p. 142)
Contusions (p. 142)

Convulsions (p. 146)
Dementia (p. 143)
Deprenyl (p. 156)
Down syndrome (p. 144)
Embolism (p. 141)
Encapsulated tumors (p. 139)
Encephalitis (p. 143)
Epidemiology (p. 151)
Epilepsy (p. 146)
Epileptic auras (p. 147)
Epileptogenesis (p. 155)
Experimental autoimmune encephalomyelitis (p. 151)
General paresis (p. 143)
Generalized seizures (p. 148)

Glutamate (p. 141)
Grand mal seizure (p. 148)
Hematoma (p. 142)
Homologous animal models (p. 154)
Huntington's disease (p. 149)
Hypoxia (p. 148)
Infiltrating tumors (p. 139)
Isomorphic animal models (p. 154)
Kindling phenomenon (p. 154)
L-DOPA (p. 148)
MPTP (p. 156)
Malignant tumors (p. 139)
Meningiomas (p. 139)

Meningitis (p. 143)
Metastatic tumors (p. 139)
Monoamine oxidase (MAO) inhibitor (p. 156)
Multiple sclerosis (MS) (p. 151)
NMDA (N-methyl-D-aspartate) receptors (p. 141)
Neurotropic infections (p. 143)
Nigrostriatal pathway (p. 148)
Pantropic infections (p. 144)
Parkinson's disease (p. 148)
Partial seizures (p. 147)

ADDITIONAL READING

I strongly recommend the following two books, both of which are collections of entertaining personal essays about neuropsychological patients:

Klawans, H. L. (1990). *Newton's madness: Further tales of clinical neurology.* New York: Harper & Row.

Sacks, O. (1985). *The man who mistook his wife for a hat and other clinical tales.* New York: Summit Books.

I also recommend the following book, which tells the stories of the MPTP patients and the science that they stimulated:

Langston, J. W., & Palfreman, J. (1996). *The case of the frozen addicts.* New York: Vintage Books.

7

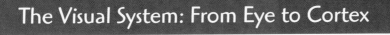

The Visual System: From Eye to Cortex

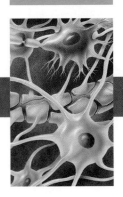

This chapter is about the visual system. Most people think their visual system has evolved to respond as accurately as possible to the patterns of light that enter their eyes. They recognize the obvious limitations in their visual system's accuracy, of course; and they appreciate those curious instances, termed *visual illusions,* in which it is "tricked" into seeing things the way they aren't. But such shortcomings are generally regarded as minor imperfections in a system that responds as faithfully as possible to the external world.

Despite its intuitive appeal, this way of thinking about the visual system is wrong. The visual system does not produce an accurate internal copy of the external world. It does much more. From the tiny, distorted, upside-down, two-dimensional retinal images projected upon the visual receptors lining the backs of our eyes, the visual system creates an accurate, richly detailed, three-dimensional perception that is—and this is the really important part—in some respects even better than the external reality from which it was created.

Regardless of what you may have heard to the contrary, "what you see is not necessarily what you get." One of my primary goals in this chapter is to help you recognize and appreciate the inherent creativity of your own visual system.

This chapter is composed of five sections. The first three sections take you on a journey from the external visual world to the visual receptors of the retina and from there over the major visual pathway to the primary visual cortex. The last two sections describe how the neurons of this pathway mediate the perception of two particularly important features of the visual world: edges and color.

You will learn in this chapter that understanding the visual system requires the integration of two types of research: (1) research that probes the visual system with sophisticated neuroanatomical, neurochemical, and neurophysiological techniques; and (2) research that focuses on the assessment of what we see. Both types of research receive substantial coverage in this chapter, but it is the second that provides you with a unique educational opportunity: the opportunity to participate in the very research you are studying. Throughout this chapter, you will be encouraged to participate in demonstrations designed to give you a taste of the excitement of scientific discovery and to illustrate the relevance of what you are learning in this chapter to life outside its pages.

7.1 Light Enters the Eye and Reaches the Retina

Everybody knows that cats, owls, and other nocturnal animals can see in the dark. Right? Wrong! Some animals have special adaptations that allow them to see under very dim illumination, but no animal can see in complete darkness. The light reflected into your eyes from the objects around you is the basis for your ability to see them; if there is no light, there is no vision.

You may recall from high-school physics that light can be thought of in two different ways: as discrete particles of energy, called *photons,* traveling through space at about 300,000 kilometers (186,000 miles) per second or as waves of energy. Both theories are useful; in some ways light behaves like a particle, and in others it behaves like a wave. Physicists have learned to live with this nagging inconsistency, and we must do the same.

Light is sometimes defined as waves of electromagnetic energy that are between 380 and 760 nanometers (billionths of a meter) in length (see Figure 7.1). There is nothing special about these wavelengths except that the human visual system responds to them. In fact, some animals can see wavelengths that we cannot. For example, rattlesnakes can see *infrared waves,* which are too long for humans to see; as a result, they can see warm-blooded prey in what for us would be complete darkness. Accordingly, if I were writing this book for rattlesnakes, I would be forced to provide another, equally arbitrary, definition of light.

Wavelength and intensity are two properties of light that are of particular interest—wavelength because it plays an important role in the perception of color, and intensity because it plays an important role in the perception of brightness. The terms *wavelength* and *color* tend to be used interchangeably in everyday speech, and so do *intensity* and *brightness.* For example, we commonly refer to an intense light with a wavelength of 700 nanometers as being a bright red light (see Figure 7.1), when in fact it is our perception of the light, not the light itself, that is bright and red. I know that these distinctions may seem trivial to you now, but by the end of the chapter you will appreciate their importance.

The amount of light reaching the retinas is regulated by the donut-shaped bands of contractile tissue, the *irises,* which give our eyes their characteristic blue or brown color (see Figure 7.2). Light enters the eye

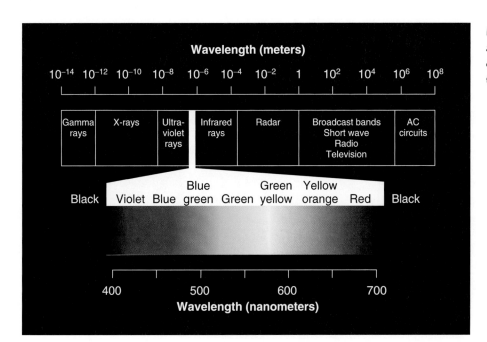

Figure 7.1 The electromagnetic spectrum and the colors associated with the frequencies of the spectrum that are visible to humans.

through the *pupil,* the hole in the iris. The adjustment of pupil size in response to changes in illumination represents a compromise between **sensitivity** (the ability to detect the presence of dimly lit objects) and **acuity** (the ability to see the details of objects). When the level of illumination is high and sensitivity is thus not important, the visual system takes advantage of the situation by constricting the pupils. When the pupils are constricted, the image falling on each retina is sharper and there is a greater *depth of focus;* that is, a greater range of depths are simultaneously kept in focus on the retinas. However, when the level of illumination is too low to adequately activate the receptors, the pupils dilate to let in more light, thereby sacrificing acuity and depth of focus.

Behind each pupil is a *lens,* which focuses incoming light on the retina (see Figure 7.3 on page 162). When we direct our gaze at something near, the tension on the ligaments holding each lens in place is reduced by the contraction of the **ciliary muscles,** and the lens assumes its natural cylindrical shape. (Be alert here: The fact that the tension on the lens is reduced by muscle contraction is counterintuitive.) This increases the ability of the lens to *refract* (bend) light and thus brings close objects into sharp focus. When we focus on a distant object, the ciliary muscles relax, and the lens is flattened. The process of adjusting the configuration of the lenses to bring images into focus on the retina is called **accommodation.**

No description of the eyes of vertebrates would be complete without a discussion of their most obvious feature: the fact that they come in pairs. One reason vertebrates have two eyes is that vertebrates have two sides: left and right. By having one eye on each side, which is by far the most common arrangement, vertebrates can see in almost every direction without moving their heads. But then why do some mammals, including humans, have their eyes mounted side by side on the front of their heads? This arrangement sacrifices the ability to see behind so that what is in front can be viewed through both eyes simultaneously—an arrangement that is an important basis for our visual system's ability to create three-dimensional perceptions (to see depth)

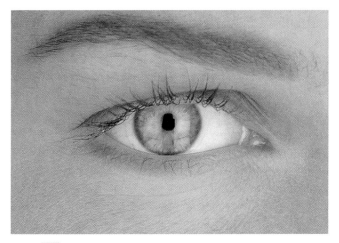

Figure 7.2 The human eye. Light enters the eye through the pupil, whose size is regulated by the iris. The iris gives the eye its characteristic brown or blue color.

Sensitivity. In vision, the ability to detect the presence of dimly lit objects.

Acuity. The ability to see the details of objects.

Ciliary muscles. The eye muscles that control the lenses.

Accommodation. The process of adjusting the configuration of the lenses to bring images into focus on the retina.

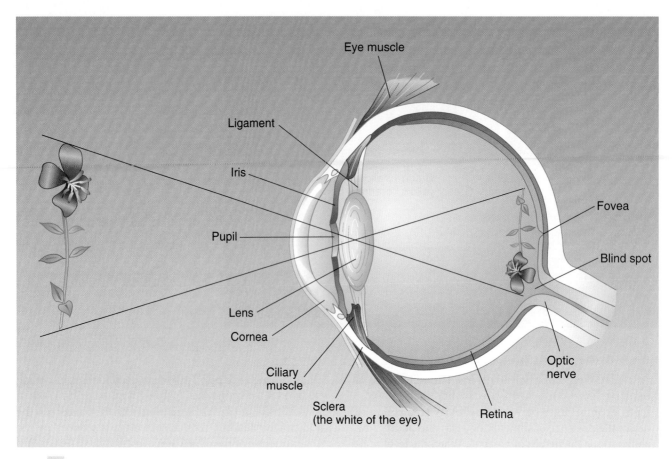

Figure 7.3 A section of the human eye.

from two-dimensional retinal images. Why do you think the two-eyes-on-the-front arrangement has evolved in some species but not in others?

The movements of your eyes are coordinated so that each point in your visual world is projected to corresponding points on your two retinas. To accomplish this, your eyes must *converge* (turn slightly inward); convergence is greatest when you are inspecting things that are close. But the positions of the retinal images on your two eyes can never correspond exactly because your two eyes do not view the world from exactly the same position (see the following demonstration).

DEMONSTRATION

The demonstration of binocular disparity and convergence is the first of the demonstrations that punctuate this chapter. If you compare the views from each eye (by quickly closing one eye and then the other) of objects at various distances in front of you—for example, your finger held at different distances—you will notice that the disparity between the two views is greater for closer objects. Now try the mysterious demonstration of the cocktail sausage. Face the farthest wall (or some other distant object) and bring the tips of your two pointing fingers together at arm's length in front of you—with the backs of your fingers away from you, unless you prefer sausages with fingernails. Now, with both eyes open, sight through the notch between your touching fingertips, but focus on the wall. Do you see the cocktail sausage between your fingertips? Where did it come from? To prove to yourself that the sausage is a product of binocularity, make it disappear by shutting one eye. Warning: Do not eat this sausage.

Binocular disparity—the difference in the position of the same images on the two retinas—is greater for close objects than for distant objects; therefore your visual system can use the degree of binocular disparity to construct one three-dimensional perception from two two-dimensional retinal images.

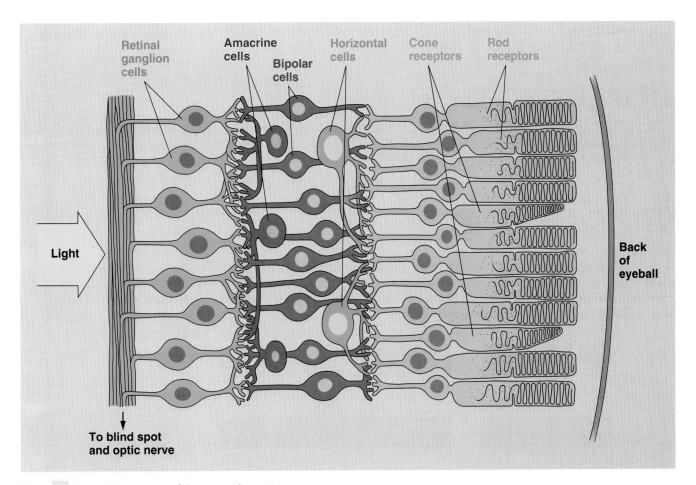

7.2 The Retina and Translation of Light into Neural Signals

Figure 7.4 illustrates the cellular structure of the retina. Notice the five different layers of cells: **receptors, horizontal cells, bipolar cells, amacrine cells,** and **retinal ganglion cells.** Notice too that the amacrine cells and horizontal cells are specialized for *lateral communication* (communication across the major channels of sensory input). The amacrine and bipolar cells release the inhibitory neurotransmitter GABA; in contrast, the receptors and bipolar cells release the excitatory neurotransmitter glutamate (see Barnstable, 1993).

Also notice in Figure 7.4 that the retina is in a sense inside-out: Light reaches the receptor layer only after passing through the other four layers. Then, once the receptors have been activated, the neural message is transmitted back out through the retinal layers to the retinal ganglion cells, whose axons project across the

Binocular disparity. The difference between the retinal image of the same object on the two retinas.

Receptors. Cells that are specialized to receive chemical, mechanical, or radiant signals from the environment.

Horizontal cells. A layer of retinal neurons whose function is lateral communication.

Bipolar cells. The cells in the middle layer of the retina.

Amacrine cells. A layer of retinal neurons whose function is lateral communication.

Retinal ganglion cells. The layer of neurons in the retina whose axons leave the eyeball.

Retinal ganglion cells

Amacrine cells

Bipolar cells

Horizontal cells

Cone receptors

Rod receptors

Light

Back of eyeball

To blind spot and optic nerve

Figure 7.4 The cellular structure of the mammalian retina.

inside of the retina before gathering together in a bundle and exiting the eyeball. This inside-out arrangement creates two visual problems. One is that the incoming light is distorted by the retinal tissue through which it must pass before reaching the receptors. The other is that for the bundle of retinal ganglion cell axons to leave the eye, there must be a gap in the receptor layer; this gap is called the **blind spot.**

The first of these two problems is minimized by the fovea (see Figure 7.5). The **fovea** is an indentation, about 0.33 centimeter in diameter, at the center of the retina; it is the area of the retina that is specialized for high-acuity vision (for seeing fine details). The thinning of the retinal ganglion cell layer at the fovea reduces the distortion of incoming light. The blind spot, the second of the two visual problems created by the inside-out structure of the retina, requires a more creative solution—which is illustrated in the demonstration below.

In this demonstration, you will experience **completion.** The visual system uses information provided by the receptors around the blind spot to fill in the gaps in your retinal images. When the visual system detects a straight bar going into one side of the blind spot and another straight bar leaving the other side, it fills in the missing bit for you; and what you see is a continuous straight bar, regardless of what is actually there. The completion phenomenon is one of the most compelling demonstrations that the visual system does much more than create a faithful copy of the external world.

It is a mistake to think that completion is merely a response to blind spots (see Ramachandran, 1992). Indeed, completion is a fundamental feature of visual system function. When you look at an object, your visual system does not conduct an image of that object from your retina to your cortex. Instead, it extracts key information about the object—primarily information about its edges and their location—and conducts that information to the cortex, where a perception of the entire object is created from that partial information. For example, the color and brightness of large unpatterned surfaces are not directly perceived but are filled in (completed) by a completion process, which in this case is called *surface interpolation.*

Cone and Rod Vision

You likely noticed in Figure 7.4 that there are two different types of receptors in the human retina: cone-shaped receptors called **cones,** and rod-shaped receptors called **rods** (see Figure 7.6). The existence of these two types of receptors puzzled researchers until 1866, when it was first noticed that species active only in the day tend to have cone-only retinas and that species active only at night tend to have rod-only retinas.

From this observation emerged the **duplexity theory** of vision—the theory that cones and rods mediate different kinds of vision. Cone-mediated vision (**photopic vision**) predominates in good lighting and pro-

---

DEMONSTRATION

First, prove to yourself that you do have areas of blindness that correspond to your retinal blind spots. Close your left eye and stare directly at the **A** below, trying as hard as you can to not shift your gaze. While keeping the gaze of your right eye fixed on the **A,** hold the book at different distances from you until the black dot to the right of the **A** becomes focused on your blind spot and disappears (at about 20 centimeters, or 8 inches).

If each eye has a blind spot, why is there not a black hole in your perception of the world when you look at it with one eye? You will discover the answer by focusing on **B** with your right eye while holding the book at the same distance as before. Suddenly, the broken line to the right of **B** will become whole. Now focus on **C** at the same distance with your right eye. What do you see?

THE VISUAL SYSTEM: FROM EYE TO CORTEX

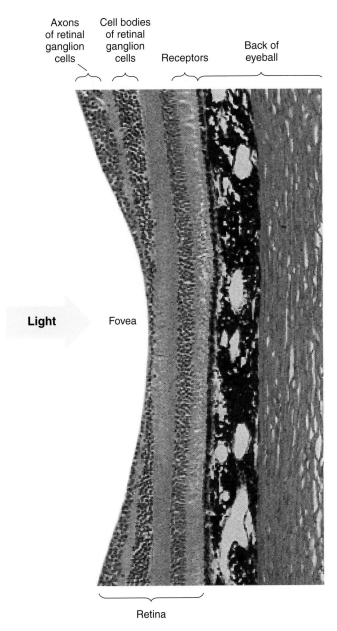

Axons of retinal ganglion cells   Cell bodies of retinal ganglion cells   Receptors   Back of eyeball

Light   Fovea

Retina

Figure 7.5 A section of the retina. The fovea is the indentation at the center of the retina; it is specialized for high-acuity vision.

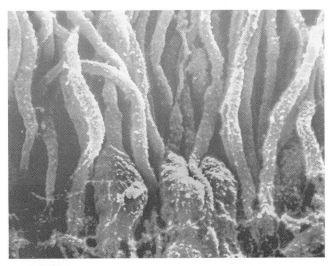

Figure 7.6 Cones and rods. The smaller, conical cells are cones; the larger, cylindrical cells are rods.

dred rods may ultimately converge on a single retinal ganglion cell, whereas it is not uncommon for a retinal ganglion cell to receive input from only a few cones. As a result, the effects of dim light simultaneously stimulating many rods can summate to influence the firing of a retinal ganglion cell onto which the output of the stimulated rods converges, whereas the effects of the same dim light applied to a sheet of cones cannot summate to the same degree, and the retinal ganglion cells may not respond to the light.

The convergent scotopic system pays for its high degree of sensitivity with a low level of acuity. When a retinal ganglion cell that receives input from hundreds of rods changes its firing, the brain has no way of knowing which portion of the rods contributed to the change. Although a more intense light is required to change the firing of a retinal ganglion cell that receives signals from cones, when it does react, there is less ambiguity about the location of the stimulus that triggered the reaction.

vides high-acuity (finely detailed) colored perceptions of the world. In dim illumination, there is not enough light to reliably excite the cones, and the more sensitive rod-mediated vision (**scotopic vision**) predominates. However, the sensitivity of scotopic vision is not achieved without cost: Scotopic vision lacks both the detail and the color of photopic vision.

The differences between photopic (cone) and scotopic (rod) vision result in part from a difference in the way the two systems are "wired." As Figure 7.7 on page 166 illustrates, there is a large difference between the two systems in *convergence*. The output of several hun-

Blind spot. The area on the retina where the axons of retinal ganglion cells gather together, penetrate the receptor layer, and leave the eye as the optic nerve.

Fovea. The central indentation of the retina, which is specialized for high-acuity vision.

Completion. The visual system's automatic use of information obtained from receptors around a blind spot to create a perception of the missing portion of the retinal image.

Cones. The visual receptors that mediate high-acuity color vision in good lighting.

Rods. The visual receptors that mediate achromatic, low-acuity vision under dim light.

Duplexity theory. The theory that cones and rods mediate photopic and scotopic vision, respectively.

Photopic vision. Cone-mediated vision, which predominates when lighting is good.

Scotopic vision. Rod-mediated vision, which predominates in dim light.

Figure 7.7 A schematic representation of the convergence of cones and rods on retinal ganglion cells. There is a low degree of convergence in cone-fed pathways and a high degree of convergence in rod-fed pathways.

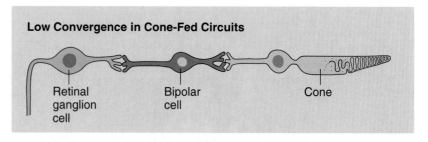

Low Convergence in Cone-Fed Circuits

Retinal ganglion cell

Bipolar cell

Cone

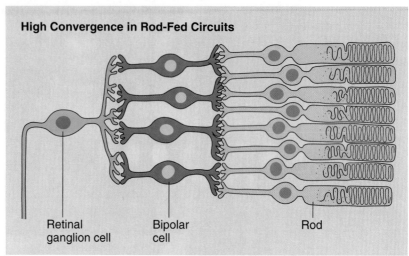

High Convergence in Rod-Fed Circuits

Retinal ganglion cell

Bipolar cell

Rod

Cones and rods differ in their distribution on the retina. As Figure 7.8 illustrates, there are no rods at all in the fovea, only cones. At the boundaries of the foveal indentation, the proportion of cones declines markedly, and there is an increase in the number of rods. The density of rods reaches a maximum at 20° from the center of the fovea. You may be puzzled by the fact that in the periphery of the retina, there are many more rods in the **nasal hemiretina** (the half of each retina next to the nose) than in the **temporal hemiretina** (the half next to the temples). The solution to this puzzle is as plain as the nose on your face. In fact, it is the nose on your face.

Figure 7.8 The distribution of cones and rods over the human retina. The figure illustrates the number of cones and rods per square millimeter as a function of distance from the center of the fovea.
(Adapted from Lindsay & Norman, 1977.)

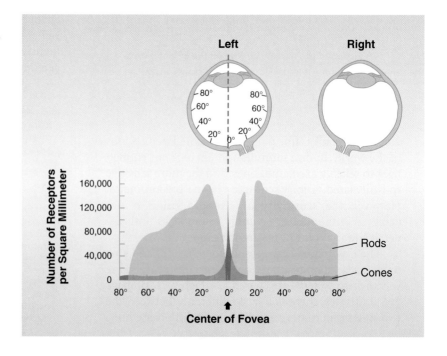

Left

Right

80°
60°
40°
20°
0°

Number of Receptors per Square Millimeter

160,000
120,000
80,000
40,000
0

80° 60° 40° 20° 0° 20° 40° 60° 80°

Rods

Cones

Center of Fovea

THE VISUAL SYSTEM: FROM EYE TO CORTEX

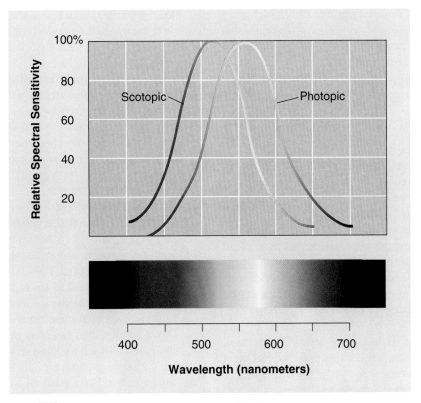

Figure 7.9 Human photopic (cone) and scotopic (rod) spectral sensitivity curves. The peak of each curve has been arbitrarily set at 100%.

Because your nose blocks the input of light onto the edges of your temporal hemiretinas, there is less need for receptors there.

Generally speaking, more intense lights appear brighter. However, wavelength also has a substantial effect on the perception of brightness. Because our visual systems are not equally sensitive to all wavelengths in the visible spectrum, lights of the same intensity but of different wavelengths can differ markedly in brightness. A graph of the relative brightness of lights of the same intensity presented at different wavelengths is called a *spectral sensitivity* curve.

By far the most important thing to remember about spectral sensitivity curves is that humans and other animals with both cones and rods have two of them: a **photopic spectral sensitivity curve** and a **scotopic spectral sensitivity curve**. The photopic spectral sensitivity of humans can be determined by having subjects judge the relative brightness of different wavelengths of light shone on the fovea. Their scotopic spectral sensitivity can be determined by asking subjects to judge the relative brightness of different wavelengths of light shone on the periphery of the retina at an intensity too low to activate the few peripheral cones that are located there.

The photopic and scotopic spectral sensitivity curves of human subjects are plotted in Figure 7.9. Notice that under photopic conditions, the visual system is maximally sensitive to wavelengths of about 560 nanometers; thus, under photopic conditions, a light at 500 nanome-

ters would have to be much more intense than one at 560 nanometers to be seen as equally bright. In contrast, under scotopic conditions, the visual system is maximally sensitive to wavelengths of about 500 nanometers; thus, under scotopic conditions, a light of 560 nanometers would have to be much more intense than one at 500 nanometers to be seen as equally bright.

Because of the difference in photopic and scotopic spectral sensitivity, an interesting visual effect can be observed during the transition from photopic to scotopic vision. In 1825, Purkinje described the following occurrence, which has become known as the **Purkinje effect** (pronounced "pur-KIN-jee"). One evening, just before dusk, while Purkinje was walking in his garden, he noticed how bright most of his yellow and red flowers appeared in relation to his blue ones. What amazed him was that just a few minutes later the relative brightness of his flowers had somehow been reversed; the entire scene, when viewed at night, appeared only in shades of gray,

Nasal hemiretina. The half of each retina next to the nose.
Temporal hemiretina. The half of each retina next to the temple.
Photopic spectral sensitivity curve. The graph of the sensitivity of cone-mediated vision to different wavelengths of light.
Scotopic spectral sensitivity curve. The graph of the sensi-

tivity of rod-mediated vision to different wavelengths of light.
Purkinje effect. In intense light, red and yellow wavelengths look brighter than blue or green wavelengths of equal intensity; in dim light, blue and green wavelengths look brighter than red and yellow wavelengths of equal intensity.

but most of the blue flowers appeared as brighter grays than did the yellow and red ones. Can you explain this shift in relative brightness by referring to the photopic and scotopic spectral sensitivity curves in Figure 7.9?

Eye Movement

If cones are in fact responsible for mediating high-acuity, color vision under photopic conditions, how can they accomplish their task when most of them are crammed into the fovea? Look around you. What you see is not a few colored details at the center of a grayish scene. You seem to see an expansive, richly detailed, lavishly colored visual world. How can such a perception be the product of a photopic system that, for the most part, is restricted to a few degrees in the center of your visual field? The demonstration below provides a clue.

What this demonstration shows is that what we see is determined not just by what is projected on the retina at that instant. Although we are not aware of it, the eye continually scans the visual field by making a series of brief fixations. About three fixations occur every second, and they are connected by very quick eye movements called **saccades.** The visual system *integrates* (adds together) the foveal images from the preceding few fixations to produce a wide-angled, high-acuity, richly colored perception (See Irwin, 1996). It is because of this *temporal integration* that the world does not vanish momentarily each time we blink.

One way of demonstrating the critical role played by eye movement in vision is to study what happens to vision when all eye movement is stopped. However, because of the risks inherent in paralyzing the eye muscles, researchers have taken an alternative approach. Rather than stopping eye movement, they have stopped the primary consequence of eye movement—the movement of the retinal image across the retina. They have accomplished this by projecting test stimuli from a tiny projector mounted on a contact lens. Each time the eye moves, the lens and the projector move with it;

this keeps the retinal image fixed on the same receptors, as if the eye had remained still.

The effect on vision of stabilizing the retinal image is dramatic (e.g., Pritchard, 1961). After a few seconds of viewing, a simple **stabilized retinal image** disappears, leaving a featureless gray field. The movements of the eyes then increase, presumably in an attempt to bring the image back. However, such movements are futile in this situation because the stabilized retinal image simply moves with the eyes. In a few seconds, the stimulus pattern, or part of it, spontaneously reappears, only to disappear once again.

Why do stabilized images disappear? The answer lies in the fact that the neurons of the visual system respond to change rather than to steady input. Most visual system neurons respond vigorously when a stimulus is presented, moved, or terminated; but they respond only weakly to a continuous, unchanging stimulus. Apparently, one function of eye movements is to keep the retinal image moving back and forth across the receptors, thus ensuring that the receptors and the neurons to which they are connected receive a continually changing pattern of stimulation. When a retinal image is stabilized, parts of the visual system stop responding to the image, and it disappears.

Visual Transduction: The Conversion of Light to Neural Signals

Transduction is the conversion of one form of energy to another. *Visual transduction* is the conversion of light to neural signals by the visual receptors. A breakthrough in the study of visual transduction came in 1876, when a red *pigment* (a pigment is any substance that absorbs light) was extracted from the predominantly rod retina of the frog. This pigment had a curious property. When the pigment (which became known as **rhodopsin**), was exposed to continuous intense light, it was *bleached* (lost its color) and lost its ability to absorb light; but when it was returned to the

DEMONSTRATION

lose your left eye, and with your right eye stare at the fixation point ✦ at a distance of about 12 centimeters (4.75 inches) from the page. Be very careful that your gaze does not shift. You will notice when your gaze is totally fixed that it is difficult to see detail and color at

20° or more from the fixation point because there are so few cones there. Now look at the page again with your right eye, but this time without fixing your gaze. Notice the difference that eye movement makes to your vision.

W		**F**	**D**	**M**		**E**	**A**	✦
50°		40°	30°	20°		10°	5°	0°

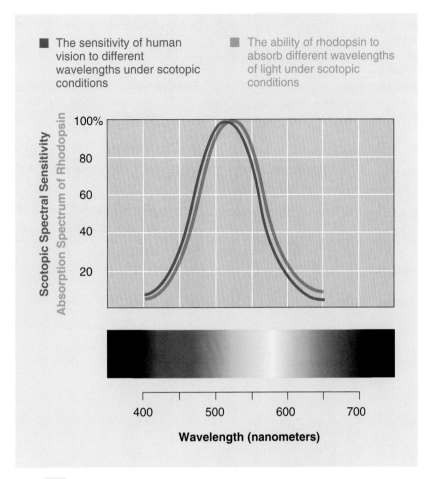

■ The sensitivity of human vision to different wavelengths under scotopic conditions

■ The ability of rhodopsin to absorb different wavelengths of light under scotopic conditions

Figure 7.10 The absorption spectrum of rhodopsin compared with the human scotopic spectral sensitivity curve.

dark, it regained both its redness and its light-absorbing capacity.

It is now clear that the absorption and bleaching of rhodopsin by light is the first step in rod-mediated vision. Evidence comes from demonstrations that the degree to which rhodopsin absorbs light in various situations predicts how humans see under the very same conditions. For example, it has been shown that the degree to which rhodopsin absorbs lights of different wavelengths is related to the ability of humans and other animals with rods to detect the presence of different wavelengths of light under scotopic conditions. Figure 7.10 illustrates the relationship between the **absorption spectrum** of rhodopsin and the human scotopic spectral sensitivity curve. The goodness of the fit leaves little doubt that, in dim light, our sensitivity to various wavelengths is a direct consequence of rhodopsin's ability to absorb them.

Rhodopsin is a G-protein linked receptor that responds to light rather than to neurotransmitter molecules (see Koutalos & Yau, 1993; Molday & Hsu, 1995). Rhodopsin receptors, like other G-protein linked receptors, initiate a cascade of intracellular chemical events when they are activated (see Figure 7.11 on page 170).

When rods are in darkness, an intracellular chemical called *cyclic GMP* (guanosine monophosphate) keeps sodium channels partially open, thus keeping the rods slightly depolarized and a steady flow of excitatory glutamate neurotransmitter molecules emanating from them. However, when rhodopsin receptors are bleached by light, the resulting cascade of intracellular chemical events deactivates the cyclic GMP; and in so doing, it closes the sodium channels and reduces the release of glutamate. The transduction of light by rods makes an important point: Signals are often transmitted through neural systems by inhibition.

Less is known about the cone photopigments than about rhodopsin. However, their structure and function appear to be similar to those of rhodopsin (see Nathans, 1989).

Saccades. The rapid movements of the eyes between fixations.
Stabilized retinal image. A retinal image that does not shift across the retina when the eye moves.
Transduction. The conversion of one type of energy to another.

Rhodopsin. The photopigment of rods.
Absorption spectrum. A graph of the ability of a substance to absorb light of different wavelengths.

Figure 7.11 The inhibitory response of rods to light. When light bleaches rhodopsin molecules, the rods' sodium channels close; as a result, the rods become hyperpolarized and release less glutamate.

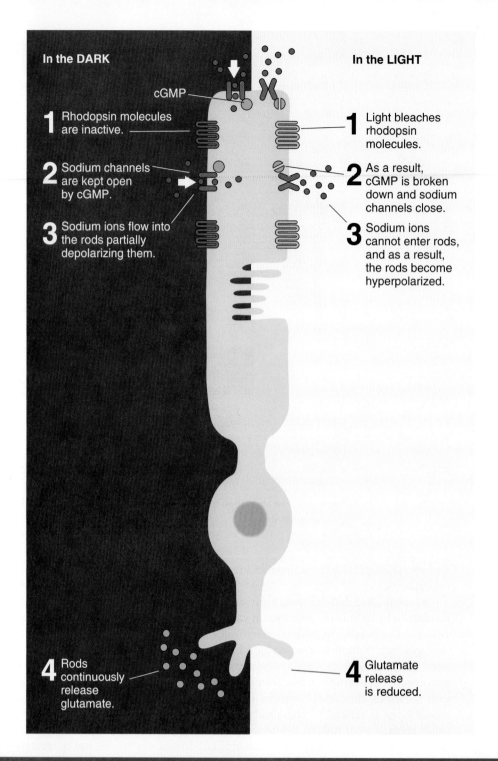

In the DARK

cGMP

1 Rhodopsin molecules are inactive.

2 Sodium channels are kept open by cGMP.

3 Sodium ions flow into the rods partially depolarizing them.

4 Rods continuously release glutamate.

In the LIGHT

1 Light bleaches rhodopsin molecules.

2 As a result, cGMP is broken down and sodium channels close.

3 Sodium ions cannot enter rods, and as a result, the rods become hyperpolarized.

4 Glutamate release is reduced.

7.3 From Retina to Primary Visual Cortex

Many pathways in the brain carry visual information. By far the largest and most thoroughly studied visual pathway is the **retina-geniculate-striate pathway,** which conducts signals from the retina to the **primary visual cortex,** or *striate cortex,* via the **lateral geniculate nuclei** of the thalamus. The organization of this retina-geniculate-striate pathway is illustrated in Figure 7.12. Examine it carefully.

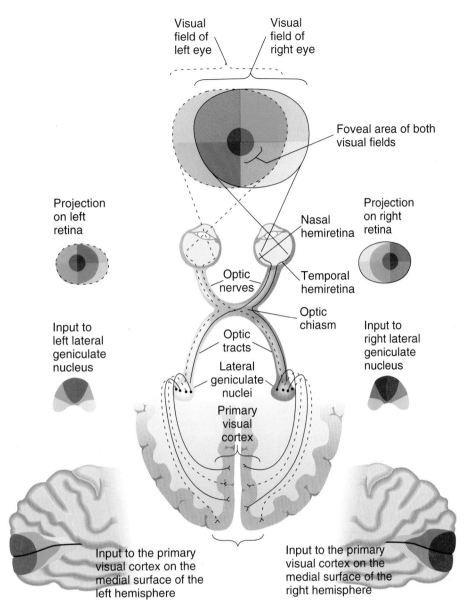

Visual field of left eye

Visual field of right eye

Foveal area of both visual fields

Projection on left retina

Nasal hemiretina

Projection on right retina

Optic nerves

Temporal hemiretina

Input to left lateral geniculate nucleus

Optic chiasm

Optic tracts

Lateral geniculate nuclei

Input to right lateral geniculate nucleus

Primary visual cortex

Input to the primary visual cortex on the medial surface of the left hemisphere

Input to the primary visual cortex on the medial surface of the right hemisphere

Figure 7.12 The retina-geniculate-striate system: The neural projections from the retinas through the lateral geniculate nuclei to the left and right primary visual cortex (striate cortex). The colors indicate the flow of information from various parts of the receptive fields of each eye to various parts of the visual system.

(Adapted from Netter, 1962.)

The main thing to notice from Figure 7.12 is that all signals from the left visual field reach the right primary visual cortex, either ipsilaterally via the *temporal hemiretina* of the right eye or contralaterally via the *nasal hemiretina* of the left eye—and that the opposite is true of all signals from the right visual field. Each lateral geniculate nucleus has six layers, and each layer receives input from all parts of the contralateral visual field of one eye. Most of the lateral geniculate neurons that project to the primary visual cortex terminate in the lower part of cortical layer IV (see Figure 3.29), pro-

ducing a characteristic stripe or striation when viewed in cross section—hence the name *striate cortex*.

Retina-geniculate-striate pathway. The major visual pathway from the retina to the striate cortex (primary visual cortex) via the lateral geniculate nuclei of the thalamus.

Primary visual cortex. The area of the cortex that receives di-

rect input from the lateral geniculate nuclei.

Lateral geniculate nucleus. The six-layered thalamic structure that receives input from the retina and transmits its output to the primary visual cortex.

Retinotopic Organization

The retina-geniculate-striate system is **retinotopic;** each level of the system is organized like a map of the retina. This means that two stimuli presented to adjacent areas of the retina excite adjacent neurons at all levels of the system. The retinotopic layout of the primary visual cortex has a disproportionate representation of the fovea; although the fovea is only a small part of the retina, a relatively large proportion of the primary visual cortex (about 25%) is dedicated to the analysis of its input.

A dramatic demonstration of the retinotopic organization of the primary visual cortex was provided by Dobelle, Mladejovsky, and Girvin (1974). They implanted an array of electrodes in the primary visual cortex of patients who were blind because of damage to their eyes. If electrical current was administered simultaneously through an array of electrodes forming a shape, such as a cross, on the surface of a patient's cortex, the patient reported "seeing" a glowing image of that shape.

The M and P Pathways

Not apparent in Figure 7.12 is the fact that the retina-geniculate-striate system is composed of two largely independent channels of communication. These two channels are most apparent in the lateral geniculate nuclei, where they are spatially segregated. One channel runs through the top four layers of each lateral geniculate nucleus. These layers are called the **parvocellular layers** (or P layers) because they are composed of neurons with small cell bodies (*parvo* means "small"). The other channel runs through the bottom two layers, which are called the **magnocellular layers** (or M layers) because they are composed of neurons with large cell bodies (*magno* means "large").

The *P pathway* is composed of the parvocellular neurons of the lateral geniculate nuclei and the retinal ganglion cells that synapse on them. The P pathway neurons, which are in the majority, are particularly responsive to color, to fine pattern details, and to stationary or slowly moving objects. In contrast, the *M pathway* is composed of the magnocellular neurons of the lateral geniculate nuclei and the retinal ganglion cells that synapse on them. The M pathway neurons are particularly responsive to movement. Cones provide the majority of the input to the P pathway, whereas rods provide the majority of the input to the M pathway.

The P and M pathways project to slightly different sites in striate cortex. The magnocellular neurons terminate just above the parvocellular nurons, both in lower layer IV.

SELF TEST

Before proceeding to the last two sections of the chapter, which describe how the visual system mediates the perception of edges and color, review what you have learned so far about the visual system by filling in the following blanks. Review material related to your errors and omissions.

1. Neural signals are carried from the retina to the lateral geniculate nuclei by the axons of _____ cells.

2. The area of the retina that mediates high-acuity vision is the _____ .

3. Cones are the receptors of the _____ system, which functions only in good lighting.

4. The photopigment of rods is _____ .

5. The most important organizational principle of the retina-geniculate-striate system is that it is laid out _____ .

6. The retinal ganglion cells from the nasal hemiretinas decussate via the _____ .

7. Evidence that rhodopsin is the scotopic photopigment is provided by the fit between the _____ spectrum of rhodopsin and the scotopic spectral sensitivity curve.

8. The high degree of _____ characteristic of the scotopic system increases its sensitivity but decreases its acuity.

9. The axons of retinal ganglion cells leave the eyeball at the _____ .

The answers are (1) retinal ganglion, (2) fovea, (3) photopic, (4) rhodopsin, (5) retinotopically, (6) optic chiasm, (7) absorption, (8) convergence, and (9) blind spot.

Seeing Edges

Edge perception (seeing edges) does not sound like a particularly important topic, but it is. Edges are the most informative features of any visual display because they define the extent and position of the various objects in it. Given the importance of perceiving visual edges and the unrelenting pressure of natural selection, it is not surprising that the visual systems of many species are particularly good at edge perception.

Before considering the visual mechanisms underlying edge perception, it is important to appreciate exactly what a visual edge is. In a sense, a visual edge is nothing: It is merely the place where two different areas of a visual image meet. Accordingly, the perception of an edge is really the perception of a *contrast* between two adjacent areas of the visual field. This section of the chapter reviews the perception of edges (the perception of contrast) between areas that differ from one another in brightness. Color contrast is discussed in the following section.

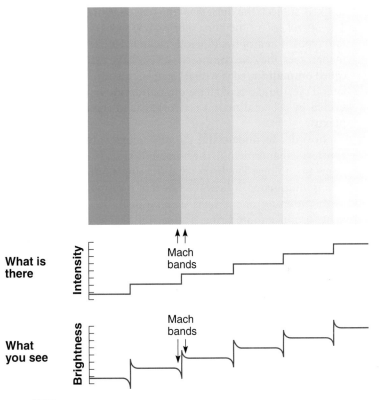

Figure 7.13 The illusory bands visible in this figure are often called Mach bands, but they were in fact discovered by French chemist M. Chevreul in the late 1800s while he was doing research on textile patterns. The Austrian physicist E. Mach discovered illusory bands in a different figure, but the term *Mach bands* is sometimes used in a general sense—as I have done here—to refer to both his and Chevreul's discoveries.

(Thanks to David Burr of the Università Degli Studi di Roma for informing me, and now you, of Chevreul's contribution—see Ross, Morrone, & Burr, 1989.)

Lateral Inhibition and Contrast Enhancement

Carefully examine the stripes in Figure 7.13. The intensity graph in the figure indicates what is there—a series of homogeneous stripes of different intensity. But this is not exactly what you see, is it? What you see is indicated in the

brightness graph. Adjacent to each edge, the brighter stripe looks brighter than it really is and the darker stripe looks darker than it really is (see the demonstration). The nonexistent stripes of brightness and darkness running adjacent to the edges are sometimes called *Mach bands*; they enhance the contrast at each edge and make the edge easier to see.

DEMONSTRATION

The Mach band demonstration is so compelling that you may be confused by it. You may think that the Mach bands in Figure 7.13 have been created by the printers of the book, rather than by your own visual system. To prove to yourself that the Mach bands are a creation of your own visual system, view each stripe individually by covering the adjacent ones with two pieces of paper, and you will see at once that each stripe is completely homogeneous. Now take the paper away and the Mach bands will suddenly reappear.

Retinotopic. Laid out according to a map of the retina.
Parvocellular layers. The layers of the lateral geniculate nuclei that are composed of small neurons; the top four layers.

Magnocellular layers. The layers of the lateral geniculate nuclei that are composed of large neurons; the bottom two layers.

It is important to appreciate that **contrast enhancement** is not something that occurs just in books. Although we are normally unaware of it, every edge we look at is highlighted for us by the contrast-enhancing mechanisms of our nervous systems. In effect, our perception of edges is better than the real thing.

The classic studies of the physiological basis of contrast enhancement were conducted on the eyes of an unlikely subject: the *horseshoe crab* (e.g., Ratliff, 1972). The *lateral eyes* of the horseshoe crab are ideal for certain types of neurophysiological research. Unlike mammalian eyes, they are composed of very large receptors, called **ommatidia,** each with its own large axon. In each lateral eye, the axons of all the ommatidia are interconnected by a lateral neural network, called the **lateral plexus.**

In order to understand the physiological basis of contrast enhancement in the horseshoe crab, you must know two things. The first is that if a single ommatidium is illuminated, it fires at a rate that is proportional to the intensity of the light striking it; more intense lights produce more firing. The second is that when a receptor fires, it inhibits its neighbors via the lateral plexus; this inhibition is called **lateral inhibition** because it spreads laterally across the array of receptors (or *mutual inhibition,* because neighboring receptors inhibit one another). The amount of lateral inhibition produced by a receptor is greatest when it is most in-

tensely illuminated, and it has its greatest effect on its immediate neighbors.

The neural basis of contrast enhancement can be understood in terms of the firing rates of the receptors on each side of an edge, as indicated in Figure 7.14. Notice that the receptor adjacent to the edge on the more intense side (receptor D) fires more than the other intensely illuminated receptors (A, B, C), while the receptor adjacent to the edge on the less-well-illuminated side (receptor E) fires less than the other receptors on that side (F, G, H). Lateral inhibition accounts for these differences. Receptors A, B, and C all fire at the same rate, because they are all receiving the same high level of stimulation and the same high degree of lateral inhibition from all their highly stimulated neighbors. Receptor D fires more than A, B, and C, because it receives as much stimulation as they do but less inhibition from its neighbors, many of whom are on the dimmer side of the edge. Now consider the receptors on the dimmer side. Receptors F, G, and H fire at the same rate, because they are all being stimulated by the same low level of light and receiving the same low level of inhibition from their neighbors. However, receptor E fires even less, because it is receiving the same excitation but more inhibition from its neighbors, many of which are on the more intense side of the edge. Now that you understand the neural basis of contrast enhancement, take another look at Figure 7.13.

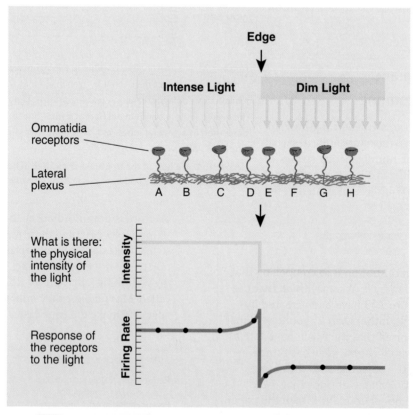

Figure 7.14 How lateral inhibition produces contrast enhancement. (Adapted from Ratliff, 1972.)

Receptive Fields of Visual Neurons

The Nobel Prize–winning research of Hubel and Wiesel is the fitting climax to this discussion of brightness contrast. Their research has revealed much about the neural mechanisms of vision, and their methods have been adopted by a generation of sensory neurophysiologists. Hubel and Wiesel's subjects are single neurons in the visual systems of cats and monkeys. First, the tip of a microelectrode is positioned near a single neuron in the visual area of interest. During testing, eye movements are blocked by *curare* (see Chapter 4), and the images on a screen in front of the subject are focused sharply on the retina by an experimenter using an adjustable lens. The next step in the procedure is to identify the receptive field of the neuron. The **receptive field** of a visual neuron is the area of the visual field within which it is possible for a visual stimulus to influence the firing of that neuron. Visual system neurons tend to be continually active; thus effective stimuli are those that either increase or decrease the rate of firing. The final step in the method is to record the responses of the neuron to various stimuli within its receptive field in order to characterize the types of stimuli that most influence its activity. Then, the electrode is advanced slightly, and the entire process of identifying and characterizing the receptive field properties is repeated for another neuron, and then for another, and another, and so on (see Kuffler, 1953). The general strategy is to begin by studying neurons near the receptors and gradually working up through "higher" and "higher" levels of the system in an effort to understand the increasing complexity of the neural responses at each level.

Receptive Fields: Neurons of the Retina-Geniculate-Striate Pathway

Hubel and Wiesel (e.g., 1979) began their studies of visual system neurons by recording from the three levels of the retina-geniculate-striate pathway: first from retinal ganglion cells, then from lateral geniculate neurons, and finally from the striate neurons of lower layer IV, the terminus of the pathway. They found little change in the receptive fields as they worked their way along the pathway.

When Hubel and Wiesel compared the receptive fields recorded from retinal ganglion cells, lateral geniculate nuclei, and lower layer IV neurons, four commonalties were readily apparent. First, at each level, the receptive fields in the foveal area of the retina were smaller than those at the periphery; this is consistent with the fact that the fovea mediates fine-grained (high-acuity) vision. Second, all the neurons (retinal ganglion cells, lateral geniculate neurons, and lower layer IV neurons, alike) had receptive fields that were circular. Third,

all the neurons were **monocular,** that is, each neuron had a receptive field in one eye but not the other. And fourth, many neurons at each of the three levels of the retina-geniculate-striate system had receptive fields that comprised an excitatory area and an inhibitory area separated by a circular boundary. It is this fourth point that is most important and most complex. Let me explain.

When Hubel and Wiesel shone a spot of white light onto the various parts of the receptive fields of neurons in the retina-geniculate-striate pathway, they discovered two different responses. The neuron responded with either "on" firing or "off" firing, depending on the location of the spot of light in the receptive field. That is, the neuron either displayed a burst of firing when the light was turned on (*"on" firing*), or it displayed an inhibition of firing when the light was turned on and a burst of firing when it was turned off (*"off" firing*).

For most neurons in the retina-geniculate-striate system, their reaction—"on" firing or "off" firing—to a light in a particular part of the receptive field was quite predictable. It depended on whether they were on-center cells or off-center cells, as illustrated in Figure 7.15 on page 176.

On-center cells respond to lights shone in the central region of their receptive fields with "on" firing and to lights shone in the periphery of their receptive fields with inhibition, followed by "off" firing when the light is turned on. **Off-center cells** display the opposite pattern; they respond with inhibition and "off" firing in response to lights in the center of their receptive fields and with "on" firing to lights in the periphery of their receptive fields.

In effect, on-center and off-center cells respond best to contrast. Figure 7.16 on page 177 illustrates this point. The most effective way to influence the firing rate of an on-center or off-center cell is to maximize the contrast between the center and the periphery of its receptive field by illuminating either the entire center or the entire surround while leaving the other region completely dark. Diffusely illuminating the entire receptive field has little effect on firing. Hubel and Wiesel thus concluded that one function of many neurons in

---

Contrast enhancement. The enhancement of the perception of edges.

Ommatidia. The visual receptors of the horseshoe crab.

Lateral plexus. The lateral neural network that interconnects the visual receptors of the horseshoe crab.

Lateral inhibition. Inhibition of adjacent neurons or receptors in a topographic array.

Receptive field. The area (e.g., on the retina) within which it is possible for the appropriate stimulus to influence the firing of the neuron.

Monocular. Involving only one eye.

On-center cells. Cells that respond to lights shone in the center of their receptive fields with "on" firing and to lights shone in the periphery of their fields with "off" firing.

Off-center cells. Neurons that respond to lights shone in the center of their receptive fields with "off" firing and to lights shone in the periphery of their fields with "on" firing.

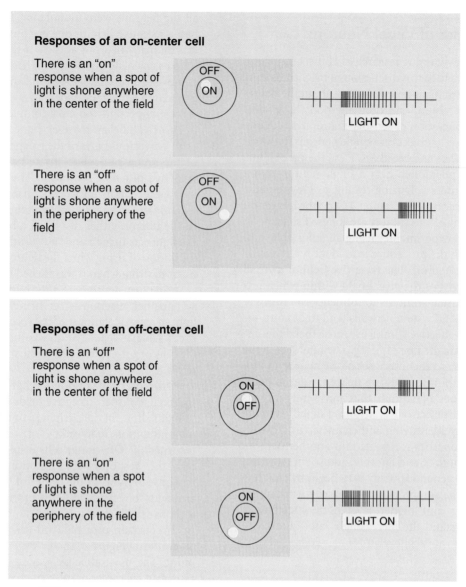

Responses of an on-center cell

There is an "on" response when a spot of light is shone anywhere in the center of the field

OFF
ON

LIGHT ON

There is an "off" response when a spot of light is shone anywhere in the periphery of the field

OFF
ON

LIGHT ON

Responses of an off-center cell

There is an "off" response when a spot of light is shone anywhere in the center of the field

ON
OFF

LIGHT ON

There is an "on" response when a spot of light is shone anywhere in the periphery of the field

ON
OFF

LIGHT ON

Figure 7.15 The receptive fields of an on-center cell and an off-center cell.

the retina-geniculate-striate system is to respond to the degree of brightness contrast between the two areas of their receptive fields (see Livingstone & Hubel, 1988).

Receptive Fields: Simple Cortical Cells

The striate cortex neurons that you just read about—that is, the neurons of lower layer IV—are exceptions. Their receptive fields are unlike the vast majority of striate neurons. The receptive fields of most primary visual cortex neurons fall into one of two classes: simple or complex. Neither of these classes includes the neurons of lower layer IV.

Simple cells, like lower layer IV neurons, have receptive fields that can be divided into antagonistic "on" and "off" regions and are thus unresponsive to diffuse light. And like lower layer IV neurons, they are all monocular. The main difference is that the borders between

the "on" and "off" regions of the cortical receptive fields of simple cells are straight lines rather than circles. Several examples of receptive fields of simple cortical cells are presented in Figure 7.17. Notice that simple cells respond best to bars of light in a dark field, dark bars in a light field, or single straight edges between dark and light areas; that each simple cell responds maximally only when its preferred straight-edge stimulus is in a particular position and in a particular orientation; and that the receptive fields of simple cortical cells are rectangular rather than circular.

Simple cells. Neurons in the visual cortex that respond maximally to straight-edge stimuli in a certain position and orientation.
Complex cells. Neurons in the visual cortex that respond

optimally to straight-edge stimuli in a certain orientation in any part of their receptive field.
Binocular. Involving both eyes.

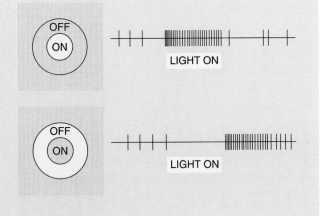

The most effective way of maximizing the firing of an on-center or off-center cell is to completely illuminate either the "on area" or the "off area" of its receptive field:

If both areas of a cell's receptive field are illuminated together, there is little reaction from the cell:

Figure 7.16 The responses of an on-center cell to contrast.

Receptive Fields: Complex Cortical Cells

Complex cells are more numerous than simple cells. Like simple cells, complex cells have rectangular receptive fields, respond best to straight-line stimuli in a specific orientation, and are unresponsive to diffuse light. However, complex cells differ from simple cells in three important ways. First, they have larger receptive fields. Second, it is not possible to divide the receptive fields of complex cells into static "on" and "off" regions: A complex cell responds to a particular straight-edge stimulus of a particular orientation regardless of its position within the receptive field of that cell. Thus, if a stimulus (e.g., a 45° bar of light) that produces "on" firing in a particular complex cell is swept across its receptive field, the cell will respond continuously to it as it moves across the field. Many complex cells respond more robustly to the movement of a straight line across their receptive fields in a particular direction. Third, unlike simple cortical cells, which are all monocular (respond to stimulation of only one of the eyes), many complex cells are **binocular** (respond to stimulation of either eye). Indeed, in monkeys over half the complex cortical cells are binocular.

If the receptive field of a binocular complex cell is measured through one eye and then through the other, the receptive fields in each eye turn out to have almost exactly the same position in the visual field, as well as

Figure 7.17 Examples of visual fields of simple cortical cells.

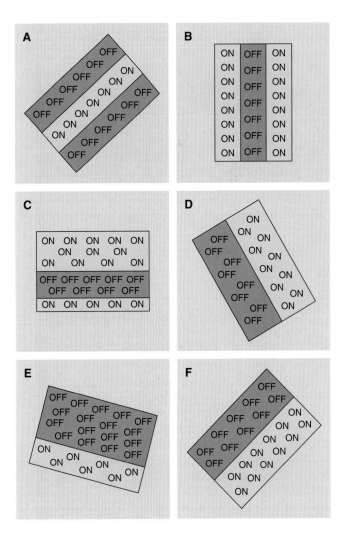

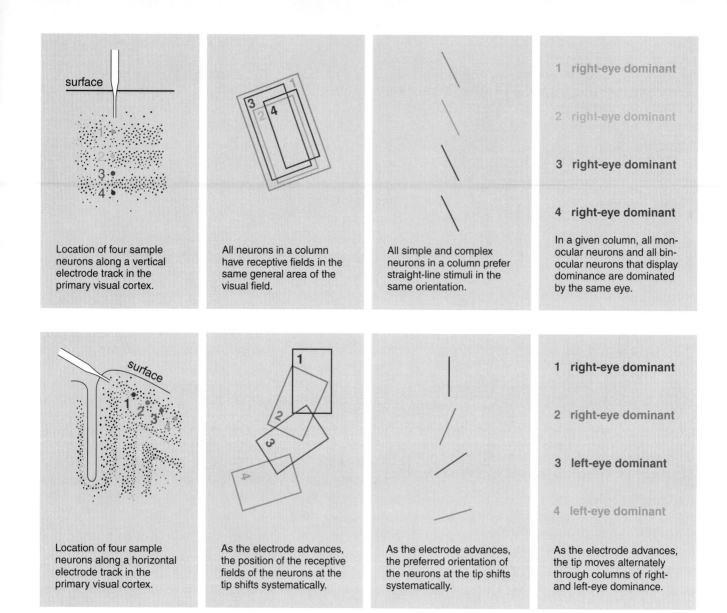

Figure 7.18 The organization of the primary visual cortex: The receptive-field properties of cells encountered along typical vertical and horizontal electrode tracks in the primary visual cortex.

the same orientation preference. In other words, what you learn about the cell by stimulating one eye is confirmed by stimulating the other. What is more, if the appropriate stimulation is applied through both eyes simultaneously, a binocular cell usually fires more robustly than if only one eye is stimulated.

Most of the binocular cells in the primary visual cortex of monkeys display some degree of *ocular dominance;* that is, they respond more robustly to stimulation of one eye than they do to the same stimulation of the other. In addition, some binocular cells fire best when the preferred stimulus is presented to both eyes at the same time but in slightly different positions on the two retinas (e.g., Bishop & Pettigrew, 1986). In other words, these cells respond best to *retinal disparity* and thus are likely to play a role in depth perception (Ohzawa, DeAngelis, & Freeman, 1990).

Columnar Organization of Primary Visual Cortex

The study of the receptive fields of primary visual cortex neurons has led to two important conclusions. The first conclusion is that the characteristics of the receptive fields of visual cortex neurons are attributable to the flow of signals from neurons with simpler receptive fields to those with more complex fields (see Reid & Alonso, 1996). Specifically, it seems that signals flow from on-center and off-center cells in lower layer IV to simple cells and from simple cells to complex cells.

The second conclusion is that primary visual cortex neurons are grouped in functional vertical columns (in this context, *vertical* means at right angles to the cortical layers). Much of the evidence for this conclusion comes from studies of the receptive fields of neurons along various vertical and horizontal electrode tracks (see Figure 7.18). If one advances an electrode vertically through the layers of the visual cortex, stopping to plot the receptive fields of many neurons along the way, each cell in the column has a receptive field in the same general area of the visual field (the area of the visual field covered by all of the receptive fields of cells in a given column is called the **aggregate field** of that column). One would also find that all the cells in a column respond best to straight lines in the very same orientation, and those neurons in a column that are either monocular or binocular with ocular dominance are all most sensitive to light in the same eye, left or right.

In contrast, if an electrode is advanced horizontally through the tissue, each successive cell encountered is likely to have a receptive field in a slightly different location and to be maximally responsive to straight lines of a slightly different orientation. And during a horizontal electrode pass, the tip passes alternately through areas of left-eye dominance and right-eye dominance.

All of the functional columns in the primary visual cortex that analyze input from one area of the retina are clustered together. Half of a cluster receives input primarily from the left eye, and half receives input primarily from the right eye. Indeed, input from the eyes has been found to enter layer IV in alternating patches. The best kind of evidence of this alternating arrangement first came from a study (LeVay, Hubel, & Wiesel, 1975) in which a radioactive amino acid was injected into one eye in sufficient quantities to cross the synapses of the retina-geniculate-striate system and show up in lower layer IV of the primary visual cortex, and to a lesser degree in the layers just above and below it. The alternating patches of radioactivity and nonradio-

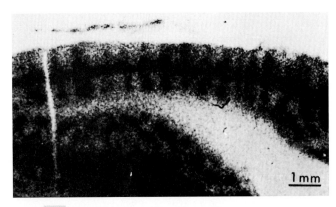

Figure 7.20 The columns of orientation specificity in the primary visual cortex of the monkey as revealed by 2-DG autoradiography.

(From "Orientation Columns in Macaque Monkey Visual Cortex Demonstrated by the 2-Deoxyglucose Autoradiographic Technique" by D. H. Hubel, T. N. Wiesel, and M. P. Stryker. Reprinted by permission from *Nature*, vol. 269, p. 329. Copyright © 1977 by Macmillan Magazines Ltd.)

activity in the autoradiograph in Figure 7.19 mark the alternating patches of input from the two eyes.

All of the clusters of functional columns that analyze input from one area of the retina are thought to include neurons with preferences for straight-line stimuli of various orientations. The columns of orientation specificity were visualized in a study (Hubel, Wiesel, & Stryker, 1977) in which radioactive 2-DG was injected into monkeys that then spent 45 minutes viewing a pattern of vertical stripes moving back and forth. As you know from previous chapters, radioactive 2-DG is taken up by active neurons and accumulates in them, thus identifying the location of neurons that are particularly active during the test period. The autoradiograph in Figure 7.20 reveals the columns of cells in the primary visual cortex that were activated by exposure to the moving vertical stripes. Notice that the neurons in lower layer IV show no orientation specificity—because they do not respond to straight-line stimuli.

Figure 7.21 on page 180 summarizes Hubel and Wiesel's theory of how the vertical columns of the primary visual cortex are organized.

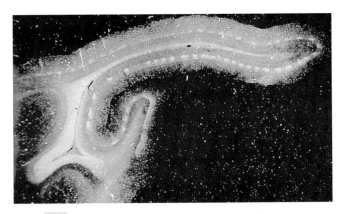

Figure 7.19 The alternation of input into lower layer IV of the primary visual cortex from the left and right eyes. Radioactive amino acids that were injected into one eye were subsequently revealed on autoradiographs of the visual cortex as patches of radioactivity alternating with patches of nonradioactivity.

(From "Brain Mechanism of Vision" by D. H. Hubel and T. N. Wiesel. Reprinted by permission of *Scientific American*, vol. 241, p. 151. Copyright © 1979 by Scientific American, Inc.)

Spatial-Frequency Theory

Hubel and Wiesel barely had time to place their Nobel Prizes on their mantels before an important qualification to their theory was proposed. DeValois, DeValois, and their colleagues (see DeValois & DeValois, 1988) proposed that the visual cortex operates on a code of

Aggregate field. The area encompassing all of the receptive fields of all of the neurons in a given column of visual cortex.

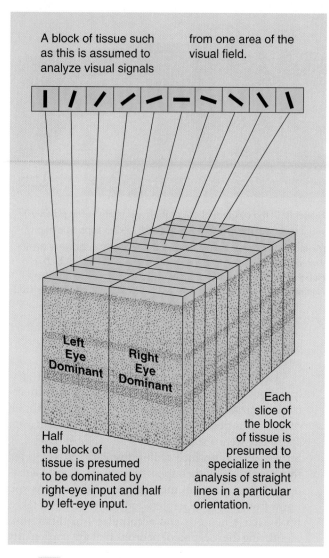

A block of tissue such as this is assumed to analyze visual signals from one area of the visual field.

Left Eye Dominant

Right Eye Dominant

Half the block of tissue is presumed to be dominated by right-eye input and half by left-eye input.

Each slice of the block of tissue is presumed to specialize in the analysis of straight lines in a particular orientation.

Figure 7.21 Hubel and Wiesel's model of the organization of functional columns in the primary visual cortex.

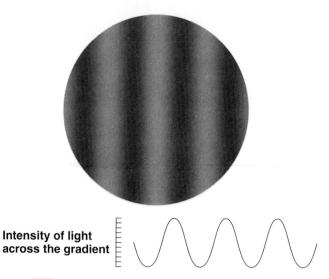

Intensity of light across the gradient

Figure 7.22 A sine-wave grating.
(Adapted from DeValois & DeValois, 1988.)

spatial frequency, not on the code of straight lines and edges hypothesized by Hubel and Wiesel.

In support of the **spatial-frequency theory** is the observation that visual cortex neurons respond even more robustly to sine-wave gratings that are placed at specific angles in their receptive fields than they do to bars or edges. A **sine-wave grating** is a set of equally spaced, parallel, alternating light and dark stripes that is created by varying the light across the grating in a sine-wave pattern—see Figure 7.22. Sine-wave gratings differ from one another in frequency (the width of their stripes), amplitude (the magnitude of the difference in intensity between the dark and light stripes), and angle.

The spatial-frequency theory is based on two physical principles. The first is that any visual stimulus can be represented by a plotting of the intensity of light along

High

Low

Intensity

Figure 7.23 A visual stimulus represented by the plotting of changes in the intensity of light along slices running through it. For example, plotted here are the changes in intensity along one slice of a scene that would interest any hungry lion.

The spatial-frequency theory of visual cortex function (see DeValois & DeValois, 1988) is that each functional module of the visual cortex performs a sort of Fourier analysis on the visual pattern in its receptive field; the neurons in each module are thought to respond selectively to various frequencies and orientations of sine-wave gratings. When all of the visual cortex neurons that are influenced by a particular scene respond together, a perception of the scene is created by the summation of its various constituent sine-wave gratings.

As I said before, the primary support for the spatial-frequency theory is that primary visual cortex neurons are more responsive to sine-wave gratings than they are to straight lines. Most neurons in the primary visual cortex respond best when a sine-wave grating of a particular frequency is presented at a particular angle in a particular location of the visual field. However, straight-edge stimuli, which have been used in most studies of visual cortex neurons, can readily be translated into component sine-wave gratings of the same orientation. Thus the research on spatial-frequency detection by visual neurons extends and complements previous research rather than refuting it.

lines running through it (see Figure 7.23). The second is that any curve, no matter how irregular, can be broken down into constituent sine waves by a mathematical procedure called **Fourier analysis** (see Figure 7.24).

Seeing Color

Color is one of the most obvious qualities of human visual experience. So far in this chapter, we have limited our discussion of vision to the so-called **achromatic colors:** black, white, and gray. Black is experienced when there is an absence of light, the perception of white is produced by an intense mixture of a wide range of wavelengths in roughly equal proportion, and the perception of gray is produced by the same mixture at lower intensities. In this section, we deal with the perception of **chromatic colors**—colors such as blue, green, and yellow. The correct term for chromatic colors is *hues,* but in everyday language they are referred to as colors; and for the sake of simplicity, I will do the same.

What is there about a visual stimulus that determines the color we perceive? To a large degree, the perception of an object's color depends on the wavelengths of light that it reflects into the eye. Figure 7.1 is an illustration of the colors associated with individual wavelengths; however, outside the laboratory, one never encounters objects that reflect single wavelengths. Sunlight and most sources of artificial light contain complex mixtures of most visible wavelengths. Most objects absorb the different wavelengths of light that strike them to varying degrees and reflect the rest. The mixture of wavelengths that objects reflect influences our perception of their color.

Spatial-frequency theory. The theory that the visual cortex encodes visual patterns in terms of their component sine-wave gratings.

Sine-wave grating. An array of equally spaced, parallel, alternating dark and light stripes that is created by varying the light across the grating in a sine-wave pattern.

Fourier analysis. A mathematical procedure for breaking down a complex wave form (e.g., an EEG signal) into component sine waves of varying frequency.

Achromatic colors. Black, white, and gray.

Chromatic colors. The hues—colors such as blue, green, and yellow.

With the development and refinement of methods for studying the responses of individual receptors and neurons in the visual system, an impressive amount has been learned in the last two or three decades about how the visual system responds to different wavelengths. However, in some ways, it is even more impressive that the basic mechanisms of color vision were derived in the last century by behaviorial scientists whose research technology was limited to their own ingenuity and observational skills. Through careful observation of the perceptual abilities of their subjects, these scientists were able to infer some of the major features of the physiological basis of color vision.

You have already encountered in this chapter many instances in which scientific gains have resulted from the convergence of behavioral, neurochemical, and neurophysiological research. However, the early advances in the study of the neural basis of color vision occurred long before it was possible to bring modern neurochemical and neurophysiological procedures to bear.

Component and Opponent Processing

The **component theory** (trichromatic theory) of color vision was proposed by Thomas Young in 1802 and refined by Hermann von Helmholtz in 1852. According to this theory, there are three different kinds of color receptors (cones), each with a different spectral sensitivity, and the color of a particular stimulus is presumed to be encoded by the ratio of activity in the three kinds of receptors. Young and Helmholtz derived their theory from the observation that any color of the visible spectrum can be matched by a mixing together of three different wavelengths of light in different proportions. This can be accomplished with any three wavelengths, provided that the color of any one of them cannot be matched by a mixing of the other two. The fact that three is normally the minimum number of different wavelengths necessary to match every color suggested that there were three types of receptors.

Another theory of color vision, the **opponent-process theory** of color vision, was proposed by Ewald Hering in 1878. He suggested that there are two different classes of cells in the visual system for encoding color and another one for encoding brightness. Hering hypothesized that each of the three classes of cells encoded two complementary color perceptions. One class of color-coding cells signaled red by changing its activity in one direction (e.g., hyperpolarization) and signaled red's complementary color, green, by changing its activity in the other direction (e.g., hypopolarization). Another class of color-coding cells was hypothesized to signal blue and its complement, yellow, in the same opponent fashion; and a class of brightness-coding cells was hypothesized to similarly signal both black and white. **Complementary colors** are pairs of colors that produce white or gray when combined in equal measure (e.g., green light and red light).

Hering based his opponent-process theory of color vision on several behavioral observations. One was that complementary colors cannot exist together: There is no such thing as bluish yellow or reddish green. Another was that the afterimage produced by staring at red is green and vice versa, and the afterimage produced by staring at yellow is blue and vice versa (see the demonstration below).

A somewhat misguided debate raged for many years between supporters of the component (trichromatic) and opponent theories of color vision. I say "misguided" because it was fueled more by the adversarial predisposition of scientists than by the incompatibility of the two theories. In fact, research subsequently proved that both color-coding mechanisms coexist in the same visual systems (see Hurlbert, 1991).

It was the development in the early 1960s of **microspectrophotometry**—a technique for measuring the absorption spectrum of the photopigment contained in a

DEMONSTRATION

Have you ever noticed complementary afterimages? To see them, stare at the fixation point in the left panel for 1 minute without moving your eyes; then quickly shift your gaze to the fixation point in the right panel. In the right panel, you will see four squares whose colors are complementary to those in the left panel.

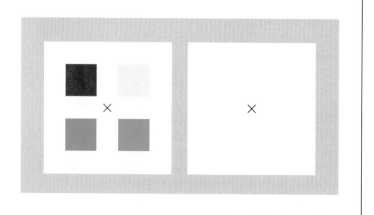

single cone—that allowed researchers to confirm the conclusion that had been reached by Young over a century and a half before (e.g., Wald, 1964). They found that there are indeed three different kinds of cones in the retinas of those vertebrates with good color vision, and they found that each of the three has a different photopigment with its own characteristic absorption spectrum. As Figure 7.25 illustrates, some cones are most sensitive to short wavelengths, some are most sensitive to medium wavelengths, and some are most sensitive to long wavelengths.

Although the coding of color by cones operates on a purely component basis, there is evidence of opponent processing of color at all subsequent levels of the retina-geniculate-striate system. That is, there are cells at all subsequent levels that respond in one direction (e.g., increased firing) to one color and in the opposite direction (e.g., decreased firing) to its complementary color. The first direct evidence of opponent processing came from a study of bipolar cells in the carp, a fish with excellent color vision (Svaetichin, 1956). Carp bipolar cells respond in one direction (hyperpolarization or depolarization) to red wavelengths and in the other direction to green wavelengths. And other retinal cells code both blue and yellow wavelengths in the same opponent fashion. Figure 7.26 on page 184 illustrates a circuit that can translate the component responses of the three types of cones into the red-green and blue-yellow opponent responses of bipolar cells.

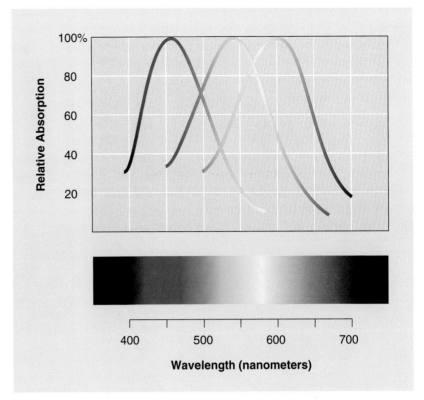

Figure 7.25 The absorption spectra of the three classes of cones.

Color Constancy and the Retinex Theory

Neither component nor opponent processing can account for the single most important characteristic of color vision: color constancy. **Color constancy** refers to the fact that the perceived color of an object is not a simple function of the wavelengths reflected by it. As I write this at 7:15 on a December morning, it is dark outside, and I am working in my office by the light of a tiny incandescent desk lamp. Later in the morning, when students start to arrive, I turn on my nasty fluorescent office lights; and then, in the afternoon, when the sun has shifted to my side of the building, I turn off the lights and work by natural light. The point is that because these light sources differ markedly in the wavelengths they contain, the wavelengths reflected by various objects in my office—my blue shirt, for example—change substantially during the course of the day. However, although the wavelengths reflected by my shirt change

markedly, its color does not. My shirt will be just as blue in midmorning and in late afternoon as it is now. Color constancy is the tendency for an object to stay the same color despite major changes in the wavelengths of light that it reflects.

Although the phenomenon of color constancy is counterintuitive, its advantage is obvious. Color constancy improves our ability to tell objects apart in a memorable way so we can respond appropriately to them; our ability to recognize objects would be greatly lessened if their color changed every time there was a change in illumination (Brou et al., 1986).

Although color constancy is an important feature of our vision, we are normally unaware of it. Under everyday conditions, we have no way of appreciating

Component theory. The theory that the relative amount of activity produced in three different classes of cones by a light determines its perceived color.

Opponent-process theory. The theory that a receptor or neuron signals one color when it responds in one way (e.g., by increasing its firing rate) and signals its complementary color when it responds in the opposite way (e.g., by decreasing its firing rate).

Complementary colors. Pairs of colors that produce white or gray when combined in equal measure; every color has a complementary color.

Microspectrophotometry. A technique that has been used to measure the absorption spectrum of the photopigment contained in a single visual receptor.

Color constancy. The tendency of an object to appear the same color even when the wavelengths that it reflects change.

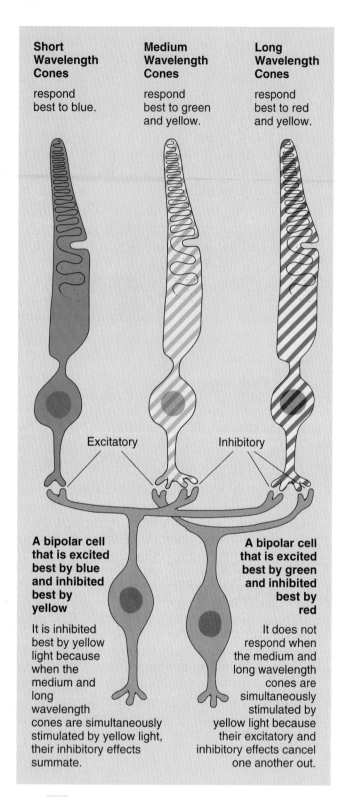

Short Wavelength Cones

respond best to blue.

Medium Wavelength Cones

respond best to green and yellow.

Long Wavelength Cones

respond best to red and yellow.

Excitatory   Inhibitory

A bipolar cell that is excited best by blue and inhibited best by yellow

It is inhibited best by yellow light because when the medium and long wavelength cones are simultaneously stimulated by yellow light, their inhibitory effects summate.

A bipolar cell that is excited best by green and inhibited best by red

It does not respond when the medium and long wavelength cones are simultaneously stimulated by yellow light because their excitatory and inhibitory effects cancel one another out.

Figure 7.26 A retinal circuit that can translate the component responses of the three types of cones into the red-green and blue-yellow opponent responses of bipolar cells.

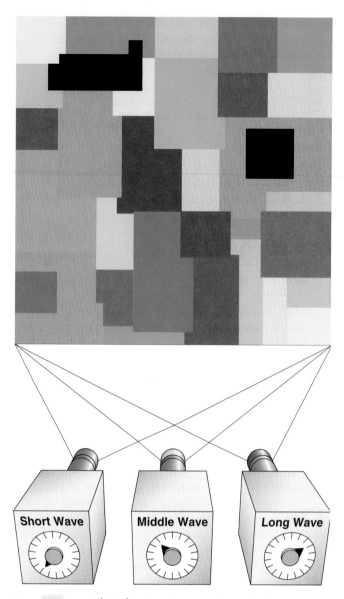

Short Wave   Middle Wave   Long Wave

Figure 7.27 Land's (1977) color-vision experiments. Subjects viewed Mondrians that were illuminated by various proportions of three different wavelengths: a short wavelength, a middle wavelength, and a long wavelength.

just how much the wavelengths reflected by an object can change without the object changing its color. It is only in the controlled environment of the laboratory that one can fully appreciate that color constancy is more than an important factor in color vision: It is the essence of color vision.

Edwin Land (1977), the inventor of the Polaroid camera, developed several dramatic laboratory demonstrations of color constancy. The following is one of them. First, Land asked subjects to adjust the intensity of light coming from each of three different projectors until they judged the mixture to be a pure white when viewed in an otherwise dark room. Each projector emitted only one wavelength of light: one a short wavelength light, one a medium wavelength light, and one a long wavelength light. Next, Land shone the three projectors on a test display like the one in Figure 7.27. (These displays are called *Mondrians* because they resemble the painting of the Dutch master painter Piet

The following visual pattern (Brou et al., 1986) illustrates how color constancy can break down when we look at displays that lack sharply defined areas of contrast. Examine it. It may surprise you to learn that the four differently colored hexagons (six-sided figures) are all exactly the same. Although you may have difficulty believing this, you can prove it to yourself by eliminating the effect of the adjacent context. Cut four holes in a piece of paper so that parts of the four hexagons, but not of the rest of the figure, will be visible through them. Place the sheet of paper over the figure and compare the four hexagons. Now do you believe me?

(Courtesy of Jerome Y. Lettvin; photo by Denice Denton and Brad Howland.)

Mondrian.) Land himself adjusted the three projectors so that the mixture of the three that was being reflected from one particular area of the Mondrian—let's say the blue rectangular shape—was the exact mixture that had been judged as white by subjects in the first stage of the demonstration. To accomplish this, Land used a *photometer* to measure the amounts of three wavelengths being reflected by the blue rectangle. Next, he repeated this process but this time for another area of the Mondrian—let's say the green rectangle—that is, he adjusted the three projectors until the mixture that had previously been judged as white was being reflected by the green rectangle.

What color was the blue rectangle when it was reflecting a pure white mixture of light, and what color was the green rectangle when it was reflecting the very same mixture of light? The answers to these questions astound many students: The blue rectangle appeared blue, and the green rectangle appeared green, even though they were reflecting the exact same mixture of white light. However, when the blue and green rectangles were viewed in isolation (not as part of a Mondrian) under the same illumination but in an otherwise dark room, they both appeared white.

The point of Land's demonstration is that blue objects stay blue, green objects stay green, and so forth, regardless of the wavelengths that they reflect. This color constancy occurs as long as the object is illumi-

nated with light that contains some short, medium, and long wavelengths (such as daylight, firelight, and virtually all manufactured lighting) and as long as the object is viewed as part of a scene, not in isolation.

According to Land's **retinex theory** of color vision, the color of an object is determined by its *reflectance*—the proportion of light of different wavelengths that a surface reflects. Although the wavelengths of light reflected by a surface change dramatically with changes in illumination, the efficiency with which a surface absorbs each wavelength and reflects the unabsorbed portion does not change. According to the retinex theory, the visual system calculates the reflectance of surfaces, and thus perceives their color, by comparing the light reflected by adjacent surfaces in three different wavelength bands (short, medium, and long), which correspond to the three classes of cones.

The detection of contrast between adjacent areas of the visual field is important in the perception of color. The demonstration above illustrates this point by showing how color constancy can break down when we look at artificial displays that lack sharply defined areas of

---

Retinex theory. Land's theory that the color of surfaces is determined by their reflectance; with the visual system calculating the reflectance of the sur- faces in a scene by comparing the ability of adjacent surfaces to reflect short, medium, and long wavelengths.

contrast. Please take the time to experience it; it is an amazing demonstration.

Why is Land's research so critical for neuroscientists trying to discover the neural mechanisms of color vision? It is important because it indicates the type of cortical neurons that are likely to be involved in color vision. If the perception of color depends on the analysis of contrast between adjacent areas of the visual field, then the critical neurons should be responsive to color contrast. And they are. For example, **dual-opponent color cells** in the monkey visual cortex respond with vigorous "on" firing when the center of their circular receptive field is illuminated with one wavelength, such as green, and the surround is simultaneously illuminated with another wavelength, such as red. And the same cells display vigorous "off" firing when the pattern of illumination is reversed—for example, red in the center and green in the surround. In essence, dual-opponent color cells respond to the contrast between wavelengths reflected by adjacent areas of their receptive field.

A major breakthrough in the understanding of the organization of the primary visual cortex came with the discovery that dual-opponent color cells are not distributed evenly throughout the primary visual cortex (see Zeki, 1993a). Livingstone and Hubel (1984) found that these neurons are distributed in the primary visual cortex in peglike columns that penetrate the layers of the primary visual cortex, with the exception of lower layer IV. The neurons in these peglike columns are particularly rich in the mitochondria enzyme **cytochrome oxidase;** thus their distribution in the primary visual cortex can be visualized if one stains slices of tissue with stains that have an affinity for this enzyme.

When a section of striate tissue is cut parallel to the cortical layers and stained in this way, the pegs are seen as "blobs" of stain scattered over the cortex (unless the section is cut from lower layer IV). To the relief of in-

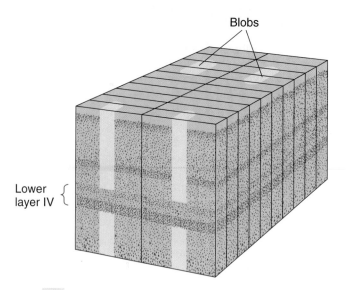

Figure 7.28 Hubel and Livingstone's model of primary visual cortex organization. The blobs are peglike columns that contain dual-opponent color cells.

structors and students alike, the term **blobs** has become the accepted scientific label for peglike, cytochrome oxidase–rich dual-opponent color columns. The blobs were found to be located in the middle of ocular dominance columns (see Figure 7.28, and compare with Figure 7.21).

Dual-opponent color cells. Neurons that respond to the differences in the wavelengths of light stimulating adjacent areas of their receptive field.
Cytochrome oxidase. An enzyme present in particularly high concentrations in the dual-opponent color cells of the visual cortex.
Blobs. Cytochrome oxidase–rich dual-opponent color columns.

CONCLUSION

This chapter began by describing the passage of light into the eye to the receptor layer of the retina (7.1). Then, it described the transduction (translation) of light into neural signals (7.2). Next, it followed the transmission of neural signals from the retinal receptors to the primary visual cortex via the retina-geniculate-striate system (7.3). It concluded by discussing the aspects of retina-geniculate-striate system structure and function that influence the perception of brightness contrast (7.4) and color (7.5).

The major theme of this chapter was that vision is a creative process. The retina-geniculate-striate pathway does not conduct intact visual images to the cortex. It conducts, via two major channels (the P channel and the M channel), information about a few critical features of the visual world—for example, information

about location, movement, brightness contrast, and color contrast; and from these bits of information, it creates a perception that is better than the retinal image in all respects and better than the external reality in some. The theme of converging operations pervades much of this book, but the study of the visual system is arguably the single best example of how major insights into the neural bases of psychological processes result from the convergence of neuroanatomical, neurochemical, neurophysiological, and behavioral research.

In this chapter, there were opportunities for you to experience firsthand the important principles of the visual process. I hope these demonstrations made you more aware of the amazing abilities of your own visual system and the relevance of what you have learned in this chapter to your everyday life.

FOOD FOR THOUGHT

1. In vision, as in photography, one frequently has to sacrifice sharpness (acuity) to increase sensitivity. Discuss.

2. Why is it so important to distinguish between intensity and brightness and between wavelength and color?

3. If you mix equal proportions of red and green light, you get something close to white or gray light, depending on the exact wavelengths of red and green (the exact complement of red is actually greenish-blue). However, if you mix equal portions of red and green paint, you get an approximation of black paint. Explain this paradox.

4. Is it appropriate to refer to the light being reflected by a red object as a red light? Why not?

KEY TERMS

Absorption spectrum (p. 169)
Accommodation (p. 161)
Achromatic colors (p. 181)
Acuity (p. 161)
Aggregate field (p. 179)
Amacrine cells (p. 163)
Binocular (p. 177)
Binocular disparity (p. 163)
Bipolar cells (p. 163)
Blind spot (p. 164)
Blobs (p. 186)
Chromatic colors (p. 181)
Ciliary muscles (p. 161)
Color constancy (p. 183)
Complementary colors (p. 182)
Completion (p. 164)
Complex cells (p. 177)

Component theory (p. 182)
Cones (p. 164)
Contrast enhancement (p. 174)
Cytochrome oxidase (p. 186)
Dual-opponent color cells (p. 186)
Duplexity theory (p. 164)
Fourier analysis (p. 181)
Fovea (p. 164)
Horizontal cells (p. 163)
Lateral geniculate nuclei (p. 170)
Lateral inhibition (p. 174)
Lateral plexus (p. 174)
Magnocellular layers (p. 172)
Microspectrophotometry (p. 182)

Monocular (p. 175)
Nasal hemiretina (p. 166)
Off-center cells (p. 175)
Ommatidia (p. 174)
On-center cells (p. 175)
Opponent-process theory (p. 182)
Parvocellular layers (p. 172)
Photopic spectral sensitivity curve (p. 167)
Photopic vision (p. 164)
Primary visual cortex (p. 170)
Purkinje effect (p. 167)
Receptive field (p. 175)
Receptors (p. 163)
Retina-geniculate-striate pathway (p. 170)
Retinal ganglion cells (p. 163)

Retinex theory (p. 185)
Retinotopic (p. 172)
Rhodopsin (p. 168)
Rods (p. 164)
Saccades (p. 168)
Scotopic spectral sensitivity curve (p. 167)
Scotopic vision (p. 165)
Sensitivity (p. 161)
Simple cells (p. 176)
Sine-wave grating (p. 180)
Spatial-frequency theory (p. 180)
Stabilized retinal image (p. 168)
Temporal hemiretina (p. 166)
Transduction (p. 168)

ADDITIONAL READING

The best introductory readings for those interested in the biopsychology of perception are *Scientific American* articles. Their large color illustrations are without rival. The following seven articles provide excellent coverage of topics discussed in this chapter:

Brou, P., Sciascia, T. R., Linden, L., & Lettvin, J. Y. (1986, September). The colors of things. *Scientific American, 255,* 84–91.

Hubel, D. H., & Wiesel, T. N. (1979, September). Brain mechanisms of vision. *Scientific American, 241,* 150–162.

Land, E. H. (1977, April). The retinex theory of color vision. *Scientific American, 237,* 108–128.

Nathans, J. (1989, February). The genes for color vision. *Scientific American, 260,* 42–49.

Ramachandran, V. (1992, May) Blind spots. *Scientific American, 266,* 86–91.

Ratliff, F. (1972, June). Contour and contrast. *Scientific American, 226,* 90–101.

Schnapf, J. L., & Baylor, D. A. (1987, April). How photoreceptor cells respond to light. *Scientific American, 256,* 40–47.

The following book is a clear summary of current knowledge about vision and the brain. It is a must for every serious student of the topic:

Zeki, S. (1993). *A vision of the brain.* Oxford: Blackwell Scientific Publications.

For those interested in learning more about the spatial-frequency theory of vision, which I could discuss only briefly in this chapter, I recommend the following book:

DeValois, R. L., & DeValois, K. K. (1988). *Spatial vision.* New York: Oxford University Press.

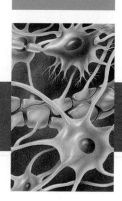

8

Mechanisms of Perception, Conscious Awareness, and Attention

here are two chapters in this text whose primary focus is sensory: Chapter 7 was the first, and this is the second. Chapter 7 described how visual signals are translated into neural signals by cones and rods, and how these neural signals are conducted by the retina-geniculate-striate system to the primary visual cortex.

This chapter differs from Chapter 7 in two major respects. First, rather than focusing on one sensory system, it discusses all five **exteroceptive sensory systems**—the five sensory systems that interpret stimuli from outside the body: vision, hearing, touch, smell, and taste. Second, rather than focusing on the conduction of sensory signals from receptors to cortex, this chapter focuses on cortical mechanisms and phenomena.

The chapter begins with three general principles of sensory system organization. Then, it returns to the story line initiated in Chapter 7: It returns to the primary visual cortex—the point of entry of visual signals into cortical visual circuits—and it follows these signals as they are subjected to analysis by other areas of visual cortex. Next, the chapter examines the other four exteroceptive sensory systems. It concludes with a discussion of the mechanisms of attention, a phenomenon important to all five of the exteroceptive sensory systems.

The disproportionate coverage of the visual system in Chapters 7 and 8 is not arbitrary. For a variety of reasons, the vast majority of research on sensory systems has focused on the visual system. As a result, far more is known about the visual system than about the other sensory systems, and most current theories of sensory system function are based on visual system research.

8.1 Principles of Sensory System Organization

The sensory areas of the cerebral cortex are of three different types: primary, secondary, and association. The **primary sensory cortex** of a system is the area of sensory cortex that receives most of its input directly from the thalamic relay nuclei of that system. For example, as you learned in Chapter 7, the primary visual cortex is the area of the cerebral cortex that receives most of its input from the lateral geniculate nucleus of the thalamus. The **secondary sensory cortex** of a system is the areas of the sensory cortex that receive most of their input from the primary sensory cortex of that system or from other areas of the secondary sensory cortex of the same system. **Association cortex** is any area of cortex that receives input from more than one sensory system. Most input to areas of association cortex comes via areas of secondary sensory cortex. The interactions among these three types of sensory cortex are characterized by three major principles: hierarchical organization, functional segregation, and parallel processing.

Hierarchical Organization

Sensory systems are characterized by **hierarchical organization**. A *hierarchy* is a system whose members can be assigned to specific levels or ranks in relation to one another. For example, the army is a hierarchical system because all soldiers are ranked with respect to their authority. In the same way, sensory structures are organized in a hierarchy on the basis of the specificity and complexity of their function (see Figure 8.1 on page 190). As one moves through a sensory system from receptors, to thalamic nuclei, to primary sensory cortex, to secondary sensory cortex, to association cortex, one finds neurons that respond optimally to stimuli of greater and greater specificity and complexity. Each level of a sensory hierarchy receives its input from lower levels and adds another layer of analysis before passing it on up the hierarchy (see Hilgetag, O'Neill, & Young, 1996).

The hierarchical organization of sensory systems is apparent from a comparison of the effects of damage to various levels: The higher the level of damage, the more specific and complex the deficit. For example, destruction of a sensory system's receptors produces a complete loss of ability to perceive in that sensory modality (e.g., total blindness or deafness); in contrast, destruc-

Exteroceptive sensory systems. The five sensory systems that interpret stimuli from outside the body: vision, hearing, touch, smell, and taste.

Primary sensory cortex. An area of sensory cortex that receives most of its input directly from the thalamic relay nuclei of one sensory system.

Secondary sensory cortex. Areas of sensory cortex that receive most of their input from the primary sensory cortex of one system or from other areas of secondary cortex of the same system.

Association cortex. Areas of the cortex that receive input from more than one sensory system.

Hierarchical organization. Organization into a series of levels that can be ranked with respect to one another; for example, primary cortex, secondary cortex, and association cortex perform progressively more detailed analyses.

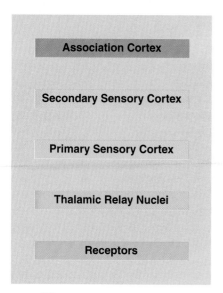

Figure 8.1 The hierarchical organization of the sensory systems. The receptors perform the simplest and most general analyses, and the association cortex performs the most complex and specific analyses.

tion of an area of association or secondary sensory cortex typically produces complex and specific sensory deficits, while leaving fundamental sensory abilities intact. Dr. P., the man who mistook his wife for a hat (Sacks, 1985), displays such a pattern of deficits:

Dr. P. was a musician of distinction, well-known for many years as a singer . . . and as a teacher. . . . It was obvious within a few seconds of meeting him that there was no trace of dementia [intellectual deterioration]. . . . He was a man of great cultivation and charm who talked well and fluently, with imagination and humour. . . .

"What seems to be the matter?" I asked him at length.

"Nothing that I know of," he replied with a smile, "but people seem to think that there's something wrong with my eyes."

"But *you* don't recognise any visual problems?"

"No, not directly, but I occasionally make mistakes." . . .

It was while examining his reflexes . . . that the first bizarre experience occurred. I had taken off his left shoe and scratched the sole of his foot with a key—a frivolous-seeming but essential test of a reflex—and then, excusing myself to screw my ophthalmoscope together, left him to put on the shoe himself. To my surprise, a minute later, he had not done this.

"Can I help?" I asked.

"Help what? Help whom?" . . .

"Your shoe," I repeated. "Perhaps you'd put it on."

He continued to look downwards, though not at the shoe, with an intense but misplaced concentration. Finally his gaze settled on his foot.

"That is my shoe, yes?" Did I mis-hear? Did I mis-see?

"My eyes," he explained, and put his hand to his foot. "This is my shoe, no?"

"No, it is not. That is your foot. *There* is your shoe."

Was he joking? Was he mad? Was he blind? If this was one of his "strange mistakes," it was the strangest mistake I had ever come across.

I helped him on with his shoe (his foot), to avoid further complication. . . . I resumed my examination. His visual acuity was good; he had no difficulty seeing a pin on the floor. . . .

He saw all right, but what did he see? . . .

"What is this?" I asked, holding up a glove.

"May I examine it?" he asked, taking it from me.

"A continuous surface," he announced at last, "infolded on itself. It appears to have"—he hesitated—"five outpouchings, if this is the word."

"Yes," I said cautiously. "You have given me a description. Now tell me what it is."

"A container of some sort?"

"Yes," I said, "and what would it contain?"

"It would contain its contents!" said Dr. P., with a laugh. "There are many possibilities. It could be a change purse, for example, for coins of five sizes. It could . . . "

"Does it not look familiar? Do you think it might contain, might fit, a part of the body?"

No light of recognition dawned on his face . . .

I must have looked aghast, but he seemed to think he had done rather well. There was a hint of a smile on his face. He also appeared to have decided the examination was over and started to look around for his hat. He reached out his hand and took hold of his wife's head, tried to lift it off, to put it on. He had apparently mistaken his wife for a hat! His wife looked as if she was used to such things.[1]

In recognition of the hierarchical organization of sensory systems, psychologists sometimes divide the general process of perceiving into two general phases: sensation and perception. **Sensation** is the process of detecting the presence of stimuli, and **perception** is the higher-order process of integrating, recognizing, and interpreting complete patterns of sensations. Dr. P.'s problem was clearly one of visual perception, not visual sensation.

Functional Segregation

It was once assumed that the primary, secondary, and association areas of a sensory system were each *func-*

---

[1]From *The Man Who Mistook His Wife for a Hat and Other Clinical Tales* (pp. 7–13) by Oliver Sacks, 1985, New York: Summit Books. Copyright © 1970, 1981, 1983, 1984, 1985 by Oliver Sacks. Reprinted by permission of Summit Books, a division of Simon & Schuster, Inc.

Sensation. The simple process of detecting the presence of stimuli.

Perception. The higher-order process of integrating, recognizing, and interpreting complex patterns of sensations.

Functional segregation. Organization into different areas, each of which performs a different function; for example, in sensory systems, different areas of secondary and association cortex analyze different aspects of the same sensory stimulus.

Parallel processing. The simultaneous analysis of a signal in different ways by the multiple parallel pathways of a neural network.

MECHANISMS OF PERCEPTION, CONSCIOUS AWARENESS, AND ATTENTION

tionally homogeneous. That is, it was assumed that all areas of cortex at any given level of a sensory hierarchy acted together to perform the same function. However, recent research has shown that **functional segregation,** rather than functional homogeneity, characterizes the organization of sensory systems. It is now clear that each of the three levels of cerebral cortex in each sensory system—primary, secondary, and association—contains several functionally distinct areas that specialize in different kinds of analysis.

Parallel Processing

It was once believed that the different levels of a sensory hierarchy were connected in a serial fashion. A *serial system* is a system in which information flows among the components over just one pathway, like a string through a strand of beads. However, recent evidence has shown that sensory systems are *parallel systems*—systems in which information flows through the components over multiple pathways. Parallel systems feature **parallel processing**—the simultaneous analysis of a signal in different ways by the multiple parallel pathways of a neural network.

An important type of parallel processing recurs throughout this chapter. There appear to be two kinds of parallel streams of analysis in our sensory systems: one that is capable of influencing our behavior without our conscious awareness and one that influences our behavior by engaging our conscious awareness (see Jeannerod et al., 1995). This finding is as counterintuitive as it is important. Pause for a moment to consider its implications. What do you think would happen if a lesion disrupted the conscious stream without disrupting its parallel unconscious stream? You will encounter patients in this chapter who have such damage: They can reach out and deftly pick up objects that they do not consciously see.

The Current Model of Sensory System Organization

Figure 8.2 summarizes the information in this section of the chapter by illustrating how thinking about the organization of sensory systems has changed. In the 1960s, sensory systems were believed to be hierarchical, functionally homogeneous, and serial. However, four decades of subsequent research have established that sensory systems are hierarchical, functionally segregated, and parallel (see Zeki, 1993a).

Sensory systems are characterized by a division of labor: multiple specialized areas, at multiple levels, interconnected by multiple parallel pathways. Yet, complex stimuli are normally perceived as integrated wholes, not as combinations of independent attributes. How does the brain combine individual sensory attributes to produce integrated perceptions? This is called the *binding problem* (see Friedman-Hill, Robertson, & Treisman, 1995).

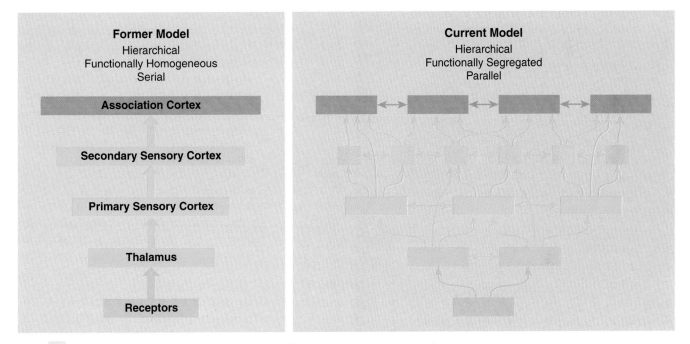

Figure 8.2 Two models of sensory system organization. The former model was hierarchical, functionally homogeneous, and serial; the current model, which is more consistent with the evidence, is hierarchical, functionally segregated, and parallel. Not shown in the current model are descending pathways that provide feedback from higher levels to lower levels.

One possible solution to the binding problem is that there is a single area of the cortex at the top of the sensory hierarchy that receives signals from all other areas of the sensory system and puts them together to form perceptions; however, there are no areas of cortex to which all areas of a single sensory system report. It seems, then, that perceptions must be a product of the combined activity of the many cortical areas of each sensory system (see Zeki, 1993a). The various cortical areas of each sensory system are richly interconnected by the major pathways ascending the sensory hierarchy, by minor descending pathways (not shown in Figure 8.2), and by a rich web of lateral connections between areas at the same level of the hierarchy.

8.2 Cortical Mechanisms of Vision

All occipital cortex as well as large areas of temporal cortex and parietal cortex are involved in vision (see Figure 8.3). The *primary visual cortex* is located in the posterior region of the occipital lobes, much of it hidden from view in the longitudinal fissure. The areas of *secondary visual cortex* are located in two general regions: in the prestriate cortex and in the inferotemporal cortex. The **prestriate cortex** is the band of tissue in the occipital lobe that surrounds the primary visual cortex. The **inferotemporal cortex** is the cortex of the inferior temporal lobe. Areas of the association cortex that receive visual input are located in several parts of the cerebral cortex, but the largest single area is in the **posterior parietal cortex.**

In keeping with the general hierarchical organization of the sensory cortex, the major flow of visual information is from the primary visual cortex to the various areas of secondary visual cortex to the areas of association cortex. As one moves up this visual hierarchy, the neurons have larger receptive fields and the stimuli to which the neurons respond are more specific and more complex (see Zeki, 1993b).

Scotomas: Completion

Damage to an area of the primary visual cortex produces a **scotoma**—an area of blindness—in the corresponding area of the contralateral visual field of both eyes (see Figure 7.12). Neurological patients with suspected damage to the primary visual cortex are usually given a **perimetry test.** While the patient's head is held motionless on a chin rest, the patient stares with one eye at a fixation point on a screen. A small dot of light is then flashed on various parts of the screen, and the patient presses a button to record when the dot is seen. Then, the entire process is repeated for the other eye. The result is a map of the visual field of each eye, which indicates any areas of blindness. Figure 8.4 illustrates the perimetric maps of the visual fields of a man with a bullet wound in his left primary visual cortex. Notice the massive scotoma in the right visual field of each eye.

Many patients with extensive scotomas are unaware of their deficits. One of the factors that contributes to this lack of awareness is the phenomenon of **completion** (see Chapter 7). A patient with a scotoma who looks at a complex figure, part of which lies in the scotoma, often reports seeing a complete image. In some cases, this completion may depend on residual visual capacities in the scotoma; however, completion also occurs in cases in which this explanation can be ruled out. For example, some **hemianopsic** patients (patients with a scotoma covering half of their visual field) see an entire face when they focus on a person's nose, even

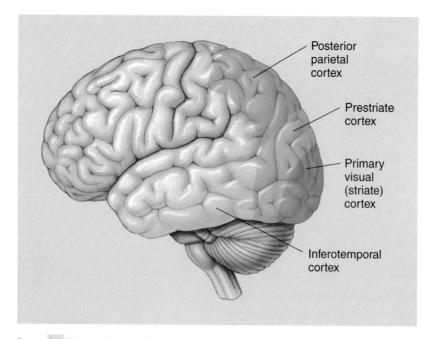

Figure 8.3 The visual areas of the human cerebral cortex.

Posterior parietal cortex

Prestriate cortex

Primary visual (striate) cortex

Inferotemporal cortex

MECHANISMS OF PERCEPTION, CONSCIOUS AWARENESS, AND ATTENTION

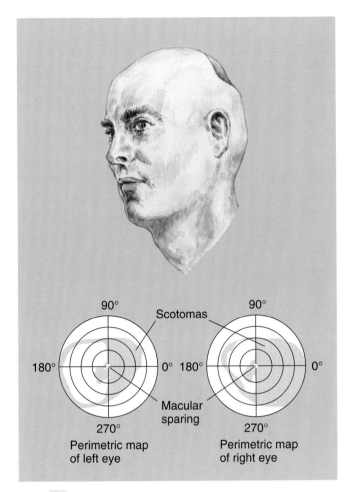

Figure 8.4 The perimetric maps of a subject with a bullet wound in his left primary visual cortex. The scotomas (areas of blindness) are indicated in gray.

(Adapted from Teuber, Battersby, & Bender, 1960.)

when the side of the face in the scotoma has been covered by a blank card.

Consider the completion phenomenon experienced by the esteemed physiological psychologist Karl Lashley (1941), who often developed a large scotoma next to his fovea during a migraine attack (see Figure 8.5 on page 194):

Talking with a friend I glanced just to the right of his face wherein his head disappeared. His shoulders and necktie were still visible but the vertical stripes on the wallpaper behind him seemed to extend down to the necktie. It was impossible to see this as a blank area when projected on the striped wallpaper of uniformly patterned surface although any intervening object failed to be seen. (p. 338)

Scotomas: Blindsight

Blindsight is another phenomenon displayed by patients with scotomas resulting from damage to primary visual cortex. Blindsight is the ability of such patients to respond to visual stimuli in their scotomas even though

they have no conscious awareness of the stimuli (Weiskrantz, 1996). For example, a subject might reach out and grab an object in her scotoma, all the while claiming not to see it. If blindsight confuses you, imagine how it confuses people who experience it. Consider, for example, the reactions to blindsight of D. B., a patient who was blind in his left visual field following surgical removal of his right occipital lobe (Weiskrantz et al., 1974):

Even though the patient had no awareness of "seeing" in his blind [left] field, evidence was obtained that (a) he could reach for visual stimuli [in his left field] with considerable accuracy; (b) could differentiate the orientation of a vertical line from a horizontal or diagonal line; (c) could differentiate the letters "X" and "O". (p. 726)

Needless to say, he was questioned repeatedly about his vision in his left half-field, and his most common response was that he saw nothing at all. . . . When he was shown his results [through his good, right-half field] he expressed surprise and insisted several times that he thought he was just "guessing." When he was shown a video film of his reaching and judging orientation of lines, he was openly astonished. (p. 721)

Islands of surviving primary visual cortex may play a role in some cases of blindsight (Wessinger, Fendrich, & Gazzaniga, 1997). However, the fact that blindsight can be demonstrated in monkeys following total surgical removal of primary visual cortex indicates that these islands are not essential for the phenomenon to occur (see Kentridge, Heywood, & Weiskrantz, 1997).

The existence of blindsight has an important theoretical implication: It suggests that not all visual information is funneled into cortical circuits through the primary visual cortex. If all visual signals were funneled through the primary visual cortex, damage to a portion of this retinotopically laid out structure should produce total blindness in the associated area of the visual field. The existence of blindsight suggests that some information is being conducted via parallel pathways directly into secondary visual cortex (see Stoerig, 1996). One such parallel pathway goes from the *superior colliculus* to the *pulvinar nucleus* of the thalamus to the prestriate cortex.

Prestriate cortex. The area of secondary visual cortex just anterior to the primary visual cortex.

Inferotemporal cortex. The cortex of the inferior temporal lobe, an area of the secondary visual cortex that is involved in object recognition.

Posterior parietal cortex. An area of association cortex that receives input from the visual, auditory, and somatosensory systems and is involved in the perception of spatial location.

Scotoma. An area of blindness in the visual field.

Perimetry test. The procedure used to map scotomas.

Completion. The visual system's automatic use of information obtained from receptors around a scotoma to create a perception of the missing portion of the retinal image.

Hemianopsic. Having a scotoma that covers half the field of vision.

Blindsight. The ability of some patients who are blind as a consequence of cortical damage to unconsciously see some aspects of their visual environments.

Figure 8.5 The completion of a migraine-induced scotoma as described by Karl Lashley.

A **B**

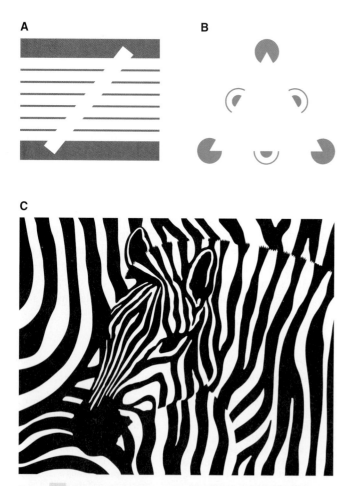

C

Figure 8.6 Subjective contours. You see the white bar in A and the white triangle in B even though they do not physically exist—they are subjective contours. Your ability to see subjective contours helps you see boundaries between objects of similar brightness, color, and pattern—for example, look at C.

Perception of Subjective Contours

Do you recall the theme of the preceding chapter—that our visual perceptions are often better than the physical reality of the visual input? Figure 8.6 illustrates this point by showing that we often see visual contours where none exist (Allbright, 1995). Perceived visual contours that do not exist are called **subjective contours.**

Why do we see subjective contours? The reason is that prestriate neurons (Peterhans & von der Heydt, 1991) and even a few primary visual cortex neurons (Sheth et al., 1996) respond as if real contours were present when subjective contours of the appropriate orientation appear in their receptive fields (see Figure 8.7).

Functional Areas of Secondary and Association Visual Cortex

Secondary visual cortex and the portions of association cortex that are involved in visual analysis are both composed of different areas, each specialized for a particular type of visual analysis. For example, in the macaque monkey, whose visual cortex has been thoroughly mapped, there are at least 30 different functional areas of visual cortex; in addition to primary visual cortex, 24 areas of secondary visual cortex and 7 areas of asso-

Subjective contours. Perceived visual contours that do not exist.

MECHANISMS OF PERCEPTION, CONSCIOUS AWARENESS, AND ATTENTION

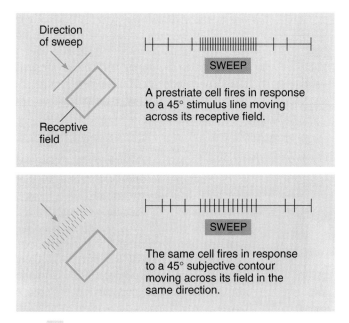

Figure 8.7 Neurons of the monkey prestriate cortex and primary visual cortex respond to subjective contours of a particular orientation. (Adapted from Peterhans & von der Heydt, 1991.)

ciation visual cortex have so far been identified. The neurons in each functional area respond most vigorously to different aspects of visual stimuli (e.g., to their color, movement, or shape); selective lesions to the different areas produce different visual losses; and there are often subtle anatomical differences among the areas (see Tanaka, 1996).

The various functional areas of secondary and association visual cortex in the macaque are prodigiously interconnected. Anterograde and retrograde tracing studies have identified over 300 interconnecting pathways (Van Essen, Anderson, & Felleman, 1992). Although connections between areas are virtually always reciprocal, the major flow of information is up the hierarchy from more simple to more complex areas.

Positron emission tomography (PET) and functional magnetic resonance imaging (fMRI) have been used to identify various areas of visual cortex in humans. The activity of the subjects' brains has been monitored while they inspect various types of visual stimuli. By identifying the areas of activation associated with various visual properties (e.g., movement or color), so far, about a dozen different functional areas of human visual cortex have been identified (Tootell et al., 1996). A map of these areas is illustrated in Figure 8.8. Most are similar in terms of location, anatomical characteristics, and function to areas in the macaque (McCourtney & Ungerleider, 1991), but each tends to be about four times the area of its macaque counterpart.

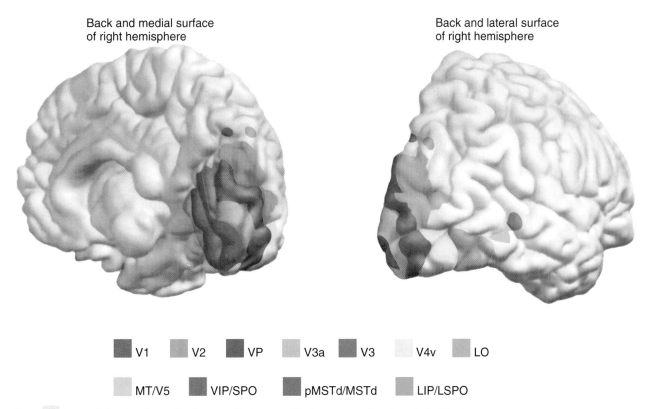

Figure 8.8 Areas of visual cortex so far discovered in humans. Their names are based on similarities to areas of visual cortex in the more thoroughly studied macaque monkey. (Based on Tootell et al., 1996.)

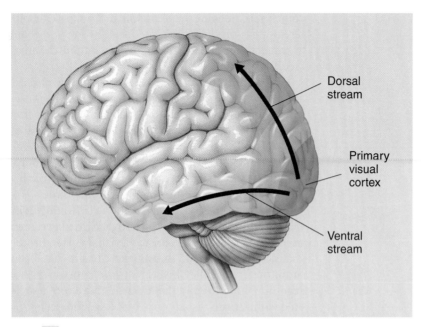

Figure 8.9 Information about particular aspects of a visual display flow out of the primary visual cortex over many pathways. The pathways can be grouped into two general streams: dorsal and ventral.

Dorsal stream

Primary visual cortex

Ventral stream

Dorsal and Ventral Streams

You learned in Chapter 7 that most visual information enters the primary visual cortex via the lateral geniculate nuclei. In the primary visual cortex, the information from the two lateral geniculate nuclei is received, combined, and then segregated into multiple pathways that project separately to the various functional areas of secondary, and then association, visual cortex (see Cabeza & Nyberg, 1997).

Many pathways that conduct information from the primary visual cortex through various specialized areas of secondary and association cortex are parts of two major streams: the dorsal stream and the ventral stream (Ungerleider & Mishkin, 1982; Courtney & Ungerleider, 1997). The **dorsal stream** flows from the primary visual cortex to the dorsal prestriate cortex to the posterior parietal cortex, and the **ventral stream** flows from the primary visual cortex to the ventral prestriate cortex to the inferotemporal cortex—see Figure 8.9.

Ungerleider and Mishkin (1982) proposed that the dorsal and ventral visual streams perform different visual functions. They suggested that the dorsal stream is involved in the perception of "where" objects are and the ventral stream is involved in the perception of "what" objects are.

The major implication of the **"where" versus "what" theory** and other parallel processing theories of vision is that damage to some areas of cortex may abolish certain aspects of vision while leaving others unaffected. Indeed,

the most convincing support for the influential "where" versus "what" theory has come from the comparison of the specific effects of damage to the dorsal and ventral streams (see Ungerleider & Haxby, 1994). Patients with damage to the posterior parietal cortex often have difficulty reaching accurately for objects that they have no difficulty describing; conversely, patients with damage to the inferotemporal cortex often have no difficulty reaching accurately for objects that they have difficulty describing.

Although the "where" versus "what" theory has many advocates, there is an alternative interpretation for the same evidence that is gaining support (Goodale, 1993; Milner & Goodale, 1993). Goodale and Milner argued that the key difference between the dorsal and ventral streams is not the kinds of information they carry but the use to which that information is put. They suggested that the function of the dorsal stream is to direct behavioral interactions with objects, whereas the function of the ventral stream is to mediate the conscious perception of objects: the "control of behavior" versus "conscious perception" theory (see Logothetis & Sheinberg, 1996).

The **"control of behavior" versus "conscious perception" theory** can readily explain the two major neuropsychological findings that are the foundation of the "where" versus "what" theory. Namely, the "control of behavior" versus "conscious perception" theory suggests that patients with dorsal stream damage may do poorly on tests of location and movement because most tests of location and movement involve performance measures; and it suggests that patients with ventral stream damage may do poorly on tests of visual recognition because most tests of visual recognition involve verbal, and thus conscious, report. Be that as it may, the major strength of the "control of behavior" versus "conscious perception" theory is its two bold and correct assertions: (1) that some patients with bilateral lesions to the ventral stream have no conscious experience of seeing and yet are able to interact with objects under visual guidance, and (2) that some patients with bilateral lesions to the dorsal stream can consciously see objects but cannot interact with them under visual guidance. The following two subsections describe two such examples.

■ THE CASE OF D. F. D. F. has bilateral damage to her ventral prestriate cortex, thus interrupting the flow of the ventral stream (Goodale et al., 1991). Amazingly, she can respond accurately to visual stimuli that she does not consciously see. Hers is the most systematically documented of such cases. Goodale and Milner (1992) describe her thusly:

> Despite her profound inability to recognize the size, shape and orientation of visual objects, DF showed strikingly accurate guidance of hand and finger movements directed at the very same objects. Thus, when she was presented with a pair of rectangular blocks of the same or different dimensions, she was unable to distinguish between them. When she was asked to indicate the width of a single block by means of her index finger and thumb, her matches bore no relationship to the dimensions of the object and showed considerable trial to trial variability. However, when she was asked simply to reach out and pick up the block, the aperture between her index finger and thumb changed systematically with the width of the object, just as in normal subjects. In other words, DF scaled her grip to the dimensions of the objects she was about to pick up, even though she appeared to be unable to [consciously] "perceive" those dimensions.
>
> A similar dissociation was seen in her responses to the orientation of stimuli. Thus, when presented with a large slot that could be placed in one of a number of different orientations, she showed great difficulty in indicating the orientation either verbally or manually (i.e., by rotating her hand or a hand-held card). Nevertheless, she was as good as normal subjects at reaching out and placing her hand or the card into the slot, turning her hand appropriately from the very onset of the movement. (p. 22)

■ **THE CASE OF A. T.** The case of A. T. is in major respects complementary to that of D. F. The patient A. T. was a woman with a lesion of the occipitoparietal region that likely interrupted the dorsal route.

> AT was able to recognize objects, and was also able to demonstrate their size with her fingers. By contrast, preshape of the hand during object-directed movements was incorrect. Correlation between object size and maximum grip size was lacking, with the consequence that objects could not be grasped between the fingertips; instead, the patient made awkward palmar grasps. The schema framework offers a compelling explanation for this deficit. Because the grasp schemas were destroyed by the lesion, or disconnected from visual input, the grip aperture did not stop at the required size, grip closure was delayed and the transport was prolonged in order to remain co-ordinated with the grasp.
>
> AT cannot preshape her hand for neutral objects like plastic cylinders, yet, when faced with a familiar object whose size is a semantic property, like a lipstick, she can grasp it with reasonable accuracy. This interaction reflects the role of the abundant anatomical interconnections between the two cortical systems. (Jeannerod et al., 1995, p. 320)

Prosopagnosia

A discussion of prosopagnosia completes this section of this chapter. It is an interesting, controversial, and important topic in its own right; but, as you will soon learn, its investigation has provided further support for the "control of behavior" versus "conscious perception" theory.

What is prosopagnosia? **Prosopagnosia,** briefly put, is visual agnosia for faces. Let me explain. **Agnosia** is a failure of recognition (*gnosis* means "to know") that is not attributable to a sensory deficit or to verbal or intellectual impairment, whereas **visual agnosia** is a specific agnosia for visual stimuli. Visual agnosics can see visual stimuli, but they don't know what they are. (Recall the case of Dr. P., the man who mistook his wife for a hat.)

Visual agnosias themselves are often specific to a particular aspect of visual input and are named accordingly; for example, *movement agnosia, object agnosia,* and *color agnosia* are difficulties in recognizing movement, objects, and color, respectively. It is presumed that each specific visual agnosia results from damage to an area of secondary visual cortex that mediates the recognition of that particular attribute. Prosopagnosics are visual agnosics with a particular difficulty in telling one face from another.

Prosopagnosics can usually recognize a face as a face, but they have difficulty telling one face from another. They often report seeing a jumble of individual facial parts (e.g., eyes, nose, chin, cheeks) that for some reason are never fused into an easy-to-recognize whole. In extreme cases, prosopagnosics cannot recognize themselves: Imagine what it would be like to stare in the mirror every morning and not recognize who is looking back.

Autopsy and structural magnetic resonance imaging (MRI) studies of prosopagnosics have linked prosopagnosia to the ventral stream: There is typically bilateral damage to the inferior prestriate area and to the adjacent portions of the inferotemporal cortex (see Gross & Sergent, 1992). Furthermore, a similar area has been shown by functional MRI to be activated in normal humans while they are viewing faces, as opposed to other pattern stimuli (see Courtney & Ungerleider, 1997).

Dorsal stream. The group of visual pathways that flows out of the primary visual cortex to the dorsal prestriate cortex to the posterior parietal cortex; according to one theory, its function is the control of visually guided behavior.

Ventral stream. The group of visual pathways that flows out of the primary visual cortex to the ventral prestriate cortex to the inferotemporal cortex; according to one theory, its function is the conscious visual perception.

"Where" versus "what" theory. The theory that the dorsal stream mediates the perception of where things are and the ventral stream mediates the perception of what things are.

"Control of behavior" versus "conscious perception" theory. The theory that the dorsal stream mediates the control of behavior by visual input and the ventral stream mediates conscious vision.

Prosopagnosia. Visual agnosia for faces.

Agnosia. The inability to consciously recognize sensory stimuli of a particular class that is not attributable to a sensory deficit or to verbal or intellectual impairment.

Visual agnosia. A failure to recognize visual stimuli that is not attributable to sensory, verbal, or intellectual impairment.

Prosopagnosia was initially assumed to result from bilateral damage to a particular area of cortex dedicated to the recognition of faces. The faces of one's conspecifics are among the most important visual stimuli for higher social primates, so it is conceivable that there is an area of the cortex specifically dedicated to face recognition. The main evidence for this interpretation is that patients who have difficulty recognizing faces have little difficulty recognizing other test objects (e.g., a chair, a pencil, or a door).

Stop reading for a moment and give this line of evidence some thought: It is seriously flawed. Because prosopagnosics have no difficulty recognizing faces as faces, the fact that they can recognize chairs as chairs, pencils as pencils, and doors as doors is not relevant. The critical question is whether they can recognize which chair, which pencil, and which door. Careful testing of some prosopagnosics has revealed that their recognition deficits are not restricted to faces: A farmer lost his ability to recognize particular cows when he became prosopagnosic, and a bird-watcher lost his ability to distinguish species of birds. These cases suggest that some prosopagnosics have a general problem recognizing specific objects that belong to complex classes of objects (e.g., particular automobiles or particular houses), not a specific problem recognizing faces. Be that as it may, some neuropsychological patients do seem to have difficulty recognizing particular faces (Farah, 1990) but not other complex objects.

Particularly convincing evidence that there is a specific region of visual cortex dedicated to the recognition of faces is provided by the case of C. K. (Moscovitch, Winocur, & Behrmann, 1997). In contrast to cases of prosopagnosia, C. K. had severe visual object agnosia but had no difficulties recognizing faces. For example, C. K. could recognize the inverted face in Figure 8.10 without being able to recognize the vegetables that compose it. C. K. had damage to his ventral stream.

Consistent with the idea that bilateral lesions in the ventral stream might produce specific deficits in facial recognition is that neurons in the macaque inferotemporal cortex seem to respond exclusively to faces (see Logothetis & Sheinberg, 1996). They do not respond to other complex shapes, to mixed-up components of faces, or to upside-down faces. Some inferotemporal neurons, as illustrated in Figure 8.11, fire only when the face is in a specific orientation (Gross et al., 1985). Moreover, PET studies have shown that an area of inferotemporal cortex—the same area implicated in prosopagnosia—becomes active in both hemispheres when human subjects view faces but not equally complex control patterns.

An interesting hypothesis about prosopagnosia can be derived from the "control of behavior" versus "conscious perception" theory. The fact that prosopagnosia results from bilateral damage to the ventral stream suggests that dorsal-stream function may be intact. In other

Figure 8.10 *The Vegetable Gardener* by Guiseppe Arcimbaldo, owned by Museo Civico Ala Ponzone, Cremona, Italy. Patient C. K. (Moscovitch, Winocur, & Behrmann, 1997) could see the face in this painting when he viewed it upside down, as could all the control subjects. But C. K. could recognize none of the vegetables that compose the face. This is evidence that prosopagnosia and visual object agnosia can be independent.

words, it suggests that prosopagnosics may be able to unconsciously recognize faces that they cannot recognize consciously. Remarkably, this is, indeed, the case.

Tranel and Damasio (1988) were the first to demonstrate unconscious facial recognition in prosopagnosics. They presented a series of photographs to each patient, some familiar to the patient, some not. The subjects claimed not to recognize any of the faces. However, when familiar, but not unfamiliar, faces were presented, the subjects displayed a large *skin conductance response,* thus indicating that the faces were being unconsciously recognized by undamaged portions of the brain.

Interim Conclusion

Before leaving the topic of visual perception, review in your mind the topics that were discussed in this section: completion, blindsight, subjective contours, func-

MECHANISMS OF PERCEPTION, CONSCIOUS AWARENESS, AND ATTENTION

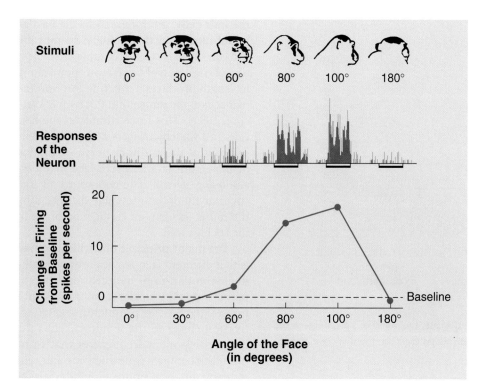

Figure 8.11 The firing rate of a monkey inferotemporal cortex neuron before, during, and after the presentation of monkey faces at different angles. The profile view (100°) was most effective in increasing the firing rate of this cell. (Adapted from Gross et al., 1985.)

tional cortical areas, dorsal and ventral streams, the cases of D. F. and A. T., and prosopagnosia. The recent increases in our understanding of these topic areas have reinforced the three principles of perceptual processing that introduced the chapter: hierarchical organization, functional segregation, and parallel processing.

8.3 Audition

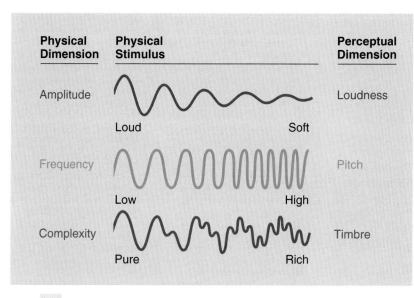

Figure 8.12 The relation between the physical and perceptual dimensions of sound.

The function of the auditory system is the perception of sound—or, more accurately, the perception of objects and events through the sounds that they make (Masterton, 1992). Sounds are vibrations of air molecules that stimulate the auditory system; humans hear only those molecular vibrations between about 20 and 20,000 hertz (cycles per second). Figure 8.12 illustrates how sounds are commonly recorded in the form of waves and the relation between the physical dimensions of sound vibrations and our perceptions of them. The *amplitude, frequency,* and *complexity* of air molecule vibrations are perceived as *loudness, pitch,* and *timbre,* respectively.

Pure tones (sine wave vibrations) exist only in laboratories and sound recording studios; in real life, sound is always associated with complex patterns of vibrations.

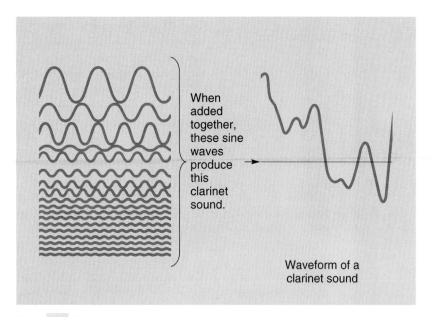

When added together, these sine waves produce this clarinet sound.

Waveform of a clarinet sound

Figure 8.13 The breaking down of a sound—in this case, the sound of a clarinet—into its component sine waves by Fourier analysis. When added together, the sine wave components produce the complex sound wave.

For example, Figure 8.13 illustrates the complex sound wave associated with one note of a clarinet. The figure also illustrates that any complex sound wave can be broken down mathematically into a series of sine waves of various frequencies and amplitudes; these component sine waves produce the original sound when they are added together. As you learned in Chapter 7, *Fourier analysis* is the mathematical procedure for breaking down complex waves into their component sine waves. One theory of audition is that the auditory system performs a Fourier-like analysis of complex sounds in terms of their component sine waves.

the **hair cells,** are mounted in the **basilar membrane,** and the **tectorial membrane** rests on the hair cells. Accordingly, a deflection of the organ of Corti at any point along its length produces a shearing force on the hair cells at the same point (Corwin & Warchol, 1991). This force stimulates the hair cells and thereby triggers action potentials in axons of the **auditory nerve**—a branch of the eighth cranial nerve (the *auditory-vestibular nerve*). The vibrations of the cochlear fluid are ultimately dissipated by the *round window,* an elastic membrane in the cochlea wall.

The major principle of cochlear coding is that different frequencies produce maximal stimulation of hair cells at different points along the basilar membrane—with higher frequencies producing greater activation closer to the windows. Thus the many component frequencies that compose each complex sound activate hair cells at many different points along the basilar membrane, and the many signals thus created by a single complex sound are carried out of the ear by many different auditory neurons. Like the cochlea, most other structures of the auditory system are arrayed according to frequency. Thus, in the same way that the organization of the visual system is primarily **retinotopic,** the organization of the auditory system is primarily **tonotopic.**

This brings us to the major unsolved mystery of auditory processing. Imagine yourself in a complex acoustic environment such as a party. The music is

The Ear

The ear is illustrated in Figure 8.14. Sound waves travel down the *auditory canal* and cause the **tympanic membrane** (the eardrum) to vibrate. These vibrations are then transferred to the three **ossicles**—the small bones of the middle ear: the *malleus* (the hammer), the *incus* (the anvil), and the *stapes* (the stirrup). The vibrations of the stapes trigger vibrations of the membrane called the **oval window,** which in turn transfers the vibrations to the fluid of the snail-shaped **cochlea** (*kokhlos* means "land snail"). The cochlea is a long, coiled tube with an internal membrane running almost to its tip. This internal membrane is the auditory receptor organ, the **organ of Corti.**

Each pressure change at the oval window travels along the organ of Corti as a wave. The organ of Corti is composed of two membranes: the basilar membrane and the tectorial membrane. The auditory receptors,

Tympanic membrane. The eardrum.

Ossicles. The three small bones of the middle ear: the malleus, the incus, and the stapes.

Oval window. The cochlear membrane that transfers vibrations from the ossicles to the fluid of the cochlea.

Cochlea. The long, coiled structure of the inner ear that houses the organ of Corti and its auditory receptors.

Organ of Corti. The auditory receptor organ, comprising the basilar membrane, the hair cells, and the tectorial membrane.

Hair cells. The receptors of the auditory system.

Basilar membrane. The membrane of the organ of Corti in which the hair cell receptors are embedded.

Tectorial membrane. The cochlear membrane that rests on the hair cells.

Auditory nerve. The branch of the eighth cranial nerve that carries auditory signals from the hair cells in the basilar membrane.

Retinotopic. Organized, like the primary visual cortex, according to a map of the retina.

Tonotopic. Organized, like the primary auditory cortex, according to the frequency of sound.

Semicircular canals. The receptive organs of the vestibular system.

Vestibular system. The sensory system that detects changes in the direction and intensity of head movements and that contributes to the maintenance of balance through its output to the motor system.

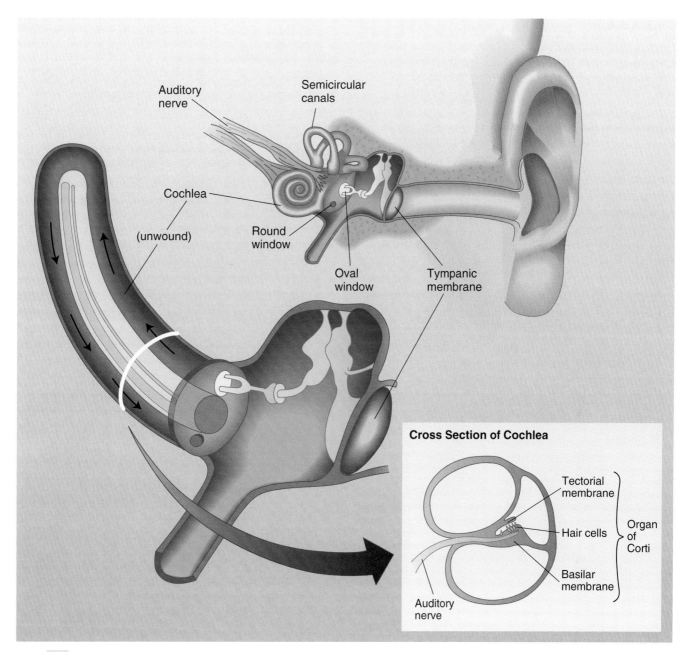

Figure 8.14 Anatomy of the ear.

playing; people are dancing, eating, and drinking; and numerous conversations are going on around you. Because the component frequencies in each individual sound activate many sites along your basilar membrane, the number of sites simultaneously activated at any one time by the party noises is enormous. But somehow your auditory system manages to sort these individual frequency messages into separate categories and combine them so that you hear each source of complex sounds independently. For example, you hear the speech of the person standing next to you as a separate sequence of sounds, despite the fact that it contains many of the same component frequencies coming from other sources.

Figure 8.14 also shows the **semicircular canals**—the receptive organs of the vestibular system. The **vestibular system** carries information about the direction and intensity of head movements, which helps us maintain our balance.

From the Ear to the Primary Auditory Cortex

There is no major auditory pathway to the cortex comparable to the retina-geniculate-striate pathway of the visual system. Instead, there is a network of auditory

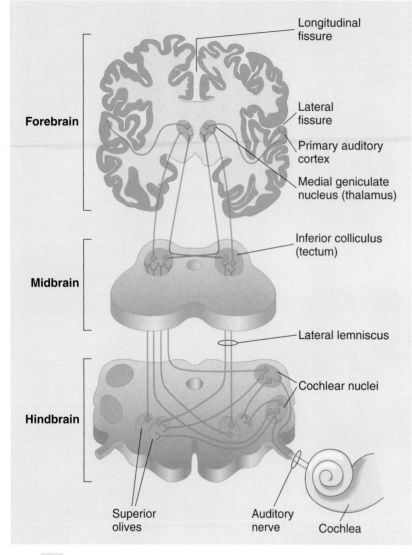

Figure 8.15 Some of the pathways of the auditory system that lead from one ear to the cortex.

tex—there are thought to be about six distinct areas of human secondary auditory cortex.

Two important principles of organization of the primary auditory cortex have been identified. First, like other areas of the cerebral cortex, the primary auditory cortex is organized in functional columns (see Schreiner, 1992): All of the neurons encountered during a vertical microelectrode penetration of the primary auditory cortex (i.e., a penetration at right angles to the cortical layers) respond optimally to sounds in the same frequency range. Second, like the cochlea, the primary auditory cortex is organized tonotopically: More anterior regions of the auditory cortex are responsive to higher frequencies, and more posterior regions are responsive to lower frequencies.

Little is known about the neurons in secondary auditory cortex because they respond weakly and inconsistently to the pure tones typically used by researchers. Rauschecker, Tian, and Hauser (1995) reasoned on the basis of what is known about the neurons of secondary visual cortex that they might have more success in studying secondary auditory cortex by using more complex stimuli—secondary visual cortex neurons respond to complex visual stimuli but respond little to dots of light. They found that monkey calls were more effective in activating secondary than primary auditory cortex neurons in monkeys. Hence, auditory cortex, like visual cortex, appears to be organized hierarchically.

pathways (see Masterton, 1992), some of which are illustrated in Figure 8.15. The axons of each *auditory nerve* synapse in the ipsilateral *cochlear nuclei,* from which many projections lead to the **superior olives** at the same level. The axons of the olivary neurons project via the *lateral lemniscus* to the **inferior colliculi,** where they synapse on neurons that project to the **medial geniculate nuclei** of the thalamus, which in turn project to the *primary auditory cortex.* Notice that signals from each ear are transmitted to both ipsilateral and contralateral auditory cortex.

Primary Auditory Cortex

In humans, the primary auditory cortex is located in the *lateral fissure* (see Figure 8.16). It is surrounded largely by several areas of secondary auditory cor-

Sound Localization

Localization of sounds in space is mediated by the lateral and medial superior olives, but in different ways. When a sound originates to our left, it reaches the left ear first, and it is louder at the left ear. Some neurons in the *medial superior olives* respond to slight differences in the time of arrival of signals from the two ears, whereas some neurons in the *lateral superior olives* respond to slight differences in the amplitude of sounds from the two ears (see Heffner & Masterton, 1990).

In mammals the medial and lateral superior olives project to the *superior colliculus,* as well as to the inferior colliculus. Those layers of the superior colliculus that receive auditory input from the superior olives are laid out according to a map of auditory space—an exception to the usual tonotopic organization of auditory

MECHANISMS OF PERCEPTION, CONSCIOUS AWARENESS, AND ATTENTION

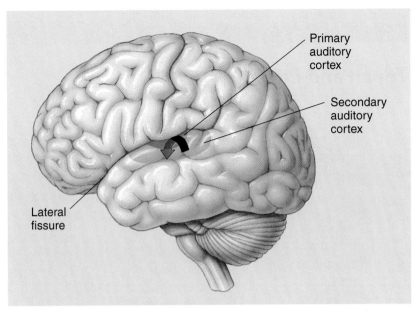

Figure 8.16 Location of the primary and secondary auditory cortex in the temporal cortex. Most of the auditory cortex is hidden in the depths of the lateral fissure.

system structures. Other layers of the superior colliculi receive visual input, and these layers are organized retinotopically.

Many researchers interested in sound localization have studied barn owls (see Figure 8.17). You see, barn owls can locate sounds in space better than any other animal whose hearing has been tested. They are nocturnal hunters and must be able to locate field mice solely by the rustling sounds the mice make in the dark.

The most striking anatomical feature of barn owls is the facial ruff, which is an effective reflector of high-fre-

quency sounds and which accounts, in part, for the owls' remarkable sound-localizing ability. Barn owls locate sounds in the horizontal dimension (horizontal to the top of the head) by comparing the loudness of sounds at the two ears (Konishi, 1993). The ability to locate sounds in the vertical dimension (at a right angle to the top of the head) is not important for most land-dwelling animals, but it is critical for barn owls because they hunt from the air. The facial ruff is the key to their ability to locate sounds in the vertical dimension. The right ear of barn owls is more sensitive to sounds above the horizontal plane because the ruff on the right is directed slightly upward; the left ear is more sensitive to sounds below the horizontal plane because the ruff on the left is directed slightly downward. This vertical difference is greater for higher frequencies because the ruff reflects higher frequencies more effectively. As a result, the barn owls' auditory system can locate sounds in the vertical dimension by comparing intensities detected at each ear for the various frequencies composing the sounds. Barn owls cannot locate single-frequency sounds in vertical space, and they cannot locate complex sounds in vertical space if their ruff has been shaved (Knudsen, 1981).

Effects of Auditory Cortex Damage

Efforts to characterize the effects of auditory cortex damage have been complicated by the fact that most human auditory cortex is deep in the lateral fissure. Consequently, it is rarely destroyed in its entirety; and if it is, there is inevitably extensive damage to surrounding tissue. As a result of this problem, efforts to understand the effects of auditory cortex damage have relied largely on the study of nonhumans.

Surprisingly, complete bilateral lesions of the primary auditory cortex in laboratory mammals produce no permanent deficits in their ability to detect the presence of sounds (e.g., Kavanagh & Kelly, 1988), even when the lesions include substantial secondary auditory cortex. However, such lesions do disrupt the ability to localize brief sounds and recognize rapid complex sequences of sound.

Figure 8.17 A barn owl. Its facial ruff is an important component of an auditory system that allows it to locate mice and other small prey in total darkness.

Superior olives. Medullary nuclei that play a role in sound localization.

Inferior colliculi. The structures of the tectum that receive auditory input from the superior olives.

Medial geniculate nuclei. The auditory thalamic nuclei that receive input from the inferior colliculi and project to primary auditory cortex.

8.4 Somatosensation: Touch and Pain

Somatosensation is a general term that refers to sensations of the body. The somatosensory system is three separate but interacting systems: (1) an *exteroceptive system,* which senses external stimuli that are applied to the skin; (2) a *proprioceptive system,* which monitors information about the position of the body that comes from receptors in the muscles, joints, and organs of balance; and (3) an *interoceptive system,* which provides general information about conditions within the body (e.g., temperature and blood pressure). This discussion deals almost exclusively with the exteroceptive system, which itself comprises three somewhat distinct divisions: a division for perceiving *mechanical stimuli* (touch), one for *thermal stimuli* (temperature), and one for *nociceptive stimuli* (pain).

Cutaneous Receptors

There are several different kinds of receptors in the skin. Figure 8.18 illustrates four that are found in both hairy skin and **glabrous skin**—hairless skin, such as that on the palms of your hands. The most simple cutaneous receptors are the **free nerve endings** (neuron endings with no specialized structures on them), which are particularly sensitive to temperature change and pain. The largest and deepest cutaneous receptors are the onionlike **Pacinian corpuscles;** because they adapt rapidly, they respond best to sudden displacements of the skin. On the other hand, *Merkel's disks* and *Ruffini endings* both adapt slowly and respond best to gradual skin indentation and gradual skin stretch, respectively.

To appreciate the functional significance of fast and slow receptor adaptation, consider what happens when a constant pressure is applied to the skin. The pressure evokes a burst of firing in all receptors, which corresponds to the sensation of being touched; however, after a few hundred milliseconds, only the slowly adapting receptors remain active, and the quality of the sensation changes. In fact, you are often totally unaware of constant skin pressure; for example, you are usually unaware of the feeling of your clothes against your body until you focus attention on it. As a consequence, when you try to identify objects by touch, you manipulate them in your hands so that the pattern of stimu-

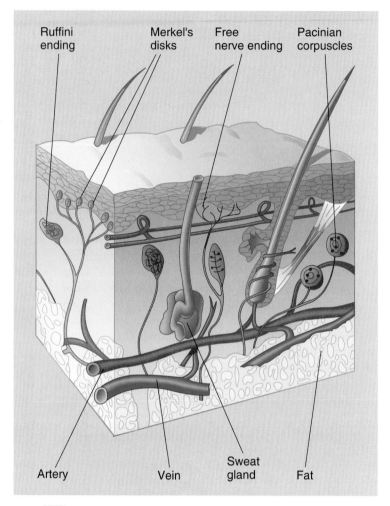

Figure 8.18 Four cutaneous receptors that occur in both hairy and glabrous skin.

lation continually changes. The identification of objects by touch is called **stereognosis.**

Dermatomes

The neural fibers that carry information from cutaneous receptors and other somatosensory receptors gather together in nerves and enter the spinal cord via the *dorsal roots.* The area of the body that is innervated by the left and right dorsal roots of a given segment of the spinal cord is called a **dermatome.** Figure 8.19 is a dermatomal map of the human body. Because there is considerable overlap between adjacent dermatomes,

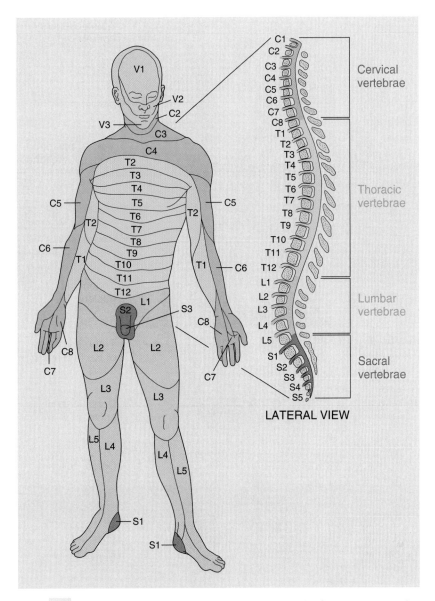

Figure 8.19 The dermatomes of the human body. S, L, T, and C refer respectively to the *sacral, lumbar, thoracic,* and *cervical* regions of the spinal cord. V1, V2, and V3 stand for the three branches of the trigeminal nerve.

destruction of a single dorsal root typically produces little somatosensory loss.

The Two Major Ascending Somatosensory Pathways

Somatosensory information ascends to the human cortex over two major somatosensory system pathways: the dorsal-column medial-lemniscus system and the anterolateral system. The **dorsal-column medial-lemniscus system** carries information about touch and proprioception. The **anterolateral system** carries information about pain and temperature.

Glabrous skin. Hairless skin.

Free nerve endings. Cutaneous receptors that are composed of nerve endings without specialized structures on them; they detect cutaneous pain and changes in skin temperature.

Pacinian corpuscles. The largest and most deeply positioned cutaneous receptors, which are sensitive to sudden displacements of the skin.

Stereognosis. The identification of objects by touch.

Dermatome. An area of the body that *is* innervated by the left and right dorsal roots of one segment of the spinal cord.

Dorsal-column medial-lemniscus system. The division of the somatosensory system that ascends in the dorsal portion of the spinal white matter and carries signals related to touch and proprioception.

Anterolateral system. The division of the somatosensory system that ascends in the anterolateral portion of spinal white matter and carries signals related to pain and temperature.

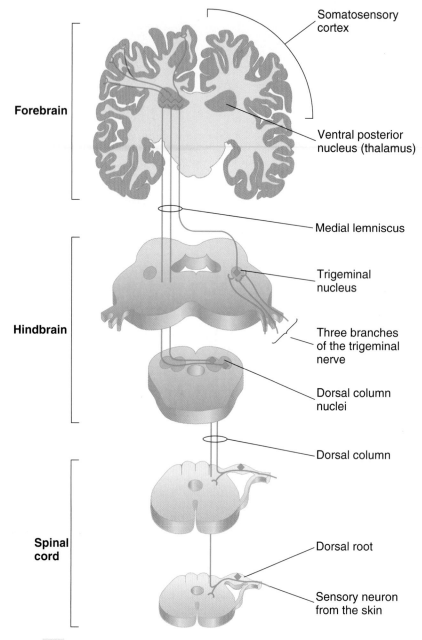

Somatosensory
cortex

Forebrain

Ventral posterior
nucleus (thalamus)

Medial lemniscus

Trigeminal
nucleus

Hindbrain

Three branches
of the trigeminal
nerve

Dorsal column
nuclei

Dorsal column

Spinal
cord

Dorsal root

Sensory neuron
from the skin

Figure 8.20 The dorsal-column medial-lemniscus system.

The dorsal-column medial-lemniscus system is illustrated in Figure 8.20. The sensory neurons of this system enter the spinal cord via a dorsal root, ascend ipsilaterally in the **dorsal columns,** and synapse in the *dorsal column nuclei* of the medulla. The axons of dorsal column nuclei neurons *decussate* (cross over to the other side of the brain) and then ascend in the **medial lemniscus** to the contralateral **ventral posterior nucleus** of the thalamus. The ventral posterior nuclei also receive input via the three branches of the *trigeminal nerve,* which carry somatosensory information from the contralateral areas of the face. Most neurons of the ventral posterior nucleus project to the *primary somatosensory cortex (SI);* others project to the *secondary*

somatosensory cortex (SII) or the posterior parietal cortex. Neuroscience trivia collectors will almost certainly want to add to their collection the fact that the dorsal column neurons that originate in the toes are the longest neurons in the human body.

The anterolateral system is illustrated in Figure 8.21. Most dorsal root neurons of the anterolateral system synapse as soon as they enter the spinal cord. The axons of most of the second-order neurons decussate and then ascend to the brain in the contralateral anterolateral portion of the spinal cord; however, some do not decussate and ascend ipsilaterally. The anterolateral system comprises three different tracts: the *spinothalamic tract,* which projects to the *ventral posterior nu-*

8 MECHANISMS OF PERCEPTION, CONSCIOUS AWARENESS, AND ATTENTION

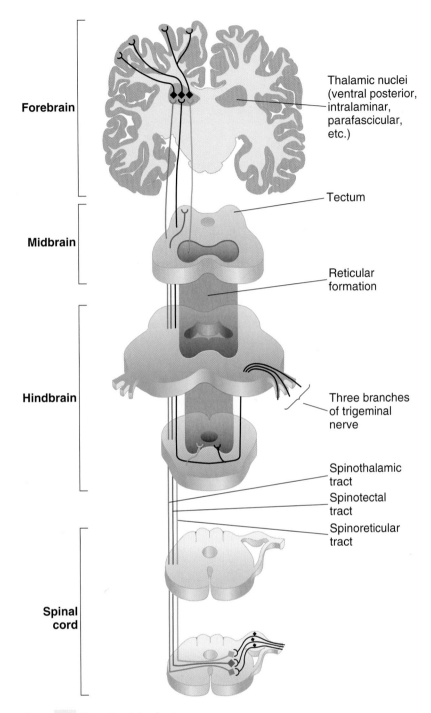

Figure 8.21 The anterolateral system.

cleus of the thalamus (as does the dorsal-column medial-lemniscus system); the *spinoreticular tract,* which projects to the *reticular formation* (and then to the *parafascicular nuclei* and *intralaminar nuclei* of the thalamus); and the *spinotectal tract,* which projects to the *tectum* (colliculi). The three branches of the trigeminal nerve carry pain and temperature information from the face to the same thalamic sites. The pain and temperature information that reaches the thalamus is then distributed to SI, SII, the posterior parietal cortex, and other parts of the brain.

Mark, Ervin, and Yakolev (1962) assessed the effects of lesions to the thalamus on the chronic pain of patients in the advanced stages of cancer. Lesions to the ventral posterior nuclei, which receive input from both

Dorsal columns. The somatosensory tracts that ascend in the dorsal portion of the spinal cord white matter.

Medial lemniscus. The somatosensory pathway between the dorsal column nuclei and the ventral posterior nucleus of the thalamus.

Ventral posterior nucleus. A thalamic relay nucleus in both the somatosensory and gustatory systems.

the spinothalamic tract and the dorsal-column medial-lemniscus system, produced some loss of cutaneous sensitivity to touch, to temperature change, and to sharp pain; but the lesions had no effect on deep, chronic pain. In contrast, lesions of the parafascicular and intralaminar nuclei, both of which receive input from the spinoreticular tract, reduced deep chronic pain without disrupting cutaneous sensitivity.

Cortical Areas of Somatosensation

In 1937, Penfield and his colleagues mapped the primary somatosensory cortex of patients during neurosurgery (see Figure 8.22). Penfield applied electrical stimulation to various sites on the cortical surface; and the patients, who were fully conscious under a local anesthetic, described what they felt. When stimulation was applied to the *postcentral gyrus,* the patients reported somatosensory sensations in various parts of their bodies. When Penfield mapped the relation between each site of stimulation and the part of the body in which the sensation was felt, he discovered that the human primary somatosensory cortex (SI) is **somatotopic**—organized according to a map of the body surface. This somatotopic map is commonly referred to as the **somatosensory homunculus** (*homunculus* means "little man").

Evidence of a second somatotopically organized area (SII) was obtained in a similar manner. SII lies just ventral to SI in the postcentral gyrus, much of it extending into the lateral fissure. SII receives much of its input from SI (Pons et al., 1987); but in contrast to SI, whose input is largely contralateral, SII receives substantial input from both sides of the body.

Much of the output of SI and SII goes to the association cortex of the *posterior parietal lobe.* Notice in Figure 8.22 that the somatosensory homunculus is distorted; the greatest proportion of the primary somatosensory cortex is dedicated to receiving input from the parts of the body that are capable of the finest tactual discriminations (e.g., hands, lips, and tongue).

Kaas et al. (1981) found that the primary somatosensory cortex is not a single area as described by Penfield. It is, in fact, four parallel strips, each with a similar, but separate, somatotopic organization. Each strip

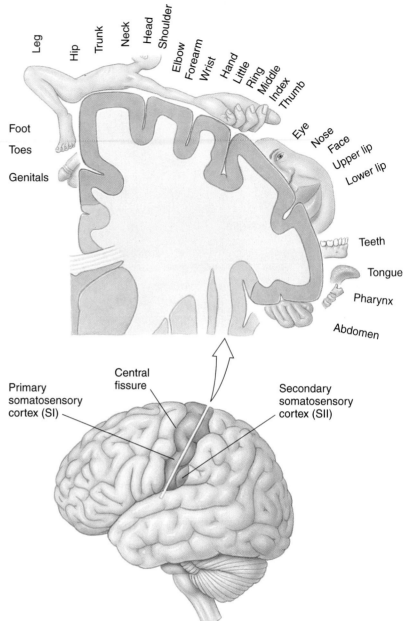

Figure 8.22 The location of human primary (SI) and secondary (SII) somatosensory cortex and an illustration of the primary somatosensory homunculus.

of primary somatosensory cortex is most sensitive to a different kind of somatosensory input (e.g., to light touch or temperature). Thus, if one were to record from neurons in a horizontal line across the four strips, one would find neurons that preferred four different kinds of tactile stimulation but all to the same part of the body.

Like the primary visual and auditory cortexes, the primary somatosensory cortex is organized in columns; each neuron in a particular cortical column responds to the same kind of somatosensory stimuli and has a receptive field on the same part of the body. The receptive fields of many neurons in the primary somatosensory cortex, like those of visual system neurons, can be di-

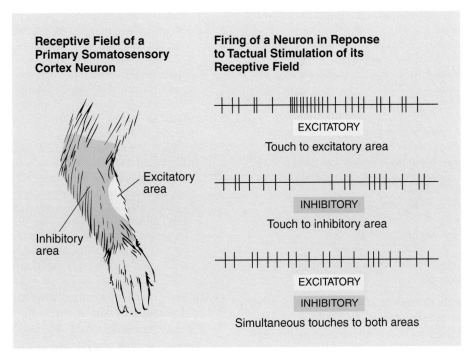

Figure 8.23 The receptive field of a neuron of the primary somatosensory cortex. Notice the antagonistic excitatory and inhibitory areas.

vided into antagonistic excitatory and inhibitory areas. Figure 8.23 illustrates the receptive field of a neuron of the primary somatosensory cortex that is responsive to light touch (Mountcastle & Powell, 1959).

Effects of Damage to the Primary Somatosensory Cortex

Like the effects of damage to the primary auditory cortex, the effects of damage to the primary somatosensory cortex are remarkably mild. Corkin, Milner, and Rasmussen (1970) assessed the somatosensory abilities of patients both before and after unilateral excision of SI for the relief of epilepsy. Following surgery, the patients displayed two minor contralateral deficits: a reduced ability to detect light touch and a reduced ability to identify objects by touch (i.e., a deficit in stereognosis). These deficits were bilateral only in those cases in which the unilateral lesion encroached on SII.

Somatosensory Agnosias

There are two major types of somatosensory agnosia. One is **astereognosia**—the inability to recognize objects by touch. Cases of pure astereognosia—those that occur in the absence of simple sensory deficits—are rare (Corkin, Miller, & Rasmussen, 1970). The other type of somatosensory agnosia is **asomatognosia**—the

failure to recognize parts of one's own body. Asomatognosia is usually unilateral, affecting only the left side of the body; and it is usually associated with extensive damage to the right posterior parietal lobe. You have already encountered one example of asomatognosia in this book, the case of the man who fell out of bed; the case of Klawans's (1990) Aunt Betty is another:

It was time to see Aunt Betty—she wasn't really my aunt, but I grew up thinking that she was. She was my mother's best friend. She had had a stroke in her right hemisphere.

As we walked to her room, one of the medical students described the case. "Left hemiplegia [left-side paralysis]," I was told.

Aunt Betty was lying on her back with her head and eyes turned to the right. "Betty," I called out. Not Aunt Betty, but Betty. I was 37; I'd dropped the "Aunt" long ago—at least 2 years earlier.

I approached her bed from the left, but Aunt Betty did not turn her head or even her eyes to look towards me.

"Hal," she called out. "Where are you?"

I turned her head gently toward me. We talked. It was clear that she had no speech problems, no memory loss, and no confusion. She was as bright as ever. But her eyes still looked to the right as if the left side of her world did not exist.

Somatotopic. Organized, like the primary somatosensory cortex, according to a map of the surface of the body.

Somatosensory homunculus. The somatotopic map that constitutes the primary somatosensory cortex.

Astereognosia. The inability to recognize objects by touch.

Asomatognosia. The failure to recognize parts of one's own body.

I picked up her right hand and held it in front of her eyes. "What's this?" I asked.

"My hand, of course," she said with an intonation that suggested what she thought of my question.

"Well then, what's this?" I said, as I held up her limp left hand where she could see it.

"A hand."

"Whose hand?"

"Your hand, I guess," she replied. She seemed genuinely puzzled. I carefully placed her hand on the bed.

"Why have you come to this hospital?" I asked.

"To see you," she replied hesitantly. I could tell that she didn't really know the answer.

"Is there anything wrong with you?"

"No."

"How about your left hand and leg?"

"They're fine," she said. "How are yours?"

"They're fine too," I replied. There was nothing else to do. Aunt Betty was in trouble. [2]

As in the case of Aunt Betty, asomatognosia is often accompanied by **anosognosia**—the failure of neuropsychological patients to recognize their own symptoms. Asomatognosia may also be accompanied by **contralateral neglect**—the tendency not to respond to stimuli that are contralateral to a right-hemisphere injury. You will learn more about contralateral neglect in the next chapter.

The Paradoxes of Pain

A paradox is a logical contradiction. The perception of pain is paradoxical in three important respects, which is why I have singled out pain for special discussion. The three paradoxes of pain are explained in the following three subsections.

■ **ADAPTIVENESS OF PAIN** One paradox of pain is that an experience that seems in every respect to be so bad is in fact extremely important for our survival. There is no special stimulus for pain; it is a response to excessive (potentially harmful) stimulation of any type (Cesare & McNaughton, 1997). The value of pain is best illustrated by a person who does not experience it:

The best documented of all cases of congenital insensitivity to pain is Miss C., a young Canadian girl who was a student at McGill University in Montreal. . . . The young lady was highly intelligent and seemed normal in every way except that she had never felt pain. As a child, she had bitten off the tip of her tongue while chewing food, and had suffered third-degree burns after kneeling on a radiator to look out of the window. . . . She felt no pain when parts of her body were subjected to strong electric shock, to hot water at temperatures that usually produce reports of burning pain, or to a prolonged ice-bath. Equally astonishing was the fact that she

showed no changes in blood pressure, heart rate, or respiration when these stimuli were presented. Furthermore, she could not remember ever sneezing or coughing, the gag reflex could be elicited only with great difficulty, and corneal reflexes (to protect the eyes) were absent. A variety of other stimuli, such as inserting a stick up through the nostrils, pinching tendons, or injections of histamine under the skin—which are normally considered as forms of torture—also failed to produce pain.

Miss C. had severe medical problems. She exhibited pathological changes in her knees, hip, and spine, and underwent several orthopaedic operations. The surgeon attributed these changes to the lack of protection to joints usually given by pain sensation. She apparently failed to shift her weight when standing, to turn over in her sleep, or to avoid certain postures, which normally prevent inflammation of joints. . . .

Miss C. died at the age of twenty-nine of massive infections . . . and extensive skin and bone trauma. [3]

■ **LACK OF CORTICAL REPRESENTATION OF PAIN** The second paradox of pain is that it has no obvious cortical representation. Removal of SI and SII in humans is not associated with any change in the threshold for pain; indeed, *hemispherectomized* patients (patients with one cerebral hemisphere removed) can still perceive pain from both sides of their bodies.

There was initial optimism that positron emission tomography (PET) and functional magnetic resonance imaging (fMRI) would easily sort out the puzzle of the cortical representation of pain: Surely, PET or fMRI recordings from patients experiencing pain would reveal the particular areas of cortex mediating the perception of pain. The initial optimism has largely dissipated.

It is now clear that the cortical representation of pain is much more complex than initially assumed. For example, the brief painful stimuli, which are commonly used in pain experiments, do not seem to activate the same cortical areas as chronic clinical pain, and many seemingly minor methodological variations seem to affect the areas of the cortex that are activated by painful stimuli (Apkarian, 1995). Apparently, pain is not mediated by cortical activity in the same way that sights, sounds, and touches are.

The one cortical area that has been most frequently linked to pain is the **anterior cingulate cortex** (see Figure 8.24). For example, Craig et al. (1996) used positron emission tomography to demonstrate increases in anterior cingulate cortex activity when subjects placed a hand on painfully cold bars, painfully hot bars, or even on alternating cool and warm bars, which produce an illusion of painful stimulation (see Figure 8.24).

Evidence suggests that the anterior cingulate cortex is involved in the emotional reaction to pain rather

---

[2]Paraphrased from pp. 12–14 of *Newton's Madness: Further Tales of Clinical Neurology* by Harold L. Klawans (New York: Harper & Row, 1990).

[3]From *The Challenge of Pain* (pp. 16–17) by Ronald Melzack and Patrick D. Wall, 1982, London: Penguin Books Ltd. Copyright © Ronald Melzack and Patrick D. Wall, 1982.

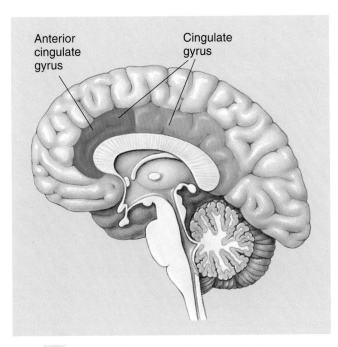

Figure 8.24 Location of anterior cingulate cortex in the cingulate gyrus.

than to the perception of pain itself. The following are two findings that support this view. First, conventional *prefrontal lobotomy,* which damages the anterior cingulate cortex and its connections, typically reduces the emotional reaction to pain without changing the threshold for pain. Second, increasing or decreasing the unpleasantness of painful stimulation by hypnosis produces corresponding changes in anterior cingulate PET activity.

■**DESCENDING PAIN CONTROL** The third paradox of pain is that this most compelling of all sensory experiences can be so effectively suppressed by cognitive and emotional factors. For example, men participating in a certain religious ceremony swing from ropes attached to giant meat hooks in their backs with little evidence of pain (Kosambi, 1967); severe wounds suffered by soldiers in battle are often associated with little pain (Beecher, 1959); and people injured in life-threatening situations frequently feel no pain until the threat is over.

Melzack and Wall (1965) proposed the **gate-control theory** to account for the ability of cognitive and emotional factors to block pain. They theorized that signals descending in centrifugal pathways (pathways conducting from higher to lower levels of a sensory hierarchy) from the brain can activate neural gating circuits in the spinal cord to block incoming pain signals.

Three important discoveries led to the identification of the descending pain-control circuit. First was the discovery that electrical stimulation of the **periaqueductal gray** (**PAG**) has analgesic (pain-blocking) effects: Reynolds (1969) was able to perform abdominal surgery

on rats with no analgesia other than that provided by PAG stimulation. Second was the discovery that the PAG and other areas of the brain contain specialized receptors for opiate analgesic drugs such as morphine, which suggested that such analgesic substances might occur naturally in the body: Why else would there be receptors for them? And third was the isolation of several endogenous (internally produced) opiate analgesics, the **endorphins,** which you learned about in Chapter 4 (e.g., Hughes et al., 1975). These three findings together suggested that analgesic drugs and psychological factors might block pain through an endorphin-sensitive circuit that descends from the PAG.

Figure 8.25 on page 212 illustrates the descending analgesia circuit first hypothesized by Basbaum and Fields (1978); see also Fields and Basbaum (1984). They proposed that the output of the PAG excites the serotonergic neurons of the *raphé nuclei* (a cluster of serotonergic nuclei in the core of the medulla), which in turn project down the dorsal columns of the spinal cord and excite interneurons that block incoming pain signals in the dorsal horn. Recent evidence suggests that several different serotonin receptor subtypes are present in the dorsal horn and that these play different roles in the inhibition of pain (see Millan, 1995).

Evidence in support of Basbaum and Field's hypothetical descending pain-control circuit has come from a variety of sources. For example, microinjection of an opiate antagonist, such as naloxone or naltrexone, into the PAG has been found to block the analgesia produced by *systemic injection* (injection into general circulation) of morphine; and activation of the raphé nucleus with electrical stimulation has been shown to inhibit pain-sensitive neurons in the dorsal horn of the spinal cord. Moreover, the analgesic effects of morphine and PAG stimulation have been attenuated by sectioning the fibers that descend from the raphé, by lesioning the raphé itself, or by depleting the raphé neurons of their serotonin neurotransmitter.

The descending analgesia circuit is not the only analgesic mechanism; it is not even the only mechanism of opiate analgesia. Opiates also act directly on a class of particularly small pain receptors by blocking their calcium channels (Taddese, Nah, & McClesky,

Anosognosia. The common failure of neurological patients to recognize their own symptoms.

Contralateral neglect. A disorder characterized by a tendency not to respond to stimuli that are contralateral to a brain injury.

Anterior cingulate cortex. The cortex of the anterior cingulate gyrus, which is involved in the emotional reaction to painful stimulation.

Gate-control theory. The theory that neural signals that descend from the brain can activate neural gating circuits in the spinal cord to block incoming pain signals.

Periaqueductal gray (PAG). The gray matter around the cerebral aqueduct, which contains opiate receptors and activates a descending analgesia circuit.

Endorphins. Endogenous (internally produced) opiate analgesics.

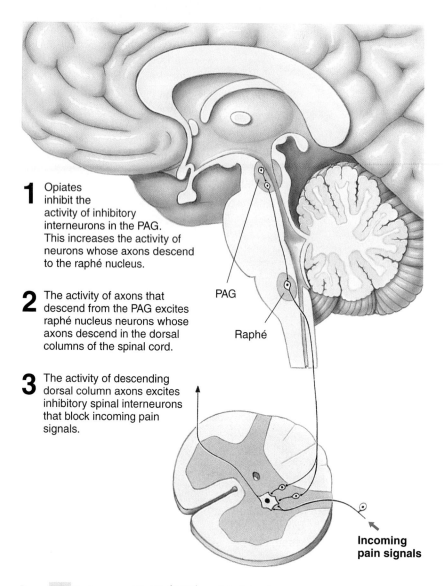

1 Opiates inhibit the activity of inhibitory interneurons in the PAG. This increases the activity of neurons whose axons descend to the raphé nucleus.

2 The activity of axons that descend from the PAG excites raphé nucleus neurons whose axons descend in the dorsal columns of the spinal cord.

3 The activity of descending dorsal column axons excites inhibitory spinal interneurons that block incoming pain signals.

PAG

Raphé

Incoming pain signals

Figure 8.25 Basbaum and Field's (1978) model of the descending analgesia circuit.

1995). These small pain receptors mediate the perception of severe chronic pain, and thus by blocking them, opiates reduce this form of pain without reducing the pain of a pinprick.

Phantom Limbs

Almost every amputee who has lost an arm or leg continues to feel the presence of the amputated limb; this perception of an amputated limb is referred to as a **phantom limb** (Melzack, 1992). The most striking feature of phantom limbs is their reality. Their existence is so compelling that a patient may try to jump out of bed onto a nonexistent leg or to lift a cup with a nonexistent hand. In most cases, the amputated limb behaves like a normal limb; for example, as an amputee walks, a phantom arm seems to swing back and forth in perfect coordination with the intact arm. However, sometimes

an amputee feels that the amputated limb is stuck in a peculiar position:

> One man felt that his phantom arm extended straight out from the shoulder, at a right angle to the body. He therefore turned sideways whenever he passed through doorways, to avoid hitting the wall. Another man, whose phantom arm was bent behind him, slept only on his abdomen or on his side because the phantom got in the way when he tried to rest on his back. (Melzack, 1992, p. 120)

About 50% of amputees experience chronic severe pain in their phantom limbs. A typical complaint is that an amputated hand is clenched so tightly that the fingernails are digging into the palm of the hand. Occasionally, this condition can be treated by having the amputee concentrate on opening the amputated hand. In phantom legs, pain is often felt as a severe cramp or as a flame being applied to the toes. The first published report of phantom limb pain described the experience of a victim of the American Civil War, who awoke from

MECHANISMS OF PERCEPTION, CONSCIOUS AWARENESS, AND ATTENTION

surgery knowing that his arm had been amputated but not knowing that his legs had been taken as well:

> [I was] suddenly aware of a sharp cramp in my left leg. I tried to get at it . . . with my single arm, but, finding myself too weak, hailed an attendant.
>
> Just rub my calf . . . if you please.
>
> Calf? . . . You ain't got none, pardner. It's took off.

A common explanation of phantom limbs and phantom limb pain is that they result from the irritation of nerves in the stump, which sends signals to those areas of the somatosensory cortex that had received input from the amputated limb prior to amputation. Accordingly, efforts to treat chronic phantom limb pain have involved surgical destruction of various parts of the neural pathway between the stump and the cortex—the peripheral nerves from the stump, the ascending anterolateral tracts, various thalamic relay nuclei—or the somatosensory cortex itself. Unfortunately, none of these surgical interventions has provided more than temporary relief from the pain (see Melzack, 1992)—and none has eliminated the phantom limb. This suggests that phantom limb pain is created in the cortex itself.

8.5 The Chemical Senses: Smell and Taste

Olfaction (smell) and *gustation* (taste) are referred to as the chemical senses because their function is to monitor the chemical content of the environment (see Bartoshuk & Beauchamp, 1994). Smell is the response of the olfactory system to airborne chemicals that are drawn by inhalation over receptors in the nasal passages, and taste is the response of the gustatory system to chemicals in the solutions of the oral cavity.

When we are eating, smell and taste act in concert. Molecules of food excite both smell and taste receptors and produce an integrated sensory impression termed **flavor.** The contribution of olfaction to flavor is often underestimated, but you won't make this mistake if you remember that people with no sense of smell have difficulty distinguishing the flavors of apples and onions.

Smell and taste have the dubious distinction of being the least understood of the exteroceptive sensory systems (see Laurent, 1997). One reason is that chemical stimuli are inherently more difficult to control and administer than are lights, tones, and touches. Another is that loss of the ability to smell and taste does not pose many serious health problems for individuals living in societies, such as ours, in which potential foods are screened by government agencies. Be that as it may, the chemical senses have attracted considerable interest in recent years.

Arguably, the single most interesting aspect of the chemical senses is their role in the social lives of many species. The members of many species release **pheromones**—chemicals that influence the behavior of *conspecifics* (members of the same species). For example, Murphy and Schneider (1970) showed that hamster sexual and aggressive behavior is under pheromonal control. Normal male hamsters attacked and killed unfamiliar males that were placed in their colonies, and they mounted and impregnated unfamiliar sexually receptive females; however, male hamsters that were unable to smell the intruders engaged in neither aggressive nor sexual behavior. Murphy and Schneider confirmed the olfactory basis of hamster aggressive and sexual behavior in a particularly devious fashion. They swabbed a male intruder with the vaginal secretions of a sexually receptive female before placing it in an unfamiliar colony; in so doing, they converted it from an object of hamster assassination to an object of hamster lust.

The possibility that humans may release sexual pheromones has received considerable attention because of its financial and recreational potential. There have been several suggestive findings. For example, (1) the olfactory sensitivity of women is greatest when they are ovulating (e.g., Doty et al., 1981); (2) the menstrual cycles of women living together tend to become synchronized (McClintock, 1971); (3) humans—particularly women—can tell the sex of a person from the breath (Doty et al., 1982) or the underarm odor (Schleidt, Hold, & Attili, 1981); and (4) men can judge the stage of a woman's menstrual cycle on the basis of her vaginal odor (Doty et al., 1975). However, there is still no direct evidence that human odors can serve as sex attractants (Doty, 1986). To put it mildly, most subjects did not find the body odors that were employed in the aforementioned studies to be particularly attractive.

Another feature of the chemical senses that has attracted attention is that they are involved in some interesting forms of learning. As you discovered in Chapter 5, animals that suffer from gastrointestinal upset after consuming a particular food develop a *conditioned*

Phantom limb. The vivid perception of an amputated limb.

Flavor. The combined impression of taste and smell.

Pheromones. Odors that are released by an animal and elicit specific patterns of behavior in its conspecifics.

taste aversion. Conversely, it has been shown that rats develop preferences for flavors that they encounter in their mother's milk (Galef & Sherry, 1973) or on the breath of conspecifics (Galef, 1989). And adult male rats that were nursed as pups by lemon-scented mothers copulate more effectively with females that smell of lemons (Fillion & Blass, 1986)—a phenomenon that has been aptly referred to as the I-want-a-girl-just-like-the-girl-who-married-dear-old-dad phenomenon (Diamond, 1986).

Olfactory System

Because we can discriminate among thousands of different odors, it has long been assumed that olfaction, like color vision (see Chapter 7), is coded according to component principles—that is, that there are a few primary receptor types, and the perception of various odors is produced by different ratios of activity in them. An alternative theory is that the olfactory system is more like the immune system—that is, that there are

a multitude of receptor types, each uniquely responsive to a particular chemical. As unlikely as this latter theory first seemed, it now appears to be largely correct: About one thousand different kinds of olfactory receptor proteins have been discovered, each maximally sensitive to a different chemical (see Buck, 1996). There is only one type of receptor protein in each olfactory receptor cell.

The olfactory system is illustrated in Figure 8.26. The olfactory receptors are located in the upper part of the nose, embedded in a layer of mucus-covered tissue called the **olfactory mucosa.** They have their own axons, which pass through a porous portion of the skull (the *cribriform plate*) and enter the **olfactory bulbs** (the first cranial nerves), where they synapse on neurons that project via the *olfactory tract* to the brain.

Taking the lead from research on other sensory systems, researchers have attempted to discover the functional principle by which the various receptors are distributed through the olfactory mucosa. If there is such a functional principle, it has not yet been discovered: Each type of receptor protein appears to be scattered almost

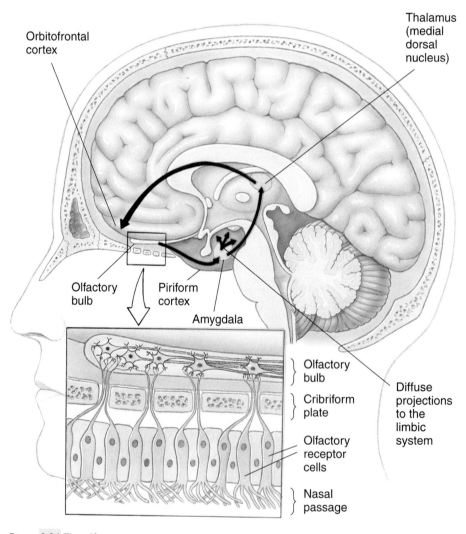

Figure 8.26 The olfactory system.

MECHANISMS OF PERCEPTION, CONSCIOUS AWARENESS, AND ATTENTION

randomly through the mucosa, providing no clue whatsoever about the organization of the system. However, all of the olfactory receptors with the same receptor protein project to the same location on the olfactory bulb (see Axel, 1995; Mombaerts, 1996; Mori, 1995).

The olfactory tract projects to several structures of the medial temporal lobes, including the amygdala and adjacent **piriform cortex**—the area of the medial temporal cortex adjacent to the amygdala. The olfactory system is thus the only sensory system whose signals do not pass through the thalamus before reaching the cerebral cortex.

Two major olfactory pathways leave the amygdala-piriform area. One projects diffusely to the limbic system, and the other projects via the **medial dorsal nuclei** of the thalamus to the **orbitofrontal cortex**—the area of cortex on the inferior surface of the frontal lobes, next to the orbits, or eye sockets. The limbic projection is thought to mediate the emotional response to odors; the thalamic-orbitofrontal projection is thought to mediate the conscious perception of odors. Little is known about how neurons receptive to different odorants are organized in the cortex.

Gustatory System

Taste receptors are found on the tongue and in parts of the oral cavity; they typically occur in clusters of 50 or so called **taste buds.** On the tongue, taste buds are often located around small protuberances called *papillae* (singular: *papilla*). The relation between taste receptors, taste buds, and papillae is illustrated in Figure 8.27. Unlike olfactory receptors, taste receptors do not have their own axons; each neuron that carries impulses away from a taste bud receives input from many receptors.

Psychologically, there are four primary tastes: sweet, sour, bitter, and salty. Consequently, it was once assumed that there are four kinds of taste receptors and that the perception of all tastes is a consequence of the relative amounts of activity in these four receptors. Although this component-processing theory of taste is consistent with some of the data, it is not without its problems. One is that many tastes cannot be created by combinations of the four primaries (Schiffman & Erickson, 1980); another is that there is no evidence that taste receptors come in just four varieties. Indeed, some *sapid* (possessing taste) substances have been shown to influence re-

Surface of Tongue

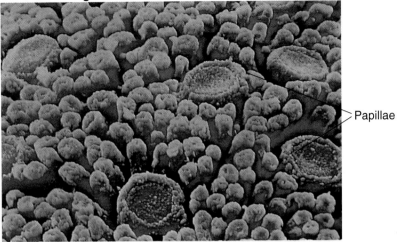

Papillae

Cross Section of a Papilla

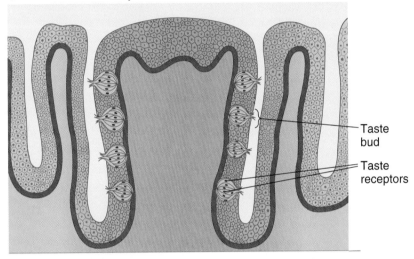

Taste bud

Taste receptors

Figure 8.27 Taste receptors, taste buds, and papillae on the surface of the tongue. Two sizes of papillae are visible in the photograph; only the larger papillae contain taste buds and receptors.

ceptor activity by acting directly on ion channels rather than receptors (see Kinnamon & Margolskee, 1996).

The major pathways over which gustatory signals are conducted to the cortex are illustrated in Figure 8.28 on page 216. Gustatory afferents leave the mouth as part of the *facial* (VII), *glossopharyngeal* (IX), and *vagus* (X) *cranial nerves,* which carry information from the front

Olfactory mucosa. The mucous membrane that lines the upper nasal passages and contains the olfactory receptor cells.

Olfactory bulbs. The first cranial nerves, whose output goes primarily to the amygdala and piriform cortex.

Piriform cortex. The area of medial temporal cortex that receives direct olfactory input.

Medial dorsal nuclei. The thalamic relay nuclei of the olfactory system.

Orbitofrontal cortex. The cortex of the inferior frontal lobes, which receives olfactory input from the thalamus.

Taste buds. Clusters of taste receptors.

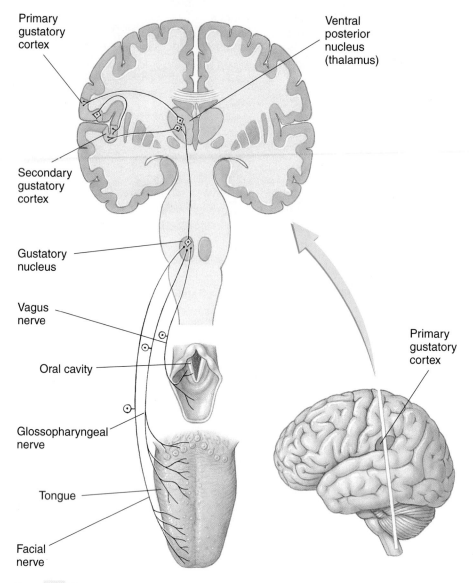

Primary gustatory cortex

Ventral posterior nucleus (thalamus)

Secondary gustatory cortex

Gustatory nucleus

Vagus nerve

Oral cavity

Glossopharyngeal nerve

Tongue

Facial nerve

Primary gustatory cortex

Figure 8.28 The gustatory system.

of the tongue, back of the tongue, and back of the oral cavity, respectively. These fibers all terminate in the **solitary nucleus** of the medulla, where they synapse on neurons that project to the *ventral posterior nucleus* of the thalamus. The gustatory axons of the ventral posterior nucleus project to the *primary gustatory cortex,* which is near the face area of the somatosensory homunculus, and to the *secondary gustatory cortex,* which is hidden from view deep in the lateral fissure. Unlike the projections of other sensory systems, the projections of the gustatory system are primarily ipsilateral.

Brain Damage and the Chemical Senses

The inability to smell is called **anosmia;** the inability to taste is called **ageusia.** The most common neurological cause of anosmia is a blow to the head that causes a dis-

placement of the brain within the skull and shears the olfactory nerves where they pass through the cribriform plate. Approximately 6% of patients hospitalized for traumatic head injuries are found to have olfactory deficits of some sort (e.g., Zusho, 1983).

In contrast to anosmia, ageusia is rare, presumably because sensory signals from the mouth are carried over three separate pathways. However, ageusia for the anterior two-thirds of the tongue on one side is sometimes observed after damage to the ear on the same side of the body. This is because the branch of the facial nerve (VII) that carries gustatory information from the anterior two-thirds of the tongue passes through the middle ear.

One noteworthy feature of ageusia and anosmia is that they sometimes occur together in neurological patients. This suggests that there is some as yet unidentified area in the brain where olfactory and gustatory information converges.

Test your knowledge of the anatomy of the sensory systems by completing each sentence with the name of the appropriate sensory system. The correct answers are provided at the bottom of this page. Before proceeding, review material related to your incorrect answers and omissions.

1. The inferotemporal cortex is an area of secondary _____ cortex.

2. The dorsal and ventral streams are part of the _____ system.

3. The primary _____ cortex is tonotopically organized.

4. The inferior colliculi and medial geniculate nuclei are components of the _____ system.

5. The dorsal-column medial-lemniscus system and the anterolateral system are pathways of the _____ system.

6. The ventral posterior nuclei, the intralaminar nuclei, and the parafascicular nuclei are all thalamic nuclei of the _____ system.

7. The periaqueductal gray and the raphé nuclei are involved in blocking the perception of _____ .

8. One pathway of the _____ system projects from the amygdala and piriform cortex, to the medial dorsal nucleus, and then to orbito-frontal cortex.

9. The ventral posterior nuclei are thalamic relay nuclei of both the somatosensory and _____ systems.

10. Unlike the projections of all other sensory systems, the projections of the _____ system are primarily ipsilateral.

8.6 Selective Attention

We consciously perceive only a small subset of the many stimuli that excite our sensory organs at any one time and largely ignore the rest. The process by which this occurs is **selective attention.**

There are two aspects to selective attention: It improves the perception of the stimuli that are its focus, and it interferes with the perception of the stimuli that are not its focus. For example, if you focus your attention on a potentially important announcement in a noisy airport, your chances of understanding it increase; but your chances of understanding a simultaneous comment from a traveling companion decrease.

The mechanisms of selective attention are of two general types: *top-down* (from higher levels to lower levels) and *bottom-up* (from lower levels to higher levels). For example, separation from a red-haired friend might focus your attention on redheads passing in the crowd—a top-down process thought to originate in decision-making circuits of frontal lobe association areas and conducted into sensory areas by centrifugal fibers (see Crick & Koch, 1992). In contrast, bottom-up attentional mechanisms are those that are triggered by the lower levels of sensory systems and conducted to higher levels. For example, a sudden movement in the periphery of your visual field will reflexively focus your attention on it.

Until recently, I underestimated the importance of selective attention. The demonstration of the following

The correct answers are (1) visual, (2) visual, (3) auditory, (4) auditory, (5) somatosensory, (6) somatosensory, (7) pain, (8) olfactory, (9) gustatory, and (10) gustatory.

Solitary nucleus. The medullary relay nucleus of the gustatory system.
Anosmia. The inability to smell.
Ageusia. The inability to taste.

Selective attention. The ability to focus on a small subset of the multitude of stimuli that are being received at any one time.

phenomenon enlightened me; I hope that my description of it enlightens you. It's called **change blindness** (Rensink, O'Regan, & Clark, 1997). Figure 8.29 illustrates how the demonstration works. The subject is shown a photographic image on a computer screen and is asked to report any change in the image as soon as it is noticed. In fact, the image is composed of two alternating images with a delay of less than a tenth of a second between. The two photographic images are identical except for one gross feature. For example, the two images of a statue in Figure 8.29 are identical except that the picture in the center of the wall is missing from one. I thought that any subject would immediately notice the picture disappearing and reappearing—and I expect that you do too. But this is not what happens: Most subjects spend many seconds staring at the image searching, as instructed, for some change before they notice the disappearing picture. Once I noticed the disappearing and reappearing picture, I could only wonder in amazement why it took me so long.

Why does change blindness occur? Change blindness occurs because, contrary to our impression, when we view a scene we have absolutely no memory for parts of the scene that are not the focus of our attention (see Enns & DiLollo, 1997). When viewing the scene in Figure 8.29, I, like other subjects, tended to attend to details of the people and did not notice when the picture disappeared, because I had no memory of it from the previous viewing. Attended parts of a scene are loaded into a memory store, and any change in them is perceived, whereas unattended parts are not remembered and are thus replaced by new parts with no conscious awareness. The change blindness phenomenon does not occur without the brief (i.e., 80 millisecond) intervals between images, although they barely produce a flicker: No memory is required without the intervals, and the changes are immediately perceived.

Desimone and Moran (1985) were the first to demonstrate the effects of attention on neural activity in the visual system (see also Spitzer, Desimone, and Moran, 1988). They trained monkeys to stare at a fixation point on the screen while they recorded the activity of neurons in a prestriate area that was part of the ventral stream and particularly sensitive to color. In one experiment, they recorded from individual neurons that responded to either red or green bars of light in their receptive fields. When the monkey was trained to perform a task that required attention to the red cue, the response to the red cue was increased, and the response to the green cue was reduced. The opposite happened when the monkey attended to green. Such attention-related changes were not recorded from neurons in the primary visual cortex (see Maunsell, 1995).

A similar experiment was conducted in the dorsal stream neurons by Treue and Maunsell (1996). When monkeys were trained to attend to movement in a particular direction, the responses of neurons to motion in that direction were enhanced, whereas responses to motion in other directions were reduced.

Experiments paralleling those in monkeys have been conducted in humans using functional brain imaging techniques (see Driver & Mattingly, 1995). For example, Corbetta et al. (1990) presented a collection of moving, colored stimuli of various shapes and asked their subjects to discriminate among the stimuli based

0.1 second

Figure 8.29 The change blindness phenomenon. These two illustrations were continually alternated, with a brief (less than 0.1 second) interval between each presentation, and the subjects were asked to report any changes that they noticed. Amazingly, it took them many seconds to notice the disappearing and reappearing picture in the center of the wall.

(Photographs prepared by James Enns, Department of Psychology, University of British Columbia.)

on either their movement, color, or shape. Attention to shape or color produced increased activity in areas of the ventral stream; attention to movement produced increased activity in an area of the dorsal stream.

In another study of attention in human subjects, Ungerleider and Haxby (1994) showed subjects a series of faces. The subjects were asked whether the faces belonged to the same person or whether they were located in the same position relative to the frame. When the subjects were attending to identity, regions of the ventral stream were more active; when the subjects were attending to position, regions of the dorsal stream were more active.

Is there a particular structure of the brain responsible for directing selective attention? Duncan, Humphreys, and Ward (1997) argued that there isn't. They argued that the brain has a limited capacity for conscious processing, and selective attention is a product of the competition among sensory signals for access to circuits mediating consciousness, not of a separate attention mechanism.

One last important characteristic of selective attention: the cocktail-party phenomenon. The **cocktail-party phenomenon** is the demonstration that even when you are focusing so intently on one conversation that you are totally unaware of the content of other conversations going on around you, the mention of your name in one of the other conversations will immediately gain access to your consciousness. This phenomenon suggests that your brain can block from consciousness all stimuli except those of a particular kind while still unconsciously monitoring the blocked-out stimuli just in case something comes up that requires attention.

Change blindness. The difficulty perceiving major changes to unattended-to parts of a visual image when the changes are introduced during brief interruptions in the presentation of the image.

Cocktail-party phenomenon. The ability to unconsciously monitor the contents of one conversation while consciously focusing on another.

CONCLUSION

This chapter began by introducing you to three important principles of sensory system organization (8.1): hierarchical organization, functional segregation, and parallel processing. Then, it reviewed each of the five exteroceptive sensory systems, with an emphasis on cortical function: the visual system (8.2), the auditory system (8.3), the somatosensory system (8.4), and the chemical sensory systems—smell and taste (8.5). It concluded with a brief discussion of selective attention (8.6). A theme that recurred throughout the chapter was that perception can occur at the unconscious level and that conscious and unconscious perception are likely mediated by different parallel systems.

Although the ultimate products of sensory systems are unitary perceptual experiences, the fundamental mechanisms by which the systems produce these unitary experiences are not unitary at all. Each sensory system conducts different aspects of its input over separate parallel pathways through a series of specialized, hierarchically organized structures, each of which performs a different analysis. In this chapter, you learned that some parallel pathways of perception influence

conscious awareness, whereas others can guide behavior in the absence of conscious awareness.

In healthy persons, independent parallel analyses are ultimately reconstituted into compelling unitary experiences, and that is why the nonunitary nature of sensory system function is often most apparent in neuropsychological patients. In this chapter, neuropsychological patients taught you much about the function of healthy sensory systems: Dr. P., the visual agnosic who mistook his wife for a hat; D. B., the man with blindsight; Karl Lashley, the physiological psychologist who used his scotoma to turn a friend's head into a wallpaper pattern; D. F., who showed by her accurate reaching that she perceived the size, shape, and orientation of objects that she could not describe; A. T., who could describe the size and shape of objects that she could not accurately reach for; C. K., the visual agnosic who could still recognize faces; Aunt Betty, the asomatognosic who lost the left side of her body; Miss C., the student who felt no pain and died as a result; and the American Civil War amputee who experienced a leg that he did not have.

FOOD FOR THOUGHT

1. Many amputees who suffer from phantom limb pain receive little or no treatment because "after all, it's all in their heads." Discuss.

2. How has this chapter changed your concept of perception?

3. Some sensory circuits directly control behavior without producing conscious perceptions, whereas others control behavior by mediating conscious perceptions. Discuss the evolutionary implications of this fact. Why did consciousness evolve?

KEY TERMS

Ageusia (*p. 216*)
Agnosia (*p. 197*)
Anosmia (*p. 216*)
Anosognosia (*p. 210*)
Anterior cingulate cortex (*p. 210*)
Anterolateral system (*p. 205*)
Asomatognosia (*p. 209*)
Association cortex (*p. 189*)
Astereognosia (*p. 209*)
Auditory nerve (*p. 200*)
Basilar membrane (*p. 200*)
Blindsight (*p. 193*)
Change blindness (*p. 218*)
Cochlea (*p. 200*)
Cocktail-party phenomenon (*p. 219*)
Completion (*p. 192*)
Contralateral neglect (*p. 210*)
"Control of behavior" versus "conscious perception" theory (*p. 196*)
Dermatome (*p. 204*)

Dorsal columns (*p. 206*)
Dorsal stream (*p. 196*)
Dorsal-column medial-lemniscus system (*p. 205*)
Endorphins (*p. 211*)
Exteroceptive sensory systems (*p. 189*)
Flavor (*p. 213*)
Free nerve endings (*p. 204*)
Functional segregation (*p. 191*)
Gate-control theory (*p. 211*)
Glabrous skin (*p. 204*)
Hair cells (*p. 200*)
Hemianopsic (*p. 192*)
Hierarchical organization (*p. 189*)
Inferior colliculi (*p. 202*)
Inferotemporal cortex (*p. 192*)
Medial dorsal nuclei (*p. 215*)
Medial geniculate nuclei (*p. 202*)
Medial lemniscus (*p. 206*)

Olfactory bulbs (*p. 214*)
Olfactory mucosa (*p. 214*)
Orbitofrontal cortex (*p. 215*)
Organ of Corti (*p. 200*)
Ossicles (*p. 200*)
Oval window (*p. 200*)
Pacinian corpuscles (*p. 204*)
Parallel processing (*p. 191*)
Perception (*p. 190*)
Periaqueductal gray (PAG) (*p. 211*)
Perimetry test (*p. 192*)
Phantom limb (*p. 212*)
Pheromones (*p. 213*)
Piriform cortex (*p. 215*)
Posterior parietal cortex (*p. 192*)
Prestrite cortex (*p. 192*)
Primary sensory cortex (*p. 189*)
Prosopagnosia (*p. 197*)
Retinotopic (*p. 200*)
Scotoma (*p. 192*)

Secondary sensory cortex (*p. 189*)
Selective attention (*p. 217*)
Semicircular canals (*p. 201*)
Sensation (*p. 190*)
Solitary nucleus (*p. 216*)
Somatosensory homunculus (*p. 208*)
Somatotopic (*p. 208*)
Stereognosis (*p. 205*)
Subjective contours (*p. 194*)
Superior olives (*p. 202*)
Taste buds (*p. 215*)
Tectorial membrane (*p. 200*)
Tonotopic (*p. 200*)
Tympanic membrane (*p. 200*)
Ventral posterior nucleus (*p. 206*)
Ventral stream (*p. 196*)
Vestibular system (*p. 201*)
Visual agnosia (*p. 197*)
"Where" versus "what" theory (*p. 196*)

ADDITIONAL READING

The following two books provide excellent summaries of research on the cortical mechanisms of perception; the first focuses on the visual system, the second on functional brain imaging studies of sensory processing:

Posner, M. I., & Raichle, M. E. (1994). *Images of mind.* New York: Scientific American Library.

Roland, P. E. (1993). *Brain activation.* New York: Wiley.

The following three review articles each provide excellent discussions of the neural mechanisms of conscious awareness:

Weiskrantz, L. (1996). Blindsight revisited. *Current Opinion in Neurobiology, 6:* 215–220.

Logothetis, N. K., & Sheinberg, D. L. (1996). Visual object recognition. *Annual Review of Neuroscience, 19:* 577–621.

Koch, C., & Braun, J. (1996). Towards the neuronal correlate of visual awareness. *Current Opinion in Neurobiology, 6:* 158–164.

9

The Sensorimotor System

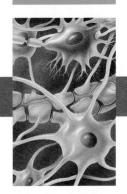

Last evening, while standing in a checkout line at the local market, I furtively scanned the headlines on the prominently displayed magazines—WOMAN GIVES BIRTH TO CAT; FLYING SAUCER LANDS IN CLEVELAND SHOPPING MALL; HOW TO LOSE 20 POUNDS IN 2 DAYS. Then, my mind began to wander, and I started to think about beginning to write this chapter. That is when I began to watch Rhonda's movements and to wonder about the neural system that controlled them. Rhonda was the cashier—the best in the place.

I was struck by the complexity of even her simplest movements. As she deftly transferred a bag of tomatoes to the scale, there was a coordinated adjustment in almost every part of her body. In addition to her obvious finger, hand, arm, and shoulder movements, coordinated movements of her head and eyes tracked her hand to the tomatoes; and there were adjustments in the muscles of her feet, legs, trunk, and other arm, which kept her from lurching forward. The accuracy of these responses suggested that they were guided in part by the patterns of visual, somatosensory, and vestibular change that they produced. The term *sensorimotor* in the title of this chapter formally recognizes the critical contribution of sensory input to guiding motor output.

As my purchases flowed through her left hand, Rhonda registered the prices with her right hand and bantered with Rick, the bagger. I was intrigued by how little of what Rhonda was doing appeared to be under her conscious control. She made general decisions about which items to pick up and where to put them, but she seemed to give no thought to the exact means by which these decisions were carried out. Each of her responses could have been made with an infinite number of different combinations of finger, wrist, elbow, shoulder, and body adjustments; but somehow she unconsciously picked one. The higher parts of her sensorimotor system—perhaps her cortex—seemed to issue conscious general commands to other parts of the system, which unconsciously produced a specific pattern of muscular responses that carried them out.

The automaticity of Rhonda's performance was a far cry from the slow, effortful responses that had characterized her first days at the market. Somehow, experience had integrated her individual movements into smooth sequences, and it seemed to have transferred the movements' control from a mode that involved conscious effort to one that did not.

I was suddenly jarred from my contemplations by a voice. "Sir, excuse me, sir, that will be $18.65," Rhonda said, with just a hint of delight at catching me in mid-daydream. I hastily paid my bill, muttered "thank you," and scurried out of the market. As I write this, I am smiling both at my own embarrassment and at the thought that Rhonda has unknowingly introduced you to three principles of sensorimotor control that are themes of this chapter: (1) The sensorimotor system is hierarchically organized. (2) Motor output is guided by sensory input. (3) Learning changes the nature and the locus of sensorimotor control.

9.1 Three Principles of Sensorimotor Function

Before getting into the details of the sensorimotor system, let's take a closer look at the three principles of sensorimotor function introduced by Rhonda. You will better appreciate these principles if you recognize that they are the very same principles that govern the operation of a large, efficient company.

The Sensorimotor System Is Hierarchically Organized

The operation of both the sensorimotor system and a large, efficient company is directed by commands that cascade down through the levels of a hierarchy (see Sakata et al., 1997)—from the association cortex or the company president (the highest levels) to the muscles or the workers (the lowest levels). Like the orders that are issued from the office of a company president, the commands that emerge from the association cortex specify general goals rather than specific plans of action. Neither the association cortex nor the company president routinely gets involved in the details. The main advantage of this *hierarchical organization* is that the higher levels of the hierarchy are left free to perform more complex functions.

Both the sensorimotor system and large, efficient companies are parallel hierarchical systems, that is, they are hierarchical systems in which signals flow between levels over multiple paths (see Rizzolatti, Fogassi, & Gallese, 1997). This parallel structure enables the association cortex or company presidents to exert control over the lower levels of the hierarchy in more than one way. For example, the association cortex may directly inhibit an eye-blink reflex to allow the insertion of a contact lens, and a company president may personally organize a delivery to an important customer.

The sensorimotor and company hierarchies are also characterized by *functional segregation*. That is, each level of the sensorimotor and company hierarchies tends to be composed of different units (neural structures or departments), each of which performs a different function.

In summary, the sensorimotor system—like the sensory systems you read about in the preceding chapter—is a parallel, functionally segregated hierarchical system. The main difference between the sensory systems and the sensorimotor system is the primary direction of information flow. In sensory systems, information mainly flows up through the hierarchy; in the sensorimotor system, information mainly flows down.

Motor Output Is Guided by Sensory Input

Efficient companies continuously monitor the effects of their own activities, and they use this information to fine-tune them. The sensorimotor system does the same. The eyes, the organs of balance, and the receptors in skin, muscles, and joints all monitor the progress of our responses; and they feed their information back into sensorimotor circuits. In most instances, this **sensory feedback** plays an important role in directing the continuation of the responses that produced it. The only responses that are not normally influenced by sensory feedback are *ballistic movements*—brief, all-or-none, high-speed movements, such as swatting a fly.

Behavior in the absence of just one kind of sensory feedback—the feedback that is carried by the somatosensory nerves of the arms—was studied in G. O., a former darts champion. An infection had selectively destroyed the somatosensory nerves of G. O.'s arms (Rothwell et al., 1982). He had great difficulty performing intricate responses such as doing up his buttons or picking up coins, even under visual guidance. Other difficulties resulted from his inability to adjust his motor output in the light of unanticipated external disturbances; for example, he could not keep from spilling a cup of coffee if somebody brushed against him. However, G. O.'s greatest problem was his inability to maintain a constant level of muscle contraction:

The result of this deficit was that even in the simplest of tasks requiring a constant motor output to the hand, G. O. would have to keep a visual check on his progress. For example, when carrying a suitcase, he would frequently glance at it to reassure himself that he had not dropped it some paces back. However, even visual feedback was of little use to him in many tasks. These tended to be those requiring a constant force output such as grasping a pen whilst writing or

holding a cup. Here, visual information was insufficient for him to be able to correct any errors that were developing in the output since, after a period, he had no indication of the pressure that he was exerting on an object; all he saw was either the pen or cup slipping from his grasp. (Rothwell et al., 1982, p. 539)

Many adjustments in motor output that occur in response to sensory feedback are controlled unconsciously by the lower levels of the sensorimotor hierarchy without the involvement of the higher levels. In the same way, large companies run more efficiently if the clerks do not have to check with the company president each time they encounter a minor problem.

Learning Changes the Nature and Locus of Sensorimotor Control

When a company is just starting up, each individual decision is made by the company president after careful consideration. However, as the company develops, many individual actions are coordinated into sequences of prescribed procedures that are routinely carried out by junior executives.

Similar changes occur during sensorimotor learning (see Halsband & Freund, 1993). During the initial stages of motor learning, each individual response is performed under conscious control; then, after much practice, individual responses become organized into continuous integrated sequences of action that flow smoothly and are adjusted by sensory feedback without conscious regulation. If you think for a moment about the sensorimotor skills you have acquired (e.g., typing, swimming, knitting, basketball playing, dancing, piano playing), you will appreciate that the organization of individual responses into continuous motor programs and the transfer of their control to lower levels of the nervous system characterizes most sensorimotor learning.

A General Model of Sensorimotor System Function

Figure 9.1 on page 224 is a model that illustrates several principles of sensorimotor system function; it is the framework of this chapter. Notice its hierarchical structure, the functional segregation of the levels (e.g., of secondary motor cortex), the parallel connections between levels, and the numerous feedback pathways.

Sensory feedback. Sensory signals that are produced by a response and are often used to guide the continuation of the response.

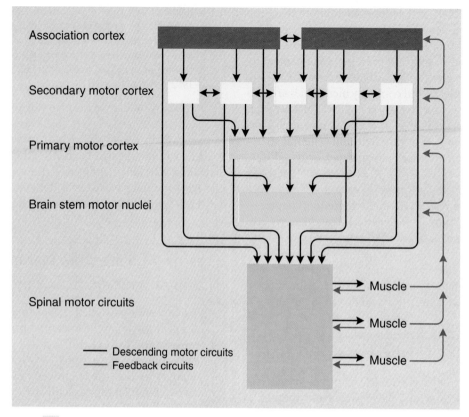

Figure 9.1 A general model of the sensorimotor system. Notice its hierarchical structure, its functional segregation, its parallel descending pathways, and its feedback circuits.

This chapter focuses on the neural structures that play important roles in the control of voluntary behavior (e.g., picking up an apple). It begins at the level of association cortex and traces major motor signals as they descend the sensorimotor hierarchy to the skeletal muscles that ultimately perform the movements.

9.2 Sensorimotor Association Cortex

Association cortex is at the top of the sensorimotor hierarchy. There are two major areas of sensorimotor association cortex. These are the posterior parietal association cortex and the dorsolateral prefrontal association cortex. Experts agree that the posterior parietal cortex and the dorsolateral prefrontal cortex are each composed of several different areas, each of which has a different function (see Ó Scalaidhe, Wilson, & Goldman-Rakic, 1997; Tanji, 1996; Wise et al., 1997); however, the experts do not yet agree on how best to divide them up.

Posterior Parietal Association Cortex

Before an effective movement can be initiated, certain information is required. The nervous system must know the original positions of the parts of the body that are to be moved, and it must know the positions of any external objects with which the body is going to interact. The **posterior parietal association cortex** plays an important role in integrating these two kinds of information (see Anderson et al., 1997). You learned in Chapter 8 that the posterior parietal cortex is classified as *association cortex* because it receives input from more than one sensory system. It receives information from the three sensory systems that play roles in the localization of the body and external objects in space: the visual system, the auditory system, and the somatosensory system. In turn, much of the output of posterior parietal cortex goes to areas of motor cortex, which are located in the frontal cortex: to the *dorsolateral prefrontal association cortex,* to the various areas of *secondary motor*

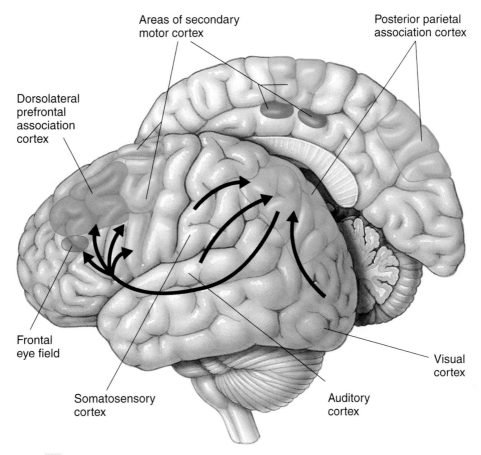

Areas of secondary
motor cortex

Posterior parietal
association cortex

Dorsolateral
prefrontal
association
cortex

Frontal
eye field

Somatosensory
cortex

Auditory
cortex

Visual
cortex

Figure 9.2 The major cortical input and output pathways of the posterior parietal association cortex. Shown are the lateral surface of the left hemisphere and the medial surface of the right hemisphere.

cortex, and to the **frontal eye field**—a small area of prefrontal cortex that controls eye movement (see Figure 9.2).

Apraxia and contralateral neglect are movement disorders that result from damage to the posterior parietal cortex. The symptoms of these two disorders are consistent with the role of the posterior parietal cortex in sensorimotor function.

Apraxia is a disorder of voluntary movement that is not attributable to a simple motor deficit (e.g., not to paralysis or weakness) or to deficits in comprehension or motivation (see Benton, 1985). Remarkably, apraxic patients have difficulty making specific movements when they are requested to do so, particularly when they are out of context; however, they can readily perform the very same movements under natural conditions. For example, an apraxic carpenter who has no difficulty at all hammering a nail during the course of her work might not be able to demonstrate hammering movements when requested to make them, particularly in the absence of a hammer. Although its symptoms are bilateral, apraxia is typically caused by unilateral damage to the left posterior parietal lobe. In contrast, lesions of the right posterior parietal lobe produce **constructional apraxia**—a bilateral disruption of movements that are

designed to assemble components of an object to form a whole. Patients with constructional apraxia have difficulty completing the block design subtest of the Wechsler Adult Intelligence Scale (WAIS), and they also have difficulty doing jigsaw puzzles, such as those of the WAIS object assembly subtest (see Chapter 5). In Figure 9.3 on page 226, an illustration drawn from a 1917 photograph, a brain-damaged war veteran is failing a test of constructional apraxia.

Contralateral neglect is a disturbance of the patient's ability to respond to visual, auditory, and somatosensory stimuli on the side of the body contralateral to the side of a brain lesion (see Rafal, 1994). The

Posterior parietal association cortex. The cortex of the posterior parietal lobe, which is thought to receive and integrate the spatial information that guides voluntary behavior.

Frontal eye field. The area of prefrontal cortex that plays a role in the control of eye movements.

Apraxia. A loss of the ability to perform voluntary movements upon request.

Constructional apraxia. The inability to perform tests of construction in the absence of primary sensory deficits or general intellectual impairment.

Contralateral neglect. A disturbance of the patient's ability to respond to visual, auditory, and somatosensory stimuli on one side of the body, usually the left side of the body following damage to the right parietal lobe.

Figure 9.3 A drawing of a 1917 photograph of a patient with constructional apraxia. This war veteran is having difficulty duplicating the stack of blocks on his left.

(Drawn from Poppelreuter, 1917.)

disturbance is often associated with large lesions of the right posterior parietal lobe (see Weintraub & Mesulam, 1989). For example, Mrs. S. suffered from contralateral neglect after a massive stroke to the posterior portions of her right hemisphere. Like many other neuropsychological patients, she developed ways of dealing with her deficiency:

> She has totally lost the idea of "left", with regard to both the world and her own body. Sometimes she complains that her portions are too small, but this is because she only eats from the right half of the plate—it does not occur to her that it has a left half as well. Sometimes, she will put on lipstick, and make up the right half of her face, leaving the left half completely neglected: it is almost impossible to treat these things, because her attention cannot be drawn to them. . . .
>
> . . . She has worked out strategies for dealing with her [problem]. She cannot look left, directly, she cannot turn left, so what she does is turn right—and right through a circle. Thus she requested, and was given, a rotating wheelchair. And now if she cannot find something which she knows should be there, she swivels to the right, through a circle, until it comes into view. . . . If her portions seem too small, she will swivel to the right, keeping her eyes to the right, until the previously missed half now comes into view; she will eat this, or rather half of this, and feel less hungry than before. But if

she is still hungry, or if she thinks on the matter, and realises that she may have perceived only half of the missing half, she will make a second rotation till the remaining quarter comes into view. (Sacks, 1985, pp. 73–74)[1]

Dorsolateral Prefrontal Association Cortex

The other large area of association cortex that has important sensorimotor functions is the **dorsolateral prefrontal association cortex** (Goldman-Rakic, Bates, & Chafee, 1992). It receives projections from posterior parietal cortex, and it sends projections to areas of *secondary motor cortex,* to *primary motor cortex,* and to the *frontal eye field* (see Figure 9.4).

In one series of experiments, the activity of dorsolateral prefrontal neurons was recorded while monkeys performed a *delayed matching-to-sample task* (Di Pelligrino & Wise, 1991). The monkeys were briefly shown a sample stimulus; then, after a delay, they were shown the sample and another stimulus. The correct response was to reach for the sample. Some dorsolateral prefrontal neurons responded to the sensory qualities of the sample both during its presentation and in the delay period—it has been suggested that such neurons store a mental representation of objects to which the subject is going to respond. Other prefrontal neurons responded before and during the response itself—there are neurons in all cortical motor areas that begin to fire in anticipation of a motor response, but those in dorsolateral prefrontal cortex fire the earliest. Thus, the decision to initiate a voluntary response may be made in the dorsolateral prefrontal association cortex on the basis of sensory information supplied to it, primarily by posterior parietal association cortex (see Goldman-Rakic, Bates, & Chafee, 1992).

In another series of studies of dorsolateral prefrontal cortex neurons (Rao, Rainier, & Miller, 1997), many of the cells responded to the location of stimuli,

---

[1]From *The Man Who Mistook His Wife for a Hat and Other Clinical Tales* (pp. 73–74) by Oliver Sacks, 1985, New York: Summit Books. Copyright © 1970, 1980, 1983, 1984, 1985 by Oliver Sacks. Reprinted by permission of Summit Books, a division of Simon & Schuster.

Dorsolateral prefrontal association cortex. The area of the prefrontal association cortex that plays a role in the initiation of complex voluntary motor responses.

Secondary motor cortex. Areas of the cerebral cortex that receive much of their input from association cortex and send much of their output to the primary motor cortex.

Supplementary motor area. The area of the secondary motor

cortex that is within and adjacent to the longitudinal fissure.

Premotor cortex. An area of the secondary motor cortex that lies between the supplementary motor area and the lateral fissure.

Cingulate motor areas. Two secondary motor areas in the cingulate gyrus of each hemisphere.

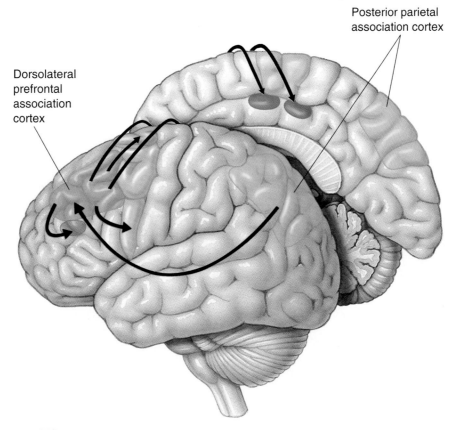

Dorsolateral
prefrontal
association
cortex

Posterior parietal
association cortex

Figure 9.4 The major cortical input and output pathways of the dorsolateral prefrontal association cortex. Shown are the lateral surface of the left hemisphere and the medial surface of the right hemisphere.

presumably on the basis of signals that they received from posterior parietal cortex. Others responded to shape, and others still responded to either shape or lo-

cation. The neurons of the dorsolateral prefrontal association cortex carry the kinds of information necessary to initiate an accurate movement.

Secondary Motor Cortex

Areas of **secondary motor cortex** are those that receive much of their input from association cortex and send much of their output to primary motor cortex (see Figure 9.5 on page 228). Until recently, only two areas of secondary motor cortex were known: the supplementary motor area and the premotor cortex. Both of these large areas are clearly visible on the lateral surface of the frontal lobe, just anterior to the *primary motor cortex.* The **supplementary motor area** wraps over the top of the frontal lobe and extends down its medial surface into the longitudinal fissure, and the **premotor cortex** runs in a strip from the supplementary motor area to the lateral fissure. However, two other areas of the secondary motor cortex—the **cingulate motor areas**—

have recently been discovered in the cortex of the cingulate gyrus of each hemisphere, just ventral to the supplementary motor area. Figure 9.5 shows the location of the supplementary motor area, the premotor cortex, and the two cingulate motor areas.

The areas of secondary motor cortex are anatomically similar to one another in the following four respects (see Dum & Strick, 1992): (1) Each sends many of its axons to primary motor cortex; (2) each receives axons back from primary motor cortex; (3) each is reciprocally connected to the other areas of secondary motor cortex; and (4) each sends axons directly into the motor circuits of the brain stem. They are functionally similar in the following three respects: (1) Electrical

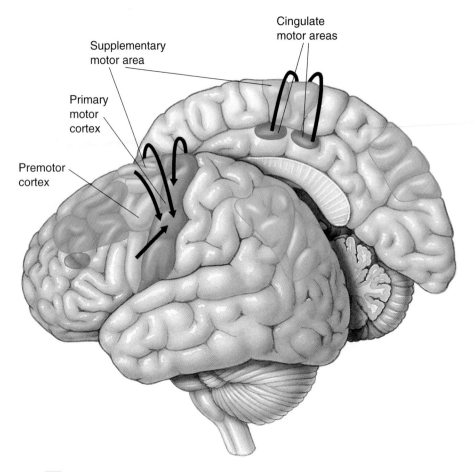

Cingulate
motor areas

Supplementary
motor area

Primary
motor
cortex

Premotor
cortex

Figure 9.5 Four areas of the secondary motor cortex—the supplementary motor area, the premotor cortex, and the two cingulate motor areas—and their output to the primary motor cortex. Shown are the lateral surface of the left hemisphere and the medial surface of the right hemisphere.

stimulation to particular sites within each area of secondary motor cortex results in complex movements of the body; (2) neurons in each area of secondary motor cortex respond prior to and during voluntary motor responses; and (3) movements of one side of the body are often associated with activation of each area of secondary motor cortex in both hemispheres.

In general, the areas of secondary motor cortex are thought to be involved in the planning and programming of movements. Evidence of such a function has come from several brain imaging studies in which the patterns of activity in the brain have been measured while the subject is either imagining his or her own performance of a particular series of movements or planning the performance of the same movements. The specific results of these studies have been quite varied depending on the particular instructions and target movements employed in the study, but bilateral increases of activity in the various areas of secondary motor cortex are often observed (see Jeannerod & Decety, 1995; Roland & Zilles, 1996). For example, Parsons et al. (1995) found that there was increased positron emission tomographic (PET) activity in the supplementary motor

area, premotor cortex, and cingulate motor areas while subjects imagined grasping and picking up an object.

Although the specific function of secondary motor cortex is commonly held to be the programming of various movements into complex sequences of behavior, modern PET studies have found extensive activation in the various areas of secondary motor cortex even during the repetition of a simple response (e.g., finger tapping), which should entail little or no response sequencing (Roland & Zilles, 1996). Complex sequences of movements do not activate additional regions of secondary motor cortex than this, but they do produce more activity in the same areas.

Similarities among the areas of secondary motor cortex aside, most effort has been put into discovering their differences. It is widely assumed that there are different areas of secondary motor cortex because the different areas play different roles in the planning, programming, and generation of movement. Efforts to identify the different functions of the various areas of secondary motor cortex have focused on the supplementary motor area and premotor cortex because the cingulate motor areas have only recently been discovered.

One hypothetical difference between the supplementary motor area and premotor cortex is that the supplementary motor area is specialized for the control of *self-generated movements,* whereas the premotor cortex is specialized for the control of *externally generated movements.* Self-generated movements are those that are initiated and controlled by an internal representation; externally generated movements are those that are initiated and guided by external stimuli. This hypothetical difference is consistent with the anatomy of these two areas: Sensory input to the supplementary motor area is primarily somatosensory, which could mediate sensory feedback from self-generated movements, whereas sensory input to the premotor cortex is primarily visual, which could provide the signals for the control of externally generated movement.

In support of this hypothetical difference, Chen et al. (1995) showed that monkeys with supplementary motor area lesions have difficulty responding appropriately in the absence of, but not in the presence of, sensory cues; and Colebatch et al. (1991) found in a positron emission tomographic study that the premotor cortex was activated when the subjects made various hand movements in time to a metronome but not when they made the same movements in the absence of any external sensory influence. Be that as it may, many studies have failed to confirm the self-generated vs. externally generated hypothesis, and the search for a better way of characterizing the specialized functions of the supplementary motor area and premotor cortex is in full swing (see Roland & Zilles, 1995; Tanji, 1996).

9.4 Primary Motor Cortex

The **primary motor cortex** is located in the *precentral gyrus* of the frontal lobe (see Figures 9.5 and 9.6). It is the major point of convergence of cortical sensorimotor signals, and it is the major point of departure of sensorimotor signals from the cerebral cortex.

In 1937, Penfield and Boldrey mapped the primary motor cortex of conscious human patients during neurosurgery by applying electrical stimulation to various points on the cortical surface and noting which part of the body moved in response to each stimulation. They found that the primary motor cortex is somatotopically organized. The **somatotopic** layout of the human primary motor cortex is commonly referred to as the **motor homunculus** (see Figure 9.6 on page 230). Notice that most of the primary motor cortex is dedicated to the control of parts of the body that are capable of intricate movements, such as the hands and mouth.

More recent research has necessitated some revisions to the original motor homunculus proposed by Penfield and Boldrey, particularly to the hand areas. Recording from individual primary motor cortex neurons in monkeys while they performed individual finger movements revealed that the control of any individual finger movement depended on the activity of a network of neurons that was widely distributed throughout the primary motor cortex hand area rather than being located in one somatotopically segregated finger area (Schieber & Hibbard, 1993). A similar pattern in the hand area of the human primary motor homunculus has also been documented using functional magnetic resonance imaging (Sanes et al., 1995).

Each area in the primary motor cortex controls the movements of particular groups of muscles, and each receives somatosensory feedback, via the somatosensory cortex, from receptors in these muscles and in the joints that they influence. One interesting exception to this general pattern of feedback has been described in monkeys: In monkeys, there are two different hand areas in the primary motor cortex of each hemisphere, and one receives input from receptors in the skin rather than from receptors in the muscles and joints. Presumably, this adaptation facilitates **stereognosis**—the process of identifying objects by touch. Close your eyes and explore an object with your hands; notice how stereognosis depends on a complex interplay between motor responses and the somatosensory stimulation produced by them.

Neurons in the arm area of the primary motor cortex fire maximally when the arm reaches in a particular direction; each neuron has a different preferred direction. Georgopoulos (1995) dissociated the direction of force and the direction of movement by applying external forces to monkeys' arms while the arms reached in various directions. The firing of primary motor cortex neurons was correlated with the direction of the re-

Primary motor cortex. The cortex of the precentral gyrus, which is the major point of departure for motor signals descending from the cortex into lower levels of the sensorimotor system.
Somatotopic. Organized according to a map of the body.

Motor homunculus. The somatotopic map in the primary motor cortex.
Stereognosis. The process of identifying objects by touch.

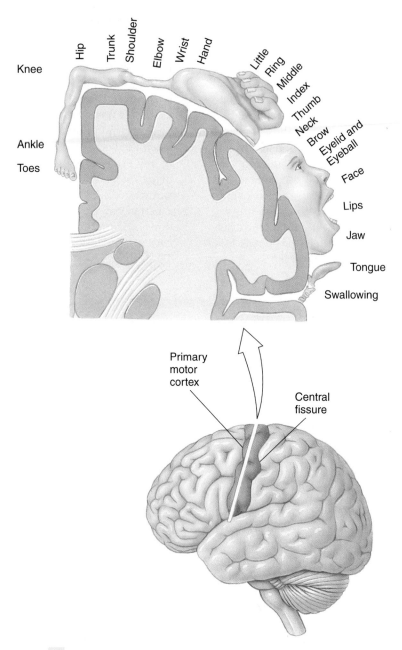

Figure 9.6 The motor homunculus: The somatotopic map of the human primary motor cortex. Stimulation of sites in the primary motor cortex elicits simple movements in the indicated parts of the body.
(Adapted from Penfield & Rasmussen, 1950.)

sulting movement rather than with the direction of the force that was generated to produce the movement. Each neuron fired most during and just before movements in a preferred direction but also fired to movements in other directions; the closer to the preferred direction, the more it fired.

Damage to the human primary motor cortex has less effect than you might expect, given that it is the major point of departure of motor fibers from the cerebral cortex. Damage to the primary motor cortex dis-

rupts a patient's ability to move one body part (e.g., one finger) independently of others (see Schieber, 1990); it produces **astereognosia** (deficits in stereognosis); and it reduces the speed, accuracy, and force of a patient's movements. It does not, however, produce paralysis, presumably because there are pathways descending directly from the secondary motor areas to subcortical motor circuits without passing through primary motor cortex (see Schwartz, 1994).

Cerebellum and Basal Ganglia

The cerebellum and the basal ganglia are both important sensorimotor structures (see Figures 3.23 and 3.31), but neither is a major part of the pathway through which signals descend the sensorimotor hierarchy. Instead, both the cerebellum and the basal ganglia interact with different levels of the sensorimotor hierarchy, and in so doing they coordinate and modulate its activities.

Cerebellum

The complexity of the cerebellum is suggested by its structure. Although it constitutes only 10% of the mass of the brain, it contains more than half of its neurons. The cerebellum receives information from the primary and secondary motor cortex, information about descending motor signals from the brain stem motor nuclei, and feedback from motor responses via the somatosensory and vestibular systems. The cerebellum is thought to compare these three sources of input and correct ongoing movements that deviate from their intended course. By performing this function, it is believed to play a major role in motor learning (see Raymond, Lisberger, & Mauk, 1996; Thach, 1996).

The consequences of diffuse cerebellar damage on motor function are devastating. The patient loses the ability to precisely control the direction, force, velocity, and amplitude of movements and the ability to adapt patterns of motor output to changing conditions. It is difficult to maintain steady postures (e.g., standing), and attempts to do so frequently lead to tremor. There are also severe disturbances in balance, gait, speech, and the control of eye movement. Learning new motor patterns is virtually impossible.

In recent years, the view that the function of the cerebellum is limited to the fine-tuning and learning of motor responses has been repeatedly challenged. The basis for this challenge has come from the observation of activity in the cerebellum by functional brain imaging during the performance of a variety of nonmotor cognitive tasks by healthy human subjects (e.g., Allen et al., 1997; Gao et al., 1996) and from the documentation of cognitive deficits in patents with cerebellar damage (e.g., Tucker et al., 1996). A variety of new theories have been proposed, but the most parsimonious of them tend to argue that the cerebellum functions in the fine-tuning and learning of cognitive responses in the same way that it functions in the fine-tuning and learning of motor responses (e.g., Leiner, Leiner, & Dow, 1995).

Basal Ganglia

The basal ganglia do not contain as many neurons as the cerebellum, but in one sense they are more complex. Unlike the cerebellum, which is organized systematically in lobes, columns, and layers, the basal ganglia are a complex heterogeneous collection of interconnected nuclei (see Graybiel et al., 1994; Mink & Thach, 1993).

The anatomy of the basal ganglia suggests that, like the cerebellum, they perform a modulatory function. They contribute no fibers to descending motor pathways; instead, they are part of neural loops that receive cortical input from various cortical areas and transmit it back via the thalamus to the various areas of motor cortex (see Goldman-Rakic & Selemon, 1990; Middleton & Strick, 1994).

In recent years, theories of basal ganglia function have changed—in much the same way that theories of cerebellar function have changed. The traditional view of basal ganglia function was that they, like the cerebellum, play a role in the modulation of motor output. This view has not changed, but it has been greatly expanded. Now, the basal ganglia are thought to be involved in a variety of cognitive functions in addition to their role in the modulation of neural output (see Brown, Schneider, & Lidsky, 1997; Graybiel, 1995). This expanded view of basal ganglia function is consistent with the fact that the basal ganglia project to cortical areas known to have cognitive functions (see Wichmann & DeLong, 1996).

In experiments on rats, the basal ganglia have been shown to participate in learning to respond correctly to learned associations, a type of response learning which characteristically progresses gradually, trial by trial (e.g., MacDonald & White, 1993). However, the basal ganglia's cognitive functions do not appear to be limited to this form of response learning. Parkinson's patients and other patients with basal ganglia damage often display difficulties in solving complex puzzles that require only a single key press to indicate the correct response (see Knowlton, Mangels, & Squire, 1996).

Astereognosia. A difficulty in recognizing objects by touch that is not attributable to a simple sensory deficit or to general intellectual impairment.

Before continuing your descent into the sensorimotor circuits of the spinal cord, review the sensorimotor circuits of the cortex, cerebellum, and basal ganglia by completing the following statements. The correct answers are provided at the bottom of this page. Before proceeding, review material related to your incorrect answers and omissions.

1. Visual, auditory, and somatosensory input converges on the _____ association cortex.

2. A small area of the frontal cortex called the frontal _____ plays a major role in the control of eye movement.

3. Contralateral neglect is often associated with large lesions of the right _____ lobe.

4. The _____ prefrontal cortex seems to play an important role in initiating complex voluntary responses.

5. The secondary motor area that is just dorsal to premotor cortex and is largely hidden from view on the medial surface of each hemisphere is the

_____

_____ .

6. Most of the direct sensory input to the supplementary motor area comes from the _____ system.

7. Most of the direct sensory input to the premotor cortex comes from the _____ system.

8. The _____ cortex is the main point of departure of motor signals from the cerebral cortex to lower levels of the sensorimotor hierarchy.

9. The foot area of the motor homunculus is in the _____ fissure.

10. Although the _____ constitutes only 10% of the mass of the brain, it contains more than half its neurons.

11. The _____ are part of neural loops that receive input from various cortical areas and transmit it back to various areas of motor cortex via the thalamus.

12. The finding that patients with _____ disease have cognitive deficits has contributed to the view that the basal ganglia are not limited to motor functions.

9.6 Descending Motor Pathways

Neural signals are conducted from the primary motor cortex to the motor neurons of the spinal cord over four different pathways. Two pathways descend in the *dorsolateral* region of the spinal cord, and two descend in the *ventromedial* region of the spinal cord.

Dorsolateral Corticospinal Tract and Dorsolateral Corticorubrospinal Tract

One group of axons that descends from the primary motor cortex descends through the *medullary pyramids*—two bulges on the ventral surface of the medulla—then it decussates and continues to descend in the contralateral dorsolateral spinal white matter. This group of axons constitutes the **dorsolateral corticospinal tract.** Most notable among its neurons are the **Betz cells**—extremely large pyramidal neurons of the primary motor cortex. Their axons terminate in the lower regions of the spinal cord on motor neurons that project to the muscles of the legs. They are thought to

The answers are (1) posterior parietal, (2) eye field, (3) parietal, (4) dorsolateral, (5) supplementary motor area, (6) somatosensory, (7) visual, (8) primary motor, (9) longitudinal, (10) cerebellum, (11) basal ganglia, and (12) Parkinson's.

be the means by which we exert rapid and powerful voluntary control over our legs.

Most axons of the dorsolateral corticospinal pathway synapse on small interneurons of the spinal gray matter, which synapse on the motor neurons of distal muscles of the wrist, hands, fingers, and toes. Primates and the few other mammals that are capable of moving their digits independently (e.g., hamsters and raccoons) have dorsolateral corticospinal tract neurons that synapse directly on digit motor neurons.

A second group of axons that descends from the primary motor cortex synapses in the *red nucleus* of the midbrain. The axons of the red nucleus cells then decussate and descend through the medulla, where some of them terminate in the nuclei of the cranial nerves that control the muscles of the face. The rest continue to descend in the dorsolateral portion of the spinal cord. This pathway is called the **dorsolateral corticorubrospinal tract** (*rubro* refers to the red nucleus). The axons of the dorsolateral corticorubrospinal tract synapse on interneurons that in turn synapse on motor neurons that project to the distal muscles of the arms and legs.

The two divisions of the dorsolateral motor pathway—the direct dorsolateral corticospinal tract and the indirect dorsolateral corticorubrospinal tract—are illustrated schematically in Figure 9.7 on page 234.

Ventromedial Corticospinal Tract and Ventromedial Cortico–Brainstem–Spinal Tract

Just as there are two major divisions of the dorsolateral motor pathway, one direct (the corticospinal tract) and one indirect (the corticorubrospinal tract), there are two major divisions of the ventromedial motor pathway, one direct and one indirect. The direct ventromedial pathway is the **ventromedial corticospinal tract,** and the indirect one—as you might infer from its cumbersome but descriptive name—is the **ventromedial cortico–brainstem–spinal tract.**

The long axons of the ventromedial corticospinal tract descend ipsilaterally from the primary motor cortex directly into the ventromedial areas of the spinal white matter. As each axon of the ventromedial corticospinal tract descends, it branches diffusely and innervates the interneuron circuits in several different spinal segments on both sides of the spinal gray matter.

The ventromedial cortico–brainstem–spinal tract comprises motor cortex axons that feed into a complex network of brain stem structures. The axons of some of the neurons in this complex brain stem motor network then descend bilaterally in the ventromedial portion of the spinal cord. Each side carries signals from both hemispheres, and each neuron synapses on the interneurons of several different spinal cord segments that control the proximal muscles of the trunk and limbs.

Which brain stem structures interact with the ventromedial cortico–brainstem–spinal tract? There are four major ones: (1) the **tectum,** which receives auditory and visual information about spatial location; (2) the **vestibular nucleus,** which receives information about balance from receptors in the semicircular canals of the inner ear; (3) the **reticular formation,** which, among other things, contains motor programs for complex species-common movements such as walking, swimming, and jumping; and (4) the motor nuclei of the cranial nerves that control the muscles of the face.

The two divisions of the descending ventromedial pathway—the direct ventromedial corticospinal tract and the indirect ventromedial cortico–brainstem–spinal tract—are illustrated in Figure 9.8 on page 235.

The Two Dorsolateral Motor Pathways and the Two Ventromedial Motor Pathways Compared

The descending dorsolateral and ventromedial pathways are similar in that each is composed of two major tracts, one whose axons descend directly to the spinal cord and the other whose axons synapse in the brain stem on neurons that in turn descend to the spinal cord. However, the two dorsolateral tracts differ from the two ventromedial tracts in two major respects:

1. The two ventromedial tracts are much more diffuse. Many of their axons innervate interneurons on both sides of the spinal gray matter and in several different

Dorsolateral corticospinal tract. The motor tract that leaves the primary motor cortex, descends to the medullary pyramids, decussates, and then descends in the contralateral dorsolateral spinal white matter.

Betz cells. Large pyramidal neurons of the primary motor cortex that synapse directly on spinal motor neurons, mainly in the lower spinal cord.

Dorsolateral corticorubrospinal tract. The descending motor tract that synapses in the red nucleus of the midbrain, decussates, and descends in the dorsolateral spinal white matter.

Ventromedial corticospinal tract. The direct ventromedial motor pathway, which descends ipsilaterally from the primary motor cortex directly into the ventromedial areas of the spinal white matter.

Ventromedial cortico–brainstem–spinal tract. The indirect ventromedial motor pathway, which descends bilaterally from the primary motor cortex to several interconnected brainstem motor structures and then descends in the ventromedial portions of the spinal cord.

Tectum. The division of the midbrain that comprises the superior and inferior colliculi and receives auditory and visual information about spatial location.

Vestibular nucleus. The brainstem nucleus that receives information about balance from the semicircular canals.

Reticular formation. A complex network of nuclei in the core of the brain stem that contains, among other things, motor programs for complex species-common movements such as walking and swimming.

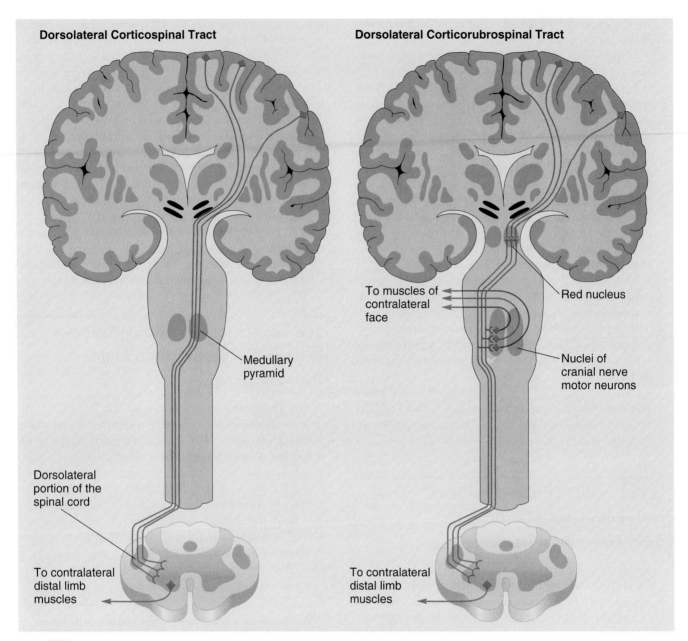

Dorsolateral Corticospinal Tract

Dorsolateral Corticorubrospinal Tract

Medullary
pyramid

Dorsolateral
portion of the
spinal cord

To contralateral
distal limb
muscles

To muscles of
contralateral
face

Red nucleus

Nuclei of
cranial nerve
motor neurons

To contralateral
distal limb
muscles

Figure 9.7 The two divisions of the dorsolateral motor pathway: The dorsolateral corticospinal tract and the dorsolateral corticorubrospinal motor tract. The projections from only one hemisphere are shown.

segments, whereas the axons of the two dorsolateral tracts terminate in the contralateral half of one segment, sometimes directly on a motor neuron.

2. The motor neurons that are activated by the two ventromedial tracts project to proximal muscles of the trunk and limbs (e.g., shoulder muscles), whereas the motor neurons that are activated by the two dorsolateral tracts project to distal muscles (e.g., finger muscles).

Because all four of the descending motor tracts originate in the cerebral cortex, they are all presumed to mediate voluntary movement; however, major differences in their routes and destinations suggest that they have different functions. This difference was demon-

strated in two experiments that were published by Lawrence and Kuypers in 1968.

In their first experiment, Lawrence and Kuypers (1968a) transected (cut through) the left and right dorsolateral corticospinal tracts of their monkey subjects in the medullary pyramids, just above their decussation. Following surgery, these monkeys could stand, walk, and climb quite normally; however, their ability to use their limbs for other activities was impaired. For example, their reaching movements were weak and poorly directed, particularly in the first few days following the surgery. Although there was substantial improvement in the monkeys' reaching ability over the ensuing weeks, two other deficits remained unabated.

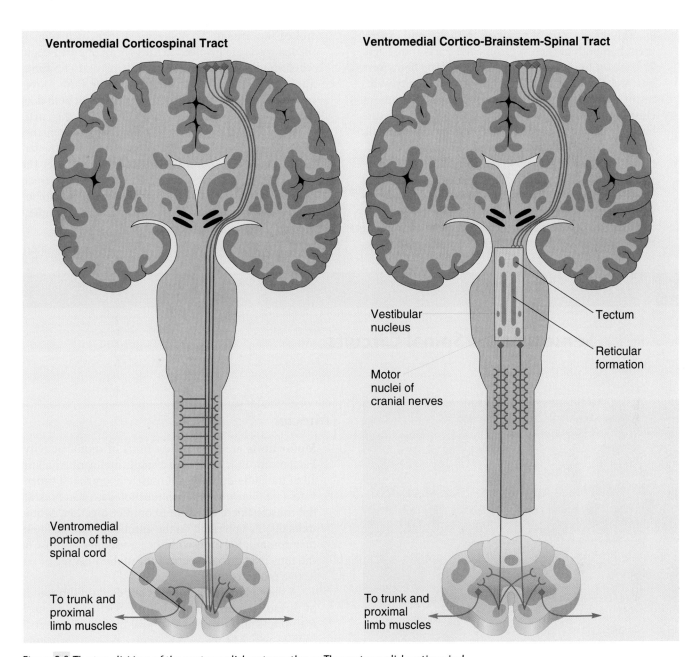

Ventromedial Corticospinal Tract

Ventromedial Cortico-Brainstem-Spinal Tract

Vestibular nucleus

Tectum

Reticular formation

Motor nuclei of cranial nerves

Ventromedial portion of the spinal cord

To trunk and proximal limb muscles

To trunk and proximal limb muscles

Figure 9.8 The two divisions of the ventromedial motor pathway: The ventromedial corticospinal tract and the ventromedial cortico—brainstem—spinal tract. The projections from only one hemisphere are shown.

First, the monkeys never regained the ability to move their fingers independently of one another; when they picked up pieces of food, they did so by using all of their fingers as a unit, as if they were glued together. And second, they never regained the ability to release objects from their grasp; as a result, once they picked up a piece of food, they often had to root for it in their hand like a pig rooting for truffles in the ground. In view of this latter problem, it is remarkable that they had no difficulty releasing their grasp on the bars of their cage when they were climbing. This point is important because it shows that the same response performed in different contexts can be controlled by different parts of the central nervous system.

In their second experiment, Lawrence and Kuypers (1968b) made additional transections in the monkeys whose dorsolateral corticospinal tracts had already been transected in their first experiment. The dorsolateral corticorubrospinal tract was transected in one group of these monkeys. The monkeys could stand, walk, and climb after this second transection; but when they were sitting, their arms hung limply by their sides (remember that monkeys normally use their arms for standing and walking). In those few instances in which the monkeys did use an arm for reaching, they used it like a rubber-handled rake—throwing it out from the shoulder and using it to draw small objects of interest back along the floor.

The other group of monkeys in the second experiment had both of their ventromedial tracts transected. In contrast to the first group, these subjects had severe postural abnormalities: They had great difficulty walking or sitting. If they did manage to sit or stand without clinging to the bars of their cages, the slightest disturbance, such as a loud noise, frequently made them fall. Although they had some use of their arms, the additional transection of the two ventromedial tracts eliminated their ability to control their shoulders. When they fed, they did so with elbow and whole-hand movements while their upper arms hung limply by their sides.

What do these experiments tell us about the roles of the various descending sensorimotor tracts in the con-trol of movement? They suggest that the two ventromedial tracts are involved in the control of posture and whole-body movements (e.g., walking and climbing) and that they can exert control over the limb movements involved in such activities. In contrast, both dorsolateral tracts—the corticospinal tract and the corticorubrospinal tract—control the reaching movements of the limbs. This redundancy was presumably the basis for the good recovery of limb movement after the initial lesions of the corticospinal dorsolateral tract. However, only the corticospinal division of the dorsolateral system is capable of mediating independent movements of the digits.

9.7 Sensorimotor Spinal Circuits

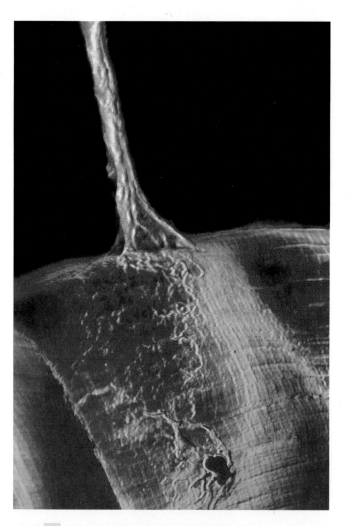

Figure 9.9 An electron micrograph of a motor unit: A motor neuron (pink) and the muscle fibers that it innervates.

Muscles

Motor units are the smallest units of motor activity. Each motor unit comprises a single motor neuron and all of the individual skeletal muscle fibers that it innervates (see Figure 9.9). When the motor neuron fires, all the muscle fibers of its unit contract together. Motor units differ appreciably in the number of muscle fibers they contain; the units with the fewest fibers—those of the fingers and face—permit the highest degree of selective motor control.

A skeletal muscle comprises hundreds of thousands of threadlike muscle fibers bound together in a tough membrane and attached to a bone by a *tendon. Acetylcholine,* which is released by motor neurons at *neuromuscular junctions,* activates the **motor end-plate** on each muscle fiber and causes the fiber to contract. All of

---

Motor units. All of the muscle fibers that are innervated by a single motor neuron.

Motor end-plate. The receptive area on a muscle fiber at a neuromuscular junction.

Motor pool. All of the motor neurons that innervate the fibers of a given muscle.

Flexors. Muscles that act to bend or flex a joint.

Extensors. Muscles that act to straighten or extend a joint.

Synergistic muscles. Pairs of muscles that produce a movement in the same direction.

Antagonistic muscles. Pairs of muscles that act in opposition.

Isometric contraction. Contraction of a muscle that increases the force of its pull but does not shorten the muscle.

Dynamic contraction. Contraction of a muscle that causes the muscle to shorten.

Golgi tendon organs. Receptors that are embedded in tendons and are sensitive to the amount of tension in the muscles to which their tendons are attached.

Muscle spindles. Receptors that are embedded in muscle tissue and are sensitive to muscle length.

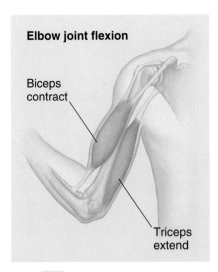

Elbow joint flexion

Biceps contract

Triceps extend

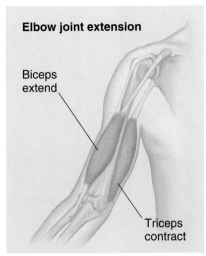

Elbow joint extension

Biceps extend

Triceps contract

Figure 9.10 The biceps and triceps, which are the flexors and extensors, respectively, of the elbow joint.

the motor neurons that innervate the fibers of a single muscle are called its **motor pool.**

Although it is an oversimplification (see Gollinick & Hodgson, 1986), skeletal muscle fibers are often considered to be of two basic types: fast and slow. *Fast muscle fibers,* as you might guess, are those that contract and relax quickly. Although they are capable of generating great force, they fatigue quickly because they are poorly vascularized (which gives them a pale color). In contrast, *slow muscle fibers,* although slower and weaker, are capable of more sustained contraction because they are more richly vascularized (and hence much redder). Muscles have different proportions of fast and slow fibers depending on their function.

Many skeletal muscles belong unambiguously to one of two categories: flexors or extensors. **Flexors** act to bend or flex a joint, and **extensors** act to straighten or extend it. Figure 9.10 illustrates the *biceps* and *triceps*—the flexors and extensors, respectively, of the elbow joint (see Chapter 4). Any two muscles whose

contraction produces the same movement, be it flexion or extension, are said to be **synergistic muscles;** those that act in opposition, like the biceps and triceps, are said to be **antagonistic muscles.**

To understand how muscles work, it is important to realize that muscles have elastic, rather than inflexible, cablelike, properties. If you think of an increase in muscle tension as being analogous to an increase in the tension of an elastic band joining two bones, you will appreciate that muscle contraction can be of two types (see Figure 9.11). Excitation of a muscle can increase the tension that it exerts on two bones without shortening and pulling them together; this is termed **isometric contraction.** Or it can shorten and pull them together; this is termed **dynamic contraction.** The tension in a muscle can be increased by increasing the number of neurons in its motor pool that are firing, by increasing the firing rates of those that are already firing, or more commonly by a combination of the two.

Receptor Organs of Tendons and Muscles

The activity of skeletal muscles is monitored by two kinds of receptors: **Golgi tendon organs** and muscle spindles. Golgi tendon organs are embedded in the *tendons,* which connect each skeletal muscle to bone; and **muscle spindles** are embedded in the muscle tissue itself. Because of their different locations, Golgi tendon organs and muscle spindles respond to different aspects of muscle contraction. Golgi tendon organs respond to increases in muscle tension (i.e., to the pull of the muscle on the tendon), but they are completely insensitive

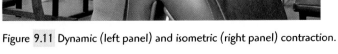

Figure 9.11 Dynamic (left panel) and isometric (right panel) contraction.

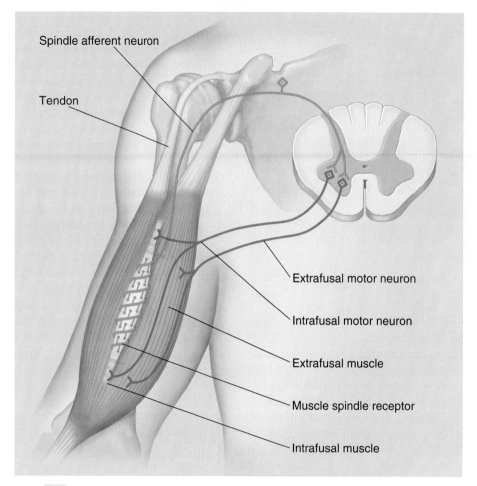

Spindle afferent neuron

Tendon

Extrafusal motor neuron

Intrafusal motor neuron

Extrafusal muscle

Muscle spindle receptor

Intrafusal muscle

Figure 9.12 The muscle-spindle feedback circuit. There are many muscle spindles in each muscle; for clarity, only one much enlarged muscle spindle is illustrated here.

to changes in muscle length. In contrast, muscle spindles respond to changes in muscle length, but they do not respond to changes in muscle tension.

Under normal conditions, the function of Golgi tendon organs is to provide the central nervous system with information about muscle tension, but they also serve a protective function. When the contraction of a muscle is so extreme that there is a risk of damage, the Golgi tendon organs excite inhibitory interneurons in the spinal cord that cause the muscle to relax.

Figure 9.12 is a schematic diagram of the *muscle-spindle feedback circuit*. Examine it carefully. Notice that each muscle spindle has its own threadlike **intrafusal muscle,** which is innervated by its own **intrafusal motor neuron.** Why would a receptor have its own muscle and motor neuron? The reason becomes apparent when you consider what would happen to a muscle spindle without them. Without its intrafusal motor input, a muscle spindle would fall slack each time its **skeletal muscle (extrafusal muscle)** contracted. In this slack state, the muscle spindle could not do its job, which is to respond to slight changes in extrafusal muscle length. As Figure 9.13 illustrates, the intrafusal

motor neuron solves this problem by shortening the intrafusal muscle each time the extrafusal muscle becomes shorter, thus keeping enough tension on the middle, stretch-sensitive portion of the muscle spindle to keep it sensitive to slight changes in the length of the extrafusal muscle.

Stretch Reflex

When the word *reflex* is mentioned, many people think of themselves sitting on the edge of their doctor's examination table having their knees rapped with a little rubber-headed hammer. The resulting leg extension is called the **patellar tendon reflex** (*patella* means "*knee*"). This reflex is a **stretch reflex**—a reflex that is elicited by a sudden external stretching force on a muscle.

When the doctor strikes the tendon of your knee, the extensor muscle running along your thigh is stretched. This initiates the chain of events that is depicted in Figure 9.14 on page 240. The sudden stretch of the thigh muscle stretches its muscle-spindle stretch receptors, which in turn initiates a volley of action potentials that

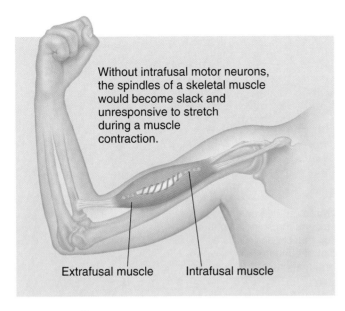

Without intrafusal motor neurons, the spindles of a skeletal muscle would become slack and unresponsive to stretch during a muscle contraction.

Extrafusal muscle   Intrafusal muscle

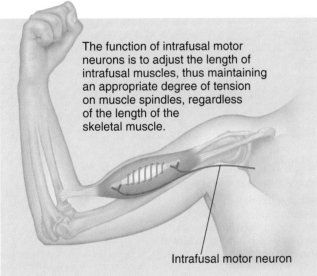

The function of intrafusal motor neurons is to adjust the length of intrafusal muscles, thus maintaining an appropriate degree of tension on muscle spindles, regardless of the length of the skeletal muscle.

Intrafusal motor neuron

Figure 9.13 The function of intrafusal motor neurons.

is carried from the stretch receptors into the spinal cord by **spindle afferent neurons** via the *dorsal root*. This volley of action potentials excites motor neurons in the *ventral horn* of the spinal cord, which respond by sending action potentials back to the muscle whose stretch originally excited them. The arrival of these impulses back at the starting point results in a compensatory muscle contraction and a sudden leg extension.

The method by which the patellar tendon reflex is typically elicited in a doctor's office—that is, by a sharp blow to the tendon of a completely relaxed muscle—is designed to make the reflex readily observable. However, it does little to communicate its functional significance. In real life situations, the function of the stretch reflex is to keep external forces from altering the intended position of the body. When an external force, such as somebody brushing against your arm while you

are holding a cup of coffee, causes an unanticipated extrafusal muscle stretch, the muscle-spindle feedback circuit produces an immediate compensatory contraction of the muscle that counteracts the force and keeps you from spilling the coffee—unless, of course, you are wearing your best clothes.

The mechanism by which the stretch reflex maintains limb stability is illustrated in Figure 9.15 on page 241. Examine it carefully because it illustrates two of the principles of sensorimotor system function that are the focus of this chapter: the important role played by sensory feedback in the regulation of motor output and the ability of lower circuits in the motor hierarchy to take care of "business details" without the involvement of higher levels.

Withdrawal Reflex

I am sure that, at one time or another, you have touched something painful—a hot pot, for example—and suddenly pulled back your hand. This is a **withdrawal reflex.** Unlike the stretch reflex, the withdrawal reflex is not *monosynaptic* (Eidelberg, 1987). When a painful stimulus is applied to the hand, the first responses are recorded in the motor neurons of the arm flexor muscles about 1.6 milliseconds later, about the time it takes a neural signal to cross two synapses. Thus the shortest route in the withdrawal-reflex circuit involves one interneuron. Other responses are recorded in the motor neurons of the arm flexor muscles after the initial volley; these responses are triggered by signals that have traveled over multisynaptic pathways—some involving the cortex (see Matthews, 1991). See Figure 9.16 on page 242.

Reciprocal Innervation

Reciprocal innervation is an important principle of spinal cord circuitry. It refers to the fact that antagonistic muscles are innervated in such a way that when one

---

Intrafusal muscle. A threadlike muscle that adjusts the tension on a muscle spindle.

Intrafusal motor neuron. A motor neuron that innervates an intrafusal muscle.

Skeletal muscle (extrafusal muscle). Striated muscle that is attached to the skeleton and is usually under voluntary control.

Patellar tendon reflex. The stretch reflex that is elicited when the patellar tendon is struck.

Stretch reflex. A reflexive counteracting reaction to an unan-

ticipated external stretching force on a muscle.

Spindle afferent neurons. Neurons that carry signals from muscle spindles into the spinal cord via the dorsal root.

Withdrawal reflex. The reflexive withdrawal of a limb when it comes in contact with a painful stimulus.

Reciprocal innervation. The principle of spinal cord circuitry that causes a muscle to automatically relax when a muscle that is antagonistic to it contracts.

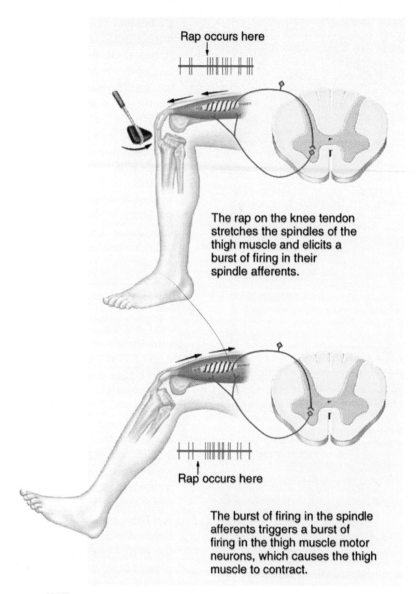

Rap occurs here

The rap on the knee tendon stretches the spindles of the thigh muscle and elicits a burst of firing in their spindle afferents.

Rap occurs here

The burst of firing in the spindle afferents triggers a burst of firing in the thigh muscle motor neurons, which causes the thigh muscle to contract.

Figure 9.14 The elicitation of a stretch reflex. All of the muscle spindles in a muscle are activated during a stretch reflex, but only a single muscle spindle is depicted here.

is contracted, the other relaxes to permit a smooth, unimpeded motor response. Figure 9.16 illustrates the role of reciprocal innervation in the withdrawal reflex. "Bad news" of a sudden painful event in the hand arrives in the dorsal horn of the spinal cord and has two effects: The signals excite both excitatory and inhibitory interneurons. The excitatory interneurons excite the motor neurons of the elbow flexors; the inhibitory interneurons inhibit the motor neurons of the elbow extensors. Thus a single sensory input produces a coordinated pattern of motor output; the activities of agonists and antagonists are automatically coordinated by the internal circuitry of the spinal cord.

Movements are quickest when there is simultaneous excitation of all agonists and complete inhibition of all antagonists; however, this is not the way voluntary movement is normally produced. Most muscles are always contracted to some degree, and movements are produced by adjustment in the level of relative cocontraction between antagonists. Movements that are produced by **cocontraction** are smooth, and they can be stopped with precision by a slight increase in the contraction of the antagonistic muscles. Moreover, cocontraction insulates us from the effects of unexpected external forces.

Recurrent Collateral Inhibition

Like most workers, muscle fibers and the motor neurons that innervate them need an occasional break, and there are inhibitory neurons in the spinal cord that make sure they get it. Each motor neuron branches just before it leaves the spinal cord, and the branch synapses

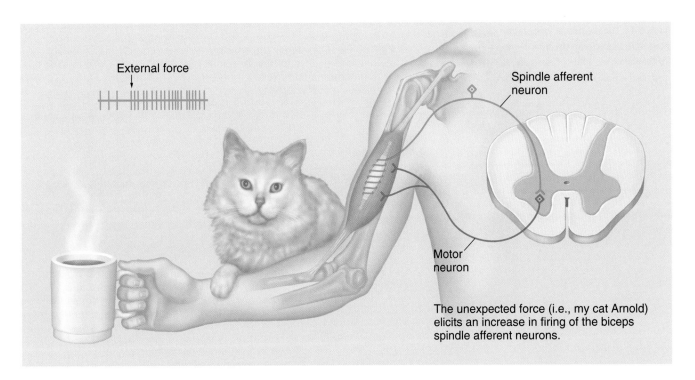

External force

Spindle afferent
neuron

Motor
neuron

The unexpected force (i.e., my cat Arnold)
elicits an increase in firing of the biceps
spindle afferent neurons.

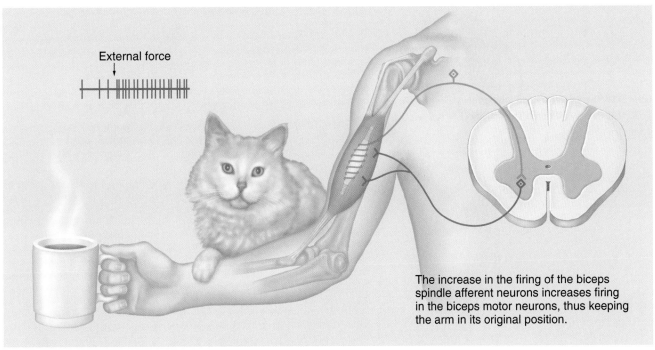

External force

The increase in the firing of the biceps
spindle afferent neurons increases firing
in the biceps motor neurons, thus keeping
the arm in its original position.

Figure 9.15 The automatic maintenance of limb position by the muscle-spindle feedback system.

on a small inhibitory interneuron, which inhibits the very motor neuron from which it receives its input. The inhibition produced by these local feedback circuits is called **recurrent collateral inhibition,** and the small inhibitory interneurons that mediate recurrent collateral inhibition are called *Renshaw cells.* As a consequence of recurrent collateral inhibition, each time a motor neuron fires, it momentarily inhibits itself and shifts the responsibility for the contraction of a particular muscle to other members of the muscle's motor pool.

Figure 9.17 on page 242 is a summary figure; it illustrates recurrent collateral inhibition and other factors that directly excite or inhibit motor neurons.

Cocontraction. The simultaneous contraction of antagonistic muscles.
Recurrent collateral inhibition. The *inhibition of a neuron that* is produced by its own activity via a collateral branch of its axon and an inhibitory interneuron.

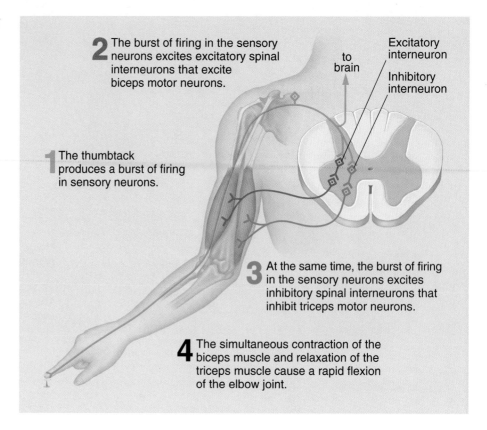

Figure 9.16 The reciprocal innervation of antagonistic muscles in the arm. During a withdrawal reflex, elbow flexors are excited, and elbow extensors are inhibited.

2 The burst of firing in the sensory neurons excites excitatory spinal interneurons that excite biceps motor neurons.

to brain

Excitatory interneuron

Inhibitory interneuron

1 The thumbtack produces a burst of firing in sensory neurons.

3 At the same time, the burst of firing in the sensory neurons excites inhibitory spinal interneurons that inhibit triceps motor neurons.

4 The simultaneous contraction of the biceps muscle and relaxation of the triceps muscle cause a rapid flexion of the elbow joint.

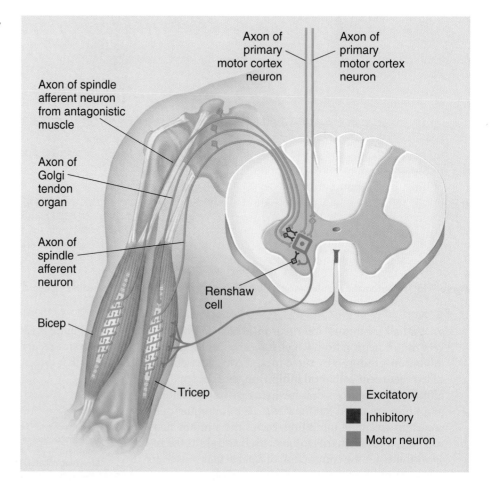

Figure 9.17 The excitatory and inhibitory signals that directly influence the activity of a motor neuron.

Axon of primary motor cortex neuron

Axon of primary motor cortex neuron

Axon of spindle afferent neuron from antagonistic muscle

Axon of Golgi tendon organ

Axon of spindle afferent neuron

Renshaw cell

Bicep

Tricep

Excitatory

Inhibitory

Motor neuron

Walking: A Complex Sensorimotor Reflex

Most reflexes are much more complex than withdrawal and stretch reflexes. Think for a moment about the complexity of the program of reflexes that is needed to control an activity such as walking. Such a program must integrate visual information from the eyes; somatosensory information from the feet, knees, hips, arms, and so on; and information about balance from the semicircular canals of the inner ears. And it must produce, on the basis of this information, an integrated series of movements that involves the muscles of the trunk, legs, feet, and upper arms. It must also be incredibly flexible; it must be able to adjust its output immediately to changes in the slope of the terrain, to instructions from the brain, or to external forces such as a bag of groceries. Nobody has yet managed to build a robot that can come close to duplicating these feats.

Grillner (1985) showed that walking is controlled largely by circuits in the spinal cord. Grillner's subjects were cats whose spinal cords had been separated from their brains by transection. He suspended the cats in a sling over a treadmill; amazingly, when the treadmill was started so that the cats received sensory feedback of the sort that normally accompanies walking, they began to walk.

9.8 Central Sensorimotor Programs

In this chapter, you have learned that the sensorimotor system is like the hierarchy of a large efficient company. You have learned how the executives—the dorsolateral prefrontal cortex, the supplementary motor area, and the premotor cortex—issue commands based on information supplied to them by the posterior parietal cortex. And you have learned how these commands are forwarded to the managing director (the primary motor cortex) for distribution over four main channels of communication (the two dorsolateral and the two ventromedial spinal motor pathways) to the metaphoric office managers of the sensorimotor hierarchy (the spinal sensorimotor circuits). Finally, you have learned how spinal sensorimotor circuits direct the activities of the workers (the muscles). The major role played by sensory feedback at each stage of the sensorimotor hierarchy has been emphasized throughout.

One theory of sensorimotor function is that the sensorimotor system comprises a hierarchy of **central sensorimotor programs** (see Brooks, 1986; Georgopoulos, 1991). The central sensorimotor program theory suggests that all but the highest levels of the sensorimotor system have certain patterns of activity programmed into them and that complex movements are produced by activating the appropriate combinations of these programs. Accordingly, if your association cortex decides that you might like to look at a magazine, it activates high-level cortical programs that in turn activate lower-level programs—perhaps in your brain stem—for walking, bending over, picking up, and thumbing through. These programs in turn activate specific spinal programs that control the various elements of the sequences and cause your muscles to complete the objective.

Once activated, each level of the sensorimotor system is capable of operating on the basis of current sensory feedback, without the direct control of higher levels. Thus, although the highest levels of your sensorimotor system retain the option of directly controlling your activities, most of the individual responses that you make are performed without direct cortical involvement, and you are barely aware of them.

In much the same way, a company president who wishes to open a new branch office simply issues the command to one of the executives, and the executive responds in the usual fashion by issuing a series of commands to the appropriate people lower in the hierarchy, who in turn do the same. Each of the executives and workers of the company knows how to complete many different tasks and executes them in the light of current conditions when instructed to do so. Good companies have mechanisms for ensuring that the programs of action at different levels of the hierarchy are well coordinated and effective. So does the sensorimotor system; this seems to be the task of the cerebellum and basal ganglia.

Central Motor Programs Can Develop without Practice

What type of experience is necessary for the normal development of central motor programs? In particular, is

---

Central sensorimotor programs. Patterns of activity that are pro- grammed into the sensorimotor system.

it necessary to practice a particular behavior for its central motor program to develop?

Although central motor programs for some behaviors can be established by practicing the behaviors, the central motor programs for many species-typical behaviors are established without explicit practice of the behaviors. This point was made clearly by the classic study of Fentress (1973). Fentress showed that adult mice raised from birth without forelimbs still made the patterns of shoulder movements typical of grooming in their species—and that these movements were well coordinated with normal tongue, head, and eye movements. For example, the mice blinked each time they made the shoulder movements that would have swept their forepaws across their eyes. Fentress's study also demonstrated the importance of sensory feedback in the operation of central sensorimotor programs. The forelimbless mice, deprived of normal tongue–forepaw contact during face grooming, would often interrupt ostensible grooming sequences to lick a cage-mate or even the floor.

Practice Creates Central Motor Programs

Although central motor programs for many species-typical behaviors develop without practice, practice is a certain way to generate or modify central motor programs. Theories of sensorimotor learning emphasize two kinds of processes that influence the learning of central motor programs: response chunking and shifting control to lower levels of the sensorimotor system.

■ **RESPONSE CHUNKING** According to the **response-chunking hypothesis,** practice combines the central control of individual response elements into individual programs that control long sequences (chunks) of behavior. In a novice typist, each response necessary to type a word is individually triggered and controlled; in a skilled typist, sequences of letters are activated as a unit, with a marked increase in speed and continuity.

An important principle of chunking is that chunks can themselves be combined into higher-order chunks. For example, the responses needed to type the individual letters and digits of one's address may be chunked into longer sequences necessary to produce the individual words and numbers, and these chunks may in turn be combined so that the entire address can be typed as a unit.

■ **SHIFTING CONTROL TO LOWER LEVELS** During the development of a central motor program, control is shifted from higher levels of the sensorimotor hierarchy to lower levels. Shifting the level of control to lower levels of the sensorimotor system during training (see Seitz et al., 1990) has two advantages. One is that it frees up the higher levels of the system to deal with more esoteric as-

pects of performance. For example, skilled pianists can concentrate on interpreting a piece of music because they do not have to consciously focus on pressing the right keys, and skilled secretaries can take dictation while performing other simple mental tasks. The other advantage of shifting the level of control is that it permits great speed because different circuits at the lower levels of the hierarchy can act simultaneously without interfering with one another. It is possible to type 120 words per minute only because the circuits responsible for activating each individual key press can become active before the preceding response has been completed.

■ **FUNCTIONAL BRAIN IMAGING AND MOTOR LEARNING**
Modern functional brain imaging techniques have provided new opportunities for studying the neural correlates of motor learning. By recording the brain activity of human subjects as they learn to perform new motor sequences, it is possible to develop hypotheses about the roles of various structures in motor learning. A good example of this approach is the PET study of Jenkins et al. (1994). Jenkins et al. recorded PET activity from human subjects who performed two different sequences of key presses. There were four different keys, and each sequence was four presses long. The presses were performed with the right hand, one every 3 seconds, and tones indicated when to press and whether or not a press was correct. There were three conditions: a rest control condition, a condition in which the subjects performed a newly learned sequence, and a condition in which the subjects performed a well-practiced sequence.

The following are six major findings of the Jenkins et al. study (see Figure 9.18). They recapitulate important points that have already been made in this chapter.

Finding 1: Posterior parietal cortex was activated during the performance of both the newly learned and well-practiced sequences, but it was more active during the newly learned sequence. This finding is consistent with the hypothesis that the posterior parietal cortex integrates sensory stimuli (in this case the tones) that are used to guide motor sequences, and it is consistent with the finding that posterior parietal cortex is more active when subjects are attending more to the stimuli, as is often the case during the early stages of motor learning.

Finding 2: Dorsolateral prefrontal cortex was activated during the performance of the newly learned sequence but not during the well-practiced sequence (see Shadmehr & Holcomb, 1997). This suggests that the dorsolateral prefrontal cortex plays a par-

Response-chunking hypothesis. The hypothesis that practice combines the central sensorimotor programs that control in-dividual responses into programs that control sequences of responses (chunks of behavior).

Sensorimotor areas activated by performing a well-practiced sequence of finger movements

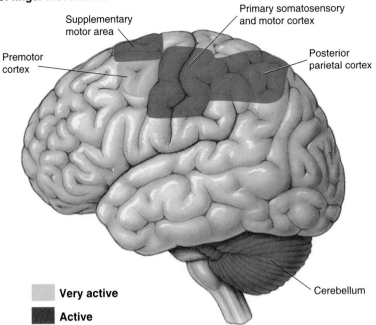

Premotor cortex

Supplementary motor area

Primary somatosensory and motor cortex

Posterior parietal cortex

Cerebellum

- Very active
- Active

Figure 9.18 The activity recorded by positron emission tomography during the performance of newly learned and well-practiced sequences of finger movements. (Adapted from Jenkins et al., 1994.)

Sensorimotor areas activated by performing a newly learned sequence of finger movements

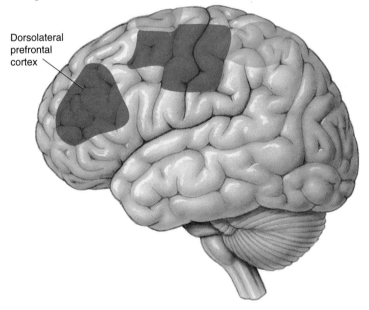

Dorsolateral prefrontal cortex

ticularly important role when motor sequences are being performed largely under conscious control, as is often the case during the early stages of motor learning.

Finding 3: The areas of secondary motor cortex responded differently. The contralateral premotor cortex was more active during the performance of the newly learned motor sequence, whereas the supplementary motor area was more active bilaterally during the well-practiced sequence. This finding is consistent with the hypothesis that the premotor cortex plays a more prominent role when performance is being largely guided by sensory stimuli, as is often the case in the early stages of motor learning, and that the supplementary motor area plays a more prominent role when performance is largely independent of sensory stimuli, as is often the case for well-practiced motor sequences, which can be run off automatically with little sensory feedback.

Finding 4: Contralateral primary motor and somato-sensory cortexes were equally activated during the performance of both the newly learned and well-practiced motor sequences. This finding is consistent with the fact that the motor elements were the same during both sequences.

Finding 5: The contralateral basal ganglia were equally activated during the performance of both the newly learned and well-practiced motor sequences. Jenkins et al. speculated that different subpopulations of basal ganglia neurons may have been active during the two conditions but went undetected because of the poor spatial resolution of PET.

Finding 6: The cerebellum was activated bilaterally during the performance of both the newly learned and well-practiced sequences, but it was more active during the newly learned sequence. This is consistent with the idea that the cerebellum plays a prominent role in motor learning (see Flament et al., 1996; Thach, 1996).

CONCLUSION

Rhonda began this chapter by illustrating three principles of sensorimotor function (9.1): The sensorimotor system is hierarchically organized, motor output is guided by sensory input, and learning changes the nature and locus of sensorimotor control. The discussion of the sensorimotor system itself began with the two major areas of the sensorimotor association cortex (9.2), the secondary motor cortex (9.3), and the primary motor cortex (9.4).

Next was the introduction to two structures—the cerebellum and the basal ganglia—both of which coordinate activities at different levels of the sensorimotor system rather than participating in the conduction of signals from the cortex to the spinal cord (9.5). Finally, the last three sections of the chapter described the four descending motor pathways (9.6), the sensorimotor circuits of the spinal cord (9.7), and the concept of central sensorimotor programs (9.8).

Recently, I stopped off to pick up a few fresh vegetables and some fish for dinner, and I once again found myself waiting in Rhonda's line. It was the longest line, but I am a creature of habit. This time, I felt rather smug as I watched her. All of the reading and thinking that had gone into the preparation of this chapter had provided me with some new insights into what she was doing and how she was doing it. I wondered whether she appreciated her own finely tuned sensorimotor system as much as I did. Then I hatched my plot—a little test of Rhonda's muscle-spindle feedback system. How would Rhonda's finely tuned sensorimotor system react to a bag that looked heavy but was in fact extremely light? Next time, I would get one of those paper bags at the mushroom counter, blow it up, drop one mushroom in it, and then fold up the top so it looked completely full. I smiled at the thought. But I wasn't the only one smiling. My daydreaming ended abruptly, and the smile melted from my face, as I noticed Rhonda's extended hand and her amused grin. Will I never learn?

FOOD FOR THOUGHT

1. Both sensorimotor systems and large businesses are complex systems trying to survive in a competitive milieu. It is no accident that they function in similar ways. Discuss.

2. We humans tend to view cortical mechanisms as preeminent, presumably because we are the species with the largest cortexes. However, one might argue from several perspectives that the lower sensorimotor circuits are more important. Discuss.

3. In this chapter, we have seen more evidence of parallel processing, with some neural circuits performing their function under conscious awareness and other circuits performing the same function in the absence of consciousness. Discuss.

KEY TERMS

Antagonistic muscles (p. 237)
Apraxia (p. 225)
Astereognosia (p. 230)
Betz cells (p. 232)
Central sensorimotor programs (p. 243)

Cingulate motor areas (p. 227)
Cocontraction (p. 240)
Constructional apraxia (p. 225)
Contralateral neglect (p. 225)

Dorsolateral corticorubro-spinal tract (p. 233)
Dorsolateral corticospinal tract (p. 232)
Dorsolateral prefrontal association cortex (p. 226)

Dynamic contraction (p. 237)
Extensors (p. 237)
Flexors (p. 237)
Frontal eye field (p. 225)
Golgi tendon organs (p. 237)

ADDITIONAL READING

The study of the sensorimotor processing is progressing rapidly, largely through the application of functional brain imaging techniques. The following are excellent reviews of this progress:

Rizzolatti, G., Fogassi, L., & Gallese, V. (1997). Parietal cortex: From sight to action. *Current Opinion in Neurobiology, 7:* 562–567.

Andersen, R. A., Snyder, L. H., Bradley, D. C., & Xing, J. (1997). Multimodal representation of space in the posterior parietal cortex and its use in planning movements. *Annual Review of Neuroscience, 20:* 303–330.

Roland, P. E., & Zilles, K. (1996). Functions and structures of the motor cortices in humans. *Current Opinion in Neurobiology, 6:* 773–781.

Tanji, J. (1996). New concepts of the supplementary motor area. *Current Opinion in Neurobiology, 6:* 782–787.

Raymond, J. L., Lisberger, S. G., & Mauk, M. D. (1996). The cerebellum: A neuronal learning machine? *Science, 272:* 1126–1131.

Brown, L. L., Schneider, J. S., & Lidsky, T. I. (1997). Sensory and cognitive functions of the basal ganglia. *Current Opinion in Neurobiology, 7:* 157–163.

Thach, W. T. (1996). On the specific role of the cerebellum in motor learning and cognition: Clues from PET activation and lesion studies in man. *Behavioral and Brain Sciences, 19:* 411–431.

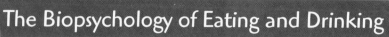

The Biopsychology of Eating and Drinking

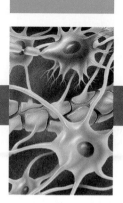

This chapter is about the biopsychology of ingestive behavior. Part 1 deals with hunger, eating, and body weight regulation, Part 2 with thirst and drinking, and Part 3 with disorders of ingestive behavior.

Eating is a behavior that is of interest to virtually everyone. We all do it; most of us derive great pleasure from it; and for many of us, it becomes a source of serious personal and health problems. Recent surveys of U.S. adults (see Brownell & Rodin, 1994) indicate that about 30% are significantly overweight, 12% grossly so; that about 45% think they are overweight; and that about 35% are currently dieting—and the figures in many other Western countries are not far behind. The incidence of obesity is greater in males, but the incidence of dieting is greater in females.

The social impact of obesity on an individual in a society obsessed with slenderness can be devastating, but the health consequences of obesity are the real tragedy. The incidence of diabetes, hypertension, cardiovascular diseases, some cancers, and thus premature death is particularly high among the obese (Bray, 1992). In addition, eating disorders such as *anorexia nervosa* and *bulimia* affect about 3% of the adolescent population, and dieting and food obsessions plague all age groups. The message is clear: At some time in your life, you or somebody you care about will almost certainly suffer from an eating-related disorder.

The massive increases in obesity and other eating-related disorders that have occurred over the last few decades in many countries stand in stark contrast to most people's thinking about hunger and eating. Most people—and I assume that this includes you—believe that hunger and eating are normally triggered when the body's energy resources fall below a prescribed optimal level or **set point:** Most people appreciate that many factors influence hunger and eating, but they assume that the hunger and eating system is designed to supply the body with just the right amount of energy. The major purpose of Part 1 of this chapter is to introduce you to a different way of thinking about hunger, eating, and weight regulation; it will almost certainly provide you with important new insights.

10.1 Digestion and Energy Flow

The primary purpose of eating is to supply the body with the energy it needs to survive and function. This section provides a brief overview of the processes by which food is digested, stored, and converted to energy.

The *gastrointestinal tract* and the process of digestion are illustrated in Figure 10.1 on page 250. **Digestion** is the gastrointestinal process of breaking down food and absorbing its constituents into the body. In order to appreciate the basics of digestion, it is useful to consider the body without its protuberances, as a simple living tube with a hole at each end. To supply itself with energy and other nutrients, the tube puts food into one of its two holes—typically the one with teeth—and passes it along its internal canal so that it can be broken down and partially absorbed from the canal into the body. The leftovers are jettisoned from the other end. Although this is not a particularly appetizing description of eating, it does serve to illustrate that, strictly speaking, food has not been consumed until it has been digested.

As a consequence of digestion, energy is delivered to the body in three forms (see Figure 10.1). These forms are (1) **lipids** (fats), (2) **amino acids** (the breakdown products of proteins), and (3) **glucose** (a simple sugar that is the breakdown product of complex *carbohydrates*, that is, of complex starches and sugars).

The body uses energy continuously, but its consumption is intermittent; therefore, it must store energy for use in the intervals between meals. Energy is stored

Set point. The value of a physiological parameter that is maintained constantly by physiological or behavioral mechanisms; for example, the body's energy resources are often assumed to be maintained at a constant optimal level by compensatory changes in hunger.
Digestion. The process by which food is broken down and absorbed through the lining of the gastrointestinal tract.
Lipids. Fats.
Amino acids. The breakdown products of proteins.
Glucose. The simple sugar breakdown product of complex starches and sugars; it is the body's primary, directly utilizable source of energy.

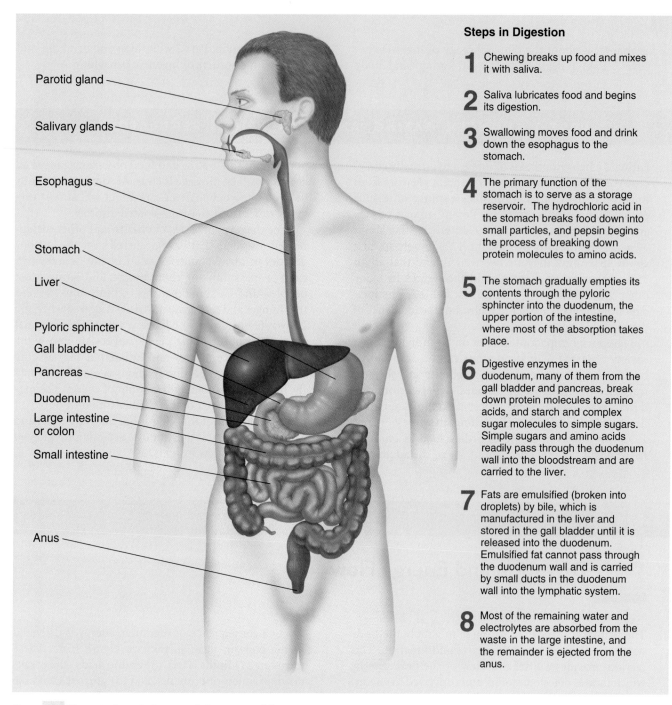

1 Chewing breaks up food and mixes it with saliva.

2 Saliva lubricates food and begins its digestion.

3 Swallowing moves food and drink down the esophagus to the stomach.

4 The primary function of the stomach is to serve as a storage reservoir. The hydrochloric acid in the stomach breaks food down into small particles, and pepsin begins the process of breaking down protein molecules to amino acids.

5 The stomach gradually empties its contents through the pyloric sphincter into the duodenum, the upper portion of the intestine, where most of the absorption takes place.

6 Digestive enzymes in the duodenum, many of them from the gall bladder and pancreas, break down protein molecules to amino acids, and starch and complex sugar molecules to simple sugars. Simple sugars and amino acids readily pass through the duodenum wall into the bloodstream and are carried to the liver.

7 Fats are emulsified (broken into droplets) by bile, which is manufactured in the liver and stored in the gall bladder until it is released into the duodenum. Emulsified fat cannot pass through the duodenum wall and is carried by small ducts in the duodenum wall into the lymphatic system.

8 Most of the remaining water and electrolytes are absorbed from the waste in the large intestine, and the remainder is ejected from the anus.

Labels on figure:
- Parotid gland
- Salivary glands
- Esophagus
- Stomach
- Liver
- Pyloric sphincter
- Gall bladder
- Pancreas
- Duodenum
- Large intestine or colon
- Small intestine
- Anus

Figure 10.1 The gastrointestinal tract and the process of digestion.

in three forms: *fats, glycogen,* and *proteins.* Most of the body's energy reserves are stored as fats, relatively little as glycogen and proteins (see Figure 10.2). Thus, changes in the body weights of adult humans are largely a consequence of changes in the amount of body fat.

Because glycogen, which is largely stored in the liver, is readily converted to glucose—the body's main directly utilizable source of energy—one might expect that glycogen would be the body's preferred mode of energy storage. There are two main reasons that fat, rather than glycogen, is the primary mode of energy storage. One is that a gram of fat can store twice as much energy as a gram of glycogen; the other is that glycogen, unlike fat, attracts and holds substantial quantities of water. Consequently, if your fat calories were all stored as glycogen, you would likely weigh well over 275 kilograms (600 pounds).

There are three phases of *energy metabolism*—the chemical changes by which energy is made available for an organism's use: the cephalic phase, the absorptive

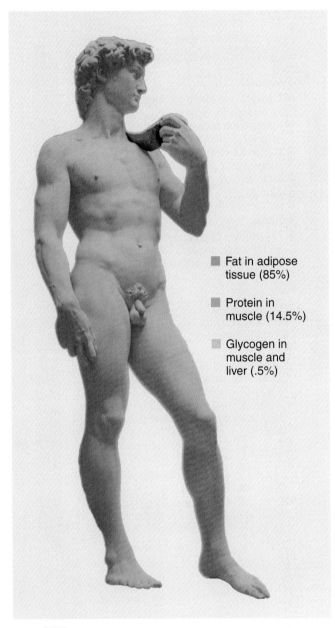

Fat in adipose
tissue (85%)

Protein in
muscle (14.5%)

Glycogen in
muscle and
liver (.5%)

Figure 10.2 Distribution of stored energy in an average person.

The flow of energy during the three phases of energy metabolism is controlled by two pancreatic hormones: insulin and glucagon. During the cephalic and absorptive phases, the pancreas releases a great deal of insulin into the bloodstream and very little glucagon. The **insulin** does three things: (1) It promotes the use of glucose as the primary source of energy by the body. (2) It promotes the conversion of blood-borne fuels to forms that can be stored: glucose to glycogen and fat, and amino acids to proteins. (3) It promotes the storage of glycogen in liver and muscle, fat in adipose tissue, and proteins in muscle. In short, the function of insulin during the cephalic phase is to lower the levels of bloodborne fuels, primarily glucose, in anticipation of the impending influx; and its function during the absorptive phase is to minimize the increasing levels of bloodborne fuels by utilizing and storing them.

In contrast to the cephalic and absorptive phases, the fasting phase is characterized by high blood levels of **glucagon** and low levels of insulin. Without high levels of insulin, glucose has difficulty entering most body cells; thus glucose stops being the body's primary fuel. In effect, this saves the body's glucose for the brain, because insulin is not required for glucose to enter most brain cells. The low levels of insulin also promote the conversion of glycogen and protein to glucose. (The conversion of protein to glucose is called **gluconeogenesis.**)

On the other hand, the high levels of fasting-phase glucagon promote the release of **free fatty acids** from adipose tissue and their use as the body's primary fuel. The high glucagon levels also stimulate the conversion of free fatty acids to **ketones,** which are used by muscles as a source of energy during the fasting phase. After a prolonged period without food, however, the brain also starts to use ketones, thus further conserving the body's resources of glucose.

Figure 10.3 on page 252 summarizes the major metabolic events associated with the three phases of energy metabolism.

phase, and the fasting phase. The **cephalic phase** is the preparatory phase; it often begins with the sight, smell, or even just the thought of food, and it ends when the food starts to be absorbed into the bloodstream. The **absorptive phase** is the period during which the energy absorbed into the bloodstream from the meal is meeting the body's immediate energy needs. The **fasting phase** is the period during which all of the unstored energy from the previous meal has been used and the body is withdrawing energy from its reserves to meet its immediate energy requirements; it ends with the beginning of the next cephalic phase. During periods of rapid weight gain, people often go directly from one absorptive phase into the next cephalic phase, without experiencing an intervening fasting phase.

Cephalic phase. The metabolic phase during which the body prepares for food that is about to be absorbed.

Absorptive phase. The metabolic phase during which the body is operating on the energy from a recently consumed meal and is storing the excess as body fat, glycogen, and proteins.

Fasting phase. The metabolic phase that begins when energy from the preceding meal is no longer sufficient to meet the immediate needs of the body and during which energy is extracted from fat and glycogen stores.

Insulin. A pancreatic hormone that facilitates the entry of glucose into cells and the conversion of bloodborne fuels to forms that can be stored.

Glucagon. A pancreatic hormone that promotes the release of free fatty acids from adipose tissue and their use as the body's primary fuel.

Gluconeogenesis. The process by which glucose is synthesized from the breakdown products of the body's protein.

Free fatty acids. Released from body fat stores, the main source of the body's energy during the fasting phase.

Ketones. Breakdown products of fat that can be used as a source of energy for the brain when glucose is in short supply.

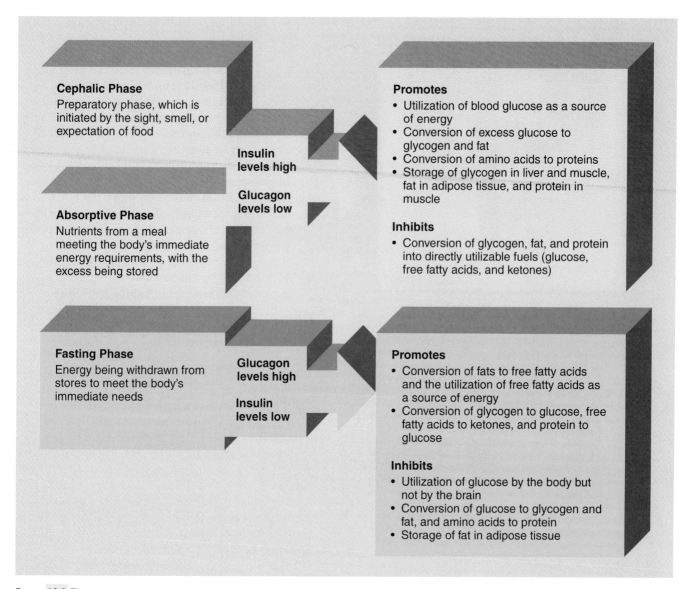

Cephalic Phase
Preparatory phase, which is initiated by the sight, smell, or expectation of food

Insulin levels high

Glucagon levels low

Absorptive Phase
Nutrients from a meal meeting the body's immediate energy requirements, with the excess being stored

Promotes
- Utilization of blood glucose as a source of energy
- Conversion of excess glucose to glycogen and fat
- Conversion of amino acids to proteins
- Storage of glycogen in liver and muscle, fat in adipose tissue, and protein in muscle

Inhibits
- Conversion of glycogen, fat, and protein into directly utilizable fuels (glucose, free fatty acids, and ketones)

Fasting Phase
Energy being withdrawn from stores to meet the body's immediate needs

Glucagon levels high

Insulin levels low

Promotes
- Conversion of fats to free fatty acids and the utilization of free fatty acids as a source of energy
- Conversion of glycogen to glucose, free fatty acids to ketones, and protein to glucose

Inhibits
- Utilization of glucose by the body but not by the brain
- Conversion of glucose to glycogen and fat, and amino acids to protein
- Storage of fat in adipose tissue

Figure 10.3 The major events associated with the three phases of energy metabolism: The cephalic, absorptive, and fasting phases.

10.2 Theories of Hunger and Eating: Set Points versus Positive Incentives

One of the main difficulties that I have in teaching the fundamentals of hunger, eating, and body weight regulation is the **set-point assumption.** Although it is ingrained in the thinking of most of my students, whether they realize it or not, it is inconsistent with most of the evidence. What exactly is the set-point assumption?

Set-Point Assumption

Most people attribute *hunger* (the motivation to eat) to the presence of an energy deficit, and they view eating as the means by which the energy resources of the body are returned to their optimal level—that is, to

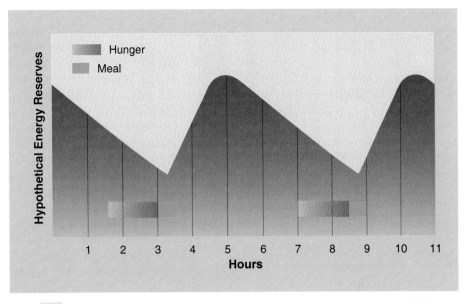

Figure 10.4 The energy set-point view that *is the basis of many people's thinking about hunger and eating.*

their *energy set point.* Figure 10.4 summarizes this set-point assumption. After a *meal* (a bout of eating), a person's energy resources are thought to be near their set point and to decline thereafter as the body uses energy to fuel its physiological processes. When the level of the body's energy resources falls far enough below the set point, a person becomes motivated by hunger to initiate another meal. The meal continues, according to the set-point assumption, until the energy level returns to its set point and the person feels *satiated* (no longer hungry).

The set-point model of hunger and eating works in much the same way as a thermostat-regulated heating system in a cool climate. The heater increases the house temperature until it reaches its set point (the thermostat setting). This turns off the heat, and then the temperature of the house gradually declines until the decline is large enough to turn the heater back on. All set-point systems have three components: a set-point mechanism, a detector mechanism, and an effector mechanism. The *set-point mechanism* defines the set point, the *detector mechanism* detects deviations from the set point, and the *effector mechanism* acts to eliminate the deviations. For example, the set-point, detector, and effector mechanisms of a heating system are the thermostat, the thermometer, and the heater, respectively.

All set-point systems are **negative feedback systems**—systems in which feedback from changes in one direction elicit compensatory effects in the opposite direction. Negative feedback systems are common in mammals because they act to maintain **homeostasis**—a constant internal environment—which is critical for the mammals' survival.

Glucostatic and Lipostatic Set-Point Theories of Hunger and Eating

In the 1940s and 1950s, researchers working under the assumption that eating is regulated by some type of set-point system speculated about the nature of the regulation. Several researchers suggested that eating is regulated by a system that is designed to maintain a blood glucose set point—the idea being that we become hungry when our blood glucose levels drop significantly below their set point and that we become satiated when eating returns our blood glucose levels to their set point. Various versions of this theory are referred to as the **glucostatic theory.** It seemed to make good sense that the main purpose of eating is to defend a blood glucose set point because glucose is the brain's primary fuel.

The **lipostatic theory** is another set-point theory that was proposed in various forms in the 1940s and 1950s. According to this theory, every person has a set point for body fat, and deviations from this set point produce compensatory adjustments in the level of eating that return levels of body fat to their set point. The most

---

Set-point assumption. The assumption that hunger is typically triggered by the decline of the body's energy reserves below their set point.

Negative feedback systems. Systems in which feedback from changes in one direction elicit compensatory effects in the opposite direction.

Homeostasis. The stability of an organism's internal environment.

Glucostatic theory. The theory that eating is controlled by deviations from a hypothetical blood glucose set point.

Lipostatic theory. The theory that eating is controlled by deviations from a hypothetical body-fat set point.

frequently cited support for the theory is the fact that the body weights of adults stay relatively constant.

The glucostatic and lipostatic theories were viewed as complementary, not mutually exclusive. The glucostatic theory was thought to account for meal initiation and termination, whereas the lipostatic theory was thought to account for long-term regulation. Thus the dominant view in the 1950s was that eating is regulated by the interaction between two set-point systems: a short-term glucostatic system and a long-term lipostatic system. The simplicity of these 1950s theories is appealing. Remarkably, they are still being presented as the latest word in some textbooks; perhaps you have encountered them.

Problems with Set-Point Theories of Hunger and Eating

Set-point theories of hunger and eating have several serious weaknesses. The following are three of them.

First, set-point theories of hunger and eating are inconsistent with basic eating-related evolutionary pressures as we understand them. The major eating-related problem faced by our ancestors was the inconsistency and unpredictability of the food supply. Thus, in order to survive, it was important for them to eat large quantities of good food when it was available so that calories could be banked in the form of body fat. Any ancestor—human or otherwise—that stopped feeling hungry as soon as immediate energy needs were met would not have survived the first hard winter or prolonged drought. For any warm-blooded species to survive under natural conditions, it needs a hunger and eating system that prevents energy deficits, rather than one that merely responds to them once they have developed. From this perspective, it is difficult to imagine how a set-point hunger and feeding system could have evolved in mammals (see Weingarten, 1985).

Second, major predictions of the set-point theories of hunger and eating have been not been confirmed. Early studies seemed to support the set-point theories by showing that large reductions in body fat, produced by starvation, or large reductions in blood glucose, produced by insulin injections, induce increases in eating in laboratory animals. The problem is that reductions of the magnitude needed to reliably induce eating rarely occur naturally. Indeed, as you have already learned in this chapter, approximately 30% of the U.S. population have a significant excess of fat deposits when they begin a meal. Conversely, efforts to reduce meal size by having subjects consume a high-calorie drink just before eating have been largely unsuccessful; indeed, beliefs about the caloric content of a premeal drink often influence the size of a subsequent meal more than does its actual caloric content (see Lowe, 1993).

Third, set-point theories of hunger and eating are deficient because they fail to recognize the major influences on hunger and eating of such important factors as taste, learning, and social factors. To convince yourself of the importance of these factors, pause for a minute and imagine the sight, smell, and taste of your favorite food. Perhaps it is a succulent morsel of lobster meat covered with melted garlic butter, a piece of chocolate cheesecake, or a plate of sizzling homemade french fries. Are you starting to feel a bit hungry? If the homemade french fries—my personal weakness—were sitting in front of you right now, wouldn't you reach out and have one, or maybe the whole plateful? Have you not on occasion felt discomfort after a large main course, only to polish off a substantial dessert? The usual positive answers to these questions lead unavoidably to the conclusion that hunger and eating are not rigidly controlled by deviations from energy set points. This same point can be easily demonstrated in laboratory rats by adding a small amount of saccharin to their laboratory chow; saccharin increases the sweetness of the chow without adding calories, and it produces a major increase in both eating and body weight.

Positive-Incentive Theory

The inability of set-point theories to account for the basic phenomena of eating and hunger has led to the development of an alternative theory. The central assertion of this new theoretical perspective, commonly referred to as the **positive-incentive theory,** is that humans and other animals are not driven to eat by internal energy deficits but are drawn to eat by the anticipated pleasure of eating—the anticipated pleasure of a behavior is called its **positive-incentive value** (see Bolles, 1980; Booth, 1981; Collier, 1980; Rolls, 1981; Toates, 1981).

The major tenet of the positive-incentive theory of eating is that eating is controlled in much the same way as sexual behavior: We engage in sexual behavior not because we have an internal deficit, but because we have evolved to enjoy it. The evolutionary pressures of unexpected food shortages have shaped us and all other warm-blooded animals, who need a continuous supply of energy to maintain their body temperatures, to take advantage of good food when it is present and eat it. According to the positive-incentive theory, it is the presence of good food, or the anticipation of it, that usually makes us hungry, not an energy deficit.

According to the positive-incentive theory, the degree of hunger that you feel at any particular time depends on the interaction of all the factors that influence the positive-incentive value of eating. These include the following: the flavor of the food that you are likely to consume, what you have learned about the effects of this food either from eating it previously or from other people, the amount of time since you last ate, the type and quantity of food in your gut, whether or not other people are present and eating, whether or not your blood glucose levels are within the normal range. This partial list illustrates one strength of the positive-incentive theory. Unlike the set-point theories, the positive-incentive theory does not single out one factor as the major determinant of hunger and ignore the others; it acknowledges that many factors interact to determine a person's hunger at any time, and it suggests that this interaction occurs through the influence of these various factors on the positive-incentive value of eating (see Cabanac, 1971).

In this section, you learned that most people think about hunger and eating in terms of energy set points, and you were introduced to an alternative: the positive-incentive theory. If you are like most people, you will have certain resistance to new ways of thinking; thus, it may be useful for you to stop now and review some of the serious problems with conventional set-point thinking: for example, the current epidemic of excessive eating and obesity, the incompatibility of set-point regulation of eating with the food-related demands of a natural environment, the fact that people in food-replete societies rarely if ever experience energy deficits, the fact that premeal calorie loads rarely reduce meal size, and the fact that set-point theories of eating do not account for the effects of factors that you know have a major effect on hunger and eating (e.g., flavor and time of day). In the next section, you will learn some of the important things that biopsychological research has taught us about eating. As you progress through it, the advantages of positive-incentive theories of eating over set-point theories of eating should become more and more apparent.

10.3 Factors That Determine What, When, and How Much We Eat

This section of the chapter describes major factors that commonly determine what we eat, when we eat, and how much we eat. Notice that energy deficits are not included among these factors. Although major energy deficits clearly increase hunger and eating, they are not a common factor in the eating behavior of people like us, who live in food-replete societies. Although you may believe that your body is short of energy just before a meal, it is not. This misconception is one that is addressed in this section.

Factors That Determine What We Eat

Certain tastes have a high positive-incentive value for virtually all members of a species. For example, most humans have a special fondness for sweet, fatty, and salty tastes. This species-typical pattern of human taste preferences is adaptive because in nature sweet and fatty tastes are typically characteristic of high-energy foods that are rich in vitamins and minerals, and salty tastes are characteristic of sodium-rich foods. In contrast, bitter tastes, for which most humans have an aversion, are often associated with toxins. Superimposed on our species-typical taste preferences and aversions, each of us has the ability to learn specific taste preferences and aversions (see Rozin & Shulkin, 1990).

■ **LEARNED TASTE PREFERENCES AND AVERSIONS** Animals learn to prefer tastes that are followed by an infusion of calories, and they learn to avoid tastes that are followed by illness (e.g., Baker & Booth, 1989; Lucas & Sclafani, 1989; Sclafani, 1990). In addition, humans and other animals learn what to eat from their conspecifics. For example, rats learn to prefer flavors that they experience in mother's milk and those that they smell on the breaths of other rats (see Galef, 1995, 1996). Similarly, in humans, many food preferences are culturally specific—for example, in some cultures various nontoxic insects are considered to be a delicacy. Galef and Wright (1995) have shown that rats reared in groups, rather than in isolation, are more likely to learn to eat a healthy diet.

■ **LEARNING TO EAT VITAMINS AND MINERALS** How do animals select a diet that provides all of the vitamins and minerals they need? To answer this question, researchers have studied how dietary deficiencies influence diet selection. Two patterns of results have emerged: one for sodium and one for the other essential vitamins and minerals. When an animal is deficient in sodium, it develops an immediate and compelling preference for the taste of sodium salt (see Rowland, 1990b). In contrast, an animal that is deficient in some vitamin or mineral other than sodium must learn to consume foods

---

Positive-incentive theory. The theory that behaviors (e.g., eating and drinking) are motivated by their anticipated pleasurable effects.

Positive-incentive value. The anticipated pleasure involved in the performance of a particular behavior, such as eating a particular food or drinking a particular beverage.

that are rich in the missing nutrient by experiencing their positive effects; this is because vitamins and minerals other than sodium normally have no detectable taste in food. For example, rats maintained on a diet deficient in *thiamine* (vitamin B$_1$) develop an aversion to the taste of that diet; and if they are offered two new diets, one deficient in thiamine and one rich in thiamine, they often develop a preference for the taste of the thiamine-rich diet over the ensuing days.

If we, like rats, are capable of learning to select diets that are rich in the vitamins and minerals we need, why are dietary deficiencies so prevalent in our society (see Willett, 1994)? One reason is that, in order to maximize profits, manufacturers produce foods with the tastes that we prefer but with most of the essential nutrients extracted from them. (Even rats prefer chocolate chip cookies to nutritionally complete rat chow.) The second reason is illustrated by the classic study of Harris and associates (1933). When thiamine-deficient rats were offered two new diets, one with thiamine and one without, almost all of them learned to eat the complete diet and avoid the deficient one. However, when they were offered ten new diets, only one of which contained the badly needed thiamine, few developed a preference for the complete diet. The number of different substances consumed each day by most people in industrialized societies is immense, and this makes it difficult, if not impossible, for their bodies to learn which foods are beneficial and which are not.

Factors That Influence When We Eat

Collier and his colleagues (see Collier, 1986) found that most mammals choose to eat many small meals (snacks) each day if they have ready access to a continuous supply of food. Only when there are physical costs involved in initiating meals—for example, having to travel a considerable distance—does an animal opt for a few large meals.

The number of times that humans eat each day is influenced by cultural norms, work schedules, family routines, personal preferences, wealth, and a variety of other factors. However, in contrast to the usual mammalian preference, most people, particularly those living in family groups, tend to eat a few large meals each day at regular times. Interestingly, each person's regular mealtimes are the very same times at which that person is likely to feel most hungry; in fact, many people experience attacks of malaise (headache, nausea, and an inability to concentrate) when they miss a regularly scheduled meal.

■**PREMEAL HUNGER** I am sure that you have experienced attacks of premeal hunger. Subjectively, they seem to provide compelling support for set-point theories. Your body seems to be crying out: "I need more energy. I

cannot function without it. Please feed me." But things are not always the way they seem. Woods has recently straightened out the confusion (see Woods, 1991; Woods & Strubbe, 1994).

According to Woods, the key to understanding hunger is to appreciate that eating meals stresses the body. Before a meal, the body's energy reserves are in reasonable homeostatic balance; then, as a meal is consumed, there is a homeostasis-disturbing influx of fuels into the bloodstream. The body does what it can to defend its homeostasis. At the first indication that a person will soon be eating—for example, when the usual mealtime approaches—the body enters the cephalic phase and takes steps to soften the impact of the impending homeostasis-disturbing influx by releasing insulin into the blood and thus reducing blood glucose. Woods's message is that the strong, unpleasant feelings of hunger that you may experience at mealtimes are not cries from your body for food; they are the sensations of your body's preparations for the expected homeostasis-disturbing meal. Mealtime hunger is caused by the expectation of food, not by an energy deficit.

As a high school student, I ate lunch at exactly 12:05 every day and was overwhelmed by hunger as the time approached. Now, my eating schedule is different, and I never experience noontime hunger pangs; I get hungry just before the time at which I usually eat. Have you had a similar experience?

■**PAVLOVIAN CONDITIONING OF HUNGER** In a clever series of Pavlovian conditioning experiments on laboratory rats, Weingarten (1983, 1984, 1985) provided strong support for the view that hunger is often caused by the expectation of food, not by an energy deficit. During the conditioning phase of one of his experiments, Weingarten presented rats with six meals per day at irregular intervals, and he signaled the impending delivery of each meal with a buzzer-and-light *conditional stimulus*. This conditioning procedure was continued for 11 days. Throughout the ensuing test phase of the experiment, the food was continuously available. Despite the fact that the subjects were never deprived during the test phase, the rats started to eat each time the buzzer and light were presented—even if they had recently completed a meal.

Factors That Influence How Much We Eat

The motivational state that causes us to stop eating a meal when there is food remaining is **satiety**. Satiety mechanisms play a major role in determining how much we eat.

■**SATIETY SIGNALS** As you will learn in the next section of the chapter, food in the gut and glucose entering the blood can induce satiety signals, which inhibit subse-

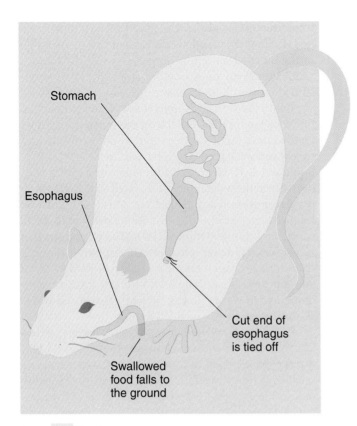

Figure 10.5 The sham-eating preparation.

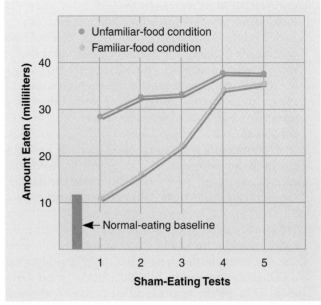

Figure 10.6 Change in the magnitude of sham eating over repeated sham-eating trials. The rats in one group sham ate the same diet they had eaten before the sham-eating phase; the rats in another group sham ate a diet different from the one they had previously eaten. (Adapted from Weingarten, 1990.)

quent consumption. These signals seem to depend on both the volume and **nutritive density** (calories per unit volume) of the food.

The effects of nutritive density have been demonstrated in studies in which laboratory rats have been maintained on a single diet. Once a stable baseline of consumption has been established, the nutritive density of the diet is changed. Many rats learn to adjust the volume of food they consume to keep their caloric intake and body weights relatively constant. However, there are limits to this adjustment: Rats often do not increase their intake sufficiently to maintain their body weights if the nutritive density of their conventional laboratory feed is reduced by more than 50%, and they do not maintain the constancy of their caloric intake if there are major changes in the diet's palatability.

■ **SHAM EATING** The study of **sham eating** indicates that satiety signals from the gut or blood are not necessary to terminate a meal. In sham-eating experiments, food is chewed and swallowed by the subject; but rather than passing down the subject's esophagus into the stomach, it passes out of the body through an implanted tube (see Figure 10.5).

Because sham eating adds no energy to the body, set-point theories predict that all sham-eaten meals should be huge. But this is not the case. Weingarten and Kulikovsky (1989) sham fed rats one of two differently fla-vored diets: one that the rats had naturally eaten many times before and one that they had never eaten before. The first sham meal of the rats that had previously eaten the diet was the same size as the previously eaten meals of that diet; then, on ensuing days they began to sham eat more and more (see Figure 10.6). In contrast, the rats that were presented with the unfamiliar diet sham ate large quantities right from the start. Weingarten and Kulikovsky concluded that the amount we eat is influenced largely by our previous experience with the particular food's postingestive effects, not by the immediate effect of the food on the body.

■ **APPETIZER EFFECT AND SATIETY** The next time you attend a dinner party, you may experience a major weakness of the set-point theory of satiety. If appetizers are served, you will experience the fact that small amounts of food consumed before a meal actually increase hunger rather than reducing it. This is the **appetizer effect**. Presumably, it occurs because the consumption of a small amount of food is particularly effective in eliciting cephalic-phase responses.

Satiety. The motivational state that terminates a meal.

Nutritive density. Calories per unit volume of food.

Sham eating. The experimental protocol in which an animal chews and swallows food, which immediately exits its body through a tube implanted in its esophagus.

Appetizer effect. The increase in hunger that is produced by the consumption of small amounts of palatable food.

■ **SOCIAL INFLUENCES AND SATIETY** Feelings of satiety depend on whether we are eating alone or with others. Redd and de Castro (1992) found that their subjects consumed 60% more when eating with others. Laboratory rats also eat substantially more when fed in groups.

In humans, social factors have also been shown to reduce consumption. Many people eat less than they would like in order to achieve their society's ideal of slenderness, and others refrain from eating large amounts in front of others so as not to appear gluttonous. Unfortunately, in our culture females are greatly influenced by such pressures, and, as you will learn later in the chapter, some develop serious eating disorders as a result.

■ **SENSORY-SPECIFIC SATIETY** The number of different tastes available at each meal has a major effect on meal size. For example, the effect of offering a laboratory rat a varied diet of highly palatable foods—a **cafeteria diet**—is dramatic. Adults rats that were offered bread and chocolate in addition to their usual laboratory diet increased their average intake of calories by 84%, and after 120 days they had increased their average body weights by 49% (Rogers & Blundell, 1980). The spectacular effects of cafeteria diets on consumption and body weight clearly run counter to the idea that satiety is rigidly controlled by internal energy set points.

The effect on meal size of cafeteria diets results from the fact that satiety is to a large degree taste-specific. As you eat one food, the positive-incentive value of all foods declines slightly, but the positive-incentive value of that particular food plummets. As a result, you soon become satiated on that food and stop eating it. However, if another food is offered to you, you will often begin eating again.

In one study of **sensory-specific satiety** (Rolls et al., 1981), human subjects were asked to rate the palatability of eight different foods, and then they ate a meal of one of them. After the meal, they were asked to rate the palatability of the eight foods once again, and it was found that their rating of the food they had just eaten had declined substantially more than had their ratings of the other seven foods. Moreover, when the subjects were offered an unexpected second meal, they consumed most of it unless it was the same as the first.

Booth (1981) asked subjects to rate the momentary pleasure produced by the flavor, the smell, the sight, or just the thought of various foods at different times after consuming a large, high-calorie, high-carbohydrate liquid meal. There was an immediate sensory-specific decrease in the palatability of foods of the same or similar flavor as soon as the meal was consumed. This was followed by a general decrease in the palatability of all substances about 30 minutes later. Thus it appears that signals from taste receptors produce an immediate decline in the positive-incentive value of similar tastes and that signals associated with the postingestive consequences of eating produce a general decrease in the positive-incentive value of all foods.

Rolls (1990) suggested that sensory-specific satiety has two kinds of effects: relatively brief effects that influence the selection of foods within a single meal and relatively enduring effects that influence the selection of foods from meal to meal. Some foods seem to be relatively immune to long-lasting sensory-specific satiety; foods such as rice, bread, potatoes, sweets, and green salads can be eaten almost every day with only a slight decline in their palatability (Rolls, 1986).

The phenomenon of sensory-specific satiety has two adaptive consequences. First, it encourages the consumption of a varied diet. If there were no sensory-specific satiety, a person would tend to eat her or his preferred food and nothing else, and the result would be malnutrition. Second, sensory-specific satiety encourages animals that have access to a variety of foods to eat a lot; an animal that has eaten its fill of one food will often begin eating again if it encounters a different one. This encourages animals to take full advantage of times of abundance, which are all too rare in nature.

10.4 Physiological Research on Hunger and Satiety

Now that you have been introduced to the set-point theory, the positive-incentive theory, and some basic eating-related facts, this section introduces you to four prominent lines of research on the physiology of hunger and satiety. Although none of these four lines involves the discovery, or even implies the existence of, a set-point mechanism, together they indicate that eating is regulated in some way.

Cafeteria diet. A diet offered to experimental animals that is composed of a wide variety of palatable foods.
Sensory-specific satiety. The fact that the consumption of a particular food produces more satiety for foods of the same taste than for other foods.

Ventromedial hypothalamus (VMH). The area of the hypothalamus that was once thought to be the satiety center.
Lateral hypothalamus (LH). The area of the hypothalamus once thought to be the feeding center.

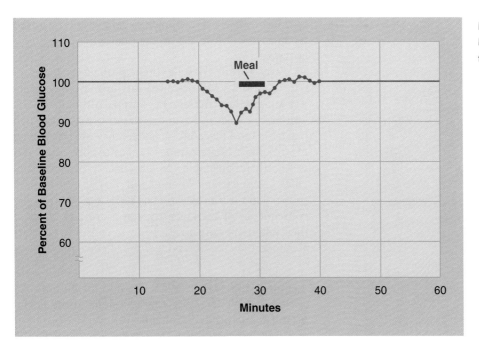

Figure 10.7 The meal-related changes in blood glucose levels observed by Campfield and Smith (1986).

Role of Blood Glucose Levels in Hunger and Satiety

As I have previously explained, efforts to link blood glucose levels to eating have been largely unsuccessful. However, the experiments of Campfield and Smith (see 1990) have renewed interest in the role of blood glucose levels in hunger and satiety. In a typical Campfield and Smith experiment, rats are housed individually with free access to a mixed diet and water, and blood glucose levels are continually monitored via chronic intravenous catheters. In this situation, baseline blood glucose levels rarely fluctuate by more than a percent or two. However, about 10 minutes before a meal is initiated, the levels suddenly drop by about 8%.

Does the finding of Campfield and Smith lend support to the glucostatic theory of hunger? I think not, for three reasons: The first is that it is a simple matter to construct a situation in which declines in blood glucose do not precede eating (e.g., Strubbe & Steffens, 1977)—for example, by unexpectedly serving a food with a high positive-incentive value. The second is that the premeal declines in blood glucose observed by Campfield and Smith seemed to be a response to the animals' intention to start eating, not the other way round. The declines of premeal blood glucose observed by Campfield and Smith were themselves preceded by an increase in blood insulin levels: This indicates that the decreases in blood glucose did not occur because the rats were running out of energy, but that the rats lowered their own blood glucose levels by releasing insulin. Also, the suddenness of the drop in blood glucose suggests that the drop was actively produced rather than being a consequence of a gradual decline in the body's energy reserves (see Figure 10.7). The third reason why I think that Campfield and Smith's data do not support the glucostatic theory is that if the expected meal is not served, blood glucose levels return to their previous homeostatic levels.

The fact that injections of insulin do not reliably induce eating in some experimental subjects unless the injections are sufficiently great to reduce blood glucose levels by 50% (see Rowland, 1981) and the fact that large premeal infusions of glucose often do not suppress eating (see Geiselman, 1987) strongly suggest that glucose deficits are not the primary cause of hunger. However, some results suggest that decreases in blood glucose can contribute to feelings of hunger. For example, Smith and Campfield (1993) induced with drugs reductions in blood glucose similar to the ones that occur spontaneously prior to meals, and they found that the reductions promoted subsequent food consumption. Conversely, Campfield, Brandon, and Smith (1985) delayed the onset of meals by infusing glucose into the blood of rats at the first sign of a premeal decline in blood glucose.

Myth of Hypothalamic Hunger and Satiety Centers

In the 1950s, experiments on rats seemed to suggest that eating behavior is controlled by two different regions of the hypothalamus: satiety by the **ventromedial hypothalamus (VMH)** and feeding by the **lateral hypothalamus (LH)**. Figure 10.8 on page 260 illustrates the locations of the VMH and the LH in the rat brain.

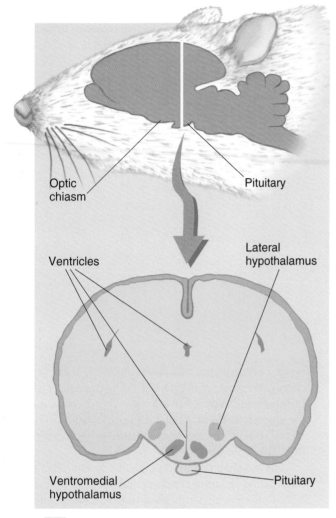

Figure 10.8 The locations in the rat brain of the ventromedial hypothalamus and the lateral hypothalamus.

tailed; conversely, if it is made to gain weight by forced feeding, it will lose the excess once forced feeding is curtailed.

Paradoxically, despite their prodigious levels of consumption, VMH-lesioned rats in some ways seem less hungry than unlesioned controls. Although VMH-lesioned rats eat much more than normal rats when palatable food is readily available, they are less willing to work for it (Teitelbaum, 1957) or to consume it if it is slightly unpalatable (Miller, Bailey, & Stevenson, 1950). Weingarten, Chang, and Jarvie (1983) have shown that the finicky eating of VMH-lesioned rats is a consequence of their obesity, not a primary effect of their lesion; they are no less likely to consume unpalatable food than are unlesioned rats of equal obesity.

■ **LH FEEDING CENTER** In 1951, Anand and Brobeck reported that bilateral electrolytic lesions to the *lateral hypothalamus* produce **aphagia**—a complete cessation of eating. Even rats that were first made hyperphagic by VMH lesions were rendered aphagic by the addition of LH lesions. Anand and Brobeck concluded that the lateral region of the hypothalamus is a feeding center. Teitelbaum and Epstein (1962) subsequently discovered two important features of the *LH syndrome*. First, they found that the aphagia was accompanied by **adipsia**—a complete cessation of drinking. Second, they found that LH-lesioned rats partially recover if they are kept alive by tube feeding. First, they begin to eat wet, palatable foods, such as chocolate chip cookies soaked in milk, and eventually they will eat dry food pellets if water is concurrently available.

■ **REINTERPRETATION OF THE EFFECTS OF VMH AND LH LESIONS** The theory of VMH satiety and LH feeding centers became very popular, and it was served up to wave after wave of students as if the evidence for it were unassailable. However, little about it is true.

The theory that the VMH is a satiety center has crumbled in the face of two lines of evidence. One of these lines has shown that the primary role of the hypothalamus is the regulation of energy metabolism, not the regulation of eating. The initial interpretation was that VMH-lesioned animals become obese because they overeat; however, the evidence suggests the converse—that they overeat because they become obese. Bilateral VMH lesions increase blood insulin levels, which increases **lipogenesis** (the production of body fat) and decreases **lipolysis** (the breakdown of body fat to utilizable forms of energy)—see Powley et al. (1980). Both are likely to be the result of the increases in insulin levels that occur following the lesion. Because the calories of VMH-lesioned rats are converted to fat at a high rate, the rats then must keep eating to ensure that they have enough calories in their blood to meet their immediate energy requirements

■ **VMH SATIETY CENTER** In 1940, it was discovered that large bilateral electrolytic lesions to the ventromedial hypothalamus produce **hyperphagia** (excessive eating) and extreme obesity in rats (Hetherington & Ranson, 1940). This *VMH syndrome* has two different phases: dynamic and static. The **dynamic phase,** which begins as soon as the subject regains consciousness after the operation, is characterized by several weeks of grossly excessive eating and rapid weight gain. However, eventually consumption gradually declines to a level that is just sufficient to maintain a stable level of obesity; this marks the beginning of the **static phase.** Figure 10.9 illustrates the weight gain and food intake of an adult rat with bilateral VMH lesions.

The most important feature of the static phase of the VMH syndrome is that the animal maintains its new body weight. If a rat in the static phase is deprived of food until it has lost a substantial amount of weight, it will regain its lost weight once deprivation is cur-

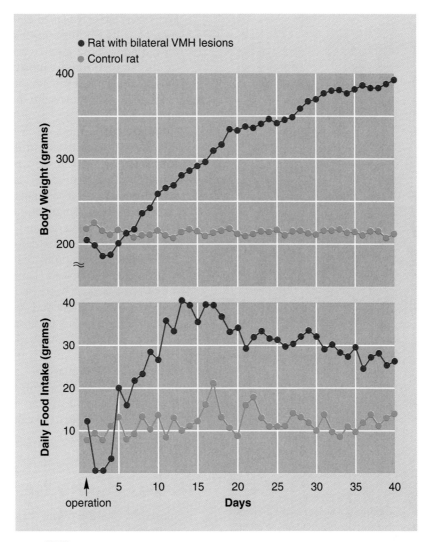

Figure 10.9 Postoperative hyperphagia and obesity in a rat with bilateral VMH lesions.
(Adapted from Teitelbaum, 1961.)

(e.g., Hustvedt & Løvø, 1972); they are like misers who run to the bank each time they make a bit of money and deposit it in a savings account from which withdrawals cannot be made.

The second line of evidence that has undermined the theory of a VMH satiety center has shown that many of the effects of VMH lesions are not attributable to VMH damage. A large fiber bundle, the *ventral noradrenergic bundle,* courses past the VMH and is thus inevitably damaged by large electrolytic VMH lesions; in particular, fibers that project from the nearby **paraventricular nuclei** of the hypothalamus are damaged (see Figure 10.10 on page 262). Bilateral lesions of the noradrenergic bundle (e.g., Gold et al., 1977) or the paraventricular nuclei (Leibowitz, Hammer, & Chang, 1981) produce hyperphagia and obesity similar to those produced by VMH lesions.

Most of the evidence against the notion of an LH feeding center has come from a thorough analysis of the effects of bilateral LH lesions. Early research fo-

cused exclusively on the aphagia and adipsia that are produced by LH lesions, but subsequent research has shown that LH lesions produce a wide range of severe motor disturbances and a general lack of responsiveness to sensory input (of which food and drink are but two examples). Because the behavioral effects of LH lesions are so general, the notion that the LH is a center specifically dedicated to feeding is untenable.

Hyperphagia. Excessive eating.
Dynamic phase. The first phase of the VMH syndrome, characterized by grossly excessive eating and weight gain.
Static phase. The second phase of the VMH syndrome, during which the grossly obese animal regulates its body weight.
Aphagia. Complete cessation of eating.

Adipsia. Complete cessation of drinking.
Lipogenesis. The production of body fat.
Lipolysis. The breakdown of body fat.
Paraventricular nuclei. Hypothalamic nuclei that play a role in eating.

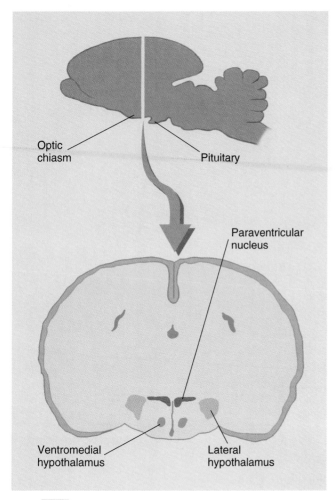

Figure 10.10 Location of the paraventricular nucleus in the rat hypothalamus. Note that the section through the hypothalamus is slightly different than the one in Figure 10.8.

Optic chiasm

Pituitary

Paraventricular nucleus

Ventromedial hypothalamus

Lateral hypothalamus

Role of the Gastrointestinal Tract in Satiety

One of the most influential early studies of hunger was published by Cannon and Washburn in 1912. It was a perfect collaboration; Cannon had the ideas, and Washburn had the ability to swallow a balloon. First, Washburn swallowed an empty balloon tied to the end of a thin tube. Then, Cannon pumped some air into the balloon and connected the end of the tube to a water-filled glass U-tube so that Washburn's stomach contractions produced a momentary increase in the level of the water at the other end of the U-tube. Washburn reported a "pang" of hunger each time that a large stomach contraction was recorded (see Figure 10.11).

Cannon and Washburn's finding led to the theory that hunger is the feeling of contractions caused by an empty stomach, whereas satiety is the feeling of stomach distention. However, support for this theory and interest in the role of the gastrointestinal tract in hunger

and satiety quickly waned with the discovery that human patients whose stomachs had been surgically removed and whose esophaguses had been hooked up directly to their **duodenums** continued to report feelings of hunger and satiety and continued to maintain their normal body weights by eating more meals of smaller size.

In the 1980s, there was a resurgence of interest in the role of the gastrointestinal tract in eating. It was stimulated by a series of experiments that indicated that the gastrointestinal tract is the source of satiety signals. For example, Koopmans (1981) transplanted an extra stomach and length of intestine into rats and then joined the major arteries and veins of the implants to the recipients' own circulatory systems (see Figure 10.12). Koopmans found that food injected into the transplanted stomach and kept there by a noose around the *pyloric sphincter* decreased eating in proportion to both its caloric content and volume. Because the transplanted stomach had no functional nerves, the gastrointestinal satiety signal had to be reaching the brain through the blood. And because nutrients are not absorbed from the stomach, the bloodborne satiety signal could not have been a nutrient. It had to be some chemical or chemicals that were released from the stomach in response to the caloric value and volume of the food.

Hunger and Satiety Peptides

Soon after the discovery that the stomach and other parts of the gastrointestinal tract release chemicals, evidence began to accumulate that these were *peptides* (see Seeley & Schwartz, 1997), short chains of amino acids that function as hormones and neurotransmitters. Ingested food interacts with receptors in the gastrointestinal tract and in so doing causes the tract to release peptides into the bloodstream. In 1973 Gibbs, Young, and Smith injected one of these gut peptides, **cholecystokinin (CCK),** into hungry rats and found that they ate smaller meals. This led to the hypothesis that circulating gut peptides provide the brain with information about the quantity and nature of food in the gastrointestinal tract and that this information plays a role in satiety.

There is now considerable support for the hypothesis that peptides can function as satiety signals (see Leibowitz, 1992). Several gut peptides have been shown to bind to receptors in the brain, and close to a dozen have been reported to reduce food intake (e.g., CCK,

Duodenum. The upper portion of the intestine through which most of the glucose and amino acids are absorbed into the bloodstream.

Cholecystokinin (CCK). A peptide that is released by the gastrointestinal tract and is thought to function as a satiety signal.

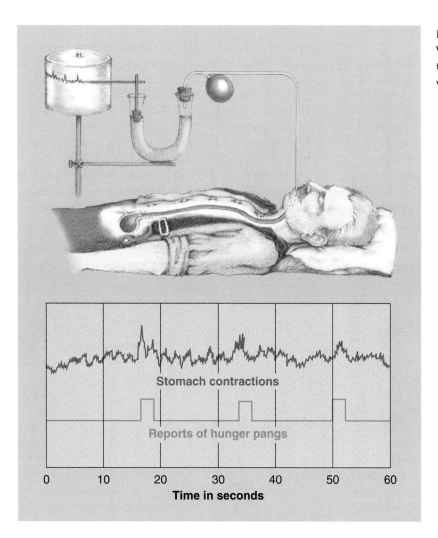

Figure 10.11 The system developed by Cannon and Washburn in 1912 for measuring stomach contractions. They found that large stomach contractions were related to pangs of hunger.

Stomach contractions

Reports of hunger pangs

Time in seconds

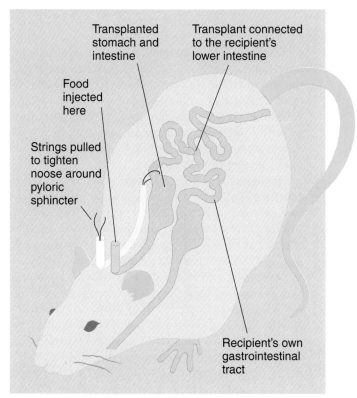

Transplanted stomach and intestine

Transplant connected to the recipient's lower intestine

Food injected here

Strings pulled to tighten noose around pyloric sphincter

Recipient's own gastrointestinal tract

Figure 10.12 Transplantation of an extra stomach and length of intestine in a rat. Koopmans (1981) implanted an extra stomach and length of intestine in each of his experimental subjects. He then connected the major blood vessels of the implanted stomachs to the circulatory systems of the recipients. Food injected into the extra stomach and kept there by a noose around the pyloric sphincter decreased eating in proportion to its volume and caloric value.

bombesin, glucagon, and somatostatin)—see Woods and Gibbs (1989).

It is conceivable that at least part of the inhibitory effect of peptides on eating is indirect—mediated by their effects on peripheral organs (see Weller, Smith, & Gibbs, 1990). For example, McHugh and Moran (1985) proposed that the inhibitory action of CCK on stomach emptying contributes to its satiety-producing effect. However, Dourish, Rycroft, and Iversen (1989) found that selective antagonists of central nervous system CCK receptors are 100 times more effective in increasing feeding than are selective antagonists of peripheral CCK receptors (see Cooper & Dourish, 1990).

Although most peptides that affect eating have proven to play an inhibitory role, there are a few exceptions: These are the hunger peptides. Most widely studied among the hunger peptides are *neuropeptide Y* (Billington & Levine, 1992) and *galanin* (Leibowitz, Akabayashi, & Wang, 1998). Both peptides increase eating when injected into the paraventricular nucleus of the hypothalamus (Leibowitz, 1992). Neuropeptide Y seems to produce a specific hunger for carbohydrates, whereas galanin seems to produce a specific hunger for fats. In addition, both peptides reduce energy metabolism and increase fat production; thus, they are likely part of a mechanism that evolved to deal with starvation.

10.5 Body Weight Regulation: Set Points versus Settling Points

One strength of the set-point theory of eating is that it also explains body-weight regulation. You have already learned that the set-point theory is largely inconsistent with the facts of eating, but how well does it account for the regulation of body weight? Certainly, most people who we have interviewed while conducting our studies of people's beliefs about hunger, eating, and weight regulation believe that body weight is regulated by a body-fat set point (Assanand, Pinel, & Lehman, 1998 a & b). They believe that when fat deposits are below a person's set point, a person becomes hungrier and eats more, which results in a return of body-fat levels to that person's set point; and conversely, they believe that when fat deposits are above a person's set point, a person becomes less hungry and eats less, which results in a return of body fat levels to their set point.

Set-Point Assumptions about Body Weight and Eating

You have already learned that set-point theories do a poor job of predicting the major properties of hunger and eating. Do they do a better job of accounting for the facts of body-weight regulation? Let's begin by looking at three lines of evidence that challenge fundamental aspects of many set-point theories of body weight regulation.

■ **VARIABILITY OF BODY WEIGHT** The set-point theory is expressly designed to explain why adult body weights remain constant. Indeed, a set-point mechanism should make it virtually impossible for an adult to gain or lose large amounts of weight. Yet, many adults experience large and lasting changes in body weight. Moreover, set-

point thinking crumbles in the face of the epidemic of obesity that is currently sweeping fast-food societies.

Set-point theories of body weight regulation suggest that the best method of maintaining a constant body weight is to eat each time that there is a motivation to eat—because the main function of these hunger motivations is to defend the set point. However, as I am sure many of you know from personal experience, many people avoid obesity only by resisting their strong drives to eat.

■ **SET POINTS AND HEALTH** One implication of set-point theories of body weight regulation is that each person's set-point is optimal for that person's health—or at least not incompatible with good health. This is why media psychologists commonly advise people to "listen to the wisdom of their bodies" and eat as much as they need to satisfy their hunger. Experimental results indicate that this common prescription for good health could not be further from the truth.

Two kinds of evidence suggest that typical *ad libitum* (free-feeding) levels of consumption are unhealthy (see Brownell & Rodin, 1994). First are the results of studies of humans who consume fewer calories than others. For example, people living on the Japanese Island of Okinawa seemed to eat so few calories that it was of concern to health officials. When they took a closer look, here is what they found (see Kagawa, 1978). Adult Okinawans were found to consume, on average, 20% fewer calories than other adult Japanese, and Okinawan schoolchildren were found to consume 38% fewer calories than recommended by public health officials. It was somewhat surprising then that the rates of morbidity and mortality and all aging-related diseases were found to be substantially lower in Okinawa than in other parts of Japan, a country in which overall levels of caloric intake and obesity are far below Western norms. For example, the death rates from stroke, cancer, and heart disease in Okinawa were only 59%, 69%, and 59%, respectively, of those in the rest of Japan. Indeed, the proportion of Okinawans living to be over 100 years of age was up to 40 times greater than that of inhabitants of various other regions of Japan.

The Okinawan study and the other studies that have reported major health benefits in humans who eat less (e.g., Manson et al., 1995; Walford & Walford, 1994) are not controlled experiments; therefore they must be interpreted with caution. For example, perhaps it is not the consumption of fewer calories per se that leads to the health and longevity; perhaps people who eat less tend to eat healthier diets. Fortunately, calorie-restriction experiments have been conducted in over a dozen different species, including monkeys, and these do not have these problems of interpretation. In each experiment, one group was allowed to eat as much as they wanted, while others maintained on the same diet had their caloric intake substantially reduced—by between 25% and 65% in various studies.

The effects of calorie-restriction are the second kind of evidence that *ad libitum* levels of consumption are unhealthy. Their results have been remarkably consistent (see Bucci, 1992; Masoro, 1988; Weindruch, 1996; Weindruch & Walford, 1988): In experiment after experiment, substantial reductions in the caloric intake of balanced diets have improved numerous indices of health and increased longevity. For example, in one experiment (Weindruch et al., 1986), groups of mice had their caloric intake of a well-balanced commercial diet reduced by either 25%, 55%, or 65% after weaning. The results indicated that all levels of dietary restriction substantially improved health and increased longevity. Moreover, the greater the degree of dietary restriction, the greater the observed improvements in health; those mice that consumed the least had the lowest incidence of cancer, the best immune responses, and the greatest maximum life span—they lived 67% longer than did subjects that ate as much as they liked.

One surprising point about the results of the *calorie-restriction experiments:* They suggested that the health benefits of restricted diets are not entirely attributable to loss of body fat (see Weindruch, 1996). The subjects were not frankly obese when they commenced their calorie-reduced diets, and thus they did not lose a lot of weight; moreover, there was no correlation between the amount of weight loss and degree of improved health. The current thinking is that some by-product of energy consumption accumulates in cells and accelerates aging with all its attendant health problems (Sohal & Weindruch, 1996).

Please stop and think about the implications of these amazing calorie-restriction experiments. They are not well known in psychology because many were published in agriculture or nutrition journals.

■ **REGULATION OF BODY WEIGHT BY CHANGES IN THE EFFICIENCY OF ENERGY UTILIZATION** Implicit in many set-point theories is the premise that body weight is largely a function of how much a person eats. Of course, how much we eat plays a role in our body weight, but it is now clear that the body controls its fat levels, to a large degree, by changing the efficiency with which it uses energy. As a person's level of body fat declines, that person starts to use energy resources more efficiently, which limits further weight loss (see Martin, White, & Hulsey, 1991); conversely, weight gain is limited by a progressive decrease in the efficiency of energy utilization. Rothwell and Stock (1982) created a group of obese rats by maintaining them on a cafeteria diet, and they found that the resting level of energy expenditure in these obese rats was 45% greater than in control rats.

This point is illustrated by the progressively declining effectiveness of weight-loss programs. Initially, low-calorie diets produce substantial weight loss. But the rate of weight loss diminishes with each successive week on the diet, until an equilibrium is achieved and little or no further weight loss occurs. Most dieters are familiar with this disappointing trend. A similar effect occurs with weight-gain programs (see Figure 10.13 on page 266).

The mechanism by which the body adjusts the efficiency of its energy utilization in response to its levels of body fat has been termed **diet-induced thermogenesis.** Increases in the levels of body fat produce increases in body temperature, which require additional energy to maintain them—and decreases in the level of body fat have the opposite effects.

There are major differences among subjects both in their **basal metabolic rate** and their ability to adjust their metabolic rate in response to changes in the levels of body fat. We all know people who remain slim even though they eat gluttonously. However, the research on calorie-restricted diets suggests that these people may not eat with impunity: There may be a health cost to pay for overeating even in the absence of obesity.

Set Points and Settling Points in Weight Control

Many investigators (see Booth, Fuller & Lewis, 1981; Wirtshafter & Davis, 1977) believe that eating is not part of a system that is designed to defend a body-fat

---

Diet-induced thermogenesis. The homeostasis-defending increases in body temperature that are associated with increases in body fat.

Basal metabolic rate. The rate at which resting individuals utilize energy to maintain their bodily processes.

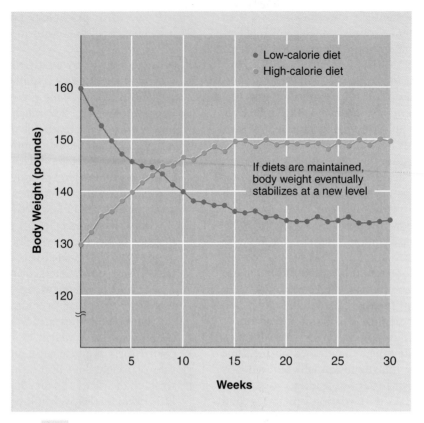

Figure 10.13 The diminishing effect on body weight of a low-calorie diet and a high-calorie diet.

set point. They argue that body weight tends to drift around a natural **settling point**—the level at which the various factors that influence body weight achieve an equilibrium. The idea is that as body-fat levels increase, changes occur that tend to limit further increases until a balance is achieved between all factors that encourage weight gain and all those that discourage it.

The settling-point model provides a loose kind of homeostatic regulation, without a set-point mechanism or mechanisms to return body weight to a set point. According to the settling-point model, body weight remains stable as long as there are no long-term changes in the factors that influence it; and if there are such changes, their impact is limited by negative feedback. In the settling-point model, the feedback merely limits further changes in the same direction, whereas in the set-point model, negative feedback triggers a return to the set point. A neuron's resting potential is a well-known biological settling point—see Chapter 4.

The seductiveness of the set-point theory is attributable in no small part to the existence of the thermostat model, which provides a vivid means of thinking about it. Figure 10.14 is a model that I like to use to think about the settling-point theory. I call it the **leaky-barrel model.** It is an analogy: (1) The amount of water entering the hose is analogous to the amount of food available to the subject; (2) the water pressure at the nozzle is analogous to the positive incentive value

of the available food; (3) the amount of water entering the barrel is analogous to the amount of energy consumed; (4) the water level in the barrel is analogous to the level of body fat; (5) the amount of water leaking from the barrel is analogous to the amount of energy being expended; and (6) the weight of the barrel on the hose is analogous to the strength of the satiety signal.

The main advantage of the settling-point theory of body weight regulation over the body-fat set-point theory is that it is more consistent with the data. Another advantage is that in those cases in which both theories make the same prediction, the settling-point theory does so more parsimoniously—that is, with a simpler mechanism that requires fewer assumptions. Let's use the leaky-barrel model to see how the two theories account for four key facts of weight regulation.

Fact 1: Body weight remains relatively constant in many adult animals. On the basis of this fact, it has been argued that body fat must be regulated around a set point. However, constant body weight does not require, or even imply, a set point. Consider the leaky-barrel model. As water from the tap begins to fill the barrel, the weight of the water in the barrel increases. This increases the amount of water leaking out of the barrel and decreases the amount of water entering the barrel by increasing the pressure of the barrel on the hose. Eventually,

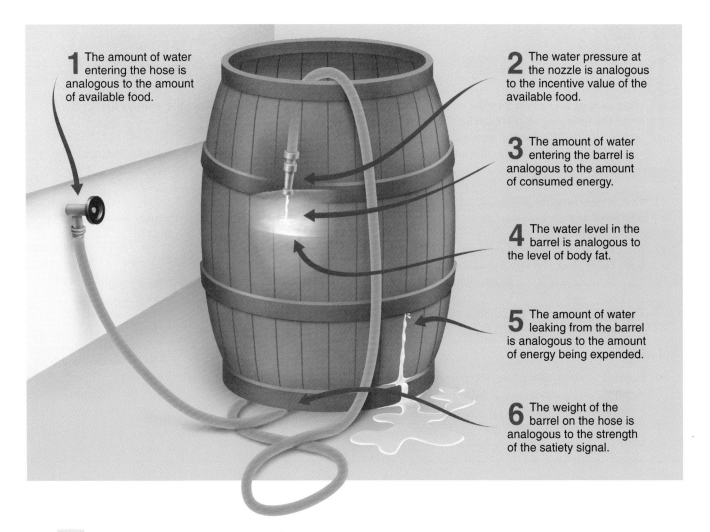

1. The amount of water entering the hose is analogous to the amount of available food.

2. The water pressure at the nozzle is analogous to the incentive value of the available food.

3. The amount of water entering the barrel is analogous to the amount of consumed energy.

4. The water level in the barrel is analogous to the level of body fat.

5. The amount of water leaking from the barrel is analogous to the amount of energy being expended.

6. The weight of the barrel on the hose is analogous to the strength of the satiety signal.

Figure 10.14 The leaky-barrel model: A settling-point model of eating and body weight homeostasis.

this system settles into an equilibrium where the water level stays constant; but because this level is neither predetermined nor actively defended, it is a settling point, not a set point.

Fact 2: Many adult animals experience enduring changes in body weight. Set-point systems are designed to maintain internal constancy in the face of fluctuations of the external environment. Thus the fact that many adult animals experience long-term changes in body weight is a strong argument against the set-point theory. In contrast, the settling-point theory predicts that when there is an enduring change in one of the parameters that affect body weight—for example, a major increase in the positive-incentive value of available food—body weight will drift to a new settling point.

Fact 3: If a subject's intake of food is reduced, metabolic changes occur that limit the loss of weight; the opposite occurs when the subject overeats. This fact is often cited as evidence for set-point regulation of body weight; however, because the metabolic changes merely limit further weight changes

rather than eliminating those that have occurred, they are more consistent with a settling-point model. For example, when water intake in the leaky-barrel model is reduced, the water level in the barrel begins to drop; but the drop is limited by a decrease in leakage and an increase in inflow attributable to the falling water pressure in the barrel. Eventually, a new settling point is achieved, but the reduction in water level is not as great as one might expect because of the loss-limiting changes.

Fact 4: After an individual has lost a substantial amount of weight (by dieting, exercise, or even **lipectomy**—the surgical removal of fat), there is a tendency for the original weight to be regained once the subject returns to the previous eating- and energy-related lifestyle. Although this finding is often offered as

---

Settling point. The point at which various factors that influence the level of some regulated function achieve an equilibrium.

Leaky-barrel model. A settling-point model of body-fat regulation.

Lipectomy. The surgical removal of body fat.

Before moving on to Part 2 of the chapter, complete the following review exercise. The correct answers are provided at the bottom of this page. Before proceeding, review material related to your incorrect answers and omissions.

1. The primary function of the _____ is to serve as a storage reservoir for undigested food.

2. Most of the absorption of nutrients into the body takes place through the wall of the _____, or upper intestine.

3. The phase of energy metabolism that is triggered by the expectation of food is the _____ phase.

4. During the absorptive phase, the pancreas releases much _____ into the bloodstream.

5. During the fasting phase, the primary fuels of the body are _____.

6. During the fasting phase, the primary fuel of the brain is _____.

7. The three components of a set-point system are a set-point mechanism, a detector, and an _____.

8. The theory that hunger and satiety are regulated by a blood glucose set point is the _____ theory.

9. The evidence suggests that hunger is a function of the current _____ value of food.

10. The evidence supports a _____ model of body weight regulation rather than a set-point model.

---

irrefutable evidence of a body weight set point, the settling-point theory readily accounts for it. When the water level in the leaky-barrel model is reduced—by temporarily decreasing input (dieting), by temporarily increasing output (exercising), or by scooping out some of the water (lipectomy)—only a temporary drop in the settling point is produced. When the original conditions are reinstated, the water level inexorably drifts back to the original settling point.

Does it really matter whether we think about body weight regulation in terms of set points or settling points—or is it just splitting hairs? It certainly matters

to biopsychologists: Understanding that body weight is regulated by a settling-point system helps them better understand and more accurately predict the changes in body weight that are likely to occur in various situations; it also indicates the kinds of physiological mechanisms that are likely to mediate them. And it should matter to you. If the set-point theory is correct, attempting to change your body weight would be a waste of time; you would inevitably be drawn back to your body weight set point. On the other hand, the leaky-barrel model suggests that it is possible to permanently change your body weight by permanently changing any of the factors that influences energy intake and output.

PART 2 / THIRST, DRINKING, AND BODY FLUID REGULATION

Part 2 of the chapter focuses on the biopsychology of thirst, drinking, and body fluid regulation. Most research on drinking is based on the premise that drinking is motivated by a deficit in the body's water resources. Like eating, some drinking is motivated by

internal deficits, but most is not. This part of the chapter begins with an introduction to the regulation of the body's fluid resources. Then, it discusses the regulation of deprivation-induced drinking and drinking in the absence of water deficits.

The answers are (1) stomach, (2) duodenum, (3) cephalic, (4) insulin, (5) free fatty acids, (6) glucose, (7) effector, (8) glucostatic, (9) positive-incentive, and (10) settling-point.

10.6 Regulation of the Body's Fluid Resources

Intracellular and Extracellular Fluid Compartments

As Figure 10.15 indicates, about two-thirds of the body's water is inside cells (*intracellular*), and about one-third is outside (*extracellular*). The water found in the extracellular compartment is in the *interstitial fluid* (the fluid in which the cells are bathed), the *blood,* and the *cerebrospinal fluid.*

Normally, the fluids in the intracellular and extracellular body fluid compartments are **isotonic solutions**—solutions of equal concentration to one another. In other words, the proportion of the intracellular fluid that is composed of *solutes* (substances dissolved in a fluid) is normally the same as the proportion of the extracellular fluid that is composed of solutes.

In the isotonic state there is no tendency for the water inside cells to be drawn out of cells, or for water in the interstitial fluid to be drawn into cells. However, if the fluid in one of the compartments is made more concentrated than the other by the addition of solutes to it or by the removal of water from it, the more concentrated fluid draws water from the less concentrated fluid through the cell membranes until the isotonicity of the fluids is reestablished. Conversely, if the concentration of the solution in one of the compartments is decreased by the addition of water to it or by the removal of solutes from it, water is drawn from it into the other compartment. The pressure that draws water from less concentrated solutions (**hypotonic solutions**) through semipermeable membranes into more-concentrated solutions (**hypertonic solutions**) is called **osmotic pressure** (see Figure 10.16 on page 270).

Isotonic solutions. Solutions that contain the same concentration of solutes as some reference solution.

Hypotonic solutions. Solutions that are less concentrated than some reference solution.

Hypertonic solutions. Solutions that are more concentrated than some reference solution.

Osmotic pressure. The pressure that draws water from a hypotonic solution to a hypertonic solution.

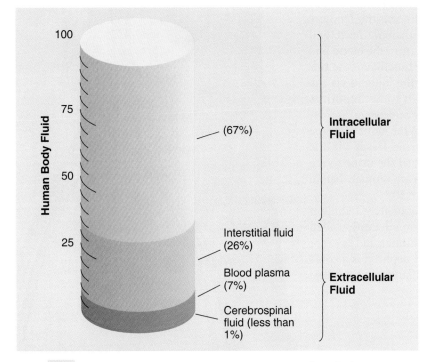

Figure 10.15 The proportion of fluid normally present in each of the fluid compartments of the human body.

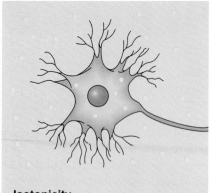

Isotonicity

The intracellular and extracellular fluids of the body are normally isotonic to one another; that is, they contain the same concentration of solutes. As a result, there is normally little or no osmotic pressure drawing water into or out of cells.

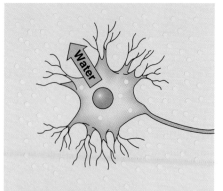

Hypertonicity

The extracellular fluid is rendered hypertonic to the intracellular fluid by the addition of solutes to the extracellular fluid or by the removal of water from it. This creates an osmotic pressure (see arrow) that draws water out of cells until isotonicity is reestablished.

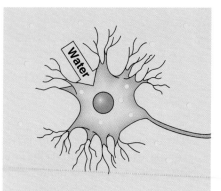

Hypotonicity

The extracellular fluid is rendered hypotonic to the intracellular fluid by the removal of solutes from the extracellular fluid or by the addition of water to it. This creates an osmotic pressure (see arrow) that draws water into cells until isotonicity is reestablished.

Figure 10.16 Isotonicity, hypertonicity, hypotonicity, and osmotic pressure.

The Kidneys: Regulation of Water and Sodium Levels

Sodium is the major solute in body fluids. Thus the regulation of water and sodium levels is intimately related. The regulation of the body's water and sodium resources is reasonably straightforward. We normally consume far more water and sodium than we need, and the excess is drawn from the blood and excreted. This is the function of the *kidneys*. Blood enters the kidneys via the *renal arteries*, where various impurities and excess sodium and water are extracted. Blood leaves the kidneys via the *renal veins*, and urine leaves via the *ureters*, which channel the urine to the *bladder* for temporary storage before excretion (see Figure 10.17).

There are approximately 1 million independent functional units, called *nephrons*, in each human kidney (see Figure 10.18). Each nephron is a complex tangle of capillaries and tubules.

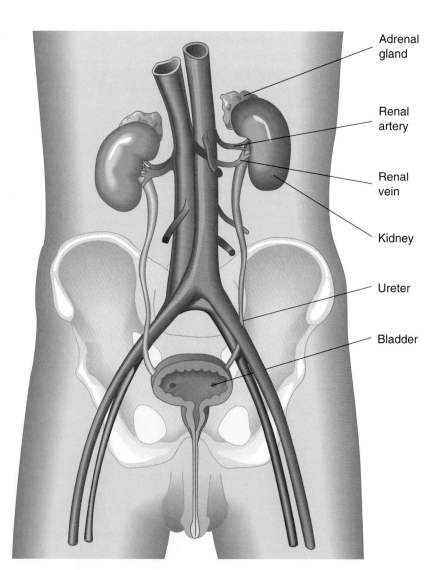

Adrenal gland

Renal artery

Renal vein

Kidney

Ureter

Bladder

Figure 10.17 The kidneys. Blood enters through the renal arteries; blood and urine exit through the renal veins and ureters, respectively.

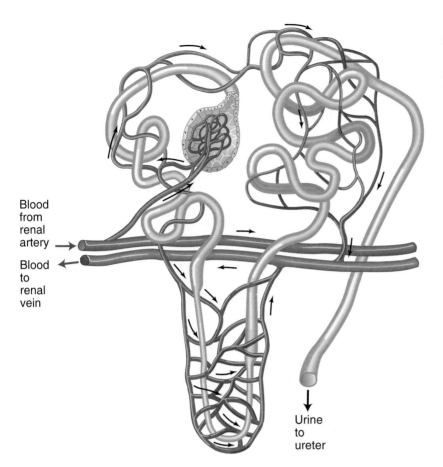

Figure 10.18 A nephron. There are approximately 1 million nephrons in each human kidney; each nephron absorbs water, sodium, and waste from the blood.

Blood from renal artery →

Blood to renal vein ←

Urine to ureter

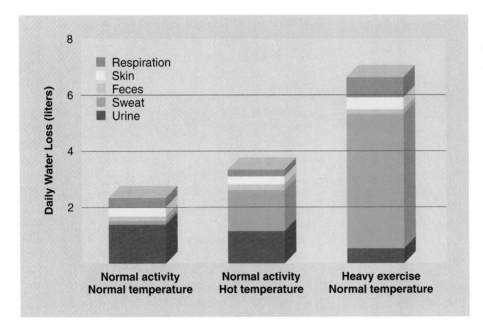

Figure 10.19 Sources of water loss from the human body.

(Adapted from Guyton, 1987.)

Daily Water Loss (liters)

■ Respiration
□ Skin
■ Feces
■ Sweat
■ Urine

Normal activity
Normal temperature

Normal activity
Hot temperature

Heavy exercise
Normal temperature

Excess water and sodium pass from the capillaries to the tubules and then to the ureters.

Urination is not the only mechanism of water loss. Significant quantities of water are also lost by perspiration, respiration, defecation, and evaporation through the skin (see Figure 10.19).

Regular water consumption is important for our survival because we humans lose water at a high rate and have a limited capacity to store excess water. In this sense, drinking is different than eating. Most people can live for many weeks without eating, but few can survive more than a few days without water.

Deprivation-Induced Drinking: Cellular Dehydration and Hypovolemia

When the body's water resources decrease significantly, the body reacts in two ways: Steps are taken to conserve the body's declining water resources, and there are increases in thirst. Two different physiological systems mediate deprivation-induced drinking: one that is sensitive to reductions in intracellular fluid volume and one that is sensitive to reductions in blood volume. A reduction in intracellular fluid volume is called **cellular dehydration** and a reduction in blood volume is called **hypovolemia.**

Cellular Dehydration and Thirst

As the bartenders who supply free salted nuts well know, salt (sodium chloride) makes one thirsty. The thirst produced by salty food is caused by cellular dehydration. Because salt does not readily pass into cells, it accumulates in the extracellular fluid, making it hypertonic and drawing water from cells into the interstitial fluid. Salt consumption has little effect on blood volume.

Cellular dehydration is usually induced in experimental animals through the injection of hypertonic solutions of salt or other solutes that do not readily pass through cell membranes (see Fitzsimons, 1972; Gilman, 1937). It can also be produced by depriving subjects of water. But because water deprivation also reduces the volume of water in the extracellular compartment, researchers interested specifically in the role of cellular dehydration usually study drinking in response to the injection of hypertonic solutions.

Most of the research on cellular dehydration has been aimed at locating the cells in the body that are responsible for detecting it. The cells that detect cellular dehydration are called **osmoreceptors.**

Evidence that osmoreceptors in the brain play a role in drinking comes from studies in which hypertonic solutions have been injected into the *carotid arteries* (arteries of the neck, which carry blood to the brain) of nondeprived animals. In one study, solutions of sodium chloride were bilaterally infused through the carotid arteries of nondeprived dogs

at concentrations that increased cerebral osmolarity without having a significant effect on the osmolarity of the body as a whole (Wood, Rolls, & Ramsay, 1977). Figure 10.20 shows that the infusions increased the dogs' water consumption during a subsequent 5-minute test and that the amount of water consumed during the test was a function of the concentration of the infused solution.

Many different kinds of studies have indicated that osmoreceptors are located in two adjacent areas of the brain: the *lamina terminalis,* a layer of structures located in the anterior wall of the third ventricle, and the adjacent *supraoptic nucleus* of the hypothalamus (see McKinley, Pennington, & Oldfield, 1996). The location of these two groups of osmoreceptors in the rat brain is illustrated in Figure 10.21.

There are two mechanisms by which osmoreceptors induce thirst: one direct and one indirect. The direct mechanism is a neural mechanism: Cellular dehydration causes the osmoreceptors to activate neural circuits that mediate the experience of thirst. The indirect mechanism is a hormonal mechanism: Cellular dehydration causes osmoreceptors to increase the release of **antidiuretic hormone (ADH)** from the posterior pituitary, and the increase in ADH levels triggers a sequence of events that results in conservation of the body's

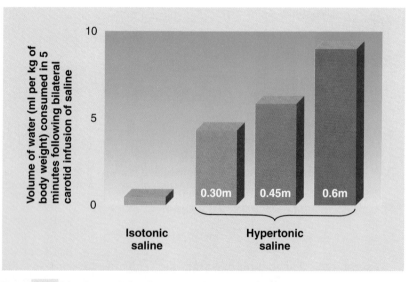

Figure 10.20 Nondeprived dogs began to drink when hypertonic sodium chloride solutions were infused through their carotid arteries. The greater the concentration of the solution, the more they drank.

(Adapted from Rolls & Rolls, 1982.)

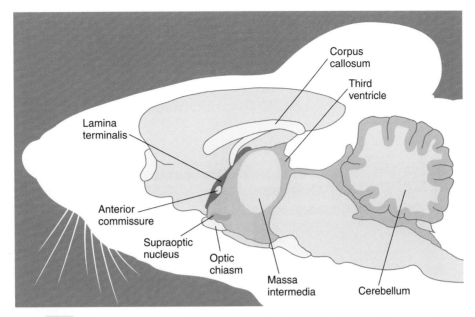

Figure 10.21 The lamina terminalis and supraoptic nucleus of the hypothalamus: Two areas that contain osmoreceptors. The location of these areas is illustrated in the rat brain, where they have been most frequently studied.

dwindling water resources and an increase in thirst. Different osmoreceptors seem to control the direct and indirect mechanisms of thirst induced by cellular dehydration; intracerebral injections of hypertonic solutions that induce drinking do not always increase ADH levels, and vice versa.

Hypovolemia and Thirst

As noted earlier in this section, in addition to producing cellular dehydration, water deprivation produces hypovolemia—a reduction in blood volume. Hypovolemia, like cellular dehydration, is an important stimulus for deprivation-induced thirst. It is selectively induced in experimental animals in one of two ways. One method is to withdraw blood from the subjects; the other is to inject a colloid substance into the peritoneal cavity. *Colloids* are gluelike substances with molecules much too large to pass through cell membranes. Thus colloids injected into the peritoneum stay there and, like sponges, draw blood plasma out of the circulatory system by osmotic pressure. Neither bleeding nor colloid injections change the osmolarity of the extracellular fluid; thus they reduce blood volume without producing cellular dehydration.

Hypovolemia is detected by **baroreceptors** (blood pressure receptors) in the wall of the heart and by **blood-flow receptors** (receptors that monitor the volume of blood flow) in the kidneys. When blood volume decreases, both the baroreceptors and the blood-flow receptors trigger changes in the kidneys that increase both thirst and the conservation of the body's water re-

sources. The baroreceptors influence kidney function by increasing the release of ADH; the blood-flow receptors influence kidney function directly.

The mechanisms by which cellular dehydration and hypovolemia increase thirst and elicit physiological reactions that conserve the body's water reserves are outlined in the following paragraphs. They are also illustrated in Figure 10.22 on page 274.

Effects of Antidiuretic Hormone

Water deprivation causes both the hypothalamic osmoreceptors and the heart baroreceptors to increase the release of antidiuretic hormone from the posterior pituitary. The ADH influences kidney function in two different ways: by reducing the volume of urine produced by the kidneys and by increasing the release of **renin** from the kidneys. The release of renin is also stimulated during water deprivation by the activity of the renal (kidney) blood-flow receptors.

Cellular dehydration. Reduction in intracellular fluid volume.

Hypovolemia. Decreased blood volume.

Osmoreceptors. Receptors sensitive to dehydration.

Antidiuretic hormone (ADH). A hormone released from the posterior pituitary that encourages the conservation of body fluids by decreasing the volume of urine produced by the kidneys; also called vasopressin.

Baroreceptors. Blood pressure receptors.

Blood-flow receptors. Receptors that monitor the volume of blood flowing through the kidneys.

Renin. A hormone that is released from the kidneys in response to increasing ADH levels or decreasing signals from cardiac baroreceptors and that stimulates the synthesis of angiotensin II.

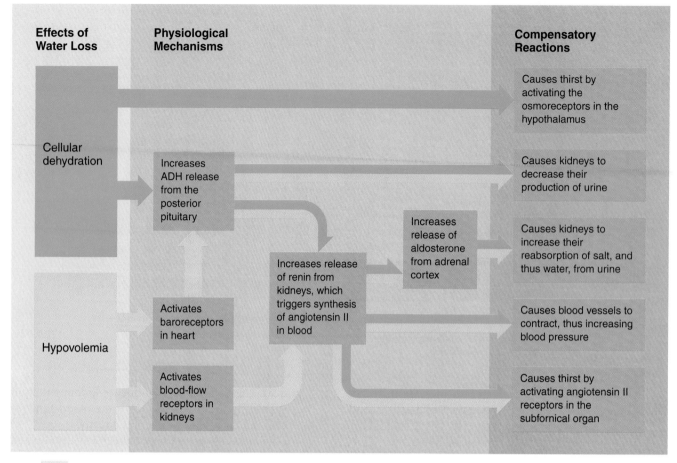

Effects of Water Loss

Physiological Mechanisms

Compensatory Reactions

Cellular dehydration

Hypovolemia

Increases ADH release from the posterior pituitary

Activates baroreceptors in heart

Activates blood-flow receptors in kidneys

Increases release of renin from kidneys, which triggers synthesis of angiotensin II in blood

Increases release of aldosterone from adrenal cortex

Causes thirst by activating the osmoreceptors in the hypothalamus

Causes kidneys to decrease their production of urine

Causes kidneys to increase their reabsorption of salt, and thus water, from urine

Causes blood vessels to contract, thus increasing blood pressure

Causes thirst by activating angiotensin II receptors in the subfornical organ

Figure 10.22 The effects of cellular dehydration and hypovolemia.

The increase of circulating renin causes the formation in the blood of the peptide hormone **angiotensin II,** and the angiotensin II in turn produces a compensatory increase in blood pressure by constricting the peripheral blood vessels and triggering the release of aldosterone from the adrenal cortexes. **Aldosterone** causes the kidneys to reabsorb much of the sodium that would otherwise have been lost in the urine. The maintenance of high levels of sodium in the blood is critical for the prevention of further decreases in blood volume; the higher the concentration of sodium in the blood, the more water the blood will retain.

Angiotensin II and Drinking

The discovery that the intraperitoneal injection of kidney extracts causes rats to drink suggested that the kidneys produce a **dipsogen**—a substance that induces drinking. This dipsogen proved to be the peptide angiotensin II, which is synthesized in the blood in response to cellular dehydration or hypovolemia. In many species, infusion of angiotensin II increases drinking without influencing other motivated behaviors (e.g., Fitzsimons & Simons, 1969).

Much of the research on the dipsogenic effect of angiotensin II has been directed at discovering its site of action in the brain. Two early clues focused attention on the **subfornical organ** (**SFO**)—the most dorsal structure of the lamina terminalis (see Figure 10.21). The first clue was that the subfornical organ is one of only a small number of sites in the brain that are not protected from blood-borne angiotensin II by the *blood–brain barrier.* The second clue was that intraventricular infusions of angiotensin II proved to be particularly effective in inducing drinking.

The following four findings subsequently confirmed the hypothesis that the subfornical organ is the site of the angiotensin II receptors that mediate hypovolemic drinking: (1) Microinjections of angiotensin II into the subfornical organ reliably elicit drinking (e.g., Simpson & Routtenberg, 1973). (2) *Saralasin,* a blocker of angiotensin II receptors, blocks the dipsogenic action of intraventricular injections of angiotensin II (Fitzsimons, Epstein, & Johnson, 1978). (3) Destruction of the subfornical organ blocks the drinking induced by intravenous injection of angiotensin II (Simpson, Epstein, & Camardo, 1978). (4) Neurons in the subfornical organ display dose-dependent increases in firing in response to microinjections of angiotensin II (Phillips & Felix, 1976).

Binding studies have shown that angiotensin II receptors exist in parts of the lamina terminalis other than the subfornical organ. It has been suggested that the cerebral angiotensin II receptors outside the subfornical organ may play a related role in salt appetite rather than thirst (Fitts & Masson, 1990). Those angiotensin II receptors located in parts of the lamina terminalis that are protected by the blood–brain barrier are assumed to respond specifically to the angiotensin II released from nerve terminals, rather than that carried in the blood.

Drinking Produced by Naturally Occurring Water Deficits

As you may have gathered from the preceding two subsections, the dipsogenic effects of intracellular and extracellular dehydration are usually studied independently of one another. However, because water deprivation simultaneously reduces the water in both the intracellular and extracellular fluid compartments, the key to understanding the drinking that results from naturally occurring water shortages lies in understanding the interaction of the deficits in the two compartments.

Rolls and her colleagues (e.g., Ramsay, Rolls, & Wood, 1977; Rolls, Wood, & Rolls, 1980) have studied the relative effects on drinking of intracellular and extracellular fluid deficits after overnight water deprivation. They injected their water-deprived subjects (rats, dogs, and monkeys) with either water or isotonic saline. The water, because it was hypotonic, was quickly taken up by the dehydrated cells; thus it eliminated the intracellular deficit without substantially influencing the extracellular deficit. Conversely, the saline, because it was isotonic, was not taken up by cells to any significant degree; thus it eliminated the extracellular deficit without substantially influencing the intracellular deficit. The elimination of the intracellular deficit reduced the drinking of the water-deprived subjects by about 75%, and the elimination of the extracellular deficit reduced drinking by about 15% (Rolls & Rolls, 1982).

10.8 Spontaneous Drinking: Drinking in the Absence of Water Deficits

Like the study of eating, the study of drinking has until recently focused almost exclusively on deficit-induced consumption. Water deficits are powerful motivators, and understanding how their motivating effects are mediated is important. However, it is also important not to lose sight of the fact that most drinking—like most eating—occurs in the absence of deficits (see Rowland, 1990a). Drinking in the absence of fluid deficits is called **spontaneous drinking.**

The fact that drinking regularly occurs in the absence of water deficits suggests that drinking is motivated by the *positive-incentive properties* of potential beverages—that is, that the motivation to drink comes from the anticipated pleasurable effects of the drinking. We tend to prefer drinks that have a pleasurable flavor (e.g., fruit juice, soda, milk) or a pleasurable pharmacologic effect (e.g., beer, coffee, tea)—or, better yet, both. According to the positive-incentive theory of drinking, water deprivation increases the positive-incentive value of virtually all salt-free beverages; after 24 hours of water deprivation, human subjects report that water itself has a pleasant taste (Rolls et al., 1980).

Flavor

The effects of flavor on drinking can be demonstrated by simply adding a bit of saccharin to the water of nondeprived rats. Their water intake skyrockets (Rolls, Wood, & Stevens, 1978). Conversely, there is a substantial decrease in fluid consumption if the palatability of a rat's water supply is reduced by the addition of a small amount of quinine to it. When rats were maintained for 60 days with quinine-adulterated water as their only source of fluid, their fluid intake decreased substantially,

---

Angiotensin II. A peptide dipsogen hormone that is synthesized in the blood in response to either cellular dehydration or hypovolemia.

Aldosterone. The hormone that is released from the adrenal cortexes in response to angiotensin II and that causes the kidneys to reabsorb much of the sodium that would otherwise be lost in the urine.

Dipsogen. A substance that induces drinking.

Subfornical organ (SFO). The most dorsal midline structure of the lamina terminalis; it is the site of the angiotensin II receptors that mediate the dipsogenic effects of angiotensin II.

Spontaneous drinking. Drinking in the absence of fluid deficits; most drinking is spontaneous drinking.

but there were no signs of ill health (Nicolaïdis & Rowland, 1975). Like humans, rats with unlimited access to water or other palatable fluids drink far more than they need.

Food

Water is required for the digestion and metabolism of food. Consequently, drinking often occurs in association with eating. Rats, for example, drink about 70% of their total water intake during meals; they drink little when they are food-deprived. Eating-related drinking is greater when the food is dry and when it is protein-rich—proteins draw large amounts of water out of the body into the digestive tract.

The release of insulin, which is associated with food consumption, may be a factor in eating-related drinking. Insulin injections have been shown to increase drinking in both rats (Novin, 1964) and humans (Brime et al., 1991).

Learning

Animals normally drink to prevent water deficits, not just to correct them. They generally drink more water than they need, and they learn to increase their drinking in anticipation of water deficits. Human joggers learn to drink before starting out on a hot day, and rats learn to drink in response to an odor that has been repeatedly paired with a subcutaneous injection of formalin, which induces temporary hypovolemia (Weisinger, 1975).

Fitzsimons and LeMagnen (1969) studied the increased water consumption of rats forced to shift to a high-protein diet. Initially, the increased drinking occurred long after the protein meal was consumed, presumably in response to the hypovolemia it created. But eventually, copious drinking occurred with each meal, rather than after. Apparently, the rats had learned to adjust their water intake to prevent the protein-produced dehydration.

10.9 Drinking and Satiety

What terminates a bout of drinking? Set-point theories suggest that it is a return to internal water-resource set points. There are three problems with this idea. The first is that the elimination of water deficits could not possibly be responsible for terminating drinking that is initiated in the absence of water deficits. The second is that even when drinking is triggered by water deprivation, it usually stops before the water has been absorbed into the body from the gastrointestinal tract. The third is that when water or other palatable liquids are readily available, animals drink far more than they need. In one study (Dicker & Nunn, 1957), rats were maintained on a daily water ration that was only about 60% of the amount they consumed when they could drink as much as they wanted to drink; urine excretion was reduced, and the rats remained healthy.

Sham Drinking

Sham-drinking preparations have been used to study the contribution of oral factors to satiety. In their first postdeprivation bout of **sham drinking,** most animals sham drink an amount that is proportional to the length of the preceding period of water deprivation; longer pe-

riods of water deprivation produce more sham drinking (see Blass & Hall, 1976), despite the fact that the water exits the gastrointestinal tract through a fistula before it can be absorbed. This result could reflect the fact that longer periods of water deprivation produce greater increases in the positive-incentive value of water.

To what degree do injections of water into the stomach or bloodstream reduce the duration of postdeprivation drinking bouts? In rats, infusions of water directly into the stomach or into the bloodstream reduced deprivation-induced drinking by only 30% of the amount injected (e.g., Rowland & Nicolaïdis, 1976); even total replenishment of an animal's water resources has only a modest inhibitory effect on deprivation-induced drinking. These findings are troublesome for any theory of satiety that is based on the

Sham drinking. The experimental protocol in which an animal drinks and swallows a fluid, which immediately exits its body through a tube implanted in its esophagus.

Saccharin elation effect. The increase in saccharin preference that occurs in nondeprived ani-

mals following a temporary interruption of access to saccharin solutions.

Schedule-induced polydipsia. Grossly excessive drinking that occurs in animals that receive a small pellet of food every minute or so.

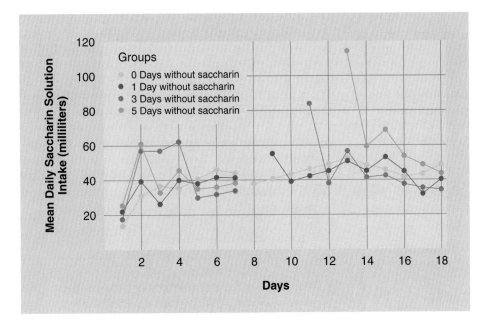

Figure 10.23 The saccharin elation effect. Four groups of rats had continuous access to water and a saccharin solution for 8 days. Then, the saccharin solution was withdrawn for 0, 1, 3, or 5 days, but the rats continued to have free access to water. Longer periods of saccharin withdrawal produced greater increases in saccharin drinking once saccharin access was reinstated.

(Adapted from Pinel & Rovner, 1977.)

premise that bouts of drinking are terminated by a return to internal fluid set points.

Drinking and Sensory-Specific Satiety

Sensory-specific satiety has a major effect on drinking—as it does on eating. This has been demonstrated in two ways. The first is by showing that animals display less preference for a beverage when it is continuously available than they do for the same beverage when it is only periodically available. For example, Figure 10.23 illustrates a phenomenon known as the **saccharin elation effect:** Rats living with continuous access to water and a saccharin solution consume large amounts of the saccharin solution, but they consume even more of it after the saccharin solution has been withdrawn for several days (e.g., Pinel & Rovner, 1977).

The second way the effect of sensory-specific satiety on drinking has been demonstrated is by showing that animals drink more when they have access to a variety of beverages. For example, Rolls and Wood (cited in Rolls, Wood, & Rolls, 1980) offered nondeprived rats access to water for 1 hour, to water with an artificial flavor added to it for 1 hour, or to water with a different artificial flavor added to it every 15 minutes during the hour. As Figure 10.24 illustrates, the addition of one flavor to the water increased intake by 88%, whereas the availability of four flavors in sequence increased intake by 182%.

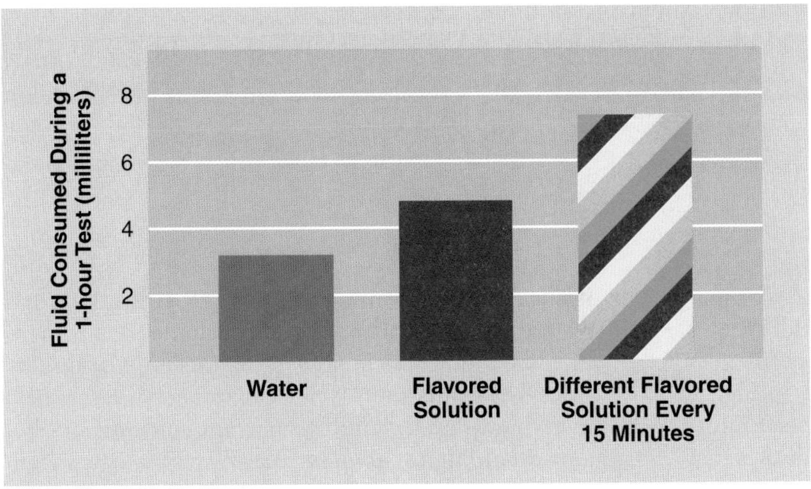

Grossly excessive drinking is referred to as *polydipsia*. One method of inducing polydipsia, as you have just seen, is to provide subjects with a variety of palatable beverages. Another is to present a small pellet of food every minute or so to subjects that have continuous access to water (Falk, 1964). In the intervals, the subjects drink huge volumes of water. For example, rats drink about 10 times more than they would if the food were given all at once during the test. This excessive drinking is called **schedule-induced polydipsia.**

Figure 10.24 The effects of variety on the fluid intake of nondeprived rats during a 1-hour test. The rats in one group had access to water for the 1 hour, the rats in another group had access to flavored water for 1 hour, and the rats in a third group were presented with a different flavor of water every 15 minutes for 1 hour.
(Adapted from Rolls, Wood, & Rolls, 1980.)

Before moving on to Part 3 of the chapter, complete the following review exercise. The correct answers are provided at the bottom of this page. Before proceeding, review material related to your incorrect answers and omissions.

1. About two-thirds of the body's water reserves is stored _____ cells.

2. Water is drawn from hypotonic to hypertonic solutions by _____ pressure.

3. Excess water is drawn from the blood by the _____ .

4. Cellular dehydration is detected in the lateral terminalis and supraoptic nucleus by cells called _____ .

5. _____ hormone is a posterior pituitary peptide that decreases urine production.

6. ADH increases the release of _____ from the kidneys.

7. High concentrations of _____ in the blood trigger the formation of angiotensin II.

8. Microinjection of angiotensin II into the _____ elicits drinking.

9. Most drinking in natural situations occurs in the absence of water deficits; such drinking is called _____ drinking.

10. The excessive drinking that is observed when a rat is offered a small pellet of food every minute or so is called schedule-induced _____ .

PART 3 / DISORDERS OF CONSUMPTION

The remainder of the chapter addresses two common human disorders of consumption: obesity and anorexia nervosa. In this chapter, you have learned to think of consumption in terms of incentive values and settling points, rather than deficits and set points. Will these new ways of thinking provide you with insights into these disorders?

10.10 Human Obesity

You have already learned that obesity is currently a major health problem in many parts of the world. What is more distressing is the rate at which the problem is growing; in the United States, for example, its incidence has more than doubled over the last century (see Kuczmarski, 1992). This rapid rate of increase indicates that environmental factors play a significant role in obesity. However, genetic factors also contribute. For example, it was estimated from a sample of U.S. twins that environmental and genetic factors contribute equally to individual differences in body fat in this population (see Price & Gottsman, 1991). Set-point theory is of no help in trying to understand the current epidemic of obesity; according to set-point theory, permanent weight gain should not occur in healthy adults.

Let's begin our analysis of obesity by considering the pressures that are likely to have led to the evolution of our eating and weight-regulation systems. During the course of evolution, inconsistent food supplies were one of the main threats to survival. As a result, the fittest individuals were those who preferred high-calorie foods,

The answers are (1) inside, (2) osmotic, (3) kidneys, (4) osmoreceptors, (5) antidiuretic, (6) renin, (7) renin, (8) subfornical organ, (9) spontaneous, (10) polydipsia.

ate to capacity when food was available, stored as many excess calories as possible in the form of body fat, and used their stores of calories as efficiently as possible. Individuals who did not have these characteristics were unlikely to survive a food shortage, and so these characteristics were passed on to future generations.

Augmenting the effects of evolution has been the development of numerous cultural practices and beliefs that promote consumption. For example, in my culture, it is commonly believed that one should eat three meals per day at regular times, whether one is hungry or not; that food should be the focus of most social gatherings; that meals should be served in courses of progressively increasing palatability; and that salt, sweets (e.g., sugar), and fats (e.g., butter) should be added to foods to improve their flavor and thus increase their consumption.

Each of us possesses an eating and weight-regulation system that evolved to deal effectively with periodic food shortages, and many of us live in cultures whose eating-related practices evolved for the same purpose. However, now we live in an environment that differs from our "natural" environment in critical food-related ways. We now live in an environment in which foods of the highest positive-incentive value are readily and continuously available. The consequence is an appallingly high level of consumption.

Why do some people become obese while others living under the same obesity-promoting conditions do not? At a superficial level, the answer is obvious: Those who are obese are those whose energy intake has grossly exceeded their energy output; those who are slim are those whose energy intake has not grossly exceeded their energy output. While this answer provides little insight, it does serve to emphasize that two kinds of individual differences play a role in obesity: those that lead to differences in energy input and those that lead to differences in energy output. Let's consider one example of each kind. First, on the intake side, Rodin (1985) has shown that obese subjects have a larger cephalic-phase insulin response to the sight, sound, and smell of a sizzling steak than do subjects who have never been obese; large cephalic insulin responses are associated with large decreases in blood glucose and high levels of subsequent food consumption. On the output side, people differ markedly from one another in the degree to which they can dissipate excess energy by diet-induced thermogenesis. In a classic study, Rose and Williams (1961) assessed the food intake of subjects of the same sex, weight, age, height, and activity level. They found that it was not uncommon for one member of a pair to be consuming twice as many calories as the other member without gaining more weight than the other.

Figure 10.25 describes the course of the typical dietary weight-loss program. Most weight-loss programs are unsuccessful in the sense that, as predicted by the

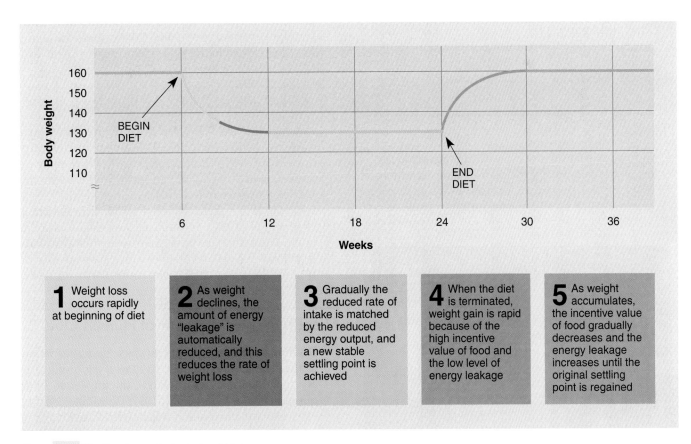

1 Weight loss occurs rapidly at beginning of diet

2 As weight declines, the amount of energy "leakage" is automatically reduced, and this reduces the rate of weight loss

3 Gradually the reduced rate of intake is matched by the reduced energy output, and a new stable settling point is achieved

4 When the diet is terminated, weight gain is rapid because of the high incentive value of food and the low level of energy leakage

5 As weight accumulates, the incentive value of food gradually decreases and the energy leakage increases until the original settling point is regained

Figure 10.25 The five stages of a typical weight-loss program.

settling-point model, most of the lost weight is regained once the program is terminated. Clearly, the key to permanent weight loss is a permanent lifestyle change. People who have difficulty controlling their weight may receive some solace by understanding that the tendency to eat large amounts of food, to accumulate body fat, and to use energy efficiently would all be highly adaptive tendencies in a natural environment. It is our current environment that is "pathological," not the people with weight problems.

Many people believe that exercise is the most effective method of losing weight; however, several studies have shown that exercise contributes little to weight loss (e.g., Sweeney et al., 1993). One reason is that physical activity normally accounts for only a small proportion of total energy expenditure: About 80% of your energy is used to maintain the resting physiological processes of your body and to digest your food (Calles-Escandon & Horton, 1992). Another reason is that after exercise, many people consume drinks and foods that contain more calories than the relatively small number that were expended during the exercise.

Severe cases of obesity are sometimes treated by wiring the jaw shut to limit consumption to liquid diets, stapling part of the stomach together to reduce the size of meals, or cutting out a section of the duodenum to reduce the absorption of nutrients from the gastrointestinal tract. The main problems with jaw wiring are that some patients do not lose weight on a liquid diet and that those who do typically regain it once the wires are removed. Problems with the other two methods include diarrhea, flatulence, vitamin and mineral deficiencies, and *nimiety*—an unpleasant feeling of excessive fullness (*nimius* means "excessive").

Mutant Obese Mice

In 1950, a genetic mutation occurred spontaneously in the mouse colony being maintained in the Jackson Laboratory at Bar Harbor, Maine. This fortuitous development may prove to be the key to understanding and treating extreme forms of human obesity. You see, the rats that were *homozygous* for this mutant gene (ob) were grossly obese, weighing up to three times normal (see Figure 10.26). These homozygous obese mice are commonly referred to as **ob/ob mice.**

Ob/ob mice eat more and convert calories to fat more efficiently than controls, and they use their fat calories more efficiently. Coleman (1979) pointed out that the ob gene would provide humans and other animals carrying it with an ability to withstand prolonged periods of food shortage, and he hypothesized that ob/ob mice lack a critical hormone that normally inhibits fat production.

Leptin: A Negative Feedback Signal from Fat

In 1994, Friedman and his colleagues characterized and cloned the gene that is mutated in ob/ob mice (Zhang et al., 1994). They found that this gene is *expressed* only in fat cells, and they characterized the protein hormone that it encodes. They named this protein **leptin.**

Research has shown that leptin satisfies three criteria of a negative feedback fat signal (Seeley & Schwartz, 1997): (1) levels of leptin in the blood have been found to be positively correlated with fat deposits in humans and other animals (Schwartz et al., 1996a); (2) injections of leptin at doses too low to be aversive have been shown to reduce eating and body fat in ob/ob mice (Campfield et al., 1995); and (3) receptors for leptin have been found in the brain (Schwartz et al., 1996b).

Insulin: Another Adiposity Feedback Signal

Although the discovery of leptin has received substantial publicity, leptin is not the only hormone to satisfy the three criteria of an adiposity negative feedback signal—it wasn't even the first. The pancreatic peptide hormone, insulin, is secreted in relation to levels of adiposity (Seeley et al., 1996); there are receptors for it in the brain (Baura et al., 1993); and infusions of insulin into the brain, at doses too low to be aversive and too low to affect blood glucose levels, reduce eating and body weight (Campfield et al., 1995; Chavez, Seeley, & Woods, 1995).

Leptin in the Treatment of Human Obesity

Do humans, like ob/ob mutant mice, have a mutation to the ob gene, and do they have low levels of the satiety signal leptin? Unfortunately, the answer to both questions is "no" (see Blum, 1997; Considine & Caro, 1996). No genetic mutations have been found in obese patients, and most have high levels of circulating leptin. Moreover, injections of leptin have not reduced the

Figure 10.26 An ob/ob mouse and a control mouse.

body fat of obese patients. These negative findings have focused the attention of researchers on leptin receptors. Perhaps, in obese people, satiety signals from fat may be inhibited by the insensitivity of leptin receptors rather low levels of leptin.

The role of the leptin system in human obesity is currently an active area of research. However, given the number of different factors that can lead to obesity, it is unlikely that a single "cure" will be discovered. Still, the possibilities are intriguing.

 ## Anorexia Nervosa

In contrast to obesity, **anorexia nervosa** is a disorder of underconsumption. Anorexics eat so little that they experience health-threatening weight loss; and despite their grotesquely emaciated appearance, they often perceive themselves as fat. About 50% of anorexics periodically engage in binges of eating, which are usually followed by purging with large doses of laxatives or by self-induced vomiting. Individuals who display the cycles of fasting, bingeing, and purging without the extreme weight loss are said to suffer from **bulimia nervosa.**

The incidence of anorexia nervosa among North American student populations is about 2.5%, with the vast majority of sufferers being female. The relatively high incidence of anorexia nervosa in young females suggests that the current societal emphasis on slimness in women may be responsible for many cases; indeed, many cases begin with severe diets. Supporting this theory is the fact that the rates of anorexia nervosa are highest among groups for whom being slim is most strongly advocated; for example, in one study of ballet dancers, the incidence was close to 10% (Szmukler et al, 1985). Unfortunately, irrespective of reports in the popular press, there are currently no proven effective treatments. In one study, only 29% of treated anorexics had shown significant recovery 20 years later. Approximately 15% die from suicide or starvation (Ratnasuriya et al., 1991).

Anorexics are ambivalent about food. On the one hand, they display a higher than normal cephalic-phase insulin response (Broberg & Bernstein, 1989), and they are often preoccupied with the discussion, purchase, and preparation of food. On the other hand, they rarely experience hunger, they are often afraid of gaining weight, they are often disgusted by fatty tastes, and they often feel ill after a meal.

In a society in which obesity is the main disorder of consumption, anorexics are out of step. People who are struggling to eat less have difficulty feeling empathy for those who are refusing to eat. Still, when you stare anorexia in the face, it is difficult not to be touched by it:

She began by telling me how much she had been enjoying the course and how sorry she was to be dropping out of the uni-

versity. She was articulate and personable, and her grades were first-class. Her problem was anorexia; she weighed only 82 pounds, and she was about to be hospitalized.

"But don't you want to eat?" I asked naively. "Don't you see that your plan to go to medical school will go up in smoke if you don't eat?"

"Of course I want to eat. I know I am terribly thin—my friends tell me I am. Believe me, I know this is wrecking my life. I try to eat, but I just can't force myself. In a strange way, I am pleased with my thinness."

She was upset, and I was embarrassed by my insensitivity. "It's too bad you're dropping out of the course before we cover the chapter on eating," I said, groping for safer ground.

"Oh, I've read it already," she responded. "It's the first chapter I looked at. It had quite an effect on me; a lot of things started to make more sense. The bit about positive incentives and learning was really good. I think my problem began when food started to lose its positive-incentive value for me—in my mind, I kind of associated food with being fat and all the boyfriend problems I was having. This made it easy to diet, but every once in a while I would get so hungry that I would lose control and eat all of the things that I shouldn't. I would eat so much that I would feel ill. So I would put my finger down my throat and make myself throw up. This made me feel a bit better, and it kept me from gaining weight, but I think it taught my body to associate my favorite foods with illness—kind of a conditioned taste aversion. Now, food has less incentive value for me. What do you think of my theory?"

Her insightfulness impressed me; it made me feel all the more sorry that she was going to discontinue her studies.

After a lengthy chat, she got up to leave, and I walked her to the door of my office. I wished her luck and made her promise to come back for a visit. I never saw her again. The image of her emaciated body walking down the hallway from my office has stayed with me.

Ob/ob mice. Mice that are homozygous for the mutant ob gene; their body fat produces no leptin, and they become very obese.

Leptin. A protein normally synthesized in fat cells; it is thought to act as an adiposity signal and reduce consumption.

Anorexia nervosa. An eating disorder that is characterized by a pathological fear of obesity and that results in health-threatening weight loss.

Bulimia nervosa. An eating disorder that is characterized by recurring cycles of fasting, bingeing, and purging without dangerous weight loss.

This student grasped an often misunderstood point about anorexia nervosa. The main question is not what causes anorexics to stop eating—these social pressures are reasonably well understood. The main question is what keeps an overpowering hunger drive from kicking in once they begin to starve; starving people generally think of little other than food, and they are driven to eat and enjoy even the most tasteless of offerings (Keys et al., 1950). Paradoxically, starving people are often made very ill by a meal, and some prisoners of war have been killed by food supplied to them by their rescuers.

CONCLUSION

Part 1 of this chapter focused on hunger, eating, and body weight regulation. In it, you learned about digestion and energy flow in the body (10.1); about set-point and positive-incentive theories of hunger and eating (10.2); about the factors that influence what, when, and how much we eat (10.3); about the neural mechanisms of hunger and satiety (10.4); and about body weight regulation (10.5). Part 2 of the chapter focused on thirst, drinking, and body fluid regulation. In it, you learned about the regulation of the body's fluid resources (10.6); about the roles of cellular dehydration and hypovolemia in deprivation-induced drinking (10.7); about spontaneous drinking (10.8); and about drinking and satiety (10.9). Lastly, Part 3 of the chapter dealt with two common disorders of consumption: obesity (10.10) and anorexia nervosa (10.11).

The primary purpose of this chapter was to provide you with new ways of thinking about ingestive behavior, ways that are more compatible with the evidence than are entrenched set-point theories. My intention was to provide you with some valuable insights into human behavior, particularly your own. Did I succeed?

FOOD FOR THOUGHT

1. Set-point theories suggest that attempts at permanent weight loss are a waste of time. On the basis of what you have learned in this chapter, design an effective weight-loss program.

2. Most of the dietary problems that people in our society face occur because the conditions in which we live are different from those in which our species evolved. Discuss.

3. There are many parallels between the regulation of eating and drinking. Describe some of them.

4. On the basis of what you have learned in this chapter, develop a feeding program for laboratory rats that would lead to obesity. Compare this program with the eating habits prevalent in those cultures in which obesity is currently a problem.

KEY TERMS

Absorptive phase *(p. 251)*
Adipsia *(p. 260)*
Aldosterone *(p. 274)*
Amino acids *(p. 249)*
Angiotensin II *(p. 274)*
Anorexia nervosa *(p. 281)*
Antidiuretic hormone (ADH) *(p. 272)*
Aphagia *(p. 260)*
Appetizer effect *(p. 257)*
Baroreceptors *(p. 273)*
Basal metabolic rate *(p. 265)*
Blood-flow receptors *(p. 273)*
Bulimia nervosa *(p. 281)*
Cafeteria diet *(p. 258)*
Cellular dehydration *(p. 272)*

Cephalic phase *(p. 251)*
Cholecystokinin (CCK) *(p. 262)*
Diet-induced thermogenesis *(p. 265)*
Digestion *(p. 249)*
Dipsogen *(p. 274)*
Duodenum *(p. 262)*
Dynamic phase *(p. 260)*
Fasting phase *(p. 251)*
Free fatty acids *(p. 251)*
Glucagon *(p. 251)*
Gluconeogenesis *(p. 251)*
Glucose *(p. 249)*
Glucostatic theory *(p. 253)*
Homeostasis *(p. 253)*

Hyperphagia *(p. 260)*
Hypertonic solutions *(p. 269)*
Hypotonic solutions *(p. 269)*
Hypovolemia *(p. 272)*
Insulin *(p. 251)*
Isotonic solutions *(p. 269)*
Ketones *(p. 251)*
Lateral hypothalamus (LH) *(p. 259)*
Leaky-barrel model *(p. 266)*
Leptin *(p. 280)*
Lipectomy *(p. 267)*
Lipids *(p. 249)*
Lipogenesis *(p. 260)*
Lipolysis *(p. 260)*
Lipostatic theory *(p. 253)*

Negative feedback systems *(p. 253)*
Nutritive density *(p. 257)*
Ob/ob mice *(p. 280)*
Osmoreceptors *(p. 272)*
Osmotic pressure *(p. 269)*
Paraventricular nuclei *(p. 261)*
Positive-incentive theory *(p. 254)*
Positive-incentive value *(p. 254)*
Renin *(p. 273)*
Saccharin elation effect *(p. 277)*
Satiety *(p. 256)*

ADDITIONAL READING

The following books and articles provide excellent coverage of current research on eating and drinking:

Blum, W. F. (1997). Leptin: The voice of adipose tissue. *Hormone Research, 48,* 2–8.

Brownell, K. D., & Rodin, J. (1994). The dieting maelstrom: Is it possible and advisable to lose weight? *American Psychologist, 49,* 781–791.

Grossman, S. P. (1990). *Thirst and sodium appetite: Physiological basis.* New York: Academic Press.

Leibowitz, S. F. (1992). Neurochemical-neuroendocrine systems in the brain controlling macronutrient intake and metabolism. *Trends in Neuroscience, 15,* 491–497.

Martin, J. R., White, B. D., & Hulsey, M. G. (1991). The regulation of body weight. *American Scientist, 79,* 528–541.

Seeley, R. J., & Schwartz, M. W. (1997). The regulation of energy balance: Peripheral hormonal signals and hypothalamic peptides. *Current Directions in Psychological Science, 6,* 39–44.

Woods, S. C., & Strubbe, J. H. (1994). The psychobiology of meals. *Psychonomic Bulletin & Review, 1,* 141–155.

Weindruch, R. (1996, January). Caloric restriction and aging. *Scientific American, 274,* 46–96.

11

Hormones and Sex

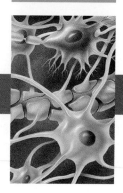

his chapter is about hormones and sex, a topic that fascinates most people. Perhaps it is because we hold our sexuality in such high esteem that we are intrigued by the fact that it is influenced by the secretions of a pair of glands that some regard as unfit topics of conversation. Perhaps it is because we each think of our gender as fundamental and immutable that we are fascinated by the fact that it can be altered with a snip or two and a few hormone injections. Perhaps what fascinates us is the idea that our sex lives might be enhanced by the application of a few hormones. For whatever reason, the topic of hormones and sex is always a hit. Some remarkable things await you in this chapter; let's go directly to them.

Hormones influence sex in two ways: (1) by influencing the development from conception to sexual maturity of the anatomical, physiological, and behavioral characteristics that distinguish one as female or male; and (2) by activating the reproduction-related behavior of sexually mature adults. The *developmental* and *activational* effects of sex hormones are dealt with in the second and third sections of this chapter; the first section prepares you for these topics by introducing the neuroendocrine system. The fourth and fifth sections discuss the role of the hypothalamus in sexual behavior and sexual orientation, respectively.

The Men-Are-Men and Women-Are-Women Attitude

Almost everybody brings to the topic of hormones and sex a piece of excess baggage, the men-are-men and women-are-women attitude—or "mamawawa." This attitude is seductive; it seems so right that we are continually drawn to it without considering alternative views. Unfortunately, it is fundamentally flawed.

The men-are-men and women-are-women attitude is the tendency to think about femaleness and maleness as discrete, mutually exclusive, complementary categories. In thinking about hormones and sex, this general attitude leads one to assume that females have female sex hormones that give them female bodies and make them do female things, and that males have male sex hormones that give them male bodies and make them do opposite male things. Despite the fact that this approach to hormones and sex is totally wrong, its simplicity, symmetry, and comfortable social implications draw us to it. That is why this chapter grapples with it throughout.

11.1 The Neuroendocrine System

This section introduces the general principles of neuroendocrine function by focusing on the glands and hormones that are directly involved in sexual development and behavior. It begins with a few basic facts about hormones, glands, and reproduction; then it describes the line of research that led to our current understanding of neuroendocrine function.

The endocrine glands are illustrated in Figure 11.1 on page 286. By convention, only the organs whose primary function is the release of hormones are referred to as endocrine glands. However, other organs (e.g., the stomach, liver, and intestine) also release hormones into general circulation (see Chapter 10), and they are thus, strictly speaking, also part of the endocrine system.

Glands

There are two types of glands: exocrine glands and endocrine glands. **Exocrine glands** (e.g., sweat glands) release their chemicals into ducts, which carry them to their targets, mostly on the surface of the body. **Endocrine glands** (ductless glands) release their chemicals, which are called **hormones,** directly into the circulatory system. Once released by an endocrine gland, a hormone travels via the circulatory system until it reaches the targets on which it normally exerts its effect (e.g., the skin, other endocrine glands, or sites in the nervous system).

Hormones

Most hormones fall into one of three categories: (1) amino acid derivatives, (2) peptides and proteins,

Exocrine glands. Glands that secrete chemicals into ducts that carry them to the surface of the body.
Endocrine glands. Ductless glands that release hormones into the general circulation of the body.
Hormones. Chemicals released by the endocrine system into general circulation.

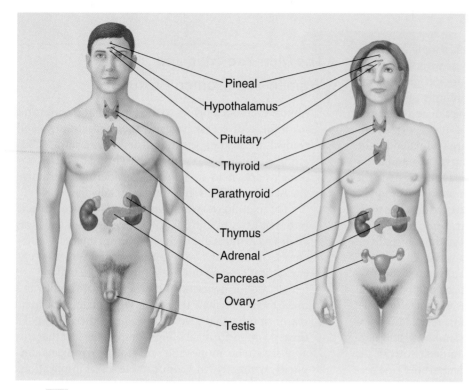

Figure 11.1 The endocrine glands.

cells and *ova*, respectively. After **copulation** (sexual intercourse), a single sperm cell may combine with an *ovum* to form a cell called a **zygote**, which contains all of the information necessary for the normal growth of a complete adult organism in its natural environment.

With the exception of ova and sperm cells, each cell of the human body has 23 pairs of chromosomes. In contrast, the ova and sperm cells contain only half that number, one member of each of the 23 pairs. Thus, when a sperm cell fertilizes an ovum, the resulting zygote ends up with the full complement of 23 pairs of chromosomes, one of each pair from the father and one of each pair from the mother.

Of particular interest in the context of this chapter is the pair of chromosomes called the **sex chromosomes,** so named because they contain the genetic programs that direct sexual development. The cells of females have two large X-shaped sex chromosomes, called *X chromosomes*. In males, one sex chromosome is an X chromosome, and the other is a small X-shaped chromosome called a *Y chromosome*. (There must be a good reason for calling a small X-shaped chromosome a Y chromosome, but I don't know what it is.) Consequently, the sex chromosome of every ovum is an X chromosome, whereas half the sperm cells have X chromosomes and half have Y chromosomes. Your gender with all its social, economic, and personal ramifications was determined by which of your father's sperm cells won the dash to your mother's ovum. If a sperm cell with an X sex chromosome won, you are a female; if one with a Y sex chromosome won, you are a male.

Writing this section reminded me of my grade 7 basketball team, "The Nads." The name puzzled our teacher because it was not at all like the names usually favored by pubescent boys—names such as the "Avengers," the "Marauders," and the "Vikings." Her puzzlement ended abruptly at our first game as our fans began to chant their support. You guessed it; "Go Nads, Go! Go Nads, Go!" My 14-year-old spotted-faced teammates and I considered this to be humor of the most mature and sophisticated sort. The teacher didn't.

and (3) steroids. **Amino acid derivative hormones** are hormones that are synthesized in a few simple steps from an amino acid molecule; an example is *epinephrine,* which is released from the *adrenal medulla* and synthesized from *tyrosine*. **Peptide hormones** and **protein hormones** are chains of amino acids—peptide hormones are short chains, and protein hormones are long chains. **Steroid hormones** are hormones that are synthesized from *cholesterol,* a type of fat molecule.

It is steroid hormones that play the major role in sexual development and behavior, and thus it is steroid hormones that are the focus of this chapter. Most other hormones exert their effects solely by binding to receptors in cell membranes. Steroids too can exert effects in this fashion; but because steroid molecules are small and fat-soluble, they readily penetrate cell membranes. Once inside cells, steroids can bind to receptors in the cytoplasm or nucleus; and by so doing, they can influence gene expression. Consequently, steroid hormones can have particularly diverse and long-lasting effects on cellular function (see Demotes-Mainard, Vernier, & Vincent, 1993; Funder, 1993; Hutchison, 1991).

Gonads

Central to any discussion of hormones and sex are the **gonads**—the male **testes** (pronounced TEST eez) and the female **ovaries** (see Figure 11.1). The primary function of the testes and ovaries is the production of *sperm*

Sex Steroids

The gonads do more than create sperm and egg cells; they also produce and release hormones. Most people are surprised to learn that the testes and ovaries release the very same hormones. The two main classes of gonadal hormones are **androgens** and **estrogens; testosterone** is the most common androgen, and **estradiol** is the most common estrogen. The fact that ovaries tend to release more estrogens than they do androgens and that testes release more androgens than they do estrogens has led to the common, but misleading, practice of referring to androgens as "the *male* sex hormones" and to estrogens as "the *female* sex hormones." This practice should be avoided because of its men-are-men and women-are-women implication that androgens produce maleness and estrogens produce femaleness. They don't.

The ovaries and testes also release a class of hormones called **progestins.** The most common progestin is **progesterone,** which in females prepares the uterus and the breasts for pregnancy. Its function in males is unclear.

Because the primary function of the **adrenal cortex**—the outer layer of the *adrenal gland* (see Figure 11.1)—is the regulation of glucose and salt levels in the blood, it is not generally thought of as a sex gland. However, in addition to its principal steroid hormones, it does release in small amounts all of the sex steroids that are released by the gonads.

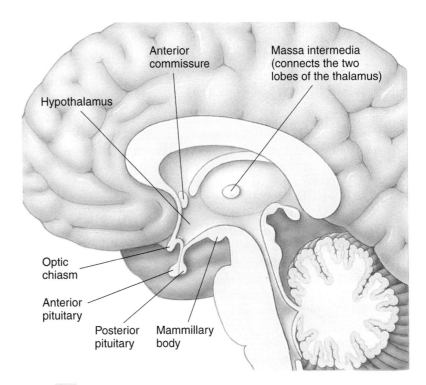

Figure 11.2 A midline view of the posterior and anterior pituitary and surrounding structures.

itary. It is the anterior pituitary that releases tropic hormones; thus it is the anterior pituitary in particular, rather than the pituitary in general, that qualifies as the master gland.

Hormones of the Pituitary

The pituitary gland is frequently referred to as the *master gland* because most of its hormones are tropic hormones. *Tropic hormones* are hormones whose primary function is to influence the release of hormones from other glands (*tropic* is an adjective that describes things that stimulate or change other things). For example, the **gonadotropins** are pituitary tropic hormones that travel through the circulatory system to the gonads, where they stimulate the release of gonadal hormones.

The pituitary gland is really two glands, the posterior pituitary and the anterior pituitary, which fuse during the course of embryological development. The **posterior pituitary** develops from a small outgrowth of hypothalamic tissue that eventually comes to dangle from the *hypothalamus* on the end of the **pituitary stalk** (see Figure 11.2). In contrast, the **anterior pituitary** begins as part of the same embryonic tissue that eventually develops into the roof of the mouth; during the course of development, it pinches off and migrates up to assume its position next to the posterior pitu-

Amino acid derivative hormones. Hormones that are simple modifications of individual amino acids.
Peptide hormones. Hormones that are short strings of amino acids.
Protein hormones. Hormones that are long strings of amino acids.
Steroid hormones. Hormones that are synthesized from cholesterol.
Gonads. The testes and ovaries.
Testes. The male gonads.
Ovaries. The female gonads.
Copulation. Sexual intercourse.
Zygote. The cell formed from the fusion of a sperm cell and an ovum.
Sex chromosomes. The pair of chromosomes (XX or XY) that contain the genetic information that directs sexual development.
Androgens. The class of steroid hormones that includes testosterone.
Estrogens. The class of steroid hormones that includes estradiol.

Testosterone. The most common androgen.
Estradiol. The most common estrogen.
Progestins. The class of gonadal hormones that includes progesterone.
Progesterone. A progestin that prepares the uterus and breasts for pregnancy.
Adrenal cortex. The outer layer of the adrenal gland, which releases gonadal hormones and hormones that regulate the salt and glucose levels of the blood.
Gonadotropins. The anterior pituitary hormones that stimulate the release of hormones from the gonads.
Posterior pituitary. The part of the pituitary gland that contains the terminals of hypothalamic neurons.
Pituitary stalk. The structure connecting the hypothalamus and the pituitary.
Anterior pituitary. The part of the pituitary gland that releases tropic hormones.

Female Gonadal Hormone Levels Are Cyclic, Male Gonadal Hormone Levels Are Steady

The major difference between the endocrine function of women and men is that in women the levels of gonadal and gonadotropic hormones go through a cycle that repeats itself every 28 days or so (see Appendix VIII). It is these more-or-less regular hormone fluctuations that control the female **menstrual cycle.** In contrast, human males are, from a neuroendocrine perspective, rather dull creatures; the levels of their gonadal and gonadotropic hormones change little from day to day. An interest in this fundamental difference between females and males was the original stimulus for a particularly fruitful line of experiments.

Because the anterior pituitary is the master gland, many early scientists assumed that an inherent difference between the male and female anterior pituitary was the basis for the difference in their patterns of gonadotropic and gonadal hormone release. However, this hypothesis was discounted by a series of clever transplant studies conducted by Geoffrey Harris in the 1950s (see Raisman, 1997). In these studies, a cycling pituitary removed from a mature female rat became a steady-state pituitary when transplanted at a suitable site in a male, and a steady-state pituitary removed from a mature male rat began to cycle once transplanted in a female. What these studies established was that anterior pituitaries are not inherently female (cyclical) or male (steady-state); their patterns of hormone release are controlled by some other part of the body. The master gland seemed to have its own master. Where was it?

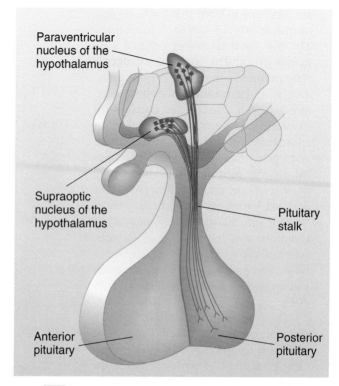

Figure 11.3 The neural connections between the hypothalamus and the pituitary. All neural input to the pituitary goes to the posterior pituitary; the anterior pituitary has no neural connections.

but how the hypothalamus controls the anterior pituitary remained a mystery. You see, the anterior pituitary, unlike the posterior pituitary, receives no neural input whatsoever from the hypothalamus, or from any other neural structure (see Figure 11.3).

Neural Control of the Pituitary

The nervous system was implicated in the control of the anterior pituitary by behavioral research on birds and other animals that breed only during a specific time of the year. It was found that the seasonal variations in the light–dark cycle triggered many of the breeding-related changes in hormone release. If the lighting conditions under which the animals lived were reversed, for example, by having the animals transported across the equator, the breeding seasons were also reversed. Somehow, visual input to the nervous system was controlling the release of tropic hormones from the anterior pituitary.

The search for the particular neural structure that controlled the anterior pituitary turned, naturally enough, to the *hypothalamus,* the structure from which the pituitary is suspended. Hypothalamic stimulation and lesion experiments quickly established that the hypothalamus is the regulator of the anterior pituitary,

Control of the Anterior and Posterior Pituitary by the Hypothalamus

There are two different mechanisms by which the hypothalamus controls the pituitary: one for the posterior pituitary and one for the anterior pituitary. The two major hormones of the posterior pituitary, **vasopressin** and **oxytocin,** are peptide hormones that are synthesized in the cell bodies of neurons in the **paraventricular nuclei** and **supraoptic nuclei** of the hypothalamus (see Figure 11.3). They are then transported along the axons of these neurons to their terminals in the posterior pituitary and are stored there until the arrival of action potentials causes them to be released into the bloodstream. (Neurons that release hormones into general circulation are called *neurosecretory cells.*) Oxytocin stimulates contractions of the uterus during labor and the ejection of milk during suckling. Vasopressin (also called *antidiuretic hormone*) facilitates the reabsorption of water by the kidneys.

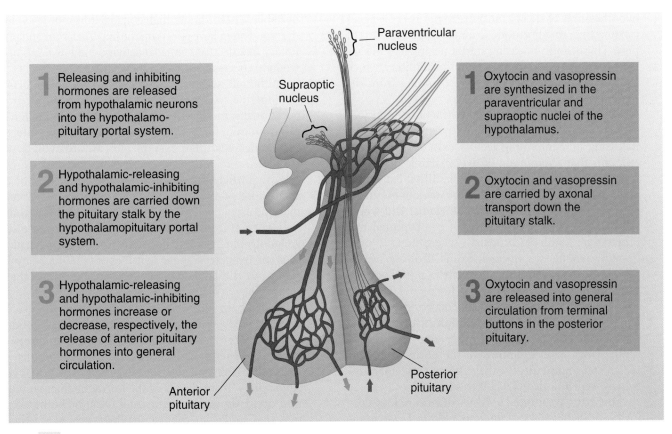

1 Releasing and inhibiting hormones are released from hypothalamic neurons into the hypothalamo-pituitary portal system.

2 Hypothalamic-releasing and hypothalamic-inhibiting hormones are carried down the pituitary stalk by the hypothalamopituitary portal system.

3 Hypothalamic-releasing and hypothalamic-inhibiting hormones increase or decrease, respectively, the release of anterior pituitary hormones into general circulation.

Paraventricular nucleus

Supraoptic nucleus

1 Oxytocin and vasopressin are synthesized in the paraventricular and supraoptic nuclei of the hypothalamus.

2 Oxytocin and vasopressin are carried by axonal transport down the pituitary stalk.

3 Oxytocin and vasopressin are released into general circulation from terminal buttons in the posterior pituitary.

Anterior pituitary

Posterior pituitary

Figure 11.4 Control of the anterior and posterior pituitary by the hypothalamus.

The means by which the hypothalamus controls the release of hormones from the neuron-free anterior pituitary was more difficult to explain. Harris (1955) suggested that the release of hormones from the anterior pituitary was itself regulated by hormones released from the hypothalamus. Two findings provided early support for this hypothesis. The first was the discovery of a vascular network, the **hypothalamopituitary portal system,** that seemed well suited to the task of carrying hormones from the hypothalamus to the anterior pituitary. As Figure 11.4 illustrates, a network of hypothalamic capillaries feeds a bundle of portal veins that carries blood down the pituitary stalk into another network of capillaries in the anterior pituitary. (A *portal vein* is a vein that connects one capillary network with another.) The second finding was the discovery that cutting the portal veins of the pituitary stalk disrupts the release of anterior pituitary hormones until the damaged veins regenerate (Harris, 1955).

Discovery of Hypothalamic Releasing Hormones

It was hypothesized that the release of each anterior pituitary hormone is controlled by a different hypothalamic hormone. The putative (hypothesized) hypothala-

mic hormones that were thought to stimulate the release of anterior pituitary hormones were referred to as **releasing factors.** Those thought to inhibit the release of an anterior pituitary hormone were referred to as **inhibitory factors.** Efforts to isolate the putative hypothalamic releasing and inhibitory factors led to a major breakthrough in 1969. Guilleman and his colleagues isolated **thyrotropin-releasing hormone** from the

Menstrual cycle. The hormone-regulated cycle in women of follicle growth, egg release, uterus lining buildup, and menstruation.

Vasopressin. One of the two major hormones of the posterior pituitary, which facilitates reabsorption of water by kidneys; also called antidiuretic hormone.

Oxytocin. One of the two major hormones of the posterior pituitary, which in females stimulates contractions of the uterus and the ejection of milk during suckling.

Paraventricular nuclei. One of the two pairs of hypothalamic nuclei in which the hormones of the posterior pituitary are synthesized.

Supraoptic nuclei. One of the two pairs of hypothalamic nuclei in which the hormones of the posterior pituitary are synthesized.

Hypothalamopituitary portal system. The vascular network that carries hormones from the hypothalamus to the anterior pituitary.

Releasing factors. Suspected (hypothesized) hypothalamic releasing hormones that have not yet been isolated.

Inhibitory factors. Hypothalamic hormones thought to regulate anterior pituitary hormones by inhibiting their release.

Thyrotropin-releasing hormone. The hypothalamic hormone that stimulates the release of thyrotropin from the anterior pituitary.

hypothalamus of sheep, and Schally and his colleagues isolated the same hormone from the hypothalamus of pigs. Thyrotropin-releasing hormone triggers the release of **thyrotropin** from the anterior pituitary, which in turn stimulates the release of hormones from the *thyroid gland.*

It is difficult to appreciate the effort that went into the initial isolation of thyrotropin-releasing hormone. Releasing and inhibiting factors exist in such small amounts that a mountain of hypothalamic tissue was required to extract even minute quantities. For example, Schally (1978) reported that the work of his group required over 1 million pig hypothalami. And where did Schally get such a quantity of pig hypothalami? From Oscar Mayer & Company—where else?

Why would two research teams dedicate over a decade of their lives to accumulate a pitifully small quantity of thyrotropin-releasing hormone? The reason was that it enabled both Guilleman and Schally to determine the chemical composition of thyrotropin-releasing hormone and then to develop methods of synthesizing larger quantities of the hormone for research and clinical use. For their efforts, Guilleman and Schally were awarded Nobel Prizes in 1977.

You may have noticed a change in terminology during the preceding discussion: from *releasing factors* to **releasing hormones.** This shift reflects the usual practice of referring to a hormone as a "factor" or "substance" until it has been isolated and its chemical structure identified.

Schally's and Guilleman's isolation of thyrotropin-releasing hormone confirmed that hypothalamic-releasing hormones control the release of hormones from the anterior pituitary and thus provided the major impetus for the isolation and synthesis of several other releasing hormones. Of direct relevance to study of sex hormones was the isolation of **gonadotropin-releasing hormone** by Schally and his group in 1970. This releasing hormone stimulates the release of both of the anterior pituitary's gonadotropins: **follicle-stimulating hormone (FSH)** and **luteinizing hormone (LH)** (Schally, Kastin, & Arimura, 1971). All releasing hormones, like all tropic hormones, have proven to be peptides.

Feedback in the Neuroendocrine System

The hypothalamus controls the anterior pituitary, and the anterior pituitary in turn controls other endocrine glands; but neuroendocrine regulation is not a one-way street. Circulating hormones often feed back on the very structures that triggered their release: the pituitary, the hypothalamus, and other sites in the brain (see McEwen et al., 1979).

Most of the feedback in the neuroendocrine system is **negative feedback,** whose function is the maintenance

of stability. Accordingly, high gonadal hormone levels in the blood often have effects on the hypothalamus and pituitary that decrease gonadal activity, and low levels often have effects that increase gonadal activity.

Although negative feedback is the rule in the neuroendocrine system, **positive feedback** can also occur; occasionally, increases in the level of a circulating hormone produce further increases, and decreases produce further decreases. For example, just before **ovulation,** (the release of a mature ovum from the package of cells, or **follicle,** in which it develops) injection of a small dose of estradiol produces an increase, rather than the usual decrease, in the release of estradiol from the ovary. It does this by stimulating the release of gonadotropin-releasing hormone from the hypothalamus and by increasing the sensitivity of the anterior pituitary to the gonadotropin-releasing hormone that reaches it.

It has been suggested that a shift from the usual negative feedback mode to a positive feedback mode may be the key factor in producing the surge in the levels of progesterone and estradiol in the blood of females that is responsible for triggering ovulation (see Appendix VIII for details of the hormone fluctuations that occur during the *menstrual cycles* of human females). A similar mechanism has been proposed to account for the surge of gonadal hormones that occurs in both males and females during puberty.

Pulsatile Hormone Release

Hormones tend to be released in pulses (Karsch, 1987); they are discharged several times per day in large surges, which typically last no more than a few minutes. Hormone levels in the blood are regulated by changes in the frequency and duration of the hormone pulses (Reame et al., 1984). One consequence of **pulsatile**

Thyrotropin. The anterior pituitary hormone that stimulates the release of hormones from the thyroid gland.

Releasing hormones. Hypothalamic hormones that stimulate the release of hormones from the anterior pituitary.

Gonadotropin-releasing hormone. The hypothalamic releasing hormone that controls the release of the two gonadotropic hormones from the anterior pituitary.

Follicle-stimulating hormone (FSH). The gonadotropic hormone that stimulates development of ovarian follicles.

Luteinizing hormone (LH). The gonadotropic hormone that causes the developing ovum to be released from its follicle.

Negative feedback. A signal from a change in one direction that results in a compensatory effect in the other direction.

Positive feedback. A signal from a change in one direction that facilitates a further change in the same direction.

Ovulation. The release of the ovum from the follicle in which it develops, which signals the beginning of the fertile period of the menstrual cycle.

Follicle. The package of cells within which each ovum begins its development in the ovary.

Pulsatile hormone release. The typical pattern of hormone release, which occurs in large pulses or surges several times a day.

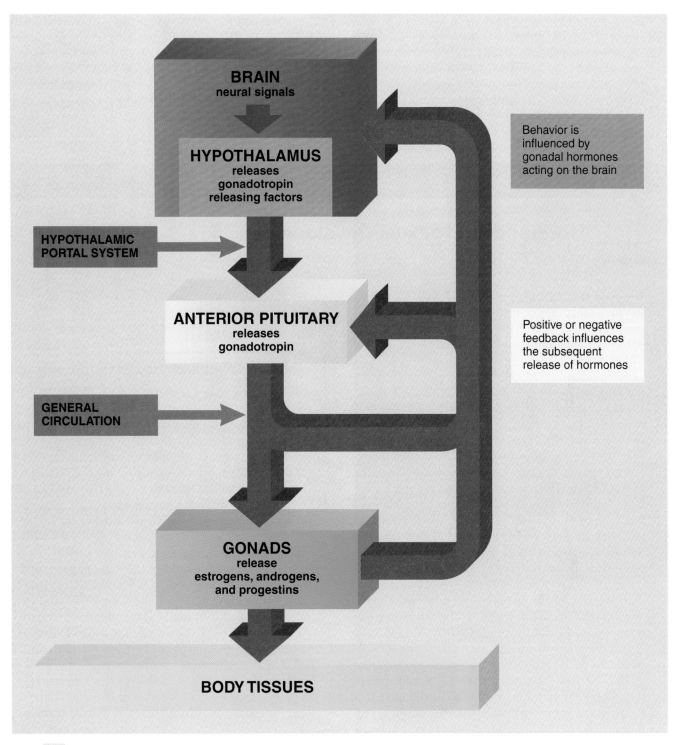

Figure 11.5 The regulation of gonadal hormones: A summary model.

hormone release is that there are often large minute-to-minute fluctuations in the levels of circulating hormones (e.g., Koolhaas, Schuurman, & Wiepkema, 1980). Accordingly, when the pattern of human male gonadal hormone release is referred to as steady, it means that there are no major systematic changes in circulating gonadal hormone levels from day to day, not that the levels never vary.

A Summary Model of Gonadal Endocrine Regulation

Figure 11.5 is a summary model of the regulation of gonadal hormones. According to this model, the brain controls the release of gonadotropin-releasing hormone from the hypothalamus into the hypothalamopituitary portal system, which carries it to the anterior pituitary. In the anterior pituitary, the gonadotropin-releasing hormone stimulates the release of gonadotropins, which are carried by the circulatory system to the gonads. In response to the gonadotropins, the gonads release androgens, estrogens, and progestins, which feed back onto the pituitary and hypothalamus to regulate subsequent gonadal hormone release.

Armed with this general perspective of neuroendocrine function, you are ready to consider how gonadal hormones direct sexual development (Section 11.2) and activate adult sexual behavior (Section 11.3), and how the hypothalamus influences sexual behavior (Section 11.4) and sexual orientation (Section 11.5).

11.2 Hormones and Sexual Development

You have undoubtedly noticed that humans are *dimorphic*—that they come in two standard models: female and male. This section describes how the development of female and male characteristics is directed by hormones.

This section concludes with three cases of exceptional sexual development. I am sure you will be intrigued by these three cases, but that is not the only reason why I have chosen to include them. My main reason is expressed by a proverb: The exception proves the rule. Most people think this proverb means that the exception "proves" the rule in the sense that it establishes its truth, but this is nonsense: The truth of a rule is challenged by, not confirmed by, exceptions to it. The word *proof* comes from the Latin *probare,* which means "to test"—as in *proving ground* or printer's *proof*—and this is the sense in which it is used in the proverb. Hence, the proverb means that the explanation of exceptional cases is a major challenge for any theory. Accordingly, the primary purpose of the three cases of exceptional sexual development that are described at the end of this section is to test the theories presented in it.

Sexual differentiation in mammals begins at fertilization with the production of one of two different kinds of zygotes: either one with an XX (female) pair of sex chromosomes or one with an XY (male) pair. It is the genetic information on these sex chromosomes that normally determines whether development will occur along female or male lines. But be cautious here: Do not fall into the seductive embrace of the men-are-men and women-are-women assumption. Do not begin by assuming that there are two parallel genetic programs for sexual development: one for female development and one for male development. As you are about to learn, sexual development unfolds according to an entirely different principle, one that many males—particularly those who still stubbornly adhere to notions of male preeminence—find unsettling. This principle is that we are all genetically programmed to develop female bodies; genetic males develop male bodies only because their fundamentally female program of development is overruled.

Fetal Hormones and the Development of Reproductive Organs

■ **GONADS** Figure 11.6 illustrates the structure of the gonads as they appear 6 weeks after fertilization. Notice that at this stage of development, each fetus, regardless of its genetic sex, has the same pair of structures, called *primordial gonads* (*primordial* means "existing at the beginning"). Each primordial gonad has an outer covering, or *cortex,* which has the potential to develop into an ovary; and each has an internal core, or *medulla,* which has the potential to develop into a testis.

Six weeks after conception, the Y chromosome of the male triggers the synthesis of **H-Y antigen** (see Haqq et al., 1994; Wang et al., 1995), and this protein causes the medulla of each primordial gonad to grow and to develop into a testis. There is no female counterpart of H-Y antigen; in the absence of H-Y antigen, the cortical cells of the primordial gonads automatically develop into ovaries. Accordingly, if H-Y antigen is injected into a genetic female fetus 6 weeks after conception, the result is a genetic female with testes; or if drugs that block the effects of H-Y antigen are injected into a male fetus, the result is a genetic male with ovaries. Such "mixed-gender" individuals expose in a dramatic fashion the weakness of "mamawawa" thinking.

■ **INTERNAL REPRODUCTIVE DUCTS** Six weeks after fertilization, both males and females have two complete sets of reproductive ducts. They have a male **Wolffian system,** which has the capacity to develop into the male reproductive ducts (e.g., the *seminal vesicles,* which hold the fluid in which sperm cells are ejaculated; and the *vas deferens,* through which the sperm cells travel to the seminal vesicles). And they have a female **Müllerian sys-

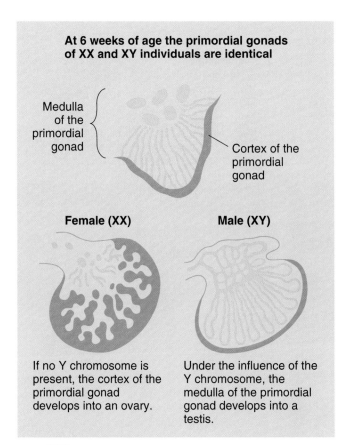

At 6 weeks of age the primordial gonads of XX and XY individuals are identical

Medulla of the primordial gonad

Cortex of the primordial gonad

Female (XX)

Male (XY)

If no Y chromosome is present, the cortex of the primordial gonad develops into an ovary.

Under the influence of the Y chromosome, the medulla of the primordial gonad develops into a testis.

Figure 11.6 The development of an ovary and a testis from the cortex and medulla, respectively, of the primordial gonadal structure that is present 6 weeks after conception.

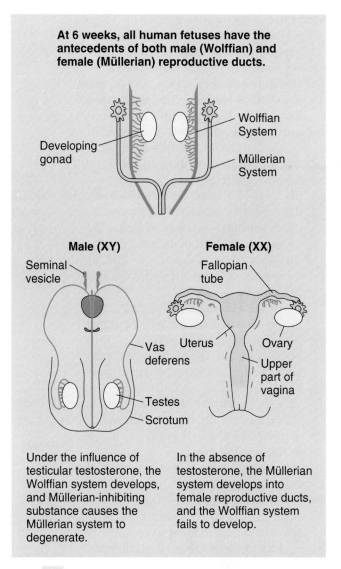

At 6 weeks, all human fetuses have the antecedents of both male (Wolffian) and female (Müllerian) reproductive ducts.

Developing gonad

Wolffian System

Müllerian System

Male (XY)

Seminal vesicle

Vas deferens

Testes

Scrotum

Female (XX)

Fallopian tube

Uterus

Ovary

Upper part of vagina

Under the influence of testicular testosterone, the Wolffian system develops, and Müllerian-inhibiting substance causes the Müllerian system to degenerate.

In the absence of testosterone, the Müllerian system develops into female reproductive ducts, and the Wolffian system fails to develop.

Figure 11.7 The development of the internal ducts of the male and female reproductive systems from the Wolffian and Müllerian systems, respectively.

tem, which has the capacity to develop into the female ducts (e.g., the *uterus;* the upper part of the *vagina;* and the *fallopian tubes,* through which ova travel from the ovaries to the uterus, where they can be fertilized).

In the third month of male fetal development, the testes secrete testosterone and **Müllerian-inhibiting substance.** As Figure 11.7 illustrates, the testosterone stimulates the development of the Wolffian system, and the Müllerian-inhibiting substance causes the Müllerian system to degenerate and the testes to descend into the **scrotum**—the sac that holds the testes outside the body cavity. Because it is testosterone—not the sex chromosomes—that triggers Wolffian development, genetic females who are injected with testosterone during the appropriate fetal period develop male reproductive ducts along with their female ones.

The differentiation of the internal ducts of the female reproductive system (see Figure 11.7) is not under the control of ovarian hormones; the ovaries are almost completely inactive during fetal development. The development of the Müllerian system occurs in any fetus that is not exposed to testosterone during the critical fetal period. Accordingly, normal female fetuses, ovariectomized female fetuses, and orchidectomized male fetuses all develop female reproductive ducts (Jost, 1972). **Ovariectomy** is the removal of the ovaries, and **orchidectomy** is the removal of the testes (*orchis* means "testicle"). **Gonadectomy,** or *castration,* is the surgical removal of gonads—either ovaries or testes.

H-Y antigen. The protein hormone that stimulates the cells of the medullary portion of the primordial gonads to proliferate and develop into testes.

Wolffian system. The embryonic precursors of the male reproductive ducts.

Müllerian system. The embryonic precursors of the female reproductive ducts.

Müllerian-inhibiting substance. The testicular hormone that causes the precursors of the female reproductive ducts to degenerate and the testes to descend.

Scrotum. The sac that holds the male testes.

Ovariectomy. The removal of the ovaries.

Orchidectomy. The removal of the testes.

Gonadectomy. The surgical removal of the gonads (testes or ovaries); castration.

■ **EXTERNAL REPRODUCTIVE ORGANS** There is a basic difference between the differentiation of the external reproductive organs and the differentiation of the internal reproductive organs (i.e., the gonads and reproductive ducts). As you have just read, every normal fetus develops separate precursors for the male (medulla) and female (cortex) gonads and for the male (Wolffian system) and female (Müllerian system) reproductive ducts; then, only one set, male or female, develops. In contrast, the male and female **genitals**—external reproductive organs—develop from the same precursor. This *bipotential precursor* and its subsequent differentiation are illustrated in Figure 11.8.

In the second month of pregnancy, the bipotential precursor of the external reproductive organs consists of four parts: the glans, the urethral folds, the lateral bodies, and the labioscrotal swellings. Then it begins to differentiate. The *glans* grows into the head of the *penis* in the male or the *clitoris* in the female, the *urethral folds* fuse in the male or enlarge to become the *labia minora* in the female, the *lateral bodies* form the shaft of the penis in the male or the hood of the clitoris in the female, and the *labioscrotal swellings* form the *scrotum* in the male or the *labia majora* in the female.

Like the development of the internal reproductive ducts, the development of the external genitals is controlled by the presence or absence of testosterone. If testosterone is present at the appropriate stage of fetal development, male external genitals develop from the bipotential precursor; if testosterone is not present, the development of the external genitals proceeds along female lines.

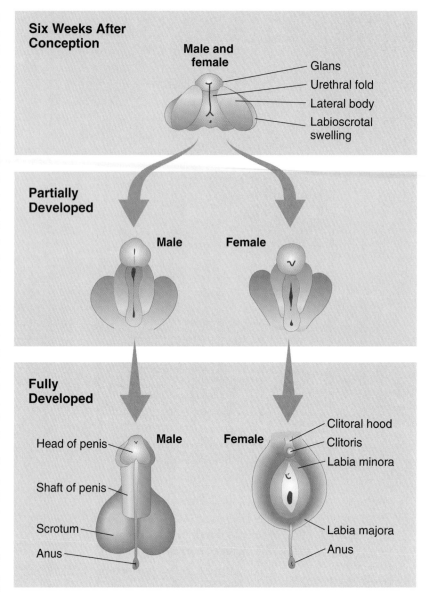

Figure 11.8 *The development of male and female external reproductive organs from the same bipotential precursor.*

Development of Sex Differences in the Brain

The brains of men and women are alike, but they are not identical. The brains of men tend to be, on the average, about 15% larger. Also, a number of more subtle anatomical differences have been documented: slight differences in the anatomy of the hypothalamus, corpus callosum, anterior commissure, and thalamus (see Breedlove, 1992). Positron emission tomography (PET) has revealed sex differences in brain function as well; for example, Gur et al. (1995) reported that men tend to have a higher level of baseline metabolic activity in several areas of the temporal lobe and limbic system, whereas women tend to have higher baseline activity in the cingulate gyrus. Presumably, some of these differences are related to differences in sexual behavior, whereas others are related to differences in cognitive and emotional function; but at the present time, the functional significance of cerebral sex differences remains a matter of conjecture.

How do sex differences in the brain develop? Most of our current understanding of the sexual differentiation of the human brain has come from experiments on rats. Rats are useful subjects for the study of brain development because they are born just 22 days after conception. At 22 days after conception, the period during which hormones can influence their genital development is largely over, but the period during which hormones can influence their brain development is just beginning. Accordingly, it is easy to study the effects of hormones on brain development, unconfounded by their effects on genital development.

■ **PERINATAL ANDROGENS AND BRAIN DIFFERENTIATION** Most of the early experiments on the development of sex differences in the brain focused on the factors that control the development of the steady and cyclic patterns of gonadotropin release in females and males, respectively. The seminal experiments were conducted by Pfeiffer in 1936. In his experiments, some neonatal rats (males and females) were gonadectomized and some were not, and some received gonad transplants (ovaries or testes) and some did not.

Remarkably, Pfeiffer found that gonadectomizing neonatal rats of either genetic sex caused them to develop into adults with the female cyclic pattern of gonadotropin release. In contrast, transplantation of testes into gonadectomized or intact female neonatal rats caused them to develop into adults with the steady male pattern of gonadotropin release. Transplantation of ovaries had no effect on the pattern of hormone release. Pfeiffer concluded that the female cyclic pattern of gonadotropin release develops unless the preprogrammed female cyclicity is overridden by testosterone during perinatal development (see Harris & Levine, 1965).

Pfeiffer incorrectly concluded that the presence or absence of testicular hormones in neonatal rats influenced the development of the pituitary because he was not aware of what we know today: that the release of gonadotropins from the anterior pituitary is controlled by the hypothalamus. Once this was discovered, it became apparent that Pfeiffer's experiments had provided the first evidence of the role of *perinatal* (around the time of birth) androgens in the sexual differentiation of the hypothalamus. Several other differences between male and female brains have been shown to be under similar hormonal control: The presence of perinatal testosterone leads to the development of male brain characteristics; its absence leads to the development of female brain characteristics, regardless of genetic sex.

■ **AROMATIZATION AND BRAIN DIFFERENTIATION** All gonadal and adrenal sex hormones are steroid hormones, which are all derived from *cholesterol*. Because all steroid hormones have similar structures, they are readily converted from one to the other. For example, a slight change to one ring of the testosterone molecule changes that ring to a benzene ring, and so doing, it converts testosterone to estradiol; this process is called **aromatization.**

There is good evidence that aromatization is a critical step in the masculinization of the brain by testosterone in some species. According to this theory, perinatal testosterone does not directly masculinize the brain;

the brain is masculinized by estradiol that has been aromatized from perinatal testosterone. Although the idea that estradiol—the alleged female hormone—masculinizes the brain is counterintuitive, there is strong evidence for it in several species. In the rat, for example, (1) the enzyme that is necessary for aromatization of testosterone is present in neonates; (2) neonatal injections of estradiol masculinize the brain; (3) **dihydrotestosterone**—an androgen that cannot be converted to estrogen—has no masculinizing effect on the brain; and (4) agents that block the aromatization of testosterone (McEwen et al., 1977) or block estrogen receptors (Booth, 1977) interfere with the masculinizing effects of testosterone on the brain.

How do genetic females of species whose brains are masculinized by estradiol keep from being masculinized by their mothers' estradiol, which circulates through the fetal blood supply? In the rat, alpha fetoprotein is the answer. **Alpha fetoprotein** is present in the blood of rats during the perinatal period, and it deactivates circulating estradiol by binding to it. How, then, does estradiol masculinize the brain of the male fetus in the presence of the deactivating effects of alpha fetoprotein? Because testosterone is immune to alpha fetoprotein, it can travel unaffected from the testes to the brain, where it enters cells and is converted there to estradiol. The estradiol is not broken down in the brain because alpha fetoprotein does not readily penetrate the blood–brain barrier.

In humans, female fetuses are protected from the masculinizing effects of the mother's estrogens by a *placental barrier*. Unfortunately, this barrier is not as effective against synthetic estrogens (e.g., *diethylstilbestrol*). As a result, the female offspring of mothers who have been exposed to synthetic estrogens while pregnant may display a variety of male characteristics (see McEwen, 1983).

Perinatal Hormones and Behavioral Development

In view of the fact that perinatal hormones influence the development of the brain, it should come as no surprise that they also influence the development of behavior. Most of the research on hormones and behavioral development has focused on the role of perinatal hormones in the development of sexually dimorphic copulatory behaviors in laboratory animals.

Genitals. The external reproductive organs.
Aromatization. The chemical process by which testosterone is converted to estradiol.
Dihydrotestosterone. An androgen that cannot be aromatized to estrogen.

Alpha fetoprotein. The protein present in the blood of perinatal rats that deactivates circulating estradiol by binding to it.

Phoenix and colleagues (1959) were among the first to demonstrate that the perinatal injection of testosterone **masculinizes** and **defeminizes** a genetic female's adult copulatory behavior. First, they injected pregnant guinea pigs with testosterone. Then, when the litters were born, they ovariectomized the female offspring. Finally, when these ovariectomized female guinea pigs reached maturity, they injected them with testosterone and assessed their copulatory behavior. Phoenix and his colleagues found that the females that had been exposed to perinatal testosterone displayed much more malelike mounting behavior in response to testosterone injections in adulthood than did adult females that had not been exposed to perinatal testosterone. And when as adults they were injected with progesterone and estradiol and mounted by males, they displayed less **lordosis**—the intromission-facilitating arched-back posture of female rodent receptivity.

In a study complementary to that of Phoenix et al., Grady, Phoenix, and Young (1965) found that the lack of early exposure of male rats to testosterone both **feminizes** and **demasculinizes** their copulatory behavior as adults. Male rats castrated shortly after birth failed to display the normal male copulatory pattern of mounting, **intromission** (penis insertion), and **ejaculation** (ejection of sperm) when they were treated with testosterone and given access to a sexually receptive female; and when they were injected with estrogen and progesterone as adults, they exhibited more lordosis than did uncastrated controls. The aromatization of perinatal testosterone to estradiol seems to be important for both the defeminization and the masculinization of rodent copulatory behavior (Goy & McEwen, 1980; Shapiro, Levine, & Adler, 1980).

Most of the research on hormones and behavioral development has focused on the copulatory act itself. As a result, we know relatively little about the role of hormones in the development of **proceptive behaviors** (solicitation behaviors) and in the development of gender-related behaviors that are not directly related to reproduction. However, testosterone has been reported to disrupt the proceptive hopping, darting, and ear wiggling of receptive female rats; to increase the aggressiveness of female mice; to disrupt the maternal behavior of female rats; and to increase rough social play in female monkeys and rats.

In thinking about hormones and behavior, it is important to remember that feminizing and demasculinizing effects do not always go together; nor do defeminizing and masculinizing effects. Hormone treatments can enhance or disrupt female behavior without affecting male behavior (e.g., Bloch, Mills, & Gale, 1995) and vice versa. It is also important to remember that timing is important. For example, the so-called "critical period" for single injections of testosterone to masculinize and defeminize the rat brain is thought to be restricted to the first 11 days after birth. However, Bloch and Mills (1995) showed that exposure of gonadectomized male rats to testosterone for 15 days beginning on day 15 was able to masculinize and defeminize their behavioral and endocrine function. Because so-called critical developmental periods are often found not to be absolutely critical, the term **sensitive period** is more appropriate.

Puberty: Hormones and the Development of Secondary Sex Characteristics

During childhood, levels of circulating gonadal hormones are low, reproductive organs are immature, and males and females differ little in general appearance. This period of developmental quiescence ends abruptly with the onset of *puberty*—the transitional period between childhood and adulthood during which fertility is achieved, the adolescent growth spurt occurs, and the secondary sex characteristics develop. **Secondary sex characteristics** are those features other than the reproductive organs that distinguish sexually mature men and women. The body changes that occur during puberty are illustrated in Figure 11.9; you are undoubtedly familiar with at least half of them.

Puberty is associated with an increase in the release of hormones by the anterior pituitary. The increase in the release of **growth hormone**—the only anterior pituitary hormone that does not have an endocrine gland as its primary target—acts directly on bone and muscle tissue to produce the pubertal growth spurt. Increases in gonadotropic hormone and **adrenocorticotropic hormone** release cause the gonads and adrenal cortex to increase their release of gonadal and adrenal hormones, which in turn initiate the maturation of the genitals and the development of secondary sex characteristics.

The general principle guiding normal pubertal sexual maturation is a simple one: In pubertal males, androgen levels are higher than estrogen levels, and masculinization is the result; in pubertal females, estro-

Masculinizes. Enhances or produces male characteristics.
Defeminizes. Suppresses or disrupts female characteristics.
Lordosis. The intromission-facilitating, arched-back, tail-to-the-side posture of female rodent receptivity.
Feminizes. Enhances or produces female characteristics.
Demasculinizes. Suppresses or disrupts male characteristics.
Intromission. Insertion of the penis into the vagina.
Ejaculation. Ejection of sperm.
Proceptive behaviors. Behaviors that serve to attract the sexual advances of the other sex.
Sensitive period. The period during the development of a particular trait, usually early in life, when a particular experience is likely to change the course of its development.
Secondary sex characteristics. Structural features, other than the reproductive organs, that distinguish men from women.
Growth hormone. The anterior pituitary hormone that acts directly on bone and muscle tissue to produce the pubertal growth spurt.
Adrenocorticotropic hormone. The anterior pituitary hormone that causes the adrenal cortex to release its hormones.
Androstenedione. The adrenal androgen that triggers the growth of pubic and axillary hair in human females.

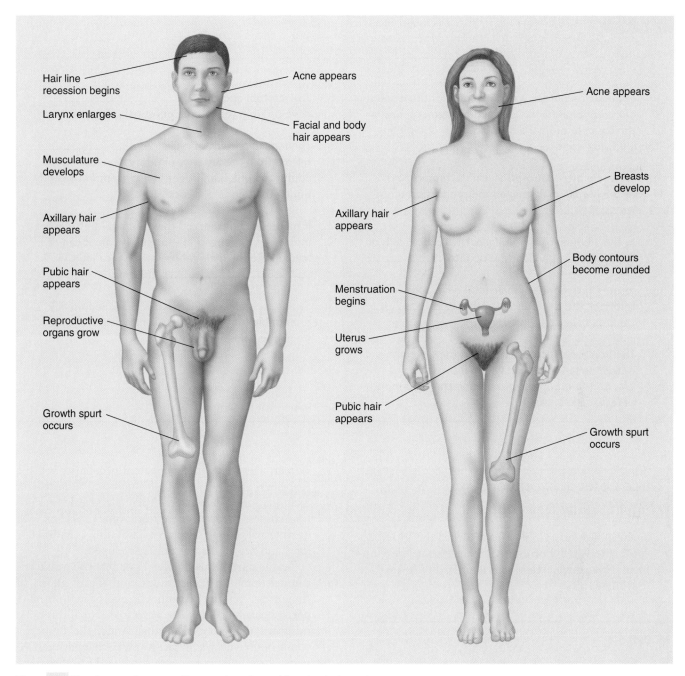

Figure 11.9 The changes that normally occur in males and females during puberty.

gen predominates, and the result is feminization. Individuals castrated prior to puberty do not become sexually mature unless they receive replacement injections of androgen or estrogen.

But even during puberty, its only major stage of relevance, the men-are-men and women-are-women assumption stumbles badly. You see, **androstenedione,** an androgen that is released primarily by the adrenal cortex, is normally responsible for the growth of pubic hair and *axillary hair* (underarm hair) in females. It is hard to take seriously the practice of referring to androgens as "male hormones" when one of them is responsible for the development of the female pattern of

pubic hair growth. The male pattern is a pyramid and the female pattern is an inverted pyramid (see Figure 11.9).

Do you remember how old you were when you started to go through puberty? In most North American and European countries, puberty begins at about 11 years of age for girls and 12 for boys. I am sure that you would have been unhappy if you had not started puberty until you were 15 or 16, but this was the norm in North America and Europe just a century and a half ago. Presumably, this 4-year acceleration of puberty has resulted from an improvement in dietary, medical, and socioeconomic conditions.

efore proceeding to a consideration of three cases of exceptional human sexual development, review the basics of normal development by completing the following exercise.

1. Six weeks after conception, the Y chromosome of the human male triggers the production of _____.

2. In the absence of H–Y antigen, the cortical cells of the primordial gonads develop into _____.

3. In the third month of male fetal development, the testes secrete testosterone and _____ _____ substance.

4. The hormonal factor that triggers the development of the human Müllerian system is the lack of _____ around the third month of fetal development.

5. The scrotum and the _____ develop from the same bipotential precursor.

6. The female pattern of cyclic _____ release from the anterior pituitary develops in adulthood unless androgens are present in the body during the perinatal period.

7. It has been hypothesized that perinatal testosterone must first be changed to estrogen before it can masculinize the male rat brain. This is called the _____ hypothesis.

8. _____ is normally responsible for pubic and axillary hair growth in human females during puberty.

Three Cases of Exceptional Human Sexual Development

So far in Section 11.2, you have learned the "rules" according to which hormones influence sexual development. Now, three exceptions are offered to "prove" (to test) these rules.

Case 1

ANDROGENIC INSENSITIVITY SYNDROME: THE CASE OF ANNE S.

Anne S., an attractive 26-year-old female, sought treatment for two sex-related disorders: lack of menstruation and pain during sexual intercourse (Jones & Park, 1971). She sought help because she and her husband of 4 years had been trying without success to have children, and she correctly surmised that her lack of a menstrual cycle was part of the problem. A physical examination revealed that Anne was a healthy young woman. Her only readily apparent peculiarity was the sparseness and fineness of her pubic and axillary hair. Examination of her external genitals revealed no abnormalities; however, there were some problems with her internal genitals. Her vagina was only 4 centimeters long, and her uterus was underdeveloped.

At the start of this chapter, I said that you would encounter some amazing things, and the diagnosis of Anne's case certainly qualifies as one of them. Anne's doctors concluded that she was a man. No, this is not a misprint; they concluded that Anne, the attractive young housewife, was in fact Anne, the happily married man. Three lines of evidence supported this diagnosis. First, analysis of cells scraped from the inside of Anne's mouth revealed that they were of the male XY type. Second, a tiny incision in Anne's abdomen, which enabled Anne's physicians to look inside, revealed a pair of internalized testes but no ovaries. Finally, hormone tests revealed that Anne's hormone levels were those of a male.

Anne suffers from **androgenic insensitivity syndrome;** all of her symptoms stem from the fact that her body lacks the ability to respond to androgens. During development, Anne's testes released normal amounts of androgens for a male, but her body could not respond to them, and her development thus proceeded as if no androgens had been released. Her external genitals, her brain, and her behavior developed along preprogrammed female lines, without the effects of androgens to override the female program, and her testes could

The answers are (1) H–Y antigen, (2) ovaries, (3) Müllerian-inhibiting, (4) androgens (or testosterone), (5) labia majora, (6) gonadotropin, (7) aromatization, and (8) androstenedione.

not descend from her body cavity with no scrotum for them to descend into. Furthermore, Anne did not develop normal internal female reproductive ducts because, like other genetic males, her testes released Müllerian-inhibiting substance; that is why her vagina was short and her uterus undeveloped. At puberty, Anne's testes released enough estrogens to feminize her body in the absence of the counteracting effects of androgens; however, adrenal androstenedione was not able to stimulate the growth of pubic and axillary hair.

Money and Ehrhardt (1972) studied the psychosexual development of 10 androgen-insensitive patients and concluded that the placidity of their childhood play, their goals, their fantasies, their sexual behavior, and their maternal tendencies—several had adopted children—all "conformed to the idealized stereotype of what constitutes femininity in our culture" (p. 112). Apparently, without the masculinizing effects of androgens, infants who look like females and are raised as females come to think and act like females—even when they are genetic males.

An interesting issue of medical ethics is raised by the androgenic insensitivity syndrome. Many people believe that physicians should always disclose all relevant findings to their patients. If you were Anne's physician, would you tell her that she is a man? Would you tell her husband? Anne's vagina was surgically enlarged, she was counseled to consider adoption, and, as far as I know, she is still happily married and unaware of her genetic sex.

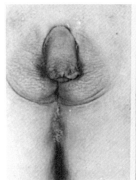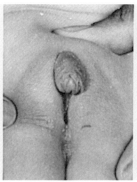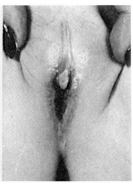

Figure 11.10 Genetic female babies with the adrenogenital syndrome displaying varying degrees of clitoral enlargement and labial fusion. The baby on your right has been surgically treated.

(Courtesy John Money, Ph.D. First published in *Johns Hopkins Medical Journal*, 122 [1968], 160–167.)

Case 2

ADRENOGENITAL SYNDROME

The **adrenogenital syndrome** is a disorder of sexual development caused by **congenital adrenal hyperplasia**—a congenital deficiency in the release of the hormone *cortisol* from the adrenal cortex, which results in compensatory adrenal hyperactivity and the excessive release of adrenal androgens. This has little effect on the development of males, other than accelerating the onset of puberty, but it has major effects on the development of genetic females. Females who suffer from the adrenogenital syndrome are usually born with an enlarged clitoris and partially fused labia, as Figure 11.10 illustrates. Their internal ducts are usually normal because the adrenal androgens are released too late to stimulate the development of the Wolffian system.

If the adrenogenital syndrome is diagnosed in a female at birth, the abnormalities of the external genitals are surgically corrected, and cortisol is administered to

reduce the levels of circulating adrenal androgens. Following early treatment, adrenogenital females grow up to be physically normal except that the onset of menstruation is likely to be later than normal. Thus they provide an excellent opportunity to study the effects of fetal androgen exposure on psychosexual development.

Adrenogenital teenage girls who have been treated with cortisol typically display a high degree of tomboyishness and little interest in maternity (e.g., Ehrhardt, Epstein, & Money, 1968). They prefer boys' clothes and toys, play mainly with boys, show little interest in handling babies, and tend to daydream about future careers rather than motherhood. It is important not to lose sight of the fact that many teenage girls in our culture display similar characteristics—and why not? Accordingly, the behavior of treated adrenogenital females, although perhaps tending toward the masculine, is well within the range considered normal by the current standards of our culture.

The most interesting questions about the development of females with adrenogenital syndrome concern their romantic and sexual preferences as adults. They seem to lag behind normal females in dating and marriage—perhaps because of the delayed onset of their menstrual cycle—but in other respects their sexual interests appear normal. Most are heterosexual, although it has been reported that they have a tendency toward bisexuality (Ehrhardt & Meyer-Bahlburg, 1981; Money,

Androgenic insensitivity syndrome. The developmental disorder of genetic males in which an insensitivity to androgens causes them to develop female bodies.

Adrenogenital syndrome. A developmental disorder in which high levels of adrenal androgens resulting from congenital adrenal hyperplasia masculinize the bodies of genetic females.

Congenital adrenal hyperplasia. A congenital deficiency in the release of cortisol from the adrenal cortex, which leads to the excessive release of adrenal androgens.

Schwartz, & Lewis, 1984). However, Zucker et al. (1996) found that although females with adrenogenital syndrome had fewer heterosexual experiences and fantasies, they had no more homosexual experiences or fantasies.

Prior to the development of cortisol therapy in 1950, genetic females with adrenogenital syndrome were left untreated. Some were raised as boys and some as girls, but the direction of their pubertal development was unpredictable. In some cases, adrenal androgens predominated and masculinized their bodies; in others, ovarian estrogens predominated and feminized their bodies. Thus some who were raised as girls were transformed at puberty into men, and some who were raised as boys were transformed into women. Money and Ehrhardt (1972) described two cases in which the sex of an untreated adrenogenital child was ostensibly changed at puberty—with devastating emotional consequences. One was referred to Money and Ehrhardt (1972) for treatment at the age of 12:

> At birth, her external genitals were somewhat ambiguous, but she was raised as a female without incident until puberty. At puberty, her sudden masculinization was the subject of great distress. . . . Treatment involved surgical enlargement of her vagina, removal of her large clitoris, and the initiation of [hormone] therapy, which suppressed androgen release and allowed her ovarian estrogens to feminize her body. She became an attractive young woman. Narrow hips and mildly short stature remained unchanged, as the *epiphyses* [the ends of bones, where bone growth takes place] of the bones had already fused under the influence of precocious masculinization. . . . The voice was husky, but so used as to be not mistaken as masculine. . . . The capacity for orgasm was not lost. The proof came fifteen years later, upon establishment of a sexual relationship and marriage. (p. 157)

Case 3

SEX REASSIGNMENT OF A TWIN
WITH ABLATIO PENIS

One of the most famous cases in the literature on sexual development is that of a male identical twin whose penis was accidentally destroyed during circumcision at the age of 7 months. Because there was no satisfactory way of surgically replacing the lost penis, a widely respected expert in such matters, John Money, recommended that the boy be castrated, that an artificial vagina be created, that the boy be raised as a girl, and that estrogen be administered at puberty to feminize the body. After a great deal of consideration and anguish, the parents followed Money's advice.

Money's (1975) report of this case of **ablatio penis** has been influential. It has been seen by some as the ultimate test of the *nature–nurture controversy* (see Chapter 2) with respect to the development of sexual identity and behavior. It seemed to pit the masculiniz-

ing effects of male genes and male hormones against the effects of being reared as a female. And the availability of a genetically identical control subject, the twin brother, made the case all the more interesting.

According to Money, the outcome of this case comes down strongly on the side of the *social-learning theory* of sexual identity. Money reported in 1975, when the patient was 12, that "she" had developed as a normal female, thus confirming his prediction that being gonadectomized, having his genitals surgically altered, and being raised as a girl would override the masculinizing effects of male genes and early androgens. Because it is such an interesting case, Money's description of it continues to be featured in many textbooks and in many television, magazine, and newspaper stories, each time carrying with it the message that the sexual identity and sexual behavior of men and women is largely a matter of upbringing.

However, a long-term follow-up study published by experts independent of the ones who initially prescribed the treatment tells an entirely different story (Diamond & Sigmundson, 1997). Despite having female genitalia and being treated as a female, John/Joan developed along male lines. Apparently, the organ that determines the course of psychosocial development is the brain, not the genitals (Reiner, 1997). The following paraphrases from Diamond and Sigmundson's report give you a glimpse of John/Joan's life.

> From a very early age, Joan tended to act in a masculine way. She preferred boys' activities and games and displayed little interest in dolls, sewing, or other conventional female activities. When she was four, she was watching her father shave and her mother put on lipstick, and she began to put shaving cream on her face. When she was told to put makeup on like her mother, she said, "No, I don't want no makeup, I want to shave."
>
> Things happened very early. As a child, I began to see that I felt different about a lot of things than I was supposed to. I suspected I was a boy from the second grade on.
>
> Despite the absence of a penis, Joan often tried to urinate while standing, and she would sometimes go to the boys' lavatory.
>
> Joan was attractive as a girl, but as soon as she moved or talked her masculinity became apparent. She was teased incessantly by the other girls, and she often retaliated violently, which resulted in her expulsion from school.
>
> Joan was put on an estrogen regimen at the age of 12 but rebelled against it. She did not want to feminize; she hated her developing breasts and refused to wear a bra.
>
> At 14, Joan decided to live as a male and switched to John. At that time, John's father tearfully revealed John's entire early history to him. "All of a sudden everything clicked. For the first time I understood who and what I was."
>
> John requested androgen treatment, a *mastectomy* (surgical removal of breasts), and *phaloplasty* (surgical creation of a penis). He became a handsome and popular young man. He married at the age of 25 and adopted his wife's children. He is strictly heterosexual.

John's ability to ejaculate and experience orgasm returned following his androgen treatments. However, his early castration permanently eliminated his reproductive capacity.

John is living a happy and productive life, but he remains bitter about his early treatment and his inability to produce offspring. He wants his story to be told to save others from his experience. Because vaginas are easier to surgically create than penises, many medical texts still advocate creating females from male infants born without a satisfactory penis.

Do current theories of hormones and sexual development pass the test of these three exceptional cases? I think so. Current theories increase our understanding of each of the three cases, and they provide an effective basis for prescribing treatment. Moreover, because each of the three people is male in some respects and female in others, each case is a serious challenge to the men-are-men and women-are-women assumption.

11.3 Effects of Gonadal Hormones on Adults

Once an individual reaches sexual maturity, gonadal hormones begin to play a role in activating reproductive behavior. These activational effects are the focus of this section, which has three parts. The first deals with the role of hormones in activating the reproduction-related behavior of men. The second deals with the role of hormones in activating the reproduction-related behavior of women. And the third deals with the epidemic of anabolic steroid use by athletes and body builders.

Male Reproduction–Related Behavior and Testosterone

The important role played by gonadal hormones in the activation of male sexual behavior is clearly demonstrated by the asexualizing effects of orchidectomy. Bremer (1959) reviewed the cases of 157 orchidectomized Norwegians. Many had committed sex-related offenses and had agreed to castration to reduce the length of their prison terms.

Two important generalizations can be drawn from Bremer's study. The first is that orchidectomy leads to a reduction in sexual interest and behavior; the second is that the rate and degree of the loss is variable. According to Bremer, about half the men became completely asexual within a few weeks of the operation; others quickly lost their ability to achieve an erection but continued to experience some sexual interest and pleasure; and a few continued to copulate successfully, although somewhat less enthusiastically, for the duration of the study. There were also body changes: a reduction of hair on the trunk, extremities, and face; the deposition of fat on the hips and chest; a softening of the skin; and a reduction in strength. Of the 102 sex offenders in the study, only 3 were reconvicted of sex offenses. Accord-

ingly, Bremer recommended castration as an effective treatment of last resort for male sex offenders.

Why do some men remain sexually active for months after orchidectomy, despite the fact that testicular hormones are cleared from their bodies within days? It has been suggested that adrenal androgens may play some role in the maintenance of sexual activity in some castrated men, but there is no direct evidence for this hypothesis.

Orchidectomy, in one fell swoop—or, to put it more precisely, in two fell swoops—removes a pair of glands that release many hormones. Because testosterone is the major testicular hormone, the major symptoms of orchidectomy have been generally attributed to the loss of testosterone, rather than to the loss of some other testicular hormone or to some nonhormonal consequence of the surgery. The therapeutic effects of **replacement injections** of testosterone have confirmed this assumption.

The very first case report of the effects of testosterone replacement therapy was that of an unfortunate 38-year-old World War I veteran, who was castrated in 1918 at the age of 19 by a shell fragment that removed his testes but left his penis undamaged. The effects were devastating:

> His body was soft; it was as if he had almost no muscles at all; his hips had grown wider and his shoulders seemed narrower than when he was a soldier. He had very little drive. . . .
>
> Just the same this veteran had married, in 1924, and you'd wonder why, because the doctors had told him he would surely be **impotent** [unable to achieve an erection]. . . . he made some attempts at sexual intercourse "for his wife's sat-

Ablatio penis. Accidental destruction of the penis.
Replacement injections. Injections of a hormone whose natural release has been curtailed by the removal of the gland that normally releases it.
Impotent. Unable to achieve a penile erection.

isfaction" but he confessed that he had been unable to satisfy her at all. . . .

Dr. Foss began injecting it [testosterone] into the feeble muscles of the castrated man. . . .

After the fifth injection, erections were rapid and prolonged. . . . But that wasn't all. During twelve weeks of treatment he had gained eighteen pounds, and all his clothes had become too small. Originally, he wore fourteen-and-a-half inch collars. Now fifteen-and-a-half were too tight. . . . testosterone had resurrected a broken man to a manhood he had lost forever. (de Kruif, 1945, pp. 97–100)

Since this first clinical trial, testosterone has breathed sexuality into the lives of many men. Testosterone does not, however, eliminate the *sterility* (inability to reproduce) of males who lack functional testes.

The fact that testosterone is necessary for male sexual behavior has led to two assumptions: (1) that the level of a man's sexuality is a function of the amount of testosterone he has in his blood, and (2) that a man's sex drive can be increased by increasing his testosterone levels. Both assumptions are incorrect.

Sex drive and testosterone levels are uncorrelated in healthy men, and testosterone injections do not increase their sex drive. It seems that each healthy male has far more testosterone than is required to activate the neural circuits that produce his sexual behavior and that having more than the minimum is of no advantage

in this respect (Sherwin, 1988). A classic experiment by Grunt and Young (1952) clearly illustrates this point. First, Grunt and Young rated the sexual behavior of each of the male guinea pigs in their experiment. Then, on the basis of the ratings, the researchers divided the male guinea pigs into three experimental groups: low, medium, and high sex drive. Following castration, the sexual behavior of all of the guinea pigs fell to negligible levels within a few weeks (see Figure 11.11), but it recovered after the initiation of a series of testosterone replacement injections. The important point is that although each subject received the same, very large replacement injections of testosterone, the injections simply returned each to its previous level of copulatory activity. The conclusion is clear: With respect to the effects of testosterone on sexual behavior, more is not necessarily better.

Dihydrotestosterone, a nonaromatizable androgen, has failed to reactivate the copulatory behavior of castrated male rats in several studies (see MacLusky & Naftolin, 1981). This suggests that in male rats the activational effects of testosterone on sexual behavior may be produced by estradiol that has been aromatized from the testosterone. However, dihydrotestosterone has proved effective in activating sexual behavior in orchidectomized primates (e.g., Davidson, Kwan, & Greenleaf, 1982).

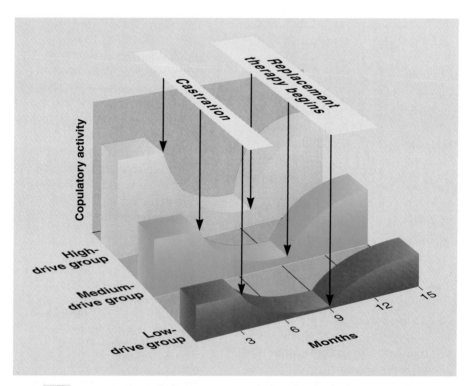

Figure 11.11 The sexual behavior of male guinea pigs with low, medium, and high sex drive. Sexual behavior was disrupted by castration and returned to its original level by very large replacement injections of testosterone.

(Adapted from Grunt & Young, 1952.)

Female Reproduction-Related Behavior and Gonadal Hormones

Sexually mature female rats and guinea pigs display 4-day cycles of gonadal hormone release. There is a gradual increase in the secretion of estrogen by the developing follicle in the 2 days prior to ovulation, followed by a sudden surge in progesterone as the egg is released. These surges of estrogen and progesterone initiate **estrus**—a period of 12 to 18 hours during which the female is *fertile, receptive* (likely to assume the lordosis posture when mounted), *proceptive* (likely to engage in behaviors that serve to attract the male), and *sexually attractive* (smelling of chemicals that attract males). The close relation between the cycle of hormone release and the **estrous cycle**—the cycle of sexual receptivity—in female rats and guinea pigs and in many other mammalian species suggests that female sexual behavior in these species is under hormonal control. The effects of ovariectomy confirm this conclusion; ovariectomy produces a rapid decline of both proceptive and receptive behaviors. Furthermore, estrus can be induced in ovariectomized rats and guinea pigs by an injection of estrogen followed a day and a half later by an injection of progesterone.

Women are not at all like female rats and guinea pigs when it comes to the hormonal control of their sexual behavior. Neither the sexual motivation nor the sexual behavior of women is inextricably linked with their menstrual cycles (see Sanders & Bancroft, 1982). Moreover, ovariectomy has surprisingly little direct effect on either their sexual motivation or sexual behavior (e.g., Martin, Roberts, & Clayton, 1980). The major consequence of ovariectomy other than sterility is a decrease in vaginal lubrication.

Paradoxically, there is evidence that the sex drive of women is under the control of androgens, not estrogens (see Sherwin, 1988). Apparently, enough androgen is released from the human adrenal glands to maintain the sexual motivation of women even after their ovaries have been removed. Support for the theory that androgens control human female sexuality has come from three sources:

1. Experiments in nonhuman female primates: Replacement injections of testosterone, but not estradiol, increase the proceptivity of ovariectomized and adrenalectomized rhesus monkeys (see Everitt & Herbert, 1972; Everitt, Herbert, & Hamer, 1971).

2. Correlational studies in healthy women: Various measures of sexual motivation are correlated with testosterone levels but not with estradiol levels (see Bancroft et al., 1983; Morris et al., 1987).

3. Clinical studies of women following ovariectomy and adrenalectomy: Replacement injections of testosterone,

but not of estradiol, rekindle their sexual motivation (see Sherwin, 1985; Sherwin, Gelfand, & Brender, 1985).

Anabolic Steroid Abuse

Anabolic steroids are steroids, such as testosterone, that have *anabolic* (growth-promoting) effects. Testosterone itself is not very useful as an anabolic drug because it is broken down soon after injection and because it has undesirable side effects. Chemists have managed to synthesize a number of potent anabolic steroids that are long-acting, but they have not managed to synthesize one that does not have side effects.

We are currently in the midst of an epidemic of anabolic steroid abuse. Many competitive athletes and bodybuilders are self-administering appallingly large doses to increase their muscularity and strength, but the problem is much more extensive than this. In recent years, the cosmetic use of steroids has reached troubling proportions. For example, a recent study in California found that 5% of boys and 3% of girls aged 12 to 14 had used anabolic steroids.

Do anabolic steroids really increase the muscularity and strength of the athletes who use them? Surprisingly, the scientific evidence is inconsistent (see Yesalis & Bahrke, 1995), even though many athletes and coaches believe that it is impossible to compete successfully at the highest levels of their sports without an anabolic steroid boost. The failure of science to confirm the benefits that seem to have been experienced by many athletes likely results from two shortcomings of the scientific research. First, the experimental studies have tended to use doses of steroids smaller than those used by athletes. Second, the experimental studies have often been conducted on subjects who are not involved in intense anabolic training. However, despite the lack of firm scientific evidence, it is difficult to ignore the successes of steroid users such as the gentleman pictured in Figure 11.12 on page 304.

It is the sex-related side effects of anabolic steroids that are of primary relevance here. However, it has proved extremely difficult to document these effects because the use of anabolic steroids without prescription is illegal in many parts of the world. Nevertheless, there is general agreement (see Yesalis & Bahrke, 1995) that people who take high doses of anabolic steroids risk the following sex-related side effects. In men, the negative feedback from high levels of anabolic steroids reduces gonadotropin release; this leads to a reduction in

---

Estrus. The portion of the estrous cycle characterized by fertility and sexual receptivity (*estrus* is a noun and *estrous* an adjective).
Estrous cycle. The cycle of sexual receptivity and nonreceptivity

displayed by many female mammals.
Anabolic steroids. Steroid drugs that are similar to testosterone and have powerful anabolic (growth-promoting) effects.

Figure 11.12 An athlete who used anabolic steroids to augment his training program.

cessive growth of body hair), growth of the clitoris, development of a masculine body shape, baldness, shrinking of the breasts, and deepening and coarsening of the voice. Unfortunately, many of the sex-related effects on women appear to be irreversible.

Both men and women who use anabolic steroids can suffer muscle spasms, muscle pains, blood in the urine, acne, general swelling from the retention of water, bleeding of the tongue, nausea, vomiting, and a variety of psychotic behaviors, including fits of depression and anger (Pope & Katz, 1987). Oral anabolic steroids produce cancerous liver tumors.

A controlled evaluation of the effects of anabolic steroid exposure was conducted in adult male mice. Mice were exposed for 6 months to a cocktail of four anabolic steroids at relative levels comparable to those used by human athletes (Bronson & Matherne, 1997). None of the mice died during the period of steroid exposure; however, by 20 months of age, 52% of the steroid-exposed mice had died, whereas only 12% of the controls had died.

The side effects of anabolic steroid abuse make two important points about hormones and sex. The first is that testosteronelike substances do not produce increases in the sexual motivation and behavior of people with testosterone levels in the normal range. The second is that the effects of hormones on the structure of the human body are not restricted to critical prenatal and pubertal periods. Although there are periods in one's life (i.e., sensitive periods) when hormones, or other agents or experiences, have a particularly great effect on development, they can also influence development outside these periods when administered in high doses.

testicular activity, which can result in *testicular atrophy* (wasting away of the testes) and sterility. *Gynecomastia* (breast growth in men) can also occur, presumably as the result of the aromatization of anabolic steroids to estrogens. In women, anabolic steroids can produce *amenorrhea* (cessation of menstruation), sterility, *hirsutism* (ex-

11.4 The Hypothalamus and Sexual Behavior

Many parts of the brain are involved in mammalian sexual behavior. However, the discovery that gonadotropin release is controlled by the hypothalamus focused the study of the neural bases of sexual behavior on this structure.

Structural Differences between the Male Hypothalamus and the Female Hypothalamus

You have already learned that the male hypothalamus and the female hypothalamus are functionally different

in their control of anterior pituitary hormones (steady versus cyclic release, respectively). In the 1970s, structural differences between the male and female hypothalamus were discovered in rats (Raisman & Field, 1971). Most notably, Gorski and his colleagues (1978) discovered a nucleus in the **medial preoptic area** of the rat hypothalamus that was several times larger in males (see Figure 11.13). They called this nucleus the **sexually dimorphic nucleus.**

At birth, the sexually dimorphic nuclei of male and female rats are the same size. In the first few days after birth, the male sexually dimorphic nuclei grow at a high rate and the female sexually dimorphic nuclei do not. The growth of the male sexually dimorphic nuclei is

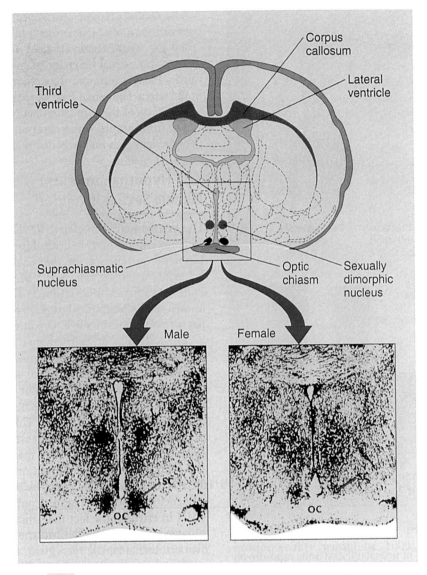

Figure 11.13 Nissl-stained coronal sections through the preoptic area of male and female rats. The sexually dimorphic nuclei (indicated by the arrows) are larger in male rats than in female rats.

(Adapted from Gorski et al., 1978.)

triggered by estradiol, which has been aromatized from testosterone (see McEwen, 1987). Accordingly, castrating day-old (but not 4-day-old) male rats significantly reduces the size of their sexually dimorphic nuclei as adults, whereas injecting neonatal (newborn) female rats with testosterone significantly increases the size of theirs (Gorski, 1980)—see Figure 11.14 on page 306. Although the overall size of the sexually dimorphic nuclei diminishes only slightly in male rats that are castrated in adulthood, specific areas of the nucleus do display significant degeneration (Bloch & Gorski, 1988).

The size of a male rat's sexually dimorphic nuclei is correlated with the rat's testosterone levels and aspects of its sexual activity (Anderson et al., 1986). However, because bilateral lesions of the sexually dimorphic nucleus have only slight effects on male rat sexual behav-

ior, it is likely that the specific function of this nucleus has yet to be established.

Since the discovery of the sexually dimorphic nuclei in rats, other sex differences in hypothalamic anatomy have been identified in rats and in other species (see Swaab & Hofman, 1995; Witelson, 1991). In humans, for example, there are nuclei in the preoptic (Swaab & Fliers, 1985), suprachiasmatic (Swaab et al., 1994), and anterior (Allen et al., 1989) regions of the hypothalamus

Medial preoptic area. The area of the hypothalamus that includes the sexually dimorphic nuclei and that plays a key role in the control of male sexual behavior.

Sexually dimorphic nucleus. The nucleus in the medial preoptic area of rats that is larger in males than in females.

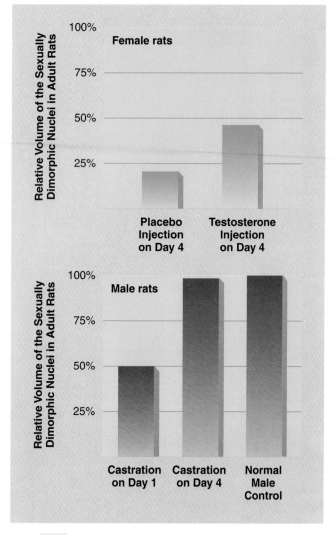

Figure 11.14 The effects of neonatal testosterone exposure on the size of the sexually dimorphic nuclei in male and female adult rats. (Adapted from Gorski, 1980.)

that are substantially larger in men than women. The gender differences in brain anatomy are a function of age; for example, the gender difference in human preoptic anatomy is not apparent in children who are less than 2 years old (Hofman & Swaab, 1989).

The Hypothalamus and Male Sexual Behavior

The medial preoptic area of the hypothalamus plays a key role in male sexual behavior. Destruction of the entire area abolishes sexual behavior in the males of many species, and selective destruction of the sexually dimorphic nuclei has been shown in some studies to reduce the sexual behavior of male rats (De Jonge et al., 1989; Turkenburg et al., 1988). In contrast, medial preoptic area lesions have no effect on female sexual be-

havior, but they do eliminate the male mounting behavior that is often observed in female rats (Singer, 1968). Thus bilateral medial preoptic lesions appear to abolish male copulatory behavior in both sexes. On the other side of the coin, electrical stimulation of the medial preoptic area elicits copulatory behavior in male rats (Malsbury, 1971), and copulatory behavior can be reinstated in castrated male rats by medial preoptic implants of testosterone (Davidson, 1980).

It is not clear why males with medial preoptic lesions stop copulating. These males vigorously approach and investigate receptive females, and they make clumsy attempts to mount them (e.g., Malsbury & Pfaff, 1974; Powers, Newman, & Bergondy, 1987). They seem to want to copulate, but for some unknown reason they can't. Everitt and Stacey (1987) confirmed this view by assessing the effects of medial preoptic lesions on male rats that had been trained to press a lever for access to receptive females, which dropped into their test chambers through a trap door in the ceiling. Following medial-preoptic-area lesions, the male rats continued to press the lever at a high rate to receive the females, but they never managed to copulate with them. In contrast, orchidectomized males stopped pressing the lever.

The medial preoptic area, in particular those regions of it that are sexually dimorphic, is dense in receptors for the neuropeptide *galanin* (Bloch, Eckersell, & Mills, 1993). Not surprisingly, then, microinjections of galanin into the male medial preoptic area elicit copulatory behavior (Bloch et al., 1993). In contrast, microinjections of endorphin into the same area block male copulatory behavior (Dornan & Malsbury, 1989; van Furth, van Ernst, & van Ree, 1995).

The medial preoptic area appears to control male sexual behavior via a tract that projects to an area of the midbrain called the *lateral tegmental field*. Destruction of this tract disrupts the sexual behavior of male rats (Brackett & Edwards, 1984). Moreover, the activity of individual neurons in the lateral tegmental field of male rats is often correlated with aspects of the copulatory act (Shimura & Shimokochi, 1990); for example, some neurons in the lateral tegmental field fire at a high rate only during intromission.

The Hypothalamus and Female Sexual Behavior

The **ventromedial nucleus** (VMN) of the hypothalamus contains circuits that are critical for female sexual behavior. Electrical stimulation of the VMN facilitates the sexual behavior of female rats, and VMN lesions reduce it (see Pfaff & Modianos, 1985). Indeed, female rats with bilateral lesions of the VMN do not display lordosis, and they are likely to attack suitors who become too ardent.

You have already learned that an injection of progesterone brings into estrus an ovariectomized female rat that received an injection of estradiol 48 hours before. Because the progesterone by itself does not induce estrus, the estradiol must in some way prime the nervous system so that the progesterone can exert its effect. This priming effect appears to be mediated by the large increase in the number of *progesterone receptors* that occurs in the VMN and surrounding area following an estradiol injection (Blaustein et al., 1988); the estradiol exerts this effect by entering VMN cells and influencing gene expression. Confirming the role of the VMN in estrus is the fact that microinjections of estradiol and progesterone directly into the VMN induce estrus in ovariectomized female rats (Pleim & Barfield, 1988).

There is evidence that the VMN mechanism that plays a role in the sexual behavior of female rats is noradrenergic. In one key experiment, levels of *norepinephrine* in the VMN were recorded by *cerebral dialysis* (see Chapter 5) in ovariectomized female rats (Vathy & Etgen, 1989). The mere presence of a male rat induced a massive release of norepinephrine in the VMN of ovariectomized female rats that had been brought into estrus by injections of estradiol and progesterone.

The influence of the VMN on the sexual behavior of female rats appears to be mediated by a tract that descends to the *periaqueductal gray (PAG)* of the tegmentum. Destruction of this tract eliminates female sexual

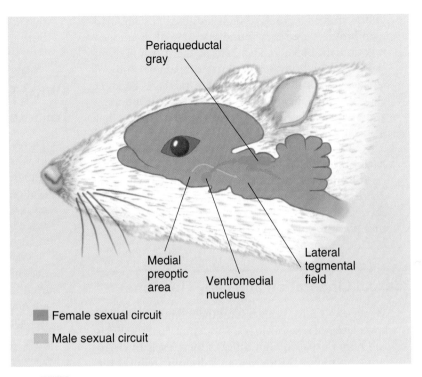

Figure 11.15 The hypothalamus–tegmentum circuits that play a role in female and male sexual behavior.

behavior (Hennessey et al., 1990), as do lesions of the PAG itself (Sakuma & Pfaff, 1979).

In summary, research on rodents suggests that tracts that run from the hypothalamus to the mesencephalon play important roles in sexual behavior. Male sexual behavior is influenced by a tract that runs from the medial preoptic area to the lateral tegmental field, and female sexual behavior is influenced by a tract that runs from the ventromedial nucleus to the periaqueductal gray (see Figure 11.15).

11.5 Sexual Orientation, Hormones, and the Brain

So far, this chapter has avoided the issue of sexual orientation. As you know, some people are **heterosexual** (sexually attracted to members of the other sex), some are **homosexual** (sexually attracted to members of the same sex), and some are **bisexual** (sexually attracted to members of both sexes). A discussion of recent research on sexual orientation is a fitting conclusion to this chapter because it brings together its hormone, hypothalamus, exception-proves-the-rule, and antimamawawa themes.

Sexual Orientation, Genes, and Hormones

Research has shown that differences in sexual orientation have a genetic basis. For example, Bailey and Pillard

---

Ventromedial nucleus. A hypothalamic nucleus that is involved in female sexual behavior.
Heterosexual. Sexually attracted to members of the other sex.

Homosexual. Sexually attracted to members of the same sex.
Bisexual. Sexually attracted to members of both sexes.

(1991) studied a group of male homosexuals who had twin brothers, and they found that 52% of the monozygotic twin brothers and 22% of the dizygotic twin brothers were homosexual. In a comparable study of female twins by the same group of researchers (Bailey et al., 1993), the concordance rates were 48% for monozygotic twins and 16% for dizygotic twins. A gene that seems to play a role in the development of male sexual orientation has been located. It is near one end of the X-chromosome (Hamer et al., 1993).

It is important not to overreact to this genetic evidence. The fact that genes influence individual differences in sexual orientation does not imply that experience plays no role.

Sexual Orientation and Early Hormones

Many people mistakenly assume that homosexuals have lower levels of sex hormones. They don't: Heterosexuals and homosexuals do not differ in their levels of circulating hormones. Moreover, orchidectomy reduces the sexual behavior of both heterosexual and homosexual males, but it does not redirect it; and replacement injections simply reactivate the preferences that existed prior to surgery.

Efforts to determine whether perinatal hormone levels influence the development of sexual orientation have focused on nonhuman species. A consistent pattern of findings has emerged from this research (see Ellis & Ames, 1987). In rats, hamsters, ferrets, pigs, zebra finches, and dogs, perinatal castration of males or testosterone treatment of females has been shown to induce same-sex preferences (see Adkins-Regan, 1988; Baum et al., 1990).

On the one hand, prudence should be exercised in applying the results of experiments on laboratory species to the development of sexual preferences in humans; it would be a mistake to ignore the profound cognitive and emotional components of human sexuality, which have no counterpart in laboratory animals. On the other hand, it would also be a mistake to think that a pattern of results that runs so consistently through so many mammalian species has no relevance to humans.

Do perinatal hormone levels influence the sexual orientation of adult humans? Although directly relevant evidence is sparse, there are some indications that the answer is yes. The strongest support for this view comes from the quasiexperimental study of Ehrhardt and her colleagues (1985). They interviewed adult women whose mothers had been exposed to *diethylstilbestrol* (a synthetic estrogen) during pregnancy. The subjects' responses indicated that they were significantly more sexually attracted to women than was a group of matched control subjects. Ehrhardt and her colleagues concluded that perinatal estrogen exposure does encourage homosexuality and bisexuality in women but

that its effect is relatively weak: The sexual behavior of all but 1 of the 30 subjects was still primarily heterosexual.

What Triggers the Development of Sexual Attraction?

The evidence indicates that most girls and boys living in Western countries experience their first feelings of sexual attraction at about 10 years of age. This finding is at odds with the usual assumption that sexual interest is triggered by puberty, which, as you have learned, currently tends to occur at 11 years of age in girls and at 12 years of age in boys.

McClintock and Herdt (1996) have suggested that the emergence of sexual attraction may be stimulated by adrenal cortex steroids. Unlike gonadal maturation, adrenal maturation occurs during childhood, at about the age of 10.

Is There a Difference in the Brains of Homosexuals and Heterosexuals?

There have been several reports of neuroanatomical, neuropsychological, and hormonal response differences between homosexuals and heterosexuals (see Gladue, 1994). Most studies have compared male heterosexuals and homosexuals; studies of lesbians are scarce. In many cases, but not all, male homosexuals have been found to be intermediate between female and male heterosexuals in their brain structure. For example LeVay (1991) compared the postmortem neuroanatomy of three groups of subjects: heterosexual men, homosexual men, and women (who were assumed to be heterosexual). Reports of gender differences in the anterior and preoptic areas of the hypothalamus of various species, including humans, focused LeVay's research on these areas. LeVay confirmed a previous report (Allen et al., 1989) that the *third interstitial nucleus of the anterior hypothalamus (INAH 3)* is more than twice as large in heterosexual men as it is in women. In addition, he found that it is more than twice as large in heterosexual men as it is in homosexual men (see Figure 11.16). LeVay's report created a kerfuffle (fuss) in both the popular and the scientific media (Byne, 1994; LeVay & Hamer, 1994).

To put LeVay's finding in proper perspective, you should ask yourself two questions about it. First: Is it reliable? You should remain a bit skeptical about any finding until it has been replicated, preferably by a different group of investigators; this is particularly true in an emotion-charged area of research such as the study of homosexuality. Second: What does it mean? LeVay's finding does not prove, as implied in many newspaper articles, that homosexuality results from a small INAH 3. Like all correlations, LeVay's observation is subject to

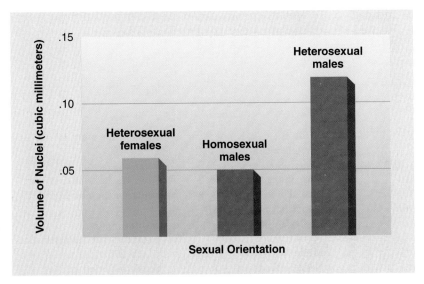

Figure 11.16 *The size of the third interstitial nucleus of the anterior hypothalamus (INAH 3) in heterosexual males and females and in homosexual males. (LeVay, 1991)*

a variety of causal interpretations. Being a homosexual may cause small INAH 3s, rather than vice versa, or some unrecognized third factor may affect both and be responsible for the correlation.

LeVay considered a third factor that might have led to the correlation, but he ruled it out: the possibility that AIDS was responsible for the correlation. Many of the homosexual brains in LeVay's study came from men who had died of AIDS, which is why LeVay was able to obtain such a large sample of male homosexual brains and why he did not include female homosexuals in his study. However, even when LeVay considered only those subjects who had died of other causes, there was still a weak correlation between sexual orientation and the size of the INAH 3.

Despite the fact that LeVay's study has proved little about the neural mechanisms of homosexuality or its causes, it is potentially of great importance. By locating a difference in the brains of male heterosexuals and homosexuals, in a part of the brain that is important for both hormonal regulation and sexual behavior, LeVay has provided a focus for the next generation of research on human sexual orientation.

CONCLUSION

The primary purpose of this chapter was to describe the role of hormones in sexual development and behavior. First, you were introduced to the principles of neuroendocrine function (11.1). Then, the effects of sex hormones on developing (11.2) and sexually mature individuals (11.3) were reviewed. Finally, the neural and hormonal factors in sexual behavior (11.4) and orientation (11.5) were discussed.

Two important subthemes ran through this chapter: (1) that exceptional cases play a particularly important role in testing scientific theory and (2) that the men-are-men and women-are-women attitude is a misleading perspective from which to consider sexual matters. If you now appreciate why exceptional cases have been so important in the study of hormones and sex, you have learned a fundamental principle that has

relevance to all fields of scientific inquiry. If you now are better able to resist the seductive appeal of the men-are-men and women-are-women attitude, you are leaving this chapter a more tolerant and understanding person than when you began it. I hope you now have an abiding appreciation of the fact that maleness and femaleness are slight, multidimensional, and at times ambiguous variations of each other.

Some stories are too good not to be told; the following is one of them. I just can't end a chapter about sex without telling it. It is about my friend's aunt, a right proper English lady. She was puzzled by "this oral sex thing" that she had been reading about in her magazines. "Good heavens," she exclaimed. "Whatever do they talk about?"

FOOD FOR THOUGHT

1. Over the last century and half, the onset of puberty has changed from age 15 or 16 to age 11 or 12, but there has been no corresponding acceleration in psychological and intellectual development. Precocious puberty is like a loaded gun in the hand of a child. Discuss.

2. Do you think sex-change operations should be permitted? Explain.

3. What should be done about the current epidemic of anabolic steroid abuse? Would you make the same recommendation if a safe anabolic steroid were developed? If a safe drug that would dramatically improve your memory were developed, would you take it?

4. Discuss LeVay's report of a difference in the brains of heterosexual and homosexual men. Discuss with re-

spect to the physiological-or-psychological and the learned-or-innate dichotomies, which were criticized in Chapter 2.

5. Heterosexuality cannot be understood without studying homosexuality. Discuss.

KEY TERMS

Ablatio penis (*p. 300*)
Adrenal cortex (*p. 287*)
Adrenocorticotropic hormone (*p. 296*)
Adrenogenital syndrome (*p. 299*)
Alpha fetoprotein (*p. 295*)
Amino acid derivative hormones (*p. 286*)
Anabolic steroids (*p. 303*)
Androgenic insensitivity syndrome (*p. 298*)
Androgens (*p. 287*)
Androstenedione (*p. 297*)
Anterior pituitary (*p. 287*)
Aromatization (*p. 295*)
Bisexual (*p. 307*)
Congenital adrenal hyperplasia (*p. 299*)
Copulation (*p. 286*)
Defeminizes (*p. 296*)
Demasculinizes (*p. 296*)
Dihydrotestosterone (*p. 295*)
Ejaculation (*p. 296*)
Endocrine glands (*p. 285*)

Estradiol (*p. 287*)
Estrogens (*p. 287*)
Estrous cycle (*p. 303*)
Estrus (*p. 303*)
Exocrine glands (*p. 285*)
Feminizes (*p. 296*)
Follicle (*p. 290*)
Follicle-stimulating hormone (FSH) (*p. 290*)
Genitals (*p. 294*)
Gonadectomy (*p. 293*)
Gonadotropin-releasing hormone (*p. 290*)
Gonadotropins (*p. 287*)
Gonads (*p. 286*)
Growth hormone (*p. 296*)
H-Y antigen (*p. 292*)
Heterosexual (*p. 307*)
Homosexual (*p. 307*)
Hormones (*p. 285*)
Hypothalamopituitary portal system (*p. 289*)
Impotent (*p. 301*)
Inhibitory factors (*p. 289*)
Intromission (*p. 296*)

Lordosis (*p. 296*)
Luteinizing hormone (LH) (*p. 290*)
Masculinizes (*p. 296*)
Medial preoptic area (*p. 304*)
Menstrual cycle (*p. 288*)
Müllerian-inhibiting substance (*p. 293*)
Müllerian system (*p. 292*)
Negative feedback (*p. 290*)
Orchidectomy (*p. 293*)
Ovariectomy (*p. 293*)
Ovaries (*p. 286*)
Ovulation (*p. 290*)
Oxytocin (*p. 288*)
Paraventricular nuclei (*p. 288*)
Peptide hormones (*p. 286*)
Pituitary stalk (*p. 287*)
Positive feedback (*p. 290*)
Posterior pituitary (*p. 287*)
Proceptive behaviors (*p. 296*)
Progesterone (*p. 287*)
Progestins (*p. 287*)
Protein hormones (*p. 286*)

Pulsatile hormone release (*p. 290*)
Releasing factors (*p. 289*)
Releasing hormones (*p. 290*)
Replacement injections (*p. 301*)
Scrotum (*p. 293*)
Secondary sex characteristics (*p. 296*)
Sensitive period (*p. 296*)
Sex chromosomes (*p. 286*)
Sexually dimorphic nucleus (*p. 304*)
Steroid hormones (*p. 286*)
Supraoptic nuclei (*p. 288*)
Testes (*p. 286*)
Testosterone (*p. 287*)
Thyrotropin (*p. 290*)
Thyrotropin-releasing hormone (*p. 289*)
Vasopressin (*p. 288*)
Ventromedial nucleus (*p. 306*)
Wolffian system (*p. 292*)
Zygote (*p. 286*)

ADDITIONAL READING

The following text provides an introduction to the general field of behavioral neuroendocrinology:

Becker, J. B., Breedlove, S. M., & Crews, D. (Eds.). (1992). *Behavioral endocrinology.* Cambridge, MA: MIT Press.

The following is an excellent review of the development of sex differences in the human brain:

Breedlove, S. M. (1994). Sexual differentiation of the human brain. *Annual Review of Psychology, 45,* 389–418.

The following is a review of the effects of anabolic steroids:

Yesalis, C. E., & Behrke, M. S. (1995). Anabolic-androgenic steroids. *Sports Medicine, 19,* 326–340.

The following article describes the tragedy of the boy whose penis was destroyed and who was subsequently raised as a girl:

Diamond, M., & Sigmundson, H. K. (1997). Sex reassignment at birth: Long-term review and clinical implications. *Archives of Pediatric and Adolescent Medicine, 151,* 298–304.

The following three articles provide coverage of research on the development of sexual orientation mainly in males; there is little comparable research in females:

Byne, W. (1994, May). The biological evidence challenged. *Scientific American, 270,* 50–55.

Gladue, B. A. (1994). The biopsychology of sexual orientation. *Current Directions in Psychological Science, 3,* 150–154.

LeVay, S., & Hamer, D. H. (1994, May). Evidence for a biological influence in male homosexuality. *Scientific American, 270,* 44–49.

Sleep, Dreaming, and Circadian Rhythms

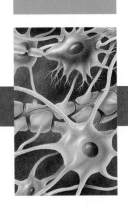

Most of us have a fondness for eating, drinking, and sex— the three highly esteemed motivated behaviors discussed in Chapters 10 and 11. But the amount of time devoted to these three behaviors by even the most amorous gourmands pales in comparison to the amount of time spent sleeping: Most of us will sleep for well over 175,000 hours in our lifetimes.

This extraordinary commitment of time implies that sleep fulfills a critical biological function. But what is it? And what about dreaming: Why do we spend so much time dreaming? And why do we tend to get sleepy at about the same time every day? Answers to these questions await you in this chapter.

Almost every time I give a lecture about sleep, somebody asks, "How much sleep do we need?" and each time, I provide the same unsatisfying answer. I explain that there are two fundamentally different answers to this question, but that neither has emerged a clear winner. One answer stresses the presumed health-promoting and recuperative powers of sleep and suggests that people need as much sleep as they can comfortably get. The other answer is that many of us sleep more than we need to and are consequently sleeping part of our lives away. Just think how your life could change if you slept 5 hours per night instead of 8. You would have an extra 21 waking hours each week, a mind-boggling 10,952 hours each decade.

As I prepared to write this chapter, I began to think of some of the personal implications of the idea that we get more sleep than we need. That is when I decided to do something a bit unconventional. While I write this chapter, I am going to be your subject in a sleep-reduction experiment. I am going to try to get no more than 5 hours of sleep per night—11:00 P.M. to 4:00 A.M.— until this chapter is written. As I begin, I am excited by the prospect of having more time to write but a little worried that this extra time might be obtained at a personal cost that is too dear.

It is the next day now—4:50 Saturday morning to be exact—and I am just beginning to write. There was a party last night, and I didn't make it to bed by 11:00; but considering that I slept for only 3 hours and 35 minutes, I feel quite good. I wonder what I will feel like later in the day. In any case, I will report my experiences to you at the end of the chapter.

The following case study challenges several common beliefs about sleep. Ponder its implications before proceeding into the body of the chapter:

Miss M . . . is a busy lady who finds her ration of twenty-three hours of wakefulness still insufficient for her needs. Even though she is now retired she is still busy in the community, helping sick friends whenever requested. She is an active painter and has recently finished a biography of William Morris, the British writer and designer. Although she becomes tired physically, when she needs to sit down to rest her legs, she does not ever report feeling sleepy. During the night she sits on her bed . . . reading, writing, crocheting or painting. At about 2:00 A.M. she falls asleep without any preceding drowsiness often while still holding a book in her hands. When she wakes about an hour later, she feels as wide awake as ever. It would be wrong to say that she woke refreshed because she did not complain of tiredness in the first place.

To test her claim we invited her along to the laboratory. She came willingly but on the first evening we hit our first snag. She announced that she did not sleep at all if she had interesting things to do, and by her reckoning a visit to a university sleep laboratory counted as very interesting. Moreover, for the first time in years, she had someone to talk to for the whole of the night. So we talked.

In the morning we broke into shifts so that some could sleep while at least one person stayed with her and entertained her during the next day. The second night was a repeat performance of the first night. . . . Things had not gone according to plan. So far we were very impressed by her cheerful response to two nights of sleep deprivation, but we had very little by way of hard data to show others.

In the end we prevailed upon her to allow us to apply EEG electrodes and to leave her sitting comfortably on the bed in the bedroom. She had promised that she would co-operate by not resisting sleep although she claimed not to be especially tired. . . . At approximately 1:30 A.M., the EEG record showed the first signs of sleep even though . . . she was still sitting with the book in her hands. . . .

The only substantial difference between her sleep and what we might have expected from any other seventy-year-old lady was that it was of short duration. . . . [After 99 minutes], she had no further interest in sleep and asked to be allowed to leave the bedroom so that she could join our company again. (Meddis, 1977, pp. 42–44)[1]

12.1 The Physiological and Behavioral Correlates of Sleep

Many changes occur in the body during sleep. This section of the chapter introduces you to the major ones.

[1]From *The Sleep Instinct* (pp. 42–44) by R. Meddis. Copyright © 1977, Routledge & Kegan Paul, London. Reprinted by permission.

The Three Standard Psychophysiological Measures of Sleep

There are major changes in the human EEG during the course of a night's sleep (Loomis, Harvey, & Hobart, 1936). Although the EEG waves that accompany sleep are generally high-voltage and slow, there are periods throughout the night that are dominated by low-voltage, fast waves similar to those of waking subjects. In 1953, Aserinsky and Kleitman discovered that *rapid eye movements (REMs)* occur under the closed eyelids of sleeping subjects during these periods of low-voltage, fast EEG activity. And in 1962, Berger and Oswald discovered that there is also a loss of electromyographic activity in the neck muscles during these same sleep periods. Subsequently, the **electroencephalogram (EEG),** the **electrooculogram (EOG),** and the neck **electromyogram (EMG)** became the three standard psychophysiological bases for defining stages of sleep (Rechtschaffen & Kales, 1968).

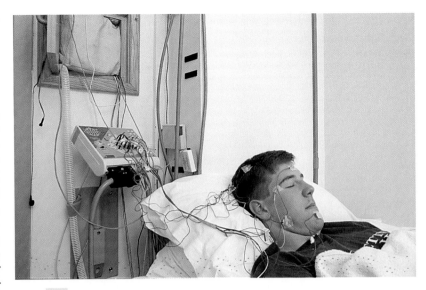

Figure 12.1 A subject participating in a sleep experiment.

Figure 12.1 depicts a subject participating in a sleep experiment. A subject's first night's sleep in a sleep laboratory is often fitful. That is why it is the usual practice to have each subject sleep several nights in the laboratory before commencing a study. The disturbance of sleep observed during the first night in a sleep laboratory is called the **first-night phenomenon.** It is well known to markers of introductory psychology examinations because of the creative definitions of it that are offered by students who forget that it is a sleep-related, rather than a sex-related, phenomenon.

Four Stages of Sleep EEG

There are four stages of sleep EEG: stage 1, stage 2, stage 3, and stage 4. Examples of each are presented in Figure 12.2 on page 314.

After the eyes are shut and a person prepares to go to sleep, **alpha waves**—waxing and waning bursts of 8- to 12-Hz EEG waves—begin to punctuate the low-voltage, high-frequency EEG of active wakefulness. Then, as the person falls asleep, there is a sudden transition to a period of stage 1 sleep EEG. The stage 1 sleep EEG is a low-voltage, high-frequency signal that is similar to, but slower than, that of active wakefulness.

There is a gradual increase in EEG voltage and a decrease in EEG frequency as the person progresses from stage 1 sleep through stages 2, 3, and 4. Accordingly, the stage 2 sleep EEG has a slightly higher amplitude and

lower frequency than the stage 1 EEG; in addition, it is punctuated by two characteristic wave forms: K complexes and sleep spindles. Each **K complex** is a single large negative wave (upward deflection) followed immediately by a single large positive wave (downward deflection). Each **sleep spindle** is a 1- to 2-second waxing and waning burst of 12- to 14-Hz waves. The stage 3 sleep EEG is defined by the occasional presence of **delta waves**—the largest and slowest EEG waves, with a frequency of 1 to 2 Hz—whereas the stage 4 sleep EEG is defined by a predominance of delta waves.

Once subjects reach stage 4 EEG sleep, they stay there for a time, and then they retreat back through the stages of sleep to stage 1. However, when they return to stage 1, things are not at all the same as they were the first time through. The first period of the stage 1 EEG during a night's sleep (**initial stage 1 EEG**) is not marked by any striking electromyographic or electrooculographic changes, whereas subsequent periods of the stage 1 sleep EEG (**emergent stage 1 EEG**) are accompanied by REMs and by a loss of tone in the muscles of the body core.

Electroencephalogram (EEG). A measure of the electrical activity of the brain, commonly recorded through scalp electrodes.

Electrooculogram (EOG). A measure of eye movement.

Electromyogram (EMG). A measure of the electrical activity of muscles.

First-night phenomenon. The sleep disturbances experienced during the first night that a subject sleeps in a laboratory.

Alpha waves. 8- to 12-Hz EEG waves that commonly punctuate the EEG of human subjects just before they fall asleep.

K complexes. The large, biphasic EEG waves that are characteristic of the stage 2 sleep EEG.

Sleep spindles. The 1- to 2-second bursts of 12- to 14-Hz EEG waves characteristic of stage 2 sleep.

Delta waves. The largest, slowest EEG waves.

Initial stage 1 EEG. The period of the stage 1 EEG that occurs at the onset of sleep; it is not associated with REM.

Emergent stage 1 EEG. All periods of stage 1 sleep EEG except initial stage 1; it is associated with REM.

Figure 12.2 The EEG of alert wakefulness, the EEG that precedes sleep onset, and the four stages of sleep EEG. Each trace is about 10 seconds long.

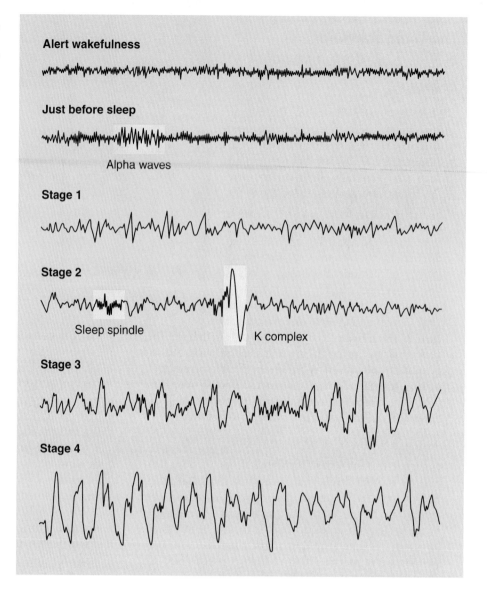

Alert wakefulness

Just before sleep

Alpha waves

Stage 1

Stage 2

Sleep spindle   K complex

Stage 3

Stage 4

After the first cycle of sleep EEG—from initial stage 1 to stage 4 and back to emergent stage 1—the rest of the night is spent going back and forth through the stages. Figure 12.3 illustrates the EEG cycles of a typical night's sleep and the close relation between emergent stage 1 sleep, REMs, and the loss of tone in core muscles. Notice that each cycle tends to be about 90 minutes long and that, as the night progresses, more and more time is spent in emergent stage 1 sleep and less and less time is spent in the other stages, particularly in stage 4. Notice also that there are brief periods during the night when the subject is awake; these periods of wakefulness are usually not remembered in the morning.

Let's pause here to get some sleep-stage terms straight. The sleep associated with emergent stage 1 EEG is often called **paradoxical sleep** because the EEG

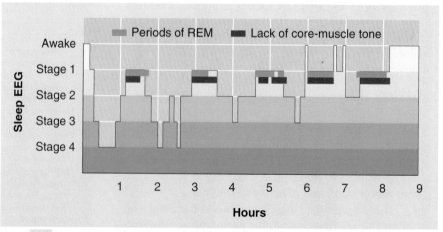

Figure 12.3 The course of EEG stages during a typical night's sleep and the relation of emergent stage 1 EEG to REMs and lack of tone in core muscles.

12 SLEEP, DREAMING, AND CIRCADIAN RHYTHMS

signal itself and the associated autonomic changes are similar to those of wakefulness, and the sleep associated with stages 3 and 4 sleep EEG is often called **delta sleep** (after the delta waves that characterize stages 3 and 4 sleep EEG). In this chapter, I follow the common practice of referring to the sleep characterized by rapid eye movements, loss of core muscle tone, and emergent stage 1 EEG as **REM sleep** and referring to stages 2, 3, and 4 together as **slow-wave sleep (SWS).**

REMs, loss of core muscle tone, and a low-amplitude, high-frequency EEG are not the only physiological correlates of REM sleep. Cerebral activity (e.g., oxygen consumption, blood flow, and neural firing) increases to waking levels in many structures, and there is a general increase in autonomic nervous system activity (e.g., in blood pressure, pulse, and respiration). Also, the muscles of the extremities occasionally twitch, and there is always some degree of clitoral or penile erection.

12.2 REM Sleep and Dreaming

Nathaniel Kleitman's laboratory was an exciting place in 1953. Kleitman's students had just discovered REM sleep, and they were driven by the fascinating implication of their discovery. With the exception of the loss of tone in the core muscles, all of the other measures suggested that REM sleep episodes were emotion-charged. Could REM sleep be the physiological correlate of dreaming? Could it provide researchers with a window into the subjective inner world of dreams? The researchers began by waking a few subjects in the middle of REM episodes and asking them if they had been dreaming. The results were remarkable:

> The vivid recall that could be elicited in the middle of the night when a subject was awakened while his eyes were moving rapidly was nothing short of miraculous. It [seemed to open] . . . an exciting new world to the subjects whose only previous dream memories had been the vague morning-after recall. Now, instead of perhaps some fleeting glimpse into the dream world each night, the subjects could be tuned into the middle of as many as ten or twelve dreams every night. (Dement, 1978, p. 37)[2]

Strong support for the theory that REM sleep is the physiological correlate of dreaming came from the observation that 80% of awakenings from REM sleep, but only 7% of awakenings from NREM (non-REM) sleep, led to dream recall. The phenomenon of dreaming, which for centuries had been the subject of wild speculation, was finally rendered accessible to scientific investigation. The following anecdote related by Dement (1978) communicates some of the excitement felt by those involved in the discovery:

> I decided to be a subject primarily out of envy; having listened with amazement and awe as many subjects recounted their dreams, I wished to enjoy the experience myself. . . .

> A hastily trained medical student . . . was monitoring the EEG and supervising my arousals. I went to sleep prepared for an exciting night and woke up with a certain urgency. . . . I searched my mind . . . I could remember nothing. . . . So I went back to sleep and was suddenly aware of being wrenched from the void once again. This time I could remember nothing except a very, very vague feeling of a name or a person. . . .

> The next time I was jolted awake—still unable to recall anything—I began to worry. Why didn't I remember a dream? I had expected to dazzle the medical student with my brilliant recall! After a fourth and fifth awakening with exactly the same results, I was really upset. . . .

> The experience had left me exhausted and extremely puzzled, and I was anxious to look at the polygraphic record of my miserable night. Upon examining the record I discovered, to my utter delight and relief, that the medical student had been mistakenly arousing me in NREM. Not once had I awakened during a REM period. . . .

> The next night, with additional instruction . . . the medical student hit the REM periods right on the button, and vivid recall flooded my mind with each awakening. (pp. 38–39)[3]

Testing Common Beliefs about Dreaming

The high correlation between REM sleep and dream recall provided an opportunity to test some common

[2]From *Some Must Watch while Some Must Sleep* by William E. Dement, published by Portable Stanford Books, Stanford Alumni Association, Stanford University. Reprinted by permission.

[3]From *Some Must Watch while Some Must Sleep* by William E. Dement, published by Portable Stanford Books, Stanford Alumni Association, Stanford University. Reprinted by permission.

Paradoxical sleep. The sleep that accompanies emergent stage 1 EEG, so called because the physiological changes associated with this stage are similar to those of wakefulness.

Delta sleep. Stages of sleep that are punctuated by delta waves (stages 3 and 4).

REM sleep. The stage of sleep characterized by rapid eye movements, loss of core muscle tone, and emergent stage 1 EEG.

Slow-wave sleep (SWS). Sleep stages 2, 3, and 4.

beliefs about dreaming. The following are five such beliefs that have been subjected to empirical tests.

1. Many people believe that external stimuli can become incorporated into their dreams. Dement and Wolpert (1958) sprayed water on sleeping subjects after they had been in REM sleep for a few minutes, and a few seconds after the spray, each subject was awakened. In 14 of 33 cases, the water was incorporated into the dream report. The following narrative was reported by a subject who had been dreaming that he was acting in a play:

   > I was walking behind the leading lady when she suddenly collapsed and water was dripping on her. I ran over to her and water was dripping on my back and head. The roof was leaking. . . . I looked up and there was a hole in the roof. I dragged her over to the side of the stage and began pulling the curtains. Then I woke up. (p. 550)

2. Some people believe that dreams last only an instant, but research suggests that dreams run on "real time." In one study (Dement & Kleitman, 1957), subjects were awakened 5 or 15 minutes after the beginning of a REM episode and asked to decide on the basis of the duration of the events in their dreams whether they had been dreaming for 5 or 15 minutes. They were correct in 92 of 111 cases.

3. Some people claim that they do not dream. However, these people have just as much REM sleep as normal dreamers. Moreover, they report dreams if they are awakened during REM episodes (Goodenough et al., 1959), although they do so less frequently than do normal dreamers.

4. Penile erections are commonly assumed to be indicative of dreams with sexual content. However, erections are no more complete during dreams with frank sexual content than during those without it (Karacan et al., 1966). Even babies have REM-related penile erections.

5. Most people believe that sleeptalking and **somnambulism** (sleepwalking) occur during dreams. This is not so; sleeptalking and somnambulism occur least frequently during dreaming, when core muscles tend to be totally relaxed. They occur most frequently during stage 4 sleep.

The Interpretation of Dreams

The idea that dreams are disguised messages has a long history. For example, the Bible describes how a dream of seven lean cattle following and devouring seven fat cattle warned that seven years of famine would follow seven years of plenty. It was Freud's theory of dreams that refined this view of dreams and gave it legitimacy.

Freud believed that dreams are triggered by unacceptable repressed wishes, many of a sexual nature. He argued that because dreams represent unacceptable wishes, the dreams we experience (our *manifest dreams*) are merely disguised versions of our real dreams (our *latent dreams*): An unconscious censor disguises and subtracts information from our real dreams so that we can endure them. Freud thus concluded that one of the keys to understanding people and dealing with their psychological problems is to expose the meaning of their latent dreams through the interpretation of their manifest dreams.

There is no convincing evidence for the Freudian theory of dreams; indeed, the brain science of the 1890s, which served as its foundation, is now obsolete. Nevertheless, the Freudian theory of dreams has been the basis for many an interesting story; as a result, it continues to be widely disseminated to the general public through the entertainment and communication media as if it were fact. Consequently, even today, the Freudian theory of dreams is deeply ingrained in many people's thinking. Many accept the notion that dreams bubble up from a troubled subconscious and that they represent repressed thoughts and wishes.

The modern alternative to the Freudian theory of dreams is Hobson's (1989) activation-synthesis theory. It is based on the observation that, during REM sleep, many brainstem circuits become active and bombard the cerebral cortex with neural signals. The essence of the **activation-synthesis theory** is that the information supplied to the cortex during REM sleep is largely random and that the resulting dream is the cortex's effort to make sense of these random signals.

Activation-synthesis theory does not deny that dreams have meaning, but it differs from Freudian theory in terms of where that meaning lies. Hobson's dreamers reveal themselves by what they add to the random jumble of brainstem signals in order to create a coherent story, not by the painful hidden message of their dreams.

Lucid Dreams

The reality of dreams is usually quite distinct from the reality of consciousness (see Williams et al., 1992). However, there are dreams, called **lucid dreams,** in which this distinction becomes blurred. These are dreams in which the dreamer is aware at the time that she or he is dreaming and can influence the course of the dream. The experience of a lucid dream is something like being awake in a dream (see Blackmore, 1991). The existence of lucid dreams has been proved by experiments in which sleeping subjects signaled to the experimenter from their dreams by a prearranged means that they were aware that they were dreaming—for example, by moving their eyes back and forth eight times (Hearne, 1978; LaBerge, 1985).

In various surveys, about 50% of respondents report having had at least one lucid dream (e.g., Gackenbach & LaBerge, 1988). However, because the concept of lucid dreaming is a difficult one to grasp, this figure is likely to be a gross overestimate.

Because many people find lucid dreams to be a positive experience, several techniques have been devised for training people to have them. One such technique involves signaling to the sleeping subject each time he or she is dreaming; a mild shock is administered to the wrist at the start of each REM period (Hearne, 1990).

People who regularly have lucid dreams have recently been used to study dreaming: It is like having a conscious person in a dream who can relay information about the dream to the conscious world. For example, in one study, the subject was instructed to draw large triangles with his right arm as soon as he got into a dream and to signal to the experimenter with eye movements just before he drew each triangle. EMG activity that was consistent with triangle drawing was recorded from the right forearm each time the eye-movement signal was received (Schatzman, Worsley, & Fenwick, 1988). In another study, a woman who could create various positive sexual encounters in her lucid dreams was found to experience real physiological orgasms during some dream encounters (LaBerge, Greenleaf, & Kedzierski, 1983).

12.3 Why Do We Sleep?

We humans have a tendency to think that most of what we do has a special, higher-order function. For example, it has been suggested that sleep helps us reprogram our complex, computerlike brains, or that it permits some kind of emotional release to maintain our mental health. However, all mammals and birds sleep, and their sleep is much like ours—characterized by high-amplitude, low-frequency EEG waves punctuated by periods of low-amplitude, high-frequency activity (see Winson, 1993). Even fish, reptiles, amphibians, and insects go through periods of inactivity and unresponsiveness that are similar to mammalian sleep.

Recuperation and Circadian Theories

The fact that sleep is so common in the animal kingdom suggests that it serves a critical survival-related function, but there is no consensus on what that function is (Rechtschaffen, 1998). There are two general theoretical approaches to the function of sleep: recuperation theories and circadian theories. The essence of the *recuperation theories* is that being awake disrupts the *homeostasis* (internal stability) of the body in some way and that sleep is required to restore it. In contrast, the *circadian theories* argue that sleep has evolved to keep animals inactive during those times of the day when they do not need to be engaging in activities necessary for their survival. According to circadian theories, prehistoric humans had enough time to get their eating, drinking, and reproducing out of the way during the daytime; and their strong motivation to sleep at

night evolved to conserve their energy resources and to make them less susceptible to mishap—e.g., predation—in the dark. In essence, recuperation theories view sleep as a nightly repairman who fixes damage produced by wakefulness, while circadian theories regard sleep as a strict parent who demands inactivity because it keeps us out of trouble.

Choosing between the recuperation and circadian approaches to sleep is the logical first step in the search for the physiological basis of sleep. Is the sleep system run by a biological clock that produces compelling urges to sleep at certain times of the day to conserve energy and protect us from mishap, or is it a homeostatic system whose function is to correct some adverse consequence of staying awake?

Table 12.1 on page 318 illustrates the average number of hours per day that various mammalian species spend sleeping. Explaining the large between-species differences in daily sleep time is one of the central challenges that must be met by any successful theory of sleep. Why do cats tend to sleep about 14 hours a day and horses only about 2?

Circadian theories have done a better job than recuperation theories of explaining the substantial between-species differences in sleep times. Recuperation

Somnambulism. Sleepwalking.
Activation-synthesis theory. The theory that dream content reflects the cerebral cortex's inherent tendency to make sense of and give form to the random

signals that it receives from the brain stem during REM sleep.
Lucid dreams. Dreams in which the dreamer is aware that she or he is dreaming and can influence the course of the dream.

Table 12.1	The Average Number of Hours Slept per Day by Various Mammalian Species	
Mammalian Species	**Hours of Sleep per Day**	
Giant Sloth	20	
Opossum, brown bat	19	
Giant armadillo	18	
Owl monkey, nine-banded armadillo	17	
Arctic ground squirrel	16	
Tree shrew	15	
Cat, golden hamster	14	
Mouse, rat, gray wolf, ground squirrel	13	
Arctic fox, chinchilla, gorilla, raccoon	12	
Mountain beaver	11	
Jaguar, vervet monkey, hedgehog	10	
Rhesus monkey, chimpanzee, baboon, red fox	9	
Human, rabbit, guinea pig, pig	8	
Gray seal, gray hyrax, Brazilian tapir	6	
Tree hyrax, rock hyrax	5	
Cow, goat, elephant, donkey, sheep	3	
Roe deer, horse	2	

Figure 12.4 Sleeping lions. After gorging themselves on a kill, African lions sleep almost continuously for 2 or 3 days. And where do they sleep? Anywhere they want.

theories predict that species that expend more energy should sleep longer, but there is no apparent correlation between a species' sleep time and its level of activity, its body size, or its body temperature. The fact that giant sloths sleep 20 hours per day is a strong argument against the theory that sleep is a compensatory reaction to energy expenditure. In contrast, circadian theories correctly predict that the daily sleep time of each species is related to how vulnerable it is while it is asleep and how much time it must spend each day to feed itself and to take care of its other survival requirements. For example, zebras must graze almost continuously to get enough to eat and are extremely vulnerable to predatory attack when they are asleep. In contrast, African lions often sleep more or less continuously for 2 or 3 days after they have gorged themselves on a kill. The photograph in Figure 12.4 says it all.

The next two sections of this chapter deal with two topics that have a bearing on the question of whether sleep is fundamentally circadian or recuperative: circadian sleep cycles and the effects of sleep deprivation.

12.4 Circadian Sleep Cycles

The world in which we live cycles from light to dark and back again once every 24 hours, and most surface-dwelling species have adapted to this regular change in their environment by developing a variety of so-called **circadian rhythms** (see Hastings, 1997). (*Circadian* means "lasting about 1 day.") For example, most species display a regular circadian sleep–wake cycle. Humans take advantage of the light of day to take care of their biological needs, and then they sleep for much of the night; *nocturnal animals*, such as rats, sleep for much of the day and stay awake at night.

Although the sleep–wake cycle is the most obvious circadian rhythm, "it is virtually impossible to find a physiological, biochemical, or behavioral process in an- imals which does not display some measure of circadian rhythmicity" (Groos, 1983, p. 19). Each day, our bodies adjust themselves in a variety of ways to meet the demands of the two environments in which we live: light and dark.

Our circadian cycles are kept on their once-every-24-hours schedule by cues in the environment. The most important of these cues for the regulation of mammalian circadian rhythms is the daily cycle of light and dark; environmental cues that can *entrain* (control the timing of) circadian rhythms are called **zeitgebers** (pronounced "ZITE gay bers"), a German word that means "time givers." In controlled laboratory environments, it is possible to lengthen or shorten circadian cycles by adjusting the duration of the light–dark cycle; for example, when exposed to alternating 10-hour periods of light and 10-hour periods of dark, subjects' circadian cycles begin to conform to a 20-hour day.

Free-Running Circadian Sleep–Wake Cycles

In a world without 24-hour cycles of light and dark, other *zeitgebers* can entrain circadian cycles. For example, the circadian sleep–wake cycles of hamsters living in continuous darkness or in continuous light can be entrained by regular daily bouts of social interaction, hoarding, eating, or exercise (see Mistlberger, 1994; Mistlberger & Rusak, 1994; Sinclair & Mistlberger, 1997). Hamsters display particularly clear circadian cycles.

What happens to circadian rhythms in an environment that is devoid of *zeitgebers*? Remarkably, under conditions in which there are absolutely no temporal cues, humans and other animals maintain all of their circadian rhythms. Circadian rhythms in constant environments are said to be **free-running rhythms,** and their duration is called the **free-running period.** Free-running periods vary in length from subject to subject, are of relatively constant duration within a given subject, and are usually longer than 24 hours—about 25 hours in most humans. It seems that we all have an internal *biological clock* that habitually runs a little slow unless it is entrained by time-related cues in the environment. A typical free-running circadian sleep–wake cycle is illustrated in Figure 12.5. Notice its regularity. Without any external cues, this man fell asleep approximately every 25.3 hours for an entire month.

The fact that the regularity of free-running circadian sleep–wake cycles is maintained despite day-to-day variations in physical and mental activity provides strong support for the dominance of circadian factors over recuperative factors in the regulation of sleep. Figure 12.6 on page 320 provides an extreme illustration of this point: A full 24 hours of sleep deprivation on day 24 had little effect on the subsequent free-running circadian sleep–wake cycle of this rat.

Perhaps the most remarkable characteristic of free-running circadian cycles is that they do not have to be learned. Even rats that are born and raised in an unchanging laboratory environment (in continuous light or in continuous darkness) display regular free-running sleep–wake cycles of about 25 hours (Richter, 1971).

The correlation between the length of a period of wakefulness and the length of the following period of sleep is negative, even when the cycle is free-running. In other words, on those occasions when a subject stays awake longer than usual, the following sleep tends to be shorter than usual (Wever, 1979). Humans appear to be programmed to have sleep–wake cycles of approximately

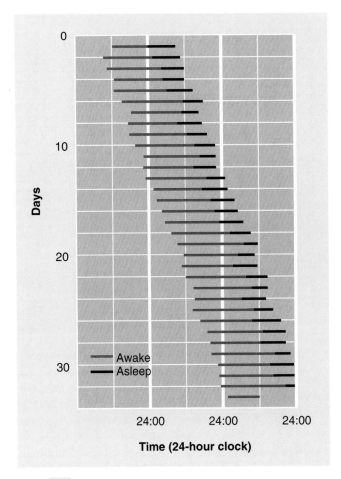

Figure 12.5 A typical free-running circadian sleep–wake cycle 25.3 hours in duration. Each day, the subject went to sleep approximately 1.3 hours later than he had the day before. (Adapted from Wever, 1979, p. 30.)

24 hours; hence, in contradiction of the main prediction of recuperation theories, the longer we stay awake during a particular cycle, the less we sleep. Recuperative theories of sleep incorrectly predict that longer periods of wakefulness will be followed by longer periods of sleep.

Many animals display a circadian cycle of body temperature that is related to their circadian sleep–wake cycle: They tend to sleep during the falling phase of their circadian body temperature cycle and awaken during its rising phase. However, when subjects are housed in constant laboratory environments, their sleep–wake and body temperature cycles sometimes break away from one another. This phenomenon is called **internal desynchronization.** For example, in one case, the free-running

Circadian rhythms. Diurnal (daily) cycles of body function.
Zeitgebers. Environmental cues, such as the light–dark cycle, that entrain circadian rhythms.
Free-running rhythms. Circadian rhythms that do not depend on environmental cues to keep them running on a regular schedule.
Free-running period. The duration of one cycle of a free-running rhythm.
Internal desynchronization. The cycling on different schedules of the free-running circadian cycles of two different processes.

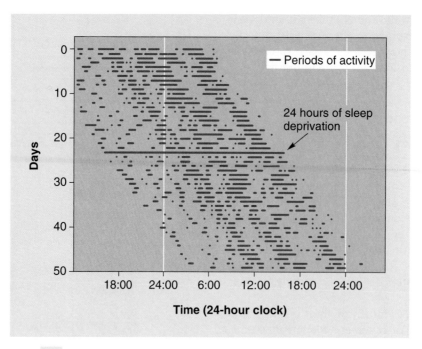

Figure 12.6 The effect of 24 hours of sleep deprivation on the free-running activity–rest circadian rhythm of a rat. Colored bars indicate periods of activity; thus long blank spaces are generally indicative of sleep. On day 24, the rat was totally deprived of sleep, yet the timing of its 25.3-hour free-running circadian rest–activity cycle was unaffected.

sleep–wake and body temperature periods of a human subject were initially both 25.7 hours; then, for some unknown reason, there was an increase in the free-running period of the sleep–wake cycle to 33.4 hours and a decrease in the free-running period of the body temperature cycle to 25.1 hours. The potential for the simultaneous existence of two different free-running periods suggests that there is more than one circadian timing mechanism (see Harrington, Rusak, & Mistlberger, 1994).

Jet Lag and Shift Work

Modern industrialized societies are faced with two different disruptions of circadian rhythmicity: jet lag and shift work. **Jet lag** occurs when the *zeitgebers* that control the phases of various circadian rhythms are accelerated during eastern flights (*phase advances*) or decelerated during western flights (*phase delays*). In *shift work,* the zeitgebers stay the same but workers are forced to adjust their natural sleep–wake cycles in order to meet the demands of changing work schedules. Both of these disruptions produce sleep disturbances, fatigue, general malaise, and deficits on tests of physical and cognitive function. The disturbances can last for many days; for example, it typically takes about 10 days to completely adjust to a Tokyo-to-Boston flight—a phase advance of 10.5 hours.

What can be done to reduce the disruptive effects of jet lag and shift work? Two behavioral approaches have been proposed for the reduction of jet lag. One is gradually shifting one's sleep–wake cycle in the days prior to the flight (see Hobson, 1989). The other is administering treatments after the flight that promote the required shift in the circadian rhythm. For example, exposure to intense light early in the morning following an eastern flight accelerates adaptation to the phase advance. Similarly, the results of a study of hamsters (Mrosovsky & Salmon, 1987) suggest that a good workout early in the morning of the first day after an eastern flight might accelerate adaptation to the phase advance; hamsters that engaged in one 3-hour bout of wheel running 7 hours before their usual period of activity adapted quickly to an 8-hour advance in their light-dark cycle (see Figure 12.7).

Companies that employ shift workers have had great success in improving the productivity and job satisfaction of their shift workers by scheduling phase delays rather than phase advances; whenever possible, shift workers are transferred from their current schedule to one that begins later in the day. It is much more difficult to go to sleep 4 hours earlier and get up 4 hours earlier (a phase advance) than it is to go to sleep 4 hours later and get up 4 hours later (a phase delay).

Jet lag. The adverse effects on body function of zeitgebers being accelerated during eastern flights or decelerated during western flights.

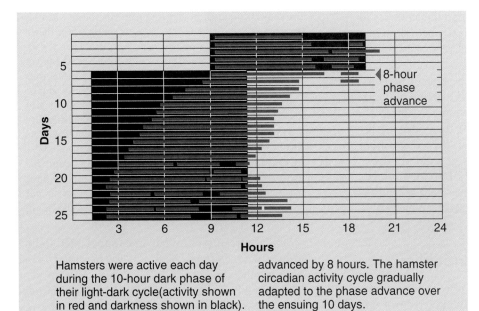

Figure 12.7 A period of forced exercise accelerates adaptation to an 8-hour phase advance in the circadian light–dark cycle. Daily activity is shown in red; periods of darkness are shown in black; and the period of forced exercise is shown in green.

(Adapted from Mrosovsky & Salmon, 1987.)

Hamsters were active each day during the 10-hour dark phase of their light-dark cycle(activity shown in red and darkness shown in black). Then, the light-dark cycle was advanced by 8 hours. The hamster circadian activity cycle gradually adapted to the phase advance over the ensuing 10 days.

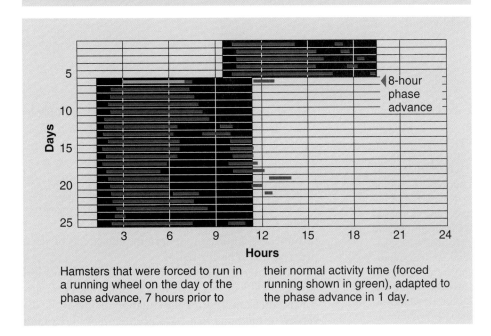

Hamsters that were forced to run in a running wheel on the day of the phase advance, 7 hours prior to their normal activity time (forced running shown in green), adapted to the phase advance in 1 day.

12.5 Effects of Sleep Deprivation

Recuperation and circadian theories of sleep make different predictions about the effects of sleep deprivation. Because recuperation theories are based on the premise that sleep is a response to the accumulation of some debilitating effect of wakefulness, they predict (1) that long periods of wakefulness will produce physiological and behavioral disturbances, (2) that these disturbances will grow steadily worse as the sleep deprivation continues, and (3) that after a period of deprivation has ended, much of the missed sleep will be regained. In contrast, the circadian theories predict (1) that there will be no debilitating effects of sleep deprivation other than those that can be attributed to an increase in the tendency to fall asleep, (2) that the increase in the desire to sleep that is produced by sleep deprivation will be greatest during the phases of the circadian cycle when the subjects normally sleep, and (3) that there will be little or no compensation for the loss of sleep once the period of deprivation has ended. Think about these predictions for a moment. On which side do you think the evidence falls?

This section begins with two classic sleep-deprivation studies. Then, the major findings of modern sleep-deprivation studies in humans and laboratory animals are summarized. Finally, the evidence for a special recuperative function for slow-wave sleep is reviewed.

Two Classic Sleep-Deprivation Studies

Kleitman's (1963) description of one of the earliest sleep-deprivation studies, which he conducted in 1922, and Dement's (1978) widely publicized case study of Randy Gardner provide strong support for the circadian theory.

■ KLEITMAN'S CLASSIC SLEEP-DEPRIVATION STUDY

While there were differences in the many subjective experiences of the sleep-evading persons, there were several features common to most. . . . [D]uring the first night the subject did not feel very tired or sleepy. He could read or study or do laboratory work, without much attention from the watcher, but usually felt an attack of drowsiness between 3 A.M. and 6 A.M. . . . Next morning the subject felt well, except for a slight malaise which always appeared on sitting down and resting for any length of time. However, if he occupied himself with his ordinary daily tasks, he was likely to forget having spent a sleepless night. During the second night . . . reading or study was next to impossible because sitting quietly was conducive to even greater sleepiness. As during the first night, there came a 2–3 hour period in the early hours of the morning when the desire for sleep was almost overpowering. . . . Later in the morning the sleepiness diminished once more, and the subject could perform routine laboratory work, as usual. It was not safe for him to sit down, however, without danger of falling asleep, particularly if he attended lectures. . . .

The third night resembled the second, and the fourth day was like the third. . . . At the end of that time the individual was as sleepy as he was likely to be. Those who continued to stay awake experienced the wavelike increase and decrease in sleepiness with the greatest drowsiness at about the same time every night. (Kleitman, 1963, pp. 220–221)

■ THE CASE OF RANDY GARDNER

As part of a 1965 science fair project, Randy Gardner and two classmates, who were entrusted with keeping him awake, planned to break the then world record of 260 hours of consecutive wakefulness. Dement read about the project in the newspaper and, seeing an opportunity to collect some important data, joined the team, much to the comfort of Randy's worried parents. Randy proved to be a friendly and coopera-

tive subject, although he did complain vigorously when his team would not permit him to close his eyes for more than a few seconds at a time. However, in no sense could Randy's behavior be considered abnormal or disturbed. Near the end of his vigil, Randy held a press conference attended by reporters and television crews from all over the United States, and he conducted himself impeccably. When asked how he had managed to stay awake for 11 days, he replied politely, "It's just mind over matter." Randy went to sleep exactly 264 hours and 12 minutes after his alarm clock had awakened him 11 days before. And how long did he sleep? Only 14 hours the first night, and thereafter he returned to his usual 8-hour schedule. Although it may seem amazing that Randy did not have to sleep longer to "catch up" on his lost sleep, the lack of substantial recovery sleep is typical of such cases.

Mrs. Maureen Weston has since supplanted Randy Gardner in the *Guinness Book of World Records*. During a rocking-chair marathon in 1977, Mrs. Weston kept rocking for 449 hours (18 days, 17 hours)—an impressive bit of "rocking around the clock." By the way, my own modest program of sleep reduction is now in its 10th day.

Experimental Studies of Sleep Deprivation in Humans

Have you experienced the effects of sleep deprivation? Many people report that they cannot function effectively without a full night's sleep. But consider this: Sleep-deprived subjects often report that they are incapable of adequate functioning even when empirical tests show their performance is normal (e.g., Van-Helder & Radominski, 1989). Clearly, careful measurements rather than subjective impressions, even yours or mine, are required to determine the effects of sleep deprivation on performance.

The interpretation of human sleep-deprivation studies is difficult because their findings have been inconsistent. Complicating the situation further is the diversity of methods that have been employed. Human sleep-deprivation experiments span three different categories (see Pilcher & Huffcutt, 1996): studies of partial deprivation (i.e., sleeping less than 5 hours in one 24-hour period), studies of short-term total sleep deprivation (i.e., no sleep for between 24 and 48 hours), and studies of long-term total sleep deprivation (i.e., no sleep for more than 48 hours). Furthermore, different sleep-deprivation studies assess performance in different ways; these measures fall into one of four general categories: measures of physiological function, measures of mood, measures of cognition, and measures of motor performance. Still, despite the variability of results and methods, some general conclusions can be drawn from human sleep-deprivation research. The following are three of them—all somewhat counterintuitive.

First, adverse effects of sleep deprivation have been more difficult to document than expected; although many studies report adverse effects (e.g., Bonnet & Arand, 1996; Dinges et al., 1997; Gilberg et al., 1996; Harrison & Horne, 1997), a surprisingly large number report few, if any. For example, Karadžić (1973), Horne (1983), and Martin (1986), all concluded that adverse physiological changes following sleep deprivation have yet to be convincingly documented. Similarly, Van Helder and Radomski (1989) reported that periods of sleep deprivation up to 72 hours had no effect on strength or motor performance, except for reducing time to exhaustion.

Second, the typical pattern of performance deficits is not what one would expect. Disturbances in the performance of simple mood and cognitive tests are often observed after sleep deprivation, whereas disturbances in the performance of complex cognitive tests are seldom observed. For example, the performance of passive, boring tests of cognitive ability—such as simple tests of vigilance (staring at a computer screen looking for signals)—is often disrupted by even a few hours of sleep reduction (Gillberg et al., 1996); whereas active, demanding tests of cognitive ability are largely immune to disruption by even long periods of sleep deprivation. For example, Percival, Horne, and Tilley (1983) found that subjects deprived of sleep for one night displayed no deficits on a battery of abstract reasoning, spatial relations, logical reasoning, and comprehension tests that were written under demanding time constraints.

Third, there is not a clear relationship between the duration of sleep deprivation and the magnitude of performance deficits. Remarkably, Pilcher and Huffcutt (1996), after analyzing the data from 19 different sleep-deprivation studies, concluded that the detrimental effects of partial sleep deprivation (sleeping fewer than 5 hours for 1 night) on performance have been greater than those of total sleep deprivation, even for several days.

Before leaving this section on studies of human sleep deprivation, I should mention one of its most reliable effects. After 2 or 3 days of sleep deprivation, it becomes very difficult for subjects to avoid microsleeps during the performance of passive tasks. **Microsleeps** are brief periods of sleep, typically about 2 or 3 seconds long, during which the eyelids droop and the subjects become less responsive to external stimuli, even though they remain sitting or even standing.

Sleep-Deprivation Studies in Laboratory Animals

Studies using a **carousel apparatus** (see Figure 12.8) to deprive rats of sleep suggest that sleep deprivation may not be as inconsequential as the research on human subjects suggests. Two rats, an experimental rat and its *yoked control,* are placed in separate chambers of the apparatus. Each time the EEG activity of the experimental

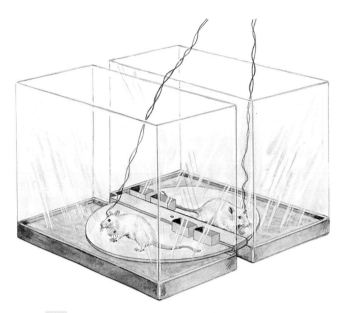

Figure 12.8 The carousel apparatus. It is used to deprive an experimental rat of sleep while a yoked control rat is exposed to the same number and pattern of disk rotations. The disk on which both rats rest rotates every time the experimental rat has a sleep EEG. If the sleeping rat does not awaken immediately, it is deposited in the water.

(Adapted from Rechtschaffen et al., 1983.)

rat indicates that it is sleeping, the disk, which serves as the floor of half of both chambers, starts to slowly rotate. As a result, if the sleeping experimental rat does not awaken immediately, it gets shoved off the disk into a shallow pool of water. The yoked control is exposed to exactly the same pattern of disk rotations; but if it is not sleeping, it can easily avoid getting dunked by walking in the direction opposite to the direction of disk rotation. The experimental rats typically died after several days, while the yoked controls stayed reasonably healthy (see Rechtschaffen & Bergmann, 1995).

The fact that human subjects have been sleep deprived for similar periods of time without dire consequences argues for caution in interpreting the results of the carousel sleep-deprivation experiments. It may be that repeatedly being awakened by the moving platform or, worse yet, being plunged into water while sleeping kills the experimental rats not because it keeps them from sleeping but because it is stressful and physically damaging. This interpretation is consistent with the pathological symptoms that were revealed in the experimental rats by postmortem examination: swollen adrenal glands, collapsed lungs, fluid in the lungs, gastric ulcers, internal bleeding, skin lesions, scrotal damage, swollen limbs, and enlarged bladders.

Microsleeps. Brief periods of sleep that occur in sleep-deprived subjects while they remain sitting or standing.	**Carousel apparatus.** An apparatus used to study the effects of sleep deprivation in laboratory rats.

REM-Sleep Deprivation

Because of its association with dreaming, REM sleep has been the subject of intensive investigation. In an effort to reveal the particular functions of REM sleep, sleep researchers have specifically deprived sleeping subjects of REM sleep by waking them up each time a bout of REM sleep begins.

REM-sleep deprivation has been shown to have two consistent effects (see Figure 12.9). First, with each successive night of deprivation, there is a greater tendency for subjects to initiate REM sequences. Thus, as REM-sleep deprivation proceeds, subjects have to be awakened more and more frequently to keep them from accumulating significant amounts of REM sleep. For example, during the first night of REM-sleep deprivation in one experiment (Webb & Agnew, 1967), the subjects had to be awakened 17 times to keep them

from having extended periods of REM sleep; but during the seventh night of deprivation, they had to be awakened 67 times. Second, following REM-sleep deprivation, subjects have more than their usual amount of REM sleep for the first two or three nights (Brunner et al., 1990).

The compensatory increase in REM sleep following a period of REM-sleep deprivation suggests that the amount of REM sleep is regulated separately from the amount of slow-wave sleep and that REM sleep serves a special function. Numerous theories of the functions of REM sleep have been proposed (see Webb, 1973; Winson, 1993). Most of them fall into one of three categories: (1) those that hypothesize that REM sleep is necessary for the maintenance of an individual's mental health, (2) those that hypothesize that REM sleep is necessary for the maintenance of normal levels of motivation, and (3) those that hypothesize that REM sleep is necessary for the processing of memories. None of

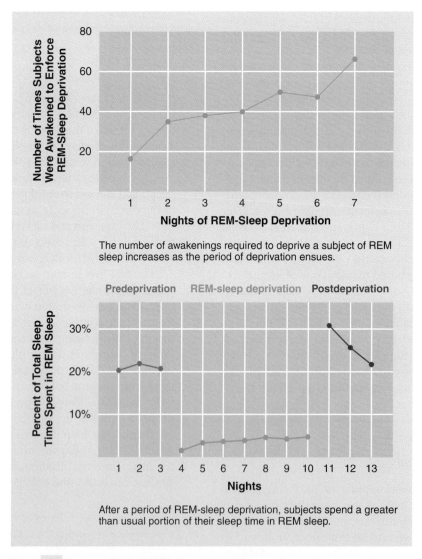

The number of awakenings required to deprive a subject of REM sleep increases as the period of deprivation ensues.

After a period of REM-sleep deprivation, subjects spend a greater than usual portion of their sleep time in REM sleep.

Figure 12.9 The two effects of REM-sleep deprivation.

these theories has emerged a clear winner. Reports that REM-sleep deprivation produces a variety of personality and motivational problems (e.g., Dement, 1960) have not proved replicable, and more recent reports that REM-sleep deprivation produces memory deficits for certain kinds of material learned the preceding day (e.g., Karni et al., 1994), while promising, have yet to be adequately assessed.

The main challenge faced by any theory of the function of REM sleep is to explain why **tricyclic antidepressant drugs** are not severely debilitating. Because tricyclic antidepressants selectively block REM sleep, patients who regularly take large doses (for depression or REM-sleep-related disorders) get little REM sleep for months at a time—and yet they experience no serious side effects that can be attributed to their REM-sleep loss.

Interpreting the Effects of Sleep Deprivation: A Special Recuperative Function for Slow-Wave Sleep

Certainly, sleep deprivation does have negative effects: Sleep-deprived people tend to feel lousy and perform monotonous cognitive tasks poorly; and a variety of other adverse effects, although less reliable, have been reported. But what does this tell us about the need for sleep? I think precious little. The problem is that virtually all conventional studies and personal experiences of sleep deprivation are confounded by stress, circadian disruptions, or both. Let me explain.

Every few months, the television news program that I watch features a story about how we all need more sleep. To support their contention, they interview an expert who explains that many people in modern society work such long hours that they sleep irregularly and suffer all kinds of adverse effects as a result (e.g., falling asleep during the day). It never seems to occur to the news reporters or to the expert that most of the people in our society who sleep irregularly do so because they are under stress and that irregular sleep often disrupts the circadian rhythms of many biological functions. Accordingly, stress and circadian disruptions might be responsible for, or at least contribute to, the adverse effects commonly attributed to loss of sleep.

Another issue that complicates the interpretation of sleep-deprivation studies is the degree to which performance deficits are attributable to microsleeps. Do sleep-deprived subjects perform more poorly when awake, or do they perform poorly because they periodically drift into microsleeps? Both recuperative and circadian theories predict that sleep deprivation will produce an increased tendency to fall asleep; only the recuperative theory predicts serious dysfunction during wakefulness.

Increase in Sleep Efficiency

One of the most important features of sleep is that the efficiency of sleep increases in response to a regular program of sleep reduction. The changes in mood, vigilance, and sleepiness that are reported by subjects when they begin to reduce their sleep time gradually disappear if the subjects adhere to their new sleep schedule (e.g., Stampi, 1992). If you have read Chapter 10, you will appreciate that there is a comparable increase in the efficiency of caloric intake when we lose weight.

The increase in sleep efficiency produced by regularly spending less time in bed each night is of two kinds. First, there is a reduction of time spent not sleeping while in bed. People who spend less time in bed fall asleep faster and wake up fewer times each night. Second, the sleep that one gets becomes more efficient; in particular, slow-wave sleep becomes much more prominent.

Slow-wave sleep seems to play a particularly important role in the recuperative effects of sleep. The following are five pieces of evidence for this view:

1. Although subjects regain only a small proportion of their total lost sleep after a period of sleep deprivation, they regain most of their lost stage 4 sleep (e.g., Borbély et al., 1981; Horne, 1976).

2. Subjects who have reduced their usual sleep time get less stage 1 and stage 2 sleep, but the amount of their stage 3 and 4 sleep remains the same as before (Mullaney et al., 1977; Webb & Agnew, 1975).

3. Short sleepers normally get as much stage 3 and 4 sleep as long sleepers (e.g., Jones & Oswald, 1966; Webb & Agnew, 1970).

4. If subjects are asked to take an extra nap in the morning after a full night's sleep, it contains little stage 3 or 4 sleep, and it does not reduce the duration of the following night's sleep (e.g., Åkerstedt & Gillberg, 1981; Hume & Mills, 1977; Karacan et al., 1970).

5. After sleep deprivation, the SWS EEG of both humans (Borbély, 1981; Borbély et al., 1981) and rats (Mistlberger, Bergmann, & Rechtschaffen, 1987) is characterized by a higher proportion of slow waves.

Consistent with the view that slow-wave sleep has a special recuperative function is the fact that it is

---

Tricyclic antidepressant drugs.
A class of drugs that are commonly prescribed for the treatment of depression and for some REM-sleep-related disorders because they selectively suppress REM sleep.

associated with a decrease in body temperature. This results in a significant savings in basal energy expenditure.

Why is the finding that sleep becomes more efficient in people who regularly sleep less such a key finding? It means that the negative consequences of loss of sleep in inefficient sleepers do not indicate whether the lost sleep was really needed: The true need for sleep can be assessed only by experiments in which sleep is regularly reduced for many weeks, to give the subjects an opportunity to adapt to less sleep by increasing their efficiency. Such studies are discussed later in the chapter.

It is an appropriate point, here at the end of the section on sleep deprivation, for me to file a brief progress report. It has now been 2 weeks since I began my 5-hours-per-night sleep schedule. Generally, things are going well. My progress on this chapter has been faster than usual. I am not having any difficulty getting up on time or in getting my work done, but I am finding that it takes a major effort to stay awake in the evening. If I try to read or watch a bit of television after 10:30, I experience attacks of microsleep. Luckily for me, my so-called friends delight in making sure that my transgressions last no more than a few seconds.

12.6 Recuperation and Circadian Theories of Sleep Combined

If you began this chapter thinking of sleep as a recuperative process, as most people do, you were probably surprised to learn that sleep is closely regulated by circadian factors and that the adverse effects of sleep deprivation are controversial. However, it is important not to overreact to this evidence. Although recuperative factors may be somewhat less important in controlling sleep than you first thought, and circadian factors somewhat more important, it is not necessarily an all-or-none issue; circadian and recuperation models are not mutually exclusive.

Borbély (1984) has proposed a model of sleep that integrates the effects of both circadian and sleep-deprivation factors. This two-process model is illustrated in Figure 12.10. The postulated circadian sleep-promoting factor is assumed to take the form of a sine wave with a minimum at about 4:00 P.M. and a maximum at about 4:00 A.M. The postulated sleep-

Figure 12.10 A model of how circadian factors and recuperative factors interact to determine the motivation to sleep. (Adapted from Borbély, 1984.)

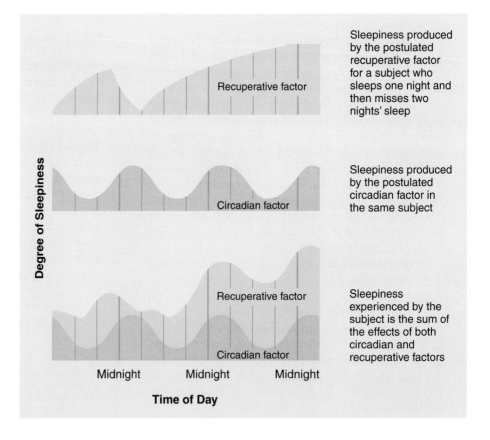

Before you proceed to the next section of the chapter, complete the following exercise to consolidate what you have learned so far. The correct answers are provided at the bottom of this page. Before proceeding, review material related to your errors and omissions.

1. The three most commonly studied psychophysiological correlates of sleep are the EEG, EMG, and _____.

2. Stage 4 sleep EEG is characterized by a predominance of _____ waves.

3. _____ stage 1 EEG is accompanied by neither REM nor loss of core muscle tone.

4. Dreaming occurs during _____ sleep.

5. The modern alternative to Freud's theory of dreaming is Hobson's _____ theory.

6. Environmental cues that can entrain circadian rhythms are called _____, or time givers.

7. In contrast to the prediction of the recuperation models of sleep, when a subject stays awake longer than usual under free-running conditions, the following period of sleep tends to be _____.

8. The most convincing evidence that REM-sleep deprivation is not debilitating comes from the study of patients taking _____.

9. After a lengthy period of sleep deprivation (e.g., several days) a subject's first night of sleep is only slightly longer than usual, but it contains a much higher proportion of _____ waves.

10. _____ sleep in particular, rather than sleep in general, appears to play the major recuperative role.

promoting effects of wakefulness are illustrated for a subject who slept one night between 11:00 P.M. and 6:00 A.M. and then missed the next two nights' sleep. The bottom trace illustrates how the effects of the circadian and wakefulness factors hypothetically combine to influence this subject's sleepiness.

12.7 Neural Mechanisms of Sleep

The first influential theory of the physiology of sleep was proposed by Bremer in 1936. He hypothesized that sleep is caused by a reduction of sensory input to the forebrain. To test his hypothesis, he severed the brain stems of cats between their *inferior colliculi* and *superior colliculi* in order to disconnect their forebrains from ascending sensory input (see Figure 12.11 on page 328) This surgical preparation is called a **cerveau isolé preparation** (pronounced "ser-VOE ees-o-LAY"—literally "isolated forebrain"). As you might well imagine, cerveau isolé preparations are not too useful for the study of behavior because the subjects are paralyzed below the level of the transection, but the preparations can be used to assess neurophysiological responses of the forebrain in the absence of ascending influences.

In support of his hypothesis, Bremer found that the cortical EEG of the isolated cat forebrains was indicative of almost continuous slow-wave sleep. Only when strong visual or olfactory stimuli were presented (the cerveau isolé has intact visual and olfactory input) could the continuous high-amplitude, slow-wave activity

The answers are (1) EOG, (2) delta, (3) Initial, (4) REM, (5) activation-synthesis, (6) zeitgebers, (7) shorter, (8) tricyclic antidepressants, (9) slow (or delta), and (10) Slow-wave (or Stage 3 and 4).

Cerveau isolé preparation. An experimental preparation in which the forebrain is disconnected from the rest of the brain by a midcollicular transection.

be changed to a **desynchronized EEG**—a low-amplitude, high-frequency EEG. However, this arousing effect barely outlasted the stimuli. Bremer's theory is classed as a *passive theory of sleep* because it postulated no mechanism of active sleep regulation; it viewed sleep as a passive consequence of a decline in sensory input to the forebrain.

Reticular Activating System Theory of Sleep

Bremer's passive sensory theory of sleep regulation was gradually replaced by the theory that sleep is actively regulated by an arousal mechanism in the *reticular formation*. This hypothetical arousal mechanism was the **reticular activating system.** Three findings contributed to the wide acceptance of the reticular activating system theory of sleep (see Figure 12.11). The first finding came from a study of the **encéphale isolé preparation** (pronounced on-say-FELL ees-o-LAY)—an experimental preparation in which the brain is disconnected from the rest of the nervous system by a transection of the caudal brain stem. Despite cutting most of the same sensory fibers as the cerveau isolé transection, the encéphale isolé transection did not disrupt the normal cycle of sleep EEG and wakefulness EEG (Bremer, 1937). This suggested that a mechanism for maintaining wakefulness was located somewhere in the brain stem between the two transections. The second finding was that partial transections at the cerveau isolé level disrupted normal sleep–wake cycles of cortical EEG only when they severed the reticular activating system core of the brain stem; when the partial transections were restricted to more lateral areas, which contain the ascending

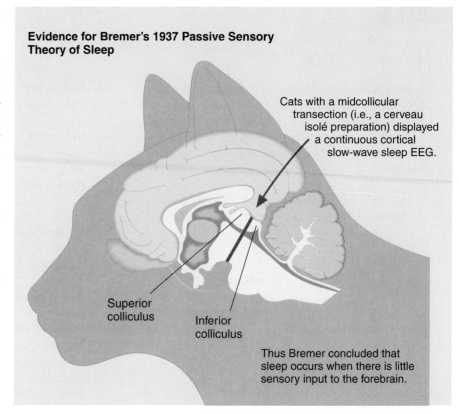

Evidence for Bremer's 1937 Passive Sensory Theory of Sleep

Cats with a midcollicular transection (i.e., a cerveau isolé preparation) displayed a continuous cortical slow-wave sleep EEG.

Superior colliculus

Inferior colliculus

Thus Bremer concluded that sleep occurs when there is little sensory input to the forebrain.

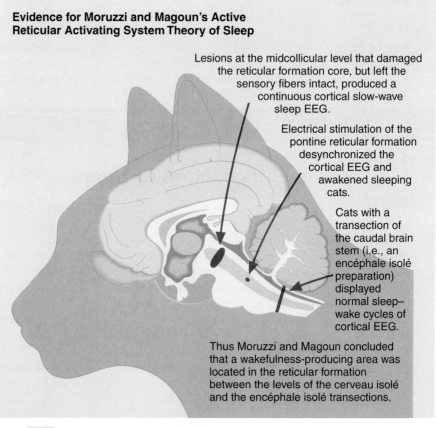

Evidence for Moruzzi and Magoun's Active Reticular Activating System Theory of Sleep

Lesions at the midcollicular level that damaged the reticular formation core, but left the sensory fibers intact, produced a continuous cortical slow-wave sleep EEG.

Electrical stimulation of the pontine reticular formation desynchronized the cortical EEG and awakened sleeping cats.

Cats with a transection of the caudal brain stem (i.e., an encéphale isolé preparation) displayed normal sleep–wake cycles of cortical EEG.

Thus Moruzzi and Magoun concluded that a wakefulness-producing area was located in the reticular formation between the levels of the cerveau isolé and the encéphale isolé transections.

Figure 12.11 Evidence for the sensory theory of sleep (a passive theory) and the reticular activating system theory (an active theory).

sensory tracts, they had little effect on the cortical EEG (Lindsey, Bowden, & Magoun, 1949). The third finding was that electrical stimulation of the reticular formation of sleeping cats awakened them and produced a lengthy period of EEG desynchronization (Moruzzi & Magoun, 1949). On the basis of these three early findings, Moruzzi and Magoun (1949) proposed that low levels of activity in the reticular formation produce sleep and that high levels produce wakefulness.

Three Important Discoveries about the Neural Basis of Sleep

The wave of research that was stimulated by the reticular activating system theory led to several discoveries. The following three are particularly important (see Steriade & Hobson, 1976).

■ **SLEEP IS NOT A STATE OF NEURAL QUIESCENCE** Because the body is inactive during sleep, it had long been assumed that sleep is a state of general neural quiescence. Neural recording and functional brain-imaging (see Hobson et al., 1998) have revealed that this is not the case. Many areas of the brain are less active during slow-wave sleep than they are during relaxed wakefulness, but the reduction in average firing rates rarely exceeds 10%—a far cry from the total inactivity that was initially assumed. Moreover, during REM sleep, the neurons in some areas become even more active than they are during relaxed wakefulness.

■ **THERE ARE SLEEP-PROMOTING CIRCUITS IN THE BRAIN** The reticular activating system theory of sleep suggested that sleep is a consequence of low levels of activity in circuits whose primary role is the maintenance of wakefulness. This view was altered by the discovery that brain stimulation can induce sleep and that brain lesions can disrupt it. Both of these findings suggest that there are structures in the brain whose function is the promotion of sleep. One such sleep-promoting structure appears to be in the caudal brain stem (i.e., in the pons and medulla). Anesthetizing (Magni et al., 1957) or cooling (Berlucchi et al., 1964) the caudal brain stem causes sleeping cats to awaken immediately.

■ **THE VARIOUS CORRELATES OF SLEEP ARE DISSOCIABLE** Most neurophysiological theories of sleep have treated REM sleep and slow-wave sleep as if each were a unitary entity—and, for simplicity, I have followed this convention in this chapter. However, evidence has accumulated that the physiological changes that go together to define REM sleep sometimes break apart and go their separate ways—and the same is true of the

changes that define slow-wave sleep. For example, during REM-sleep deprivation, penile erections, which normally occur during REM sleep, begin to occur during slow-wave sleep. And during total sleep deprivation, slow waves, which normally occur only during slow-wave sleep, begin to occur during wakefulness. This suggests that REM sleep, slow-wave sleep, and wakefulness are not each controlled by a single mechanism; each state seems to result from the interaction of a variety of mechanisms that are capable under certain conditions of operating independently of one another.

The classic example of the dissociation between the behavioral and EEG indexes of slow-wave sleep is the study of Feldman and Waller (1962), who compared the effects of lesions to the cat midbrain reticular formation with those of lesions to the adjacent posterior hypothalamus. The hypothalamic lesions produced behavioral sleep that persisted even when the cats' desynchronized cortical EEG suggested that they were awake. In contrast, the midbrain reticular formation lesions produced a high-amplitude slow-wave cortical EEG that persisted even when the cats were fully alert (see Vanderwolf & Robinson, 1981).

Brain Areas That Have Been Implicated in Controlling Sleep and Dreaming

Several areas of the brain have been implicated in sleep. The following are three of them: the raphé nuclei, the basal forebrain region, and the REM-sleep circuits in the caudal reticular formation.

■ **RAPHÉ NUCLEI** The **raphé** (pronounced "ra-FAY") **nuclei** are a cluster of serotonin-producing nuclei running in a thin strip down the midline of the caudal reticular formation (see Figure 12.12 on page 330). Lesions that destroyed 80 to 90% of the raphé nuclei in cats produced complete insomnia for 3 or 4 days, and then there was a partial recovery that never exceeded more than 2.5 hours of sleep per day, all slow-wave sleep (Jouvet & Renault, 1966). Cats normally sleep about 14 hours per day, which is why they are favored as subjects in sleep experiments.

The theory that the raphé nuclei promote sleep received initial support from the observation that an

---

Desynchronized EEG. Low-amplitude, high-frequency EEG.
Reticular activating system. The hypothetical arousal system in the reticular formation.
Encéphale isolé preparation. An experimental preparation in which the brain is separated from the rest of the nervous system by a transection of the caudal brain stem.
Raphé nuclei. A cluster of serotonin-producing nuclei running in a thin strip down the midline of the caudal reticular formation.

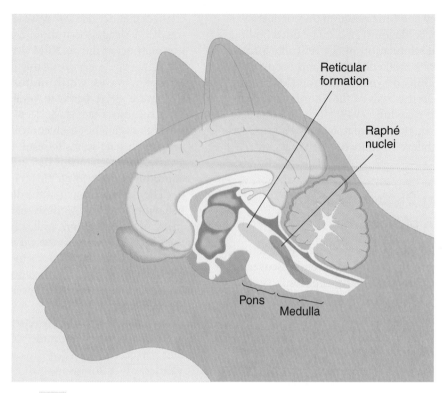

Figure 12.12 The location of the raphé nuclei in the caudal reticular formation.

injection of **parachlorophenylalanine (PCPA)** — a chemical that temporarily blocks the synthesis of serotonin—produced temporary insomnia in cats (Mouret, Bobillier, & Jouvet, 1968). However, when PCPA was injected every day, both REM sleep and slow-wave sleep eventually recovered to 80% of their normal levels despite the fact that serotonin levels remained low (Dement, Mitler, & Henriksen, 1972). Further challenges to the raphé nucleus–serotonin theory of sleep came from the discovery that serotonin injections do not induce sleep and the discovery that PCPA injections do not disrupt sleep in species other than cats (see Vanderwolf, 1988).

■ **BASAL FOREBRAIN REGION** Although much of the research on the physiology of sleep has focused on the brain stem, there is some evidence that the **basal forebrain region**—the area of the forebrain just in front of the hypothalamus—is also involved. As Figure 12.13 shows, bilateral lesions of this area in cats produce a substantial reduction of daily sleep time that is maximal 2 weeks after the lesion but recovers somewhat thereafter (McGinty & Sterman, 1968). However, LoPiccolo (1977) found no indication that basal forebrain stimulation promotes sleep in cats.

■ **CAUDAL RETICULAR FORMATION REM-SLEEP CIRCUITS** REM sleep appears to be controlled from a variety of

sites scattered throughout the caudal reticular formation. Each site is responsible for controlling one of the major indexes of REM sleep (Siegel, 1983; Vertes, 1983)—a site for the reduction of core muscle tone, a site for EEG desynchronization, and a site for rapid eye movements, and so on. The approximate location in the caudal brain stem of each of these putative REM-sleep centers is illustrated in Figure 12.14 on page 332.

The coordinated activation of the REM-sleep centers is controlled by cholinergic mechanisms in the pontine portion of the caudal reticular formation. Microinjections of cholinergic agonists into this site elicit immediate and prolonged REM sleep in cats (Qualtrochi et al., 1989). In sleeping human subjects, the intravenous infusion of cholinergic agonists increases REM sleep, and the intravenous infusion of cholinergic antagonists decreases REM sleep (Sitaram, Moore, & Gillin, 1978).

In contrast, neurons in two areas of the caudal reticular formation seem to play a role in inhibiting REM sleep: the *noradrenergic neurons* of the **locus coeruleus** (Lydic, McCarley, & Hobson, 1983) and the *serotonergic neurons* of the **dorsal raphé nuclei** (Trulson & Jacobs, 1979). Neurons in both areas are active during slow-wave sleep but are almost totally quiescent during REM sleep. This finding has contributed to the view (see Hobson, 1989) that the recurring cycle of REM sleep is controlled in the caudal reticular forma-

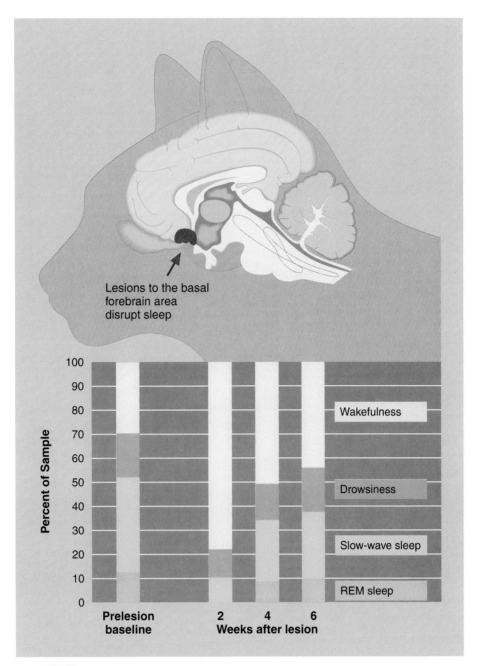

Figure 12.13 The effects of basal forebrain lesions on the sleep of cats.
(Adapted from McGinty & Sterman, 1968.)

tion by a reciprocal interaction between excitatory cholinergic neurons and inhibitory noradrenergic and serotonergic neurons.

In summary, we now understand that the cycles of REM sleep are controlled by interactions among circuits in the caudal reticular formation. However, our understanding of the circuits that cause us to fall asleep is less developed. The theory that sleep results from a general decrease in reticular activating system activity is out of step with the current knowledge of the intricacy and specificity of reticular formation circuits, and

support for hypothetical basal forebrain and raphé sleep mechanisms has been inconsistent.

Parachlorophenylalanine (PCPA). A chemical that blocks the synthesis of serotonin and produces insomnia in cats.
Basal forebrain region. The area of the forebrain just in front of the hypothalamus.

Locus coeruleus. A noradrenergic nucleus of the caudal reticular formation that is thought to inhibit REM sleep.
Dorsal raphé nuclei. Serotonergic nuclei of the dorsal raphé, which are thought to inhibit REM sleep.

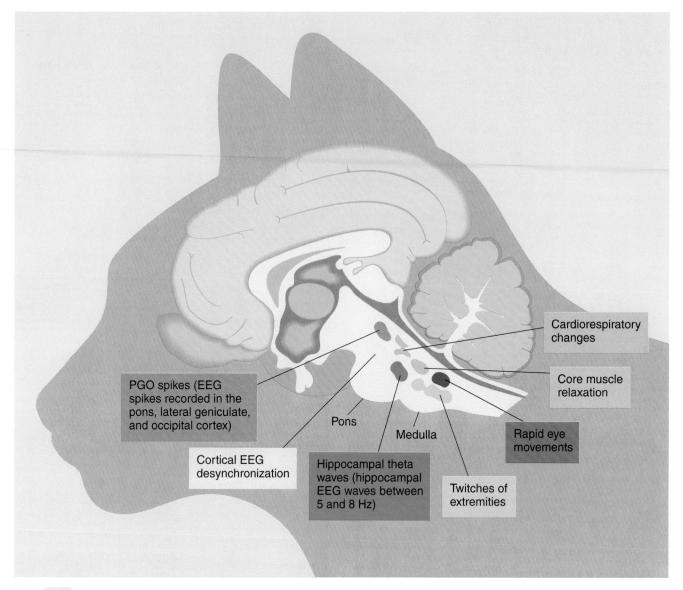

Figure 12.14 A sagittal section of the brain stem of the cat illustrating the areas that control the various physiological indexes of REM sleep.

(Adapted from Vertes, 1983.)

The Circadian Clock: Neural and Molecular Mechanisms

The fact that circadian sleep–wake cycles persist in the absence of circadian signals from the environment indicates that the physiological systems that regulate sleep are controlled by an internal timing mechanism—the **circadian clock.** Where is this timing mechanism?

Location of the Circadian Clock in the Suprachiasmatic Nuclei

The first breakthrough in the search for the circadian clock was Richter's 1967 discovery that large medial hypothalamic lesions disrupt circadian cycles of eating, drinking, and activity in rats. Next, specific lesions of the **suprachiasmatic nuclei** (SCN) of the medial hypothalamus were shown to disrupt various circadian cycles, including cycles of sleep. Although SCN lesions do not reduce the amount of time mammals spend sleeping, they do abolish its circadian periodicity.

Further support for the conclusion that the suprachiasmatic nuclei contain a circadian timing mechanism comes from the observation that the nuclei display circadian cycles of electrical, metabolic, and biochemical activity (e.g., Moore, 1982)—even when they have been surgically isolated from the rest of the brain by circular knife cuts (Groos & Hendricks, 1982; Inouye & Kawamura, 1982). Also, electrical stimulation of the SCN has been shown to produce phase shifts in free-running rhythms (Rusak & Groos, 1982).

If there was any lingering doubt about the location of the circadian clock, it was eliminated by the brilliant experiment of Ralph and his colleagues (1990). They removed the SCN from the fetuses of a strain of mutant hamsters that had an abnormally short (20-hour) free-running sleep–wake cycle. Then, they transplanted these SCN into normal adult hamsters whose free-running sleep–wake cycles of 25 hours had been abolished by SCN lesions. These transplants restored free-running sleep–wake cycles in the recipients; but, remarkably, the cycles were about 20 hours long rather than the original 25 hours. Transplants in the other direction—that is, from normal hamster fetuses to SCN-lesioned adult mutants—had the complementary effect: They restored free-running sleep–wake cycles that were about 25 hours long rather than the original 20 hours.

Although the suprachiasmatic nuclei are unquestionably the major circadian clocks, they are not the only ones. Evidence for this conclusion comes from two sources. First, under certain conditions, bilateral SCN lesions have been shown to leave some circadian rhythms unaffected while abolishing others (e.g., Boulos & Terman, 1980). Second, bilateral SCN lesions do not eliminate the ability of all environmental stimuli to entrain circadian rhythms; for example, in hamsters, SCN lesions block entrainment by light but not by food or water availability (Abe & Rusak, 1992; Mistlberger, 1993).

Genetics of Circadian Rhythms

Several genes that influence circadian rhythms have been discovered in invertebrates (see Gillette, 1997), and these have now been cloned and characterized. The first circadian gene to be discovered in mammals was the spontaneous mutation called *tau*, which shortens the free-running circadian rhythms of hamsters. Unfortunately little progress has been made in the study of *tau* because there is so little background information about the hamster genome.

The major breakthrough in the study of mammalian circadian genes came with the discovery and localization of *clock* (for circadian locomotor output cycles kaput), a genetic mutation in mice (Vitanerna et al., 1994). When placed in constant darkness, mice carrying the *clock* gene initially have longer than normal free-running rhythms, and they eventually lose all circadian rhythmicity. King et al. (1997) recently cloned and characterized *clock,* so it is likely that the mechanism by which *clock* disrupts circadian rhythms will soon be identified, and this information should provide some important clues about the molecular mechanisms of normal circadian rhythms.

Mechanisms of Entrainment

How does the 24-hour light–dark cycle entrain the sleep–wake cycle and other circadian rhythms? To answer this question, researchers began at the obvious starting point: the eyes. They tried to identify and track the specific neurons that left the eyes and carried the information about light and dark that entrained the biological clock. Cutting the *optic nerves* before they reached the *optic chiasm* eliminated the ability of the light–dark cycle to entrain circadian rhythms; however, when the *optic tracts* were cut at the point where they left the optic chiasm, the ability of the light–dark cycle to entrain circadian rhythms was unaffected. As Figure 12.15 on page 334 illustrates, these two findings indicated that visual axons critical for the entrainment of circadian rhythms branch off from the optic nerve in the vicinity of the optic chiasm. This finding led to the discovery of the *retinohypothalamic tracts,* which leave the optic chiasm and project to the adjacent suprachiasmatic nuclei.

The nature of the molecular mechanism by which activity in the retinohypothalamic tracts influences circadian rhythms was revealed by Rusak and his colleagues (1990). They studied the mechanism by which 30 minutes of intense artificial light during the night initiates a phase advance in the circadian sleep–wake cycles of rats and hamsters. They found that exposure of their subjects to light at times that induced phase advances triggered the immediate and transient expression of a gene called *c-fos* in the SCN. *C-fos* controls the production of *fos* protein, which in turn regulates the expression of other genes. This finding suggests that light influences circadian rhythms by controlling gene expression in the SCN.

Circadian clock. An internal timing mechanism that is capable of maintaining daily cycles of physiological change, even when there are no temporal cues from the environment.

Suprachiasmatic nuclei (SCN). Nuclei of the hypothalamus that control the circadian cycles of various body functions.

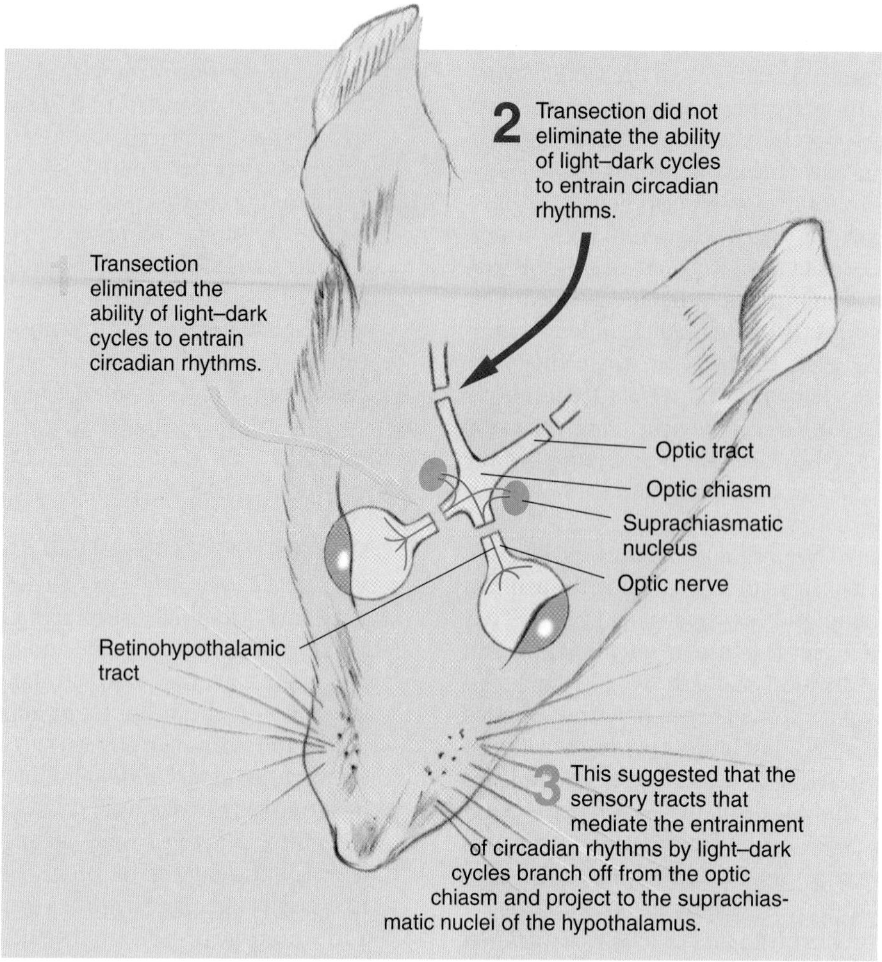

2 Transection did not eliminate the ability of light–dark cycles to entrain circadian rhythms.
1 Transection eliminated the ability of light–dark cycles to entrain circadian rhythms.
Optic tract
Optic chiasm
Suprachiasmatic nucleus
Optic nerve
Retinohypothalamic tract
3 This suggested that the sensory tracts that mediate the entrainment of circadian rhythms by light–dark cycles branch off from the optic chiasm and project to the suprachiasmatic nuclei of the hypothalamus.

Figure 12.15 The discovery of the retinohypothalamic tracts. Neurons from each retina project to both suprachiasmatic nuclei.

12.9 Drugs That Affect Sleep

Most drugs that influence sleep fall into two different classes: hypnotic and antihypnotic. **Hypnotic drugs** are drugs that increase sleep; **antihypnotic drugs** are drugs that reduce sleep. A third class of sleep-influencing drugs comprises those that influence its circadian rhythmicity; the main drug of this class is **melatonin.**

Hypnotic Drugs

The **benzodiazepines** (e.g., Valium and Librium) were developed and tested for the treatment of anxiety, yet they are the most commonly prescribed hypnotic medications. In the short term, they increase drowsiness, decrease the time it takes to fall asleep, reduce the number of awakenings during a night's sleep, and increase

Hypnotic drugs. Sleep-promoting drugs.
Antihypnotic drugs. Sleep-reducing drugs.
Melatonin. A hormone synthesized from serotonin in the pineal gland.
Benzodiazepines. A class of anxiolytic drugs that are often prescribed as sleeping pills.
5-hydroxytryptophan (5-HTP). The precursor of serotonin.
Pineal gland. The endocrine gland that is the human body's sole source of melatonin.

total sleep time. Thus they can be effective in the treatment of occasional difficulties in sleeping.

Although benzodiazepines can be effective therapeutic hypnotic agents in the short term, their prescription for the treatment of chronic sleep difficulties is ill-advised. Still, they are commonly prescribed for this purpose—primarily by general practitioners. Following are four complications associated with the chronic use of benzodiazepines as hypnotic agents: First, tolerance develops to the hypnotic effects of benzodiazepines; thus patients must take larger and larger doses to maintain their efficacy. Second, cessation of benzodiazepine therapy after chronic use causes *insomnia* (sleeplessness), which can exacerbate the very problem that the benzodiazepines were intended to correct. Third, chronic benzodiazepine use is addictive. Fourth, benzodiazepines distort the normal pattern of sleep: They increase the duration of sleep by increasing the duration of stage 2 sleep, but they actually decrease the duration of stage 4 and REM sleep.

Evidence that the raphé nuclei play a role in sleep suggested that serotonergic drugs might be effective hypnotics. Efforts to demonstrate the hypnotic effects of such drugs have focused on **5-hydroxytryptophan (5-HTP)**—the precursor of serotonin—because 5-HTP, but not serotonin, readily passes through the blood–brain barrier. Injections of 5-HTP do reverse the insomnia produced both in cats and in rats by the serotonin antagonist PCPA; however, they are of no therapeutic benefit in the treatment of human insomnia (see Borbély, 1983).

Antihypnotic Drugs

There are two main classes of antihypnotic drugs: *stimulants* (e.g., cocaine and amphetamine) and *tricyclic antidepressants*. Both stimulants and antidepressants increase the activity of catecholamines (norepinephrine, epinephrine, and dopamine) either by increasing their release, by blocking their reuptake from the synapse, or by both mechanisms. From the perspective of the treatment of sleep disorders, the most important property of antihypnotic drugs is that they act preferentially on REM sleep. They can totally suppress REM sleep even at doses that have little effect on total sleep time.

Using stimulant drugs to treat chronic excessive sleepiness is a risky proposition. Most are highly addictive, and they produce a variety of adverse side effects, such as loss of appetite. Moreover, unless stimulants are taken at just the right doses and at just the right times, there is a danger that they will interfere with normal sleep.

Melatonin

Melatonin is a hormone that is synthesized from the neurotransmitter serotonin in the **pineal gland** (see Moore, 1996). The pineal gland is an inconspicuous gland that Descartes once believed to be the seat of the soul; it is located on the midline of the brain just ventral to the rear portion of the corpus callosum (see Figure 12.16).

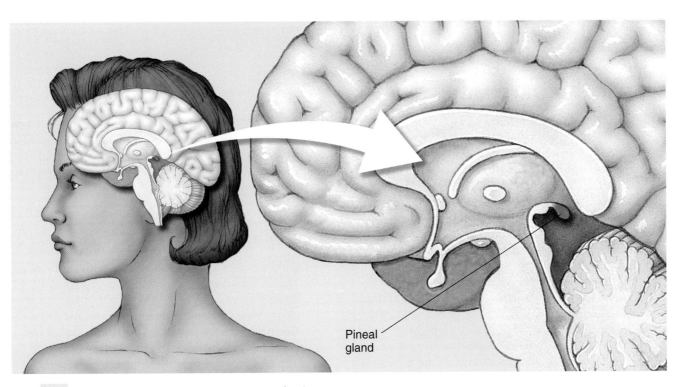

Figure 12.16 The location of the pineal gland, the source of melatonin.

Pineal gland

The pineal gland has important functions in birds, reptiles, amphibians, and fish (see Cassone, 1990). The pineal gland of these species has inherent timing properties and regulates circadian rhythms and seasonal changes in reproductive behavior through its release of melatonin. In humans and other mammals, however, the functions of the pineal gland and melatonin are not so apparent.

In humans and other mammals, circulating levels of melatonin display circadian rhythms under control of the suprachiasmatic nucleus (see Gillette & McArthur, 1996), with the highest levels being associated with darkness and sleep (see Foulkes et al., 1997). On the basis of this correlation, it has long been assumed that melatonin plays a role in promoting sleep or in regulating its timing in mammals. Despite the fact that melatonin is currently in widespread use by the general public, largely because of irresponsible reporting by the news media, its effects in mammals are only now emerging.

In order to keep the facts about melatonin in perspective, it is important to keep one significant point firmly in mind. In mammals, pinealectomy and the consequent elimination of melatonin has no adverse effects on adult mammals—or at least none that have been apparent. The pineal plays a role in the development of mammalian sexual maturity, but its functions after puberty are not at all obvious.

Does *exogenous* (externally produced) melatonin improve sleep, as widely believed? The evidence is mixed and certainly does not warrant melatonin's use for this reason. Early studies reported that subjects taking melatonin at bedtime felt more sleepy and that they slept better, but subsequent objective studies failed to find EEG, EMG, or REM indices of improved sleep. However, a recent study (Haimov & Lavie, 1995) has shown that melatonin capsules taken at various times during the day, when *endogenous* (internally produced) levels of melatonin are low, produce quicker and better sleep during nap tests 2 hours after drug administration.

In contrast to the controversy over the soporific (sleep-promoting) effects of exogenous melatonin in mammals, there is good evidence that it can influence mammalian circadian cycles (see Lewy, Ahmed, & Sack, 1996). Exposure to exogenous melatonin acts much like exposure to a period of darkness, which makes sense because high levels of endogenous melatonin are associated with darkness. Thus, a dose of melatonin before dusk can help jet-lagged travelers adapt to eastern flights, whereas a dose after dawn can help adaptation to western flights. The shift in circadian rhythms is, however, typically slight—less than an hour.

Exogenous melatonin has been shown to have a therapeutic potential in the treatment two types of sleep problems. Melatonin before sleep time has been shown to improve the sleep of insomniacs who are melatonin deficient (e.g., Haimov et al., 1995) and of blind patients who have sleep problems attributable to the lack of the synchronizing effects of the light–dark cycle (e.g., Lapierre & Dumont, 1995).

12.10 Sleep Disorders

Many sleep disorders fall into one of two complementary categories: insomnia and hypersomnia. **Insomnia** includes all disorders of initiating and maintaining sleep, whereas **hypersomnia** includes disorders of excessive sleep or sleepiness. A third major class of sleep disorders includes all those disorders that are specifically related to REM-sleep dysfunction.

In various surveys, approximately 30% of the respondents report significant sleep-related problems. However, it is important to recognize that complaints of sleep problems often come from people whose sleep appears normal in laboratory sleep tests. For example, many people who complain of insomnia actually sleep a reasonable amount (e.g., 6 hours a night), but they believe that they should sleep more (e.g., 8 hours a night). As a result, they spend more time in bed than they should and have difficulty getting to sleep. Often, the anxiety associated with their inability to sleep makes it even more difficult for them to sleep. Such patients can often be helped by counseling that convinces them to go to bed only when they are very sleepy (see Anch et al., 1988). Others with disturbed sleep face more serious problems.

Insomnia

Many cases of insomnia are **iatrogenic**—physician-created. Paradoxically, sleeping pills (e.g., benzodiazepines) prescribed by well-intentioned physicians are a major cause of insomnia. At first, hypnotic drugs are effective in increasing sleep, but soon the patient is trapped in a rising spiral of drug use, as *tolerance* to the drug develops and progressively more drug is required to produce its original hypnotic effect. Soon, the patient cannot stop taking the drug without running the risk of experiencing *withdrawal symptoms,* which include insomnia. The following case study illustrates this problem:

> Mr. B. was studying for a civil service exam, the outcome of which would affect his entire future. He was terribly worried about the test and found it difficult to get to sleep at night. Feeling that the sleep loss was affecting his ability to study, he consulted his physician for the express purpose of getting "something to make me sleep." His doctor prescribed a moderate dose of barbiturate at bedtime, and Mr. B. found that this medication was very effective . . . for the first several nights. After about a week, he began having trouble sleeping again and decided to take two sleeping pills each night. Twice more the cycle was repeated, until on the night before the exam he was taking four times as many pills as his doctor had prescribed. The next night, with the pressure off, Mr. B. took no medication. He had tremendous difficulty falling asleep, and when he did, his sleep was terribly disrupted. . . . Mr. B. now decided that he had a serious case of insomnia, and returned to his sleeping pill habit. By the time he consulted our clinic several years later, he was taking approximately 1,000 mg sodium amytal every night, and his sleep was more disturbed than ever. . . . Patients may go on for years and years—from one sleeping pill to another—never realizing that their troubles are caused by the pills. (Dement, 1978, p. 80)[4]

Sleep apnea is another common cause of insomnia. In sleep apnea, the patient stops breathing many times each night. Each time, the patient awakens, begins to breathe again, and drifts back to sleep. Sleep apnea usually leads to a sense of having slept poorly and is thus often diagnosed as insomnia. However, some patients are totally unaware of their multiple awakenings and instead complain of excessive sleepiness during the day, which leads to a diagnosis of *hypersomnia.*

Sleep apnea disorders are thought to be of two types: (1) those resulting from obstruction of the respiratory passages by muscle spasms or *atonia* (lack of muscle tone) and (2) those resulting from the failure of the central nervous system to stimulate respiration. Sleep apnea is most common in males, in the overweight, and in the elderly.

Two other causes of insomnia—nocturnal myoclonus and restless legs—both involve the legs. **Nocturnal myoclonus** is a periodic twitching of the body, usually the legs, during sleep. Most patients suffering from this disorder complain of poor sleep and daytime sleepiness but are unaware of the nature of their problem. In contrast, people with **restless legs** are all too aware of their problem. They complain of a hard-to-describe tension or uneasiness in their legs that keeps them from falling asleep. Benzodiazepines are often prescribed in cases of nocturnal myoclonus and restless legs because of their hypnotic, *anxiolytic* (antianxiety), muscle relaxant, and anticonvulsant properties; however, they are rarely effective.

---

[4]From *Some Must Watch while Some Must Sleep* by William E. Dement, published by Portable Stanford Books, Stanford Alumni Association, Stanford University. Reprinted by permission.

In one study, insomniacs claimed to take an average of 1 hour to fall asleep and to sleep an average of only 4.5 hours per night; but when they were tested in a sleep laboratory, they were found to have an average sleep latency of only 15 minutes and an average nightly sleep duration of 6.5 hours. It used to be common medical practice to assume that people who claimed to suffer from insomnia but slept more than 6.5 hours per night were neurotic. However, this practice stopped when some of those diagnosed as *neurotic pseudoinsomniacs* were subsequently found to be suffering from sleep apnea, nocturnal myoclonus, or other sleep-disturbing problems. Insomnia is not necessarily a problem of too little sleep; it is often a problem of too little undisturbed sleep.

Hypersomnia

Narcolepsy is the most well-understood disorder of hypersomnia. It is characterized by repeated, brief (10- to 15-minute) daytime sleep attacks. Narcoleptics typically sleep only about an hour per day more than average; it is the inappropriateness of their sleep episodes that defines their condition. Most of us occasionally fall asleep on the beach, in front of the television, or in the most *soporific* (sleep-promoting) of all daytime sleep sites: the large, dimly lit lecture hall. But narcoleptics fall asleep in the middle of a conversation, while eating, while making love, or even while scuba diving. Narcolepsy is treated with stimulants, taken in the morning.

REM-Sleep-Related Disorders

As well as being a disorder of hypersomnia, narcolepsy is classified as a *REM-sleep-related disorder.* Narcoleptics, unlike normal people, often go directly into REM sleep when they fall asleep, and narcoleptic attacks appear to be instances in which REM-sleep phenomena encroach on wakefulness.

Cataplexy, another REM-sleep-related disorder, is often associated with narcolepsy. Cataplexy is characterized by recurring losses of muscle tone during wakefulness, often triggered by emotional experiences. In its mild form, it may simply require that the patient sit down for a few seconds until it passes. In its extreme

Insomnia. Disorders of initiating and maintaining sleep.
Hypersomnia. Disorders characterized by excessive sleep or sleepiness.
Iatrogenic. Physician-created.
Sleep apnea. A condition in which sleep is repeatedly disturbed by momentary interruptions in breathing.
Nocturnal myoclonus. Periodic sleep-disrupting twitching of the legs during sleep.

Restless legs. Tension or uneasiness in the legs that keeps people from falling asleep.
Narcolepsy. A disorder of hypersomnia characterized by repeated, brief daytime sleep attacks.
Cataplexy. A disorder that is characterized by sudden losses of muscle tone during wakefulness and is often seen in cases of narcolepsy.

form, the patient drops to the ground as if shot and remains there for a minute or two, fully conscious. An attack of cataplexy occurs when the lack of core muscle tone, which normally accompanies REM sleep, occurs during wakefulness.

Research on the mechanisms of cataplexy has focused on the cells of the caudal reticular formation that control muscle relaxation during REM sleep: the cells of the **nucleus magnocellularis.** Recently, Siegel et al. (1991) recorded the activity of these cells in dogs that experienced cataplectic attacks when they became excited. Of the cells of the caudal reticular formation that were active during REM sleep, only those of the nucleus magnocellularis were also active during cataplectic attacks. This suggests that cataplectic attacks result from the encroachment of REM-related atonia into wakefulness.

Because both narcolepsy and cataplexy are disorders of REM sleep, they are often treated with *tricyclic antidepressants.* As mentioned previously, tricyclic antidepressants suppress REM sleep.

Occasionally, patients are discovered who have little or no REM sleep. Although this disorder is rare, it is important because of its theoretical implications. Lavie et al. (1984) described a patient who had suffered a brain injury that presumably involved damage to the REM-sleep generator in the pontine reticular formation. The most important finding of this case study was that the patient did not appear to be adversely affected by his lack of REM sleep. After receiving his injury, he completed high school, college, and law school and now has a thriving law practice.

Some patients experience REM sleep without core muscle atonia. It has been suggested that the function of REM-sleep atonia is to prevent the acting out of dreams. This theory receives support from case studies of people who suffer from this disorder:

> I was a halfback playing football, and after the quarterback received the ball from the center he lateraled it sideways to me and I'm supposed to go around end and cut back over tackle and—this is very vivid—as I cut back over tackle there is this big 280-pound tackle waiting, so I, according to football rules, was to give him my shoulder and bounce him out of the way. . . . [W]hen I came to I was standing in front of our dresser and I had [gotten up out of bed and run and] knocked lamps, mirrors and everything off the dresser, hit my head against the wall and my knee against the dresser. (Schenck et al., 1986, p. 294)

Presumably, REM sleep without atonia is caused by damage to the nucleus magnocellularis or to an interruption of its output. Supporting this hypothesis is the fact that lesions of the caudal reticular formation often induce a similar disorder in cats:

> To a naive observer, the cat, which is standing, looks awake since it may attack unknown enemies, play with an absent mouse, or display flight behavior. There are orienting movements of the head or eyes toward imaginary stimuli, although the animal does not respond to visual or auditory stimuli. These extraordinary episodes . . . are a good argument that "dreaming" occurs during REM sleep in the cat. (Jouvet, 1972, pp. 236–237)

Have you ever experienced a period of paralysis or a vivid dreamlike state just as you are falling asleep or waking up? Many people have. These experiences are called **sleep paralysis** and **hypnagogic hallucinations,** respectively. Both are thought to result from the encroachment of REM-sleep phenomena into wakefulness, and both are common in cases of narcolepsy.

12.11 The Effects of Long-Term Sleep Reduction

You have already learned in this chapter that answering the question of how much sleep we need requires a particular kind of research. Studies of short-term (i.e., a few days) sleep reduction provide little insight, because short-term sleep reduction is typically associated with stress and circadian disturbances and because most people are inefficient sleepers at the beginning of a sleep-reduction study. Clearly, the only way to explore the boundary of minimal sleep requirements is to study healthy human subjects voluntarily following regular, long-term programs of reduced sleep. Because they are so time-consuming, few of these critical studies have been conducted; but there have been enough of them for a clear pattern to have emerged. I think you will by amazed by the results.

There have two kinds of long-term sleep-reduction studies: studies in which the subjects sleep nightly and studies in which subjects sleep by napping. Following a brief discussion of these two kinds of studies, the chapter concludes with my own personal experiences of sleep reduction.

Long-Term Sleep Reduction: Nightly Sleep

There have been two studies in which healthy subjects have reduced their nightly sleep for several weeks or longer. In one (Webb & Agnew, 1974), a group of 16 subjects slept for only 5.5 hours per night for 60 days, with only one detectable deficit on an extensive battery of mood, medical, and performance tests: a slight deficit on a test of auditory vigilance.

In the other systematic study of long-term sleep reduction (Friedman et al., 1977; Mullaney et al., 1977), 8 subjects reduced their nightly sleep by 30 minutes every 2 weeks until they reached 6.5 hours per night, then by 30 minutes every 3 weeks until they reached 5 hours, and then by 30 minutes every 4 weeks thereafter. After a subject indicated a lack of desire to reduce sleep further, the person slept for 1 month at the shortest duration of nightly sleep that was achieved, then for 2 months at the shortest duration plus 30 minutes. Finally, each subject slept each night for 1 year for however long the person preferred. The minimum duration of nightly sleep achieved during this experiment was 5.5 hours for 2 subjects, 5.0 hours for 4 subjects, and an impressive 4.5 hours for 2 subjects. In each of the subjects, a reduction in sleep time was associated with an increase in sleep efficiency: a decrease in the amount of time it took the subjects to fall asleep after going to bed, a decrease in the number of nighttime awakenings, and an increase in the proportion of stage 4 sleep. After the subjects had reduced their sleep to 6 hours per night, they began to experience daytime sleepiness, and this became a problem as sleep time was further reduced. Nevertheless, there were no deficits on any of the mood, medical, or performance tests given to the subjects throughout the experiment. The most encouraging result was that during a follow-up 1 year later, all subjects were sleeping less than they had previously—between 7 and 18 hours less each week—with no excessive sleepiness.

Long-Term Sleep Reduction by Napping

Most mammals and human infants display **polyphasic sleep cycles**; that is, they regularly sleep more than once per day. In contrast, most adult humans display **monophasic sleep cycles**; that is, they sleep once per day. Nevertheless, most adult humans do display polyphasic cycles of sleepiness, with periods of sleepiness occurring in late afternoon and late morning (Stampi, 1992). Have you ever experienced them?

Do adult humans need to take sleep in one continuous period per day, or can they sleep effectively in several naps as infants and other mammals do? Which of the two sleep patterns is more efficient? Research has shown that naps have recuperative powers out of proportion with their brevity (e.g., Horne & Reyner, 1996; Naitoh, 1992), thus suggesting that polyphasic sleep might be particularly efficient.

Interest in the value of polyphasic sleep was stimulated by the legend that Leonardo da Vinci managed to generate a steady stream of artistic and engineering accomplishments during his life by napping for 15 min-

utes every 4 hours, thereby limiting his sleep to 1.5 hours per day. As unbelievable as this may seem, it has been replicated in several experiments (see Stampi, 1992). Here are the main findings of these truly mind-boggling experiments. First, the subjects required a long time, about 2 weeks, to adapt to a polyphasic sleep schedule. Second, once adapted to polyphasic sleep, the subjects were content and displayed no deficits on the performance tests that they received. Third, Leonardo's 4-hour schedule works quite well, but in unstructured working situations (e.g., as in around-the-world solo sailboat races), subjects often vary the duration of the cycle without feeling negative consequences. Fourth, most subjects display a strong preference for particular sleep durations (e.g., 25 minutes) and refrain from sleeping too little, which leaves them unrefreshed, or too much, which leaves them groggy for several minutes when they awake—an effect called *sleep inertia*. Fifth, at first most of the sleep is slow-wave sleep, but eventually the subjects return to their usual relative proportions of REM and slow-wave sleep; however, REM and slow-wave sleep seldom occur during the same nap.

The following are the words of artist Giancarlo Sbragio, who adopted Leonardo's sleep schedule:

> . . . this schedule was difficult to follow at the beginning. . . . It took about 3 wk to get used to it. But I soon reached a point at which I felt a natural propensity for sleeping at this rate, and it turned out to be a thrilling and exciting experience.
>
> . . . How beautiful my life became: I discovered dawns, I discovered silence, and concentration. I had more time for studying and reading—far more than I did before. I had more time for myself, for painting, and for developing my career. (Sbragia, 1992, p. 181)

Long-Term Sleep Reduction: A Personal Case Study

I began this chapter 4 weeks ago with both zeal and trepidation. I was fascinated by the idea that I could wring 2 or 3 extra hours of living out of each day by sleeping less, and I hoped that adhering to a sleep-reduction program while writing about sleep would create an enthusiasm for the subject that would color my writing and be passed on to you. On the other hand, I

Nucleus magnocellularis. The nucleus of the caudal reticular formation that promotes relaxation of the core muscles during REM sleep and during cataleptic attacks.

Sleep paralysis. A sleep disorder characterized by attacks of paralysis just as a person is falling asleep.

Hypnagogic hallucinations. Vivid dreamlike states that some people occasionally experience just as they are falling asleep.

Polyphasic sleep cycles. Sleep cycles that regularly involve more than one period of sleep per day.

Monophasic sleep cycles. Sleep cycles that regularly involve only one period of sleep per day, typically at night.

was more than a little concerned about the negative effect that losing 3 hours of sleep per night might have on me.

Rather than using the gradual step-wise reduction method of Friedman and his colleagues, I jumped into my 5-hours-per-night sleep schedule with both feet. This proved to be less difficult than you might think. I took advantage of a trip to the East Coast from my home on the West Coast to reset my circadian clock. While I was in the East, I got up at 7:00 A.M., which is 4:00 A.M. on the West Coast, and I just kept on the same schedule when I got home. I decided to add my extra waking hours to the beginning of my day rather than to the end so there would be no temptation for me to waste them; there are not too many distractions around this university at 5:00 A.M.

Figure 12.17 is a record of my sleep times for the 4-week period that it took me to write a first draft of this chapter. I didn't quite meet my goal of sleeping less than 5 hours every night, but I didn't miss by much: My overall mean was 5.05 hours per night. Notice that in the last week, there was a tendency for my circadian clock to run a bit slow; I began sleeping in until 4:30 A.M. and staying up until 11:30 P.M.

What were the positives and negatives of my experience? The main positive was the time to do things that it created: Having an extra 21 hours per week was wonderful. Furthermore, because my daily routine was out of synchrony with everybody else's, I spent little time sitting in rush-hour traffic. The only negative of the experience was sleepiness. It was no problem during the day, when I was active. However, staying awake during the last hour before I went to bed—an hour during which I usually engaged in sedentary activities, such as reading—was at times a problem. This is when I be-

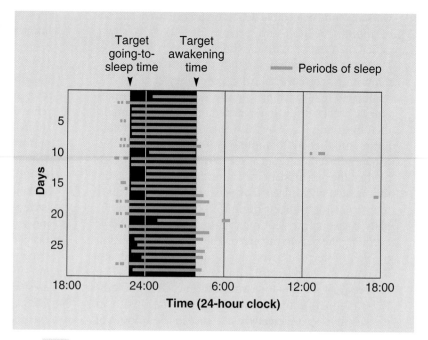

Figure 12.17 Sleep record of JPJP during a 4-week sleep-reduction program.

came personally familiar with the phenomenon of microsleep, and it was then that I required some assistance in order to stay awake. Going to bed and falling asleep each night became a fleeting but satisfying experience.

I began this chapter with the question: How much sleep do we need? Then, I gave you my best professorial it-could-be-this, it-could-be-that answer. However, that was a month ago. Now, after experiencing sleep reduction firsthand, I am less inclined toward wishy-washiness on the topic of sleep. The fact that most committed subjects who are active during the day can reduce their sleep to about 5.5 hours per night without great difficulty or major adverse consequences suggested to me that the answer is 5.5 hours of sleep. But that was before I reviewed the recent research on napping and polyphasic sleep schedules. Now, I must revise my estimate downward—substantially.

CONCLUSION

This chapter has introduced you to the fundamentals of sleep, dreaming, and circadian rhythms. It began by describing the physiological and behavioral correlates of sleep (12.1), with an emphasis on REM sleep and dreaming (12.2). Then, the next four sections introduced you to the recuperation and circadian theories of sleep (12.3); to two different lines of research that have a bearing on these theories—circadian sleep-cycle research (12.4) and sleep-deprivation research (12.5);

and to a model of sleep that combines both recuperation and circadian factors (12.6). Following discussion of the recuperation and circadian theories, the chapter discussed the neural mechanisms of sleep (12.7), the neural and molecular mechanisms of the circadian clock (12.8), sleep-affecting drugs (12.9), and sleep disorders (12.10). Finally, the chapter ended with a discussion of research on sleep reduction and its personal implications (12.11).

FOOD FOR THOUGHT

1. Do you think that your life could be improved by changing when or how long you sleep each day? In what ways? What negative effects do you think such changes might have on you?

2. Some people like to stay up late, some people like to get up early, others like to do both, and still others like to do neither. Design a sleep-reduction program that is tailored to your own biology and lifestyle and that is consistent with the research literature on circadian cycles and sleep deprivation. The program should produce the greatest benefits for you with the least discomfort.

3. How has reading about sleep research changed your views about sleep? Give three specific examples.

4. Given the evidence that the long-term use of benzodiazepines actually contributes to the problems of insomnia, why are they so commonly prescribed for its treatment?

5. Your friend tells you that everybody needs 8 hours of sleep per night; she points out that every time she stays up late to study, she feels lousy the next day. Convince her that she is wrong.

KEY TERMS

Activation-synthesis theory (p. 316)
Alpha waves (p. 313
Antihypnotic drugs (p. 334)
Basal forebrain region (p. 330)
Benzodiazepines (p. 334)
Carousel apparatus (p. 323)
Cataplexy (p. 337)
Cerveau isolé preparation (p. 327)
Circadian clock (p. 332)
Circadian rhythms (p. 318)
Delta sleep (p. 315)
Delta waves (p. 313)
Desynchronized EEG (p. 328)
Dorsal raphé nucleus (p. 330)
Electroencephalogram (EEG) (p. 313)
Electromyogram (EMG) (p. 313)

Electrooculogram (EOG) (p. 313)
Emergent stage 1 EEG (p. 313)
Encéphale isolé preparation (p. 328)
First-night phenomenon (p. 313)
Free-running period (p. 319)
Free-running rhythms (p. 319)
5-hydroxytryptophan (5-HTP) (p. 335)
Hypersomnia (p. 336)
Hypnagogic hallucinations (p. 338)
Hypnotic drugs (p. 334)
Iatrogenic (p. 336)
Initial stage 1 EEG (p. 313)
Insomnia (p. 336)
Internal desynchronization (p. 319)

Jet lag (p. 320)
K complexes (p. 313)
Locus coeruleus (p. 330)
Lucid dreams (p. 316)
Melatonin (p. 334)
Microsleeps (p. 323)
Monophasic sleep cycles (p. 339)
Narcolepsy (p. 337)
Nocturnal myoclonus (p. 337)
Nucleus magnocellularis (p. 338)
Parachlorophenylalanine (PCPA) (p. 330)
Paradoxical sleep (p. 314)
Pineal gland (p. 335)
Polyphasic sleep cycles (p. 339)
REM sleep (p. 315)
Raphé nuclei (p. 329)

Restless legs (p. 337)
Reticular activating system (p. 328)
Sleep apnea (p. 337)
Sleep paralysis (p. 338)
Sleep spindles (p. 313)
Slow-wave sleep (SWS) (p. 315)
Somnambulism (p. 316)
Suprachiasmatic nuclei (SCN) (p. 333)
Tricyclic antidepressant drugs (p. 325)
Zeitgebers (p. 318)

ADDITIONAL READING

There are several classic introductions to the topic of sleep; the following four are my favorites:

Dement, W. C. (1978). *Some must watch while some must sleep.* New York: Norton.

Hartmann, E. L. (1973). *The functions of sleep.* Westford, MA: Murray Printing.

Hobson, J. A. (1989). *Sleep.* New York: Scientific American Library.

Meddis, R. (1977). *The sleep instinct.* London: Henley and Boston.

The following book is a must for anybody interested in the question of how much we need to sleep:

Stampi, C. (1992). *Why we nap: Evolution, chronobiology, and functions of polyphasic and ultrashort sleep.* Boston: Birkhäuser.

The following book raises some interesting ethical and legal issues; it describes a reasonable, kind man who killed his father-in-law while under the influence of a sleep disorder.

Callwood, J. (1990). *The sleepwalker.* Toronto: Lester & Orpen Dennys.

13

Drug Addiction and Reward Circuits in the Brain

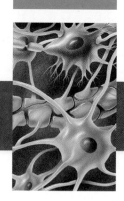

Drug addiction is a serious problem in most parts of the world. For example, in the United States alone, about 60 million people are addicted to nicotine, alcohol, or both; 5.5 million are addicted to illegal drugs; and many millions more are addicted to prescription drugs (see Holloway, 1991). Pause for a moment and think about the sheer magnitude of the grief represented by such figures—hundreds of millions of sick and suffering people worldwide. Think also about what these figures may mean for you personally. The incidence of drug addiction is so high that it is almost certain that you, or somebody dear to you, will be adversely affected by drugs. Perhaps it has happened already.

This chapter introduces you to some basic pharmacological principles and concepts; it compares the effects of five common addictive drugs; and it reviews recent research on the neural mechanisms of addiction. You likely already have strong views about drug addiction; thus, as you progress through this chapter, it is particularly important that you do not let your thinking be clouded by preconception. In particular, it is important that you do not fall into the trap of assuming that a drug's legal status has much to say about its safety. You will be less likely to assume that legal drugs are safe and illegal drugs are dangerous if you remember that most laws governing drug abuse in various parts of the world were enacted in the early 1900s or before, long before there was any scientific research on the topic (see Musto, 1991).

People's tendency to equate drug legality with drug safety was recently illustrated to me in a particularly ironic fashion: I was invited to address a convention of high school teachers on the topic of drug abuse. When I arrived at the convention center to give my talk, I was escorted to a special suite, where I was encouraged to join the executive committee in a round of drug taking—the drug being a special high-proof single-malt whiskey. Later, the irony of the situation had its full impact. As I stepped to the podium under the influence of a psychoactive drug (the whiskey), I looked out through the haze of cigarette smoke at an audience of educators who had invited me to speak to them because they were concerned about the unhealthy impact of drugs on their students. The welcoming applause gradually gave way to the melodic tinkling of ice cubes in liquor glasses, and I began. They did not like what I had to say.

13.1 Basic Principles of Drug Action

This section focuses on the basic principles of drug action, with an emphasis on **psychoactive drugs**—drugs that influence subjective experience and behavior by acting on the nervous system.

Drug Administration and Absorption

Drugs are usually administered in one of four ways: by oral ingestion, by injection, by inhalation, or by absorption through the mucous membranes of the nose, mouth, or rectum. The route of administration influences the rate at which and the degree to which the drug reaches its sites of action.

■ INGESTION The oral route is the preferred route of administration for many drugs. Once they are swallowed, drugs dissolve in the fluids of the stomach and are carried to the intestine, where they are absorbed into the bloodstream. However, some drugs readily pass through the stomach wall (e.g., alcohol), and these take effect sooner because they do not have to reach the intestine to be absorbed. Drugs that are not readily absorbed from the digestive tract or that are broken down into inactive metabolites before they can be absorbed must be taken by some other route.

The two main advantages of the oral route of administration over other routes are its ease and relative safety. Its main disadvantage is its unpredictability: Absorption from the digestive tract into the bloodstream can be greatly influenced by such difficult-to-gauge factors as the amount and type of food in the stomach.

■ INJECTION Drug injection is common in medical practice because the effects of injected drugs are large, rapid, and predictable. Drug injections are typically made **subcutaneously (SC)** into the fatty tissue just beneath the skin, **intramuscularly (IM)** into the large muscles, or **intravenously (IV)** directly into veins at points where

---

Psychoactive drugs. Drugs that influence subjective experience and behavior by acting on the nervous system.
Subcutaneously (SC). Under the skin.
Intramuscularly (IM). Into a muscle.
Intravenously (IV). Into a vein.

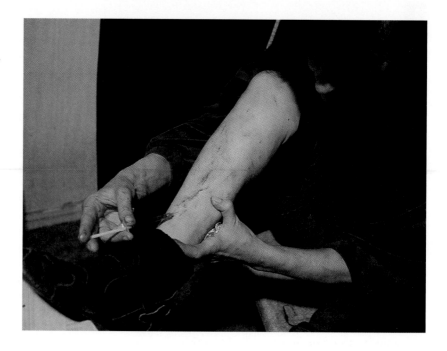

Figure 13.1 Scar tissue associated with chronic intravenous drug use. Many addicts who administer their drugs intravenously develop scar tissue, infections, and collapsed veins at the few sites where large veins course near the body surface.

they run just beneath the skin. Many addicts prefer the intravenous route because the bloodstream delivers the drug directly to the brain. However, the speed and directness of the intravenous route are mixed blessings; after an intravenous injection, there is little or no opportunity to counteract the effects of an overdose, an impurity, or an allergic reaction. Furthermore, many addicts develop scar tissue, infections, and collapsed veins at the few sites on their bodies where there are large accessible veins (see Figure 13.1).

■ INHALATION   Some drugs can be absorbed into the bloodstream through the rich network of capillaries in the lungs. Many anesthetics are usually administered by *inhalation,* as are tobacco and marijuana. The two main shortcomings of this route are that it is difficult to precisely regulate the dose of inhaled drugs, and many chronically inhaled substances damage the lungs.

■ ABSORPTION THROUGH MUCOUS MEMBRANES   Some drugs can be administered through the mucous membranes of the nose, mouth, and rectum. Cocaine, for example, is commonly self-administered through the nasal membranes (snorted)—but not without damaging them.

Penetration of the Central Nervous System by Drugs

Once a drug enters the bloodstream, it is carried in the blood to the blood vessels of the central nervous system. Fortunately, a protective filter, the *blood–brain*

barrier, makes it difficult for many potentially dangerous blood-borne chemicals to pass from the blood vessels of the CNS into CNS neurons.

Mechanisms of Drug Action

Psychoactive drugs influence the nervous system in many ways (see Koob & Bloom, 1988). Some of these drugs (e.g., alcohol and many of the general anesthetics) act diffusely on neural membranes throughout the CNS. Others act in a less general way: by binding to particular synaptic receptors; by influencing the synthesis, transport, release, or deactivation of particular neurotransmitters; or by influencing the chain of chemical reactions elicited in postsynaptic neurons by the activation of their synaptic receptors (see Chapter 4). Accordingly, some drugs are much more selective in their actions than others.

Drug metabolism. The conversion of a drug from its active form to a nonactive form.

Drug tolerance. A state of decreased susceptibility to a drug that develops as a result of exposure to the drug.

Cross tolerance. Tolerance that develops to the effects of one drug as the result of exposure to another drug.

Sensitization. An increase in the sensitivity to a drug effect that develops as the result of exposure to the drug.

Metabolic tolerance. Tolerance that results from a reduction in the amount of a drug getting to its sites of action.

Functional tolerance. Tolerance resulting from a reduction in the reactivity of the nervous system (or other sites of action) to a drug.

Withdrawal syndrome. The illness brought on by the elimination from the body of a drug on which the person is physically dependent.

Physically dependent. Being in a state from which the discontinuation of drug taking will induce withdrawal effects.

Drug Metabolism and Elimination

The actions of most drugs are terminated by enzymes synthesized by the liver. These liver enzymes stimulate the conversion of active drugs to nonactive forms—a process referred to as **drug metabolism.** In many cases, drug metabolism eliminates a drug's ability to pass through lipid membranes so that it can no longer penetrate the blood–brain barrier. In addition to the deactivating effects of drug metabolism, small amounts of some psychoactive drugs are deactivated by being passed from the body in urine, sweat, feces, breath, and mother's milk.

Drug Tolerance

Drug tolerance is a state of decreased sensitivity to a drug that develops as a result of exposure to it. Drug tolerance can be demonstrated in two ways: by showing that a given dose of the drug has less effect than it had before drug exposure or by showing that it takes more of the drug to produce the same effect. In essence, what this means is that tolerance is a shift in the *dose-response curve* (a graph of the magnitude of the effect of different doses of the drug) to the right (see Figure 13.2).

There are three important points to remember about the specificity of drug tolerance. The first is that exposure to one drug can produce tolerance to other drugs that act by the same mechanism; this is known as **cross tolerance.** The second is that tolerance often develops to some effects of a drug but not to others. Failure to understand this second point can have tragic consequences for people who think that because they have become tolerant to some effects of a drug (e.g., to the nauseating effects of alcohol or tobacco), they are tolerant to all of them. In fact, tolerance may develop to some effects of a drug while the sensitivity to other effects increases; the increases in sensitivity are called

sensitization (Robinson, 1991). The third important point about the specificity of drug tolerance is that drug tolerance is not a unitary phenomenon; that is, there is no single mechanism that underlies all examples of it. When a drug is administered at active doses, many kinds of adaptive changes can occur to reduce the effect of the drug.

Two categories of changes underlie drug tolerance: metabolic and functional. Drug tolerance that results from changes that reduce the amount of drug getting to its sites of action is called **metabolic tolerance.** Drug tolerance that results from changes that reduce the reactivity of the sites of action to the drug is called **functional tolerance.**

Tolerance to psychoactive drugs is largely functional. Functional tolerance to psychoactive drugs can result from several different types of neural changes. For example, exposure to a psychoactive drug can reduce the number of receptors for it, decrease the efficiency with which it binds to existing receptors, or diminish the impact of receptor binding on the activity of the cell.

Drug Withdrawal Effects and Physical Dependence

After significant amounts of a drug have been in the body for a period of time (e.g., several days), its sudden elimination can trigger an illness called a **withdrawal syndrome.** The effects of drug withdrawal are virtually always opposite to the initial effects of the drug. For example, the withdrawal of anticonvulsant drugs often triggers convulsions, and the withdrawal of sleeping pills often produces insomnia. Individuals who suffer withdrawal reactions when they stop taking a drug are said to be **physically dependent** on that drug.

The fact that withdrawal effects are frequently opposite to the initial effects of the drug suggests that withdrawal effects may be produced by the same neural

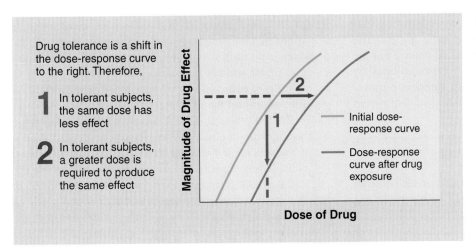

Figure 13.2 Drug tolerance: A shift in the dose-response curve to the right as a result of exposure to the drug.

Drug tolerance is a shift in the dose-response curve to the right. Therefore,

1 In tolerant subjects, the same dose has less effect

2 In tolerant subjects, a greater dose is required to produce the same effect

Magnitude of Drug Effect

Dose of Drug

Initial dose-response curve

Dose-response curve after drug exposure

Figure 13.3 The relation between drug tolerance and withdrawal effects. The same adaptive neurophysiological changes that develop in response to drug exposure and produce drug tolerance manifest themselves as withdrawal effects once the drug is removed. As the neurophysiological changes develop, tolerance increases; and as they subside, the severity of the withdrawal effects decreases.

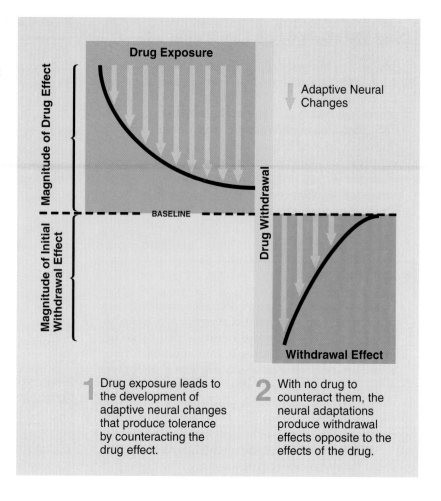

Adaptive Neural Changes

1 Drug exposure leads to the development of adaptive neural changes that produce tolerance by counteracting the drug effect.

2 With no drug to counteract them, the neural adaptations produce withdrawal effects opposite to the effects of the drug.

changes that produce drug tolerance (see Figure 13.3). According to this theory, exposure to a drug produces compensatory changes in the nervous system that offset the drug's effects and produce tolerance. Then, when the drug is eliminated from the body, these compensatory neural changes, without the drug to offset them, manifest themselves as withdrawal symptoms opposite to the initial effects of the drug.

The severity of withdrawal symptoms depends on the particular drug in question, on the duration and degree of the preceding drug exposure, and on the speed with which the drug is eliminated from the body. In general, longer exposure to greater doses followed by more rapid elimination produces greater withdrawal effects.

Addiction: What Is It?

Addicts are habitual drug users, but not all habitual drug users are addicts. **Addicts** are those habitual drug users who continue to use a drug despite its adverse effects on their health and social life and despite their repeated efforts to stop using it.

The greatest confusion about the nature of addiction concerns its relation to physical dependence. Many people equate the two: They see addicts as people who are trapped on a merry-go-round of drug taking, withdrawal symptoms, and further drug taking to combat the withdrawal symptoms. Although appealing in its simplicity, this conception of drug addiction is wrong. Addicts sometimes take drugs to prevent or alleviate withdrawal symptoms, but this is rarely the primary motivating factor in their addiction. If it were, addicts could be easily cured by hospitalizing them for a few days, until their withdrawal symptoms subsided. However, most addicts renew their drug taking even after months of enforced abstinence. This is an important issue; we will return to it later in the chapter.

When physical dependence was believed to be the major cause of addiction, the term *psychological dependence* was coined to refer to exceptions to this general rule. **Psychological dependence** was said to be the cause of any compulsive drug taking that occurred in the absence of physical dependence. However, now that it is clear that physical dependence is not the major motivating factor in addiction, there is little need for a special category of psychological dependence.

13.2 Role of Learning in Drug Tolerance and Drug Withdrawal Effects

An important line of psychopharmacologic research has shown that learning plays a major role in both drug tolerance and drug withdrawal. This research has contributed substantially to our understanding of tolerance and withdrawal, but its impact has been more far-reaching: It has emphasized that efforts to understand the effects of psychoactive drugs without considering the experience and behavior of the subjects will provide only partial answers.

Research on the role of learning in drug tolerance has focused on three phenomena: contingent drug tolerance, conditioned drug tolerance, and conditioned withdrawal effects. These phenomena are discussed in the following subsections.

Contingent Drug Tolerance

Contingent drug tolerance refers to demonstrations that tolerance develops only to drug effects that are actually experienced. Most studies of contingent drug tolerance employ the **before-and-after design.** In before-and-after experiments, two groups of subjects receive the same series of drug injections and the same series of repeated tests, but the subjects in one group receive the drug before each test of the series and those in the other group receive the drug after each test. At the end of the experiment, all subjects receive the same dose of the drug followed by the test so that the degree to which the drug disrupts test performance in the two groups can be compared.

My colleagues and I (e.g., Pinel, Mana, & Kim, 1989) have used the before-and-after design to study contingent tolerance to the anticonvulsant effect of alcohol. In our study, two groups of rats received exactly the same regimen of alcohol injections: one injection every 2 days for the duration of the experiment. During the tolerance development phase, the rats in one group received each alcohol injection 1 hour before a mild convulsive amygdala stimulation so that the anticonvulsant effect of the alcohol could be experienced on each trial. The rats in the other group received their injections 1 hour after each convulsive stimulation so that the anticonvulsant effect could not be experienced. At the end of the experiment, all of the subjects received a test injection of alcohol, followed 1 hour later by a convulsive stimulation so that the amount of tolerance to the anticonvulsant effect of alcohol could be compared in the two groups. As Figure 13.4 on page 348 illustrates, the rats that received alcohol on each trial before a convulsive stimulation became almost totally tolerant to alcohol's anticonvulsant effect, whereas those that received the same injections and stimulations in the reverse order developed no tolerance whatsoever to alcohol's anticonvulsant effect.

Contingent drug tolerance has been demonstrated to many drug effects (see Poulos & Cappell, 1991). For example, tolerance to the disruptive effects of alcohol on the sexual behavior of male rats was greater in rats that engaged in sexual behavior after each alcohol injection (Pinel, Pfaus, & Christensen, 1991), tolerance to the anorexic effect of cholecystokinin on food consumption was greater in rats that ate after each cholecystokinin injection (Goodison & Siegel, 1995), and the disruptive effects of alcohol on maze running was greater in rats that ran the maze after each alcohol injection (Chen, 1968).

Contingent tolerance must be a very basic phenomenon indeed because it can be demonstrated even at the level of the synapse. Traynor, Schlapfer, and Barondes (1980) found that tolerance to the disruptive effect of alcohol on synaptic transmission in the abdominal ganglion of a marine snail (*Aplysia*) did not occur unless the synapse was activated during the period of alcohol exposure. Apparently, functional drug tolerance, like all forms of neural adaptation, is triggered by the experience of disruptions of particular patterns of neural activity, rather than by mere exposure to the disrupting agent.

Conditioned Drug Tolerance

Whereas studies of contingent drug tolerance focus on what subjects do while they are under the influence of drugs, studies of conditioned drug tolerance focus on

Addicts. Habitual drug users who continue to use a drug despite the adverse effects of the drug on their health and life and despite their repeated efforts to stop using it.

Psychological dependence. Compulsive drug taking that occurs in the absence of physical dependence.

Contingent drug tolerance. Drug tolerance that develops as a reaction to the experience of the effects of drugs rather than to drug exposure alone.

Before-and-after design. The experimental design used to demonstrate contingent drug tolerance; the experimental group receives the drug before each of a series of behavioral tests and the control group receives the drug after each test.

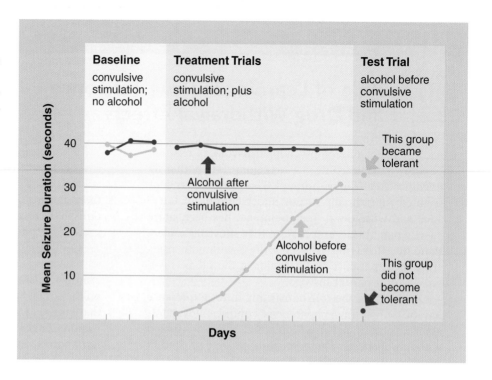

Figure 13.4 Contingent tolerance to the anticonvulsant effect of alcohol. The rats that received alcohol on each trial before a convulsive stimulation became tolerant to its anticonvulsant effect; those that received the same injections after a convulsive stimulation on each trial did not become tolerant.

(Adapted from Pinel, Mana, & Kim, 1989.)

the situations in which drugs are taken. **Conditioned drug tolerance** refers to demonstrations that tolerance effects are maximally expressed only when a drug is administered in the same situation in which it has pre-

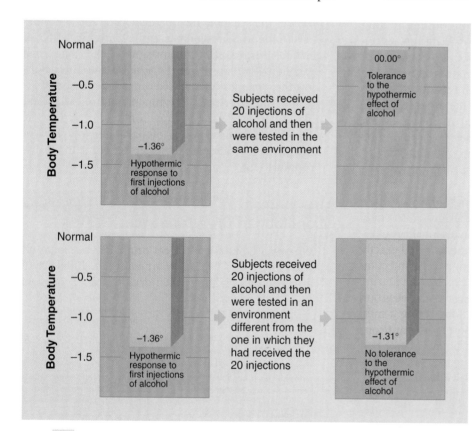

Figure 13.5 The situational specificity of tolerance to the hypothermic effects of alcohol.
(Adapted from Crowell et al., 1981.)

viously been administered. For example, in one demonstration of conditioned drug tolerance (Crowell, Hinson, & Siegel, 1981), two groups of rats received 20 alcohol and 20 saline injections in an alternating sequence, 1 injection every other day. The only difference between the two groups was that the rats in one group received all 20 alcohol injections in a distinctive test room and the 20 saline injections in their colony room, while the rats in the other group received the alcohol in the colony room and the saline in the distinctive test room. At the end of the injection period, the tolerance of all rats to the **hypothermic** (temperature-reducing) effects of alcohol was assessed in both environments. As Figure 13.5 illustrates, tolerance was observed only when the rats were injected in the environment that had previously been paired with alcohol administration. This demonstration of the *situational specificity of drug tolerance* may surprise you; however, it is a general effect that has been repeatedly demonstrated to a variety of drug effects.

The numerous demonstrations of the situational specificity of drug tolerance led Siegel and his colleagues to propose that addicts may be particularly susceptible to the lethal effects of a drug *overdose* when the drug is administered in a new context. Their hypothesis is that addicts become tolerant when they repeatedly self-administer their drug in the same environment and, as a result, begin taking larger and larger doses to counteract the diminution of drug effects. Then, if the addict administers the usual massive dose in an unusual situation, tolerance effects are not present to counteract the effects of the drug, and there is a greater risk of death from overdose. In support of this hypothesis, Siegel and colleagues (1982) found that many more heroin-tolerant rats died following a high dose of heroin administered in a novel environment than in their usual injection environment. Heroin kills by suppressing respiration.

Of the several noteworthy theories that have been proposed to account for the situational specificity of drug tolerance (see Baker & Tiffany, 1985; Eikelboom & Stewart, 1982; Paletta & Wagner, 1986), Siegel's theory has been the most influential. Siegel views each incidence of drug administration as a Pavlovian conditioning trial in which various environmental stimuli that regularly predict the administration of the drug (e.g., pubs, washrooms, needles, other addicts) are conditional stimuli and the drug effects are unconditional stimuli. The central assumption of the theory is that conditional stimuli that predict drug administration come to elicit conditional responses opposite to the unconditional effects of the drug. Siegel has termed these hypothetical opposing conditional responses **conditioned compensatory responses.** The theory is that as the stimuli that repeatedly predict the effects of a drug come to elicit greater and greater conditioned compensatory responses, they increasingly counteract the unconditional effects of the drug and produce situationally specific tolerance.

Although tolerance develops to many drug effects, sometimes the opposite happens: sensitization. Drug sensitization, like drug tolerance, can be situation specific. For example, Anagnostaras and Robinson (1996) demonstrated the situational specificity of sensitization to the motor stimulant effects of amphetamine. They found that 10 amphetamine injections, 1 every 3 or 4 days, greatly increased the ability of amphetamine to activate the motor activity of rats but only when the rats were injected and tested in the same environment in which they had experienced the previous amphetamine injections.

Conditioned Withdrawal Effects

As you have just learned, Siegel's conditioned compensatory response theory suggests that when a drug is repeatedly administered in the same environment, that environment begins to elicit responses that counteract

the drug effects and lead to the development of tolerance. One prediction of this theory is that in the absence of the drug, the drug environment should elicit effects opposite to the original effects of the drug. Withdrawal effects that are elicited by the drug environment or by other drug-associated cues are **conditioned withdrawal effects.**

There have been many demonstrations of conditioned withdrawal effects. For example, Krank and Perkins (1993) administered two injections each day to three groups of rats. One group of rats received a morphine injection each day in a distinctive test environment and a saline injection in their home cages; another group received saline injections in the test environment and morphine injections in their home cages; and the third group received saline injections in both the test environment and their home cages. After 10 injection days (i.e., after 20 injections), the rats were placed undrugged in the distinctive test environment and morphine withdrawal reactions were assessed. The results are illustrated in Figure 13.6 on page 350. The rats that had received their morphine injections in the distinctive test environment displayed substantially more morphine withdrawal symptoms than did the rats that had received their morphine injections in their home cages and the rats that had received only saline injections.

Thinking about Drug Conditioning

In any situation in which drugs are repeatedly administered, conditioning effects are inevitable. That is why it is particularly important to understand them. However, most theories of drug conditioning have a serious problem: They have difficulty predicting their direction. For example, Siegel's conditioned compensatory response theory predicts that conditioned drug effects will always be opposite to the unconditional effects of the drug, but there are many documented instances in which conditional stimuli elicit responses similar to those of the drug.

Ramsay and Woods (1997) contend that much of the confusion about conditioned drug effects stems from a misunderstanding of Pavlovian conditioning. In particular, they criticize the common assumption

Conditioned drug tolerance. Tolerance effects that are maximally expressed only when the drug is administered in situations in which it has previously been administered.
Hypothermic. Temperature-reducing.
Conditioned compensatory responses. Physiological responses opposite to the effects of a drug that are elicited by stimuli that are regularly associated with experiencing the drug effects.
Conditioned withdrawal effects. Withdrawal effects that are elicited by the drug environment or by other drug-associated cues.

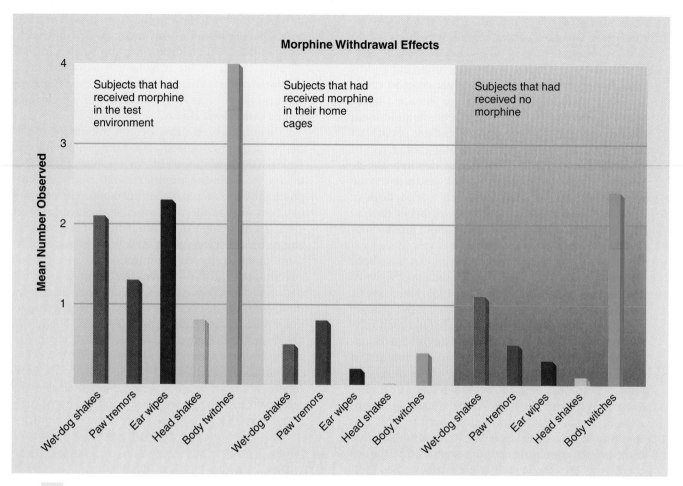

Figure 13.6 Conditioned morphine withdrawal effects in rats. Being placed in an environment in which they had previously experienced the effects of morphine elicited morphine withdrawal effects in rats. (Adapted from Krank & Perkins, 1993.)

that the unconditional stimulus in a drug-tolerance experiment is the drug and that the unconditional response is whatever change in physiology or behavior the experimenter happens to be recording. They cogently argue instead that the unconditional stimulus (i.e., the stimulus to which the subject reflexively reacts) is the disruption of neural functioning that has been directly produced by the drug, and that the unconditional responses are the various neurally mediated compensatory reactions to the unconditional stimulus.

This new perspective makes a big difference. For example, in the previously described alcohol tolerance experiment by Crowell et al. (1981), alcohol was designated as the unconditional stimulus and the resulting hypothermia as the unconditional response. Instead Ramsay and Woods would argue that the unconditional stimulus was the hypothermia directly produced by the exposure to alcohol, whereas the compensatory changes that tended to increase body temperature were the unconditional responses. The important point

about all of this is that once one determines the unconditional stimulus and response, it is easy to predict the conditional response in any drug-conditioning experiment: The conditional response is always similar to the unconditional response. Moreover, they argue that when the unconditional response counteracts the unconditional stimulus, as is usually the case, conditioning produces tolerance; whereas when the unconditional response augments the unconditional stimulus, conditioning produces sensitization.

Nicotine. The major psychoactive ingredient of tobacco.
Smoker's syndrome. The chest pain, labored breathing, wheezing, coughing, and heightened susceptibility to infections of the respiratory tract commonly observed in tobacco smokers.

Buerger's disease. A nicotine-produced disease in which blood flow to the legs is restricted, the ultimate result being gangrene and amputation.

13 DRUG ADDICTION AND REWARD CIRCUITS IN THE BRAIN

13.3 Five Commonly Abused Drugs

This section is about five commonly abused drugs: tobacco, alcohol, marijuana, cocaine, and the opiates.

Tobacco

Next to caffeine, tobacco is the most widely used psychoactive drug in our society. When a cigarette is smoked, **nicotine**—the major psychoactive ingredient of tobacco—and some 4,000 other chemicals, collectively referred to as *tar*, are absorbed through the lungs. Because considerable tolerance develops to some of the immediate adverse effects of tobacco, the effects of smoking a cigarette on nonsmokers and smokers can be quite different. Nonsmokers often respond to a few puffs of a cigarette with various combinations of nausea, vomiting, coughing, sweating, abdominal cramps, dizziness, flushing, and diarrhea. In contrast, smokers report that they are more relaxed, more alert, and less hungry after a cigarette.

There is no question that heavy smokers are drug addicts in every sense of the word (Jones, 1987). The compulsive drug craving, which is the major defining feature of addiction, is readily apparent in any heavy smoker who has run out of cigarettes or who is forced by circumstance to refrain from smoking for several hours. Furthermore, heavy smokers who stop smoking experience a variety of withdrawal effects, such as de-

pression, anxiety, restlessness, irritability, constipation, and difficulties in sleeping and concentrating.

About 70% of all people who experiment with smoking become addicted—this figure compares unfavorably with 10% for alcohol and 30% for heroin. Moreover, only about 20% of all attempts to stop smoking are successful for 2 years or more (Schelling, 1992). Can you think of any other psychoactive drug that is self-administered almost continually—even while the addicts are walking along the street or drinking coffee?

The consequences of long-term tobacco use are alarming. **Smoker's syndrome** is characterized by chest pain, labored breathing, wheezing, coughing, and a heightened susceptibility to infections of the respiratory tract. Chronic smokers are highly susceptible to a variety of potentially lethal lung disorders, including pneumonia, *bronchitis* (chronic inflammation of the bronchioles of the lungs), *emphysema* (loss of elasticity of the lung from chronic irritation), and lung cancer. Although the increased risk of lung cancer receives the greatest publicity, smoking also increases the risk of cancer of the larynx (voice box), mouth, esophagus, kidneys, pancreas, bladder, and stomach. Smokers also run a greater risk of developing a variety of cardiovascular diseases, which may culminate in heart attack or stroke. According to the Surgeon General of the United States, about 400,000 Americans die each year from smoking-related disorders (Schelling, 1992).

Sufferers from Buerger's disease provide a shocking illustration of the addictive power of nicotine. **Buerger's disease** is a condition in which the blood vessels, especially those supplying the legs, are constricted whenever nicotine enters the bloodstream:

> If a patient with this condition continues to smoke, gangrene may eventually set in. First a few toes may have to be amputated, then the foot at the ankle, then the leg at the knee, and ultimately at the hip. Somewhere along this gruesome progression gangrene may also attack the other leg. Patients are strongly advised that if they will only stop smoking, it is virtually certain that the otherwise inexorable march of gangrene up the legs will be curbed. Yet surgeons report that it is not at all uncommon to find a patient with Buerger's disease vigorously puffing away in his hospital bed following a second or third amputation operation. (Brecher, 1972, pp. 215–216)

The adverse effects of tobacco smoke are unfortunately not restricted to those who smoke. There is now strong evidence that individuals who live or work with smokers are more likely to develop heart disease and cancer than those who don't. Even the unborn are vulnerable: Smoking during pregnancy increases the likelihood of miscarriage, stillbirth, and early death of the child. The levels of nicotine in the blood of breast-fed infants are often as great as those in the blood of the mother.

Because there are many active ingredients in tobacco, its mechanism of action has been difficult to identify. One current hypothesis is that free radicals are the culprits in many tobacco-related disorders. **Free radicals** are chemicals with one or more unpaired electrons; they are particularly dangerous because they can break down many biological molecules, including DNA, by *oxidation* (the removal of hydrogen atoms from a compound). Indeed, the urine of smokers has been shown to contain elevated levels of a by-product of DNA oxidation (Fischer-Nielson, Loft, & Gjervig Jensen, 1993). This raises the possibility that some of the adverse effects of smoking might be negated by *antioxidants* (compounds, such as vitamin C and beta-carotene, that block oxidation). In one study, a 14-week program of beta-carotene supplements reduced by 30% the fragments of faulty genetic material coughed up by smokers (van Poppel, Spanhaak, & Ockhuizen, 1993).

Alcohol

Approximately two-thirds of the population of the United States consume alcoholic beverages (see Musto, 1996; Vallee, 1998), and of these about 15 million are addicted. Alcohol is currently involved in roughly 3% of all deaths in the United States, including deaths from birth defects, ill health, accidents, and violence (see Hunt, 1993).

Because alcohol molecules are small and soluble in both fat and water, they invade all parts of the body. Alcohol is classified as a **depressant** because at moderate-to-high doses it depresses neural firing; however, at low doses it can stimulate neural firing and facilitate social interaction.

At moderate doses, the alcohol drinker experiences various degrees of cognitive, perceptual, verbal, and motor impairment, as well as a loss of control that can lead to a variety of socially unacceptable actions. High doses result in unconsciousness; and if blood levels reach 0.5%, there is a risk of death from respiratory depression. The telltale red facial flush of alcohol intoxication is produced by the dilation of blood vessels in the skin; this dilation increases the amount of heat that is lost from the blood to the air and leads to a decrease in body temperature (hypothermia). Alcohol is also a **diuretic;** that is, it increases the production of urine by the kidneys.

Alcohol, like many addictive drugs, produces both tolerance and physical dependence. The livers of heavy drinkers metabolize alcohol more quickly than do the livers of nondrinkers, but this increase in metabolic efficiency contributes only slightly to overall alcohol tolerance; most alcohol tolerance is functional. Alcohol withdrawal often produces a mild syndrome of headache, nausea, vomiting, and tremulousness, which is euphemistically referred to as a *hangover.*

A full-blown alcohol withdrawal syndrome comprises three phases. The first phase begins about 5 or 6 hours after the cessation of a long bout of heavy drinking and is characterized by severe tremors, agitation, headache, nausea, vomiting, abdominal cramps, profuse sweating, and sometimes hallucinations. The defining feature of the second phase, which typically occurs between 15 and 30 hours after cessation of drinking, is convulsive activity. The third phase, which usually begins a day or two after the cessation of drinking and lasts for 3 or 4 days, is called **delirium tremens (DTs).** The DTs are characterized by disturbing hallucinations, bizarre delusions, agitation, confusion, *hyperthermia* (high temperature), and *tachycardia* (rapid heartbeat). The convulsions and the DTs produced by alcohol withdrawal can be lethal.

Alcohol attacks almost every tissue in the body (see Anderson et al., 1993). Chronic alcohol consumption produces extensive brain damage (Hayakawa et al., 1992) and **Korsakoff's syndrome**—a neuropsychological disorder that is characterized by severe memory loss, sensory and motor dysfunction, and severe *dementia* (intellectual deterioration). It also causes extensive scarring, or **cirrhosis,** of the liver, which is the major cause of death among heavy alcohol users. Alcohol erodes the muscles of the heart and thus increases the risk of heart attack. It irritates the lining of the digestive tract and, in so doing, increases the risk of oral and liver cancer, stomach ulcers, *pancreatitis* (inflammation of the pancreas), and *gastritis* (inflammation of the stomach). And not to be forgotten is the carnage that it produces on our highways and in our homes.

Like nicotine, alcohol readily penetrates the placental membrane and affects the fetus. The result is that the off-

13 DRUG ADDICTION AND REWARD CIRCUITS IN THE BRAIN

spring of mothers who consume substantial quantities of alcohol during their pregnancy can develop **fetal alcohol syndrome (FAS)** (see Mattson, Barron, & Riley, 1988). The FAS child suffers from some or all of the following symptoms: mental retardation, poor coordination, poor muscle tone, low birth weight, retarded growth, and physical deformity. In rats, a single day of alcohol exposure during the fetal brain growth spurt can significantly reduce adult brain weight (Goodlett, Marcussen, & West, 1990).

Alcohol has multiple mechanisms of action (see Hunt, 1993). For example, it reduces the flow of calcium into neurons by acting on calcium channels, increases the action of the inhibitory neurotransmitter GABA by acting on the GABA receptor complex, increases the number of binding sites for the excitatory neurotransmitter glutamate, reduces the effects of glutamate at some of its receptor subtypes, and interferes with second messenger systems inside neurons.

Marijuana

Marijuana is the name commonly given to the dried leaves and flowers of *Cannabis sativa*—the common hemp plant. The usual mode of consumption is to smoke these leaves in a *joint* (a cigarette of marijuana) or pipe; but it is also effective when ingested orally, if first baked into an oil-rich substrate, such as a chocolate brownie, to promote absorption from the gastrointestinal tract.

The psychoactive effects of marijuana are largely attributable to a constituent called **THC** (delta-9-tetrahydrocannabinol). However, marijuana contains over 80 *cannabinoids* (chemicals of the same chemical class as THC), which may also be psychoactive (see Kephalas et al., 1976). Most of the cannabinoids are found in a sticky resin covering the leaves and flowers of the plant, which can be extracted and dried to form a dark, corklike material called **hashish**. The hashish can be further processed into an extremely potent product called *hash oil*.

Written records of marijuana use go back 6,000 years in China, where its stem was used to make rope, its seeds were used as a grain, and its leaves and flowers were used for their psychoactive and medicinal effects.

In the Middle Ages, cannabis cultivation spread from the Middle East into Western Europe; however, in Europe, it was grown primarily for the manufacture of rope, and its psychoactive properties were largely forgotten. During the period of European imperialism, rope was in high demand for sailing vessels. In 1611, the American colonies responded to this demand by growing cannabis as a cash crop; George Washington was one of the more notable cannabis growers.

The practice of smoking the leaves of the cannabis plant and the word *marijuana* itself seem to have been introduced to the southern United States in the early part of the 1900s by Mexican immigrants; and its use gradually became popular among certain subgroups, such as the poor in city ghettos and jazz musicians. In 1926, an article appeared in a New Orleans newspaper exposing the "menace of marijuana," and soon similar stories were appearing in newspapers all over the United States under titles such as "The Evil Weed," "The Killer Drug," and "Marijuana Madness." The population was told that marijuana turns normal people into violent, drug-crazed criminals who rapidly become addicted to heroin.

Free radicals. Chemicals with one or more unpaired electrons.

Depressant. A drug that depresses neural activity and behavior.

Diuretic. A drug that increases the production of urine.

Delirium tremens (DTs). The phase of the alcohol withdrawal syndrome characterized by hallucinations, delusions, and extremely agitated behavior.

Korsakoff's syndrome. The severe memory loss and dementia that is commonly associated with alcohol addiction.

Cirrhosis. Scarring, typically of the liver.

Fetal alcohol syndrome (FAS). A syndrome produced by prenatal exposure to alcohol and characterized by mental retardation, low birth weight, and a variety of other physical abnormalities.

Cannabis sativa. The common hemp plant and the source of marijuana.

THC. Delta-9-tetrahydrocannabinol, the main psychoactive ingredient of marijuana.

Hashish. The processed resin of *Cannabis sativa*.

The result of the misrepresentation of the effects of marijuana by the U.S. news media was the enactment of many laws against the drug. In many states, marijuana was legally classified a **narcotic** (a legal term generally used to refer to opiates), and punishment was dealt out accordingly. However, the structure of marijuana and its physiological and behavioral effects bear no resemblance to those of the other narcotics; thus legally classifying marijuana as a narcotic was akin to passing a law that red is green.

The popularization of marijuana smoking among the middle and upper classes in the 1960s stimulated a massive program of research; yet there is still considerable confusion about marijuana among the general population. One of the difficulties in characterizing the effects of marijuana is that they are subtle, difficult to measure, and greatly influenced by the social situation:

> At low, usual "social" doses, the intoxicated individual may experience an increased sense of well-being: initial restlessness and hilarity followed by a dreamy, carefree state of relaxation; alteration of sensory perceptions including expansion of space and time; and a more vivid sense of touch, sight, smell, taste, and sound; a feeling of hunger, especially a craving for sweets; and subtle changes in thought formation and expression. To an unknowing observer, an individual in this state of consciousness would not appear noticeably different. (National Commission on Marijuana and Drug Abuse, 1972, p. 68)

Although the effects of typical social doses of marijuana are subtle, extraordinarily high doses do impair psychological functioning. Short-term memory is impaired, and the ability to carry out tasks involving multiple steps to reach a specific goal declines. Speech becomes slurred, and meaningful conversation becomes difficult. A sense of unreality, emotional intensification, sensory distortion, and motor impairment are also common. However, even after very high doses, an unexpected knock at the door can often bring about the return of a reasonable semblance of normal behavior.

In the light of the documented effects of marijuana, the earlier claims that marijuana would trigger a wave of violent crimes in the youth of America seem absurd. It is difficult to imagine how anybody could believe that the red-eyed, gluttonous, sleepy, giggling products of common social doses of marijuana would be likely to commit violent criminal acts. In fact, marijuana actually curbs aggressive behavior (Tinklenberg, 1974).

There is one effect of marijuana that warrants special mention because of its serious consequences. Marijuana-intoxicated drivers can stop as quickly as normal drivers, but they are not always as quick to notice the things for which they should stop (Moskowitz, Hulbert, & McGlothin, 1976).

What are the hazards of long-term marijuana use (see Zimmer & Morgan, 1997)? The main risk appears to be lung damage. Those who regularly smoke marijuana tend to have deficits in respiratory function (e.g., Tilles et al., 1986), and they are more likely to develop a chronic cough, bronchitis, and asthma (Abramson, 1974).

Some authors list four other adverse effects of regular marijuana use; however, in each case, the evidence is either indirect, inconsistent, or incomplete (see Mendelson, 1987). First, there have been reports that chronic marijuana smoking lowers the plasma *testosterone* levels of males (e.g., Kolodny et al., 1974); but several studies have failed to replicate them. Second, there has been some suggestion that marijuana can adversely influence the *immune system*, but it has yet to be demonstrated that marijuana smokers are more susceptible to infection than are comparable nonsmokers. Third, because *tachycardia* (rapid heart rate) is one effect of marijuana, there has been some concern that chronic marijuana consumption might cause cardiovascular problems; but again there is no direct evidence for this hypothesis. Fourth, many people have hypothesized that the relaxation produced by marijuana could reach pathological proportions and produce what is generally referred to as the **amotivational syndrome.** The evidence that occasional marijuana use causes a significant amotivational syndrome is far from strong (see Mendelson et al., 1976): No significant difference was found between the grade point averages of marijuana smokers and nonsmokers in a study of 2,000 college students (Brill & Christie, 1974). Nevertheless, it seems likely that continual marijuana use would be associated with some decline in productivity, assuming that the user was a productive person in the first place.

The addiction potential of marijuana is low. Most people who use marijuana do so only occasionally, and most who use it as youths curtail their use in their 30s and 40s. Tolerance to marijuana develops during periods of sustained use (Babor et al., 1975); however, withdrawal symptoms (e.g., nausea, diarrhea, sweating, chills, tremor, restlessness, sleep disturbance) are extremely rare, except in contrived laboratory situations in which massive oral doses are administered.

Some effects of marijuana have been shown to be of clinical benefit (see Cohen & Stillman, 1976). It has been used, often illegally, to block the nausea of cancer patients undergoing chemotherapy and to stimulate the appetites of patients who have lost their appetites. *Nabilone,* a synthetic cannabis analogue, is now some-

---

Narcotic. A legal classification of certain drugs, mostly opiates.

Amotivational syndrome. Chronic lack of motivation produced by drug use.

Stimulants. Drugs that produce general increases in neural and behavioral activity.

Cocaine. Cocaine hydrochloride, a strong stimulant drug that is highly addictive.

Crack. A potent, cheap, smokable base form of cocaine.

Cocaine sprees. Binges of cocaine use.

Cocaine psychosis. Psychotic behavior observed during a cocaine spree, similar in many respects to schizophrenic behavior.

times prescribed with chemotherapy (Lemberger & Rowe, 1975). Marijuana has also been shown to block seizures (Corcoran, McCaughran, & Wada, 1978), to dilate the bronchioles of asthmatics, and to decrease the severity of *glaucoma* (a disorder characterized by an increase in the pressure of the fluid inside the eye); but it is not normally prescribed for these purposes.

Because THC is fat-soluble, it was initially assumed that it influenced the brain by inserting itself directly into neural membranes. However, we now know that THC binds to receptors that are particularly dense in the basal ganglia, hippocampus, cerebellum, and neocortex (Howlett et al., 1990); presumably, it exerts most of its effects through this mechanism. The cloning of the gene for the THC receptor (Matsuda et al., 1990) triggered a search for an endogenous THC-like chemical that binds to it. Such a chemical has been isolated, and its structure has been characterized (Devane et al., 1992). The chemical has been named *anandamide* (which means "internal bliss").

Cocaine and Other Stimulants

Stimulants are drugs whose primary effect is to produce general increases in neural and behavioral activity. Although stimulants all have a similar profile of effects, they differ greatly in their potency. Coca-Cola is a mild commercial stimulant preparation consumed by many people around the world. Today, its stimulant action is attributable to *caffeine*, but when it was first introduced, "the pause that refreshes" packed a real wallop in the form of small amounts of cocaine. **Cocaine** and its derivatives are the most commonly abused stimulants, and thus they are the focus of discussion here.

Cocaine is prepared from the leaf of the coca bush, which is found primarily in Peru and Bolivia. For centuries, a crude extract called *coca paste* has been made

directly from the leaves and eaten. Today, it is more common to treat the coca paste and extract *cocaine hydrochloride,* the nefarious white powder that is simply referred to as *cocaine.* Cocaine is typically consumed by snorting or by injection. Cocaine hydrochloride may be converted to its base form by boiling it in a solution of baking soda until the water has evaporated. The impure residue of this process is **crack,** which is a potent, cheap, smokable form of cocaine. Crack has thus rapidly become the preferred form of the drug by many cocaine users. However, because crack is impure, variable, and consumed by smoking, it is difficult to study and most research on cocaine derivatives has thus focused on cocaine hydrochloride.

Cocaine hydrochloride is an effective local anesthetic, and it was once widely prescribed as such until it was supplanted by synthetic analogues such as *procaine* and *lidocaine.* It is not, however, cocaine's anesthetic actions that are of interest to users. People eat, smoke, snort, or inject cocaine or its derivatives in order to experience its psychological effects. Users report being swept by a wave of well-being; they feel self-confident, alert, energetic, friendly, outgoing, fidgety, and talkative; and they have less than their usual desire for food and sleep.

Like alcohol, cocaine hydrochloride is frequently consumed in *binges* (see Gawin, 1991). Cocaine addicts tend to go on so-called **cocaine sprees,** binges in which extremely high levels of intake are maintained for periods of a day or two. During a cocaine spree, users become increasingly tolerant to the euphoria-producing effects of cocaine. Accordingly, larger and larger doses are often administered to maintain the initial level of euphoria. The spree usually ends when the cocaine is gone or when it begins to have serious toxic effects.

Extremely high blood levels of cocaine are reached during cocaine sprees. The results commonly include sleeplessness, tremors, nausea, and psychotic behavior. The syndrome of psychotic behavior observed during cocaine sprees is called **cocaine psychosis.** It is similar to, and has often been mistakenly diagnosed as, *paranoid schizophrenia.*

During cocaine sprees, there is a risk of loss of consciousness and death from seizures (Earnest, 1993), respiratory arrest, or stroke (Kokkinos & Levine, 1993). Although tolerance develops to most effects of cocaine (e.g., to the euphoria), repeated cocaine exposure sensitizes subjects (i.e., makes them even more responsive) to its motor and convulsive effects (see Robinson & Berridge, 1993).

Fatalities from cocaine overdose are most likely following IV injection. Cocaine snorting can damage the nasal membranes, and cocaine smoking can damage the lungs; but both routes are safer than IV injection.

Although cocaine is extremely addictive, the withdrawal effects triggered by abrupt termination of a cocaine spree are mild (Miller, Summers, & Gold, 1993). Common cocaine withdrawal symptoms include a negative mood swing and insomnia.

Cocaine facilitates catecholaminergic transmission. It does this by blocking the reuptake of *catecholamines* (dopamine, norepinephrine, and epinephrine) into presynaptic neurons. In particular, its agnostic effects on dopaminergic transmission seem to play the major role in mediating its euphoria-inducing effects.

Cocaine and its various derivatives are not the only commonly abused stimulant drugs. **Amphetamine** (speed) and its relatives also constitute major health problems. Amphetamine has been in wide illicit use since the 1960s—it is usually been consumed orally in its potent *d-amphetamine* (dextroamphetamine) form. The effects of *d*-amphetamine are comparable to those of cocaine; for example, it produces a syndrome of psychosis called *amphetamine psychosis.*

In the past decade, *d*-amphetamine has been supplanted as the favored amphetaminelike drug by several new, more potent relatives. One is *methamphetamine* (see Cho, 1990), a much more potent drug than *d*-amphetamine. Methamphetamine (meth) is commonly used in its even more potent, smokable, crystalline form (ice or crystal). Another potent relative of amphetamine is *3,4-methylenedioxymethamphetamine* (MDMA or ecstasy), which is taken orally. Relatively little is known about the particular dangers of new amphetaminelike drugs; however, both methamphetamine and ecstasy have been shown to destroy serotonergic neurons in animal models. Because it is associated with the "rave" culture, ecstasy is commonly associated with the adverse consequences of overexercise on the dance floor: dehydration, exhaustion, muscle breakdown, overheating, and convulsions (Wills, 1997; Julien, 1996).

The Opiates: Heroin and Morphine

Opium—the sap that exudes from the seeds of the opium poppy—has several psychoactive ingredients. Most notable are **morphine** and **codeine,** its weaker relative. Morphine, codeine, and other drugs that have similar structures or effects are commonly referred to as the **opiates.** The opiates have a Jekyll-and-Hyde problem of major proportions. On their Dr. Jekyll side, opiates are unmatched as **analgesics** (painkillers), and they are also extremely effective in the treatment of cough and diarrhea. But unfortunately, the kindly Dr. Jekyll always brings with him the evil Mr. Hyde—the risk of addiction.

Archeological evidence suggests that the practice of eating opium became popular in the Middle East sometime before 4000 B.C., and then it spread throughout Africa, Europe, and Asia (see Berridge & Edwards, 1981; Latimer & Goldberg, 1981). Three historic events fanned the flame of opiate addiction. First, in 1644, the Emperor of China banned tobacco smoking, and many Chinese tobacco smokers tried smoking opium and liked it. Because smoking opium has a greater effect on the brain than does eating it, many more people became addicted to opium as the practice of opium smoking slowly spread to other countries. Second, morphine, the most potent constituent of opium, was isolated from opium in 1803, and in the 1830s it became available commercially. Third, the hypodermic needle was invented in 1856, and soon injured soldiers (e.g., those of the American Civil War) were introduced to morphine through a needle; during this era, morphine addiction was known as *soldiers' disease.*

Most people are surprised to learn that until the early 1900s, opium was legally available and consumed in great quantity in many parts of the world, including Europe and North America. Opium was available in cakes, candies, and wines, as well as in a variety of over-the-counter medicinal offerings. Opium potions such as *laudanum* (a very popular mixture of opium and alcohol), *Godfrey's Cordial,* and *Dalby's Carminative* were very popular. (The word *carminative* should win first prize for making a sow's ear at least sound like a silk purse: A carminative is a drug that expels gas from the digestive tract, thus reducing stomach cramps and flatulence. *Flatulence* is the obvious pick for second prize.) There were even over-the-counter opium potions just for baby. Potions such as *Mrs. Winslow's Soothing Syrup* and the aptly labeled *Street's Infant Quietness* were popular in many households. Although pure morphine could not be purchased without a prescription in the early 1900s, it was so frequently prescribed by physicians for so many different maladies that morphine addiction was common among those who could afford doctors.

The **Harrison Narcotics Act,** passed in 1914, made it illegal to sell or use opium, morphine, or cocaine in the United States. However, the act did not include the semisynthetic opiate **heroin.** Heroin had been synthesized in 1870 by the addition of two acetyl groups to the morphine molecule, which greatly increased its ability to penetrate the blood–brain barrier. In 1898, heroin was marketed by the Bayer Drug Company; it was freely available without prescription and was widely advertised as a super aspirin. Tests showed that it was a more potent analgesic than morphine and that it was less likely to induce nausea and vomiting. Moreover, the Bayer Drug Company, on the basis of flimsy evidence, claimed that heroin was not addictive; this is why it was not covered by the Harrison Narcotics Act.

The consequence of this omission was that opiate addicts in the United States, forbidden by law to use opium or morphine, turned to the readily available and much more potent heroin; and the flames of addiction were further fanned. In 1924, the U.S. Congress made it illegal for anybody to possess, sell, or use heroin. Unfortunately, the laws enacted to stamp out opiate addiction in the United States have been far from successful: An estimated 2 million Americans currently use heroin, and organized crime flourishes on the proceeds.

The effect of opiates most valued by opiate addicts is the *rush* that follows intravenous injection. The *heroin rush* is a wave of intense abdominal, orgasmic pleasure that evolves into a state of serene, drowsy euphoria. Many opiate users, drawn by these pleasurable effects, begin to use the drug more and more frequently. Then, once they reach a point where they keep themselves drugged much of the time, tolerance and physical dependence develop and contribute to the problem. Opiate tolerance encourages addicts to progress to higher doses, to more potent drugs (e.g., heroin), and to more direct routes of administration (e.g., IV injection); and physical dependence adds to the already high motivation to take the drug.

Although opiates are highly addictive, the direct health hazards of chronic exposure are surprisingly minor. The main risks are constipation, pupil constriction, menstrual irregularity, and reduced libido (sex drive). Many opiate addicts have taken large doses of pure heroin or morphine for years with no serious ill

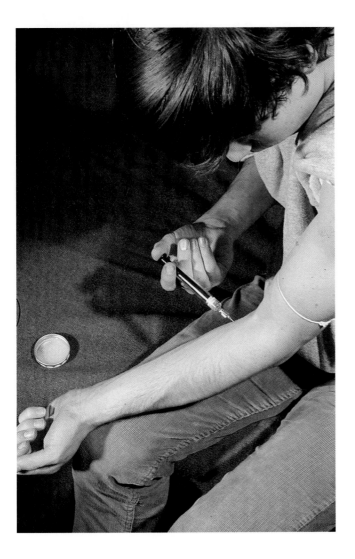

effects. In fact, opiate addiction is more prevalent among doctors, nurses, and dentists than among other professionals (e.g., Brewster, 1986):

> An individual tolerant to and dependent upon an opiate who is socially or financially capable of obtaining an adequate supply of good quality drug, sterile syringes and needles, and other paraphernalia may maintain his or her proper social and occupational functions, remain in fairly good health, and suffer little serious incapacitation as a result of the dependence. (Julien, 1981, p. 117)

> One such individual was Dr. William Steward Halsted, one of the founders of Johns Hopkins Medical School and one of the most brilliant surgeons of his day . . . known as "the father of modern surgery." And yet, during his career he was addicted to morphine, a fact that he was able to keep secret from all but his closest friends. In fact, the only time his habit caused him any trouble was when he was attempting to reduce his dosage. (McKim, 1986, p. 197)

The classic opiate withdrawal syndrome usually begins 6 to 12 hours after the last dose. The first withdrawal sign is typically an increase in restlessness; the addict begins to pace and fidget. Watering eyes, running nose, yawning, and sweating are also common during the early stages of opiate withdrawal. Then, the addict often falls into a fitful sleep, which typically lasts for several hours. After the sleep is over, the original symptoms may be joined in extreme cases by chills, shivering, profuse sweating, gooseflesh, nausea, vomiting, diarrhea, cramps, pains, dilated pupils, tremor, and muscle spasms. The gooseflesh skin and leg spasms of the opiate withdrawal syndrome are the basis for the expressions "going cold turkey" and "kicking the habit." The symptoms of opiate withdrawal are typically most severe in the second or third day after the last injection, and by the seventh day they have all but disappeared.

The symptoms of opiate withdrawal (see Koob, Maldonado, & Stinus, 1992) are not trivial, but their severity has been widely exaggerated. Opiate withdrawal is about as serious as a bad case of the flu—a far cry from the convulsions, delirium, and risk of death associated with alcohol withdrawal:

> Opiate withdrawal is probably one of the most misunderstood aspects of drug use. This is largely because of the image of withdrawal that has been portrayed in the movies and popular literature for many years. . . . Few addicts . . . take

Amphetamine. A stimulant drug whose effects are similar to those of cocaine.

Opium. The sap that exudes from the opium poppy.

Morphine. The major psychoactive ingredient in opium.

Codeine. A weak psychoactive ingredient of opium.

Opiates. Morphine, codeine, heroin, and other chemicals with similar structures or effects.

Analgesics. Drugs that reduce pain.

Harrison Narcotics Act. The act, passed in 1914, that made it illegal to sell or use opium, morphine, or cocaine in the United States.

Heroin. A powerful semisynthetic opiate.

enough drug to cause the . . . severe withdrawal symptoms that are shown in the movies. Even in its most severe form, however, opiate withdrawal is not as dangerous or terrifying as withdrawal from barbiturates or alcohol. (McKim, 1986, p. 199)

Most risks of opiate addiction are indirect—that is, not a consequence of the drug itself. Many are risks that arise out of the battle between the relentless addictive power of opiates and the attempts of governments to eradicate addiction by making drugs illegal. The opiate addicts who cannot give up their habit—treatment programs report success rates of only 10%—are caught in the middle. Because most opiate addicts must purchase their morphine and heroin from illicit dealers at greatly inflated prices, those who are not wealthy become trapped in a life of poverty and petty crime. They are poor, they are undernourished, they receive poor medical care, they are often driven to prostitution, and they run great risk of contracting AIDS and other infections from unsafe sex and unsterile needles. Moreover, they never know for sure what they are injecting: Some street drugs are poorly processed, and virtually all have been *cut* (stretched by the addition of some similar-appearing substance) to some unknown degree.

A case in point is death from heroin overdose, the most common cause of heroin-related death. Overdose deaths are a risk any time addictive drugs are routinely administered via the intravenous route, but it is clear that the very laws designed to prevent heroin addiction are complicit in heroin-overdose deaths. The laws force addicts to buy their drugs from unreliable sources, and, as a result, waves of overdose deaths occur when shipments of contaminated drugs hit the street. Paradoxically, similar waves of deaths occur when shipments of particularly pure heroin hit the street—because addicts select doses on the basis of their previous experience with heroin that has been heavily cut.

The opiates, like marijuana, seem to exert their effects by binding to particular receptors whose normal function is to bind to *endogenous* chemicals. The endogenous chemicals that bind to opiate receptors are called *endorphins*, and about 20 different kinds have been identified. There are three classes of opiate receptors; one of them, the *delta opioid receptor*, has been cloned and its structure characterized (Evans et al., 1992).

Comparison of the Hazards of Tobacco, Alcohol, Marijuana, Cocaine, and Heroin

One way of comparing the adverse effects of tobacco, alcohol, marijuana, cocaine, and heroin is to compare the prevalence of their use in society as a whole. In terms of this criterion, it is clear that tobacco and alcohol have a far greater negative impact than do marijuana, cocaine, and heroin (see Figure 13.7).

But what about the individual drug user? Who is taking greater health risks: the cigarette smoker, the alcohol drinker, the marijuana smoker, the cocaine user, or the heroin user? You now have the information to answer this question. First, in the Self Test (on page 360), list all of the demonstrated major health hazards of each of the five drugs; be sure to focus on direct hazards of the drug, not on indirect hazards created by its legal and social status. Then, on the basis of your five lists, rank the five drugs in terms of their overall health risks. Would you have ranked the drugs in the same way before you began this chapter?

The Drug Dilemmas: Striking the Right Balance

Drug abuse is currently a serious problem. In the United States alone, recreational drugs contribute to several hundred thousand deaths each year, and the public must bear the brunt of the crime and violence

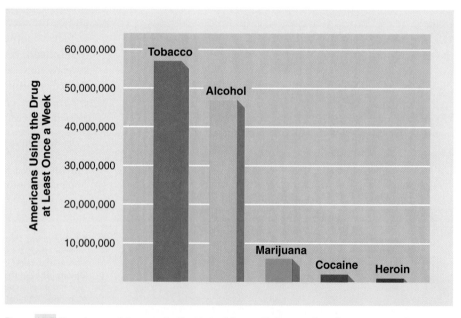

Figure 13.7 Prevalence of drug use in the United States. Figures are based on a survey of people 12 years of age and over who live in households.

(Adapted from Goldstein & Kalant, 1990.)

that is perpetrated by addicts who are forced to steal and prostitute themselves to fuel their expensive habits. Also, the public must bear the economic burdens of increased medical care, increased law enforcement, and decreased productivity—an estimated $86 billion annually (see Hunt, 1993).

Several eminent psychopharmacologists and political scientists have evaluated the U.S. approach to drug control in the light of current data; they all recommended sweeping changes (see Goldstein & Kalant, 1990; Jarvik, 1990; Nadelman, 1989). Each of these experts concluded that the current system of drug control is both poorly conceived and ineffective. The following quotes provide glimpses of their disenchantment with a system that treats addiction as a crime, rather than a disease, and that tries to combat it by reducing the supply and punishing the users:

> The investment of more than 70% of the federal [U.S.] drug control money into supply reduction seems misplaced. . . . Curtailing the supply of demanded drugs has been compared to squeezing a balloon: constrict it in one place and it expands somewhere else. . . . An example is the expansion of the California marijuana crop after the availability of Mexican marijuana was reduced. (Jarvik, p. 339)

> The greatest beneficiaries of the drug laws are . . . drug traffickers. More than half of all organized crime revenues are believed to derive from the illicit drug business. (Nadelman, p. 941)

> Drug treatment programs remain notoriously underfunded, turning away tens of thousands of addicts seeking help even as increasing billions of dollars are spent to arrest, prosecute, and imprison illegal drug . . . users. (Nadelman, p. 942)

The experts recommend solutions to the drug problem that are different than the ones preferred by the American public. The experts say (1) that there is no way of stopping the supply—every major drug bust merely increases the street prices of drugs and encourages more illicit suppliers to enter the market; (2) that it makes little sense to persecute and punish the sick and the weak; and (3) that it is hypocritical to take Draconian measures against some drugs while allowing others that are more dangerous to be openly advertised. In contrast to the views of the experts, recent surveys suggest that the U.S. public, frustrated with the drug problem and not understanding the issues, wants even more money to be spent on the approaches that are currently proving so ineffective.

Here are some of the specific recommendations that have been made by the experts:

1. The only way of reducing recreational drug use is by reducing the demand. Some of the billions that are currently being spent on arresting and supporting drug users in crowded jails would be better spent on education, research, and social programs.

2. More emphasis should be placed on caring for addicts than on persecuting them.

3. Unlike the current laws, the laws that govern drug use should be enforceable and should be tailored to the hazards of each drug.

4. Judges should be given greater discretion in sentencing. For example, the current 5-year minimum sentence for anybody caught sharing a small amount of heroin or cocaine with a friend is unduly harsh.

5. All cigarette and alcohol advertising should be curtailed.

6. The possession of small amounts of marijuana for personal use has been legalized in some parts of the country; the effects of this legalization should be carefully monitored. If it does not lead to a significant increase in use, other states should follow suit to allow the legal system to focus on more serious problems.

7. Experimental clinics should be established. In them, addicts, as a first step in their treatment, should be provided with small maintenance doses of their drug. The potential advantages of such programs are many: They would encourage addicts to enter treatment; they would bring addicts in contact with health care professionals who are experienced in dealing with the health problems of addicts (e.g., AIDS and malnutrition); they would allow some addicts who have not been able to shake their habits to live reasonably normal, productive lives; and they would reduce the amount of drug-related crime.

8. Finally, lessons should be learned from countries that have taken approaches to drug control that are more in tune with the preceding recommendations. For example, in 1976 Holland removed criminal penalties for possession and small-scale sales of marijuana, with no resulting increases in the use of marijuana or more dangerous drugs (see MacCoun & Reuter, 1997).

One does not normally find a discussion of legal and social policy in a biopsychology textbook. Please excuse my digression, but I believe that the drug problem is a serious one and that biopsychologists have important things to say about it. They have a responsibility to bring the relevant research literature to the attention of policy makers and the educated public. I hope that I have interested you enough to pursue the issue further; the articles of Goldstein and Kalant (1990), Jarvik (1990), Nadelman (1989), and MacCoun and Reuter (1997) are a good place to start.

List the major direct health hazards of the following five drugs. Omit indirect hazards that result from the drugs' legal or social status.

Tobacco	Alcohol	Marijuana	Cocaine	Heroin
1. _____	1. _____	1. _____	1. _____	1. _____
2. _____	2. _____	2. _____	2. _____	2. _____
3. _____	3. _____	3. _____	3. _____	3. _____
4. _____	4. _____	4. _____	4. _____	4. _____
5. _____	5. _____	5. _____	5. _____	5. _____
6. _____	6. _____	6. _____	6. _____	6. _____

On the basis of comparisons among your five lists, rank the five drugs in terms of the overall danger of their direct health hazards.

Most Hazardous 1. _____

2. _____

3. _____

4. _____

Least Hazardous 5. _____

13.4 Biopsychological Theories of Addiction

This section of the chapter introduces two diametrically different theories of addiction: Are addicts driven to take drugs by an internal need, or are they drawn to take drugs by their anticipated positive effects? I am sure you will recognize from preceding chapters that this is the same fundamental question that has been the focus of biopsychological research on the motivation to eat, drink, and sleep.

Physical-Dependence Theories of Addiction

Early attempts to explain the phenomenon of drug addiction attributed it to physical dependence. According to the **physical-dependence theory of addiction,** physical dependence traps addicts in a vicious circle of drug taking and withdrawal symptoms. The idea was that drug users whose intake has reached a level sufficient to induce physical dependence are driven by their withdrawal symptoms to self-administer the drug each time they attempt to curtail their intake.

Early drug addiction treatment programs were based on the physical-dependence theory of addiction. They attempted to break the vicious circle of drug taking by gradually withdrawing drugs from addicts in a hospital environment. (Gradual withdrawal produces less severe withdrawal symptoms than does sudden withdrawal.) Unfortunately, once discharged, almost all detoxified addicts return to their former drug-taking habits—**detoxified addicts** are addicts who have no drugs in their bodies and who are no longer experiencing withdrawal symptoms.

The failure of detoxification as a treatment for addiction is not surprising, for two reasons. First, some highly addictive drugs, such as cocaine and amphetamine, do not produce severe withdrawal distress (see Gawin, 1991). Second, the pattern of drug taking routinely displayed by many addicts involves an alternating cycle of binges and detoxification (Mello & Mendelson, 1972). There are a variety of reasons for this pattern of drug use. For example, some addicts adopt it because weekend binges are compatible with their work schedules, others adopt it because they do not have enough money to use drugs continuously, others have it forced on them because their binges often land them in jail, and others have it forced on them by their repeated unsuccessful efforts to shake their habit. However, whether detoxification is by choice or necessity, it does not stop addicts from renewing their drug-taking habits (see Leshner, 1997).

Modern physical-dependence theories of drug addiction attempt to account for the fact that addicts frequently relapse after lengthy drug-free periods by postulating that withdrawal symptoms can be conditioned (Koob et al., 1993). According to this theory, when addicts who have remained drug-free for a considerable period of time return to a situation in which they have previously experienced the drug, conditioned withdrawal effects opposite to the effects of the drug (conditioned compensatory responses) are elicited. These effects are presumed to result in a powerful craving for the drug to counteract them.

The theory that *relapse* is motivated primarily by an attempt to counteract conditioned withdrawal effects encounters two major problems (see Eikelboom & Stewart, 1982; Zelman, Tiffany, & Baker, 1985). One is that many of the effects elicited by environments that have previously been associated with drug administration are similar to those of the drug rather than being antagonistic to them (Stewart & Eikelboom, 1982). The second is that experimental animals and addicts often display a preference for drug-predictive cues, even when no drug is forthcoming (e.g., Bozarth & Wise,

1981; Mucha et al., 1982; White, Sklar, & Amit, 1977). For example, some detoxified heroin addicts called *needle freaks* derive pleasure from sticking an empty needle into themselves. It therefore seems unlikely that conditioned withdrawal effects could be the primary motivating factor in drug relapse. In accordance with this conclusion, Krank and Perkins (1993) found that conditioned morphine withdrawal effects in rats did not increase their morphine self-administration.

Positive-Incentive Theories of Addiction

The failure of physical-dependence theories to account for the major aspects of addiction has lent support to the theory that the primary reason most addicts take drugs is not to escape or avoid the unpleasant consequences of withdrawal or conditioned withdrawal, but rather to obtain the drugs' positive effects. This **positive-incentive theory of addiction** acknowledges that addicts may sometimes self-administer drugs to suppress withdrawal symptoms or to escape from other unpleasant aspects of their existence, but it holds that the primary factor in most cases of addiction is the craving for the positive-incentive (pleasure-producing) properties of the drugs (McAuliffe et al., 1986; Stewart, de Wit, & Eikelboom, 1984). Anecdotal support for this view comes from the statements of some addicts—for example:

> I'm just trying to get high as much as possible. I would have to spend $25 a day on heroin to avoid withdrawal, but I actually use about $50 worth. If I could get more money, I would spend it all on drugs. All I want is to get loaded. I just really like shooting dope. I don't have any use for sex; I'd rather shoot dope. I like to shoot dope better than anything else in the world. I have to steal something every day to get my dope.

One recent positive-incentive theory of addiction is based on the idea that the positive-incentive value of addictive drugs increases (i.e., is sensitized) with drug use. Robinson and Berridge (1993) have suggested that in addiction-prone individuals, the use of drugs sensitizes their positive-incentive value, thus rendering the user highly motivated to consume drugs and to seek drug-associated stimuli. A key point of Robinson and Berridge's *incentive-sensitization theory* deserves emphasis: They argue that it isn't the pleasure of drug taking per se that is the basis of addiction; it is the anticipated pleasure of drug taking (i.e., the drug's positive-incentive

---

Physical-dependence theory of addiction. The theory that the main factor that motivates drug addicts to take drugs is the prevention or termination of withdrawal symptoms.

Detoxified addicts. Addicts who have none of the drug to which they are addicted in their body

and who are no longer experiencing withdrawal symptoms.

Positive-incentive theory of addiction. The theory that the primary factor in most cases of addiction is a craving for the pleasure-producing effects of drugs.

value). Initially, a drug's positive-incentive value is closely tied to its pleasurable effects; but tolerance often develops to the pleasurable effects, whereas the addict's wanting for the drug is sensitized. Thus, in chronic addicts, the positive-incentive value of the drug is often out of proportion with the pleasure actually derived from it: Many addicts are miserable, their lives are in ruins, and the drug effects are not that great anymore; but they crave the drug more than ever (see Berridge & Robinson, 1995; Ness & Berridge, 1997).

13.5 Reward Circuits in the Brain

Rats (Olds & Milner, 1954), humans (Bishop, Elder, & Heath, 1963), and many other species will perform a response, such as pressing a lever, in order to administer brief bursts of electrical stimulation to specific sites in their own brains (see Figure 13.8). This phenomenon is known as **intracranial self-stimulation (ICSS).**

Olds and Milner, the discoverers of intracranial self-stimulation, argued that the specific brain sites that mediate self-stimulation are those that normally mediate the pleasurable effects of natural rewards (e.g., food, water, and sex). Accordingly, researchers have studied the self-stimulation of various brain sites in order to map the neural circuits that mediate the experience of pleasure. Because the pleasure-producing effects of drugs are now believed to play a major causal role in addiction, this section of the chapter focuses on these cerebral pleasure circuits.

Intracranial Self-Stimulation: Fundamental Characteristics

It was initially assumed that intracranial self-stimulation was a unitary phenomenon—that is, that its fundamental properties were the same regardless of the site of stimulation. Most early studies of intracranial self-stimulation involved septal or lateral hypothalamic stimulation because the rates of self-stimulation from these sites are spectacularly high: Rats typically press a lever thousands of times per hour for stimulation of these sites, stopping only after they become exhausted. However, the self-stimulation of many other brain structures has now been documented; Figure 13.9 illustrates the intracranial self-stimulation sites in the rat brain.

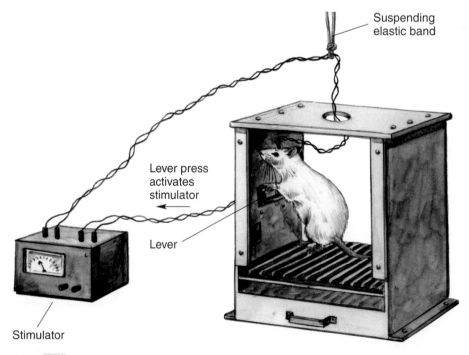

Figure 13.8 A rat pressing a lever for rewarding brain stimulation.

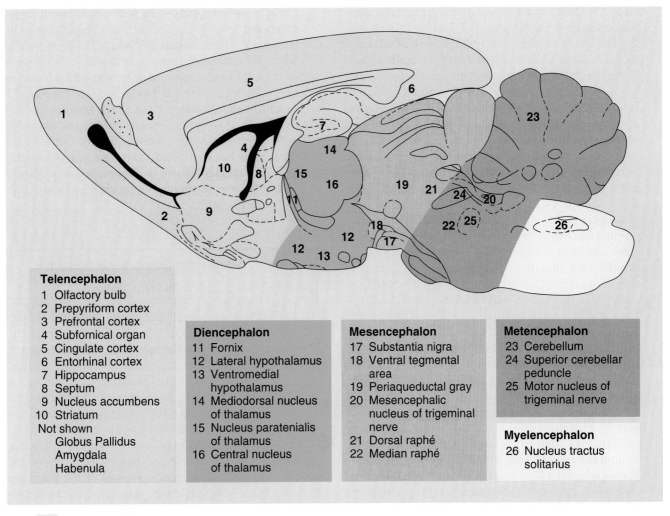

Telencephalon

1 Olfactory bulb
2 Prepyriform cortex
3 Prefrontal cortex
4 Subfornical organ
5 Cingulate cortex
6 Entorhinal cortex
7 Hippocampus
8 Septum
9 Nucleus accumbens
10 Striatum
Not shown
    Globus Pallidus
    Amygdala
    Habenula

Diencephalon

11 Fornix
12 Lateral hypothalamus
13 Ventromedial
    hypothalamus
14 Mediodorsal nucleus
    of thalamus
15 Nucleus paratenialis
    of thalamus
16 Central nucleus
    of thalamus

Mesencephalon

17 Substantia nigra
18 Ventral tegmental
    area
19 Periaqueductal gray
20 Mesencephalic
    nucleus of trigeminal
    nerve
21 Dorsal raphé
22 Median raphé

Metencephalon

23 Cerebellum
24 Superior cerebellar
    peduncle
25 Motor nucleus of
    trigeminal nerve

Myelencephalon

26 Nucleus tractus
    solitarius

Figure 13.9 The major intracranial self-stimulation sites in the rat brain.
(Adapted from Phillips & Fibiger, 1989.)

Early studies of intracranial self-stimulation suggested that lever pressing for brain stimulation was fundamentally different from lever pressing for natural reinforcers such as food or water. Two puzzling observations contributed to this view. First, despite their extremely high response rates, many rats stopped pressing the self-stimulation lever almost immediately when the current delivery mechanism was shut off. This finding was puzzling because high rates of operant responding are generally assumed to indicate that the reinforcer is particularly pleasurable, whereas rapid rates of extinction are usually assumed to indicate that it is not. Would you stop pressing a lever that had been delivering $100 bills the first few times that a press did not produce one? Second, experienced self-stimulators often did not recommence lever pressing when they were returned to the apparatus after being briefly removed from it. In such cases, the rats had to be **primed** to get them going again: The experimenter simply pressed the lever a couple of times, to deliver a few free stimula-

tions, and the hesitant rat immediately began to self-stimulate at a high rate once again.

These differences between lever pressing for rewarding lateral hypothalamic or septal stimulation and lever pressing for food or water seemed to discredit Olds and Milner's original theory that intracranial self-stimulation involves the activation of natural reward circuits in the brain. Accordingly, many of the investigators who studied self-stimulation in the 1950s and 1960s viewed it as some kind of artifact—albeit a particularly interesting one. However, since then, the pendulum of opinion has swung back to its original position: The current consensus seems to be that the

Intracranial self-stimulation (ICSS). The repeated performance of a response that delivers electrical stimulation to certain sites in the brain.

Primed. Induced to resume self-stimulation by a few "free" stimulations.

circuits mediating intracranial self-stimulation phenomena are reward circuits.

The return to the reward-circuit view of intracranial self-stimulation was based on four kinds of evidence. First, brain stimulation through electrodes that mediate self-stimulation often elicits natural motivated behaviors such as eating, drinking, maternal behavior, and copulation in the presence of the appropriate goal objects. Second, producing increases in natural motivation (for example, by food or water deprivation, by hormone injections, or by the presence of prey objects) often increases self-stimulation rates (e.g., Caggiula, 1970). Third, lever pressing for stimulation at some brain sites (other than the lateral hypothalamus and septum, on which the early studies focused) is often quite similar to lever pressing for natural rewards (i.e., acquisition is slow, response rates are low, extinction is slow, and priming is not necessary). And fourth, it became clear that subtle differences between the situations in which rewarding brain stimulation and natural rewards were usually studied contributes to the impression that their rewarding effects are qualitatively different. For example, comparisons between lever pressing for food and lever pressing for brain stimulation are usually confounded by the fact that subjects pressing for brain stimulation are nondeprived and by the fact that the lever press delivers the reward directly and immediately. In contrast, in studies of lever pressing for natural rewards, subjects are often deprived, and they press a lever for a food pellet or drop of water that they then must approach and consume to experience rewarding effects.

In a clever experiment, Panksepp and Trowill (1967) compared lever pressing for brain stimulation with lever pressing for a natural reinforcer in a situation in which the usual confounds were absent. In the absence of the confounds, some of the major differences between lever pressing for food and lever pressing for brain stimulation disappeared. When nondeprived rats lever pressed to inject a small quantity of chocolate milk directly into their mouths through an intraoral tube, they behaved remarkably like self-stimulating rats: They quickly learned to lever press, they pressed at high rates, they extinguished quickly, and some even had to be primed.

Mesotelencephalic Dopamine System and Intracranial Self-Stimulation

The mesotelencephalic dopamine system has been shown to play an important role in intracranial self-stimulation. The **mesotelencephalic dopamine system** is a system of dopaminergic neurons that projects from the mesencephalon (the midbrain) into various regions of the telencephalon. As Figure 13.10 indicates, the neurons that compose the mesotelencephalic dopamine system have their cell bodies in two midbrain nuclei—the **substantia nigra** and the **ventral tegmental area;** and their axons project to a variety of telencephalic sites, including specific regions of the prefrontal neocortex, the limbic cortex, the olfactory tubercle, the amygdala, the septum, the striatum, and in particular

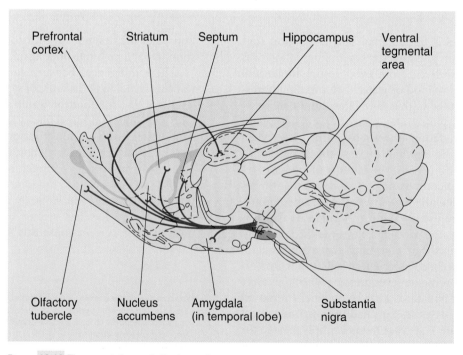

Figure 13.10 The mesotelencephalic dopamine system.

the **nucleus accumbens,** which is a widely studied nucleus of the ventral striatum.

It was originally believed that two entirely separate dopamine pathways project from the mesencephalon to the telencephalon: one from the substantia nigra to the striatum (the *nigrostriatal pathway*) and one from the ventral tegmental area to the cortex and limbic system (the *mesocorticolimbic pathway*). However, it is now clear that there is considerable intermingling of the neurons of these two pathways (Björklund & Lindvall, 1986; White, 1996). Still, it is the particular neurons that project from the ventral tegmental area to the nucleus accumbens that have been most frequently implicated in the effects of rewarding brain stimulation, natural rewards, and addictive drugs.

Several kinds of studies have supported the view that the mesotelencephalic dopamine system plays an important role in intracranial self-stimulation (see Chen, 1993). Prominent among these are (1) mapping studies, (2) microdialysis studies, (3) dopamine agonist and antagonist studies, and (4) lesion studies.

■ **MAPPING STUDIES** The first evidence of the involvement of the mesotelencephalic dopamine system in intracranial self-stimulation came from the discovery that many brain sites at which self-stimulation occurs are part of the mesotelencephalic dopamine system (see Routtenberg, 1978). For example, the mapping of self-stimulation sites in the mesencephalon revealed that most are located in the substantia nigra and ventral tegmental area (e.g., Routtenberg & Malsbury, 1969). Moreover, Corbett and Wise (1980) found that the mesencephalic self-stimulation sites at which the response rates were the highest and the current thresholds the lowest were those with the greatest concentrations of dopaminergic fibers.

Some self-stimulation sites do not contain large numbers of dopaminergic neurons. However, several nondopaminergic self-stimulation sites have been shown to project directly to the mesotelencephalic dopamine system (see Shizgal & Murray, 1989; Yeomans, Mathur, & Tampakeras, 1993).

■ **CEREBRAL DIALYSIS STUDIES** In *cerebral dialysis studies,* samples of extracellular fluid are continuously drawn from a particular area of the brain as the subject behaves, and the fluid is later subjected to chemical analysis. (It takes about 15 minutes to get a large enough sample for analysis.) Several investigators have used the cerebral dialysis technique to show that self-stimulation is often

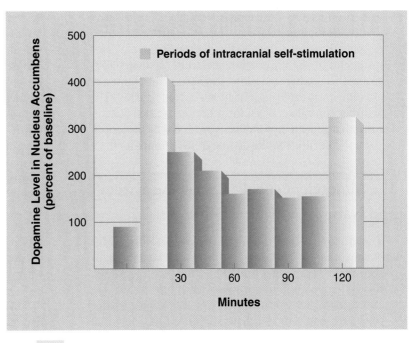

Figure 13.11 The increase in dopamine release from the nucleus accumbens during consecutive periods of intracranial self-stimulation.
(Adapted from Phillips et al., 1992.)

associated with an increase in dopamine release. For example, Phillips and colleagues (1992) and Fiorino et al. (1993) found an increase in dopamine release in the nucleus accumbens when rats engaged in ventral tegmental area self-stimulation (see Figure 13.11).

■ **DOPAMINE AGONIST AND ANTAGONIST STUDIES** Several studies have shown that dopamine agonists increase self-stimulation and dopamine antagonists decrease self-stimulation. For example, microinjections of the dopamine agonist *amphetamine* into the nucleus accumbens increase lateral hypothalamic self-stimulation rates (Colle & Wise, 1988), and microinjections of the dopamine antagonist *spiroperidol* into the nucleus accumbens decrease ventral tegmental area self-stimulation rates (Mogenson et al., 1979).

■ **LESION STUDIES** Lesions of the mesotelencephalic dopamine system disrupt self-stimulation. For example, in one experiment (Fibiger et al., 1987), selective unilateral lesions of the mesotelencephalic dopamine system

Mesotelencephalic dopamine system. The ascending projections of dopamine-releasing neurons from the substantia nigra and ventral tegmental area of the mesencephalon into various regions of the telencephalon.

Substantia nigra. The midbrain nucleus of the mesotelencephalic dopamine system that is a major source of

dopaminergic projections to the striatum.

Ventral tegmental area. The midbrain nucleus of the mesotelencephalic dopamine system that is a major source of dopaminergic projections to limbic and cortical structures.

Nucleus accumbens. A nucleus of the ventral striatum and a major terminal of the mesencephalic dopamine system.

were produced by unilateral injections of the selective toxin *6-hydroxydopamine (6-OHDA)* into the ventral tegmental area. Lesions to the ventral tegmental area ipsilateral to a stimulation electrode reduced self-stimulation, whereas lesions to the ventral tegmental area contralateral to a stimulation electrode did not. The fact that contralateral lesions produced no deficit indicated that general motor deficits produced by the lesions did not contribute to the decline in self-stimulation.

The Mesotelencephalic Dopamine System and Natural Motivated Behaviors

The discovery that the mesotelencephalic dopamine system plays an important role in intracranial self-stimulation stimulated interest in the possible role of this system in natural motivated behaviors (see Fibiger, 1993; Robbins & Everitt, 1996). The following are three of the experiments that have supported the view that the mesotelencephalic dopamine system is involved in natural motivated behaviors. In one experiment, Nomikos and colleagues (see Fibiger, 1993) confined rats for 20 minutes to one compartment of a two-compartment test box; then, the compartment door was opened so that the rats could enter the other compartment, which contained a palatable liquid diet. After several such daily training sessions, dopamine release in the nucleus accumbens was measured by *microdialysis* during the test session, and dopamine levels were found to become elevated once the rats gained access to the compartment with the liquid diet. In a second experiment, Pfaus and colleagues (1990) found that levels of extracellular dopamine measured in the nucleus accumbens of male rats by *electrochemistry* increased on the test day once a divider screen was raised to provide the subjects with access to a receptive female rat. In a third experiment, Schultz (1997) recorded the electrical activity of dopaminergic neurons of the ventral tegmental area and substantia nigra in monkeys. He found that dopaminergic neurons responded to rewards only when they were presented unpredictably—as in the early stages of a conditioning experiment. If the reward was expected—as in the late stages of a conditioning experiment—the reward itself did not increase the activity of dopaminergic neurons, but the conditional stimulus that predicted the reward did.

Studies of the correlation between dopaminergic activity and natural motivated behaviors have focused on the issue of whether dopamine release is correlated with consummatory behaviors or preparatory behaviors. **Consummatory behaviors** (pronounced "con SUHM a tor ee," not "con SUME a tor ee," because it is derived from the verb *consummate,* not the verb *consume*) are behaviors, such as copulation or eating, that consummate or complete a sequence of motivated behaviors. **Preparatory behaviors** (also referred to as *appetitive, instrumental,* or *anticipatory behaviors*) are behaviors, such as approaching a sex partner or searching for food, that enable an organism to subsequently perform a consummatory behavior.

Most of the recent evidence suggests that dopamine release increases during the preparation for reward, thus supporting the view that dopamine plays a specific role in incentive motivation (see Robbins & Everitt, 1996). There is, however, often a further increase in dopamine release during the consummatory phase (e.g., Fiorino, Coury, & Phillips, 1997).

13.6 Neural Mechanisms of Addiction

Evidence that the mesotelencephalic dopamine system mediates the rewarding effects of intracranial stimulation and natural motivated behaviors suggests that it may also mediate the rewarding effects of addictive drugs (see Chen, 1993; Wise, 1996). And so we return to our discussion of drug addiction.

Two behavioral paradigms have been used extensively in the study of the neural mechanisms of addiction (Stolerman, 1992): the drug self-administration paradigm (see Yokel, 1987) and the conditioned place-preference paradigm (see White & Hiroi, 1993). They are illustrated in Figure 13.12. In experiments involving the **drug self-administration paradigm,** laboratory rats or primates press a lever to inject drugs into themselves through implanted cannulas. They readily learn to self-administer intravenous injections of drugs to which humans become addicted. Furthermore, once they have learned to self-administer an addictive drug, their drug taking often mimics in major respects the drug taking of human addicts. Studies in which microinjections have been self-administered directly into particular brain structures have proved particularly enlightening.

In experiments involving the **conditioned place-preference paradigm,** rats repeatedly receive a drug in one compartment (the *drug compartment*) of a two-

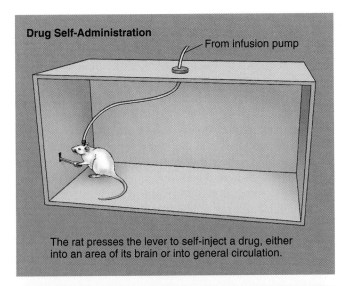

Drug Self-Administration

From infusion pump

The rat presses the lever to self-inject a drug, either into an area of its brain or into general circulation.

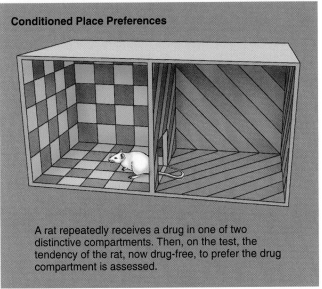

Conditioned Place Preferences

A rat repeatedly receives a drug in one of two distinctive compartments. Then, on the test, the tendency of the rat, now drug-free, to prefer the drug compartment is assessed.

Figure 13.12 Two behavioral paradigms that are used extensively in the study of the neural mechanisms of addiction: The drug self-administration paradigm and the conditioned place-preference paradigm.

compartment box. Then, during the test phase, the rat is placed in the box drug-free, and the proportion of time it spends in the drug compartment, as opposed to the equal-sized but distinctive *control compartment,* is measured. Rats usually prefer the drug compartment over the control compartment when the drug compartment has been associated with the effects of drugs to which humans become addicted. The main advantage of the conditioned place-preference paradigm is that the subjects are tested drug-free, which means that the measure of the incentive value of a drug is not confounded by other effects the drug might have on behavior (see Carr, Fibiger, & Phillips, 1989; Van der Kooy, 1987).

Evidence of the Involvement of the Mesotelencephalic Dopamine System in Drug Addiction

Several lines of evidence support the view that the mesotelencephalic dopamine system—particularly the mesocorticolimbic pathway from the ventral tegmental area to the nucleus accumbens—mediates the motivating effects of drugs (see Wise, 1996). Most of this evidence comes from studies of morphine, cocaine, and amphetamine; however, the mesotelencephalic dopamine system has also been implicated in the rewarding effects of other drugs (e.g., alcohol, nicotine, and THC). The following are five of the major lines of evidence.

First, laboratory animals self-administer microinjections of addictive drugs directly into various structures of the mesotelencephalic dopamine system but not usually into other brain regions. For example, laboratory animals have been shown to self-administer microinjections of morphine into the ventral tegmental area, the nucleus accumbens, and the septum (see Chen, 1993).

Second, microinjections of drugs directly into various structures of the mesotelencephalic dopamine system lead to the development of conditioned place preferences. For example, in one series of studies (see White & Hiroi, 1993), microinjections of amphetamine directly into the nucleus accumbens produced a preference for the compartment in which the drug was injected, whereas microinjections into other mesotelencephalic structures (the striatum, amygdala, or olfactory tubercle) did not.

Third, addictive drugs, but not nonaddictive drugs, have been shown to increase the rewarding effects of electrical stimulation to the mesotelencephalic dopamine system (see Wise et al., 1992). For example, in one study, opiates with abuse potential reduced the current threshold for self-stimulation in mesotelencephalic structures, whereas opiates with no abuse potential did not (Kornetsky & Esposito, 1979).

Fourth, disruption of mesotelencephalic function, either by lesions or by dopamine antagonists, has been shown to reduce the rewarding effects of addictive drugs injected *systemically* (into general circulation). For example, lesions to either the ventral tegmental

Consummatory behaviors. Behaviors that complete (consummate) a sequence of motivated behavior.
Preparatory behaviors. Behaviors that prepare or enable an organism to perform a consummatory response.
Drug self-administration paradigm. A test of the addictive potential of drugs in which animals can inject drugs into themselves by pressing a lever.
Conditioned place-preference paradigm. A test that assesses an animal's preference for environments in which it has previously experienced drug effects.

area (Roberts & Koob, 1982) or the nucleus accumbens (Roberts et al., 1980)—but not to the other terminal structures of the mesotelencephalic dopamine system (Roberts & Zito, 1987)—have been shown to disrupt intravenous self-administration of amphetamine. Also, both dopamine antagonists (Phillips, Spyraki, & Fibiger, 1982) and lesions to the nucleus accumbens (Kelsey, Carlezon, & Falls, 1989) have been shown to prevent the development of conditioned place preferences associated with systemic morphine injections.

Fifth, electrochemical and cerebral dialysis recordings from the nucleus accumbens, the striatum, and other terminals of the mesotelencephalic dopamine system have shown that the systemic self-administration of most addictive drugs is associated with increased dopamine release (see Wise, 1993). For example, the levels of extracellular dopamine have been found to be elevated in the nucleus accumbens during cocaine, heroin, and THC self-administration (Pettit & Justice, 1991; Tanda, Pontieri, & Chiara, 1997).

The study of the mesotelencephalic dopamine system has greatly increased our understanding of the neural basis of addiction, but what has it done for addicts? Not much, at least not yet. The challenge is to develop selective dopamine antagonists that can substantially reduce the positive-incentive value of drugs in addicts without reducing the positive-incentive value of natural motivated behaviors.

CONCLUSION

In the first four sections of this chapter, you were introduced to the basic principles of drug action (13.1), to the role of learning in drug tolerance and drug withdrawal effects (13.2), to five commonly abused drugs (13.3), and to two fundamentally different ways of thinking about drug addiction (13.4). Then, you were introduced to the reward circuit of the brain—the mesotelencephalic dopamine system and its role in intracranial self-stimulation and natural motivated behaviors (13.5). Finally, you were presented with evidence that the mesotelencephalic dopamine system mediates the rewarding effects of addictive drugs (13.6).

To illustrate in a more personal way some of the things you have learned about addiction, this chapter concludes with a series of quotations that describe the interactions of one drug addict with two drugs of abuse: cocaine and tobacco. The addict was Sigmund Freud, a man of very special significance to psychology. Freud's battles with these two drugs have sobering implications. The following excerpts are from a report written in 1972 by Edward Brecher:

> The chief ingredient in coca leaves, the alkaloid cocaine, was isolated in pure form in 1844. Little use was made of it in Europe, however, until 1883, when a German army physician . . . issued it to Bavarian soldiers during their autumn maneuvers. . . .
>
> Among those who read [the] . . . account with fascination was a poverty-stricken twenty-eight-year-old Viennese neurologist, Dr. Sigmund Freud. . . . "I have been reading about cocaine, the essential ingredient of coca leaves, which some Indian tribes chew to enable them to resist privations and hardships," Freud wrote his fiancée, Martha Bernays, on April 21, 1884. "I am procuring some myself and will try it. . . ."
>
> In addition to taking cocaine himself, Freud offered some to his friend and associate, Dr. Ernst von Fleischl-Marxow, who was suffering from an exceedingly painful disease of the nervous system, and who was addicted to morphine. . . .
>
> Freud even sent some of this precious cocaine to Martha. . . . "[H]e pressed it on his friends and colleagues, both for themselves and their patients; he gave it to his sis-

> ters. In short, looked at from the vantage point of present knowledge, he was rapidly becoming a public menace." (pp. 272–273)

Freud's famous essay "Song of Praise," to cocaine, was published in July 1884. In this article, Freud wrote in such glowing terms about his own personal experiences with cocaine that he created a wave of interest in the drug. But within a year, there was a critical reaction to Freud's premature advocacy:

> In July 1885, a German authority on morphine addiction named Erlenmeyer launched the first of a series of attacks on cocaine as an addicting drug. In January 1886 Freud's friend Obersteiner, who had first favored cocaine, reported that it

produced severe mental disturbances [later called cocaine psychosis]. . . . Other attacks soon followed; and Freud was subjected to "grave reproaches." Freud continued to praise cocaine as late as July 1887. . . . But soon thereafter he discontinued all use of it both personally and professionally. Despite the fact that he had been taking cocaine periodically over a three-year span, he appears to have had no difficulty in stopping. (p. 274)

Some 9 years later, in 1894, when Freud was 38, his physician and close friend ordered him to stop smoking because it was causing a heart arrhythmia. Freud was a heavy smoker; he smoked approximately 20 cigars per day:

Freud did stop for a time . . . but his subsequent depression and other withdrawal symptoms proved unbearable. . . .

Within seven weeks, Freud was smoking again.

On a later occasion, Freud stopped smoking for fourteen very long months. . . .

More than fifteen years later, at the age of fifty-five, Freud was still smoking twenty cigars a day—and still struggling against his addiction. [In a letter written at the time, he commented on the sudden intolerance of his heart for tobacco.]

Four years later he wrote . . . that his passion for smoking hindered his analytic studies. Yet he kept on smoking.

In February 1923, at the age of sixty-seven, Freud noted sores on his right palate and jaw that failed to heal. They were cancers. An operation was performed—the first of thirty-three operations for cancer of the jaw and oral cavity which he endured during the sixteen remaining years of his life. "I am still out of work and cannot swallow," he wrote shortly after his first operation. "Smoking is accused as the etiology [cause] of this tissue rebellion." Yet he continued to smoke.

In addition to his series of cancers . . . Freud now suffered attacks of "tobacco angina" [heart pains] whenever he smoked. . . . Yet he continued to smoke.

At seventy-three, Freud was ordered to retire to a sanitarium for his heart condition. He made an immediate recovery [because he stopped smoking] . . . for twenty-three days. Then he started smoking one cigar a day. Then two. Then three or four. . . .

In 1936, at the age of seventy-nine . . . Freud had more heart trouble. . . . His jaw had by then been entirely removed and an artificial jaw substituted; he was in almost constant pain; often he could not speak and sometimes he could not chew or swallow. Yet at the age of eighty-one, Freud was still smoking what . . . , his close friend at this period, calls, "an endless series of cigars."

Freud died of cancer in 1939. (pp. 214–215)

FOOD FOR THOUGHT

1. There are many misconceptions about drug abuse. Describe three. What do you think are the reasons for these misconceptions?

2. A man who had been a heroin user for many years was found dead of an overdose at a holiday resort. He appeared to have been in good health, and no foul play was suspected. What factors might have led to his death?

3. If you had an opportunity to redraft the current legislation related to drug abuse in the light of what you have learned in this chapter, what changes would you make? Explain.

4. Speculate. How might recent advances in the study of the mesotelencephalic dopamine system eventually lead to effective treatments?

KEY TERMS

Addicts (p. 346)
Amotivational syndrome (p. 354)
Amphetamine (p. 356)
Analgesics (p. 356)
Before-and-after design (p. 347)
Buerger's disease (p. 351)
Cannabis sativa (p. 353)
Cirrhosis (p. 352)
Cocaine (p. 355)
Cocaine psychosis (p. 355)
Cocaine sprees (p. 355)
Codeine (p. 356)
Conditioned compensatory responses (p. 349)

Conditioned drug tolerance (p. 348)
Conditioned place-preference paradigm (p. 366)
Conditioned withdrawal effects (p. 349)
Consummatory behaviors (p. 366)
Contingent drug tolerance (p. 347)
Crack (p. 355)
Cross tolerance (p. 345)
Delirium tremens (DTs) (p. 352)
Depressant (p. 352)
Detoxified addicts (p. 361)
Diuretic (p. 352)

Drug metabolism (p. 345)
Drug self-administration paradigm (p. 366)
Drug tolerance (p. 345)
Fetal alcohol syndrome (FAS) (p. 353)
Free radicals (p. 352)
Functional tolerance (p. 345)
Harrison Narcotics Act (p. 356)
Hashish (p. 353)
Heroin (p. 356)
Hypothermic (p. 348)
Intracranial self-stimulation (ICSS) (p. 362)
Intramuscularly (IM) (p. 343)
Intravenously (IV) (p. 343)

Korsakoff's syndrome (p. 352)
Mesotelencephalic dopamine system (p. 364)
Metabolic tolerance (p. 345)
Morphine (p. 356)
Narcotic (p. 354)
Nicotine (p. 351)
Nucleus accumbens (p. 365)
Opiates (p. 356)
Opium (p. 356)
Physical-dependence theory of addiction (p. 360)
Physically dependent (p. 345)
Positive-incentive theory of addiction (p. 361)
Preparatory behaviors (p. 366)
Primed (p. 363)

ADDITIONAL READING

A number of paperbacks provide interesting introductions to the topic of drug abuse. The following two are my current favorites:

Grilly, D. M. (1998). *Drugs and Human Behavior* (3rd ed.). Boston: Allyn & Bacon.

Wills, S. (1997). *Drugs of abuse.* London: Pharmaceutical Press.

The following four articles, all published in *Science,* one of the world's most respected scientific journals, are essential reading for anybody interested in the development of more effective approaches to dealing with the drug problem:

Goldstein, A., & Kalant, H. (1990). Drug policy: Striking the right balance. *Science, 249,* 1513–1519.

Jarvik, M. E. (1990). The drug dilemma: Manipulating the demand. *Science, 250,* 387–392.

MacCoun, R., & Reuter, P. (1997). Interpreting Dutch Cannabis Policy: Reasoning by analogy in the legalization debate. *Science, 278,* 47–52.

Nadelmann, E. A. (1989). Drug prohibition in the United States: Costs, consequences, and alternatives. *Science, 245,* 939–947.

For reviews of recent research on the biopsychology of addiction, I recommend the following journal issues, which are dedicated entirely to the topic:

Trends in Pharmacological Science, 13 (May 1992).

Seminars in the Neurosciences, 5 (October 1993).

Seminars in Neuroscience, 9 (Issue 3/4, 1997).

14

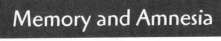

Memory and Amnesia

Memory is the brain's ability to store the learned effects of its experience. It is one of the brain's most fundamental abilities; it is difficult to imagine human existence without it. Without memory, each moment would be like waking from a lifelong sleep: Each person would be a stranger, each act a new challenge, and each word incomprehensible.

Even simple invertebrate nervous systems display elementary forms of memory; however, in this chapter, the emphasis will be on the memory systems of the human brain. In particular, this chapter will focus on what has been learned about the mechanisms of human memory from the assessment of brain-damage–produced amnesia in human neuropsychological patients and in animal models of human amnesic disorders.

14.1 Amnesic Effects of Bilateral Medial Temporal Lobectomy

Ironically, the person who has contributed more than any other to our understanding of the neuropsychology of memory is not a neuropsychologist. In fact, although he has collaborated on dozens of studies of memory, he has no formal research training and not a single degree to his name. He is H. M., a man who in 1953, at the age of 27, had the medial portions of his temporal lobes removed for the treatment of a severe case of epilepsy. Just as the Rosetta Stone has provided archaeologists with important clues to the meaning of Egyptian hieroglyphics, H. M.'s memory deficits have been instrumental in the achievement of our current understanding of the neural bases of memory.

Early Theories of Memory Storage

In order to put the scientific contributions of H. M.'s case in perspective, let's first consider two ideas about the neural bases of memory that were prominent in the 1950s, when the first reports of H. M.'s case began to appear. First, the field of memory research was reeling from Karl Lashley's fruitless search for the location of the engram—the hypothetical change in the brain responsible for storing a memory.

Lashley, the most influential physiological psychologist of his era, had spent 35 years (1915 to 1950) training rats, cats, and monkeys to perform complex learning tasks and then cutting, destroying, or removing specific parts of their brains in a vain attempt to erase the memory of their training. For example, in one series of studies, rats received lesions of various sizes to different parts of the cerebral cortex after they had learned a maze task. Ten days later, their retention of the task was assessed. Lashley found that only large cortical lesions disrupted retention and that the particular site of the lesion was of little consequence: Cortical lesions of equal size produced similar effects regardless of their location.

On the basis of his findings, Lashley concluded that memories for complex tasks are stored diffusely throughout the neocortex (the **principle of mass action**) and that all parts of the neocortex play an equal role in their storage (the **principle of equipotentiality**). Although Lashley conceded that certain areas of the neocortex may play a more important role than other areas in the storage of certain memories—for example, the visual cortex may play a more important role in the storage of memories of visual stimuli—he argued that memories were stored diffusely and equally throughout these functional areas. Thus one effect of Lashley's work was to discourage theories of memory that assigned specific **mnemonic** (pertaining to memory) abilities to specific parts of the brain.

The second idea about the physiological bases of memory that was prominent in the 1950s was the theory that there are two different memory storage mechanisms: a *short-term system* and a *long-term system*. According to this theory, which is still widely accepted, each memory is held in short-term storage while the physiological changes necessary for long-term storage are taking place. For example, in order to remember a new phone number, we hold it in short-term storage by actively thinking about it until its presence in short-term storage produces the physiological changes that underlie its long-term storage. The hypothetical transfer of a memory from short-term to long-term storage is called **consolidation.**

According to the most influential theory of consolidation (Hebb, 1949), the memory for a particular event is stored in the short-term mode by *reverberating neural activity* (neural activity that goes around and around in closed-loop circuits), which eventually produces long-term structural changes in the synapses that facilitate the

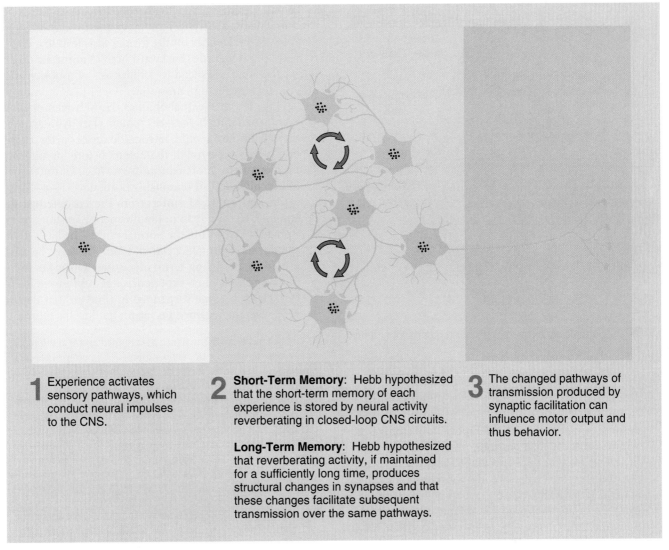

1 Experience activates sensory pathways, which conduct neural impulses to the CNS.

2 **Short-Term Memory**: Hebb hypothesized that the short-term memory of each experience is stored by neural activity reverberating in closed-loop CNS circuits.

Long-Term Memory: Hebb hypothesized that reverberating activity, if maintained for a sufficiently long time, produces structural changes in synapses and that these changes facilitate subsequent transmission over the same pathways.

3 The changed pathways of transmission produced by synaptic facilitation can influence motor output and thus behavior.

Figure 14.1 Hebb's (1949) theory of consolidation: How short-term memories were thought to be stored by reverberating neural activity that eventually becomes consolidated into long-term structural synaptic changes.

later occurrence of the same pattern of activity. These structural synaptic changes are the putative mechanism of long-term memory storage (see Figure 14.1).

The major prediction of Hebb's theory of consolidation is that those experiences that are not held in short-term reverberatory storage for a sufficient period of time by conscious consideration will not become integrated into the store of long-term structural memories. The classic example of this prediction is the loss of recall that is experienced by people when they are distracted just after they have looked up a new phone number.

Bilateral Medial Temporal Lobectomy

During the 11 years preceding his surgery, H. M. suffered an average of one generalized convulsion each week and many partial convulsions each day, despite massive doses of anticonvulsant medication. Electroencephalography suggested that H. M.'s convulsions arose from foci in the medial portions of both his left and right temporal lobes. Because the removal of one medial temporal lobe had proved to be an effective treatment for patients with a unilateral temporal lobe focus, the decision was made to

Memory. The brain's ability to store the learned effects of its experiences.
Engram. The hypothetical change in the brain responsible for the storage of a memory.
Principle of mass action. Lashley's idea that memories for complex tasks are stored diffusely throughout the neocortex.

Principle of equipotentiality. Lashley's idea that all parts of the neocortex play an equal role in the storage of memories for complex tasks.
Mnemonic. Pertaining to memory.
Consolidation. The hypothetical process by which a memory is transferred from short-term storage to long-term storage.

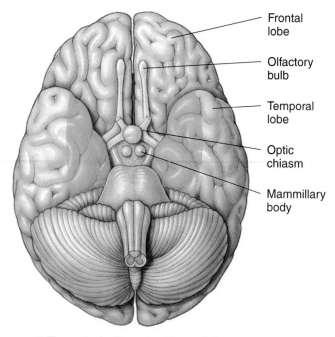

Figure 14.2 *Medial temporal lobectomy. The portions of the medial temporal lobes that were removed from H. M.'s brain are illustrated in a view of the inferior surface of the brain.*

Frontal lobe

Olfactory bulb

Temporal lobe

Optic chiasm

Mammillary body

■ Tissue typically excised in medial-temporal lobectomy

perform a **bilateral medial temporal lobectomy**—the removal of the medial portions of both temporal lobes, including most of the **hippocampus, amygdala,** and adjacent cortex (see Figure 14.2). (A **lobectomy** is an operation in which a lobe, or a major part of one, is removed from the brain; a **lobotomy** is an operation in which a lobe, or a major part of one, is separated from the rest of the brain by a large cut but is not removed.) The location and extent of H. M.'s bilateral medial temporal lobectomy was recently confirmed by magnetic resonance imaging (Corkin et al., 1997).

In several respects, H. M.'s bilateral medial temporal lobectomy was an unqualified success. His generalized convulsions were all but eliminated, and the incidence of his minor seizures was reduced to one or two per day, even though the level of his anticonvulsant medication was substantially reduced. Furthermore, H. M. entered surgery a reasonably well-adjusted individual with normal perceptual and motor abilities and superior intelligence, and he left it in the same condition. Indeed, H. M.'s IQ increased from 104 to 118 as a result of his surgery, presumably because of the decline in the incidence of his seizures. Be that as it may, H. M. was the last patient to receive a bilateral medial temporal lobectomy—because of its devastating amnesic effects.

H. M.'s Postsurgery Memory Deficits

In assessing the amnesic effects of brain surgery, it is usual to administer tests of the patient's ability to re-

member things learned before the surgery and tests of the patient's ability to remember things learned after the surgery. Deficits on the former tests lead to a diagnosis of **retrograde** (backward-acting) **amnesia;** those on the latter tests lead to a diagnosis of **anterograde** (i.e., forward-acting) **amnesia.**

Like his intellectual abilities, H. M.'s memory for events predating his surgery remains largely intact. Although he has a mild retrograde amnesia for those events that occurred in the 2 years before his surgery, his memory for more remote events (e.g., for the events of his childhood) is reasonably normal.

In contrast, H. M. suffers from a severe anterograde amnesia. His ability to hold information in short-term storage is well within the normal range—he has a **digit span** of six digits (Wickelgren, 1968); however, he cannot form new long-term memories. Once he stops thinking about a new experience, it is lost forever. In effect, H. M. became suspended in time on that day in 1953 when he regained his health but lost his future:

As far as we can tell, this man has retained little if anything of events subsequent to the operation. . . . Ten months before I examined him, his family had moved from their old house to a new one a few blocks away on the same street. He still had not learned the new address (though remembering the old one perfectly), nor could he be trusted to find his way home alone. He did not know where objects in constant use were kept, and his mother stated that he would read the same magazines over and over again without finding their contents familiar. . . . [F]orgetting occurred the instant the patient's focus of attention shifted. (Milner, 1965, pp. 104–105)

During three of the nights at the Clinical Research Center, the patient rang for the night nurse, asking her, with many apolo-

Bilateral medial temporal lobectomy. The removal of the medial portions of both temporal lobes, including the hippocampus, the amygdala, and the adjacent cortex.

Hippocampus. A structure of the medial temporal lobes that plays a role in memory for spatial location.

Amygdala. A structure of the medial temporal lobe that plays a role in the memory for the emotional significance of experiences.

Lobectomy. An operation in which a lobe, or a major part of one, is removed from the brain.

Lobotomy. An operation in which a lobe, or a major part of one, is separated from the rest of the brain by a large cut but is not removed.

Retrograde amnesia. Loss of memory for information learned before the amnesia-inducing brain injury.

Anterograde amnesia. Loss of memory for events occurring af-

ter the amnesia-inducing brain injury.

Digit span. The maximum number of random digits that a subject can successfully repeat 50% of the time—the standard measure of verbal short-term memory.

Digit span + 1 test. A measure of verbal memory in which each time the subject correctly repeats a sequence of digits, the next test item is the same sequence with an additional digit added to the end of it.

Block-tapping memory span test. A nonverbal equivalent of the digit span test.

Global amnesia. Amnesia for information in all sensory modalities.

Matching-to-sample test. A memory test in which a sample stimulus is momentarily presented, followed by a delay, at which point the subject must select the sample stimulus from a group of test stimuli.

gies, if she would tell him where he was and how he came to be there. He clearly realized that he was in a hospital but seemed unable to reconstruct any of the events of the previous day. On another occasion he remarked "Every day is alone in itself, whatever enjoyment I've had, and whatever sorrow I've had." Our own impression is that . . . events fade for him long before the day is over. He often volunteers stereotyped descriptions of his own state, by saying that it is "like waking from a dream." His experience seems to be that of a person who is just becoming aware of his surroundings without fully comprehending the situation, because he does not remember what went before.

He still fails to recognize people who are close neighbours or family friends but who got to know him only after the operation. When questioned, he tries to use accent as a clue to a person's place of origin and weather as a clue to the time of year. Although he gives his date of birth unhesitatingly and accurately, he always underestimates his own age and can only make wild guesses as to the date. (Milner, Corkin, & Teuber, 1968, pp. 216–217)

H. M. has lived in a nursing home for many years. He spends much of each day doing crossword puzzles; his progress on a crossword puzzle is never lost because it is written down.

Formal Assessment of H. M.'s Anterograde Amnesia

This subsection describes H. M.'s performance on several objective tests of memory.

■ **DIGIT SPAN + 1 TEST** H. M.'s inability to form long-term memories is illustrated by his performance on the **digit span + 1 test.** H. M. was asked to repeat 5 digits that were read to him at 1-second intervals. He repeated the sequence correctly. On the next trial, the same 5 digits were presented in the same sequence with 1 new digit added to the end. This same 6-digit sequence was presented a few times until he got it right, and then another

digit was added to the end of it, and so on. After 25 trials, H. M. had not managed to repeat the 8-digit sequence. Normal subjects can repeat about 15 digits after 25 digit span + 1 trials (Drachman & Arbit, 1966).

■ **BLOCK-TAPPING MEMORY-SPAN TEST** Milner (1971) demonstrated that H. M.'s amnesia was not restricted to verbal material by assessing his performance on the + 1 version of the **block-tapping memory span test.** An array of 9 blocks was spread out on a board in front of H. M., and he was asked to watch the neuropsychologist touch a sequence of them and then to repeat the same sequence of touches. H. M. had a *block-tapping span* of 5 blocks, which is in the normal range; but he could not learn to correctly touch a sequence of 6 blocks, even when the same sequence was repeated 12 times. H. M. has **global amnesia**—amnesia for information presented in all sensory modalities.

■ **MATCHING-TO-SAMPLE TESTS** H. M.'s reliance on active rehearsal to remember new experiences was illustrated by a comparison of his performance on verbal and nonverbal matching-to-sample tests. On each trial of a **matching-to-sample test,** a sample item is presented. Then, after a delay, an array of test items is presented. From this array, the subject must select the one item that matches (is the same as) the sample. Sidman, Stoddard, and Mohr (1968) tested H. M. with verbal and nonverbal forms of this test (see Figure 14.3). When the stimuli were sequences of three consonants, H. M. had

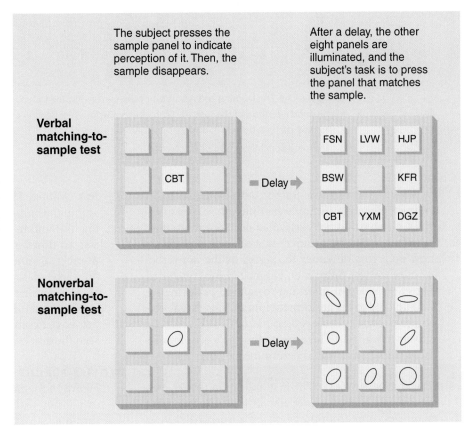

Figure 14.3 The verbal and nonverbal matching-to-sample tests given to H. M. by Sidman, Stoddard, and Mohr (1968). Although H. M. performed the verbal form of the test without error up to the 40-second retention interval, he could not perform the nonverbal form at intervals of greater than 5 seconds, presumably because of the difficulty of actively rehearsing the nonverbal stimuli.

The subject presses the sample panel to indicate perception of it. Then, the sample disappears.

After a delay, the other eight panels are illuminated, and the subject's task is to press the panel that matches the sample.

Verbal matching-to-sample test

CBT → ■ Delay ➡

FSN | LVW | HJP
BSW | | KFR
CBT | YXM | DGZ

Nonverbal matching-to-sample test

→ ■ Delay ➡

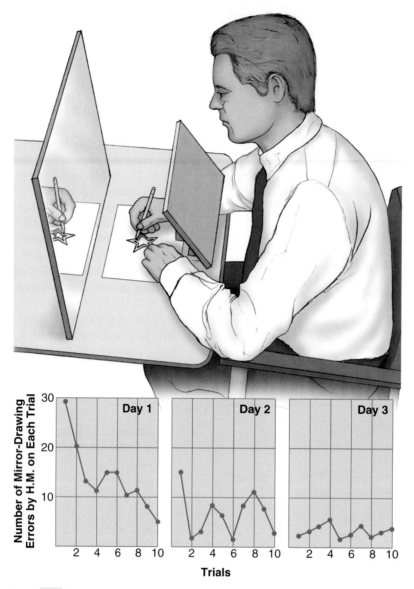

Figure 14.4 The learning and retention of the mirror-drawing task by H. M. Despite his good retention of the task, H. M. had no conscious recollection of having performed the task before.

(Adapted from Milner, 1965.)

no difficulty at even the longest, 40-second, delay. In contrast, when the stimuli were different shapes of ellipses, H. M. could not perform at delays of more than 5 seconds. A control group of schoolchildren made almost no errors on either the verbal or the nonverbal forms of the test. Sidman and his colleagues concluded that H. M.'s verbal matching-to-sample performance was superior to his performance on the nonverbal version of the test because letters, but not ellipses, can be actively rehearsed. (There are no English words for different ellipses that would permit their rehearsal.)

■ MIRROR-DRAWING TEST The first indication that H. M.'s anterograde amnesia does not involve all long-term memories came from the results of a **mirror-drawing test** (Milner, 1965). H. M.'s task was to draw a line within the boundaries of a star-shaped target by watching his hand in a mirror. H. M. was asked to trace the star 10 times on each of 3 consecutive days, and the number of times that he went outside the boundaries on each trial was recorded. As Figure 14.4 shows, H. M.'s performance improved over the 3 days, which indicates retention of the task. However, despite his improved performance, H. M. could not recall ever having seen the task before.

■ ROTARY-PURSUIT TEST In the **rotary-pursuit test** (see Figure 14.5), the subject tries to keep the tip of a stylus in contact with a target that rotates on a revolving turntable. Corkin (1968) found that H. M.'s perfor-

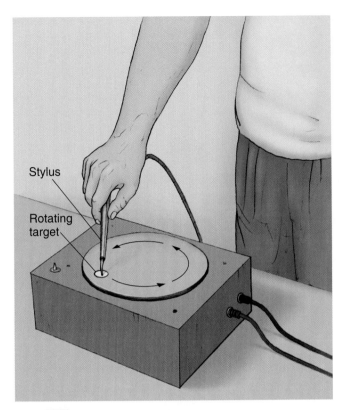

Stylus

Rotating target

Figure 14.5 The rotary-pursuit task. The subject tries to keep the stylus in contact with the rotating target, and time-on-target is automatically recorded. H. M. learned and retained this task although he had no conscious recollection of the learning trials.

mance of the rotary-pursuit task improved significantly over 9 daily practice sessions, despite the fact that H. M. claimed each day that he had never seen the pursuit rotor before. His improved performance was retained over a 7-day retention interval.

■ **INCOMPLETE-PICTURES TEST** The discovery that H. M. is capable of forming long-term memories for reverse mirror drawing and rotary pursuit suggested that sensorimotor tasks were the one exception to his inability to form long-term memories. However, this view was challenged by the demonstration that H. M. could also form new long-term memories for the **incomplete-pictures test** (Gollin, 1960)—a nonsensorimotor test of memory that employs five sets of fragmented drawings. Each set contains drawings of the same 20 objects, but they differ in their degree of sketchiness; set 1 contains the most fragmented drawings, and set 5 contains the complete drawings. The subject is asked to identify the 20 objects from the sketchiest set (set 1); then, those objects that go unrecognized are presented in their set 2 versions, and so on until all 20 items have been identified. Figure 14.6 on page 378 illustrates the performance of H. M. on this test and his improved performance 1 hour later (Milner, Corkin, & Teuber, 1968).

Despite his improved performance, H. M. could not recall previously performing the task.

■ **LANGUAGE-COMPREHENSION TEST** Early tests of H. M.'s language abilities suggested that they were unaffected by his surgery. However, H. M. was subsequently found to have difficulty identifying ambiguous sentences and in explaining them once they had been pointed out to him (McKay, Stewart, & Burke, 1998). This suggests that language comprehension and memory may have some cognitive elements in common.

■ **PAVLOVIAN CONDITIONING** H. M. learned a trace eyeblink Pavlovian conditioning task, albeit at a retarded rate (Woodruff-Pak, 1993). *Trace conditioning* is conditioning in which there is an interval (in this case, 0.5 seconds) between the termination of the conditional stimulus (in this case, a tone) and the onset of the unconditional stimulus (in this case, a puff of air to the eye). Two years later, H. M. retained the conditioned response almost perfectly although he had no conscious recollection of the training.

Scientific Contributions of H. M.'s Case

H. M.'s case is a story of personal tragedy, but its contributions to the study of the neural basis of memory have been immense. Following are five of them:

1. By showing that the medial temporal lobes play a particularly important role in memory, H. M.'s case challenged the view that memory functions are diffusely and equivalently distributed throughout the brain. H. M.'s case thus renewed efforts to relate particular brain structures to particular mnemonic processes.

2. By implicating the hippocampus in memory, H. M.'s case spawned a massive research effort aimed at clarifying the mnemonic functions of the hippocampus and other medial temporal lobe structures.

3. The discovery that bilateral medial temporal lobectomy abolished H. M.'s ability to form certain kinds of long-term memories without disrupting his performance on tests of short-term memory supported the theory that there are different modes of storage for short-term and long-term memory.

Mirror-drawing test. A test in which the subject traces a star while watching her or his hand in a mirror.
Rotary-pursuit test. A test in which the subject tries to keep the end of a stylus in contact with a target rotating on a turntable.
Incomplete-pictures test. A test of memory involving the improved ability to identify fragmented figures that have been previously observed.

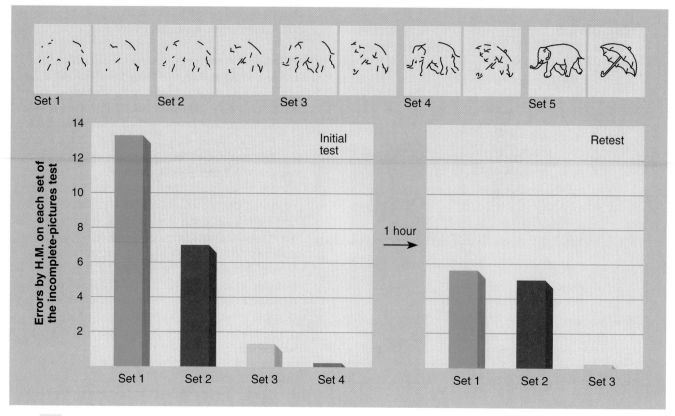

Figure 14.6 Two items from the incomplete-pictures test. H. M.'s memory for the 20 items of the test was indicated by his ability to recognize the more fragmented versions of them when he was retested. Nevertheless, he had no conscious awareness of having previously seen the items.

4. The pattern of H. M.'s memory deficits suggested that the medial temporal lobes play a role in memory consolidation. H. M.'s capacity to store short-term memories has remained intact, as has his capacity to store most of his long-term memories that were formed before his operation. His specific problem appears to be the transfer of short-term explicit memories to long-term storage.

5. H. M.'s case study was the first to reveal that an amnesic patient might claim no recollection of a previous experience, while demonstrating memory for it by improved performance. Conscious memories that can be expressed by declaration are called **explicit** (declarative) **memories,** whereas memories that are expressed by improved test performance without conscious awareness are called **implicit** (procedural) **memories** (see Graf & Schacter, 1987; Schacter, Chiu, & Ochsner, 1993).

Medial Temporal Lobe Amnesia

Neuropsychological patients with a profile of mnemonic deficits similar to those of H. M., with preserved intellectual functioning, and with evidence of medial temporal lobe damage are said to suffer from **medial temporal lobe amnesia.** Because their brain damage is typically a consequence of tumors, strokes, or other disease processes, it is typically not restricted to the medial temporal lobes. Still, the study of these patients has provided some indication about the effects of medial temporal lobe damage, which complements what is being learned from the study of H. M. The following are three fruitful lines of research on medial temporal lobe amnesics.

■ **PAVLOVIAN CONDITIONING IN MEDIAL TEMPORAL LOBE AMNESICS** One interesting series of studies of medial temporal lobe amnesics examined their reaction to Pavlovian conditioning. The pattern of findings was initially puzzling: The medial temporal lobe amnesics responded as well as normal control subjects to *delay conditioning* (Clarke & Squire, 1998) but had serious difficulties learning with *trace conditioning* procedures (McGlinchey-Berroth et al., 1997). This was puzzling because delay and trace conditioning are not very different: In delay conditioning, the unconditional stimulus comes on while the conditional stimulus is still on and both go off together; whereas in trace conditioning, there is a brief delay between the offset of the conditional stimulus and the onset of the unconditional stimulus.

A solution to this puzzle was suggested by an experiment on healthy volunteers. Clark and Squire (1998) found that delay conditioning proceeds automatically (i.e., requires implicit memory), whereas trace conditioning requires conscious involvement (i.e., requires explicit memory), of which medial temporal lobe amnesics are incapable. Healthy subjects who were not aware that the conditional stimulus predicted the unconditional stimulus in trace conditioning did not condition, whereas delay conditioning did not require conscious awareness.

■ SEMANTIC AND EPISODIC MEMORY IN MEDIAL TEMPORAL LOBE AMNESICS H. M.'s radical medial-temporal lobectomy has left him with minor retrograde and severe anterograde problems with explicit (i.e., declarative) memory. Research on medial temporal lobe amnesics has shown that one particular type of explicit memories is selectively disrupted by medial temporal lobe damage. The semantic memories of medial temporal lobe amnesics are often quite normal, whereas episodic memories are largely absent (see Eichenbaum, 1997). **Semantic memories** are explicit memories for general facts or information, whereas **episodic memories** are explicit memories for the particular events or experiences of one's life.

The special susceptibility of medial temporal lobe amnesics to episodic, as opposed to semantic, memory deficits was demonstrated in a particularly well-documented study by Vargha-Khadem and colleagues (1997). They managed to identify three individuals who had experienced bilateral medial temporal lobe damage early in life; then they assessed the memory problems experienced by these amnesics as they developed. Remarkably, despite the fact that they remembered few of the experiences that they had during their daily lives (episodic memory), they progressed through mainstream schools and acquired reasonable levels of language ability and factual knowledge (semantic memory).

■ WHY TWO MEMORY SYSTEMS: IMPLICIT AND EXPLICIT? The symptoms of medial temporal lobe amnesia raise an important question: Why do we have two parallel memory systems, one conscious (explicit) and one unconscious (implicit)? Presumably, the implicit system was the first to evolve, so the question is, "What advantage was there in having a second, conscious system?" Two recent experiments, one in amnesic patients (Reber, Knowlton, & Squire, 1996) and one in amnesic monkeys with medial temporal lobe lesions (Buckley & Gaffan, 1998), suggest that the answer is "flexibility." In both experiments, the amnesic subjects learned an implicit learning task as well as control subjects; however, if they were asked to use their implicit knowledge in a

different way or in a different context, they failed miserably. Presumably, the evolution of explicit memory systems provided for the flexible use of information.

Because many human amnesics—not just medial temporal lobe amnesics—display deficits in explicit memory but not in implicit memory, tests of implicit memory have played an important role in the study of human amnesia. Tests of implicit memory are called **repetition priming tests.** The incomplete-pictures test is an example, but repetition priming tests that involve memory for words are more common. First, the subjects are asked to peruse a list of words; they are not asked to learn or remember anything. Later they are shown a series of word fragments (e.g., _ O B S _ E R) of words from the original list, and they are simply asked to complete them. Control subjects who have seen the original words perform well. Surprisingly, amnesic subjects often perform equally well, even though they have no explicit memory of seeing the original list.

R. B.: Effects of Selective Hippocampal Damage

One particular case study of medial temporal lobe amnesia, the case study of R. B. (Zola-Morgan, Squire, & Amaral, 1986), has had a major impact on theories of memory. R. B.'s case seemed to confirm Scoville and Milner's (1957) initial impression that the amnesic effects of bilateral medial temporal lobectomy are largely a consequence of the hippocampal damage.

At the age of 52, R. B.'s brain was damaged during cardiac bypass surgery. An equipment malfunction interrupted the flow of blood to R. B.'s brain, and the resulting **ischemic brain damage**—brain damage produced by ischemia (an interruption of the blood supply)—left R. B. amnesic.

Explicit memories. Conscious memories that can be expressed by declaration; declarative memories.

Implicit memories. Memories that are expressed by improved performance without conscious recall or recognition; procedural memories.

Medial temporal lobe amnesia. Amnesia associated with bilateral damage to the medial temporal lobes; its major feature is anterograde amnesia for explicit memories in combination with preserved intellectual functioning.

Semantic memories. Explicit memories of general facts and knowledge.

Episodic memories. Explicit memories of the particular events and experiences of one's life.

Repetition priming tests. Tests of implicit memory; in one example, a list of words is presented, then fragments of the original words are presented and the subject is asked to complete the fragments with any appropriate word that comes to mind.

Ischemic brain damage. Brain damage caused by ischemia—by an interruption of the blood supply to the affected area.

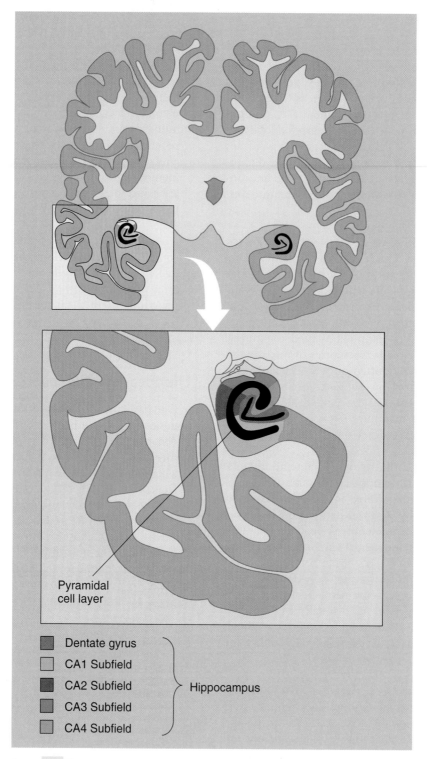

Figure 14.7 The major components of the hippocampus: CA1, CA2, CA3, and CA4 subfields and the dentate gyrus. R. B.'s brain damage appeared to be restricted largely to the pyramidal cell layer of the CA1 subfield.

Although R. B.'s amnesia was not as severe as H. M.'s, it was comparable in many aspects. R. B. died in 1983 of a heart attack, and a detailed postmortem examination of his brain was carried out with the permission of his family. Obvious brain damage was restricted largely to the **pyramidal cell layer** of just one part of the hippocampus—the **CA1 subfield** (see Figure 14.7). R. B.'s case suggested that hippocampal damage by itself can produce amnesia; however, this conclusion has been seriously challenged—as you will learn later in this chapter.

14.2 Amnesia of Korsakoff's Syndrome

As you have learned in previous chapters, **Korsakoff's syndrome** is a disorder of memory that is common in people who consume large amounts of alcohol. In its advanced stages, it is characterized by a variety of sensory and motor problems, extreme confusion, personality changes, and a risk of death from liver, gastrointestinal, or heart disorders. Postmortem examination typically reveals lesions to the *medial diencephalon* (the medial thalamus and the medial hypothalamus) and diffuse damage to several other brain structures, most notably the neocortex and the cerebellum.

The amnesia of Korsakoff's syndrome is similar to medial temporal lobe amnesia in major respects. In particular, Korsakoff patients experience an anterograde amnesia for explicit memories, which is largely restricted to deficits in episodic explicit memories during its early stages of development. However, unlike medial temporal lobe amnesia, Korsakoff amnesia is also associated with a severe retrograde amnesia that in advanced cases typically extends back into the events of their childhood.

The gradual, insidious onset and progressive development of Korsakoff's syndrome complicates the study of retrograde amnesia. It is never entirely clear to what extent Korsakoff amnesia for recent events reflects the retrograde disruption of existing memories or the gradually increasing anterograde blockage of the formation of new ones.

Medial Diencephalic Damage and Korsakoff Amnesia

Because the brain damage associated with Korsakoff's syndrome is diffuse, it has not been easy to identify the portion of it that is specifically responsible for the amnesia. The first hypothesis, which was based on several small postmortem studies, was that damage to the **mammillary bodies** of the hypothalamus was responsible for the memory deficits of Korsakoff patients; however, subsequent studies revealed cases of Korsakoff's amnesia with no mamillary body damage. But in all of these exceptional cases, however, there was damage to another pair of medial diencephalic nuclei: the **mediodorsal nuclei** of the thalamus. The occurrence of amnesia in stroke patients with small ischemic lesions to the mediodorsal nuclei provides additional evidence of their important mnemonic function (e.g., Graff-Radford et

al., 1985; Winocur et al., 1984). Be that as it may, it is unlikely that the memory deficits of Korsakoff patients are entirely attributable to the damage of any single diencephalic structure (see Butters & Stuss, 1989).

Medial Diencephalic Amnesia: The Case of N. A.

After a year of junior college, N. A. joined the U.S. Air Force; he served as a radar technician until his accident in December of 1960. On that fateful day, N. A.

> was assembling a model airplane in his barracks room. His roommate had removed a miniature fencing foil from the wall and was making thrusts behind N. A.'s chair. N. A. turned suddenly and was stabbed through the right nostril. The foil penetrated the cribriform plate [the thin bone around the base of the frontal lobes], taking an upward course to the left into the forebrain. (Squire, 1987, p. 177)

> The examiners . . . noted that at first he seemed to be unable to recall any significant personal, national or international events for the two years preceding the accident, but this extensive retrograde amnesia appeared to shrink. . . . Two-and-a-half years after the accident, the retrograde amnesia was said to involve a span of perhaps two weeks immediately preceding the injury, but the exact extent of this retrograde loss was (and remains) impossible to determine. . . .

> During . . . convalescence (for the first six to eight months after the accident), the patient's recall of day-to-day events was described as extremely poor, but "occasionally some items sprang forth uncontrollably; he suddenly recalled something he seemed to have no business recalling." His physicians thus gained the impression that his memory was patchy; he appeared to have difficulty in calling up at will many things that at other times emerged spontaneously. . . .

> Since his injury, he has been unable to return to any gainful employment, although his memory has continued to improve, albeit slowly. (Teuber, Milner, & Vaughan, 1968, pp. 268–269)

Pyramidal cell layer. The major layer of cell bodies in the hippocampus.

CA1 subfield. The region of the hippocampus that is commonly damaged by cerebral ischemia.

Korsakoff's syndrome. A memory disorder that is often associated with chronic alcohol consumption.

Mammillary bodies. A pair of hypothalamic nuclei, damage to which was originally thought to be critical for many of the memory deficits associated with Korsakoff's syndrome.

Mediodorsal nuclei. A pair of medial thalamic nuclei, damage to which is thought to be responsible for many of the memory deficits associated with Korsakoff's syndrome.

A CAT scan of N. A.'s brain was taken in the late 1970s (Squire & Moore, 1979). The scan revealed a lesion that seemed to be restricted to the left mediodorsal nucleus of the thalamus—this seemed to confirm that mediodorsal nucleus damage causes Korsakoff's amnesia. However, a subsequent magnetic resonance imaging study (Squire et al., 1989) revealed extensive medial diencephalic damage, including damage to the mammillary bodies. Accordingly, the case of N. A. is important because it illustrates the type of amnesia that can result from damage restricted to the medial diencephalon (i.e., *medial diencephalic amnesia*), rather than to any one of its particular nuclei.

14.3 Memory Deficits Associated with Prefrontal Cortex Damage

The **prefrontal cortex** has traditionally been assumed to be the seat of our most complex intellectual functions. Nevertheless, neuropsychological patients with damage restricted to the prefrontal cortex often do not display deficits on conventional tests of memory (see Petrides, 1996). They do, however, have two kinds of memory problems that involve temporal order.

The first temporal-order memory problem experienced by patients with prefrontal-lobe damage is a difficulty in remembering the sequence of events. This problem was clearly demonstrated in a classic study by Corsi and Milner (see Milner, 1971). Patients with prefrontal pathology were shown a series of stimulus cards, each with a different image. Occasionally, a card with two images would appear, and the subject would be asked which of the two images had appeared previously—or, if both had appeared previously, which had appeared more recently. Unlike medial temporal lobe or medial-diencephalic amnesics, the patients with prefrontal damage readily identified images that they had seen before; however, they had great difficulty in judging which of two familiar images had appeared more recently.

The second temporal-order memory problem experienced by patients with prefrontal-lobe damage is a difficulty in performing **self-ordered tasks**—these are tasks in which subjects must remember which of a series of responses they have performed and which remain to be done. In one self-ordered task, patients are shown a series of cards each with the same group of images but in a different arrangement. The subject's task is to touch one item on each card, always an item that has not been touched before, until all items have been touched. Patients with prefrontal damage have difficulty performing this task (see Petrides, 1996).

In contrast to H. M. and N. A., many Korsakoff patients display deficits in memory for temporal order (Squire, 1982). Presumably, this is because they usually have diffuse prefrontal cortex damage in addition to their diencephalic damage.

The prefrontal cortex is a large heterogeneous structure. It is composed of numerous anatomically distinct areas, which have different connections and, presumably, different functions. The particular mnemonic functions of individual prefrontal areas has yet to be elucidated (see Petrides, 1994).

14.4 Amnesia of Alzheimer's Disease

Alzheimer's disease is the most common cause of *dementia* (general intellectual deterioration); close to 5% of all people over 65 suffer from it. It is progressive and terminal.

Autopsy reveals three kinds of pathological changes in the brains of Alzheimer patients: extensive neural degeneration, **neurofibrillary tangles** (threadlike tangles in the neural cytoplasm), and **amyloid plaques** (spherical clumps of scar tissue composed of degenerating neurons interspersed with an abnormal protein called *amyloid*). Although they are distributed diffusely throughout the brain, these pathological changes are particularly prevalent in the temporal, frontal, and parietal cortex; in the structures of the medial temporal lobe; and in the structures of the basal forebrain.

The first sign of Alzheimer's disease is usually a mild deterioration of memory. Then, the symptoms grow progressively more severe and diverse until the patient is incapable of even simple activities (e.g., eating, speaking, recognizing a spouse, or even controlling the bladder). Efforts to understand the neural basis of Alzheimer's amnesia have focused on the testing of Alzheimer patients who have yet to reach the advanced stages of the disorder.

The memory deficits associated with predementia Alzheimer's disease are more general than those associated with medial temporal lobe damage, medial diencephalic damage, and Korsakoff's syndrome (see Butters & Delis, 1995). In addition to major anterograde and retrograde deficits in tests of explicit memory, predementia Alzheimer patients often display deficits in short-term memory and in some types of implicit memory: Implicit memory for verbal and perceptual material is often deficient, whereas implicit memory for sensorimotor learning is not (see Gabrieli et al., 1993; Postle, Corkin, & Growdon, 1996).

Early studies of the biochemistry of Alzheimer's disease focused on the large reduction in cholinergic activity that occurs in the brains of Alzheimer's patients: There is less acetylcholine, less *choline acetyltransferase* (the enzyme that stimulates the synthesis of acetylcholine), and less *acetylcholinesterase* (the enzyme that breaks down acetylcholine in synapses). This reduction of cholinergic activity results from the degeneration of neurons of the **basal forebrain,** which are the brain's major source of acetylcholine. The three main cholinergic structures of the basal forebrain are the *nucleus basalis of Meynert,* the *diagonal band of Broca,* and the *medial septal nucleus.* The nucleus basalis of Meynert projects widely to the frontal, temporal, and parietal cortexes, whereas the diagonal band of Broca and the medial septal nucleus project to the structures of the medial temporal lobe.

The discovery that acetylcholine depletion is a symptom of Alzheimer's disease led to the hypothesis that acetylcholine depletion is the specific cause of Alzheimer's amnesia (see Everitt & Robbins, 1997). There is some support for the idea that acetylcholine plays a role in memory: For example, amnesia commonly occurs in neuropsychological patients with damage restricted to the basal forebrain (Morris et al., 1992). However, several observations question whether acetylcholine is the single major factor in the amnesia of Alzheimer's disease (see Fibiger, 1991; Zola-Morgan & Squire, 1993). For example, levels of other cerebral neurotransmitters (e.g., norepinephrine and serotonin) have also been found to be reduced in Alzheimer's patients (see Coyle, 1987); Alzheimer's patients have been found to have medial temporal lobe damage, which could account for many of their memory problems (see Hyman, Van Hoesen, & Damasio, 1990); cholinergic agonists have been unable to forestall the inexorable progression of Alzheimer's amnesia; and basal forebrain damage produces deficits in attention, which could easily be mistaken for memory deficits in some tests of memory (see Robbins et al., 1989).

The cholinergic hypothesis of Alzheimer's amnesia has spawned numerous attempts to show that acetylcholine agonists can function as **nootropics**—memory-improving drugs. However, despite some promising results in laboratory animals (e.g., Meck, Smith, & Williams, 1989), claims of drug-induced memory enhancement in healthy humans are best viewed with skepticism at the present time. On the other hand, the ability of muscarinic cholinergic antagonists (e.g., scopolamine) to impair long-term object-recognition memory is well established (e.g., Aigner, Walker, & Mishkin, 1991).

14.5 Amnesia after Concussion

Blows to the head that do not penetrate the skull but are severe enough to produce *concussion* (a temporary disturbance of consciousness produced by a nonpenetrating head injury) are the most common causes of amnesia (see Levin, 1989). Amnesia following a nonpenetrating blow to the head is called **posttraumatic amnesia (PTA).**

The *coma* (pathological state of unconsciousness) following a severe blow to the head usually lasts a few seconds or minutes, but in severe cases it can last weeks. Then, once the patient regains consciousness, there is a period of confusion. Victims of concussion are typically not tested by a neuropsychologist until after the period

Prefrontal cortex. The area of the frontal cortex anterior to the motor cortex, damage to which disrupts memory for temporal order and release from proactive interference.

Self-ordered tasks. Tasks in which subjects must remember which of a series of responses they have already performed and which remain to be done.

Neurofibrillary tangles. Abnormal threadlike tangles in the neural cytoplasm of patients with Alzheimer's disease.

Amyloid plaques. Scars composed of degenerating neural fibers and amyloid protein that are found in the brains of patients with Alzheimer's disease.

Basal forebrain. The cholinergic area at the base of the forebrain that is damaged in Alzheimer's disease and includes the nucleus basalis of Meynert, the diagonal band of Broca, and the medial septal nucleus.

Nootropics. Hypothetical memory-improving drugs.

Posttraumatic amnesia (PTA). Amnesia produced by a nonpenetrating head injury (e.g., by a blow to the head that does not penetrate the skull).

of confusion—if they are tested at all. Testing usually reveals that the patient has a permanent retrograde amnesia for the events that led up to the blow and a permanent anterograde amnesia for many of the events that occurred during the subsequent period of confusion.

The anterograde memory deficits that follow a nonpenetrating head injury are often quite puzzling to the friends and relatives who have talked to the patient during the period of confusion—for example, during a hospital visit. The patient may seem reasonably lucid at the time, because short-term memory is normal, but later may have no recollection whatsoever of the conversation.

Figure 14.8 summarizes the effects of a closed-head injury on memory. Note that the duration of the period of confusion and anterograde amnesia is typically longer than that of the coma, which is typically longer than the period of retrograde amnesia. More severe blows to the head tend to produce longer comas, longer periods of confusion, and longer periods of amnesia (Levin, Papanicolaou, & Eisenberg, 1984). Not illustrated in Figure 14.8 are **islands of memory**—memories that sometimes survive for isolated events that occurred during periods that have otherwise been wiped out.

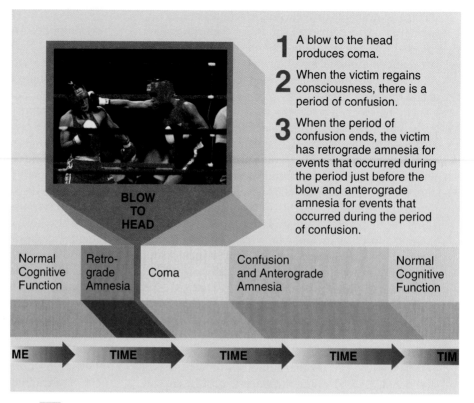

1 A blow to the head produces coma.

2 When the victim regains consciousness, there is a period of confusion.

3 When the period of confusion ends, the victim has retrograde amnesia for events that occurred during the period just before the blow and anterograde amnesia for events that occurred during the period of confusion.

BLOW TO HEAD

Normal Cognitive Function | Retrograde Amnesia | Coma | Confusion and Anterograde Amnesia | Normal Cognitive Function

ME TIME | TIME | TIME | TIM

Figure 14.8 The retrograde amnesia and anterograde amnesia that are associated with a concussion-producing blow to the head.

Electroconvulsive Shock and Gradients of Retrograde Amnesia

Electroconvulsive shock (ECS) is an intense, brief, seizure-inducing current that is administered to the brain through large electrodes attached to the scalp. It is used in the treatment of severe depression, and one of its side effects is posttraumatic amnesia.

ECS seemed to provide a method of studying memory consolidation. The rationale was that by disrupting neural activity, ECS would erase from storage only those memories that had not yet been converted to structural synaptic changes; the length of the period of retrograde amnesia produced by an ECS would thus provide an estimate of the amount of time needed for memory consolidation.

In one such study, thirsty rats were placed for 10 minutes on each of 5 consecutive days in a test box that contained a small niche. By the 5th of these habituation sessions, most rats explored the niche only 1 or 2 times per session. On the 6th day, a water spout was placed in the niche, and each rat was allowed to drink for 15 seconds after it discovered the spout. This was the learning trial. Then, 10 seconds, 1 minute, 10 minutes, 1 hour, or 3 hours later, each experimental rat received a single ECS. Some control rats received no learning trial, whereas others received the learning trial but no ECS. The next day, the retention of all subjects was assessed on the basis of how many times each explored the niche when the water spout was not present. The control rats that experienced the learning trial but received no ECS explored the empty niche an average of 10 times during the 10-minute test session, thereby indicating that they remembered their discovery of water the previous day. The rats that had received ECS 1 hour or 3 hours after the learning trial also explored the niche about 10 times. In contrast, the rats that received the ECS 10 seconds, 1 minute, or 10 minutes after the learning trial explored the empty niche significantly less on the test day. This result suggested that the consolidation of the memory of the learning trial took between 10 minutes and 1 hour (see Figure 14.9).

Numerous variations of this experiment were conducted in the 1950s and 1960s, with different learning

Islands of memory. Memories for isolated events that occurred during periods for which a person is otherwise totally amnesic.

Electroconvulsive shock (ECS). A diffuse electric shock to the brain that induces a convulsion.

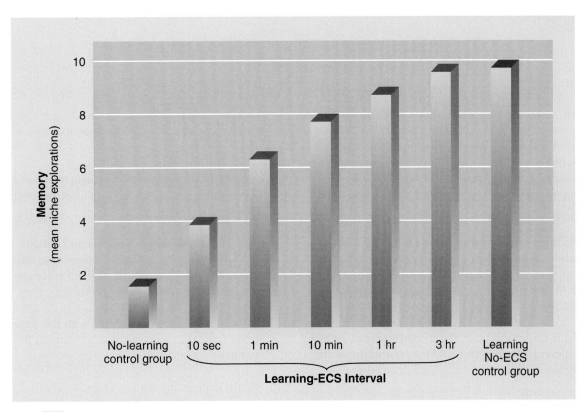

Figure 14.9 Retention of one-trial appetitive learning by control rats and by groups of rats that received ECS at various intervals after the learning trial. Only the rats that received ECS within 10 minutes of the learning trial displayed significant retrograde amnesia for it.

(Adapted from Pinel, 1969.)

tasks, different species, and different numbers and intensities of electroconvulsive shocks. Initially, there was some consistency in the findings: Most seemed to suggest a rather brief consolidation time of a few minutes or less (e.g., Chorover & Schiller, 1965). But then researchers began to observe very long gradients of ECS-produced retrograde amnesia. For example, Squire, Slater and Chace (1975) measured the memory of a group of ECS-treated patients for television shows that had played for only one season in different years prior to their electroconvulsive therapy. They tested each subject twice on different forms of the test, once before they received a series of five electroconvulsive

shocks and once after. The difference between the before-and-after scores served as an estimate of memory loss for the events of each year. Figure 14.10 illustrates

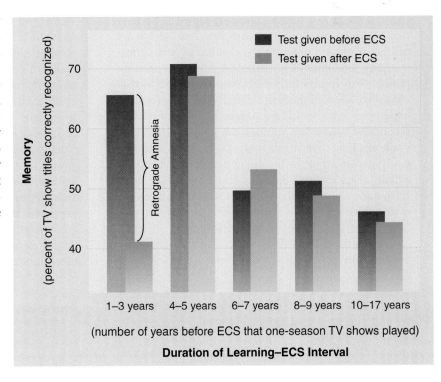

Figure 14.10 A demonstration of ECS-produced amnesia. A series of five electroconvulsive shocks produced retrograde amnesia for television shows that played for only one season in the 3 years before the shocks; however, the shocks did not produce amnesia for one-season shows that had played prior to that.

(Adapted from Squire et al., 1975.)

This chapter soon moves from the discussion of human amnesia to a consideration of animal models of human amnesia. Finish reading this section, then review what you have learned about human amnesia by completing the following exercise. The correct answers are provided at the bottom of this page. Before proceeding, review the material related to your errors and omissions.

1. The transfer of a memory from short-term storage to long-term storage is termed _____.

2. H. M. had his _____ temporal lobes removed.

3. The rotary-pursuit test, the incomplete-picture test, the mirror-drawing test, and the repetition-priming test are all tests of _____ memory.

4. H. M. appears incapable of forming new long-term _____ memories.

5. Support for the view that hippocampal damage can by itself cause amnesia comes from the study of R. B., a subject who suffered _____ damage to the pyramidal cells of his CA1 hippocampal subfield.

6. The current view is that damage to the _____ diencephalon is responsible for most of the memory deficits of people with Korsakoff's disease.

7. Initially, N. A. was thought to have selective damage to the _____ nucleus of the thalamus.

8. Patients with Korsakoff's disease and patients with _____ cortex damage have difficulty remembering the temporal order of events and display deficits on self-ordered tasks.

9. Alzheimer's disease is associated with the degeneration of _____ neurons in the basal forebrain.

10. Posttraumatic amnesia can be induced with _____ shock, which is used in the treatment of depression.

11. Because some gradients of retrograde amnesia are extremely long, it is unlikely that memory consolidation is mediated by _____ neural activity, as hypothesized by Hebb.

that five electroconvulsive shocks disrupted the retention of television shows that had played in the 3 years prior to treatment but not those that had played earlier.

Long gradients of retrograde amnesia are incompatible with Hebb's theory of consolidation. It is reasonable to think of the neural activity resulting from an experience reverberating through the brain for a few seconds or even a few minutes; but gradients of retrograde amnesia covering days, weeks, or years cannot be easily accounted for by the disruption of reverberatory activity (e.g., Squire & Spanis, 1984). Long gradients of retrograde amnesia indicate that the resistance of memories to disruption can continue to increase for a very long time after learning, if not indefinitely.

The discovery that H. M. suffers from a temporally graded retrograde amnesia led Scoville and Milner (1957) to suggest that the hippocampus and related structures play a role in consolidation. They suggested that memories are temporarily stored in the hippocampus until they can be transferred to a more stable cortical storage system—a widely held theory that has changed little over the years (see Squire & Alvarez, 1995).

Nadel and Moscovitch (1997) recently proposed a theory of consolidation that is more consistent with long gradients of retrograde amnesia and with case reports of retrograde amnesia that is not temporally graded. Nadel and Moscovitch propose that the hippocampus and related structures are involved in storing explicit episodic memories for as long as the memories exist. When a conscious experience occurs, it is rapidly and sparsely encoded in a distributed fashion throughout the hippocampus. The function of the

The answers are (1) consolidation, (2) medial, (3) implicit (or procedural), (4) explicit (or declarative), (5) ischemic, (6) medial, (7) mediodorsal, (8) prefrontal, (9) cholinergic, (10) electroconvulsive, and (11) reverberating.

Nonrecurring-items delayed nonmatching-to-sample test. A test in which the subject is presented with an unfamiliar sample object and then, after a delay, is presented with a choice between the sample object and another unfamiliar object—the correct choice being the non-sample object.

hippocampus is to link the cortical circuits that store the information and to provide spatial context to the memory, which gives it its episodic quality. Memories become more resistant to partial hippocampal damage because each time a similar experience occurs or the original memory is recalled, *new memory traces* (engrams) are established throughout the hippocam-

pus, which are linked to the original trace making the memory easier to recall and the trace more difficult to disrupt. Total bilateral hippocampectomy (including related structures) would be expected to disrupt all episodic memories irrespective of their age (see Knowlton & Fanselow, 1998; Moscovitch & Nadel, 1998).

14.6 Neuroanatomy of Object-Recognition Memory

As interesting and informative as the study of amnesic patients can be, it has major limitations. Many important questions about the neural bases of memory and amnesia cannot be answered by studying amnesic patients because controlled experiments are necessary for answering them. For example, in order to identify the particular structures of the brain that participate in various kinds of memory, it is necessary to make precise lesions in various structures and to control what and when the subjects learn, and how and when their retention is tested. Because such experiments are not feasible in human subjects, there has been a major effort to develop animal models of human brain-damage-produced amnesia to complement the study of human cases.

The first reports of H. M.'s case in the 1950s triggered a massive effort to develop an animal model of his disorder so that it could be subjected to experimental analysis. In its early years, this effort was a dismal failure; lesions of medial temporal lobe structures did not produce severe anterograde amnesia in either rats or monkeys. The failure led some researchers to suggest that the memory systems of humans differ from those of their mammalian relatives; however, this has proved not to be the case.

In retrospect, there were two major reasons for the initial difficulty in developing an animal model of medial temporal lobe amnesia. First, it was not initially apparent that H. M.'s anterograde amnesia did not extend to all kinds of long-term memory—that is, that it was specific to explicit (declarative) long-term memories; and most animal memory tests that were widely used in the 1950s and 1960s were tests of implicit (procedural) memory (e.g., Pavlovian and operant conditioning). Second, it was incorrectly assumed that the amnesic effects of medial temporal lobe lesions were largely, if not entirely, attributable to hippocampal damage; and most efforts to develop animal models of medial temporal lobe amnesia thus focused exclusively on hippocampal lesions.

Monkey Model of Object-Recognition Amnesia: The Nonrecurring-Items Delayed Nonmatching-to-Sample Test

H. M. does not learn to recognize objects that he encounters for the first time after his operation. Indeed, virtually all amnesics display anterograde object-recognition deficits. A major breakthrough in the study of the neural mechanisms of memory was the development in the mid 1970s of a monkey model of these object-recognition deficits (Gaffan, 1974; Mishkin & Delacour, 1975).

It was discovered that bilateral medial temporal lobe lesions in monkeys produce severe deficits in the **nonrecurring-items delayed nonmatching-to-sample test.** In this test, a monkey is presented with a distinctive object (i.e., the *sample* object), under which it finds food (e.g., a banana pellet). Then, after a delay, the monkey is presented with two test objects: the sample object and an unfamiliar object. The monkey must remember the sample object so that it can select the unfamiliar object to obtain food concealed beneath it. New objects (i.e., nonrecurring items) are used on each trial. The correct performance of a trial is illustrated in Figure 14.11 on page 388. Intact well-trained monkeys perform correctly on about 90% of the trials when the retention intervals are a few minutes or less.

The deficits of monkeys with bilateral medial temporal lobe lesions on the nonrecurring-items delayed nonmatching-to-sample test model the object-recognition deficits of H. M. in key respects. The monkeys' performance is normal at brief delays (delays of a few seconds); it falls off to near chance levels at delays of several minutes (see Figure 14.12 on page 389); and it is extremely susceptible to the disruptive effects of distraction (Squire & Zola-Morgan, 1985). Indeed, human amnesics have been tested on the nonrecurring-items delayed nonmatching-to-sample test—their

1 The monkey moves the sample object to obtain food from the well beneath it.

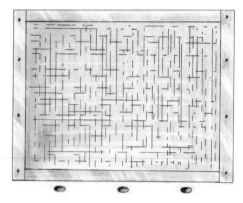

2 A screen is lowered in front of the monkey during the delay period.

3 The monkey is confronted with the sample object and an unfamiliar object.

4 The monkey must remember the sample object and then select the unfamiliar object to obtain the food beneath it.

Figure 14.11 The correct performance of a nonrecurring-items delayed nonmatching-to-sample trial. (Adapted from Mishkin & Appenzeller, 1987.)

rewards were coins rather than banana pellets—and their performance mirrored the performance of amnesic monkeys (Aggleton et al., 1988; Squire, Zola-Morgan, & Chen, 1988).

Further support for the monkey nonrecurring-items delayed nonmatching-to-sample model comes from the demonstration that performance of the nonrecurring-items delayed nonmatching-to-sample test by monkeys is also disrupted by medial diencephalic lesions (Aggleton & Mishkin, 1983). The fact that deficits can be produced by discrete lesions of the medial dorsal nuclei (Zola-Morgan & Squire, 1985), but not by lesions of the mammillary bodies (Aggleton & Mishkin, 1983) supports the view that mediodorsal nucleus damage plays a greater role than mammillary body damage in Korsakoff's amnesia.

Other tests have been developed for modeling human object-recognition deficits in monkeys. However, the nonrecurring-items delayed nonmatching-to-sample test has proved most useful and influential.

Early Monkey Studies of Medial Temporal Lobe Damage and Object-Recognition Amnesia

Figure 14.13 illustrates the location in the monkey brain of three of the structures of the medial temporal lobe: the hippocampus, the amygdala, and the rhinal cortex. (The **rhinal cortex** is composed of two areas of medial temporal cortex located around the *rhinal fis-*

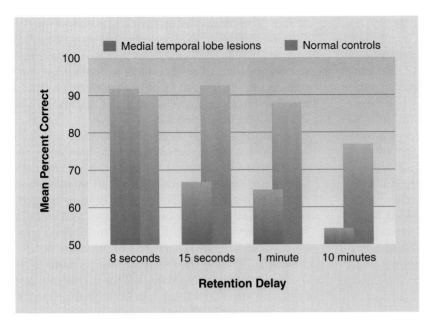

Figure 14.12 The deficits of monkeys with large bilateral medial temporal lobe lesions on the nonrecurring-items delayed nonmatching-to-sample test. There were significant deficits at all but the shortest retention interval. These deficits parallel the memory deficits of human medial temporal lobe amnesics on the same task.

(Adapted from Squire & Zola-Morgan, 1991.)

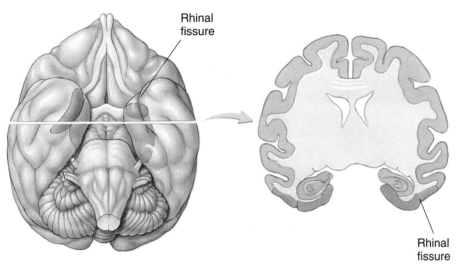

Figure 14.13 The three major structures of the medial temporal lobe, illustrated in the monkey brain: The hippocampus, the amygdala, and the rhinal cortex. The rhinal cortex is composed of the entorhinal cortex and the perirhinal cortex.

sure: the *entorhinal cortex* and the *perirhinal cortex*.) The hippocampus, amygdala, and rhinal cortex are all severely damaged by bilateral medial temporal lobectomy. The monkey nonrecurring-items delayed nonmatching-to-sample model provided a means of testing the assumption that the resulting amnesia was specifically a consequence of the hippocampal damage.

In the late 1970s and much of the 1980s, research on the monkey nonrecurring-items delayed nonmatching-to-sample model of medial temporal lobe amnesia focused on the contributions of hippocampal and amygdalar damage. Almost everybody accepted that the hippocampus played the major role in object-recognition memory, and the research focused on whether amygdalar damage contributed to the effects of hippocampal damage. To answer this question, the effects of hippocampal aspiration lesions on nonrecurring-items delayed nonmatching-to-sample tests were compared to the effects of combined hippocampal and amygdalar aspiration. The results were mixed: Some studies seemed to suggest that amygdalar damage did not contribute significantly to the amnesic effects of hippocampal damage; others seemed to suggest that it contributed significantly, and still others seemed to suggest that it played a critical role, with few memory deficits occurring unless both the hippocampus and the amygdala were aspirated.

Rhinal cortex. The area of medial temporal cortex around the rhinal fissure; it comprises the entorhinal cortex and perirhinal cortex.

In retrospect, the source of the early confusion about the relative contributions of hippocampal and amygdalar damage to anterograde object-recognition amnesia is clear (see Murray, 1992). Until the late 1980s, the focus on the contributions of hippocampal and amygdalar damage was so great that researchers gave little consideration to the possible contributions of damage to the underlying rhinal cortex, which was always removed in order to expose the hippocampus and amygdala for aspiration. Then, in the late 1980s, two important developments took place in the study of the neural basis of object-recognition amnesia. First, researchers working with the monkey model began to assess the effects of rhinal cortex lesions. And second, a rat model of object-recognition amnesia that is directly comparable to the monkey model was developed.

Rat Model of Object-Recognition Amnesia: The Nonrecurring-Items Delayed Nonmatching-to-Sample Test

Monkeys have a major advantage over laboratory rats when it comes to modeling human brain-damage-produced amnesia: The monkey brain is more similar than the rat brain to the human brain. However, laboratory rats have two advantages of their own. The first is that it is possible to conduct large-scale studies of amnesia in rats that are not feasible in monkeys for ethical and economic reasons. The second is that the hippocampus—the major neuroanatomical focus of research on memory—is more accessible to selective lesions in rats because of its smaller size and more dorsal location.

Figure 14.14 illustrates the usual methods of making hippocampal aspiration lesions in monkeys and rats. As a result of the size and location of the hippocampus, almost all studies of hippocampal lesions in monkeys have involved *aspiration* (suction) of large portions of the rhinal cortex in addition to the hippocampus, whereas in rats the extraneous damage associated with aspiration lesions of the hippocampus is typically limited to a small area of parietal neocortex. Furthermore, the rat hippocampus is small enough that it can readily be lesioned electrolytically or with intracerebral neurotoxin injections; in either case there is little extraneous damage.

Several versions of the rat nonrecurring-items delayed nonmatching-to-sample test have been developed (see Aggleton, 1985; Rothblat & Hayes, 1987). The

Figure 14.14 Aspiration lesions of the hippocampus in monkeys and rats. Because of differences in the size and location of the hippocampus in monkeys and rats, hippocampectomy in monkeys, but not in rats, typically involves the removal of large amounts of rhinal cortex.

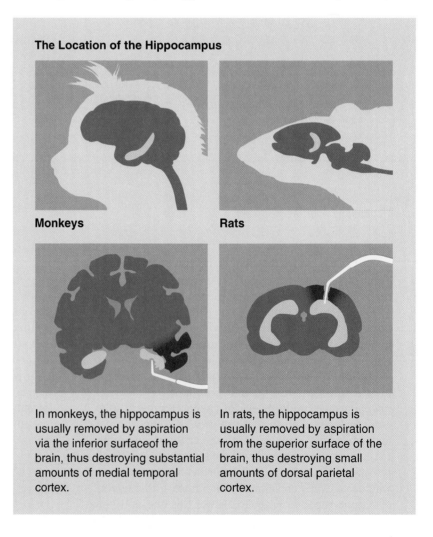

The Location of the Hippocampus

Monkeys

Rats

In monkeys, the hippocampus is usually removed by aspiration via the inferior surfaceof the brain, thus destroying substantial amounts of medial temporal cortex.

In rats, the hippocampus is usually removed by aspiration from the superior surface of the brain, thus destroying small amounts of dorsal parietal cortex.

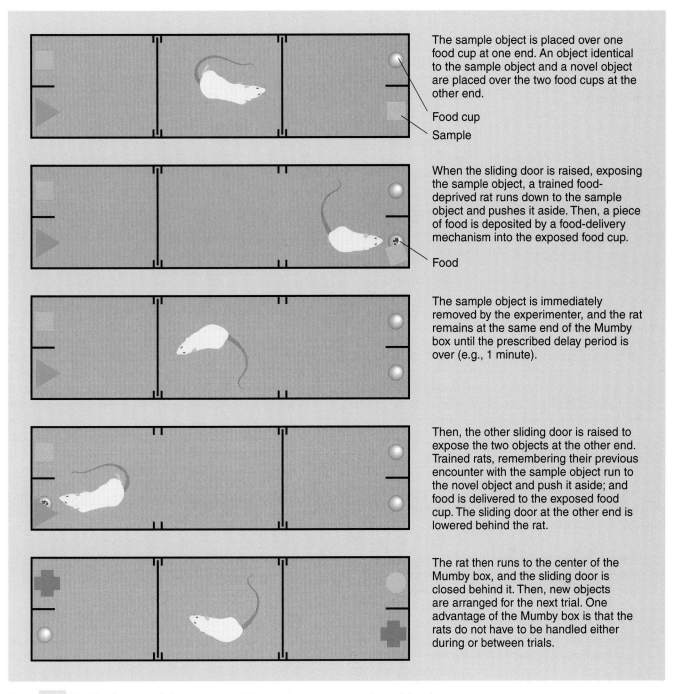

The sample object is placed over one food cup at one end. An object identical to the sample object and a novel object are placed over the two food cups at the other end.

Food cup

Sample

When the sliding door is raised, exposing the sample object, a trained food-deprived rat runs down to the sample object and pushes it aside. Then, a piece of food is deposited by a food-delivery mechanism into the exposed food cup.

Food

The sample object is immediately removed by the experimenter, and the rat remains at the same end of the Mumby box until the prescribed delay period is over (e.g., 1 minute).

Then, the other sliding door is raised to expose the two objects at the other end. Trained rats, remembering their previous encounter with the sample object run to the novel object and push it aside; and food is delivered to the exposed food cup. The sliding door at the other end is lowered behind the rat.

The rat then runs to the center of the Mumby box, and the sliding door is closed behind it. Then, new objects are arranged for the next trial. One advantage of the Mumby box is that the rats do not have to be handled either during or between trials.

Figure 14.15 The Mumby box and the rat version of the monkey nonrecurring-items delayed nonmatching-to-sample paradigm.

version that most closely resembles the monkey test was developed by Mumby using an apparatus that has become known as the **Mumby box.** This version of the rat nonrecurring-items delayed nonmatching-to-sample test is illustrated in Figure 14.15.

It was once assumed that rats could not perform a task as complex as nonrecurring-items delayed nonmatching-to-sample; Figure 14.16 on page 392 indicates otherwise. Rats perform almost as well as monkeys at delays up to 1 minute (Mumby, Pinel, & Wood, 1989).

The validity of the rat nonrecurring-items delayed nonmatching-to-sample test has been established by studies of the effects of medial temporal lobe and mediodorsal nucleus lesions. Bilateral lesions of the rat hippocampus that also involve the amygdala and the rhinal cortex produce major retention deficits at all but

Mumby box. An apparatus that is used to test nonrecurring- items delayed nonmatching-to-sample in rats.

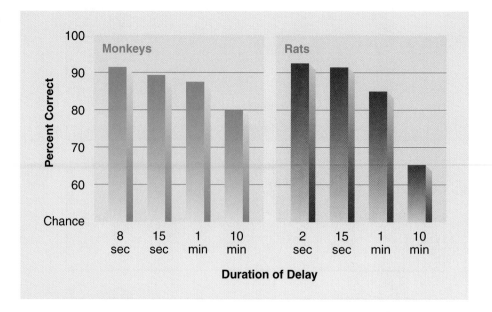

Figure 14.16 A comparison of the performance of intact monkeys (Zola-Morgan, Squire, & Mishkin, 1982) and intact rats (Mumby, Pinel, & Wood, 1989) on the nonrecurring-items delayed nonmatching-to-sample task.

the shortest retention intervals (Mumby, Wood, & Pinel, 1992), and the same is true of bilateral lesions of the mediodorsal nuclei (Mumby, Pinel, & Dastur, 1993). Thus the effects of medial temporal lobe and mediodorsal nucleus lesions on the performance of nonrecurring-items delayed nonmatching-to-sample tests is comparable in rats, monkeys, and humans.

Neuroanatomical Basis of the Object-Recognition Deficits Resulting from Medial Temporal Lobectomy

There is no better demonstration of the value of the comparative approach in biopsychological research than the surprising resolution to the question that has been the focus of research and speculation since the first reports of H. M.'s case: To what extent are the object-recognition deficits associated with bilateral medial temporal lobectomy a consequence of hippocampal damage? The results of experiments using the monkey and rat nonrecurring-items delayed nonmatching-to-sample models tell a consistent story that contradicts the long-held theory that the hippocampus and perhaps the amygdala play the major roles in the consolidation of explicit long-term memories.

The following two surprising findings have triggered a reevaluation of the relative contributions of the various medial temporal lobe structures to memory (see Duva, Kornecook, & Pinel, in press; Murray, 1996). First, lesions of the hippocampus or amygdala that do not extend into the rhinal cortex have been found to produce few, if any, deficits in nonrecurring-items delayed nonmatching-to-sample in either monkeys or rats (Murray & Mishkin, 1998). For example, in one monkey study, selective lesions of the hippocampus produced a deficit at only

the longest (10-minute) test interval (Alvarez, Zola-Morgan, & Squire, 1995); and in one rat study, lesions of the hippocampus and amygdala combined produced a deficit at only the longest (5-minute) test interval (Mumby, Wood, & Pinel, 1992). Second, lesions of the rhinal cortex that do not extend into the hippocampus or amygdala have been found to produce major deficits in nonrecurring-items delayed nonmatching-to-sample in both monkeys (Meunier et al., 1990; Zola-Morgan et al., 1989) and rats (Mumby & Pinel, 1994). Figure 14.17 compares the effects of rhinal cortex lesions and hippocampus plus amygdala lesions in rats.

Ischemia-Produced Brain Damage and Object-Recognition Deficits

The recent reports that object-recognition memory is severely disrupted by rhinal cortex lesions but not by hippocampal lesions have led to a resurgence of interest in the case of R. B. Earlier in this chapter, you learned that R. B. was left amnesic following an ischemic accident that occurred during heart surgery and that subsequent analysis of his brain revealed that obvious cell loss was restricted largely to the pyramidal cell layer of his CA1 hippocampal subfield (see Figure 14.7). This result has been replicated in both monkeys and rats. In both monkeys (Zola-Morgan et al., 1992) and rats (Wood et al., 1993), cerebral ischemia leads to a loss of CA1 hippocampal pyramidal cells and severe deficits in nonrecurring-items delayed nonmatching-to-sample.

The relation between ischemia-produced hippocampal damage and object-recognition deficits in humans, monkeys, and rats seems to provide strong support for the theory that the hippocampus plays a key role in object-recognition memory. But there is a gnawing

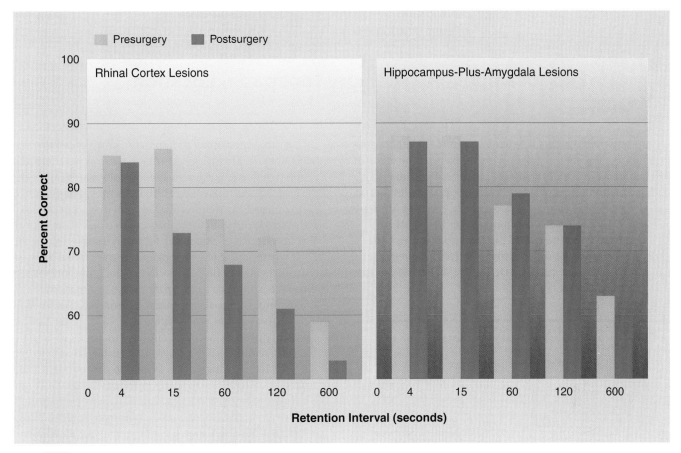

Figure 14.17 Effects of rhinal cortex lesions and hippocampus plus amygdala lesions in rats. Lesions of the rhinal cortex, but not of the hippocampus and amygdala combined, produced severe deficits in nonrecurring–items delayed nonmatching–to–sample in rats.

(Adapted from Mumby, Wood, & Pinel, 1992; Mumby & Pinel, 1994.)

problem with this line of evidence: How can ischemia-produced lesions to one small part of the hippocampus be associated with severe deficits in nonrecurring-items delayed nonmatching-to-sample in both monkeys and rats when the deficits associated with total removal of the hippocampus are only minor?

Mumby and his colleagues (1996) conducted an experiment that appears to resolve this paradox. They hypothesized the following: (1) that the ischemia-produced hyperactivity of CA1 pyramidal cells damages neurons outside the hippocampus, possibly through the excessive release of excitatory amino acids by the hyperactive CA1 cells; (2) that this extrahippocampal damage is not readily detectable by conventional histological analysis (i.e., it does not involve cell loss); and (3) that this extrahippocampal damage is largely responsible for the object-recognition deficits that are produced by cerebral ischemia. Mumby and colleagues supported these hypotheses by showing that bilateral hippocampectomy actually blocks the development of ischemia-produced deficits in nonrecurring-items delayed nonmatching-to-sample. First, they produced cerebral ischemia in rats by temporarily tying off their

carotid arteries. Then, one group of the ischemic rats received a bilateral hippocampectomy 1 hour later, a second group received a bilateral hippocampectomy 1 week later, and a third group received no bilateral hippocampectomy. Following recovery, the latter two groups of ischemic rats displayed severe object-recognition deficits, whereas the rats whose hippocampus had been removed 1 hour after ischemia did not. Explaining how hippocampectomy can prevent the development of the object-recognition deficits normally produced by cerebral ischemia is a major problem for the theory that the hippocampus plays a major role in object-recognition memory.

Support for the theory that the object-recognition deficits of ischemic patients result from extra-hippocampal disturbances comes from functional brain imaging studies. Widespread cerebral dysfunction is commonly observed in neuroanatomically intact areas distant from sites of ischemic cell loss (e.g., Baron, 1989). Consequently, cases of ischemia-produced amnesia with hippocampal cell loss (cases such as R. B.) do not provide evidence that the hippocampus plays a major role in object-recognition memory.

14.7 Hippocampus and Memory for Spatial Location

Because H. M.'s case seemed to point to the hippocampus as a key memory structure, it has been the focus of a massive amount of research. Numerous studies have assessed the effects of bilateral hippocampal lesions on the performance of many kinds of memory tests by laboratory animals—primarily rats. The most consistent finding has been that hippocampal lesions disrupt the performance of tests that involve the retention of spatial locations (e.g., McDonald & White, 1993)—see O'Keefe (1993).

Tests of Spatial Memory in Rats

Many tests of rat behavior involve the rat walking through the test environment, and thus they have a spatial memory component. However, the discovery that hippocampal damage disrupts spatial memory stimulated the development of tests expressly designed for its assessment. Two widely used tests of rat spatial memory are the Morris water maze test and the radial arm maze test.

In the **Morris water maze test,** intact rats placed at various locations in a circular pool of murky water rapidly learn to swim to an invisible stationary platform just below the surface. Rats with hippocampal lesions learn this simple task with great difficulty.

In the **radial arm maze test,** several arms (e.g., eight arms) radiate out from a central starting chamber, and the same few arms are baited with food each day. Intact rats readily learn to visit only those arms that contain food, without visiting the same arm more than once each day. The ability to visit only the baited arms of the radial arm maze is a measure of **reference memory**—memory for the general principles and skills that are required to perform a task; and the ability to refrain from visiting an arm more than once in a given day is a measure of **working memory**—temporary memory necessary for the successful performance of tasks on which one is currently working. Rats with hippocampal lesions display major deficits on both the reference memory and the working memory measures of radial arm maze performance.

Place Cells

Consistent with the observation that the hippocampal lesions disrupt spatial memory tasks in rats is the fact that rat hippocampal pyramidal neurons are **place cells** (O'Keefe & Dostrovsky, 1971)—neurons that respond only when a subject is in specific locations (i.e., in the *place fields* of the neuron). For example, when a rat is first placed in an unfamiliar test environment, none of its hippocampal neurons have a place field in that environment; then, as the rat familiarizes itself with the environment, each hippocampal pyramidal neuron acquires a place field in it—that is, each fires only when the rat is in a particular part of the test environment. Each hippocampal pyramidal neuron has a place field in many different environments.

By placing a rat in an ambiguous situation in a familiar test environment, it is possible to determine where the rat thinks it is from the route that it then follows to get to the location in the environment where it has previously been rewarded. Using this strategy (O'Keefe & Speakman, 1987; Wilson & McNaughton, 1993), it has been shown that the firing of a rat's place cells indicates where the rat "thinks" it is in the test environment.

Two recent studies have examined the effects of *NMDA* (N-methyl-D-aspartate) receptors on the establishment of hippocampal place fields. Kentros and colleagues (1998) found that an NMDA antagonist did not interfere with the establishment of hippocampal place fields in rats, but it did disrupt their long-term stability. Wilson and Tonegawa (1997) tested gene knockout mice with no $NMDA_1$ receptors (a subtype of NMDA receptors), and they found that the mice performed poorly in the Morris water maze and had abnormally unspecific (abnormally large) place fields.

Comparative Studies of the Hippocampus and Spatial Memory

Although most of the evidence that the hippocampus plays a role in spatial memory comes from research on rats, the hippocampus seems to perform a similar function in many other species. Most noteworthy has been the research in food-caching birds. Food-caching birds must have remarkable spatial memories, because in order to survive, they must remember the location of hundreds of food caches scattered around their territories. In one study, Sherry and colleagues (1989) found the food-caching species tended to have larger hippocampuses than related non-food-caching species.

Although research in a variety of species indicates that the hippocampus does play a role in spatial memory, the evidence from primate studies has been inconsistent. The hippocampal pyramidal cells of primates do have place fields (Rolls, Robertson, & Georges-François, 1995), but the effects of hippocampal damage on the performance of spatial memory tasks have been mixed (e.g., Maguire et al., 1998; Pigott & Milner, 1993). The problem may be that in humans and monkeys spatial memory is typically tested in stationary subjects making judgments of location on computer screens; whereas in rats, mice, and birds, spatial memory is typically studied in subjects navigating through controlled test environments.

Theories of Hippocampal Function

As you have already learned, the first theory of the hippocampus's role in memory—based on the study of H. M.—is that the hippocampus was a consolidation center for all explicit memories. This theory is no longer tenable in view of the fact that the hippocampus seems to play little or no role in object recognition.

Based on the observation of spatial memory deficits in animals with hippocampal damage and on the discovery that the hippocampus contains place cells, O'Keefe and Nadel (1978) proposed the **cognitive map theory** of hippocampal function. According to this theory, there are several systems in the brain that specialize in the memory for different kinds of information, and the specific function of the hippocampus is the storage of memories for spatial location. Specifically, Nadel and O'Keefe proposed that the hippocampus constructs and stores allocentric maps of the external world from the sensory input that it receives. *Allocentric* refers to representations of space based on relations among external objects and landmarks; in contrast, *egocentric* refers to representations based on relations to one's own position.

Another influential theory of hippocampal function is the *configural association theory* of Rudy and Sutherland (1992). The configural association theory is based on the observation that hippocampal damage sometimes disrupts the performance of tasks that do not appear to be spatial, and it is based on the premise that spatial memory is one specific manifestation of the hippocampus's more general function. The configural association theory is that the hippocampus plays a role in the long-term retention of interrelations among cues (in the retention of the behavioral significance of combinations of stimuli but not of individual stimuli). For example, according to this theory, the hippocampus is involved in remembering that a flashing light in a particular context (i.e., at a particular location or time) signals food but not that a flashing light signals food ir-

respective of the context. There is substantial support for this theory; however, there have also been several notable failures to disrupt the performance of nonspatial configural tasks with hippocampal lesions (e.g., Bussey et al., 1998; Whishaw & Tomie, 1995).

Another theory of hippocampal function is the *path-integration theory* (see Whishaw, McKenna, & Maaswinkel, 1997). Specifically, the path integration theory is that the hippocampus mediates path integration—the calculation of current location, past locations, and future locations from one's own movements.

A demonstration that rats are capable of path integration will clarify the concept for you (Whishaw & Tomie, 1996). Rats were tested on a large round platform with eight identical holes equally spaced around the perimeter. A rat's cage was placed under one hole so that it could climb up through the hole onto the platform and forage for a food pellet hidden in one of the other holes. Once the rat found the pellet, it took it in a straight line back to its cage where it consumed it. How do rats return in a straight line to their cage hole? They typically navigate by using allocentric cues in the room (e.g., doors, lights); however, they can also use egocentric cues. This can be demonstrated by blindfolding them. Blindfolded rats still run straight to their home hole with their newfound morsel. Clearly these blindfolded rats must have performed a complex path integration as they moved about foraging, and from this they "calculated" the angle of the straight line back to their starting point.

The key finding in the present context is that rats with hippocampal lesions are capable of making an accurate straight-line return journey by using allocentric cues, but they are incapable of returning by path integration (see McDonald & White, 1995). This suggests that the hippocampus plays a role in path integration but does not rule out the possibility that it performs other functions.

Morris water maze test. A widely used test of spatial memory in which rats must learn to swim directly to an invisible platform hidden just beneath the surface of a circular pool of murky water.

Radial arm maze test. A widely used test of rats' spatial ability in which the same arms are baited on each trial, and the rats must learn to visit only the baited arms only one time on each trial.

Reference memory. Memory for the general principles and skills that are required to perform a task.

Working memory. Temporary memory necessary for the successful completion of the task on which one is currently working.

Place cells. Neurons that develop place fields—that is, that come to fire rapidly only when the subject is in a particular place in a familiar test environment.

Cognitive map theory. The theory that the main function of the hippocampus is to store memories of spatial location.

Memory Structures of the Brain: A Summary

Figure 14.18 illustrates the structures of the brain that have been implicated in memory (see Mishkin & Murray, 1994; Tulving & Markowitsch, 1997); you have already encountered most of them in this chapter. This section completes the chapter by briefly summarizing the putative mnemonic functions of each structure.

jor role in the formation of new long-term explicit memories for objects. The fact that the retrograde amnesia that is produced by rhinal cortex lesions leaves remote memories unaffected suggests that memories for objects are not stored in the rhinal cortex (Kornecook, 1998; Wiig, Cooper, & Bear, 1996).

Rhinal Cortex

Recent studies of nonrecurring-items delayed non-matching-to-sample in monkeys and rats with rhinal cortex lesions indicate that the rhinal cortex plays a ma-

Hippocampus

Hippocampal lesions disrupt the performance of tasks that require the long-term retention of spatial information. The fact that they block the formation of new

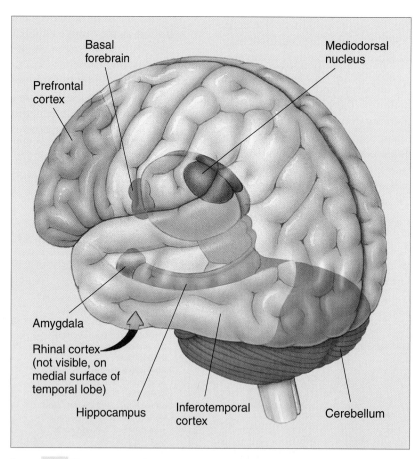

Figure 14.18 The structures of the brain that have been shown to play a role in memory. Because they would have blocked the view of other structures, the basal ganglia are not included. See Figure 3.31.

memories for spatial location but do not eliminate memories for spatial location that were acquired long before the lesions suggests that the hippocampus is involved in the consolidation of long-term memories for spatial location, not their storage. The role of the hippocampus in spatial memory has been supported by the discovery that many hippocampal neurons have place fields. The remaining question, however, is whether or not the hippocampus also performs functions that are not primarily spatial in nature and what these functions are (see Wallenstein, Eichenbaum, & Hasselmo, 1998).

Amygdala

Like the hippocampus, the amygdala was initially thought to play a role in long-term object-recognition memory; however, the discovery that amygdalar lesions that do not damage the underlying rhinal cortex produce no deficits in nonrecurring-items delayed nonmatching-to-sample has challenged this theory. The current view is that the amygdala plays a specific role in memory for the emotional significance of experiences. Rats with amygdalar lesions, unlike intact rats, do not respond with fear to a neutral stimulus that has been repeatedly followed by painful electric footshocks (see LeDoux, 1992). Bechara and colleagues (1995) reported the case of a neuropsychological patient with bilateral damage to the amygdala who could not acquire conditioned autonomic startle responses to various visual or auditory stimuli but had good declarative memory for them.

Inferotemporal Cortex

The retrograde amnesia produced by medial temporal lobectomy does not affect remote memories (see Zola-Morgan & Squire, 1990). This suggests that the medial temporal lobe structures play a role in the consolidation of long-term memories but are not the ultimate sites of their storage. So where in the brain are long-term memories stored? Current evidence suggests that long-term memories are stored in those cortical circuits that mediated their original experience—that is, in secondary sensory cortex and association cortex (see Tanaka, 1997).

Most of the research on the storage of long-term memories has focused on visual memories and their storage in the secondary visual cortex of the inferotemporal lobe. For example, Buffalo and colleagues (1998) found that monkeys with **inferotemporal cortex** damage could not learn a *concurrent discrimination task* (a task in which several pairs of different objects are repeatedly presented to the subject in sequence and the subject must remember which object of each pair is always associated with reward). Similarly, the *posterior*

parietal cortex is believed to store memories of spatial location, *secondary somatosensory cortex* is believed to store memories of tactile patterns, and *secondary auditory cortex* is believed to store auditory memories.

Cerebellum and Striatum

Just as explicit memories of experiences are presumed to be stored in the circuits of the brain that mediated their original perception, implicit memories of sensorimotor learning are presumed to be stored in sensorimotor circuits (see Salmon & Butters, 1995). Most research on the neural mechanisms of memory for sensorimotor tasks have focused on two structures: the **cerebellum** and the **striatum** (the dopaminergic structure composed of the caudate and putamen).

The cerebellum is thought to store the memories of learned sensorimotor skills. Its role in the Pavlovian conditioning of the eye-blink response has been intensively investigated (see Daum & Schugens, 1996). For example, Krupa, Thompson, and Thompson (1993) conditioned rabbits by repeatedly pairing a tone with a puff of air to the eye. Control subjects learned to blink in response to the tone and retained this Pavlovian conditioning over a series of daily test sessions. There were two experimental groups, each of which had an important structure of the eye-blink-conditioning circuit deactivated during training by microinfusions of the GABA agonist *muscimol*. The rabbits in one experimental group had their *red nuclei* deactivated; these rabbits displayed no behavior during conditioning; but when they were tested the next day without the muscimol, they showed that they had learned and retained the conditioning. This indicated that the memory for the conditioning was being formed at some point in the eye-blink-conditioning circuit before the red nucleus. The cerebellum is the structure in the eye-blink-conditioning circuit that projects to the red nucleus. The rabbits in the second experimental group had their cerebellums deactivated during the conditioning trials; and when their retention was assessed without the muscimol, they showed no retention whatsoever.

The striatum is thought to store memory for consistent relationships between stimuli and responses—the type of memories that develop incrementally over many trials (see White, 1997). For example, Knowlton,

---

Inferotemporal cortex. The area of secondary visual cortex in the inferior temporal lobe, where memories of visual images are thought to be stored.

Cerebellum. The metencephalic structure that has been shown to mediate the retention of Pavlovian eye-blink conditioning.

Striatum. A structure of the basal ganglia that is damaged in Parkinson patients; it seems to play a role in memory for consistent relationships between stimuli and responses in multiple-trial tasks.

Mangels, and Squire (1996) found that Parkinson patients with striatal damage could not solve a probabilistic discrimination problem designed to prevent explicit memory. The problem was a computer "weather forecasting" game, and the task of the subjects was to correctly predict the weather by pressing one of two keys, rain or shine. They based their predictions on stimulus cards presented on the screen—each card had a different probability of leading to sunshine. The Parkinson patients did not improve over 50 trials although they displayed normal explicit (conscious) memory for the training episode. In contrast, amnesic patients with medial temporal lobe or medial diencephalic damage displayed marked improvement in performance but later had no explicit memory of their training.

Prefrontal Cortex

Patients with bilateral prefrontal damage are not grossly amnesic; however, they do have specific memory problems. Their major problems are a difficulty in remembering the temporal order of events, even though they have no difficulty remembering the events themselves, and a related difficulty in performing self-ordered tasks.

The results of functional brain-imaging studies suggest that studies of brain-damage-produced amnesia underestimate the role of prefrontal lobes in memory. Functional brain images recorded in humans performing various memory tasks commonly reveal major increases in prefrontal activity even though, as you have learned, prefrontal damage seems to produce only a few selective effects on memory in human patients (see Buckner, 1996; Nyberg, Cabeza, & Tulving, 1996). Equally paradoxical is the fact that functional brain-imaging studies often do not detect activity in the classic medial diencephalic and medial temporal-lobe areas (see Fletcher, Frith, & Rugg, 1997).

The spatial resolution of functional brain-imaging techniques has improved to the point that it is possible to localize changes in activity to particular areas of prefrontal cortex. For example, the retrieval of semantic and episodic memories from long-term storage has been shown to activate different areas of prefrontal cortex. In several studies, the retrieval of information from semantic memory has activated the left inferior prefrontal cortex (e.g., Gabrieli et al., 1996), whereas the retrieval of memories of past experiences from episodic

memory has activated the right anterior prefrontal cortex (see Buckner & Petersen, 1996).

Mediodorsal Nucleus

The discovery that the mediodorsal nuclei are involved in memory came from the observation that they are virtually always damaged in cases of Korsakoff amnesia. Additional support for this view has come from two sources. First, circumscribed lesions of the mediodorsal nuclei produce nonrecurring-items delayed nonmatching-to-sample deficits in both monkeys (Aggleton & Mishkin, 1983) and rats (Mumby, Pinel, & Dastur, 1993). And second, exposure of rats to *pyrithiamine,* an antithiamine drug, produces mediodorsal nucleus damage and deficits on a variety of memory tests (Mair et al., 1991a).

One theoretical issue that has been the focus of considerable debate is whether the amnesia produced by damage to the medial diencephalon is qualitatively different from the amnesia produced by damage to the medial temporal lobe. So far, no major qualitative difference between medial diencephalic and medial temporal lobe amnesia has been delineated in human patients. This suggests that the two areas are components of the same memory circuit.

Basal Forebrain

The role of the basal forebrain in memory is somewhat controversial. The original suggestion that the basal forebrain is involved in memory came from the observation of basal forebrain damage in patients with Alzheimer's disease. However, this line of evidence was seriously challenged by the finding that Alzheimer's patients typically have widespread brain damage, including damage to structures that could account for their memory problems (e.g., prefrontal cortex, medial temporal lobes, medial diencephalon). However, the fact that localized basal forebrain strokes or tumors often produce amnesia suggests that the basal forebrain does play a role in memory.

The mnemonic functions of the basal forebrain are not well understood. This may be because only some of its structures (the medial septum, the diagonal band of Broca, and the nucleus basalis of Meynert) have mnemonic functions (see Everitt & Robbins, 1997).

CONCLUSION

This chapter began by introducing you to the amnesias associated with medial temporal lobe damage (14.1), Korsakoff's syndrome (14.2), prefrontal cortex damage (14.3), Alzheimer's disease (14.4), and concussion

(14.5). The study of each of these amnesic syndromes has provided important clues about the neural basis of memory, but it is the experimental study of animal models of brain-damage-produced amnesia that has led to most of the recent progress in this field. In particular, the study of animal models has led to recent advances in our understanding of the neural basis of object-recognition memory (14.6) and memory for spatial location (14.7). Current evidence suggests that the following brain structures play important roles in memory (14.8): the rhinal cortex, the hippocampus, the amygdala, the inferotemporal cortex (and other areas of secondary sensory and association cortex), the cerebellum, the striatum, the prefrontal cortex, the mediodorsal nucleus, and the basal forebrain.

This chapter began with the case of H. M.; it ends with the case of another amnesic, R. M. What makes R. M.'s case particularly ironic is that he is a biopsychologist. R. M. fell on his head while skiing; and when he regained consciousness, he was suffering from both retrograde and anterograde amnesia. For several hours, he could recall little of his previous life: He could not remember if he was married, where he lived, or where

he worked. Also, many of the things that happened to him in the hours after his accident were forgotten as soon as his attention was diverted from them. His was a classic case of posttraumatic amnesia. Like H. M., he was trapped in the present, with only a cloudy past and seemingly no future. The irony of the situation was that during those few hours, when R. M. could recall few of the events of his own life, his thoughts repeatedly drifted to one person—a person whom he remembered hearing about somewhere in his muddled past. Through the haze, he remembered H. M., his fellow prisoner of the present; and he wondered if the same fate lay in store for him.

R. M. is now fully recovered and looks back on what he can recall of his experience with relief and with a feeling of empathy for H. M. Unlike H. M., R. M. received a reprieve; but his experience left him with a better appreciation for the situation of those amnesics, like H. M., who are serving life sentences.

FOOD FOR THOUGHT

1. The study of the anatomy of memory has come a long way since H. M.'s misfortune. What kind of research on this topic do you think will prove to be most important in the next decade?

2. Using examples from your own experience, compare implicit and explicit memory.

3. What are the advantages and shortcomings of animal models of amnesia? Compare the usefulness of monkey and rat models.

4. Studies of brain-damaged humans, monkeys, and rats suggest that the medial diencephalon and medial temporal lobes play critical roles in memory. Paradoxically, functional brain-imaging studies have often not found increased activity in these areas in healthy humans performing memory tasks. Suggest an explanation for this paradox. [Hint: A possible explanation focuses on the poor temporal resolution of conventional functional brain-imaging techniques.]

KEY TERMS

Amygdala (p. 374)
Amyloid plaques (p. 382)
Anterograde amnesia (p. 374)
Basal forebrain (p. 383)
Bilateral medial temporal lobectomy (p. 374)
Block-tapping memory span test (p. 375)
CA1 subfield (p. 380)
Cerebellum (p. 397)
Cognitive-map theory (p. 395)
Consolidation (p. 372)
Digit span (p. 374)
Digit span + 1 test (p. 375)
Electroconvulsive shock (ECS) (p. 384)
Engram (p. 372)
Episodic memories (p. 379)

Explicit memories (p. 378)
Global amnesia (p. 375)
Hippocampus (p. 374)
Implicit memories (p. 378)
Incomplete-pictures test (p. 377)
Inferotemporal cortex (p. 397)
Ischemic brain damage (p. 379)
Islands of memory (p. 384)
Korsakoff's syndrome (p. 381)
Lobectomy (p. 374)
Lobotomy (p. 374)
Mammillary bodies (p. 381)
Matching-to-sample test (p. 375)
Medial temporal lobe amnesia (p. 378)

Mediodorsal nuclei (p. 381)
Memory (p. 372)
Mirror-drawing test (p. 376)
Mnemonic (p. 372)
Morris water maze test (p. 394)
Mumby box (p. 391)
Neurofibrillary tangles (p. 382)
Nonrecurring-items delayed nonmatching-to-sample test (p. 387)
Nootropics (p. 383)
Place cells (p. 394)
Posttraumatic amnesia (PTA) (p. 383)
Prefrontal cortex (p. 382)

Principle of equipotentiality (p. 372)
Principle of mass action (p. 372)
Pyramidal cell layer (p. 380)
Radial arm maze test (p. 394)
Reference memory (p. 394)
Repetition priming tests (p. 379)
Retrograde amnesia (p. 374)
Rhinal cortex (p. 388)
Rotary-pursuit test (p. 376)
Self-ordered tasks (p. 382)
Semantic memories (p. 379)
Striatum (p. 397)
Working memory (p. 394)

ADDITIONAL READING

The following articles provide readable reviews of much of the material in this chapter:

Buckner, R. L., & Petersen, S. E. (1996). What does neuroimaging tell us about the role of prefrontal cortex in memory retrieval? *Seminars in the Neurosciences, 8,* 47–55.

O'Keefe, J. (1993). Hippocampus, theta, and spatial memory. *Current Opinion in Neurobiology, 3,* 917–924.

Nadel, L., & Moscovitch, M. (1997). Memory consolidation, retrograde amnesia and the hippocampal complex. *Current Opinion in Neurobiology, 7,* 217–227.

Murray, E. A. (1996). What have ablation studies told us about the neural substrates of stimulus memory? *Seminars in the Neurosciences, 8,* 13–22.

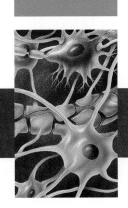

Neuroplasticity: Development, Learning, and Recovery from Brain Damage

Most of us tend to think of the nervous system as a three-dimensional array of neural elements "wired" together in a massive network of circuits. The sheer magnitude and complexity of this wiring-diagram concept of the nervous system is staggering, but it sells the nervous system short by failing to capture one of its most important features. The nervous system is not a static network of interconnected elements as is implied by the wiring-diagram model. It is a plastic, living organ that grows and changes continuously in response to its genetic programs and its interactions with its environment.

Neuroplasticity is the subject of this chapter. In it, you will learn about the neuroplastic processes involved in neural development, in learning and memory, and in recovery from brain damage. The chapter ends with a discussion of one of the most exciting fields of modern neuroscientific research: neurotransplantation.

Along with research on human subjects, you will encounter in this chapter studies that at first may appear to be strange fodder for students of biopsychology: studies of fish, frogs, salamanders, and snails. Why have some lines of research on neuroplasticity focused on such creatures? The answer in one word is "simplicity." There is an advantage in studying neuroplasticity in neural circuits that are complex enough to mediate behavioral change but simple enough to be analyzed neuron by neuron. This approach to the study of neuroplasticity is called the **simple-systems approach.**

15.1 Phases of Neural Development

In the beginning, there is a *zygote,* a single cell formed by the amalgamation of an *ovum* and a *sperm.* The zygote divides to form two daughter cells. These two divide to form four, the four divide to form eight, and so on, until a mature organism is produced. Of course, there must be more to development than this; if there were not, each of us would have ended up like a bowl of rice pudding: an amorphous mass of homogeneous cells.

To save us from this fate, three things other than cell multiplication must occur. First, cells must *differentiate;* some must become muscle cells, some must become multipolar neurons, some must become glial cells, and so on. Second, cells must make their way to appropriate sites and align themselves with the cells around them to form particular structures. And third, cells must establish appropriate functional relations with other cells. Section 15.1 describes how developing neurons accomplish these things in five phases: (1) induction of the neural plate, (2) neural proliferation, (3) migration and aggregation, (4) axon growth and synapse formation, and (5) neuron death and synapse rearrangement.

Induction of the Neural Plate

Three weeks after conception, the tissue that is destined to develop into the human nervous system becomes recognizable as the **neural plate**—a small patch of ectodermal tissue on the dorsal surface of the developing embryo. The ectoderm is the outermost of the three layers of embryo cells: *ectoderm, mesoderm,* and *endoderm.* The development of the neural plate is the first major stage of neural development.

As Figure 15.1 illustrates, the neural plate folds to form the *neural groove,* and then the lips of the neural

Simple-systems approach. Studying the neural basis of complex processes, such as learning and memory, in simple neural systems.

Neural plate. A small patch of embryonic ectodermal tissue from which the neural groove, the neural tube, and ultimately the mature nervous system develops.

Neural tube. The tube that is formed in the embryo when the edges of the neural groove fuse; it develops into the central nervous system.

Totipotential. Capable of developing into any type of body cell if transplanted to the appropriate site of the developing embryo.

Mesoderm layer. The middle of the three cell layers in the developing embryo.

Induction. The process of causing an enduring change in the nervous system.

Neural proliferation. The rapid increase in the number of neurons that occurs following the formation of the neural tube.

Ventricular zone. The zone adjacent to the ventricle in the developing neural tube; the zone where neural proliferation occurs.

Stem cells. Newly created, undifferentiated cells that have the potential to develop into various kinds of mature cells; stem cells in the developing nervous system can develop into various kinds of neurons or glial cells.

Migration. The movement of cells from their site of creation in the ventricular zone of the neural tube to their ultimate location in the mature nervous system.

Radial glial cells. Glial cells that exist in the neural tube only during the period of neural migration; they form a matrix along which developing neurons migrate.

groove fuse to form the **neural tube.** The inside of the neural tube eventually becomes the *cerebral ventricles* and *spinal canal.* By 40 days of age, three swellings are visible at the anterior end of the neural tube; these swellings ultimately develop into the *forebrain, midbrain,* and *hindbrain* (see Figure 3.21).

Prior to the development of the neural plate, each of the cells of the dorsal ectoderm is **totipotential**—having the potential to develop into any type of body cell. However, with the development of the neural plate, they lose their totipotency: Neural plate cells develop into neurons or glial cells even if they are transplanted to a different part of the embryo.

The development of the neural plate seems to be induced by chemical signals from the underlying **mesoderm layer** (see Kessler & Melton, 1994). Tissue taken from the dorsal mesoderm of one embryo (i.e., the *donor*) and implanted beneath the ventral ectoderm of another embryo (i.e., the *host*) induces the development of an extra neural plate on the ventral surface of the host.

One of the most fanciful demonstrations of **induction** is one that may require the abandonment of the expression "as scarce as hen's teeth." Kollar and Fisher (1980) induced teeth to grow from the ectodermal cells of chick embryos by implanting beneath them a tiny piece of mouse embryo mesoderm taken from beneath the portion of the ectoderm that would have normally developed into the mouse's mouth.

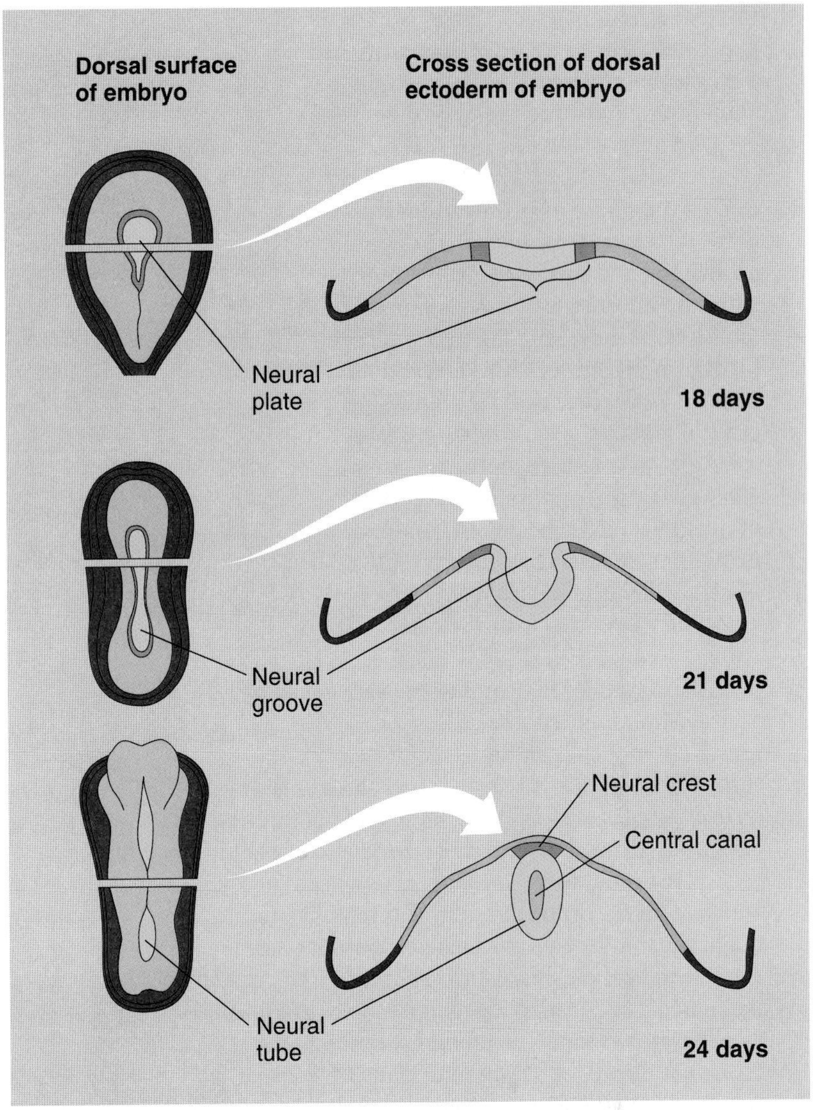

Figure 15.1 How the neural plate develops into the neural tube during the third and fourth weeks of human embryological development.
(Adapted from Cowan, 1979.)

Neural Proliferation

Once the lips of the neural groove have fused to create the neural tube, the cells of the tube begin to *proliferate* (increase greatly in number). This **neural proliferation** does not occur simultaneously or equally in all parts of the tube. In each species, the cells in different parts of the neural tube proliferate in a characteristic sequence that is responsible for the pattern of swelling and folding that gives each brain its species-characteristic shape. Most cell division in the neural tube occurs in the **ventricular zone**—the region adjacent to the *ventricle* (the fluid-filled center of the tube).

When the cells are first created they are called **stem cells** (McKay, 1997). Stem cells have the potential to develop into various kinds of mature cells; stem cells in the developing nervous system can develop into various kinds of neurons or glial cells.

Migration and Aggregation

■ **MIGRATION** Once cells have been created through cell division in the ventricular zone of the neural tube, they migrate to an appropriate location. During the period of **migration,** a temporary network of glial cells, called **radial glial cells** (see Figure 15.2 on page 404), is present in the developing neural tube. Migrating neurons mainly move outward along these radial glial cells to their destinations (see Herrup & Silver, 1994), but there are also significant *tangential migrations,* migrations at right angles to the radial glial cells (Pearlman et al., 1998).

The first neurons to be created during the phase of proliferation migrate to the *intermediate zone* of the growing neural tube (see Figure 15.3). After the intermediate zone is well established, some of the migrating cells form a layer between the *ventricular zone* and the intermediate zone. The cells that migrate to this *subventricular zone* are destined to become either glial cells or interneurons. In the forebrain, new cells begin to migrate through these layers to establish a layer of cells called the *cortical plate,* which eventually develops into the cerebral cortex. Because the cells of the deepest of the six layers of neocortex arrive at their destination first, the cells of progressively higher layers must migrate through them; this is referred to as the *inside-out pattern of cortical development.* When the migration of cells away from the ventricular zone is complete, the cells remaining there develop into *ependymal cells,* which form the lining of both the cerebral ventricles of the brain and the central canal of the spinal cord.

The **neural crest** is a structure that is situated just dorsal to the neural tube (see Figure 15.1). It is formed from cells that break off from the neural tube as it is being formed. Neural crest cells develop into the neurons and glial cells of the peripheral nervous system, and thus many of them must migrate over considerable distances. What directs them to their destinations? Their migration is directed by the media through which they travel, rather than information contained within the cells themselves. Consequently, cells transplanted from one part of the neural crest to another adopt the route characteristic of their new location. A host of chemicals have been discovered that guide migrating neurons by either attracting or repelling them (see Goldman & Luskin, 1998).

■ AGGREGATION   Once developing neurons have migrated, they must align themselves with other developing neurons that have migrated to the same area to form the structures of the ner-

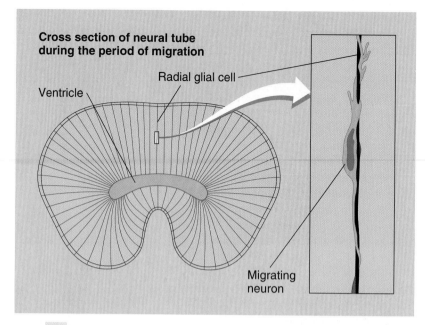

Figure 15.2 Newly created neurons migrate away from the ventricular zone along a network of radial glial cells.

vous system. This process is called **aggregation.** Both migration and aggregation are thought to be mediated by **cell-adhesion molecules (CAMs),** which are located on the surface of the neurons and other cells. Cell-adhesion molecules have the ability to recognize molecules on other cells and adhere to them (see Fazeli & Walsh, 1996).

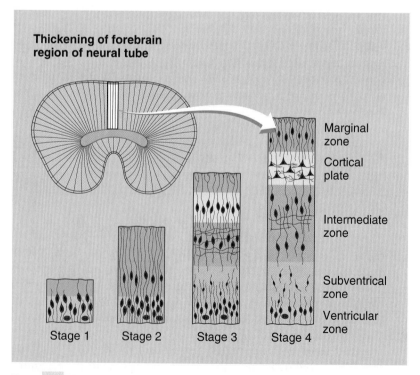

Figure 15.3 Neurons migrating out from the ventricular zone of the neural tube, creating new layers of cells. Illustrated here is the growth of the forebrain area of the neural tube.

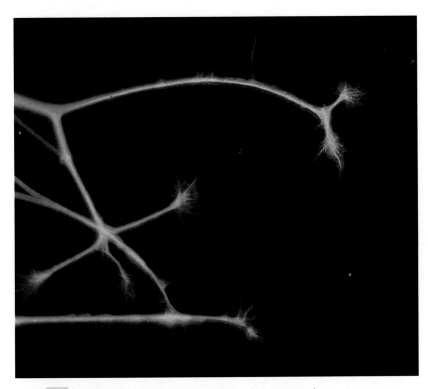

Figure 15.4 Growth cones. The cytoplasmic fingers (the filopodia) of growth cones seem to grope for the correct route.

(Courtesy of Naweed I. Syed, Ph.D., Departments of Anatomy and Medical Physiology, the University of Calgary.)

Axon Growth and Synapse Formation

Once neurons have migrated to their appropriate positions and aggregated into neural structures, axons and dendrites begin to grow from them. For the nervous system to function, these neural projections must grow to appropriate targets. At each growing tip of an axon or dendrite is an amoebalike structure called a **growth cone** (see Stirling & Dunlop, 1995), which extends and retracts fingerlike cytoplasmic extensions called *filopodia* (see Figure 15.4), as if searching for the correct route. Three hypotheses have been proposed to explain how growth cones find their way to their appropriate destinations: the chemoaffinity hypothesis, the blueprint hypothesis, and the topographic gradient hypothesis.

■ **CHEMOAFFINITY HYPOTHESIS** In 1943, Sperry conducted a classic series of experiments on the growth of axons in the frog visual system. In one of them, he cut the optic nerves of frogs, rotated their eyeballs 180°, and waited for the axons of the **retinal ganglion cells,** which compose the optic nerve, to *regenerate* (grow again). (Frogs, unlike mammals, have retinal ganglion cells that regenerate.) Once regeneration was complete, Sperry used a convenient behavioral test to assess the frogs' visual capacities (see Figure 15.5 on page 406). When he dangled a lure behind the frogs, they struck forward, thus indicating that their visual world, like

their eyes, had been rotated 180°. Frogs whose eyes had been rotated but whose optic nerves had not been cut responded in exactly the same way. This was strong evidence that each retinal ganglion cell had grown back to the same part of the **optic tectum** to which it had originally been connected.

On the basis of his studies of regeneration, Sperry proposed the **chemoaffinity hypothesis** of axonal development (see Sperry, 1963). He hypothesized that each postsynaptic surface in the nervous system releases a specific chemical label and that each growing axon is attracted by the label to its postsynaptic target during both neural development and regeneration. Strong support for the chemoaffinity hypothesis has come from two important discoveries. First, it has been shown that in some cases developing neurons will grow to their normal targets *in vitro* (in tissue culture) (see Bolz, 1994); this supports the chemoaffinity hypothesis because none of the spatial cues that might guide axon growth *in vivo* (in living organisms) would be present in a tissue culture. Second, numerous chemicals that either attract or repel growth cones have been isolated from extracellular neural tissue (see Cook, Tannahill, & Keynes, 1998; Stoekli & Landmesser, 1998).

The chemoaffinity hypothesis accounts for many aspects of axon growth (see Tessier-LaVigne & Placzek, 1991), but it cannot explain why targets transplanted to novel positions sometimes become incorrectly innervated. For example, when Whitelaw and Hollyday (1983) implanted an extra thigh segment in the legs of developing chick embryos so that the sequence was thigh, thigh, calf, foot—instead of the normal thigh, calf, foot—the second thigh segment became innervated by axons that normally would have innervated the calf. Also, the chemoaffinity hypothesis has difficulty explaining how some axons manage to follow exactly the same circuitous route to their target in every member

Neural crest. The structure formed by cells breaking off from the neural groove during the formation of the neural tube; it develops into the PNS.

Aggregation. The alignment of cells during development to form the various structures of the body.

Cell-adhesion molecules (CAMs). Molecules on the surface of cells that have the ability to recognize specific molecules on the surface of other cells and bind to them.

Growth cone. The structure at the tip of each growing axon or

dendrite that guides its growth to its appropriate target.

Retinal ganglion cells. The neurons whose axons compose the optic nerve.

Optic tectum. The main destination of visual neurons in lower vertebrates.

Chemoaffinity hypothesis. The hypothesis that each postsynaptic surface in the nervous system releases a specific chemical to which particular growing axons are attracted during development.

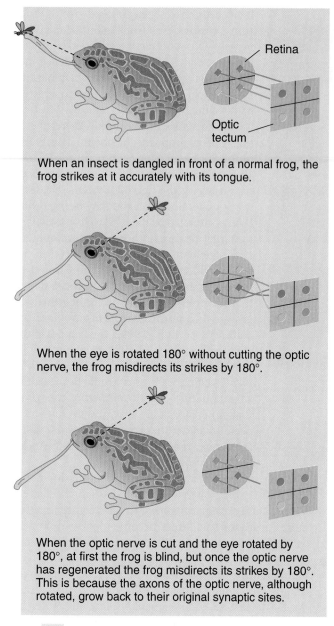

When an insect is dangled in front of a normal frog, the frog strikes at it accurately with its tongue.

When the eye is rotated 180° without cutting the optic nerve, the frog misdirects its strikes by 180°.

When the optic nerve is cut and the eye rotated by 180°, at first the frog is blind, but once the optic nerve has regenerated the frog misdirects its strikes by 180°. This is because the axons of the optic nerve, although rotated, grow back to their original synaptic sites.

Figure 15.5 Sperry's classic study of eye rotation and regeneration.

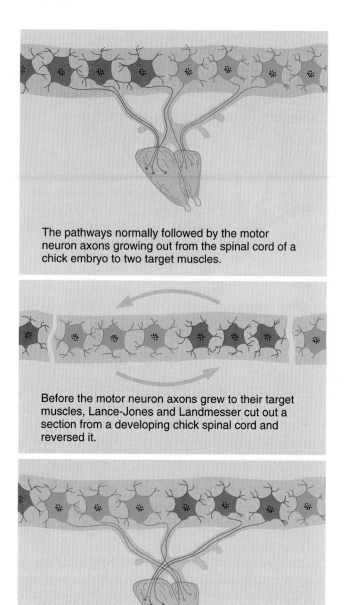

The pathways normally followed by the motor neuron axons growing out from the spinal cord of a chick embryo to two target muscles.

Before the motor neuron axons grew to their target muscles, Lance-Jones and Landmesser cut out a section from a developing chick spinal cord and reversed it.

Although the cell bodies of the motor neurons were then in an abnormal position, they grew out to their appropriate muscle.

Figure 15.6 Evidence against the blueprint hypothesis. When a section of spinal cord was cut from a chick embryo, inverted, and implanted back in the same location, the motor neuron axons grew out to their original target muscles.

(Adapted from Lance-Jones & Landmesser, 1980.)

of a species, rather than growing directly to the target (Bastiani et al., 1985; Kuwada, 1986).

■ BLUEPRINT HYPOTHESIS   The inability of the chemo-affinity hypothesis to account for certain aspects of axon development led to the proposal of the blueprint hypothesis. According to the **blueprint hypothesis,** the undeveloped nervous system contains specific chemical or mechanical trails that growing axons follow to their destinations. **Pioneer growth cones**—the first growth cones to travel along a particular route in a developing nervous system—are presumed to follow the correct trail by interacting with the *cell-adhesion molecules* of cells along the route (see Tessier-La Vigne & Goodman, 1996; Van Vactor, 1998). Then, subsequent growth cones embarking on the same journey follow the routes blazed by the pioneers. The tendency of growing axons to grow along the same paths established by preceding axons is called **fasciculation.** When pioneer axons in the fish spinal cord were destroyed with a laser, subsequent axons of the same nerves did not reach their usual destinations.

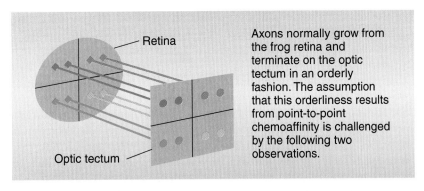

Axons normally grow from the frog retina and terminate on the optic tectum in an orderly fashion. The assumption that this orderliness results from point-to-point chemoaffinity is challenged by the following two observations.

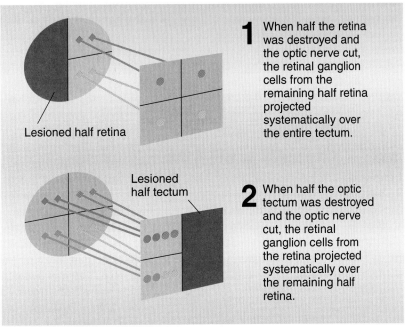

1 When half the retina was destroyed and the optic nerve cut, the retinal ganglion cells from the remaining half retina projected systematically over the entire tectum.

2 When half the optic tectum was destroyed and the optic nerve cut, the retinal ganglion cells from the retina projected systematically over the remaining half retina.

Figure 15.7 The regeneration of the optic nerve of the frog after portions of either the retina or the optic tectum have been destroyed: support for the topographic gradient hypothesis.

Although the blueprint hypothesis can account for some aspects of axon growth, it cannot account for the ability of some developing axons to reach their correct destinations in tissue culture. Nor can it account for the ability of some developing axons to reach their correct destinations in vivo when their starting points have been surgically shifted. For example, when Lance-Jones and Landmesser (1980) cut a small portion of the spinal cord from a chick embryo, inverted it, and implanted it back into the same embryo, the axons grew out to their original target muscles despite the fact that they started from a new location (see Figure 15.6).

■ **TOPOGRAPHIC GRADIENT HYPOTHESIS** Much of the axonal growth in complex nervous systems involves growth from one topographic array of neurons to another. The neurons on one array project to another, maintaining the same topographic relation they had on the first; for example, the topographic map of the retina is maintained on the optic tectum (see Figure 15.7).

It was initially assumed that the integrity of topographical relations in the developing nervous system was maintained by point-to-point chemoaffinity. Although this may be the primary mechanism of axon growth in invertebrate nervous systems, research on the development of vertebrate visual systems has led to the **topographic gradient hypothesis** (Easter et al., 1985). According to this hypothesis, axons that have grown out from one sheet of cell bodies (e.g., the retina) to another (e.g., the optic tectum) arrange their synaptic

Blueprint hypothesis. The hypothesis that developing axons grow to their correct targets by following chemical or mechanical trails through the developing nervous system.

Pioneer growth cones. The first growth cones to grow along a particular route in the developing nervous system.

Fasciculation. The tendency of growing axons to follow the route of preceding axons.

Topographic gradient hypothesis. The hypothesis that axonal growth is guided by the relative position of the cell bodies on intersecting gradients, rather than by point-to-point coding of neural connections.

terminals according to the relative positions of their cell bodies on the original sheet, as defined by two intersecting right-angle gradients (e.g., an up-down gradient and a left-right gradient).

Support for the topographic gradient hypothesis has come both from studies of development and from studies of regeneration. For example, in studies of visual system development, it was found that the synaptic connections between eyes and tectums are established long before either reach their full size; then, as the eyes and the optic tectums grow at different rates, the initial synaptic connections shift to other tectal neurons so that the retina is always faithfully mapped onto the tectum, regardless of their relative sizes (Gaze et al., 1979; Reh & Constantine-Paton, 1984).

In studies of visual system regeneration (e.g., Gaze & Sharma, 1970; Yoon, 1971), the optic nerves of mature frogs were cut and their pattern of regeneration was assessed after parts of either the retina or the optic tectum had been destroyed. In both cases, the axons did not grow out to their original points of connection (as the chemoaffinity and blueprint hypotheses predicted they would); instead they grew out to fill the available space in an orderly fashion. Axons growing from the remaining portion of a lesioned retina "spread out" in an orderly fashion to fill all of the space on an intact tectum. Conversely, axons growing from an intact retina "squeeze in" in an orderly fashion to fill the remaining space on a lesioned tectum. These results are illustrated schematically in Figure 15.7.

■ **AXON GROWTH AND SYNAPSE FORMATION: CONCLUSION** Over half a century of research on the miraculous ability of developing axons to grow to their correct targets has led to the conclusion that no single mechanism can account for all instances (see Holt & Harris, 1998). The main guiding force appears to be the growth cones' attraction to specific chemical signals that are released by their targets, but there are well-documented instances in which the growth cones follow specific circuitous routes through the cellular matrix, presumably by following trails of cell-adhesion molecules in the substrate. Furthermore, the ability of growing axons to establish topographic gradients seems to require a spatially graded chemical signal from the target structure and a gradient-related mechanism of axon–axon interaction.

Neuron Death and Synapse Rearrangement

■ **NEURON DEATH** Neuron death is a normal and important part of neural development. Neural development seems to operate on the principle of survival of the fittest: Many more neurons—about 50% more—are produced than are required, and only the fittest survive.

Large-scale death is not a time-limited stage of development; it occurs in waves in various parts of the brain throughout development.

Three findings suggest that developing neurons die because of their failure to compete successfully for **neurotrophins**—life-preserving chemicals that are supplied to neurons by their targets. First, the implantation of extra target sites decreases neuron death. For example, Hollyday and Hamburger (1976) grafted an extra limb on one side of a chick embryo and fewer motor neurons on that side died. Second, destroying some of the neurons growing into an area before the period of cell death increases the survival rate of the remaining neurons (e.g., Pilar, Landmesser, & Burstein, 1980). Third, increasing the number of axons that initially innervate a target decreases the proportion that survive.

Nerve growth factor (NGF) was the first neurotrophic factor to be isolated (see Levi-Montalcini, 1952, 1975). Nerve growth factor is synthesized and released by the targets of *sympathetic neurons* during the period of cell death, and it is taken up by the sympathetic neurons and promotes their survival. Since the discovery of nerve growth factor, there has been a major effort to isolate neurotrophins that promote the survival of other neurons; such factors may have major therapeutic value in halting the course of neurodegenerative diseases. Several substances that promote the survival of certain kinds of neurons have been identified, and work is now being directed at trying to understand their actions (see Nishi, 1994).

Neuron death was initially assumed to be a passive process. It was assumed that the appropriate neurotrophins are needed for the survival of neurons and that without them neurons passively degenerate and die. However, it is now clear that cell death can sometimes be an active process: The absence of the appropriate neurotrophins can trigger a genetic program inside neurons that causes them to actively commit suicide. Passive cell death is called **necrosis** (ne KROE sis); active cell death is called **apoptosis** (a poe TOE sis).

Necrotic cell death is dangerous. Necrotic cells break apart and spill their contents into extracellular fluid, and the consequence is potentially harmful inflammation. In contrast, in apoptotic cell death, DNA and other internal structures are cleaved apart and packaged in membranes before the cell membrane disintegrates; consequently, no inflammation occurs (see Ashkenazi & Dixit, 1998; Green & Reed, 1998).

Most of the cell death associated with the early development of the nervous system is apoptotic. It prunes tissues by removing cells in a safe, neat, and orderly way. But apoptosis has a dark side as well. If genetic programs for apoptotic cell death are inhibited, the consequence can be cancer; if the programs are inappropriately activated, the consequence can be neurodegenerative disease (Adams & Cory, 1998; Evan & Littlewood, 1998).

Fill in the blanks in the following chronological list of the major stages in the development of the nervous system after you have finished reading this section. The correct answers are provided at the bottom of this page. Before proceeding, review material related to your errors and omissions.

1. Induction of the neural _____.

2. Formation of the _____ tube.

3. Neural _____.

4. Neural _____.

5. _____ aggregation.

6. Growth of _____.

7. Formation of _____.

8. Neuron _____ and synapse _____.

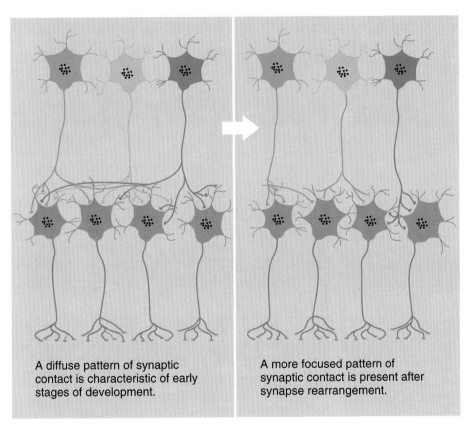

A diffuse pattern of synaptic contact is characteristic of early stages of development.

A more focused pattern of synaptic contact is present after synapse rearrangement.

Figure 15.8 The effect of neuron death and synapse rearrangement on the selectivity of synaptic transmission. The synaptic contacts of each axon become focused on a smaller number of cells.

■ **SYNAPSE REARRANGEMENT** During the period of cell death, neurons that have established incorrect connections are particularly likely to die. As they die, the space that they vacate on postsynaptic membranes is filled by the sprouting axon terminals of surviving neurons. Thus cell death results in a massive rearrangement of synap-

tic connections. Synapse rearrangement focuses the output of each neuron on a smaller number of postsynaptic cells, thus increasing the selectivity of transmission (see Figure 15.8).

The answers are (1) plate, (2) neural, (3) proliferation, (4) migration, (5) Neural, (6) neural processes (axons and dendrites), (7) synapses, and (8) death; rearrangement.

Neurotrophins. Substances that promote the survival of neurons.
Nerve growth factor (NGF). A neurotrophin that attracts the growing axons of the sympathetic nervous system and promotes their survival.

Necrosis. Passive cell death, which is characterized by inflammation.
Apoptosis. Cell death that is actively induced by genetic programs.

Effects of Experience on Neural Development

Genetic programs of neural development do not act in a vacuum. Neural development unfolds through interactions between neurons and their environment. You learned in the previous section how factors in a neuron's immediate environment (e.g., neurotrophins and cell-adhesion molecules) can influence its development. In contrast, this section focuses on how a neuron's interactions with the external environment can influence its development. The main principle that governs the effects of experience on neural development is simple: Neurons and synapses that are not activated by experience do not usually survive (see Hockfield & Kalb, 1993; Kalil, 1989).

Early Studies of Experience and Neural Development

Many of the first demonstrations of the impact of early experience on neural development came from two lines of research: from the study of the effects of early visual deprivation and from the study of early exposure to enriched environments. For example, animals reared in the dark were found to have fewer synapses and fewer dendritic spines in their primary visual cortexes, and they were found to have deficits in depth and pattern vision as adults. Conversely, rats that were raised in enriched (complex) group cages rather than by themselves in barren cages were found to have thicker cortexes with greater dendritic development and more synapses per neuron.

Competitive Nature of Experience and Neural Development

Experience promotes the development of active neural circuits, but there is a competitive aspect to this. This competitive aspect is clearly illustrated by the disruptive effects of early monocular deprivation.

Depriving only one eye of input early in life blocks the development of vision in the deprived eye, but this does not happen if the other eye is also blindfolded. When only one eye is blindfolded during early development, the ability of that eye to activate the visual cortex is reduced or eliminated, whereas the ability of the other eye is increased. Both these effects occur because early monocular deprivation changes the pattern of synaptic input into layer IV of the primary visual cortex.

In newborn cats and monkeys, the input into layer IV from the left and right eyes is intermingled; then, during the course of normal development, it becomes segregated into equal-size alternating columns of ocular dominance (see Figure 7.19). Early monocular deprivation decreases the width of the columns of input from the deprived eye and increases the width of the columns of input from the nondeprived eye (Hata & Stryker, 1994; Hubel, Wiesel, & LeVay, 1977).

It takes only a few days of early monocular deprivation to produce significant reductions in the proportion of visual cortex neurons that can be activated by stimulation of the deprived eye. These changes were thought to be too rapid to be mediated by structural changes; however, this has proved not to be the case. Antonini and Stryker (1993) found that a few days of monocular deprivation produces a massive decrease in the axonal branching of the lateral geniculate nucleus neurons that normally carry signals from the deprived eye to layer IV of the primary visual cortex (see Figure 15.9).

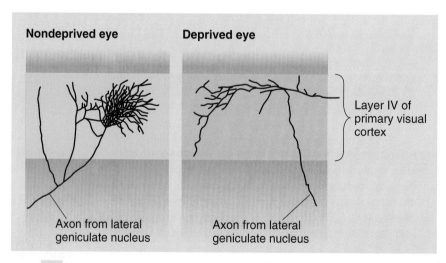

Figure 15.9 The effect of a few days of early monocular deprivation on the structure of axons projecting from the lateral geniculate nucleus into layer IV of the primary visual cortex. Axons carrying information from the deprived eye displayed substantially less branching. (Adapted from Antonini & Stryker, 1993.)

The competitive nature of the effects of neural activity on synapse rearrangement has also been demonstrated in experiments on motor neurons and muscle cells. In *neonates* (newborns), each muscle cell is normally innervated by several motor neurons, and then all but one are eliminated during the course of development. Lo and Poo (1991) developed an in vitro preparation in which one developing muscle cell was innervated by two developing motor neurons. Applying pulses of electrical stimulation to one of them caused a rapid degradation in the synaptic contacts of the other. Apparently, motor neurons compete with one another for synaptic contacts on muscle cells, and active synapses take precedence.

Colman, Nabekura, and Lichtman (1997) studied the mechanism by which neonatal synapses on each muscle are reduced to one. They found a gradual increase in the neurotransmitter released at synapses that subsequently survived and a decrease at synapses that were subsequently eliminated.

Effects of Experience on the Development of Topographic Sensory Cortex Maps

Some of the most remarkable demonstrations of the effects of experience on neural development come from lines of research on the development of cortical topographic maps of the sensory systems. The following are three of them.

First, Roe and colleagues (1990) caused the developing axons of ferret retinal ganglion cells to synapse in the medial geniculate nuclei of the auditory system instead of in the lateral geniculate nuclei of the visual system. Remarkably, once the ferrets matured, their auditory cortex responded to visual stimuli, and it was laid out retinotopically.

Second, Knudsen and Brainard (1991) raised barn owls with vision-displacing prisms over their eyes. This led to a corresponding change in the auditory spatial map in the tectum. For example, an owl that was raised wearing prisms that shifted its visual world 23° to the right had an auditory map that was also shifted 23° to

the right, so that objects were heard to be where they were seen to be (Knudsen, 1991).

Third, Weliky and Katz (1997) periodically disturbed the spontaneous optic nerve activity of neonatal ferrets that had yet to open their eyes. This disrupted the development of the orientation and direction selectivity of the ferrets' primary visual cortex neurons. Thus, it appears that patterns of spontaneous neural activity emanating from fetal eyes prior to the onset of vision play a role in the development of the visual cortex (see Katz & Shatz, 1996). Although visual cortex is largely developed in primates when they are born, subsequent lack of visual input leads to its deterioration (Crair, Gillespie, & Stryker, 1998).

Mechanisms of Experiential Effects on Neural Development

As you have just learned, it is now well established that experience affects neural development; however, the mechanisms by which this occurs are not well understood. Be that as it may, recent experiments have revealed several mechanisms by which experience might affect neural development. The following are three of them.

First, neural activity has been shown to regulate the expression of genes that direct the synthesis of cell adhesion molecules. Thus, by influencing neural activity, experience can produce changes in cell adhesion (Fields & Itoh, 1996; Itoh et al., 1995).

Second, neural activity has been shown to regulate the release of neurotrophins from neural dendrites (Thoenen, 1995). Thus, by influencing neural activity, experience can promote and direct the growth of presynaptic neurons and influence their survival.

Third, some neurotransmitter systems (e.g., monoamine systems) are functional early in the course of brain development, and the activity of these systems is necessary for subsequent brain development to progress normally. Thus, by influencing the activity of the early-developing neurotransmitter systems, experience can influence the course of brain development (see Levitt et al., 1997).

15.3 Neural Bases of Learning and Memory in Simple Systems

So far, this chapter has focused on the plasticity of developing nervous systems. Now the emphasis changes to the plasticity of adult nervous systems. This section discusses how experience induces adaptive changes in

adult nervous systems and how these changes are maintained and later expressed. In other words, this section focuses on the neural bases of learning and memory. Learning and memory refer to different aspects of the same neuroplastic phenomena: **Learning** is the induction by experience of behavior-related neural changes, and **memory** is their maintenance and expression in the form of behavioral change.

This section of the chapter focuses on two influential lines of research, both of which feature the simple-systems approach. The first deals with the neural basis of learning and memory in *Aplysia*, a simple marine invertebrate; the second deals with long-term potentiation, a learning- and memory-related phenomenon of the mammalian brain.

Learning in the Aplysia Gill-Withdrawal Reflex Circuit

The **Aplysia** is a marine snail that spends its life oozing along the ocean floor eating seaweed and avoiding predation by tasting as bad as it looks (see Figure 15.10). The Aplysia *siphon* is a small, fleshy spout that is used to expel seawater and waste. When the siphon is touched, it and the adjoining gill are reflexively drawn up under a protective *mantle*. This response to touch is the Aplysia's *gill-withdrawal reflex.*

The neural circuit that mediates the Aplysia gill-withdrawal reflex is relatively simple. The skin of the siphon contains 24 sensory neurons that synapse on 6 motor neurons that are responsible for retracting the siphon and gill. The sensory neurons also activate interneurons that in turn synapse on the motor neurons. This circuit is illustrated schematically in Figure 15.11.

■ NONASSOCIATIVE LEARNING IN APLYSIA A change in behavior that results from the repeated experience of a single stimulus or of two or more different stimuli that are not spatially or temporally related is called **nonassociative learning.** The two most commonly studied forms of nonassociative learning are habituation and sensitization.

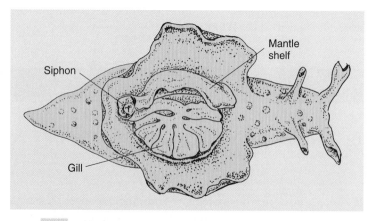

Figure 15.10 An Aplysia.

Habituation is the progressive decrease in the strength of the behavioral reaction to a stimulus that is repeatedly presented. For example, if the Aplysia siphon is touched once every 30 seconds, the gill-withdrawal reflex becomes less and less vigorous. Habituation of the Aplysia gill-withdrawal reflex lasts 2 or 3 hours following a single 10-stimulus habituation session, but several such sessions can produce habituation that lasts for weeks (Carew, Pinsker, & Kandel, 1972).

What is the neural mechanism of habituation in the Aplysia gill-withdrawal reflex circuit? The first clue came from the discovery that habituation is associated with a decline in the number of action potentials that are elicited in the gill motor neurons by each siphon touch (Castellucci et al., 1970). Because the responsiveness of the motor neurons to the neurotransmitter released by the sensory neurons did not decline during habituation (Castellucci & Kandel, 1974), it was concluded that the progressive decline in the number of motor neuron action potentials must have resulted from a decline in the release of neurotransmitter from the sensory neurons.

What causes the siphon sensory neurons to release progressively less neurotransmitter in response to each successive siphon touch during the course of habituation? There are two possibilities. One is that less neurotransmitter is released because progressively fewer action potentials are elicited in the siphon sensory neurons by each successive touch; the other is that there is a decline in the amount of neurotransmitter that is released in response to each action potential. The discovery that the number of sensory neuron action potentials does not decline during the course of habituation supported the latter alternative.

Once it became clear that the habituation of the Aplysia gill-withdrawal reflex results from a decrease in the amount of neurotransmitter that is released from siphon sensory neurons in response to each of their own action potentials, researchers began the search for the mechanism of this decrease. The search focused on calcium ions because it is the influx of calcium ions into the terminal buttons that causes synaptic vesicles to fuse with the presynaptic membrane and release their contents into the synapse. It was soon established that the decrease in siphon sensory neuron neurotransmitter release during habituation of the gill-withdrawal reflex results in part from a decrease in the number of calcium ions entering the terminal buttons of the siphon sensory neurons in response to each action potential (e.g., Klein, Shapiro, & Kandel, 1980). Subsequently, it was shown that depletion of the neurotransmitter pools in the sensory neuron also contribute substantially to the decrease in neurotransmitter release (Gingrich & Byrne, 1985).

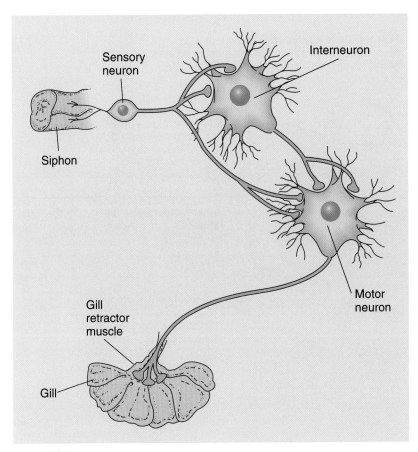

Figure 15.11 A schematic illustration of the components of the neural circuit that mediates the Aplysia gill-withdrawal reflex.

neurons in response to their own action potentials (Castellucci & Kandel, 1976).

How does tail shock cause the siphon sensory neurons to increase their release of neurotransmitter onto the gill motor neurons? The mechanism is **presynaptic facilitation.** Sensory fibers from the Aplysia tail synapse on facilitatory *serotonergic* (serotonin-releasing) interneurons, which in turn synapse on the buttons of siphon sensory neurons (see Mercer, Emptage, & Carew, 1991). It is via these serotonergic interneurons that the tail shock changes the siphon sensory neuron buttons so that each action potential arriving there from the siphon results in a greater influx of calcium ions and a greater release of neurotransmitter onto the motor neurons (see Figure 15.12). Applications of serotonin to Aplysia sensorimotor synapses in vitro produce sensitization lasting from several minutes to several days (see Byrne & Kandel, 1996).

Cleary, Lee, and Byrne (1998) studied the neuronal mechanisms of long-term sensitization. They found changes in the sensory neurons that were consistent with the conventional view that sensitization results from an increased release of neurotransmitter from sensory neurons. However, they also observed some lasting increases in the motor neuron excitability. It seems therefore that at least the long-term variety of sensitization has multiple mechanisms.

The following theory of habituation learning in the Aplysia gill-withdrawal reflex has emerged from this line of research (see Figure 15.12 on page 414). With repeated elicitation of the gill-withdrawal reflex, each siphon touch continues to fully activate the sensory neurons, sending the same full barrage of action potentials down their axons. However, because fewer calcium ions enter the synaptic terminals in response to each successive barrage of action potentials and because the neurotransmitter pools become partially depleted, less and less neurotransmitter is released from the sensory neurons into the synapses, fewer and fewer action potentials are elicited in the motor neurons, and the contraction of the gill muscle in response to each siphon touch grows weaker and weaker.

Sensitization is the general increase in an animal's responsiveness to stimuli that occurs following a noxious stimulus. Sensitization of the Aplysia gill-withdrawal reflex lasts for several minutes following a single tail shock, but it can last for weeks following a series of tail shocks administered over several days. In contrast to the mechanism of habituation, sensitization has been shown to result from an increase in the amount of neurotransmitter that is released by the siphon sensory

■ **ASSOCIATIVE LEARNING IN APLYSIA** The Aplysia gill-withdrawal reflex circuit is capable of *Pavlovian conditioning*—of learning an association between a conditional stimulus and an unconditional stimulus. If a light touch of the siphon (the conditional stimulus) is paired with a strong shock to the tail (the unconditional stimulus) every few minutes for several trials, the light touch by itself begins to elicit a robust gill-withdrawal response similar to that elicited by the tail shock. The associative nature of this effect is shown by the fact that

Learning. The induction of behavior-related neural changes by sensory experience.

Memory. The maintenance and later expression as a change in behavior of experience-induced neural changes.

Aplysia. A simple marine snail whose gill-withdrawal reflex is capable of simple forms of nonassociative and associative learning.

Nonassociative learning. A change in behavior that results from the repeated experience of a single stimulus or of two or

more stimuli that are not temporally or spatially related.

Habituation. The progressive decrease in the strength of the behavioral reaction to a repeatedly presented stimulus.

Sensitization. The general increase in an animal's responsiveness to stimuli following the experience of a noxious stimulus.

Presynaptic facilitation. The cellular mechanism thought to underlie sensitization and Pavlovian conditioning in the Aplysia gill-withdrawal circuit.

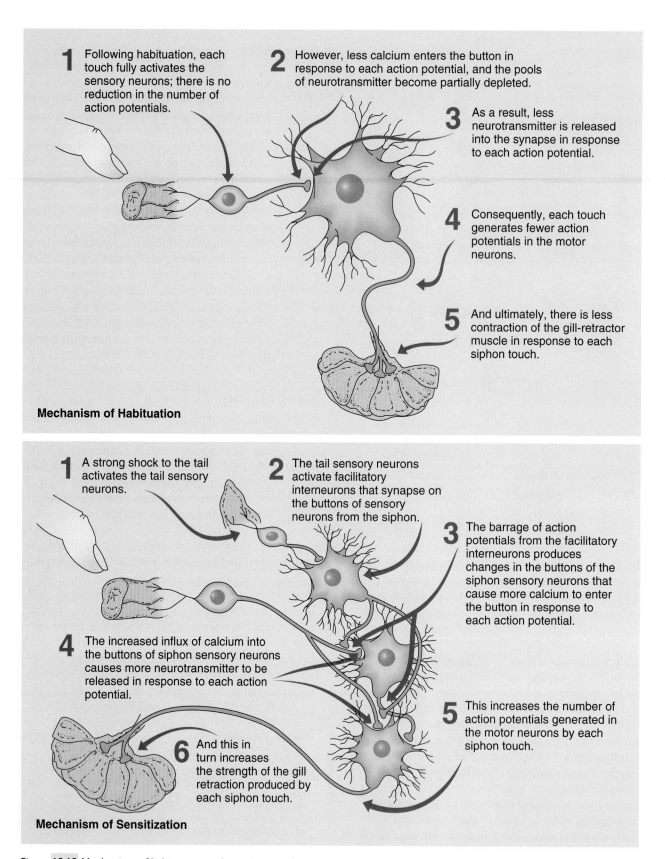

1 Following habituation, each touch fully activates the sensory neurons; there is no reduction in the number of action potentials.

2 However, less calcium enters the button in response to each action potential, and the pools of neurotransmitter become partially depleted.

3 As a result, less neurotransmitter is released into the synapse in response to each action potential.

4 Consequently, each touch generates fewer action potentials in the motor neurons.

5 And ultimately, there is less contraction of the gill-retractor muscle in response to each siphon touch.

Mechanism of Habituation

1 A strong shock to the tail activates the tail sensory neurons.

2 The tail sensory neurons activate facilitatory interneurons that synapse on the buttons of sensory neurons from the siphon.

3 The barrage of action potentials from the facilitatory interneurons produces changes in the buttons of the siphon sensory neurons that cause more calcium to enter the button in response to each action potential.

4 The increased influx of calcium into the buttons of siphon sensory neurons causes more neurotransmitter to be released in response to each action potential.

5 This increases the number of action potentials generated in the motor neurons by each siphon touch.

6 And this in turn increases the strength of the gill retraction produced by each siphon touch.

Mechanism of Sensitization

Figure 15.12 Mechanisms of habituation and sensitization of the Aplysia gill-withdrawal reflex.

the increase in the intensity of the reflex is not nearly so great if the two stimuli are presented in an unpaired fashion (Carew, Walters, & Kandel, 1981); unpaired presentations produce sensitization but no conditioning. The conditional response is typically retained for several days after 20 conditioning trials.

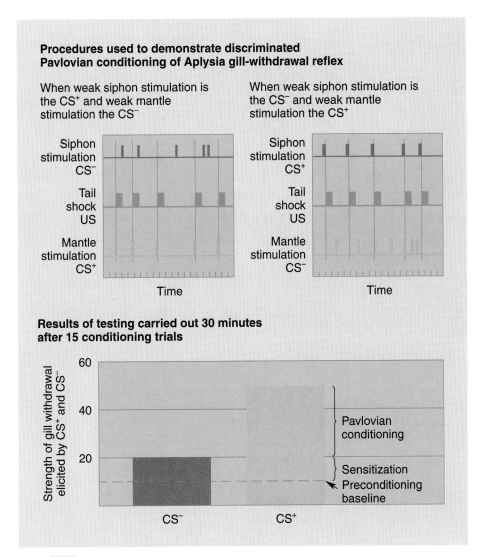

Procedures used to demonstrate discriminated Pavlovian conditioning of Aplysia gill-withdrawal reflex

When weak siphon stimulation is the CS$^+$ and weak mantle stimulation the CS$^-$

When weak siphon stimulation is the CS$^-$ and weak mantle stimulation the CS$^+$

Siphon stimulation CS$^-$

Tail shock US

Mantle stimulation CS$^+$

Time

Siphon stimulation CS$^+$

Tail shock US

Mantle stimulation CS$^-$

Time

Results of testing carried out 30 minutes after 15 conditioning trials

Strength of gill withdrawal elicited by CS$^+$ and CS$^-$

60

40

20

CS$^-$ CS$^+$

Pavlovian conditioning

Sensitization

Preconditioning baseline

Figure 15.13 Discriminated Pavlovian conditioning of the Aplysia gill-withdrawal reflex. (Adapted from Carew, Hawkins, & Kandel, 1983.)

The Aplysia gill-withdrawal reflex is capable of *discriminated Pavlovian conditioning*—Pavlovian conditioning to the conditional stimulus but not to another stimulus (see Figure 15.13). In an experiment by Carew, Hawkins, and Kandel (1983), two conditional stimuli were administered: mild stimulation to the mantle and mild stimulation to the siphon. Both elicited a weak gill-withdrawal response. During training, one of the conditional stimuli (called the CS$^+$) was always paired with the unconditional stimulus, a severe tail shock, whereas the other conditional stimulus (called the CS$^-$) was not. At the end of training, the CS$^+$ elicited a strong withdrawal reaction, whereas the CS$^-$ elicited a weak withdrawal reaction. Optimal conditioning occurred when the CS$^+$ preceded the unconditional stimulus by 0.5 second, and it didn't occur at all when the CS$^+$ followed the unconditional stimulus.

Pavlovian conditioning of the gill-withdrawal reflex can be thought of as a special case of sensitization. In effect, it is a demonstration that tail shock has the great-

est sensitizing effect on reflexes that are active during the shock. This relation between sensitization and Pavlovian conditioning is reflected in one model that has been proposed to explain Pavlovian conditioning (see Figure 15.14 on page 416). Like sensitization, Pavlovian conditioning of the gill-withdrawal reflex is assumed to be mediated by the action of tail-shock-activated interneurons on the sensory neurons that normally activate the reflex. However, unlike sensitization, Pavlovian conditioning depends on the temporal relation between the activation of the interneuron by tail shock and the activation of the sensory neuron by the CS$^+$. The greatest increase in the release of neurotransmitter from the CS$^+$ sensory neurons is produced following trials in which they are in the act of firing at the time when input reaches their presynaptic terminals from the tail-shock-activated interneurons. Accordingly, the synaptic facilitation that mediates this form of Pavlovian conditioning has been termed **activity-dependent enhancement** (see Glanzman, 1995).

The activity-dependent-enhancement model of Pavlovian conditioning of the gill-withdrawal reflex assumes that the key changes occur in the siphon sensory neuron, and there is substantial evidence for this view. However, there is also evidence of conditioning-related changes in the motor neuron, thus suggesting that there may be more than a single mechanism (see Lechner & Byrne, 1998).

■ **ROLE OF SECOND MESSENGERS AND STRUCTURAL CHANGES** Earlier in this text, you learned that there are two modes of synaptic transmission: one mode that produces rapid momentary changes in postsynaptic neurons and one that produces slow, enduring changes in postsynaptic neurons. The first mode acts through *ion-channel linked receptors,* and the second acts through *G-protein linked receptors* and second messengers. *Second messengers* are chemicals that are created inside postsynaptic neurons in response to a neurotransmitter

Activity-dependent enhancement. Enhancement of synaptic transmission whose induction depends on the presynaptic neuron being active during the enhancement-inducing presynaptic input.

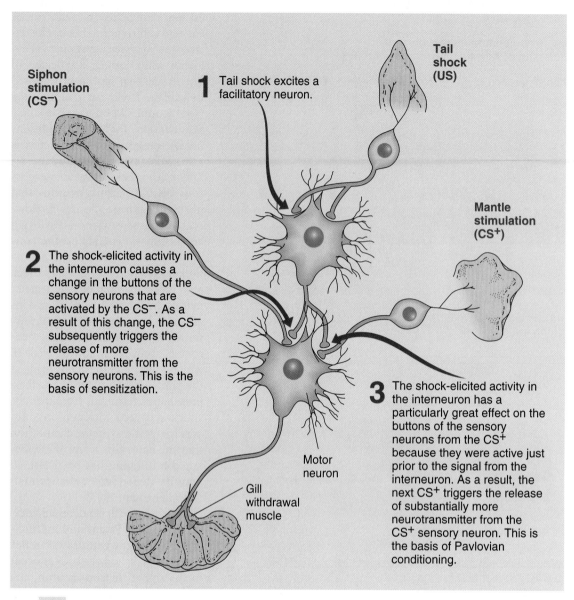

Siphon stimulation (CS⁻)

1 Tail shock excites a facilitatory neuron.

Tail shock (US)

Mantle stimulation (CS⁺)

2 The shock-elicited activity in the interneuron causes a change in the buttons of the sensory neurons that are activated by the CS⁻. As a result of this change, the CS⁻ subsequently triggers the release of more neurotransmitter from the sensory neurons. This is the basis of sensitization.

3 The shock-elicited activity in the interneuron has a particularly great effect on the buttons of the sensory neurons from the CS⁺ because they were active just prior to the signal from the interneuron. As a result, the next CS⁺ triggers the release of substantially more neurotransmitter from the CS⁺ sensory neuron. This is the basis of Pavlovian conditioning.

Motor neuron

Gill withdrawal muscle

Figure 15.14 The activity–dependent–enhancement model, which has been proposed to explain discriminated Pavlovian conditioning of the gill-withdrawal reflex.

(Adapted from Kandel, 1985.)

binding to a G-protein linked receptor. Once created, second messengers can induce lasting changes in neural structure and function in a variety ways—for example, by interacting with the genetic material of the neuron. Not surprisingly, given their ability to produce lasting changes, second messengers have been implicated in memory storage (see Byrne et al., 1993; Krasne & Glanzman, 1995).

Cyclic AMP (cyclic adenosine monophosphate) is an example of one second messenger that has been found to play a role in the sensitization of the Aplysia gill-withdrawal reflex. The tail-shock-produced release of serotonin onto the buttons of the siphon sensory neurons increases the levels of cyclic AMP in the buttons. The cyclic AMP in turn activates another enzyme, *protein kinase A*—protein kinases are a family of cellular

enzymes that regulate protein synthesis. Protein kinase A closes many of the potassium channels in the buttons, which increases the duration of each action potential. This increase in the duration of each action potential increases the influx of calcium and thus the release of neurotransmitter in response to each touch of the siphon. Byrne and Kandel (1996) reported that this mechanism largely accounts for short-term synaptic facilitation, but that long-term facilitation depends on a second cascade of changes mediated by protein kinase C.

Research on learning in the Aplysia gill-withdrawal reflex suggests that although long-term and short-term memories are stored at the same synapses, their mode of storage is different. Long-term storage requires that second messengers stimulate protein synthesis in the neuron cell body, whereas short-term storage does not have this requirement. Accordingly, inhibitors of protein synthesis block the formation of long-term memories but not short-term memories (see Castellucci et al., 1989). This difference suggests that short-term memories can be expressed at individual terminal buttons, whereas long-term memories, because of their reliance on the synthesis of nuclear protein, are expressed throughout the entire neuron (Emptage & Carew, 1993).

The protein synthesis that is involved in the formation of long-term memories can lead to structural changes in the neuron. Bailey and Chen (1983, 1988) observed by *electron microscopy* that long-term habituation and long-term sensitization induce structural changes in the synaptic terminals of the siphon sensory neurons. The sensory neurons of the habituated subjects had fewer active zones of neurotransmitter release, smaller active zones of neurotransmitter release, and fewer synaptic vesicles than those of control subjects. In contrast, the sensory neurons of the sensitized subjects had more active zones of neurotransmitter release, larger active zones of neurotransmitter release, and more synaptic vesicles than those of control subjects. Such structural changes cannot occur rapidly enough to account for short-term retention of sensitization and habituation; thus they are presumed to be mechanisms of long-term storage.

Long-Term Potentiation in Mammalian Hippocampus

Not all attempts to identify the cellular mechanisms of learning and memory have focused on learning in simple nervous systems. A different strategy has been to study neuroplastic phenomena in simple circuits that are components of complex nervous systems. Long-term potentiation is the most widely studied neuroplastic phenomenon of the mammalian nervous system.

Long-term potentiation (LTP) is the enduring facilitation of synaptic transmission that occurs following activation of a synapse by intense high-frequency stimulation of the presynaptic neurons (Bliss & Lømø, 1973). Long-term potentiation has been demonstrated in many neural structures, but it has been most frequently studied at three synapses in the hippocampus: (1) the synapses of perforant path axons from the entorhinal cortex on the granule cells of the hippocampal dentate gyrus, (2) the synapses of dentate granule cell axons on the pyramidal cells of the CA3 subfield, and (3) the synapses of CA3 pyramidal cell axons on the pyramidal cells of the CA1 subfield (see Figure 15.15 on page 418). LTP has been studied in freely moving animals, in anesthetized animals, and in *hippocampal slice preparations*—slices of hippocampal tissue that have been cut from a living brain and maintained alive in a saline bath.

Figure 15.16 on page 419 is a demonstration of LTP in the granule cell layer of the hippocampal dentate gyrus. First, a single low-intensity pulse of current was delivered to the perforant path, and the response was recorded through an extracellular multiple-unit electrode in the granule cell layer of the hippocampal dentate gyrus; the purpose of this initial stimulation was to determine the initial response baseline. Second, 10 seconds of intense high-frequency stimulation was delivered to the perforant path to induce the LTP. Third, the granule cell responses to single pulses of the low-intensity current were measured after various delays to determine their magnitude. It is apparent in Figure 15.16 that the transmission at the granule cell synapse was still potentiated 1 week after the potentiating stimulation.

■ **RELATION OF LTP TO LEARNING AND MEMORY** The reason long-term potentiation is one of the most widely studied neuroscientific phenomena goes back to 1949 and D. O. Hebb. Hebb argued that the facilitation of synaptic transmission is the fundamental mechanism of learning and memory. He believed that each experience triggers a unique pattern of neural activity that reverberates through cerebral circuits, that the reverberating activity is the mode of short-term memory storage, that the reverberating activity causes structural changes in the synapses of the repeatedly activated circuits, and that these structural changes facilitate subsequent transmission across the same synapses. Hebb believed that the facilitation of synaptic transmission is the neural mechanism of long-term memory. Could the synaptic changes that were hypothesized by Hebb to underlie long-term memory be related to the changes that underlie LTP?

LTP has two key properties that Hebb hypothesized to be characteristics of the physiological mechanisms of learning and memory. First, LTP can last for a long time—for many weeks after multiple stimulations. Second, LTP develops only if the firing of the presynaptic neuron is followed by the firing of the postsynaptic neuron; it does not develop when the presynaptic neuron fires and the postsynaptic neuron does not, and it does not develop when the postsynaptic neuron fires and the presynaptic neuron does not (e.g., Kelso, Ganong, & Brown, 1986; Sastry, Goh, & Auyeung, 1986). The **co-occurrence** of firing in presynaptic and postsynaptic cells is now recognized as the critical factor in several forms of neural plasticity, and the assumption that

Cyclic AMP. Cyclic adenosine monophosphate; a second messenger involved in sensitization of the Aplysia gill-withdrawal reflex.

Long-term potentiation (LTP). The enduring facilitation of synaptic transmission that occurs following activation of a synapse by intense high-frequency stim-

ulation of the presynaptic neurons.

Co-occurrence. The assumption that facilitatory changes at the synapses between two neurons occur only if the firing of the presynaptic neuron causes the postsynaptic neuron to fire.

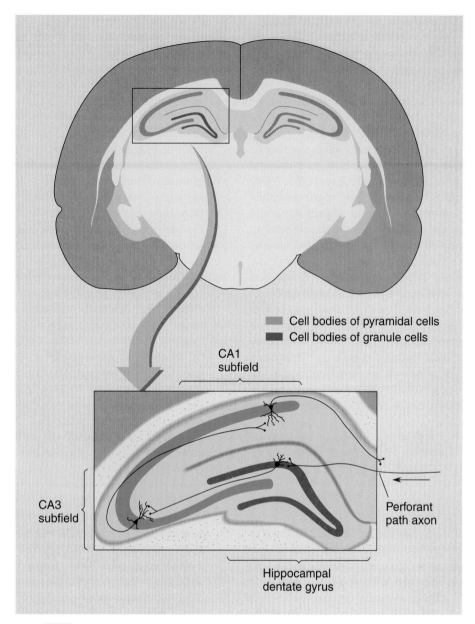

Figure 15.15 A slice of hippocampal tissue that illustrates the three synapses at which LTP is most commonly studied: (1) the dentate granule cell synapse, (2) the CA3 pyramidal cell synapse, and (3) the CA1 pyramidal cell synapse. *CA* stands for *cornu ammonis,* another name for the hippocampus.

co-occurrence is a physiological necessity for learning is often referred to as *Hebb's postulate for learning.*

Additional support for the idea that LTP is related to the neural mechanism of learning and memory has come from several observations: (1) LTP can be elicited by low levels of stimulation that mimic normal neural activity; (2) LTP effects are most prominent in structures that have been implicated in learning and memory—structures such as the hippocampus; (3) behavioral conditioning can produce LTP-like changes in the hippocampus (e.g., Iriki et al., 1989); (4) many drugs that influence learning and memory have parallel effects on LTP (e.g., Brown et al., 1988; Skelton et al.,

1987); (5) the induction of maximal LTP blocks the learning of a Morris water maze until the LTP has subsided (Castro et al., 1989); and (6) mutant mice that display little hippocampal LTP have difficulty learning the Morris water maze (Silva et al., 1992). Still, it is important to keep in mind that all this evidence is indirect and that LTP as induced in the laboratory by electrical stimulation is at best a caricature of the subtle cellular events that underlie learning and memory (see Cain, 1997; Eichenbaum, 1996; Shors & Matzel, 1997).

■INDUCTION OF LTP LTP has been studied most extensively at synapses at which the NMDA receptor is pre-

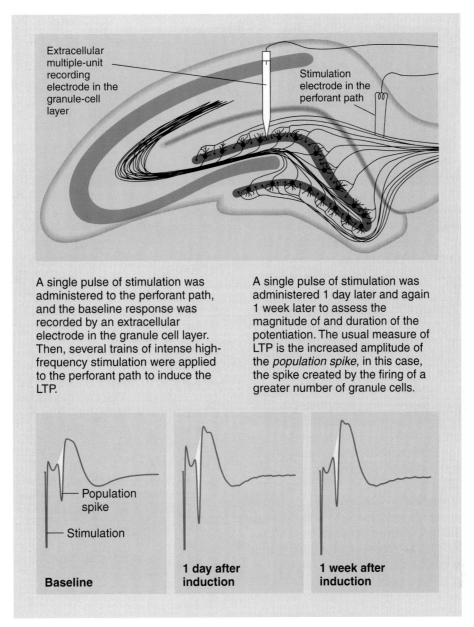

A single pulse of stimulation was administered to the perforant path, and the baseline response was recorded by an extracellular electrode in the granule cell layer. Then, several trains of intense high-frequency stimulation were applied to the perforant path to induce the LTP.

A single pulse of stimulation was administered 1 day later and again 1 week later to assess the magnitude of and duration of the potentiation. The usual measure of LTP is the increased amplitude of the *population spike*, in this case, the spike created by the firing of a greater number of granule cells.

Figure 15.16 Long-term potentiation in the granule cell layer of the hippocampal dentate gyrus. (Traces courtesy of Michael Corcoran, Department of Psychology, University of Saskatchewan.)

dominant. The **NMDA** (N-methyl-D-aspartate) **receptor** is a receptor for **glutamate**—the main excitatory neurotransmitter of the brain. The NMDA receptor has a special property. It does not respond maximally unless two events occur simultaneously: Glutamate must bind to it, and the postsynaptic neuron must already be partially depolarized. This dual requirement stems from the fact that the calcium channels that are linked to NMDA receptors allow only small numbers of calcium ions to enter the neuron unless the neuron is already depolarized when glutamate binds to the receptor; it is the influx of calcium ions that triggers action potentials and the cascade of events in the postsynaptic

neuron that induces LTP. The study of calcium influx has been greatly facilitated by the development of *optical imaging* techniques for visualizing it (see Figure 15.17 on page 420).

An important characteristic of the induction of LTP at glutaminergic synapses stems from the nature of the NMDA receptor and LTP's requirement for co-occurrence. This characteristic is not obvious under the

NMDA receptor. N-methyl-D-aspartate receptor; a glutamate receptor subtype that plays an important role in long-term potentiation at some synapses.

Glutamate. The main excitatory neurotransmitter of the brain.

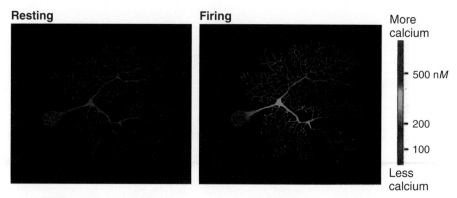

Figure 15.17 The influx of calcium into active neurons. This influx can now be visualized with microfluorometric techniques. Notice that the greatest influx occurs in the axon terminal branches. (Courtesy of Tank et al., 1988.)

usual, but unnatural, experimental condition in which LTP is induced by high-intensity, high-frequency stimulation, which always activates the postsynaptic neurons through massive temporal and spatial summation. However, when a more natural, low-intensity stimulation is applied, the postsynaptic neurons do not fire and thus LTP is not induced—unless the postsynaptic neurons are already partially depolarized so that their calcium channels open wide when glutamate binds to their NMDA receptors.

The requirement for the postsynaptic neurons to be partially depolarized when the glutamate binds to them is an extremely important characteristic of LTP because it permits neural networks to learn associations. Let me explain. If one glutaminergic neuron were to fire by itself and release its glutamate neurotransmitter across a synapse onto the NMDA receptors of a postsynaptic neuron, there would be no potentiation of transmission at that synapse because the postsynaptic cell would not fire. However, if the postsynaptic neuron were partially depolarized by input from other neurons when the presynaptic neuron fires, the binding of the glutamate to the NMDA receptors would open wide the calcium channels, calcium ions would flow into the postsynaptic neuron, and transmission across the synapses between the presynaptic and postsynaptic neuron would be potentiated. Accordingly, the requirement for co-occurrence and the dependence of NMDA receptors on simultaneous binding and partial depolarization means that, under natural conditions, synaptic facilitation records the fact that there has been simultaneous activity in at least two converging inputs to the postsynaptic neuron—such as would be produced by the simultaneous presentation of a conditional stimulus and an unconditional stimulus.

The exact mechanisms by which calcium influx induces LTP are unclear; however, there is substantial evidence that calcium exerts its effects by activating protein kinases in the neural cytoplasm (see Grant & Silva, 1994; Linden & Routtenberg, 1989). A consistent find-

ing has been that protein kinase inhibitors block the induction of LTP (see Bashir & Collingridge, 1992). Figure 15.18 summarizes the induction of NMDA-receptor-mediated LTP.

■ MAINTENANCE AND EXPRESSION OF LTP Although there is a consensus that the chemical events that induce LTP occur in postsynaptic neurons, it is still not clear whether the mechanisms responsible for its maintenance and expression are presynaptic or postsynaptic (Edwards, 1995). Do LTP maintenance and expression depend on changes in presynaptic neurons that increase their release of the neurotransmitter or on changes in postsynaptic neurons that increase their responsiveness to the neurotransmitter? The difficulty in answering this question stems from the current difficulty in measuring neurotransmitter release at individual synapses (Malinow, 1994).

Although it is still not clear whether the maintenance and expression of LTP are presynaptic or postsynaptic, progress in understanding the mechanisms of maintenance and expression has recently been made on three fronts.

1. Whether LTP is presynaptic or postsynaptic, there must be some mechanism to account for the fact that its maintenance and expression are restricted to specific synapses on the postsynaptic neuron (see Malgaroli et al., 1995). Recent research suggests that the specificity of LTP is attributable to **dendritic spines;** calcium that enters one dendritic spine does not diffuse out of it and thus exerts its effects locally (see Harris & Kater, 1994).

2. Whether LTP is presynaptic or postsynaptic, it seems likely that its maintenance over long intervals (weeks) would require the synthesis of neural protein. Recent studies of NMDA-receptor-mediated LTP have shown that blocking protein synthesis immediately after stimulation has no effect on the maintenance of LTP for 1

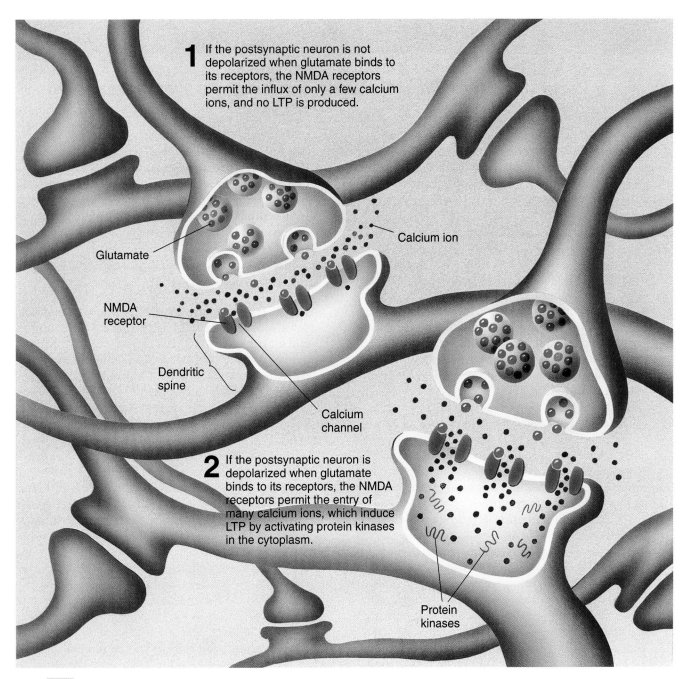

1 If the postsynaptic neuron is not depolarized when glutamate binds to its receptors, the NMDA receptors permit the influx of only a few calcium ions, and no LTP is produced.

Calcium ion

Glutamate

NMDA receptor

Dendritic spine

Calcium channel

2 If the postsynaptic neuron is depolarized when glutamate binds to its receptors, the NMDA receptors permit the entry of many calcium ions, which induce LTP by activating protein kinases in the cytoplasm.

Protein kinases

Figure 15.18 The induction of NMDA-receptor-mediated LTP.

or 2 hours but blocks its maintenance for longer periods (e.g., Nguyen, Abel, & Kandel, 1994).

3. If the maintenance and expression is presynaptic while the induction is postsynaptic, there must be some signal that passes from the postsynaptic neuron back to the presynaptic neuron. Recent evidence suggests that the soluble gas neurotransmitter **nitric oxide** serves this function; it appears to be synthesized in the postsynaptic neuron in response to calcium influx and then diffuses back into the presynaptic button (see Harris, 1995; Larkman & Jack, 1995). Injection of nitric oxide

inhibitors into the postsynaptic neuron during stimulation limits the maintenance of LTP to 1 hour (Haley, Wilcox, & Chapman, 1992) at synapses where nitric oxide has been found near the postsynaptic membrane (Haley et al., 1996).

Dendritic spines. Tiny buds on dendrites, which are the location of many dendritic synapses; their function seems to be to restrict certain synaptic effects in the postsynaptic neuron to the vicinity of the synapse.

Nitric oxide. A soluable gas neurotransmitter that is thought to serve as a retrograde messenger in the production of LTP-maintaining changes in presynaptic neurons.

15.4 Neural Degeneration, Regeneration, and Reorganization

This section of the chapter is about three neuroplastic responses of the nervous system to damage: degeneration, regeneration, and reorganization. Each is discussed in a separate subsection.

Neural Degeneration

After **axotomy**—the severing of an axon or bundle of axons—two kinds of neural degeneration (deterioration) occur: anterograde degeneration and retrograde degeneration. **Anterograde degeneration** is the degeneration of the **distal segment**—the segment of a cut axon between the cut and the synaptic terminals. **Retrograde degeneration** is the degeneration of the **proximal segment**—the segment of a cut axon between the cut and the cell body.

Anterograde degeneration occurs quickly following axotomy, because the cut separates the distal segment of the axon from the cell body, which is the metabolic center of the neuron. The entire distal segment becomes badly swollen within a few hours, and within a few days it breaks into fragments.

The course of retrograde degeneration is different; it progresses gradually back from the cut to the cell body. In about 2 or 3 days, major changes become apparent in the cell bodies of most axotomized neurons. These early cell body changes are either degenerative or regenerative. Early degenerative changes (e.g., a decrease in size) suggest that the neuron will ultimately die. Early regenerative changes (e.g., an increase in size) indicate that the cell body is involved in a massive synthesis of the proteins that will be used to replace the degenerated axon. But early regenerative changes in the cell body do not guarantee the long-term survival of the neuron; if the regenerating axon does not manage to make synaptic contact with an appropriate target, the neuron eventually dies.

Following damage to the central nervous system (CNS), **astroglia** proliferate and absorb most of the resulting debris. This reaction is termed **phagocytosis,** and astroglia are thus referred to as *phagocytes*. In the peripheral nervous system (PNS), phagocytosis of dead neurons is largely carried out by the **Schwann cells** that compose the myelin sheaths of the degenerated axons.

Sometimes, degeneration spreads from damaged neurons to neurons that are linked to them by synapses; this is called *transneuronal degeneration*. In some cases, degeneration spreads from damaged neurons to the neurons on which they synapse; this is called **anterograde transneuronal degeneration.** And in some cases, degeneration spreads from damaged neurons to the neurons that synapse on them; this is called **retrograde transneuronal degeneration.** Neural and transneuronal degeneration are illustrated in Figure 15.19.

Neural Regeneration

Neural regeneration—the regrowth of damaged neurons—does not proceed as successfully in mammals and other higher vertebrates as it does in most invertebrates and lower vertebrates. For some reason, the capacity for accurate axon growth, which is possessed by higher vertebrates during their original development, is lost once they reach maturity. Regeneration is virtually nonexistent in the CNS of adult mammals, and regeneration in their PNS is at best a hit-or-miss affair.

In the mammalian PNS, regrowth from the proximal stump of a damaged nerve begins 2 or 3 days after the damage. What happens next depends on the nature of the injury (see Tonge & Golding, 1993); there are three possibilities. First, if the original Schwann cell myelin sheaths remain intact, the regenerating peripheral axons grow through them to their original targets at a rate of a few millimeters per day. Second, if the peripheral nerve is severed and the cut ends become separated by a few millimeters, regenerating axon tips often grow into incorrect sheaths and are guided by them to incorrect destinations; that is why it is often difficult to regain the coordinated use of a limb affected by nerve damage even if there has been substantial regeneration. And third, if the cut ends of a severed

---

Axotomy. Severing an axon or a bundle of axons.

Anterograde degeneration. The degeneration of the distal segment of a cut axon.

Distal segment. The segment of a cut axon between the cut and the axon terminals.

Retrograde degeneration. Degeneration of the proximal segment of a cut axon.

Proximal segment. The segment of a cut axon between the cut and the cell body.

Astroglia. Glial cells that absorb debris at sites of neural damage in the CNS.

Phagocytosis. The act of absorbing cellular debris or foreign cells in the body.

Schwann cells. The satellite cells that compose the myelin sheaths of PNS axons and promote their regeneration.

Anterograde transneuronal degeneration. The degeneration of a neuron caused by damage to neurons that synapse on it.

Retrograde transneuronal degeneration. The degeneration of a neuron caused by damage to neurons on which it synapses.

Neural regeneration. The regrowth of damaged neurons.

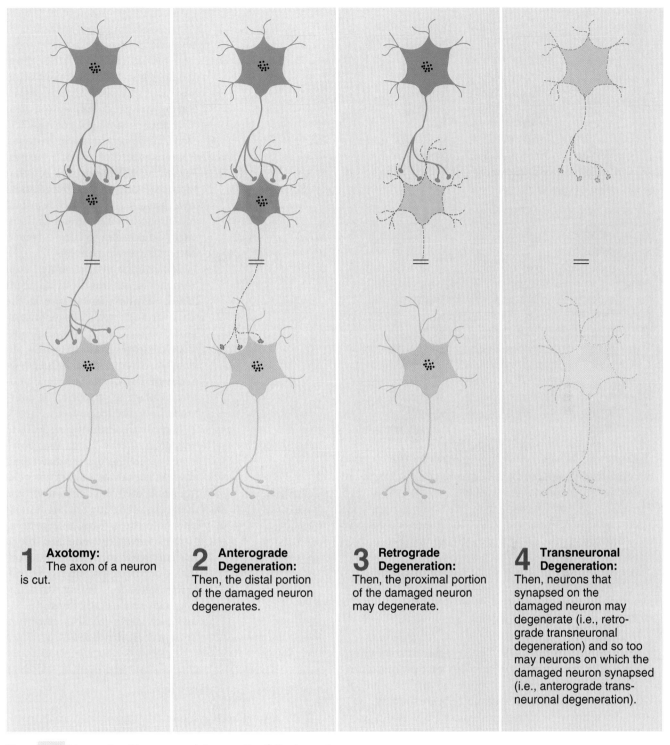

1 **Axotomy:**
The axon of a neuron is cut.

2 **Anterograde Degeneration:**
Then, the distal portion of the damaged neuron degenerates.

3 **Retrograde Degeneration:**
Then, the proximal portion of the damaged neuron may degenerate.

4 **Transneuronal Degeneration:**
Then, neurons that synapsed on the damaged neuron may degenerate (i.e., retrograde transneuronal degeneration) and so too may neurons on which the damaged neuron synapsed (i.e., anterograde transneuronal degeneration).

Figure 15.19 Neuronal and transneuronal degeneration following axotomy.

mammalian peripheral nerve become widely separated or if a lengthy section of the nerve is damaged, there may be no meaningful regeneration at all; regenerating axon tips grow in a tangled mass around the proximal stump, and the neurons ultimately die. These three patterns of mammalian peripheral nerve regeneration are illustrated in Figure 15.20 on page 424.

Why do mammalian PNS neurons regenerate, and mammalian CNS neurons do not? The obvious answer is that PNS neurons are inherently capable of regeneration while CNS neurons are not, but this answer has proved to be incorrect. CNS neurons are capable of regeneration if they are transplanted to the PNS, whereas PNS neurons are not capable of regeneration if they are

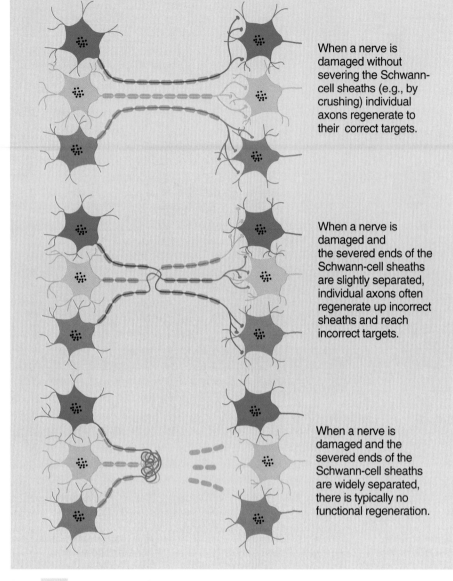

When a nerve is damaged without severing the Schwann-cell sheaths (e.g., by crushing) individual axons regenerate to their correct targets.

When a nerve is damaged and the severed ends of the Schwann-cell sheaths are slightly separated, individual axons often regenerate up incorrect sheaths and reach incorrect targets.

When a nerve is damaged and the severed ends of the Schwann-cell sheaths are widely separated, there is typically no functional regeneration.

Figure 15.20 Three patterns of axonal regeneration in mammalian peripheral nerves.

transplanted to the CNS. Clearly, there is something about the environment of the PNS that promotes regeneration and something about the environment of the CNS that does not. Schwann cells are the key.

Schwann cells, which myelinate PNS axons, promote regeneration in the mammalian PNS by producing both neurotrophic factors and cell-adhesion molecules. The neurotrophic factors released by Schwann cells stimulate the growth of new axons, and the cell-adhesion molecules on the cell membranes of Schwann cells provide the paths along which regenerating PNS axons grow (see Aubert, Ridet, & Gage, 1995; Son, Trachtenberg, & Thompson, 1996). In contrast, **oligo-dendroglia,** which myelinate CNS axons, do not stimulate or guide regeneration; indeed, they release factors that actively block regeneration (Filbin, 1995).

In contrast to neural regeneration in mammals, regeneration in lower vertebrates is extremely accurate. It is accurate in both the central and peripheral nervous systems, and it is accurate even when the regenerating axons do not grow into remnant Schwann cell sheaths. The accuracy of regeneration in lower vertebrates offers hope of a medical breakthrough: If the factors that promote accurate regeneration in lower vertebrates can be identified and applied to the human brain, it might be possible to cure currently untreatable brain injuries.

When an axon degenerates, axon branches grow out from adjacent healthy axons and synapse at the sites vacated by the degenerating axon; this is called **collateral sprouting.** Collateral sprouts may grow out from the axon terminal branches or nodes of Ranvier of adjacent neurons. Collateral sprouting is illustrated in Figure 15.21.

Collateral sprouting appears to be triggered by a factor that is released from the denervated target tissue. One can induce motor neuron axons to grow collateral sprouts merely by rendering the target muscle inactive (e.g., Brown & Ironton, 1977); conversely, one can block the collateral sprouting that normally occurs from motor neuron axons following damage to adjacent axons by electrically stimulating the target muscle (Ironton, Brown, & Holland, 1978).

Neural Reorganization

It has long been assumed that major changes in mammalian nervous systems were limited to the period of early development: Adult mammalian nervous systems were thought to be limited to the subtle functional changes that mediate learning. This assumption was supported by several influential early reports. For example, Hubel, Wiesel, and LeVay (1977) found that monocular deprivation influences the development of ocular dominance columns in visual cortex only if it occurs in the first few weeks of life. However, it is now clear that the mature mammalian brain retains the ability to undergo substantial reorganization.

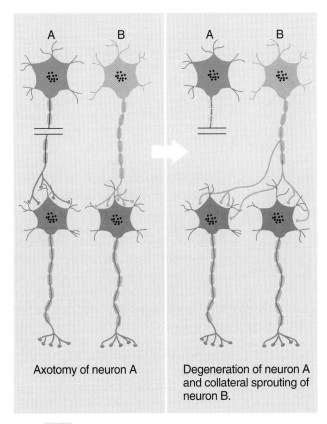

Figure 15.21 Collateral sprouting after neural degeneration.

Axotomy of neuron A	Degeneration of neuron A and collateral sprouting of neuron B.

Most studies of neural reorganization in adulthood have focused on the ability of adult sensory and motor systems to reorganize themselves in response to either damage or experience (see Donoghue, 1995). Primary sensory and primary motor cortexes are ideally suited to the study of neural reorganization because of their topographic layout. Most studies of neural reorganization have been conducted in nonhumans, but several studies have been conducted in humans using functional brain imaging techniques.

■ PRIMARY SENSORY CORTEX The reorganization of adult mammalian primary sensory cortex has been induced in three ways: by damaging sensory pathways, by damaging sensory cortex itself, or by distorting sensory experience. Examples of each of these three methods of inducing reorganization in sensory systems follow.

The following two studies illustrate the reorganization of adult primary sensory cortex that can be induced by damaging sensory pathways. Kaas et al. (1990) assessed the effect of making a small lesion in one retina and removing the other. Several months after the retinal lesions were made, primary visual cortex neurons that originally had receptive fields in the lesioned area of the retina were found to have receptive fields in the area of the retina next to the lesion; remarkably, this change began within minutes of the lesion (Gilbert &

Wiesel, 1992). In a similar study, Pons and colleagues (1991) mapped the primary somatosensory cortex of monkeys whose contralateral arm sensory neurons had been cut 10 years before. They found that the cortical face representation had systematically expanded into the original arm area. This study created a stir because the scale of the reorganization was far greater than had been assumed to be possible: The primary somatosensory cortex face area had expanded its border by well over a centimeter, likely as a consequence of the particularly long (10-year) interval between surgery and testing.

The reorganization of sensory cortex can be induced by damaging the sensory cortex itself. Jenkins and Merzenich (1987) removed the area of monkey somatosensory cortex that responded to touches of the palm of the contralateral hand. Several weeks later, they found that neurons adjacent to the lesion now responded to touches of the palm.

The following two studies illustrate the reorganization of sensory cortex that can be induced by altering sensory experience. Recanzone and colleagues (1992) trained monkeys to detect differences in the frequency of vibrating stimuli by feeling them with their middle finger; and over several weeks, as their performance improved, the area of primary somatosensory cortex receiving input from that finger expanded. Pettet and Gilbert (1992) created the experience of a *scotoma* (a blind spot) without damaging the visual system by occluding a small area of one retina while applying visual stimulation to the remainder of the retina. Remarkably, after only several minutes of this treatment, primary visual cortex neurons with receptive fields in the occluded area had expanded the size of their receptive fields several-fold.

Several functional neuroimaging studies have confirmed in humans the results of experiments on sensory cortex in laboratory animals. For example, Elbert et al. (1995) found that the area of somatosensory cortex receiving input from the fingers of the left hand was greater in a group of experienced musicians who played stringed instruments than in control subjects. Apparently, the amount of representation of different parts of the body in the primary somatosensory cortex depends on use.

■ PRIMARY MOTOR CORTEX Reorganization of the primary motor cortex has been observed following damage to motor neurons. Sanes, Suner, and Donoghue (1990) transected the motor neurons of rats that controlled the muscles of their *vibrissae* (whiskers). A few

Oligodendroglia. The glial cells that myelinate CNS axons.
Collateral sprouting. The growth of axon branches from mature neurons, usually to postsynaptic sites abandoned by adjacent axons that have degenerated.

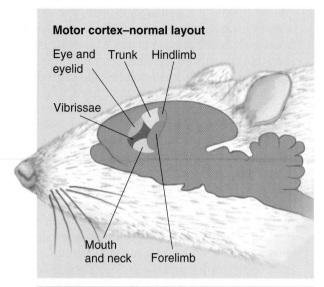

Motor cortex–normal layout

Eye and eyelid · Trunk · Hindlimb

Vibrissae

Mouth and neck · Forelimb

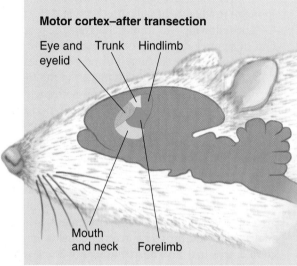

Motor cortex–after transection

Eye and eyelid · Trunk · Hindlimb

Mouth and neck · Forelimb

Figure 15.22 Reorganization of the rat motor cortex following transection of the motor neurons that control movements of the vibrissae. The motor cortex was mapped by brain stimulation before transection and then again a few weeks after.

(Adapted from Sanes, Suner, & Donoghue, 1990.)

weeks later, stimulation of the area of motor cortex that had previously elicited vibrissae movement now activated other muscles of the face. This result is illustrated in Figure 15.22.

Primary motor cortex reorganization has also been induced by experience. Following are two examples. In one experiment (Sanes, Wang, & Donoghue, 1992), regions of adult rat primary motor cortex that did not normally produce forelimb movement when stimulated did so after the forelimb had been kept extended for 30 minutes. In another (Nudo, Jenkins, & Merzenich, 1990), the area of primary motor cortex from which a particular movement could be elicited was expanded in just 1 hour by repeated elicitation of the movement with primary motor cortex stimulation.

Several functional neuroimaging studies have confirmed in humans the results of experiments on the plasticity of motor cortex in laboratory animals. For example, Halligan, Marshall, and Wade (1994) found that a greater area of motor cortex was associated with the shoulder movements of amputated arms than of intact arms. This indicates that the remaining arm muscles of amputated arms acquired a larger area of motor cortex representation.

■ **FUNCTIONS AND MECHANISMS OF NEURAL REORGANIZATION** Recent studies of neural reorganization in adult mammals have made two important points. First, either experience or neural damage can induce reorganizational changes very quickly; and second, if given sufficient time, they can induce reorganizational changes of substantial magnitude (see Gilbert, 1993; Weinberger, 1993). The current view is that the primary function of slow changes is to compensate for nervous system damage, whereas the primary function of the rapid changes is to tune the brain to changes in experience. The ability of the neocortex to rapidly expand or contract its representations of various classes of stimuli and responses depending on its experience could be one of the neural mechanisms of sensorimotor learning.

Two kinds of mechanisms have been proposed to account for the reorganization of neural circuits: a strengthening of existing connections through release from inhibition and the establishment of new connections by collateral sprouting (see O'Leary, Ruff, & Dyck, 1994). Support for the first mechanism comes from two observations: Reorganization often occurs too quickly to be explained by neural growth, and rapid reorganization never involves changes of more than 2 millimeters of cortical surface. Support for the second mechanism comes from the observation that the magnitude of long-term reorganization can be too great to be explained by changes in existing connections. Figure 15.23 illustrates how these two mechanisms might account for the reorganization that occurs after damage to a peripheral somatosensory nerve.

A recent experiment may prove to be an important breakthrough in understanding the mechanisms of cortical plasticity (see Juliano, 1998). Kilgard and Merzenich (1998) found that repeatedly presenting a tone to a rat over several weeks greatly increased the area of auditory cortex activated by the tone; in fact, it led to a reorganization of the entire auditory cortex. The important point is that this reorganization occurred only if the tone was paired with electrical stimulation of the *basal forebrain*—an area of the brain that plays a role in memory and attention.

■ **NEURAL REORGANIZATION AND RECOVERY OF FUNCTION AFTER BRAIN DAMAGE** The role of neural reorganization in recovery of function after brain damage is controversial. It seems likely that neural reorganization

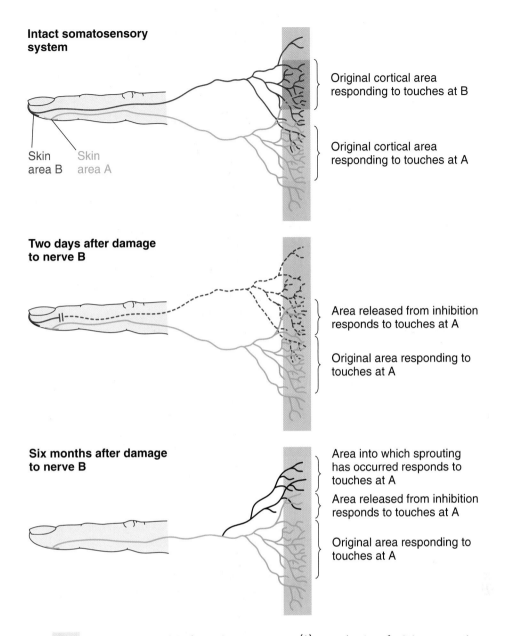

Intact somatosensory system

} Original cortical area responding to touches at B

} Original cortical area responding to touches at A

Skin area B   Skin area A

Two days after damage to nerve B

} Area released from inhibition responds to touches at A

} Original area responding to touches at A

Six months after damage to nerve B

} Area into which sprouting has occurred responds to touches at A

} Area released from inhibition responds to touches at A

} Original area responding to touches at A

Figure 15.23 The two-stage model of neural reorganization: (1) strengthening of existing connections through release from inhibition and (2) establishment of new connections by sprouting.

contributes to recovery from brain damage, but so far the only evidence for this hypothesis has been indirect. In fact, little is known for sure about recovery from brain damage. The problem is that brain damage produces a variety of changes that can easily be confused with bona fide recovery of function. For example, any improvement in the week or two after damage could reflect a decline in *cerebral edema* (brain swelling) rather than a recovery from the neural damage per se, and any gradual improvement in the months after damage could reflect the learning of new cognitive and behavioral strategies rather than the return of lost abilities.

Despite the difficulties in studying recovery of function, three general conclusions have emerged from its investigation (Kolb & Whishaw, 1990). One is that bona fide recovery of function is less common and less complete than most people believe. Think of patient H. M. from the last chapter; his memory has not improved in over 40 years. A second is that small lesions are more likely than large lesions to be associated with recovery. And a third is that the likelihood of recovery is greater in young patients than in old patients (see Figure 15.24). The fact that neural reorganization is also greater when lesions are small (Jenkins & Merzenich, 1987) and subjects young (Gall, McWilliams, & Lynch, 1980) supports the hypothesis that neural reorganization plays a significant role in recovery of function.

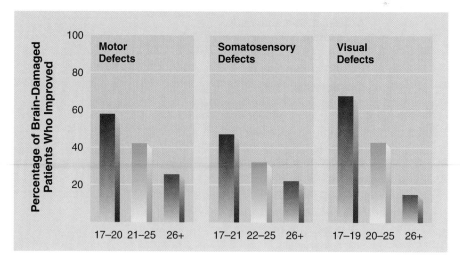

Figure 15.24 Percentage of patients showing improvement following brain injury. Teuber (1975) assessed the deficits of brain-damaged soldiers within a week of their injury and again 20 years later.

15.5 Therapeutic Implications of Neuroplasticity

Brain damage—whether produced by accident, surgery, or neurodegenerative disease—inevitably involves degenerative changes and sometimes regenerative changes, which may or may not be accompanied by recovery. Consequently, research on neuroplasticity is leading to the development of promising new therapeutic approaches. These are the focus of this, the final section of the chapter.

Promotion of Recovery from Brain Damage by Rehabilitative Training

Small strokes typically produce a core of brain damage, which is often followed by a gradually expanding loss of neural function around this core. Nudo et al. (1996) have shown that this spread of dysfunction can be reduced in the motor cortex by rehabilitative training.

Nudo and colleagues produced small *ischemic lesions* (lesions produced by an interruption of blood supply) in the hand area of the motor cortexes of monkeys. Then, 5 days later, a program of hand training and practice was initiated. During the ensuing 3 or 4 weeks, the monkeys plucked hundreds of tiny food pellets from food wells of different size. This practice substantially reduced the expansion of the loss of motor cortex hand representation around the *ischemic infarct* (the area of damage produced by ischemia). The monkeys that received rehabilitative training also showed greater recovery in the use of their affected hand.

It has already been shown that highly stereotyped repetitive training of the same movement is therapeutically superior to conventional physiotherapy (see Freund, 1996). However, much more needs to be known about the mechanisms and parameters of rehabilitative training before therapeutic potential can be fully realized.

Have you forgotten that I am currently recovering from a brain tumor (see the ironic case of Professor P. in Chapter 6)? My motor problems are largely facial in nature (e.g., making facial expressions and speaking). Influenced by Nudo and colleagues, I decided to return to my work environment almost immediately after surgery (3 weeks), knowing full well that I would get little work done but that I would be forced to do a lot of talking and smiling. There is no way of knowing for sure, but I like to think that this strategy has been in part responsible for my good recovery.

Rehabilitative training is already being used to treat spinal injuries (see Muir & Steeves, 1997). In one approach, patients incapable of walking were supported by a harness over a moving treadmill. With most of their weight supported and the treadmill providing appropriate feedback, the patients gradually learned to make walking movements. Then, as they improved, the amount of support was gradually reduced. In one study using this training technique, over 90% of the trained patients eventually became independent walkers, compared with only 50% of those receiving conventional physiotherapy.

Promotion of Recovery from Brain Damage by Genetic Engineering

Numerous neurotrophins have been isolated, and the genes that orchestrate their synthesis have been identified and cloned. Because various neurotrophins have the ability to save damaged cells from death and to promote and direct regeneration, their potential in treating brain damage is great (see Doering, 1996). However, before neurotrophins can be used effectively, a method of initiating their steady release from particular sites in the brain has to be developed. Two solutions are currently emerging: one involving stem cells and one involving viruses.

Stem cells (embryo cells that still have the potential to develop into a variety of different cell types depending on their environment) can be maintained in cell culture and treated so that they become locked in a cycle of continual cell division. This creates a limitless supply of stem cells whose genetic material can be altered so that, when mature, they release a particular neurotrophin. These can then be injected into a patient's brain and become incorporated into the tissue at the injection site (see Martinez-Serrano & Björklund, 1997; Snyder & Macklis, 1996).

The second approach to introducing neurotrophin-synthesizing genes into the brain involves the injection of viruses genetically altered to produce neurotrophins (see Neve & Geller, 1996). These are injected into the target site, where they infect resident cells, depositing their genetic material inside them.

Although the therapeutic benefits of the genetic engineering of neurotrophin synthesis are yet unrealized, the results of several experiments on laboratory animals illustrate its potential. In one of them (Choi-Lundberg et al., 1997), the neurotoxin *6-hydroxydopamine* was injected into the striatum of rats, where it selectively destroyed many of the dopaminergic neurons of control subjects. Injection along with the 6-hydroxydopamine of a virus containing the genetic material for the synthesis of a particular neurotrophin tripled the survival rate of the dopaminergic neurons.

Promotion of Recovery from Brain Damage by Neurotransplantation

Every time I read an article about neurotransplantation, I remember how I was introduced to the concept. Perhaps you were introduced to it in the same way: by television cartoons. In one cartoon, a mad scientist places a wired helmet on the head of one animal subject and another wired helmet on the head of another animal of a different species. Then he throws a massive switch. There are some sparks, a puff of smoke, and voilà, the brains of the two subjects have been switched. This is good for a few laughs, but the highlight of the cartoon comes when the scientist accidentally gets one of the helmets on his own head, and his brain ends up in the body of a chicken and vice versa. It is ironic that this childhood fantasy is now one of the most exciting lines of research in neuroscience.

In 1971, it was first demonstrated that the neural tissue of *donor* rats would survive in the brains of *host* rats (Das & Altman, 1971). Subsequent research established that rejection of CNS transplants is rare if the tissue is taken from fetal donors of the same species.

Raisman, Morris, and Zhou (1987) took advantage of the highly regular arrangement of cell bodies and connections in the hippocampus to show that tiny hippocampal transplants establish reasonably normal connections. Figure 15.25 on page 430 is a photograph of a slice taken through a granule cell implant that was labeled with horseradish peroxidase. Notice that axons from the implant grew to their usual target in the CA3 subfield of the hippocampal pyramidal cell layer.

Efforts to develop neurotransplantation protocols for the treatment of neurological disorders have used two different strategies. First is the transplantation for the purpose of stimulating and directing regeneration; second is the replacement of dysfunctional tissue with new tissue.

■ **PROMOTION OF REGENERATION IN THE CNS BY NEUROTRANSPLANTATION** One approach to the development of therapeutic neurotransplantation circuits has been to transplant sections of myelinated nerves from the PNS into the CNS. The axons die, leaving a bundle of Schwann-cell sheaths, which stimulate regeneration and provide guide shafts for regenerating CNS axons. This technique was developed by Aguayo and his colleagues. In one study (Bray, Vidal-Sanz, & Aguayo, 1987), the optic nerve of a rat was cut, and a segment of myelinated peripheral nerve was grafted between the stump of the optic nerve and the superior colliculus. Four months later, axons of retinal ganglion cells had regenerated along the graft from the eye to the superior colliculus (see Figure 15.26 on page 431).

Cheng, Cao, and Olson (1996) extended the experiments of Aguayo. Theirs was a tremendous accomplishment (Wise, 1996). They demonstrated for the first time that the transplantation of sections of nerve to the CNS could lead to functional recovery—that is, to regeneration that led to the return of behavioral function. First, they rendered rats *paraplegic* (paralyzed in the posterior portion of their bodies). Then, in some of the rats, they transplanted sections of peripheral nerve across the transection, from white matter on the anterior side to gray matter on the posterior side. CNS neurons regenerated through the implanted Schwann-cell sheaths; and

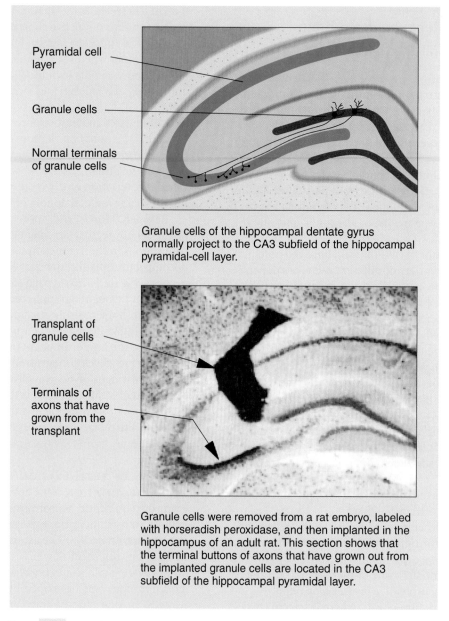

Pyramidal cell layer

Granule cells

Normal terminals of granule cells

Granule cells of the hippocampal dentate gyrus normally project to the CA3 subfield of the hippocampal pyramidal-cell layer.

Transplant of granule cells

Terminals of axons that have grown from the transplant

Granule cells were removed from a rat embryo, labeled with horseradish peroxidase, and then implanted in the hippocampus of an adult rat. This section shows that the terminal buttons of axons that have grown out from the implanted granule cells are located in the CA3 subfield of the hippocampal pyramidal layer.

Figure 15.25 Axons from a granule cell implant in the rat hippocampus. These axons grew out to their normal targets: the pyramidal cells of the CA3 hippocampal subfield.

with the regeneration, the rats regained use of their hindquarters. A similar finding was subsequently reported by Li, Field, and Raisman (1997).

■ NEUROTRANSPLANTATION OF REPLACEMENT PARTS IN THE BRAIN The second experimental approach to the treatment of CNS damage by transplantation has been to replace damaged tissue with healthy donor tissue. Most noteworthy have been efforts to treat Parkinson's disease by transplanting dopamine-releasing cells in the striatum of the host (see Brüstle & McKay, 1996)— the symptoms of Parkinson's disease (e.g., rigidity, tremor at rest, and lack of spontaneous movement) result from the degeneration of the dopamine-releasing

neurons that project from the substantia nigra to the striatum.

Bilateral transplantation of fetal substantia nigra cells has proved successful in alleviating parkinsonian symptoms induced in monkeys by intramuscular injections of MPTP (Bankiewicz et al., 1990; Sladek et al., 1987). (You may recall that MPTP was discovered when a group of drug addicts developed Parkinson's disease after they self-administered a synthetic opiate that contained the MPTP toxin.) Fetal substantia nigra transplants survived in the MPTP-treated monkeys; they innervated adjacent striatal tissue; they released dopamine; and, most importantly, they alleviated the severe poverty of movement, tremor, and rigidity pro-

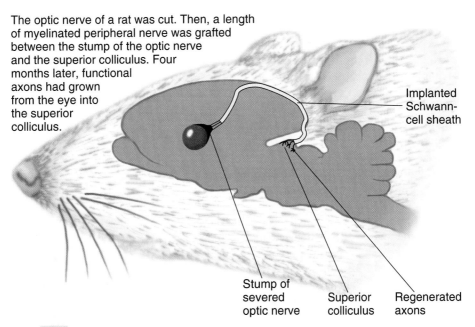

The optic nerve of a rat was cut. Then, a length of myelinated peripheral nerve was grafted between the stump of the optic nerve and the superior colliculus. Four months later, functional axons had grown from the eye into the superior colliculus.

Implanted Schwann-cell sheath

Stump of severed optic nerve

Superior colliculus

Regenerated axons

Figure 15.26 *The stimulation and guidance of axonal regeneration from the eye to the superior colliculus by an implanted Schwann-cell sheath.* (Adapted from Bray, Vidal-Sanz, & Aguayo, 1987.)

duced by the MPTP. The fact that the degree of improvement observed in each monkey was related to the degree to which dopaminergic axons from the graft invaded the striatum suggested that the innervation of the striatum by the implant was the critical factor in their improvement.

Soon after the promising effects of neurotransplants on laboratory animals were reported, neurotransplantation was offered as a treatment for Parkinson's disease at major research hospitals. The evaluations have been promising. The fetal substantia nigra implants have survived, and they have released dopamine into the host striatum (see Sawle & Myers, 1993). More importantly, many of the patients have improved: They have become more active, and their rigidity has declined, particularly on the side contralateral to the transplant.

Autotransplantation—transplanting tissue from one part of a patient's body to another site in the same patient—circumvents the practical and ethical problems of obtaining donor tissue for transplantation. Parkinson's disease has been treated by autotransplanting extracts of the adrenal medulla into the donor's own striatum. (Adrenal medulla extracts release small amounts of dopamine.) A positive early report stimulated considerable interest in this treatment (Madrazo et al., 1987). However, subsequent studies have found the clinical benefits of adrenal medulla autotransplants to be modest (e.g., Goetz et al., 1989), and it has been largely abandoned as an experimental therapy.

In Chapter 4, you were introduced to the roller-coaster case of Roberto Garcia d'Orta—the Lizard.

D'Orta, who suffered from Parkinson's disease, initially responded to L-DOPA therapy; but after 3 years of therapy, his condition worsened. Then he responded to treatment with a dopamine agonist, but again the improvement was only temporary. D'Orta was in a desperate state when he heard about adrenal medulla autotransplantation, and he demanded this treatment from his doctor. When his doctor refused, on the ground that the effectiveness of autotransplantation was still in doubt, d'Orta found himself another doctor—a neurosurgeon who was not nearly so cautious:

> Roberto flew to Juarez. The neurosurgeon there greeted him with open arms. As long as Roberto could afford the cost, he'd be happy to do an adrenal implant on him. . . .
>
> Were there any dangers?
>
> The neurosurgeon seemed insulted by the question. If Señor d'Orta didn't trust him, he could go elsewhere. . . .
>
> Roberto underwent the procedure.
>
> He flew back home two weeks later. He was no better. He was told that it took time for the cells to grow and make the needed chemicals. . . .
>
> Then I received an unexpected call from Roberto's wife. Roberto was dead. . . .
>
> He'd died of a stroke. . . . Had the stroke been a complication of his surgery? It was more than a mere possibility. (Klawans, 1990, pp. 63–64)

Autotransplantation. Transplanting tissue from one part of a patient's body to another site in the same patient.

CONCLUSION

Neuroplasticity in its various manifestations was the subject of this chapter. This chapter described the neural changes that occur during the development of the nervous system (15.1); the effects of experience on neural development (15.2); the neural bases of learning and memory in simple neural systems (15.3); the neural degeneration, regeneration, and reorganization that occur in adult mammals (15.4); and the therapeutic procedures that are being developed from these lines of research (15.5).

The final section of this chapter on neurotransplantation began with the image of a cartoon scientist running about clucking like a chicken, and the chapter ends on a similar, but less frivolous, note. It ends with the incredible experiment of Balaban, Teillet, and LeDouarin (1988). They removed from the neural tubes of chicken fetuses the segment that would have normally developed into the mesencephalon and diencephalon, and they replaced it with tissue from the corresponding segment of Japanese quail neural tubes. A few days after the chicks had hatched, Balaban and his colleagues performed a spectrographic analysis of the chicks' crowing sounds. All of the chicks made abnormal crowing sounds, and most of them made sounds unmistakably like those of Japanese quail. Transplantation of other segments of the neural tube did not have this effect. With this experiment, the cross-species transfer of behavior by neurotransplantation has left the realm of childhood fantasy. The possibilities of this procedure boggle the imagination.

After the furor died down, the rooster moved to New York and became a regular on the talkshow circuit. Dr. Cain quit his job and wandered out West, where he was arrested for making lewd comments to chickens.

FOOD FOR THOUGHT

1. Neurotransplants are now being used in the treatment of Parkinson's disease. Suggest some other potential clinical applications of this procedure.

2. Do you think it will ever be possible to transplant memories? How might this be done? Design an experiment to demonstrate memory transplantation.

3. How has this chapter changed your concept of the brain?

KEY TERMS

Activity-dependent enhancement (p. 415)
Aggregation (p. 404)
Anterograde degeneration (p. 422)
Anterograde transneuronal degeneration (p. 422)
Aplysia (p. 412)
Apoptosis (p. 408)
Astroglia (p. 422)
Autotransplantation (p. 431)
Axotomy (p. 422)

Blueprint hypothesis (p. 406)
Cell-adhesion molecules (CAMs) (p. 404)
Chemoaffinity hypothesis (p. 405)
Collateral sprouting (p. 424)
Co-occurrence (p. 417)
Cyclic AMP (p. 416)
Dendritic spines (p. 420)
Distal segment (p. 422)
Fasciculation (p. 406)
Glutamate (p. 419)

Growth cone (p. 405)
Habituation (p. 412)
Induction (p. 403)
Learning (p. 412)
Long-term potentiation (LTP) (p. 417)
Memory (p. 412)
Mesoderm layer (p. 403)
Migration (p. 403)
Necrosis (p. 408)
Nerve growth factor (NGF) (p. 408)

Neural crest (p. 404)
Neural plate (p. 402)
Neural proliferation (p. 403)
Neural regeneration (p. 422)
Neural tube (p. 403)
Neurotrophins (p. 408)
Nitric oxide (p. 421)
NMDA receptor (p. 419)
Nonassociative learning (p. 412)
Oligodendroglia (p. 424)
Optic tectum (p. 405)

ADDITIONAL READING

The following review articles provide up-to-date readable introductions to various aspects of neuroplasticity:

Brüstle, O., & McKay, R. D. G. (1996). Neuronal progenitors as tools for cell replacement in the nervous system. *Current Opinion in Neurobiology, 6,* 689–695.

Cain, D. P. (1997). LTP, NMDA, genes and learning. *Current Opinion in Neurobiology, 7,* 235–242.

Glanzman, D. L. (1995). The cellular basis of classical conditioning in *Aplysia californica*—It's less simple than you think. *Trends in Neurosciences, 18,* 30–36.

Herrup, K., & Silver, J. (1994). Cortical development and topographic maps: Patterns of cell dispersion in developing cerebral cortex. *Current Opinion in Neurobiology, 4,* 108–111.

Krasne, F. B., & Glanzman, D. L. (1995). What we can learn from invertebrate learning. *Annual Review of Psychology, 46,* 585–624.

Lechner, H. A., & Byrne, J. H. (1998). New perspectives on classical conditioning: A synthesis of Hebbian and non-Hebbian mechanisms. *Neuron, 20,* 355–358.

O'Leary, D. D. M., Ruff, N. L., & Dyck, R. H. (1994). Development, critical period plasticity, and adult reorganizations of mammalian somatosensory systems. *Current Opinion in Neurobiology, 4,* 535–544.

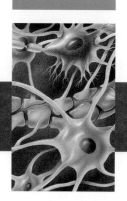

16

Lateralization, Language, and the Split Brain

ith the exception of a few midline orifices, we have two of almost everything—one on the left and one on the right. Even the brain, which most people view as the unitary indivisible basis of self, reflects this general principle of bilateral duplication. In its upper reaches, the brain comprises two structures, the left and right cerebral hemispheres, which are entirely separate except for the **cerebral commissures** connecting them. The fundamental duality of the human forebrain and the location of the cerebral commissures are illustrated in Figure 16.1.

Although the left and right hemispheres are similar in appearance, there are major differences between them in function. This chapter is about these differences, a topic commonly referred to as **lateralization of function.** The study of **split-brain patients**—patients whose left and right hemispheres have been separated by **commissurotomy**—is a major focus of discussion.

Another focus of discussion is the cortical localization of language abilities in the left hemisphere; language abilities are the most highly lateralized of all cognitive abilities.

You will learn in this chapter that your left and right hemispheres have different abilities, and you will learn that they have the capacity to function independently—to have different thoughts, memories, and emotions. Accordingly, this chapter will challenge the concept you have of yourself as a unitary being. I hope you both enjoy it.

Cerebral commissures. Tracts that connect the left and right cerebral hemispheres.
Lateralization of function. The unequal representation of a particular psychological func-

tion in the two hemispheres of the brain.
Split-brain patients. Commissurotomized patients.
Commissurotomy. Severing of the cerebral commissures.

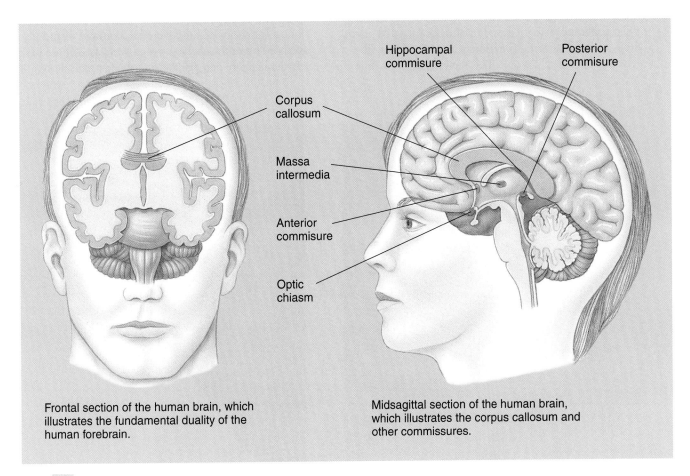

Hippocampal commisure

Posterior commisure

Corpus callosum

Massa intermedia

Anterior commisure

Optic chiasm

Frontal section of the human brain, which illustrates the fundamental duality of the human forebrain.

Midsagittal section of the human brain, which illustrates the corpus callosum and other commissures.

Figure 16.1 The cerebral hemispheres and cerebral commissures.

16.1 Lateralization of Function: Methods and Basic Findings

In 1836, Dax, an unknown country doctor, presented a short report at a medical society meeting in France. It was his first and only scientific presentation. Dax was struck by the fact that of the 40 or so brain-damaged patients with speech problems whom he had seen during his career, not a single one had damage restricted to the right hemisphere. His report aroused little interest, and Dax died the following year unaware that he had anticipated one of today's most important areas of neuropsychological research.

Aphasia, Apraxia, and Left-Hemisphere Damage

One reason Dax's paper had little impact was that most of his contemporaries believed that the brain acted as a whole and that specific functions could not be attributed to particular parts of it. This view began to change

25 years later, when Paul Broca reported his postmortem examination of two aphasic patients. **Aphasia** is a brain-damage-produced deficit in the ability to produce or comprehend language.

Both of Broca's patients had a left-hemisphere lesion that involved an area in the frontal cortex just in front of the face area of the primary motor cortex. Broca at first did not realize that there was a relation between aphasia and the side of the brain damage; he had not heard of Dax's report. However, by 1864, Broca had performed postmortem examinations on seven more aphasic patients, and he was struck by the fact that, like his first two, they all had damage to the *inferior prefrontal cortex* of the left hemisphere—which by then had become known as **Broca's area** (see Figure 16.2).

In the early 1900s, another example of lateralization of function was discovered. Liepmann found that **apraxia,** like aphasia, is almost always associated with left-hemisphere damage, despite the fact that its symp-

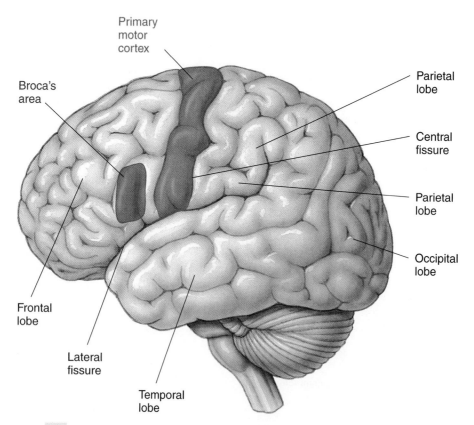

Figure 16.2 The location of Broca's area. It is located in the inferior left prefrontal cortex, just anterior to the face area of the left primary motor cortex.

toms are *bilateral* (involving both sides of the body). Apraxic patients have difficulty performing movements when asked to perform them out of context, even though they often have no difficulty performing the same movements when they are not thinking about it.

The combined impact of the evidence that the left hemisphere plays a special role in both language and voluntary movement led to the concept of *cerebral dominance*. According to this concept, one hemisphere—usually the left—assumes the dominant role in the control of all complex behavioral and cognitive processes and the other plays only a minor role. This concept led to the practice of referring to the left hemisphere as the **dominant hemisphere** and the right hemisphere as the **minor hemisphere.**

Tests of Language Lateralization

Early research on the lateralization of language abilities compared the effects of left-hemisphere and right-hemisphere lesions. However, other techniques were subsequently developed expressly for measuring language lateralization; the sodium amytal test and the dichotic listening test are two of the most widely used. Functional brain imaging, although not expressly designed for the purpose of studying language lateralization, has also proven useful for this purpose.

■ **SODIUM AMYTAL TEST** The **sodium amytal test** of language lateralization (Wada, 1949) is often given to patients prior to neurosurgery. The neurosurgeon uses the results of the test to plan the surgery; every effort is made to avoid damaging areas of the cortex that are likely to be involved in language. The sodium amytal test involves the injection of a small amount of sodium amytal into the carotid artery on one side of the neck. The injection anesthetizes the hemisphere on that side for a few minutes, thus allowing the capacities of the other hemisphere to be assessed. During the test, the patient is asked to recite well-known series (e.g., letters of the alphabet, days of the week, months of the year) and to name pictures of common objects. Then, an injection is administered to the other side, and the test is repeated. When the hemisphere that is dominant for speech, usually the left hemisphere, is anesthetized, the patient is rendered completely mute for a minute or two; then once the ability to talk returns, there are errors of serial order and naming. In contrast, when the minor speech hemisphere, usually the right, is anesthetized, mutism often does not occur at all, and errors are few.

■ **DICHOTIC LISTENING TEST** Unlike the sodium amytal test, the **dichotic listening test** is noninvasive; thus it can be administered to healthy subjects. In the standard dichotic listening test (Kimura, 1961), three pairs of spoken digits are presented through earphones; the digits of each pair are presented simultaneously, one to each ear. For example, a subject might hear the sequence 3, 9, 2 through one ear and at the same time 1, 6, 4 through the other. The subject is then asked to report all of the digits. Kimura found that most people report more of the digits presented to the right ear than to the left, which is indicative of left-hemisphere dominance for language. In contrast, Kimura found that all the patients who had been identified by the sodium amytal test as right-hemisphere dominant for language performed better with the left ear than the right.

Why does the superior ear on the dichotic listening test indicate the dominance of the contralateral hemisphere? Kimura argued that although the sounds from each ear are projected to both hemispheres, the contralateral connections are stronger and take precedence when two different sounds are simultaneously competing for access to the same cortical auditory centers.

■ **FUNCTIONAL BRAIN IMAGING AND LANGUAGE LATERALIZATION** Recently, lateralization of function has been studied using functional brain-imaging techniques. While the subject engages in some language-related activity, such as reading, the activity of the brain is monitored by positron emission tomography (PET) or functional magnetic resonance imaging (fMRI). On language tests, functional brain-imaging techniques typically reveal greater activity in the language areas of the left hemisphere than in the right hemisphere (e.g., Belin et al., 1998).

Speech Laterality and Handedness

Two early large-scale lesion studies clarified the relation between the lateralization of speech and handedness. One study was of military personnel who suffered brain damage in World War II (Russell & Espir, 1961), and the other was of neurological patients who underwent unilateral excisions for the treatment of neurological disorders (Penfield & Roberts, 1959). In both studies, approximately 60% of **dextrals** (right-handers) with

---

Aphasia. A disturbance in the ability to use or comprehend language.

Broca's area. The area of the inferior prefrontal cortex of the left hemisphere hypothesized by Broca to be the center of speech production.

Apraxia. A disorder in which patients have great difficulty performing movements when asked to do so out of context but can readily perform them spontanously in natural situations.

Dominant hemisphere. A term used in the past to refer to the left hemisphere, based on the incorrect assumption that the left hemisphere is dominant in all complex activities.

Minor hemisphere. A term used in the past to refer to the right hemisphere, based on the incorrect assumption that the left hemisphere is dominant in all complex activities.

Sodium amytal test. A test of language lateralization in which each hemisphere is anesthetized with sodium amytal so that the speech abilities of the other hemisphere can be assessed.

Dichotic listening test. A test of language lateralization in which two sequences of three spoken digits are presented simultaneously to each ear and the subject is asked to report all of the digits heard.

Dextrals. Right-handers.

left-hemisphere lesions and 2% of those with right-hemisphere lesions were diagnosed as aphasic; the comparable figures for **sinestrals** (left-handers) were about 30% and 24%, respectively. These results indicate that the left hemisphere is dominant for language-related abilities in almost all dextrals and in the majority of sinestrals; they also indicate that sinestrals are more variable than dextrals with respect to language lateralization.

Results of the sodium amytal test have confirmed the relation between handedness and language lateralization that was first observed in early lesion studies. For example, Milner (1974) found that almost all right-handed patients without early left-hemisphere damage were left-hemisphere dominant for speech (92%), that most left-handed and ambidextrous patients without early left-hemisphere damage were left-hemisphere dominant for speech (69%), and that early left-hemisphere damage decreased left-hemisphere dominance for speech in left-handed and ambidextrous patients (30%). In interpreting these results, it is important to remember that sodium amytal tests are administered only to people who are experiencing brain dysfunction, that early brain damage can cause the lateralization of speech to shift to the other hemisphere (see Maratsos & Matheny, 1994), and that many more people are left-hemisphere dominant to start with. Considered together, these points suggest that Milner's findings likely underestimate the proportion of left-hemisphere dominant individuals among healthy members of the general population.

Sex Differences in Brain Lateralization

Interest in the possibility that the brains of females and males differ in their degree of lateralization was stimulated by McGlone's (1977, 1980) studies of unilateral stroke victims. McGlone found that male victims of unilateral strokes were three times more likely to suffer from aphasia than female victims. She found that male victims of left-hemisphere strokes had deficits on the Wechsler Adult Intelligence Scale (WAIS) verbal subtests, whereas male victims of right-hemisphere strokes had deficits on the WAIS performance subtests. And she found that female victims of unilateral strokes had the same deficits on the WAIS regardless of the side of the stroke. On the basis of these three findings, McGlone concluded that the brains of males are more lateralized than the brains of females.

McGlone's hypothesis of a sex difference in brain lateralization has been widely embraced, and it has been used to explain almost every imaginable behavioral difference between the sexes. Be that as it may, others have failed to confirm McGlone's findings. Indeed, Inglis and Lawson (1982) reviewed 16 studies of unilateral brain lesions and concluded that there was no evidence that left-hemisphere lesions differentially affect the performance of females and males on verbal tests. Also, Hier and Kaplan (1980) and De Renzi (1980) found the incidence of aphasia to be only slightly greater in males than in females.

It is important to recognize that ostensible differences between females and males in brain laterality could merely reflect differences in the strategies that they use to solve problems. For example, if females tend to use both verbal and nonverbal strategies in the solution of particular problems that are solved by males entirely by nonverbal means, the disruptive effects of unilateral lesions on the performance of these problems would appear less lateralized in females—even if there were no sex differences in lateralization.

16.2 The Split Brain

In the early 1950s, the **corpus callosum**—the largest cerebral commissure—constituted a paradox of major proportions. Its size, an estimated 200 million axons, and its central position, right between the two cerebral hemispheres, implied that it performed an extremely important function; yet research in the 1930s and 1940s seemed to suggest that it did nothing at all. The corpus callosum had been cut in monkeys and in several other laboratory species, but the animals seemed no different after the surgery than they had been before. Similarly, human patients who were born without a corpus callosum seemed perfectly normal. In the early 1950s, Roger Sperry and his colleagues were attracted by this paradox.

Groundbreaking Experiment of Myers and Sperry

The solution to the puzzle of the corpus callosum was provided in 1953 by an experiment on cats by Myers and Sperry. The experiment made two astounding theoretical points. First, it showed that one function of the corpus callosum is to transfer learned information from one hemisphere to the other. Second, it showed that when the corpus callosum was cut, each hemisphere could function independently; each split-brain cat appeared to have two brains. If you find the thought of a cat with two brains provocative, you will almost certainly be bowled over by similar observations about split-brain humans. But I am getting ahead of myself. Let's first consider the research on cats.

In their experiment, Myers and Sperry trained cats to perform a simple visual discrimination. On each trial, each cat was confronted by two panels, one with a circle on it and one with a square on it. The relative positions of the circle and square (right or left) were varied randomly from trial to trial, and the cats had to learn which symbol to press in order to get a food reward. Myers and Sperry correctly surmised that the key to split-brain research was to develop procedures for teaching and testing one hemisphere at a time. Figure 16.3 illustrates the method they used to isolate visual-discrimination learning in one hemisphere of the cats. There are two routes by which visual information can cross from one eye to the contralateral hemisphere: via the corpus callosum or via the optic chiasm. Accordingly, in their key experimental group, Myers and Sperry *transected* (cut completely through) both the optic chiasm and the corpus callosum of each cat and put a patch on one eye. This restricted all incoming visual information to the hemisphere ipsilateral to the uncovered eye.

The results of Myers and Sperry's experiment are illustrated in Figure 16.4 on page 440. In the first phase of the study, all cats learned the task with a patch on one eye. The cats in the key experimental group (those with both the optic chiasm and the corpus callosum transected) learned the simple discrimination as rapidly as did unlesioned control cats or control cats with either the corpus callosum or the optic chiasm transected, despite the fact that cutting the optic chiasm produced a **scotoma**—an area of blindness—involving the entire medial half of each retina. This result suggested that one hemisphere working alone can learn simple tasks as rapidly as two hemispheres working together.

More surprising were the results of the second phase of Myers and Sperry's experiment, during which

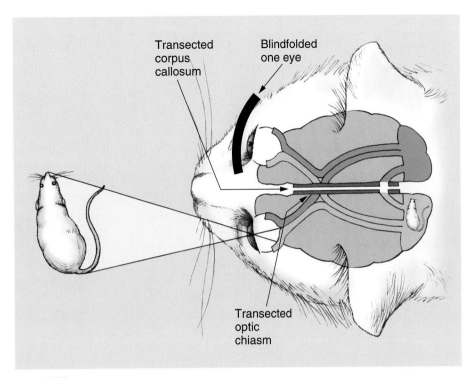

Figure 16.3 Restricting visual information in cats to one hemisphere. To restrict visual information to one hemisphere, Myers and Sperry (1) cut the corpus callosum, (2) cut the optic chiasm, and (3) blindfolded one eye. This restricted the visual information to the hemisphere ipsilateral to the uncovered eye.

the patch was transferred to the other eye. The transfer of the patch had no effect on the performance of the intact control cats or of the control cats with either optic chiasm or the corpus callosum transected; these subjects continued to perform the task with close to 100% accuracy. In contrast, transferring the eye patch had a devastating effect on the performance of the experimental cats. In effect, it blindfolded the hemisphere that had originally learned the task and tested the knowledge of the other hemisphere, which had been blindfolded during initial training. When the patch was transferred, the performance of the experimental cats dropped immediately to baseline (i.e., to 50% correct); and then the cats relearned the task with no savings whatsoever, as if they had never seen it before. Myers and Sperry concluded that each cat brain has the capacity to act as two separate brains and that the function of the corpus callosum is to transmit information between them.

Myers and Sperry's startling conclusions about the fundamental duality of the brain and the information-transfer function of the corpus callosum have been confirmed in a variety of species with a variety of test

Sinestrals. Left-handers.
Corpus callosum. The largest cerebral commissure.

Scotoma. An area of blindness produced by damage to, or disruption of, part of the visual system.

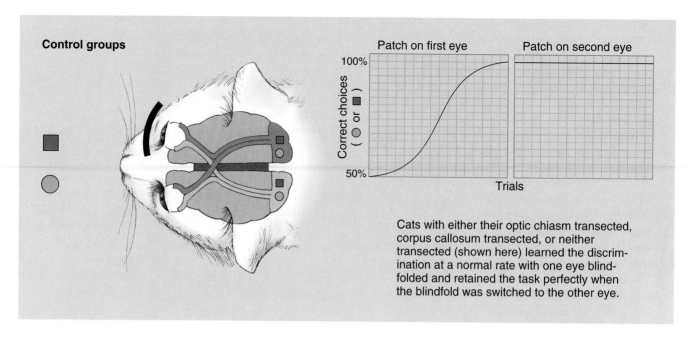

Control groups

Patch on first eye

Patch on second eye

Correct choices (○ or ■)

100%

50%

Trials

Cats with either their optic chiasm transected, corpus callosum transected, or neither transected (shown here) learned the discrimination at a normal rate with one eye blindfolded and retained the task perfectly when the blindfold was switched to the other eye.

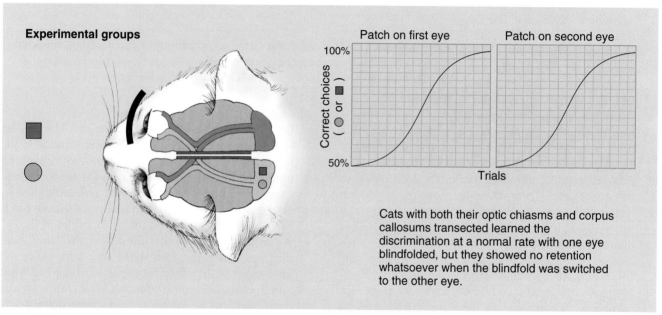

Experimental groups

Patch on first eye

Patch on second eye

Correct choices (○ or ■)

100%

50%

Trials

Cats with both their optic chiasms and corpus callosums transected learned the discrimination at a normal rate with one eye blindfolded, but they showed no retention whatsoever when the blindfold was switched to the other eye.

Figure 16.4 Schematic illustration of Myers and Sperry's (1953) groundbreaking split-brain experiment. There were four groups: (1) the key experimental group with both the optic chiasm and corpus callosum transected, (2) a control group with only the optic chiasm transected, (3) a control group with only the corpus callosum transected, and (4) an unlesioned control group. The performance of the three control groups did not differ, so they are illustrated here as one.

procedures. For example, split-brain monkeys cannot perform tasks requiring fine tactual discriminations (e.g., rough versus smooth) or fine motor responses (e.g., unlocking a puzzle) with one hand if they have learned them with the other—provided that they are not allowed to watch their hands, which would allow the information to enter both hemispheres. There is no transfer of fine tactual and motor information in split-brain monkeys because the somatosensory and motor

fibers involved in fine sensory and motor discriminations are all contralateral.

Commissurotomy in Human Epileptics

In the first half of the 20th century, when the normal function of the corpus callosum was still a mystery, it was known that epileptic discharges often spread from one hemisphere to the other through the corpus callosum. This fact and the fact that cutting the corpus callosum had proven in numerous studies to have no obvious effect on performance outside the contrived conditions of Sperry's laboratory led two neurosurgeons, Vogel and Bogen, to initiate a program of *commissurotomy* for the treatment of severe intractable cases of epilepsy. The rationale underlying this treatment—which typically involves transecting the corpus callosum and leaving the smaller commissures intact—was that the severity of the patient's convulsions might be reduced if the discharges could be limited to the hemisphere of their origin. The therapeutic benefits of commissurotomy turned out to be even greater than anticipated: Despite the fact that commissurotomy is performed in only the most severe cases, many commissurotomized patients do not experience another major convulsion.

The evaluation of the split-brain patient's neuropsychological status was placed in the capable hands of Sperry and his associate Gazzaniga. They began by developing a battery of tests based on the same methodological strategy that had proved so informative in their studies of laboratory animals: delivering information to one hemisphere while keeping it out of the other.

They could not use the same visual-discrimination procedure that had been used in studies of split-brain laboratory animals (i.e., cutting the optic chiasm and blindfolding one eye) because cutting the optic chiasm produces a scotoma. Instead, they employed the procedure that is illustrated in Figure 16.5. Each patient was asked to fixate on the center of a display screen; then, visual stimuli were flashed onto the left or right side of the screen for 0.1 second. The 0.1-second exposure time was long enough for the subjects to perceive the stimuli but short enough to preclude the confounding effects of eye movement. All stimuli thus presented in the left visual field were transmitted to the right visual cortex, and all stimuli thus presented in the right visual field were transmitted to the left visual cortex.

Fine tactual and motor tasks were performed by each hand under a ledge. This procedure was used so that the nonperforming hemisphere, that is, the ipsilateral hemisphere, could not monitor the performance via the visual system.

The results of the tests on split-brain patients have confirmed the research with split-brain laboratory animals in one major respect, but not in another. Like split-brain laboratory animals, human split-brain patients seem to have two independent brains, each with its own stream of consciousness, abilities, memories, and emotions (e.g., Gazzaniga, 1967; Gazzaniga & Sperry, 1967; Sperry, 1964). But unlike the brains of

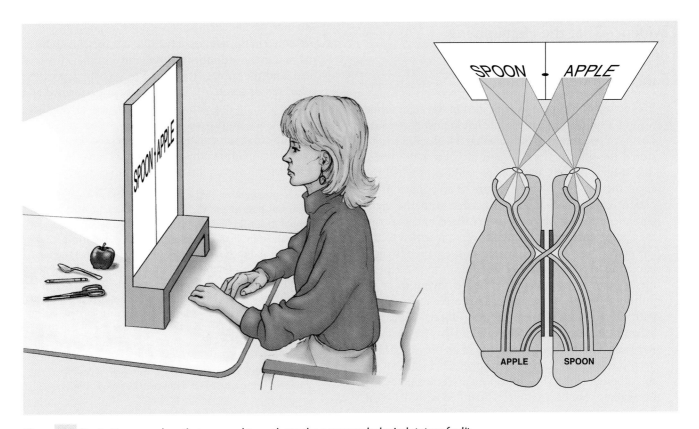

Figure 16.5 The testing procedure that was used to evaluate the neuropsychological status of split-brain patients. Visual input goes from each visual field to the contralateral hemisphere; fine tactual input goes from each hand to the contralateral hemisphere; and each hemisphere controls the fine motor movements of the contralateral hand.

split-brain laboratory animals, the brains of split-brain patients are far from equal in their ability to perform certain tasks. Most notably, the left hemisphere of most split-brain patients is capable of speech, whereas the right hemisphere is not.

Before I recount some of the key results of the tests on split-brain humans, let me give you some advice. Some students become confused by the results of these tests because their tendency to think of the human brain as a single unitary organ is deeply engrained. If you become confused, think of each split-brain patient as two separate subjects: Ms. or Mr. Right Hemisphere, who understands a few simple instructions but cannot speak, who receives sensory information from the left visual field and left hand, and who controls the fine motor responses of the left hand; and Ms. or Mr. Left Hemisphere, who is verbally adept, who receives sensory information from the right visual field and right hand, and who controls the fine motor responses of the right hand. In everyday life, the behavior of split-brain subjects is reasonably normal because their two brains go through life together and acquire much of the same information; however, in the neuropsychological laboratory, major discrepancies in what the two hemispheres learn can be created. As you are about to find out, this situation has some interesting consequences.

Evidence That the Hemispheres of Split-Brain Patients Function Independently

If a picture of an apple were flashed in the right visual field of a split-brain patient, the left hemisphere could do one of two things to indicate that it had received and stored the information. Because it is the hemisphere that speaks, the left hemisphere could simply tell the experimenter that it saw a picture of an apple. Or the patient could reach under the ledge with the right hand, feel the test objects that are there, and pick out the apple. Similarly, if the apple were presented to the left hemisphere by being placed in the patient's right hand, the left hemisphere could indicate to the experimenter that it was an apple either by saying so or by putting the apple down and picking out another apple with the right hand from the test objects under the ledge. If, however, the nonspeaking right hemisphere were asked to indicate the identity of an object that has been presented to the left hemisphere, it could not do so. Although objects that have been presented to the left hemisphere can be accurately identified with the right hand, performance is no better than chance with the left hand.

When test objects are presented to the right hemisphere either visually (in the left visual field) or tactually (in the left hand), the pattern of responses is entirely different. A patient asked to name an object flashed in the left visual field is likely to claim that nothing appeared on the screen. (Remember that it is the left hemisphere who is talking and the right hemisphere who has seen the stimulus.) A patient asked to name an object placed in the left hand is usually aware that something is there, presumably because of the crude tactual information carried by ipsilateral somatosensory fibers, but is unable to say what it is. Amazingly, all the while the patient is claiming (i.e., all the while that the left hemisphere is claiming) the inability to identify a test object presented in the left visual field or left hand, the left hand (i.e., the right hemisphere) can identify the correct object. Imagine how confused the patient must become when, in trial after trial, the left hand can feel an object and then fetch another just like it from a collection of test items under the ledge, while the left hemisphere is vehemently claiming that it does not know the identity of the test object.

Cross-Cuing

Although the two hemispheres of a split-brain subject have no means of direct neural communication, they sometimes communicate with each other indirectly by a method called **cross-cuing.** An example of cross-cuing occurred during a series of tests designed to determine whether the left hemisphere could respond to colors presented in the left visual field. To test this possibility, a red or a green stimulus was presented in the left visual field, and the subject was asked to verbally report the color: red or green. At first, the patient performed at a chance level on this task (50% correct); but after a time, performance improved appreciably, thus suggesting that the color information was somehow being transferred over neural pathways from the right hemisphere to the left. However, this proved not to be the case:

> We soon caught on to the strategy the patient used. If a red light was flashed and the patient by chance guessed red, he would stick with that answer. If the flashed light was red, and the patient by chance guessed green, he would frown, shake his head and then say, "Oh no, I meant red." What was happening was that the right hemisphere saw the red light and heard the left hemisphere make the guess "green." Knowing that the answer was wrong, the right hemisphere precipitated a frown and a shake of the head, which in turn cued in the left hemisphere to the fact that the answer was wrong and that it had better correct itself! . . . The realization that the neurological patient has various strategies at his command emphasizes how difficult it is to obtain a clear neurological description of a human being with brain damage. (Gazzaniga, 1967, p. 27)

Learning Two Things at Once

In most of the classes that I teach, there is a student who fits the following stereotype. He sits—or rather sprawls—near the back of the class; and despite good grades, he tries to create the impression that he is above it all by making sarcastic comments. I am sure you recognize him—and it is almost always a him. Such a student inadvertently triggered an interesting discussion in one of my classes. His comment went something like this: "If getting my brain cut in two could create two separate brains, perhaps I should get it done so that I could study for two different exams at the same time."

The question raised by this comment is a good one. If the two hemispheres of a split-brain patient are capable of total independence, then they should be able to learn two different things at the same time. Can they? Indeed they can. For example, in one test two different visual stimuli appeared simultaneously on the test screen—let's say a pencil in the left visual field and an orange in the right visual field. The subject was asked to simultaneously reach into two bags—one with each hand—and grasp in each hand the object that was on the screen. After grasping the objects, but before withdrawing them, the subject was asked to tell the experimenter what was in the two hands; the subject (i.e., the left hemisphere) replied, "Two oranges." Much to the bewilderment of the verbal left hemisphere, when the hands were withdrawn, there was an orange in the right hand and a pencil in the left. The two hemispheres of the split-brain subject had learned two different things at exactly the same time.

In another test in which two visual stimuli were presented simultaneously—again let's say a pencil to the left visual field and an orange to the right—the subjects were asked to pick up the presented object from an assortment of objects on a table, this time in full view. As the right hand reached out to pick up the orange under the direction of the left hemisphere, the right hemisphere saw what was happening and thought an error was being made (remember that the right hemisphere saw a pencil). On some trials, the right hemisphere dealt with this problem in the only way that it could: The left hand shot out, grabbed the right hand away from the orange, and redirected it to the pencil. This response is called the **helping-hand phenomenon.**

Yet another example of simultaneous learning in the two hemispheres involves the phenomenon of **visual completion.** As you may recall, subjects with scotomas are often unaware of them because their brains have the capacity to fill them in (to complete them) by using information from the surrounding areas of the visual field. In a sense, each hemisphere of a split-brain patient is a subject with a scotoma covering the entire ipsilateral visual field.

The ability of each hemisphere of a split-brain subject to simultaneously and independently engage in completion has been demonstrated in studies using the **chimeric figures test**—named after *Chimera*, a mythical monster composed of the combined parts of differ-

ent animals. Levy, Trevarthen, and Sperry (1972) flashed photographs composed of the fused half faces of two different people onto the center of a screen in front of their split-brain subjects. The subjects were then asked to describe what they saw or to indicate what they saw by pointing to it in a series of photographs of intact faces. Amazingly, each subject (i.e., each left hemisphere) reported seeing a complete, bilaterally symmetrical face, even when asked such leading questions as, "Did you notice anything peculiar about what you just saw?" When the subjects were asked to describe what they saw, they usually described a completed version of the half that had been presented to the right visual field (i.e., the left hemisphere). In contrast, when the subjects were asked to point out the correct face from a series of possibilities, they usually pointed to the completed version of the half that had been presented to the left visual field (i.e., the right hemisphere), regardless of which hand was used for pointing. Pointing is a crude motor response, and thus it can be controlled by either the contralateral or the ipsilateral hemisphere. Clearly, each hemisphere of a split-brain patient is capable of visual completion, and each can see a different face in exactly the same place at exactly the same time.

The Z Lens

Once it was firmly established that the two hemispheres of each split-brain patient can function independently, it became clear that the study of split-brain patients provided a unique opportunity to compare the abilities of left and right hemispheres. However, early studies of the lateralization of function in split-brain patients were limited by the fact that visual stimuli requiring more than 0.1 second to perceive could not be studied using the conventional method for restricting visual input to one hemisphere. This methodological barrier was eliminated by Zaidel in 1975. Zaidel developed a lens, called the **Z lens,** that limits visual input to one hemisphere of split-brain patients while they scan complex visual material such as the pages of a book. As Figure 16.6 on page 444 illustrates, the Z lens is a contact lens that is opaque on one side. Because it moves with the eye, it permits visual input to

---

Cross-cuing. Nonneural communication between hemispheres that have been separated by commissurotomy.

Helping-hand phenomenon. The redirection of one hand of a split-brain patient by the other hand.

Visual completion. The completion or filling in of a scotoma by the brain.

Chimeric figures test. The test of visual completion in split-brain subjects that uses pictures composed of the left and right halves of two different faces.

Z lens. A contact lens that is opaque on one side and thus allows visual input to enter only one hemisphere of a split-brain subject, irrespective of eye movement.

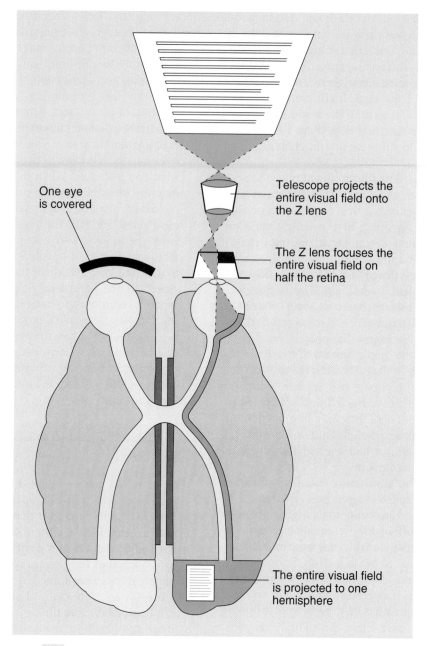

One eye
is covered

Telescope projects the
entire visual field onto
the Z lens

The Z lens focuses the
entire visual field on
half the retina

The entire visual field
is projected to one
hemisphere

Figure 16.6 The Z lens, which was developed by Zaidel to study functional asymmetry in split-brain patients. It is a contact lens that is opaque on one side, so that visual input reaches only one hemisphere.

enter only one hemisphere, irrespective of eye movement. Zaidel used the Z lens to compare the ability of the left and right hemispheres of split-brain patients to perform various tests.

The usefulness of the Z lens is not restricted to purely visual tests. For example, here is how it has been used to compare the ability of the left and right hemispheres to comprehend speech. Because each ear projects to both hemispheres, it is not possible to present spoken words to only one hemisphere. Thus, to assess the ability of a hemisphere to comprehend spoken words

or sentences, Zaidel presented them to both ears, and then he asked the subject to pick the correct answer or to perform the correct response under the direction of visual input to only that hemisphere. For example, to test the ability of the right hemisphere to understand oral commands, the subjects were given an oral instruction (such as, "put the green square under the red circle"), and then the right hemisphere's ability to comprehend the direction was tested by allowing only the right hemisphere to observe the colored tokens while the task was being completed.

Differences between the Left and Right Hemispheres

So far in this chapter, you have learned about the discovery of lateralization of function, about some of the methods used to study it, about the left-hemisphere dominance in the control of language and fine movement, and about split brains. This section takes a more systematic look at some of the differences that have been discovered between the left and right cerebral hemispheres. Because the verbal and motor abilities of the left hemisphere are readily apparent, most recent research on the lateralization of function has focused on uncovering the abilities of the right hemisphere.

Table 16.1 Abilities that Display Cerebral Lateralization of Function

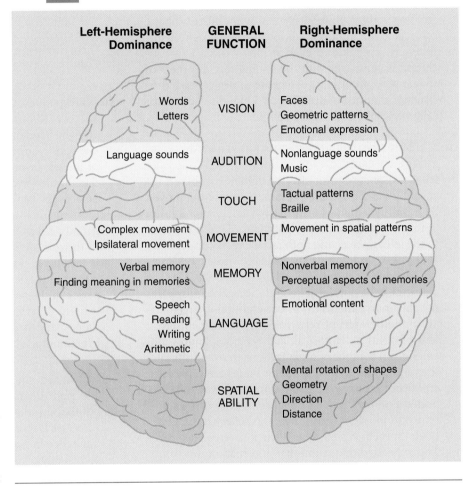

Left-Hemisphere Dominance	GENERAL FUNCTION	Right-Hemisphere Dominance
Words Letters	VISION	Faces Geometric patterns Emotional expression
Language sounds	AUDITION	Nonlanguage sounds Music
	TOUCH	Tactual patterns Braille
Complex movement Ipsilateral movement	MOVEMENT	Movement in spatial patterns
Verbal memory Finding meaning in memories	MEMORY	Nonverbal memory Perceptual aspects of memories
Speech Reading Writing Arithmetic	LANGUAGE	Emotional content
	SPATIAL ABILITY	Mental rotation of shapes Geometry Direction Distance

Some Examples of Lateralization of Function

Table 16.1 lists some of the abilities that have been shown to be lateralized. They appear in two columns: those that are controlled more by the left hemisphere and those that are controlled more by the right hemisphere. The study of lateralization of function has put the archaic notion of left-hemisphere dominance to rest. The right hemisphere has been shown to be functionally superior to the left in several respects. The three best-documented domains of right-hemisphere superiority are spatial ability, emotion, and musical ability. Also, the right hemisphere is superior in performing some memory tasks. Before discussing these four superiorities of the right hemisphere, let's take a look at an unexpected superiority of the left hemisphere.

■ **SUPERIORITY OF THE LEFT HEMISPHERE IN CONTROL-
LING IPSILATERAL MOVEMENT** One interesting and unexpected lateralized function was recently revealed by functional brain imaging studies (see Haaland &

Harrington, 1996). When complex, cognitively driven movements are made by one hand, most of the activity is observed in the *contralateral* hemisphere, as expected. However, some activation is also observed in the *ipsilateral* hemisphere, and these ipsilateral effects are substantially greater in the left hemisphere than in the right (Kim et al., 1993). Consistent with this observation is the fact that left-hemisphere lesions are more likely than right-hemisphere lesions to be associated with ipsilateral motor problems.

■ **SUPERIORITY OF THE RIGHT HEMISPHERE IN SPATIAL
ABILITY** Levy (1969) placed a three-dimensional block of a particular shape in either the right hand or the left

hand of her split-brain subjects. Then, after they had thoroughly *palpated* (tactually investigated) it, she asked them to point to the two-dimensional test stimulus that best represented what the three-dimensional block would look like if it were made of cardboard and unfolded. She found a right-hemisphere superiority on this task, and she found that the two hemispheres seemed to go about the task in different ways. The performance of the left hand and right hemisphere was rapid and silent, whereas the performance of the right hand and left hemisphere was hesitant and often accompanied by a running verbal commentary that was difficult for the subjects to inhibit. Levy concluded that the right hemisphere is superior to the left at spatial tasks. This conclusion is consistent with the finding that disorders of spatial perception (e.g., contralateral neglect and constructional apraxia—see Chapter 9) tend to be specifically associated with right-hemisphere damage.

■ SUPERIORITY OF THE RIGHT HEMISPHERE IN THE EXPERIENCE OF EMOTION
According to the old concept of left-hemisphere dominance, the right hemisphere is incapable of emotion. This presumption has been proven false. Indeed, analysis of the effects of unilateral brain lesions indicates that the right hemisphere is superior to the left at perceiving both facial expression (Bowers et al., 1985) and mood (Tompkins & Mateer, 1985).

Sperry, Zaidel, and Zaidel (1979) used the Z lens to assess the behavioral reactions of the right hemispheres of split-brain patients to various emotion-charged images: photographs of relatives; of pets; of themselves; and of political, historical, and religious figures and emblems. Their behavioral reactions were appropriate, thus indicating that right hemispheres are capable of emotional expression. In addition, there was an unexpected finding: The emotional content of images presented to the right hemisphere was reflected in the patients' speech as well as in their nonverbal behavior. This suggested that emotional information was somehow being passed from the right to the verbal left hemisphere of the split-brain subjects. The ability of emotional reactions, but not visual information, to be passed from the right hemisphere to the left hemisphere created a bizarre situation. A subject's left hemisphere often reacted with the appropriate emotional verbal response to an image that had been presented to the right hemisphere, even though it did not know what the image was.

Consider the following remarkable exchange (paraphrased from Sperry, Zaidel, & Zaidel, 1979, pp. 161–162). The patient's right hemisphere was presented with an array of photos, and the patient was asked if one was familiar. He pointed to the photo of his aunt.

Experimenter: "Is this a neutral, a thumbs-up, or a thumbs-down person?"

Patient: With a smile, he made a thumbs-up sign and said, "This is a happy person."

Experimenter: "Do you know him personally?"

Patient: "Oh, it's not a him, it's a her."

Experimenter: "Is she an entertainment personality or an historical figure?"

Patient: "No, just . . . "

Experimenter: "Someone you know personally?"

Patient: He traced something with his left index finger on the back of his right hand, and then he exclaimed, "My aunt, my Aunt Edie."

Experimenter: "How do you know?"

Patient: "By the E on the back of my hand."

Pause and think about the experiences and thoughts of these two hemispheres as each struggled to perform the task.

■ SUPERIORITY OF THE RIGHT HEMISPHERE IN MUSICAL ABILITY
Kimura (1964) compared the performance of 20 right-handers on the standard, digit version of the dichotic listening test with their performance on a version of the test involving the dichotic presentation of melodies. In the melody version of the test, Kimura simultaneously played two different melodies—one to each ear—and then asked the subjects to identify the two they had just heard from four that were subsequently played to them through both ears. The right ear (i.e., the left hemisphere) was superior in the perception of digits, whereas the left ear (i.e., the right hemisphere) was superior in the perception of melodies. This is consistent with the observation that right temporal lobe lesions are more likely to disrupt music discriminations than are left temporal lobe lesions.

■ HEMISPHERIC DIFFERENCE IN MEMORY
Both the left and right hemispheres have the ability to remember, but they go about the task of remembering in different ways (see Gazzaniga, 1998). Although this hemispheric difference in memory style has been demonstrated in several ways, it is particularly well illustrated by the performance of split-brain patients on the following task. In this task, the left or right hemispheres of split-brain patients are required to guess which of two lights will come on in each trial: top light or bottom light? The top light comes on 80% of the time in random sequence, but the subjects are not given this information. The fact that the top light comes on more than the bottom is quickly discovered by intact control subjects; however, because they try to figure out the nonexistent rule that predicts the exact sequence, they are correct only 68% of the time—even though they could score 80% if they always selected the top light.

The left hemispheres of split-brain subjects perform like intact controls: They attempt to find deeper meaning in their memories and as a result perform poorly on this task. In contrast, right hemispheres, like rats, do not try to interpret their memories and readily learn to maximize their correct responses by always selecting the top light. The left hemisphere attempts to place its experiences in a larger context, while the right hemisphere attends strictly to the perceptual aspects of the stimulus (Metcalfe, Funnell, & Gazzaniga, 1995).

Statistical versus All-or-None Hemispheric Differences

Studies of lateralization of function involve statistical comparisons of large groups of left-hemisphere and right-hemisphere measurements. For most measures, no statistically significant differences are found; lateralization of function is the exception rather than the rule. And when statistically significant hemisphere differences are found, they tend to be slight biases in favor of one hemisphere or the other—not absolute differences (see Brown & Kosslyn, 1993). Be that as it may, the pop psychology media inevitably portray left–right cerebral differences as absolute. As a result, it is widely believed that various abilities reside exclusively in one hemisphere or the other. For example, it is widely believed that the left hemisphere has exclusive control over language and the right hemisphere has exclusive control over emotion and creativity. The most disturbing thing about this misrepresentation is that modern educational programs are sometimes inspired by it.

Language-related abilities provide a particularly good illustration of the fact that lateralization of function is statistical rather than absolute. Language is the most lateralized of all cognitive abilities. Yet, even in this most extreme case, lateralization is far from total; there is substantial language-related activity in the right hemisphere. Following are three illustrations of this point:

1. In the dichotic listening test, the right ear tends to identify more digits than the left ear in subjects who are left-hemisphere dominant for language, but the right-ear advantage is only slight (e.g., 55% to 45%).

2. In brain-imaging studies, language-related activities produce greater overall activation in the left hemisphere than in the right, but there is a substantial activation in the right hemisphere (see Roland, 1993).

3. Z-lens studies of split-brain patients have shown that the right hemisphere can understand many spoken or written words, and it can also understand simple sentences (see Zaidel, 1983, 1987). Although there is considerable variability among split-brain patients in the ability of their right hemispheres to perform tests of language comprehension (Gazzaniga, 1998), the language abilities of many right hemispheres are comparable to those of a preschool child.

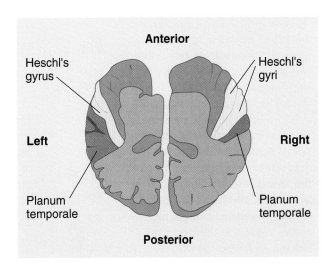

Figure 16.7 Two language areas of the cerebral cortex that display neuroanatomical asymmetry: The planum temporale (Wernicke's area) and Heschl's gyrus (primary auditory cortex).

Neuroanatomical Asymmetries

Casual inspection suggests that the left and right hemispheres are mirror images of one another, but they are not; many anatomical differences between them have been documented. Most effort has been expended trying to document anatomical asymmetries in areas of the cortex that are important for language. Three of these areas are the planum temporale, Heschl's gyrus, and the frontal operculum (see Figure 16.7). The **planum temporale** is the area of temporal lobe cortex that lies in the posterior region of the lateral fissure; it is thought to play a role in the comprehension of language and is often referred to as *Wernicke's area.* **Heschl's gyrus** is located in the lateral fissure just anterior to the planum temporale in the temporal lobe; it is the location of primary auditory cortex. The **frontal operculum** is the area of frontal lobe cortex that lies just in front of the face area of the primary motor cortex; in the left hemisphere, it is the location of Broca's area.

Because the planum temporale, Heschl's gyrus, and the frontal operculum are all involved in language-related activities, one might expect that they would all be larger in the left hemisphere than in the right in most subjects; but they aren't. The left planum temporale does tend to be larger on the left, but only in 65% of human brains (Geschwind & Levitsky, 1968). In contrast, the cortex of Heschl's gyrus tends to be larger on

---

Planum temporale. An area of the temporal lobe that in the left hemisphere roughly corresponds to Wernicke's area.
Heschl's gyrus. The temporal lobe gyrus that *is* the location of primary auditory cortex.

Frontal operculum. The neuroanatomical designation for the area of prefrontal cortex that in the left hemisphere roughly corresponds to Broca's area.

the right, primarily because there are often two Heschl's gyri in the right hemisphere and only one in the left. The laterality of the frontal operculum is less clear. The area of the frontal operculum that is visible on the surface of the brain tends to be larger on the right; but when the cortex buried within sulci of the frontal operculum is considered, there tends to be a greater volume of frontal operculum cortex on the left (Falzi, Perrone, & Vignolo, 1982).

A word of caution is in order. It is tempting to conclude that the tendency for the planum temporale to be larger in the left hemisphere predisposes the left hemisphere for language dominance. Indeed, the finding that the left planum temporale is larger than the right in fetal brains (Wada, Clarke, & Hamm, 1975) is consistent with this view. However, because most studies of neuroanatomical asymmetry are conducted at autopsy, there is no evidence that people with well-developed anatomical asymmetries tend to have more lateralized language functions. In fact, there is a substantial discrepancy between the proportion of the population that has been reported to have a larger left planum temporale (about 65%) and the proportion that is left-hemisphere dominant for language (over 90%).

Schlaug et al. (1995) recently used structural magnetic resonance imaging (MRI) to measure the asymmetry of the planum temporale and relate it to the presence of *perfect pitch* (the ability to identify the pitch of individual musical notes). The planum temporale was found to be more lateralized to the left hemisphere in musicians with perfect pitch than in nonmusicians or in musicians without perfect pitch (see Figure 16.8). Because several other musical abilities have been found to be lateralized in the right hemisphere, the discovery that perfect pitch is associated with a larger left planum temporale suggests that the categories we use to think about lateralization of function—categories such as language, musical ability, and spatial ability—are too crude.

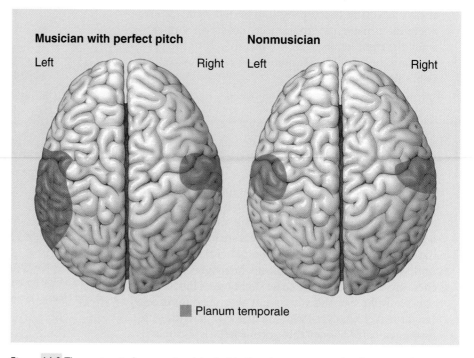

Musician with perfect pitch   **Nonmusician**

Left   Right   Left   Right

Planum temporale

Figure 16.8 The anatomical asymmetry detected in the planum temporale of musicians by magnetic resonance imaging. In most people, the planum temporale is larger in the left hemisphere than in the right; this difference was found to be greater in musicians with perfect pitch than in either musicians without perfect pitch or control subjects.

(Adapted from Schlaug et al., 1995.)

Theories of Cerebral Asymmetry

Several theories have been proposed to explain why cerebral asymmetry evolved. All of them are based on the same general premise: that it is advantageous for areas of the brain that perform similar functions to be located in the same hemisphere. However, each theory of cerebral asymmetry postulates a different distinction between left and right hemisphere function. The following are three prominent theories of cerebral asymmetry.

■**ANALYTIC–SYNTHETIC THEORY** One theory of cerebral asymmetry is the analytic–synthetic theory. The *analytic–synthetic theory of cerebral asymmetry* holds that there are two basic modes of thinking, an analytic mode and a synthetic mode, which have become segregated during the course of evolution in the left and right hemispheres, respectively. According to this theory,

> . . . the left hemisphere operates in a more logical, analytical, computerlike fashion, analyzing stimulus information input sequentially and abstracting the relevant details, to which it attaches verbal labels; the right hemisphere is primarily a synthesizer, more concerned with the overall stimulus configuration, and organizes and processes information in terms of gestalts, or wholes. (Harris, 1978, p. 463)

Although the analytic–synthetic theory has been the darling of pop psychology, its vagueness is a problem. Because it is not possible to specify the degree to which any task requires either analytic or synthetic processing, it has been difficult to subject the analytic–synthetic theory to empirical tests.

■**MOTOR THEORY** A second theory of cerebral asymmetry is the motor theory (see Kimura, 1979). According to the *motor theory of cerebral asymmetry,* the left hemisphere is specialized not for the control of speech per se but for the control of fine movements, of which speech is only one category. Support for this theory comes from reports that lesions that produce aphasia also produce other motor deficits. For example, Kimura (1987) found a correlation between the disruption of language abilities by lesions and their disruption of voluntary nonspeech oral movements; Kimura and Watson (1989) found that left frontal lesions produced deficits in the ability to make both individual speech sounds and individual facial movements, whereas left temporal and parietal lesions produced deficits in the ability to make sequences of speech sounds and sequences of facial movements; and Wolff et al. (1990) found that subjects with reading disabilities also have difficulty performing a finger-tapping test.

■ **LINGUISTIC THEORY** A third theory of cerebral asymmetry is the linguistic theory. The *linguistic theory of cerebral asymmetry* posits that the primary role of the left hemisphere is language—in contrast to the analytic–synthetic and motor theories that view language as a secondary specialization residing in the left hemisphere because of its primary specialization for synthetic thought and skilled motor activity, respectively.

The linguistic theory of cerebral asymmetry is based to a large degree on the study of deaf people who use American Sign Language (a sign language with a structure similar to spoken language) and then suffer unilateral brain damage. W. L. was such a case (Corina et al., 1992). W. L. experienced a specific loss in his ability to use or understand American Sign Language after suffering a major left-hemisphere stroke that damaged parts of his frontal, temporal, and parietal lobes. The fact that he could produce and understand complex pantomime gestures suggested that his sign-language aphasia was not the result of motor or sensory deficits, and the fact that he showed no deficits on a battery of cognitive tests suggested that it was not the result of general cognitive deficits. The fact that left-hemisphere damage disrupts the use of American Sign Language as well as the use of conventional language argues that the fundamental specialization of the left hemisphere is language.

Evolution of Cerebral Lateralization

Cerebral lateralization is often assumed to be an exclusive feature of the hominid brain. One theory of the evolution of cerebral asymmetry is based on the motor theory of cerebral asymmetry: Left-hemisphere dominance for motor control is thought to have evolved in early hominids in response to their use of tools, and then the subsequent evolution of the propensity for vocal language is thought to have evolved in the left hemisphere because of its greater motor dexterity. This theory of the evolution of cerebral lateralization of function is challenged by reports of handedness in nonhuman primates.

The first studies of hand preference in nonhuman primates found that some individual monkeys tended to use one hand more than the other but that there was no general tendency for the right to be preferred over the left. However, more recently, there have been several reports that some nonhuman primates display a right-hand preference for certain tasks (see Hopkins, 1996). For example, Hopkins (1995) found that chimpanzees tended to use their right hands to extract peanut butter from a transparent tube, and Westergaard and Suomi (1996) using the same task found a right-hand preference in rhesus monkeys but not in tufted capuchins. Also, the control of communicative vocalizations has been found to be lateralized in the left hemisphere of some nonhuman primates (see Owren, 1990), and the left hemisphere of macaque monkeys has been shown to play the dominant role in the discrimination of macaque vocalizations (Heffner & Heffner, 1984). The results of these studies suggest that the evolution of cerebral lateralization may have preceded the evolution of hominids.

16.4 Cortical Localization of Language: The Wernicke-Geschwind Model

So far, this chapter has focused on the functional asymmetry of the brain, with an emphasis on the lateralization of language-related functions. At this point, it shifts its focus from language lateralization to language localization. In contrast to language lateralization, which refers to the relative control of language-related functions by the left and right hemispheres, *language localization* refers to the location within the hemispheres of the circuits that participate in language-related activities.

Like most introductions to language localization, the following discussion begins with the **Wernicke-Geschwind model.** Although this model has proved to be inconsistent with the findings of many of the studies that it has spawned, it has been the single most influential theory of language localization. Because most of the research on the localization of language has been conducted and interpreted within the context of this model, reading about the localization of language without a basic understanding of the Wernicke-Geschwind model would be like watching a game of chess without knowing the rules—not a very fulfilling experience.

Historic Antecedents of the Wernicke-Geschwind Model

The history of the localization of language and the history of the lateralization of function began at the same point, with Broca's assertion that a small area in the inferior portion of the left prefrontal cortex (Broca's area) is the center for speech production. Broca hypothesized that programs of articulation are stored within this area and that speech is produced when these programs activate the adjacent area of the precentral gyrus, which controls the muscles of the face and oral cavity. According to Broca, damage restricted to Broca's area should disrupt speech production without producing deficits in language comprehension.

The next major event in the study of the cerebral localization of language occurred in 1874, when Wernicke (pronounced "VER-ni-key") concluded on the basis of 10 clinical cases that there is a language area in the left temporal lobe just posterior to the primary auditory cortex (i.e., in the left planum temporale). This second language area, which Wernicke argued was the cortical area of language comprehension, subsequently became known as **Wernicke's area.**

Wernicke suggested that selective lesions of Broca's area produce a syndrome of aphasia whose symptoms are primarily **expressive**—characterized by normal comprehension of both written and spoken language and by speech that retains its meaningfulness despite being slow, labored, disjointed, and poorly articulated. This hypothetical form of aphasia became known as **Broca's aphasia.** In contrast, Wernicke suggested that selective lesions of Wernicke's area produce a syndrome of aphasia whose deficits are primarily **receptive**—characterized by poor comprehension of both written and spoken language and speech that is meaningless but still retains the superficial structure, rhythm, and intonation of normal speech. This hypothetical form of aphasia became known as **Wernicke's aphasia,** and the normal-sounding but nonsensical speech of Wernicke's aphasia became known as **word salad.**

The following are examples of the kinds of speech that are presumed to be associated with selective damage to Broca's and Wernicke's areas (Geschwind, 1979, p. 183):

Broca's Aphasia: A patient who was asked about a dental appointment replied haltingly and indistinctly: "Yes . . . Monday . . . Dad and Dick . . . Wednesday nine o'clock . . . 10 o'clock . . . doctors . . . and . . . teeth."

Wernicke's Aphasia: A patient who was asked to describe a picture that showed two boys stealing cookies reported smoothly: "Mother is away here working her work to get her better, but when she's looking the two boys looking in the other part. She's working another time."

Wernicke reasoned that damage to the pathway connecting Broca's and Wernicke's areas—the **arcuate fasciculus**—would produce a third type of aphasia, one that he called **conduction aphasia.** He contended that comprehension and spontaneous speech would be intact in patients with damage to the arcuate fasciculus but that there would be difficulty in repeating words that had just been heard.

The left **angular gyrus**—the area of left temporal and parietal cortex just posterior to Wernicke's area—is another cortical area that has been implicated in language. Its role in language was recognized in 1892 by Dejerine on the basis of the postmortem examination of one special patient. The patient suffered from **alexia** (the inability to read) and **agraphia** (the inability to write). What made this case special was that the alexia and agraphia were exceptionally pure: Although the patient could not read or write, he had no difficulty speaking or understanding speech. Dejerine's postmortem examination revealed damage in the pathways connecting the visual cortex with the left angular gyrus. He con-

---

Wernicke-Geschwind model. An influential cortical model of language localization.

Wernicke's area. The area of the left temporal cortex hypothesized by Wernicke to be the center of language comprehension.

Expressive. Pertaining to the generation of language; that is, pertaining to writing or talking.

Broca's aphasia. A hypothetical disorder of speech production with no associated deficits in language comprehension.

Receptive. Pertaining to the comprehension of language.

Wernicke's aphasia. A hypothetical disorder of language comprehension with no associated deficits in speech production.

Word salad. Speech that has the overall sound and flow of fluid speech but is totally incomprehensible.

Arcuate fasciculus. The major neural pathway between Broca's area and Wernicke's area.

Conduction aphasia. Aphasia that is thought to result from damage to the neural pathway between Broca's area and Wernicke's area.

Angular gyrus. The gyrus of the posterior cortex at the boundary between the temporal and parietal lobes, which in the left hemisphere is thought to play a role in reading.

Alexia. A specific inability to read, one that does not result from general visual, motor, or intellectual deficits.

Agraphia. A specific inability to write, one that does not result from general visual, motor, or intellectual deficits.

cluded that the left angular gyrus is responsible for comprehending language-related visual input, which is received directly from the adjacent left visual cortex and indirectly from the right visual cortex via the corpus callosum.

During the era of Broca, Wernicke, and Dejerine, there were many influential neuroscientists who opposed their attempts to localize various language-related abilities to specific neocortical areas (e.g., Freud, Head, and Marie). In fact, these advocates of the holistic approach to brain function gradually gained the upper hand, and interest in the cerebral localization of language waned. However, in 1965, Geschwind revived the old localizationist ideas of Broca, Wernicke, and Dejerine; added some new data and insightful interpretation; and melded the mix into a powerful theory: the Wernicke-Geschwind model.

Wernicke-Geschwind Model

The following are the seven components of the Wernicke-Geschwind model: primary visual cortex, angular gyrus, primary auditory cortex, Wernicke's area, arcuate fasciculus, Broca's area, and primary motor cortex—all in the left hemisphere. They are shown in Figure 16.9.

The following two examples illustrate how the Wernicke-Geschwind model is presumed to work (see Figure 16.10). First, when you are having a conversation, the auditory signals triggered by the speech of the other person are received by your primary auditory cortex and conducted to Wernicke's area, where they are comprehended. If a response is in order, Wernicke's area generates the neural representation of the thought underlying the reply, and it is transmitted to Broca's area via the left arcuate fasciculus. In Broca's area, this signal activates the appropriate program of articulation that drives the appropriate neurons of your primary motor cortex and ultimately your muscles of articulation. Second, when you are reading aloud, the signal received by your primary visual cortex is transmitted to your left angular gyrus, which translates the visual form of the word into its auditory code and transmits it to Wernicke's area for comprehension. Wernicke's area then triggers the

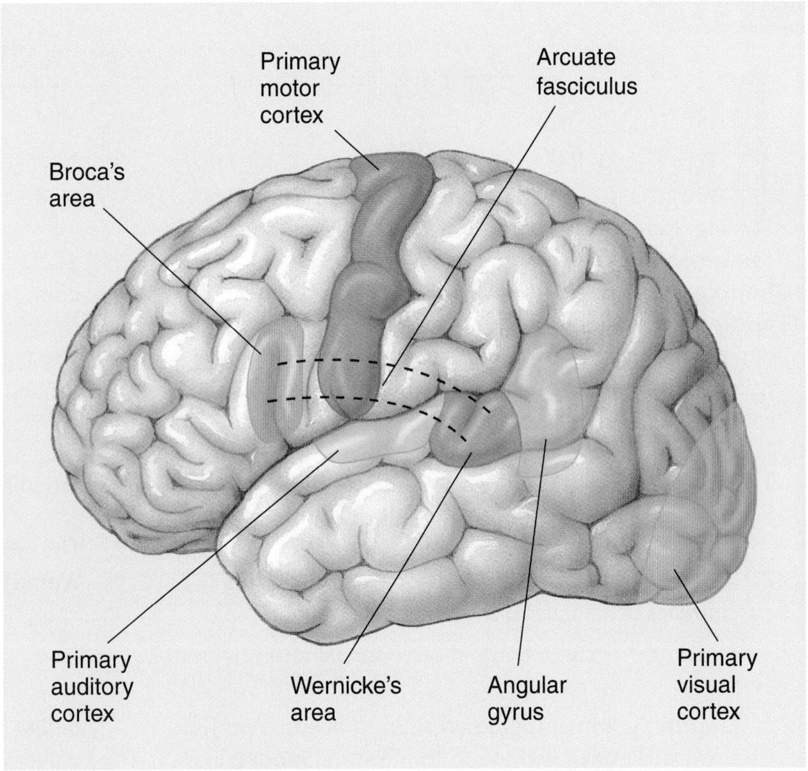

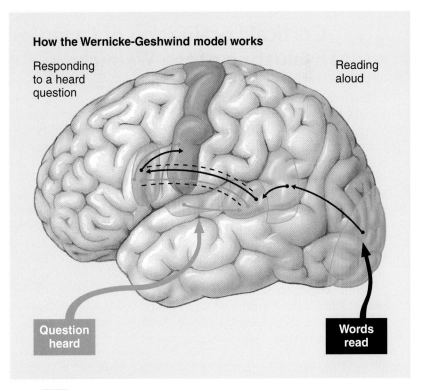

Figure 16.9 The seven components of the Wernicke-Geschwind model.

appropriate responses in your arcuate fasciculus, Broca's area, and motor cortex, respectively, to elicit the appropriate speech sounds.

How the Wernicke-Geshwind model works

Responding to a heard question

Reading aloud

Question heard

Words read

Figure 16.10 How the Wernicke-Geschwind model works: How it responds to a heard question and how it reads aloud.

Before proceeding to the following discussion of the Wernicke-Geschwind model, complete the following exercise to confirm that you understand its fundamentals. The correct answers are provided at the bottom of this page. Review material related to your errors and omissions.

According to the Wernicke-Geschwind model, the following seven areas of the left cerebral cortex play a role in language-related activities:

1. The _____ gyrus translates the visual form of a read word into an auditory code.

2. The _____ cortex controls the muscles of articulation.

3. The _____ cortex perceives the written word.

4. _____ area is the center for language comprehension.

5. The _____ cortex perceives the spoken word.

6. _____ area contains the programs of articulation.

7. The left _____ carries signals from Wernicke's area to Broca's area.

From the foregoing description, it is apparent that the Wernicke-Geschwind model is a **serial model:** Each process that it mediates involves a chain of responses that are triggered in linear sequence, like a single line of falling dominoes. **Parallel models** are those that involve two or more simultaneous routes of activity (e.g., a dual-route model).

16.5 Cortical Localization of Language: Evaluation of the Wernicke-Geschwind Model

Unless you are reading this text from back to front, you should have read the preceding description of the Wernicke-Geschwind model with some degree of skepticism. By this point in the text, you will almost certainly recognize that any model of a complex cognitive process that involves a few localized neocortical centers joined in a serial fashion by a few arrows is sure to have major shortcomings, and you will appreciate that the neocortex is not divided into neat compartments whose cognitive functions conform to vague concepts such as language comprehension, speech motor programs, and conversion of written language to auditory language.

Initial skepticism aside, the ultimate test of a theory's validity is the degree to which its predictions are consistent with the empirical evidence. Before we examine this evidence, three confusing points require clarification.

First, the Wernicke-Geschwind model was initially based on case studies of aphasic patients with strokes, tumors, and penetrating brain injuries. Damage in such cases is almost always diffuse, and it inevitably encroaches on subcortical fibers coursing through the lesion site to other areas of the brain (see Bogen & Bogen, 1976). For example, illustrated in Figure 16.11 is the extent of the cortical damage in one of Broca's two original cases (see Mohr, 1976).

Second, Broca's and Wernicke's aphasias probably do not exist in their pure forms as defined by Wernicke and Geschwind. Aphasia virtually always involves both expressive and receptive symptoms (see Benson, 1985). Accordingly, the terms *Broca's aphasia* and *Wernicke's aphasia* are commonly used to designate aphasic disorders that are largely expressive or receptive, respectively.

Third, Broca's aphasia and Wernicke's aphasia do not necessarily result from damage to Broca's and Wernicke's areas. This is a prediction of the model, not a description of the evidence.

The answers are (1) angular, (2) primary motor, (3) primary visual, (4) Wernicke's, (5) primary auditory, (6) Broca's, and (7) arcuate fasciculus.

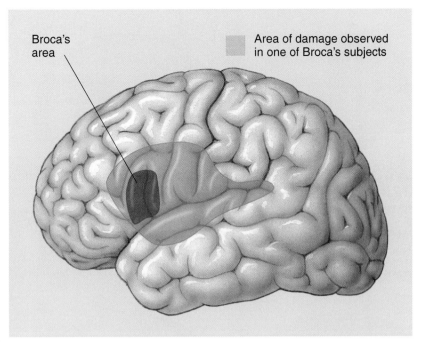

Broca's area

Area of damage observed in one of Broca's subjects

Figure 16.11 The extent of brain damage in one of Broca's two original patients. Like this patient, most aphasic patients have diffuse brain damage. It is thus difficult to determine from their investigation the precise location of particular cortical language areas. (Adapted from Mohr, 1976.)

Effects of Damage to Various Areas of Cortex on Language-Related Abilities

In view of the fact that the Wernicke-Geschwind model grew out of the study of patients with cortical damage, it is appropriate to begin evaluating it by assessing its ability to predict the language-related deficits produced by damage to various parts of the cortex.

■ **SURGICAL REMOVAL OF CORTICAL TISSUE** The study of patients in whom discrete areas of cortex have been surgically removed has proved particularly informative in the study of the cortical localization of language. This is because the location and extent of their lesions can be derived with reasonable accuracy from the surgeon's report.

The study of neurosurgical patients has not confirmed the predictions of the Wernicke-Geschwind model by any stretch of the imagination. See the six cases summarized in Figure 16.12 on page 454.

Surgery that destroys all of Broca's area but little surrounding tissue typically has no lasting effects on speech (Penfield & Roberts, 1959; Rasmussen & Milner, 1975; Zangwill, 1975). Some speech problems have been observed after Broca's excisions, but their temporal course suggests that they were products of postsurgical *edema* (swelling) in the surrounding neural tissue rather than from the *excision* (cutting out) of Broca's area per se: Prior to the use of effective anti-inflammatory drugs,

patients with excisions of Broca's area often regained consciousness with their language abilities fully intact only to have serious language-related problems develop over the next few hours and then subside in the following weeks. Similarly, permanent speech difficulties are not produced by discrete surgical lesions to the arcuate fasciculus, and permanent alexia and agraphia are not produced by surgical lesions restricted to the cortex of the angular gyrus (Rasmussen & Milner, 1975).

The consequences of the surgical removal of Wernicke's area are less well documented; surgeons have been hesitant to remove it in light of Wernicke's dire predictions. Nevertheless, in some cases, a good portion of Wernicke's area has been removed without lasting language-related deficits (e.g., Ojemann, 1979; Penfield & Roberts, 1959).

Supporters of the Wernicke-Geschwind model argue that despite the precision of surgical excision, negative evidence obtained from the study of the effects of brain surgery should be discounted. They argue that the brain pathology that warranted the surgery may have reorganized the control of language by the brain.

■ **ACCIDENTAL OR DISEASE-RELATED BRAIN DAMAGE** Hécaen and Angelergues (1964) rated the articulation, fluency, comprehension, naming ability, ability to repeat spoken sentences, reading, and writing of 214 right-handed patients with small, medium, or large accidental or disease-related lesions to the left hemisphere. The extent and location of the damage in each case was estimated by either postmortem histological examination or visual inspection during subsequent surgery. Figure 16.13 on page 455 summarizes the deficits found by Hécaen and Angelergues in patients with relatively localized damage to one of five different regions of left cerebral cortex.

Hécaen and Angelergues found that small lesions to Broca's area seldom produced lasting language deficits and that those restricted to Wernicke's area sometimes did not. Medium-sized lesions did produce some deficits; but in contrast to the predictions of the Wernicke-Geschwind model, problems of articulation were just as likely to occur following medium-sized parietal or temporal lesions as they were following comparable lesions in the vicinity of Broca's area. All other symptoms that were produced by medium-sized lesions were

---

Serial model. A model that involves a single chain of responses triggered in linear sequence.

Parallel models. Models involving two or more simultaneous routes of activity.

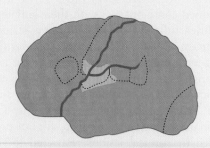

Case J.M. No speech difficulties for 2 days after his surgery, but by Day 3 he was almost totally aphasic; 18 days after his operation he had no difficulty in spontaneous speech, naming, or reading, but his spelling and writing were poor.

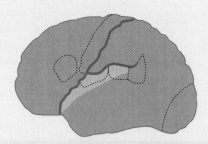

Case H.N. After his operation, he had a slight difficulty in spontaneous speech, but 4 days later he was unable to speak; 23 days after surgery, there were minor deficits in spontaneous speech, naming, and reading aloud, and a marked difficulty in oral calculation.

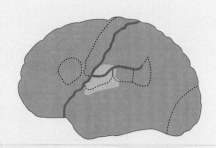

Case J.C. There were no immediate speech problems; 18 hours after his operation he became completely aphasic, but 21 days after surgery, only mild aphasia remained.

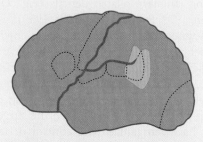

Case P.R. He had no immediate speech difficulties; 2 days after his operation, he had some language-related problems, but they cleared up.

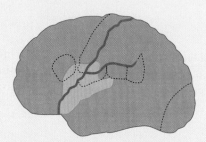

Case D.H. This operation was done in two stages; following completion of the second stage, no speech-related problems were reported.

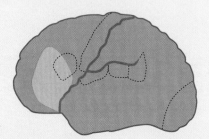

Case A.D. He had no language-related problems after his operation, except for a slight deficit in silent reading and writing.

Figure 16.12 The lack of permanent disruption of language-related abilities after surgical excision of the classic Wernicke–Geschwind language areas.

(Adapted from Penfield & Roberts, 1959.)

more likely to appear following parietal or temporal lesions than following frontal damage.

The only observation from Hécaen and Angelergues's study that is consistent with the Wernicke-Geschwind model came from the analysis of the effects of large lesions (those involving three lobes). Large lesions of the anterior brain were more likely to be associated with articulation problems than were large lesions of the posterior brain. It is noteworthy that none of the 214 subjects displayed specific syndromes of expressive aphasia (Broca's aphasia) or receptive aphasia (Wernicke's aphasia) implied by the Wernicke-Geschwind model.

■ CT AND STRUCTURAL MRI SCANS OF APHASIC PATIENTS
Since the development of *computed tomography (CT)* and structural *magnetic resonance imaging (MRI)*, it has been possible to visualize the brain damage of living

aphasic patients (see Damasio, 1989). In the CT studies by Mazzocchi and Vignolo (1979) and Naeser and colleagues (1981), none of the aphasic patients had cortical damage restricted to Broca's and Wernicke's areas, and all had extensive damage to subcortical white matter. In both studies, large anterior lesions of the left hemisphere were more likely to produce deficits in language expression than were large posterior lesions, and large posterior lesions were more likely to produce deficits in language comprehension than were large anterior lesions. Also, in both studies, **global aphasia**—a severe disruption of all language-related abilities—was associated with very large left-hemisphere lesions that involved both the anterior and posterior cortex and substantial portions of subcortical white matter.

The findings of Damasio's (1989) structural MRI study were similar to those of the aforementioned CT studies, with one important addition. Damasio found a

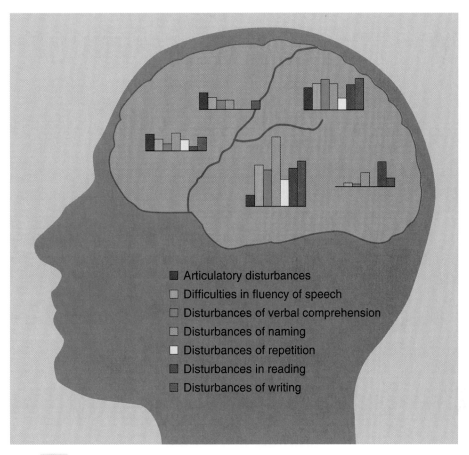

Figure 16.13 The relative effects on language-related abilities of damage to one of five general areas of left-hemisphere cortex.

(Adapted from Hécaen & Angelergues, 1964.)

Articulatory disturbances
Difficulties in fluency of speech
Disturbances of verbal comprehension
Disturbances of naming
Disturbances of repetition
Disturbances in reading
Disturbances of writing

few aphasic patients whose damage was restricted to the medial frontal lobes (to the supplementary motor area and the anterior cingulate cortex), an area not included in the Wernicke-Geschwind model. Similarly, several CT and MRI studies have found cases of aphasia resulting from damage to subcortical structures (see Alexander, 1989)—for example, to the left subcortical white matter, the left basal ganglia, or the left thalamus (e.g., Naeser et al., 1982).

Electrical Stimulation of the Cortex and Localization of Language

The first large-sale electrical brain-stimulation studies of humans were conducted by Penfield and his colleagues in the 1940s at the Montreal Neurological Institute (see Feindel, 1986). One purpose of the studies was to map the language areas of each patient's brain so that tissue involved in language could be avoided during the surgery. The mapping was done by assessing the responses of conscious patients under local anesthetic to stimulation applied to various points on the cortical surface. The description of the effects of

each stimulation were dictated to a stenographer—this was before the days of tape recorders—and then a tiny numbered card was dropped on the stimulation site for subsequent photography.

Figure 16.14 on page 456 illustrates the responses to stimulation of a 37-year-old right-handed epileptic patient. He had started to have seizures about 3 months after receiving a blow to the head; and at the time of his operation, in 1948, he had been suffering from seizures for 6 years, despite efforts to control them with medication. In considering his responses, remember that the cortex just posterior to the central fissure is primary somatosensory cortex and that the cortex just anterior to the central fissure is primary motor cortex.

Because electrical stimulation of the cortex is much more localized than a brain lesion, it has been a useful method of testing predictions of the Wernicke-Geschwind model. Penfield and Roberts (1959) published the first large-scale study of the effects of cortical stimulation on speech. They found that sites at which stimulation blocked or disrupted speech in conscious

Global aphasia. Almost total elimination of all language-related abilities.

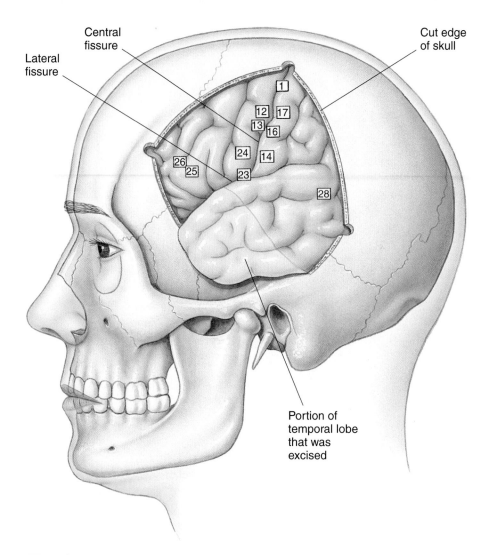

1 Tingling in the right thumb and a slight movement

12 Quivering of the jaw in a sidewise manner

13 Pulling of jaw to right

14 Sensation in the jaw and lower lip

16 Tingling in the right side of tongue

17 Sensation in right upper lip

23 Stimulation, applied while the patient was talking, stopped his speech. After cessation of stimulation, he said that he had been unable to speak despite trying.

24 The patient tried to talk, his mouth moved, but he made no sound.

25 The patient had initial difficulty, but eventually he named a picture of a butterfly.

26 The patient said, "Oh, I know what it is" in response to a picture of a foot. "That is what you put in your shoes." After termination of the stimulation, he said, "foot."

28 The patient became unable to name the pictures as soon as the electrode was placed here. The EEG revealed seizure activity in the temporal lobe. When the seizure discharges stopped, the patient spoke at once. "Now I can talk," he said, and he correctly identified the picture of a butterfly.

Figure 16.14 The responses of the left hemisphere of a 37-year-old epileptic to electrical stimulation. Numbered cards were placed on the brain during surgery to mark the sites where brain stimulation had been applied.

(Adapted from Penfield & Roberts, 1959.)

neurosurgical patients were scattered throughout a large expanse of frontal, temporal, and parietal cortex, rather than being restricted to the Wernicke-Geschwind areas (see Figure 16.15). They also found no tendency for particular kinds of speech disturbances to be elicited from particular areas of the cortex: Sites at which stimulation produced disturbances of pronunciation, confusion of counting, inability to name objects, or mis-

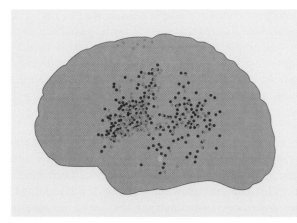

Figure 16.15 The wide distribution of left hemisphere sites where cortical stimulation either blocked speech or disrupted it. (Adapted from Penfield & Roberts, 1959.)

- Sites at which stimulation produced a complete arrest of speech

- Sites at which stimulation disrupted speech but did not block it completely

naming of objects were pretty much intermingled. Right-hemisphere stimulation almost never disrupted speech.

In a more recent series of cortical stimulation studies, Ojemann and his colleagues (see Ojemann, 1983) assessed naming, reading of simple sentences, short-term verbal memory, ability to mimic orofacial movements, and the ability to recognize **phonemes**—individual speech sounds—during cortical stimulation. In contrast to the predictions of the Wernicke-Geschwind model, they found (1) that the areas of the cortex at which stimulation could disrupt language extended far beyond the boundaries of the Wernicke-Geschwind language areas, (2) that all of the specific language abilities were represented at both anterior and posterior sites, and (3) that there were major differences among the subjects in the organization of language abilities.

Because the disruptive effects of stimulation at a particular site were frequently quite specific (i.e., disrupting only a single test), Ojemann suggested that the language cortex might be organized like a mosaic, with the discrete columns of tissue performing a particular function being widely distributed throughout the language area of the cortex.

Mateer and Cameron (1989), in contrast to the findings of Ojemann, found that stimulation of the cortex around the lateral fissure tended to disrupt **phonological analysis** (analysis of the sound of language) more than other aspects of language. They also found that the control of both **grammatical analysis** (analysis of the structure of language) and **semantic analysis** (analysis of the meaning of language) was distributed throughout the other cortical language areas.

Cortical Localization of Language: Evidence from Dyslexia

Approximately 15% of males and 5% of females fail to learn to read and write despite normal or superior intelligence (Shaywitz, 1996). This disorder is termed **dyslexia.** The inability of dyslexic subjects to read aloud has been subjected to intensive investigation, and the findings have implications for theories of cortical localization of language abilities (e.g., Stein & Walsh, 1997). The Wernicke-Geschwind model is a serial model, whereas the model of language that has emerged from the study of dyslexia is a *dual-route parallel model*—a model in which two types of processing of the same input occur simultaneously over two different neural pathways.

■ **DUAL-ROUTE PARALLEL MODEL** According to the dual-route parallel model of reading aloud, reading aloud is simultaneously mediated by a lexical procedure and a nonlexical procedure. The **lexical procedure** is based on specific stored information that we have acquired about the written words in our vocabulary, and the **nonlexical procedure** is based on general rules of pronunciation that allow us to pronounce unfamiliar words or nonwords such as *spleemer* and *twipple*.

Evidence in support of the idea that reading aloud is mediated by parallel lexical and nonlexical pathways comes from cases of dyslexia in which either the lexical or nonlexical procedure is impaired while the other is not (see Hinton, Plaut, & Shallice, 1993). Dyslexics in whom the lexical route appears to be dysfunctional while the nonlexical route remains functional are said to be suffering from **surface dyslexia;** conversely, dyslexics in whom the nonlexical route appears to be

Phonemes. Individual speech sounds.
Phonological analysis. Sound-related analysis of a language.
Grammatical analysis. Analysis of a language in terms of its rules of sentence structure.
Semantic analysis. Meaning-related analysis of a language.
Dyslexia. A specific pathological difficulty in reading, one that does not result from general visual, motor, or intellectual deficits.

Lexical procedure. A procedure for reading aloud that is based on information acquired about the pronunciation of specific written words.
Nonlexical procedure. A procedure for reading aloud that is based on the general rules of pronunciation of a language.
Surface dyslexia. A reading disorder in which the lexical procedure is disrupted while the nonlexical procedure is not.

dysfunctional while the lexical route remains functional are said to be suffering from **deep dyslexia.**

In cases of surface dyslexia, patients have lost their ability to pronounce words based on their specific memories of the words (i.e., they have lost their lexical procedure), but they can still apply rules of pronunciation in their reading (i.e., they can still use their nonlexical procedure). Accordingly, they retain their ability to pronounce words whose pronunciation is consistent with common rules (e.g., *fish, river,* or *glass*) and their ability to pronounce nonwords according to common rules of pronunciation (e.g., *spleemer* or *twipple*); but they have great difficulty pronouncing words that do not follow common rules of pronunciation (e.g., *have, lose,* or *steak*). The errors they make often involve the misapplication of common rules of pronunciation; for example, *have, lose,* and *steak* are typically pronounced as if they rhyme with *cave, hose,* and *beak.*

In cases of deep dyslexia, patients have lost their ability to apply rules of pronunciation in their reading (i.e., they have lost their nonlexical procedure), but they can still pronounce familiar concrete words based on their specific memories of them (i.e., they can still use their lexical procedure). Accordingly, they are completely incapable of pronouncing nonwords and have difficulty pronouncing uncommon words and words whose meaning is abstract. In attempting to pronounce words, patients with deep dyslexia try to react to them by using various lexical strategies, such as responding to the overall look of the word, the meaning of the word, or the derivation of the word. This leads to a characteristic pattern of errors. A patient with deep dyslexia might say "quill" for *quail* (responding to the overall look of the word), "hen" for *chicken* (responding to the meaning of the word), or "wise" for *wisdom* (responding to the derivation of the word).

Coltheart (1980) believes that the mechanisms mediating the nonlexical procedure of reading aloud are lateralized in the left hemisphere. The most striking support for Coltheart's hypothesis has come from the study of a dyslexic patient who had a left **hemispherectomy**—removal of the left cerebral hemisphere—at the age of 14 (Patterson, Vargha-Khadem, & Polkey, 1989). Performing with only her right hemisphere, she was capable of pronouncing familiar concrete words, but she could not pronounce simple nonwords (e.g., *neg*), and her errors indicated that she was reading on the basis of the meaning and appearance of words rather than by translating letters into sounds (e.g., when presented with the word *fruit,* she responded, "Juice . . . it's apples and pears and . . . fruit"). In other words, she suffered from a severe case of deep dyslexia.

■ **DYSLEXIA AND BRAIN ABNORMALITIES** Many differences between the brains of dyslexics and normal readers have been reported (see Farmer & Klein, 1995). These differences include the following: absence of the usual left-larger-than-right asymmetry in the size of the planum temporale, reduced size of the magnocellular neurons of the lateral geniculate nuclei, and reduced size of neurons in the left medial geniculate nucleus.

It has been suggested that the pattern of abnormalities produced in the brains of dyslexics may have been caused in infancy by exposure to a virus or toxic substance and that these brain abnormalities are the basis of the disorder. However, recent studies of neural plasticity suggest that there is another possibility: Perhaps some or all of the brain abnormalities are the result, rather than the cause, of the disorder. In other words, maybe lack of reading experience causes the brains of dyslexics to develop differently than those of normal readers.

Before we leave the topic of dyslexia, I must keep a promise I made to one of my students. I promised him I would tell you about a dyslexic woman he knows who is also an insomniac and an agnostic. According to my student, this dyslexic woman stays awake every night wondering if there really is a doG.

Interim Conclusion

Studies of aphasia following surgical or accidental brain damage, of language difficulties associated with electrical brain stimulation, and of dyslexia all suggest that the Wernicke-Geschwind is seriously flawed. However, our analysis of the Wernicke-Geschwind model does not stop here. The next, and final, section of the chapter focuses on modern functional brain-imaging of language, and this research has much to say about the Wernicke-Geschwind model.

16.6 Cortical Localization of Language: Functional Brain-Imaging Research

Modern functional brain-imaging techniques have revolutionized the study of the localization of language. In the last decade, there have been numerous PET and functional MRI studies of subjects engaging in various language-related activities. Two of the best are Petersen and colleagues' (1989) positron emission tomography study of hearing or seeing single words and Bavelier and colleagues' (1997) functional MRI study of reading sentences.

A PET Study of Hearing or Seeing Single Words

Petersen and colleagues (1989) used PET to measure language-related changes in patterns of cerebral blood flow under two sets of conditions: visual and auditory. Each set comprised four conditions of progressively increasing complexity. In the four visual conditions, the subjects were asked to do the following: (1) to fixate on (stare at) a crosshair on a blank display screen, (2) to fixate on the crosshair while printed nouns were presented on the screen, (3) to fixate on the crosshair while reading aloud the printed nouns, and (4) to fixate on the crosshair while saying an appropriate verb to go with the printed noun (e.g., cake: eat; radio: listen). The four auditory conditions were identical to the four visual conditions except that tape-recorded nouns were played to the subjects while they stared at the crosshair.

After the data in these visual and auditory tests had been collected, three levels of subtraction were performed on the images recorded during the tests. The activity during the fixation-only condition was subtracted from that during the passive-noun condition to get a measure of the activation produced by passively observing or hearing the nouns. The activity during the passive-noun condition was subtracted from that during the saying-noun condition to get a measure of the activation produced by saying the noun. And the activity during the saying-noun condition was subtracted from that during the verb-association condition to get a measure of the activation produced by the cognitive processes involved in forming the association. Then, the difference scores for each area of the brain were averaged over all the subjects. In short, they used the *paired-image subtraction technique,* which was described in Chapter 5.

The results of Petersen et al.'s study are summarized in Figures 16.16 on page 460 and 16.17 on page 461. First, the presentation of printed nouns added activity in the secondary visual cortex of both hemispheres, and the presentation of auditory nouns added activity in the secondary auditory cortex of both hemispheres. Second, regardless of whether the nouns were presented in printed or auditory form, repeating them aloud added activity in the somatosensory and motor areas along the central fissures of both hemispheres and along the lateral fissure of the right hemisphere. And third, regardless of whether the words were presented in a printed or auditory form, the verb-association condition added activity in the prefrontal cortex of the left hemisphere just in front of Broca's area and in the medial cortex of both hemispheres just above the

front of the corpus callosum (i.e., in the cortex of the cingulate gyrus).

Petersen and his colleagues assumed that adding a level of complexity to their behavioral tasks would merely add additional areas of cortical activity to those associated with the simpler tasks. However, they found that the activation that occurred along the lateral fissure in the visual and auditory noun-repetition conditions was largely absent in the respective verb-association conditions (see Fiez & Petersen, 1993). On the basis of this observation, they proposed the following dual-route theory: When subjects perform a highly practiced verbal response, such as simply repeating a written or spoken noun, processing moves from sensory areas to motor areas through the association cortex of the lateral fissure. In contrast, when subjects are performing a verbal task that requires a more complex analysis, such as in the verb-association tasks, processing moves from sensory to motor areas via frontal and cingulate cortex. To test this dual-route theory, Raichle and colleagues (1991) assessed the effects of practice on the cerebral activity that mediated the performance of the verb-association tasks. In support of the theory, they found that just a few minutes of practice producing verb associations for the same list of nouns changed the pattern of activation from one involving frontal and cingulate areas to one involving areas along the lateral fissure.

An fMRI Study of Reading

Bavelier and colleagues used fMRI to measure the cerebral blood flow of subjects as they read sentences. Their methodology was noteworthy in two respects: First, they used a new fMRI procedure that allowed them to identify areas of activity with more accuracy than in most previous studies and without having to average the scores of several subjects; second, they recorded activity during reading sentences—rather than during the more simple, controllable, and unnatural activities used in most other functional brain-imaging studies of language.

The subjects in Bavelier and colleagues' study viewed sentences displayed one word at a time on a screen. Interposed between periods of silent reading were control periods during which the subjects were presented with strings of consonants. The differences in activity during the reading and control periods served as the basis for calculating the areas of cortical activity associated with reading. Only the lateral cortical surfaces were monitored.

Let's begin by considering the findings observed in individual subjects, before any averaging took place.

Deep dyslexia. A reading disorder in which the nonlexical procedure is disrupted while the lexical procedure is not.

Hemispherectomy. The removal of one cerebral hemisphere.

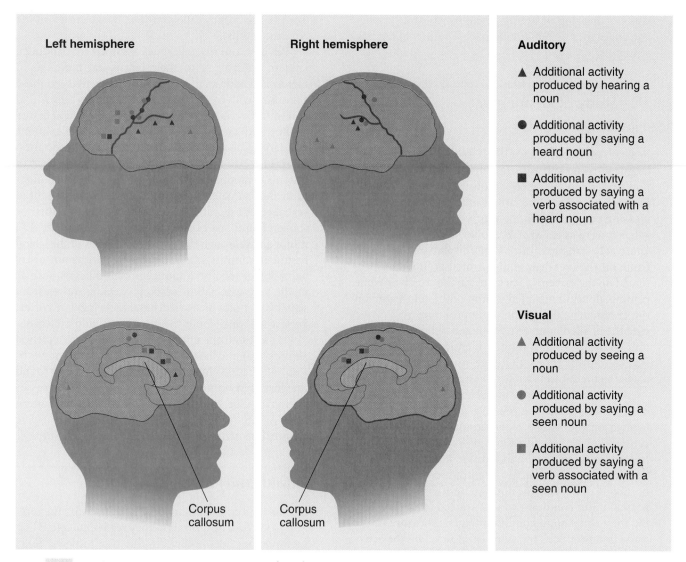

Left hemisphere

Right hemisphere

Auditory

▲ Additional activity produced by hearing a noun

● Additional activity produced by saying a heard noun

■ Additional activity produced by saying a verb associated with a heard noun

Visual

▲ Additional activity produced by seeing a noun

● Additional activity produced by saying a seen noun

■ Additional activity produced by saying a verb associated with a seen noun

Corpus callosum

Corpus callosum

Figure 16.16 A summary of the results of Petersen et al.'s (1989) PET scan study of language localization.

Three important points emerged from this analysis. First, the areas of activity were patchy; that is, they were tiny areas of activity separated by areas of inactivity. Second, the patches of activity were variable; that is, the areas of activity differed from subject to subject and even from trial to trial in the same subject. Third, although some activity was observed in the classic Wernicke-Geschwind regions, it was widespread over the lateral surfaces of the brain. Notice that these findings are consistent with the findings of modern brain stimulation studies, which we have already discussed.

Figure 16.18 on page 462 illustrates the reading-related increases of activity averaged over all of the subjects in the Bavelier et al. study. The averaging creates the false impression that large expanses of tissue were active during reading, whereas patches of activity included only between 5% and 10% of the illustrated areas on any given trial. Nevertheless, the following two findings are readily apparent: first, greater activity in the left rather than the right hemisphere; and second,

activity in many areas of the left frontal and temporal cortex, including Broca's area, Wernicke's area, and the angular gyrus.

Summary of the Findings of Functional Brain-Imaging Studies of Language

Although the specific functions of the various language areas of the brain are still not well understood, substantial progress has been made in the last few years, largely through the application of functional brain-imaging techniques. You have just learned about two prominent functional brain-imaging studies of language, but there are many more. The chapter concludes with a brief overview of what functional brain-imaging research has taught us about the classic Wernicke-Geschwind language areas (see Binder, 1997; Chertkow & Murtha, 1997).

Patterns of Activity
Identified by the
Three Auditory Subtractions

Patterns of Activity
Identified by the
Three Visual Subtractions

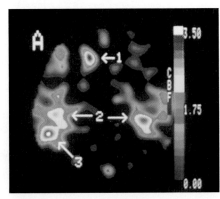

Additional activity produced by
hearing a noun

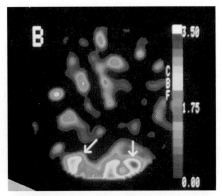

Additional activity produced by
seeing a noun

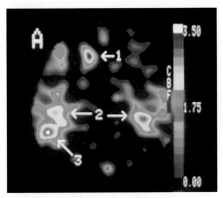

Additional activity produced by
saying a heard noun

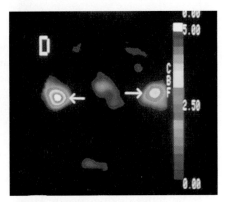

Additional activity produced by
saying a seen noun

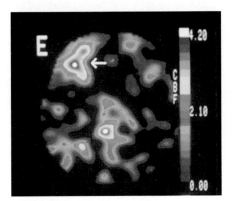

Additional activity produced by
saying a verb associated with a
heard noun

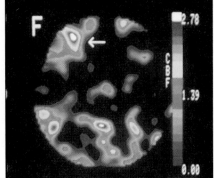

Additional activity produced by
saying a verb associated with a
seen noun

Figure 16.17 PET scan computer images of the subtracted patterns of blood flow from the experiment of Petersen et al. (1989). Each image represents a horizontal section of the brain averaged over all of the subjects in that condition. Anterior is toward the top of the page; the
right hemisphere is on your right, and the left hemisphere is on your left. As shown by the adjacent scales, the highest levels of activity are indicated by yellow, orange, red, and white (the
very highest).

(Courtesy of Steve Petersen.)

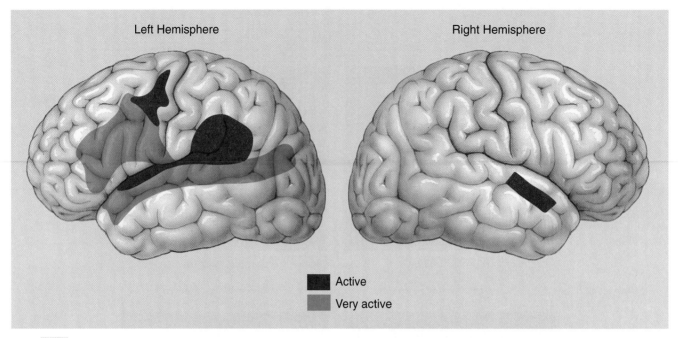

Figure 16.18 The areas in which reading-associated increases in activity were observed in the fMRI study of Bavelier et al. (1997). These maps were derived by averaging the scores of all subjects, each of whom displayed patchy increases of activity in 5 to 10% of the indicated areas on any particular trial.

■ **BROCA'S AREA** Broca's area has traditionally been thought of as a center for speech production, and it is commonly found to be active during speech. However, several functional brain-imaging studies—such as the study of Bavelier et al. (see Figure 16.18)—have found the area to be active during the silent viewing of words. Moreover, Broca's area is also active when deaf subjects watch American Sign Language (Neville et al., 1995). Complicating the picture further is that activity is often observed in the corresponding area of the right hemisphere during language tasks. Clearly, Broca's area is important for language, but speech production does not appear to be its specific function.

■ **WERNICKE'S AREA** Wernicke's area has generally been thought of as a center for speech reception and interpretation. Indeed, listening to speech typically produces activity in a large area of left superior temporal cortex that includes Wernicke's area, as well as in the same area of the right hemisphere—as in the study of Petersen et al. (see Figure 16.16). However, the Wernicke-Geschwind model also predicts that written words will activate Wernicke's area (after being translated into an auditory code by the angular gyrus), and such activation is often not observed—it was not observed by Petersen et al. (see Figure 16.16) but was by Bavelier et al. (see Figure 16.18).

■ **ARCUATE FASCICULUS** According to the Wernicke-Geschwind model, the left arcuate fasciculus plays a major role in language. In particular, it has been thought to mediate the ability of people to repeat a heard word. However, activity of the arcuate fasciculus has usually not been observed during such tasks—for example, see Petersen et al. (Figure 16.16).

■ **ANGULAR GYRUS** According to convention, the angular gyrus is a center for reading. However, activity in the angular gyrus has rarely been observed in functional brain images taken during reading—for example, Petersen et al. did not observe such activity (see Figure 16.16). The problem may be that most studies have typically focused on the reading of individual words: Bavelier et al. (see Figure 16.18) observed angular gyrus activity in subjects reading sentences.

Interim Conclusion

The use of functional brain imaging is in its infancy; methods are still being improved and testing protocols being refined. Still, important progress has been made.

One important contribution of functional brain-imaging studies of language is that they have tested some of the claims of the Wernicke-Geschwind model.

These studies suggest that the Wernicke-Geschwind model is basically correct with respect to Wernicke's area, but only if one also includes the surrounding cortex. However, functional brain-imaging studies suggest that the Wernicke-Geschwind model is totally wrong about Broca's area and the arcuate fasciculus. The situation regarding the angular gyrus is currently unclear.

Perhaps the major contribution of functional brain-imaging studies of language is that they have demonstrated that language functions are not limited to the classic Wernicke-Geschwind areas. Indeed, large areas of frontal and temporal cortex, both on the lateral and medial surfaces, appear to play a role in language—see Figures 16.16, 16.17, and 16.18.

CONCLUSION

This chapter has been the story of two theories, one largely right and one largely wrong, but both extremely important. On the one hand, Sperry's theory of brain duality and asymmetry has withstood the empirical challenge of the research it has generated. Study after study has confirmed and extended its basic tenets: that the two hemispheres of the human brain can function independently and that they possess different capacities that are normally integrated by the cerebral commissures. On the other hand, the empirical evidence has been less kind to the strict localizationist theories of language organization proposed by Broca, Wernicke, and Geschwind. Lesion, brain-stimulation, and brain-imaging studies have all failed to confirm most of their specific predictions.

The positive impact of the Wernicke-Geschwind model illustrates a frequently misunderstood point: Theories are important because they are useful, and they do not have to be right to be useful. The strengths of the Wernicke-Geschwind model lie in its clarity and testability. Because it is clear, scientists and students alike have found it to be a useful vehicle for organizing their thinking about the localization of language. And because it is so eminently testable, its predictions have stimulated and guided much of the research in the field. Considering that it was one of the first steps toward the solution of an extremely difficult problem, it is not at all surprising that it turned out to be flawed; but it is the mass of research that it has generated that will stand as the ultimate testimonial to its worth.

FOOD FOR THOUGHT

1. Design an experiment to show that it is possible for a human split-brain student to study for an English exam and a geometry exam at the same time by using the Z lens.

2. The decision to perform commissurotomies on epileptic patients turned out to be a good one; the decision to

perform prefrontal lobotomies on mental patients (see Chapter 1) turned out to be a bad one. Was this just the luck of the draw? Discuss.

3. Design a fMRI study to identify the areas of the brain involved in comprehending speech.

KEY TERMS

Agraphia (p. 450)
Alexia (p. 450)
Angular gyrus (p. 450)
Aphasia (p. 436)
Apraxia (p. 436)
Arcuate fasciculus (p. 450)
Broca's aphasia (p. 450)
Broca's area (p. 436)
Cerebral commissures (p. 435)
Chimeric figures test (p. 443)

Commissurotomy (p. 435)
Conduction aphasia (p. 450)
Corpus callosum (p. 438)
Cross-cuing (p. 442)
Deep dyslexia (p. 458)
Dextrals (p. 437)
Dichotic listening test (p. 437)
Dominant hemisphere (p. 437)
Dyslexia (p. 457)
Expressive (p. 450)

Frontal operculum (p. 447)
Global aphasia (p. 454)
Grammatical analysis (p. 457)
Helping-hand phenomenon (p. 443)
Hemispherectomy (p. 458)
Heschl's gyrus (p. 447)
Lateralization of function (p. 435)
Lexical procedure (p. 457)

Minor hemisphere (p. 437)
Nonlexical procedure (p. 457)
Parallel models (p. 452)
Phonemes (p. 457)
Phonological analysis (p. 457)
Planum temporale (p. 447)
Receptive (p. 450)
Scotoma (p. 439)
Semantic analysis (p. 457)
Serial model (p. 452)

ADDITIONAL READING

The following papers provide reviews of some of the current issues in the study of cerebral laterality and language localization:

Brown, H. D., & Kosslyn, S. M. (1993). Cerebral lateralization. *Current Opinion in Neurobiology, 3,* 183–186.

Chertkow, H., & Murtha, S. (1997). PET activation and language. *Clinical Neuroscience, 4,* 78–86.

Fiez, J. A., & Petersen, S. E. (1993). PET as part of an interdisciplinary approach to understanding processes involved in reading. *Psychological Science, 4,* 287–293.

Gazzaniga, M. S. (1998, July). The split brain revisited. *Scientific American, 279,* 50–55.

Maratsos, M., & Matheny, L. (1994). Language specificity and elasticity: Brain and clinical syndrome studies. *Annual Review of Psychology, 45,* 487–516.

17

Biopsychology of Stress and Illness

This chapter is about the biopsychology of stress and illness. However, it begins with a general introduction to biopsychology of emotion that gradually begins to focus on the darker end of the emotional spectrum: fear and anxiety. Biopsychological research on emotions has concentrated on these negative *affective* (emotional) states, not because biopsychologists are a perverse lot but because of the major impact that the stress associated with these emotions has on our health and well-being.

The stress associated with chronic fear and anxiety can increase our susceptibility to a wide range of physical diseases, regardless of their causes. These include physical disorders such as ulcers and infections and numerous psychological disorders (see Stout & Nemeroff, 1994), including the three that you will learn about in this chapter: schizophrenia, affective disorders, and anxiety disorders.

17.1 Biopsychology of Emotion

This section provides a general introduction to the biopsychology of emotion. It describes several of the classic early discoveries, and then it discusses the role of the autonomic nervous system in emotional experience, the facial expression of emotion, and the effects of cortical damage on emotion.

Early Progress in the Biopsychological Study of Emotion

The early study of the biopsychology of emotions featured the following topics: Darwin's theory of the evolution of emotion, the James-Lange and Cannon-Bard theories of emotion, sham rage, the limbic system, and the Kluver-Bucy syndrome. These topics are discussed in this subsection.

■ **DARWIN'S THEORY OF THE EVOLUTION OF EMOTION**
The first major event in the study of the biopsychology of emotion was the publication in 1872 of Darwin's book *The Expression of Emotions in Man and Animals.* In it, Darwin argued, largely on the basis of anecdotal evidence, that particular emotional responses, such as human facial expressions, tend to accompany the same emotional states in all members of a species.

Darwin believed that expressions of emotion, like other behaviors, are products of evolution; he therefore tried to understand them by comparing them in different species. From such interspecies comparisons, Darwin developed a theory of the evolution of emotional expression that was composed of three main ideas: (1) that expressions of emotion evolve from behaviors that indicate what an animal is likely to do next; (2) that if the signals provided by such behaviors benefit the animal that displays them, they will evolve in

ways that enhance their communicative function, and their original function may be lost; and (3) that opposite messages are often signaled by opposite movements and postures (the *principle of antithesis*).

Consider how Darwin's theory accounts for the evolution of *threat displays*. Originally, facing one's enemies, rising up, and exposing one's weapons were the components of the early stages of combat. But once enemies began to recognize these behaviors as signals of impending aggression, a survival advantage accrued to attackers that could communicate their aggression most effectively and intimidate their victims without actually fighting. As a result, elaborate threat displays evolved and actual combat declined.

To be most effective, signals of aggression and submission must be clearly distinguishable; thus they tended to evolve in opposite directions. For example, gulls signal aggression by pointing their beaks at one another and submission by pointing their beaks away from one another, and primates signal aggression by staring and submission by averting their gaze. Figure 17.1 is a reproduction of the actual woodcuts that Darwin used in his 1872 book to illustrate this principle of antithesis in dogs.

■ **JAMES-LANGE AND CANNON-BARD THEORIES** The first physiological theory of emotion was proposed independently by James and Lange in 1884. According to the **James-Lange theory,** emotion-inducing sensory stimuli are received and interpreted by the cortex, which triggers changes in the visceral organs via the autonomic nervous system and in the skeletal muscles via the somatic nervous system. Then, the autonomic and somatic responses trigger the experience of emotion in the brain. In effect, what the James-Lange theory did was to reverse the usual commonsense way of thinking about the causal relation between the experience of

Aggression

Submission

Figure 17.1 Two woodcuts from Darwin's 1872 book, *The Expression of Emotions in Man and Animals*, that he used to illustrate the principle of antithesis. The aggressive posture of dogs features ears forward, back up, hair up, and tail up; the submissive posture features ears back, back down, hair down, and tail down.

emotion and its expression. James and Lange argued that the autonomic activity and behavior that are triggered by the emotional event (e.g., rapid heartbeat and running away) produce the feeling of emotion, not vice versa.

In the early 1900s, Cannon proposed an alternative to the James-Lange theory of emotion, and it was subsequently extended and promoted by Bard. According to the **Cannon-Bard theory,** emotional stimuli have two independent excitatory effects: They excite both the feeling of emotion in the brain and the expression of emotion in the autonomic and somatic nervous systems. Accordingly, the Cannon-Bard theory, in contrast to the James-Lange theory, views emotional experience and emotional expression as parallel processes that have no direct causal relation.

The James-Lange and Cannon-Bard theories make different predictions about the role of feedback from autonomic and somatic nervous system activity in emotional experience. According to the James-Lange theory, emotional experience depends entirely on feedback from autonomic and somatic nervous system activity; according to the Cannon-Bard theory, emotional experience is totally independent of such feedback. Both extreme positions have proved to be incorrect. On the one hand, it seems that the autonomic and somatic feedback is not necessary for the experience of emotion: Human patients whose autonomic and somatic feedback has been largely eliminated by a broken neck are capable of a full range of emotional experiences (e.g., Lowe & Carroll, 1985). On the other hand, there have been numerous reports—some of which you will soon encounter—that autonomic and somatic responses

to emotional stimuli can influence emotional experience. Failure to find unqualified support for either the James-Lange or the Cannon-Bard theory has led to the view that each of the three principal factors in an emotional response—the perception of the emotion-inducing stimulus, the autonomic and somatic responses to the stimulus, and the experience of the emotion—influences the other two (see Figure 17.2 on page 468).

■ **SHAM RAGE** In the late 1920s, Bard (1929) discovered that **decorticate** cats—cats whose cortex has been removed—respond aggressively to the slightest provocation: After a light touch, they arch their backs, erect their hair, growl, hiss, and expose their teeth. The aggressive responses of decorticate animals are abnormal in two respects: They are inappropriately severe, and they are not directed at particular targets. Bard referred to the exaggerated, poorly directed aggressive responses of decorticate animals as **sham rage.**

Sham rage can be elicited in cats whose cerebral hemispheres have been removed down to, but not including, the hypothalamus; but it cannot be elicited if the hypothalamus is also removed. On the basis of this observation, Bard concluded that the hypothalamus is

James-Lange theory. The theory that emotional experience results from the brain's perception of the pattern of autonomic and somatic nervous system responses elicited by emotional stimuli.

Cannon-Bard theory. The theory that emotional experience and emotional expression are parallel processes that have no direct causal relation.
Decorticate. Lacking a cortex.
Sham rage. The exaggerated, poorly directed aggressive responses of decorticate animals.

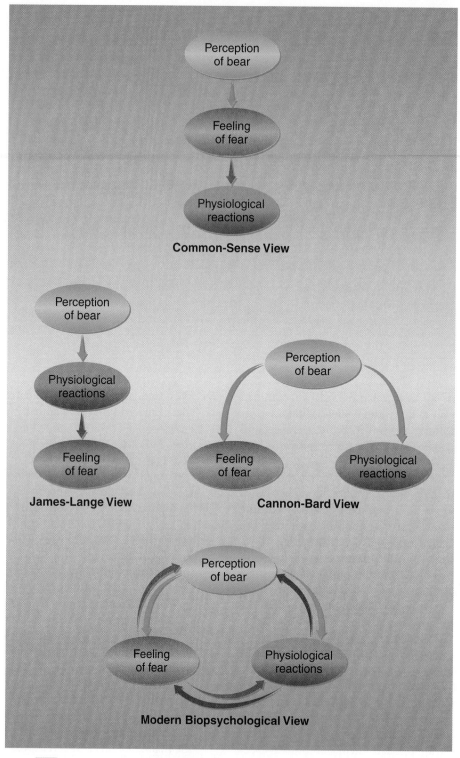

Figure 17.2 Four ways of thinking about the relations among the perception of emotion–inducing stimuli, the autonomic and somatic responses to the stimuli, and the emotional experience.

critical for the expression of aggressive responses and that the function of the cortex is to inhibit and direct these responses.

■LIMBIC SYSTEM AND EMOTION In 1937, Papez (pronounced "Payps") proposed that emotional expression is controlled by several interconnected neural structures that he referred to as the limbic system. The **limbic system** is a collection of nuclei and tracts that borders the thalamus (*limbic* means "border"). Figure 17.3 illustrates some of its key structures: the amygdala, mammillary body, hippocampus, fornix, cingulate cor-

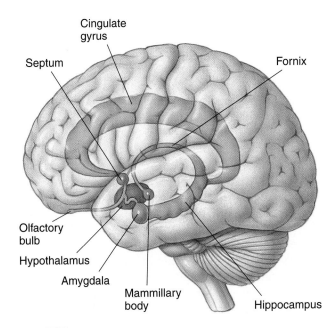

Figure 17.3 The location of the major limbic system structures; in general they are arrayed near the midline in a ring around the thalamus. (See also Figure 3.30.)

Labels in figure: Cingulate gyrus, Septum, Fornix, Olfactory bulb, Hypothalamus, Amygdala, Mammillary body, Hippocampus

tex, septum, olfactory bulb, and hypothalamus (see Macchi, 1989). Papez proposed that emotional states are expressed through the action of the other limbic structures on the hypothalamus and that they are experienced through the action of the limbic structures on the cortex.

■ **KLUVER-BUCY SYNDROME** In 1939, Kluver and Bucy observed a striking *syndrome* (pattern of behavior) in monkeys that had had their anterior temporal lobes removed. This syndrome, which is commonly referred to as the **Kluver-Bucy syndrome,** includes the following behaviors: the consumption of almost anything that is edible, increased sexual activity often directed at inappropriate objects, a tendency to repeatedly investigate familiar objects, a tendency to investigate objects with the mouth, and a lack of fear. Monkeys that could not be handled before surgery were transformed by bilateral anterior temporal lobectomy into tame subjects that showed no fear whatsoever—even in response to snakes, which terrify normal monkeys. In primates, most of the symptoms of the Kluver-Bucy syndrome appear to result from amygdala damage.

The Kluver-Bucy syndrome has been observed in several species. Following is a description of the syndrome in a human patient with a brain infection:

He exhibited a flat affect, and although originally restless, ultimately became remarkably placid. He appeared indifferent to people or situations. He spent much time gazing at the television, but never learned to turn it on; when the set was off, he tended to watch reflections of others in the room on the glass screen. On occasion he became facetious, smiling inappropriately and mimicking the gestures and actions of

others. Once initiating an imitative series, he would perseverate copying all movements made by another for extended periods of time. . . . He engaged in oral exploration of all objects within his grasp, appearing unable to gain information via tactile or visual means alone. All objects that he could lift were placed in his mouth and sucked or chewed. . . .

Although vigorously heterosexual prior to his illness, he was observed in hospital to make advances toward other male patients. . . . [H]e never made advances toward women, and, in fact, his apparent reversal of sexual polarity prompted his fiancée to sever their relationship. (Marlowe, Mancall, & Thomas, 1985, pp. 55–56)

Emotions and the Autonomic Nervous System

Research on the role of the autonomic nervous system (ANS) in emotion has focused on two issues: the degree to which specific patterns of ANS activity are associated with specific emotions and the effectiveness of ANS measures in polygraphy (lie detection).

■ **EMOTIONAL SPECIFICITY OF THE AUTONOMIC NERVOUS SYSTEM** The James-Lange and Cannon-Bard theories differ in their views of the emotional specificity of the autonomic nervous system. The James-Lange theory is that different emotional stimuli induce different patterns of ANS activity and that these different patterns produce different emotional experiences. In contrast, the Cannon-Bard theory is that all emotional stimuli produce the same general pattern of sympathetic activation, which prepares the organism for action (i.e., increased heart rate, increased blood pressure, pupil dilation, increased flow of blood to the muscles, increased respiration, and increased release of epinephrine and norepinephrine from the adrenal medulla).

The experimental evidence suggests that the specificity of ANS reactions lies somewhere between the extremes of total specificity and total generality. There is ample evidence that not all emotions are associated with the same pattern of ANS activity (see Ax, 1955); however, there is insufficient evidence to make a strong case for the view that each emotion is characterized by a different pattern of ANS activity.

■ **POLYGRAPHY** **Polygraphy** is a method of interrogation that employs autonomic nervous system indexes of emotion to infer the truthfulness of the subject's responses.

Limbic system. A collection of interconnected nuclei and tracts that circles the thalamus and plays a role in emotion.
Kluver-Bucy syndrome. The syndrome of behavioral changes (e.g., lack of fear and hypersexuality) that is induced in primates by bilateral damage to the anterior temporal lobes.
Polygraphy. A method of interrogation in which autonomic nervous system indexes of emotion are used to infer the truthfulness of the responses.

Polygraph tests administered by skilled examiners can be useful additions to normal interrogation procedures, but they are not infallible (Iacono & Patrick, 1987).

The main problem in evaluating the effectiveness of polygraphy is that it is rarely possible in real-life situations to know for certain whether the suspect is guilty or innocent. Consequently, many studies of polygraphy have employed the *mock-crime procedure:* Volunteer subjects participate in a mock crime and are then subjected to a polygraph test by an examiner who is unaware of their "guilt" or "innocence." The usual interrogation method is the **control-question technique.** In this technique, the physiological response to the target question (e.g., Did you steal that purse?) is compared with the responses to control questions whose answers are known (e.g., Have you ever been in jail before?). The assumption is that lying will be associated with greater sympathetic activation. The average success rate in various mock-crime studies using the control-question technique is about 80%.

Despite being commonly referred to as *lie detection,* polygraphy detects emotions, not lies. Consequently, it is likely more difficult to detect lies in real life than in experiments. In real-life situations, questions such as "Did you steal that purse?" are likely to elicit a reaction from all suspects, regardless of their guilt or innocence, making it difficult to detect deception. Lykken (1959) developed the **guilty-knowledge technique** to circumvent this problem. In order to use this technique, the polygrapher must have a piece of information concerning the crime that would be known only to the guilty person. Rather than attempting to catch the suspect in a lie, the polygrapher simply assesses the suspect's reaction to a list of actual and contrived details of the crime. Innocent parties, because they have no knowledge of the crime, react to all such details in the same way; the guilty react differently.

In one study of the guilty-knowledge technique (Lykken, 1959), subjects waited until the occupant of an office went to the washroom. Then, they entered her office, stole her purse from her desk, removed the money, and left the purse in a locker. The critical part of the interrogation went something like this: "Where do you think that we found the purse? In the washroom? . . . In a locker? . . . Hanging on a coat rack? . . . " Even though electrodermal activity was the only measure of ANS activity used in this study, 88% of the mock criminals were correctly identified, and, more importantly, none of the innocent parties was judged guilty.

Emotions and Facial Expression

Ekman and his colleagues have been preeminent in the study of facial expression (see Ekman, 1992, 1993). They began in the 1960s by analyzing hundreds of films and photographs of people experiencing various real emotions. From these, they compiled an atlas of the facial expressions that are normally associated with different emotions (Ekman & Friesen, 1975). The facial expressions in Ekman and Friesen's atlas are not photographs of people experiencing genuine emotions. They are photographs of models who were instructed to contract specific facial muscles on the basis of Ekman and Friesen's analysis. For example, to produce the facial expression for surprise, models were instructed to pull their brows upward so as to wrinkle their forehead, to open their eyes wide so as to reveal white above the iris, to slacken the muscles around their mouth, and to drop their jaw. Try it.

■ **UNIVERSALITY OF FACIAL EXPRESSION** Despite Darwin's assertion that people in all parts of the world make similar facial expressions, it was widely believed that facial expressions are learned and culturally variable. Then, several empirical studies showed that people of different cultures do indeed make similar facial expressions in similar situations and that they can correctly identify the emotional significance of facial expressions displayed by people of other cultures (e.g., Ekman, Sorenson, & Friesen, 1969; Izard, 1971). The most convincing of these studies was a study of the members of an isolated New Guinea tribe who had had little or no contact with the outside world (Ekman & Friesen, 1971). Although these findings support Darwin's view of the universality of facial expressions, they do not deny the possibility of minor cultural differences.

■ **PRIMARY FACIAL EXPRESSIONS** Ekman and Friesen concluded that the facial expressions of the following six emotions are primary: surprise, anger, sadness, disgust, fear, and happiness. They further concluded that all other facial expressions of genuine emotion are composed of predictable mixtures of the six primaries. In Figure 17.4, Ekman himself illustrates the six primary facial expressions and their combination to form a nonprimary expression.

■ **FACIAL FEEDBACK** Is there any truth to the old idea that putting on a happy face can make you feel better? Research suggests that there is (see Adelmann & Zajonc, 1989). The hypothesis that our facial expressions influence our emotional experience is called the **facial feedback hypothesis.**

Control-question technique. A lie-detection technique in which the polygrapher compares the responses to target questions with the responses to control questions.

Guilty-knowledge technique. A lie-detection technique in which the polygrapher records autonomic nervous system responses to control and crime-related information known only to the criminal and the examiners.

Facial feedback hypothesis. The hypothesis that our facial expressions can influence how we feel.

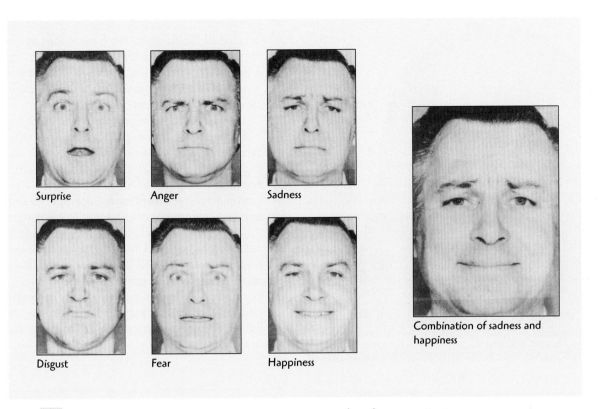

Figure 17.4 Examples of the six facial expressions that Ekman and Friesen (1975) considered to be primary: surprise, anger, sadness, disgust, fear, and happiness. All other emotional facial expressions were considered to be combinations of these six. For example, shown here on the right is an expression you might make while visiting a sick friend; it is a combination of sadness in the upper half of the face and happiness in the lower half.

In a test of the facial feedback hypothesis, Rutledge and Hupka (1985) instructed subjects to assume one of two patterns of facial contractions while they viewed a series of slides; the patterns corresponded to happy or angry faces, although the subjects were unaware of it. The subjects reported that the slides made them feel more happy and less angry when they were making happy faces, and less happy and more angry when they were making angry faces (see Figure 17.5). Why don't you try it? Pull your eyebrows down and together; raise your upper eyelids and tighten your lower eyelids, and narrow your lips and press them together. Now, hold this expression for a few seconds. If it makes you feel slightly angry, you have just experienced the effect of facial feedback.

■ **VOLUNTARY CONTROL OF FACIAL EXPRESSION** Because we can exert voluntary control over our facial muscles, it is possible to inhibit true facial expressions and to substitute false ones. There are many reasons for choosing to put on a false facial expression. Some of them are positive (e.g., putting on a false smile to reassure a worried friend), and some are negative (e.g., putting on a false smile to disguise a lie). In either case, it is difficult to fool an expert.

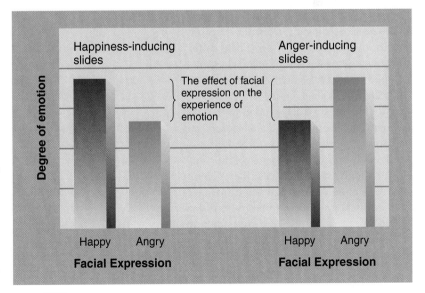

Figure 17.5 The effects of facial expression on the feeling of emotion. Subjects reported feeling more happy and less angry when they viewed slides while making a happy face, and less happy and more angry when they viewed slides while making an angry face. (Adapted from Rutledge & Hupka, 1985.)

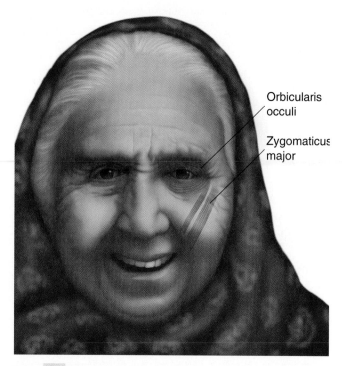

Orbicularis occuli

Zygomaticus major

Figure 17.6 The orbicularis oculi and zygomaticus major, two muscles that contract during genuine (Duchenne) smiles. Because the lateral portion of the orbicularis oculi is difficult for most people to contract voluntarily, fake smiles usually lack this component.

There are two ways of distinguishing true expressions from false ones (Ekman, 1985). First, *microexpressions* (brief facial expressions) of the real emotion often break through the false one. Such microexpressions last only about 0.05 second, but with practice they can be detected without the aid of slow-motion photography. Second, there are often subtle differences between genuine facial expressions and false ones that can be detected by skilled observers.

The most widely studied difference between a genuine and a false facial expression was first described by the French anatomist Duchenne in 1862. Duchenne said that the smile of enjoyment could be distinguished from deliberately produced smiles by consideration of the two facial muscles that are contracted during genuine smiles: *orbicularis oculi*, which encircles the eye and pulls the skin from the cheeks and forehead toward the eyeball, and *zygomaticus major*, which pulls the lip corners up (see Figure 17.6). According to Duchenne, the zygomaticus major can

be controlled voluntarily, whereas the orbicularis oculi is normally contracted only by genuine pleasure. Thus inertia of the orbicularis oculi in smiling unmasks a false friend—a fact you would do well to remember. Ekman named the genuine smile the **Duchenne smile** (see Ekman & Davidson, 1993).

Not all emotions are accompanied by changes in facial expression—as any good poker player will tell you. However, *facial electromyography (EMG)* can detect changes in the motor input to facial muscles that are too slight to produce observable changes in muscle contraction (see Tassinary & Cacioppo, 1992). For example, Cacioppo and colleagues (1986) recorded the EMG activity of several facial muscles while the subjects viewed slides. Although facial expressions were seldom evoked, the EMG activity was related to how much the subjects reported that they liked each slide. For example, the smile muscles—the orbicularis oculi and the zygomaticus major—tended to be more active while the subjects were viewing slides that they judged to be pleasant.

Effects of Cortical Damage on Human Emotion

The study of emotion in patients with cortical damage has led to two general findings. First, the prefrontal cortex plays an important role in emotion. You may recall from the description of the prefrontal-lobotomy epi-

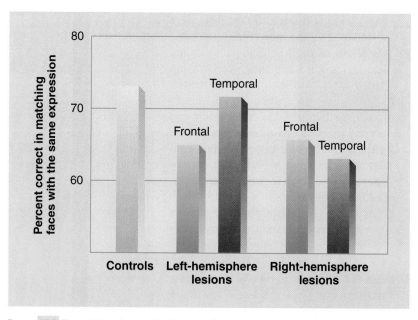

Figure 17.7 The ability of control subjects and patients with cortical damage to match photographs of faces on the basis of expression.
(Adapted from Kolb & Taylor, 1988.)

sode in Chapter 1 that one of the effects of prefrontal lobotomy was a general emotional blunting, which dismayed the family and friends of many lobotomized patients. Second, there is a general tendency for the cortex of the right hemisphere to play a greater role in emotion than the cortex of the left hemisphere. Notwithstanding these two general points, it is important to recognize that cortical involvement in emotion depends on the particular manifestation of emotion under consideration. For example, different areas of cortex control the perception of emotion than those that control the expression of emotion.

■ **CORTICAL DAMAGE AND PERCEPTION OF EMOTION**
There is evidence (see Bowers et al., 1987; Etcoff, 1989) of right-hemisphere dominance for the perception of both facial expression and **prosody** (emotional tone of voice); for example, right-hemisphere lesions tend to disrupt the perception of both facial expression and prosody more than left-hemisphere lesions. However, this does not mean that the left hemisphere does not play a role. Kolb and Taylor (1988) found that the perception of facial expression was disrupted equivalently by right temporal, right frontal, and left frontal lesions (see Figure 17.7).

■ **CORTICAL DAMAGE AND EXPRESSION OF EMOTION**
Some studies of patients with unilateral brain damage have found a right-hemisphere dominance for emotional expression (e.g., Caltagirone et al., 1989; Tucker, 1981), but many have not. Studies by Kolb and his colleagues suggest that whether or not right-hemisphere lesions disrupt emotional expression more than left-hemisphere lesions depends on the location of the lesions within the hemispheres. For example, they found no right-hemisphere dominance for the decrease in facial expressions produced by frontal lesions: Both left- and right-hemisphere damage produced similar reductions.

■ **LATERALIZATION OF FACIAL EXPRESSION** Strong support for the right-hemisphere dominance of emotional expression comes from a study of facial expression (see Figure 17.8). For example, Hauser (1993) conducted a frame-by-frame analysis of the facial expressions of free-ranging rhesus monkeys. He found that the formation of each expression began on the left side of the face, and then milliseconds later similar changes occurred on the right side of the face. Furthermore, at peak amplitude, the changes on the left side of the face were of greater amplitude than those on the right.

Hauser's study adds to the evidence of right-hemisphere dominance of emotional expression in humans. It also is strong evidence that lateralization of function is not restricted to the human species—a point made in the preceding chapter.

Figure 17.8 A frame-by-frame illustration of a fear grimace in a rhesus monkey (redrawn with permission of Hauser, 1993). Notice that the expression begins on the left side and is of greater magnitude there, thus suggesting right-side dominance for facial expression.

Duchenne smile. A genuine smile, one that includes contraction of the orbicularis oculi muscles.

Prosody. Emotional tone of voice.

Fear, Defense, and Aggression

Biopsychological research on emotion has focused to a large degree on fear and defensive behaviors. One reason for this focus—as will become more apparent as the chapter progresses—is the major role played by the stressful effects of chronic fear in the development of disease (see Adamec, 1997). **Fear** is the emotional reaction to threat; it is the motivating force for defensive behaviors. **Defensive behaviors** are behaviors whose primary function is to protect the organism from threat or harm. In contrast, **aggressive behaviors** are behaviors whose primary function is to threaten or harm.

Types of Aggressive and Defensive Behaviors

Considerable progress in the understanding of aggressive and defensive behaviors has come from **ethoexperimental research**—research that focuses on the systematic description of behavior sequences observed in controlled laboratory environments that have been structured to mimic key features of the subjects' natural environment (see Blanchard et al., 1989). Ethoexperimental research has shown that aggressive and defensive behaviors in the same species come in a variety of standard forms, each of which occurs in different situations, serves different functions, and has different neural and hormonal bases.

The research of Blanchard and Blanchard (see 1989, 1990a, 1990b) on the *colony-intruder model of aggression and defense* is an excellent example of ethoexperimental research in the rat. Blanchard and Blanchard have derived rich descriptions of rat intraspecific aggressive and defensive behaviors by studying the interactions between the **alpha male**—the dominant male—of an established mixed-sex colony and a small male intruder:

The alpha approaches the stranger and sniffs at its perianal area. . . . If the intruder is an adult male, the alpha's sniff leads to piloerection. . . .

Shortly after piloerecting, the alpha male usually bites the intruder, and the intruder runs away. The alpha chases after it, and after one or two additional bites, the intruder stops running and turns to face its attacker. It rears up on its hind legs, using its forelimbs to push off the alpha. . . . However, rather than standing nose to nose with the "boxing" intruder, the attacking rat abruptly moves to a lateral orientation, with the long axis of its body perpendicular to the front of the defending rat. . . . It moves sideways toward the intruder, crowding and sometimes pushing it off balance. If the defending rat stands solid against this "lateral attack" movement, the alpha may make a quick lunge forward and around the defender's body to bite at its back. In response to such a lunge, the defender usually pivots on its hind feet, in the same direction as the attacker is moving, continuing its frontal orientation to the attacker. If the defending rat moves quickly enough, no bite will be made.

However, after a number of instances of the lateral attack, and especially if the attacker has succeeded in biting the intruder, the stranger rat may roll backward slowly from the boxing position, to lie on its back. The attacker then takes up a position on top of the supine animal, digging with its forepaws at the intruder's sides. If the attacker can turn the other animal over, or expose some portion of its back, . . . it bites. In response to these efforts, the defender usually moves in the direction of the attacker's head, rolling slightly on its back to continue to orient its ventrum [front] toward the alpha, and continuing to push off with both forelimbs and hindlimbs. Although all four legs and abdomen of the defending rat are exposed, the attacker does not bite them. This sequence of bites, flight, chasing, boxing, lateral attack, lying on the back, and standing on top is repeated . . . until the stranger rat is removed. (Blanchard & Blanchard, 1984, pp. 8–9)[1]

Another excellent example of ethoexperimental research on defense and aggression is the study of Pellis and colleagues (1988). They began by videotaping interactions between cats and mice. They found that different cats reacted to mice in different ways: Some were efficient mouse killers, some reacted defensively, and some seemed to play with the mice. Careful analysis of the "play" sequences led to two important conclusions. The first conclusion was that, in contrast to the common belief, cats do not play with their prey; the cats that appeared to be playing with the mice were simply vacillating between attack and defense. The second conclusion was that one can best understand each cat's interactions with mice by locating the interactions on a linear scale, with total aggressiveness at one end, total defensiveness at the other, and various proportions of the two in between.

Pellis and colleagues tested their conclusions by reducing the defensiveness of the cats with an antianxiety drug. As predicted, the drug moved each cat along the

[1]From "Affect and Aggression: An Animal Model Applied to Human Behavior," by D. C. Blanchard and R. J. Blanchard, in *Advances in the Study of Aggression,* Vol. 1, 1984, edited by D. C. Blanchard and R. J. Blanchard. San Diego: Academic Press. Copyright 1984 by Academic Press. Reprinted by permission.

Table 12.1 Categories of Aggressive and Defensive Behavior in the Rat

AGGRESSIVE BEHAVIORS

Predatory aggression	The stalking and killing of members of other species for the purpose of eating them. Rats kill prey, such as mice and frogs, by delivering bites to the back of the neck.
Social aggression	Unprovoked aggressive behavior that is directed at a conspecific for the purpose of establishing, altering, or maintaining a social hierarchy. In mammals, social aggression occurs primarily among males. In rats, it is characterized by piloerection, lateral attack, and bites directed at the defender's back.

DEFENSIVE BEHAVIORS

Intraspecific defense	Defense against social aggression. In rats, it is characterized by freezing and flight and by various behaviors, such as boxing, that are specifically designed to protect the back from bites.
Defensive attacks	Attacks that are launched by animals when they are cornered by threatening conspecifics or members of other species. In rats, they include lunging, shrieking, and biting attacks that are usually directed at the face of the attacker.
Freezing and flight	Responses that many animals use to avoid attack. For example, if a human approaches a wild rat, it will often freeze until the human penetrates its safety zone, whereupon it will explode into flight.
Maternal defensive behaviors	The behaviors by which mothers protect their young. Despite their defensive function, they are similar to male social aggression in appearance.
Risk assessment	Behaviors that are performed by animals in order to obtain specific information that helps them defend themselves more effectively. For example, rats that have been chased by a cat into their burrow do not emerge until they have spent considerable time at the entrance scanning the surrounding environment.
Defensive burying	Rats and other rodents spray sand and dirt ahead with their forepaws to bury dangerous objects in their environment, to drive off predators, and to construct barriers in burrows.

scale toward more efficient killing. Cats that avoided mice before the injection played with them after the injection, those that played with them before the injection killed them after the injection, and those that killed them before the injection killed them more quickly after the injection. The next time you play with a cat, take the opportunity to analyze the cat's behavior in the light of Pellis's observations.

The defensive and aggressive behaviors of rats have been divided into categories on the basis of three different criteria: (1) their *topography* (form), (2) the situations that elicit them, and (3) their apparent function. Several of these categories are described in Table 17.1.

The ethoexperimental analysis of aggressive and defensive behavior has led to the development of the **target-site concept**—the idea that the aggressive and defensive behaviors of an animal are often designed to attack specific sites on the body of another animal while protecting specific sites on its own. For example, the behavior of a socially aggressive rat (e.g., lateral attack) appears to be designed to deliver bites to the defending rat's back and to protect its own face, the likely target of a defensive attack. Conversely, most of the maneuvers of the defending rat (e.g., boxing) appear to be designed to protect the target site on its back. The emergence of the target-site concept illustrates what ethoexperimental analysis is all about. Ethoexperimentalists study the details of behavioral sequences not to accumulate libraries full of behavioral minutiae but to extract simple explanatory principles (see Pellis & Pellis, 1993).

The discovery that aggressive and defensive behaviors occur in a variety of stereotypical species-common forms was the necessary first step in the identification of their neural bases. Because the different categories of aggressive and defensive behavior are mediated by different neural circuits, little progress was made in identifying these circuits before the categories were delineated (see Davis, Rainnie, & Cassell, 1994; Kalin, 1993). For example, the lateral septum was once believed to inhibit all aggression, because lateral septal lesions rendered laboratory rats notoriously difficult to handle—the behavior of the septal rats was commonly referred to as *septal aggression* or *septal rage*. However, we now know that lateral septal lesions do not increase experimenter-directed aggression: Rats with lateral septal lesions do not initiate more attacks at the experimenter if they are left undisturbed. However, they do initiate

Fear. The emotion that is normally elicited by the presence or expectation of threatening stimuli.

Defensive behaviors. Behaviors whose primary function is protection from threat or harm.

Aggressive behaviors. Behaviors whose primary function is to threaten or harm other organisms.

Ethoexperimental research. The systematic analysis of behavioral sequences in seminatural laboratory environments.

Alpha male. The dominant male of a colony.

Target-site concept. The idea that many of the species-specific sequences of attack and defense can be reduced to the fact that animals are trying to attack a specific site on the other animal's body, to protect a specific site on their own, or both.

more defensive attacks and predatory aggression, but less social aggression.

Aggression and Testosterone

The fact that social aggression in many species occurs more commonly among males than among females is usually explained with reference to the organizational and activational effects of testosterone. The brief period of testosterone release that occurs around birth in genetic males is thought to organize their nervous systems along masculine lines and hence to create the potential for male patterns of social aggression to be activated by the high testosterone levels that are present after puberty. These organizational and activational effects have been demonstrated in many nonprimate mammalian species. For example, neonatal castration of male mice eliminates the ability of testosterone injections to induce social aggression in adulthood, and adult castration eliminates social aggression in males that do not receive testosterone replacement injections.

In contrast to the research on nonprimates, attempts to demonstrate the organizational and activational effects of testosterone on the aggressive behavior of humans have been mixed. In human males, aggressive behavior does not increase at puberty as testosterone levels increase, it is not eliminated by castration, and it is not increased by testosterone injections (see Albert, Walsh, & Jonik, 1993). However, a few studies have found that violent male criminals and aggressive male athletes tend to have slightly higher testosterone levels than normal (see Bernhardt, 1997). This weak correlation may reflect that aggressive encounters increase testosterone, rather than vice versa (see Archer, 1991).

The fact that human aggression is testosterone-independent could mean that its hormonal and neural regulation differs from the regulation in nonprimate mammalian species. However, Albert, Walsh, and Jonik (1993) believe that the evidence favors a different conclusion. They contend that the confusion has arisen because the researchers who study human aggression often fail to appreciate the difference between defensive aggression and social aggression. Most aggressive outbursts in humans are overreactions to real or perceived threat, and they are thus more appropriately viewed as defensive attack than social aggression. Consequently, the failure to find positive correlations between human aggressive behavior and testosterone levels is consistent with the failure to find positive correlations between defensive attack and testosterone levels in other species.

Neural Mechanisms of Conditioned Fear

The amygdala plays a key role in the experience and expression of fear—the amygdala is located in the ante-

rior temporal lobe, just anterior to the hippocampus. This subsection examines three lines of evidence that have implicated the amygdala in the mediation of fear.

■ AMYGDALA AND THE STUDY OF CONDITIONED FEAR

Many studies of the neural mechanisms of fear have focused on the study of **fear conditioning.** In the usual fear-conditioning experiment, the subject, typically a rat, hears a tone and then receives a mild electric shock to its feet. After several pairings of the tone conditional stimulus and the shock unconditional stimulus, the rat responds to the tone with a variety of defensive behaviors (e.g., freezing and increased susceptibility to startle) and sympathetic nervous system responses (e.g., increased heart rate and blood pressure). LeDoux and his colleagues have mapped the neural system that mediates this form of auditory fear conditioning (see Armony et al., 1995; LeDoux, 1995).

LeDoux and his colleagues began their search for the neural mechanisms of auditory fear conditioning by making lesions in the auditory pathways. They found that bilateral lesions to the *medial geniculate nucleus* (the auditory relay nucleus of the thalamus) blocked fear conditioning to a tone, but bilateral lesions to auditory cortex did not. This indicated that for auditory fear conditioning to occur, it is necessary for signals elicited by the tone to reach the medial geniculate nucleus but not the auditory cortex. It also indicated that a pathway from the medial geniculate nucleus to a structure other than the auditory cortex plays a key role in fear conditioning. This pathway proved to be the pathway from the medial geniculate nucleus to the amygdala. Lesions of the amygdala, like lesions of the medial geniculate nucleus, blocked fear conditioning. The amygdala receives input from all sensory systems, and it is believed to be the structure in which the emotional significance of sensory signals is learned and retained.

Several pathways carry signals from the amygdala to structures that control the various emotional responses. For example, a pathway to the periaqueductal gray of the midbrain elicits appropriate defensive responses (see Bandler & Shipley, 1994), whereas another pathway to the lateral hypothalamus elicits appropriate sympathetic responses.

The fact that auditory cortex lesions do not disrupt fear conditioning to simple tones does not mean that the auditory cortex is not involved in auditory fear conditioning. There are two pathways from the medial geniculate nucleus to the amygdala: the direct one, which you have already learned about, and an indirect one that projects via the auditory cortex (Romanski & LeDoux, 1992). Both routes are capable of mediating fear conditioning to simple sounds; if only one is destroyed, conditioning progresses normally. However, only the cortical route is capable of mediating fear conditioning to complex sounds (Jarrell et al., 1987).

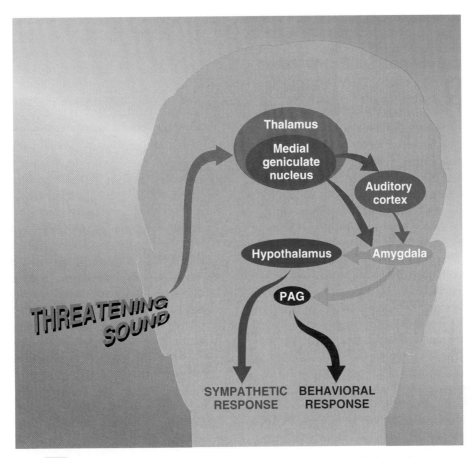

Figure 17.9 The structures that are thought to mediate the sympathetic and behavioral responses conditioned to an auditory conditional stimulus.

Figure 17.9 illustrates the circuit of the brain that is thought to mediate fear conditioning to auditory conditional stimuli (see LeDoux, 1994). Sound signals from the medial geniculate nucleus of the thalamus reach the amygdala either directly or via the auditory cortex. The amygdala assesses the emotional significance of the sound on the basis of previous encounters with it, and then the amygdala activates the appropriate sympathetic and behavioral response circuits in the hypothalamus and periaqueductal gray, respectively. It is important to recognize, however, that the amygdala is composed of several different nuclei, and their respective functions have yet to be delineated (see Pitkänen, Savander, & LeDoux, 1997).

Amygdalectomy and Human Fear

The discovery that bilateral anterior temporal lobectomy produces a syndrome of tameness (the Kluver-Bucy syndrome) initiated a search for the specific anterior temporal lobe damage that produces taming. The discovery that bilateral damage restricted to the amygdala is sufficient to produce a general insensitivity to fear-inducing stimuli in several mammalian species, including humans (see Aggleton, 1993) led to the pre-

scription of *amygdaledectomy* (surgical destruction of the amygdala) for the psychosurgical treatment of human violence. Amygdalectomy has proven effective in reducing violent behavior (largely defensive attack) in some patients; nevertheless, there are good reasons for questioning its use (see Aggleton, 1993). One reason is that amygdalectomy does not reduce violent behavior in all patients; another is that it has a variety of adverse effects, including a general blunting of emotion.

Bilateral amygdalectomy produces a variety of emotion-related effects (see Gallagher & Chiba, 1996). For example, bilateral (Adolphs et al., 1994; Young et al., 1995), but not unilateral (Adolphs et al., 1995), amygdala damage reduces the ability of human patients to recognize fearful facial expressions as fearful. This effect occurs in the absence of any difficulty in identifying faces. Also, human subjects with amygdalar damage have difficulty in *fear conditioning,* that is, in learning to react to neutral stimuli that predict fear-inducing stimuli. A conditional stimulus that repeatedly predicted a loud noise did not acquire the ability to elicit a galvanic skin response in amygdalectomized subjects.

Fear conditioning. Establishing fear of a neutral conditional stimulus by repeatedly pairing it with an aversive unconditional stimulus.

Irwin and colleagues (1996) recorded functional magnetic resonance images of the brains of subjects as the subjects viewed emotion-inducing material. The subjects viewed a series of pictures, some affectively neutral and some affectively negative. In each subject, the viewing of the affectively negative pictures produced bilateral amygdalar activation.

17.3 Stress and Psychosomatic Disorders

When the body is exposed to harm or threat, the result is a cluster of physiological changes that is generally referred to as *the stress response*—or just **stress.** All *stressors,* whether psychological (e.g., dismay at the loss of one's job) or physical (e.g., long-term exposure to cold), produce a similar core pattern of physiological changes; however, it is chronic psychological stress that has been most frequently implicated in ill health.

The Stress Response

Hans Selye (pronounced "SELL-yay") first described the stress response in the 1950s, and he quickly recognized its dual nature. In the short term, it produces adaptive changes that help the animal respond to the stressor (e.g., mobilization of energy resources, inhibition of inflammation, and resistance to infection); in the long term, however, it produces changes that are maladaptive (e.g., enlarged adrenal glands).

Selye attributed the stress response to the activation of the *anterior-pituitary adrenal-cortex system.* He concluded that stressors acting on neural circuits (see Herman & Cullinan, 1997) stimulate the release of **adrenocorticotropic hormone (ACTH)** from the anterior pituitary, that the ACTH in turn triggers the release of **glucocorticoids** from the **adrenal cortex,** and that the glucocorticoids produce many of the effects of the stress response. The level of circulating glucocorticoids is the most commonly employed physiological measure of stress.

With his emphasis on the role of the anterior pituitary adrenal cortex system in stress, Selye largely ignored the contributions of the sympathetic nervous system. Stressors also activate the sympathetic nervous system, which increases the release of epinephrine and norepinephrine from the **adrenal medulla.** Most modern theories of stress (see Stanford & Salmon, 1993) acknowledge the major roles of both systems (see Figure 17.10).

The magnitude of the stress response depends not only upon the stressor and the individual; it depends on the strategies that the individual adopts to cope with the stress (McEwen, 1994). For example, in a study of women awaiting surgery for possible breast cancer, the levels of stress were lower in those who had convinced themselves to think about their problem in certain ways. Those who had convinced themselves either that they could not possibly have cancer, that their prayers were certain to be answered, or that it was counterproductive to worry about it experienced less stress (Katz et al., 1970).

From the perspective of psychological science, the major contribution of Selye's discovery of the stress re-

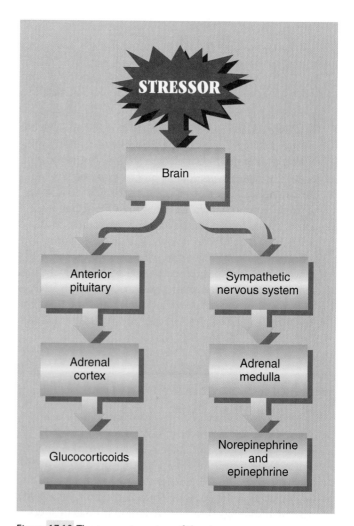

Figure 17.10 The two-system view of the stress response.

sponse was that it provided a mechanism by which psychological factors can influence physical illness: All kinds of common psychological stressors (e.g., losing a job, preparing for an examination, ending a relationship) are associated with high circulating levels of glucocorticoids, epinephrine, and norepinephrine (see Burns, 1990); and these in turn have been implicated in many physical disorders (e.g., hypertension, strokes, and diabetes). The following two sections describe two such *psychosomatic disorders* (disorders whose symptoms are primarily physical but whose development is influenced by psychological factors): gastric ulcers and infections.

Stress and Gastric Ulcers

Gastric ulcers are painful lesions to the lining of the stomach and duodenum, which in extreme cases can be life threatening. In the United States alone, 500,000 new cases are reported each year (see Livingston & Guth, 1992). Several studies have found a higher incidence of gastric ulcers in people living in stressful situations. However, the most convincing evidence that stress can be a causal factor in gastric ulcers comes from experiments in laboratory animals. Many experiments have shown that stressors (e.g., confinement to a restraint tube for a few hours) can produce ulcers in some laboratory animals.

Gastric ulcers have for decades been regarded as the prototypical psychosomatic disease—the physical disease with incontrovertible evidence of a psychological cause. However, all of this seemed to change with the report that gastric ulcers are caused by bacteria. Indeed, it has been claimed that the ulcer-causing bacteria (*Helicobacter pylori*) are responsible for all cases except those caused by nonsteroidal anti-inflammatory agents such as aspirin (Blaser, 1996). This seemed to rule out stress as a causal factor in gastric ulcers, but a careful consideration of the evidence suggests otherwise (Overmier & Murison, 1997).

The facts do not deny that *H. pylori* damages the stomach wall or that antibiotic treatment of gastric ulcers helps many sufferers. The facts do, however, suggest that *H. pylori* infection alone is insufficient to produce the disorder in most people. Although it is true that most patients with gastric ulcers display signs of *H. pylori* infection, so too do 75% of healthy control subjects. Also, although it is true that antibiotics improve the condition of many patients with gastric ulcers, so do psychological treatments—and they do it without reducing signs of *H. pylori* infection. Apparently, in most cases, there is another factor that increases the susceptibility of the stomach wall to damage from *H. pylori*, and this factor is likely to be stress. The evidence suggests that gastric ulcers are most likely to occur when both causal factors are present.

The study of the mechanisms of stress-induced gastric ulcers has focused on the amygdala because of the key role it plays in fear and defensive behavior (see Henke, 1992). Electrical stimulation of some areas of the amygdala increases the release of hydrochloric acid and decreases blood flow in the stomach wall. As a result, stimulation of these areas of the amygdala for only a few hours can produce gastric ulcers.

Psychoneuroimmunology: Stress and Infections

A major breakthrough in the study of stress and health came with the discovery that stress can reduce a person's resistance to infection. This finding had a great impact on the field of psychology, because it showed that stress could play a role in infectious diseases, which up to that point had been regarded as "strictly physical." In so doing, it opened up a vast area of medicine to psychological input (see Cohen, 1996; Cohen & Herbert, 1996). The theoretical and clinical implications of the finding that stress can increase susceptibility to infection were so great that the discovery led in the early 1980s to the emergence of a new field of biopsychological research. That field is **psychoneuroimmunology**—the study of interactions among psychological factors, the nervous system, and the immune system (see Maier, Watkins, & Fleshner, 1994). Psychoneuroimmunological research has focused on three important questions, which will be discussed later in this section; but first is an introduction to the immune system.

■ **IMMUNE SYSTEM** Microorganisms of every description revel in the warm, damp, nutritive climate of your body (see Ploegh, 1998). Your **immune system** keeps your body from being overwhelmed by these invaders. Before it can take any action against an invading microorganism, the immune system must have some way of distinguishing foreign cells from body cells. That is why **antigens**—protein molecules on the surface of a cell

Stress. The physiological response to physical or psychological threat.

Adrenocorticotropic hormone (ACTH). The anterior pituitary hormone that triggers the release of glucocorticoids from the adrenal cortex.

Glucocorticoids. Steroid hormones that are released from the adrenal cortex in response to stressors.

Adrenal cortex. The cortex of the adrenal glands, which releases glucocorticoids in response to stressors.

Adrenal medulla. The core of the adrenal glands, which releases epinephrine and norepinephrine in response to stressors.

Gastric ulcers. Lesions to the lining of the stomach or duodenum, a common consequence of stress.

Psychoneuroimmunology. The study of interactions among psychological factors, the nervous system, and the immune system.

Immune system. The system that protects the body against infectious microorganisms.

Antigens. Proteins on the surface of cells that identify them as native or foreign.

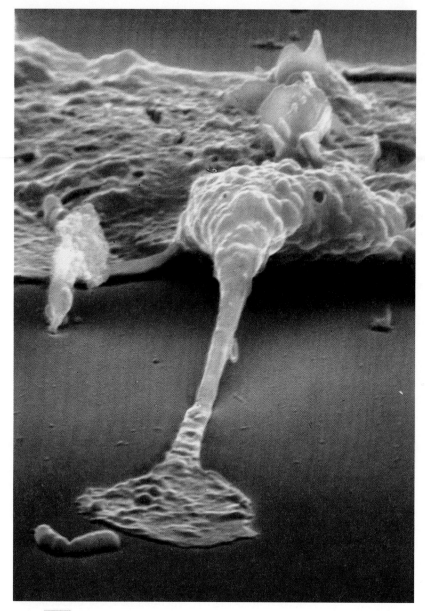

Figure 17.11 Phagocytosis: A macrophage hunts down and destroys a bacterium.

duced in bone marrow and are stored in the lymphatic system. **Cell-mediated immunity** is directed by **T cells** (T lymphocytes); **antibody-mediated immunity** is directed by **B cells** (B lymphocytes).

The cell-mediated immune reaction begins when a **macrophage**—a type of large phagocyte—ingests a foreign microorganism. The macrophage then displays the microorganism's antigens on the surface of its cell membrane (see Figure 17.11), and this attracts T cells. Each T cell has two kinds of receptors on its surface, one for molecules that are normally found on the surface of macrophages and other body cells and one for a specific foreign antigen. There are millions of different receptors for foreign antigens on T cells, but there is only one kind on each T cell and there are only a few T cells with each kind of receptor. After the microorganism has been ingested and its antigens have been displayed, a T cell with a receptor for the foreign antigen binds to the surface of the infected macrophage, which initiates a series of reactions. Among these reactions is the multiplication of the bound T cell, which creates more T cells with the specific receptor necessary to destroy all invaders that contain the target antigens and all body cells that have been infected by the invaders.

The antibody-mediated immune reaction begins when a B cell binds to a foreign antigen for which it contains an appropriate receptor. This causes the B cell to multiply and to synthesize a lethal form of its receptor molecules. These lethal receptor molecules, called **antibodies,** are released into the intracellular fluid, where they bind to the foreign antigens and destroy or deactivate the microorganisms that possess them. Memory B cells for the specific antigen are also produced during the pro-

that identify it as native or foreign—play a major role in specific immune reactions (see Beck & Habicht, 1996; Nossal, 1993).

Immune system barriers to infection are of two sorts. First, there are nonspecific barriers: barriers that act generally and quickly against most invaders. These barriers include mucous membranes, which destroy many foreign microorganisms, and **phagocytosis**—the process by which foreign microorganisms and debris are consumed and destroyed by *phagocytes* (specialized body cells that consume foreign microorganisms and debris)—see Figure 17.11. Second, there are specific barriers: barriers that act specifically against particular strains of invaders. The specific barriers are of two types—cell-mediated and antibody-mediated—each defended by a different class of lymphocytes. **Lymphocytes** are specialized white blood cells that are pro-

Phagocytosis. The consumption of dead tissue and invading microorganisms by specialized body cells (phagocytes).

Lymphocytes. Specialized white blood cells that play important roles in the body's immune reactions.

Cell-mediated immunity. The immune reaction by which T cells destroy invading microorganisms.

T cells. T lymphocytes; lymphocytes that bind to foreign microorganisms and cells that contain them and, in so doing, destroy them.

Antibody-mediated immunity. The immune reaction by which B cells destroy invading microorganisms.

B cells. B lymphocytes; lymphocytes that manufacture antibodies against antigens they encounter.

Macrophage. A large phagocyte that plays a role in cell-mediated immunity.

Antibodies. Proteins that bind specifically to antigens on the surface of invading microorganisms and in so doing promote the destruction of the microorganisms.

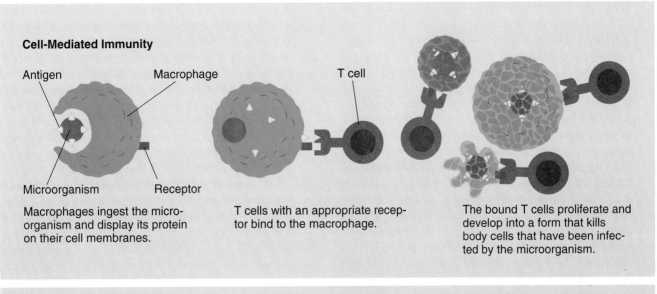

Cell-Mediated Immunity

Antigen   Macrophage   T cell

Microorganism   Receptor

Macrophages ingest the micro-organism and display its protein on their cell membranes.

T cells with an appropriate receptor bind to the macrophage.

The bound T cells proliferate and develop into a form that kills body cells that have been infected by the microorganism.

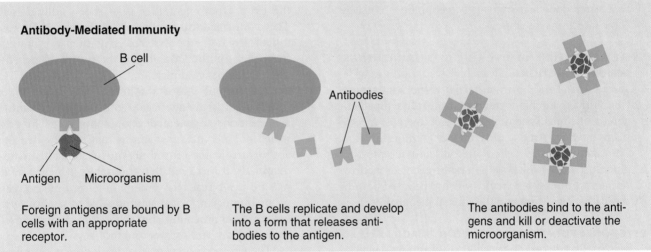

Antibody-Mediated Immunity

B cell

Antibodies

Antigen   Microorganism

Foreign antigens are bound by B cells with an appropriate receptor.

The B cells replicate and develop into a form that releases antibodies to the antigen.

The antibodies bind to the antigens and kill or deactivate the microorganism.

Figure 17.12 *Specific barriers to infection: Cell-mediated immunity and antibody-mediated immunity. In cell-mediated immunity, microorganisms or body cells that they have invaded are killed by T cells; in antibody-mediated immunity, microorganisms are killed by antibodies produced by B cells.*

cess; these cells have a long life and accelerate antibody-mediated immunity if there is a subsequent infection by the same organism (see Ahmed & Gray, 1996).

Cell-mediated immunity and antibody-mediated immunity are illustrated in Figure 17.12. Both processes take several days the first time a particular foreign antigen is recognized, but responses to subsequent invasions of microorganisms with the same antigen are much faster thanks to the memory T cells and B cells. This is why *inoculation* (the injection of small samples of an infective microorganism into healthy individuals) is often an effective preventive measure against the effects of subsequent infection.

Now that you have been introduced to the immune system, it is time to turn to a consideration of psychoneuroimmunological research. It has focused on the following three questions.

■ **DOES STRESS DISRUPT IMMUNE FUNCTION?** Numerous studies have documented the adverse effects of stress on various aspects of immune function, both in humans and in laboratory animals (see Auphan et al., 1995; Maier, Watkins, & Fleshner, 1994). In laboratory animals, electric shocks, social defeat, overcrowding, the odor of stressed conspecifics, loud noise, and maternal separation have all been shown to depress immune function. In humans, the list includes final examinations, sleep deprivation, divorce, bereavement, and caring for a relative with Alzheimer's disease.

■ **ARE STRESS-RELATED DECREASES IN IMMUNE FUNCTION LARGE ENOUGH TO BE OF CLINICAL SIGNIFICANCE?** Although stress has been shown to suppress many aspects of immune function, it has been harder than you might think to prove that these effects are large enough to increase the rate or severity of infectious diseases in humans. True, numerous studies have reported positive correlations between stress and ill health in human subjects; for example, students in one study reported more respiratory infections during their final examination period (Glaser et al., 1987). However, the causal interpretation of such correlations is never straightforward: Stressed subjects may report more illness during times of stress because they expect to be more ill, because the experience of illness during times of stress is more unpleasant, or because the stress caused illness-inducing changes in their behavior (e.g., changes in diet, drug use, or sleep patterns). Be that as it may, the causal effect of stress on the susceptibility to infectious diseases has been demonstrated in many well-controlled experiments on laboratory animals. Together the two lines of evidence—the human correlational studies and the controlled laboratory experiments—leave little doubt that stress does increase our susceptibility to at least some infectious diseases.

■ **WHAT IS THE MECHANISM BY WHICH STRESS INFLUENCES IMMUNE FUNCTION?** Given that stress produces widespread neural and hormonal activity through the anterior pituitary adrenal cortex system and the sympathetic adrenal medulla system, there are innumerable mechanisms by which stress could influence immune function. For example, both T cells and B cells have receptors for glucocorticoids, which are released by the adrenal cortex, and for norepinephrine, which is released both by sympathetic neurons and the adrenal medulla.

■ **PSYCHONEUROIMMUNOLOGY: CONCLUSION** We have just briefly touched on psychoneuroimmunological research here. Cohen and Herbert (1996) after reviewing the entire field reached the following three conclusions: First, numerous neural mechanisms by which stress might increase susceptibility to infection have been identified; second, stressors have been shown to disrupt immune function in a variety of ways; and third, there is already evidence that that stress increases susceptibility to several infectious diseases (e.g., colds, influenza, herpes).

Effects of Stress on the Hippocampus

Before leaving the topic of stress, I would be remiss if I did not tell you about two related lines of research that have generated considerable interest among biopsychologists. Both involve the hippocampus, which has a particularly dense population of glucocorticoid receptors.

The first of these two lines of research began with the discovery that handling rat pups for a few minutes per day during the first few weeks of their lives has a variety of salutary (health-promoting) effects (see Sapolsky, 1997). Among these salutary effects was a decrease in glucocorticoids. This handling-produced decrease in glucocorticoids created a stir among neuroscientists, because elevated levels of glucocorticoids had been shown to adversely affect the brain—for example, by accelerating neural loss during aging. Indeed, rats handled as pups were found to have less hippocampal degeneration and fewer memory deficits in old age (Meaney et al., 1988). The reduction of circulating glucorticoid levels seems to be a consequence of the increased negative feedback resulting from an increase in the number of glucocorticoid receptors in the hippocampus.

It is remarkable that a few hours of handling early in life could have such a significant and lasting effect on the development of the nervous system. However, handling itself does not directly produce the effect. Liu et al. (1997) found that handled rats were groomed (licked) more by their mothers, and they hypothesized that the salutary effects of handling were stimulated by the extra grooming rather than the handling itself. They confirmed this hypothesis by showing that those unhandled rat pups that received intense grooming from their mothers developed the profile of benefits observed in handled pups.

The second important line of stress-and-hippocampus experiments began with the observation of an exception to a general developmental rule: This rule, which now requires revision, is that no new neurons are formed in the central nervous systems of mature mammals. It turns out that thousands of new *granule cells* are created each day in the adult *dentate gyrus* (part of the hippocampus). It is impossible to say how general this phenomenon is; but so far, it has been demonstrated in rats, tree shrews, and monkeys.

The effects of stress on the development of granule cells in adulthood may explain how stress or excessive exposure to glucocorticoids causes hippocampal damage (see Sapolsky, 1996; Yehuda, 1997). Gould and colleagues (1998) found that stress blocks the normal creation of new hippocampal granule cells in adulthood. They exposed male monkeys to stress by placing them for 1 hour in an unfamiliar monkey colony, where they were targets of social aggression from the high-ranking male residents, and this was sufficient to substantially reduce the number of developing hippocampal granule cells. Thus, stress and glucocorticoids may produce hippocampal damage by blocking the creation of new neurons rather than by damaging existing ones.

These two findings about stress and the hippocampus—the finding that glucocorticoid-reducing neonatal maternal contact can prevent hippocampal degeneration in adulthood and the finding that glucocorticoid-increasing stress in adulthood can disrupt the normal generation of new neurons—have generated excitement among both brain scientists and clinicians. If stress can adversely affect the anatomy of the brain, is it any wonder that stress has been implicated in the *etiology* (cause) of several psychological disorders?

Before proceeding to a discussion of stress and psychological disorders, review your introduction to emotion, fear, and stress by filling in the following blanks with the most appropriate term. The correct answers are provided at the bottom of this page. Review material related to your errors and omissions.

1. The theory that the subjective experience of emotion is triggered by ANS responses is called the _____ theory.

2. The pattern of aggressive responses observed in decorticate animals is called _____ .

3. Between the amygdala and the fornix in the limbic ring is the _____ .

4. A Duchenne smile, but not a false smile, involves contraction of the _____ .

5. Aggression directed by the alpha male of a colony at a male intruder is called _____ aggression.

6. The usual target site of rat defensive attacks is the _____ of the attacking rat.

7. Bilateral lesions of the medial geniculate nucleus or the _____ block fear conditioning to auditory conditional stimuli.

8. The _____ of the midbrain elicits the appropriate behavioral responses to fear-inducing stimuli.

9. Glucocorticoids are released from the _____ _____ as part of the stress response.

10. Stressors increase the release of epinephrine and norepinephrine from the _____ _____ .

11. The study of the interactions among psychological factors, the nervous system, and the immune system is called _____ .

12. T cells and B cells are involved in cell-mediated and _____ immune reactions, respectively.

17.4 Schizophrenia

So far, the focus has been on emotions, particularly on the stress resulting from negative emotions and its causal role in psychosomatic disorders. Now the focus shifts to three classes of psychiatric disorder: schizophrenia, affective disorders, and anxiety disorders. This is a fitting continuation to our discussion of stress in two ways: First, negative emotional symptoms are prominent features of most psychological disorders; second, stress can be an important causal factor in psychological disorders—just as it is in psychosomatic disorders.

It would be a mistake to think that stress is the primary cause of psychological disorders: There is no evidence for this, although it is a point of view that is often presented as fact. Instead, stress seems to exacerbate the symptoms of individuals who already have a psychological disorder or a susceptibility to it—its causal role in psychiatric disorders thus appears to be no different than its causal role in psychosomatic disorders.

The answers are (1) James-Lange, (2) sham rage, (3) hippocampus, (4) orbicularis oculi, (5) social, (6) face, (7) amygdala, (8) periaqueductal gray, (9) adrenal cortex, (10) adrenal medulla, (11) psychoneuroimmunology, and (12) antibody-mediated.

One widely held theory of psychiatric illness is the **diathesis–stress model** (pronounced die ATH e sis): the theory that psychological disorders are caused by the interaction of a genetic propensity (diathesis) and stress (see Eley & Plomin, 1997). The search for particular genes that predispose people to psychological disorders is now in full swing. Although there have been several recent reports of linkage between particular chromosomal sites and the susceptibility to particular psychological disorders, none has yet been convincingly replicated (Leboyer et al., 1998).

Now that you have been generally oriented to the diathesis–stress model, let's turn to schizophrenia, the psychiatric disorder that is the focus of this section. The term **schizophrenia** means the splitting of psychic functions. It was coined in the early 1900s to describe what was assumed to be the primary symptom of the disorder: the breakdown of integration among emotion, thought, and action. It is the disease that is most commonly associated with the concept of madness. It attacks about 1% of individuals of all races and cultural groups, typically beginning in adolescence or early adulthood.

The major difficulty in studying and treating schizophrenia is accurately defining it. Its symptoms are complex and diverse; they overlap greatly with those of other psychiatric disorders, and they frequently change during the progression of the disorder (see Andreasen, 1994; Heinrichs, 1993). As a result, there have been many attempts to break the diagnosis of schizophrenia down into several disorders, but none of these attempts has proved successful. The following are the symptoms of schizophrenia, but none of them appears in all cases; indeed, the recurrence of only one of them is grounds for the diagnosis of schizophrenia:

Bizarre delusions. Delusions of being controlled (e.g., "Martians are making me think evil thoughts"), delusions of persecution (e.g., "My mother is trying to poison me"), delusions of grandeur (e.g., "Michael Jordan admires my sneakers").

Inappropriate affect. Failure to react with an appropriate level of emotionality to positive or negative events.

Hallucinations. Imaginary voices telling the person what to do or commenting negatively on the person's behavior.

Incoherent thought. Illogical thinking, peculiar associations among ideas, or belief in supernatural forces.

Odd behavior. Long periods with no movement (*catatonia*), a lack of personal hygiene, talking in rhymes, avoiding social interaction.

Causal Factors in Schizophrenia

In the first half of the 20th century, the cloak of mysticism began to be removed from mental illness by a se-

ries of studies that established schizophrenia's genetic basis. First, it was discovered that although only 1% of the population develops schizophrenia, the probability of schizophrenia occurring in a close biological relative (i.e., in a parent, child, or sibling) of a schizophrenic is about 10%, even if the relative was adopted shortly after birth by a healthy family (e.g., Kendler & Gruenbert, 1984; Rosenthal et al., 1980). Then, it was discovered that the concordance rates for schizophrenia are higher in identical twins (45%) than in fraternal twins (10%)—see Holzman and Matthyse (1990) and Kallman (1946).

The fact that the concordance rate for schizophrenia in identical twins is substantially less than 100% suggests that differences in experience contribute significantly to differences among people in the development of schizophrenia. The current view is that some people inherit a potential for schizophrenia, which may or may not be activated by experience. Supporting this view is a recent comparison of the offspring of a large sample of identical twins who were themselves discordant for schizophrenia (i.e., one had the disorder and one did not); the incidence of schizophrenia was as great in the offspring of the nonschizophrenic twins as in the offspring of the schizophrenic twins (Gottesman & Bertelsen, 1989).

Several types of experience have been hypothesized to play a key role in activating schizophrenic symptoms in people with an inherited susceptibility; however, much of the recent evidence has implicated exposure to stress as the major factor. Several studies have found

17 BIOPSYCHOLOGY OF STRESS AND ILLNESS

that exposure to stressors is common just before a schizophrenic attack, and several have found correlations between the severity of the stressors and the severity of the resulting schizophrenic symptoms (see Norman & Malla, 1993).

Discovery of the First Antischizophrenic Drugs

The first major breakthrough in the study of the biochemistry of schizophrenia was the accidental discovery in the early 1950s of the first antischizophrenic drug, **chlorpromazine.** Chlorpromazine was developed by a French drug company as an antihistamine. Then, in 1950, a French surgeon noticed that chlorpromazine given prior to surgery to counteract swelling had a calming effect on some of his patients, and he suggested that it might have a calming effect on difficult-to-handle psychotic patients. His suggestion proved to be incorrect, but the clinical trials it triggered led to the discovery that chlorpromazine alleviates schizophrenic symptoms: Agitated schizophrenics were calmed by chlorpromazine, and emotionally blunt schizophrenics were activated by it. Don't get the idea that chlorpromazine cures schizophrenia. It doesn't. But in many cases it reduces the severity of schizophrenic symptoms enough to allow institutionalized patients to be discharged.

Shortly after the antischizophrenic action of chlorpromazine was first documented, an American psychiatrist became interested in reports that the snakeroot plant had long been used in India for the treatment of mental illness. He gave **reserpine**—the active ingredient of the snakeroot plant—to his schizophrenic patients and confirmed its antischizophrenic action. Reserpine is no longer used in the treatment of schizophrenia because it produces a dangerous decline in blood pressure at antischizophrenic doses.

Although the chemical structures of chlorpromazine and reserpine are dissimilar, their antischizophrenic effects are similar in two major respects. First, the antischizophrenic effect of both drugs is manifested only after a patient has been medicated for 2 or 3 weeks. Second, the onset of the antischizophrenic effect of the medication is usually associated with motor effects similar to the symptoms of Parkinson's disease: tremors at rest, muscular rigidity, and a general decrease in voluntary movement. These similarities suggested to researchers that chlorpromazine and reserpine were acting through the same mechanism, one that was related to Parkinson's disease.

Dopamine Theory of Schizophrenia

Paradoxically, the next major breakthrough in the study of schizophrenia came from research on Parkinson's disease. In 1960, it was reported that the *striatums* (caudates plus putamens) of persons dying of Parkinson's disease had been depleted of dopamine (Ehringer & Hornykiewicz, 1960). This finding suggested that a disruption of dopaminergic transmission might produce Parkinson's disease; and because of the relation between Parkinson's disease and the antischizophrenic effects of chlorpromazine and reserpine, it suggested that antischizophrenic drug effects might be produced in the same way. Thus was born the *dopamine theory of schizophrenia*—the theory that schizophrenia is caused by too much dopamine and, conversely, that antischizophrenic drugs exert their effects by decreasing dopamine levels.

Lending instant support to the dopamine theory of schizophrenia were two already well-established facts. First, the antischizophrenic drug reserpine was known to deplete the brain of dopamine and other monoamines by breaking down their synaptic vesicles. Second, drugs such as amphetamine and cocaine, which can trigger schizophrenic episodes in normal subjects, were known to increase the extracellular levels of dopamine and other monoamines in the brain.

An important step in the evolution of the dopamine theory of schizophrenia came in 1963, when Carlsson and Lindqvist assessed the effects of chlorpromazine on extracellular levels of dopamine and its *metabolites* (molecules that are created when another molecule is broken down). They expected to find that chlorpromazine, like reserpine, depletes the brain of dopamine; but they didn't. The extracellular levels of dopamine were unchanged by chlorpromazine, and the extracellular levels of its metabolites were increased. They concluded that both chlorpromazine and reserpine antagonize transmission at dopamine synapses but that they do it in different ways—reserpine by depleting the brain of dopamine and chlorpromazine by binding to dopamine receptors. They argued that chlorpromazine is a **false transmitter** (receptor blocker) at dopamine synapses—that is, that it binds to dopamine receptors without activating them and that, in so doing, keeps dopamine from activating them (see Figure 17.13 on page 486). They further postulated that the lack of activity at postsynaptic dopamine receptors

Diathesis–stress model. The theory that psychological disorders are caused by the interaction of genetic propensity (diathesis) and stress.

Schizophrenia. A psychosis that is characterized by the recurrence of any of the following symptoms: bizarre delusions, inappropriate affect, hallucinations, incoherent thought, and odd behavior.

Chlorpromazine. The first antischizophrenic drug.

Reserpine. The first monoamine antagonist to be used in the treatment of schizophrenia; it is the active ingredient of the snakeroot plant.

False transmitter. A receptor blocker, a chemical that binds to a synaptic receptor without activating it and, in so doing, blocks the action of the neurotransmitter.

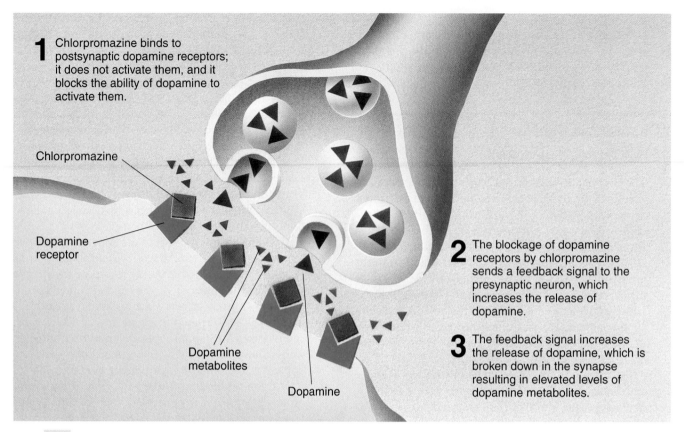

1 Chlorpromazine binds to postsynaptic dopamine receptors; it does not activate them, and it blocks the ability of dopamine to activate them.

Chlorpromazine

Dopamine receptor

Dopamine metabolites

Dopamine

2 The blockage of dopamine receptors by chlorpromazine sends a feedback signal to the presynaptic neuron, which increases the release of dopamine.

3 The feedback signal increases the release of dopamine, which is broken down in the synapse resulting in elevated levels of dopamine metabolites.

Figure 17.13 Chlorpromazine, a false transmitter at dopamine synapses.

sent a feedback signal to the presynaptic cells that increased their release of dopamine, which was broken down in the synapses. This explained why dopaminergic activity was reduced while extracellular dopamine levels stayed about the same and the extracellular levels of its metabolites were increased. Carlsson and Lindqvist's findings led to an important revision of the dopamine theory of schizophrenia: Rather than high dopamine levels per se, the main factor in schizophrenia was presumed to be high levels of activity at dopamine receptors.

In the mid-1970s, Snyder and his colleagues (Creese, Burt, & Snyder, 1976) assessed the degree to which the various antischizophrenic drugs that had been developed by that time bind to dopamine receptors. First, they added radioactively labeled dopamine to samples of dopamine-receptor-rich neural membrane obtained from calf striatums. Then, they rinsed away the unbound dopamine molecules from the samples and measured the amount of radioactivity left in them to obtain a measure of the number of dopamine receptors. Next, in other samples, they measured each drug's ability to block the binding of radioactive dopamine to the sample, the assumption being that the drugs with a high affinity for dopamine receptors would leave fewer sites available for the dopamine. In general, they found that chlorpromazine and the other effective antischizophrenic drugs had a high affinity for dopamine receptors, whereas inef-

fective antischizophrenic drugs had a low affinity. There were, however, several major exceptions, one of them being haloperidol. Although **haloperidol** was one of the most potent antischizophrenic drugs of its day, it had a relatively low affinity for dopamine receptors.

A solution to the haloperidol puzzle came with the discovery that dopamine binds to more than one receptor subtype—five have now been identified (Hartmann & Civelli, 1997). It turned out that chlorpromazine and the other antischizophrenic drugs in the same chemical class (the **phenothiazines**) all bind effectively to both D_1 and D_2 receptors, whereas haloperidol and the other antischizophrenic drugs in its chemical class (the **butyrophenones**) all bind effectively to D_2 receptors but not to D_1 receptors.

This discovery of the selective binding of butyrophenones to D_2 receptors led to an important revision in the dopamine theory of schizophrenia. It suggested that schizophrenia is caused by hyperactivity specifi-

Haloperidol. A butyrophenone antischizophrenic drug.
Phenothiazines. A class of antischizophrenic drugs that bind effectively to both D_1 and D_2 receptors.
Butyrophenones. A class of antischizophrenic drugs that bind primarily to D_2 receptors.

Neuroleptics. Drugs that alleviate schizophrenic symptoms.
Clozapine. An antischizophrenic drug that does not produce many of the side effects of conventional neuroleptics and does not bind to D_2 receptors.

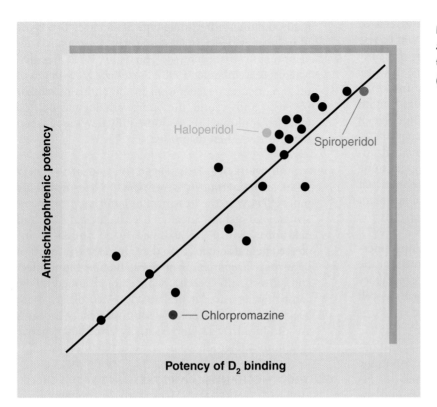

Antischizophrenic potency

Haloperidol

Spiroperidol

Chlorpromazine

Potency of D_2 binding

cally at D_2 receptors, rather than at dopamine receptors in general. Snyder and his colleagues (see Snyder, 1978) subsequently confirmed that the degree to which **neuroleptics**—antischizophrenic drugs—bind to D_2 receptors is highly correlated with their effectiveness in suppressing schizophrenic symptoms (see Figure 17.14). For example, they found that the butyrophenone *spiroperidol* had the greatest affinity for D_2 receptors and the most potent antischizophrenic effect.

The D_2 receptor version of the dopamine theory is currently the most widely recognized theory of the neural basis of schizophrenia. The major events in its development are summarized in Table 17.2.

Current Research on the Neural Basis of Schizophrenia

Although the evidence implicating D_2 receptors in schizophrenia is strong, the dopamine theory as it currently stands has some major weaknesses. Following are five major questions about the theory that have been the focus of recent research.

■ **ARE D_2 RECEPTORS THE ONLY RECEPTORS INVOLVED IN SCHIZOPHRENIA?** The development of *atypical neuroleptic drugs* (antischizophrenic drugs that are not D_2 receptor blockers) has challenged the view that D_2 receptors are the only receptors involved in schizophrenia. For example, **clozapine** is effective in the treatment of schizophrenia; yet, unlike conventional neuroleptics,

it does not have a high affinity for D_2 receptors or produce parkinsonian side effects (see Meltzer et al., 1990). The effectiveness of clozapine and other atypical neuroleptics thus suggests that D_2 receptors are not the only receptors involved in schizophrenia; clozapine has a high affinity for D_1 receptors, D_4 receptors, and several serotonin receptors.

Table 17.2 The Key Events That Led to the Development and Refinement of the Dopamine Theory of Schizophrenia

Early 1950s	The antischizophrenic effects of both chlorpromazine and reserpine were documented and related to their parkinsonian side effects.
Late 1950s	The brains of recently deceased Parkinson's patients were found to be depleted of dopamine.
Early 1960s	It was hypothesized that schizophrenia was associated with excessive activity at dopaminergic synapses.
1960s and 1970s	Chlorpromazine and other clinically effective neuroleptics were found to act as false transmitters at dopamine synapses.
Mid-1970s	The affinity of neuroleptics for dopamine receptors was found to be only roughly correlated with their antischizophrenic potency.
Late 1970s	The binding of existing antischizophrenic drugs to D_2 receptors was found to be highly correlated with their antischizophrenic potency.

■ **WHY DOES IT TAKE SEVERAL WEEKS OF NEUROLEPTIC THERAPY TO AFFECT SCHIZOPHRENIC SYMPTOMS?** The dopamine theory of schizophrenia has difficulty explaining why it takes several weeks of neuroleptic therapy to alleviate schizophrenic symptoms when dopaminergic transmission is effectively blocked within hours. This discrepancy indicates that the blockage of dopamine receptors is not the specific mechanism by which schizophrenic symptoms are alleviated. It appears that blocking dopamine receptors triggers some slow-developing compensatory change in the brain that is the key factor in the therapeutic effect. One recent theory is that this critical slow-acting change is the *dopamine-cell depolarization block* (Grace et al., 1997). Neuroleptics initially increase the firing of dopaminergic neurons, but eventually, at about the time that the therapeutic effects are manifested, there is a general decrease in their firing. This decrease is the dopamine-cell depolarization block.

■ **WHAT PARTS OF THE BRAIN ARE INVOLVED IN SCHIZOPHRENIA?** Brain-imaging studies of schizophrenic patients typically reveal widespread abnormalities, including an abnormally small cerebral cortex and abnormally large cerebral ventricles (see Frith & Dolan, 1998). Surprisingly, however, there is yet no direct evidence of structural damage to dopaminergic circuits (see Egan & Weinberger, 1997). One major question about the brain pathology of schizophrenics is whether or not it is developmental: Do the brains of schizophrenics develop abnormally, or do they develop normally and then suffer some type of damage? Two types of indirect evidence suggest that schizophrenia is a developmental disorder (see Harrison, 1997; Raedler, Knable, & Weinberger, 1998): First, there are no signs of ongoing neural degeneration in the brains of schizophrenics; and second, the brain pathology associated with schizophrenia seems to be fully developed when the disorder is first diagnosed.

■ **WHY ARE NEUROLEPTICS EFFECTIVE AGAINST ONLY SOME SCHIZOPHRENIC SYMPTOMS?** Neuroleptics are more effective in the treatment of *positive schizophrenic symptoms* (such as incoherence, hallucinations, and delusions), which are assumed to be caused by increased neural activity, than they are in the treatment of *negative schizophrenic symptoms* (such as blunt affect and poverty of speech), which are assumed to be caused by decreased neural activity. Accordingly, it has been suggested that positive schizophrenic symptoms are produced by D_2 hyperactivity and that negative symptoms are produced by structural pathology.

■ **BY WHAT MECHANISM CAN STRESS ACTIVATE SCHIZOPHRENIC SYMPTOMS?** Stress activates dopaminergic projections to the prefrontal cortex, which dampen responses to stress in other circuits. One theory is that the abnormal development of prefrontal cortex that occurs in many schizophrenics (Winn, 1994) results in exaggerated responses to stressors, and in so doing, contributes to the activation of schizophrenic symptoms (Jaskiw & Weinberger, 1992).

17.5 Affective Disorders: Depression and Mania

All of us have experienced depression. Depression is a normal reaction to grievous loss such as the loss of a loved one, the loss of self-esteem, the loss of personal possessions, or the loss of health. However, there are people whose tendency toward depression is out of proportion. These people repeatedly fall into the depths of despair, often for no apparent reason; and their depression can be so extreme that it is almost impossible for them to meet the essential requirements of their daily lives—to keep a job, to maintain social contacts, or even to maintain an acceptable level of personal hygiene. It is these people who are said to be suffering from clinical **depression.**

Many people who suffer from clinical depression also experience periods of mania. **Mania** is at the other end of the scale of mood. During periods of mild mania, people are talkative, energetic, impulsive, positive, and very confident. In this state, they can be very effective at certain jobs and can be great fun to be with. But when mania becomes extreme, it is a serious clinical problem. The florid manic often awakens in a state of unbridled enthusiasm, with an outflow of incessant chatter that careens nonstop from topic to topic. No task is too difficult. No goal is unattainable. This confidence and grandiosity, coupled with high energy, distractibility, and a leap-before-you-look impulsiveness, result in a continual series of disasters: Mania leaves behind it a trail of unfinished projects, unpaid bills, and broken relationships. Depression and mania are considered to be disorders of *affect* (emotion).

Depression is often divided into two categories: **reactive depression,** which is triggered by an obvious negative experience, and **endogenous depression,** which is not. Not all depressive patients experience periods of

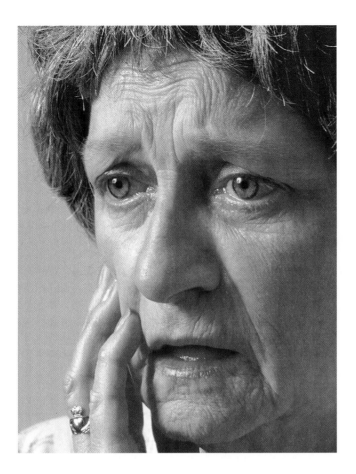

mania. Those that do not are said to suffer from **unipolar affective disorder;** those that do are said to suffer from **bipolar affective disorder.**

The incidence of affective disorders in industrialized Western societies has been well documented. About 6% of people suffer from unipolar affective disorder at one point in their lives, and about 1% suffer from bipolar affective disorder. Moreover, unipolar affective disorder tends to be twice as prevalent in women as in men; there is no sex difference in the incidence of bipolar affective disorder; and about 10% of those suffering from affective disorders commit suicide (see Culbertson, 1997; Weissman & Olfson, 1995). In contrast, the incidence of affective disorders in other societies appears to be variable. For example, in Chile and China, the incidence of depression appears to be many times greater in women than in men (see Kleinman & Cohen, 1997).

Causal Factors in Affective Disorders

Genetic factors contribute to differences among people in the development of affective disorders (see MacKinnon, Jamison, & DePaulo, 1997). Twin studies of affective disorders suggest a concordance rate of about 60% for identical twins and 15% for fraternal twins, whether they are reared together or apart. Although there are many exceptions, there is a tendency for affected twins to suffer from the same disorder, unipolar or bipolar;

and the concordance rates for bipolar disorders tend to be higher than those for unipolar disorders.

Most of the research on the causal role of experience in affective disorders has focused on the role of stress in the etiology of depression. Several studies have shown that stressful experiences can trigger attacks of depression in already depressed individuals. For example, Brown (1993) found that over 84% of a large sample of patients seeking treatment for depression had experienced severe stress in the preceding year, in comparison to 32% of a group of control subjects. However, it has been more difficult to confirm the hypothesis that early exposure to stress increases likelihood of developing depression in adulthood (Kessler, 1997).

Discovery of Antidepressant Drugs

Four classes of drugs have been developed for the treatment of affective disorders: monoamine oxidase inhibitors, tricyclic antidepressants, lithium, and selective monoamine-reuptake inhibitors.

■ **MONOAMINE OXIDASE INHIBITORS Iproniazid,** the first antidepressant drug, was originally developed for the treatment of tuberculosis, and as such it proved to be a dismal flop. However, interest in the antidepressant potential of the drug was kindled by the observation that iproniazid left patients with tuberculosis less depressed about their disorder. As a result, iproniazid was tested on a mixed group of psychiatric patients and was found to be effective against depression. It was first marketed as an antidepressant drug in 1957.

Iproniazid is a monoamine agonist; it increases the levels of monoamines (e.g., norepinephrine and serotonin) by inhibiting the activity of *monoamine oxidase (MAO)*, the enzyme that breaks down monoamine neurotransmitters in the cytoplasm of the neuron. **MAO inhibitors** have several side effects; the most dangerous is known as the **cheese effect.** Foods such as cheese, wine,

---

Depression. A normal reaction to grievous loss; when depression is excessive, disruptive, and recurring, it is classified as a psychiatric disorder.

Mania. An affective disorder in which the patient is impulsive, overconfident, highly energetic, and distractible.

Reactive depression. Depression that is precipitated by a negative experience.

Endogenous depression. Depression that appears not to have been triggered by a negative experience.

Unipolar affective disorder. A depressive disorder in which the patient does not experience periods of mania.

Bipolar affective disorder. A disorder of emotion in which the patient experiences periods of mania interspersed with periods of depression.

Iproniazid. The first antidepressant drug, a monoamine oxidase inhibitor.

MAO inhibitors. Drugs that increase the level of monoamine neurotransmitters by inhibiting the action of monoamine oxidase.

Cheese effect. The surges in blood pressure that occur when individuals taking MAO inhibitors consume tyramine-rich foods.

and pickles contain an amine called *tyramine,* which is a potent elevator of blood pressure. Normally, these foods have little effect on blood pressure, because tyramine is rapidly metabolized in the liver by MAO. However, people who take MAO inhibitors and consume tyramine-rich foods run the risk of strokes caused by surges in blood pressure.

■ **TRICYCLIC ANTIDEPRESSANTS** The **tricyclic antidepressants** are so named because of their antidepressant action and because their chemical structures include a three-ring chain. **Imipramine,** the first tricyclic antidepressant, was initially thought to be an antischizophrenic drug. However, when its effects on a mixed sample of psychiatric patients were assessed, its antidepressant effect was immediately obvious. Tricyclic antidepressants block the reuptake of both serotonin and norepinephrine, thus increasing their levels in the brain. They are a safer alternative to MAO inhibitors.

■ **LITHIUM** The discovery of the ability of **lithium**—a simple metallic ion—to block mania is yet another important pharmacological breakthrough that was made by accident. Cade, an Australian psychiatrist, mixed the urine of manic patients with lithium to form a soluble salt; then he injected the salt into a group of guinea pigs to see if it would induce mania. As a control, he injected lithium into another group. Instead of inducing mania, the urine solution seemed to calm the guinea pigs; and because the lithium control injections had the same effect, Cade concluded that lithium, not uric acid, was the calming agent. In retrospect, Cade's conclusion was incredibly foolish. We now know that at the doses used by Cade, lithium salts produce extreme nausea. To Cade's untrained eye, his subjects' inactivity may have looked like calmness. But the subjects weren't calm; they were sick. Be that as it may, flushed with what he thought was the success of his guinea pig experiments, in 1954 Cade tried lithium on a group of 10 manic patients, and it proved remarkably effective.

There was little immediate reaction to Cade's report. Few scientists were impressed by Cade's scientific credentials, and few drug companies were interested in spending millions of dollars to evaluate the therapeutic potential of a metallic ion that could not be protected by a patent. Accordingly, the therapeutic potential of lithium was not fully appreciated until the late 1960s, when it was discovered that lithium is effective against depression as well as mania (Angst et al., 1970; Baastrup & Schou, 1967). Today, lithium is the treatment of choice for bipolar affective disorder. Its therapeutic effects are thought to be mediated by its agonist effects on serotonin function.

■ **SELECTIVE MONOAMINE-REUPTAKE INHIBITORS** *Fluoxetine,* which is marketed under the name **Prozac,** is an offspring of the tricyclic antidepressants. It is a slight structural variation of tricyclic antidepressants that se-

lectively blocks serotonin reuptake, rather than blocking both serotonin and norepinephrine reuptake (see Figure 17.15). Accordingly, Prozac and other drugs of its class (Paxil, Zoloft, Luvox) are called *selective serotonin-reuptake inhibitors.*

Prozac was introduced for clinical use in the 1980s. Although it is no more effective against depression than imipramine, it has already been prescribed for more than 10 million people. There are two reasons for its remarkable popularity (see Barondes, 1994). First, it has few side effects; and second, it has proved effective against a wide range of psychological disorders other than depression. Because Prozac is so effective against disorders that were once considered to be the exclusive province of psychotherapy (e.g., lack of self-esteem, fear of failure, excessive sensitivity to criticism, and inability to experience pleasure), it has had a major impact on the fields of psychiatry and clinical psychology.

Recently, *selective norepinephrine-reuptake inhibitors* (e.g., *reboxetine*) have been introduced for the treatment of depression. They seem to be as effective as selective serotonin-reuptake inhibitors.

Neural Mechanisms of Depression

The search for the neural mechanisms of affective disorders has focused on depression; however, the fact that lithium is effective against both depression and mania suggests that the mechanisms of the two are closely related.

■ **MONOAMINE THEORY OF DEPRESSION** The dominant theory of depression is the *monoamine theory.* It is based on the fact that monoamine oxidase inhibitors, tricyclic antidepressants, selective serotonin-reuptake inhibitors, and selective norepinephrine-reuptake inhibitors are all agonists of serotonin, norepinephrine, or both. The monoamine theory of depression is that depression is associated with underactivity at serotonergic and noradrenergic synapses.

The monoamine theory of depression has been supported by the results of autopsy studies (see Nemeroff, 1998). Certain subtypes of norepinephrine and serotonin receptors have been found to be elevated in depressed individuals who have not received pharmacological treatment. This implicates a deficit in monoamine release: When insufficient neurotransmitter is released at a synapse, there are usually compensatory increases in the number of receptors for that neurotransmitter. This process of compensatory receptor proliferation is called **up-regulation.**

Another line of support for the monoamine theory of depression comes from the development of an improved drug protocol for the treatment of depression. Normally, any increased levels of serotonin in synapses are dampened by presynaptic **autoreceptors** that detect

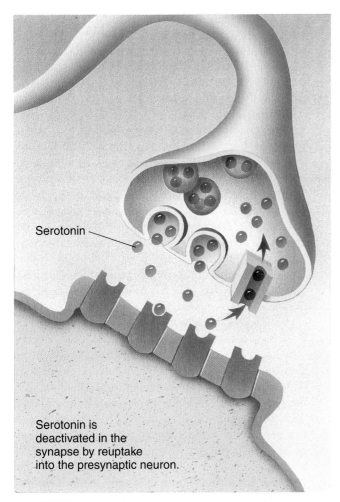

Serotonin

Serotonin is
deactivated in the
synapse by reuptake
into the presynaptic neuron.

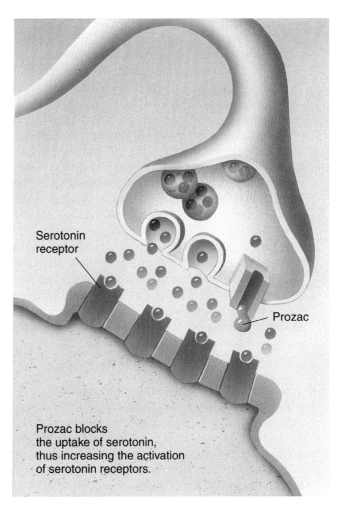

Serotonin
receptor

Prozac

Prozac blocks
the uptake of serotonin,
thus increasing the activation
of serotonin receptors.

Figure 17.15 Blockade of serotonin reuptake by fluoxetine (Prozac).

the increased levels and trigger a reduction in subsequent serotonin release. Artigas and colleagues (1996) blocked the autoreceptor-mediated dampening of the increases in extracellular serotonin that are produced by selective serotonin-reuptake inhibitors by administering a serotonin autoreceptor blocker (pindolol) in combination with a selective serotonin-reuptake inhibitor. The autoreceptor blocker allowed the selective serotonin-reuptake inhibitor to produce a greater increase in extracellular serotonin, and, as predicted by the monoamine theory, it increased the antidepressant effect of the selective serotonin-reuptake inhibitor.

■ HYPOTHALAMUS-PITUITARY-ADRENAL THEORY OF DE-
PRESSION Other theories of depression have focused on abnormalities of the hormonal response to stress. Depressed individuals synthesize more hypothalamic *corticotropin-releasing hormone* from the hypothalamus, release more *adrenocorticotropic hormone* from the anterior pituitary, and release more *glucocorticoids* from the adrenal cortex. Moreover, injections of *dexamethasone*, a synthetic glucocorticoid, do not reduce glucocorticoid release by negative feedback in many depressed patients as they do in normal subjects.

The fact that dysfunctions of the hypothalamus anterior-pituitary adrenal-cortex system are commonly observed in depressed patients suggests that they may play a causal role in the disorder. However, it is also possible that dysfuctions of the hypothalamus anterior-pituitary adrenal-cortex system are the result, rather than the cause, of depression. Supporting the theory that hypothalamus anterior-pituitary adrenal-cortex pathology is a cause, rather than a result, of depression are reports that injections of corticotropin-releasing hormone can induce signs of depression (insomnia, decreased appetite, decreased sexual activity, anxiety) in laboratory animals.

Tricyclic antidepressants. Drugs with an antidepressant action and a three-ring structure.

Imipramine. The first tricyclic antidepressant drug.

Lithium. A metallic ion that is used in the treatment of bipolar affective disorder.

Prozac. The trade name of fluoxetine, the widely prescribed selective serotonin-reuptake inhibitor that is effective against depression and various anxiety disorders.

Up-regulation. The increase in a neurotransmitter's receptors in response to decreased release of that neurotransmitter.

Autoreceptors. Receptors in the presynaptic membrane that are sensitive to a neuron's own neurotransmitter.

■ DIATHESIS–STRESS MODEL OF DEPRESSION It is not yet clear how genetic, monaminergic, and hormonal factors combine in the production of depression. One possibility is suggested by the diathesis–stress model.

According to the diathesis–stress model of depression (see Nemeroff, 1998), some people inherit a tendency to develop depression—possibly because their monoaminergic systems are hypoactive, their hypothalamus anterior-pituitary adrenal-cortex systems are hyperactive, or both. The central idea of the diathesis–stress model is that this inherited susceptibility to depression is usually incapable of inducing the disorder by itself. However, if susceptible individuals are exposed to stress early in life, their systems become permanently sensitized and over-react to mild stressors for the rest of their lives. Support for the diathesis–stress model of depression comes from the observation that early stress produced in rat pups by separation from their mothers causes increases in circulating corticotropic-releasing, adrenocorticotropic, and corticosteroid hormones that persist into adulthood (see Nemeroff, 1998).

■ NEURAL MECHANISMS OF DEPRESSION: REMAINING QUESTIONS Although the monoamine theory, the hypothalmus-pituitary-adrenal theory, and diathesis–stress model together provide a general framework for understanding the neural mechanisms of depression, there are several key questions that they do not address. The following are four of them.

Why does it take weeks for monoamine oxidase inhibitors, tricyclic antidepressants, and selective mono-amine-reuptake blockers to begin to exert a therapeutic effect, when monoamine levels become elevated within minutes of the first drug administration? It seems that some slow-developing consequence of increased monoamine levels, rather than increased monoamine levels per se, is the key antidepressant effect.

How do drugs that do not appear to influence monoaminergic activity reduce depression? Kramer, et al. (1998) found that MK-869, an antagonist of the neuropeptide *substance P*, is an effective antidepressant. Although MK-869 does not appear to influence monoaminergic activity, the fact that it takes 2 or 3 weeks of MK-869 therapy to produce an antidepressant effect suggests that MK-869 and monoamine agonists may exert their therapeutic effects through a common mechanism (Wahlestedt, 1998).

Why do some monoamine agonists not produce antidepressant effects? For example, both cocaine and amphetamine are powerful monoamine agonists, yet they are ineffective as antidepressant agents.

How does sleep deprivation induce its antidepressant effect? One of the most remarkable facts about depression is that more than 50% of depressed patients display dramatic improvement after one night of sleep deprivation (Kuhs & Tölle, 1991; Wu & Bunney, 1990). This finding is of little therapeutic relevance because the depression returns once patients return to their normal sleep pattern; however, it is a reliable antidepressant effect that may provide an indication of the neural mechanism of antidepressant action. The antidepressant effect of sleep deprivation remains unexplained by current theories of depression.

17.6 Anxiety Disorders

Anxiety—chronic fear that persists in the absence of any direct threat—is a common psychological correlate of stress. Anxiety is adaptive if it motivates effective coping behaviors; however, when it becomes so severe that it disrupts normal functioning, it is referred to as an **anxiety disorder.** All anxiety disorders are associated with feelings of anxiety (e.g., fear, worry, despondency) and with a variety of physiological stress reactions—for example, *tachycardia* (rapid heartbeat), *hypertension* (high blood pressure), nausea, breathing difficulty, sleep disturbances, and high glucocorticoid levels. Anxiety disorders are the most prevalent of all psychiatric disorders; in Great Britain, for example, 1 in 5 women and 1 in 10 men take antianxiety medication each year (Dunbar, Perera, & Jenner, 1989).

The four major classes of anxiety disorders are generalized anxiety disorders, phobic anxiety disorders, panic disorders, and obsessive-compulsive disorders. **Generalized anxiety disorders** are characterized by stress responses and extreme feelings of anxiety that occur in the absence of any obvious precipitating stimulus. **Phobic anxiety disorders** are similar to generalized anxiety disorders except that they are triggered by exposure to particular objects (e.g., birds, spiders) or situations (e.g., crowds, darkness). **Panic disorders** are characterized by rapid-onset attacks of extreme fear and severe symptoms of stress (e.g., choking, heart palpitations, shortness of breath); they are often components of generalized anxiety and phobic disorders, but they also occur as separate disorders. **Obsessive-compulsive**

disorders are characterized by frequently recurring, uncontrollable, anxiety-producing thoughts (obsessions) and impulses (compulsions). Responding to them—for example, by repeated compulsive hand washing—is a means of dissipating the anxiety associated with them.

Pharmacological Treatment of Anxiety Disorders

Two classes of drugs are effective against anxiety disorders: benzodiazepines and serotonin agonists.

■ **BENZODIAZEPINES** Benzodiazepines such as *chlordiazepoxide* (Librium) and *diazepam* (Valium) are widely prescribed for the treatment of anxiety disorders. They are also prescribed as hypnotics (sleep-inducing drugs), anticonvulsants, and muscle relaxants. Indeed, benzodiazepines are the most widely prescribed psychoactive drugs; approximately 10% of adult North Americans are currently taking them. The benzodiazepines have several adverse side effects: sedation, ataxia (disruption of motor activity), tremor, nausea, addiction, and a withdrawal reaction that includes rebound anxiety.

The behavioral effects of benzodiazepines are thought to be mediated by their agonistic action on the $GABA_A$ receptor. Benzodiazepines bind to the $GABA_A$ receptor at a different site than the one at which GABA molecules bind and, in so doing, increase the binding of GABA molecules to the receptor (see Figure 4.20). The $GABA_A$ receptor is distributed widely throughout the brain.

■ **SEROTONIN AGONISTS** Buspirone is another drug available for the clinical treatment of anxiety disorders. Unlike the benzodiazepines, buspirone is a serotonin agonist; it acts selectively on one serotonin receptor subtype, the $5-HT_{1A}$ receptor. The main advantage of buspirone is that it produces *anxiolytic* (antianxiety) effects without producing ataxia, muscle relaxation, or sedation—which are common side effects of benzodiazepines. Presumably, the selectivity of its behavioral effects is attributable to its selective pattern of binding. Other serotonin agonists (e.g., monoamine oxidase inhibitors, tricyclic antidepressants, and selective serotonin-reuptake inhibitors) also have anxiolytic effects.

Animal Models of Anxiety

Animal models of anxiety have played an important role in the study of anxiety and in the assessment of the anxiolytic potential of new drugs (see Green, 1991; Treit, 1985). These models typically involve animal defensive behaviors, the implicit assumption being that defensive behaviors are motivated by fear and that fear and anxiety are similar states. Three animal behaviors

that model anxiety are elevated-plus-maze performance, defensive burying, and risk assessment.

In the *elevated-plus-maze test,* rats are placed on a four-armed plus-sign-shaped maze that is 50 centimeters above the floor. Two arms have sides and two arms have no sides, and the measure of anxiety is the proportion of time the rats spend in the enclosed arms, rather than venturing onto the exposed arms (see Pellow et al., 1985).

In the *defensive-burying test* (see Figure 5.26), rats are shocked by a wire-wrapped wooden dowel mounted on the wall of a familiar test chamber. The measure of anxiety is the amount of time the rats spend spraying bedding material from the floor of the chamber at the shock source with forward thrusting movements of their head and forepaws (see Treit et al., 1993).

In the *risk-assessment test,* after a single brief exposure to a cat on the surface of a laboratory burrow system, rats flee to their burrows and freeze. Then, they engage in a variety of risk-assessment behaviors (e.g.,

Anxiety. Fear that persists in the absence of direct threat.

Anxiety disorder. Anxiety that is so extreme and so pervasive that it disrupts normal functioning.

Generalized anxiety disorders. Anxiety disorders that are not precipitated by any obvious event.

Phobic anxiety disorders. Anxiety disorders characterized by extreme, largely irrational fears of specific objects or situations.

Panic disorders. Anxiety disorders characterized by recurring rapid-onset attacks of extreme fear that are often associated with choking, heart palpitations, and shortness of breath.

Obsessive-compulsive disorders. Anxiety disorders characterized by recurring uncontrollable thoughts and impulses.

Benzodiazepines. The major class of anxiolytic drugs, including chlordiazepoxide (Librium) and diazepam (Valium).

Buspirone. A serotonin agonist that is an effective anxiolytic drug.

scanning the surface from the mouth of their burrow or exploring the surface in a cautious stretched posture) before their behavior returns to normal (see Blanchard, Blanchard, & Rodgers, 1991; Blanchard et al., 1990). The measures of anxiety are the amounts of time that the rats spend in freezing and in risk assessment.

The elevated-plus-maze, defensive-burying, and risk-assessment models of anxiety have all been validated by demonstrations that benzodiazepines reduce the various indexes of anxiety in these models, whereas nonanxiolytic drugs usually do not. There is a potential problem with this line of evidence, however. The potential problem stems from the fact that many cases of anxiety do not respond well to benzodiazepine therapy. Accordingly, existing animal models of anxiety may be models of benzodiazepine-sensitive anxiety rather than of anxiety in general, and thus the models may not be sensitive to anxiolytic drugs that act by a different (i.e., a nonGABAergic) mechanism. For example, the atypical anxiolytic buspirone does not have a reliable anxiolytic effect in the elevated-plus-maze test.

Neural Bases of Anxiety Disorders

Like current theories of the neural bases of schizophrenia and depression, current theories of the neural bases of anxiety disorders rest heavily on the analysis of the effects of therapeutic drug effects. The fact that many anxiolytic drugs are agonists at either $GABA_A$ receptors

(e.g., the benzodiazepines) or serotonin receptors (e.g., buspirone and Prozac) has focused attention on the possible role in anxiety disorders of deficits in both GABAergic and serotonergic transmission. However, there is little additional evidence to support either mechanism.

Recent speculations about the brain structures involved in anxiety disorders have focused on the amygdala because of the central role it plays in fear and defensive behavior (see LeDoux, 1995). In support of the involvement of the amygdala in anxiety disorders are the following findings: The amygdala has a high concentration of $GABA_A$ receptors, local infusion of benzodiazepines into the amygdala produces anxiolytic effects in laboratory animals, and local injections of GABA antagonists into the amygdala can block the anxiolytic effects of *systemic* (into general circulation) injections of benzodiazepines (see Davis, Rainnie, & Cassell, 1994).

Brain-imaging studies have not revealed obvious structural pathology in cases of anxiety disorder. In contrast, many functional changes have been reported, but so far none has been consistently replicated (e.g., Wilson, 1998). One likely problem may be that crude diagnostic categories inevitably cloud brain images that are obtained by averaging observations from several subjects. Thus, the recent improvements in brain-imaging technology that decrease the reliance on averaging could lead to significant advances in our understanding of anxiety disorders—and other psychological disorders—over the next few years.

CONCLUSION

The chapter began with a general overview of some of the major early research on the biopsychology of emotion (17.1), before focusing on the study of fear, defense, and aggression (17.2). Then, the focus shifted to the negative impact on health of stress and anxiety, first on physical disorders such as ulcers and infections (17.3) and finally on three major classes of psychological disorders: schizophrenia (17.4), affective disorders (17.5), and anxiety disorders (17.6). The chapter continually emphasized that emotions and illness are topics of mutual relevance: that the stress associated with negative emotions can trigger both physical and psychological disorders in predisposed individuals, and conversely that emotional dysfunction is a common symptom of psychological disorders.

It is fitting for me to be writing the last few words of a chapter about emotion at a time that is such an emotional one. I feel relieved to be finishing the project that I began several years ago, and I am excited by the prospect of being able to speak through my writing to so many students like you. You must also feel relieved to be finishing this book; still, I hope that you feel a tiny bit of regret that our time together is over. We have experienced much together, but our mutual experiences have transcended space and time. Right now, I am sitting at my desk looking out over the Pacific Ocean, as the neighborhood finches celebrate completion of this edition with a song. It is 8:00 A.M. on Sunday, April 4, 1999. Where and when are you?

FOOD FOR THOUGHT

1. With practice, you could become an expert in the production and recognition of facial expressions. How could you earn a living with these skills?

2. Does the concept of target sites have any relevance to human aggression, defense, and play fighting?

3. Blunder often plays an important role in scientific progress. Discuss this with respect to the development of drugs for the treatment of psychiatric disorders.

4. The mechanism by which a disorder is alleviated is not necessarily opposite to the mechanism by which it was caused. Discuss this with respect to current theories of schizophrenia, depression, and anxiety.

5. Discuss the diathesis–stress model of psychological disorders. Design an experiment to test the model.

KEY TERMS

Adrenal cortex (p. 478)
Adrenal medulla (p. 478)
Adrenocorticotropic hormone (ACTH) (p. 478)
Aggressive behaviors (p. 474)
Alpha male (p. 474)
Antibodies (p. 480)
Antibody-mediated immunity (p. 480)
Antigens (p. 479)
Anxiety (p. 492)
Anxiety disorder (p. 492)
Autoreceptors (p. 490)
B cells (p. 480)
Benzodiazepines (p. 493)
Bipolar affective disorder (p. 489)
Buspirone (p. 493)
Butyrophenones (p. 486)
Cannon-Bard theory (p. 467)
Cell-mediated immunity (p. 480)
Cheese effect (p. 489)
Chlorpromazine (p. 485)

Clozapine (p. 487)
Control-question technique (p. 470)
Decorticate (p. 467)
Defensive attacks (p. 475)
Defensive behaviors (p. 474)
Defensive burying (p. 475)
Depression (p. 488)
Diathesis–stress model (p. 484)
Duchenne smile (p. 472)
Endogenous depression (p. 488)
Ethoexperimental research (p. 474)
Facial feedback hypothesis (p. 470)
False transmitter (p. 485)
Fear (p. 474)
Fear conditioning (p. 476)
Freezing and flight (p. 475)
Gastric ulcers (p. 479)
Generalized anxiety disorders (p. 492)

Glucocorticoids (p. 478)
Guilty-knowledge technique (p. 470)
Haloperidol (p. 486)
Imipramine (p. 490)
Immune system (p. 479)
Intraspecific defense (p. 475)
Iproniazid (p. 489)
James-Lange theory (p. 466)
Kluver-Bucy syndrome (p. 469)
Limbic system (p. 468)
Lithium (p. 490)
Lymphocytes (p. 480)
MAO inhibitors (p. 489)
Macrophage (p. 480)
Mania (p. 488)
Maternal defensive behaviors (p. 475)
Neuroleptics (p. 487)
Obsessive-compulsive disorders (p. 493)
Panic disorders (p. 493)
Phagocytosis (p. 480)

Phenothiazines (p. 486)
Phobic anxiety disorders (p. 492)
Polygraphy (p. 469)
Predatory aggression (p. 475)
Prosody (p. 473)
Prozac (p. 490)
Psychoneuroimmunology (p. 479)
Reactive depression (p. 488)
Reserpine (p. 485)
Risk assessment (p. 475)
Schizophrenia (p. 484)
Sham rage (p. 467)
Social aggression (p. 475)
Stress (p. 478)
T cells (p. 480)
Target-site concept (p. 475)
Tricyclic antidepressants (p. 490)
Unipolar affective disorder (p. 489)
Up-regulation (p. 490)

ADDITIONAL READING

The following articles provide excellent up-to-date reviews of research on the biopsychology of emotion, stress, and mental illness:

Albert, D. J., Walsh, M. L., & Jonik, R. H. (1993). Aggression in humans: What is its biological foundation? *Neuroscience and Biobehavioral Reviews, 17,* 405–425.

Barondes, S. H. (1994). Thinking about Prozac. *Science, 263,* 1102–1104.

Cohen, S., & Herbert, T. B. (1996). Health psychology: Psychological factors and physical disease from the perspective of human psychoneuroimmunology. *Annual Review of Psychology, 47,* 113–142.

Egan, M. F., & Weinberger, D. R. (1997). Neurobiology of schizophrenia. *Current Opinion in Neurobiology, 7,* 701–707.

Ekman, P. (1993). Facial expression and emotion. *American Psychologist, 48,* 384–392.

LeDoux, J. E. (1994, June). Emotion, memory, and the brain. *Scientific American, 270,* 50–57.

Nemeroff, C. B. (1998, June). The neurobiology of depression. *Scientific American, 278,* 42–49.

Overmier, J. B., & Murison, R. (1997). Animal models reveal the "psych" in the psychosomatics of peptic ulcers. *Current Directions in Psychological Science, 6,* 180–184.

EPILOGUE

Biopsychology is a fascinating discipline. I have tried to convince you of this by peeling away its complexities and serving up its fundamentals with big helpings of clear writing, good humor, and personal implications. If you liked my approach, let your instructor know so that it can benefit future students at your university.

Like good friends, we have shared good times and bad. We have shared the fun and wonder of Rhonda, the dexterous cashier; the Nads basketball team; people who rarely sleep; the mamawawa theme; split brains; and brain transplantation. And together we have been touched by the personal tragedies of Alzheimer's disease; MPTP poisoning; the lost mariner; H. M.; the man who mistook his wife for a hat; and let's not forget Professor P., the biopsychologist who experienced brain surgery from the other side of the knife. Thank you for allowing me to share *Biopsychology* with you. I hope you have found it to be an enriching experience.

If you have any comments or suggestions, write to me at the Department of Psychology, University of British Columbia, Vancouver, B. C., Canada V6T 1Z4, or send me E-mail (jpinel@cortex.psych.ubc.ca)—or better yet, if you are ever on campus, stop by for a visit.

APPENDICES

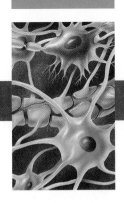

The Autonomic Nervous System

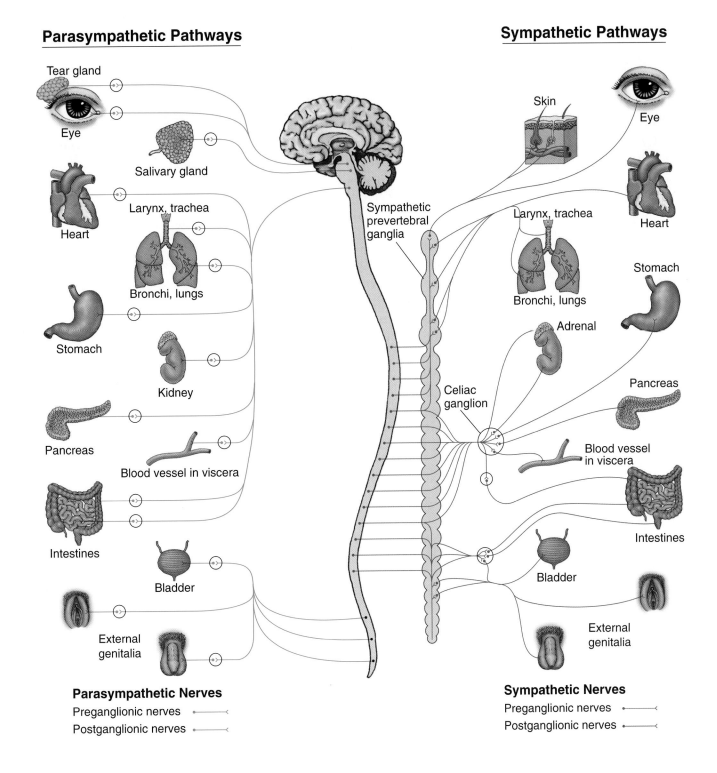

Parasympathetic Pathways

Tear gland

Eye

Salivary gland

Heart

Larynx, trachea

Bronchi, lungs

Stomach

Kidney

Pancreas

Blood vessel in viscera

Intestines

Bladder

External genitalia

Sympathetic Pathways

Skin

Eye

Larynx, trachea

Heart

Bronchi, lungs

Stomach

Sympathetic prevertebral ganglia

Adrenal

Pancreas

Celiac ganglion

Blood vessel in viscera

Intestines

Bladder

External genitalia

Parasympathetic Nerves

Preganglionic nerves

Postganglionic nerves

Sympathetic Nerves

Preganglionic nerves

Postganglionic nerves

Some Functions of Sympathetic and Parasympathetic Neurons

Organ	Sympathetic effect	Parasympathetic effect
Salivary gland	Decreases secretion	Increases secretion
Heart	Increases heart rate	Decreases heart rate
Blood vessels	Constricts blood vessels in most organs	Dilates blood vessels in a few organs
Penis	Ejaculation	Erection
Iris radial muscles	Dilates pupils	No effect
Iris sphincter muscles	No effect	Constricts pupils
Tear gland	No effect	Stimulates secretion
Sweat gland	Stimulates secretion	No effect
Stomach and intestine	No effect	Stimulates secretion
Lungs	Dilates bronchioles; inhibits mucous secretion	Constricts bronchioles; stimulates mucous secretion
Arrector pili muscles	Erects hair and creates gooseflesh	No effect

The Cranial Nerves

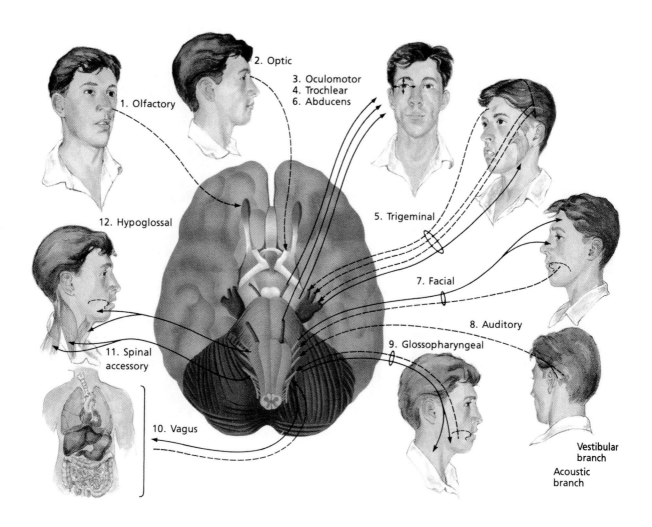

1. Olfactory
2. Optic
3. Oculomotor
4. Trochlear
6. Abducens
5. Trigeminal
7. Facial
8. Auditory
9. Glossopharyngeal
10. Vagus
11. Spinal accessory
12. Hypoglossal

Vestibular branch
Acoustic branch

Functions of the Cranial Nerves

Number	Name	General Function	Specific Functions
1	Olfactory	Sensory	Smell
2	Optic	Sensory	Vision
3	Oculomotor	Motor Sensory	Eye movement and pupillary constriction Sensory signals from certain eye muscles
4	Trochlear	Motor Sensory	Eye movement Sensory signals from certain eye muscles
5	Trigeminal	Sensory Motor	Facial sensations Chewing
6	Abducens	Motor Sensory	Eye movement Sensory signals from certain eye muscles
7	Facial	Sensory Motor	Taste from anterior two-thirds of tongue Facial expression, secretion of tears, salivation, cranial blood vessel dilation
8	Auditory-Vestibular	Sensory	Audition; sensory signals from the organs of balance in the inner ear
9	Glossopharyngeal	Sensory Motor	Taste from posterior third of tongue Salivation, swallowing
10	Vagus	Sensory Motor	Sensations from abdominal and thoracic organs Control over abdominal and thoracic organs and muscles of the throat
11	Spinal Accessory	Motor Sensory	Movement of neck, shoulders, and head Sensory signals from muscles of the neck
12	Hypoglossal	Motor Sensory	Tongue movements Sensory signals from tongue muscles

Nuclei of the Thalamus

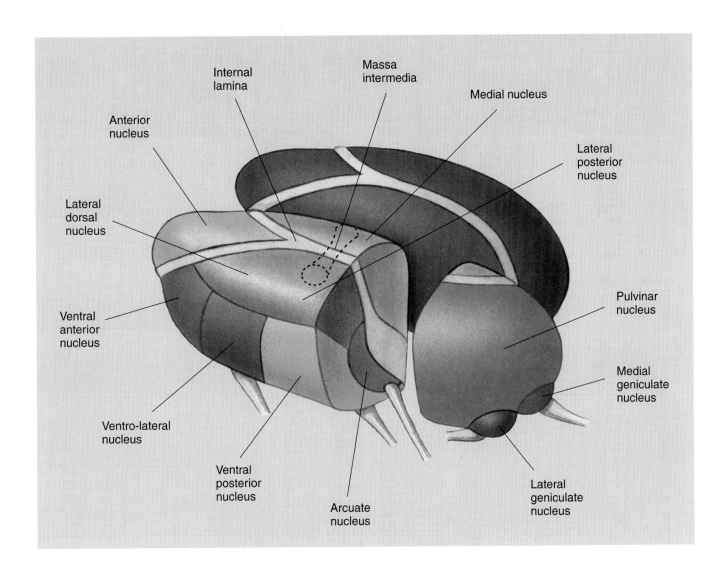

Nuclei of the Hypothalamus

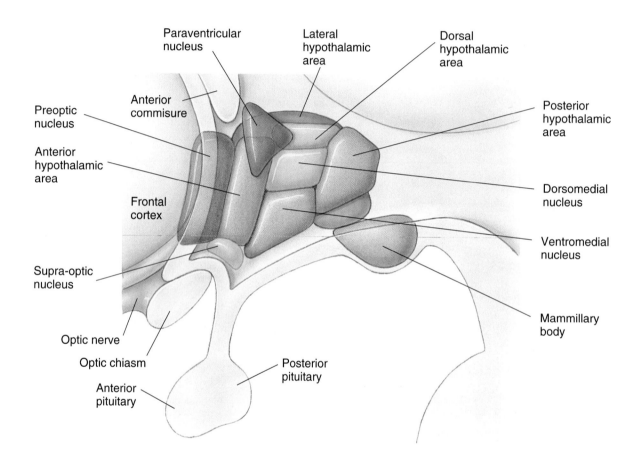

Some of the Peptides That Have Been Found in Mammalian Neurons

Major Neuropeptides

Pituitary Peptides

Corticotropin

Growth hormone

Lipotropin

α-Melanocyte stimulating hormone

Oxytocin

Prolactin

Vasopressin

Gut Peptides

Cholecystokinin

Gastrin

Motilin

Pancreatic polypeptide

Secretin

Substance P

Vasoactive intestinal polypeptide

Miscellaneous Peptides

Angiotensin

Bombesin

Bradykinin

Carnosine

Glucagon

Insulin

Neuropeptide Y

Neurotensin

Proctolin

Hypothalamic Peptides

Luteinizing hormone-releasing hormone

Somatostatin

Thyrotropin-releasing hormone

Endorphins

Dynorphin

β-Endorphin

Met Enkephalin

Leu Enkephalin

Phases of the Human Menstrual Cycle

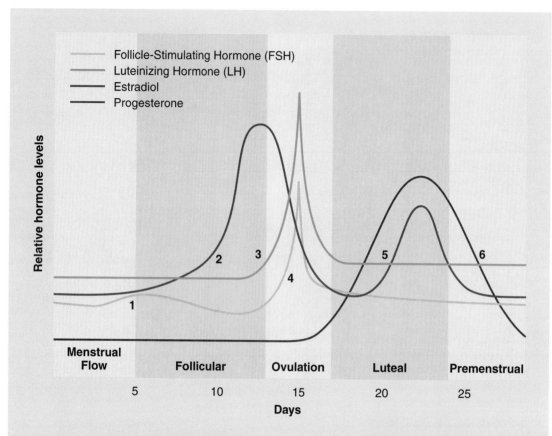

1 In response to an increase in FSH, small spheres of cells called ovarian follicles begin to grow around individual egg cells (ova).

2 The follicles begin to release estrogens such as estradiol.

3 The estrogens stimulate the hypothalamus to increase the release of LH and FSH from the anterior pituitary.

4 In response to the LH surge, one of the follicles ruptures and releases its ovum.

5 The ruptured follicle under the influence of LH develops into a corpus luteum (yellow body) and begins to release progesterone, which prepares the lining of the uterus for the implantation of a fertilized ovum.

6 Meanwhile, the ovum is moved into the fallopian tube by the rowing action of ciliated cells. If the ovum is not fertilized, progesterone and estradiol levels fall, the walls of the uterus are sloughed off as menstrual flow, and the cycle begins once again.

REFERENCES

Abe, H., & Rusak, B. (1992). Anticipatory activity and entrainment of circadian rhythms in Syrian hamsters exposed to restricted palatable diets. *American Journal of Physiology, 263,* 116–124.

Abramson, H. A. (1974). Editorial: Respiratory disorders and marijuana use. *Journal of Asthma Research, 11,* 97.

Acker, W., Ron, M. A., Lishman, W. A., & Shaw, G. K. (1984). A multivariate analysis of psychological, clinical and CT scanning measures in detoxified chronic alcoholics. *British Journal of Addiction, 79,* 293–301.

Adamec, R. (1990). Kindling, anxiety and limbic epilepsy: Human and animal perspectives. In J. A. Wada, (Ed.), *Kindling 4* (pp. 329–341). New York: Plenum Press.

Adamec, R. (1997). Introduction to neurobiology of defense. *Neuroscience and Biobehavioral Reviews, 21*(6), 729–731.

Adams, J. M., & Cory, S. (1998). The Bcl-2 protein family: Arbiters of cell survival. *Science, 281,* 1322–1326.

Adelmann, P. K., & Zajonc, R. B. (1989). Facial efference and the experience of emotion. *Annual Review of Psychology, 40,* 249–280.

Adkins-Regan, E. (1988). Sex hormones and sexual orientation in animals. *Psychobiology, 16,* 335–347.

Adolphs, R., Tranel, D., Damasio, H., & Damasio, A. (1994). Impaired recognition of emotion in facial expressions following bilateral damage to the human amygdala. *Nature, 372,* 669–672.

Adolphs, R., Tranel, D., Damasio, H., & Damasio, A. R. (1995). Fear and the human amygdala. *The Journal of Neuroscience, 15*(9), 5879–5891.

Aggleton, J. P. (1985). One-trial object recognition by rats. *Quarterly Journal of Experimental Psychology, 37b,* 279–294.

Aggleton, J. P. (1993). The contribution of the amygdala to normal and abnormal emotional states. *Trends in Neurosciences, 16,* 328–333.

Aggleton, J. P., & Mishkin, M. (1983). Visual recognition impairment following medial thalamic lesions in monkeys. *Neuropsychologia, 21,* 189–197.

Aggleton, J. P., Nicol, R. M., Huston, A. E., & Fairbairn, A. F. (1988). The performance of amnesic subjects on tests of experimental amnesia in animals: Delayed matching-to-sample and concurrent learning. *Neuropsychologia, 26,* 265–272.

Ahmed, R., & Gray, D. (1996). Immunological memory and protective immunity: Understanding their relation. *Science, 272,* 54–60.

Aigner, T. G., Walker, D. L., & Mishkin, M. (1991). Comparison of the effects of scopolamine administered before and after acquisition in a test of visual recognition memory in monkeys. *Behavioral and Neural Biology, 55,* 61–67.

Åkerstedt, R., & Gillberg, M. (1981). The circadian variation of experimentally displaced sleep. *Sleep, 4*(2), 159–169.

Albert, D. J., Walsh, M. L., & Jonik, R. H. (1993). Aggression in humans: What is its biological foundation? *Neuroscience and Biobehavioral Reviews, 17,* 405–425.

Albin, R. L., & Tagle, D. A. (1995). Genetics and molecular biology of Huntington's disease. *Trends in Neurosciences, 18,* 11–14.

Albright, T. D. (1995). 'My most true mind thus makes mine eye untrue.' *Trends in Neurosciences, 18,* 331–333.

Allegretta, M., Nicklas, J. A., Sriram, S., & Albertini, R. J. (1990). T cells responsive to myelin basic protein in patients with multiple sclerosis. *Science, 247,* 718–720.

Allen, G., Buxton, R. B., Wong, E. C., & Courchesne, E. (1997). Attentional activation of the cerebellum independent of motor involvement. *Science, 275,* 1940–1943.

Allen, L. S., Hines, M., Shryne, J. E., & Gorski, R. A. (1989). Two sexually dimorphic cell groups in the human brain. *Journal of Neuroscience, 9,* 497–506.

Alvarez, P., Zola-Morgan, S., & Squire, L. R. (1995). Damage limited to the hippocampal region produces long-lasting memory impairment in monkeys. *Journal of Neuroscience, 15,* 3796–3807.

Ameisen, J. C. (1996). The origin of programmed cell death. *Science, 272,* 1278–1279.

Anagnostaras, S. G., & Robinson, T. E. (1996). Sensitization to the psychomotor stimulant effects of amphetamine: Modulation by associative learning. *Behavioral Neuroscience, 110*(6), 1397–1414.

Anand, B. K., & Brobeck, J. R. (1951). Localization of a "feeding center" in the hypothalamus of the rat. *Proceedings of the Society for Experimental Biology and Medicine, 77,* 323–324.

Anch, A. M., Browman, C. P., Mitler, M. M., & Walsh, J. K. (1988). *Sleep: A scientific perspective.* Englewood Cliffs, NJ: Prentice Hall.

Anderson, P., Cremona, A., Paton, A., Turner, C., & Wallace, P. (1993). The risk of alcohol. *Addiction, 88,* 1493–1508.

Andersen, R. A., Snyder, L. H., Bradley, D. C., & Xing, J. (1997). Multimodal representation of space in the posterior parietal cortex and its use in planning movements. *Annual Review of Neuroscience, 20,* 303–330.

Anderson, R. H., Fleming, D. E., Rhees, R. W., & Kinghorn, E. (1986). Relationships between sexual activity, plasma testosterone, and the volume of the sexually dimorphic nucleus of the preoptic area in prenatally stressed and non-stressed rats. *Brain Research, 370,* 1–10.

Andreasen, N. C. (1994). The mechanisms of schizophrenia. *Current Opinion in Neurobiology, 4,* 245–251.

Andreassi, J. L. (1989). *Psychophysiology: Human behavior and physiological response.* Hillsdale, NJ: Erlbaum.

Angst, J., Weis, P., Grof, P., Baastrup, P. G., & Schou, M. (1970). Lithium prophylaxis in recurrent affective disorders. *British Journal of Psychiatry, 116*, 604–614.

Antonini, A., & Stryker, M. P. (1993). Rapid remodeling of axonal arbors in the visual cortex. *Science, 260*, 1819–1821.

Apkarian, A. V. (1995). Functional imaging of pain: New insights regarding the role of the cerebral cortex in human pain perception. *Seminars in the Neurosciences, 7*, 279–293.

Archer, J. (1991). The influence of testosterone on human aggression. *British Journal of Psychology, 82*, 1–28.

Armony, J. L., Cohen, J. D., Servan-Schreiber, D., & LeDoux, J. E. (1995). An anatomically constrained neural network model of fear conditioning. *Behavioral Neurosciences, 109*(2), 246–257.

Artigas, F., Romero, L., de Montigny, C., & Biller, P. (1996). Acceleration of the effect of selected antidepressant drugs in major depression by 5-HT$_{1A}$ antagonists. *Trends in Neurosciences, 19*, 378–383.

Aserinsky, E., & Kleitman, N. (1953). Regularly occurring periods of eye motility and concomitant phenomena, during sleep. *Science, 118*, 273–274.

Ashkenazi, A., & Dixit, V. M. (1998). Death receptors: Signaling and modulation. *Science, 281*, 1305–1308.

Assanand, S., Pinel, J. P. J., & Lehman, D. R. (1998). Personal theories of hunger and eating. *Journal of Applied Social Psychology, 28*(11), 998–1015.

Assanand, S., Pinel, J. P. J., & Lehman, D. R. (1998). Teaching theories of hunger and eating: Overcoming students' misconceptions. *Teaching of Psychology, 25*(1), 44–46.

Aubert, I., Ridet, J-L., & Gage, F. H. (1995). Regeneration in the adult mammalian CNS: Guided by development. *Current Opinion in Neurobiology, 5*, 625–635.

Auerbach, S. H., Allard, T., Naeser, M., Alexander, M. P., & Albert, M. L. (1982). Pure word deafness: Analysis of a case with bilateral lesions and a defect at the prephonemic level. *Brain, 105*, 271–300.

Auphan, N., DiDonato, J. A., Rosette, C., Helmberg, A., & Karin, M. (1995). Immunosuppression by glucocorticoids: Inhibition of NF-$_K$B activity through induction of I$_K$B synthesis. *Science, 270*, 286–290.

Ax, A. F. (1955). The physiological differentiation between fear and anger in humans. *Psychosomatic Medicine, 15*, 433–442.

Axel, R. (1995, October). The molecular logic of smell. *Scientific American, 273*, 154–159.

Baastrup, P. C., & Schou, M. (1967). Lithium as a prophylactic agent. *Archives of General Psychiatry, 16*, 162–172.

Babor, T. F., Mendelson, J. H., Greenberg, I., & Kuehnle, J. C. (1975). Marijuana consumption and tolerance to physiological and subjective effects. *Archives of General Psychiatry, 32*, 1548–1552.

Bailey, C. H., & Chen, M. C. (1983). Morphological basis of long-term habituation and sensitization in Aplysia. *Science, 220*, 91–93.

Bailey, C. H., & Chen, M. C. (1988). Long-term memory in Aplysia modulates the total number of varicosities of single identified sensory neurons. *Proceedings of the National Academy of Sciences (USA), 85*, 2373–2377.

Bailey, J. M., Pillard, R. C., Neale, M. C., & Agyei, Y. (1993). Heritable factors influence sexual orientation in women. *Archives of General Psychiatry, 50*, 217–223.

Bailey, M. J., & Pillard, R. C. (1991). A genetic study of male sexual orientation. *Archives of General Psychiatry, 48*, 1089–1096.

Baker, B. J., & Booth, D. A. (1989). Preference conditioning by concurrent diets with delayed proportional reinforcement. *Physiology & Behavior, 46*, 585–590.

Baker, T. B., & Tiffany, S. T. (1985). Morphine tolerance as habituation. *Psychological Review, 92*, 78–108.

Balaban, E., Teillet, M. A., & Le Douarin, N. (1988). Application of the quail-chick chimera system to the study of brain development and behavior. *Science, 241*, 1339–1342.

Ballard, P. A., Tetrud, J. W., & Langston, J. W. (1985). Permanent human parkinsonism due to 1-methyl-4-phenyl-1,2,3,6-tetrahydropyridine (MPTP): Seven cases. *Neurology, 35*, 949–956.

Bancroft, J., Sanders, D., Davidson, D., & Warner, P. (1983). Mood, sexuality, hormones and the menstrual cycle: III. Sexuality and the role of androgens. *Psychosomatic Medicine, 45*, 509–516.

Bandler, R., & Shipley, M. T. (1994). Columnar organization in the midbrain periaqueductal gray: Modules for emotional expression? *Trends in Neurosciences, 17*, 379–389.

Bankiewicz, K. S., Plunkett, R. J., Jaconowitz, D. M., Porrino, L., di Porzio, U., London, W. T., Kopin, I. J., & Oldfield, E. H. (1990). The effect of fetal mesencephalon implants on primate MPTP-induced parkinsonism: Histochemical and behavioral studies. *Journal of Neuroscience, 72*, 231–244.

Bard, P. (1929). The central representation of the sympathetic system. *Archives of Neurology and Psychiatry, 22*, 230–246.

Barnstable, C. J. (1993). Glutamate and GABA in retinal circuitry. *Current Opinion in Neurobiology, 3*, 520–525.

Baron, J. C. (1989). Depression of energy metabolism in distant brain structures: Studies with positron emission tomography in stroke patients. *Seminars in Neurology, 9*, 281–285.

Barondes, S. H. (1994). Thinking about Prozac. *Science, 263*, 1102–1104.

Bartoshuk, L. M., & Beauchamp, G. K. (1994). Chemical senses. *Annual Review of Psychology, 45*, 419–449.

Basbaum, A. I., & Fields, H. L. (1978). Endogenous pain control mechanisms: Review and hypothesis. *Annals of Neurology, 4*, 451–462.

Bashir, Z. I., & Collingridge, G. L. (1992). Synaptic plasticity: long-term potentiation in the hippocampus. *Current Opinion in Neurobiology, 2*, 328–335.

Bastiani, M. J., Doe, C. Q., Helfand, S. L., & Goodman, C. S. (1985). Neuronal specificity and growth cone guidance in grasshopper and Drosophila embryos. *Trends in Neurosciences, 8*, 257–266.

Baum, M. J., Erskine, M. S., Kornberg, E., & Weaver, C. E. (1990). Prenatal and neonatal testosterone exposure interact to affect differentiation of sexual behavior and partner preference in female ferrets. *Behavioral Neuroscience, 104*(1), 183–198.

Baura, G., Foster, D., Porte, D., Kahn, S. E., Bergman, R. N., Cobelli, C., & Schwartz, M. W. (1993). Saturable transport of insulin from plasma into the central nervous system of dogs in vivo: A mechanism for regulated insulin delivery to the brain. *Journal of Clinical Investigations, 92*, 1824–1830.

Bavelier, D., Corina, D. Jessard, P., Padmanabhan, S., Clark, V. P., Karni, A., Prinster, A., Braun, A., Lalwani, A., Rauschecker, J. P., Turner, R., & Neville, H. (1997). Sentence reading: A functional MRI study at 4 Telsa. *Journal of Cognitive Neuroscience, 9*(5), 664–686.

Beardsley, T. (1996, March). Trends in human genetics: Vital data. *Scientific American, 274*, 100–105.

Bechara, A., Tranel, D., Damasio, H., Adolphs, R., Rockland, C., & Damasio, A. R. (1995). Double dissociation of conditioning and declarative knowledge relative to the amygdala and hippocampus in humans. *Science, 269*, 1115–1118.

Beck, G., & Habicht, G. S. (1996, November). Immunity and invertebrates. *Scientific American, 275*, 60–66.

Becker, J. B., Breedlove, S. M., & Crews, D. (Eds.) (1992). *Behavioral endocrinology.* Cambridge, MA: MIT Press.

Beecher, H. K. (1959). *Measurement of subjective responses: Quantitative effects of drugs.* New York: Oxford University Press.

Belin, P., Silbovicius, M., Crozier, S., Thivard, L., Masure, M.-C., & Samson, Y. (1998). Lateralization of speech and auditory temporal processing. *Journal of Cognitive Neuroscience, 10*(4), 536–540.

Bennett, E. L., Diamond, M. C., Krech, D., & Rosenzweig, M. R. (1964). Chemical and anatomical plasticity of brain. *Science, 146,* 610–619.

Bennett, M. K. (1997). Ca^{2+} and the regulation of neurotransmitter secretion. *Current Opinion in Neurobiology, 7,* 316–351.

Benson, D. F. (1985). Aphasia. In K. M. Heilman & E. Valenstein (Eds.), *Clinical neuropsychology* (pp. 17–47). New York: Oxford University Press.

Benton, A. (1985). Visuoperceptual, visuospatial, and visuoconstructive disorders. In K. M. Heilman and E. Valenstein (Eds.), *Clinical neuropsychology* (pp. 15–185). New York: Oxford University Press.

Benton, A. L. (1994). Neuropsychological assessment. *Annual Review of Psychology, 45,* 1–23.

Berger, R. J., & Oswald, I. (1962). Effects of sleep deprivation on behaviour, subsequent sleep, and dreaming. *Journal of Mental Science, 106,* 457–465.

Berlucchi, G., Maffei, L., Moruzzi, G., & Strata, P. (1964). EEG and behavioral effects elicited by cooling of medulla and pons. In A. Mosso, V. Aducco, & G. Moruzzi (Eds.), *Archives Italiennes de biologie, 102,* (pp. 373–392). Pisa: Universita Degli Studi.

Bernhardt, P. C. (1997). Influences of serotonin and testosterone in aggression and dominance: Convergence with social psychology. *Current Directions in Psychological Science, 6*(2), 44–48.

Bernstein, I. L., & Webster, M. M. (1980). Learned taste aversion in humans. *Physiology & Behavior, 25,* 363–366.

Berridge, K. C., & Robinson, T. E. (1995). The mind of an addicted brain: Neural sensitization of wanting versus liking. *Current Directions in Psychological Science, 4*(3), 71–76.

Berridge, V., & Edwards, G. (1981). *Opium and the people: Opiate use in nineteenth-century England.* New York: St. Martin's Press.

Billington, C. J., & Levine, A. S. (1992). Hypothalamic neuropeptide Y regulation of feeding and energy metabolism. *Current Opinion in Neurobiology, 2,* 847–851.

Binder, J. R. (1997). Neuroanatomy of language processing studied with functional MRI. *Clinical Neuroscience, 4,* 87–94.

Bishop, M. P., Elder, S. T., & Heath, R. G. (1963). Intracranial self-stimulation in man. *Science, 140,* 394–396.

Bishop, P. O., & Pettigrew, J. D. (1986). Neural mechanisms of binocular vision. *Vision Research, 26,* 1587–1600.

Björklund, A., & Lindvall, O. (1986). Catecholaminergic brainstem regulatory systems. In V. B. Mountcastle, F. E. Bloom, & S. R. Geiger (Eds.), *Handbook of physiology: The nervous system* (Vol. 4, pp. 155–236). Bethesda, MD: American Physiological Society.

Blackmore, S. (1991). Lucid dreaming: Awake in your sleep? *Skeptical Inquirer, 15,* 362–370.

Blaha, C. D., Coury, A., Fibiger, H. C., & Phillips, A. G. (1990). Effects of neurotensin on dopamine release and metabolism in the rat striatum and nucleus accumbens: Cross-validation using in vivo voltammetry and microdialysis. *Neuroscience, 34,* 669–705.

Blaha, C. D., & Jung, M. E. (1991). Electrochemical evaluation of stearate-modified graphite paste electrodes: Selective detection of dopamine is maintained after exposure to brain tissue. *Journal of Electroanalytical Chemistry, 310,* 317–334.

Blanchard, D. C., & Blanchard, R. J. (1984). Affect and aggression: An animal model applied to human behavior. In D. C. Blanchard & R. J. Blanchard (Eds.), *Advances in the study of aggression* (pp. 1–62). Orlando, FL: Academic Press.

Blanchard, D. C., & Blanchard, R. J. (1988). Ethoexperimental approaches to the biology of emotion. *Annual Review of Psychology, 39,* 43–68.

Blanchard, D. C., & Blanchard, R. J. (1990a). Behavioral correlates of chronic dominance-subordination relationships of male rats in a seminatural situation. *Neuroscience and Biobehavioral Reviews, 14,* 455–462.

Blanchard, D. C., Blanchard, R. J., & Rodgers, R. J. (1991). Risk assessment and animal models of anxiety. *Animal Models in Psychopharmacology: Advances in Pharmacological Sciences.* Basel: Birkhauser Verlag.

Blanchard, D. C., Blanchard, R. J., Tom, P., & Rodgers, R. J. (1990). Diazepam changes risk assessment in an anxiety/defense test battery. *Psychopharmacology, 101,* 511–518.

Blanchard, R. J., & Blanchard, D. C. (1989). Anti-predator defensive behaviors in a visible burrow system. *Journal of Comparative Psychology, 103,* 70–82.

Blanchard, R. J., & Blanchard, D. C. (1990b). Anti-predator defense as models of animal fear and anxiety. In P. F. Brain, S. Parmigiani, R. J. Blanchard, and D. Mainardi (Eds.), *Fear and defense* (pp. 89–108). New York: Harwood Academic Publishers.

Blanchard, R. J., Brain, P. F., Blanchard, D. C., & Parmigiani, S. (Eds.). (1989). *Ethoexperimental approaches to the study of behavior.* Dordrecht, The Netherlands: Kluwer Academic Publishers.

Blaser, M. J. (1996, February). The bacteria behind ulcers. *Scientific American, 275,* 104–107.

Blass, E. M., & Hall, W. G. (1976). Drinking termination: Interactions between hydrational, orogastric and behavioral controls in rats. *Psychological Review, 183,* 356–374.

Blaustein, J. D., King, J. C., Toft, D. O., & Turcotte, J. (1988). Immunocytochemical localization of estrogen-induced progestin receptors in guinea pig brain. *Brain Research, 474,* 1–15.

Blessing, W. W. (1997). Inadequate frameworks for understanding bodily homeostasis. *Trends in Neurosciences, 20,* 235–239.

Bliss, T. V. P., & Lømø, T. (1973). Long-lasting potentiation of synaptic transmission in the dentate area of the anaesthetized rabbit following stimulation of the perforant path. *Journal of Physiology, 232,* 331–356.

Bloch, G. J., & Gorski, R. A. (1988). Cytoarchitectonic analysis of the SDN-POA of the intact and gonadectomized rat. *Journal of Comparative Neurology, 275,* 604–612.

Bloch, G. J., Eckersell, C., & Mills, R. (1993). Distribution of galanin-immunoreactive cells within sexually dimorphic components of the medial preoptic area of the male and female rat. *Brain Research, 620,* 259–268.

Bloch, G. J., & Mills, R. (1995). Prepubertal testosterone treatment of neonatally gonadectomized male rats: Defeminization and masculinization of behavioral and endocrine function in adulthood. *Neuroscience and Behavioral Reviews, 19*(2), 187–200.

Bloch, G. J., Mills, R., & Gale, S. (1995). Prepubertal testosterone treatment of female rats: Defeminization of behavioral and endocrine function in adulthood. *Neuroscience and Biobehavioral Reviews, 19*(2), 177–186.

Blum, W. F. (1997). Leptin: The voice of the adipose tissue. *Hormonal Research, 48*(4), 2–8.

Bogen, J. G., & Bogen, G. M. (1976). Wernicke's region—Where is it? *Annals of the New York Academy of Science, 280*, 834–843.

Bolles, R. C. (1980). Some functionalistic thought about regulation. In F. M. Toates & T. R. Halliday (Eds.), *Analysis of motivational processes* (pp. 63–75). London: Academic Press.

Bolz, J. (1994). Cortical circuitry in a dish. *Current Opinion in Neurobiology, 4*, 545–549.

Bonnet, M. H., & Arand, D. L. (1996). Insomnia—Nocturnal sleep disruption—Daytime fatigue: The consequences of a week of insomnia. *Sleep, 19*(6), 453–461.

Booth, D. A. (1981). The physiology of appetite. *British Medical Bulletin, 37*, 135–140.

Booth, D. A., Fuller, J., & Lewis, V. (1981). Human control of body weight: Cognitive or physiological? Some energy-related perceptions and misperceptions. In L. A. Cioffi (Ed.), *The body weight regulatory system: Normal and disturbed systems* (pp. 305–314). New York: Raven Press.

Booth, J. E. (1977). Sexual behaviour of male rats injected with the anti-oestrogen MER-25 during infancy. *Physiology & Behavior, 19*, 35–39.

Borbély, A. A. (1981). The sleep process: Circadian and homeostatic aspects. *Advances in Physiological Sciences, 18*, 85–91.

Borbély, A. A. (1983). Pharmacological approaches to sleep regulation. In A. R. Mayes (Ed.), *Sleep mechanisms and functions in humans and animals* (pp. 232–261). Wokingham, England: Van Nostrand Reinhold.

Borbély, A. A. (1984). Sleep regulation: Outline of a model and its implications for depression. In A. Borbély & J. L. Valatx (Eds.), *Sleep mechanisms* (pp. 272–284). Berlin: Springer-Verlag.

Borbély, A. A., Baumann, F., Brandeis, D., Strauch, I., & Lehmann, D. (1981). Sleep deprivation: Effect on sleep stages and EEG power density in man. *Electroencephalography and Clinical Neurophysiology, 51*, 483–493.

Bouchard, T. J., Jr. (1994). Genes, environment, and personality. *Science, 264*, 1700–1701.

Bouchard, T. J., Jr., Lykken, D. T., McGue, M., Segal, N. L., & Tellegen, A. (1990). Sources of human psychological differences: The Minnesota study of twins reared apart. *Science, 250*, 223–228.

Boucsein, W. (1992). *Electrodermal activity.* New York: Plenum Press.

Boulos, Z., & Terman, M. (1980). Food availability and daily biological rhythms. *Neuroscience and Biobehavioral Reviews, 4*, 119–131.

Bowers, D., Bauer, R. M., Coslett, H. B., & Heilman, K. M. (1985). Processing of face by patients with unilateral hemisphere lesions. I. Dissociations between judgements of facial affect and facial identity. *Brain Cognition, 4*, 258–272.

Bowers, D., Coslett, H. B., Bauer, K. M., Speedie, L. J., & Heilman, K. M. (1987). Comprehension of emotional prosody following unilateral hemispheric lesions: Processing defect versus distraction defect. *Neuropsychologia, 25*, 317–328.

Bozarth, M. A., & Wise R. A. (1981). Heroin reward is dependent on a dopaminergic substrate. *Life Sciences, 29*, 1881–1886.

Brackett, N. L., & Edwards, D. A. (1984). Medial preoptic connections with the midbrain tegmentum are essential for male sexual behavior. *Physiology & Behavior, 32*, 79–84.

Brady, J. V. (1993). Behavior analysis applications and interdisciplinary research strategies. *American Psychologist, 48*, 435–440.

Brainard, M. S. (1994). Neural substrates of sound localization. *Current Opinion in Neurobiology, 4*, 557–562.

Bray, G. A. (1992). Pathophysiology of obesity. *American Journal of Clinical Nutrition, 55*, 488–494.

Bray, G. M., Vidal-Sanz, M., & Aguayo, A. J. (1987). Regeneration of axons from the central nervous system of adult rats. In F. J. Seil, E. Herbert, and B. M. Carlson (Eds.), *Progress in brain research*, Vol. 71 (pp. 373–378). New York: Elsevier.

Brecher, E. M. (1972). *Licit and illicit drugs.* Boston: Little, Brown & Co.

Breedlove, S. M. (1992). Sexual differentiation of the brain and behavior. In J. B. Becker, S. M. Breedlove, and D. Crews (Eds.), *Behavioral endocrinology* (pp. 39–70). Cambridge, MA: MIT Press.

Breedlove, S. M. (1994). Sexual differentiation of the human nervous system. *Annual Review of Psychology, 45*, 389–418.

Breitner, J. C. S. (1990). Life table methods and assessment of familial risk in Alzheimer's disease. *Archives of General Psychiatry, 47*, 395–396.

Bremer, F. (1936). Nouvelles recherches sur le mécanisme du sommeil. *Comptes Rendus de la Société de Biologie, 22*, 460–464.

Bremer, F. L. (1937). L'activité cérébrale au cours du sommeil et de la narcose. Contribution à l'étude du mécanisme du sommeil. *Bulletin de l'Académie Royale de Belgique, 4*, 68–86.

Bremer, J. (1959). *Asexualization.* New York: Macmillan Publishing Co.

Brenman, J. E., & Bredt, D. S. (1997). Synaptic signaling by nitric oxide. *Current Opinion in Neurobiology, 7*, 374–378.

Brewster, J. M. (1986). Prevalence of alcohol and other drug problems among physicians. *Journal of the American Medical Association, 255*, 1913–1920.

Bridgeman, B., Van der Heijden, A. H. C., & Velichkovsky, B. M. (1994). A theory of visual stability across saccadic eye movements. *Behavioral and Brain Sciences, 17*, 247–292.

Brill, N. Q., & Christie, R. L. (1974). Marihuana use and psychosocial adaptation. *Archives of General Psychiatry, 31*, 713–719.

Brime, J. I., Lopez-Sela, P., Bernado, R., Costales, M., Diaz, F., Marin, B., & Vijande, M. (1991). Psychological aspects of insulin-induced thirst. *Physiology & Behavior, 49*, 153–154.

Broberg, D. J., & Bernstein, I. L. (1989). Cephalic insulin release in anorexic women. *Physiology & Behavior, 45*, 871–875.

Bronson, F. H., & Matherne, C. M. (1997). Exposure to anabolic-androgenic steroids shortens life span of male mice. *Medicine and Science in Sports and Exercise, 29*, 615–619.

Brooks, V. B. (1986). *The neural basis of motor control.* New York: Oxford.

Brou, P., Sciascia, T. R., Linden, L., & Lettvin, J. Y. (1986, September). The colors of things. *Scientific American, 255*, 84–91.

Brown, G. W. (1993). The role of life events in the aetiology of depressive and anxiety disorders. In S. C. Stanford & S. Salmon (Eds.) *Stress: From Synapse to Syndrome* (pp. 23–50). San Diego: Academic Press.

Brown, H. D., & Kosslyn, S. M. (1993). Cerebral lateralization. *Current Opinion in Neurobiology, 3*, 183–186.

Brown, L. L., Schneider, J. S., & Lidsky, T. I. (1997). Sensory and cognitive functions of the basal ganglia. *Current Opinion in Neurobiology, 7*, 157–163.

Brown, M. C., & Ironton, R. (1977). Motor neurone sprouting induced by prolonged tetrodotoxin block of nerve action potentials. *Nature, 265*, 459–461.

Brown, T. H., Chapman, P. F., Kairiss, E. W., & Keenan, C. L. (1988). Long-term synaptic potentiation. *Science, 242*, 724–728.

Brownell, K. D., & Rodin, J. (1994). The dieting maelstrom: Is it possible and advisable to lose weight? *American Psychologist, 49,* 781–791.

Brunner, D. P., Dijk, D.-J., Tobler, I., & Borbély, A. A. (1990). Effect of partial sleep deprivation on sleep stages and EEG power spectra: Evidence for non-REM and REM sleep homeostasis. *Electroencephalography and Clinical Neurophysiology, 75,* 492–499.

Brüstle, O., & McKay, R. D. G. (1996). Neuronal progenitors as tools for cell replacement in the nervous system. *Current Opinion in Neurobiology, 6,* 688–695.

Bucci, T. J. (1992). Dietary restriction: Why all the interest? An overview. *Laboratory Animal, 21,* 29–34.

Buck, L. B. (1996). Information coding in the vertebrate olfactory system. *Annual Reviews in Neuroscience, 19,* 517–544.

Buckley, M. J., & Gaffan, D. (1998). Perirhinal cortex ablation impairs visual object identification. *The Journal of Neuroscience, 18*(6), 2268–2275.

Buckner, R. L. (1996). Beyond HERA: Contributions of specific prefrontal brain areas to long-term memory retrieval. *Pychonomic Bulletin & Review, 3*(2), 149–158.

Buckner, R. L., & Petersen, S. E. (1996). What does neuroimaging tell us about the role of prefrontal cortex in memory retrieval? *Seminars in the Neurosciences, 8,* 47–55.

Buffalo, E. A., Stefanacci, L., Squire, L. R., Zola, S. M. (1998). A reexamination of the concurrent discrimination learning task: The importance of anterior inferotemporal cortex, Area TE. *Behavioral Neuroscience, 112*(1), 3–14.

Burke, A. C., & Feduccia, A. (1997). Developmental patterns and the identification of homologies in the avian hand. *Science, 278,* 666–668.

Burke, J. F., & Benson, P. J. (1997). Web alert motor systems. *Current Opinion in Neurobiology, 7,* 765.

Burns, R. S., Chiueh, C. C., Markey, S. P., Ebert, M. H., Jacobowitz, D. M., & Kopin, I. J. (1983). A primate model of Parkinsonism: Selective destruction of dopaminergic neurons in the pars compacta of the substantia nigra by N-methyl-4-phenyl-1,2,3,6-tetrahydropyridine. *Proceedings of the National Academy of Sciences (USA), 80,* 4546–4550.

Burns, S. L. (1990). *How to survive unbearable stress.* Huntington Beach, CA: I-MED Press.

Bussey, T. J., Warburton, E. C., Aggleton, J. P., & Muir, J. L. (1998). Fornix lesions can facilitate acquisition of the transverse patterning task: A challenge for "configural" theories of hippocampal function. *The Journal of Neuroscience, 18*(4), 1622–1631.

Butters N., & Stuss, D. T. (1989). Diencephalic amnesia. In F. Boller & J. Grafman (Eds.), *Handbook of neuropsychology* (3rd ed., pp. 107–148). New York: Elsevier.

Butters, N., & Delis, D. C. (1995). Clinical assessment of memory disorders in amnesia and dementia. *Annual Review of Psychology, 46,* 493–523.

Butterworth, R. F., Kril, J. J., & Harper, C. G. (1993). Thiamine-dependent enzyme changes in the brains of alcoholics: Relationship to the Wernicke-Korsakoff syndrome. *Alcoholism: Clinical and Expermental Research, 17,* 1084–1088.

Byne, W. (1994, May). The biological evidence challenged: Even if genetic and neuroanatomical traits turn out to be correlated with sexual orientation, causation is far from proved. *Scientific American, 270,* 50–55.

Byrne, J. H., & Kandel, E. R. (1996). Presynaptic facilitation revisited: State and time dependence. *The Journal of Neuroscience, 15,* 425–435.

Byrne, J. H., Zwartjes, R., Homayouni, R., Critz, S. D., & Eskin, A. (1993). Roles of second messenger pathways in neuronal plasticity and in learning and memory: Insights gained from Aplysia. In S. Shenolikar and A. C. Nairn (Eds.), *Advances in second messenger and phosphoprotein research* (Vol. 27, pp. 47–108). New York: Raven Press.

Cabanac, M. (1971). Physiological role of pleasure. *Science, 173,* 1103–1107.

Cabeza, R., & Nyberg, L. (1997). Imaging cognition: An empirical review of PET studies with normal subjects. *Journal of Cognitive Neuroscience, 9*(1), 1–26.

Cacioppo, J. T., Petty, R. E., Losch, M., & Kim, H. S. (1986). Electromyographic activity over facial muscle regions can differentiate the valence and intensity of emotional reactions. *Journal of Personality and Social Psychology, 50,* 260–268.

Cade, J. F. J. (1949). Lithium salts in treatment of psychotic excitement. *Medical Journal of Australia, 2,* 349–352.

Caggiula, A. R. (1970). Analysis of the copulation-reward properties of posterior hypothalamic stimulation in male rats. *Journal of Comparative and Physiological Psychology, 70,* 399–412.

Cain, D. P. (1986). The transfer phenomenon in kindling. In J. A. Wada, (Ed.), *Kindling 3* (pp. 231–245). New York: Raven Press.

Cain, D. P. (1997). LTP, NMDA, genes and learning. *Current Opinion in Neurobiology, 7,* 235–242.

Calles-Escandon, J., & Horton, E. S. (1992). The thermogenic role of exercise in the treatment of morbid obesity: A critical evaluation. *American Journal of Clinical Nutrition, 55,* 533S–537S.

Callwood, J. (1990). *The sleepwalker.* Toronto: Lester & Orpen Dennys Ltd.

Calne, S., Schoenberg, B., Martin, W., Uitti, J., Spencer, P., & Calne, D. B. (1987). Familial Parkinson's disease: Possible role of environmental factors. *Canadian Journal of Neurological Sciences, 14,* 303–305.

Caltagirone, C., Zoccolotti, P., Originale, G., Daniele, A., & Mammucari, A. (1989). Autonomic reactivity and facial expression of emotion in brain damaged patients. In G. Gainotti and C. C. Caltagirone (Eds.), *Emotion and dual brain.* New York: Springer Verlag.

Campfield, L. A., & Smith, F. J. (1990). Transient declines in blood glucose signal meal initiation. *International Journal of Obesity, 14* (Supplement 3), 15–33.

Campfield, L. A., Brandon, P., & Smith, F. J. (1985). On-line continuous measurement of blood glucose and meal pattern in free-feeding rats: The role of glucose in meal initiation. *Brain Research Bulletin, 14,* 605–616.

Campfield, L. A., Smith, F. J., Gulsez, Y., Devos, R., & Burn, P. (1995). Mouse OB protein: Evidence for a peripheral signal linking adiposity and central neural networks. *Science, 269,* 546–550.

Cannon, W. B., & Washburn, A. L. (1912). An explanation of hunger. *American Journal of Physiology, 29,* 441–454.

Carew, T. J., Hawkins, R. D., & Kandel, E. R. (1983). Differential classical conditioning of a defensive withdrawal reflex in *Aplysia californica. Science, 219,* 397–400.

Carew, T. J., Pinsker, H. M., & Kandel, E. R. (1972). Long-term habituation of a defensive withdrawal reflex in Aplysia. *Science, 175,* 451–454.

Carew, T. J., Walters, E. T., & Kandel, E. R. (1981). Associative learning in Aplysia: Cellular correlates supporting a conditioned fear hypothesis. *Science, 211,* 501–503.

Carlson, N. R. (1994). *Physiology of behavior* (5th ed.). Boston, MA: Allyn and Bacon.

Carlsson, A., & Linqvist, M. (1963). Effect of chlorpromazine or haloperidol on formation of 3-methoxytyramine and normetanephrine in mouse brains. *Acta Pharmacologica et Toxicologica, 20,* 140–144.

Carr, G. D., Fibiger, H. C., & Phillips, A. G. (1989). Conditioned place preference as a measure of drug reward. In J. M. Liebman & S. J. Cooper (Eds.), *The neuropharmacological basis of reward* (pp. 264–319). Oxford: Clarendon Press.

Carroll, D. (1984). *Biofeedback in practice.* New York: Longman Group.

Cassone, V. M. (1990). Effects of melatonin on vertebrate circadian systems. *Trends in Neurosciences, 13*(11), 457–467.

Castellucci, V., & Kandel, E. R. (1974). A quantal analysis of the synaptic depression underlying habituation of the gill-withdrawal reflex in Aplysia. *Proceedings of the National Academy of Sciences (USA), 71,* 5004–5008.

Castellucci, V., & Kandel, E. R. (1976). Presynaptic sensitization as a mechanism for behavioral sensitization in Aplysia. *Science, 194,* 1176–1178.

Castellucci, V., Pinsker, H., Kupfermann, I., & Kandel, E. R. (1970). Neuronal mechanisms of habituation and dishabituation of the gill-withdrawal reflex in Aplysia. *Science, 167,* 1745–1748.

Castellucci, V. F., Blumenfeld, H., Goelet, P., & Kandel, E. R (1989). Inhibitor of protein synthesis blocks long-term behavioral sensitization in the isolated gill-withdrawal reflex of Aplysia. *Journal of Neurobiology, 20,* 1–9.

Castro, C. A., Silbert, L. H., McNaughton, B. L., & Barnes, C. A. (1989). Recovery of spatial learning deficits after decay of electrically induced synaptic enhancement in the hippocampus. *Nature, 342,* 545–548.

Cesare, P., & McNaughton, P. (1997). Peripheral pain mechanisms. *Current Opinion in Neurobiology, 7,* 493–499.

Chan-Ling, T., & Stone, J. (1991). Factors determining the morphology and distribution of astrocytes in the cat retina: A 'contact-spacing' model of astrocyte interaction. *The Journal of Comparative Neurology, 303,* 387–399.

Changeux, J.-P. (1993, November). Chemical signaling in the brain. *Scientific American, 269,* 58–62.

Chavez, M., Seeley, R. J., & Woods, S. C,.(1995). A compaarison between the effects of intraventricular insulin and intraperitoneal LiCl on three measures sensitive to emetic agents. *Behavioral Neuroscience, 109,* 547–550.

Chen, C. S. (1968). A study of the alcohol-tolerance effect and an introduction of a new behavioral technique. *Psychopharmacology, 12,* 433–440.

Chen, J. (1993). Dopaminergic mechanisms and brain reward. *Seminars in the Neurosciences, 5,* 315–320.

Chen, Y.-C., Thaler, D., Nixon, P. D., Stern, C. E., & Passingham, R. E. (1995). The functions of the medial premotor cortex II. The timing and selection of learned movements. *Experimental Brain Research, 102,* 461–473.

Cheney, D. L., & Seyfarth, R. M. (1992). Précis of how monkeys see the world. *Behavioral and Brain Sciences, 15,* 135–182.

Cheng, J., Cao, Y., & Olson, L. (1996). Spinal cord repair in adult paraplegic rats: Partial restoration of hind limb function. *Science, 273,* 510–451.

Chertkow, H., & Murtha, S. (1997). PET activation and language. *Clinical Neuroscience, 4,* 78–86.

Cho, A. K. (1990). Ice: A new dosage form of an old drug. *Science, 249,* 631–634.

Choi, D. W. (1996). Ischemia-induced neuronal apoptosis. *Current Opinion in Neurobiology, 6,* 667–672.

Choi-Lundberg, D. L., Lin, Q., Chang, Y.-N., Chiang, Y. L., Hay, C. M., Mohajeri, H., Davidson, B. L., & Bohn, M. C. (1997). Dopaminergic neurons protected from degeneration by GDNF gene therapy. *Science, 275,* 838–930.

Chorover, S. L., & Schiller, P. H. (1965). Short-term retrograde amnesia in rats. *Journal of Comparative and Physiological Psychology, 59,* 73–78.

Clapham, D. E. (1994). Direct G protein activation of ion channels. *Annual Review of Neuroscience, 17,* 441–464.

Clarke, R. E., & Squire, L. R. (1998). Classical conditioning and brain systems: The role of awareness. *Science, 280,* 77–81.

Cleary, L. J., Lee, W. L., & Byrne, J. H. (1998). Cellular correlates of long-term sensitization in Aplysia. *The Journal of Neuroscience, 18*(15), 5988–5998.

Clements, J. D., Lester, R. A. J., Tong, G., Jahr, C. E., & Westbrook, G. L. (1992). The time course of glutamate in the synaptic cleft. *Science, 258,* 1498–1501.

Cohen, M. S., & Bookheimer, S. Y. (1994). Localization of brain function using magnetic resonance imaging. *Trends in Neurosciences, 17,* 268–277.

Cohen, S. (1996). Psychological stress, immunity, and upper respiratory infections. *Current Directions in Psychological Science, 5*(3), 86–90.

Cohen, S., & Herbert, T. B. (1996). Health psychology: Psychological factors and physical disease from the perspective of human psychoneuroimmunology. *Annual Review of Psychology, 47,* 113–142.

Cohen, S., & Stillman, R. C. (Eds.) (1976). *The therapeutic potential of marihuana.* New York: Plenum Medical Book Company.

Colebatch, J. G., Deiber, M.-P., Passingham, R. E., Friston, K. J., & Frakowiak, R. S. J. (1991). Regional cerebral blood flow during voluntary arm and hand movements in human subjects. *Journal of Neurophysiology, 65,* 1392–1401.

Coleman, D. L. (1979). Obesity genes: beneficial effects in heterozygous mice. *Science, 203,* 663–665.

Colle, L. M., & Wise, R. A. (1988). Effects of nucleus accumbens amphetamine on lateral hypothalamic brain stimulation reward. *Brain Research, 459,* 361–368.

Collier, G. (1986). The dialogue between the house economist and the resident physiologist. *Nutrition and Behavior, 3,* 9–26.

Collier, G. H. (1980). An ecological analysis of motivation. In F. M. Toates & T. R. Halliday (Eds.), *Analysis of motivational processes* (pp. 125–151). London: Academic Press.

Colman, H., Nabekura, J., & Lichtman, J. W. (1997). Alterations in synaptic strength preceding axon withdrawal. *Science, 275,* 356–362.

Coltheart, M. (1980). Deep dyslexia: A right hemisphere hypothesis. In M. Coltheart, K. Patterson, and J. C. Marshall (Eds.), *Deep dyslexia* (pp. 326–380). London: Routledge.

Considine, R. V., & Caro, J. F. (1996). Leptin: Genes, concepts and clinical perspective. *Hormonal Research, 46,* 249–256.

Cook, G., Tannahill, D., & Keynes, R. (1998). Axon guidance to and from choice points. *Current Opinion in Neurobiology, 8,* 64–72.

Cooper, R. M., & Zubek, J. P. (1958). Effects of enriched and restricted early environments on the learning ability of bright and dull rats. *Canadian Journal of Psychology, 12,* 159–164.

Cooper, S. J., & Dourish, C. T. (1990). Multiple cholecystokinin (CCK) receptors and CCK-monoamine interactions are instrumental in the control of feeding. *Physiology & Behavior, 48,* 849–857.

Coppens, Y. (1994, May). East side story: The origin of humankind. *Scientific American, 270,* 88–95.

Corbett, D., & Wise, R. A. (1980). Intracranial self-stimulation in relation to the ascending dopaminergic systems of the midbrain: A moveable electrode mapping study. *Brain Research, 185,* 1–15.

Corbetta, M., Miezin, F. M., Dobmeyer, S., Shulman, G. L., & Petersen, S. E. (1990). Attentional modulation of neural processing of shape, color, and velocity in humans. *Science, 248,* 1556–1559.

Corcoran, M., McCaughran, J. A., Jr., & Wada, J. A. (1978). Antiepileptic and prophylactic effects of tetrahydrocannabinols in amygdaloid kindled rats. *Epilepsia, 19,* 47–55.

Corcoran, M. E., McCaughran, J. A., Jr., & Wada, J. A. (1973). Acute anti-epileptic effects of D9-tetrahydrocannabinol in rats with kindled seizures. *Experimental Neurology, 40,* 471–483.

Corina, D. P., Poizner, H., Bellugi, U., Feinberg, T., Dowd, D., & O'Grady-Batch, L. (1992). Dissociation between linguistic and nonlinguistic gestureal systems: A case for compositionality. *Brain and Language, 43,* 414–447.

Corkin, S. (1968). Acquisition of motor skill after bilateral medial temporal-lobe excision. *Neuropsychologia, 6,* 255–265.

Corkin, S., Amaral, D. G., Gonzalez, R. G., Johnson, K. A., & Hyman, B. T. (1997). H. M.'s medial temporal lobe lesion: Findings from magnetic resonance imaging. *Journal of Neuroscience, 17*(10), 3964–3979.

Corkin, S., Milner, B., & Rasmussen, R. (1970). Somatosensory thresholds. *Archives of Neurology, 23,* 41–59.

Corsi, P. I. (1991). *The enchanted loom: Chapters in the history of neuroscience.* New York: Oxford.

Corwin, J. T., & Warchol, M. E. (1991). Auditory hair cells. *Annual Review of Neuroscience, 14,* 301–333.

Courtney, S. M., & Ungerleider, L. G. (1997). What fMRI has taught us about human vision. *Current Opinion in Neurobiology, 7,* 554–561.

Coyle, J. T. (1987). Alzheimer's disease. In G. Adelman (Ed.), *Encyclopedia of neuroscience* (pp. 29–31). Boston: Birkhäuser.

Craig, A. D., Reiman, E. M., Evans, A., & Bushnell, M. C. (1996). Functional imaging of an illusion of pain. *Nature, 384,* 258–260.

Crair, M. C., Gillespie, D. C., & Stryker, M. P. (1998). The role of visual experience in the development of columns in cat visual cortex. *Science, 279,* 566–570.

Creese, I., Burt, D. R., & Snyder, S. H. (1976). Dopamine receptor binding predicts clinical and pharmacological potencies of antischizophrenic drugs. *Science, 192,* 481–483.

Cremona, O., & De Camilli, P. (1997). *Current Opinion in Neurobiology 7,* 323–330.

Crick, F., & Koch, C. (1992, September). The problem of consciousness. *Scientific American, 267,* 153–159.

Crowell, C. R., Hinson, R. E., & Siegel, S. (1981). The role of conditional drug responses in tolerance to the hypothermic effects of ethanol. *Psychopharmacology, 73,* 51–54.

Crusio, W. M. (1996). Gene-targeting studies: New methods, old problems. *Trends in Neurosciences, 19,* 186–187.

Culbertson, F. M. (1997). Depression and gender. *American Psychologist, 52*(1), 25–31.

Daly, M., & Wilson, M. (1983). *Sex, evolution, and behavior.* Boston, MA: Allard Grant Press.

Damasio, H. (1989). Neuroimaging contributions to the understanding of aphasia. In F. Boller & J. Grafman (Eds.), *Handbook of neuropsychology,* Vol. 2 (pp. 3–46). New York: Elsevier.

Darnell, J. E., Jr. (1997). STATS and gene regulation. *Science, 277,* 1630–1635.

Das, G. D., & Altman, J. (1971). Transplanted precursors of nerve cells: Their fate in the cerebellums of young rats. *Science, 173,* 637–638.

Daum, I., & Schugens, M. M. (1996). On the cerebellum and classical conditioning. *Current Directions in Psychological Science, 5*(2), 58–61.

Davidson, J. M. (1980). Hormones and sexual behavior in the male. In D. T. Krieger and J. C. Hughes (Eds.), *Neuroendocrinology* (pp. 232–238). Sunderland, MA: Sinauer Associates.

Davidson, J. M., Kwan, M., & Greenleaf, W. J. (1982). Hormonal replacement and sexuality in men. *Clinics in Endocrinology and Metabolism, 11,* 599–623.

Davis, H. P., Rosenzweig, M. R., Becker, L. A., & Sather, K. J. (1988). Biological psychology's relationships to psychology and neuroscience. *American Psychologist, 43,* 359–371.

Davis, M., Rainnie, D., & Cassell, M. (1994). Neurotransmission in the rat amygdala related to fear and anxiety. *Trends in Neurosciences, 17,* 208–214.

Deadwyler, S. A., & Hampson, R. E. (1995). Ensemble activity and behavior: What's the code? *Science, 270,* 1316–1318.

De Jonge, F. H., Louwerse, A. L., Ooms, M. P., Evers, P., Endert, E., & van de Poll, N. E. (1989). Lesions of the SDN-POA inhibit sexual behavior of male Wistar rats. *Brain Research Bulletin, 23,* 483–492.

de Kruif, P. (1945). *The male hormone.* New York: Harcourt, Brace and Co.

Dement, W. C. (1960). The effect of dream deprivation. *Science, 131,* 1705–1707.

Dement, W. C. (1978). *Some must watch while some must sleep.* New York: W. W. Norton.

Dement, W. C., & Kleitman, N. (1957). The relation of eye movement during sleep to dream activity: An objective method for the study of dreaming. *Journal of Experimental Psychology, 53,* 339–553.

Dement, W. C., Mitler, M., & Henriksen, S. (1972). Sleep changes during chronic administration of parachorophenylalanine. *Revue Canadienne de Biologie, 31,* 239–246.

Dement, W. C., & Wolpert, E. A. (1958). The relation of eye movements, body motility and external stimuli to dream content. *Journal of Experimental Psychology, 55,* 543–553.

Demotes-Mainard, J., Vernier, P., & Vincent, J.-D. (1993). Hormonal control of neural function in the adult brain. *Current Opinion in Neurobiology, 3,* 989–996.

De Renzi, E. (1980). The influence of sex and age on the incidence and type of aphasia. *Cortex, 16,* 627–630.

De Renzi, E. (1982). *Disorders of space exploration and cognition.* New York: Wiley.

DeValois, R. L., & DeValois, K. K. (1988). *Spatial vision.* New York: Oxford University Press.

Devane, W. A., Hanus, L., Breuer, A., Pertwee, R. G., Stevenson, L. A., Griffin, G., Gibson, D., Mandelbaum, A., Etinger, A., & Mechoulam, R. (1992). Isolation and structure of a brain constituent that binds to the cannabinoid receptor. *Science, 258,* 1946–1949.

Dewji, N. N., & Singer, S. J. (1996). Genetic clues to Alzheimer's disease. *Science, 271,* 159–160.

Dewsbury, D. A. (1990). *Contemporary issues in comparative psychology.* Sunderland, MA: Sinauer.

Dewsbury, D. A. (1991). Psychobiology. *American Psychologist, 46,* 198–205.

Diamond, A., Prevor, A., Callender, G., & Druin, D. P. (1997). *Prefrontal cortex cognitive deficits in children treated early and continuously for PKU.* Chicago: University of Chicago Press.

Diamond, M., & Sigmundson, H. K. (1997). Sex reassignment at birth: Long-term review and clinical implications. *Archives of Pediatric and Adolescent Medicine, 151,* 298–304.

Diamond, M. C. (1986). I want a girl just like the girl . . . *Discover, 7,* 65–68.

Dicker, S. E., & Nunn, J. (1957). The role of antidiuretic hormone during water deprivation in rats. *Journal of Physiology, 136,* 235–248.

DiFiglia, M., Sapp, E., Chase, K. O., Davies, S. W., Bates, G. P., Vonsattel, J. P., & Aronin, N. (1997). Aggregation of Huntingtin in neuronal intranuclear inclusions and dystrophic neurites in brain. *Science, 277,* 1990–1993.

Dinges, D. F., Pack, F., Williams, K., Gillen, K. A., Powell, J. W., Ott, G. E., Aptowicz, C., & Pack, A. I. (1997). Cumulative sleepiness, mood disturbance, and psychomotor vigilance performance decrements during a week of sleep restricted to 4–5 hours per night. *Sleep, 20*(4), 267–277.

Di Pelligrino, G. D., & Wise, S. P. (1991). Neurophysiological comparison of three distinct regions in the primate frontal lobe. *Brain, 114,* 951–978.

Dobelle, W. H., Mladejovsky, M. G., & Girvin, J. P. (1974). Artificial vision for the blind: Electrical stimulation of visual cortex offers hope for a functional prosthesis. *Science, 183,* 440–444.

Doering, L. C. (1996). Towards gene therapy in the nervous system. *Clinical Neuroscience, 3,* 259–261.

Donoghue, J. P. (1995). Plasticity of adult sensorimotor representations. *Current Opinion in Neurobiology, 5,* 749–754.

Dornan, W. A., & Malsbury, C. W. (1989). Neuropeptides and male sexual behavior. *Neuroscience and Biobehavioral Reviews, 13,* 1–5.

Doty, R. L. (1986). Gender and endocrine-related influences on human olfactory perception. In H. Meiselman & R. S. Rivlin (Eds.), *Clinical measurement of taste and smell* (pp. 377–413). New York: Macmillan Publishing Co.

Doty, R. L., Ford, M., Preti, G., & Huggins, G. R. (1975). Changes in the intensity and pleasantness of human vaginal odors during the menstrual cycle. *Science, 190,* 1316–1318.

Doty, R. L., Green, P. A., Ram, C., & Yankell, S. L. (1982). Communication of gender from human breath odors: Relationship to perceived intensity and pleasantness. *Hormones and Behavior, 16,* 13–22.

Doty, R. L., Snyder, P. J., Huggins, G. R., & Lowry, L. D. (1981). Endocrine, cardiovascular, and psychological correlates of olfactory sensitivity changes during the human menstrual cycle. *Journal of Comparative and Physiological Psychology, 95,* 45–60.

Doupe, A. J. (1993). A neural circuit specialized for vocal learning. *Current Opinion in Neurobiology, 3,* 104–110.

Dourish, C. T., Rycroft, W., & Iversen, S. D. (1989). Postponement of satiety by blockade of brain cholecystokinin (CCK-B) receptors. *Science, 245,* 1509–1511.

Drachman, D. A., & Arbit, J. (1966). Memory and the hippocampal complex. *Archives of Neurology, 15,* 52–61.

Driver, J., & Mattingly, J. B. (1996). Selective attention in humans: Normality and pathology. *Current Opinion in Neurobiology, 5,* 191–197.

Duff, K. (1997). Alzheimer transgenic mouse models come of age. *Trends in Neuroscience, 20,* 279–280.

Duke, R. C., Ojcius, D. M., & Young, J. D.-E. (1996, December). Cell suicide in health and disease. *Scientific American, 275,* 80–87.

Dum, R. P., & Strick, P. L. (1992). Medial wall motor areas and skeletomotor control. *Current Opinion in Neurobiology, 2,* 836–839.

Dunbar, G. C., Perera, M. H., & Jenner, F. A. (1989). Patterns of benzodiazepine use in Great Britain as measured by a general population survey. *British Journal of Psychiatry, 155,* 836–841.

Duncan, J., Humphreys, G., & Ward, R. (1997). Competitive brain activity in visual attention. *Current Opinion in Neurobiology, 7,* 255–261.

Duva, C. A., Kornecook, T. J., & Pinel, P. J. P. (in press). Animal models of medial temporal lobe amnesia: The myth of the hippocampus. In C. M. Haug and R. E. Whalen (Eds.), *Brain, behavior, and cognition: Animal models and human studies.* Washington: APA Books.

Duvoisin, R. C., Heikkila, R. E., Nicklas, W. J., & Hess, A. (1986). Dopaminergic neurotoxicity of MPTP in the mouse: A murine model of parkinsonism. In S. Fahn, C. D. Marsden, P. Jenner, & P. Teychenne (Eds.), *Recent developments in Parkinson's disease* (pp. 147–154). New York: Raven Press.

Earnest, M. P. (1993). Seizures. *Neurologic Complications of Drug and Alcohol Abuse, 11*(3), 563–575.

Easter, S. S., Jr., Purves, D., Rakic, P., & Spitzer, N. C. (1985). The changing view of neural specificity. *Science, 230,* 507–511.

Edwards, F. A. (1995). LTP—a structural model to explain the inconsistencies. *Trends in Neurosciences, 18,* 250–255.

Egan, M. F., & Weinberger, D. R. (1997). Neurobiology of schizophrenia. *Current Opinion in Neurobiology, 7,* 701–707.

Ehrhardt, A. A., Epstein, R., & Money, M. (1968). Fetal androgens and female gender identity in the early-treated androgenital syndrome. *Johns Hopkins Medical Journal, 122,* 160–167.

Ehrhardt, A. A., & Meyer-Bahlberg, H. F. L. (1981). Effects of prenatal sex hormones on gender-related behavior. *Science, 211,* 1312–1317.

Ehrhardt, A. A., Meyer-Bahlburg, H. F. L., Rosen, L. R., Feldman, J. F., Veridiano, N. P., Zimmerman, I., & McEwen, B. S. (1985). Sexual orientation after prenatal exposure to exogenous estrogen. *Archives of Sexual Behavior, 14,* 57–77.

Ehringer, H., & Hornykiewicz, O. (1960). Verteilung von Noradrenalin und Dopamin (3-Hydroxytyramin) im gehirn des Menschen und ihr Verhalten bei Erkrankungen des Extrapyramidalen Systems. *Klinische Wochenschrift, 38,* 1236–1239.

Eichenbaum, H. (1996). Learning from LTP: A comment on recent attempts to identify cellular and molecular mechanisms of memory. *Learning & Memory, 3,* 61–73.

Eichenbaum, H. (1997). How does the brain organize memories? *Science, 277,* 330–332.

Eidelberg, E. (1987). Flexion reflexes. In G. Adelman (Ed.), *Encyclopedia of neuroscience, I* (pp. 431–432). Boston, MA: Birkhäuser.

Eikelboom, R., & Stewart, J. (1982). Conditioning of drug-induced physiological responses. *Psychological Review, 89,* 507–528.

Eilers, J., & Konnerth, A. (1997). Dendritic signal integration. *Current Opinion in Neurobiology, 7,* 385–390.

Ekman, P. (1985). *Telling lies.* New York: Norton.

Ekman, P. (1992). Facial expressions of emotion: New findings, new questions. *Psychological Science, 3,* 34–38.

Ekman, P. (1993). Facial expression and emotion. *American Psychologist, 48,* 384–392.

Ekman, P., & Davidson, R. J. (1993). Voluntary smiling changes regional brain activity. *Psychological Science, 4,* 342–345.

Ekman, P., & Friesen, W. V. (1971). Constants across cultures in the face and emotion. *Journal of Personality and Social Psychology, 17*, 124–129.

Ekman, P., & Friesen, W. V. (1975). *Unmasking the face: A guide to recognizing emotions from facial clues.* Englewood Cliffs, NJ: Prentice-Hall.

Ekman, P., Sorenson, E. R., & Friesen, W. V. (1969). Pan-cultural elements in facial displays of emotions. *Science, 164*, 86–88.

Elbert, T., Pantev, C., Wienbruch, C., Rockstroh, B., & Taub, E. (1995). Increased cortical representation of the fingers of the left hand in string players. *Science, 270*, 305–307.

Elena, S. F., Cooper, V. S., Lenski, R. E. (1996). Punctuated evolution cased by selection of rare beneficial mutations. *Science, 272*, 1802–1807.

Eley, T. C., & Plomin, R. (1997). Genetic analysis of emotionality. *Current Opinion in Neurobiology, 7*, 279–284.

Ellis, L., & Ames, M. A. (1987). Neurohormonal functioning and sexual orientation: A theory of homosexuality-heterosexuality. *Psychological Bulletin, 101*, 233–258.

Emptage, N. J., & Carew, T. J. (1993). Long-term synaptic facilitation in the absence of short-term facilitation in Aplysia neurons. *Science, 262*, 253–256.

Enns, J. T., & DiLollo, V. (1997). Object substitution: A new form of masking in unattended visual locations. *Psychological Science, 8*, 135–139.

Etcoff, N. L. (1989). Asymmetries in recognition of emotion. In F. Boller and J. Grafman (Eds.), *Handbook of neuropsychology* (3rd ed., pp. 363–402). New York: Elsevier.

Evan, G., & Littlewood, T. (1998). A matter of life and cell death. *Science, 281*, 1317–1320.

Evans, C. J., Keith, D. E., Jr., Morrison, H., Magendzo, K., & Edwards, R. H. (1992). Cloning of delta opioid receptor by functional expression. *Science, 258*, 1952–1955.

Everitt, B. J., & Herbert, J. (1972). Hormonal correlates of sexual behavior in sub-human primates. *Danish Medical Bulletin, 19*, 246–258.

Everitt, B. J., Herbert, J., & Hamer, J. D. (1971). Sexual receptivity of bilaterally adrenalectomized female rhesus monkeys. *Physiology & Behavior, 8*, 409–415.

Everitt, B. J., & Robbins, T. W. (1997). Central cholinergic systems and cognition. *Annual Review of Psychology, 48*, 649–84.

Everitt, B. J., & Stacey, P. (1987). Studies of instrumental behavior with sexual reinforcement in male rats (*Rattus norvegicus*): II Effects of preoptic area lesions, castration, and testosterone. *Journal of Comparative Psychology, 101*, 407–419.

Falk, J. L. (1964). Production of polydipsia in normal rats by an intermittent food schedule. *Science, 133*, 195–196.

Falzi, G., Perrone, P., & Vignolo, L. A. (1982). Right–left asymmetry in anterior speech region. *Archives of Neurology, 39*, 239–240.

Farah, M. J. (1990). *Visual agnosia: Disrders of object recognition and what they tell us about normal vision.* Cambridge, MA: MIT Press.

Farmer, M. E., & Klein, R. M. (1995). The evidence for a temporal processing deficit linked to dyslexia: A review. *Psychonomic Bulletin and Review, 2*(4), 460–493.

Fazeli, S., & Walsh, F. S. (1996). The role of cell adhesion molecules during the development and regeneration of the neuromuscular system. *Seminars in the Neurosciences, 8*, 367–377.

Feindel, W. (1986). Electrical stimulation of the brain during surgery for epilepsy—Historical highlights. In G. P. Varkey (Ed.), *Anesthetic considerations for craniotomy in awake patients* (pp. 75–87). Boston: Little, Brown and Company.

Feldman, S. M., & Waller, H. J. (1962). Disassociation of electrocortical activation and behavioral arousal. *Nature, 196*, 1320–1322.

Fentress, J. C. (1973). Development of grooming in mice with amputated forelimbs. *Science, 179*, 704–705.

Fibiger, H. C. (1991). Cholinergic mechanisms in learning, memory and dementia: A review of recent evidence. *Trends in Neurosciences, 14*, 20–223.

Fibiger, H. C. (1993). Mesolimbic dopamine: An analysis of its role in motivated behavior. *Seminars in the Neurosciences, 5*, 321–327.

Fibiger, H. C., LePiane, F. G., Jakubovic, A., & Phillips, A. G. (1987). The role of dopamine in intracranial self-stimulation of the ventral tegmental area. *Journal of Neuroscience, 7*, 3888–3896.

Fields, H. L., & Basbaum, A. I. (1984). Endogenous pain control mechanisms. In P. D. Wall & R. Melzack (Eds.), *Textbook of pain* (pp. 142–152). Edinburgh: Churchill Livingstone.

Fields, R. D., & Itoh, K. (1996). Neural cell adhesion molecules in activity-dependent development and synaptic plasticity. *Trends in Neurosciences, 19*, 473–480.

Fiez, J. A., & Petersen, S. E. (1993). PET as part of an interdisciplinary approach to understanding processes involved in reading. *Psychological Science, 4*, 287–293.

Filbin, M. T. (1995). Myelin-associated glycoprotein: A role in myelination and in the inhibition of axonal regeneration? *Current Opinion in Neurobiology, 5*, 588–595.

Fillion, T. J., & Blass, E. M. (1986). Infantile experience with suckling odors determines adult sexual behavior in male rats. *Science, 231*, 729–731.

Finger, S., Le Vere, T. E., Almli, C. R., & Stein, D. G. (1988). *Brain injury and recovery: Theoretical and controversial issues.* New York: Plenum.

Finlay, B. L., & Darlington, R. B. (1995). Linked regularities in the development and evolution of mammalian brains. *Science, 268*, 1578–1584.

Fiorino, D. F., Coury, A., Fibiger, H. C., & Phillips, A. G. (1993). Electrical stimulation of reward sites in the ventral tegmental area increases dopamine transmission in the nucleus accumbens of the rat. *Behavioural Brain Research, 55*, 131–141.

Fiorino, D. F., Coury, A., & Phillips, A. G. (1997). Dynamic changes in nucleus accumbens dopamine efflux during the Coolidge effect in male rats. *The Journal of Neuroscience, 17*(12), 4849–4855.

Fischer-Nielson, S., Loft, S., & Gjervig Jensen, K. (1993). Effect of ascorbate and 5-aminosalicylic acid on light-induced 8-hydroxydeoxyguanosine formation in V79 Chinese hamster cells. *Carcinogenesis, 14*, 2431–2433.

Fitts, D. A., & Masson, D. B. (1990). Preoptic angiotensin and salt appetite. *Behavioral Neuroscience, 104*, 643–50.

Fitzsimons, J. T. (1972). Thirst. *Physiological Reviews, 52*, 468–561.

Fitzsimons, J. T., Epstein, A. N., & Johnson, A. K. (1978). Peptide antagonists of the renin-angiotensin system in the characterisation of receptors for angiotensin-induced drinking. *Brain Research, 153*, 319–331.

Fitzsimons, J. T., & LeMagnen, J. (1969). Eating as a regulatory control of drinking in the rat. *Journal of Comparative and Physiological Psychology, 67*, 273–283.

Fitzsimons, J. T., & Simons, B. J. (1969). The effect on drinking in the rat of intravenous infusion of angiotensin, given alone or in combination with other stimuli of thirst. *Journal of Physiology, 203*, 45–57.

Flament, D., Ellermann, J. M., Kim, S.-G., Uğurbil, K., & Ebner, T. J. (1996). Functional magnetic resonance imaging of cerebellar activation during the learning of a visuomotor dissociation task. *Human Brain Mapping, 4,* 210–226.

Fletcher, P. C., Frith, C. D., & Rugg, M. D. (1997). The functional neuroanatomy of episodic memory. *Trends in Neurosciences, 20,* 213–218.

Floresco, S. B., Seamans, J. K., & Phillips, A. G. (1997). Selective roles for hippocampal, prefrontal cortical, and ventral striatal circuits in radial-arm maze tasks with or without a delay. *The Journal of Neuroscience 17*(5), 1880–1890.

Foulkes, N. S., Borjigin, J., Snyder, S. H., & Sassone-Corsi, P. (1997). Rhythmic transcription: The molecular basis of circadian melatonin synthesis. *Trends in Neurosciences, 20,* 487–492.

Freund, H.-J. (1996). Remapping the brain. *Science, 272,* 1754.

Friedman, J., Globus, G., Huntley, A., Mullaney, D., Naitoh, P., & Johnson, L. (1977). Performance and mood during and after gradual sleep reduction. *Psychophysiology, 14,* 245–250.

Friedman-Hill, S. R., Robertson, L. C., & Treisman, A. (1995). Parietal contributions to visual feature binding: Evidence from a patient with bilateral lesions. *Science, 269,* 853–855.

Frith, C., & Dolan, R. J. (1998). Images of psychopathology. *Current Opinion in Neurobiology, 8,* 259–262.

Funder, J. W. (1993). Mineralocorticoids, glucocorticoids, receptors and response elements. *Science, 259,* 1132–1133.

Gabrieli, J. D. E., Corkin, S., Mickel, S. F., & Growdon, J. H. (1993). Intact acquisition and long-term retention of mirror-tracing skill in Alzheimer's disease and in global amnesia. *Behavioral Neuroscience, 107,* 899–910.

Gabrieli, J. D. E., Desmond, J. E., Demb, J. B., Wagner, A. D., Stone, M. V., Vaidya, C. J., & Glover, G. H. (1996). Functional magnetic resonance imaging of semantic memory processes in the frontal lobes. *Psychological Science, 7*(5), 278–283.

Gackenbach, J., & LaBerge, S. (Eds.). (1988). *Conscious mind, sleeping brain.* New York: Plenum.

Gaffan, D. (1974). Recognition impaired and association in the memory of monkeys after transection of the fornix. *Journal of Comparative and Physiological Psychology, 86,* 1100–1109.

Galef, B. G. (1989). Laboratory studies of naturally-occurring feeding behaviors: Pitfalls, progress and problems in ethoexperimental analysis. In R. J. Blanchard, P. F. Brain, D. C. Blanchard, and S. Parmigiani (Eds.), *Ethoexperimental approaches to the study of behavior* (pp. 51–77). Dordrecht, The Netherlands: Kluwer Academic Publishers.

Galef, B. G. (1995). Food selection: problems in understanding how we choose foods to eat. *Neuroscience and Biobehavioral Reviews, 20,* 67–73.

Galef, B. G. (1996). Social enhancement of food preferences in Norway rats: A brief review. In *Social learning in animals: The roots of culture,* pp. 49–64. New York: Academic Press.

Galef, B. G., & Sherry, D. F. (1973). Mother's milk: A medium for transmission of cues reflecting the flavor of mother's diet. *Journal of Comparative and Physiological Psychology, 83,* 374–378.

Galef, B. G., & Wright, T. J. (1995). Groups of naive rats learn to select nutritionally adequate foods faster than do isolated naive rats. *Animal Behavior, 49,* 403–409.

Gall, C., McWilliams, R., & Lynch, G. (1980). Accelerated rates of synaptogenesis by "sprouting" afferents in the immature hippocampal formation. *Journal of Comparative Neurology, 193,* 1047–1061.

Gallagher, M., & Chiba, A. A. (1996). The amygdala and emotion. *Current Opinion in Neurobiology, 6,* 221–227.

Gallup, G. G., Jr. (1983). Toward a comparative psychology of mind. In R. L. Mellgren (Ed.), *Animal cognition and behavior* (pp. 473–505). New York: North-Holland Publishing.

Gao, J.-H., Parsons, L. M., Bower, J. M., Xiong, J., Li, J., & Fox, P. T. (1996). Cerebellum implicated in sensory acquisition and discrimination rather than motor control. *Science, 272,* 545–547.

Garcia, J., & Koelling, R. A. (1966). Relation of cue to consequence in avoidance learning. *Psychonomic Science, 4,* 123–124.

Gawin, F. H. (1991). Cocaine addiction: Psychology and neurophysiology. *Science, 251,* 1580–1586.

Gaze, R. M., Keating, M. J., Ostberg, A., & Chung, S. H. (1979). The relationship between retinal and tectal growth in larval Xenopus: Implications for the development of the retino-tectal projection. *Journal of Embryology and Experimental Morphology, 53,* 103–143.

Gaze, R. M., & Sharma, S. C. (1970). Axial differences in the reinnervation of the goldfish optic tectum by regenerating optic nerve fibres. *Experimental Brain Research, 10,* 171–181.

Gazzaniga, M. S. (1967, August). The split brain in man. *Scientific American, 217,* 24–29.

Gazzaniga, M. S. (1998, July). Groundbreaking work that began more than a quarter of a century ago has led to ongoing insights about brain organization and consciousness. *Scientific American, 278,* 51–55.

Gazzaniga, M. S., & Sperry, R. W. (1967). Language after section of the cerebral commissure. *Brain, 90,* 131–148.

Geiselman, P. J. (1987). Carbohydrates do not always produce satiety: An explanation of the appetite- and hunger-stimulating effects of hexoses. *Progress in Psychobiology and Physiological Psychology, 12,* 1–46.

Georgopoulos, A. P. (1991). Higher order motor control. *Annual Review of Neuroscience, 14,* 361–377.

Georgopoulos, A. P. (1995). Current issues in directional motor control. *Trends in Neurosciences, 18,* 506–510.

Gerlai, R. (1996). Gene-targeting studies of mammalian behavior: Is it the mutation or the background genotype? *Trends in Neurosciences, 19,* 177–181.

Geschwind, N. (1965). The organization of language and the brain. *Science, 170,* 940–944.

Geschwind, N. (1979, September). Specializations of the human brain. *Scientific American, 241,* 180–199.

Geschwind, N., & Levitsky, W. (1968). Human brain: Left–right asymmetries in temporal speech region. *Science, 161,* 186–187.

Gevins, A., Leong, H., Smith, M. E., Le, J., & Du, R. (1995). Mapping cognitive brain function with modern high-resolution electroencephalography. *Trends in Neurosciences, 18,* 429–436.

Gibbs, J., Young, R. C., & Smith, G. P. (1973). Cholecystokinin decreases food intake in rats. *Journal of Comparative and Physiological Psychology, 84,* 488–495.

Gilbert, C. D. (1993). Rapid dynamic changes in adult cerebral cortex. *Current Opinion in Neurobiology, 3,* 100–103.

Gilbert, C. D., & Wiesel, T. N. (1992). Receptive field dynamics in adult primary visual cortex. *Nature, 356,* 150–152.

Gillberg, M., Kecklund, G., Axelsson, J., & Åkerstedt, T. (1996). The effects of a short daytime nap after restricted night sleep. *Sleep, 19*(7), 570–575.

Gillette, M. U. (1997). Cellular and biochemical mechanisms underlying circadian rhythms in vertebrates. *Current Opinion in Neurobiology, 7,* 797–804.

Gillette, M. U., & McArthur, A. J. (1996). Circadian actions of melatonin at the suprachiasmatic nucleus. *Behavioural Brain Research, 73,* 135–139.

Gilliam, T. C., Gusella, J. F., & Lehrach, H. (1987). Molecular genetic strategies to investigate Huntington's disease. *Advances in Neurology, 48*, 17–29.

Gilman, A. (1937). The relation between blood osmotic pressure, fluid distribution and voluntary water intake. *American Journal of Physiology, 120*, 323–328.

Gingrich, K. J., & Byrne, J. H. (1985). Simulation of synaptic depression, potentiation potentiation, and presynaptic facilitation of synaptic potentials from sensory neurons mediating gill-withdrawal reflex in *Aplysia*. *Journal of Neurophysiology, 53*, 652–669.

Gladue, B. A. (1994). The biopsychology of sexual orientation. *Current Directions in Psychological Science, 3*(5), 150–154.

Glanzman, D. L. (1995). The cellular basis of classical conditioning in *Aplysia californica*—Less simple than you think. *Trends in Neurosciences, 18*, 30–36.

Glaser, R., Rice, J., Sheridan, J., Fertel, R., Stout, J., Speicher, C., Pinsky, D., Koture, M., Post, A., Beck, M., & Kiecolt-Glaser, J. K. (1987). Stress-related immune suppression: Health implications. *Brain, Behavior & Immunity, 1*, 7–20.

Goate, A., Chartier-Harlin, M.-C., Mullan, M., Brown, J., Crawford, F., Fidani, L., Giuffra, L., Haynes, A., Irving, N., James, L., Mant, R., Newton, P., Rooke, K., Roques, P., Talbot, C., Pericak-Vance, M., Roses, A., Williamson, R., Rossor, M., Wen, M., & Hardy, J. (1991). Segregation of a missense mutation in the amyloid precursor protein gene with familial Alzheimer's disease. *Nature, 349*, 704–706.

Goddard, G. V., McIntyre, D. C., & Leech, C. K. (1969). A permanent change in brain function resulting from daily electrical stimulation. *Experimental Neurology, 25*, 295–330.

Goedert, M. (1993). Tau protein and the neurofibrillary pathology of Alzheimer's disease. *Trends in Neurosciences, 16*, 460–465.

Goetz, C. G., Olanow, C. W., Koller, W. C., Penn, R. D., Cahill, D., Morantz, R., Stebbins, G., Tanner, C. M., Klawans, H. L., Shannon, K. M., Comella, C. L., Witt, T., Cox, C., Waxman, M., & Gauger, L. (1989). Multicenter study of autologous adrenal medullary transplantation to the corpus striatum in patients with advanced Parkinson's disease. *The New England Journal of Medicine, 320*, 337–341.

Gold, R. M., Jones, A. P., Sawchenko, P. E., & Kapatos, G. (1977). Paraventricular area: Critical focus of a longitudinal neurocircuitry mediating food intake. *Physiology & Behavior, 18*, 1111–1119.

Goldman, S. A., & Luskin, M. B. (1998). Strategies utilized by migrating neurons of the postnatal vertebrate forebrain. *Trends in Neurosciences, 21*, 107–114.

Goldman-Rakic, P. S., Bates, J. F., & Chafee, M. V. (1992). The prefontal cortex and internally generated motor acts. *Current Opinion in Neurobiology, 2*, 830–835.

Goldman-Rakic, P. S., & Selemon, L. D. (1990). New frontiers in basal ganglia research. *Trends in Neurosciences, 13*, 241–244.

Goldstein, A., & Kalant, H. (1990). Drug policy: Striking the right balance. *Science, 249*, 1513–1521.

Goldstein, G. W., & Betz, A. L. (1986, September). The blood–brain barrier. *Scientific American, 255*, 74–83.

Gollin, E. S. (1960). Developmental studies of visual recognition of incomplete objects. *Perceptual Motor Skills, 11*, 289–298.

Gollinick, P. D., & Hodgson, D. R. (1986). The identification of fiber types in skeletal muscle: A continual dilemma. *Exercise and Sport Sciences Reviews, 14*, 81–104.

Goodale, M. A. (1993). Visual pathways supporting perception and action in the primate cerebral cortex. *Current Opinion in Neurobiology, 3*, 578–585.

Goodale, M. A., & Milner, A. D. (1992). Separate visual pathways for perception and action. *Trends in Neurosciences, 15*, 20–25.

Goodale, M. A., Milner, A. D., Jakobson, L. S., & Carey, D. P. (1991). A neurological dissociation between perceiving objects and grasping them. *Nature, 349*, 154–156.

Goodenough, D. R., Shapiro, A., Holden, M., & Steinschriber, L. (1959). A comparison of 'dreamers' and 'nondreamers': Eye movements, electroencephalograms, and the recall of dreams. *Journal of Abnormal and Social Psychology, 59*, 295–303.

Goodison, T., & Siegal, S. (1995). Learning and tolerance to the intake suppressive effect of cholecystokinin in rats. *Behavioral Neuroscience, 109*, 62–70.

Goodlett, C. R., Marcussen, B. L., & West, J. R. (1990). A single day of alcohol exposure during the brain growth spurt induces brain weight restriction and cerebellar Purkinje cell loss. *Alcohol, 7*, 107–114.

Gorski, R. A. (1980). Sexual differentiation in the brain. In D. T. Krieger & J. C. Hughes (Eds.), *Neuroendocrinology* (pp. 215–222). Sunderland, MA: Sinauer.

Gorski, R. A., Gordom, J. H., Shryne, J. E., & Southam, A. M. (1978). Evidence for a morphological sex difference within the medial preoptic area of the rat brain. *Brain Research, 148*, 333–346.

Gottesmann, I. I., & Bertelsen, A. (1989). Confirming unexpressed genotypes for schizophrenia. *Archives of General Psychiatry, 46*, 867–872.

Gottlieb, D. I. (1988, February). GABAergic neurons. *Scientific American, 258*, 82–89.

Gould, E., Tanapat, P., McEwen, B. S., Flügge, G., & Fuchs, E. (1998). Proliferation of granule cell precursors in the dentate gyrus of adult monkeys is diminished by stress. *Proceedings of the National Academy of Science, 99*, 3168–3171.

Goy, R. W., & McEwen, B. S. (1980). *Sexual differentiation of the brain.* Cambridge, MA: MIT Press.

Grace, A., Bunney, B. S., Moore, H., & Todd, C. L. (1997). Dopamine-cell depolarization block as a model for the therapeutic actions of antipsycholitc drugs. *Trends in Neuroscience, 20*, 31–37.

Grady, K. L., Phoenix, C. H., & Young, W. C. (1965). Role of the developing rat testis in differentiation of the neural tissues mediating mating behavior. *Journal of Comparative and Physiological Psychology, 59*, 176–182.

Graf, P., & Schacter, D. J. (1987). Selective effects of interference on implicit and explicit memory for new associations. *Journal of Experimental Psychology: Learning, Memory, and Cognition, 13*, 45–53.

Graff-Radford, N., Damasio, H., Yamada, T., Eslinger, P. J., & Damasio, A. R. (1985). Nonhaemorrhagic thalamic infarction. *Brain, 108*, 485–516.

Grant, P. R. (1991, October). Natural selection and Darwin's finches. *Scientific American, 265*, 82–87.

Grant, S. G. N., & Silva, A. J. (1994). Targeting learning. *Trends in Neurosciences, 17*, 71–79.

Graybiel, A. M. (1995). Building action repertoires: Memory and learning functions of the basal ganglia. *Current Opinion in Neurobiology, 5*, 733–741.

Graybiel, A. M., Aosaki, T., Flaherty, A. W., & Kimura, M. (1994). The basal ganglia and adaptive motor control. *Science, 265*, 1826–1831.

Green, D. R., & Reed, J. C. (1998). Mitochondria and apoptosis. *Science, 281,* 1309–1316.

Green, S. (1991). Benzodiazepines, putative anxiolytics and animal models of anxiety. *Trends in Neurosciences, 14,* 101–103.

Grillner, S. (1985). Neurobiological bases of rhythmic motor acts in vertebrates. *Science, 228,* 143–149.

Groos, G. (1983). Regulation of the circadian sleep–wake cycle. *Sleep 1982, 6th European Congress on Sleep Research* (Zurich, 1982) (pp. 19–29). Basel: Karger.

Groos, G., & Hendricks, J. (1982). Circadian rhythms in electrical discharge of rat suprachiasmatic neurones recorded in vitro. *Neuroscience Letters, 34,* 283–288.

Gross, C. G., & Sergent, J. (1992). Face recognition. *Current Opinion in Neurobiology, 2,* 156–161.

Gross, C. G., Desimone, R., Albright, T. X., & Schwarz, E. L. (1985). Inferior temporal cortex and pattern recognition. In C. Chagas, R. Gattass, & C. Gross (Eds.), *Pattern recognition mechanisms* (pp. 179–201). Berlin: Springer-Verlag.

Grossman, S. P. (1990). *Thirst and sodium appetite: Physiological basis.* San Diego: Academic Press.

Grunt, J. A., & Young, W. C. (1952). Differential reactivity of individuals and the response of the male guinea pig to testosterone propionate. *Endocrinology, 51,* 237–248.

Gur, R. C., Mozley, L. H., Mozley, P. D., Resnick, S. M., Karp, J. S., Alavi, A., Arnold, S. E., & Gur, R. E. (1995). Sex differences in regional cerebral glucose metabolism during a resting state. *Science, 267,* 528–531.

Haaland, K. Y., & Harrington, D. L. (1996). Hemispheric asymmetry of movement. *Current Opinion in Neurobiology, 6,* 796–800.

Haimov, I., & Lavie, P. (1996). Melatonin—A soporific hormone. *Current Directions in Psychological Science, 5*(4), 106–111.

Haley, J. E., Schaible, E., Pavlidis, P., Murdock, A., & Madison, D. V. (1996). Basal and apical synapses of CA 1 pyramidal cells employ different LTP induction mechanisms. *Learning & Memory, 3,* 289–295.

Haley, J. E., Wilcox, G. L., & Chapman, P. F. (1992). The role of nitric oxide in hippocampal synaptic potentiation. *Neuron, 8,* 211–216.

Halligan, P. W., Marshall, J. C., Wade, D. T. (1994). Sensory disorganization and perceptual plasticity after limb amputation: A follow-up study. *Neuroreport, 5,* 1341–1345.

Halsband, U., & Freund, H.-J. (1993). Motor learning. *Current Opinion in Neurobiology, 3,* 940–949.

Hamer, D. H., Hu, S., Magnuson, V. L., Hu, N., & Pattatucci, A. M. L. (1993). A linkage between DNA markers on the chromosome and male sexual orientation. *Science, 261,* 321–327.

Hammond, P. H., Merton, P. A., & Sutton, G. G. (1956). Nervous gradation of muscular contraction. *British Medical Bulletin, 12,* 214–218.

Haqq, C. M., King, C.-Y., Ukiyama, E., Falsafi, S., Haqq, T. N., Donahoe, P. K., & Weiss, M. A. (1994). Molecular basis of mammalian sexual determination: Activation of Müllerian inhibiting substance gene expression by SRY. *Science, 266,* 1494–1500.

Harrington, M. E., Rusak, B., & Mistlberger, R. E. (1994). Anatomy and physiology of the mammalian circadian system. In M. H. Kryger, T. Roth, and W. C. Dement (Eds.), *Principles and practise of sleep medicine* (2nd ed., pp. 286–300). Philadelphia: W. B. Saunders Co.

Harris, G. W. (1955). *Neural control of the pituitary gland.* London: Edward Arnold (Pub.) Ltd.

Harris, G. W., & Levine, S. (1965). Sexual differentiation of the brain and its experimental control. *Journal of Physiology, 181,* 379–400.

Harris, K. M. (1995). How multiple-synapse boutons could preserve input specificity during an interneuronal spread of LTP. *Trends in Neurosciences, 18,* 365–369.

Harris, K. M., & Kater, S. B. (1994). Dendritic spines: Cellular specializations imparting both stability and flexibility to synaptic function. *Annual Review of Neuroscience, 17,* 341–371.

Harris, L. J. (1978). Sex differences in spatial ability: Possible environmental, genetic, and neurological factors. In M. Kinsbourne (Ed.), *Asymmetrical function of the brain* (p. 463). Cambridge, U.K.: Cambridge University Press.

Harris, L. J., Clay, J., Hargreaves, F. J., & Ward, A. (1933). Appetite and choice of diet: The ability of the vitamin B deficient rat to discriminate between diets containing and lacking the vitamin. *Proceedings of the Royal Society of London, (B), 113,* 161–190.

Harrison, P. J. (1997). Schizophrenia: A disorder of neurodevelopment? *Current Opinion in Neurobiology, 7,* 285–289.

Harrison, Y., & Horne, J. A. (1997). Sleep deprivation affects speech. *Sleep, 20*(10) 871–877.

Hartmann, D. S., & Civelli, O. (1997). Dopamine receptor diversity: molecular and pharmacological perspectives. *Progressive Drug Research, 48,* 173–194.

Hartmann, E. L. (1973). *The functions of sleep.* Westford, MA: Murray Printing Company.

Harvey, P. H., & Krebs, J. R. (1990). Comparing brains. *Science, 249,* 140–145.

Hastings, M. H. (1997). Central clocking. *Trends in Neuroscience, 20,* 459–464.

Hata, Y., & Stryker, M. P. (1994). Control of thalamocortical afferent rearrangement by postsynaptic activity in developing visual cortex. *Science, 265,* 1732–1735.

Hauser, M. D. (1993). Right hemisphere dominance for the production of facial expression in monkeys. *Science, 261,* 475–478.

Hayakawa, K., Kumagai, H., Suzuki, Y., Furusawa, N., Haga, T., Hoshi, T., Fujiwara, Y., & Yamaguchi, K. (1992). MR imaging of chronic alcoholism. *Acta Radiologica, 33,* 201–206.

Hearne, K. (1978). Lucid dreams: An electrophysiological and psychological study. Unpublished Ph.D. thesis, University of Hull, Hull, England.

Hearne, K. (1990). *Lucid dreams.* London: Hamish Hamilton.

Hebb, D. O. (1949). *The organization of behavior.* New York: John Wiley & Sons, Inc.

Hécaen, H., & Angelergues, R. (1964). Localization of symptoms in aphasia. In A. V. S. de Reuck & M. O'Connor (Eds.), *CIBA foundation symposium on the disorders of language* (pp. 222–256). London: Churchill Press.

Heffner, H. E., & Heffner, R. S. (1984). Temporal lobe lesions and perception of species-specific vocalizations by macaques. *Science, 226,* 75–76.

Heffner, H. E., & Masterton, R. B. (1990). Sound localization in mammals: Brainstem mechanisms. In M. Berkley and W. Stebbins (Eds.), *Comparative perception, Vol. I: Discrimination.* New York: Wiley & Sons.

Heinrichs, R. W. (1994). Schizophrenia and the brain. *American Psychologist, 48*(3), 221–233.

Henke, P. G. (1992). Stomach pathology and the amygdala. In J. P. Aggleton (Ed.), *The amygdala: Neurobiological aspects of emotion, memory, and mental dysfunction* (pp. 323–338). New York: Wiley-Liss, Inc.

Hennessey, A. C., Camak, L., Gordon, F., & Edwards, D. A. (1990). Connections between the pontine central gray and the ventromedial hypothalamus are essential for lordosis in female rats. *Behavioral Neuroscience, 104,* 477–488.

Herman, J. P., & Culliman, W. E. (1997). Neurocircuitry of stress: Central control of the hypthalamo-pituitary-adrenocortical axis. *Trends in Neuroscience, 20,* 78–84.

Herrup, K., & Silver, J. (1994) Cortical development and topographic maps: Patterns of cell dispersion in developing cerebral cortex. *Current Opinion in Neurobiology, 4,* 108–111.

Herzberg, C., & Diamond, A. (1993). Impaired contrast sensitivity in children with treated PKU, presumably due to dopaminergic deficiency. *Society for Neuroscience Abstracts, 19,* 772.

Hetherington, A. W., & Ranson, S. W. (1940). Hypothalamic lesions and adiposity in the rat. *Anatomical Record, 78,* 149–172.

Hier, D. B., & Kaplan, J. (1980). Are sex differences in cerebral organization clinically significant? *Behavioral and Brain Sciences, 3,* 238–239.

Hilgetag, C.-C., O'Neill, M. A., & Young, M. P. (1996). Indeterminate organization of the visual system. *Science, 271,* 776–777.

Hinton, G. E., Plaut, D. C., & Shallice, T. (1993, October). Simulating brain damage. *Scientific American, 269,* 76–82.

Hobson, J. A. (1989). *Sleep.* New York: Scientific American Library.

Hobson, J. A., Pace-Schott, E. F., Stickgold, R., & Kahn, (1998). To dream or not to dream? Relevant data from new neuroimaging and electrophysiological studies. *Current Opinion in Neurobiology, 8*(2), 239–244.

Hockfield, S., & Kalb, R. G. (1993). Activity-dependent structural changes during neuronal development. *Current Opinion in Neurobiology, 3,* 87–92.

Hofman, M. A., & Swaab, D. F. (1989). The sexually dimorphic nucleus of the preoptic area in the human brain: A comparative morphometric study. *Journal of Anatomy, 164,* 55–72.

Holloway, M. (1991, March). Rx for addiction. *Scientific American, 264,* 95–103.

Hollyday, M., & Hamburger, V. (1976). Reduction of the naturally occurring motor neuron loss by enlargement of the periphery. *Journal of Comparative Neurology, 170,* 311–320.

Hölscher, C. (1997). Nitric oxide, the enigmatic neuronal messenger: Its role in synaptic plasticity. *Trends in Neurosciences, 20,* 298–303.

Holt, C. E., & Harris, W. A. (1998). Target selection: Invasion, mapping and cell choice. *Current Opinion in Neurobiology, 8,* 98–105.

Holtzman, P. S., & Matthyse, S. (1990). The genetics of schizophrenia: A review. *American Psychological Society, 1,* 279–286.

Hopkins, W. D. (1995). Chimpanzee handedness revisited: 55 years since Finch (1941). *Psychonomic Bulletin & Review, 3*(4), 449–457.

Hopkins, W. D. (1996). Hand preferences for a coordinated bimanual task in 110 chimpanzees (*Pan troglodytes*): Cross-sectional analysis. *Journal of Comparative Psychology, 109*(3), 291–297.

Horne, J. A. (1976). Recovery sleep following different visual conditions during total sleep deprivation in man. *Biological Psychology, 4,* 107–118.

Horne, J. A. (1983). Mammalian sleep function with particular reference to man. In A. R. Mayes (Ed.), *Sleep mechanisms and functions in humans and animals* (pp. 262–312). Wokingham, England: Van Nostrand Reinhold.

Horne, J. A., & Reyner, L. A. (1996). Counteracting driver sleepiness: Effects of napping, caffeine, and placebo. *Psychophysiology, 33,* 306–309.

Howlett, A. C., Bidaut-Russell, M., Devane, W. A., Melvin, L. S., Johnson, M. R., & Herkenham, M. (1990). The cannabinoid

receptor: Biochemical, anatomical and behavioral characterization. *Trends in Neurosciences, 13,* 420–423.

Hsiao, K., Chapman, P., Nilsen, S., Eckman, C., Harigaya, Y., Younkin, S., Yang, F., & Cole, G. (1996). Correlative memory deficits, Aß elevation, and amyloid plaques in transgenic mice. *Science, 274,* 99–102.

Hubel, D. H., & Wiesel, T. N. (1979, September). Brain mechanisms of vision. *Scientific American, 249,* 150–162.

Hubel, D. H., Wiesel, T. N., & LeVay, S. (1977). Plasticity of ocular dominance columns in the monkey striate cortex. *Philosophical Transactions of the Royal Society of London, 278,* 377–409.

Hubel, D. H., Wiesel, T. N., & Stryker, M. P. (1977). Orientation columns in macaque monkey visual cortex demonstrated by the 2-deoxyglucose autoradiographic technique. *Nature, 269,* 328–330.

Hugdahl, K. (1996). Cognitive influences on human autonomic nervous system function. *Current Opinion in Neurobiology, 6,* 252–258.

Hughes, J., Smith, T. W., Kosterlitz, H. W, Fothergill, L. A., Morgan, B. A., & Morris, H. R. (1975). Identification of two related pentapeptides from the brain with potent opiate agonist activity. *Nature, 258,* 577–581.

Hume, K. I., & Mills, J. N. (1977). Rhythms of REM and slowwave sleep in subjects living on abnormal time schedules. *Waking and Sleeping, 1,* 291–296.

Hunt, W. A. (1993). Neuroscience research: How has it contributed to our understanding of alcohol abuse and alcoholism? A review. *Alcoholism: Clinical and Experimental Research, 17,* 1055–1065.

Huntington's Disease Collaborative Research Group (1993). A novel gene containing a trinucleotide repeat that is expanded and unstable on Huntington's disease chromosomes. *Cell, 72,* 971–983.

Hunton, D. L., Miezin, F. M., Buckner, R. L., van Mier, H. I., Raichle, M. E., & Petersen, S. E. (1996). An assessment of functional–anatomical variability in neuroimaging studies. *Human Brain Mapping, 4,* 122–139.

Hurlbert, A. (1991). Deciphering the colour code. *Nature, 349,* 191–193.

Hustvedt, B. E., & Løvø, A. (1972). Correlation between hyperinsulinemia and hyperphagia in rats with ventromedial hypothalamic lesions. *Acta Physiologica Scandinavica, 84,* 29–33.

Hutchison, J. B. (1991). Hormonal control of behaviour: Steroid action in the brain. *Current Opinion in Neurobiology, 1,* 562–572.

Hyman, B. T., Van Hoesen, G. W., & Damasio, A. R. (1990). Memory-related neural systems in Alzheimer's disease: An anatomic study. *Neurology, 40,* 1721–1730.

Iacono, W. G. (1985). Psychophysiologic markers in psychopathology: A review. *Canadian Psychology, 26,* 96–111.

Iacono, W. G., & Koenig, W. G. R. (1983). Features that distinguish the smooth-pursuit eye-tracking performance of schizophrenic, affective-disorder, and normal individuals. *Journal of Abnormal Psychology, 92,* 29–41.

Iacono, W. G., & Patrick, C. J. (1987). What psychologists should know about lie detection. In I. B. Weiner and A. K. Hess (Eds.), *Handbook of forensic psychology* (pp. 460–489). New York: John Wiley & Sons.

Iadecola, C. (1993). Regulation of the cerebral microcirculation during neural activity: Is nitric oxide the missing link? *Trends in Neurosciences, 16,* 206–214.

Inglis, J., & Lawson, J. S. (1982). A meta-analysis of sex-differences in the effects of unilateral brain damage on intelligence test results. *Canadian Journal of Psychology, 36*, 670–683.

Inouye, S. I., & Kawamura, H. (1982). Characteristics of a circadian pacemaker in the suprachiasmatic nucleus. *Journal of Comparative Psychology, 146*, 153–160.

Institute of Laboratory Animal Resources: Commission on Life Sciences (1996). *Guide for the care and use of laboratory animals.* Washington: National Academy Press.

Iriki, A., Pavlides, C., Keller, A., & Asanuma, H. (1989). Long-term potentiation in the motor cortex. *Science, 245*, 1385–1387.

Ironton, R., Brown, M. C., & Holland, R. L. (1978). Stimuli to intramuscular nerve growth. *Brain Research, 156*, 351–354.

Irwin, D. E. (1996). Integrating information across saccadic eye movements. *Current Directions in Psychological Science, 5*, 94–100.

Irwin, W., Davidson, R. J., Lowe, M. J., Mock, B. J., Sorenson, J. A., & Turski, P. A. (1996). Human amygdala activation detected with echo-planar functional magnetic resonance imaging. *NeuroReport, 7*, 1765–1769.

Itoh, K., Stevens, B., Schachner, M., & Fields, R. D. (1995). Regulated expression of the neural cell adhesion molecule L1 by specific patterns of neural impulses. *Science, 270*, 1369–1372.

Izard, C. E. (1971). *The face of emotion.* New York: Appleton-Century-Crofts.

Jacobs, W., Blackburn, J. R., Buttrick, M., Harpur, T. J., Kennedy, D., Mana, M. J., MacDonald, M. A., McPherson, L. M., Paul, D., & Pfaus, J. G. (1988). Observations. *Psychobiology, 16*, 3–9.

Jahn, R., & Südhof, T. C. (1994). Synaptic vesicles and exocytosis. *Annual Review of Neuroscience, 17*, 219–246.

Jarrell, T. W., Gentile, C. G., Romanski, L. M., McCabe, P. M., & Schneiderman, N. (1987). Involvement of cortical and thalamic auditory regions in retention of differential bradycardia conditioning to acoustic conditioned stimuli in rabbits. *Brain Research, 412*, 285–294.

Jarvik, M. E. (1990). The drug dilemma: Manipulating the demand. *Science, 250*, 387–392.

Jaskiw, G. E., & Weinberger, D. R. (1992). Dopamine and schizophrenia—A cortically corrective perspective. *The Neurosciences, 4*, 179–188.

Jeannerod, M., Arbib, M. A., Rizzolatti, G., & Sakarta, H. (1995). Grasping objects: The cortical mechanisms of visuomotor transformation. *Trends in Neurosciences, 18*(7), 314–327.

Jeannerod, M., & Decety, J. (1995). Mental motor imagery: A window into the representational stages of action. *Current Opinion in Neurobiology, 5*, 727–732.

Jenkins, I. H., Brooks, D. J., Bixon, P. D., Frackowiak, R. S. J., & Passingham, R. E. (1994). Motor sequence learning: A study with positron emission tomography. *The Journal of Neuroscience, 14*(6), 3775–3790.

Jenkins, W. M., & Merzenich, M. M. (1987). Reorganization of neocortical representations after brain injury: A neurophysiological model of the bases of recovery from stroke. *Progressive Brain Research, 71*, 249–266.

Johnston, T. D. (1987). The persistence of dichotomies in the study of behavioral development. *Developmental Review, 7*, 149–182.

Jones, H. S., & Oswald, I. (1966). Two cases of healthy insomnia. *Electroencephalography and Clinical Neurophysiology, 24*, 378–380.

Jones, H. W., & Park, I. J. (1971). A classification of special problems in sex differentiation. In D. Bergsma (Ed.), *The clinical delineation of birth defects. Part X: The endocrine system* (pp. 113–121). Baltimore: The Williams and Wilkins Company.

Jones, R. T. (1987). Tobacco dependence. In H. Y. Meltzer (Ed.), *Psychopharmacology: The third generation of progress* (pp. 1589–1596). New York: Raven Press.

Jost, A. (1972). A new look at the mechanisms controlling sex differentiation in mammals. *Johns Hopkins Medical Journal, 130*, 38–53.

Jouvet, M. (1972). The role of monoamines and acetylcholine-containing neurons in the regulation of the sleep–waking cycle. *Ergebnisse der Physiologie, 64*, 166–307.

Jouvet, M., & Renault, J. (1966). Insomnie persistante aprés lésions des noyaux du raphé chez le chat. *Comptes Rendus de la Société de Biologie (Paris), 160*, 1461–1465.

Juliano, S. L. (1998). Mapping the sensory mosaic. *Science, 279*, 1653–1654.

Julien, R. M. (1981). *A primer of drug action.* San Francisco: W. H. Freeman.

Julien, R. M. (1996). *A primer of drug action: A concise, nontechnical guide to the actions, uses, and side effects of psychoactive drugs* (7th ed.). W. H. Freeman and Company: New York.

Jung, L. J., & Scheller, R. H. (1991). Peptide processing and targeting in the neuronal secretory pathway. *Science, 251*, 1330–1335.

Juusola, M., French, A. S., Uusitalo, R. O., & Weckström, M. (1996). Information processing by graded-potential transmission through tonically active synapses. *Trends in Neurosciences, 19*, 292–297.

Kaas, J. H., Krubtzer, L. A., Chino, Y. M., Langston, A. L., Polley, E. H., & Blair, N. (1990). Reorganization of retinotopic cortical maps in adult mammals after lesions of the retina. *Science, 248*, 229–231.

Kaas, J. H., Nelson, R. J., Sur, M., & Merzenich, M. M. (1981). Organization of somatosensory cortex in primates. In F. O. Schmitt, F. G. Worden, G. Adelman, & S. G. Dennis (Eds.), *The organization of the cerebral cortex* (pp. 237–261). Cambridge, MA: MIT Press.

Kagawa, Y. (1978). Impact of westernization on the nutrition of Japanese: Changes in physique, cancer, longevity, and centenarians. *Preventive Medicine, 7*, 205–217.

Kalil, R. E. (1989, December). Synapse formation in the developing brain. *Scientific American, 261*, 76–85.

Kalin, N. H. (1993, May). The neurobiology of fear. *Scientific American, 268*, 94–101.

Kallman, F. J. (1946). The genetic theory of schizophrenia: An analysis of 691 schizophrenic twin index families. *American Journal of Psychiatry, 103*, 309–322.

Kalynchuk, L. E., Pinel, J. P. J., Treit, D., & Kippin, T. E. (1997). Changes in emotional behavior produced by long-term amygdala kindling in rats. *Biological Psychiatry, 41*, 438–451.

Kandel, E. R. (1985). Cellular mechanisms of learning and the biological basis of individuality. In E. R. Kandel and J. H. Schwartz (Eds.), *Principles of neural science* (pp. 816–833). New York: Elsevier.

Kandel, E. R., & Schwartz, J. H. (Eds). (1991). *Principles of neural science* (2nd ed.). New York: Elsevier.

Karacan, I., Goodenough, D. R., Shapiro, A., & Starker, S. (1966). Erection cycle during sleep in relation to dream anxiety. *Archives of General Psychiatry, 15*, 183–189.

Karacan, I., Williams, R. L., Finley, W. W., & Hursch, C. J. (1970). The effects of naps on nocturnal sleep: Influence on the need for stage-1 REM and stage-4 sleep. *Biological Psychiatry, 2*, 391–399.

Karadžić, V. T. (1973). Physiological changes resulting from total sleep deprivation. *1st European Congress on Sleep Research (Basel, 1972)* (pp. 165–174). Basel: Karger.

Karni, A., Tanne, D., Rubenstein, B. S., Askenasy, J. J. M., & Sagi, D. (1994). Dependance on REM sleep of overnight improvement of a perceptual skill. *Science, 265,* 679–682.

Karsch, F. J. (1987). Central actions of ovarian steroids in the feedback regulation of pulsatile secretion of luteinizing hormone. *Annual Review of Physiology, 49,* 365–382.

Katz, J. L., Ackamn, P., Rothwax, Y., Sachar, E. J., Weiner, H., Hellman, L., & Gallagher, T. F. (1970). Psychoendocrine aspects of cancer of the breast. *Psychosomatic Medicine, 32,* 1–18.

Katz, L. C., & Shatz, C. J. (1996). Synaptic activity and the construction of cortical circuits. *Science, 274,* 1133–1138.

Kavanagh, G. L., & Kelly, J. B. (1988). Hearing in the ferret (Mustela putorius): Effects of primary auditory cortical lesions on thresholds for pure tone detection. *Journal of Neurophysiology, 60,* 879–888.

Kelsey, J. E., Carlezon, W. A., Jr., & Falls, W. A. (1989). Lesions of the nucleus accumbens in rats reduce opiate reward but do not alter context-specific opiate tolerance. *Behavioral Neuroscience, 103,* 1327–1334.

Kelso, S. R., Ganong, A. H., & Brown, T. H. (1986). Hebbian synapses in hippocampus. *Proceedings of the National Academy of Sciences (USA), 83,* 5326–5330.

Kendler, K. S., & Gruenberg, A. M. (1984). An independent analysis of the Danish adoption study of schizophrenia: VI. The relationship between psychiatric disorders as defined by DSM-III in the relatives and adoptees. *Archives of General Psychiatry, 41,* 555–564.

Kentridge, R. W., Heywood, C. A., & Weiskrantz, L. (1997). Residual vision in multiple retinal locations within a scotoma: Implications for blindsight. *Journal of Cognitive Neuroscience, 9*(2), 191–202.

Kentros, C., Hargreaves, E., Hawkins, R. D., Kandel, E. R., Shapiro, M., & Muller, R. V. (1998). Abolition of long-term stability of new hippocampal place cell maps by NMDA receptor blockade. *Science, 280,* 2121–2126.

Kephalas, T. A., Kiburis, J., Michael, C. M., Miras, C. J., & Papadakis, D. P. (1976). Some aspects of cannabis smoke chemistry. In G. G. Nahas (Ed.), *Marihuana: Chemistry, biochemistry, and cellular effects* (pp. 39–49). New York: Springer-Verlag.

Kerr, R. A. (1996). New mammal data challenge evolutionary pulse theory. *Science, 273,* 431–432.

Kessler, D. S., & Melton, D. A. (1994). Vertebrate embryonic induction: Mesodermal and neural patterning. *Science, 266,* 596–604.

Kessler, R. C. (1997). The effects of stressful life events on depression. *Annual Review of Psychology, 48,* 191–214.

Keys, A., Brož, J., Henschel, A., Mickelsen, O., & Taylor, H. L. (1950). *The biology of human starvation.* Minneapolis: The University of Minnesota Press.

Kilgard, M. P., & Merzenich, M. M. (1998). Cortical map reorganization enabled by nucleus basalis activity. *Science, 279,* 1714–1718.

Killacky, H. P. (1995). Evolution of the human brain: A neuroanatomical perspective. In M. S. Gazzaniga (Ed.), *The cognitive neurosciences.* Cambridge, MA: MIT Press.

Kim, S.-G., Ashe, J., Hendrich, K., Ellermann, J. M., Merkle, H., Uğurbil, K., & Georgopoulos, A. P. (1993). Functional magnetic resonance imaging of motor cortex: Hemispheric asymmetry and handedness. *Science, 261,* 615–617.

Kimble, G. A. (1989). Psychology from the standpoint of a generalist. *American Psychologist, 44,* 491–499.

Kimelberg, H. K., & Norenberg, M. D. (1989, April). Astrocytes. *Scientific American, 260,* 66–76.

Kimura, D. (1961). Some effects of temporal-lobe damage on auditory perception. *Canadian Journal of Psychology, 15,* 156–165.

Kimura, D. (1964). Left–right differences in the perception of melodies. *Quarterly Journal of Experimental Psychology, 16,* 355–358.

Kimura, D. (1973, March). The asymmetry of the human brain. *Scientific American, 228,* 70–78.

Kimura, D. (1979). Neuromotor mechanisms in the evolution of human communication. In H. E. Steklis & M. J. Raleigh (Eds.), *Neurobiology of social communication in primates* (pp. 197–219). New York: Academic Press.

Kimura, D. (1987). Sex differences, human brain organization. In G. Adelman (Ed.), *Encyclopedia of neuroscience, Vol. II.* Boston: Birkhäuser.

Kimura, D., & Watson, N. (1989). The relation between oral movement control and speech. *Brain and Language, 37,* 565–690.

King, A. P., & West, M. J. (1990). Variation in species-typical behavior: A contemporary issue for comparative psychology. In D. A. Dewsbury (Ed.), *Contemporary issues in comparative psychology* (pp. 321–339). Sunderland, MA: Sinauer.

King, D. P., Zhao, Y., Sangoram, A. M., Wilsbacher, L. D., Tanaka, M., Antoch, M. P., Steeves, T. D. L., Vitaterna, M. H., Kornhauser, J. M., Lowrey, P. L., Turek, F. W., & Takahashi, J. S. (1997). Positional cloning of the mouse circadian *clock* gene. *Cell, 89,* 641–653.

Kinnamon, S. C., & Margolskee, R. F. (1996). Mechanisms of taste transduction. *Current Opinion in Neurobiology, 6,* 506–513.

Klawans, H. L. (1990). *Newton's madness: Further tales of clinical neurology.* New York: Harper & Row.

Klein, M., & Kandel, E. R. (1978). Presynaptic modulation of voltage-dependent Ca^{2+} current: Mechanism for behavioral sensitization in Aplysia californica. *Proceedings of the National Academy of Sciences (USA), 75,* 3512–3516.

Klein, M., Shapiro, E., & Kandel, E. R. (1980). Synaptic plasticity and the modualtion of the Ca^{2+} current. *Journal of Experimental Biology, 89,* 117–157.

Kleinman, A., & Cohen, A. (1997, March). Psychiatry's global challenge: An evolving crisis in the developing world signals the need for a better understanding of the links between culture an mental disorders. *Scientific American, 276,* 86–89.

Kleitman, N. (1963). *Sleep and wakefulness.* Chicago: University of Chicago.

Kluver, H., & Bucy, P. C. (1939). Preliminary analysis of the temporal lobes in monkeys. *Archives of Neurology and Psychiatry, 42,* 979–1000.

Knoth, R. L., & Mair, R. G. (1991). Response latency and accuracy on a pretrained nonmatching-to-sample task in rats recovered from pyrithiamine-induced thiamine deficiency. *Behavioral Neuroscience, 105,* 375–385.

Knowlton, B. J., & Fanselow, M. S. (1998). The hippocampus, consolidation and on-line memory: Discussion point. *Current Opinion in Neurobiology, 8,* 293–296.

Knowlton, B. J., Mangels, J. A., & Squire, L. R. (1996). A neostriatal habit learning system in humans. *Science, 273,* 1399–1402.

Knudsen, E. I. (1981, December). The hearing of the barn owl. *Scientific American, 245,* 113–125.

Knudsen, E. I. (1991). Dynamic space codes in the superior colliculus. *Current Opinion in Neurobiology, 1,* 628–632.

Knudsen, E. I., & Brainard, M S. (1991). Visual instruction of the neural map of auditory space in the developing optic tectum. *Science, 253,* 85–87.

Koch, C., & Braun, J. (1996). Towards the neuronal correlate of visual awareness. *Current Opinion in Neurobiology, 6,* 158–164.

Kogure, T., & Kogure, K. (1997). Molecular and biochemical events within the brain subjected to cerebral ischemia (targets for therapeutic intervention). *Clinical Neuroscience, 4,* 179–183.

Kokkinos, J., & Levine, S. R. (1993). Stroke. *Neurologic Complications of Drug and Alcohol Abuse, 11*(3), 577–590.

Kolb, B. (1989). Brain development, plasticity, and behavior. *American Psychologist, 44,* 1202–212.

Kolb, B., & Taylor, L. (1988). Facial expression and the neocortex. *Society for Neuroscience Abstracts, 14,* 219.

Kolb, B., & Whishaw, I. Q. (1990). *Fundamentals of human neuropsychology* (3rd ed.). New York: Freeman.

Kolb, B., & Whishaw, I. Q. (1996). *Fundamentals of human neuropsychology* (4th ed.). New York: Freeman.

Kollar, E. J., & Fisher, C. (1980). Tooth induction in chick epithelium: Expression of quiescent genes for enamel synthesis. *Science, 207,* 993–995.

Kolodny, R. C., Masters, W. H., Kolodner, R. M., & Toro, G. (1974). Depression of plasma testosterone levels after chronic intensive marihuana use. *New England Journal of Medicine, 290,* 872–874.

Konishi, M. (1993, April). Listening with two ears. *Scientific American, 268,* 66–73.

Koob, G. F., & Bloom, F. E. (1988). Cellular and molecular mechanisms of drug dependence. *Science, 242,* 715–723.

Koob, G. F., Maldonado, R., & Stinus, L. (1992). Neural substrates of opiate withdrawal. *Trends in Neurosciences, 15*(5), 186–191.

Koob, G. F., Markou, A., Weiss, F., & Schulteis, G. (1993). Opponent process and drug dependence: Neurobiological mechanisms. *Seminars in the Neurosciences, 5,* 351–358.

Koolhaas, J. M., Schuurman, T., & Wiepkema, P. R. (1980). The organization of intraspecific agonistic behaviour in the rat. *Progress in Neurobiology, 15,* 247–268.

Koopmans, H. S. (1981). The role of the gastrointestinal tract in the satiation of hunger. In L. A. Cioffi, W. B. T. James, & T. B. Van Italie (Eds.), *The body weight regulatory system: Normal and disturbed mechanisms* (pp. 45–55). New York: Raven Press.

Kornecook, T. J. (1998). Comparison of the amnesic deficits associated with damage to the medial temporal lobe, medial diencephalon, or basal forebrain in rats. Unpublished doctoral dissertation, University of British Columbia.

Kornetsky, C. (1977). Animal models: Promises and problems. In I. Hanin & E. Usdin (Eds.), *Animal models of psychiatry and neurology* (pp. 1–7). Oxford, U.K.: Pergamon Press.

Kornetsky, C., & Esposito, R. U. (1979). Euphorigenic drugs: Effects on the reward pathways of the brain. *Federation Proceedings, 38,* 2473–2476.

Kosambi, D. D. (1967, February). Living prehistory in India. *Scientific American, 216,* 105–114.

Kosslyn, S. M., & Andersen, R. A. (1992). *Frontiers in cognitive neuroscience.* Cambridge, MA: MIT Press.

Koutalos, Y., & Yau, K.-W. (1993). A rich complexity emerges in phototransduction. *Current Opinion in Neurobiology, 3,* 513–519.

Kramer, M. S., Cutler, N., Feighner, J., Shrivastava, R., Carman, J., Sramek, J. J., Reines, S. A., Liu, G., Snavely, D., Wyatt-Knolwes, E., Hale, J. J., Mills, S. G., MacCoss, M., Swain, C. J., Harrison, T., Hill, R. G., Hefti, F., Scolnick, E. M., Cascieri, M. A., Chicchi, G. G., Sadowski, S., Williams, A. R., Hewson, L., Smith, D., Carlson, E. J., Hargreaves, R. J., & Rupniak, N. M. J. (1998). Distinct mechanism for antidepressant activity by blockade of central substance P receptors. *Science, 281,* 1640–1645.

Krank, M. D., & Perkins, W. L. (1993). Conditioned withdrawal signs elicited by contextual cues for morphine administration. *Psychobiology, 21,* 113–119.

Krasne, F. B., & Glanzman, D. L. (1995) What we can learn from invertebrate learning. *Annual Review of Psychology, 46,* 585–624.

Krieglstein, J. (1997). Mechanisms of neuroprotective drug actions. *Clinical Neuroscience, 4,* 184–193.

Krupa, D. J., Thompson, J. K., & Thompson, R. F. (1993). Localization of a memory trace in the mammalian brain. *Science, 260,* 989–991.

Kuczmarski, R. J. (1992). Prevalence of overweight and weight gain in the United States. *American Journal of Clinical Nutrition, 55,* 495S–502S.

Kuffler, S. W. (1953). Discharge patterns and functional organization of mammalian retina. *Journal of Neurophysiology, 16,* 37–68.

Kuhs, H., & Tölle, R. (1991). Sleep deprivation therapy. *Biological Psychiatry, 29,* 1129–1148.

Kuwada, J. Y. (1986). Cell recognition by neuronal growth cones in a simple vertebrate embryo. *Science, 233,* 740–746.

LaBerge, S. (1985). *Lucid dreaming.* Los Angeles: Tarcher.

LaBerge, S., Greenleaf, W., & Kedzierski, B. (1983). Physiological responses to dreamed sexual activity during lucid REM sleep. *Psychophysiology, 20,* 454–455.

Lance-Jones, C., & Landmesser, L. (1980). Motorneuron projection patterns in the chick hind limb following early partial spinal cord reversals. *Journal of Physiology, 302,* 559–580.

Land, E. H. (1977, April). The retinex theory of color vision. *Scientific American, 237,* 108–128.

Lander, E. S. (1996). The new genomics: Global views of biology. *Science, 274,* 536–539.

Langston, J. W. (1985). MPTP and Parkinson's disease. *Trends in Neurosciences, 8,* 79–83.

Langston, J. W. (1986). MPTP-induced parkinsonism: How good a model is it? In S. Fahn, C. P. Marsden, P. Jenner, & P. Teychenne (Eds.), *Recent developments in Parkinson's disease* (pp. 119–126). New York: Raven Press.

Langston, J. W., & Palfreman, J. (1996). *The case of the frozen addicts.* New York: Vintage Books.

Langston, J. W., Forno, L. S., Robert, C. S., & Irwin, I. (1984). Selective nigral toxicity after systemic administration of 1-methyl-4-phenyl-1,2,3,6-tetrahydropyridine (MPTP) in the squirrel monkey. *Brain Research, 292,* 390–394.

Lapierre, O., & Dumont, M. (1995). Melatonin treatment of a non-24-hour sleep-wake cycle in a blind retarded child. *Biological Psychiatry, 38,* 119–122.

Larkman, A. U., & Jack, J. J. B. (1995). Synaptic plasticity: Hippocampal LTP. *Current Opinion in Neurobiology, 5,* 324–334.

Lashley, K. S. (1941). Patterns of cerebral integration indicated by the scotomas of migraine. *Archives of Neurology and Psychiatry, 46,* 331–339.

Lathe, R. (1996). Mice, gene-targeting and behaviour: More than just genetic background. *Trends in Neurosciences, 19,* 183–186.

Latimer, D., & Goldberg, J. (1981). *Flowers in the blood.* New York: Franklin Watts.

Laurent, G. (1997). Olfactory processing: Maps, time and codes. *Current Opinion in Neurobiology, 7,* 7547–553.

Lavie, P., Pratt, H., Scharf, B., Peled, R., & Brown, J. (1984). Localized pontine lesion: Nearly total absence of REM sleep. *Neurology, 34,* 1118–1120.

Lawrence, D. G., & Kuypers, H. G. J. M. (1968a). The functional organization of the motor system in the monkey: I. The effects of bilateral pyramidal lesions. *Brain, 91,* 1–14.

Lawrence, D. G., & Kuypers, H. G. J. M. (1968b). The functional organization of the motor system in the monkey: II. The effects of lesions of the descending brain-stem pathways. *Brain, 91,* 15–36.

Le Douarin, N. M. (1993). Embryonic neural chimaeras in the study of brain development. *Trends in Neurosciences, 16,* 64–72.

Leakey, M., & Walker, A. (1997, June). Early hominid fossils from Africa: A new species of Australopithecus, the ancestor of Homo, pushes back the origins of bipedalism to some four million years ago. *Scientific American, 276,* 7479.

Leboyer, M., Bellivier, F., Nosten-Bertrand, M., Jouvent, R., Pauls, D., & Mallet, J. (1998). Psychiatric genetics: Search for phenotypes. *Trends in Neurosciences, 21,* 102–105.

Lechner, H. A., & Byrne, J. H. (1998). New perspectives on classical conditioning: A synthesis of Hebbian and non-Hebbian mechanisms. *Neuron, 20,* 355–358.

LeDoux, J. E. (1992). Brain mechanisms of emotion and emotional learning. *Current Opinion in Neurobiology, 2,* 191–197.

LeDoux, J. E. (1994, June). Emotion, memory and the brain. *Scientific American, 270,* 50–57.

LeDoux, J. E. (1995). Emotion: Clues from the brain. *Annual Review of Psychology, 46,* 209–235.

Leech, C. K., & McIntyre, D. C. (1976). Kindling rates in inbred mice: An analog to learning? *Behavioral Biology, 16,* 439–452.

Leibowitz, S. F. (1992). Neurochemical-neuroendocrine systems in the brain controlling macronutrient intake and metabolism. *Trends in Neurosciences, 15,* 491–497.

Leibowitz, S. F., Akabayashi, A., & Wang, J. (1998). Obesity on a high-fat diet: Role of hypothalamic galanin in neurons of the anterior paraventricular nucleus projecting to the median eminence. *The Journal of Neuroscience, 18*(7), 2709–2719.

Leibowitz, S. F., Hammer, N. J., & Chang, K. (1981). Hypothalamic paraventricular nucleus lesions produce overeating and obesity in the rat. *Physiology & Behavior, 27,* 1031–1040.

Leiner, H. C., Leiner, A. L., & Dow, R. S. (1995). The underestimated cerebellum. *Human Brain Mapping, 2,* 244–254.

Lemberger, L., & Rowe, H. (1975). Clinical pharmacology of nabilone, a cannabinol derivative. *Clinical Pharmacology and Therapeutics, 18,* 720–726.

Lennox, W. G. (1960). *Epilepsy and related disorders.* Boston: Little, Brown and Co.

Leshner, A. I. (1997). Addiction is a brain disease, and it matters. *Science, 278,* 45–46.

Lester, G. L. L., & Gorzalka, B. B. (1988). Effect of novel and familiar mating partners on the duration of sexual receptivity in the female hamster. *Behavioral and Neural Biology, 49,* 398–405.

LeVay, S. (1991). A difference in hypothalamic structure between heterosexual and homosexual men. *Science, 253,* 1034–1037.

LeVay, S., & Hamer, D. H. (1994, May). Evidence for a biological influence in male homosexuality. *Scientific American, 270,* 44–49.

LeVay, S., Hubel, D. H., & Wiesel, T. N. (1975). The pattern of ocular dominance columns in macaque visual cortex revealed by a reduced silver stain. *Journal of Comparative Neurology, 159,* 559–576.

Levi-Montalcini, R. (1952). Effects of mouse motor transplantation on the nervous system. *Annals of the New York Academy of Science, 55,* 330–344.

Levi-Montalcini, R. (1975). NGF: An uncharted route. In F. G. Worden, J. P. Swazey, & G. Adelman (Eds.), *The neurosciences: Paths of discovery* (pp. 245–265). Cambridge, MA: MIT Press.

Levin, H. S. (1989). Memory deficit after closed-head injury. *Journal of Clinical and Experimental Neuropsychology, 12,* 129–153.

Levin, H. S., Papanicolaou, A., & Eisenberg, H. M. (1984). Observations on amnesia after non-missile head injury. In L. R. Squire & N. Butters (Eds.), *Neuropsychology of memory* (pp. 247–257). New York: Guilford Press.

Levitt, P., Harvey, J. A., Friedman, E., Simansky, K., & Murphy, E. H. (1997). New evidence for neurotransmitter influences on barren development. *Trends in Neurosciences, 20,* 269–274.

Levy, J. (1969). Possible basis for the evolution of lateral specialization of the human brain. *Nature, 224,* 614–615.

Levy, J., Trevarthen, C., & Sperry, R. W. (1972). Perception of bilateral chimeric figures following hemispheric deconnection. *Brain, 95,* 61–78.

Lewy, A. J., Ahmed, S., & Sack, R. L. (1996). Phase shifting the human circadian clock using melatonin. *Behavioural Brain Research, 73,* 131–134.

Li, Y., Field, P., Raisman, G. (1997). Repair of adult rat corticospinal tract by transplants of olfactory ensheathing cells. *Science, 277,* 2000–2002.

Linden, D. J., & Routtenberg, A. (1989). The role of protein kinase C in long-term potentiation: A testable model. *Brain Research Reviews, 14,* 279–296.

Linder, M. E., & Gilman, A. G. (1992, July). G proteins. *Scientific American, 267,* 56–65.

Lindsey, D. B., Bowden, J., & Magoun, H. W. (1949). Effect upon the EEG of acute injury to the brain stem activating system. *Electroencephalography and Clinical Neurophysiology, 1,* 475–486.

Lishman, W. A. (1990). Alcohol and the brain. *British Journal of Psychiatry, 156,* 635–644.

Liu, D., Diorio, J., Tannenbaum, B., Caldji, C., Francis, D., Plotsky, M. J., & Meaney, M. J. (1997). Maternal care, hippocampal glucocorticoid receptors, and hypothalamic-pituitary-adrenal responses to stress. *Science, 277,* 1659–1662.

Livingston, E. H., & Guth, P. H. (1992). Peptic ulcer disease: Wounds in the walls of the stomach develop only after elaborate cellular and molecular defensive mechanisms are breached. *American Scientist, 80,* 592–598.

Livingstone, M. S., & Hubel, D. H. (1984). Anatomy of physiology of a color system in the primate visual cortex. *Journal of Neuroscience, 4,* 309–356.

Livingstone, M. S., & Hubel, D. S. (1988). Segregation of form, color, movement, and depth: Anatomy, physiology, and perception. *Science, 240,* 740–749.

Llinás, R., & Welsh, J. P. (1993). On the cerebellum and motor learning. *Current Opinion in Neurobiology, 3,* 958–965.

Lo, Y.-J. & Poo, M.-M. (1991). Activity-dependent synaptic competition in vitro: Heterosynaptic suppression of developing synapses. *Science, 254,* 1019–1022.

Logothetis, N. K., & Sheinberg, D. L. (1996). Visual object recognition. *Annual Review of Neuroscience, 19,* 577–621.

Loomis, A. L., Harvey, E. N., & Hobart, G. (1936). Electrical potentials of the human brain. *Journal of Experimental Psychology, 19,* 249–279.

LoPiccolo, M. A. (1977). Behavioral and neuronal effects of EEG synchronizing stimuli in the cat. Unpublished doctoral dissertation. McMaster University, Hamilton, Ontario, Canada.

Lowe, J., & Carroll, D. (1985). The effects of spinal injury on the intensity of emotional experience. *British Journal of Clinical Psychology, 24,* 135–136.

Lowe, M. R. (1993). The effects of dieting on eating behavior: A three-factor model. *Psychological Bulletin, 114,* 100–121.

Lucas F., & Sclafani, A. (1989). Flavor preferences conditioned by intragastric fat infusions in rats. *Physiology & Behavior, 46,* 403–412.

Lui, D., Dorio, J., Tannenbaum, B., Caldji, C., Francis, D., Freedman, A., Sharma, S., Pearson, D., Plotsky, P. M., & Meaney, M. J. (1997). Maternal care, hippocampal glucocorticoid receptors, and hypothalamic-pituitary-adrenal responses to stress. *Science, 277,* 1659–1662.

Luria, A. R. (1972). *The history of a brain wound. The man with a shattered world.* Cambridge, MA: Harvard University Press.

Lydic, R., McCarley, R. W., & Hobson, J. A. (1983). The time-course of dorsal raphé discharge, PGO waves, and muscle tone averaged across multiple sleep cycles. *Brain Research, 274,* 365–370.

Lykken, D. T. (1959). The GSR in the detection of guilt. *Journal of Applied Psychology, 43,* 385–388.

Macchi, G. (1989). Anatomical substrate of emotional reactions. In F. Boller and J. Grafman (Eds.), *Handbook of neuropsychology, Vol. 3* (pp. 283–304). New York: Elsevier.

MacCoun, R., & Reuter, P. (1997). Interpreting Dutch cannabis policy: Reasoning by analogy in the legalization debate. *Science, 278,* 47–52.

MacDonald, M. E., & Gusella, J. F. (1996). Huntington's disease: Translating a CAG repeat into a pathogenic mechanism. *Current Opinion in Neurobiology, 6,* 638–643.

Macdonald, R. L., & Olsen, R. (1994). GABA$_A$ receptor channels. *Annual Review of Neuroscience, 17,* 569–602.

MacKinnon, D. F., Jamison, K. R., & DePaulo, J. R. (1997). Genetics of manic depressive illness. *Annual Review of Neuroscience, 20,* 355–373.

MacLusky, N. J., & Naftolin, F. (1981). Sexual differentiation of the central nervous system. *Science, 211,* 1294–1302.

Madrazo, I., Drucker-Colin, R., Diaz, V., Martinez-Mata, J., Torres, C., & Becerril, J. J. (1987). Open microsurgical autograft of adrenal medulla to the right caudate nucleus in two patients with intractable Parkinson's disease. *New England Journal of Medicine, 316,* 831–834.

Magni, F., Moruzzi, G., Rossi, G. F., & Zanchetti, A. (1957). EEG arousal following inactivation of the lower brain stem by selective injection of barbiturate into the vertebral circulation. *Archives Italiennes de Biologie, 95,* 33–46.

Maguire, E. A., Frith, C. D., Burgess, N., Donnett, J. G., & O'Keefe, J. (1998). Knowing where things are: Parahippocampal involvement in encoding object locations in virtual large-scale space. *Journal of Cognitive Neuroscience, 19*(10), 61–76.

Maier, S. R., Watkins, L. R., & Fleshner, M. (1994). Psychoneuroimmunology: The interface between behavior, brain, and immunity. *American Psychologist, 49,* 1004–1017.

Mair, R. G., Knoth, R. L., Rabenchuk, S. A., & Langlais, P. J. (1991). Impairment of olfactory, auditory, and spatial serial reversal learning in rats recovered from pyrithiamine-induced thiamine deficiency. *Behavioral Neuroscience, 105,* 360–374.

Mair, R. G., Otto, T. A., Knoth, R. L., & Langlais, P. J. (1991). Analysis of aversively conditioned learning and memory in rats recovered from pyrithiamine-induced thiamine deficiency. *Behavioral Neuroscience, 105,* 351–359.

Malgaroli, A., Ting, A. E., Wendland, B., Bergamaschi, A., Villa, A., Tsien, R. W., & Scheller, R. H. (1995). Presynaptic component of long-term potentiation visualized at individual hippocampal synapses. *Science, 268,* 1624–1628.

Malinow, R. (1994). LTP: Desperately seeking resolution. *Science, 266,* 1195–1196.

Malsbury, C. W. (1971). Facilitation of male rat copulatory behavior by electrical stimulation of the medial preoptic area. *Physiology & Behavior, 7,* 797–805.

Malsbury, C. W., & Pfaff, D. W. (1974). Neural and hormonal determinants of mating behavior in adult male rats. A review. In L. V. DiCara (Ed.), *Limbic and autonomic nervous system research* (pp. 85–136). New York: Plenum Press.

Manson, J. E., Willett, W. C., Stampfer, M. J., Colditz, G. A., Hunter, D. J., Hankinson, S. E., Hennekens, C. H., & Speizer, F. E. (1995). Body weight and mortality among women. *New England Journal of Medicine, 333,* 677–685.

Maratsos, M., & Matheny, L. (1994). Language specificity and elasticity: Brain and clinical syndrome studies. *Annual Review of Psychology, 45,* 487–516.

Mark, V. H., Ervin, F. R., & Yakolev, P. I. (1962). The treatment of pain by stereotaxic methods. 1st International Symposium on Stereoencephalotomy (Philadelphia, 1961), *Confina Neurologica, 22,* 238–245.

Marks, W. B., Dobelle, W. H., & MacNichol, E. F. (1964). Visual pigments of single primate cones. *Science, 143,* 1181–1183.

Marler, P. (1991). Song learning behavior: The interface with neuroethology. *Trends in Neurosciences, 14,* 199–206.

Marler, P., & Nelson, D. (1992). Neuroselection and song learning in birds: Species universals in a culturally transmitted behavior. *Seminars in the Neurosciences, 4,* 415–423.

Marlowe, W. B., Mancall, E. L., & Thomas, J. J. (1985). Complete Kluver-Bucy syndrome in man. *Cortex, 11,* 53–59.

Marshall, E. (1995). Gene therapy's growing pains. *Science, 269,* 1050–1055.

Martin, B. J. (1986). Sleep deprivation and exercise. In K. B. Pandolf (Ed.), *Exercise and sport sciences reviews* (pp. 213–229). New York: Macmillan Pub. Co.

Martin, J. B. (1987). Molecular genetics: Applications to the clinical neurosciences. *Science, 238,* 765–772.

Martin, R. J., White, B. D., & Hulsey, M. G. (1991). The regulation of body weight. *American Scientist, 79,* 528–541.

Martin, R. L., Roberts, W. V., & Clayton, P. J. (1980). Psychiatric status after a one-year prospective follow-up. *Journal of the American Medical Association, 244,* 350–353.

Martinez-Serrano, A., & Björklund, A. (1997). Immortalized neural progenitor cells for CNS gene transfer and repair. *Trends in Neurosciences, 20,* 530–538.

Masoro, E. J. (1988). Minireview: Food restriction in rodents: An evaluation of its role in the study of aging. *Journal of Gerontology, 43,* 59–64.

Masterton, R. B. (1992). Role of the central auditory system in hearing: The new direction. *Trends in Neurosciences, 15,* 280–285.

Mateer, C. A., & Cameron, P. A. (1989). Electrophysiological correlates of language: Stimulation mapping and evoked potential studies. In F. Boller and J. Grafman (Eds.), *Handbook of neuropsychology, Vol. 2* (pp. 91–116). New York: Elsevier.

Matsuda, L. A., Lolait, S. J., Brownstein, M. J., Young, A. C., & Bonner, T. I. (1990). Structure of a cannabinoid receptor and functional expression of the cloned DNA. *Nature, 346,* 561–564.

Matteoli, M., & De Camilli, P. (1991). Molecular mechanisms in neurotransmitter release. *Current Opinion in Neurobiology, 1,* 91–97.

Matthews, G. (1996). Neurotransmitter release. *Annual Review of Neuroscience, 19,* 219–233.

Matthews, G., & von Gersdorff, H. (1996). Calcium dependence of neurotransmitter release. *The Neurosciences, 8,* 329–334.

Matthews, P. B. C. (1991). The human stretch reflex and the motor cortex. *Trends in Neurosciences, 3,* 87–91.

Mattson, S. N., Barron, S., & Riley, E. P. (1988). The behavioral effects of prenatal alcohol exposure. In K. Kuriyama, A. Takada, & H. Ishii (Eds.), *Biomedical and social aspects of alcohol and alcoholism* (pp. 851–853). Tokyo: Elsevier.

Maunsell, J. H. R. (1995). The brain's visual world: Representation of visual targets in cerebral cortex. *Science, 270,* 764–768.

Mayford, M., Bach, M. E., Huang, Y.-Y., Wang, L., Hawkins, R. D., & Kandel, E. R. (1996). Control of memory formation through regulated expression of CMKII transgene. *Science, 274,* 1678–1680.

Mazzocchi, F., & Vignolo, L. A. (1979). Localisation of lesions in aphasia: Clinical-CT scan correlations in stroke patients. *Cortex, 15,* 627–654.

McAuliffe, W. E., Feldman, B., Friedman, R., Launer, E., Magnuson, E., Mahoney, C., Santangelo, S., Ward, W., & Weiss, R. (1986). Explaining relapse to opiate addiction following successful completion of treatment. In F. M. Tims and C. G. Leukefield (Eds.), *Relapse and recovery in drug abuse: National Institute on Drug Abuse Research Monograph Series* (Vol. 72, pp. 136–156). Rockville, MD: National Institute on Drug Abuse Research Monograph Series 72.

McCann, T. S. (1981). Aggression and sexual activity of male southern elephant seals, Mirounga leonina. *Journal of Zoology, 195,* 295–310.

McClearn, G. E., Johansson, B., Berg, S., Pedersen, N. L., Ahern, F., Petrill, S. A., & Plomin, R. (1997). *Science, 276,* 1560–1563.

McClintock, M. K. (1971). Menstruation synchrony and suppression. *Nature, 229,* 244–245.

McClintock, M. K., & Herdt, G. (1996). Rethinking puberty: The development of sexual attraction. *Current Directions in Psychological Science, 5*(6), 178–183.

McDonald, R. J., & White, N. M. (1993). Triple dissociation of memory systems: Hippocampus, amygdala, and dorsal striatum. *Behavioral and Neural Biology, 59,* 107–119.

McDonald, R. J., & White, N. M. (1995). Hippocampal and nonhippocampal contributions to place learning in rats. *Behavioral Neuroscience, 109,* 579–593.

McEwen, B. (1994). Introduction: Stress and the nervous system. *Seminars in the Neurosciences, 6,* 195–196.

McEwen, B. S. (1983). Gonadal steroid influences on brain development and sexual differentiation. In R. O. Greep (Ed.), *Reproductive physiology IV.* Baltimore, MD: University Park Press.

McEwen, B. S. (1987). Sexual differentiation. In G. Adelman (Ed.), *Encyclopedia of neuroscience, Vol. II* (pp. 1086–1088). Boston, MA: Birkhäuser.

McEwen, B. S., Davis, P. G., Parsons, B., & Pfaff, D. W. (1979). The brain as a target for steroid hormone action. *Annual Reviews in Neuroscience, 2,* 65–112.

McEwen, B. S., Lieberburg, I., Chaptal, C., & Krey, L. C. (1977). Aromatization: Important for sexual differentiation of the neonatal rat brain. *Hormones and Behavior, 9,* 249–263.

McGeer, P. L., Schulzer, M., & McGeer, E. G. (1996). Arthritis and anti-inflammatory agents as possible protective factors for Alzheimers's disease: A review of 17 epidemiologic studies. *Neurology, 47,* 425–431.

McGinty, D. J., & Sterman, M. B. (1968). Sleep suppression after basal forebrain lesions in the cat. *Science, 160,* 1253–1255.

McGlinchey-Berroth, R., Carrillo, M. C., Gabrieli, J. D. E., Brawn, C. M., & Disterhoft, J. F. (1997). Impaired trace eyeblink conditioning in bilateral, medial-temporal lobe amnesia. *Behavioral Neuroscience, 111*(3), 873–882.

McGlone, J. (1977). Sex differences in the cerebral organization of verbal functions in patients with unilateral brain lesions. *Brain, 100,* 775–793.

McGlone, J. (1980). Sex differences in human brain asymmetry: A critical survey. *Behavioral and Brain Sciences, 3,* 215–263.

McHugh, P. R., & Moran, T. H. (1985). The stomach: A conception of its dynamic role in satiety. In J. M. Sprague and A. N. Epstein (Eds.), *Progress in psychobiology and physiological psychology, 11,* 197–232.

McKay, D. G., Stewart, R., & Burke, D. M. (1998). H. M. revisited: Relations beteen language comprehension, memory, and the hippocampal system. *Journal of Cognitive Neuroscience, 10*(3), 377–394.

McKay, R. (1997). Stem cells in the central nervous system. *Science, 276,* 66–69.

McKim, W. A. (1986). *Drugs and behavior: An introduction to behavioral pharmacology.* Englewood Cliffs, NJ: Prentice-Hall.

McKinley, M. J., Pennington, G. L., & Oldfield, B. J. (1996). Anteroventral wall of the third ventricle and dorsal lamina terminalis: Headquarters for control of body fluid homeostasis? *Clinical and Experimental Pharmacology and Physiology, 23,* 271–281.

Meaney, M. J., Aitken, D. H., van Berkel, C., Bhatnagar, S., & Sapolsky, R. M. (1988). Effect of neonatal handling on age-related impairments associated with the hippocampus. *Science, 239,* 766–768.

Meaney, M. J., & Stewart, J. (1981). Neonatal androgens influence the social play of prepubescent rats. *Hormones and Behavior, 15,* 197–213.

Meck, W. H., Smith, R. A., & Williams, C. L. (1989). Organizational changes in cholinergic activity and enhanced visuospatial memory as a function of choline administered prenatally or postnatally or both. *Behavioral Neuroscience, 103,* 1234–1241.

Meddis, R. (1977). *The sleep instinct.* London: Routledge & Kegan Paul.

Mello, N. K., Mendelson, J. H. (1972). Drinking patterns during work-contingent and noncontingent alcohol acquisition. *Psychosomatic Medicine, 34,* 139–165.

Meltzer, H. Y., Alphs, L. D., Bartani, B., Ramirez, L. F., & Kwon, K. (1991). Clinical efficacy of clozapine in the treatment of schizophrenia. *Pharmacopsychiatry, 24*(2), 44–45.

Melzack, R. (1992, April). Phantom limbs. *Scientific American, 266,* 120–126.

Melzack, R., & Wall, P. D. (1965). Pain mechanisms: A new theory. *Science, 150,* 971–979.

Mendelson, J. H. (1987). Marijuana. In H. Y. Meltzer (Ed.), *Psychopharmacology: The third generation of progress* (pp. 1565–1571). New York: Raven Press.

Mendelson, J. H., Kuehnle, J. C., Greenberg, I., & Mello, N. K. (1976). The effects of marihuana use on human operant behavior: Individual data. In M. C. Braude and S. Szara (Eds.), *The pharmacology of marihuana* (pp. 643–653). New York: Raven Press.

Mercer, A. R., Emptage, N. J., & Carew, T. J. (1991). Pharmacological dissociation of modulatory effects of serotonin in Aplysia sensory neurons. *Science, 254,* 1811–1813.

Metcalfe, J., Funnell, M., & Gazzaniga, M. S. (1995). Right hemisphere memory veridicality: Studies of a split-brain patient. *Psychological Science, 6,* 157–165.

Meunier, M., Murray, E. A., Bachevalier, J., & Mishkin, M. (1990). Effects of perirhinal cortical lesions on visual recognition memory in rhesus monkeys. *Society for Neuroscience Abstracts, 17,* 337.

Middleton, F. A., & Strick, P. L. (1994). Anatomical evidence for cerebellar and basal ganglia involvement in higher cognitive function. *Science, 266,* 458–461.

Millan, M. J. (1995). Serotonin (5-HT) and pain: A reappraisal of its role in the light of receptor multiplicity. *Seminars in the Neurosciences, 7,* 409–419.

Miller, N. E., Bailey, C. J., & Stevenson, J. A. F. (1950). Decreased "hunger" but increased food intake resulting from hypothalamic lesions. *Science, 112,* 256–259.

Miller, N. S., Summers, G. L., & Gold, M. S. (1993). Cocaine dependence: Alcohol and other drug dependence and withdrawal characteristics. *Journal of Addictive Diseases, 12,* 25–35.

Milner, B. (1965). Memory disturbances after bilateral hippocampal lesions. In P. Milner & S. Glickman (Eds.), *Cognitive processes and the brain* (pp. 104–105). Princeton, NJ: D. Van Nostrand Co. Inc.

Milner, B. (1971). Interhemispheric differences in the localization of psychological processes in man. *British Medical Bulletin, 27,* 272–277.

Milner, B. (1974). Hemispheric specialization: Scope and limits. In F. O. Schmitt and F. G. Worden (Eds.), *The neurosciences: Third study program* (pp. 75–89). Cambridge, MA: MIT Press.

Milner, B., Corkin, S., & Teuber, H. L. (1968). Further analysis of the hippocampal amnesic syndrome: 14-year follow-up study of H. M. *Neuropsychologia, 6,* 317–338.

Milner, D., & Goodale, M. A. (1993). Visual pathways to perception and action. *Progress in Brain Research, 95,* 317–337.

Milner, P. M. (1993, January). The mind and Donald O. Hebb. *Scientific American, 268,* 124–129.

Milner, P. M., & White, N. M. (1987). What is physiological psychology? *Psychobiology, 15,* 2–6.

Mink, J. W., & Thach, W. T. (1993). Basal ganglia intrinsic circuits and their role in behavior. *Current Opinion in Neurobiology, 3,* 950–957.

Mishkin, M. (1978). Memory in monkeys severely impaired by combined but not by separate removal of amygdala and hippocampus. *Nature, 273,* 297–298.

Mishkin, M., & Delacour, J. (1975). An analysis of short-term visual memory in the monkey. *Journal of Experimental Psychology: Animal Behavior Processes, 1,* 326–334.

Mishkin, M., & Murray, E. A. (1994). Stimulus recognition. *Current Opinion in Neurobiology, 4,* 200–206.

Mistlberger, R., Bergmann, B., & Rechtschaffen, A. (1987). Period-amplitude analysis of rat electroencephalogram: Effects of sleep deprivation and exercise. *Sleep, 10,* 508–522.

Mistlberger, R. E. (1993). Circadian properties of anticipatory activity to restricted water access in suprachiasmatic-ablated hamsters. *American Journal of Physiology, 263,* 22–29.

Mistlberger, R. E. (1994). Circadian food-anticipatory activity: Formal models and physiological mechanisms. *Neuroscience and Biobehavioral Reviews, 18*(2), 171–195.

Mistlberger, R. E., & Rusak, B. (1994). Circadian rhythms in mammals: Formal properties and environmental influences. In M. H. Kryger, T. Roth, and W. C. Dement (Eds.), *Principles and practice of sleep medicine* (2nd ed., pp. 277–285). Philadelphia: W. B. Saunders Co.

Mogenson, G. J., Takigawa, M., Robertson, A., & Wu, M. (1979). Self-stimulation of the nucleus accumbens and ventral tegmental area of Tsai attenuated by microinjections of spiroperidol into the nucleus accumbens. *Brain Research, 171,* 247–259.

Mohr, J. P. (1976). Broca's area and Broca's aphasia. In H. Whitaker & H. A. Whitaker (Eds.), *Studies in neurolinguistics: Volume 1* (pp. 201–235). New York: Academic Press.

Molday, R. S., & Hsu, Y.-T. (1995). The cGMP-gated channel of photoreceptor cells: Its structural properties and role in phototransduction. *Behavioral and Brain Sciences, 18,* 441–451.

Mombaerts, P. (1996). Targeting olfaction. *Current Opinion in Neurobiology, 6,* 481–486.

Money, J. (1975). Ablation penis: Normal male infant sex-reassigned as a girl. *Archives of Sexual Behavior, 4*(1), 65–71

Money, J. (1987). Sin, sickness, or status? Homosexual gender identity and psychoneuroendocrinology. *American Psychologist, 42,* 384–399.

Money, J., & Ehrhardt, A. A. (1972). *Man & woman, boy & girl.* Baltimore: Johns Hopkins University Press.

Moonen, C. T. W., van Zijl, P. C. M., Frank, J. A., Le Bihan, D., & Becker, E. D. (1990). Functional magnetic resonance imaging in medicine and physiology. *Science, 250,* 53–61.

Moore, R. Y. (1982). The suprachiasmatic nucleus and the organization of a circadian system. *Trends in Neurosciences, 5,* 404–407.

Moore, R. Y. (1996). Neural control of the pineal gland. *Behavioural Brain Research, 73,* 125–130.

Moran, J., & Desimone, R. (1985). Selective attention gates visual processing in the extrastriate cortex. *Science, 229,* 782–784.

Mori, K. (1995). Relation of chemical structure to specificity of response in olfactory glomeruli. *Current Opinion in Neurobiology, 5,* 467–474.

Mori, N., & Wada, J. A. (1990). Does electrical and excitatory amino acid kindling share a common neurobiological mechanism? In J. A. Wada (Ed.), *Kindling 4* (pp. 209–222). New York: Plenum Press.

Morris, M. K., Bowers, D., Chatterjee, A., & Heilman, K. M. (1992). Amnesia following a discrete basal forebrain lesion. *Brain, 115,* 1827–1847.

Morris, N. M., Udry, J. R., Khan-Dawood, F., & Dawood, M. Y. (1987). Marital sex frequency and midcycle female testosterone. *Archives of Sexual Behavior, 16,* 27–37.

Morris, R. G. M. (1981). Spatial localization does not require the presence of local cues. *Learning and Motivation, 12,* 239–260.

Moruzzi, G., & Magoun, H. W. (1949). Brain stem reticular formation and activation of the EEG. *Electroencephalography and Clinical Neurophysiology, 1,* 455–473.

Moscovitch, M., & Nadel, L. (1998). Consolidation and the hippocampal complex revisited: In defense of the multiple-trace model. *Current Opinion in Neurobiology, 8,* 297–300.

Moscovitch, M., Winocur, G., & Behrmann, M. (1997). What is special about face recognition? Nineteen experiments on a person with visual object agnosia & dyslexia but normal face recognition. *Journal of Cognitive Neuroscience, 9*(5), 555–604.

Moskowitz, H., Hulbert, S., & McGlothin, W. H. (1976). Marihuana: Effects on simulated driving performance. *Accident Analysis and Prevention, 8,* 45–50.

Mountcastle, V. B., & Powell, T. P. S. (1959). Neural mechanisms subserving cutaneous sensibility with special references to the role of afferent inhibition in sensory perception and discrimination. *Bulletin of Johns Hopkins Hospital, 105,* 201–232.

Mouret, J., Bobillier, P., & Jouvet, M. (1968). Insomnia following parachlorophenylalanin in the rat. *European Journal of Pharmacology, 5,* 17–22.

Mrosovsky, N., & Salmon, P. A. (1987). A behavioral method for accelerating re-entrainment of rhythms to new light–dark cycles. *Nature, 330,* 372–373.

Mucha, R. F., Van der Kooy, D., O'Shaughnessy, M., & Bucenieks, P. (1982). Drug reinforcement studied by the use of place conditioning in rat. *Brain Research, 243,* 91–105.

Muir, G. D., & Steeves, J. D. (1997). Sensorimotor stimulation to improve locomotor recovery after spinal cord injury. *Trends in Neurosciences, 20,* 72–77.

Mullaney, D. J., Johnson, L. C., Naitoh, P., Friedman, J. K., & Globus, G. G. (1977). Sleep during and after gradual sleep reduction. *Psychophysiology, 14,* 237–244.

Mumby, D. G., & Pinel, J. P. J. (1994). Rhinal cortex lesions impair object recognition in rats. *Behavioral Neuroscience, 108,* 11–18.

Mumby, D. G., Pinel, J. P. J., & Dastur, F. N. (1993). Mediodorsal thalamic lesions and object recognition in rats. *Psychobiology, 21,* 27–36.

Mumby, D. G., Pinel, J. P. J., & Wood, E. R. (1989). Nonrecurring items delayed nonmatching-to-sample in rats: A new paradigm for testing nonspatial working memory. *Psychobiology, 18,* 321–326.

Mumby, D. G., Wood, E. R., Duva, C. A., Kornecook, T. J., Pinel, J. P. J., & Phillips, A. G. (1996). Ischemia-induced object-recognition deficits in rats are attenuated by hippocampal ablation before or soon after ischemia. *Behavioral Neuroscience, 110*(2), 266–281.

Mumby, D. G., Wood, E. R., & Pinel, J. P. J. (1992). Object-recognition memory is only mildly impaired in rats with lesions of the hippocampus and amygdala. *Psychobiology, 20,* 18–27.

Murphy, M. R., & Schneider, G. E. (1970). Olfactory bulb removal eliminates mating behavior in the male golden hamster. *Science, 157,* 302–304.

Murray, E. A. (1992). Medial temporal lobe structures contributing to recognition memory: The amygdaloid complex versus the rhinal cortex. In J. Aggleton (Ed.), *The amygdala: Neurobiological aspects of emotion, memory, and mental dysfunction* (pp. 453–470). New York: Wiley & Sons.

Murray, E. A. (1996). What have ablation studies told us about the neural substrates of stimulus memory? *Seminars in the Neurosciences, 8,* 13–22.

Murray, E. A., & Mishkin, M. (1998). Object recognition and location memory in monkeys with excitation lesions of the amygdala and hippocampus. *The Journal of Neuroscience, 18*(16), 6568–6582.

Musto, D. F. (1991, July). Opium, cocaine and marijuana in American history. *Scientific American, 265,* 40–47.

Musto, D. F. (1996). Alcohol in American history. *Scientific American, 274,* 78–83.

Myers, R. E., & Sperry, R. W. (1953). Interocular transfer of a visual form discrimination habit in cats after section of the optic chiasma and corpus callosum. *American Association of Anatomists: Abstracts of Papers from Platform,* p. 351.

Nadel, L., & Moscovitch, M. (1997). Memory consolidation, retrograde amnesia and the hippocampal complex. *Current Opinion in Neurobiology, 7,* 217–227.

Nadelman, E. A. (1989). Drug prohibition in the United States: Costs, consequences, and alternatives. *Science, 245,* 939–947.

Naeser, M. A., Alexander M. P., Helm-Estabrooks, N., Levine, H. L., Laughlin, S. A., & Geschwind, N. (1982). Aphasia with predominantly subcortical lesion sites. *Archives of Neurolinguistics, 39,* 2–14.

Naeser, M. A., Hayward, R. W., Laughlin, S. A., & Zatz, L. M. (1981). Quantitative CT scan studies in aphasia. *Brain and Language, 12,* 140–164.

Naitoh, P. (1992). Minimal sleep to maintain performance: The search for sleep quantum in sustained operations. In C. Stampi (Ed.), *Why we nap: Evolution, chronobiology, and functions of polyphasic and ultrashort sleep.* Boston: Birkhaüser.

Nathans, J. (1989, February). The genes for color vision. *Scientific American, 260,* 42–49.

National Commission on Marijuana and Drug Abuse (1972). R. P. Schafer, Chairman. *Marijuana: A signal of misunderstanding.* New York: New American Library.

National Institutes of Health, Publication No. 85–23 (Revised 1985), 9000 Rockville Pike, Besthesda, MD 20892.

Nauta, W. J. H., & Feirtag, M. (1986). *Fundamental neuroanatomy.* New York: W. H. Freeman.

Neher, E., & Sakmann, B. (1992, March). The patch clamp technique. *Scientific American, 266,* 44–51.

Nemeroff, C. B. (1998, June). The neurobiology of depression. *Scientific American, 278,* 42–49.

Ness, R. M., & Berridge, K. C. (1997). Psychoactive drug use in evolutionary perspective. *Science, 278,* 63–66.

Netter, F. H. (1962). *The CIBA collection of medical illustrations: Vol. 1. The nervous system.* New York: CIBA.

Neve, R. L., & Geller, A. I. (1996). A defective herpes simplex virus vector system for gene delivery into the brain: Comparison with alternative gene delivery systems and usefulness for gene therapy. *Clinical Neuroscience, 3,* 262–267.

Neville, H., Corina, D., Bavelier, D., Clark, V. P., Jezzard, P., Prinster, A., Padmanabhan, S., Braun, A., Rauschecker, J., & Turner, R. (1995). Effects of early experience on cerebral organization for language: An fMRI study of sentence processing in English and ASL by hearing and deaf subjects. *Human Brain Mapping, Supplement 1,* 278.

Newsom-Davis, J., & Vincent, A. (1991). Antibody-medicated neurological disease. *Current Opinion in Neurobiology, 1,* 430–435.

Nguyen, P. V., Abel, T., & Kandel, E. R. (1994). Requirement of a critical period of transcription for induction of a late phase of LTP. *Science, 265,* 1104–1106.

Nicolaïdis, S., & Rowland, N. (1975). Regulatory drinking in rats with permanent access to a bitter fluid source. *Physiology & Behavior, 14,* 819–824.

Nicoletti, F., Bruno, V., Copani, A., Casabona, G., & Knöpfel, T. (1996). Metabotropic glutamate receptors: A new target for the therapy of neurodegenerative disorders? *Trends in Neurosciences, 19,* 267–271.

Nishi, R. (1994). Neurotrophic factors: Two are better than one. *Science, 265,* 1052–1053.

Nordeen, K. W., & Nordeen, E. J. (1992). Auditory feedback is necessary for the maintenance of stereotyped song in adult zebra finches. *Behavioral and Neural Biology, 57,* 58–66.

Norman, R. M. G., & Malla, A. K. (1993). Stressful life events and schizophrenia I: A review of the research. *British Journal of Psychiatry, 162,* 161–166.

Nossal, G. J. V. (1993, September). Life, death and the immune system. *Scientific American, 269,* 53–62.

Nottebohm, F. (1991). Reassessing the mechanisms and origins of vocal learning in birds. *Trends in Neurosciences, 14,* 206–211.

Novin, D. (1964). The effects of insulin on water intake in the rat. In M. J. Wayner (Ed.), *Proceedings of the 1st international symposium in the regulation of body water* (pp. 177–184). Oxford, U.K.: Pergamon Press.

Nudo, R. J., Jenkins, W. M., & Merzenich, M. M. (1996). Repetitive microstimulation alters the cortical representation of movements in adult rats. *Somatosensory Motor Research, 7,* 463–483.

Nyberg, L., Cabeza, R., & Tulving, E. (1996). PET studies of encoding and retrieval: The HERA model. *Psychonomic Bulletin & Review, 3*(2), 149–158.

O'Banion, M. K., Coleman, P. D., & Callahan, L. M. (1994), Regional neuronal loss in aging and Alzheimer's disease: A brief review. *Seminars in the Neurosciences, 6,* 307–314.

O'Callaghan, M. A. J., & Carroll, D. (1982). *Psychosurgery: A scientific analysis.* Ridgewood, NJ: George A. Bogdaen & Son.

Ohzawa, I., DeAngelis, G. C., & Freeman, R. D. (1990). Stereoscopic depth discrimination in the visual cortex: Neurons ideally suited as disparity detectors. *Science, 249,* 1037–1040.

Ojemann, G. A. (1979). Individual variability in cortical localization of language. *Journal of Neurosurgery, 50,* 164–169.

Ojemann, G. A. (1983). Brain organization for language from the perspective of electrical stimulation mapping. *Behavioral and Brain Sciences, 2,* 189–230.

O'Keefe, J. (1993). Hippocampus, theta, and spatial memory. *Current Opinion in Neurobiology, 3,* 917–924.

O'Keefe, J., & Nadel, L. (1978). *The hippocampus as a cognitive map.* Oxford, U.K.: The Clarendon Press.

O'Keefe, J., & Speakman, A. (1987). Single unit activity in the rat hippocampus during a spatial memory task. *Experimental Brain Research, 68,* 1–27.

O'Keefe, J., & Dostrovsky, J. (1971). The hippocampus as a spatial map. Preliminary evidence from unit activity in the freely-moving rat. *Brain Research, 34,* 171–175.

Olds, J., & Milner, P. (1954). Positive reinforcement produced by electrical stimulation of septal area and other regions of rat brain. *Journal of Comparative and Physiological Psychology, 47,* 419–427.

O'Leary, A. (1990). Stress, emotion, and human immune function. *Psychological Bulletin, 108,* 363–382.

O'Leary, D. D. M., Ruff, N. L., & Dyck, R. H. (1994). Development, critical period plasticity, and adult reorganization of mammalian somatosensory systems. *Current Opinion in Neurobiology, 4,* 535–544.

Olton, D. S., & Samuelson, R. J. (1976). Remembrance of places: Spatial memory in rats. *Journal of Experimental Psychology: Animal Behavior Processes, 2,* 97–116.

O'Neill, L., Murphy, M., & Gallager, R. B. (1994). What are we? Where did we come from? Where are we going? *Science, 263,* 181–184.

Ó Scalaidhe, S. P., Wilson, F. A. W., & Goldman-Rakic, P. S. (1997). Areal segregation of face-processing neurons in prefrontal cortex. *Science, 278,* 1135–1138.

Overmier, J. B., & Murison, R. (1997). Animal models reveal the "psych" in the psychosomatics of peptic ulcers. *Current Directions in Psychological Science, 6*(6), 180–184.

Owren, M. J. (1990). Acoustic classification of alarm calls by vervet monkeys (*Cercopithecus aethiops*) and humans (*Homo sapiens*): II. Synthetic calls. *Journal of Comparative Psychology, 104,* 29–40.

Pääbo, S. (1995). The Y chromosome and the origin of all of us (men). *Science, 268,* 1141–1142.

Paletta, M. S., & Wagner, A. R. (1986). Development of context specific tolerance to morphine: Support for a dual-process interpretation. *Behavioral Neuroscience, 100,* 611–623.

Panksepp, J., & Trowill, J. A. (1967). Intraoral self-injection: II. The simulation of self-stimulation phenomena with a conventional reward. *Psychonomic Science, 9,* 407–408.

Papez, J. W. (1937). A proposed mechanism of emotion. *Archives of Neurology and Psychiatry, 38,* 725–743.

Parker, S. T., Mitchell, R. W., & Boccia, M. L. (1994). *Self-awareness in animals and humans: Developmental perspectives.* New York: Cambridge University Press.

Parsons, L. M., Fox, P. T., Downs, J. H., Glass, T., Hirsch, T. B., Martin, C. C., Jerabek, P. A., & Lancaster, J. L. (1995). Use of implicit motor imagery for visual shape discrimination as revealed by PET. *Nature, 375,* 54–58.

Patterson, K., Vargha-Khadem, F., & Polkey, C. E. (1989). Reading with one hemisphere. *Brain, 112,* 39–63.

Paulson, H. L., & Fischbeck, K. H. (1996). Trinucleiotide repeats in neurogenetic disorders. *Annual Review of Neuroscience, 19,* 79–107.

Paxinos, G. (Ed.). (1990). *The human nervous system.* New York: Harcourt Brace Jovanovich.

Pearlman, A. L., Faust, P. L., Hatten, M. E., & Brunstrom, J. E. (1998). New directions for neuronal migration. *Current Opinion in Neurobiology, 8,* 45–54.

Pellis, S. M., O'Brien, D. P., Pellis, V. C., Teitelbaum, P., Wolgin, D. L., & Kennedy, S. (1988). Escalation of feline predation along a gradient from avoidance through 'play' to killing. *Behavioral Neuroscience, 102,* 760–777.

Pellis, S. M., & Pellis, V. C. (1993). Influence of dominance on the development of play fighting in pairs of male Syrian golden hamsters (*Mesocricetus auratus*). *Aggressive Behavior, 19,* 293–302.

Pellow, S., Chopin, P., File, S. E., & Briley, M. (1985). Validation of open:closed arm entries in an elevated plus-maze as a measure of anxiety in the rat. *Journal of Neuroscience Methods, 14,* 149–167.

Penfield, W., & Boldrey, E. (1937). Somatic motor and sensory representations in cerebral cortex of man as studied by electrical stimulation. *Brain, 60,* 389–443.

Penfield, W., & Rasmussen, T. (1950). *The cerebral cortex of man: A clinical study of the localization of function.* New York: Macmillan Pub. Co.

Penfield, W., & Roberts, L. (1959). *Speech and brain mechanisms* (pp. 133–191). Princeton, NJ: Princeton University Press.

Percival, J. E., Horne, J. A, & Tilley, A. J. (1983). Effects of sleep deprivation on tests of higher cerebral functioning. *Sleep 1982. 6th European Congress on Sleep Research (Zurich, 1982)* (pp. 390–391). Basel: Karger.

Pert, C. B., Snowman, A. M., & Snyder, S. H. (1974). Localization of opiate receptor binding in presynaptic membranes of rat brain. *Brain Research, 70,* 184–188.

Peterhans, E., & von der Heydt, R. (1991). Subjective contours—Bridging the gap between psychophysics and physiology. *Trends in Neurosciences, 14,* 112–119.

Peters, M., & Brooke, J. (1998). Conduction velocity in muscle and cutaneous afferents in humans. *Journal of Motor Behavior, 30,* 285–287.

Peters, M., Jäncke, L., Staiger, J. F., Schlaug, G., Huang, Y., & Steinmetz, H. (1998). Unsolved problems in comparing brain sizes in *Homo sapiens*. *Brain and Cognition, 37,* 254–285.

Petersen, S. E., Fox, P. T., Mintun, M. A., Posner, M. I., & Raichle, M. E. (1989). Studies of the processing of single words using averaged positron emission tomographic measurements of cerebral blood flow change. *Journal of Cognitive Neuroscience, 1,* pp. 153–170.

Petersen, S. E., Fox, P. T., Posner, M. I., Mintun, M., & Raichle, M. E. (1988). Positron emission tomographic studies of the cortical anatomy of single-word processing. *Nature, 331,* 585–589.

Petrides, M. (1994). Frontal lobes and behavior. *Current Opinion in Neurobiology, 4,* 207–211.

Petrides, M. (1996). Lateral frontal cortical contribution to memory. *Seminars in the Neurosciences, 8,* 57–63.

Petrinovich, L. (1990). Avian song development: Methodological and conceptual issues. In D. A. Dewsbury (Ed.), *Contemporary issues in comparative psychology* (pp. 321–339). Sunderland, MA: Sinauer.

Pettet, M. W., & Gilbert, C. D. (1992). Dynamic changes in receptive field size in cat primary visual cortex. *Procedures of the National Academy of Sciences (USA), 89,* 8366–8370.

Pettit, H. O., & Justice, J. B. (1991). Effect of dose on cocaine self-administration as studied by in vivo microdialysis. *Pharmacology Biochemistry & Behavior, 34,* 899–904.

Pfaff, D., & Modianos, D. (1985). Neural mechanisms of female reproductive behavior. In N. Adler, D. Pfaff, and R. W. Goy (Eds.), *Handbook of behavioral neurobiology, Vol. 7, Reproduction* (pp. 423–493). New York: Plenum Press.

Pfaus, J. G., Damsma, G., Nomikos, G. G., Phillips, A. G., & Fibiger, H. C. (1990). Sexual behavior enhances central dopamine transmission in the male rat. *Brain Research, 530,* 345–348.

Pfaus, J. G., & Pinel, J. P. J. (1989). Alcohol inhibits and disinhibits sexual behavior in the male rat. *Psychobiology, 17,* 195–201.

Pfeiffer, C. A. (1936). Sexual differences of the hypophyses and their determination by the gonads. *American Journal of Anatomy, 58,* 195–225.

Phelps, M. E., & Mazziotta, J. C. (1985). Positron emission tomography: Human brain function and biochemistry. *Science, 288,* 782–799.

Phillips, A. G., Coury, A., Fiorino, D., LePiane, F. G., Brown, E., & Fibiger, H. C. (1992). Self-stimulation of the ventral tegmental area enhances dopamine release in the nucleus accumbens: A microdialysis study. *Annals of the New York Academy of Sciences, 654,* 199–206.

Phillips, A. G., Spyraki, C., & Fibiger, H. C. (1982). Conditioned place preference with amphetamine and opiates as reward stimuli: Attenuation by haloperidol. In B. G. Hoebel and D. Novin (Eds.), *The neural basis of feeding and reward* (pp. 455–464). Brunswick, MN: Haer Institute.

Phillips, D. P. (1989). Neurobiology relevant to some central auditory processing disorders. *Journal of Speech-Language Pathology and Audiology (Human Communication Canada), 13,* 17–34.

Phillips, M. I., & Felix, D. (1976). Specific angiotensin II receptive neurons in the cat subfornical organ. *Brain Research, 109,* 531–540.

Phoenix, C. H., Goy, R. W., Gerall, A. A., & Young, W. C. (1959). Organizing action of prenatally administered testosterone proprionate on the tissues mediating mating behavior in the female guinea pig. *Endocrinology, 65,* 369–382.

Pigott, S., & Milner, B. (1993). Memory for different aspects of complex visual scenes after unilateral temporal- or frontal-lobe resection. *Neuropsychologia, 31,* 1–15.

Pilar, G., Landmesser, L., & Burstein, L. (1980). Competition for survival among developing ciliary ganglion cells. *Journal of Neurophysiology, 43,* 233–254.

Pilcher, J. J., & Huffcutt, A. I. (1996). Effects of sleep deprivation on performance: A meta-analysis. *Sleep, 19*(4), 318–326.

Pinel, J. P. J. (1969). A short gradient of ECS-produced amnesia in a one-trial appetitive learning situation. *Journal of Comparative and Physiological Psychology, 68,* 650–655.

Pinel, J. P. J. (1981). Spontaneous kindled motor seizures in rats. In J. A. Wada (Ed.), *Kindling 2* (pp. 179–192). New York: Raven Press.

Pinel, J. P. J., Jones, C. H., & Whishaw, I. Q. (1992). Behavior from the ground up: Rat behavior from the ventral perspective. *Psychobiology, 20,* 185–188.

Pinel, J. P. J., Kim, C. K., & Mana, M. J. (1990). Contingent tolerance to the anticonvulsant effects of drugs on kindled convulsions. In J. A. Wada (Ed.), *Kindling 4* (pp. 283–297). New York: Plenum Press.

Pinel, J. P. J., & Mana, M. J. (1989). Adaptive interactions of rats with dangerous inanimate objects: Support for a cognitive theory of defensive behavior. In R. J. Blanchard, P. F. Brain, D. C. Blanchard, & S. Parmigiani (Eds.), *Ethoexperimental approaches to the study of behavior* (pp. 137–150). Dordrecht, The Netherlands: Kluwer Academic Publishers.

Pinel, J. P. J., Mana, M. J., & Kim, C. K., (1989). Effect-dependent tolerance to ethanol's anticonvulsant effect on kindled seizures. In R. J. Porter, R. H. Mattson, J. A. Cramer, & I. Diamond (Eds.), *Alcohol and seizures: Basic mechanisms and clinical implications* (pp. 115–125). Philadelphia: F. A. Davis.

Pinel, J. P. J., Pfaus, J. G., & Christensen, B. K. (1991). Contingent tolerance to the disruptive effects of alcohol on the copulatory behavior of male rats. *Pharmacology Biochemistry & Behavior, 41,* 133–137.

Pinel, J. P. J., & Rovner, L. I. (1977). Saccharin elation effect. *Bulletin of the Psychonomic Society, 9,* 275–278.

Pinel, J. P. J., Symons, L. A., Christenson, B. K., & Tees, R. C. (1989). Development of defensive burying in *Rattus norvegicus:* Experience and defensive responses. *Journal of Comparative Psychology, 103,* 359–365.

Pinel, J. P. J., & Treit, D. (1978). Burying as a defensive response in rats. *Journal of Comparative and Physiological Psychology, 92,* 708–712.

Pitkänen, A., Savander, V., & LeDoux, J. E. (1997). Organization of intra-amygdaloid circuitries in the rat: An emerging framework for understanding functions of the amygdala. *Trends in Neurosciences, 20,* 517–523.

Pleim, E. T., & Barfield, R. J. (1988). Progesterone versus estrogen facilitation of female sexual behavior by intracranial administration to female rats. *Hormones and Behavior, 22,* 150–159.

Ploegh, H. L. (1998). Viral strategies of immune evasion. *Science, 280,* 248–252.

Plomin, R. (1990). *Nature and nurture: An introduction to human behavioral genetics.* Pacific Grove, CA: Brooks/Cole.

Plomin, R. (1995). Molecular genetics and psychology. *American Psychological Society, 4*(4), 114–117.

Plomin, R., DeFries, J. C., McClearn, G. E., & Rutter, M. (1997). *Behavioral genetics* (3rd ed.). New York: Freeman.

Plomin, R., & Neiderhiser, J. M. (1992). Genetics and experience. *Current Directions in Psychological Science, 1,* 160–163.

Plomin, R., Owen, M. J., & McGuffin, P. (1994). The genetic basis of complex human behaviors. *Science, 264,* 1733–1739.

Plum, F. (1997). Extension of fundamental stroke research into clinical care. *Clinical Neuroscience, 4,* 175–178.

Polymeropoulos, M. H., Lavedan, C., Leroy, E., Ide, S. E., Dehejia, A., Dutra, A., Pike, B., Root, H., Rubenstein, J., Boyer, R., Stenroos, E. S., Chandrasekharappa, S., Athanassiadou, A., Papapetropoulos, T., Johnson, W. G., Lazzarini, A. M., Duvoisin, R. C., Iorio, G. D., Golbe, L. I., & Nussbaum, R. L. (1997). Mutation in the α-synuclein gene identified in families with Parkinson's disease. *Science, 276,* 2045–2047.

Pons, T. P., Garraghty, P. E., Friedman, D. P., & Mishkin, M. (1987). Physiological evidence for serial processing in somatosensory cortex. *Science, 237,* 417–420.

Pons, T. P., Garraghty, P. E., Ommaya, A. K., Kaas, J. H., Taub, E., & Mishkin, M. (1991). Massive cortical reorganization after sensory deafferentation in adult macaques. *Science, 252,* 1857–1860.

Pope, H. G., & Katz, D. L. (1987). Bodybuilder's psychosis. *Lancet, 1*(8537), 863.

Poppelreuter, W. (1917). *Die psychischen Schädigungen durch Kopfschuss im Kriege 1914–1916: Die Störungen der niederen und höheren Sehleistungen durch Verletzungen des Okzipitalhirns.* Leipzig: Voss.

Posner, M. I., & Raichle, M. E. (1994). *Images of the mind.* New York: Scientific American Library.

Post, R. M., Weiss, S. R. B., Clark, M., Nakajima, T., & Pert, A. (1990). Amygdala versus local anesthetic kindling: Differential anatomy, pharmacology, and clinical implications. In J. A. Wada (Ed.), *Kindling 4* (pp. 357–369). New York: Plenum Press.

Postle, B. R., Corkin, S., & Growdon, J. H. (1996). Intact implicit memory for novel patterns in Alzheimer's disease. *Learning & Memory, 3,* 305–312.

Potts, R. (1996). Evolution and climate variability. *Science, 273,* 922.

Poulos, C. X., & Cappell, H. (1991). Homeostatic theory of drug tolerance: A general model of physiological adaptation. *Psychological Review, 98,* 390–408.

Powers, J. B., Newman, S. W., & Bergondy, M. L. (1987). MPOA and BNST lesions in male Syrian hamsters: Differential effects on copulatory and chemoinvestigatory behaviors. *Behavioral Brain Research, 23,* 181–195.

Powley, T. L., Opsahl, C. A., Cox, J. E., & Weingarten, H. P. (1980). The role of the hypothalamus in energy homeostasis. In P. J. Morgane & J. Panksepp (Eds.), *Handbook of the hypothalamus—3A: Behavioral studies of the hypothalamus* (pp. 211–298). New York: Marcel Dekker.

Preuss, T. M. (1995). The argument from animals to humans in cognitive neuroscience. In M. S. Gazzaniga (Ed.), *The cognitive neurosciences.* Cambridge: MIT Press.

Price, R. A., & Gottesman, I. I. (1991). Body fat in identical twins reared apart: Roles for genes and environment. *Behavioral Genetics, 21,* 1–7.

Pritchard, R. M. (1961, June). Stabilized images on the retina. *Scientific American, 204,* 72–78.

Pusey, A., Williams, J., & Goodall, J. (1997). The influence of dominance rank on the reproductive success of female chimpanzees. *Science, 277,* 828–830.

Qualtrochi, J. J., Mamelak, A. N., Madison, R. D., Macklis, J. D., & Hobson, J. A. (1989). Mapping neuronal inputs to REM sleep induction sites with carbachol-fluorescent microspheres. *Science, 245,* 984–986.

Racine, R. J. (1972). Modification of seizure activity by electrical stimulation: II. Motor seizure. *Electroencephalography and Clinical Neurophysiology, 32,* 281–294.

Racine, R. J. (1978). Kindling: The first decade. *Neurosurgery, 3,* 234–252.

Racine, R. J., & Burnham, W. M. (1984). The kindling model. In P. A. Schwartzkroin & H. Wheal (Eds.), *Electrophysiology of epilepsy* (pp. 153–171). London: Academic Press.

Racine, R. J., Burnham, W. M., Gartner, J. G., & Levitan, D. (1973). Rates of motor seizure development in rats subjected to electrical brain stimulation: Strain and interstimulation interval effects. *Electroencephalography and Clinical Neurophysiology, 35,* 553–556.

Racine, R. J., Livingston, K., & Joaquin, A. (1975). Effects of procaine hydrochloride, diazepam, and diphenylhydantoin on seizure development in cortical and subcortical structures in rats. *Electroencephalography and Clinical Neurophysiology, 38,* 355–365.

Raedler, T. J., Knable, M. B., & Weinberger, D. R. (1998). Schizophrenia as a developmental disorder of the cerebral cortex. *Current Opinion in Neurobiology, 8,* 157–161.

Rafal, R. D. (1994). Neglect. *Current Opinion in Neurobiology, 4,* 231–236.

Raichle, M. E. (1994, April). Visualizing the mind. *Scientific American, 2,* 58–64.

Raichle, M. E., Fiez, J., Videen, T. O., Fox, P. T., Pardo, J. V., & Petersen, S. E. (1991). Practice-related changes in human brain functional anatomy. *Society for Neuroscience Abstracts, 17,* 21.

Rainville, P., Duncan, G. H., Price, D. D., Carrier, B., & Bushnell, M. C. (1997). Pain affect encoded in human anterior cingulate but not somatosensory cortex. *Science, 277,* 968–971.

Raisman, G. (1997). An urge to explain the incomprehensible: Geoffrey Harris and the discovery of the neural control of the pituitary gland. *Annual Review of Neuroscience, 20,* 533–566.

Raisman, G., & Field, P. M. (1971). Sexual dimorphism in the neuropil of the preoptic area of the rat and its dependence on neonatal androgens. *Brain Research, 54,* 1–29.

Raisman, G., Morris, R. J., & Zhou, C. F. (1987). Specificity in the reinnervation of adult hippocampus by embryonic hippocampal transplants. In F. J. Seil, E. Herbert, & B. M. Carlson (Eds.), *Progress in brain research* (Vol. 71, pp. 325–333). New York: Elsevier.

Rakic, P. (1979). Genetic and epigenetic determinants of local neuronal circuits in the mammalian central nervous system. In F. O. Schmitt & F. G. Worden (Eds.), *The neurosciences: Fourth study program.* Cambridge, MA: MIT Press.

Ralph, M. R., Foster, T. G., Davis, F. C., & Menaker, M. (1990). Transplanted suprachiasmatic nucleus determines circadian period. *Science, 247,* 975–978.

Ramachandran, V. S. (1992, May). Blind spots. *Scientific American, 260,* 86–91.

Ramsay, D. J., Rolls, B. J., & Wood, R. J. (1977). Body fluid changes which influence drinking in the water deprived rat. *Journal of Physiology, 266,* 453–469.

Ramsay, D. S., & Woods, S. C. (1997). Biological consequences of drug administration: Implications for acute and chronic tolerance. *Psychological Review, 104*(1), 170–193.

Rao, S. C., Rainer, G., & Miller, E. K. (1997). Integration of what and where in the primate prefrontal cortex. *Science, 276,* 821–824.

Rasmussen, T., & Milner, B. (1975). Excision of Broca's area without persistent aphasia. In K. J. Zulch, O. Creutzfeldt, & G. C. Galbraith (Eds.), *Cerebral localization* (pp. 258–263). New York: Springer-Verlag.

Ratliff, F. (1972, June). Contour and contrast. *Scientific American, 226,* 90–101.

Ratnasuriya, R. H., Eisler, I., Szmukler, G. I., & Russell, G. F. M. (1991). Anorexia nervosa: Outcome and prognostic factors after 20 years. *British Journal of Psychiatry, 158,* 495–502.

Rauschecker, J. P., Tian, B., & Hauser, M. (1995). Processing of complex sounds in the macaque nonprimary auditory cortex. *Science, 268,* 111–114.

Raymond, J. L., Lisberger, S. G., & Mauk, M. D. (1996). The cerebellum: A neuronal learning machine? *Science, 272,* 1126–1131.

Reame, N., Sauder, S. E., Kelch, R. P., & Marshall, J. C. (1984). Pulsatile gonadotropin secretion during the human menstrual cycle: Evidence for altered frequency of gonadotropin releasing hormone secretion. *Journal of Clinical Endocrinology and Metabolism, 59,* 328.

Reber, P. J., Knowlton, B. J., & Squire, L. R. (1996). Dissociable properties of memory system: Differences in the flexibility of declarative and nondeclarative knowledge. *Behavioral Neuroscience, 110*(5), 861–871.

Recanzone, G. H., Merzenich, M. M., Jenkins, W. M., Kamil, A. G., & Dinse, H. R. (1992). Topographic reorganization of the hand representation in cortical area 3b of owl monkeys trained in a frequency-discrimination task. *Journal of Neurophysiology, 67,* 1031–1056.

Rechtschaffen, A. (1998). Current perspectives on the function of sleep. *Perspectives in Biology and Medicine, 41*(3), 359–390.

Rechtschaffen, A., & Bergmann, B. M. (1995). Sleep deprivation in the rat by the disk-over-water method. *Behavioural Brain Research, 69,* 55–63.

Rechtschaffen, A., & Kales, A. (1968). *A manual of standardized terminology, techniques and scoring systems for sleep stages of human subjects.* Washington, DC: U.S. Government Printing Office.

Redd, M., & de Castro, J. M. (1992). Social facilitation of eating: Effects of social instruction on food intake. *Physiology & Behavior, 52,* 749–754.

Reh, T. A., & Constantine-Paton, M. (1984). Retinal ganglion cell terminals change their projection sites during larval development of Rana pipiens. *Journal of Neuroscience, 4,* 442–457.

Reid, R. C., & Alonso, J.-M. (1996). The processing and encoding of information in the visual cortex. *Current Opinion in Neurobiology, 6,* 475–480.

Reiner, W. (1997). To be male or female—That is the question. *Archives of Pediatry and Adolescent Medicine, 151,* 224–225.

Rensink, R. A., O'Regan, J. K., & Clark, J. J. (1997). To see or not to see: The need for attention to perceive changes in scenes. *Psychological Science, 8*(5), 368–373.

Revusky, S. H., & Garcia, J. (1970). Learned associations over long delays. In G. H. Bower & J. T. Spence (Eds.), *The psychology of learning and motivation* (Vol. 4, pp. 1–85). New York: Academic Press.

Reynolds, D. V. (1969). Surgery in the rat during electrical analgesia induced by focal brain stimulation. *Science, 164,* 444–445.

Rice, W. R. (1994). Degeneration of a nonrecombining chromosome. *Science, 263,* 230–232.

Richter, C. P. (1967). Sleep and activity: Their relation to the 24-hour clock. *Proceedings of the Association for Research on Nervous and Mental Disorders, 45,* 8–27.

Richter, C. P. (1971). Inborn nature of the rat's 24-hour clock. *Journal of Comparative and Physiological Psychology, 75,* 1–14.

Rindi, G. (1989). Alcohol and thiamine of the brain. *Alcohol & Alcoholism, 24,* 493–495.

Rizzolatti, G., Fogassi, L., & Gallese, V. (1997). Parietal cortex: From sight to action. *Current Opinion in Neurobiology, 7,* 562–567.

Robbins, T. W., & Everitt, B. J. (1996). Neurobehavioural mechanisms of reward and motivation. *Current Opinion in Neurobiology, 6,* 228–236.

Robbins, T. W., Everitt, B. J., Ryan, C. N., Marston, H. M., Jones, G. H., & Page, K. J. (1989). Comparative effects of quisqualic and ibotenic acid-induced lesions of the substantia innominata and globus pallidus on attentional function in the rat: Further implications for the role of the cholinergic neurons of the nucleus basalis in cognitive processes. *Behavioral Brain Research, 35,* 221–240.

Roberts, D. C. S., & Koob, G. F. (1982). Disruption of cocaine self-administration following 6-hydroxydopamine lesions of the ventral tegmental area in rats. *Pharmacology, Biochemistry & Behavior, 17,* 901–904.

Roberts, D. C. S., Koob, G. F., Klonoff, P., & Fibiger, H. C. (1980). Extinction and recovery of cocaine self-administration following 6-hydroxydopamine lesions of the nucleus accumbens. *Pharmacology, Biochemistry & Behavior, 12,* 781–787.

Roberts, D. C. S., & Zito, K. A. (1987). Interpretation of lesion effects on stimulant self-administration. In M. A. Bozarth (Ed.), *Methods of assessing the reinforcing properties of abused drugs* (pp. 87–103). New York: Springer-Verlag.

Robinson, T. E. (1991). Persistent sensitizing effects of drugs on brain dopamine systems and behavior: Implications for addiction and relapse. In J. Barchas and S. Korenman (Eds.), *The biological basis of substance abuse and its therapy.* New York: Oxford University Press.

Robinson, T. E., & Berridge, K. C. (1993). The neural basis of drug craving: An incentive-sensitization theory of addiction. *Brain Research Reviews, 18,* 247–291.

Robinson, T. E., & Justice, J. B. (Eds.). (1991). *Microdialysis in the neurosciences. Vol. 7, Techniques in the neural and behavioral sciences.* Elsevier: Amsterdam.

Rodin, J. (1985). Insulin levels, hunger, and food intake: An example of feedback loops in body weight regulation. *Health Psychology, 4,* 1–24.

Roe, A. W., Pallas, S. L., Hahm, J.-O., & Sur, M. (1990). A map of visual space induced in primary auditory cortex. *Science, 250,* 818–820.

Rogers, P. J., & Blundell, J. E. (1980). Investigation of food selection and meal parameters during the development of dietary induced obesity. *Appetite, 1,* 85–88.

Roland, P. E. (1993). *Brain activation.* New York: Wiley-Liss.

Roland, P. E., & Zilles, K. (1996). Functions and structures of the motor cortices in humans. *Current Opinion in Neurobiology, 6,* 773–781.

Rolls, B. J. (1986). Sensory-specific satiety. *Nutrition Reviews, 44,* 93–101.

Rolls, B. J. (1990). The role of sensory-specific satiety in food intake and food selection. In E. D. Capaldi and T. L. Powley (Eds.), *Taste, experience, & feeding* (pp. 28–42). Washington, DC: American Psychological Association.

Rolls, B. J., Rolls, E. T., Rowe, E. A., & Sweeney, K. (1981). Sensory specific satiety in man. *Physiology & Behavior, 27,* 137–142.

Rolls, B. J., Wood, R., Rolls, E. T., Lind, H., Lind, R., & Ledingham, J. G. (1980). Thirst following water deprivation in humans. *American Journal of Physiology, 239,* 476–482.

Rolls, B. J., Wood, R. J., & Rolls, R. M. (1980). Thirst: The initiation, maintenance, and termination of drinking. In J. M. Sprague and A. N. Epstein (Eds.), *Progress in psychology and physiological psychology.* New York: Academic Press.

Rolls, B. J., Wood, R. J., & Stevens, R. M. (1978). Effects of palatability on body fluid homeostasis. *Physiology & Behavior, 20,* 15–19.

Rolls, E. T. (1981). Central nervous mechanisms related to feeding and appetite. *British Medical Bulletin, 37,* 131–134.

Rolls, E. T., Robertson, R. G., & Georges-François, P. (1995). The representation of space in the primate hippocampus. *Society for Neuroscience Abstracts, 21,* 1492.

Rolls, E. T., & Rolls, B. J. (1982). Brain mechanisms involved in feeding. In L. M. Barker (Ed.), *The psychobiology of human food selection* (pp. 33–65). Westport, CT: AVI Pub. Co.

Romanski, L. M., & LeDoux, J. E. (1992). Equipotentiality of thalamo-cortico-amygdala projections as auditory conditioned stimulus pathways. *Journal of Neuroscience, 12,* 4501–4509.

Rose, G. A., & Williams, R. T. (1961). The psychobiology of meals. *British Journal of Nutrition, 15,* 1–9.

Rosenthal, D., Wender, P. H., Kety, S. S., Welner, J., & Schulsinger, F. (1980). The adopted-away offspring of schizophrenics. *American Journal of Psychiatry, 128,* 87–91.

Roses, A. D. (1996). The Alzheimer diseases. *Current Opinion in Neurobiology, 6,* 644–650.

Rothblat, L. A., & Hayes, L. L. (1987). Short-term object recognition memory in the rat: Nonmatching with trial-unique junk stimuli. *Behavioral Neuroscience, 101,* 587–590.

Rothman, J. E., & Orci, L. (1996, March). Budding vesicles in living cells. *Scientific American, 274,* 70–75.

Rothman, S. M. (1994). Excitotoxic neuronal death: Mechanisms and clinical relevance. *Seminars in the Neurosciences, 6,* 315–322.

Rothwell, J. C., Traub, M. M., Day, B. L., Obeso, J. A., Thomas, P. K., & Marsden, C. D. (1982). Manual motor performance in a deafferented man. *Brain, 105,* 515–542.

Rothwell, N. J., & Stock, M. J. (1982). Energy expenditure derived from measurements of oxygen consumption and energy balance in hyperphagic, "cafeteria"-fed rats. *Journal of Physiology, 324,* 59–60.

Routtenberg, A. (1978, November). The reward system of the brain. *Scientific American, 239,* 154–164.

Routtenberg, A., & Malsbury, C. (1969). Brainstem pathways of reward. *Journal of Comparative and Physiological Psychology, 68,* 22–30.

Rowen, L., Mahairas, G., & Hood, L. (1997). Sequencing the human genome. *Science, 278,* 605–607.

Rowland, N. (1981). Glucoregulatory feeding on cats. *Physiology & Behavior, 26,* 901–903.

Rowland, N., & Nicolaïdis, S. (1976). Metering of fluid intake and determinants of ad libitum drinking in rats. *American Journal of Physiology, 231,* 1–8.

Rowland, N. E. (1990a). On the waterfront: Predictive and reactive regulatory descriptions of thirst and sodium appetite. *Physiology & Behavior, 48,* 899–903.

Rowland, N. E. (1990b). Sodium appetite. In E. D. Capaldi and T. L. Powley (Eds.), *Taste, experience, and feeding* (pp. 94–104). Washington, DC: American Psychological Association.

Rozin, P. N., & Schulkin, J. (1990). Food selection. In E. M. Stricker (Ed.), *Handbook of behavioral neurobiology* (pp. 297–328). New York: Plenum Press.

Rudy, J. W., & Sutherland, R. J. (1992). Configural and elemental associations and the memory coherence problem. *Journal of Cognitive Neuroscience, 4,* 208–216.

Rusak, B., & Groos, G. (1982). Suprachiasmatic stimulation phase shifts rodent circadian rhythms. *Science, 215,* 1407–1409.

Rusak, B., Robertson, H. A., Wisden, W., & Hunt, S. P. (1990). Light pulses that shift rhythms induce gene expression in the suprachiasmatic nucleus. *Science, 248,* 1237–1240.

Russell, W. R., & Espir, M. I. E. (1961). *Traumatic aphasia—A study of aphasia in war wounds of the brain.* London: Oxford University Press.

Rutledge, L. L., & Hupka, R. B. (1985). The facial feedback hypothesis: Methodological concerns and new supporting evidence. *Motivation and Emotion, 9,* 219–240.

Rutter, M. L. (1997). Nature–nurture integration: The example of antisocial behavior. *American Psychologist, 52*(4), 390–398.

Sacks, O. (1985). *The man who mistook his wife for a hat and other clinical tales.* New York: Summit Books.

Sager, R. (1989). Tumor suppressor genes: The puzzle and the promise. *Science, 246,* 1406–1412.

Sakai, K., & Miyashita, Y. (1993). Memory and imagery in the temporal lobe. *Current Opinion in Neurobiology, 3,* 166–170.

Sakata, H., Taira, M., Kusunoki, M., Murata, A., & Tanaka, Y. (1997). The TINS lecture. The parietal association cortex in depth perception and visual control of hand action. *Trends in Neurosciences, 20,* 350–357.

Sakuma, Y., & Pfaff, D. W. (1979). Mesencephalic mechanisms for the integration of female reproductive behavior in the rat. *American Journal of Physiology, 237,* 285–290.

Salmon, D. P., & Butters, N. (1995). Neurobiology of skill and habit learning. *Current Opinion in Neurobiology, 5,* 184–190.

Sanders, D., & Bancroft, J. (1982). Hormones and the sexuality of women—The menstrual cycle. *Clinics in Endocrinology and Metabolism, 11,* 639–659.

Sanes, J. N., Donoghue, J. P., Thangaraj, V., Edelman, R. R., & Warach, S. (1995). Shared neural substrates controlling hand movements in human motor cortex. *Science, 268,* 1775–1777.

Sanes, J. N., Suner, S., & Donoghue, J. P. (1990). Dynamic organization of primary motor cortex output to target muscles in adult rats. I. Long-term patterns of reorganization following motor or mixed peripheral nerve lesions. *Experimental Brain Research, 79,* 479–491.

Sanes, J. N., Wang, J., & Donoghue, J. P. (1992). Immediate and delayed changes of rat motor cortical output representation with new forelimb configurations. *Cerebral Cortex, 2,* 141–152.

Sapolsky, R. M. (1996). Why stress is bad for your brain. *Science, 273,* 749–750.

Sapolsky, R. M. (1997). The importance of a well-groomed child. *Science, 277,* 1620–1622.

Sarter, M., Berntson, G. G., & Cacioppo, J. T. (1996). Brain imaging and cognitive neuroscience toward strong inference in attributing function to structure. *American Psychologist, 51,* 13–21.

Sastry, B. R., Goh, J. W., & Auyeung, A. (1986). Associative induction of posttetanic and long-term potentiation in CA1 neurons of rat hippocampus. *Science, 232,* 988–990.

Sawle, G. V., & Myers, R. (1993) The role of positron emission tomography in the assessment of human neurotransplantation. *Trends in Neurosciences, 16,* 172–176.

Sbragia, G. (1992). Leonardo da Vinci and ultrashort sleep: Personal experience of an eclectic artist. In C. Stampi (Ed.), *Why we nap:*

Evolution, chronobiology, and functions of polyphasic and ultrashort sleep. Boston: Birkhäuser.

Schacter, D. L., Chiu, C.-Y. P., & Ochsner, K. N. (1993). Implicit memory: A selective review. *Annual Review of Neuroscience, 16,* 159–182.

Schally, A. V. (1978). Aspects of hypothalamic regulation of the pituitary gland. *Science, 202,* 18–28.

Schally, A. V., Kastin, A. J., & Arimura, A. (1971). Hypothalamic follicle-stimulating hormone (FSH) and luteinizing hormone (LH)-regulating hormone: Structure, physiology, and clinical studies. *Fertility and Sterility, 22,* 703–721.

Schatzman, M., Worsley, A., & Fenwich, P. (1988). Correspondence during lucid dreams between dreamed and actual events. In J. Gackenbach and S. LaBerge (Eds.), *Conscious mind, sleeping brain* (pp. 67–103). New York: Plenum.

Schelling, T. C. (1992). Addictive drugs: The cigarette experience. *Science, 255,* 430–433.

Schenck, C. H., Bundlie, S. R., Ettinger, M. G., & Mahowald, M. W. (1986). Chronic behavioral disorders of human REM sleep: A new category of parasomnia. *Sleep, 9,* 293–308.

Schieber, M. H. (1990). How might the motor cortex individuate movements? *Trends in Neurosciences, 13,* 440–445.

Schieber, M. H., & Hibbard, L. S. (1993). How somatotopic is the motor cortex hand area? *Science, 261,* 489–492.

Schiffman, S. S., & Erikson, R. P. (1980). The issue of primary tastes versus a taste continuum. *Neuroscience and Biobehavioral Reviews, 4,* 109–117.

Schlaug, G., Jäncke, L., Huang, Y., & Steinmetz, H. (1995). In vivo evidence of structural brain asymmetry in musicians. *Science, 267,* 699–701.

Schleidt, M., Hold, B., & Attili, G. (1981). A cross-cultural study on the attitude towards personal odors. *Journal of Chemical Ecology, 7,* 19–31.

Schlundt, D. G., & Johnson, W. G. (1990). *Eating disorders: Assessment and treatment.* Boston, MA: Allyn and Bacon.

Schnapf, J. L., & Baylor, D. A. (1987, April). How photoreceptor cells respond to light. *Scientific American, 256,* 40–47.

Schousboe, A., Belhage, B., & Frandsen, A. (1997). Role of Ca^{++} and other second messengers in excitatory amino acid receptor mediated neurodegeneration: Clinical perspectives. *Clinical Neuroscience, 4,* 194–198.

Schreiner, C. E. (1992). Functional organization of the auditory cortex: Maps and mechanisms. *Current Opinion in Neurobiology, 2,* 516–521.

Schultz, W. (1997). Dopamine neurons and their role in reward mechanisms. *Current Opinion in Neurobiology, 7,* 191–197.

Schuman, E. M., & Madison, D. V. (1994). Nitric oxide and synaptic function. *Annual Review of Neurosciences, 17,* 153–183.

Schwartz, A. B. (1994). Distributed motor processing in cerebral cortex. *Current Opinion in Neurobiology, 4,* 840–846.

Schwartz, M. W., Peskind, E., Raskind, M., Nicolson, M., Moore, J., Morawiecki, A., Boyko, E. J., & Porte, D. J. (1996a). Cerebrospinal fluid leptin levels: Relationship to plasma levels and to adiposity in humans. *Nature Medicine, 2,* 589–593.

Schwartz, M. W., Seeley, R. J., Campfield, L. A., Burn, P., & Baskin, D. G. (1996b). Identification of hypothalamic targets of leptin action. *Journal of Clinical Investigation, 98,* 1101–1106.

Sclafani, A. (1990). Nutritionally based learned flavor preferences in rats. In E. D. Capaldi and T. L. Powley (Eds.), *Taste, experience, and feeding* (pp. 139–156). Washington, DC: American Psychological Association.

Scoville, W. B., & Milner, B. (1957). Loss of recent memory after bilateral hippocampal lesions. *Journal of Neurology, Neurosurgery and Psychiatry, 20,* 11–21.

Searle, L. V. (1949). The organization of hereditary maze-brightness and maze-dullness. *Genetic Psychology Monographs, 39,* 279–325.

Seeley, R. J., & Schwartz, M. W. (1997). The regulation of energy balance: Peripheral hormonal signals and hypothalamic neuropeptides. *American Psychological Society, 6,* 39–44.

Seeley, R. J., van Dijk, G., Campfield, L. A., Smith, F. J., Nelligan, J. A., Bell, S. M., Baskin, D. G., Woods, S. C., & Schwartz, M. W. (1996). The effect of intraventricular administration of leptin (OB protein) in food intake and body weight in the rat. *Hormone and Metabolic Research, 28,* 664–668.

Seitz, R. J., Roland, P. E., Bohm, C., Greitz, T., & Stone-Elanders, S. (1990). Motor learning in man: A positron emission tomographic study. *NeuroReport, 1,* 17–20.

Sejnowski, T. J. (1997). The year of the dendrite. *Science, 275,* 178–213.

Selkoe, D. J. (1991, November). Amyloid protein and Alzheimer's. *Scientific American, 265,* 68–78.

Selkoe, D. J. (1997). Alzheimer's disease: Genotypes, phenotype, and treatments. *Science, 275,* 630–631.

Shadmehr, R., & Holcomb, H. H. (1997). Neural correlates of motor memory consolidation. *Science, 277,* 821–825.

Shapiro, B. H., Levine, D. C., & Adler, N. T. (1980). The testicular feminized rat: A naturally occurring model of androgen independent brain masculinization. *Science, 209,* 418–420.

Shaywitz, S. E. (1996, November). Dyslexia. *Scientific American, 275,* 98–104.

Sherry, D. F., Vaccarino, A. L., Buckenham, K., & Herz, R. S. (1989). The hippocampal complex of food-storing birds. *Brain, Behavior and Evolution, 34,* 308–317.

Sherwin, B. B. (1985). Changes in sexual behavior as a function of plasma sex steroid levels in post-menopausal women. *Maturitas, 7,* 225–233.

Sherwin, B. B. (1988). A comparative analysis of the role of androgen in human male and female sexual behavior: Behavioral specificity, critical thresholds, and sensitivity. *Psychobiology, 16,* 416–425.

Sherwin, B. B., Gelfand, M. M., & Brender, W. (1985). Androgen enhances sexual motivation in females: A prospective cross-over study of sex steroid administration in the surgical menopause. *Psychosomatic Medicine, 47,* 339–351.

Sheth, B. R., Sharma, J., Chenchal Rao, S., & Sur, M. (1996). Orientation maps of subjective contours in visual cortex. *Science, 274,* 2110–2115.

Shimura, T., & Shimokochi, M. (1990). Involvement of the lateral mesencephalic tegmentum in copulatory behavior of male rats: Neuron activity in freely moving animals. *Neuroscience Research, 9,* 173–183.

Shizgal, P., & Murray, B. (1989). Neuronal basis of intracranial self-stimulation. In J. M. Liebman and S. J. Cooper (Eds.), *The neuropharmacological basis of reward* (pp. 106–163). Oxford, U.K.: Clarendon Press.

Shors, T. J., & Matzel, L. D. (1997). Long-term potentiation: What's learning got to do with it? *Behavioral and Brain Sciences, 20,* 597–655.

Shousboe, A., Belhage, B., & Frandsen, A. (1997). Role of Ca^{++} and other second messengers in excitatory amino acid receptor mediated neurodegeneration; clinical perspectives. *Clinical Neuroscience, 4,* 194–198.

Shouse, M. N., King, A., Langer, J., Vreeken, T., King, K., & Richkind, M. (1990). The ontogeny of feline temporal lobe epilepsy: Kindling a spontaneous seizure disorder in kittens. *Brain Research, 525,* 215–224.

Shultz, W. (1997). Dopamine neurons and their role in reward mechanisms. *Current Opinion in Neurobiology, 7,* 191–197.

Sidman, M., Stoddard, L. T., & Mohr, J. P. (1968). Some additional quantitative observations of immediate memory in a patient with bilateral hippocampal lesions. *Neuropsychologia, 6,* 245–254.

Siegel, J. M. (1983). A behavioral approach to the analysis of reticular formation unit activity. In T. E. Robinson (Ed.), *Behavioral approaches to brain research* (pp. 94–116). New York: Oxford University Press.

Siegel, J. M., Nienhuis, R., Fahringer, H. M., Paul, R., Shiromani, P., Dement, W. C., Mignot, E., & Chui, C. (1991). Neuronal activity in narcolepsy: Identification of cataplexy-related cells in the medial medulla. *Science, 252,* 1315–1318.

Siegel, S., Hinson, R. E., Krank, M. D., & McCully, J. (1982). Heroin "overdose" death: Contribution of drug-associated environmental cues. *Science, 216,* 436–437.

Silva, A. J., Paylor, R., Wehner, J. M., & Tonegawa, S. (1992). Impaired spatial learning in α-calcium-calmodulin kinase II mutant mice. *Science, 257,* 206–211.

Simpson, J. B., Epstein, A. N., & Camardo, J. S. (1978). Localization of receptors for the dipsogenic action of angiotensin II in the subfornical organ of rat. *Journal of Comparative and Physiological Psychology, 92,* 581–608.

Simpson, J. B., & Routtenberg, A. (1973). Subfornical organ: Site of drinking elicitation by angiotensin II. *Science, 181,* 1172–1175.

Sinclair, S. V., & Mistlberger, R. E. (1997). Scheduled activity reorganizes circadian phase of Syrian hamsters under full and skeleton photoperiods. *Behavioural Brain Research, 87,* 127–137.

Singer, J. (1968). Hypothalamic control of male and female sexual behavior. *Journal of Comparative and Physiological Psychology, 66,* 738–742.

Sitaram, N., Moore, A. M., & Gillin, J. C. (1978). Experimental acceleration and slowing of REM sleep ultradian rhythm by cholinergic agonist and antagonist. *Nature, 274,* 490–492.

Skelton, R. W., Scarth, A. S., Wilkie, D. M., Miller, J. J., & Phillips, A. G. (1987). Long-term increases in dentate granule cell responsivity accompany operant conditioning. *Journal of Neuroscience, 7,* 3081–3087.

Sladek, J. R., Jr., Redmond, D. E., Jr., Collier, T. J., Haber, S. N., Elsworth, J. D., Deutch, A. Y., & Roth, R. H. (1987). Transplantation of fetal dopamine neurons in primate brain reverses MPTP induced parkinsonism. In F. J. Seil, E. Herbert, & B. M. Carlson (Eds.), *Progress in brain research* (Vol. 71, pp. 309–323). New York: Elsevier.

Smith, F. J., & Campfield, L. A. (1993). Meal initiation occurs after experimental induction of transient declines in blood glucose. *American Journal of Physiology, 265,* 1423–1429.

Snyder, E. Y., & Macklis, J. D. (1996). Multipotent neural progenitor or stem-like cells may be uniquely suited for therapy for some neurodegenerative conditions. *Clinical Neuroscience, 3,* 310–316.

Snyder, S. H. (1978). Neuroleptic drugs and neurotransmitter receptors. *Journal of Clinical and Experimental Psychiatry, 133,* 21–31.

Snyder, S. H. (1992). Synaptic signalling by nitric oxide. *Current Opinion in Neurobiology, 2,* 323–327.

Sohal, R. S., & Weindruch, R. (1996). Oxidative stress, caloric restriction, and aging. *Science, 273,* 59–68.

Spector, R., & Johanson, C. E. (1989, November). The mammalian choroid plexus. *Scientific American, 261,* 68–74.

Sperry, R. W. (1963). Chemoaffinity in the orderly growth of nerve fiber patterns and connections. *Proceedings of the National Academy of Sciences (USA), 50,* 703–710.

Sperry, R. W. (1964, January). The great cerebral commissure. *Scientific American, 210,* 42–52.

Sperry, R. W., Zaidel, E., & Zaidel, D. (1979). Self recognition and social awareness in the deconnected minor hemisphere. *Neuropsychologia, 17,* 153–166.

Spitzer, H., Desimone, R., & Moran, J. (1988). Increased attention enhances both behavioral and neuronal performance. *Science, 240,* 338–340.

Squire, L. R. (1982). Comparisons between forms of amnesia: Some deficits are unique to Korsakoff's syndrome. *Journal of Experimental Psychology: Learning, Memory, and Cognition, 8,* 560–571.

Squire, L. R. (1987). *Memory and brain* (p. 139). New York: Oxford University Press.

Squire, L. R., Amaral, D. G., Zola-Morgan, S., Kritchevsky, M., & Press, G. (1989). Description of brain injury in the amnesic patient N. A. based on magnetic resonance imaging. *Experimental Neurology, 105,* 23–35.

Squire, L. R., & Moore, R. Y. (1979). Dorsal thalamic lesion in a noted case of human memory dysfunction. *Annals of Neurology, 6,* 503–506.

Squire, L. R., & Spanis, C. W. (1984). Long gradient of retrograde amnesia in mice: Continuity with the findings in humans. *Behavioral Neuroscience, 98,* 345–348.

Squire, L. R., Slater, P. C., & Chace, P. M. (1975). Retrograde amnesia: Temporal gradient in very long term memory following electroconvulsive therapy. *Science, 187,* 77–79.

Squire, L. R., & Zola-Morgan, S. (1985). The neuropsychology of memory: New links between humans and experimental animals. *Annals of the New York Academy of Sciences, 444,* 137–149.

Squire, L. R., Zola-Morgan, S., & Chen, K. (1988). Human amnesia and animal models of amnesia: Performance of amnesic patients on tests designed for the monkey. *Behavioral Neuroscience, 102,* 210–221.

Squire, R., & Alvarez, P. (1995). Retrograde amnesia and memory consolidation: A neurobiological perspective. *Current Opinion in Neurobiology, 5,* 169–177.

Stampi, C. (1992a). Evolution, chronobiology, and functions of polyphasic and ultrashort sleep: Main issues. In C. Stampi (Ed.), *Why we nap: Evolution, chronobiology, and functions of polyphasic and ultrashort sleep.* Boston: Birkhäuser.

Stampi, C. (Ed.) (1992b). *Why we nap: Evolution, chronobiology, and functions of polyphasic and ultrashort sleep.* Boston: Birkhäuser.

Stanford, S. C., & Salmon, P. (1993). *Stress: From synapse to syndrome.* London: Academic Press.

Stein, J., & Walsh, V. (1997). To see but not to read; the magnocellular theory of dyslexia. *Trends in Neurosciences, 20,* 147–152.

Steriade, M., & Hobson, J. A. (1976). Neuronal activity during the sleep-waking cycle. *Progress in Neurobiology, 6,* 155–376.

Stewart, J., de Wit, H., & Eikelboom, R. (1984). Role of unconditioned and conditioned drug effects in the self-administration of opiates and stimulants. *Psychological Review, 91,* 251–268.

Stewart, J., & Eikelboom, R. (1982). Conditioned drug effects. In L. L. Iversen, S. D. Iversen, and S. H. Snyder (Eds.), *Handbook of psychopharmacology, Vol. 19. New directions in behavioral pharmacology* (pp. 1–57). New York: Plenum Press.

Stirling, R. V., & Dunlop, S. A. (1995). The dance of the growth cones—Where to next? *Trends in Neurosciences, 18,* 111–115.

Stoekli, E. T., & Landmesser, L. T. (1998). Axon guidance at choice points. *Current Opinion in Neurobiology, 8,* 73–79.

Stoerig, P. (1993). Sources of blindsight. *Science, 261,* 493–494.

Stolerman, I. (1992). Drugs of abuse: Behavioural principles, methods and terms. *Trends in Neurosciences, 13,* 170.

Stout, S. C., & Nemeroff, C. B. (1994). Stress and psychiatric disorders. *Seminars in the Neurosciences, 6,* 271–280.

Strange, P. G. (1992). *Brain biochemistry and brain disorders.* Oxford: Oxford University Press.

Strubbe, J. H., & Steffens, A. B. (1977). Blood glucose levels in portal and peripheral circulation and their relation to food intake in the rat. *Physiology & Behavior, 19,* 303–307.

Susman, R. L. (1994). Fossil evidence for early hominid tool use. *Science, 265,* 1570–1573.

Sutton, S., & Ruchkin, D. S. (1984). The late positive complex: Advances and new problems. In R. Karrer, J. Cohen, & P. Teuting (Eds.), *Brain and information: Event-related potentials* (pp. 1–23). In *Annals of the New York Academy of Sciences, Vol. 425.* New York: New York Academy of Sciences.

Svaetichin, G. (1956). Spectral response curves from single cones. *Acta Physiologica Scandinavica, 39,* 17–46.

Swaab, D. F., & Hofman, M. A. (1995). Sexual differentiation of the human hypothalamus in relation to gender and sexual orientation. *Trends in Neuroscience, 18,* 264–270.

Swaab, D. F., & Fliers, E. (1985). A sexually dimorphic nucleus in the human brain. *Science, 188,* 1112–1115.

Swaab, D. F., Zhou, J. N., Ehlhart, T., & Hofman, M. A. (1994). Development of vasoactive intestinal polypeptide neurons in the human suprachiasmatic nucleus in relation to birth and sex. *Developmental Brain Research, 79,* 249–259.

Sweeney, M. E., Hill, P. A., Baney, R., & DiGirolamo, M. (1993). Severe vs. moderate energy restriction with and without exercise in the treatment of obesity: Efficiency of weight loss. *American Journal of Clinical Nutrition, 57,* 127–134.

Szatkowski, M., & Attwell, D. (1994). Triggering and execution of neuronal death in brain ischaemia: Two phases of glutamate release by different mechanisms. *Trends in Neuroscience, 17,* 359–365.

Szmukler, G. I., Eisler, I., Gillies, C., & Hayward, M. E. (1985). The implications of anorexia nervosa in a ballet school. *Journal of Psychiatric Research, 19,* 177–181.

Taddese, A., Nah, S.-Y., McCleskey, E. W. (1995). Selective opioid inhibition of small nociceptive neurons. *Science, 270,* 1366–1368.

Tanaka, A. (1972). A progressive change of behavioral and electroencephalographic response to daily amygdaloid stimulations in rabbits. *Fukuoka Acta Medica, 63,* 152–163.

Tanaka, K. (1996). Inferotemporal cortex and object vision. *Annual Review of Neuroscience, 19,* 109–139.

Tanaka, K. (1997). Mechanisms of visual object recognition: Monkey and human studies. *Current Opinion in Neurobiology, 7,* 523–529.

Tanda, G., Pontieri, F. E., & Chiara, G. D. (1997). Cannabinoid and heroin activation of mesolimbic dopamine transmission by a common μ opioid receptor mechanism. *Science, 276,* 2048–2049.

Tanji, J. (1996). New concepts of the supplementary motor area. *Current Opinion in Neurobiology, 6,* 782–787.

Tassinary, L. G., & Cacioppo, J. T. (1992). Unobservable facial actions and emotion. *Psychological Science, 3,* 28–33.

Tattersall, I. (1997, April). Out of Africa again . . . and again? *Scientific American, 276,* 60–67.

Taylor, J. R., Elsworth, J. D., Roth, J. R., Sladek, J. R., & Redmond, D. E., Jr., (1990). Cognitive and motor deficits in the acquisition of an object retrieval/detour task in MPTP-treated monkeys. *Brain, 113,* 617–637.

Teitelbaum, P. (1957). Random and food-directed activity in hyperphagic and normal rats. *Journal of Comparative and Physiological Psychology, 50,* 486–490.

Teitelbaum, P., & Epstein, A. N. (1962). The lateral hypothalamic syndrome: Recovery of feeding and drinking after lateral hypothalamic lesions. *Psychological Review, 69,* 74–90.

Tessier-LaVigne, M., & Goodman, C. S. (1996). The molecular biology of axon guidance. *Science, 274,* 1123–1132.

Tessier-Lavigne, M., & Placzek, M. (1991). Target attraction: Are developing axons guided by chemotropism? *Trends in Neurosciences, 14,* 303–310.

Tetrud, J. W., & Langston, J. W. (1989). The effect of deprenyl (Selegiline) on the natural history of Parkinson's disease. *Science, 245,* 519–522.

Teuber, H.-L., Battersby, W. S., & Bender, M. B. (1960a). Recovery of function after brain injury in man. In *Outcome of severe damage to the nervous system. Ciba Foundation Symposium 34.* Amsterdam: Elsevier North-Holland.

Teuber, H.-L., Battersby, W. S., & Bender, M. B. (1960b). *Visual field defects after penetrating missile wounds of the brain.* Cambridge, MA: Harvard University Press.

Teuber, H.-L., Milner, B., & Vaughan, H. G., Jr. (1968). Persistent anterograde amnesia after stab wound of the basal brain. *Neuropsychologia, 6,* 267–282.

Thach, W. T. (1996). On the specific role of the cerebellum in motor learning and cognition: Clues from PET activation and lesion studies in man. *Behavioral and Brain Sciences, 19,* 411–431.

Thoenen, H. (1995). Neurotrophins and neuronal plasticity. *Science, 270,* 593–598.

Thureson-Klein, A. K., & Klein, R. L. (1990). Exocytosis from neuronal large dense-cored vesicles. *International Review of Cytology, 121,* 67–126.

Tilles, D., Goldenheim, P., Johnson, D. C., Mendelson, J. H., Mello, N. K., & Hales, C. A. (1986). Marijuana smoking as cause of reduction in single-breath carbon monoxide diffusing capacity. *American Journal of Medicine, 80,* 601–606.

Timberlake, W. (1993). Animal behavior: A continuing synthesis. *Annual Review of Psychology, 44,* 675–708.

Tinbergen, N., & Perdeck, A. C. (1950). On the stimulus situation releasing the begging response in the newly hatched herring gull chick (*Larus argentatus argentatus* Pont). *Behavior, 3,* 1–39.

Tinklenberg, J. R. (1974). Marijuana and human aggression. In L. L. Miller (Ed.), *Marijuana, effects on human behavior* (pp. 339–358). New York: Academic Press.

Toates, F. M. (1981). The control of ingestive behaviour by internal and external stimuli—A theoretical review. *Appetite, 2,* 35–50.

Tompkins, C. A., & Mateer, C. A. (1985). Right hemisphere appreciation of intonational and linguistic indications of affect. *Brain and Language, 24,* 185–203.

Tonge, D. A., & Golding, J. P. (1993). Regeneration and repair of the peripheral nervous system. *Seminars in the Neurosciences, 5,* 385–390.

Tooby, J., & Cosmides, L. (1995). Mapping of the evolved functional organization of mind and brain. In M. S. Gazzaniga (Ed.), *The cognitive neurosciences*. Cambridge, MA: MIT Press.

Tootell, R. B. H., Dale, A. M., Sereno, M. I., & Malach, R. (1996). New images from human visual cortex. *Trends in Neurosciences, 19*, 481–489.

Tranel, D., & Damasio, A. R. (1985). Knowledge without awareness: An autonomic index of facial recognition by prosopagnosics. *Science, 228*, 1453–1454.

Traynor, A. E., Schlapfer, W. T., & Barondes, S. J. (1980). Stimulation is necessary for the development of tolerance to a neural effect of ethanol. *Journal of Neurobiology, 11*, 633–637.

Treit, D. (1985). Animal models for the study of anti-anxiety agents: A review. *Neuroscience and Biobehavioral Reviews, 9*, 203–222.

Treit, D. (1987). RO 15-1788, CGS 8216, picrotoxin, pentylenetetrazol: Do they antagonize anxiolytic drug effects through an anxiogenic action? *Brain Research Bulletin, 19*, 401–405.

Treit, D., Robinson, A., Rotzinger, S., & Pesold, C. (1993). Anxiolytic effects of serotonergic interventions in the shock-probe burying test and the elevated plus-maze test. *Behavioural Brain Research, 54*, 23–34.

Treue, S., & Maunsell, J. H. R. (1996). Attentional modulation of visual motion processing in cortical areas MT and MST. *Nature, 382*, 539–541.

Trulson, M. E., & Jacobs, B. L. (1979). Raphe unit activity in freely moving cats: Correlation with level of behavioral arousal. *Brain Research, 163*, 135–150.

Tryon, R. C. (1934). Individual differences. In F. A. Moss (Ed.), *Comparative Psychology* (pp. 409–448). New York: Prentice-Hall Inc.

Tucker, D. M. (1981). Lateral brain function, emotion, and conceptualization. *Psychological Bulletin, 89*, 19–46.

Tucker, J., Nixon, P. D., Rushworth, M., Harding, A. E., Jahanshahi, M., Quinn, N. P., Thompson, P. D., & Passingham, R. E. (1996). Associative learning in patients with cerebellar ataxia. *Behavioral Neuroscience, 110*(6), 1229–1234.

Tulving, E., & Markowitsch, J. J. (1997). Memory beyond the hippocampus. *Current Opinion in Neurobiology, 7*, 209–216.

Turkenburg, J. L., Swaab, D. F., Endert, E., Louwerse, A. L., & van de Poll, N. E. (1988). Effects of lesions of the sexually dimorphic nucleus on sexual behavior of testosterone-treated female Wistar rats. *Brain Research Bulletin, 329*, 195–203.

Turner, R. (1995). Functional mapping of the human brain with magnetic resonance imaging. *Seminars in the Neurosciences, 7*, 179–195.

Ulrich, R. E. (1991). Commentary: Animal rights, animal wrongs and the question of balance. *Psychological Science, 2*, 197–201.

Ungerleider, L. G., & Haxby, J. V. (1994). "What" and "where" in the human brain. *Current Opinion in Neurobiology, 4*, 157–165.

Ungerleider, L. G., & Mishkin, M. (1982). Two cortical visual systems. In D. J. Ingle, M. A. Goodale, & R. J. W. Mansfield (Eds.), *Analysis of visual behavior* (pp. 549–586). Cambridge, MA: MIT Press.

Valenstein, E. S. (1973). *Brain control.* New York: John Wiley and Sons.

Valenstein, E. S. (1980). *The psychosurgery debate: Scientific, legal, and ethical perspectives.* San Francisco: W. H. Freeman and Co.

Valenstein, E. S. (1986). *Great and desperate cures: The rise and decline of psychosurgery and other radical treatments for mental illness.* New York: Basic Books.

Vallee, B. L. (1998, June). Alcohol in the western world. *Scientific American, 278*, 80–85.

Vallee, R. B., & Bloom, G. S. (1991). Mechanisms of fast and slow axonal transport. *Annual Review of Neuroscience, 14*, 59–92.

Valverde, F. (1971). Rate and extent of recovery from dark rearing in the visual cortex of the mouse. *Brain Research, 33*, 1–11.

Van der Kooy, D. (1987). Place conditioning: A simple and effective method for assessing the motivational properties of drugs. In M. A. Bozarth (Ed.), *Methods of assessing the reinforcing properties of abused drugs* (pp. 229–240). New York: Springer-Verlag.

Vanderwolf, C. H. (1988). Cerebral activity and behavior: Control by central cholinergic and serotonergic systems. *International Review of Neurobiology, 30*, 225–340.

Vanderwolf, C. H., & Robinson, T. E. (1981). Reticulo-cortical activity and behavior: A critique of the arousal theory and a new synthesis. *Behavioral and Brain Sciences, 4*, 459–514.

Van Essen, D. C., Anderson, C. H., & Felleman, D. J. (1992). Information processing in the primate visual system: An integrated systems perspective. *Science, 255*, 419–423.

Van Furth, W. R., van Emst, M. G., & van Ree, J. M. (1995). Opioids and sexual behavior of male rats: Involvement of the medial preoptic area. *Behavioral Neurosciences, 109*(1), 125–134.

VanHelder, T., & Radomski, M. W. (1989). Sleep deprivation and the effect on exercise performance. *Sports Medicine, 7*, 235–247.

van Poppel, G., Spanhaak, S., & Ockhuizen, T. (1993). Effect of ß-carotene on immunological indexes in healthy male smokers. *The American Journal of Clinical Nutrition, 57*, 402–407.

van Vactor, D. (1998). Adhesion and signaling in axonal fasciculation. *Current Opinion in Neurobiology, 8*, 80–86.

Vargha-Khadem, F., Gadian, D. G., Watkins, K. E., Connelly, A., van Paesschen, W., & Mishkin, M. (1997). Differential effects of early hippocampal pathology on episodic and semantic memory. *Science, 277*, 376–380.

Vathy, I. U., & Etgen, A. M. (1989). Hormonal activation of female sexual behavior is accompanied by hypothalamic norepinephrine release. *Journal of Neuroendocrinology, 1*, 383–388.

Vermeij, G. J. (1996). Animal origins. *Science, 274*, 525–526.

Vertes, R. P. (1983). Brainstem control of the events of REM sleep. *Progress in Neurobiology, 22*, 241–288.

Vessie, P. R. (1932). On the transmission of Huntington's chorea for 300 years—The Bures family group. *The Journal of Nervous and Mental Disease, 76*, 553–573.

Vicario, D. S. (1991). Neural mechanisms of vocal production in songbirds. *Current Opinion in Neurobiology, 1*, 595–600.

Victor, M., Adams, R. D., & Collins, G. H. (1971). *The Wernicke syndrome* (p. 22). Philadelphia: F. A. Davis.

Vitaterna, M. H., King, D. P., Chang, A.-M., Korhauser, J. M., Lowrey, P. L., McDonald, J. D., Dove, W. J., Pinto, L. H., Turek, F. W., & Takahashi, J. S. (1994). Mutagenesis and mapping of a mouse gene, clock, essential for circadian behavior. *Science, 264*, 719–725.

Wada, J. A. (1949). A new method for the determination of the side of cerebral speech dominance. *Igaku to Seibutsugaku, 14*, 221–222.

Wada, J. A. (1990a). Erosion of kindled epileptogenesis and kindling-induced long-term seizure suppressive effect in primates. In J. A. Wada (Ed.), *Kindling 4* (pp. 382–394). New York: Plenum Press.

Wada, J. A. (Ed.). (1990b). *Kindling 4.* New York: Plenum Press.

Wada, J. A., Clarke, R., & Hamm, A. (1975). Cerebral hemispheric asymmetry in humans. *Archives of Neurology, 32,* 239–246.

Wada, J. A., & Sato, M. (1974). Generalized convulsive seizures induced by daily electrical stimulation of the amygdala in cats: Correlative electrographic and behavioral features. *Neurology, 24,* 565–574.

Wada, J. A., Sato, M., & Corcoran, M. E. (1974). Persistent seizure susceptibility and recurrent spontaneous seizures in kindled cats. *Epilepsia, 15,* 465–478.

Wahlestedt, C. (1998). Reward for persistence in substance P research. *Science, 281,* 1624–1625.

Wald, G. (1964). The receptors of human color vision. *Science, 145,* 1007–1016.

Walford, R. L., & Walford, L. (1994) *The anti-aging plan.* New York: Four Walls Eight Windows.

Wallace, D. C. (1997, August). Mitochondrial DNA in aging and disease. *Scientific American, 277,* 40–47.

Wallenstein, G. V., Eichenbaum, H., & Hasselmo, M. E. (1998). The hippocampus as an associator of discontiguous events. *Trends in Neurosciences, 21,* 317–323.

Wang, W., Meadows, L. R., den Haan, J. M. M., Sherman, N. E., Chen, Y., Blokland, E., Shabanowitz, J., Agulnik, A. I., Hendrickson, R. C., Bishop, C. E., Hunt, D. F., Goulmy, E., & Engelhard, V. H. (1995). Human H-Y: A male-specific histocompatibility antigen derived from the SMCY protein. *Science, 269,* 1588–1590.

Watson, J. B. (1930). *Behaviorism.* New York: W. W. Norton.

Wauquier, A., Ashton, D., & Melis, W. (1979). Behavioral analysis of amygdaloid kindling in beagle dogs and the effects of clonazepam, diazepam, phenobarbital, diphenylhydantoin, and flunarizine on seizure manifestion. *Experimental Neurology, 64,* 579–586.

Webb, W. B. (1973). Selective and partial deprivation of sleep. In W. P. Koella & P. Levin (Eds.), *Sleep: Physiology, biochemistry, psychology, pharmacology, clinical implications* (pp. 176–204). Basel: Karger.

Webb, W. B., & Agnew, H. W. (1967). Sleep cycling within the twenty-four hour period. *Journal of Experimental Psychology, 74,* 167–169.

Webb, W. B., & Agnew, H. W. (1970). Sleep stage characteristics of long and short sleepers. *Science, 163,* 146–147.

Webb, W. B., & Agnew, H. W. (1974). The effects of a chronic limitation of sleep length. *Psychophysiology, 11,* 265–274.

Webb, W. B., & Agnew, H. W. (1975). The effects on subsequent sleep of an acute restriction of sleep length. *Psychophysiology, 12,* 367–370.

Weinberg, R. A. (1991). Tumor suppressor genes. *Science, 254,* 1138–1145.

Weinberger, N. M. (1993). Learning-induced changes of auditory receptive fields. *Current Opinion in Neurobiology, 3,* 570–577.

Weindruch, R. (1996, January). Caloric restriction and aging. *Scientific American, 274,* 46–52.

Weindruch, R., & Walford, R. L. (1988). *The retardation of aging and disease by dietary restriction.* Springfield, IL: Charles C. Thomas.

Weindruch, R., Walford, R. L., Fligiel, S., & Guthrie, D. (1986). The retardation of aging in mice by dietary restriction: Longevity, cancer, immunity, and lifetime energy intake. *Journal of Nutrition, 116,* 641–654.

Weingarten, H. P. (1983). Conditioned cues elicit feeding in sated rats: A role for learning in meal initiation. *Science, 220,* 431–433.

Weingarten, H. P. (1984). Meal initiation controlled by learned cues: Basic behavioral properties. *Appetite, 5,* 147–158.

Weingarten, H. P. (1985). Stimulus control of eating: Implications for a two-factor theory of hunger. *Appetite, 6,* 387–401.

Weingarten, H. P. (1990). Learning, homeostasis, and the control of feeding behavior. In E. D. Capaldi and T. L. Powley (Eds.), *Taste, experience, and feeding* (pp. 14–27). Washington, DC: American Psychological Association.

Weingarten, H. P., Chang, P. K., & Jarvie, K. R. (1983). Reactivity of normal and VMH-lesion rats to quinine-adulterated foods: Negative evidence for negative finickiness. *Behavioral Neuroscience, 97,* 221–233.

Weingarten H. P., & Kulikovsky, O. T. (1989). Taste-to-postingestive consequence conditioning: Is the rise in sham feeding with repeated experience a learning phenomenon? *Physiology & Behavior, 45,* 471–476.

Weintraub, S., & Mesulam, M.-M. (1989). Neglect: Hemispheric specialization, behavioral components and anatomical correlates. In F. Boller & J. Grafman (Eds.), *Handbook of neuropsychology, 2.* New York: Elsevier Science Publishers.

Weisinger, R. S. (1975). Conditioned and pseudoconditioned thirst and sodium appetite. In G. Peters, J. T. Fitzsimons, & L. Peters-Haefeli (Eds.), *Control mechanisms of drinking* (pp. 149–154). New York: Springer-Verlag.

Weiskrantz, L. (1996). Blindsight revisited. *Current Opinion in Neurobiology, 6,* 215–220.

Weiskrantz, L., Warrington, E. K., Sanders, M. D., & Marshall, J. (1974). Visual capacity in the hemianopic field following a restricted occipital ablation. *Brain, 97,* 709–728.

Weissman, M. M., & Olfson, M. (1995). Depression women: Implications for health care research. *Science, 269,* 799–801.

Wekerle, H. (1993). Experimental autoimmune encephalomyelitis as a model of immune-mediated CNS disease. *Current Opinion in Neurobiology, 3,* 779–784.

Weliky, M., & Katz, C. (1997). Disruption of orientation tuning in visual cortex by artificially correlated neuronal activity. *Nature, 386,* 680–685.

Weller, A., Smith, G. P., & Gibbs, J. (1990). Endogenous cholecystokinin reduces feeding in young rats. *Science, 247,* 1589–1590.

Wessinger, C. M., Fendrich, R., & Gazzaniga, M. S. (1997). Islands of residual vision in hemianopic patients. *Journal of Cognitive Neuroscience, 9*(2), 203–221.

Westergaard, G. C., & Suomi, S. J. (1996). Hand preference for a bimanual task in tufted capuchins (*Cebus apella*) and rhesus macaques (*Macaca mullata*). *Journal of Comparative Psychology, 110*(4), 406–411.

Westerink, B. H. C., & Justice, J. B., Jr. (1991). Microdialysis compared with other in vivo release models. In T. E. Robinson and J. B. Justice, Jr. (Eds.), *Microdialysis in the neurosciences. Vol. 7, Techniques in the neural and behavioral sciences* (pp. 23–43). Amsterdam: Elsevier.

Wever, R. A. (1979). *The circadian system of man.* New York: Springer-Verlag.

Wexler, N. S., Rose, E. A., & Housman, D. E. (1991). Molecular approaches to hereditary diseases of the nervous system: Huntington's disease as a paradigm. *Annual Review of Neuroscience, 14,* 503–529.

Whishaw, I. Q., & Tomie, J. (1995). Rats with fimbria-fornix lesions can acquire and retain a visual-tactile transwitching (configural) task. *Behavioral Neuroscience, 109*(4), 607–612.

Whishaw, I. Q., & Tomie, J. (1996). Impairments on a movement integration task in rats with fimbria-fornix lesions. *Society of Neuroscience Abstracts*, 680.

Whishaw, I. Q., Kolb, B., & Sutherland, R. J. (1983). The analysis of behavior in the laboratory rat. In T. E. Robinson (Ed.), *Behavioral approaches to brain research* (pp. 141–211). New York: Oxford University Press.

Whishaw, I. Q., McKenna, J. E., & Maaswinkel, H. (1997). Hippocampal lesions and path integration. *Current Opinion in Neurobiology, 7,* 228–234.

White, F. J. (1996). Synaptic regulation of mesocorticolimbic dopamine neurons. *Annual Review of Neuroscience, 19,* 405–36.

White, N., Sklar, L., & Amit, Z. (1977). The reinforcing action of morphine and its paradoxical side effect. *Psychopharmacology, 52,* 63–66.

White, N. M. (1997). Mnemonic functions of the basal ganglia. *Current Opinion in Neurobiology, 7,* 164–169.

White, N. M., & Hiroi, N. (1993). Amphetamine conditioned cue preference and the neurobiology of drug seeking. *Seminars in the Neurosciences, 5,* 329–336.

Whitelaw, V., & Hollyday, M. (1983). Position-dependent motor innervation of the chick hindlimb following serial and parallel duplications of limb segments. *Journal of Neuroscience, 3,* 1216–1225.

Wichmann, T., & DeLong, M. R. (1996). Functional and pathophysiological models of the basal ganglia. *Current Opinion in Neurobiology, 6,* 751–758.

Wickelgren, W. A. (1968). Sparing of short-term memory in an amnesic patient: Implications for strength theory of memory. *Neuropsychologia, 6,* 235–244.

Wiig, K. A., Cooper, L. N., & Bear, M. F. (1996). Temporally graded retrograde amnesia following separate and combined lesions of the perirhinal cortex and fornix in the rat. *Learning & Memory, 3,* 313–325.

Wilhelm, P. (1983). *The Nobel prize.* London: Springwood Books.

Willett, W. C. (1994). Diet and health: What should we eat? *Science, 264,* 532–537.

Williams, J., Merritt, J., Rittenhouse, C., & Hobson, J. A. (1992). Bizarreness in dreams and fantasies: Implications for the activation-synthesis hypothesis. *Consciousness and Cognition, 1,* 172–185.

Wills, S. (1997). *Drugs of abuse.* Cambridge: Pharmaceutical Press.

Wilson, K. D. (1998). Issues surrounding the cognitive neuroscience of obsessive-compulsive disorder. *Psychonomic Bulletin & Review, 5*(2), 161–172.

Wilson, M. A., & McNaughton, B. L. (1993). Dynamics of the hippocampal ensemble code for space. *Science, 261,* 1055–1058.

Wilson, M. A., & Tonegawa, S. (1997). Synaptic plasticity, place cells and spatial memory: Study with second generation knockouts. *Trends in Neurosciences, 20,* 1102–106.

Wiltstein, W. (1995, October 26). Quarry KO'd by dementia. *The Vancouver Sun,* 135.

Winn, P. (1994). Schizophrenia research moves to the prefrontal cortex. *Trends in Neurosciences, 17,* 265–268.

Winocur, G., Oxbury, S., Roberts, R., Agnetti, V., & Davis, C. (1984). Amnesia in patients with bilateral lesions to the thalamus. *Neuropsychologia, 22,* 123–143.

Winson, J. (1993). The biology and function of rapid eye movement sleep. *Current Opinion in Neurobiology, 3,* 243–248.

Wirtshafter, D., & Davis, J. D. (1977). Set points, settling points, and the control of body weight. *Physiology & Behavior, 19,* 75–78.

Wise, R. A. (1993). In vivo estimates of extracellular dopamine and dopamine metabolite levels during intravenous cocaine or heroin self-administration. *Seminars in the Neurosciences, 5,* 337–342.

Wise, R. A. (1996). Neurobiology of addition. *Current Opinion in Neurobiology, 6,* 243–251.

Wise, R. A., Bauco, P., Carlezon, W. A., & Trojniar, W. (1992). Self-stimulation and drug reward mechanisms. *Annals of the New York Academy of Science, 654,* 192–198.

Wise, S. P., Boussaoud, D., Johnson, P. B., & Caminiti, R. (1997). Premotor and parietal cortex: Corticocortical connectivity and combinatorial computations. *Annual Review of Neuroscience, 20,* 25–42.

Witelson, S. F. (1991). Neural sexual mosaicism: Sexual differentiation of the human temporo-parietal region for functional asymmetry. *Psychoneuroendocrinology, 16,* 133–153.

Wodak, A., Richmond, R., & Wilson, A. (1990). Thiamin fortification and alcohol. *The Medical Journal of Australia, 152,* 97–99.

Wolf, M. E., & Goodale, M. A. (1987). Oral asymmetries during verbal and non-verbal movements of the mouth. *Neuropsychologia, 25,* 375–396.

Wolff, P. H., Michel, G. F., Ovrut, M., & Drake, C. (1990). Rate and timing precision of motor coordination in developmental dyslexia. *Developmental Psychology, 26,* 349–359.

Wood, E. R., Mumby, D. G., Pinel, J. P. J., & Phillips, A. G. (1993). Impaired object recognition memory in rats following ischemia-induced damage to the hippocampus. *Behavioral Neuroscience, 107,* 51–62.

Wood, R. J., Rolls, B. J., & Ramsay, D. J. (1977). Drinking following intracarotid infusions of hypertonic solutions in dogs. *American Journal of Physiology, 1,* R88–R91.

Woodruff-Pak, D. S. (1993). Eyeblink classical conditioning in H. M.: Delay and trace paradigms. *Behavioral Neuroscience, 107,* 911–925.

Woods, S. C. (1991). The eating paradox: How we tolerate food. *Psychological Review, 98,* 488–505.

Woods, S. C., & Gibbs, J. (1989). The regulation of food intake by peptides. The psychobiology of human eating disorders: Preclinical and clinical perspectives. *Annals of the New York Academy of Sciences, 75,* 236–242.

Woods, S. C., & Strubbe, J. H. (1994). The psychology of meals. *Psychonomic Bulletin & Review, 1,* 141–155.

Wu, J. C., & Bunney, W. E. (1990). The biological basis of an antidepressant response to sleep deprivation and relapse: Review and hypothesis. *American Journal of Psychiatry, 147*(1), 14–21.

Wu, L.-G., & Saggau, P. (1997). Presynaptic inhibition of elicited neurotransmitter release. *Trends in Neurosciences, 20,* 204–212.

Yaqub, B. A., Gascon, G. G., Al-Nosha, M., & Whittaker, H. (1988). Pure word deafness (acquired verbal auditory agnosia) in an Arabic speaking patient. *Brain, 111,* 457–466.

Yehuda, R. (1997). Stress and glucocorticoid. *Science, 275,* 1662–1664.

Yeomans, J. S., Mathur, A., & Tampakeras, M. (1993). Rewarding brain stimulation: Role of tegmental cholinergic neurons that activate dopamine neurons. *Behavioral Neuroscience, 107,* 1077–1087.

Yesalis, C. E., & Bahrke, M. S. (1995). Anabolic-androgenic steroids: Current issues. *Sports Medicine, 19*(5), 326–340.

Yokel, R. A. (1987). Intravenous self-administration: Response rates, the effects of pharmacological challenges, and drug preference. In M. A. Bozarth (Ed.), *Methods of assessing the reinforcing properties of abused drugs* (pp. 1–33). New York: Springer-Verlag.

Yoon, M. (1971). Reorganization of retinotectal projection following surgical operations on the optic tectum in goldfish. *Experimental Neurology, 33,* 395–411.

Youdim, M. B. H., & Riederer, P. (1997, January). Understanding Parkinson's disease. *Scientific American, 276,* 52–59.

Young, A. W., Aggleton, J. P., Hellawell, D. J., Johnson, M., & Broks, P. (1995). Face processing impairments after amygdalotomy. *Brain, 118,* 15–24.

Young, W. (1996). Spinal cord regeneration. *Science, 273,* 451–452.

Young-Jin, S., Trachtenberg, J. T., & Thompson, W. J. (1996). Schwann cells induce and guide sprouting and reinnervation of neuromuscular junctions. *Trends in Neurosciences, 19,* 280–285.

Zaidel, E. (1975). A technique for presenting lateralized visual input with prolonged exposure. *Vision Research, 15,* 283–289.

Zaidel, E. (1983). Disconnection syndrome as a model for laterality effects in the normal brain. In J. B. Hellige (Ed.), *Cerebral hemisphere asymmetry: Method, theory, and application* (pp. 95–151). New York: Praeger Press.

Zaidel, E. (1987). Language in the disconnected right hemisphere. In G. Adelman (Ed.), *Encyclopedia of neuroscience* (pp. 563–564). Cambridge, MA: Birkhäuser.

Zangwill, O. L. (1975). Excision of Broca's area without persistent aphasia. In K. J. Zulch, O. Creutzfeldt, & G. C. Galbraith (Eds.), *Cerebral localization* (pp. 258–263). New York: Springer-Verlag.

Zeki, S. (1993a). *A vision of the brain.* Oxford, UK.: Blackwell Scientific Publications.

Zeki, S. (1993b). The visual association cortex. *Current Opinion in Neurobiology, 3,* 155–159.

Zelman, D. C., Tiffany, S. T., & Baker, T. B. (1985). Influence of stress on morphine induced pyrexia: Relevance to a pavlovian model of tolerance development. *Behavioral Neuroscience, 99,* 122–144.

Zetterström, R. H., Solomin, L., Jansson, L., Hoffer, B. J., Olson, L., & Perlmann, T. (1997). Dopamine neuron agenesis in Nurr1-deficient mice. *Science, 276,* 248–250.

Zhang, Y., Proenca, R., Maffie, M., Barone, M., Leopold, L., & Friedman, J. M. (1994). Positional cloning of the mouse obese gene and its human homologue. *Nature, 372,* 425–432.

Zimitat, C., Kril, J., Harper, C. G., & Nixon, P. F. (1990). Progression of neurological disease in thiamin-deficient rats is enhanced by ethanol. *Alcohol, 7,* 493–501.

Zimmer, L., & Morgan, J. P. (1997). *Marijuana myths, marijuana facts: A review of the scientific evidence.* New York: Lindesmith Center.

Zivin, J. A., & Choi, D. W. (1991, July). Stroke therapy. *Scientific American, 265,* 56–63.

Zola-Morgan, S., & Squire L. R. (1985). Medial temporal lesions in monkeys impair memory on a variety of tasks sensitive to human amnesia. *Behavioral Neuroscience, 99,* 22–34.

Zola-Morgan, S., & Squire, L. R. (1993). Neuroanatomy of memory. *Annual Review of Neuroscience, 16,* 547–563.

Zola-Morgan, S., Squire, L. R., & Amaral, D. G. (1986). Human amnesia and the medial temporal region: Enduring memory impairment following a bilateral lesion limited to field CA1 of the hippocampus. *Journal of Neuroscience, 6,* 2950–2967.

Zola-Morgan, S., Squire, L. R., Rempel, N. L., Clower, R. P., & Amaral, D. G. (1992). Enduring memory impairment in monkeys after ischemic damage to the hippocampus. *Journal of Neuroscience, 12,* 2582–2596.

Zola-Morgan, S. M., & Squire, L. R. (1990). The primate hippocampal formation: Evidence for a time-limited role in memory storage. *Science, 250,* 288–290.

Zola-Morgan, S. M., Squire, L. R., Amaral, D. G., & Suzuki, W. A. (1989). Lesions of perirhinal and parahippocampal cortex that spare the amygdala and hippocampal formation produce severe memory impairment. *Journal of Neuroscience, 9,* 4355–4370.

Zucker, K. J., Bradley, S. J., Oliver, G., Blake, J., Fleming, S., & Hood, J. (1996). Psychosexual development of women with congential adrenal hyperplasia. *Hormones and Behavior, 30,* 300–318.

Zusho, H. (1983). Posttraumatic anosmia. *Archives of Ontolaryngology, 4,* 252–256.

CREDITS

PHOTO CREDITS

Fig. 1.1, Med. Ills. SBHA/Tony Stone Images; Fig. 1.4, Corbis; Fig. 2.5, Dale and Marion Zimmerman/Animals Animals; Fig. 2.6, Sid Bhart/Photo Researchers, Inc.; Fig. 2.7, Tom Meyers/Photo Researchers, Inc.; Fig. 2.8, Kevin Shafer/Peter Arnold, Inc.; Erwin & Peggy Bauer/Bruce Coleman, Inc.; A. Comoost/Peter Arnold, Inc.; Erwin & Peggy Bauer/Bruce Coleman, Inc.; John Curtis/Offshoot Stock; Fig. 2.10, Ken Fisher/Tony Stone Images; Fig. 2.11, John Reader/Photo Researchers, Inc.; Fig. 2.15, David Phillips/Photo Researchers, Inc.; Fig. 2.19, Peter Arnold, Inc.; page 49, K. Wanstall/The Image Works; Fig. 3.11, Ed Reschke ©/ Peter Arnold, Inc.; page 77, Peter Arnold, Inc.; Fig. 5.1, Science Photo Library/Photo Researchers, Inc.; Fig. 5.3, CNRI/PhotoTake, NY; Fig. 5.4, Scott Carmazine/Photo Researchers, Inc.; Fig. 5.9, Photo Researchers, Inc.; Fig. 6.4, Volker Steger/Peter Arnold, Inc.; Fig. 6.6, © 1996 Scott Carmazine; Fig. 6.8, Dr. David Rosenbaum/ Phototake; Fig. 6.11, James Stevens/Science Photo Library/Photo Researchers, Inc.; Fig. 6.12, Cecil Fox/Photo Researchers, Inc.; Fig. 7.2, Oscar Burriel/Science Photo Library/Photo Researchers, Inc.; Fig. 7.5, Science Photo Library/Photo Researchers, Inc.; Fig. 7.6, Ralph C. Eagle/Photo Researchers, Inc.; Fig. 7.23, M. Bruce/Picture Cube; Fig. 8.10, Erich Lessing/Art Resource, NY; Fig. 8.17, John Shaw/Bruce Coleman, Inc.; Fig. 9.9, SecchiLecaque/ Roussel-UCLA/Photo Researchers, Inc.; Fig. 9.11, Bonnie Kamin; Fig. 10.2, Richard Reinauer/Color-Pic, Inc.; Fig. 10.26, The Jackson Lab, Bar Harbor, ME; Fig. 11.12, Gabo/Focus/Trivel/ Woodfin Camp & Associates; Fig. 12.1, Hank Morgan/Photo Researchers, Inc.; Fig. 12.4, Animals/Animals; Fig. 13.1, A. Ramey/Woodfin Camp & Associates; page 351, Dratch/The Image Works; page 352, Will Hart; page 353, Mark K. Walker, Picture Cube; page 355, Will Hart; page 357, E. R. Degginger/Color-Pic, Inc.; page 368, Corbis; Fig. 14.8, Corbis/Kevin R. Morris; Fig. 17.4, Reprinted by permission of the Human Interaction Laboratory/Dr. Eckman and Dr. Friesen (1975); Fig. 17.11, Lennert Nillson/Bonnier Alba; page 484, Jan Halaska/Photo Researchers, Inc.; page 489, SIU School of Medicine/Bruce Coleman, Inc.; page 493, Elena Dorfman/Offshoot Stock

ILLUSTRATION CREDITS

Chapter 1
Fig. 1.3, 1.5, Schneck-DePippo Graphics; Fig. 1.6, 1.7, 1.8, 1.10, Frank Forney; Fig. 1.9, 1.11, William C. Ober and Claire W. Garrison

Chapter 2
Fig. 2.1, William C. Ober and Claire W. Garrison; Fig. 2.3, 2.4, 2.12, 2.13, 2.14, 2.16, 2.17, 2.23, 2.24, 2.26, 2.27, page 49, Schneck-DePippo Graphics; Fig. 2.9, Leo Harrington; Fig. 2.18, 2.20, 2.21, Illustrious Interactive; Fig. 2.22, Frank Forney

Chapter 3
Fig. 3.1, Adrienne Lehmann; Fig. 3.2, 3.4, 3.5, 3.7, 3.16, 3.17, 3.19, 3.22, 3.31, 3.32, Schneck-DePippo Graphics; Fig. 3.3, 3.18, 3.20, 3.23, 3.24, 3.25, 3.26, 3.27, 3.28, 3.30, William C. Ober and Claire Garrison; Fig. 3.6, 3.8, 3.9, 3.10, Mark Lefkowitz

Chapter 4
Fig. 4.1, 4.2, 4.4, 4.5, 4.6, 4.7, 4.8, 4.9, 4.16, 4.17, Schneck-DePippo Graphics; Fig. 4.3, Illustrious Interactive; Fig. 4.10, 4.11, 4.13, 4.14, 4.18, 4.19, Frank Forney; Fig. 4.12, 4.20, Mark Lefkowitz

Chapter 5
Fig. 5.2, 5.8, 5.10, 5.11, 5.14, 5.16, 5.17, 5.19, 5.27, Schneck-DePippo Graphics; Fig. 5.12, 5.18, 5.25, Frank Forney; Fig. 5.15, Adrienne Lehmann

Chapter 6
Fig. 6.5, Mark Lefkowitz; Fig. 6.9, 6.10, 6.13, 6.14, Schneck-DePippo Graphics

Chapter 7
Fig. 7.1, 7.8, 7.11, 7.12, 7.13, 7.14, 7.15, 7.16, 7.17, 7.18, 7. 22, 7.23, 7.24, Schneck-DePippo Graphics; Fig. 7.4, 7.7, 7.9, 7.10, 7.21, 7.25, 7.26, 7.27, 7.28, Celadon Digital Studios

Chapter 8
Fig. 8.1, 8.2, 8.4, Leo Harrington; Fig. 8.3, 8.16, 8.22, 8.24, 8.28, William C. Ober and Claire W. Garrison; Fig. 8.5, Academy Artworks; Fig. 8.6, 8.13, 8.15, 8.19, 8.27, Illustrious Interactive; Fig. 8.7, 8.9, 8.11, 8.12, 8.21, 8.23, 8.25, 8.26, Schneck-DePippo Graphics; Fig. 8.8, Frank Forney; Fig. 8.14, 8.18, Adrienne Lehmann

Chapter 9
Fig. 9.1, Leo Harrington; **Fig. 9.2, 9.7, 9.8, 9.16,** Schneck-DePippo Graphics; **Fig. 9.3, 9.4, 9.5, 9.10, 9.12, 9.13, 9.14, 9.15, 9.17,** Frank Forney; **Fig. 9.6,** William C. Ober and Claire W. Garrison

Chapter 10
Fig. 10.1, Gale Mueller; **Fig. 10.2, 10.3, 10.4, 10.5, 10.6, 10.7, 10.9, 10.12, 10.13, 10.15, 10.19, 10.20, 10.22, 10.23, 10.24, 10.25,** Schneck-DePippo Graphics; **Fig. 10.8, 10.10, 10.11,** Academy Artworks; **Fig. 10.14, 10.21,** Frank Forney; **Fig. 10.16,** Illustrious Interactive; **Fig. 10.17, 10.18,** Adrienne Lehmann

Chapter 11
Fig. 11.1, 11.5, 11.7, 11.11, 11.14, 11.16, Schneck-DePippo Graphics; **Fig. 11.2,** William C. Ober and Claire W. Garrison; **Fig. 11.3, 11.4,** Adrienne Lehmann; **Fig. 11.6, 11.13,** Illustrious Interactive; **Fig. 11.8,** Frank Forney; **Fig. 11.9,** Gale Mueller; **Fig. 11.15,** Academy Artworks

Chapter 12
Fig. 12.2, 12.7, 12.8, 12.9, 12.10, 12.11, 12.12, 12.13, 12.14, 12.15, 12.17, Schneck-DePippo Graphics; **Fig. 12.3, 12.5, 12.6,** Illustrious Interactive; **Fig. 12.16,** Frank Forney

Chapter 13
Fig. 13.2, 13.3, 13.4, 13.5, 13.6, 13.7, 13.8, 13.11, Schneck-DePippo Graphics; **Fig. 13.9, 13.10,** Illustrious Interactive; **Fig. 13.12,** Frank Forney

Chapter 14
Fig. 14.1, 14.7, Illustrious Interactive; **Fig. 14.2, 14.3, 14.6, 14.8, 14.9, 14.10, 14.11, 14.12, 14.15, 14.16, 14.17, 14.18,** Schneck-DePippo Graphics; **Fig. 14.4, 14.5, 14.14,** Frank Forney; **Fig. 14.12,** William C. Ober and Claire W. Garrison

Chapter 15
Fig. 15.1, 15.2, 15.3, 15.5, 15.8, 15.9, 15.11, 15.19, 15.20, 15.21, Illustrious Interactive; **Fig. 15.6,** Frank Forney; **Fig. 15.7, 15.10, 15.12, 15.13, 15.14, 15.15, 15.16, 15.23, 15.24, 15.25,** Schneck-DePippo Graphics; **Fig. 15.18,** Mark Lefkowitz; **Fig. 15.22, 15.26,** Academy Artworks

Chapter 16
Fig. 16.1, 16.2, 16.9, 16.10, 16.11, William C. Ober and Claire W. Garrison; **Fig. 16.3, 16.4, 16.5, 16.6, 16.18, Table 16.1,** Frank Forney; **Fig. 16.7, 16.13, 16.16,** Illustrious Interactive; **Fig. 16.8, 16.12, 16.14, 16.15,** Schneck-DePippo Graphics

Chapter 17
Fig. 17.1, 17.2, 17.5, 17.7, 17.10, 17.12, 17.14, Schneck-DePippo Graphics; **Fig. 17.3,** William C. Ober and Claire W. Garrison; **17.6, 17.8,** Frank Forney; **Fig. 17.9,** Illustrious Interactive; **Fig. 17.13, 17.15,** Mark Lefkowitz

Appendixes
Appendix I, Frank Forney; **Appendix VIII,** Schneck-DePippo Graphics

SUBJECT INDEX

Auditory nerve, 200
Auditory system, 199
    the ear, 200–201
    effects of damage, 203
    from ear to primary auditory cortex, 201–202
    sound localization, 202–203
Autonomic nervous system (ANS), 10, 11, 52, 53
    emotions and, 469–470
Autoradiography, 122, 123
Autoreceptors, 96, 97, 490–491
Autotransplantation, 431
Axodendritic synapses, 91
Axonal conduction, 91
Axon growth, 405–408
Axon hillock, 86, 87
Axosomatic synapses, 91
Axotomy, 422

Bacterial infections, 143
Baroreceptors, 273
Basal forebrain, 330, 331, 383, 398
Basal ganglia, 74–75, 231
Basal metabolic rate, 265
Basilar membrane, 200
Before-and-after design, 347
Behavior
    evolution and, 27–28
    genetics, 11
    model of, 24
    nature-nurture issue, 21–22, 23–24
    perinatal hormones and development of, 295–296
    physiological versus psychological, 21
Behavioral biology, defined, 3
Behavioral paradigm
    of animal behavior, 132–135
    defined, 126, 127
Behaviorism, 22
Benign tumors, 138, 139
Benzodiazepines, 102–103, 334–335, 493
Between-subject design, 6, 7
Betz cells, 232, 233
Bilateral medial temporal lobectomy, 373–374
Binding problem, 191–182
Binocular, 176, 177
Binocular disparity, 163
Biopsychology
    animal behavior and, 132–135
    defined, 3–4
    divisions of, 9–11
    errors in, 15–17
    other names for, 3
    relation with other disciplines, 4
Bipolar affective disorder, 489
Bipolar cells, 163
Bipolar neuron, 56
Birdsong, development of, 45–47
Bisexual, 307
Blindsight, 193

Blind spot, 164, 165
Blobs, 186
Block-tapping memory span test, 374, 375
Blood-brain barrier, 55–56
Blood-flow receptors, 273
Blood glucose, hunger and satiety and, 259
Blood pressure, 116
Blood volume, 116
Blueprint hypothesis, 406–407
Body fluid regulation, 269–271
    See also Drinking
Body weight, set points and, 264–268
Brain
    See also Lateralization of function; Split brain
    controlling sleep and dreaming and role of, 329–331
    development of sex differences in, 294–295
    differences between left and right hemispheres, 445–449
    divisions of, 66–67
    evolution of human, 32–34
    locating neurotransmitters and receptors in, 123–124
    major structures of, 67–76
    measuring chemical activity of, 122–123
    memory structures of, 396–398
    methods of visualizing, 107–111
    reward circuits in the, 362–366
    stem, 33, 66, 67
Brain damage
    neural reorganization after damage to, 426–427
    therapeutic approaches for, 428–431
Brain damage, causes of
    cerebrovascular disorders, 140–141
    chemical senses and, 216
    closed-head injuries, 141–143
    genetic factors, 144–145
    infections, 143–144
    neurotoxins, 144
    programmed cell death, 145
    tumors, 139–140
Brain tumors, 139–140
Bregma, 117
Broca's aphasia, 450
Broca's area, 436, 437, 450, 461
Buerger's disease, 350, 351
Bulimia nervosa, 281
Buspirone, 493
Butyrophenones, 486

Cafeteria diet, 258
Cannabis sativa, 353
Cannula, 122, 123
Cannon-Bard theory, 467
CA1 subfield, 380, 381
Carbon monoxide, 99
Cardiovascular activity, 116
Carousel apparatus, 323
Cartesian dualism, 21

Case studies, 7–8
Cataplexy, 337–338
Catecholamines, 98
Caudal reticular formation, 330–331
Caudate, 75
Cell-adhesion molecules (CAMs), 404, 405
Cell-mediated immunity, 480
Cells of the nervous system, 56–61
Cellular dehydration, 272–273
Central canal, 53
Central fissure, 72
Central nervous system (CNS), 52, 53
    penetration of drugs by, 344
Central sensorimotor programs, 243–246
Cephalic phase, 251
Cerebellum, 69, 231, 397–398
Cerebral angiography, 107
Cerebral aqueduct, 55, 69
Cerebral asymmetry, 448–449
Cerebral commissures, 72, 435
Cerebral cortex, 9, 72–74
Cerebral dialysis, 123
    studies, 365
Cerebral hemorrhage, 140, 141
Cerebral ischemia, 140–141
Cerebral lateralization, 449
Cerebral ventricles, 53
Cerebrospinal fluid (CSF), 53, 55
Cerebrovascular disorders, 140–141
Cerebrum, 33
Cerveau isolé preparation, 327
Change blindness, 218, 219
Cheese effect, 489–490
Chemical lesions, 122
Chemical senses, 213–216
Chemoaffinity hypothesis, 405–406
Chimeric figures test, 443
Chlorpromazine, 485
Cholecystokinin (CCK), 262, 264
Chordates, 28
Choroid plexuses, 55
Chromatic colors, 181
Chromosomes
    defined, 35
    division of, 35–36
    sex, 36–38
    structure and replication, 38–39
Ciliary muscles, 161
Cingulate cortex, 75
Cingulate gyrus, 75
Cingulate motor areas, 226, 227
Circadian clock, 332–333
Circadian rhythms, 318, 319
Circadian sleep cycles, 318–321
Cirrhosis, 352, 353
Clozapine, 486, 487
Cocaine, 102, 103, 354, 355–356
Cocaine psychosis, 354, 355
Cocaine sprees, 354, 355
Cochlea, 200
Cocktail-party phenomenon, 219
Cocontraction, 240, 241

Codeine, 356, 357
Codon, 39–40
Coexistence, 94, 95
Cognition, 10, 11
Cognitive map theory, 395
Cognitive neuroscience
    behavioral methods of, 131–132
    defined, 10–11, 130, 131
Collateral sprouting, 424, 425
Colony-intruder paradigm, 132, 133
Color, seeing, 181–186
Color constancy, 183–186
Columnar organization, 74, 75
Commissurotomy, 435
    in epileptics, 440–442
Comparative approach, 5, 34, 35
Comparative psychology, 11
Complementary colors, 182, 183
Completion, 164, 165, 192–193
Complex cells, 176, 177–178
Complex partial seizures, 147
Component theory, 182, 183
Computed tomography (CT), 107–108,
    454–455
Concussion, 143
Conditioned compensatory responses, 349
Conditioned defensive burying, 135
Conditioned drug tolerance, 347–349
Conditioned place-preference paradigm,
    366–367
Conditioned taste aversion, 133–134
Conditioned withdrawal effects, 349
Conditioning paradigms, 133
Conduction aphasia, 450
Cones, 164, 165
Cones and rod vision, 164–168
Configural association theory, 395
Confounded variable, 6, 7
Congenital, 140, 141
Congenital adrenal hyperplasia, 299–300
Consolidation, 372, 373
Conspecifics, 28
Constituent cognitive processes, 130, 131
Constructional apraxia, 225
Consummatory behaviors, 366, 367
Contingent drug tolerance, 347
Contralateral, 70, 71
Contralateral neglect, 210, 211, 225–226
Contrast enhancement, 173–174, 175
Contrast X-ray techniques, 107
Contrecoup injuries, 142, 143
"Control of behavior" versus "conscious
    perception" theory, 196, 197
Control-question technique, 470
Contusions, 142, 143
Convergent evolution, 32, 33
Converging operation, 12, 13
Convolutions, 33–34
Convulsions, 146, 147
Co-occurrence, 417–418
Coolidge effect, 6, 7
Copulation, 286, 287

Corpus callosum, 72, 438, 439
Cortical areas of somatosensation,
    208–209
Cortical localization of language
    functional brain-imaging research,
        458–463
    Wernicke-Geschwind model, 449–458
Cortical mechanisms of vision, 192–199
Courtship display, 27–28
Crack, 354, 355
Cranial nerves, 53
Cross-cuing, 442, 443
Crossing over, 36
Cross section, 64
Cross tolerance, 344, 345
Cryogenic blockade, 119
Curare, 103–104
Cutaneous receptors, 204
Cyclic AMP, 416, 417
Cytochrome oxidase, 186

Decorticate, 467
Decussate, 70, 71
Deep dyslexia, 458, 459
Defeminizes, 296
Defensive behavior
    defined, 474, 475
    testing of, 132–133
    types of, 474–475
Delirium tremens (DTs), 352, 353
Delta sleep, 315
Delta waves, 313
Demasculinizes, 296
Dementia, 143
Dendritic spines, 91, 420, 421
Dendrodendritic synapses, 91
Deoxyribonucleic acid (DNA), 38, 39
    -binding proteins, 39
    mitochondrial, 42
Dependent variable, 6, 7
Depolarize, 84, 85
Deprenyl, 156
Depressant, 352, 353
Depression
    defined, 488, 489
    drugs for, 489–490
    genetics and, 489
    neural mechanisms of, 490–492
Dermatomes, 204–205
Desynchronized (EEG), 328, 329
Detoxified addicts, 361
Dextrals, 437
Diathesis-stress model, 484, 485, 492
Dichotic listening test, 129, 437
Dichotomous traits, 34, 35
Diencephalon, 70–71
Diet-induced thermogenesis, 265
Digestion, energy flow and, 249–252
Digit span, 374
Digit span + 1 test, 374, 375
Digit-span test, 128, 129
Dihydrotestosterone, 295

Dipsogen, 274, 275
Directed synapses, 92
Distal segment, 422
Diuretic, 352, 353
DNA. See Deoxyribonucleic acid
Dominant hemisphere, 437
Dominant trait, 34, 35
Dopamine, 81, 98, 123, 148
    agonist and antagonist studies, 365
    schizophrenia and, 485–487
Dorsal, 64
Dorsal-column medial-lemniscus system,
    205, 206
Dorsal columns, 206, 207
Dorsal horns, 66, 67
Dorsal raphé nuclei, 330, 331
Dorsal stream, 196–197
Dorsolateral corticorubrospinal tract,
    232–233
Dorsolateral corticospinal tract, 232–233
Dorsolateral prefrontal association cortex,
    226–227
Down syndrome, 39, 144, 145
Dreaming, 315–317
Drinking
    angiotensis II, 274–275
    cellular dehydration, 272–273
    deprivation-induced, 272–275
    hypovolemia, 272, 273
    satiety and, 276–277
    spontaneous, 275–276
Drug(s)
    administration absorption routes,
        121–122, 343–344
    affects on synaptic transmission,
        101–104
    antidepressant, 489–490
    antischizophrenic, 485–487
    for anxiety disorders, 493
    brain reward circuits and, 362–366
    commonly abused, 351–359
    metabolism, 344, 345
    psychoactive, 101–104
    research methods using, 121–124
    sleep affected by, 334–336
Drug abuse
    prevalence of, 358–359
    recommendations for dealing with, 359
Drug action, principles of, 343–346
Drug addiction
    biopsychological theories of, 360–362
    defined, 346
    neural mechanisms of, 366–369
    role of learning in drug tolerance and
        withdrawal effects, 347–350
Drug self-administration paradigm, 133,
    366, 367
Drug tolerance
    conditioned, 347–349
    contingent, 347
    defined, 344, 345
    role of learning in, 347–350

Dual-opponent color cells, 186
Duchenne smile, 472, 473
Duodenum, 262
Duplexity theory, 164, 165
Dura mater, 53
Dynamic contraction, 236, 237
Dynamic phase, 260, 261
Dyslexia, 457–458

Ear, 200–201
Eating
    factors that influence, 255–258
    set points and, 264–268
    theories of, 252–255
Edge perception, 173–181
Efferent nerves, 52, 53
Ejaculates, 133
Ejaculation, 296
Electrical stimulation, 120
Electrocardiogram (ECG/EKG), 116, 117
Electrochemistry, 123
Electoconvulsive shock (ECS), 384–387
Electroencephalogram (EEG), 10, 11, 120, 313
Electroencephalography, 112–114
Electromyogram (EMG), 313
Electromyography, 114–115
Electron microscopy, 62
Electrooculogram (EOG), 313
Electrooculography, 115
Elevated plus maze, 132–133
Embolism, 141
Emergent stage 1 EEG, 313
Emotion(s)
    autonomic nervous system and, 469–470
    biopsychology of, 466–473
    cortical damage and, 472–473
    facial expressions and, 470–472
    lateralized function and experience of, 446
    limbic system and, 468–469
Encapsulated tumors, 138, 139
Encéphale isolé preparation, 328, 329
Encephalitis, 143
Endocrine glands, 285
Endogenous depression, 488, 489
Endorphins, 100, 211
Energy flow, digestion and, 249–252
Engram, 372, 373
Enzymatic degradation, 96, 97–98
Enzymes, 98, 99
Epidemiology, 151
Epilepsy, 146–148
Epileptic auras, 147
Epileptics, commissurotomy in, 440–442
Epileptogenesis, 155
Epinephrine, 98
Episodic memory, 379
Estradiol, 287
Estrogens, 287
Estrous cycle, 303

Estrus, 303
Ethoexperimental research, 474, 475
Ethological research, 11
Ethology, 22, 23
Event-related potentials (ERPs), 113
Evolution, 24–34
    behavior and, 27–28
    course of human, 28–31
    evidence supporting, 25–26
    of human brain, 32–34
Evolve, 24, 25
Excitatory postsynaptic potentials (EPSPs), 84, 85–86
Exocrine glands, 285
Exocytosis, 94, 95
Experience, effects on neural development, 410–411
Experimental autoimmune encephalomyelitis, 151
Experiments, role and types of, 5–7
Explicit memory, 378, 379
Expression of Emotions in Man and Animals, The (Darwin), 466
Expressive, 450
Extensors, 236, 237
Exteroceptive sensory systems, 189
Extracellular unit recordings, 120
Extrafusal muscle, 238, 239
Eye(s)
    See also Visual system
    movement, 115, 168
    parts of, 163

Facial expressions, emotions and, 470–472
Facial feedback hypothesis, 470–471
False transmitter, 485
Far-field potentials, 113
Fasciculation, 406, 407
Fasting phase, 251
Fear
    amygdalectomy and, 477–478
    conditioning, 476, 477
    defined, 474, 475
    neural mechanisms of conditioned, 476–477
Feminizes, 296
Fetal alcohol syndrome (FAS), 353
First-night phenomenon, 313
Fissures, 72
Fitness, 26, 27
5-hydroxytryptophan (5-HTP), 334, 335
Flavor, 213
Flexors, 236, 237
Follicle, 290
Follicle-stimulating hormone (FSH), 290
Fornix, 75
Fourier analysis, 181, 200
Fovea, 164, 165
Fraternal twins, 48, 49
Free fatty acids, 251
Free nerve endings, 204, 205
Free radicals, 352, 353

Free-running period, 319
Free-running rhythms, 319
Frontal eye field, 225
Frontal lobe, 72
Frontal-lobe function, 130
Frontal operculum, 447
Frontal sections, 64
Functional approach, 34, 35
Functional brain-imaging research, 458–463
Functional MRI, 110, 195, 459–460
Functional segregation, 190–191
Functional tolerance, 344, 345

Gametes, 35
Gamma-aminobutyric acid (GABA), 98, 102–103, 353
Ganglia, 56
Gastric ulcers, 479
Gastrointestinal tract, satiety and, 262
Gate-control theory, 211
Gene(s), 34, 35
    expression, 39
    knockout techniques, 125
    maps, 36
    sexual orientation and, 307–309
Generalizability, 8, 9
Generalized anxiety disorders, 492, 493
Generalized seizures, 148, 149
General paresis, 143
Gene replacement techniques, 125
Genetic code, 39–40
Genetic engineering, 125, 429
Genetics
    brain damage and, 144–145
    of circadian rhythms, 333
    chromosomes, reproduction, and linkage, 35–36
    chromosome structure and replication, 38–39
    depression and, 489
    genetic code and gene expression, 39–40
    human genome project, 40–42
    interaction of experience and, 43–47
    Mendelian, 34–35
    mitochondrial DNA, 42
    psychological differences and, 47–49
    sex chromosomes and sex-linked traits, 36–38
Genitals, 294, 295
Genotype, 34, 35
Glabrous skin, 204, 205
Glands, 285
Glial cells, 56–60
Global amnesia, 374, 375
Global aphasia, 454, 455
Globus pallidus, 75
Glucagon, 251
Glucocorticoids, 478, 479
Gluconeogenesis, 251
Glucose, 249

Glucostatic theory, 253, 254
Glutamate, 98, 141, 419
Glycine, 98
Golgi complex, 92
Golgi stain, 61
Golgi tendon organs, 236, 237–238
Gonadal endocrine regulation, summary model of, 291–292
Gonadal hormones, effects on adults, 301–304
Gonadectomy, 293
Gonadotropin-releasing hormone, 290
Gonadotropins, 287
Gonads, 286, 287, 292
Graded responses, 84, 85
Grammatical analysis, 457
Grand mal seizure, 148, 149
Gray matter, 65
Growth cone, 405
Growth hormone, 296
Guilty-knowledge technique, 470
Gustatory system, 213–214, 215–216
Gyri, 72

Habituation, 412, 413
Hair cells, 200
Haloperidol, 486
Halstead-Reitan Neuropsychological Test Battery, 127
Handedness, 437–438
Harrison Narcotics Act (1914), 356, 357
Hashish, 353
Head injuries, closed-, 141–143
Heart rate, 116
Helping-hand phenomenon, 443
Hematoma, 142, 143
Hemianopsic patients, 192–193
Hemispherectomy, 458, 459
Heritability estimate, 48, 49
Heroin, 356, 357
Herpes, 144
Heschl's gyrus, 447
Heterosexual, 307, 308–309
Heterozygous, 35
Hierarchical organization, 189–190, 222–223
Hippocampus
    defined/role of, 74, 374, 396–397
    long-term potentiation, 417–421
    memory for spatial location and, 394–395
    stress and, 482
Homeostasis, 253
Hominids, 30, 31
Homo erectus, 30, 31
Homologous, 32, 33
    animal models, 154, 155
Homosexual, 307, 308–309
Homozygous, 35
Horizontal cells, 163
Horizontal sections, 64

Hormones
    See also Sexual development and hormones
    categories of, 285–286
    defined, 285
    effects of gonadal hormones on adults, 301–304
    neuroendocrine system, 285–292
    perinatal hormones and behavioral development, 295–296
    of the pituitary, 287
    pulsatile hormone release, 290–291
    released by hypothalamus, 289–290
    sexual orientation and, 307–309
Human genome project, 40–42
Humankind, emergence of, 30–31
Human subjects, 5
Hunger
    physiological research on, 258–264
    theories of, 252–255
Huntington's disease, 144, 149–151
H-Y antigen, 292, 293
Hydrocephalus, 55
Hyperphagia, 260, 261
Hyperpolarize, 84, 85
Hypersomnia, 336, 337
Hypertension, 116, 117
Hypertonic solutions, 269
Hypnagogic hallucinations, 338, 339
Hypnotic drugs, 334–335
Hypothalamopituitary portal system, 289
Hypothalamus, 70
    control of the pituitary, 288–289
    hormones released by, 289–290
    hunger and satiety and, 259–262
    sexual behavior and, 304–307
Hypothalamus-pituitary-adrenal theory of depression, 491–492
Hypothermic, 348, 349
Hypotonic solutions, 269
Hypovolemia, 272, 273
Hypoxia, 148, 149

Iatrogenic, 336, 337
Identical twins, 47–48
Imipramine, 490, 491
Immune system, 479
Immunocytochemistry, 124, 125
Implicit memory, 378, 379
Impotent, 301
Incomplete-pictures test, 377
Independent variable, 6, 7
Indolamines, 98
Induction, 402, 403
Infections, brain, 143–144
Inferior, 64
Inferior colliculi, 69, 202, 203
Inferotemporal cortex, 192, 193, 397
Infiltrating tumors, 138, 139
Inhibitory factors, 289
Inhibitory postsynaptic potentials (IPSPs), 84, 85–86

Initial stage 1 EEG, 313
In situ hybridization, 124, 125
Insomnia, 336–337
Instinctive behaviors, 22, 23
Insulin, 251, 280
Integration, 86, 87
Intelligence testing, 128
Internal desynchronization, 319–320
Interneurons, 56, 91
Intracellular unit recordings, 120
Intracranial self-stimulation (ICSS), 362–366
Intrafusal motor neuron, 238, 239
Intrafusal muscle, 238, 239
Intramuscularly (IM), 343
Intravenously (IV), 343
Intromission, 133, 296
Invasive research methods, 117–121
Ion channels, 83
    voltage-activated, 88, 89
Ionic basis
    of action potentials, 89
    of resting potential, 83–85
Ionotropic receptors, 95
Ions, 83
Iproniazid, 489
Ipsilateral, 70, 71
Ipsilateral movement, lateralized function and, 445
Ischemic brain damage, 379
Islands of memory, 384
Isometric contraction, 236, 237
Isomorphic animal models, 154, 155
Isotonic solutions, 269

Jacksonian seizures, 147
James-Lange theory, 466–467
Jet lag, 320

K complex, 313
Ketones, 251
Kidneys, 270–271
Kindling phenomenon, 154–155
Kluver-Bucy syndrome, 469
Knife cuts, 118–119
Korsakoff's syndrome, 12–13, 352, 353, 381–382

Language
    cortical localization of (functional brain-imaging research), 458–463
    cortical localization of (Wernicke-Geschwind model), 449–458
    lateralization, 129, 437
    testing, 129, 130, 377
Lateral, 64
Lateral fissure, 72
Lateral geniculate nuclei, 70, 170, 171
Lateral hypothalamus (LH), 258, 259–261
Lateral inhibition, 173–174, 175

Neuroanatomical
  asymmetries, 447–448
  directions, 63–64
  techniques, 61–63
  tracing techniques, 63
Neuroanatomy, 4, 5
  of object-recognition memory, 387–393
Neurochemistry, 4, 5
Neuroendocrine system, 285–292
Neuroendocrinology, 4, 5
Neurofibrillary tangles, 382, 383
Neuroleptics, 486, 487
Neuromuscular junctions, 104
Neuron cell membrane, 56
Neurons
  action potentials, conduction of, 89–91
  action potentials, generation of, 86–88
  anatomy of, 56
  conduction in, without axons, 91
  death and synapse rearrangement,
    408–409
  defined, 2, 3
  membrane potential, 81–85
  postsynaptic potentials, generation and
    conduction of, 85–86
  synaptic transmission, 91–98
Neuropathology, 4, 5
Neuropeptides, 100
Neuropharmacology, 4, 5
Neurophysiology, 4, 5
Neuroplasticity. See Neural development/
  neuroplasticity
Neuropsychological diseases
  animal models of human, 154–156
  types of, in humans, 146–152
Neuropsychological testing
  customizied-test-battery approach,
    127–130
  single-test approach, 127
  standardized-test-battery approach,
    127
Neuropsychology, 9–10
Neuroscience, 2, 3
Neurotoxins, 122, 123, 144
Neurotransmitters
  acetylcholine, 99–100
  activation of receptors by, 94–97
  amino acids, 98
  locating in the brain, 123–124
  monoamine, 98–99
  neuropeptides, 100
  release of molecules, 94
  reuptake, enzymatic degradation, and
    recycling, 97–98
  soluble-gas, 99
  synthesis, packaging, and transport of
    molecules, 92–94
Neurotransplantation, 429–431
Neurotrophins, 408, 409
Neurotropic infections, 143–144
Nicotine, 350, 351
Nigrostriatal pathway, 148, 149

Nissl stain, 61–62
Nitric oxide, 99, 421
NMDA (N-methyl-D-aspartate) receptors,
  141, 394, 419–420
Nobel Prizes awarded for studies of the
  nervous system or behavior, 8
Nocturnal myoclonus, 337
Nodes of Ranvier, 90, 91
Nonassociative learning, 412–413
Nondirected synapses, 92
Nonlexical procedure, 457
Nonrecurring-items delayed
  nonmatching-to-sample test, 386, 387
Nootropics, 383
Norepinephrine, 98
Nuclei, 56
Nucleotide bases, 38, 39
Nucleus accumbens, 365
Nucleus magnocellularis, 338, 339
Nutritive density, 257

Obesity, 249, 278–281
Object-recognition memory, 387–393
Ob/ob mice, 280, 281
Obsessive-compulsive disorders, 493
Occipital lobe, 73
Off-center cells, 175
Olfactory bulbs, 214, 215
Olfactory mucosa, 214, 215
Olfactory system, 213–215
Oligodendroglia (oligodendrocyte), 59, 61,
  424, 425
Ommatidia, 174, 175
On-center cells, 175
On the Origins of Species (Darwin), 24
Ontogeny, 43
Open-field test, 132, 133
Operant conditioning paradigm, 133
Operator gene, 39
Opiates, 356–358
Opium, 356, 357
Opponent-process theory, 182, 183
Optic chiasm, 70
Optic tectum, 405
Orbitofrontal cortex, 215
Orchidectomy, 293, 301
Organization of Behavior (Hebb), 3
Organ of Corti, 200
Orthodromic conduction, 90, 91
Oscilloscope, 82, 83
Osmoreceptors, 272, 273
Osmotic pressure, 269
Ossicles, 200
Oval window, 200
Ovariectomy, 293
Ovaries, 286, 287
Overweight. See Obesity
Ovulation, 290
Oxytocin, 288, 289

Pacinian corpuscles, 204, 205
Pain. See Somatosensation

Paired-image subtraction technique, 130,
  131
Panic disorders, 493
Pantropic infections, 144, 145
Parachlorophenylalanine (PCPA), 330, 331
Paradoxical sleep, 314–315
Parallel models, 452, 453
Parallel processing, 190, 191
Parasympathetic nerves, 53
Paraventricular nuclei, 261, 288, 289
Parietal lobe, 72–73
Parkinson's disease, 75, 81, 148–149, 485
  MPTP model of, 156
Partial seizures, 147–148
Parvocellular layers, 172, 173
Patellar tendon reflex, 238, 239
Path-integration theory, 395
Pavlovian conditioning, 377, 378–379
  Aplysia gill-withdrawal reflex, 413, 415
  of hunger, 256
  paradigm, 133
Peptide hormones, 286, 287
Peptides, 92
  hunger and satiety, 262–264
Perception, 190
Periaqueductal gray (PAG), 69, 211
Perimetry test, 192, 193
Peripheral nervous system (PNS), 52, 53
Petit mal seizure, 148, 149
Phagocytosis, 422, 480
Phantom limbs, 212–213
Pharmacology. See Drugs
Phenothiazines, 486
Phenotype, 34, 35
Phenylketonuria (PKU), 44–45, 144
Phenylpyruvic acid, 44, 45
Pheromones, 213
Phobic anxiety disorders, 492–493
Phonemes, 457
Phonological analysis, 457
Photopic spectral sensitivity curve, 167
Photopic vision, 164–165
Phylogeny, 43
Physical-dependence theory of addiction,
  360–361
Physically dependent, 344, 345–346
Physiological activity, recording, 112–117
Physiological correlates of sleep, 312–315
Physiological psychology, 9
Physiological research on hunger and
  satiety, 258–264
Pia mater, 53
Pineal gland, 334, 335–336
Pioneer growth cones, 406, 407
Piriform cortex, 215
Pituitary gland, 70
  hormones of, 287
  hypothalamus control of, 288–289
  neural control of, 288
Pituitary stalk, 287
Place cells, 394, 395
Planum temporale, 447

Plethysmography, 116, 117
Pneumoencephalography, 107
Polydipsia, 277
Polygraphy, 469–470
Polyphasic sleep cycles, 339
Pons, 69
Positive feedback, 290
Positive-incentive theory, 254–255
    of addiction, 361–362
Positive-incentive value, 254, 255
Positron emission tomography (PET),
    109, 131–132, 195, 228, 244, 459
Postcentral gyri, 73
Posterior, 64
Posterior parietal association cortex,
    224–226
Posterior parietal cortex, 192, 193
Posterior pituitary, 287
Postsynaptic inhibition, 91
Postsynaptic potentials, generation and
    conduction of, 85–86
Posttraumatic amnesia (PTA), 383–384
Precentral gyri, 73
Predictive animal models, 154, 155
Prefrontal cortex, 398
    damage, memory deficits and, 382, 383
Prefrontal lobes, 16, 17
Prefrontal lobotomy, 16, 17
Premotor cortex, 226, 227
Preparatory behaviors, 366, 367
Prestriate cortex, 192, 193
Presynaptic facilitation, 413
Presynaptic inhibition, 91
Primary auditory cortex, 201–202
Primary motor cortex, 229–230,
    425–426
Primary sensory cortex, 189, 425
Primary visual cortex, 170–172
Primates, 28, 29
Primed, 363
Principle of equipotentiality, 372, 373
Principle of mass action, 372, 373
Proceptive behaviors, 298
Progesterone, 287
Progestins, 287
Programmed cell death, 145
Prosody, 473
Prosopagnosia, 197–198
Protein hormones, 286, 287
Proteins, 39
Proximal segment, 422
Prozac, 490, 491
Psychoactive drugs, 101–104, 343
Psychological dependence, 346, 347
Psychological differences, genetics and,
    47–49
Psychology, defined, 3
Psychomotor attack, 147
Psychoneuroimmunology, 479–482
Psychopharmacology, 9
Psychophysiology, 10, 11
P300 wave, 113

Puberty and secondary sex characteristics,
    296–297
Pulsatile hormone release, 290–291
Punch-drunk syndrome, 143
Pure research, 8, 9
Purkinje effect, 167–168
Putamen, 75
Pyramidal cell layer, 380, 381
Pyramidal cells, 73

Quasiexperimental studies, 7

Rabies, 144
Radial arm maze, 134, 135, 394, 395
Radial glial cells, 402, 403
Radio-frequency lesions, 118
Raphé nuclei, 329–330
Reactive depression, 488, 489
Receptive, 450
Receptive fields
    complex cortical cells, 177–178
    defined, 175
    neurons of the retina-geniculate-striate
        pathway, 175–176
    simple cortical cells, 176
Receptor organs of muscles and tendons,
    237–238
Receptors, 94–95, 163
    cutaneous, 204
Receptor subtype, 95
Recessive trait, 34, 35
Reciprocal innervation, 239–240
Recurrent collateral inhibition,
    240–241
Red nucleus, 69
Reference memory, 394, 395
Refractory periods, 88, 89–90
Rehabilitative training, 428
Relative refractory period, 88, 89
Releasing factors, 289
Releasing hormones, 290
REM sleep
    defined, 315
    deprivation, 324–325
    dreaming and, 315–317
    related disorders, 337–338
Renin, 273
Renshaw cells, 241
Repetition priming tests, 129, 379
Replacement injections, 301
Replication, 39
Reproductive ducts, internal, 292–293
Reproductive organs, external, 294
Reptiles, 28
Research
    ethological, 11
    experiments versus nonexperiments,
        5–8
    human and nonhuman subjects, 5
    invasive methods, 117–121
    pharmacological, 121–124
    pure and applied, 8

Reserpine, 485
Response-chunking hypothesis, 244
Resting potential
    defined, 83
    ionic basis of, 83–85
Restless legs, 337
Reticular activating system theory of sleep,
    328–329
Reticular formation, 68, 233
Retina
    cellular structure of, 163
    how light enters the eye and reaches the,
        160–163
    from retina to primary visual cortex,
        170–172
    translation of light into neural signals,
        163–170
Retina-geniculate-striate pathway, 170,
    171, 175–176
Retinal ganglion cells, 163, 405
Retinex theory, 185
Retinohypothalamic tracts, 333
Retinotopic organization, 172, 173, 200
Retrograde amnesia, 374, 386
Retrograde degeneration, 422
Retrograde transneuronal degeneration,
    422
Reuptake, 96, 97–98
Rhinal cortex, 388–389, 396
Rhodopsin, 168, 169
Ribonucleic acid (RNA), 39
    messenger, 39
    transfer, 40
Ribosomes, 39
RNA. *See* Ribonucleic acid
Rods, 164, 165
Rod vision, cones and, 164–168
Rotary-pursuit test, 376–377

Saccades, 168, 169
Saccharin elation effect, 276, 277
Sagittal sections, 64
Saltatory conduction, 90, 91
Satellite cells, 56
Satiety
    appetizer effect and, 257
    defined, 256–257
    drinking and, 276–277
    physiological research on, 258–264
    sensory-specific, 258, 277
    social influences and, 258
Schedule-induced polydipsia,
    276, 277
Schizophrenia, 483
    causal factors in, 484–485
    current research on, 487–488
    defined, 484, 485
    discovery of first antischizophrenic
        drugs, 485
    dopamine theory of, 485–487
Schwann cells, 61, 422
Scientific inference, 13–15

Synapses
    axon growth and formation of, 405–408
    neuron death and rearrangement of,
        408–409
    structure of, 91–92
Synaptic transmission
    activation of receptors by
        neurotransmitter molecules, 94–97
    description of, 91–98
    pharmacology of, 101–104
    release of neurotransmitter molecules,
        94
    reuptake, enzymatic degradation, and
        recycling, 97–98
    structure of synapses, 91–92
    synthesis, packaging, and transport of
        neurotransmitter molecules, 92–94
Synaptic vesicles, 92
Synergistic muscles, 236, 237
Syphilis, 143

Tardive dyskinesia (TD), 144, 145
Target-site concept, 475
Taste, 213–214, 215–216
Taste buds, 215
T cells, 480
Tectorial membrane, 200
Tectum, 69, 233
Tegmentum, 69
Telencephalon, 71–75
Temporal hemiretina, 166, 167
Temporal lobe, 73
Temporal summation, 87
Tendons, receptor organs of, 237–238
Testes, 286, 287
Testosterone, 287, 476
Thalamus, 70
THC, 353
Thigmotaxic, 132, 133
Thirst. *See* Drinking
3-per-second spike-and-wave discharge,
    148, 149
Threshold of excitation, 86, 87
Thrombosis, 140–141
Thyrotropin, 290
Thyrotropin-releasing hormone,
    289–290

Tobacco, 351–352
Token test, 129
Tonotopic, 200
Topographic gradient hypothesis,
    407–408
Totipotential, 402, 403
Touch. *See* Somatosensation
Toxic psychosis, 144, 145
Tracts, 56
Transduction, visual, 168–170
Transfer RNA, 40
Transgenic mice, 125
    model of Alzheimer's disease, 155–156
Transorbital lobotomy, 17
Tricyclic antidepressant drugs, 325, 490,
    491
True-breeding lines, 34, 35
Tumor
    brain, 139–140
    defined, 138, 139
Twins
    types of, 47–48
    Minnesota study of, 48–49
    multiple sclerosis in, 151
2-deoxyglucose (2-DG), 109, 122
Tympanic membrane, 200

Unipolar affective disorder, 489
Unipolar neuron, 56
Up-regulation, 490, 491

Vasopressin, 288, 289
Ventral, 64
    horns, 66, 67
    posterior nuclei, 70, 206, 207
    stream, 196–197
    tegmental area, 364, 365
Ventricular zone, 402, 403
Ventromedial cortico-brainstem-spinal
    tract, 233
Ventromedial corticospinal tract, 233
Ventromedial hypothalamus (VMH), 258,
    259–261
Ventromedial nucleus (VMN), 306–307
Vertebrates, evolution of, 28, 31
Vestibular nucleus, 233
Vestibular system, 200, 201

Viral infections, 143–144
Vision, cortical mechanisms of,
    192–199
Visual agnosia, 197
Visual completion, 443
Visual system
    cones and rod vision, 164–168
    how light enters the eye and reaches the
        retina, 160–163
    from retina to primary visual cortex,
        170–172
    seeing color, 181–186
    seeing edges, 173–181
    translation of light into neural signals,
        163–170
Voltage-activated ion channels, 88, 89

Walking, 243
Wechsler Adult Intelligence Scale (WAIS),
    128, 129, 225
Wernicke-Geschwind model, 449
    description of, 451–452
    evaluation of, 452–458
    historic antecedents of, 450–451
Wernicke's aphasia, 450
Wernicke's area, 450, 461
"Where" versus "what" theory, 196, 197
White matter, 65
Wisconsin Card Sorting Test, 130
Withdrawal reflex, 239
Withdrawal syndrome/effects
    conditioned, 349
    defined, 344, 345–345
    role of learning in, 347–350
Within-subjects design, 6, 7
Wolffian system, 292, 293
Word salad, 450
Working memory, 394, 395

X-rays
    computed tomography, 107–108
    contrast, 107

Zeitgebers, 318, 319
Zeitgeist, 21, 26
Z lens, 443–444
Zygote, 36, 286, 287